Designed for the Internal Medicine Clerkship

IM Essentials ☑

A Medical Knowledge Self-Assessment Program® (MKSAP®) for Students

Philip A. Masters, MD, FACP
Senior Physician Educator
American College of Physicians
Editor-in-Chief

American College of Physicians

CDIM

Clerkship Directors in Internal Medicine

Foreword

Welcome to IM Essentials, an educational resource for learning internal medicine developed specifically for students!

IM Essentials is a suite of educational materials produced collaboratively by the American College of Physicians (ACP), the national practice society for internal medicine, and the Clerkship Directors in Internal Medicine (CDIM), the national organization of individuals responsible for teaching internal medicine to medical students.

The IM Essentials suite consists of IM Essentials Text, an abbreviated textbook of internal medicine organized by traditional topic areas, IM Essentials Questions, containing over 500 detailed self-assessment and study questions, and IM Essentials Online, a digital version available on multiple platforms that combines the textbook and self-assessment content and provides multiple additional features for use in learning internal medicine. Be sure to explore the special features of IM Essentials Online (available even if you are using the print version of either book) created specifically to optimize your studying, such as electronic flashcards and the ability to create custom quizzes.

The content in the IM Essentials suite has been developed by over 90 CDIM-member internal medicine clerkship directors and clerkship faculty representing 70 medical schools. Combined with the educational knowledge and expertise of the ACP, IM Essentials represents an authoritative, evidence-based resource that can be trusted to help you learn internal medicine.

As with the previous versions of these materials (Internal Medicine Essentials for Clerkship Students and MKSAP for Students), the content in IM Essentials is based on the Society of General Internal Medicine/CDIM core curriculum for the internal medicine clerkship, and focuses on the key internal medicine concepts and factual information that are evaluated on both the end-of-clerkship and USMLE Step 2 examinations.

As in the past, we hope to receive your feedback to help us improve future editions – please let us know your thoughts about IM Essentials and how it may best fit your learning needs.

Thank you for using IM Essentials, and enjoy learning internal medicine!

Philip A. Masters, MD, FACP
Editor-in-Chief
Senior Physician Educator
American College of Physicians

Editor-in-Chief

Philip A. Masters, MD, FACP
Senior Physician Educator
American College of Physicians
Philadelphia, Pennsylvania

Associate Editors

Jonathan S. Appelbaum, MD, FACP
Associate Professor, Clinical Sciences Department
Director, Internal Medicine Education
Florida State University College of Medicine
Tallahassee, Florida

Thomas M. De Fer, MD, FACP
Professor of Medicine
Director, Internal Medicine Clerkship
Washington University School of Medicine
Saint Louis, Missouri

Susan T. Hingle, MD, FACP
Associate Professor of Medicine
Internal Medicine Clerkship Director
Southern Illinois University School of Medicine
Springfield, Illinois

Robert Trowbridge, MD, FACP
Assistant Professor of Medicine
Tufts University School of Medicine
Director of Undergraduate Medical Education
Department of Medicine
Maine Medical Center
Portland, Maine

T. Robert Vu, MD, FACP
Associate Professor of Clinical Medicine
Director, Internal Medicine Clerkship
Indiana University School of Medicine
Indianapolis, Indiana

ACP Editorial Staff

Edward Warren
Project Manager

Lisa Levine
Editorial Production

Rosemarie Houton
Editorial Production

ACP Principal Staff

Patrick C. Alguire, MD, FACP
Senior Vice President, Medical Education

Sean McKinney
Vice President, Medical Education

CDIM Principal Staff

Sheila T. Costa
AAIM Director of Development and Communications
Alliance for Academic Internal Medicine

Acknowledgments

The American College of Physicians (ACP) gratefully acknowledges the special contributions to the development and production of the 1st edition of IM Essentials made by the following people:

Graphic Services: Michael Ripca (Graphics Technical Administrator/ Graphic Designer), Barry Moshinski (Art Director, Graphics Services), Thomas Malone (Graphics Production Supervisor)

Production/Systems: Dan Hoffmann (Director, Web Services & Systems Development), Scott Hurd (Manager, Content Systems), Neil Kohl (Senior Architect), Chris Patterson (Senior Architect) and Robert Guthy (Systems Analyst/Developer).

IM Essentials Online: Under the direction of Steven Spadt, Vice President, ACP Digital Products & Services, the online version of IM Essentials was developed within the ACP's Digital Product Development department, led by Brian Sweigard (Director). Other members of the team included Dan Barron (Senior Systems Analyst/Developer), Chris Forrest (Senior Software Developer/Design Lead), Kara Kronenwetter (Senior Web Developer), Brad Lord (Senior Web Application Developer), John McKnight (Senior Web Developer), and Nate Pershall (Senior Web Developer).

The College also wishes to acknowledge that many other persons, too numerous to mention, have contributed to the production of this program. Without their dedicated efforts, this program would not have been possible.

Disclosure Policy

It is the policy of the American College of Physicians (ACP) to ensure balance, independence, objectivity, and scientific rigor in all its educational activities. To this end, and consistent with the policies of the ACP and the Accreditation Council for Continuing Medical Education (ACCME), contributors to all ACP continuing medical education activities are required to disclose all relationships with any entity producing, marketing, re-selling, or distributing health care goods or services consumed by, or used on, patients. Contributors are required to use generic names in the discussion of therapeutic options and are required to identify any unapproved, off-label, or investigative use of commercial products or devices. Where a trade name is used, all available trade names for the same product type are also included. If trade-name products manufactured by companies with whom contributors have relationships are discussed, contributors are asked to provide evidence-based citations in support of the discussion. If necessary, adjustments to topics or contributors' roles in content development are made to balance the discussion. The editors of IM Essentials have ensured that content is based on best evidence and updated clinical care guidelines, when such evidence and guidelines were available. Contributors' disclosure information is reviewed by the editors and every effort was made to resolve any conflicts presented. Further, all readers of this text are asked to evaluate the content for evidence of commercial bias so that future decisions about content and contributors can be made in light of this information.

Educational Disclaimer

The editors and publisher of IM Essentials recognize that the development of new material offers many opportunities for error. Despite our best efforts, some errors may persist in print. Drug dosage schedules are, we believe, accurate and in accordance with current standards. Readers are advised, however, to ensure that the recommended dosages in IM Essentials concur with the information provided in the product information material. This is especially important in cases of new, infrequently used, or highly toxic drugs. Application of the information in IM Essentials remains the professional responsibility of the practitioner.

The primary purpose of IM Essentials is educational. Information presented, as well as publications, technologies, products, and/or services discussed, is intended to inform subscribers about the knowledge, techniques, and experiences of the contributors. A diversity of professional opinion exists, and the views of the contributors are their own and not those of the ACP. Inclusion of any material in the program does not constitute endorsement or recommendation by the ACP. The ACP does not warrant the safety, reliability, accuracy, completeness, or usefulness of and disclaims any and all liability for damages and claims that may result from the use of information, publications, technologies, products, and/or services discussed in this program.

For order information in the U.S. or Canada call 800-523-1546, extension 2600. All other countries call 215-351-2600. Fax inquiries to 215-351-2799 or email to custserv@acponline.org.

Contributing Authors

Gauri Agarwal, MD, FACP
Assistant Regional Dean for Medical Curriculum
Clerkship Director, Integrated Medicine
University of Miami Miller School of Medicine
Miami, Florida

Erik K. Alexander, MD, FACP
Director, Medical Student Education
Brigham and Women's Hospital
Associate Professor of Medicine
Harvard Medical School
Boston, Massachusetts

Irene Alexandraki, MD, MPH, FACP
Assistant Professor of Medicine
University of Central Florida College of Medicine
Orlando, Florida

Alpesh N. Amin, MD, MBA, FACP
Professor of Medicine
Medicine Clerkship Director
University of California, Irvine
Orange, California

Joel Appel, DO
Director, Ambulatory and Subinternship Programs
Section Chief Hematology/Oncology
Sinai-Grace Hospital
Wayne State University School of Medicine
Detroit, Michigan

Jonathan S. Appelbaum, MD, FACP
Education Director
Professor of Internal Medicine
Florida State University College of Medicine
Tallahassee, Florida

Mary Jane Barchman, MD, FACP, FASN
Professor of Medicine
Internal Medicine Clerkship Director
Section of Nephrology and Hypertension
Brody School of Medicine at East Carolina University
Greenville, North Carolina

Gonzalo Bearman, MD, MPH
Professor of Medicine
Associate Hospital Epidemiologist
Virginia Commonwealth University
Richmond, Virginia

Jennifer Bequette, MD, FACP
Assistant Professor, Department of Medicine
Continuing Care Clinic Clerkship Director
University of Missouri at Kansas City School of Medicine
Kansas City, Missouri

Jennifer Bierman, MD, FACP
Primary Care Clerkship Director
Northwestern University Feinberg School of Medicine
Chicago, Illinois

Matthew J. Burday, DO, FACP
Associate Program Director
Internal Medicine Residency Program Director
Medical Student Programs
Department of Medicine, Christiana Care Health System
Newark, Delaware

Cynthia A. Burns, MD, FACP
Assistant Professor
Internal Medicine Clerkship Director
Department of Internal Medicine
Section on Endocrinology & Metabolism
Wake Forest University School of Medicine
Winston-Salem, North Carolina

Danelle Cayea, MD, MS
Assistant Professor of Medicine
Johns Hopkins University School of Medicine
Baltimore, Maryland

Dennis T. Chang, MD
Assistant Professor, Department of Medicine
Co-Director, Medicine-Geriatrics Clerkship
Division of Hospital Medicine
Mount Sinai Health System
New York, New York

Joseph Charles, MD, FACP, FHM
Assistant Professor of Medicine
Division Education Coordinator
Department of Hospital Internal Medicine
4th year Clerkship Director
Mayo Clinic Hospital
Phoenix, Arizona

Mark D. Corriere, MD, FACP
Johns Hopkins University
Division of Endocrinology, Diabetes, and Metabolism
Baltimore, Maryland

Feroza Daroowalla, MD, MPH
Associate Professor, Department of Medicine
Stony Book University
Stony Brook, New York

Thomas M. DeFer, MD, FACP
Professor of Medicine
Clerkship Director
Washington University School of Medicine
Saint Louis, Missouri

Matthew J. Diamond, DO, MS, FACP
Associate Professor of Medicine, Section of Nephrology,
    Hypertension, and Transplant Medicine
The Medical College of Georgia at Georgia Regents University
Augusta, Georgia

Gretchen Diemer, MD, FACP
Assistant Professor of Internal Medicine
Director of Undergraduate Medical Education
Program Director, Internal Medicine Residency
Thomas Jefferson University
Philadelphia, Pennsylvania

Reed E. Drews, MD, FACP
Program Director, Hematology-Oncology
Beth Israel Deaconess Medical Center
Boston, Massachusetts

Maria Dungo, MD
Associate Professor
David Geffen School of Medicine, UCLA
Division of Medical Oncology and Hematology
Harbor-UCLA Medical Center
Torrance, California

Anne Eacker, MD, FACP
Associate Professor
Medicine Associate Dean, Student Affairs
University of Washington School of Medicine
Seattle, Washington

Richard S. Eisenstaedt, MD, MACP
Chair, Department of Medicine
Abington Memorial Hospital
Abington, Pennsylvania

D. Michael Elnicki, MD, FACP
Ambulatory Clerkship Director
University of Pittsburgh School of Medicine
Pittsburgh, Pennsylvania
Assistant Professor of Medicine
Clerkship Director, Medicine
Weill Cornell Medical College
New York, New York

Mark J. Fagan, MD, FACP
Internal Medicine Clerkship Director
Professor of Medicine
Alpert Medical School of Brown University
Providence, Rhode Island

Sara B. Fazio, MD, FACP
Associate Professor, Harvard Medical School
Division of General Internal Medicine
Beth Israel Deaconess Medical Center
Boston, Massachusetts

Jane P. Gagliardi, MD, MHS, FACP, FAPA
Assistant Professor of Psychiatry & Behavioral Sciences
Assistant Professor of Medicine
Duke University School of Medicine
Durham, North Carolina

Susan Glod MD, FACP
Assistant Professor of Medicine
Penn State College of Medicine
Hershey, Pennsylvania

Roderick Go, DO
Medicine Subinternship Director
Medicine Clerkship Co-Director
Stony Book University School of Medicine
Stony Brook, New York

Alda Maria R. Gonzaga, MD, MS, FACP, FAAP
Associate Professor of Internal Medicine and Pediatrics
Program Director, Internal Medicine-Pediatrics Residency
University of Pittsburgh School of Medicine
Pittsburgh, Pennsylvania

Eric Goren
Assistant Professor of Medicine
Perelman School of Medicine
University of Pennsylvania
Philadelphia, Pennsylvania

Eric H. Green, MD, MSc, FACP
Program Director, Internal Medicine
Clinical Associate Professor of Medicine
Mercy Catholic Medical Center
Drexel University College of Medicine
Philadelphia and Darby, Pennsylvania

David V. Gugliotti, MD, FACP, SFHM
Internal Medicine Discipline Leader/Clerkship Director
Clinical Assistant Professor of Medicine, Cleveland Clinic
Lerner College of Medicine of Case Western Reserve University
Cleveland, Ohio

Heather Harrell, MD, FACP
Clinical Associate Professor and Clerkship Director
Department of Medicine
University of Florida College of Medicine
Gainesville, Florida

Amy Hayton, MD, MPH
Assistant Professor of Medicine
Medicine Associate Clerkship Director
Loma Linda University School of Medicine
Loma Linda, California

Brian S. Heist, MD
Assistant Professor of Medicine
University of Pittsburgh School of Medicine
Pittsburgh, Pennsylvania

Scott Herrle, MD, MS, FACP
Assistant Professor of Medicine
University of Pittsburgh School of Medicine
VA Pittsburgh Healthcare System
Pittsburgh, Pennsylvania

Susan T. Hingle, MD, FACP
Professor of Medicine
Interim Chair, Department of Medicine
Medicine Clerkship Director
Southern Illinois University School of Medicine
Springfield, Illinois

Martha L. Hlafka, MD
Assistant Professor, Department of Internal Medicine
Associate Director, Internal Medicine Clerkship
Southern Illinois University School of Medicine
Springfield, Illinois

Eric Hsieh, MD, FACP
Program Director, Internal Medicine Residency
Assistant Professor of Clinical Medicine
Keck School of Medicine
University of Southern California
Los Angeles, California

Nadia Ismail, MD, MPH, MEd
Internal Medicine Clerkship Director
Baylor College of Medicine
Houston, Texas

Asra R. Khan, MD, FACP
Associate Professor of Clinical Medicine
Associate Program Director, Internal Medicine
Clerkship & Sub-I Director, Internal Medicine
Course Director, Essentials of Clinical Medicine
University of Illinois College of Medicine
Chicago, Illinois

Karen E. Kirkham, MD, FACP
Vice-Chair for Undergraduate Medical Education
Department of Internal Medicine
Boonshoft Wright State School of Medicine
Dayton, Ohio

Christopher A. Klipstein, MD
Professor of Medicine
Director, Medicine Inpatient Clerkship
University of North Carolina School of Medicine
Chapel Hill, North Carolina

Norra Kwong, MD
Endocrine Fellow
Brigham and Women's Hospital
Harvard Medical School
Boston, Massachusetts

Amalia M. Landa-Galindez, MD
Assistant Professor of Medicine
Assistant Clerkship Director, Internal Medicine
Florida International University
Herbert Wertheim College of Medicine
Miami, Florida

Valerie J. Lang, MD, FACP
Associate Professor of Medicine
Director, Inpatient Internal Medicine Clerkship
University of Rochester School of Medicine and Dentistry
Rochester, New York

Lawrence Loo, MD, MACP
Vice Chair for Education and Faculty Development
Professor of Medicine, Department of Medicine
Loma Linda University School of Medicine
Loma Linda, California

Fred A. Lopez, MD, MACP
Richard Vial Professor and Vice Chair
Department of Medicine
Louisiana State University Health Sciences Center
New Orleans, Louisiana

Merry Jennifer Markham, MD, FACP
Assistant Professor, Division of Hematology-Oncology
Co-Course Director, Medicine Clerkship
University of Florida College of Medicine
Gainesville, Florida

Lianne Marks, MD, PhD, FACP
Assistant Dean for Educational Development
Regional Chair of Internal Medicine
Texas A & M College of Medicine
Baylor Scott & White Health
Round Rock, Texas

Kevin M. McKown, MD, FACP
Professor of Medicine
University of Wisconsin School of Medicine and Public Health
Madison, Wisconsin

Alyssa C. McManamon, MD, FACP
Associate Clerkship Director, Department of Medicine
Uniformed Services University of the Health Sciences
Bethesda, Maryland

Chad S. Miller, MD, FACP
Director, Student Programs
Associate Program Director, Residency
Department of Internal Medicine
Tulane University Health Sciences Center
New Orleans, Louisiana

Nina Mingioni, MD, FACP, MD
Clerkship Director, Internal Medicine
Associate Program Director, Internal Medicine Residency
Jefferson Medical College
Thomas Jefferson University
Philadelphia, Pennsylvania

Lynda Misra, DO, FACP, MEd
Associate Dean, Undergraduate Clinical Education
Assistant Professor, Internal Medicine and Neurology
Oakland University William Beaumont School of Medicine
Rochester, Michigan

Liana Nikolaenko, MD
Fellow, Department of Hematology-Oncology
Harbor-UCLA Medical Center
Torrance, California

L. James Nixon, MD, MHPE
Professor of Medicine & Pediatrics
Vice Chair for Education, Department of Medicine
University of Minnesota Medical School
Minneapolis, Minnesota

Kendall Novoa-Takara, MD, FACP
Medicine Clerkship Site Director
University of Arizona College of Medicine
Phoenix, Arizona

Isaac O. Opole, MD, PhD, FACP
Associate Professor of Medicine
Assistant Dean for Student Affairs
Internal Medicine Clerkship Director
Department of Internal Medicine
University of Kansas School of Medicine
Kansas City, Kansas

Carlos Palacio, MD, MPH, FACP
Associate Professor of Medicine, Department of Medicine
University of Florida College of Medicine-Jacksonville
Jacksonville, Florida

Robert Pargament, MD, FACP
Program Director
Internal Medicine Residency Program
York Hospital
York, Pennsylvania

Michael Picchioni, MD
Assistant Professor of Medicine
Clerkship Site Director
Baystate Medical Center
Tufts University School of Medicine
Springfield, Massachusetts

Seth Politano, DO, FACP
Associate Program Director, Office of Educational Affairs
Assistant Professor of Clinical Medicine
Keck School of Medicine of the University of Southern California
Los Angeles, California

Nora L. Porter, MD, MPH, FACP
Professor of Medicine Co-Director, Internal Medicine Clerkship
Saint Louis University School of Medicine
Saint Louis, Missouri

Joseph Rencic, MD, FACP
Associate Professor of Medicine
Tufts Medical Center
Tufts University School of Medicine
Boston, Massachusetts

Juan Reyes, MD, MPH
Assistant Professor of Medicine
Clerkship Director Internal Medicine
George Washington University School of Medicine
Washington, DC

Robert Robinson, MD, FACP
Associate Professor of Clinical Medicine
Department of Internal Medicine
Southern Illinois University School of Medicine
Springfield, Illinois

Kathleen F. Ryan, MD, FACP
Associate Professor of Medicine
Department of Medicine
Drexel University College of Medicine
Philadelphia, Pennsylvania

Mysti D.W. Schott, MD, FACP
Clinical Associate Professor of Medicine
Department of Medicine, Division of General Medicine
University of Texas Health Science Center
San Antonio School of Medicine
San Antonio, Texas

Monica Ann Shaw, MD, FACP
Professor of Medicine
Associate Dean for Medical Education
University of Louisville School of Medicine
Louisville, Kentucky

Patricia Short, MD, FACP
Assistant Professor of Medicine
Program Director, Internal Medicine Residency
Uniformed Services University of the Health Sciences
Madigan Army Medical Center
Tacoma, Washington

Leigh Simmons, MD
Assistant Professor
Clerkship Director
Harvard Medical School
Massachusetts General Hospital
Boston, Massachusetts

Madhusree Singh, MD
Associate Clinical Professor
VA San Diego Health System
University of California, San Diego
San Diego, California

Karen Szauter, MD, FACP
Co-Director, Internal Medicine Clerkship
University of Texas Medical Branch
Galveston, Texas

Harold M. Szerlip, MD, FACP, FCCP, FASN, FNKF
Professor, Department of Medicine
University of North Texas Health Sciences Center
Fort Worth, Texas

Gary Tabas, MD, FACP
Transitional Year Program Director
University of Pittsburgh School of Medicine
UPMC Shadyside
Pittsburgh, Pennsylvania

Kimberly M. Tartaglia, MD, FACP
Assistant Professor – Clinical
Ohio State University College of Medicine
Ohio State University Wexner Medical Center
Columbus, Ohio

Bipin Thapa, MD, MS, FACP
Assistant Professor, Department of Medicine
Associate Clerkship Director, Internal Medicine Clerkship
Medical College of Wisconsin
Milwaukee, Wisconsin

David C. Tompkins, MD
Interim Chair, Department of Medicine
Director of Medical Education
Lutheran Medical Center
Brooklyn, New York

Robert L. Trowbridge, MD, FACP
Division Director, General Internal Medicine
Director of Student Education, Department of Medicine
Maine Medical Center
Portland, Maine

Corina Ungureanu, MD
Assistant Professor-Clinical, General Internal Medicine
Ambulatory Internal Medicine Clerkship Director
Ohio State University
Columbus, Ohio

John Varras, MD
Chairman
Department of Internal Medicine
University of Nevada School of Medicine
Las Vegas, Nevada

H. Douglas Walden, MD, MPH, FACP
Professor of Medicine
Co-Director, Internal Medicine Clerkship
Saint Louis University School of Medicine
Saint Louis, Missouri

John A. Walker, MD, FACP
Professor and Vice-Chair for Education
Department of Medicine
Medicine Clerkship Director
Rutgers Robert Wood Johnson Medical School
New Brunswick, New Jersey

Sarita Warrier, MD, FACP
Assistant Professor of Medicine
Division of General Internal Medicine
Warren Alpert Medical School of Brown University
Providence, Rhode Island

Joseph T. Wayne, MD, MPH, FACP
Internal Medicine Clerkship Director
Department of Internal Medicine
Albany Medical College
Albany, New York

Sean A. Whelton, MD
Associate Professor of Medicine (Rheumatology)
Clerkship Director, Internal Medicine
Georgetown University School of Medicine
Washington, DC

Jenny Wright, MD
Assistant Professor of Medicine
University of Washington School of Medicine
Seattle, Washington

Contents

9 Oncology

10 Pulmonary Medicine

11 Rheumatology

Previous Author Acknowledgments

ACP would like to thank the following people who contributed to earlier versions of the chapters listed below.

Cardiovascular Medicine
Chapter 2: Dr. Anna C. Maio
Chapter 5: Dr. Charin L. Hanlon
Chapter 6: Dr. Steven J. Durning, Dr. Mark C. Haigney,
   and Dr. Suma Pokala
Chapter 7: Dr. James L. Sebastian

Endocrinology and Metabolism
Chapter 15: Dr. Melissa A. McNeil and Dr. Janine M. Frank

Gastroenterology and Hepatology
Chapter 16: Dr. Priya Radhakrishnan
Chapter 17: Dr. Brown J. McCallum
Chapter 18: Dr. Brown J. McCallum and Dr. Shalini Reddy
Chapter 19: Dr. Brown J. McCallum
Chapter 26: Dr. Brown J. McCallum

General Internal Medicine
Chapter 34: Dr. Lawrence I. Kaplan and Dr. Rosa Lee
Chapter 37: Dr. Hugo A. Alvarez
Chapter 40: Dr. Lawrence I. Kaplan
Chapter 43: Dr. Ivonne Z. Jiménez-Velázquez
Chapter 46: Dr. Hanah Polotsky and Dr. Robert Jablonover

Hematology
Chapter 50: Dr. Mark M. Udden
Chapter 51: Dr. Mark M. Udden
Chapter 52: Dr. Diane C. Sliwka

Infectious Disease
Chapter 56: Dr. Robert W. Nelson, Jr.
Chapter 64: Dr. Charin L. Hanlon

Nephrology
Chapter 69: Dr. Tomoko Tanabe

Pulmonary Medicine
Chapter 89: Dr. Kevin D. Whittle

Rheumatology
Chapter 102: Dr. Kathryn A. Naus, Dr. Kyla Lokitz,
   and Dr. Seth Mark Berny
Chapter 103: Dr. Saba Khan and Dr. Seth Berney

High Value Care Recommendations

The High Value Care initiative of the American College of Physicians is an effort to improve health care outcomes by encouraging physicians to provide care with proven benefit and to reduce harms and costs by avoiding unnecessary interventions. The initiative integrates the important concept of health care value (balancing clinical benefit with costs and harms) for a given intervention into various educational materials to address the needs of medical students, trainees, practicing physicians, and patients.

To incorporate high value care principles into IM Essentials, we have highlighted high value care recommendations throughout this book (**in bold**) that meet the definition below. In addition, we have aggregated each section's recommendations at the beginning of the section so that they can be reviewed in one location.

High Value Care Recommendation: A recommendation to choose diagnostic and management strategies for patients in specific clinical situations that balance clinical benefit with cost and harms with the goal of improving patient outcomes.

Section I
Cardiovascular Medicine

Associate Editor – Robert Trowbridge, MD, FACP

High Value Care Recommendations

- Use of antioxidant vitamins or hormone replacement therapy in postmenopausal women is not recommended for coronary artery disease (CAD) risk reduction.

- Testing homocysteine levels should not be performed as part of routine cardiovascular risk assessment.

- The American Heart Association and Centers for Disease Control and Prevention do not recommend routine measurement of highly-sensitive C-reactive protein (hs-CRP), but measurement may be useful in patients with a moderate (10%-20%) 10-year risk of a first CAD event.

- Asymptomatic patients without cardiovascular risk factors should not undergo routine screening for CAD, either with electrocardiography or stress testing.

- Computed tomography (CT)-based coronary artery calcium scoring is an evolving technology with unclear benefit in predicting cardiovascular risk relative to traditional risk-prediction tools; it should therefore not be used routinely.

- Patients with a low probability of CAD do not require stress testing, and patients with a high probability of CAD should be started immediately on medical management, with consideration of coronary angiography if there is no response to therapy or if severe disease is suspected.

- Positron emission tomography (PET) with CT is a complex and expensive diagnostic modality and its appropriate role in evaluating chronic stable angina remains to be established.

- Patients with an abnormal stress test who do not have factors suggestive of severe CAD may benefit from initial medical management.

- Percutaneous coronary intervention (PCI; angioplasty and stent placement) has not been shown to reduce mortality or cardiovascular events in patients with stable CAD, but it has been shown to reduce angina and to improve quality of life. PCI is most appropriately used in patients who do not respond to medical therapy.

- Routine resting electrocardiograms (ECGs) are not recommended if there have been no changes in symptoms, examination findings, or medications. A repeat stress test is indicated if there is a change in symptoms but should not be performed routinely.

- Although newer oral anticoagulant medications do not require routine monitoring of their anticoagulation effect and may have several other potential advantages, they are significantly more expensive than warfarin.

- Echocardiography should not be used to screen for heart failure in asymptomatic patients without murmurs.

- Do not routinely measure B-type natriuretic peptide (BNP) in patients with typical signs and symptoms of heart failure.

- Once heart failure is diagnosed, serial chest radiographs are not sensitive to small changes in pulmonary vascular congestion and are not recommended.

- Combined treatment with an angiotensin-converting enzyme (ACE) inhibitor and an angiotensin receptor blocker (ARB) is not recommended as additional benefit of using these two medications together is not well established.

- Spironolactone is usually first-line therapy due to clinical experience and cost considerations; however, the more receptor-specific eplerenone may be useful in individuals developing gynecomastia with spironolactone.

- Echocardiographic reassessment of ejection fraction is most useful when there is a notable change in clinical status rather than at regular or arbitrary intervals.

- Not all systolic murmurs are pathologic. Short, soft systolic murmurs (grade <3) that are asymptomatic often do not require further investigation.

- Routine serial echocardiography is not needed in asymptomatic patients with prosthetic heart valves.

- For most patients, imaging studies are not needed for routine monitoring of peripheral artery disease (PAD), but may be indicated if intervention is felt to be needed.

- In patients with a low likelihood of disease, D-dimer testing may be useful in excluding the diagnosis of dissection.

- Screening for carotid stenosis is not recommended in the general population.

- Carotid artery stenting is usually associated with a higher risk of stroke than surgery and is not routinely performed in patients with carotid stenosis.

- Patients with a low clinical likelihood of deep vein thrombosis (DVT) should undergo testing with D-dimer as the combination of a low clinical probability, and negative D-dimer rules out DVT.

- There is no indication for routine screening for DVT in asymptomatic patients at risk for venous thromboembolism (VTE).

- Newer oral anticoagulation medications tend to be very expensive and their long-term safety remains to be established.

Chapter 1

Approach to Chest Pain

Eric Goren, MD

Chest pain is one of the most common complaints in internal medicine. The differential diagnosis of chest pain includes cardiac, pulmonary, gastrointestinal, musculoskeletal, and psychiatric causes (Table 1). In outpatients, the most common cause is musculoskeletal chest pain, although up to 12% of patients may have chest pain secondary to myocardial ischemia. A prudent approach to treating patients with acute chest pain focuses the initial evaluation on six potentially lethal conditions (the "serious six"): acute coronary syndrome, pulmonary embolism (PE), pericarditis/pericardial tamponade, pneumothorax, aortic dissection, and esophageal rupture.

Cardiac Causes

Acute coronary syndrome (ACS) is an important cause of acute chest pain. Although only 15% to 30% of patients presenting to emergency departments with nontraumatic chest pain have ACS, the 28-day mortality rate of ACS may be as high as 10%. ACS refers to a spectrum of diseases, including unstable angina, non-ST-segment elevation myocardial infarction, and ST-segment elevation myocardial infarction, based on electrocardiographic (ECG) changes and the presence of cardiac biomarkers (see Chapter 3). Patients with acute cardiac ischemia classically present with substernal pressure, tightness, or heaviness, with radiation to the jaw, shoulders, back, or arms. The pain may be accompanied by dyspnea, diaphoresis, and nausea. Up to 30% of patients, particularly those with diabetes mellitus, women, and the elderly, may present with atypical symptoms, such as dyspnea without chest pain. ACS should be particularly suspected in patients with atherosclerotic disease risk factors such as diabetes, hypertension, and hyperlipidemia.

The most powerful clinical features that increase the probability of myocardial infarction (MI) include chest pain that simultaneously radiates to both arms (positive likelihood ratio = 9.7) and an S_3 (positive likelihood ratio = 3.2). Pain that increases with exertion is

Table 1. Differential Diagnosis of Chest Pain

Disorder	Clinical Features/Notes
The "Serious Six"	
Acute coronary syndrome (see Chapter 3)	Frequent but not always exertional chest pain that is often not sharp or positional and radiates to both arms. Pain not easily reproducible. An S_3 is occasionally present. ECG changes or elevated cardiac enzymes in initial workup followed by stress testing or catheterization.
Pulmonary embolism (see Chapter 96)	Pleuritic chest pain and shortness of breath in patients at risk for thromboembolism. Clinical probability determined using Wells criteria. In low-probability patients, a normal D-dimer can exclude the diagnosis. If intermediate or high probability, ventilation-perfusion scan or spiral CT is indicated.
Pericarditis	Substernal chest discomfort that can be sharp, dull, or pressure-like in nature, often relieved with sitting forward; usually pleuritic. ECG changes may include ST-segment elevation (usually diffuse) or more specifically (but less commonly) PR-segment depression.
Pneumothorax (see Chapter 90)	Sudden onset of pleuritic chest pain and dyspnea in a smoker or COPD patient. Chest radiograph or CT scan confirms the diagnosis.
Aortic dissection (see Chapter 9)	Substernal chest pain with radiation to the back or midscapular region; often described as "tearing" or "ripping" pain. Pulse or blood pressure differential useful but uncommonly present. Chest radiograph may show a widened mediastinal silhouette, pleural effusion, or both.
Esophageal rupture	Intense retrosternal pain after vomiting; often associated with ethanol use. Pneumomediastinum on CXR can be seen.
Other Causes	
Aortic stenosis (see Chapter 8)	Chest pain with exertion, heart failure, syncope. Typical systolic murmur at the base of the heart radiating to the neck.
Panic attack	May be indistinguishable from angina. Often diagnosed after a negative evaluation for ischemic heart disease. Often associated with palpitations, sweating, and anxiety.
Musculoskeletal pain	Typically more reproducible chest pain. Includes muscle strain, costochondritis, and fracture. Should be a diagnosis of exclusion.
Esophagitis (see Chapter 18)	Burning-type chest discomfort usually precipitated by meals and not related to exertion. It is often worse upon lying down and improved with sitting.

COPD = chronic obstructive pulmonary disease; CT = computed tomography; CXR = chest x-ray; ECG = electrocardiographic; MI = myocardial infarction; VTE = venous thromboembolism.

also suggestive of ACS. Features that make an ischemic cause less likely include a normal ECG result (negative likelihood ratio = 0.1-0.3), chest pain that is positional (negative likelihood ratio = 0.3), chest pain reproduced by palpation (negative likelihood ratio = 0.2-0.4), or chest pain that is sharp or stabbing (negative likelihood ratio = 0.3). Patients suspected of having ACS are hospitalized and evaluated with serial ECGs and cardiac biomarkers. Low-risk patients without evidence of MI are evaluated with exercise or pharmacologic stress testing, as indicated. Higher-risk patients or those with ST-segment elevations undergo urgent cardiac catheterization.

Cocaine use can cause chest pain and ST-segment changes due to vasospasm, even in patients without significant occlusive coronary artery disease, and may result in myocardial injury.

Pericarditis is characterized by sudden onset of sharp, stabbing, substernal chest pain with radiation along the trapezius ridge. Often, the pain is worse with inspiration and lying flat and is alleviated with sitting and leaning forward. A pericardial friction rub is present in 85% to 100% of cases at some time during the course of pericarditis. Given the ephemeral nature of the friction rub, its absence does not rule out pericarditis. The classic rub consists of three components: occurring during atrial systole, ventricular systole, and ventricular diastole. A confirmatory ECG reading will show diffuse ST-segment elevation and P-R segment depression, findings that are specific but not sensitive (Figure 1). An echocardiogram may be helpful if there is suspicion of significant pericardial effusion or pericardial tamponade. Acute pericarditis secondary to infection (viral or bacterial) may be preceded or accompanied by symptoms of an upper respiratory tract infection and fever. In patients with acute pericarditis, hospitalization is prompted by an associated MI, pyogenic infection, or tamponade. Outpatient management is appropriate if other potentially serious causes of chest pain are excluded, hemodynamic status is normal, and a moderate or large pericardial effusion is excluded by echocardiography. In the absence of a specific cause for acute peri-

carditis, anti-inflammatory therapy with nonsteroidal anti-inflammatory drugs (NSAIDs) is the mainstay of treatment.

Patients with dissection of the thoracic aorta typically present with abrupt onset of severe, sharp, or "tearing" chest pain often radiating to the abdomen, or with back pain. Although dissection is fairly rare compared to other chest pain causes (an incidence of 3 per 100,000 patients per year), it can be rapidly life threatening. Aortic dissection can be associated with syncope due to decreased cardiac output, stroke, and MI caused by carotid or coronary artery occlusion/dissection, cardiac tamponade, and sudden death due to rupture of the aorta. Hypertension is present in 50% of patients and is not helpful diagnostically. A pulse differential (diminished pulse compared with the contralateral side) on palpation of the carotid, radial, or femoral arteries is one of the most useful findings but is uncommon (sensitivity of 30%; positive likelihood ratio = 5.7). An early diastolic murmur due to acute aortic insufficiency may be heard, particularly if the dissection involves the ascending aorta, but the presence or absence of a diastolic murmur is not useful in ruling in or ruling out dissection. Focal deficits on neurologic examination can be present in a few patients but are highly suggestive in the proper clinical context (positive likelihood ratio = 6.6-33.0).

In patients with dissection of the thoracic aorta, a wide mediastinum on a chest radiograph is the most common initial finding (sensitivity of 85%); the absence of this finding helps but does not completely rule out dissection (negative likelihood ratio = 0.3). When aortic dissection is suspected, imaging the aorta is indicated. Computed tomography or magnetic resonance imaging of the chest, transesophageal echocardiography, and aortic root angiography all have a high sensitivity and specificity for detecting a dissection flap; the specific diagnostic modality chosen depends on how quickly the examination can be performed and the patient's stability. Because of an increased risk of coronary artery dissection and tamponade with dissection progression, dissections involving the ascending aorta and

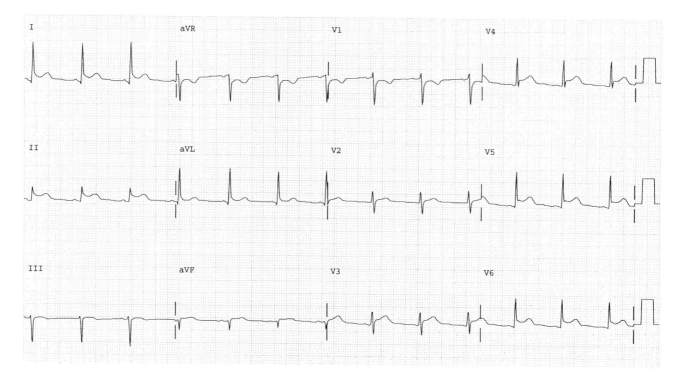

Figure 1. Electrocardiogram showing sinus rhythm with diffuse ST-segment elevation consistent with acute pericarditis. Note also the PR-segment depression in leads I, II, and V_4-V_6.

aortic arch are surgical emergencies. Dissections distal to the sub-clavian artery are usually treated medically to reduce the patient's blood pressure (intravenous β-blockers followed by sodium nitro-prusside, fenoldopam, or enalaprilat).

Aortic stenosis is a cause of exertional chest pain and may also be accompanied by dyspnea, palpitations, and exertional syncope due to a diminished cardiac output (see Chapter 8). Physical examina-tion reveals a systolic, crescendo-decrescendo murmur best heard at the second right intercostal space, with radiation to the right carotid artery. A transthoracic echocardiogram is the diagnostic test of choice for patients with suspected aortic stenosis.

Pulmonary Causes

Patients with PE may present with acute pleuritic chest pain (45% to 75% of cases), dyspnea, and, less often, cough and hemoptysis (see Chapter 96). Physical examination findings are nonspecific but may include tachypnea and tachycardia. ECG readings may also show findings of right ventricular strain, but the most common finding is sinus tachycardia. Wells criteria can help precisely define pretest probability of PE and dictate further testing. A negative D-dimer, a test for PE with a high specificity but low sensitivity, can exclude the diagnosis when clinical suspicion is low. When suspicion is moder-ate or high, however, a spiral computed tomography scan or a ven-tilation-perfusion lung scan is an appropriate initial approach

Pleuritic chest pain can also be a manifestation of pneumonia and is associated with fever, chills, cough, purulent sputum, and dyspnea (see Chapter 57). The physical examination may show wheezing or crackles and signs of consolidation, such as dullness to percussion, egophony, and bronchophony. Chest x-ray is considered the gold stan-dard for pneumonia diagnosis and is an appropriate initial diagnos-tic test for any case of chest pain with a possible pulmonary etiology.

Pneumothorax should be considered in any patient with sudden onset of pleuritic chest pain and dyspnea (see Chapter 90). It is most common in smokers, especially those with chronic obstructive pul-monary disease. The physical examination may reveal decreased breath sounds on the affected side; if a tension pneumothorax is present, hypotension and tracheal deviation to the opposite side of the pneumothorax may be noted. Chest radiography shows a lack of lung markings on the affected side. In tension pneumothorax, there is a shift of the mediastinum away from the side of the pneumotho-rax, whereas hydropneumothorax is identified by the presence of concomitant pleural fluid.

Gastrointestinal Causes

Gastroesophageal reflux disease (GERD) can also cause chest pain. Although sometimes difficult to differentiate from ischemic cardiac chest pain, GERD pain often lasts minutes to hours and resolves spontaneously or with antacids (see Chapter 18). Chest discomfort associated with GERD may also depend on the patient's position, being worse when lying down and after meals or upon awakening the patient from sleep. Other symptoms may include heartburn, regurgitation, chronic cough, sore throat, and hoarseness. On phys-ical examination, patients may exhibit wheezing, halitosis, dental erosions, and pharyngeal erythema. In unclear cases, it is most appropriate to exclude cardiac causes of chest pain before evaluating gastrointestinal causes. For patients with a high probability of GERD, empiric treatment with a proton pump inhibitor for 4 to 6 weeks is an appropriate initial diagnostic and therapeutic approach.

Patients with spontaneous esophageal rupture typically have severe retching and vomiting followed by excruciating retrosternal chest and upper abdominal pain. These symptoms are followed by the rapid development of odynophagia, tachypnea, dyspnea, cyanosis, fever, and shock. Many cases are related to excessive alcohol inges-tion. Chest radiography may show pneumomediastinum, although computed tomography is more sensitive for making this diagnosis.

Patients with acute cholecystitis frequently present with right upper quadrant and lower chest pain that may radiate to the right shoulder and is associated with nausea, vomiting, and fever (see Chapter 23). On physical examination, deep palpation during inspi-ration can elicit pain in the right upper quadrant and cause inspira-tory arrest (Murphy sign).

Musculoskeletal Causes

Musculoskeletal causes of chest pain are more common in women than in men. Frequent causes of musculoskeletal chest pain include costochondritis, arthritis, and shoulder rotator cuff injuries. Musculoskeletal chest pain has an insidious onset and may last for hours to weeks. It is most recognizable when sharp and localized to a specific area of the chest; however, it can also be poorly localized. The pain may be worsened by turning, deep breathing, or arm move-ment. Chest pain may or may not be reproducible by chest palpa-tion; pain reproduced by palpation does not exclude ischemic heart disease. The cardiovascular examination often is normal. For mus-culoskeletal chest pain, the history and physical examination are keys to the diagnosis; selected radiographic studies and laboratory tests may be indicated depending on the clinical circumstances.

Psychiatric Causes

Chest pain can be a manifestation of severe anxiety and panic attacks. Patients may complain of sweating, trembling, or shaking; sensations of choking, shortness of breath, or smothering; nausea or abdominal distress; or feeling dizzy, unsteady, or lightheaded. On physical exam-ination, tachycardia and tachypnea may be present, but the cardio-vascular and pulmonary examinations are otherwise unremarkable. Generalized anxiety and panic attacks may be treated with cognitive behavioral therapy and selective serotonin reuptake inhibitors or ven-lafaxine. Panic disorder stands alone among the anxiety spectrum disorders as a condition for which there is evidence that the combi-nation of cognitive behavioral therapy and pharmacotherapy is supe-rior to either treatment modality alone. Psychosomatic chest pain is a clinical diagnosis; other causes of chest pain are usually excluded by a careful history and physical examination.

Skin Causes

Herpes zoster can present in thoracic dermatomes and lead to chest pain. Pain is classically described as intense, burning, and localized to the dermatome involved. Physical exam reveals unilateral vesicu-lar lesions, although pain often precedes the appearance of these classic lesions. Pain persisting after the disappearance of the skin findings (postherpetic neuralgia) is also common.

Bibliography

Lee TH, Goldman L. Evaluation of the patient with acute chest pain. N Engl J Med. 2000;342:1187-1195. [PMID: 10770985]

McConaghy JR, Oza RS. Outpatient diagnosis of acute chest pain in adults. Am Fam Physician. 2013;87(3):177-182. [PMID: 23418761]

Chapter 2

Chronic Stable Angina

John Varras, MD

Angina is a sensation of chest discomfort secondary to myocardial ischemia, which classically occurs with exertion and is relieved by rest. Chronic stable angina often occurs with a predictable amount of exertion and is relieved by a predictable amount of rest or nitroglycerin, but it can vary based on several factors. Conditions that provoke angina do so by increasing myocardial oxygen demand, decreasing myocardial oxygen supply, or both. Myocardial oxygen demand is determined by heart rate, systolic blood pressure (afterload), myocardial contractility, and left ventricular wall stress, which is proportional to left ventricular end-diastolic volume (preload) and myocardial mass. Myocardial oxygen supply depends on coronary blood flow and perfusion pressure. The subendocardium, which is at greatest risk for ischemia, receives most of its blood supply during diastole; tachycardia, which shortens diastole, may cause ischemia. Some patients may not present with classic chest pain but may have other symptoms referred to as *anginal equivalents*. These symptoms can include dyspnea, weakness, syncope, and mental status changes. Dyspnea is the most frequent anginal equivalent and is difficult to differentiate from heart failure or pulmonary disease. The pathogenesis is an elevated left ventricular filling pressure induced by ischemia, which leads to vascular congestion. The most common cause of angina is coronary artery disease (CAD). Angina may also be present in the absence of coronary artery obstruction; these patients may have coronary vasospasm, aortic stenosis, hypertrophic cardiomyopathy, or systemic arterial hypertension.

Prevention

Cardiovascular risk factors should be identified and modified. Risk reduction efforts are particularly important in patients at high risk for CAD. Smoking cessation should be encouraged in all patients who smoke. Testing for dyslipidemia is recommended for men and women beginning at age 20 years if they have increased risk for CAD, defined as tobacco use, diabetes, hypertension, obesity (body mass index ≥30), a personal history of cardiovascular disease, or a family history of premature cardiovascular disease (before age 50 in male relatives and before age 50 in female relatives). Blood pressure should be checked at each office visit in patients 18 years of age and older to identify and treat hypertension. In patients with diabetes mellitus, risk factors for CAD should be treated aggressively; strict blood pressure and lipid control appear to provide additional benefits to patients with diabetes above those seen in the general population. The Framingham Risk Score (http://cvdrisk.nhlbi.nih.gov/calculator.asp[0]) allows estimation of the 10-year risk of CAD using age, gender, and other risk factors. A newer risk calculator, the Pooled Cohort Risk Equations (http://my.americanheart.org/professional/StatementsGuidelines/PreventionGuidelines/PreventionGuidelines_UCM_457698_SubHomePage.jsp), based on several additional patient databases in addition to the Framingham study cohort, has been developed to assess 10-year risk for atherosclerotic cardiovascular disease.

Primary prevention with aspirin (75-325 mg/day) should be considered in asymptomatic patients with a moderate (10%-20%) 10-year absolute risk of a first CAD event, barring any contraindication or risk factors for bleeding. All patients should be encouraged to engage in regular physical activity, such as brisk walking for ≥30 minutes 5 to 7 times per week. Dietary advice to all patients should include limiting refined sugars, cholesterol, and fat, particularly saturated fats, and eating a diet rich in fruits, vegetables, and fiber and low in sodium. **Use of antioxidant vitamins or hormone replacement therapy in postmenopausal women is not recommended for CAD risk reduction.** Although elevated homocysteine levels are associated with coronary events, reducing homocysteine levels has not been shown to improve outcomes. **Testing homocysteine levels should not be performed as part of routine cardiovascular risk assessment.** Cohort studies of healthy individuals have shown that the concentration of C-reactive protein measured by high-sensitivity assay (hs-CRP) modestly correlates with future risk of CAD independent of conventional risk factors. **The American Heart Association and Centers for Disease Control and Prevention do not recommend routine measurement of hs-CRP, but measurement may be useful in patients with a moderate (10%-20%) 10-year risk of a first CAD event.** Measurement of hs-CRP has been found to reclassify up to 30% of moderate-risk patients to either low- or high-risk status.

Screening

Asymptomatic patients without cardiovascular risk factors should not undergo routine screening for CAD, either with electrocardiography or stress testing. Although exercise testing may identify individuals with CAD, two factors limit the utility of routine stress testing in asymptomatic adults: false-positive results are common, and abnormalities of exercise testing do not accurately predict major cardiac events. **CT-based coronary artery calcium scoring is an evolving technology with unclear benefit in predicting cardiovascular risk relative to traditional risk-prediction tools; it should therefore not be used routinely.** It may be reasonable to use calcium scoring in select patients with an estimated 10% to 20% 10-year risk of coronary events, based on the possibility that such patients might be reclassified to a higher risk status and offered more aggressive risk management interventions.

Diagnosis

The pretest probability for CAD can be estimated (Table 1) based on the type of chest pain, patient age and gender, and presence of cardiac risk factors. Typical angina consists of three components: (1) substernal chest pain or discomfort of a usual duration and quality, (2) provocation by exertion or stress, and (3) relief by rest or nitroglycerin. Atypical angina has two of the three components, and

Table 1. Clinical Assessment of Pretest Probability of Coronary Artery Disease

| | Pretest Probability | | | | | |
| | Noncardiac Chest Pain[a] | | Atypical Chest Pain[b] | | Typical Chest Pain[c] | |
Age (y)	Men	Women	Men	Women	Men	Women
30-39	4	2	34	12	76	26
40-49	13	3	51	22	87	55
50-59	20	7	65	31	93	73
60-69	27	14	72	51	94	86

[a]Noncardiac chest pain has one or none of the components for typical chest pain.
[b]Atypical chest pain has two of the three components for typical chest pain.
[c]Typical chest pain has three components: (1) substernal chest pain or discomfort, (2) provocation by exertion or emotional stress, and (3) relief by rest and/or nitroglycerin.

Data from Diamond GA, Forrester JS. Analysis of probability as an aid in the clinical diagnosis of coronary artery disease. N Engl J Med. 1979;300:1350-1358. [PMID: 440357]

nonanginal chest pain has one or none of the components. Physical examination findings suggesting peripheral vascular or cerebrovascular disease increase the likelihood of CAD. Patients should be assessed for conditions that increase myocardial oxygen demand (eg, aortic stenosis, hypertrophic cardiomyopathy, uncontrolled hypertension, tachyarrhythmias, hyperthyroidism), conditions that diminish tissue oxygenation (eg, anemia, hypoxemia), and conditions that cause hyperviscosity (eg, polycythemia), all of which may precipitate angina in the setting of nonocclusive CAD. A complete blood count, thyroid-stimulating hormone level, or drug screen (eg, cocaine) should be obtained as indicated by the clinical situation.

A resting electrocardiogram (ECG) is obtained in all patients without a clearly nonanginal cause of chest pain. Chest radiography is useful in all patients with signs or symptoms of heart failure, valvular heart disease, pericardial disease, aortic dissection, or aneurysm. Standard echocardiography is obtained in patients with possible valvular disease, signs or symptoms of heart failure, or a history of myocardial infarction (MI).

Cardiac stress testing is the primary diagnostic method for evaluating angina (Figure 1). **Patients with a low probability of CAD do not require stress testing, and patients with a high probability of CAD should be started immediately on medical management, with consideration of coronary angiography if there is no response to therapy or if severe disease is suspected.** Noninvasive tests provide the most diagnostic information about patients with a moderate probability of CAD.

The choice of stress test is based on the patient's pretest probability of CAD, ability to exercise, and baseline ECG reading (Table 2). Exercise electrocardiography involves analysis of ECG tracings during physical exertion. In patients with significant resting ECG abnor-

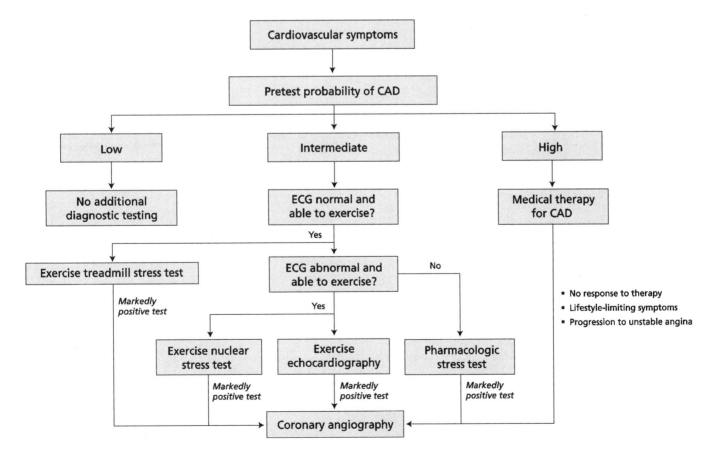

Figure 1. Diagnosis of coronary artery disease (CAD). ECG = electrocardiogram.

Table 2. Choice of Diagnostic Stress Test

Test	Notes
Exercise electrocardiography without imaging	Obtain in patients who have a moderate probability of CAD and are able to exercise, including patients with <1-mm ST-segment depression or complete right bundle branch block on resting ECG. Left ventricular hypertrophy with repolarization abnormality on resting ECG reduces the specificity of exercise treadmill testing.
Exercise electrocardiography with myocardial perfusion imaging or exercise echocardiography	Obtain in patients who have a moderate probability of CAD, are able to exercise, and have pre-excitation (Wolff-Parkinson-White syndrome) or >1-mm ST-segment depression on resting ECG. Also appropriate in patients with a moderate probability of CAD and a history of previous revascularization (PCI or CABG).
Pharmacologic stress myocardial perfusion imaging or dobutamine echocardiography	Obtain in patients with a moderate probability of CAD and an electronically paced ventricular rhythm or left bundle branch block. Also appropriate in patients with a moderate probability of CAD who are unable to exercise.

CABG = coronary artery bypass grafting; CAD = coronary artery disease; ECG = electrocardiogram; PCI = percutaneous coronary intervention.

malities on their baseline ECG that would make interpretation difficult, myocardial perfusion imaging using a radionuclide to indicate areas of ischemia or echocardiography to identify wall motion abnormalities caused by ischemia are used. In patients unable to perform adequate physical activity, pharmacologic agents (such as dipyridamole for myocardial perfusion imaging or dobutamine for echocardiography) are used to simulate stress conditions.

Exercise electrocardiography has a sensitivity of 65% to 70% and a specificity of 70% for diagnosing CAD; the sensitivity increases to 85% in patients with a completely normal baseline ECG reading. Exercise stress testing is preferred whenever possible because it provides additional prognostic information relating to the level of exercise attained. The greater degree of exercise performed improves the long-term prognosis, regardless of whether ischemia is detected. Myocardial perfusion imaging or stress echocardiography has similar sensitivity (80%-85%) and specificity (77%-88%). Pharmacologic stress tests are used in patients who cannot exercise or in patients with a left bundle branch block. In general, patients with normal results on exercise electrocardiography, myocardial perfusion imaging, or stress echocardiography have a good prognosis. Patients with indeterminate results or suspicious clinical histories may require additional testing based on the clinical scenario. Those with markedly abnormal stress tests indicating multivessel disease should be considered for cardiac catheterization and possible revascularization.

CT angiography (CTA) is a newer modality that can provide information about the coronary anatomy but does not assess ischemia. Although noninvasive, CTA requires intravenous contrast, exposes the patient to significant radiation, and is prone to discovering incidental findings (such as lung nodules). Trials of CTA in detecting significant CAD show good sensitivity (85%-96%) and specificity (74%-90%), and current guidelines suggest CTA as an option in moderate-risk patients; however, the appropriate role of this test in evaluating chronic stable angina is continuing to evolve.

Positron emission tomography (PET) with CT is another imaging option that combines myocardial perfusion imaging with anatomical imaging. Initial data show good sensitivity (92%) and specificity (85%), and it may be particularly useful in obese patients. **PET with CT is a complex and expensive diagnostic modality and its appropriate role in evaluating chronic stable angina remains to be established.**

Coronary angiography is the gold standard that should be considered in patients at high risk for severe CAD, patients with inconclusive results on noninvasive testing, patients with chronic angina that is increasing in severity, patients with markedly abnormal stress test results, and patients with an episode of sudden cardiac death or

ventricular tachycardia. Severe coronary artery disease includes two- or three-vessel disease, which would be amenable to invasive treatments, such as percutaneous coronary interventions or coronary artery bypass grafting. **Patients with an abnormal stress test who do not have factors suggestive of severe CAD may benefit from initial medical management.** Risks associated with angiography include use of contrast, cholesterol emboli, and bleeding.

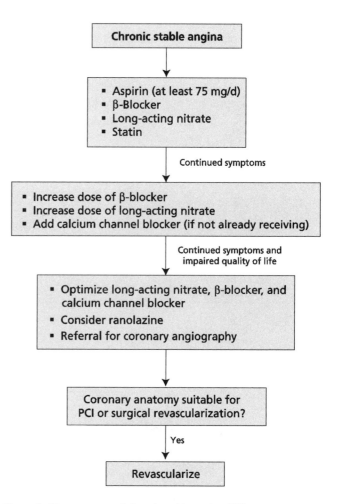

Figure 2. Management of chronic stable angina. PCI = percutaneous coronary intervention.

Therapy

Risk factor modification is vital to the treatment of patients with chronic stable angina. Patients who smoke should be advised to stop smoking. All patients should be encouraged to engage in at least 30 to 60 minutes of moderate physical activity 5 to 7 days a week and to maintain a healthy body weight. In addition, all patients should be encouraged to eat a heart-healthy diet low in saturated fat and cholesterol and rich in plant stanols/sterols.

The goals of medical therapy include reducing episodes of angina, preventing progression of atherosclerotic lesions, preventing cardiovascular events, and improving survival. Medical therapy has been shown to be as effective as early revascularization. Drug therapy can be divided into antianginal medications (eg, β-blockers, calcium channel blockers, nitrates) and vascular protective medications (eg, antiplatelet agents, statins, angiotensin-converting enzyme [ACE] inhibitors) (Figure 2).

β-Blockers are first-line therapy in most patients with chronic stable angina; these medications reduce angina severity and frequency by reducing heart rate and myocardial contractility. β-Blockers have been shown to reduce mortality after MI and are used to treat heart failure. Absolute contraindications include severe bradycardia and decompensated heart failure. β-Blockers are often well tolerated by patients with mild to moderate chronic obstructive pulmonary disease, asthma, and diabetes.

Calcium channel blockers are indicated for patients who cannot tolerate β-blockers or whose symptoms are inadequately controlled with β-blockers. Calcium channel blockers produce vasodilation, increase coronary blood flow, and reduce myocardial contractility.

Non-dihydropyridine agents (eg, verapamil, diltiazem) have a greater effect on myocardial contractility and conduction and should be avoided in patients with heart failure or bradycardia. Dihydropyridine agents have a greater vasodilatory effect and can be used together with β-blockers and in patients with heart failure. Short-acting calcium channel blockers are contraindicated because of their association with increased risk of MI and, possibly, mortality.

Long-acting nitrates can be used in combination with or instead of β-blockers or calcium channel blockers (if these agents are not tolerated). Nitrates alleviate symptoms of angina by causing dilation of epicardial coronary vessels and increasing capacitance of the venous system, resulting in diminished cardiac preload and myocardial oxygen demand. Nitrates are usually withheld overnight to mitigate nitrate tolerance. Nitrates must be avoided in patients taking phosphodiesterase-5 inhibitors (eg, sildenafil, vardenafil, and tadalafil).

Ranolazine is a selective inhibitor of a late sodium channel that may lead to favorable effects on diastolic function in patients with severe chronic angina. It is generally reserved for patients with inadequate response to standard antianginal therapy and has been shown to reduce angina by about one episode per week without affecting the heart rate or blood pressure. Aspirin is prescribed unless there is a history of significant gastrointestinal bleeding or aspirin allergy. Aspirin reduces platelet aggregation and acute coronary events and decreases the risk of MI and death. It should be used in all patients with CAD, especially those who have had an MI.

Thienopyridine derivatives (eg, clopidogrel, ticlopidine, and prasugrel) should be used in patients who have contraindications to aspirin or who have other indications (eg, recent stent placement, acute coronary syndrome). The data do not provide convincing sup-

Table 3. Drug Treatment of Chronic Stable Angina

Agent	Notes
β-Blockers	First-line agents. Reduce heart rate, myocardial contractility, and arterial pressure, resulting in decreased myocardial oxygen demand. Used in patients with a history of MI and in stable heart failure.
Dihydropyridine calcium channel blockers (eg, amlodipine, felodipine, nifedipine)	Second-line agents. Reduce blood pressure; do not affect heart rate and can be used with β-blockers. Avoid short-acting agents (such as nifedipine).
Nondihydropyridine calcium channel blockers (verapamil, diltiazem)	Second-line agents. Reduce blood pressure; negative chronotropy and inotropy reduce myocardial oxygen demand. Mostly used in patients who cannot take β-blockers. Avoid in patients with heart failure; use with caution in patients taking β-blockers (bradycardia).
ACE inhibitors	Reduce blood pressure and afterload by a reduction in peripheral vascular resistance. Reduce ventricular remodeling and fibrosis after infarction. Improve long-term survival in patients with LVEF ≤40% and, possibly, in patients with high cardiovascular risk (eg, diabetes mellitus, PVD). Side effects include cough, hyperkalemia, kidney failure, and angioedema.
Long-acting nitrates	Second-line agents. Can be used with β-blockers and calcium channel blockers. Tachyphylaxis occurs with continued use; requires nitrate-free period (8-12 h/d). Side effects include headache. Avoid in patients taking PDE-5 inhibitors.
Short-acting nitrates	Dilate coronary arteries and reduce preload. Indicated for all patients with chronic stable angina for use on an as-needed basis.
Ranolazine	Indicated as add-on therapy for patients not responding to standard therapy; used in combination with a nitrate, β-blocker, or calcium channel blocker. Avoid using with verapamil or diltiazem (prolongs QT interval).
Aspirin	Indicated for all patients with stable angina, barring contraindications; reduces major cardiovascular events by 33%.
Thienopyridine derivatives (eg, clopidogrel, ticlopidine, prasugrel)	Aspirin alternatives, but significantly more expensive. Improve outcomes in patients with recent ACS or stent placement. In patients with stable CAD, thienopyridine derivatives do not improve outcomes.
Statins	In patients with mild to moderate elevations in total and LDL cholesterol and a history of MI, statins are associated with a 24% risk reduction for fatal and nonfatal MI.

ACE = angiotensin-converting enzyme; ACS = acute coronary syndrome; CAD = coronary artery disease; LDL = low-density lipoprotein; LVEF = left ventricular ejection fraction; MI = myocardial infarction; PDE-5 = phosphodiesterase-5; PVD = peripheral vascular disease.

port for the use of these agents in patients with chronic stable angina, in which the risk of bleeding may outweigh the benefits.

In patients with CAD, high-intensity statin therapy (to lower the low-density lipoprotein [LDL] cholesterol level by ≥50%) should be prescribed for patients ≤75 years; moderately intensive statin therapy (to reduce the LDL cholesterol level by 30% to <50%) should be given to patients older than 75 years.

Treatment with an ACE inhibitor reduces mortality most dramatically in patients with heart failure and reduced left ventricular function (ejection fraction <40%). Treatment also reduces mortality and cardiovascular events in high-risk patients with vascular disease, diabetes, and other risk factors as well as patients with stable CAD and preserved left ventricular function who are at higher risk. Table 3 summarizes drug treatment options for patients with chronic stable angina.

Percutaneous coronary intervention (PCI; angioplasty and stent placement) has not been shown to reduce mortality or cardiovascular events in patients with stable CAD, but it has been shown to reduce angina and to improve quality of life. PCI is most appropriately used in patients who do not respond to medical therapy. It may also be used in patients who are at increased risk of complications after CABG or who those prefer PCI.

Coronary artery bypass grafting (CABG) is used to treat patients with extensive CAD who are at increased risk of complications. It has been shown to improve mortality in patients with left main coronary artery stenosis, three-vessel disease, and, possibly, two-vessel disease (if it includes the left anterior descending coronary artery). In patients with diabetes, CABG is associated with improved clinical outcomes (eg, death, MI, stroke, revascularization) as compared with PCI.

Follow-Up

Regular follow-up visits should address angina symptoms, medication use, and modifiable risk factors; patients should be seen every 4 to 12 months, depending on their stability. **Routine resting ECGs are not recommended if there have been no changes in symptoms, examination findings, or medications. A repeat stress test is indicated if there is a change in symptoms but should not be performed routinely.**

Bibliography

Qaseem A, Fihn SD, Williams S, et al. Diagnosis of stable ischemic heart disease: summary of a clinical practice guideline from the American College of Physicians/American College of Cardiology Foundation/American Heart Association/American Association for Thoracic Surgery/Preventive Cardiovascular Nurses Association/Society of Thoracic Surgeons. Ann Intern Med. 2012;157(10):729-734. [PMID: 23165664]

Qaseem A, Fihn SD, Dallas P, et al. Management of stable ischemic heart disease: summary of a clinical practice guideline from the American College of Physicians/American College of Cardiology Foundation/American Heart Association/American Association for Thoracic Surgery/Preventive Cardiovascular Nurses Association/Society of Thoracic Surgeons. Ann Intern Med. 2012;157(10):735-743. [PMID: 23165665]

Chapter 3

Acute Coronary Syndrome

Michael Picchioni, MD

The term *acute coronary syndrome* (ACS) refers collectively to the set of clinical scenarios involving acute myocardial ischemia. The ACS spectrum encompasses unstable angina (UA), non–ST-segment elevation myocardial infarction (NSTEMI), and ST-segment elevation myocardial infarction (STEMI); because UA and NSTEMI represent a continuum and may be difficult to distinguish clinically, they may be referred to as non-ST segment elevation acute coronary syndromes (NSTE-ACS).

The common pathophysiology of ACS is characterized by atherosclerotic plaque rupture leading to the formation of a platelet and fibrin thrombus and local release of vasoactive substances. UA and NSTEMI are most commonly caused by a nonocclusive thrombus, while STEMI usually involves complete vessel occlusion. Additional causes of ACS include spontaneous vasospasm of an epicardial coronary artery (variant or Prinzmetal angina) or spasm due to cocaine use. Myocardial cell death can also develop when there is significant "demand" ischemia, such as when illness or arrhythmia leads to marked tachycardia or if there is sufficient hypoxemia or anemia. Such situations usually involve some degree of underlying coronary stenosis without the dynamic and threatening nature of clot formation and infrequently result in significant cardiac complications. The management of each form of ACS is based on the pathophysiology of the underlying condition.

Patients with STEMI exhibit a clinical presentation consistent with individuals who have acute myocardial infarction (MI) and electrocardiogram (ECG) evidence of ST-segment elevation. UA and NSTEMI are closely related and differ only in the severity of ischemia. NSTEMI is associated with elevated biomarkers of myocardial injury,

whereas UA is not; however, the principles of risk stratification and therapy are identical for both. It is critical to distinguish between STEMI and UA/NSTEMI because of the immediate implications for management. Patients with STEMI benefit from immediate reperfusion therapy consisting of coronary angiography, angioplasty, and stenting (percutaneous coronary intervention [PCI]), or thrombolysis. Patients with UA or NSTEMI angina require immediate medical therapy followed by risk stratification to determine the risk for nonfatal MI or death, which determines the need for angiography versus a more conservative approach with medical therapy alone.

Prevention and Screening

The principles of primary prevention and screening for ACS are discussed in Chapter 2, Chronic Stable Angina.

Diagnosis

Recognizing ACS is crucial to reduce morbidity and mortality. Unfortunately, the presentation can be quite variable. The pain of ACS is often described as a pressure or discomfort that is retrosternal in location. It may radiate to the shoulders, arms, or neck and may be associated with diaphoresis or shortness of breath. Typical angina is also characterized by onset with exertion and relief with rest or administration of nitroglycerin. Gastrointestinal symptoms such as nausea and vomiting can be experienced, particularly with an inferior MI, and patients often confuse chest pain from coronary

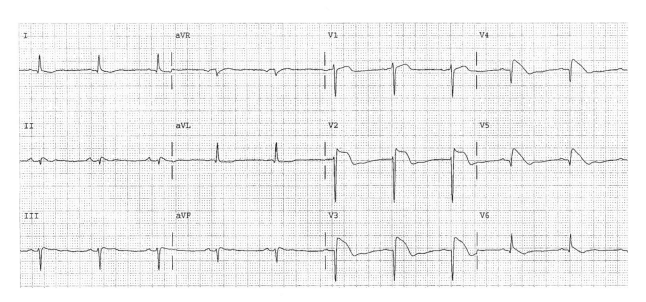

Figure 1. Electrocardiogram showing abnormal Q waves in leads V_3-V_5 and ST-segment elevation in leads V_2-V_5. The T waves are beginning to invert in leads V_3-V_6. This pattern is most consistent with a recent anterolateral myocardial infarction.

ischemia with heartburn or indigestion. The most common reason for failure to diagnose ACS is that the patient presents with atypical symptoms such as dyspnea, fatigue, nausea, abdominal discomfort, or syncope; thus, any of these symptoms, with or without chest discomfort, should always prompt consideration of ACS. Up to 25% of patients with ACS–particularly women, older persons, and patients with diabetes–present with atypical symptoms. Chest pain that is pleuritic, sharp, stabbing, or positional significantly decreases the likelihood of ACS.

The physical examination should focus on conditions that can mimic ACS (eg, pericarditis, aortic dissection) and conditions that influence prognosis and treatment decisions (eg, heart failure). Physical examination in patients with ACS is often normal, but hypotension, asymmetric blood pressures, distended neck veins, a new murmur, a pericardial friction rub, an S_3 gallop, and dependent pulmonary crackles are important findings to identify. A new murmur may suggest valvular incompetence caused by papillary muscle dysfunction or rupture. Heart failure may be present if ischemia results in left ventricular dysfunction or valvular incompetence and is associated with high risk for death.

The initial ECG is an extremely important yet limited tool in evaluating patients with possible ACS (Figure 1). The ECG may be nondiagnostic in half of patients; therefore, serial ECGs are recommended (eg, every 20 minutes for 2 hours). The diagnostic yield of the ECG is improved if a tracing can be recorded during an episode of chest discomfort. Diagnostic criteria for STEMI are outlined in Table 1. These typically include ST-segment elevations >1 mm in two or more contiguous leads, a new left bundle branch block, or evidence of true posterior infarction on ECG. NSTEMI is defined by elevated cardiac biomarkers and absence of diagnostic ST-segment elevation. NSTEMI is often associated with ST-segment depression or T-wave changes. The anatomic location and involved vasculature may be suggested by ECG findings (Table 2). A persistently normal ECG result decreases the probability of ACS but does not rule it out.

With prolonged ischemia, cardiac myocytes lose membrane integrity and leak specific proteins (eg, cardiac troponins) into the serum. By serially measuring these proteins at 0, and 3 to 6 hours, evidence of myocardial damage within the previous 24 hours can be detected. Measurement of cardiac troponin T or troponin I, which peak at 3 to 6 hours and remain elevated for days, is indicated for diagnosis. Cardiac troponins, and particularly troponin T, may be elevated in patients with kidney failure. In that setting, use of troponin I is preferred; alternatively, the rise in troponin level can be more meaningful than the absolute value when baseline levels are elevated. In patients with acute ST-segment elevations, reperfusion therapy should not be delayed pending the return of biomarker studies.

Coronary angiography provides detailed information about the coronary anatomy and facilitates invasive management of occluded coronary arteries. PCI is the preferred reperfusion therapy in specific subsets of patients with ACS (ie, STEMI, new left bundle branch block, or true posterior infarction). Early cardiac catheterization during hospitalization for ACS should be considered for patients with recurrent ischemic symptoms, serious complications, or other intermediate- to high-risk features (eg, heart failure, left ventricular dysfunction, ventricular arrhythmias). These complications and high-risk features are associated with more severe coronary artery disease and subsequent cardiac events. Cardiac catheterization also is routinely indicated for stable high-risk patients following successful thrombolytic therapy.

Therapy

The primary goals of therapy for patients with ACS are to reduce the amount of myocardial injury with preservation of left ventricular function as well as preventing and treating major complications. Preserving left ventricular function is accomplished by eliminating or minimizing ischemia by addressing both the supply and demand of oxygen within myocardial cells. Major complications include arrhythmia, pulmonary edema, and cardiogenic shock. To detect these early, all patients with ACS should be admitted for continuous cardiac monitoring.

Multiple medical therapies are given to most patients with ACS. Effective analgesia early in the course of ACS is an important therapeutic intervention. Morphine sulfate reduces sympathetic tone through a centrally mediated anxiolytic affect. Morphine also reduces myocardial oxygen demand by reducing preload and through a vagally mediated reduction in pulse rate.

Unless there are compelling contraindications, all patients presenting with presumed ACS should be treated with dual antiplatelet therapy. Patients should chew an aspirin tablet to rapidly achieve therapeutic blood levels. Thienopyridines (eg, clopidogrel, prasugrel, ticagrelor) block the adenosine diphosphate $P2Y_{12}$ receptor on platelets, preventing aggregation. A loading dose followed by a maintenance dose of thienopyridine should be added to background aspirin therapy (162-325 mg/day).

Patients should also receive a β-blocker or calcium channel blocker. Cardioselective β-blockers should be given to all patients except those with decompensated heart failure, systolic blood pressure <90 mm Hg, pulse rate <50 bpm, or second-degree atrioventricular block. Oral β-blockers are typically used for most patients. Calcium channel blockers, with the exception of nifedipine, can be used in patients with contraindications to β-blockers and in those with continued angina despite optimal doses of β-blockers and nitrates. β-Blockers should not be used in patients with STEMI precipitated by cocaine or those with variant angina because of the risk of potentiating coronary artery spasm.

Table 1. ECG Criteria for STEMI

ECG Change	Two or More Contiguous ECG Leads	Comments
ST-segment elevation	II, III, aVF	≥0.1 mV[a] at J-point for most leads
	V_1-V_3	≥0.15 mV for V_2-V_3 for women
	V_4-V_6	≥0.2 mV for V_2-V_3 for men ≥40 y
	I, aVL	≥0.25 mV for V_2-V_3 for men <40 y
ST-segment depression (indicates true posterior wall MI)	V_1-V_3	≥0.1 mV [b]; often has tall R waves in V_1-V_3
New LBBB	n/a	New finding or presumed new

[a]0.1 mV = 1 mm on standard ECG tracing.
[b]Alternatively may have ST-elevation in "extended leads" (V_7-V_9) placed posteriorly.
ECG = electrocardiographic; LBBB = left bundle branch block; MI = myocardial infarction; n/a = not applicable; STEMI = ST-segment elevation myocardial infarction.

Table 2. ECG Leads and Anatomic Correlates

Indicative ECG Leads	Anatomic Location	Coronary Artery
II, III, aVF	Inferior	RCA
V_1-V_3	Anteroseptal	LAD
V_4-V_6; possible elevations in I and aVL	Lateral and apical	LCx
V_1-V_3 (ST depression)	Posterior wall[a]	"Dominant" vessel (RCA or LCx)
V_4R[b]	Right ventricle[a]	Right coronary artery

[a]Often associated with inferior and/or lateral ST-elevation infarctions and tall R wave in V_1.
[b]Indicates a precordial lead placed at the V_4 position on the right side of the chest.
ECG = electrocardiographic; LAD = left anterior descending artery; LCx = left circumflex artery, RCA = right coronary artery.

Nitrates have several mechanisms of action that can be beneficial. Although they decrease vasospasm, their primary benefit in ACS is reduction of myocardial oxygen consumption by reducing preload. Sublingual nitroglycerin should be given to all patients with ACS experiencing chest pain; an exception is that in individuals with an inferior STEMI and presumed right ventricular infarction, treatment-related hypotension may occur. Intravenous nitroglycerin should be initiated for patients with continued chest pain without hypotension. Transdermal or oral nitrates should be used for patients with UA or NSTEMI who have had recent episodes of chest pain but have no active symptoms at presentation.

Because thrombus is a major part of the pathophysiology of ACS, anticoagulants are an important adjunct to antiplatelet therapy. All but low-risk patients with concern for ACS are treated with heparin. Advantages of low-molecular-weight heparin (LMWH) include twice-daily subcutaneous administration and achievement of predictable levels of anticoagulation without the need for laboratory monitoring. LMWH should be avoided in patients who are obese or those with chronic kidney disease. Patients treated with stenting also require heparin therapy; unfractionated heparin is often preferred to LMWH in patients receiving thrombolytics or undergoing PCI because of the ease with which the degree of anticoagulation can be monitored or reversed. Once started, therapeutic anticoagulation is usually continued for at least 48 hours.

In patients with STEMI, reperfusion therapy is the mainstay of treatment. PCI is preferred because it is associated with a lower 30-day mortality rate compared with thrombolytic therapy. PCI in patients with STEMI should ideally be performed within 90 minutes of presentation to a facility with PCI capability or within 120 minutes if the patient requires transfer from a non–PCI-capable hospital. PCI is also indicated in patients with a contraindication to thrombolytic therapy and in patients with cardiogenic shock. PCI is most effective if completed within 12 hours of chest pain onset; the earlier the intervention, the better the outcome. PCI may still be reasonable in selected patients beyond this window.

PCI is a catheter-based, nonsurgical mechanical opening of an occluded vessel, often with the placement of a stent to maintain patency of the artery. Stents may be bare metal or drug eluting, which is a metallic stent with a polymer covering containing an antirestenotic drug that is released over a period of 14 to 30 days. Because of their greater effectiveness, drug-eluting stents have further increased the clinical advantage of PCI over thrombolytic therapy. The drug also impedes the process of epithelialization, however, requiring dual antiplatelet therapy for a longer period of time to prevent stent occlusion. For this reason, bare metal stents are preferred if there is a high risk of bleeding or if the patient will be unlikely to tolerate the prolonged period of dual antiplatelet therapy. Glycoprotein IIb/IIIa inhibitors (eg, tirofiban, eptifibatide, abcix-imab) act by occupying platelet receptors that would otherwise bind with fibrinogen, thus preventing platelet aggregation. They are also extremely beneficial in patients undergoing PCI, and early administration improves coronary patency.

In the United States, approximately 70% of patients with STEMI present to hospitals without onsite PCI capabilities; therefore, thrombolytic therapy is the predominant method of reperfusion in those who are unable to be transported to a PCI-capable facility within 120 minutes. By lysing the clot that is limiting blood flow to the myocardium, thrombolytics restore perfusion to the ischemic area, reduce infarct size, and improve survival. Thrombolytics should be administered within 12 hours after the onset of chest pain; the earlier the administration, the better the outcome. Patients receiving thrombolytic therapy require concomitant heparin therapy. Absolute contraindications to thrombolytic therapy include any prior intracerebral hemorrhage, known cerebrovascular lesions (eg, tumor or arteriovenous malformation), suspected aortic dissection, active bleeding or bleeding diathesis, significant closed head or facial trauma within 3 months, and ischemic stroke within 3 months. Relative contraindications include uncontrolled hypertension at presentation (blood pressure >180 mm Hg systolic and/or >110 mm Hg diastolic), history of ischemic stroke more than 3 months previously, traumatic or prolonged (>10 minutes) cardiopulmonary resuscitation, major surgery within the preceding 3 weeks, internal bleeding within the preceding 2 to 4 weeks, or an active peptic ulcer.

In patients with UA or NSTEMI, urgent PCI or thrombolysis do not improve outcomes. Instead, the 14-day risk for nonfatal MI or death in patients presenting with UA or NSTEMI is usually estimated using the Thrombolysis in Myocardial Infarction (TIMI) risk score (Table 3). The TIMI risk score identifies patients who will derive the greatest benefit from aggressive medical therapy or an early invasive treatment approach. TIMI scores of 0 to 2 are considered low risk and are typically treated with a conservative approach with medical therapy and predischarge cardiac stress testing; coronary angiography is performed if the stress test result is abnormal. Intermediate (3-4) and high-risk (5-7) TIMI scores identify patients who may benefit from addition of a glycoprotein IIb/IIIa inhibitor to standard medical therapy and consideration for early coronary angiography.

The role of coronary artery bypass graft surgery in the treatment of ACS is limited to patients with STEMI who have coronary anatomy that is not amenable to PCI or those with ongoing ischemia, cardiogenic shock, or severe heart failure. An intra-aortic balloon pump is indicated for patients who have ACS with cardiogenic shock unresponsive to medical therapy, acute mitral regurgitation secondary to papillary muscle dysfunction, ventricular septal rupture, or refractory angina. The intra-aortic balloon pump reduces afterload during ventricular systole and increases coronary perfusion during diastole.

Table 3. TIMI Risk Score for Unstable Angina/Non–ST-Segment Elevation Myocardial Infarction

Prognostic Variables

Age ≥65 y

≥3 traditional CAD risk factors[a]

Documented CAD with ≥50% diameter stenosis

ST-segment deviation

≥2 anginal episodes in the past 24 h

Aspirin use in the past wk

Elevated cardiac biomarkers (creatine kinase–MB or troponin)

TIMI Risk Score (Sum of Prognostic Variables)

0-2 low risk

3-4 intermediate risk

5-7 high risk

[a]Family history of CAD, hypertension, hypercholesterolemia, diabetes mellitus, being a current smoker.
Data from Antman EM, Cohen M, Bernink PJ, et al. The TIMI risk score for unstable angina/non-ST elevation MI: a method for prognostication and therapeutic decision making. JAMA. 2000;284(7):835-842. [PMID: 10938172]
CAD = coronary artery disease.

The final phase of hospital therapy for patients with ACS includes initiation of angiotensin-converting enzyme (ACE) inhibitor therapy, statin therapy, and, in certain individuals, an aldosterone antagonist. ACE inhibitors can attenuate ventricular remodeling, resulting in a reduction in the development of heart failure and risk of death. ACE inhibitors may also reduce the risk of recurrent infarction and other vascular events. They should be given within 24 hours in all patients with heart failure or a left ventricular ejection fraction ≤40%. In patients who cannot tolerate an ACE inhibitor, an angiotensin-receptor blocker is a reasonable alternative. Early statin therapy appears to improve endothelial function and to reduce the risk of future coronary events. The concept of plaque stabilization and improvement in endothelial function suggests that there is a benefit to statin therapy in ACS beyond reducing low-density lipoprotein cholesterol. Aldosterone antagonists (eg, spironolactone, eplerenone) have favorable effects on the neurohumoral profile and limit collagen formation and ventricular remodeling. They are recommended for use following ACS in patients with a left ventricular ejection fraction ≤40% and clinical heart failure or diabetes. They should be used with great caution, however, or not at all in patients with kidney disease (creatinine >2.5 mg/dL [88.4 µmol/L]) or pre-existing hyperkalemia (potassium >5.0 meq/L [5 mmol/L]).

Mechanical complications of STEMI and NSTEMI occur between days 2 and 7. These complications include ventricular septal defect, papillary muscle rupture leading to acute mitral valve regurgitation, and left ventricular free wall rupture leading to cardiac tamponade.

Ventricular septal defect and papillary muscle rupture usually lead to a new, loud systolic murmur and acute pulmonary edema or hypotension. Diagnosis is critical because the 24-hour survival rate is approximately 25% with medical therapy alone but increases to 50% with emergency surgical intervention. Pericardial tamponade from free wall rupture usually leads to sudden hypotension, pulseless electrical activity on electrocardiography, and death.

Follow-Up

Early cardiac catheterization during hospitalization for ACS should be considered for patients with recurrent ischemic symptoms, serious complications, or other intermediate- to high-risk features (eg, heart failure, left ventricular dysfunction, ventricular arrhythmias). Cardiac catheterization is also routinely indicated for stable high-risk patients following successful thrombolytic therapy. Nonemergent bypass surgery is preferred in patients who are found to have a large amount of myocardium at ischemic risk due to proximal left main disease or multivessel disease, especially if the left ventricular ejection fraction is reduced. Post-MI exercise testing in patients without high-risk features is performed as a prognostic assessment. By doing stress testing early post-MI, the clinician can assess functional capacity, evaluate efficacy of the patient's current medical regimen, and assess the risk of future cardiac events.

Secondary prevention measures are an essential component of outpatient management following ACS and include management of hypertension and diabetes, lipid lowering, smoking cessation, and an exercise program. Aspirin, β-blockers, and ACE inhibitors should be continued indefinitely. High-dose statin therapy should also be continued indefinitely. A thienopyridine should be continued for at least 1 year for patients who receive medical or thrombolytic therapy. Patients with coronary stents should take aspirin and a thienopyridine for at least 1 month for a bare metal stent and for at least 1 year following placement of a drug-eluting stent.

Studies indicate that approximately 20% of patients experience depression after acute MI and that depression is associated with increased risk for recurrent hospitalization and death. Post-MI, patients should be screened for depression.

Bibliography

O'Gara PT, Kushner FG, Ascheim DD, et al. 2013 ACCF/AHA Guideline for the Management of ST-Elevation Myocardial Infarction: Executive Summary: A Report of the American College of Cardiology Foundation/American Heart Associate Task Force on Practice Guidelines. Circulation. 2013;127:529-555. [PMID: 23247303]

Amsterdam EA, Wenger NK, Brindis RG, et al. 2014 AHA/ACC Guideline for the Management of Patients With Non-ST-Elevation Acute Coronary Syndromes: A Report of the American College of Cardiology/American Heart Association Task Force on Practice Guidelines. Circulation. 2014 Sep 23. [PMID: 25249585]

Chapter 4

Conduction Blocks and Bradyarrhythmias

Robert Trowbridge, MD

Cardiac conduction defects and bradyarrhythmias are most commonly the result of idiopathic degeneration of the conduction system, myocardial disease (eg, coronary artery disease, amyloidosis, Lyme disease, hypertension), or medication effects (eg, calcium channel blockers, β-blockers, digoxin, cholinesterase inhibitors). Any level of the conduction system may be affected, including the sinoatrial (SA) node, the atrioventricular (AV) node, and the ventricular system (eg, bundle of His, right and left bundle branches). Depending on the level and severity of the conduction defect, clinical manifestations range from electrocardiographic abnormalities without clinical effects (eg, right bundle branch block [RBBB], first-degree AV block) to symptomatic bradycardia manifesting as lightheadedness, syncope, and sudden death.

Bradyarrhythmias

Evaluation of bradyarrhythmia centers on identifying underlying cardiac and systemic disease as well as assessing potential medication effects. Accordingly, therapy includes removing offending agents, treating underlying disorders, and considering permanent pacemaker placement. In general, pacemaker placement is not appropriate unless symptoms are present or if there is a high likelihood of progression to symptomatic disease (Table 1).

SA node disease is common in the elderly as a result of idiopathic degeneration of the cardiac conducting system. The spectrum of SA node disease includes sinus bradycardia, sinus arrest, and the bradycardia-tachycardia (brady-tachy) syndrome (sometimes called "sick sinus syndrome"). Sinus bradycardia is often asymptomatic but, if severe, may manifest as lightheadedness, weakness, or syncope. Most cases do not require intervention. Sinus arrest appears as prolonged sinus pauses of 2 seconds or more on electrocardiography and may also cause syncope. Brady-tachy syndrome is a subtype of SA node disease in which bradycardia or pauses occur following episodes of supraventricular tachyarrhythmias, most commonly atrial fibrillation. SA node disease may require pacemaker implantation if symptomatic. Brady-tachy syndrome requires concomitant therapy for the tachycardia as well as pacemaker placement.

Atrioventricular Block

AV block is classified as first-degree, second-degree, or third-degree. First-degree AV block may occur at several levels in the conduction system and is defined as prolongation of the PR interval to >200 msec. First-degree AV block is asymptomatic but associated with an increased risk of heart failure and death in some patient populations. It usually does not require intervention.

There are two types of second-degree AV block, both recognized electrocardiographically by the presence of a P wave that is not followed by a ventricular complex. Mobitz type I block (Wenckebach block) manifests as a progressive prolongation of the PR interval until there is a dropped ventricular beat (Figure 1). Mobitz type I block is usually secondary to a block at the level of the AV node and only rarely causes symptoms or progresses to higher-grade AV block. Mobitz type II block manifests as dropped ventricular beats without antecedent PR prolongation (Figure 2). In contrast to the defect in Mobitz type I, the conduction defect in Mobitz type II block is usu-

Table 1. Selected Indications for Permanent Pacing
Symptomatic bradycardia (heart rate <40 bpm) or sinus pauses
Symptomatic complete heart block or second-degree heart block (type 1 or 2)
Asymptomatic complete heart block or advanced second-degree heart block
Atrial fibrillation with pauses of ≥5 seconds
Alternating bundle branch block

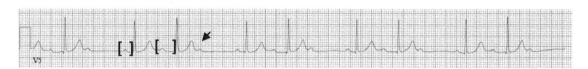

Figure 1. Electrocardiogram showing Mobitz type I second-degree atrioventricular block (Wenckebach block). Note prolongation of PR intervals (*brackets*) followed by nonconducted P waves (*arrow*).

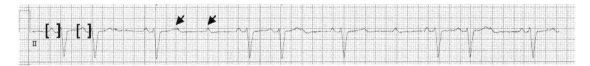

Figure 2. Electrocardiogram showing Mobitz type II second-degree atrioventricular block. Note absence of PR prolongation (*brackets*) and successive nonconducted P waves (*arrows*).

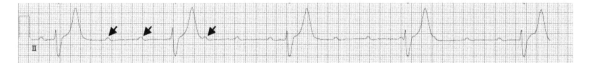

Figure 3. Electrocardiogram showing complete heart block. Note stable R-R intervals and lack of relation of P waves (*arrows*) to the QRS complex.

ally infranodal (eg, within the ventricular conduction system). Mobitz type II block is often accompanied by an intraventricular conduction delay (which manifests as a widened QRS complex) or a left bundle branch block (LBBB) and typically progresses to third-degree AV block. Patients with Mobitz type I block usually do not require therapy, but Mobitz type II block is an indication for permanent pacemaker placement.

Third-degree AV block (complete heart block) occurs when there is no conduction of the atrial beats to the ventricles, resulting in the two chambers beating asynchronously. The atrial and ventricular rates are independent, and the QRS complex may be wide or narrow, depending on the origin of the ventricular escape rhythm (Figure 3). The conduction defect in third-degree AV block may be at the level of the AV node but more typically is within the infranodal system. It is often associated with significant bradycardia (pulse rates near 30 bpm) and, if untreated, may result in lightheadedness, syncope, and death. Third-degree AV block is an indication for permanent pacemaker placement.

Bundle Branch and Fascicular Blocks

Conduction defects at the level of the individual components of the ventricular conduction system may also be electrocardiographically apparent without causing bradycardia. LBBB manifests electrocardiographically as a wide QRS complex (>120 msec), loss of Q waves in leads V_5 and V_6, and wide R waves in the lateral leads (I, V_5, and V_6) (Figure 4). LBBB is common in the elderly and, as with other manifestations of conduction disease, may reflect degeneration of the conduction system or myocardial disease. LBBB is usually asymptomatic, but when new may be the electrocardiographic representation of an acute anterior wall myocardial infarction in patients with an acute coronary syndrome; specific criteria (eg, Sgarbossa criteria) can be used to help determine the likelihood of acute myocardial infarction in patients with LBBB. Blocks may also occur in the anterior or posterior divisions (fascicles) of the left bundle; these are termed fascicular blocks (or hemiblocks). Left anterior fascicular block (LAFB) is recognized by a positive QRS in lead I and a negative

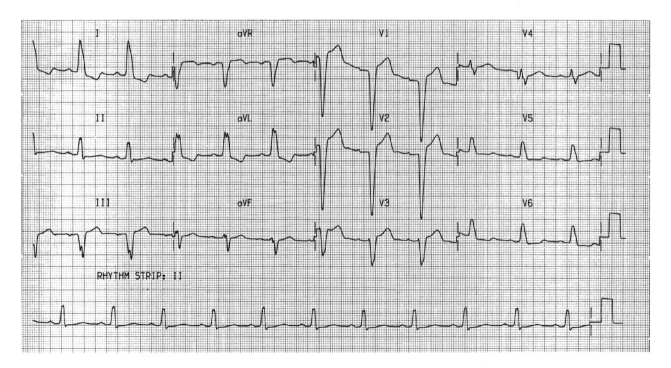

Figure 4. Electrocardiogram showing left bundle branch block pattern, including a wide QRS complex (>120 msec), absent Q waves in leads V_5 and V_6, and wide R waves in leads I, V_5, and V_6.

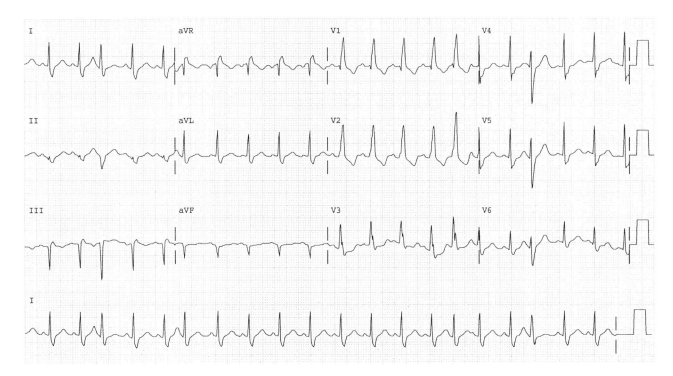

Figure 5. Electrocardiogram showing right bundle branch block pattern, including a wide QRS complex (>120 msec), RSR' pattern in lead V_1, and a wide negative S wave in leads I, V_5, and V_6.

QRS in aVF. Left posterior fascicular block (LPFB) is recognized by a negative QRS in lead I and a positive QRS in aVF. The QRS duration is normal in both LAFB and LPFB. Isolated LAFB or LPFB is asymptomatic but may indicate underlying myocardial disease.

RBBB is diagnosed by a widened QRS complex (>120 msec), an RSR' pattern (small initial upward deflection followed by a small downward deflection, then a large upward deflection) in lead V_1, and a wide negative S wave in leads I, V_5, and V_6 (Figure 5). RBBB is asymptomatic and may be the result of degenerative disease. It can also be a marker of right heart strain secondary to primary arterial hypertension, chronic obstructive or restrictive pulmonary disease, congenital heart disease, or pulmonary embolism. No specific therapy is indicated for RBBB.

Bifascicular block refers to the combination of RBBB with either LAFB or LPFB. Trifascicular block refers to the combination of RBBB, LAFB or LPFB, and first-degree AV block. Bifascicular block and trifascicular block can both progress to third-degree AV block but are not an indication for pacemaker placement in the absence of symptoms.

Bibliography

Da Costa D, Brady WJ, Edhouse J. Bradycardias and atrioventricular conduction block. BMJ. 2002;324:535-538. [PMID: 11872557]

Chapter 5

Supraventricular Arrhythmias

Chad S. Miller, MD

Supraventricular tachycardias (SVTs) are a group of arrhythmias that arise in atrial tissue or the atrioventricular (AV) node. Because conduction of supraventricular impulses below the AV node are conducted normally, the electrocardiogram (ECG) in SVT usually reveals a narrow complex tachycardia, although the QRS complexes can be wide (>120 msec) in the presence of bundle branch block, aberrancy, pacing, or anterograde accessory pathway conduction (eg, antidromic tachycardia).

SVTs include abnormal electrical activity arising in the atrium (eg, premature atrial contractions, atrial tachycardia, atrial fibrillation and flutter, multifocal atrial tachycardia), or AV node (eg, junctional tachycardia, AV nodal reentrant tachycardia [AVNRT], atrioventricular reciprocating tachycardia [AVRT]).

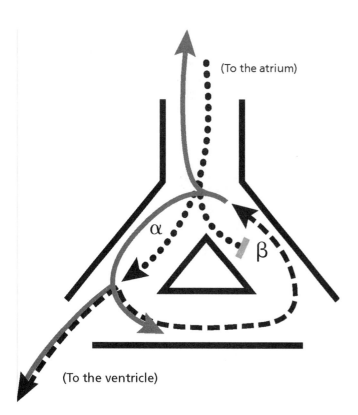

Figure 1. Initiation of AV nodal reentrant tachycardia (AVNRT). The α pathway has a short refractory period, and the β pathway has a long refractory period. The *dotted line* represents antegrade conduction down the α pathway; conduction does not occur down the β pathway because it is refractory. The *dashed line* represents impulse conduction into the ventricle and retrograde up the β pathway, which is no longer refractory. The *grey line* represents completion of the circuit, with activation of the atria and ventricles.

Enhanced automaticity and reentry are the mechanisms responsible for most episodes of SVT. Enhanced automaticity is the accelerated generation of an action potential, which occurs normally in the sinoatrial (SA) node but also can occur abnormally in diseased myocardial tissue. Enhanced automaticity is responsible for atrial tachycardia, a subtype of SVT. Reentry is responsible for most other forms of SVT and is characterized by an electrical circuit that continuously reexcites the myocardium. Re-entry usually depends on the presence of two interconnected conduction pathways (Figure 1). The first pathway is initially refractory to new impulse conduction because of a recent depolarization, whereas an alternative pathway is able to conduct the impulse. The conduction down the alternative pathway is slow enough to allow the first pathway to recover from its refractory period from the prior conducted impulse and become susceptible to depolarization by the impulse conducted by the alternative pathway. The reentrant circuit is completed when the conduction along the first pathway restimulates the alternative pathway to form a repeating electrical loop. Reentrant SVTs are classified by their conduction within or around the AV node. AVNRT describes a reentrant circuit within the AV node, whereas atrioventricular reciprocating tachycardia (AVRT) describes a circuit that may involve the AV node but is not entirely contained within the node itself. SVTs may also be further categorized as regular or irregular (Figure 2). Multifocal atrial tachycardia and atrial fibrillation are the most common irregular supraventricular tachyarrhythmias.

Diagnosis

Symptoms of SVT include palpitations, syncope, chest pain, dyspnea, and fatigue. The objective for diagnosing any arrhythmia is to document the heart rhythm at the time of symptoms with electrocardiography or another recording device. If a suspected arrhythmia cannot be documented on a resting ECG or cardiac monitor during initial evaluation, the cardiac rhythm may be recorded for a full 24 or 48 hours using portable monitoring devices. Unless the abnormal rhythm occurs during this time frame, however, this study may be nondiagnostic. A cardiac event monitor is a device that the patient activates at the time of symptoms, and it records the heart rhythm during or around the time of the episode. For symptoms that are very brief or prevent the patient from activating the event monitor (eg, syncope), a continuous loop recorder activated by the patient after the event will save cardiac rhythm data from the previous 30 seconds to 2 minutes. If symptoms are very infrequent, an implantable recorder can be used. This small device is placed subcutaneously, although there are no leads placed directly into the heart; cardiac rhythm data can be retrieved noninvasively.

Treatment for SVT is variable and depends on the underlying rhythm. Except for sinus tachycardia, however, electrical cardioversion is indicated for any rhythm that results in hemodynamic instability.

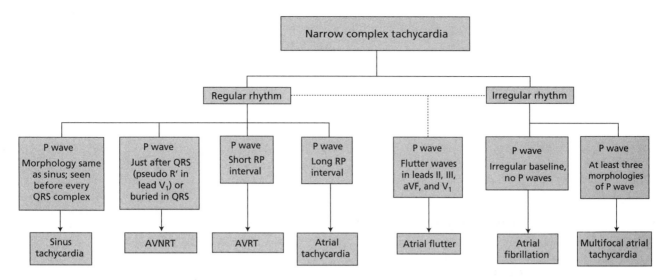

Figure 2. Classification of narrow-complex tachycardias. AVNRT = atrioventricular nodal reentrant tachycardia; AVRT = atrioventricular reentrant tachycardia.

Sinus Tachycardia

Sinus tachycardia is the result of increased automaticity at the SA node. The most common causes are normal physiologic responses to exercise and increased sympathetic activity. Because sinus tachycardia originates from the SA node and propagates normally through the AV node to the ventricles, it is generally not included in the SVT category. Heart rate is between 100/min and 150/min. The onset and conclusion of sinus tachycardia are gradual, in contrast to SVTs, which tend to begin and end suddenly. The P wave has normal morphology but may be difficult to identify with very rapid rates; slowing the heart rate with carotid sinus massage may allow identification of the normal P wave morphology and help establish the diagnosis. Fever, exercise, anxiety, pain, anemia, thyrotoxicosis, hypoxemia, cocaine use, and alcohol withdrawal are common causes of sinus tachycardia. Treatment is guided by the underlying cause.

Atrial Tachycardia

Atrial tachycardia usually results from increased automaticity of a group of atrial cells separate from the SA node. Heart rate is between 150/min and 200/min. The P wave morphology is abnormal, often upright, biphasic, or inverted in the inferior leads, and the PR interval is often short because the origin of the depolarizing impulse is typically located closer to the ventricles than the SA node. Atrial tachycardia commonly occurs in patients with coronary artery disease or cor pulmonale. Other causes include pulmonary embolization, thyrotoxicosis, digitalis toxicity, and acute noncardiac illness. Atrial tachycardia is occasionally seen in patients without structural heart disease.

Atrial tachycardia often terminates without intervention once the underlying cause is treated. First-line drug therapies for stable atrial tachycardia are β-blockers and non-dihydropyridine calcium channel blockers (eg, verapamil, diltiazem). Adenosine and electrical cardioversion are relatively ineffective. If atrial tachycardia fails to respond to first-line therapy, more advanced antiarrhythmic therapy may be needed with agents such as amiodarone, flecainide, and sotalol. These drugs have significant side effects and can be proarrhythmic. For refractory cases, radiofrequency catheter ablation of the abnormal impulse generation site is an option.

Atrioventricular Nodal Reentrant Tachycardia

AVNRT accounts for approximately 60% of all SVTs that present as a regular rhythm. AVNRT is diagnosed by its characteristic findings on an ECG; the P wave either is seen just after the QRS complex, which accounts for a short RP interval or is concealed within the QRS complex (no visible P wave) (Figure 3). Heart rate is typically between 120/min and 220/min. AVNRT often occurs in the absence of structural heart disease and is typically benign.

AVNRT may be terminated by maneuvers to increase vagal tone, such as Valsalva or unilateral carotid massage (after careful carotid artery auscultation for bruits). Intravenous adenosine, a non-dihydropyridine calcium channel blocker, and β-blockers are often successful in terminating AVNRT not responding to vagal maneuvers. Intravenous adenosine has a very rapid onset and is extremely short-acting, with a half-life of 10 seconds, making it an excellent first therapeutic choice. Adenosine is contraindicated in patients with severe bronchospastic disease. β-Blockers and non-dihydropyridine calcium channel blockers can also be used long term to prevent frequent recurrence of AVNRT. In refractory cases, catheter radiofrequency ablation is between 95% and 99% successful in preventing AVNRT recurrence.

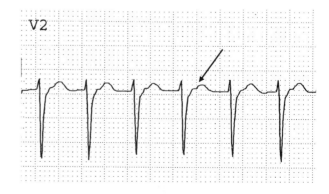

Figure 3. Atrioventricular nodal reentrant tachycardia is a narrow complex tachycardia with P waves buried in the T wave, most easily seen in lead V$_2$.

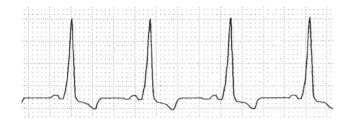

Figure 4. Preexcitation pattern typical of the Wolff-Parkinson-White syndrome showing a delta wave (upsloping of initial QRS wave), causing widening of the QRS complex and short PR interval.

Atrioventricular Reciprocating Tachycardia

AVRT is associated with an accessory pathway between the atria and ventricle that is not contained within the AV node itself. The presence of an accessory pathway may be seen on a resting electrocardiograph by the presence of two characteristics: a short PR interval and the presence of a delta wave (a sloping upstroke initiating the QRS complex, which may be wide due to sequential rather than parallel depolarization of the ventricles) (Figure 4). This pattern on ECG is referred to as *preexcitation*, and when present with symptomatic tachycardia, it is called the *Wolff-Parkinson-White syndrome*. During tachycardia, the reentrant impulses may travel antegrade (from atria to ventricles) down the AV node and then retrograde (from ventricles to atria) via the accessory pathway (orthodromic AVRT), or they may travel anterograde down the accessory pathway and back up to the atria via the AV node (antidromic AVRT). An accessory pathway that conducts impulses antidromically cannot be identified on routine electrocardiography. In a given patient, the defining features of Wolff-Parkinson-White syndrome may not be present at all times and can even vary from beat to beat. Heart rate is typically between 140/min and 250/min. Because the accessory pathway may be capable of rapid antegrade conduction, patients who develop atrial fibrillation can experience a very rapid ventricular response that can degenerate into ventricular fibrillation. The risk of sudden cardiac death in these patients is 0.15% to 0.39% over 3 to 10 years.

Patients with narrow-complex AVRT are treated in the same manner as those with AVNRT. AV nodal-blocking drugs are contraindicated when AVRT is associated with a wide QRS complex secondary to antegrade conduction over the accessory pathway, as these medications are associated with accelerated conduction down the bypass tract, and administration may result in rapid ventricular rates and possible induction of ventricular arrhythmias. Catheter radiofrequency ablation has similar success rates as in AVNRT and can prevent sudden death associated with AVRT. If antiarrhythmic medications are used, procainamide is the drug of choice for patients with wide-complex AVRT because it increases refractoriness in the accessory pathway.

Multifocal Atrial Tachycardia

Multifocal atrial tachycardia (MAT) is diagnosed by the presence of three or more morphologically distinct P waves and a heart rate between 100/min and 140/min. MAT is caused by multiple areas of increased automaticity or triggered activity within the atria. Underlying pulmonary disease usually triggers MAT. It occurs most often in patients with severe chronic obstructive pulmonary disease (COPD), but it may also occur in patients with pulmonary embolism, congestive heart failure, and hypoxemia. The treatment of these potential precipitating causes is the primary therapy for MAT and minimizing or discontinuing agents that may precipitate MAT (such as β-agonist therapy). If MAT persists despite the appropriate treatment of underlying causes, metoprolol or even high-dose magnesium may improve the tachycardia.

Atrial Fibrillation

Atrial fibrillation is associated with loss of sinus node function, leading to uncoordinated atrial activity. The ECG is characterized by absent P waves and irregularity of the ventricular response (Figure 5). Atrial fibrillation is classified as paroxysmal (lasting <7 days), persistent (lasting >7 days), or long-standing persistent (permanent) (lasting >1 year or associated with failed cardioversion). Most cases of atrial fibrillation are associated with structural heart disease, such as valvular disease (especially mitral valve disease), dilated cardiomyopathy, hypertension, and coronary artery disease. Heart failure, pulmonary hypertension, and increasing age are also strongly associated with atrial fibrillation. Noncardiac causes include substance abuse (eg, alcohol, caffeine, cocaine, amphetamines), inhaled β-agonists, hypoxemia, COPD, pulmonary embolization, obstructive sleep apnea, and hyperthyroidism. Lone atrial fibrillation is a form of atrial fibrillation occurring in young patients within an otherwise normal heart in the absence of precipitating or predisposing factors.

Treatment of atrial fibrillation is guided by three basic principles: rate control, restoration/maintenance of sinus rhythm, and stroke prevention. Atrial fibrillation with a rapid ventricular rate and hemodynamic compromise is treated acutely with electrical cardioversion; stable patients with a rapid ventricular rate may be treated with intravenous non-dihydropyridine calcium channel blockers or β-blockers. For stable patients with atrial fibrillation requiring a lower degree of rate control, initiating an oral non-dihydropyridine calcium channel blocker or β-blocker is the usual first step in therapy. The goal of rate control is to reduce the ventricular rate to <110/min at rest as long as there is normal ventricular function. Digitalis is not recommended as a single agent for rate control due to its slower onset, increased toxicity, and lack of efficacy for controlling the ventricular rate during exercise, although it may be a useful adjunctive therapy in patients with relative hypotension or systolic heart failure. Other options to control ventricular rate include full or partial catheter radiofrequency ablation of the AV node, which may require concomitant pacemaker placement. In patients with long-standing, uncontrolled ventricular rates >130/min, a tachycardia-related cardiomyopathy can develop.

In most patients, an approach in which rate control coupled with stroke prevention (rate control approach) is preferred to attempting to return and maintain the cardiac rhythm to normal sinus (rhythm control approach). Use of a rate control strategy in patients aged >65 years results in fewer hospitalizations and serious drug reactions to

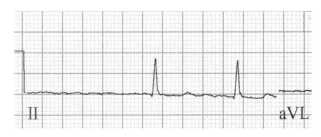

Figure 5. Atrial fibrillation showing atrial fibrillatory waves, best seen in lead II, and an irregular ventricular response.

Table 1. Assessment of Stroke Risk in Atrial Fibrillation Patients

CHADS$_2$	Score	CHA$_2$DS$_2$-VAS$_c$	Score
Congestive heart failure	1	**C**ongestive heart failure	1
Hypertension	1	**H**ypertension	1
Age >75 y	1	**A**ge >75 y	2
Diabetes mellitus	1	**D**iabetes mellitus	1
Stroke	2	**S**troke	2
		Vascular disease (prior MI, PAD, or aortic plaque)	1
		Aged 65 to 74 y	1
		Sex (female)	1

For both scoring systems, a score of 0 indicates a low risk of stroke and no treatment or aspirin is indicated. Those with a score of 1 have an intermediate stroke risk, and either anticoagulation or antiplatelet therapy is indicated based on physician and patient preference. For a score of 2 or greater, oral anticoagulation is recommended for prevention of stroke.

MI = myocardial infarction; PAD= peripheral artery disease.

antiarrhythmic medications. Restoring sinus rhythm in some patients, typically those who are younger, however, may be associated with improved quality of life.

If a rhythm control strategy is pursued, synchronized direct-current cardioversion and pharmacologic therapy (eg, dofetilide, flecainide, ibutilide) are both effective methods for converting atrial fibrillation to sinus rhythm. For atrial fibrillation of <48 hours' duration, cardioversion can proceed safely without anticoagulation. For atrial fibrillation of >48 hours' or of unknown duration, cardioversion is performed after therapeutic anticoagulation for at least 3 weeks. If cardioversion is desired more quickly, a transesophageal echocardiogram can be performed to evaluate for the presence of left atrial thrombus. In the absence of thrombus, the patient is anticoagulated with heparin, cardioverted, and maintained on therapeutic anticoagulation for at least 4 weeks. The antiarrhythmic agents amiodarone, flecainide, ibutilide, propafenone, and sotalol are used to maintain patients in sinus rhythm following cardioversion. Amiodarone is the antiarrhythmic drug of choice in patients with underlying heart disease because of its relatively low proarrhythmic potential compared to other agents. Even with antiarrhythmic drugs, the long-term (>1 year) recurrence rate of symptomatic atrial fibrillation is 20% to 50%.

An emerging strategy is to use pulmonary vein catheter radiofrequency ablation to prevent recurrent atrial fibrillation. Foci for atrial fibrillation are commonly located around the ostia of the pulmonary veins and can be isolated with catheter radiofrequency ablation. Up to 80% of patients with paroxysmal atrial fibrillation will remain arrhythmia free after pulmonary vein catheter radiofrequency ablation. This procedure is commonly used in patients with lone atrial fibrillation. Alternatively, the "maze" procedure is an open surgical procedure that may be considered in patients undergoing heart surgery for other reasons. It consists of multiple atrial incisions to reduce effective atrial size and prevent the formation of atrial fibrillation wavelets and is 70% to 95% effective.

Systemic embolization is a major adverse event, of which stroke is the most common manifestation. Ineffectual atrial contraction results in stasis of blood, especially in the atrial appendages, allowing for the formation of thrombi, which may embolize to other organs. The annual risk of stroke in patients with atrial fibrillation is estimated to be around 4% per year, with the risk being significantly higher in patients with atrial fibrillation caused by valvular disease (mitral stenosis) or a prior stroke or transient ischemic attack (TIA). Several scoring systems are available to estimate the stroke risk given a particular patient's risk factors to help guide treatment decisions. The CHADS$_2$ risk score is used to predict the likelihood of

stroke in patients with nonvalvular atrial fibrillation. The CHADS$_2$ score uses individual stroke risk factors (ie, **C**ongestive heart failure, **H**ypertension, **A**ge >75 years, **D**iabetes mellitus, and prior **S**troke or TIA). Patients are assigned 2 points for a previous stroke or TIA and 1 point for each of the other risk factors. The higher the CHADS$_2$ score, the greater the risk of stroke will be. Recently, the CHADS$_2$ score was updated to the CHA$_2$DS2-VAS$_c$ score, which better recognizes the influence of gender and the presence of established vascular disease as stroke risk factors, and also weights age more heavily as a risk factor. For a score of 1 using either risk estimating system, either anticoagulation or antiplatelet therapy is indicated. For a score of 2 or greater, oral anticoagulation is recommended for stroke prevention (Table 1).

For patients at intermediate risk for stroke (CHA$_2$DS2-VAS$_c$ score of 1), the need for anticoagulation therapy should be assessed individually, taking into account the risk of major hemorrhage and patient preference. The HAS-BLED score (Table 2) can be used to

Table 2. Assessment of Bleeding Risk (HAS-BLED) in Atrial Fibrillation Patients

HAS-BLED	Score
Hypertension (systolic blood pressure >160 mm Hg)	1
Abnormal renal or liver function (1 point each)[a]	1 or 2
Stroke	1
Bleeding tendency/predisposition[b]	1
Labile INR (if on warfarin)[c]	1
Elderly (age >65 y)	1
Drugs or alcohol (1 point each)[d]	1 or 2

A HAS-BLED score of ≥3 indicates that caution and close observation are warranted when prescribing oral anticoagulation.

[a]Abnormal kidney function is classified as the presence of long-term dialysis, renal transplantation, or serum creatinine ≥2.26 mg/dL (200 mmol/L). Abnormal liver function includes chronic hepatic disease or biochemical evidence of significant hepatic derangement (eg, bilirubin two to three times the upper limit of normal, aspartate aminotransferase alanine aminotransferase elevations three times the upper limit of normal).

[b]History of bleeding or predisposition (anemia).

[c]Labile INR = time in therapeutic range <60%.

[d]Concomitant antiplatelet or nonsteroidal anti-inflammatory drugs, or excess alcohol.

INR = international normalized ratio.

Data from Lane DA, Lip GY. Use of the CHA$_2$DS2VASc and HAS-BLED scores to aid decision making for thromboprophylaxis in nonvalvular atrial fibrillation. Circulation. 2012;126:860-865. [PMID: 22891166]

identify patients at high risk of bleeding. Caution is warranted for any patient with a score of ≥3 when prescribing anticoagulants. Most of these patients will benefit from anticoagulant therapy, although aspirin may be a reasonable choice in those with a $CHA_2DS2-VAS_c$ score of 1. In patients in whom full anticoagulation is contraindicated, aspirin decreases stroke risk by 22%. In patients with a $CHA_2DS2-VAS_c$ score of 0, the risk of stroke is low, and anticoagulation is not required. Long-term anticoagulation is also considered if there is a high risk for recurrence of atrial fibrillation following successful cardioversion, evidence of intracardiac thrombus, or other risk factors for thromboembolism.

Warfarin (target international normalized ratio [INR] of 2.0-3.0) reduces the risk of stroke by an average of 64% in patients with nonvalvular atrial fibrillation. Its use, however, requires frequent monitoring of the INR, and it is often difficult to maintain patients in the therapeutic range. Recently, several newer oral agents have been approved for stroke prevention in patients with atrial fibrillation. **Although newer oral anticoagulant medications do not require routine monitoring of their anticoagulation effect and may have several other potential advantages, they are significantly more expensive than warfarin.** Additionally, no reliable method for reversing the anticoagulation effect of newer oral anticoagulant medications is currently available if major bleeding occurs. Therefore, their use should be based on an assessment of their potential risks and benefits relative to the more established agent, warfarin. Dabigatran, a direct thrombin inhibitor, is effective but appears to be associated with a higher risk of gastrointestinal bleeding than warfarin. Rivaroxaban, a factor Xa inhibitor, has the advantage that it is not affected by food, antacids, or nonsteroidal anti-inflammatory drugs as is warfarin and has few interactions with common cardiac medications. Apixaban, another factor Xa inhibitor, has a similar increased risk for gastrointestinal bleeding as dabigatran. These three medications have not been studied in patients with valvular atrial fibrillation or mechanical heart valves. Warfarin remains the drug of choice for these patients. Also, limited data are available on the efficacy of these new oral anticoagulants in renal failure.

Atrial Flutter

Atrial flutter is characterized by regular atrial contractions (flutter waves) on electrocardiography (Figure 6). The atrial rate is between 240/min and 300/min and is usually associated with a 2:1 or 3:1 AV block, resulting in a ventricular rate of approximately 100/min to 150/min. The rhythm is typically due to a reentrant electrical loop in the right atrium around the cavotricuspid isthmus. Sustained atrial flutter is uncommon, and flutter typically converts to atrial fibrillation over time; these two rhythms frequently coexist. The underlying causes of atrial flutter are similar to those for atrial fibrillation and often result from atrial dilation. Typical causes include pulmonary embolism, septal defects, mitral or tricuspid valve disease, and chronic left ventricular failure. Atrial flutter may occur in patients without underlying heart disease, however, such as those with thyrotoxicosis or alcoholism.

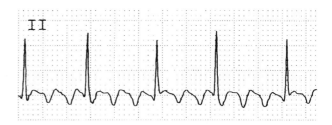

Figure 6. Electrocardiogram showing an irregular rate and a saw-tooth pattern in lead II, characteristic of atrial flutter.

Treatment of atrial flutter follows the same principles as atrial fibrillation. Patients with hemodynamic instability due to atrial flutter should be immediately electrically cardioverted. In others, rate control involves the use of a non-dihydropyridine calcium channel blocker or a β-blocker. Because it is more difficult to control the rate in atrial flutter compared to atrial fibrillation, cardioversion (either electrical or pharmacological) and radiofrequency ablation are more valuable treatment options. Recurrence of atrial flutter is common; radiofrequency ablation of the reentrant circuit is the definitive treatment to prevent recurrence. Preventing stroke and cardiac embolization is identical to atrial fibrillation as mentioned previously.

Follow-Up

In patients on antiarrhythmic drugs, a 12-lead ECG should be obtained to assess for significant adverse drug effects (such as QT prolongation), serum drug levels should be monitored if appropriate, and patients should be followed for potential side effects of antiarrhythmic drug therapy. In particular, amiodarone has several potentially serious side effects including hyperthyroidism, hypothyroidism, hepatitis, and pulmonary fibrosis. Therefore, monitoring usually includes periodic thyroid function and liver chemistry tests and careful observation for possible pulmonary side effects. Procainamide can cause agranulocytosis, so periodic blood counts should be checked.

In patients with atrial fibrillation, assess rate control by asking about easy fatigability and exertional dyspnea, and measure their heart rate after walking. If the heart rate is >110/min, the degree of AV nodal blockade should be increased. Maintain the INR at 2.0 to 3.0 in patients with nonvalvular atrial fibrillation or at 2.5 to 3.5 in patients with valvular atrial fibrillation.

Bibliography

Delacrétaz E. Clinical practice. Supraventricular tachycardia. N Engl J Med. 2006;354:1039-1051. [PMID: 16525141]

Lane DA, Lip GY. Use of the $CHA_2DS2-VAS_c$ and HAS-BLED Scores to aid decision making for thromboprophylaxis in nonvalvular atrial fibrillation. Circulation. 2012;126:860-865. [PMID: 22891166]

Chapter 6

Ventricular Arrhythmias

Robert Trowbridge, MD

Ventricular arrhythmias are the most important causes of sudden cardiac death, particularly in patients with structural heart disease and a low ventricular ejection fraction. In general, the ventricular arrhythmias associated with structural heart disease are more malignant than those associated with a structurally normal heart. Ventricular arrhythmias can be categorized into premature ventricular contractions (PVCs), ventricular tachycardia (VT), and ventricular fibrillation (VF).

PVCs are extraventricular beats that occur individually or as couplets. Although PVCs may be a marker of underlying heart disease, they have minimal prognostic significance if left ventricular function is preserved. VT is a potentially life-threatening arrhythmia due to rapid, depolarizing impulses originating from the His-Purkinje system, the ventricular myocardium, or both. VT often accompanies structural heart disease, most commonly ischemic heart disease, and it is associated with electrolyte disorders (eg, hypokalemia, hypomagnesemia), drug toxicity, valvular heart disease, nonischemic cardiomyopathy, and long QT syndrome. VT is subdivided into sustained VT and nonsustained VT. VT is sustained when it persists >30 seconds or requires termination due to hemodynamic collapse. Nonsustained VT has ≥3 beats but is <30 seconds in duration. VT is also categorized by the morphology of the QRS complexes. VT is monomorphic if QRS complexes in the same leads do not vary in contour (Figure 1). VT is polymorphic if the QRS complexes in the same leads vary in contour (Figure 2). Proper use of these terms and the patient context in which VT occurs are essential for accurate diagnosis and therapy.

The pathophysiology of VT most commonly relates to abnormalities of impulse conduction, usually involving a reentrant pathway. Reentry occurs when an impulse fails to extinguish after normal activation of myocardial tissue and continues to propagate after the refractory period. Once the reentrant pathway is initiated, repetitive circulation of the impulse over the loop can produce VT. VT may also arise through abnormal impulse formation, such as enhanced automaticity or triggered activity. Enhancement of normal automaticity in latent pacemaker fibers or the development of abnormal automaticity due to partial resting membrane depolarization can serve as a nidus for VT. Triggered activity does not occur spontaneously; it requires a change in cardiac electrical frequency as a trigger, such as early depolarization (ie, PVCs).

VF reflects a lack of organized ventricular activity and, unless terminated, results in sudden death. VF may occur as a primary event, or it may result from degeneration of VT.

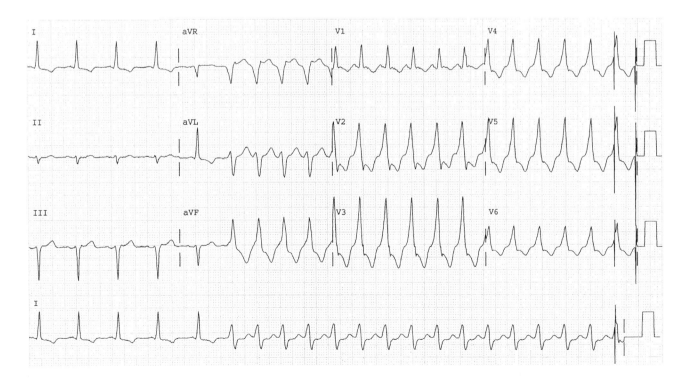

Figure 1. Approximately one quarter of the way into this electrocardiogram, monomorphic ventricular tachycardia begins; it is associated with an abrupt change in the QRS axis.

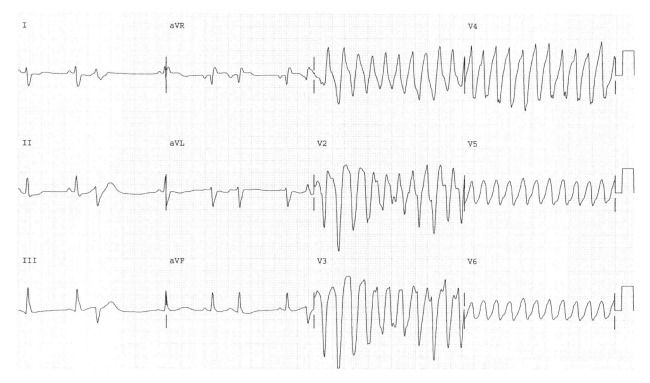

Figure 2. Electrocardiogram showing degeneration of sinus rhythm into polymorphic ventricular tachycardia.

Prevention

Because VT and VF often occur in the setting of ischemic heart disease, identification and reduction of risk factors for coronary artery disease are indicated. Care should be taken in prescribing medications that prolong the QT interval, and prescribing more than one such medication should be avoided when possible. Common medications that prolong the QT interval include antimicrobials (eg, extended-spectrum fluoroquinolones and macrolides, fluconazole), antiarrhythmic agents, antipsychotics, and methadone.

Screening

Routine screening for VT in asymptomatic persons is not recommended. A screening electrocardiogram (ECG) is reasonable in asymptomatic persons with a family history of sudden cardiac death, however, as these individuals may have long QT syndrome, arrhythmogenic right ventricular dysplasia, or Brugada syndrome (an ion channel disorder associated with incomplete right bundle branch block).

Diagnosis

Symptoms depend on several factors, including the ventricular rate, the duration of tachycardia, and the presence of underlying heart disease. Patients with PVCs rarely have symptoms but may complain of palpitations or a sensation that the heart has stopped, owing to the post-PVC compensatory pause. Patients with nonsustained VT usually are asymptomatic but may experience palpitations, dizziness, or syncope. Patients with sustained VT usually present with syncope or near syncope and can also present with sudden cardiac death. Patients with VF usually present with sudden cardiac death.

VTs are characterized by wide-complex QRS morphology (QRS >120 msec) and ventricular rate >100/min. In patients with VT, the ventricular rate typically ranges from 140/min to 250/min; in those with VF, the rate is typically >300/min. In patients with torsades de pointes, a special subset of polymorphic VT, the ventricular rate ranges from 200/min to 300/min. Torsades de pointes is associated with long QT syndrome, which may be congenital or acquired. Long QT syndrome is characterized by prolonged ventricular repolarization and a predisposition to the development of polymorphic VT and sudden cardiac death. Patients can be diagnosed after presenting with syncope, or a prolonged QT interval (>500 msec, corrected for heart rate) can be an incidental finding on an ECG. Risk factors for acquired long QT syndrome include female sex, hypokalemia, hypomagnesemia, structural heart disease, and a history of previous long QT or drug-induced arrhythmias. An extensive list of agents that can cause torsades de pointes can be found at www.crediblemeds.org.

Supraventricular tachycardia with a wide QRS complex can mimic VT and is usually due to coexisting bundle branch block or preexcitation syndrome (Wolff-Parkinson-White syndrome). Differentiating VT from supraventricular tachycardia with aberrant conduction is important, because the treatment differs markedly. VT is more common than supraventricular tachycardia with aberrancy, particularly in patients with structural heart disease. A key point is that any wide QRS tachycardia should be considered to be VT until proven otherwise (Figure 3). The most important differentiating point is a history of ischemic heart disease. In the presence of known structural heart disease, particularly a prior myocardial infarction (MI), the diagnosis of VT is almost certain. Another clue is more profound hemodynamic deterioration in patients with VT; however, a normal blood pressure does not rule out VT. Additionally, supraventricular tachycardia and VT may be distinguished at times by looking for evidence of atrioventricular dissociation on physical examination, which is present in patients with VT. The presence of cannon *a* waves (large *a* waves) in the jugular venous pulsations and varying intensity of S_1 support atrioventricular dissociation and the diagno-

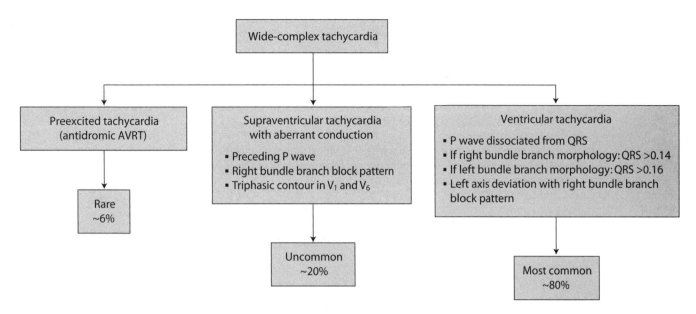

Figure 3. Differentiating ventricular tachycardia from supraventricular tachycardia with aberrancy. AVRT = atrioventricular reentrant tachycardia.

sis of VT. At times, physical examination and electrocardiography are insufficient to identify the cause of a wide-complex tachycardia; electrophysiologic testing provides definitive diagnosis and is indicated in these patients. In the absence of immediate expert consultation, it is always preferable to assume the patient has VT and to treat accordingly with immediate cardioversion.

The key points in the evaluation of VT include (1) reviewing the patient's history for evidence of ischemic heart disease, (2) examining prior ECGs for evidence of long QT syndrome and baseline electrocardiographic abnormalities (eg. prior MI, Wolff-Parkinson-White syndrome), and (3) searching for reversible causes, including electrolyte abnormalities, heart failure, and drug toxicity.

Therapy

Immediate cardioversion is the treatment of choice for hemodynamically unstable patients (regardless of the rhythm disorder) and is often the safest choice even in hemodynamically stable patients, particularly those with wide-complex tachycardia. Survival in cardiac arrest is proportional to the time to intervention (cardioversion or defibrillation). Epinephrine or vasopressin is recommended for hemodynamic support, and amiodarone has largely replaced other antiarrhythmic agents for resistant VT in the acute setting, although lidocaine can be useful in patients with coronary ischemia. After termination of the arrhythmia, the ECG can provide clues regarding the presence of a prior MI, left ventricular hypertrophy, or long QT syndrome; an ECG also provides evaluation for structural heart disease and assessment of left ventricular function. Exercise testing can screen for significant coronary artery disease and provoke exercise-associated tachycardias. In newly diagnosed cardiomyopathy, cardiac catheterization is often necessary to evaluate for coronary artery disease as the cause of myocardial dysfunction.

The treatment of VT is complicated and must take into account the type of VT present (nonsustained or sustained) and the presence of concomitant structural heart disease. Options include medical (antiarrhythmic) therapy, placement of an implantable cardioverter-defibrillator (ICD) and catheter-radiofrequency ablation. An ICD is an internal defibrillator that senses dangerous cardiac arrhythmias

and automatically converts the rhythm to sinus rhythm by either administering a high-energy shock or delivering a short series of paced beats. Catheter-directed radiofrequency ablation involves destroying the region of the heart from which the abnormal impulses are initiated.

In general, medical therapy does not improve survival in patients with nonsustained VT, and thus pharmacologic therapy is avoided unless the patient has a history of structural heart disease or long QT syndrome or (rarely) intolerable symptoms. β-Blockers are the mainstay of treatment for those with symptomatic nonsustained VT, although non–dihydropyridine calcium channel blockers may also be used in patients with structurally normal hearts. If needed, the most frequently used antiarrhythmic agents are amiodarone and sotalol. Patients in whom drug therapy for nonsustained VT fails or is not tolerated can be referred for catheter-directed radiofrequency ablation. ICD placement may also be appropriate in selected patients, especially those with a depressed left ventricular ejection fraction.

As is the case with nonsustained VT, the utility of pharmacologic therapy of sustained VT is limited, and its use frequently depends on the presence or absence of structural heart disease. Sustained, symptomatic VT in patients with ischemic or nonischemic cardiomyopathy is an adverse prognostic indicator with a high risk of recurrence. Although ICD placement is usually the primary treatment for these patients, pharmacologic therapy may be useful in individuals who refuse ICD placement or who have frequent shocks from their ICDs. Sustained VT in the absence of structural heart disease may be more amenable to pharmacologic therapy, and an expert in electrophysiology usually directs this care. For patients presenting with hemodynamically unstable sustained VT, electrical cardioversion is indicated. For hemodymically stable patients with sustained VT, first-line treatment is an intravenous antiarrhythmic agent such as amiodarone. Procainamide and sotalol are also acceptable, and lidocaine can be used as a second-line agent.

ICD placement has largely supplanted pharmacologic therapy in VT, as it has been shown to improve survival rates in many patients with VT. It is indicated in patients with sustained VT in the setting of structural heart disease or when a completely reversible risk factor cannot be identified (such as in patients with hypertrophic cardiomyopathy at increased risk for sudden cardiac death). ICD placement is also indicated for the primary prevention of sudden cardiac death in patients with (1) NYHA Class II or III heart failure and an ejection fraction of less than 35% or (2) a prior MI and an ejection fraction of less than 30% (after a waiting period of 40 days) (see Chapter 7).

Catheter-directed radiofrequency ablation of VT is useful in patients with idiopathic VT (those without structural heart disease or another clear etiology) as well as those with frequent recurrences of VT.

An important distinction concerns patients presenting with VT within 48 hours of an acute coronary syndrome or reperfusion therapy. These patients, although at increased risk for overall mortality, should not be treated with long-term therapy (antiarrhythmic medications, ICD placement) unless the arrhythmia recurs after 48 hours. In all patients with coronary artery disease and VT, however, management includes treatment of reversible ischemia.

In contrast to sustained VT, polymorphic VT is commonly related to an underlying genetic defect predisposing to often-fatal cardiac arrhythmias. The treatment of torsades de pointes is complex and requires consultation with a specialist. Recommendations that have strong supporting evidence include withdrawal of any offending drugs, correction of electrolyte abnormalities, and initiating β-blocker therapy for patients with congenital prolonged QT syndrome. Patients who continue to have recurrent arrhythmias despite β-blocker therapy should be considered for ICD placement.

The treatment of PVCs is less aggressive than that of VT and VF. Among persons with no evidence of heart disease, frequent PVCs are of uncertain significance. Among persons with a depressed ejection fraction, frequent PVCs are associated with increased mortality, but suppression of PVCs with antiarrhythmic drugs does not improve mortality. If symptoms can be clearly correlated with PVCs, treatment may be appropriate, although many patients respond well to reassurance. If symptoms are intolerable, first-line therapy almost always is a β-blocker or a non-dihydropyridine calcium channel blocker. Class IC and class III antiarrhythmic agents can also be useful but have a high incidence of side effects; class IC drugs are proarrhythmic in patients with coronary artery disease. Radiofrequency ablation may be appropriate for patients with severe symptoms that are refractory to drug therapy.

Follow-Up

Appropriate follow-up for ventricular arrhythmias depends on the nature of the arrhythmia, the presence or absence of structural heart disease, and the risk for sudden cardiac death. In many cases, care is provided along with a cardiologist specializing in electrophysiology.

Bibliography

Thavendiranathan P, Bagai A, Khoo C, Dorian P, Choudhry NK. Does this patient with palpitations have a cardiac arrhythmia? JAMA. 2009; 302:2135-2143. [PMID: 19920238]

John RM, Tedrow UB, Albert CM, et al. Ventricular arrhythmias and sudden cardiac death. Lancet. 2012;380:1520-1529. [PMID: 23101719]

Chapter 7

Heart Failure

Alpesh N. Amin, MD

Heart failure is a complex clinical syndrome resulting from a structural or functional abnormality that impairs the ability of the ventricles to fill with or eject blood. New-onset systolic heart failure often results from acute pump dysfunction caused by myocardial ischemia or infarction. In chronic systolic heart failure, the left ventricle dilates and/or hypertrophies, causing the chamber to become more spherical in a process called *ventricular remodeling*. The geometric changes that affect the left ventricle increase wall stress, depress myocardial performance, and activate various neurohormonal compensatory responses that result in salt and water retention despite the presence of excess intravascular volume. In addition to causing peripheral vasoconstriction, elevated levels of circulating neurohormones (eg, epinephrine, aldosterone, angiotensin II) may exert direct toxic effects on cardiac cells by promoting further hypertrophy, stimulating myocardial fibrosis, and triggering programmed cell death (apoptosis).

Heart failure with preserved systolic function (previously termed *diastolic dysfunction* or *diastolic heart failure*) is diagnosed when signs and symptoms of systolic heart failure are present but an echocardiogram reveals a normal left ventricular ejection fraction and the absence of significant valvular or pericardial abnormalities. Heart failure with preserved systolic function is common, especially in elderly patients and in conditions causing significant left ventricular hypertrophy (eg, hypertension, aortic stenosis, hypertrophic cardiomyopathy).

Factors contributing to the development of heart failure include coronary heart disease, (62%), cigarette smoking (17%), hypertension (10%), increased body weight (8%), diabetes (3%), and valvular heart disease (2%).

Prevention

Controlling risk factors for coronary artery disease is an important preventive measure because it is a significant risk factor for the development of heart failure (see Chapter 2). Aggressive blood pressure and lipid control appears to provide benefits to patients with diabetes above those seen in the general population. Angiotensin-converting enzyme (ACE) inhibitors and angiotensin-receptor blockers (ARBs) may prevent the development of heart failure and also provide kidney protection in patients with diabetes.

Patients should be advised to avoid exposure to cardiotoxic substances such as alcohol, tobacco, and illicit drugs, particularly cocaine. Alcohol is a direct myocardial toxin and can cause heart failure. In some patients, abstinence from alcohol can reverse left ventricular dysfunction. Cocaine has both direct and indirect effects on the myocardium that increase the risk of heart failure and sudden cardiac death.

Prolonged tachycardia may be associated with the development of a reversible form of left ventricular systolic dysfunction. Control of rapid ventricular responses in patients with atrial fibrillation and other supraventricular tachycardias can prevent the development of tachycardia-induced cardiomyopathy.

Screening

Echocardiography should be used to screen for valvular heart disease and heart failure in patients with significant murmurs, including a diastolic, holosystolic, or grade 3 or greater midsystolic heart murmur. **Echocardiography should not be used to screen for heart failure in asymptomatic patients without murmurs.**

Unexplained heart failure, sudden cardiac death, and progressive heart failure in young family members should prompt a search for familial causes of heart failure. Dilated cardiomyopathies may be familial in a significant percentage of cases. A personal or family history of hemochromatosis, hypertrophic cardiomyopathy, or amyloidosis may warrant echocardiographic or genetic screening of asymptomatic family members.

Diagnosis

Among patients presenting to the emergency department with dyspnea, several signs and symptoms influence the likelihood of heart failure. Features that increase the likelihood of heart failure include the presence of paroxysmal nocturnal dyspnea (>twofold likelihood) and the presence of an S_3 (11 times greater likelihood). The likelihood of heart failure is decreased 50% by the absence of dyspnea on exertion and by the absence of crackles on pulmonary auscultation. Elevated jugular venous pressure and an S_3 are independently associated with adverse outcomes, including progression of heart failure. Clinical findings to evaluate for heart failure and their test characteristics are listed in Table 1.

Symptoms are used to assess functional capacity. Functional capacity is most commonly expressed in terms of the New York Heart Association (NYHA) classification, which describes the effort needed to elicit symptoms (Table 2). Such classification schemes are used to determine prognosis and to guide therapy.

Laboratory Evaluation

A resting 12-lead electrocardiogram should be obtained in any patient with new-onset heart failure or an exacerbation of preexisting heart failure to identify the cardiac rhythm and determine the presence of ischemia, prior infarction, left ventricular hypertrophy, and/or conduction system abnormalities. In addition, the electrocardiogram may be used in decision making regarding cardiac resynchronization therapy.

Initial laboratory evaluation should include serum electrolytes, kidney and liver function testing, a complete blood count, and, if indicated, assessment of thyroid function along with tests to screen

Table 1. Clinical Signs of Heart Failure

Finding	Sensitivity[a]	Specificity[a]
Jugular venous distention	0.39	0.92
S_3 gallop	0.13	0.99
Pulmonary crackles	0.60	0.78
Hepatojugular reflux	0.24	0.96
Ascites	0.01	0.97
Edema	0.50	0.78

[a]Among patients presenting with dyspnea to the emergency department.

Data from Wang CS, FitzGerald JM, Schulzer M, Mak E, Ayas NT. Does this dyspneic patient in the emergency department have congestive heart failure? JAMA. 2005;294(15):1944-56. [PMID: 16234501].

Table 2. Clinical Stages of Chronic Heart Failure

NYHA Functional Class	Estimated 1-Year Mortality
I (asymptomatic)	5%-10%
II (symptomatic; slight limitation of physical activity)	15%-30%
III[a] (symptomatic; marked limitation of physical activity)	15%-30%
III[a] (symptomatic; marked limitation of physical activity)	15%-30%
IV (inability to perform any physical activity without symptoms)	50%-60%

NYHA = New York Heart Association.

for specific cardiomyopathies (eg, hemochromatosis) if suggested by the history or clinical presentation.

Measurement of serum B-type natriuretic peptide (BNP), a sensitive marker of ventricular pressure and volume overload, should be reserved for differentiating heart failure from noncardiac causes of dyspnea in the acute care setting when the diagnosis is not clear. **Do not routinely measure BNP in patients with typical signs and symptoms of heart failure.** A BNP level >100 pg/mL is 90% sensitive and 73% specific in the diagnosis of patients with heart failure in the emergency department. Patients with chronic heart failure may have BNP levels <100 pg/mL. Other conditions that raise BNP levels include acute myocardial infarction, pulmonary embolism, chronic kidney disease, older age, and female sex. BNP is reduced by obesity.

Common radiographic findings in patients with heart failure include cardiomegaly (positive likelihood ratio = 4; negative likelihood ratio = 0.26), cephalization (positive likelihood ratio = 9.4; negative likelihood ratio = 0.61), and interstitial edema (positive likelihood ratio = 12.7; negative likelihood ratio = 0.72). Chest radiography may be helpful in determining the cause of dyspnea. **Once heart failure is diagnosed, serial chest radiographs are not sensitive to small changes in pulmonary vascular congestion and are not recommended.**

Echocardiography can help identify specific causes of heart failure, including hypertensive heart disease, ischemic disease, hypertrophic or infiltrative cardiomyopathy, and primary valvular heart disease. Echocardiography is necessary for distinguishing systolic heart failure from heart failure with preserved systolic function.

Coronary artery disease, which is the underlying cause of systolic heart failure in about two thirds of patients, may show echocardiographic evidence of regional wall motion abnormalities and/or post-myocardial infarction ventricular remodeling. Ischemia may also be an exacerbating factor in patients with preexisting heart failure. In appropriate patients, revascularization can result in improved ventricular function, reduced symptoms, and increased survival.

Evaluation for the presence of ischemia is necessary in almost all patients with new-onset or worsening heart failure, unless the clinical evidence strongly suggests a cause other than ischemia. The American College of Cardiology/American Heart Association guidelines recommend coronary angiography for patients with new-onset heart failure who have angina or significant ischemia and are potential candidates for revascularization. For patients with known coronary disease who present with heart failure, noninvasive imaging to assess for myocardial ischemia and viability is reasonable.

Cardiomyopathies

Specific cardiomyopathies may require specific testing or treatment beyond that generally recommended for individuals with systolic heart failure. A diagnosis of dilated cardiomyopathy requires evidence of dilatation and impaired contraction of the left ventricle or both ventricles. Dilated cardiomyopathy has many causes, with the most common being idiopathic (50%), myocarditis (9%), ischemic (7%), peripartum (4%), and toxic (3%). Idiopathic cardiomyopathy is diagnosed if there is no evidence of coronary artery obstruction, myocarditis, or a primary or secondary form of heart muscle disease. Acute myocarditis is immunologically mediated damage to the myocardium; cardiac troponin levels are typically elevated, indicating some degree of myocardial necrosis, and ventricular dysfunction may be global or regional. Peripartum cardiomyopathy occurs during the last trimester of pregnancy or up to 6 months postpartum in the absence of an identifiable cause. Peripartum cardiomyopathy is a major cause of pregnancy-related death in North America; maternal death is related to heart failure, thromboembolic events, and arrhythmias. Left ventricular function improves within 6 months after delivery in approximately 50% of women with peripartum cardiomyopathy. Subsequent pregnancies are associated with a high risk of recurrence, however.

Restrictive cardiomyopathy is a disease of ventricular myocardium that typically results in delayed diastolic relaxation, decreased compliance, and elevated filling pressures with nondilated ventricles and is often due to an infiltrative process. Amyloidosis is the most common diagnosis when a cause can be identified; other common causes include sarcoidosis and hemochromatosis. Prominent symptoms of restrictive cardiomyopathy include fatigue, weakness, anorexia, and edema. Physical examination may reveal peripheral edema, jugular venous distention, hepatojugular reflux, and Kussmaul sign (an increase in jugular venous distention during inspiration). The apical impulse may be forceful, a loud S_3 usually is present, and regurgitant murmurs are common.

Amyloidosis is suggested by neuropathy, marked proteinuria, and hepatomegaly disproportionate to other signs of right-sided heart failure. Characteristic echocardiographic features of amyloidosis include increased ventricular wall thickness, thickened atrioventricular valves, a thickened atrial septum, and pericardial effusion. The combination of low voltage on electrocardiogram and thick ventricular walls on echocardiogram suggests amyloidosis (or another infiltrative process). Bilateral hilar lymphadenopathy with or without pulmonary reticular opacities and skin, joint, or eye lesions are common presenting signs of sarcoidosis. In patients with sarcoidosis, cardiac involvement is suggested by the presence of arrhythmias, conduction blocks, or heart failure. Cardiac symptoms are the initial presentation of hemochromatosis in up to 15% of patients. In patients with hemochromatosis and restrictive cardiomyopathy by echocardiography, a presumptive diagnosis of myocardial hemochromatosis is appropriate.

Hypertrophic cardiomyopathy (HCM) is typically asymptomatic in childhood and adolescence. Symptoms that develop in HCM include angina, dyspnea, palpitations, fatigue, dizziness, and syncope. Symptoms may be caused by diastolic dysfunction, myocardial ischemia, outflow obstruction with or without associated mitral regurgitation, or atrial fibrillation. The most common pattern of hypertrophy is asymmetric septal hypertrophy. In this type, a midsystolic murmur caused by left ventricular outflow tract obstruction may be evident. Maneuvers that decrease preload (Valsalva maneuver) enhance the murmur, and those that augment venous return (leg elevation) diminish the murmur. Within 10 years of diagnosis, 25% of patients with HCM with no or mild symptoms will develop debilitating symptoms. Atrial fibrillation is present in 5% of patients at diagnosis and develops in 10% to 22% of patients over the ensuing 5 to 9 years after diagnosis. Atrial fibrillation may precipitate heart failure or stroke. HCM progresses to dilated cardiomyopathy in 5% to 10% of patients as a result of fibrosis and ventricular remodeling. As this occurs, left ventricular obstruction, if originally present, is lost. Causes of cardiovascular death in patients with HCM include sudden death, heart failure, and stroke. Sudden death is infrequent but is more common in the young (aged 15 to 35 years).

Therapy

Limiting dietary sodium to 2 g daily and fluid to 2 liters per day and recording daily weights results in fewer hospitalizations for patients with decompensated heart failure. Because exercise may improve both physical and psychological well-being, it is important to encourage patients to participate in a long-term aerobic exercise program that is tailored to their functional capacity. Exercise conditioning also improves metabolic and hemodynamic indices in patients with heart failure.

Sleep-disordered breathing, especially sleep apnea and Cheyne-Stokes breathing (a cyclic pattern with progressive, alternating increasing and decreasing respiratory frequency and tidal volume), is common in patients with heart failure. Effective treatment of sleep-disordered breathing and optimization of fluid status is associated with significant improvement in exercise capacity, blood pressure control, and quality of life, as well as decreased rates of disease progression and rehospitalization for heart failure.

Drug Therapy

Table 3 outlines medical therapies for patients with chronic heart failure by functional status. ACE inhibitors are indicated for treatment of all NYHA functional classes of systolic heart failure, including asymptomatic (NYHA Class I) disease. ACE inhibitors delay the onset of clinical heart failure in patients with asymptomatic left ventricular dysfunction, and they reduce morbidity and mortality. Overall, ACE inhibitor therapy reduces mortality by about 20%, risk for myocardial infarction by about 20%, and risk for hospitalization for heart failure by 30% to 40%. ARBs also reduce morbidity and mortality in patients with systolic heart failure. The primary reason to use an ARB instead of an ACE inhibitor is to avoid the side effect of cough. **Combined treatment with an ACE inhibitor and an ARB is not recommended as additional benefit of using these two medications together is not well established.** Furthermore, concurrent therapy is significantly associated with an increased risk of worsening kidney function, hyperkalemia, and hypotension.

As with ACE inhibitors, β-blockers are indicated for treatment of patients with systolic heart failure of any NYHA functional class, including asymptomatic (NYHA Class I) and severe (NYHA Class IV) disease. Treatment with a β-blocker is consistently associated with a 30% reduction in total mortality. Both sudden death and death due to pump failure are reduced. In the United States, carvedilol and extended-release metoprolol (metoprolol succinate) are approved for the treatment of heart failure. In general, β-blockers should not be initiated when a patient is acutely decompensated (hypotensive or volume overloaded), as initiation of therapy is associated with a transient

Table 3. Medical Therapy for Systolic Heart Failure by Functional Status

Initial Therapy

All NYHA classes (I-IV)

ACE inhibitor (if ACE inhibitor is not tolerated because of cough, an ARB can be used; if ACE inhibitor is contraindicated because of hyperkalemia or renal insufficiency, combined hydralazine and isosorbide dinitrate can be used)

β-Blocker

Additional Therapy

NYHA class I or II (asymptomatic or mild symptoms)

Diuretic as needed to maintain euvolemia

NYHA class III or IV (moderate to severe symptoms)

Spironolactone (if gynecomastia occurs, eplerenone can be used)

Combined hydralazine and isosorbide dinitrate (for black patients)

Digoxin

Diuretic as needed to maintain euvolemia

ACE = angiotensin-converting enzyme; ARB = angiotensin-receptor blocker; NYHA = New York Heart Association.

decline in cardiac output. β-Blockers can be initiated and tolerated once euvolemia or near-euvolemia has been established. The risk of exacerbating bronchospastic pulmonary disease with β-blockers is low except in patients with the most refractory pulmonary disease. If reactive airway disease is a concern, more cardioselective (β₁-receptor–selective) agents such as metoprolol should be used.

Diuretics are used to manage volume overload and are typically needed acutely to achieve euvolemia before starting β-blocker therapy and on a long-term basis to prevent recurrent volume overload. In general, loop diuretics (eg, furosemide, bumetanide, torsemide) are used for volume management in patients with heart failure because of their superior natriuretic effects compared with other classes of diuretics.

Aldosterone antagonists (eg, spironolactone, eplerenone) have been shown to improve survival in specific patients with systolic heart failure, decrease symptoms, and improve functional level, likely due to blockade of the deleterious effects of aldosterone on the heart and their potassium-sparing effect that may avoid hypokalemia. Their use is generally recommended for patients with NYHA Class III or IV symptoms and a left ventricular ejection fraction of ≤35%. These drugs, however, may cause hyperkalemia and should be used with caution or avoided in patients with kidney failure or baseline hyperkalemia. **Spironolactone is usually first-line therapy due to clinical experience and cost considerations; however, the more receptor-specific eplerenone may be useful in individuals developing gynecomastia with spironolactone.**

In patients in sinus rhythm, digoxin is used primarily for symptom control. Treatment with digoxin has not been shown to affect mortality but has been shown to reduce hospitalizations.

One study demonstrated that black patients with severe heart failure (NYHA Class III or IV) had a significant (approximately 40%) reduction in mortality with the addition of hydralazine and isosorbide dinitrate to standard heart failure therapy (ie, ACE inhibitor or ARB, β-blocker, spironolactone, digoxin, and diuretics).

First-generation calcium channel blockers (eg, nifedipine) have been shown to increase the risk of heart failure decompensation and hospitalization; however, second-generation dihydropyridine calcium channel blockers do not appear to increase the risk of decompensation or to adversely affect mortality. These agents can be used in patients with heart failure to manage hypertension or angina not adequately controlled with other agents (eg, ACE inhibitors, β-blockers) but are generally not used to treat heart failure itself.

Managing peripartum cardiomyopathy includes early delivery and standard medical therapy with β-blockers, digoxin, and diuretics prior to delivery. Because of teratogenicity, ACE inhibitors and ARBs are withheld until after delivery.

Managing patients with heart failure and preserved left ventricular function is based largely on theoretical concepts and extrapolation from trials in individuals with low ejection fractions. There is general agreement that the approach to such patients includes control of heart rate and blood pressure, maintenance of normal sinus rhythm, and identification and management of myocardial ischemia. Furthermore, in diastolic dysfunction, it is ideal to minimize using agents that decrease preload and avoid the use of digoxin.

Device Therapy and Cardiac Transplantation

Patients with NYHA Class III or IV heart failure, an ejection fraction ≤35%, and a prolonged QRS duration (>150 msec and perhaps >120 msec) on electrocardiography may benefit from cardiac resynchro-

Table 4. Indications for Device Therapy in Heart Failure

Implantable Cardioverter-Defibrillator

NYHA Class II or III while on optimal medical therapy[a] *and*
Life expectancy >1 year *and*
Either of the following:
Ischemic or nonischemic cardiomyopathy with ejection fraction ≤35% (primary prevention)
History of hemodynamically significant ventricular arrhythmia or cardiac arrest (secondary prevention)

Cardiac Resynchronization Therapy

All of the following:
NYHA Class III or IV
Ejection fraction ≤35%
Ventricular dyssynchrony (QRS duration >120 msec)

NYHA = New York Heart Association.

[a] NYHA Class I and ejection fraction ≤30% is also an accepted indication.

Recommendations from Epstein AE, Dimarco JP, Ellenbogen KA, et al; American College of Cardiology; American Heart Association Task Force on Practice Guidelines; American Association for Thoracic Surgery; Society of Thoracic Surgeons. ACC/AHA/HRS 2008 Guidelines for device-based therapy of cardiac rhythm abnormalities [published erratum appears in Heart Rhythm. 2009;6:e2]. Heart Rhythm. 2008;5:e1-62. [PMID: 18534360]

nization therapy, which is pacing of both the right and left ventricles that improves pump function cause by dyssynchrony because of the conduction delay. Cardiac resynchronization therapy in these patients improves functional capacity, quality of life, and mortality.

In patients with sustained significant left ventricular systolic dysfunction (ejection fraction ≤35% for >40 days), NYHA Class II or III heart failure (but not Class IV) while on optimal medical therapy, and life expectancy >1 year, implantation of a cardioverter-defibrillator is associated with a reduction in mortality regardless of whether the underlying cardiomyopathy is secondary to an ischemic or nonischemic cause (Table 4).

Device therapy is not recommended for patients who have heart failure with preserved left ventricular function.

Cardiac transplantation improves survival, functional status, and quality of life in patients with NYHA Class III or IV heart failure. Relative contraindications to cardiac transplantation include age >65 years, end-organ damage from diabetes or vascular disease, malignancy, previous stroke, lack of psychosocial support, or active psychiatric illness.

Follow-Up

Once the diagnosis and underlying cause of heart failure are established, factors responsible for any symptomatic exacerbations should be identified and corrected. Common reasons for an increase in symptoms or a decline in functional status include myocardial ischemia or infarction, cardiac arrhythmias (ie, atrial fibrillation), severe hypertension, worsening kidney function, and nonadherence with medications or dietary recommendations. In general, any condition that causes tachycardia (eg, fever, infection, anemia, thyrotoxicosis) has the potential to worsen heat failure symptoms by shortening diastole and impairing left ventricular filling. It is important to be aware that concomitant use of noncardiac medications (eg, NSAIDs, thiazolidinediones) may cause significant fluid retention and worsen heart failure.

Serial measurements of a patient's weight will determine clinical stability or the need to adjust diuretic doses. Electrolyte disturbances in heart failure are common due to the effect of medications as well as the pathophysiology of heart failure. **Echocardiographic reassessment of ejection fraction is most useful when there is a notable change in clinical status rather than at regular or arbitrary intervals.**

Bibliography

Goldberg LR. Heart failure. Ann Intern Med. 2010;152:ITC61-15; quiz ITC616. [PMID: 20513825]

Chapter 8

Valvular Heart Disease

H. Douglas Walden, MD

Prevention

Antibiotic treatment of group A streptococcal infections and long-term prophylactic antibiotic therapy for patients with a history of rheumatic carditis may decrease the likelihood of rheumatic valvular heart disease.

Screening

Routine screening for valvular heart disease is not recommended, although a high degree of suspicion is appropriate whenever a patient presents with chest pain, heart failure, arrhythmias, congenital abnormalities (eg, Marfan syndrome), or a history of rheumatic fever.

Approach to Cardiac Murmurs

Cardiac murmurs result from increased blood flow across a normal orifice (eg, anemia, thyrotoxicosis, pregnancy, atrial septal defect), turbulent flow through a narrowed orifice (eg, aortic stenosis, mitral stenosis), or regurgitant flow through an incompetent valve (eg, aortic regurgitation, mitral regurgitation). Timing in the cardiac cycle, chest wall location, radiation, intensity (Table 1), configuration, duration, and pitch all assist in the differential diagnosis (Table 2). **Not all systolic murmurs are pathologic. Short, soft systolic murmurs (grade <3) that are asymptomatic often do not require further investigation.** The presence of any diastolic or continuous murmur, cardiac symptoms (eg, chest pain, dyspnea, syncope), or abnormalities on examination (eg, clicks, abnormal S_2, abnormal pulses) requires evaluation by echocardiography.

Various interventions may alter the intensity of murmurs. The murmur of hypertrophic cardiomyopathy may increase with standing or Valsalva maneuver (both maneuvers decrease venous return, which decreases left ventricular chamber size and increases the degree of obstruction). The click and murmur of mitral valve pro-

lapse may move earlier in systole and increase in intensity with standing or Valsalva maneuver (mitral prolapse occurs earlier and is louder with decreased ventricular volume and chamber size).

Aortic outflow murmurs increase in intensity in the beat following a premature ventricular contraction (due to increased left ventricular volume). Murmurs of mitral regurgitation, ventricular septal defect, and aortic regurgitation increase with handgrip (because of increased cardiac output and peripheral resistance). Right-sided heart murmurs may increase during inspiration (due to increased venous return).

Characteristics of the S_2 may assist in determining the diagnosis or the severity of a valvular lesion. A fixed split of S_2 (present during inspiration and expiration instead of only inspiration) results from a delay in right ventricular emptying and is strongly associated with atrial septal defect. A paradoxical split of S_2 (present during expiration) indicates a delay in left ventricular emptying (such as severe aortic stenosis). Presence of a physiologic split (present during inspiration) is helpful for excluding severe aortic stenosis.

Aortic Stenosis

In adults, aortic stenosis occurs as a result of rheumatic heart disease (patients aged 30-40 years), degeneration of a congenital bicuspid valve (patients aged 50-60 years), or age-related degeneration of a normal trileaflet valve (patients aged ≥70 years). A prolonged asymptomatic period of many years marked by progressive left ventricular hypertrophy is followed by a shorter symptomatic period (1-3 years) characterized by angina, syncope, and heart failure. Surgical valve replacement is the definitive therapy.

Diagnosis

Exercise intolerance is an early symptom; symptoms of more advanced disease include dyspnea, angina, or exertional syncope. Physical examination reveals a crescendo-decrescendo systolic murmur loudest at the second right intercostal space, with radiation to the carotid arteries. The murmur becomes longer and peaks later in systole with more advanced disease. It may soften in the presence of left ventricular dysfunction; the intensity of the murmur does not correlate with disease severity. The S_2 may be diminished in intensity, as the valve loses mobility in patients with calcific disease. In younger patients with mild to moderate aortic stenosis due to a bicuspid valve, S_2 may be accentuated and associated with an aortic ejection click heard best at the right upper sternal border just prior to the murmur. An S_4 gallop may accompany left ventricular hypertrophy. Pulsus parvus et tardus (dampened and delayed carotid pulsations) may be present, but carotid upstrokes can be brisk in elderly patients with noncompliant vessels.

Chest radiographs are often normal but may demonstrate a boot-shaped silhouette of left ventricular hypertrophy. Electrocardiograms (ECGs) may demonstrate changes consistent with left atrial or left

Table 1. Grading the Intensity of Cardiac Murmurs

Grade	Description
1	Murmur heard with the stethoscope, but not at first
2	Faint murmur heard with the stethoscope on the chest wall
3	Murmur heard with the stethoscope on the chest wall; louder than grade 2 but without a thrill (a vibration felt on palpation over the heart)
4	Murmur associated with a thrill
5	Murmur heard with just the rim of the stethoscope held against the chest
6	Murmur heard with the stethoscope held close to but not touching the chest wall

Table 2. Cardiac Murmurs and Associated Findings

Cause of Murmur	Characteristic	Location	Radiation	Associated Findings
Systolic Murmurs				
Innocent flow murmur	Soft, midsystolic	Base	None	Normal splitting of S_2
Aortic stenosis	Crescendo-decrescendo, midsystolic	Base	Carotids	Single S_2, pulsus parvus, S_4
Hypertrophic obstructive cardiomyopathy	Crescendo, mid- or late systolic	Lower left sternal border	Carotids	Bifid carotid impulse; murmur decreases with passive leg elevation or handgrip, increases with Valsalva
Mitral regurgitation	Holo- or late systolic	Apex	Axilla or back	Murmur increases with isometric exercise; best heard with patient in left lateral decubitus position
Mitral valve prolapse mitral regurgitation	Late systolic	Apex	Axilla	With Valsalva, midsystolic click and murmur move closer to S_1, and murmur increases in intensity
Tricuspid regurgitation	Holosystolic	Lower left sternal border	Lower right sternal border	Prominent *v* waves in neck; murmur increases with inspiration
Diastolic Murmurs				
Aortic regurgitation	Decrescendo	Second right or third to left intercostal space	None	Widened pulse pressure, fourth bounding carotid pulses; murmur best heard with patient in upright position, leaning forward, at end-expiration
Pulmonic regurgitation	Mid-diastolic	Upper left sternal border	None	Loud S_2 if pulmonary hypertension is present
Mitral stenosis	Low-pitched rumble	Apex	None	Murmur best heard with patient in left lateral decubitus position; opening snap

ventricular enlargement. Echocardiograms often demonstrate thickened and calcified aortic valve leaflets with restricted motion. Doppler studies can estimate the transvalvular pressure gradient and aortic valve area. CT can be helpful in evaluating the aortic root to exclude aortic aneurysm, which is particularly common in patients with a bicuspid aortic valve. A coronary angiogram is usually obtained before aortic valve surgery in patients with concomitant coronary artery disease and those at risk for it (men aged ≥35 years, postmenopausal women and women aged ≥35 years with risk factors) to enable treatment at the time of valve replacement.

Therapy

Surgical aortic valve replacement is the definitive therapy for patients with symptomatic severe disease (valve area <1.0 cm²). Left ventricular failure is associated with an increased mortality rate but is not a contraindication to surgery. Ventricular function often improves after valve replacement. Surgical aortic valve replacement may be considered for patients with asymptomatic severe valvular stenosis (valve area <0.60 cm²), those with rapid progression of disease, and those requiring open-heart surgery for other reasons (coronary artery disease or other valvular disease).

Transcatheter aortic valve replacement involves percutaneous placement of a bioprosthetic valve over the native stenotic valve and is a therapeutic option for patients too frail for surgical aortic valve replacement. Although improved survival has been documented, its use is limited to this patient group as its effectiveness in lower-risk patients has not been established.

Balloon aortic valvuloplasty does not improve survival and is associated with a high rate of restenosis but can be considered as a temporizing or bridging measure in select patients who have other noncardiac disease that is considered life-limiting.

Hemodynamically unstable patients may benefit from the use of sodium nitroprusside and intra-aortic balloon counterpulsation before surgical intervention. Atrial fibrillation is often poorly tolerated due to loss of the atrial contractile kick and inadequate diastolic filling with faster heart rates. Cardioversion or atrioventricular nodal blocking agents (eg, calcium channel or β-blockers) are used to manage heart rate in patients with atrial fibrillation. Use of ACE inhibitors, digoxin, and diuretics may result in symptomatic improvement in heart failure but are of limited value if surgical therapy is not possible and may cause hemodynamic collapse.

Follow-Up

Asymptomatic patients with mild disease typically remain stable for years. The degree of aortic valve calcification, the presence of coronary disease, and more severe valvular disease predict worse outcomes without surgery. A history and physical examination and transthoracic echocardiography are often performed annually, with more frequent clinical evaluations in patients with more advanced disease.

Aortic Insufficiency

Acute and chronic disease differ in clinical presentation. Acute aortic insufficiency is caused by infective endocarditis, aortic dissection, or trauma; it often presents as cardiogenic shock and usually requires emergent valve replacement. Chronic aortic insufficiency may result from rheumatic heart disease, previous endocarditis, a bicuspid aortic valve, aortic root disease, or tertiary syphilis.

Diagnosis

The diagnosis of acute aortic insufficiency is suggested in patients with rapid onset of dyspnea, exercise intolerance, or chest pain (aortic dissection). Physical findings include tachycardia, hypotension, a soft S_1 (due to premature closure of the mitral valve), an S_3 gallop, an accentuated pulmonic valve closure sound (P_2), and pulmonary crackles. Heart size may be normal, and pulse pressure may not be widened. The typical murmur of aortic insufficiency may not be prominent in acute disease, as aortic and left ventricular diastolic pressures equilibrate quickly, resulting in a short and soft (sometimes inaudible) diastolic murmur.

Symptoms of chronic disease include dyspnea on exertion, orthopnea, paroxysmal nocturnal dyspnea, angina, and palpitations. Some patients remain asymptomatic for long periods as the left ventricle insidiously dilates. Physical findings include cardiomegaly, tachycardia, a widened pulse pressure, a thrill at the base of the heart, a soft S_1 and sometimes absent aortic valve closure sound (A_2), and an S_3 gallop. The characteristic high-pitched diastolic murmur begins immediately after S_2 and is heard at the second right or third left intercostal space; it is heard best with the patient seated and leaning forward at end-expiration. Manifestations of the widened pulse pressure may include Traube sign (pistol shot sounds over the peripheral arteries), Musset sign (head bobs with each heartbeat), Duroziez murmur (systolic and diastolic murmur heard over the femoral artery), and Quincke pulse (systolic plethora and diastolic blanching in the nail bed with nail compression).

Chest radiographs may reveal cardiomegaly, valve calcification, enlargement of the aortic root, or pulmonary congestion. ECG findings can include left axis deviation and left ventricular hypertrophy. Tertiary syphilis should be excluded with appropriate serological testing (ie, VDRL, rapid plasma reagin). Doppler echocardiography with color flow can confirm the presence and severity of disease and help assess the cause.

Therapy

Immediate aortic valve replacement is indicated in acute disease because a normal left ventricle cannot accommodate the large regurgitant volume. Sodium nitroprusside or intravenous nitroglycerin leads to augmentation of forward cardiac output, reduction of regurgitant flow, and an improved ejection fraction and can be used as a bridge to valve replacement. Intravenous diuretics and inotropic agents (dobutamine) may also support blood pressure and improve cardiac contractility. The use of an intra-aortic balloon pump is contraindicated in acute aortic insufficiency because this will increase regurgitant flow.

Aortic valve replacement is also the treatment of choice for patients with severe chronic disease. Left ventricular systolic function is the most important determinant of survival. Valve replacement is indicated for all patients with more than mild symptoms, patients with progressive left ventricular dilatation, and patients with a left ventricular ejection fraction of <50%. The use of vasodilators such as dihydropyridine calcium channel blockers, hydralazine, an ACE inhibitor, or angiotensin-receptor blocker may be helpful as a short-term measure in symptomatic patients or for patients with left ventricular dysfunction unable to undergo surgical valve replacement. Prognosis for asymptomatic patients with a preserved ejection fraction is excellent without drug therapy; there is no clear benefit of vasodilators in this group.

Follow-Up

A history and physical examination and transthoracic echocardiography are often performed annually in asymptomatic patients with normal left ventricular size and function. Evaluation every 6 to 12 months is needed in asymptomatic patients with severe aortic insufficiency and in patients with dilated left ventricles. Transthoracic echocardiography should also be obtained in patients with new or changing symptoms, worsening exercise tolerance, or clinical findings suggestive of progressive disease.

Mitral Stenosis

Nearly all cases of mitral stenosis in adults are due to rheumatic heart disease. Rare causes include malignant carcinoid syndrome, systemic lupus erythematosus, rheumatoid arthritis, and amyloidosis. Thickening and calcification of the valve impair flow from the left atrium to the left ventricle, leading to pulmonary hypertension and right-sided heart failure. Symptoms develop after years of valvular dysfunction. Surgical valve repair is the definitive treatment of severe disease.

Diagnosis

Symptoms of mitral stenosis include dyspnea, fatigue, edema, orthopnea, paroxysmal nocturnal dyspnea, cough, hemoptysis, hoarseness, chest pain, palpitations, and symptoms suggestive of systemic embolism. Exertional symptoms often develop when the valve area is <1.5 cm^2, whereas resting symptoms can be present when the valve area is <1.0 cm^2. Symptoms may develop with larger valve areas during exercise, pregnancy, infection, or atrial fibrillation. Physical findings include a prominent a wave in the jugular pulse (decreased right ventricular compliance with pulmonary hypertension), a palpable thrill at the apex, a right ventricular heave, and signs of right-sided heart failure (eg, jugular venous distention, hepatomegaly, ascites, edema). Cardiac auscultation reveals an accentuated P_2 (evidence of elevated pulmonary artery pressure), an opening snap (a high-pitched apical sound best heard with the diaphragm), and a low-pitched, rumbling diastolic murmur best heard at the apex using the bell, with the patient in the left lateral decubitus position. Presystolic accentuation of the murmur may be present in both sinus rhythm and atrial fibrillation. As the severity of the stenosis worsens, the opening snap moves closer to S_2 as a result of increased left atrial pressure, and the murmur increases in duration.

A chest radiograph may reveal chamber enlargement and interstitial edema. ECG findings often include rhythm abnormalities (ie, atrial fibrillation in 30% of symptomatic patients), right axis deviation, and left atrial and right ventricular enlargement. Transthoracic Doppler echocardiography can assess mitral valve morphology, involvement of other valves, chamber size and function, presence of a left atrial thrombus, and can exclude other conditions that mimic mitral stenosis. The valve area, the pressure gradient across the valve, and concomitant mitral regurgitation can be determined using Doppler techniques.

Therapy

Mitral valvotomy or valve replacement is the treatment of choice in symptomatic patients. Percutaneous balloon valvotomy is suitable in symptomatic patients with moderate to severe disease and pliable noncalcified leaflets with minimal mitral regurgitation. Valve replacement is recommended for patients with moderate or severe disease (marked limitation of physical activity or inability to perform any physical activity) who are not candidates for valvotomy or valve repair, or for patients with significantly increased pulmonary arterial pressures. Mortality associated with mitral valve replacement depends on functional status, age, left ventricular function, and the presence of coronary artery disease but can be as high as 10% to 20% in older patients with comorbidities.

β-Blockers or calcium channel blockers with negative chronotropic properties increase diastolic filling time and are used for patients with symptoms associated with tachycardia. Diuretics are useful if pulmonary vascular congestion is present. Atrial fibrillation is usually treated with anticoagulants and atrioventricular nodal blocking agents to control heart rate, but antiarrhythmic agents or cardioversion may be considered for worsening symptoms. Warfarin therapy (goal international normalized ratio [INR] of 2.0-3.0) is recommended for patients with a history of prior embolic events and for patients with atrial fibrillation, sinus rhythm and an enlarged left atrium, or left atrial thrombi.

Follow-Up

Asymptomatic and mildly symptomatic patients are evaluated annually with a history and physical examination, electrocardiography, and chest radiography. Patients who have undergone percutaneous or surgical mitral valvuloplasty are evaluated with postprocedure echocardiography and an annual evaluation thereafter. An echocardiogram is obtained if symptoms recur or if a change is noted on physical examination.

Mitral Regurgitation

Acute mitral regurgitation may result from chordae tendineae rupture, papillary muscle rupture or dysfunction in patients with acute coronary syndrome, myxomatous degeneration (pathologic weakening of the valve associated with accumulation of glycosaminoglycans), infective endocarditis, trauma, or acute myocardial ischemia. Mitral valve prolapse currently is the most common cause of chronic disease, followed by ischemic mitral valve disease and damage from infective endocarditis. Mitral annular calcification is a common cause of mitral regurgitation in older patients, whereas rheumatic heart disease is now a relatively uncommon cause.

Diagnosis

Acute, severe mitral regurgitation causes abrupt onset of dyspnea, pulmonary edema, or cardiogenic shock. Physical findings may include hypotension, an apical holosystolic murmur radiating to the axilla (the murmur may be short or absent), an S_3 or S_4 gallop, pulmonary crackles, and signs of right-sided heart failure (eg, jugular venous distention, hepatomegaly, edema).

Chronic mitral regurgitation results in exercise intolerance, dyspnea, or fatigue. Physical findings include brisk carotid upstrokes, a laterally displaced apical impulse, decreased intensity of S_1, increased intensity of P_2, a widely split S_2 during inspiration, and an S_3 gallop. The holosystolic murmur is best heard with the diaphragm at the apex, with the patient in the left lateral decubitus position; the murmur may radiate to the left axilla and left scapular region. In advanced cases, chest radiographs may reveal cardiomegaly and pulmonary vascular congestion. An ECG may demonstrate an abnormal rhythm (ie, atrial fibrillation) and findings consistent with left atrial enlargement and left ventricular hypertrophy. Doppler echocardiography allows for assessment of left atrial and left ventricular volumes, ejection fraction, and other valvular disease. The left ventricular ejection fraction may be normal or falsely elevated due to systolic ejection of a portion of left ventricular volume into the low-pressure left atrium.

Therapy

Repair or replacing the mitral valve is indicated in symptomatic patients with acute disease. Vasodilators (eg, sodium nitroprusside, nitroglycerin) and diuretics reduce pulmonary congestion and improve forward cardiac output. An inotropic agent (dobutamine) may be used if hypotension develops. Intra-aortic balloon counterpulsation can improve coronary perfusion and reduce afterload in hemodynamically unstable patients as a bridge to valve replacement.

In long-term disease, survival depends on left ventricular function, and surgery is most effective prior to the development of heart failure, atrial fibrillation, and pulmonary hypertension. Patients who display echocardiographic features of left ventricular dilatation and/or depressed function are candidates for surgical intervention. Valve repair has advantages over replacement, including the avoidance of anticoagulants and future mechanical valve complications or failure. A percutaneously placed clip that focally approximates the edges of the mitral valve leaflets to reduce regurgitation is available for patients considered too frail to tolerate surgery. In chronic mitral regurgitation with depressed left ventricular function, diuretics, β-blockers, and ACE inhibitors (or angiotensin-receptor blockers) are indicated. Anticoagulants and atrioventricular nodal blocking agents are used in patients with atrial fibrillation.

Follow-Up

Annual history, physical examination, and echocardiography are appropriate for patients with mild disease. More frequent monitoring is indicated for advanced disease. Patients with evidence of progressive left ventricular dysfunction require surgical intervention.

Mitral Valve Prolapse

Mitral valve prolapse results from myxomatous degeneration and is the most common congenital valvular abnormality, with a prevalence of up to 4% to 5%. Many patients are asymptomatic, others require symptomatic treatment, and occasional patients may progress to severe mitral regurgitation requiring valve replacement or repair.

Diagnosis

Patients may experience chest pain, palpitations, dizziness, syncope, dyspnea, fatigue, or symptoms of embolic phenomena. Many symptoms cannot be attributed directly to valvular dysfunction. Auscultation may reveal a high-pitched, midsystolic click sometimes followed by a late systolic murmur that is loudest at the apex. The click and murmur are accentuated and move earlier into systole as left ventricular volume decreases (standing or Valsalva maneuver).

Chest radiographs may reveal chamber enlargement, thoracic aneurysm formation, and skeletal abnormalities (eg, pectus excavatum or carinatum, abnormalities of the thoracic spine). An ECG may reveal a prolonged QT interval and arrhythmias. Echocardiography is used to assess the severity of mitral regurgitation, mitral leaflet morphology, and left ventricular size and function. Severe regurgitation, thick and redundant leaflets, flail leaflets, and left atrial and left ventricular enlargement are associated with adverse outcomes.

Therapy

Dietary and lifestyle modifications (ie, restriction of alcohol and caffeine intake, smoking cessation) are the initial treatment for palpitations, chest pain, anxiety, and fatigue. If symptoms persist, β-blockers are used. Anticoagulation with warfarin is indicated if structural cardiac disease and atrial fibrillation are present. Surgical intervention (mitral valve repair or replacement) is indicated for severe mitral regurgitation.

Follow-Up

Serial echocardiograms are useful for patients with thickened, redundant mitral leaflets, chest pain, syncope, or left ventricular dysfunction/mitral regurgitation. Development of significant mitral regurgitation may ultimately lead to the need for mitral valve surgery.

Tricuspid Valve Disease

Tricuspid valve regurgitation is almost always an acquired process, not a primary valvular disease. Pulmonary hypertension due to chronic lung disease or left-sided heart failure causes right ventricular enlargement, with stretching of the tricuspid annulus. Other causes may include carcinoid heart disease, irradiation, and drug exposure (eg, fenfluramine, dexfenfluramine, pergolide, ergotamine, methysergide).

Diagnosis

Most patients with mild to moderate tricuspid regurgitation are asymptomatic. Dyspnea, ascites, and edema can appear with severe regurgitation. Examination reveals a systolic murmur, which is loudest at the lower left sternal border and may increase with inspiration. An ECG may reveal right axis deviation and changes consistent with right atrial enlargement and right ventricular enlargement. Echocardiography can confirm the diagnosis.

Treatment

Diuretics may be helpful for the management of ascites and edema. Valve replacement or repair is usually not required but may be needed in refractory cases.

Pregnancy

The increased plasma volume and increased heart rate present during pregnancy may lead to cardiac decompensation in patients with impaired left ventricular function or moderate to severe valvular heart disease. Regurgitant lesions may be tolerated, but stenotic lesions often pose clinical problems due to inadequate diastolic filling with faster heart rates. Mitral stenosis, in particular, may first come to attention during pregnancy. For women with prosthetic heart valves, issues pertaining to anticoagulation during pregnancy require careful attention and discussion among the patient, obstetrician, and cardiologist.

Prosthetic Heart Valves

Decisions regarding the timing of surgical intervention for valvular disease can be difficult and are best made in consultation with a cardiologist and cardiac surgeon. Preservation of left ventricular function is important to optimal cardiac function after surgery, particularly in patients with mitral valve disease.

The choice of a bioprosthetic valve (a valve constructed from human or animal tissue) or a mechanical prosthetic valve is an individualized decision based primarily on patient age and suitability or desirability of warfarin anticoagulation. Mechanical valves are more durable than bioprostheses, but they require long-term warfarin anticoagulation to a goal INR of 2.5 to 3.5 (with the addition of aspirin, assuming no contraindication to its use). Bioprostheses are reasonable choices for older patients but may also be used in younger patients who understand the potential future need for a second valve procedure. The development and future use of less invasive techniques of valve replacement (eg, percutaneous catheter-based aortic valve replacement) may make selection of bioprostheses even more reasonable as an initial choice. Patients with bioprostheses in the aortic or mitral position and without known risk factors for embolic events (eg, atrial fibrillation, left ventricular dysfunction, previous thromboembolism, hypercoagulable state) may be treated with aspirin without the addition of warfarin. All patients with prosthetic heart valves should receive antibiotic prophylaxis for the prevention of infective endocarditis.

Patients with prosthetic valves should be monitored clinically for evidence of valvular dysfunction. Findings that suggest prosthetic aortic valvular dysfunction can include loss of a sharp valve click and development of the diastolic murmur of aortic regurgitation. A systolic ejection murmur secondary to turbulent flow is common after aortic valve replacement and is not evidence of valvular dysfunction. Evidence suggesting prosthetic mitral valvular dysfunction includes loss of a sharp valve click and development of the blowing murmur of mitral regurgitation. **Routine serial echocardiography is not needed in asymptomatic patients with prosthetic heart valves.** Echocardiography is indicated when clinical symptoms or clinical examination suggests the presence of prosthetic valvular dysfunction.

Bibliography

Etchells E, Bell C, Robb K. Does this patient have an abnormal systolic murmur? JAMA. 1997;277:564-571. [PMID: 9032164]

Choudhry NK, Etchells EE. Does this patient have aortic regurgitation? JAMA. 1999;281:2231-2238. [PMID: 10376577]

Maganti K, Rigolin, VH, Sarano ME, et al. Valvular heart disease. Mayo Clin Proc. 2010;85(5):483-500. [PMID: 20435842]

Chapter 9

Vascular Disease

Leigh Simmons, MD
Robert Trowbridge, MD

Lower Extremity Peripheral Arterial Disease

Lower extremity peripheral arterial disease (PAD) refers to the atherosclerotic obstruction of blood flow to the arteries supplying the lower extremities, including the aorta. Lower extremity ischemia may also result from clot embolization, most commonly in patients with atrial fibrillation or congestive heart failure.

Diagnosis

The patients at highest risk for PAD are those with known atherosclerosis or atherosclerosis risk factors including hyperlipidemia, hypertension, and cigarette use. Patients commonly present with pain or fatigue in the legs when walking. The pain may be present anywhere from the buttocks to the feet with location being a reflection of the level of arterial blockage. Patients with critical limb ischemia may present with acute onset of pain or pain at rest.

The examination should include inspection of the lower legs and feet for hair loss and shiny skin, skin breakdown or ulceration in the feet, and documentation of pulses. The femoral, popliteal, dorsalis pedis, and posterior tibial pulses may be diminished. Patients with critical limb ischemia may present with some or all of the "6 P's" (pain, poikilothermia [variation in temperature], paresthesias, pulselessness, pallor, paralysis). If the patient's history or physical examination suggests PAD, further testing is indicated.

The ankle-brachial index (ABI) is an excellent initial test for PAD in the patient without critical limb ischemia. It is performed by examining the patient while fully supine and using palpation or a Doppler ultrasound to locate the dorsalis pedis pulse and the posterior tibial pulse on each side. A blood pressure cuff is applied to the lower leg above the malleolus and inflated to occlude blood flow; the cuff is deflated, and the blood pressure at which arterial flow is detected in each artery is recorded. The brachial artery pressure in both arms is measured in the same way. The ABI is calculated by the highest ankle pressure of either side divided by the highest brachial pressure of either side. An ABI of ≤0.90 establishes PAD; an ABI of ≤0.40 suggests severe PAD. If the ABI is >1.40, this suggests noncompressible (calcified) vessels, and the results are not interpretable. Furthermore, if the ABI is borderline or normal but the patient has a high pretest probability of PAD, then performing an ABI with exercise can be done. If the ABI decreases by 20% or more after exercise, significant PAD is suggested.

Computed tomography angiography or magnetic resonance angiography may be performed to determine anatomy for patients who are candidates for surgical intervention. Both require intravenous contrast and must be used carefully in patients with chronic kidney disease. Conventional angiography is generally reserved for those undergoing surgery but is performed emergently if critical limb ischemia is suspected.

Therapy

Medical therapy centers on risk factor modification. Smoking cessation is critical for limiting progression of PAD and to protect surgical bypass grafts in patients treated surgically for PAD. Hypertension and dyslipidemia should be treated aggressively. Statin therapy reduces risk of cardiovascular events and for some patients will have modest benefit for pain-free walking distance. All patients with symptomatic PAD should receive antiplatelet therapy, usually aspirin or clopidogrel for patients who do not tolerate aspirin. Combination treatment with aspirin and warfarin, or warfarin alone, is not generally warranted for PAD.

A regular walking program that includes 30 to 45 minutes of exercise three times weekly has been shown to improve symptoms. Cilostazol, a phosphodiesterase inhibitor that has antiplatelet and vasodilatory properties, can be used to increase pain-free walking time, although a walking program is more effective.

Many patients have stable disease or respond to medical therapy. Patients with significant pain and debility, however, should be considered for revascularization. If anatomically amenable, endovascular stenting (ie, the placement of a stent percutaneously using a catheter) is the treatment of choice for aortoiliac disease and is superior to angioplasty (dilating stenosed vessels) alone. Patients with critical limb ischemia must undergo immediate revascularization, which may be accomplished through surgical bypass, angioplasty, or thrombolysis.

Follow-Up

Patients with PAD should have regular examinations that include a review of symptoms, including questions about claudication, rest pain, and weakness, and regular vascular examinations to inspect pulses and signs of arterial insufficiency. **For most patients, imaging studies are not needed for routine monitoring of PAD, but may be indicated if intervention is felt to be needed.**

Aortic Disease

Aortic Dissection

Aortic dissection results from a tear in the aortic intima with formation of a flap and migration of blood into the media of the artery. Propagation of the dissection causes many of the additional complications of aortic dissection, including ischemia, cardiac tamponade, massive hemorrhage, and aortic regurgitation.

Diagnosis

Risk factors for acute aortic dissection include hypertension, atherosclerosis, preexisting aneurysm, vasculitis, collagen disorders, and bicuspid aortic valve. Aortic dissections are classically defined by the Stanford system as type A (involving the ascending aorta) and type

B (all others). The syndrome of aortic dissection usually presents with sharp or tearing chest and/or back pain, may be accompanied by syncope, heart failure, or stroke, and is rarely asymptomatic. Chest pain with concomitant acute ischemia in a distant arterial bed (eg, stroke, limb ischemia) should prompt consideration of dissection. Key clinical findings with acute aortic dissection include the abrupt onset of pain with a sharp, tearing character, mediastinal or aortic widening on chest radiography, and variation in pulse (eg, absence of proximal extremity or carotid pulse) and/or blood pressure (>20 mm/Hg difference in systolic pressure between the arms).

In patients with a low likelihood of disease, D-dimer testing may be useful in excluding the diagnosis of dissection. If indicated, immediate imaging using chest computed tomography (CT), transesophageal echocardiography, or chest magnetic resonance imaging (MRI) may all be used in the initial evaluation of patients with suspected thoracic aortic aneurysm.

Therapy

Therapy for patients with aortic dissection depends on the area of aorta involved. Emergent surgical intervention is always indicated for patients with type A dissection involving the ascending aorta because of the high risk of complications and death. For stable patients who have an uncomplicated aortic dissection confined to the descending thoracic aorta, medical therapy with reduction of systolic blood pressure to <100 to 120 mm Hg is appropriate; a β-blocker is preferred to minimize aortic wall stress. Intervention may also be indicated with type B dissection if there is end-organ ischemia, persistent pain, or propagation of the dissection; endovascular stent grafting may be an option in stable patients.

Follow-Up

Long-term management of patients with aortic dissection involves minimizing aortic wall stress with lifelong β-blocker therapy and avoidance of strenuous physical activity. Patients are followed with serial chest CT or MRI scans at regular and initially frequent intervals. Some patients may require reoperation if they have recurrence or extension of the aneurysm, or any evidence of graft problems.

Aortic Aneurysm

Thoracic Aortic Aneurysm

Thoracic aortic aneurysms (TAAs) can be related to heritable conditions, including Marfan syndrome and congenital aortic valvular disease. More commonly, they are acquired and related to atherosclerotic disease. TAAs will less commonly result from infections such as syphilis or inflammation such as Takayasu arteritis.

Diagnosis

TAAs are most commonly noted incidentally on chest radiography performed for other purposes. If TAAS are suspected, patients should undergo CT, MRI, or echocardiography to determine aortic cross-sectional area. Patients with physical characteristics suggestive of Marfan syndrome (eg, tall stature, arachnodactyly), family history of TAA, or a known bicuspid aortic valve, are candidates for additional testing. Other patients may have symptoms such as hoarseness or dysphagia that prompt imaging for TAAs.

Therapy

All patients with TAAs should have treatment to lower blood pressure, and those with degenerative atherosclerotic aneurysms should have cardiovascular disease risk factor modification. Patients with

Marfan syndrome should be treated with β-blockers to reduce the rate of aneurysm expansion; angiotensin-receptor blockers may be similarly effective in these patients.

Not all TAAs will require repair, with the decision to repair depending on size, presence of an underlying genetic etiology, and trajectory of aneurysm expansion. Repair requires high-risk surgery and may include aortic valve replacement; endovascular stent repair is currently under study.

Follow-Up

Patients with TAAs require regular monitoring of their aneurysm size depending on the cause of the aneurysm and rate of expansion.

Abdominal Aortic Aneurysm

The abdominal aorta is the most common site of arterial aneurysms. Risk factors for development of abdominal aortic aneurysms (AAAs) include age, male sex, tobacco use, family history of AAA in a first-degree relative, atherosclerosis, and Ehlers-Danlos syndrome.

Diagnosis

Most AAAs are discovered incidentally or on screening examination. All men aged 65 to 75 years who have ever smoked or have a first degree relative with a treated or ruptured AAA should be screened once with ultrasound (see Chapter 30). Patients may present with symptoms related to aneurysm expansion or leakage, including back or abdominal pain. Occasionally, patients may have symptoms related to aneurysm-related thrombosis, especially in the lower extremities. Patients with a ruptured AAA are often hypotensive, and a pulsatile mass may be palpated in some patients. The lack of a pulsatile mass, however, is not reliable in excluding the diagnosis, especially in obese patients.

AAAs can be adequately evaluated either by ultrasound or by CT angiography. CT angiography is generally indicated for hemodynamically stable patients with suspected rupture, as the CT can provide additional information about aortic anatomy that will assist in intervention.

Therapy

There are no proven medical treatments to reduce the rate of AAA expansion; however, all patients with AAAs should have aggressive treatment of hypertension, hyperlipidemia, and especially tobacco dependence, as associated cardiovascular disease is very common in patients with AAAs.

Surgical treatment of asymptomatic patients who have a life expectancy of >2 years is performed when the AAA has reached a diameter of 5.5 cm or is expanding at a rate of >0.5 cm in 6 months. Patients who present with abdominal or back pain in association with AAAs should be evaluated closely to determine whether the symptoms are related to the AAA. Urgent open surgical or endovascular repair is always indicated for ruptured AAAs, although the optimal procedure (open surgical or endovascular) requires assessment of individual patient risks and benefits.

Follow-Up

Most patients with AAAs do not require intervention at the time of diagnosis. Patients with AAAs <5.5 cm in diameter should undergo regular monitoring with ultrasound. Moderate exercise is indicated for best cardiovascular health, although heavy lifting and other activities that cause the Valsalva maneuver should be avoided.

Patients with small abdominal aortic aneurysms (<4.5 cm) are generally monitored annually with ultrasound, and those with larger aneurysms may be monitored every 3 to 6 months depending on rate of expansion.

Carotid Artery Stenosis

Carotid artery stenosis refers to atherosclerotic blockage of one or both carotid arteries. Cerebral embolization of unstable carotid plaque is an important cause of ischemic stroke. Complete occlusion of a carotid artery may also cause stroke, although the redundant cerebral circulation and the circle of Willis provides some protection against this mechanism of stroke.

Diagnosis

Screening for carotid stenosis is not recommended in the general population. Carotid artery stenosis is usually diagnosed as part of the evaluation for an ischemic stroke or transient ischemic attack (TIA). Such ischemic events occur in the distribution of the anterior cerebral circulation, most commonly that of the middle cerebral arteries. It may also be discovered as part of the evaluation for a carotid bruit.

Radiographic evaluation is centered on identifying patients with high-grade (>70%) stenosis, as these patients may benefit from surgical intervention. Duplex ultrasonography is commonly used for detecting and quantifying carotid artery stenosis because it is safe, effective, and relatively inexpensive. Magnetic resonance angiography and CT angiography may have slightly improved test characteristics than ultrasound but are more expensive; CT angiography requires the use of potentially nephrotoxic contrast dye. Conventional cerebral arteriography is the gold standard study but is now rarely performed, as it incurs a small risk of stroke.

Therapy

All patients with carotid artery stenosis should undergo aggressive risk factor modification with treatment of hypertension and cessation of tobacco use. All patients should additionally be aggressively treated with antiplatelet therapy and lipid-lowering agents, specifically statins.

The decision to pursue surgical therapy is controversial and depends on whether the patient is symptomatic, the degree of arterial stenosis, the surgical risk, and the skill of the surgeon. In asymptomatic patients, surgical carotid endarterectomy may be considered in patients with stenosis of 70% to 99%. This is not an absolute indication, however, and medical therapy is also reasonable, even in patients with low surgical risk.

Symptomatic patients are those with a transient ischemic event or completed minor stroke in the cerebral vascular distribution distal to the atherosclerotic blockage. The presence of symptoms increases the risk of subsequent stroke, and thus treatment is usually more aggressive. Carotid endarterectomy is often recommended for most patients with symptomatic disease and stenosis >70% with the threshold dropping to >50% in men. **Carotid artery stenting is usually associated with a higher risk of stroke than surgery and is not routinely performed in patients with carotid stenosis.** Stenting may be an option in patients with a limited life expectancy or severe comorbidities, but there is little evidence supporting this approach.

Renal Artery Stenosis

Renal artery stenosis is usually associated with atherosclerotic disease but may be secondary to fibromuscular dysplasia, especially in young women.

Diagnosis

The presentation of renal artery stenosis is variable. It typically presents in a patient with known arterial disease with progressive renal insufficiency and hypertension, which is often severe and refractory to treatment. It may also be associated with acute onset pulmonary edema and intolerance of angiotensin-converting enzyme inhibitors or angiotensin receptor blockers. In young patients with fibromuscular dysplasia, hypertension is usually the presenting complaint.

Diagnosis is made via imaging. Doppler ultrasonography has excellent test characteristics but is highly operator dependent. CT angiography and magnetic resonance angiography are also reasonable diagnostic options but are limited by cost and the need for intravenous contrast media.

Therapy

Carefully selected patients may benefit from renal artery angioplasty or stenting, but most patients should be treated medically. Medical treatment centers on controlling hypertension; an exception is patients with fibromuscular dysplasia who respond well to angioplasty.

Venous Disease

Venous Stasis

Venous stasis occurs most commonly in the lower extremities and is usually the result of venous insufficiency caused by chronic insufficiency of the dependent venous system (varicose veins), or damage to veins due to prior inflammation (post-phlebitic syndrome).

Diagnosis

Patients with venous stasis typically present with progressive lower extremity edema with achy pain in the legs that may be worse with prolonged standing. Examination reveals edema with shiny, atrophic skin as well as cutaneous telangiectasia. Varicose veins may also be present. In severe cases, there is breakdown of skin or ulceration, especially around the medial malleolus.

Lower extremity edema secondary to venous stasis must be differentiated from other causes including congestive heart failure, mechanical venous obstruction, liver failure, and chronic kidney disease. Venous stasis may also be confused with cellulitis, although cellulitis is rarely bilateral, and the erythema associated with cellulitis is blanching.

Therapy

External compression, most often through the use of specialized stockings, is the first line of treatment in addition to behavior modification (eg, eliminating prolonged periods of standing, leg elevation). When varicosities are present, consideration can be given to radiofrequency or laser ablation, although the efficacy of these procedures in reducing stasis is unclear. Avoiding systemic volume overload is desirable, although diuresis in otherwise euvolemic patients is not usually an effective treatment.

Ulcers secondary to chronic venous stasis are difficult to treat and often recur. Unna boots are specialized compressive dressings treated with agents to decrease edema and promote healing, although they must be applied periodically by medical professionals. Aspirin may also be effective.

Deep Venous Thrombosis

Deep venous thrombosis (DVT) and pulmonary embolism (PE) are manifestations of the same disease, collectively referred to as *venous*

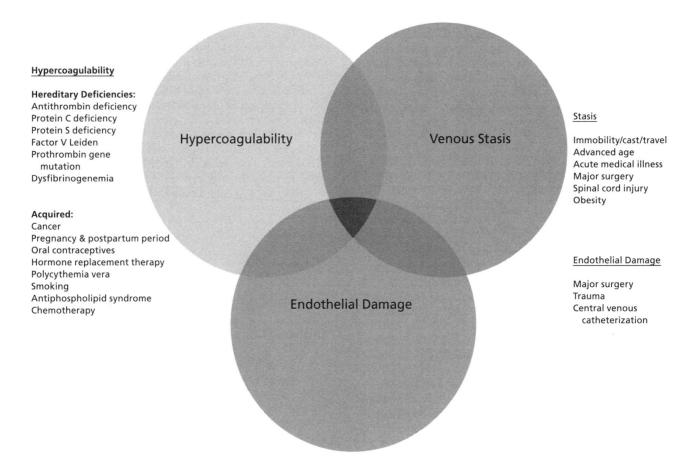

Hypercoagulability

Hereditary Deficiencies:
Antithrombin deficiency
Protein C deficiency
Protein S deficiency
Factor V Leiden
Prothrombin gene
  mutation
Dysfibrinogenemia

Acquired:
Cancer
Pregnancy & postpartum period
Oral contraceptives
Hormone replacement therapy
Polycythemia vera
Smoking
Antiphospholipid syndrome
Chemotherapy

Stasis

Immobility/cast/travel
Advanced age
Acute medical illness
Major surgery
Spinal cord injury
Obesity

Endothelial Damage

Major surgery
Trauma
Central venous
  catheterization

Figure 1. Risk factors for pulmonary embolism: Virchow triad. Data from Tapson VF. Acute pulmonary embolism. N Engl J Med. 2008;358(10):1037-1052. [PMID: 18322285]

thromboembolism (VTE). Venous stasis, hypercoagulability, and endothelial damage are the underlying predisposing conditions for VTE (Figure 1). PE is discussed in the Pulmonary Vascular Diseases chapter (see Chapter 96). The syndrome of DVT includes thrombosis of the proximal leg veins and large veins of the upper extremities. DVT of the upper extremities is rising in incidence, in large part secondary to increasing use of indwelling venous catheters.

Diagnosis

Patients with lower extremity DVT often present with erythema, swelling, and tenderness of the affected limb, although the clinical manifestations may be variable and need to be differentiated from other potential causes (Table 1). Homan sign (conventionally known as pain in the calf on forced dorsiflexion of the foot) is neither sensitive nor specific for DVT. The initial and most important step in evaluating a possible DVT is estimating the clinical likelihood of disease, as this will determine the proper testing. Clinical prediction rules, such as the Wells score (Table 2), are useful for initial assessment. **Patients with a low clinical likelihood of DVT should undergo testing with D-dimer as the combination of a low clinical probability, and negative D-dimer rules out DVT.** If the D-dimer is positive, or if the clinical likelihood is high, then duplex ultrasonography should be performed. This test has an excellent sensitivity and specificity for DVT such that the gold standard test (venography) is rarely performed.

Prevention

Patients with known thrombophilic conditions with an indication for treatment should receive prophylaxis for VTE (see Chapter 53). All hospitalized patients with VTE risk factors and no significant con-

Table 1. Differential Diagnosis of Lower Extremity Deep Venous Thromboembolism

Disorder	Notes
Venous insufficiency (venous reflux)	Usually due to venous hypertension from such causes as venous reflux or obesity. Obtain ultrasound to diagnose venous reflux.
Muscle strain, tear, or trauma	Pain occurring with range of motion more characteristic of orthopedic problem due to trauma.
Ruptured Baker cyst	Pain localized to popliteal region of leg. Diagnosed with ultrasonography.
Cellulitis	Skin tenderness, erythema, and warmth. Normal ultrasound result.
Lymphedema	Toe edema is more characteristic of lymphedema than of venous edema. Lymphedema can occur in one leg or both legs.

Table 2. Wells Criteria for Deep Venous Thrombosis

Clinical Characteristic	Score
Active cancer (patient receiving treatment for cancer within 6 mo or currently receiving palliative treatment)	1
Paralysis, paresis, or recent plaster cast immobilization of the lower extremities	1
Recently bedridden for 3 days or more, or major surgery within the previous 12 weeks requiring general or regional anesthesia	1
Localized tenderness along the distribution of the deep venous system	1
Entire leg swollen	1
Calf swelling at least 3 cm larger than the asymptomatic side (measured 10 cm below the tibial tuberosity)	1
Pitting edema confined to the symptomatic leg	1
Collateral superficial veins (nonvaricose)	1
Previously documented deep venous thrombosis	1
Alternative diagnosis at least as likely as deep venous thrombosis	-2

A score of less than 2 indicates that a deep venous thrombosis is unlikely. A score of 2 points or higher indicates that a deep venous thrombosis is likely.

Data from Wells PS, Anderson DR, Rodger M, et al. Evaluation of D-dimer in the diagnosis of suspected deep-vein thrombosis. N Engl J Med. 2003;349(13):1227-1235. [PMID: 14507948]

traindications should receive risk-appropriate venous thromboembolism prophylaxis to decrease their risk of VTE (Table 3). Pharmacologic prophylaxis is the most effective treatment and is preferred in these patients; mechanical prophylaxis measures (eg, pneumatic compression stockings) are not well studied in medical patients, and the use of graduated compression stockings is discouraged because of unproven efficacy and the risk of lower extremity skin damage. **There is no indication for routine screening for DVT in asymptomatic patients at risk for VTE.**

Therapy

All patients with established DVT and no contraindications should undergo immediate anticoagulation. Intravenous unfractionated heparin may be used, but many patients are treated with low-molecular-weight heparin, which facilitates outpatient treatment.

Longer-term anticoagulation is usually with warfarin, which may be initiated simultaneously with heparin, and both therapies are overlapped for a minimum of 5 days and until the international normalized ration (INR) has reached the therapeutic range (2.0 to 3.0) for two measurements taken 24 hours apart. Multiple newer oral anticoagulant agents are available (eg, dabigatran, rivaroxaban, apix-

aban, edoxaban). In general, they have a rapid onset of action, do not require routine monitoring of their anticoagulant effect, do not require overlap with heparin, and have minimal interactions with food or other medications. Most cannot be used in patients with significant kidney failure, however, and there is a lack of reliable reversal agents if bleeding occurs. **Newer oral anticoagulation medications tend to be very expensive and their long-term safety remains to be established.** Table 4 lists the available pharmacologic options for VTE therapy.

Patients with extensive thrombosis may be considered for thrombolytic therapy, including catheter-directed therapy. The proper role of thrombolysis, however, is poorly defined.

Once a patient is on stable anticoagulation, therapy should be continued for a duration based on his or her risk factor profile (Table 5); all patients should be treated for a minimum of 3 months of anticoagulation.

If there are strong contraindications to anticoagulation, an inferior vena cava filter should be placed. These filters decrease the likelihood PE in the short term, but they may actually increase the long-term risk of recurrent DVT. If the contraindication to anticoagulation is temporary, consider initiating a standard course of anticoagulation as well as filter removal.

Table 3. VTE Risk Factors and Prophylaxis

VTE Risk Factors	Prophylaxis Options	Contraindications to Pharmacologic Prophylaxis
NYHA Class III/IV HF	Unfractionated heparin, 5000 units SC every 8-12 h	Active or high risk for bleeding
Acute respiratory failure	Enoxaparin, 40 mg SC every 24 h	Coagulopathy (abnormal aPTT or PT not due to lupus anticoagulant)
Active cancer	Dalteparin, 5000 units SC every 24 h	
Stroke with paresis	Fondaparinux, 2.5 mg SC every 24 h	Thrombocytopenia (platelets <50,000/μL [50 × 10⁹/L])
History of VTE	or	
Acute infectious illness	Intermittent pneumatic compression devices if pharmacologic prophylaxis is contraindicated	
Age >60 y		
Thrombophilia		
Acute rheumatic disease		
Inflammatory bowel disease		
Immobility		

aPTT = activated partial thromboplastin time; HF = heart failure; PT = prothrombin time; NYHA = New York Heart Association; SC = subcutaneous; VTE = venous thromboembolism.

Note: In patients with stroke, active cancer, and surgery, low-molecular-weight heparin is superior to unfractionated heparin.

Table 4. Anticoagulation Agents

Agent	Comments
Initial Therapy	
Unfractionated heparin	Much experience in use, requires monitoring and usually IV access for continuous infusion, inexpensive
Low-molecular-weight heparins (eg, dalteparin, enoxaparin)	Generally no coagulation monitoring required, renal clearance, less reliable dosing in very obese patients, less experience treating PE with hemodynamic instability, expensive
Parenteral factor Xa inhibitors (eg, fondaparinux)	Synthetic pentasaccharide; no coagulation monitoring required; renal clearance; less experience treating PE with hemodynamic instability; expensive, but generic version available
Parenteral direct thrombin inhibitors (eg, bivalirudin, argatroban)	Not used for primary treatment, may be used for acute anticoagulation in patients with HIT, expensive
Long-Term Therapy	
Vitamin K antagonists (warfarin)	Oral, much experience in use, requires 4-5 d of heparin therapy before continuing warfarin alone, less predictable dosing requires close INR monitoring, many drug-drug and diet-drug interactions may reduce efficacy and/or increase toxicity, inexpensive
Factor Xa inhibitors (eg, rivaroxaban, apixaban, edoxaban)	No coagulation monitoring required, partial hepatic metabolism and renal clearance requiring dose modification or avoidance in patients with advanced kidney or hepatic impairment, expensive
Oral direct thrombin inhibitors (eg, dabigatran)	No coagulation monitoring required, prompt therapeutic effect, long half-life, no clear antidote for toxicity and bleeding, expensive

CVA = cerebrovascular accident; DVT = deep venous thrombosis; HIT = heparin-induced thrombocytopenia; IV = intravenous; PE = pulmonary embolism.

Table 5. Duration of Treatment of Patients With VTE[a]

Type of VTE	Duration of Therapy
Associated with a transient reversible risk factor	3-6 mo of anticoagulation
Associated with major continuing risk factor	≥6-12 mo of anticoagulation with consideration of long-term, indefinite anticoagulation
Associated with major thrombophilic defect (APS, AT, or PC deficiency)	Same as above
Recurrent	Same as above
Idiopathic	Same as above
Associated with cancer	3-6 mo of anticoagulation with LMWH followed by warfarin if anticoagulation still required

APS = antiphospholipid syndrome; AT = antithrombin; LMWH = low-molecular-weight heparin; PC = protein C; VTE = venous thromboembolism.

[a]Patients must be assessed regularly for indefinite or long-term anticoagulation, and the duration is determined by assessing the risk of bleeding while undergoing anticoagulation versus the risk for recurrent VTE after stopping anticoagulation.

Bibliography

Bounameaux H, Perrier A, Righini M. Diagnosis of venous thromboembolism: an update. Vasc Med. 2010;15:399-406. [PMID: 20926499]

von Kodolitsch Y, Schwartz AG, Nienaber CA. Clinical prediction of acute aortic dissection. Arch Intern Med. 2000; 160:2977.

Section 2
Endocrinology and Metabolism

Associate Editor – T. Robert Vu, MD, FACP

High Value Care Recommendations

- In the absence of clinical findings, testing only for serum prolactin may be appropriate for microadenomas.

- Screening for hyperthyroidism is not recommended for the general population.

- Thyroid-stimulating hormone (TSH) receptor antibody tests lack sensitivity and specificity in Graves disease and are minimally useful for initial diagnosis.

- Patients with subclinical hypothyroidism may not require treatment if they are asymptomatic or are women not desiring pregnancy or currently pregnant.

- An annual evaluation of serum TSH levels is recommended in patients receiving levothyroxine therapy; studies have demonstrated that up to 30% of such patients may be unintentionally under- or overtreated.

- For patients with a history of hypoglycemia, a limited life expectancy, and advanced macrovascular complications, a target hemoglobin A_{1c} (HbA_{1c}) goal of 8.0% may be reasonable.

- There is no advantage of newer bisphosphonates compared to older forms available as generics (ie, oral alendronate).

- Teriparatide is 10 times more expensive than other therapies for osteoporosis and cannot be continued beyond 24 months because of concern about a potential risk for osteosarcoma.

- Because of potential side effects and expense, denosumab is considered second-line therapy for patients unable to take or tolerate bisphosphonate therapy.

- For patients with a normal or low normal bone mineral density (BMD), repeat dual-energy x-ray absorptiometry (DEXA) scans need not occur for 10 to 15 years.

Chapter 10

Hypothalamic and Pituitary Disorders

Eric Goren, MD

The hypothalamic-pituitary-adrenal axis serves as a key link between the nervous and endocrine systems and controls the secretion of hormones essential for numerous functions throughout the body.

As the name implies, the hypothalamus sits directly below the thalamus and above the brainstem and optic chiasm. Some of the neurons that begin in the hypothalamus have axonal terminations in the posterior pituitary. These neurons are responsible for the secretion of antidiuretic hormone (ADH) and oxytocin. The anterior pituitary is not directly connected to the hypothalamus. However, neurons in the hypothalamus are able to secrete messenger molecules into the hypothalamo-hypophyseal portal vessels to control hormone release from the anterior pituitary. The hypothalamus produces hormones that stimulate the release of a corresponding anterior pituitary hormone with the exception of prolactin release, which is under the tonic inhibitory control of dopamine (Table 1). This chapter reviews the disease states when hormones are over- or underproduced by the hypothalamus and the posterior and anterior pituitary.

Hypothalamic Disorders

The hypothalamus also has key roles outside of its control of the anterior and posterior pituitary. It helps control satiety and regulates body temperature and other autonomic functions. Because of this, when conditions damage or destroy the hypothalamus, patients often present with diffuse manifestations such as weight gain and body temperature dysregulation. They may also have one or more of the anterior and posterior pituitary hormone deficiency states described below.

In most cases, damage to the hypothalamus is idiopathic, although an autoimmune process may ultimately be the cause. Neurosurgical procedures, particularly those with a transsphenoidal approach, cranial irradiation, and central nervous system tumors such as craniopharyngiomas, can also lead to hypothalamic damage.

Posterior Pituitary Diseases

The posterior pituitary is responsible for the release of 2 hormones: ADH (also known as arginine vasopressin) and oxytocin. ADH acts on the kidney to promote free water re-absorption; deficiency leads to central diabetes insipidus (DI), and its excess leads to the syndrome of inappropriate antidiuretic hormone secretion (SIADH).

Central DI

When stimulated by elevated osmolality or hypovolemia, ADH released from the posterior pituitary acts on the kidney to promote greater water reabsorption. Nephrogenic DI (see Chapter 67) is caused by a failure of released ADH to act on the kidney. This leads to increased urination (polyuria) and results in an increased sense of thirst (polydipsia) to maintain sodium concentrations and osmolality. If patients are allowed adequate access to water, they will maintain a high-normal osmolality and serum sodium. Central DI presents with the same symptoms but is caused by decreased ADH secretion. The cause of decreased secretion is mostly idiopathic. Some tumors (craniopharyngiomas) and some neurosurgical procedures can also result in diminished ADH release. Central DI is usually treated with desmopressin (1-desamino-8-D-arginine vasopressin, or DDAVP), an ADH analogue that replaces the deficient hormone.

Central SIADH

Many medications as well as several central nervous system conditions (such as trauma, stroke, or infection, and even certain psychiatric disorders (such as psychosis) can lead to excess release of ADH, which leads to increased free water retention and hyponatremia (see Chapter 67).

Anterior Pituitary Diseases

Pituitary Masses

Masses are frequently detected in the pituitary gland when magnetic resonance imaging (MRI) or computed tomography (CT) scanning is performed for other reasons. In most cases, these lesions are nonfunctioning adenomas and are considered incidental findings ("incidentalomas"). These lesions are classified by their size on imaging, with masses <10 mm in size considered microadenomas and those ≥10 mm considered macroadenomas. Given the pituitary's place-

Table 1. Hypothalamic-Anterior Pituitary Axis		
Hypothalamic Hormone/Action	**Anterior Pituitary Hormone**	**Hormone Target**
Corticotropin-releasing hormone (CRH)/(+)	Adrenocorticotropic hormone (ACTH)	Adrenal cortex
Gonadotropin-releasing hormone (GnRH)/(+)	Follicle-stimulating hormone (FSH) Luteinizing hormone (LH)	Ovaries, testicles
Growth hormone-releasing hormone (GHRH)/(+)	Growth hormone (GH)	Various
Thyrotropin-releasing hormone (TRH)/(+)	Thyroid-stimulating hormone (TSH)	Thyroid
Dopamine/(-)	Prolactin	Various

(+) indicates that it stimulates release of anterior pituitary hormone; (-) indicates that it inhibits release of anterior pituitary hormone.

ment near the optic chiasm, visual field testing should be performed for all lesions ≥10 mm; patients with these larger lesions may have headache or visual field defects.

When a pituitary lesion is identified, clinical evidence of pituitary hormone hypersecretion or dysfunction should be sought. **In the absence of clinical findings, testing only for serum prolactin may be appropriate for microadenomas.** Hormonal testing of anterior pituitary hormones is recommended for all macroadenomas. For nonfunctioning lesions, monitoring with pituitary MRI at 6- to 12-month intervals for at least 3 years is warranted for a microadenoma to detect an enlarging tumor that may require surgery, with more frequent and protracted monitoring of any macroadenoma.

Hormone Underproduction

In the majority of cases, the underproduction of anterior pituitary hormones is caused by the presence of a pituitary tumor (most commonly a prolactinoma; see below), which crowds out hormone-producing cells. One feared complication of these often benign tumors is pituitary apoplexy. In pituitary apoplexy, hemorrhagic infarction of a pituitary tumor causes sudden-onset headache and visual field defects (bitemporal hemianopsia) and impairment in anterior pituitary hormone release. Resection of pituitary tumors can also damage anterior pituitary function. The pathophysiology, symptoms, diagnosis, and treatment of deficiency of 5 of the anterior pituitary hormones are discussed below.

Adrenocorticotropic Hormone Deficiency

Adrenocorticotropic hormone (ACTH) stimulates the release of cortisol from the adrenal glands. Like other anterior pituitary hormone deficiencies, ACTH deficiency can be caused by a pituitary mass or pituitary apoplexy, although this is not a common cause. Deficiency in ACTH is most often due to the administration of high-dose, long-term glucocorticoids that suppress corticotropin-releasing hormone from the hypothalamus through negative feedback. Other medications that can suppress corticotropin-releasing hormone include megestrol or opioids.

Decreased ACTH secretion leads to central (secondary) adrenal insufficiency, which differs in several key features from primary adrenal insufficiency in which there is direct failure of the adrenal glands. In central adrenal insufficiency, decreased production of the ACTH precursor proopiomelanocortin does not allow skin hyperpigmentation to develop, which is a characteristic associated with primary adrenal insufficiency. In addition, in central adrenal insufficiency, the significant alterations in sodium, potassium, and volume status are not seen, as ACTH does not regulate mineralocorticoid production from the adrenal zona glomerulosa cells. The clinical presentation, diagnosis, and treatment of adrenal insufficiency are discussed in the Adrenal Disease chapter (see Chapter 12).

Gonadotropin Deficiency

Gonadotropin-releasing hormone (GnRH), released in pulsatile fashion from the hypothalamus, stimulates follicle-stimulating hormone (FSH) and luteinizing hormone (LH) production in the anterior pituitary. Severe stress and malnutrition, as seen in patients with eating disorders, can lead to suppression of GnRH release. Severe illness and intense exercise can also inhibit GnRH release. Excess prolactin release, as seen in prolactinomas, also inhibits GnRH release.

Loss of GnRH stimulation of gonadotropic cells in the anterior pituitary leads to decreased FSH and LH release and secondary hypogonadism (as opposed to primary hypogonadism where the testes or ovaries fail). Hypogonadism presents with decreased libido, erectile dysfunction, loss of skeletal muscle mass, and anemia in men, and amenorrhea, breast atrophy, vaginal dryness, and diminished libido in women.

Although FSH and LH may be measured directly, in patients with suspected pituitary deficiency, evaluation depends on the sex of the patient. In men, measurement of the serum testosterone level is the usual initial diagnostic step. If repeatedly low, the LH concentration helps define the cause, with the level being elevated in testicular failure (primary hypogonadism) and low or low-normal in pituitary insufficiency (secondary hypogonadism).

In women, the presence of normal menses excludes central hypogonadism, as normal cycles require an intact hypothalamic-pituitary-gonadal axis. With amenorrhea or oligomenorrhea, measurement of FSH and LH levels is obtained; elevated levels usually represent ovarian failure. Low or low-normal levels, particularly if associated with a low serum estradiol level or failure to bleed after a trial of medroxy-progesterone, are consistent with gonadotropin deficiency.

Gonadotropin deficiency is treated with testosterone in men and estrogen in women, depending on individual clinical circumstances.

Growth Hormone Deficiency

Adult-onset growth hormone (GH) deficiency is the most common pituitary deficiency associated with a pituitary tumor that has been treated with neurosurgical intervention or cranial irradiation; isolated idiopathic adult-onset GH deficiency is rare. Because GH has a variety of effects in adults, the manifestation of GH deficiency is somewhat nonspecific. Patients may note a decrease in libido, energy, or stamina. Muscle mass and bone density may decrease, while fat mass may increase.

Growth hormone is secreted in a pulsatile manner, so measuring its level alone does not diagnose deficiency. Among its many effects, GH stimulates the release of insulin-like growth factor-1 (IGF-1) from the liver, which is a more reliable indicator of GH secretion. Therefore, a low IGF-1 level in a patient with known pituitary disease confirms the diagnosis.

While some evidence supports the use of recombinant human GH for adult-onset disease, no mortality benefit has yet been shown and conflicting evidence exists on improvement in bone density or exercise capacity.

Thyroid-Stimulating Hormone Deficiency

Central thyroid-stimulating hormone (TSH) deficiency is rarely seen in isolation, as it almost always presents with absence of other anterior pituitary hormones. Low TSH levels lead to low thyroxine (T_4) production by the thyroid. As in thyroid organ disease, T_4 deficiency leads to a variety of symptoms and clinical findings that are discussed in the Thyroid Disease chapter (see Chapter 11).

Measured T_4 levels will always be low. In hypothyroidism caused by thyroid organ disease, feedback from the low T_4 levels will cause the anterior pituitary to produce high levels of TSH to compensate and increase the level of hormone production back to the setpoint; therefore, TSH levels will be elevated. However, in central TSH deficiency, TSH levels will remain low or inappropriately low-normal despite the low T_4 levels. As in primary thyroid disease–mediated hypothyroidism, exogenous thyroid hormone is given.

It is important to recognize that although measurement of TSH is the most reliable indicator of the adequacy of thyroid function in patients with an intact hypothalamic-pituitary axis, in the presence of central hypothyroidism the TSH no longer reflects the appropriateness of thyroid hormone production. In this case, measurement of circulating thyroid hormone must be used to evaluate thyroid status.

Hormone Overproduction

Hyperprolactinemia and Prolactinoma

Prolactin release from the anterior pituitary is under the tonic inhibition of dopamine, which, in turn, is released from the pituitary stalk. While a prolactinoma is the most common cause of hyperprolactinemia, not all patients with hyperprolactinemia have prolactinomas. Table 2 lists the many physiologic, pathologic, and medication-induced causes of hyperprolactinemia. Some physiologic causes of hyperprolactinemia include pregnancy, nipple stimulation, exercise, and food intake. Hyperprolactinemia is commonly found in patients with hypothyroidism, chronic liver disease, and chronic kidney disease. Many medications can increase prolactin secretion by blocking dopamine release or action. The most common medications include typical and atypical antipsychotics, antidepressants (tricyclic antidepressants, monoamine oxidase inhibitors, fluoxetine), opiates, metoclopramide, and certain antihypertensive agents.

Prolactinomas are the most common form of functioning pituitary adenomas. Because one of the primary roles of prolactin is to stimulate lactation, overproduction can lead to galactorrhea in women. However, prolactinomas frequently interfere with the production of other anterior pituitary hormones such as FSH/LH, leading to oligomenorrhea, amenorrhea, and hirsutism. In men, prolactinomas may cause hypogonadotropic hypogonadism, resulting in decreased libido and infertility. In more rare cases, production of other anterior pituitary hormones may be affected, leading to deficiency states.

Initial diagnosis is by measurement of serum prolactin levels. As many factors influence prolactin secretion (eg, sleep, exercise, breast stimulation, drugs, and hypothyroidism), marginally elevated levels should be measured again. Prolactinomas are confirmed by the presence of an adenoma seen on MRI (Plate 1).

Treatment decisions are based on the size of the adenoma and symptoms associated with hyperprolactinemia. Treatment is essential if the adenoma is large enough to cause neurologic symptoms, such as visual impairment or headache. In patients requiring treatment for symptoms, dopamine agonist agents (bromocriptine or cabergoline) are used as first-line therapy; they result in decreased prolactin production and usually shrink the adenoma. Withdrawal of treatment may be possible with prolonged normalization of the prolactin level and disappearance of the adenoma on imaging.

ACTH-Secreting Adenomas

Pituitary adenomas may involve ACTH-producing cells. Hypersecretion of ACTH leads to hypercortisolism. Hypercortisolism of any cause is frequently referred to as Cushing syndrome; when it results from an ACTH-secreting adenoma, this condition may be termed Cushing disease. Clinical presentation, diagnosis, and treatment are discussed in the Adrenal Disease chapter (see Chapter 12).

GH-Secreting Adenomas

In adults, hypersecretion of GH leads to acromegaly. Clinical features of acromegaly include frontal bossing; prognathism, with dental malocclusion and increased spacing between the teeth; enlargement of the nose, lips, and tongue; skin tags; arthritis; carpal tunnel syndrome; sleep apnea; and excess sweating. The facial features of acromegaly can often best be appreciated by comparing a patient's current appearance to that of old photos.

Similarly with GH deficiency, random measurement of GH is not diagnostically helpful because of its pulsatile release. Instead, the diagnosis is made from an elevated IGF-1 level. Treatment typically involves transsphenoidal resection of the pituitary gland, which lowers GH secretion in many patients. However, some patients may also require adjuvant treatment with a somatostatin analogue (octreotide or lanreotide), which leads to further diminished GH secretion. Although treatment may improve soft tissue changes, any bony changes usually persist.

TSH-Secreting Tumors

These are the rarest pituitary adenomas. When present, they produce the same signs and symptoms of hypothyroidism (see Chapter 11). The diagnosis is made by the presence of elevated T_4 levels in association with elevated TSH levels; the diagnosis should then be further confirmed with a pituitary MRI since these tumors are often microadenomas. Treatment involves the transsphenoidal resection of the pituitary.

Table 2. Causes of Hyperprolactinemia

Cause	Result
Pituitary disease	Prolactinomas
	Growth hormone-secreting tumors (cosecretion of prolactin or pituitary stalk effects)
	Nonfunctioning pituitary tumors (pituitary stalk effects)
	Lymphocytic hypophysitis (pituitary stalk effects)
	Empty sella syndrome (pituitary stalk effects)
	Cushing disease (cosecretion of prolactin or pituitary stalk effects)
Nonpituitary sellar and parasellar lesions	Craniopharyngioma
	Hypothalamic disease (sarcoidosis, Langerhans cell histiocytosis, lymphoma)
	Metastatic tumors to pituitary/hypothalamus
	Meningiomas
	Dysgerminomas
	Irradiation
Neurogenic	Chest wall or spinal cord disease
	Breast stimulation/lesions
Drugs	Psychotropic agents (butyrophenones and phenothiazines, monoamine oxidase inhibitors, tricyclic antidepressants, fluoxetine, molindone, risperidone, cocaine)
	Antihypertensive agents (verapamil, methyldopa, reserpine)
	Metoclopramide
	(Estrogen in conventionally used doses does not cause hyperprolactinemia.)
Other	Pregnancy
	Physiologic cause (coitus, nipple stimulation, strenuous exercise, stress)
	Hypothyroidism
	Chronic kidney failure
	Cirrhosis
	Macroprolactinoma
	Idiopathic
	Adrenal insufficiency
	Ectopic secretion

Bibliography

Klibanski A. Clinical practice. Prolactinomas. N Engl J Med. 2010;362(13): 1219-1226. [PMID: 20357284]

Melmed S. Medical progress: acromegaly. N Engl J Med. 2006;355(24): 2558-2573. [PMID: 17167139]

Chapter 11

Thyroid Disease

Norra Kwong, MD
Erik K. Alexander, MD

The thyroid gland releases 2 forms of thyroid hormone: thyroxine (T_4) and triiodothyronine (T_3). All T_4 in the body is made within the thyroid gland, whereas 80% of T_3 is derived from the peripheral conversion of T_4. The synthesis and release of thyroid hormone are controlled by pituitary-derived thyroid-stimulating hormone (TSH) under the influence of thyrotropin-releasing hormone (TRH) from the hypothalamus. In addition, TSH stimulates basic thyrocyte functions, such as iodine uptake and organification. Conversion of T_4 to T_3 is down-regulated during the course of nonthyroid illness and by various medications, including propranolol, glucocorticoids, propylthiouracil, and amiodarone. Both T_3 and T_4 are predominantly bound to circulating carrier proteins (thyroxine-binding globulin [TBG], transthyretin, and albumin); binding serves to prevent excessive tissue uptake and maintain a readily accessible reserve of thyroid hormone. Several medications (eg, estrogens and glucocorticoids) affect levels of TBG without affecting the levels of free (unbound) thyroid hormone.

Screening

Screening for hyperthyroidism is not recommended for the general population. However, it should be considered for certain higher-risk populations. It is reasonable to screen women aged >50 years using a sensitive TSH test, given the increased prevalence of hypothyroidism in this population. It is also appropriate to measure TSH in the following high-risk individuals, even in the absence of symptoms:

- Patients with a first-degree relative with Hashimoto disease or Graves disease
- Patients with other autoimmune diseases such as type 1 diabetes mellitus
- Patients with a history of any prior thyroid dysfunction
- Patients taking amiodarone or lithium
- Patients living in an iodine-deficient region of the world
- Patients who are obese with a body mass index >30 kg/m²
- Women who are anticipating a pregnancy or are currently pregnant

Young women on thyroid replacement for hypothyroidism should be counseled to contact their physician as soon as pregnancy is suspected or confirmed, so that the levothyroxine dose can be adjusted to maintain a euthyroid state. The daily thyroid hormone requirement increases by approximately 40% beginning very early in gestation. Inadequate supplementation results in maternal (and possibly fetal) hypothyroidism. For this reason, screening for hypothyroidism is important in women who are or are planning to become pregnant.

Diagnosis

Physical Examination

Effective examination of the thyroid is critical for accurate diagnosis of nodules or a simple goiter. Examination of the thyroid includes anterior and lateral inspection and palpation. To enhance visualization, patients should tilt their head back slightly, which stretches the tissues overlying the thyroid. On the lateral view, there should be a smooth, straight contour from the cricoid cartilage to the suprasternal notch; disruption of this smooth contour suggests thyroid enlargement. Movement of the thyroid should be observed when the patient swallows a sip of water. Next, the location of the thyroid isthmus should be located by the physician standing behind the patient and palpating between the cricoid cartilage and suprasternal notch. The sternocleidomastoid muscle should be moved aside with one hand, and the opposite hand should be used to palpate the thyroid fullness beneath the sternocleidomastoid muscle, and again while swallowing a sip of water.

Laboratory Studies

Multiple tests are available to assess thyroid function and anatomy (Table 1). It is important to understand each study and its appropriate use to optimize diagnosis of potential thyroid disease and avoid inappropriate or excessive testing.

TSH, Total T_4, Total T_3, Free T_4, Free T_3 – In patients with an intact hypothalamic-pituitary axis, measurement of the TSH is the most effective study for assessing thyroid function and is usually the first step in evaluation. Free T_4 represents the prohormone available for conversion to active T_3. When serum TSH is abnormal, free T_4 should be measured to assess the degree of hyper- or hypothyroidism. A free T_4 test should also be conducted to detect secondary hypothyroidism in patients with hypothyroidism and TSH levels that are low or inappropriately normal. Because total T_4 levels are greatly affected by variation in binding protein levels, they may not accurately reflect free T_4 levels. In most cases, serum T_3 (or free T_3) testing is not helpful.

Thyroglobulin – Thyroglobulin is a glycoprotein integral in follicular storage of thyroid hormone. Thyroglobulin levels can be elevated in both hyperthyroidism and destructive thyroiditis. Levels are suppressed by intake of exogenous thyroid hormone, making thyroglobulin measurement useful to detect thyrotoxicosis caused by surreptitious use of thyroid hormone.

Thyroid Peroxidase Antibody – Thyroid peroxidase antibody (TPO-Ab) is an excellent marker of autoimmune thyroid disease. A positive titer is associated with Hashimoto thyroiditis.

TSH Receptor Antibodies – Thyroid-stimulating hormone receptor antibodies, including thyroid-stimulating immunoglobulin and thyrotropin-binding inhibitor immunoglobulin, are elevated in Graves disease. They can be used as an adjunctive method to establish the diagnosis of Graves disease if the diagnosis is clinically

Table 1. Common Tests of Thyroid Function

Measurement	Reference Range	Indication
Serum TSH	0.5-5.0 µU/mL (0.5-5.0 mU/L)	Suspected thyroid dysfunction
Serum free T_4	0.9-2.4 ng/dL (12-31 pmol/L)	Suspected thyroid dysfunction with concern for pituitary dysfunction, or evidence of TSH abnormality
Serum free T_3	3.6-5.6 ng/L (5.6-8.6 pmol/L)	Rarely used except when T_3 thyrotoxicosis is suspected
Serum thyroglobulin	3-40 ng/mL (3-40 µg/L)	Suspected subacute thyroiditis or suspected surreptitious ingestion of thyroid hormone or analogues; followed as a tumor marker in patients with well-differentiated thyroid cancer
Thyroid receptor antibodies		
Serum TSI	0%-125%	Graves disease; (euthyroid) ophthalmopathy
Serum TBII	<10%	Similar to TSI
Antithyroid peroxidase antibodies	<2 units/mL	Suspected Hashimoto thyroiditis
Radioactive iodine uptake	10%-30% of dose at 24 hours	Determination of the cause of thyrotoxicosis; contraindicated during pregnancy and breastfeeding

T_3 = triiodothyronine; T_4 = thyroxine; TBII = thyrotropin-binding inhibitory immunoglobulin; TSH = thyroid-stimulating hormone; TSI = thyroid-stimulating immunoglobulin.

uncertain and radioactive iodine uptake (RAIU) is contraindicated. **TSH receptor antibody tests lack sensitivity and specificity in Graves disease and are minimally useful for initial diagnosis.** Measurement of TSH receptor antibodies can be helpful during pregnancy in patients with Graves disease since antibodies can cross the placenta and may affect fetal thyroid function.

Imaging Studies

Thyroid Scan – Thyroid scans are nuclear medicine studies that show the locations of radioactive iodine uptake within the thyroid gland (eg, diffusely in Graves disease or focally within autonomous nodules). Radionuclide studies should not be performed during pregnancy or in women who are breastfeeding.

RAIU – Radioactive iodine uptake measures thyroid gland iodine uptake over a timed period, usually 24 hours. Patients with hyperthyroidism typically have an elevated RAIU. Conversely, in patients with thyroiditis or exposure to exogenous thyroid hormone, the RAIU will be low (<5%) despite biochemical hyperthyroidism.

Thyroid Ultrasonography – Thyroid ultrasound is most useful in the evaluation of thyroid nodules.

Thyrotoxicosis

The term *thyrotoxicosis* encompasses all forms of excess thyroid hormone, whether endogenous or exogenous. Most thyrotoxicosis is caused by excess thyroid hormone production (hyperthyroidism) or by increased thyroid hormone release from a damaged thyroid (thyroiditis). The most common cause of hyperthyroidism is Graves disease. Rarely, a toxic ("hot") adenoma, toxic multinodular goiter, factitious hyperthyroidism due to thyroid hormone consumption, or a struma ovarii may be the cause. Certain drugs such as amiodarone or lithium can also cause thyrotoxicosis, usually by inducing thyroiditis.

Table 2. Signs and Symptoms of Hyperthyroidism and Hypothyroidism

Hyperthyroidism (% frequency)	Hypothyroidism (% frequency)
Common symptoms	**Common symptoms**
Nervousness or emotional lability (99)	Sluggish affect or depression (91)
Increased sweating (91)	Fatigue (87)
Heat intolerance (89)	Cold intolerance (70)
Palpitations (89)	Constipation (70)
Fatigue (88)	Weight gain (56)
Weight loss (85)	Alopecia (44)
Hyperdefecation (33)	**Common signs**
Menstrual irregularity (22)	Dry, coarse skin and hair (75)
Common signs	Periorbital puffiness (75)
Tachycardia or atrial fibrillation (100)	Bradycardia (55)
Goiter (99)	Slow movements and speech (53)
Tremor (97)	Hoarseness (50)
Proptosis of the eyes or extraocular muscle palsy (40)	Diastolic hypertension (30)
Stare, lid lag, or signs of optic neuropathy (40)	Goiter (27)
Pretibial myxedema (NA)	Loss of the lateral portion of the eyebrow (NA)
	Delayed deep tendon reflexes (NA)

NA = not available.

Consider the diagnosis of hyperthyroidism in patients with signs or symptoms of thyrotoxicosis (Table 2) or in those with diseases known to be caused or aggravated by thyrotoxicosis (eg, atrial fibrillation, osteoporosis, weight loss, and anxiety). A diagnostic approach to thyrotoxicosis is indicated in Figure 1. In hyperthyroidism, serum TSH is low or undetectable and free T_4 is elevated. If TSH is suppressed and free T_4 is normal, the serum T_3 concentration should be measured. Triiodothyronine thyrotoxicosis (suppressed TSH, normal T_4, and elevated T_3) is occasionally seen in patients with toxic multinodular goiter and autonomously functioning thyroid nodules. Look for "apathetic thyrotoxicosis" in elderly patients, a condition characterized by a lower frequency of goiter, fewer hyperadrenergic symptoms, and cardiac findings including heart failure and atrial fibrillation. Patients with a low TSH but a normal free T_4 have subclinical hyperthyroidism. This distinction is important because subclinical hyperthyroidism can be followed with periodic thyroid function tests in otherwise healthy patients aged <60 years. The optimal test to differentiate between hyperthyroidism and thyroiditis is RAIU. An elevated RAIU is consistent with hyperthyroidism, whereas a suppressed RAIU (usually <5%) is consistent with thyroiditis.

The risks of hyperthyroidism are primarily related to cardiac function and arrhythmias, osteoporosis, and a hypermetabolic state. Graves ophthalmopathy (soft tissue inflammation, proptosis, extraocular muscle dysfunction, and optic neuropathy) is present in 10% to 25% of affected patients, although up to 70% of patients may have subclinical enlargement of extraocular muscles without overt eye disease. Pretibial myxedema (infiltrative dermopathy characterized by nonpitting scaly thickening and induration of the skin) is a rare complication of Graves disease. Once hyperthyroidism is treated effectively, the overall risks associated with hyperthyroidism can be substantially diminished.

Hypothyroidism

Hypothyroidism has a wide range of clinical signs and symptoms (see Table 2). Serum TSH levels are elevated (>10 µU/mL [10 mU/L]) in primary hypothyroidism (thyroid gland failure), whereas TSH is low or normal in conjunction with a low free T_4 in rare cases of hypothyroidism due to pituitary or hypothalamic disease (secondary hypothyroidism). Patients with a mildly elevated TSH (5-10 µU/mL [5-10 mU/L]) and a normal free T_4 have subclinical hypothyroidism. **Patients with subclinical hypothyroidism may not require treatment if they are asymptomatic or are women not desiring pregnancy or currently pregnant.**

The most common causes of hypothyroidism are chronic lymphocytic thyroiditis (Hashimoto disease), post-thyroidectomy, and

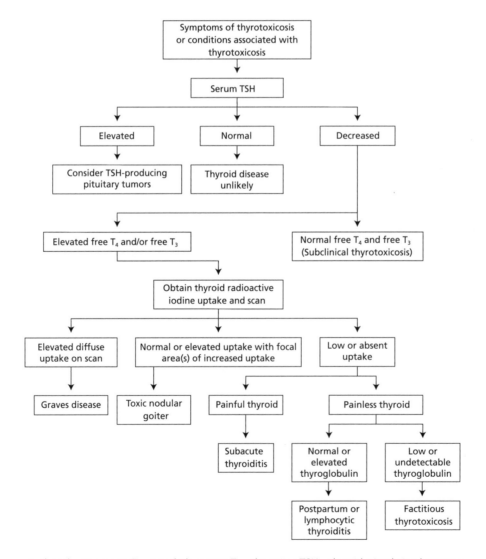

Figure 1. Diagnostic approach to thyrotoxicosis. T_3 = triiodothyronine; T_4 = thryoxine; TSH = thyroid-stimulating hormone.

prior radioiodine therapy (Table 3). Hashimoto disease is an autoimmune disease that may present at any time but increases in prevalence with age. Onset is usually insidious and associated with a goiter. The presence of TPO-Ab is highly correlated with Hashimoto disease, though confirmation of the diagnosis with measurement of TPO-Ab is usually not necessary. However, measurement of TPO-Ab may be helpful in patients with subclinical hypothyroidism. In these patients, increased TPO-Ab titers confer an increased risk of hypothyroidism (approximately 4% per year), which escalates as TSH levels rise above the reference range. These patients warrant close monitoring. Subacute or painful thyroiditis can also lead to hypothyroidism. Most patients demonstrate a triphasic thyroid hormone response: mild hyperthyroidism, followed by mild hypothyroidism, followed by a return to normal thyroid function. If the final phase of thyroid normalization is not attained, TSH will remain elevated and hypothyroidism will persist.

Effects of Nonthyroid Illness on Thyroid Function

Patients with acute nonthyroid illness may have TSH suppression that is part of the "euthyroid sick syndrome" and not due to underlying thyrotoxicosis. Most commonly, T_3 levels decline sharply and T_4 levels remain relatively unchanged, although low T_4 levels have been reported in patients with prolonged severe illness. The TSH response is less consistent, with low, normal, or elevated levels reported. The thyroid hormone patterns associated with nonthyroid illness appear to be an adaptive response to mitigate catabolism associated with severe stress. Thyroid hormone therapy is not beneficial or indicated. Thyroid hormone levels typically normalize 4 to 8 weeks after recovery from the nonthyroid illness.

Therapy

Thyrotoxicosis

Thyrotoxicosis due to thyroiditis is often self-limited and managed conservatively. β-Blockers can be used to control sympathomimetic symptoms (tachycardia, tremor, and anxiety). Nonsteroidal antiinflammatory drugs and, rarely, glucocorticoids are administered to reduce inflammation and discomfort.

Graves disease and autonomously functioning thyroid nodules can be treated with antithyroid drugs or radioiodine, although patient preference, age, comorbidities, severity of thyrotoxicosis, and the presence of Graves ophthalmopathy must be taken into account. Antithyroid drugs (methimazole or propylthiouracil) are preferred to radioiodine in the presence of severe Graves ophthalmopathy and thyroid storm. Between 20% and 40% of patients with Graves disease will achieve drug-free remission rates after 1 year of treatment with antithyroid drugs. Methimazole is generally recommended as first-line antithyroid therapy, as propylthiouracil has been associated with a higher rate of serious adverse effects on the liver. However, in women in the first trimester of pregnancy, methimazole is avoided as it has been associated with possible teratogenicity. With either drug, patients should be counseled about the risk of the rare, but severe, side effects of agranulocytosis, vasculitis, and severe hepatic necrosis.

Most patients select radioiodine as therapy for thyrotoxicosis caused by Graves disease, toxic multinodular goiter, or autonomously functioning thyroid nodules. Radioiodine is also indicated in patients failing to achieve remission after a course of antithyroid drugs. Thyroidectomy is a reasonable choice in thyrotoxic patients with concomitant suspicious (malignant) nodules and in patients who cannot tolerate or refuse radioiodine or antithyroid drugs.

Hypothyroidism

Levothyroxine is the preferred treatment of hypothyroidism. Levothyroxine is converted to T_3 primarily in peripheral tissues at an appropriate rate for overall metabolic needs. Treatment with a combination of T_4 and T_3 is not recommended. Although all patients with overt hypothyroidism should be treated, most nonpregnant patients with subclinical hypothyroidism can be safely monitored with TSH measurements every 4 to 6 months. This recommendation excludes women seeking pregnancy or currently pregnant, who should be treated once TSH rises above 2.5 IU/L. For pregnant women, baseline levothyroxine dosing should be increased by approximately 30% as soon as pregnancy is confirmed. Thyroid function should be measured every 4 weeks through midpregnancy, as subsequent adjustments of the levothyroxine dose may be required. In general, serum TSH levels should be maintained at <2.5 µU/mL (2.5 mU/L) throughout gestation.

Follow-Up

Following treatment for hyperthyroidism, TSH and free T_4 levels are monitored every 3 to 6 months for the first year and every 6 to 12 months thereafter. Therapeutic radioiodine is likely to cause permanent thyroid destruction, requiring lifelong levothyroxine therapy.

Table 3. Differential Diagnosis of Hypothyroidism

Cause	Notes
Hashimoto disease	TSH high; positive family history for hypothyroidism; TPO antibodies present; slowly progressive
Iodine deficiency	TSH high; iodine-deficient area; rare in United States
Postpartum thyroiditis (hypothyroid phase)	TSH triphasic (low, high, normal) over 2-4 mo but often ultimately elevated; recent pregnancy
Silent thyroiditis	TSH triphasic (low, high, normal) over 2-4 mo; self-limited in most cases
Subacute thyroiditis	TSH triphasic (low, high, normal) over 2-4 mo; ESR elevated; TPO antibody negative; painful thyroid
Drug-induced hypothyroidism	TSH high; use of amiodarone, lithium, sunitinib, interferon, iodine, or thioamides in past 1-6 mo
Pituitary/hypothalamic mass (central hypothyroidism)	TSH low or normal; free T_4 low; headaches; most often a pituitary or sellar lesion noted on MRI/CT scan or evidence of prior pituitary surgery
Pituitary/hypothalamic radiation therapy	TSH low or normal; free T_4 low; history of cranial radiation therapy

CT = computed tomography; ESR = erythrocyte sedimentation rate; MRI = magnetic resonance imaging; T_4 = thyroxine; TPO = thyroid peroxidase; TSH = thyroid-stimulating hormone.

Once initiated for the treatment of hypothyroidism, levothyroxine therapy is lifelong. Serum TSH levels should be monitored 6 to 8 weeks after initiating therapy, with adjustments in levothyroxine dose made to achieve a TSH value within the reference range. A full replacement dose of levothyroxine is approximately 1.7 μg/kg, although many patients require a lower dose because of partial thyroid function. **An annual evaluation of serum TSH levels is recommended in patients receiving levothyroxine therapy; studies have demonstrated that up to 30% of such patients may be unintentionally under- or overtreated.**

Thyroid Nodules and Multinodular Goiter

Thyroid nodules usually occur in euthyroid patients and are often benign. Clinically, the focus is on detecting the few thyroid nodules that are malignant. Factors associated with increased cancer risk include young age (<30 years), male sex, a history of head or neck irradiation, a family history of thyroid cancer (especially medullary thyroid cancer), rapid nodule growth, larger nodules, and hoarseness. Evaluation of serum TSH levels is recommended to diagnose functional ("toxic" or "hot") nodules; these nodules are rarely malignant (<1% cancer risk). All euthyroid patients with possible nodular disease should undergo thyroid ultrasonography. Ultrasonography allows accurate detection and sizing of all thyroid nodules, and ultrasound characteristics can be used to further delineate cancer risk. According to several guidelines, biopsy of any nodule greater than 1 cm in diameter is reasonable (10%-15% cancer risk), and biopsy of smaller nodules should be considered in patients with thyroid cancer risk factors. Patients with a cytologically benign nodule >1 cm should be monitored after biopsy with a repeat evaluation performed within 2 to 4 years. Historically, management options for nodules with indeterminate cytology involve diagnostic surgical resection. However, molecular characterization of indeterminate fine needle aspirates that either detect molecular markers for malignancy or measure the expression of specific genes (gene expression classifier) is an emerging technology that may further help risk stratify and guide management of these nodules. Nodules with malignant cytology should undergo surgery (see section *Thyroid Cancer* below).

A goiter refers to enlargement of the thyroid gland. The enlargement can be nodular or diffuse with variations in associated thyroid function, including euthyroid (nontoxic goiter), hyperthyroid (toxic goiter), or hypothyroid. Goitrous enlargement may result from various etiologies: stimulation from elevated TSH levels as seen in iodine deficiency and Hashimoto disease, TSH-receptor antibodies/agonists as in Graves disease, or unclear etiology such as in nontoxic multinodular goiter. The progression of goiter is usually slow and patients are often asymptomatic, although some may present with symptoms of obstruction due to compression of vital structures in the neck or upper thoracic cavity. Work-up should be focused on identifying the etiology, and obtaining serum TSH levels should be the initial diagnostic step. If thyroid dysfunction is identified, correction of hyperthyroidism or hypothyroidism will usually reduce the goiter size. However, no consensus currently exists for treatment of asymptomatic nontoxic (normal TSH) diffuse or multinodular goiter. Many physicians opt for conservative monitoring. Unfortunately, medical intervention (such as TSH suppressive therapy) for nontoxic multinodular goiter is minimally effective and substantially increases the risk of adverse effects.

Thyroid Emergencies

Thyroid storm is a life-threatening condition characterized by exaggerated clinical signs and symptoms of thyrotoxicosis accompanied by systemic decompensation. Thyroid storm is usually caused by rapid release of thyroid hormone (eg, following a large iodine load, withdrawal of antithyroid drugs, or treatment with radioactive iodine) in the setting of other conditions such as surgery, infection, or trauma. Thyroid storm is a clinical diagnosis; there is no diagnostic thyroid hormone concentration. Common symptoms include tachycardia, hyperpyrexia, altered mental status ranging from agitation to coma, and gastrointestinal symptoms. Early recognition and prompt treatment are crucial. Treatment is directed at reducing thyroid hormone level/activity and providing supportive care while correcting for the underlying disorder that prompted the thyroid storm. In severe cases, combinations of β-blockers (propranolol), thionamides (propylthiouracil or methimazole), and inorganic iodine (saturated solution of potassium iodide), with or without glucocorticoids, are commonly used. Surgical resection is reserved for patients in whom acute medical therapy is contraindicated or when it failed to control symptoms.

Myxedema coma is caused by severe hypothyroidism and has been associated with a high mortality rate. Similar to thyroid storm, there is no concentration of thyroid hormone that is diagnostic. Mental status changes and hypothermia are hallmark findings of myxedema coma. Additional findings are hypoxemia, hypercapnia, and hyponatremia. Myxedema coma is a medical emergency, and early treatment with thyroid hormone replacement and supportive care is essential. Patients with thyroid disorders are also at risk for concurrent adrenal insufficiency. Until adrenal insufficiency can be excluded, prophylactic steroid treatment should be provided before initiating thyroid hormone therapy in order to prevent adrenal crisis.

Thyroid Cancer

Thyroid cancer accounts for approximately 2% of all malignancies in the United States. The incidence of thyroid cancer has increased dramatically in recent years, accounting for the largest annual increase of any cancer in the United States. The majority of thyroid cancers are papillary carcinomas (80%-85%), while follicular carcinomas (10%-15%), medullary thyroid carcinomas (<5%), and anaplastic carcinomas (<1%) make up the remainder. Papillary carcinoma and follicular carcinoma are considered differentiated thyroid cancers (DTC), which are usually slow growing and detected as thyroid nodules on physical examination or incidentally through imaging. The mainstay therapy for DTC is surgical resection with possible radioiodine therapy and thyroid hormone suppressive therapy. Patients with treated DTC have an excellent prognosis when compared to other types of cancers. The 5-year disease-specific survival rate for patients with early stage papillary carcinoma is nearly 100%. Age is an especially important prognostic factor. Patients younger than 45 years of age have a low mortality rate, even in cases of advanced or metastatic disease. Importantly, despite an excellent long-term survival, patients with DTC can suffer recurrent disease. Thus, it is important to maintain close follow-up. Medullary thyroid carcinoma is a more aggressive cancer and can be inherited in a familial pattern as a part of the multiple endocrine neoplasia type 2 syndrome. It is characterized by production of calcitonin by the parafollicular or "C" cells of the thyroid gland. Anaplastic carcinoma is the least common thyroid cancer but is one of the most aggressive tumors. It usually presents with symptoms of rapid growth. Unfortunately, current therapy is minimally effective and patients have a median survival of only 5 months following diagnosis.

Bibliography

Brent GA. Clinical practice. Graves' disease. N Engl J Med. 2008;358(24): 2594-2605. [PMID: 18550875]

Cooper DS, Doherty GM, Haugen BR, et al; American Thyroid Association (ATA) Guidelines Taskforce on Thyroid Nodules and Differentiated Thyroid Cancer. Revised American Thyroid Association management guidelines for patients with thyroid nodules and differentiated thyroid cancer. Thyroid. 2009;19(11):1167-1214. [PMID: 19860577]

Garber JR, Cobin RH, Gharib H, et al; American Association of Clinical Endocrinologists and American Thyroid Association Taskforce on Hypothyroidism In Adults. Clinical practice guidelines for hypothyroidism in adults: cosponsored by the American Association of Clinical Endocrinologists and the American Thyroid Association. Thyroid. 2012;22(12):1200-1235. [PMID: 22954017]

Jin J, Phitayakorn R, Wilhelm SM, McHenry CR. Advances in management of thyroid cancer. Curr Probl Surg. 2013;50(6):241-289. [PMID: 23672743]

McDermott MT. In the clinic. Hypothyroidism. Ann Intern Med. 2009;151(11):ITC61. [PMID: 19949140]

Chapter 12

Adrenal Disease

Cynthia A. Burns, MD

This chapter reviews 4 types of adrenal disease: adrenal insufficiency, hyperadrenocorticism (Cushing syndrome), hyperaldosteronism, and pheochromocytoma. Adrenal nodules discovered incidentally on imaging are also reviewed.

Physiologic Regulation of Adrenal Function

The adrenal cortex is composed of 3 layers: the zona glomerulosa, the zona fasciculata, and the zona reticularis. Glucocorticoids and adrenal androgens are produced in the zona fasciculata and zona reticularis, and mineralcorticoids are produced in the zona glomerulosa. The renin-angiotensin system regulates aldosterone production. Pituitary production of adrenocorticotropic hormone (ACTH), which is regulated by hypothalamic production of corticotropin-releasing hormone (CRH), regulates cortisol and dehydroepiandrosterone (DHEA)/DHEA sulfate (DHEAS) production; this is termed the hypothalamic-pituitary-adrenal (HPA) axis (Figure 1).

Adrenal Insufficiency

Primary adrenal insufficiency results in deficiencies of cortisol, aldosterone, and adrenal androgens, whereas central insufficiency causes only isolated cortisol deficiency. Autoimmune adrenalitis is the most common cause of primary adrenal insufficiency in the United States; exogenous glucocorticoid (GC) therapy is the most common cause of central/secondary adrenal insufficiency due to suppression of endogenous CRH and ACTH production. Patients treated with supraphysiologic GC for <3 weeks will not have suppression of the HPA axis, and GC tapering is not necessary. Patients with >3 weeks of GC therapy will require tapering to allow for recovery of the HPA axis. Chronic suppression (>1 year) of the HPA axis by exogenous GC therapy may eventually lead to atrophy of the zonae fasciculata and reticularis, which requires lifelong daily GC replacement therapy.

Diagnosis

The presentation of adrenal insufficiency may be acute or slowly progressive and should be suspected in patients with suggestive signs and symptoms and those at increased risk. Acute adrenal crisis (often presenting with shock) most commonly occurs in patients with primary adrenal insufficiency who have concurrent illness or stress, such as surgery or trauma, due to the loss of both GC and aldosterone production. Adrenal crisis is unlikely in patients with secondary insufficiency due to the intact renin-angiotensin system, although milder clinical findings of adrenal insufficiency may occur due to the inability to produce adequate GC under stressful situations. Following discontinuation of long-term GC therapy, patients are vulnerable for adrenal insufficiency for up to 1 year. Other settings associated with adrenal insufficiency include sepsis, autoimmune disease, adrenal hemorrhage/infarction, granulomatous disease (tuberculosis or sarcoidosis), AIDS, and, rarely, pituitary/hypothalamic disease (see Chapter 10) (Table 1).

Table 1. Causes of Adrenal Insufficiency

Primary Adrenal Insufficiency

Autoimmune adrenalitis

Infection (tuberculosis, mycosis, bacterial, or human immunodeficiency virus-associated)

Metastatic cancer

Adrenal hemorrhage (acute disease)

Medications (such as etomidate, ketoconazole, mitotane, and metyrapone)

Secondary (Central) Adrenal Insufficiency

Exogenous glucocorticoid therapy (oral, intramuscular, intra-articular, inhaled, or intravenous)

Hypothalamic/pituitary diseases or surgery

Cranial irradiation

Chronic administration of drugs with glucocorticoid activity (such as megestrol)

Unexplained weight loss, anorexia, weakness, nausea, abdominal pain, arthralgias, fatigue, and malaise should be observed in most patients with adrenal insufficiency. Orthostatic hypotension and salt craving can be prominent in primary insufficiency due to aldosterone deficiency leading to profound volume depletion. In secondary insufficiency, there may be a small decrease in blood pressure (BP) due to the loss of the slight vasoconstrictive effect of cortisol. Hyperpigmentation is often present in primary insufficiency due to elevated ACTH levels. Hyperkalemia, hyponatremia, and azotemia are often found in primary insufficiency, while hypoglycemia and eosinophilia may be present in both (Table 2).

Measuring a random or morning cortisol level will not detect insufficiency. A cosyntropin (ACTH) stimulation test establishes the diagnosis of adrenal insufficiency. Cortisol and ACTH values are obtained at baseline and at 30 and 60 minutes following administration of cosyntropin. A rise of serum cortisol by ≥18 µg/dL (496.6 nmol/L) rules out adrenal insufficiency. However, these values may not apply to critically ill patients who have low concentrations of albumin and cortisol-binding globulin due to the false lowering of the total cortisol level; in these patients, serum free cortisol concentrations should be measured.

To distinguish primary from secondary adrenal insufficiency, plasma ACTH and cortisol levels should be measured at 8 AM. In primary adrenal insufficiency, ACTH is elevated by >100 pg/mL (22 pmol/L), while ACTH is low or inappropriately normal in central adrenal insufficiency. A pituitary magnetic resonance imaging (MRI) scan should be obtained in secondary insufficiency, and other pituitary axes, such as thyroid and reproductive function, should be assessed.

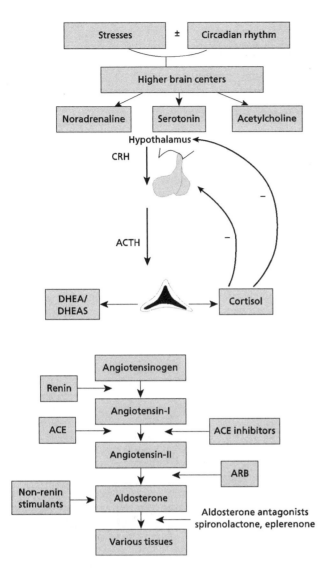

Figure 1. Regulation of hypothalamic-pituitary-adrenal function and the renin-angiotensin system. *Top,* hypothalamic secretion of CRH is mediated by several neurotransmitters in response to changes in stress levels and circadian rhythm. Adrenocorticotropic hormone stimulates the zona fasciculata of the adrenal cortex to synthesize cortisol, which in turn feeds back centrally by negatively inhibiting CRH and ACTH secretion. In addition, ACTH stimulates zona reticularis to synthesize the adrenal androgens DHEA and DHEAS, but these hormones do not participate in the feedback mechanism. *Bottom,* regulation of the renin-angiotensin system involves aldosterone being secreted by the outermost layer of the adrenal cortex (zona glomerulosa) as a result of angiotensin II stimulation. The site of action of commonly used drugs that interfere with the system is shown. ACE = angiotensin-converting enzyme; ACTH = adrenocorticotropic hormone; ARB = angiotensin-receptor blocker; CRH = corticotropin-releasing hormone; DHEA = dehydroepiandrosterone; DHEAS = DHEA sulfate.

Therapy

If acute adrenal crisis is suspected, serum ACTH and cortisol levels should be obtained immediately. While awaiting results, high-dose GC and large-volume intravenous saline should be given. Dexamethasone is the preferred GC therapy because it does not interfere with serum cortisol assays. For less critically ill patients, oral GC should be promptly administered for primary or secondary adrenal insufficiency; delay is potentially life threatening. Fludrocortisone is required in primary but not secondary insufficiency, but stress dosing is not required; in the acute phase, intravenous saline is required because several days of therapy are necessary for the effects of fludrocortisone to be seen. Mild stress (eg, fever or gastroenteritis) requires doubling or tripling of the daily GC dose, and severe illness requires hospitalization for high-dose intravenous GC therapy. Oral GC used for daily replacement therapy are prednisone, hydrocortisone, and dexamethasone (Table 3).

Follow-Up

Patients are advised to wear a medical alert bracelet indicating their diagnosis, and they need to understand and be able to articulate how to increase their GC dose during illness. Adequacy of GC replacement is assessed by looking for signs and symptoms of cortisol insufficiency (under-replacement), such as afternoon fatigue, weight loss, or malaise, or Cushing syndrome (over-replacement), such as weight gain, hyperglycemia, or hypertension. Adjustment of the replacement mineralocorticoid dose is based on the plasma renin activity (PRA) or the patient's symptoms. Patients experiencing lightheadedness upon standing or who are orthostatic on examination may need more fludrocortisone, whereas patients with peripheral edema or increased BP may need less. Mineralocorticoid replacement does not need to be increased for acute illness.

Hypercortisolism

Excess cortisol (hypercortisolism, or Cushing syndrome) is usually secondary to exogenous GC therapy for other medical conditions, such as chronic obstructive pulmonary disease, systemic lupus erythematosus, or rheumatoid arthritis. The most common endogenous cause is an ACTH-secreting pituitary tumor (Cushing disease); adrenocortical tumors and ectopic ACTH-secreting malignant tumors each account for 10% of endogenous cases (Table 4). When the syndrome is due to an ectopic ACTH-secreting tumor, symptoms of weight loss, muscle weakness, and profound hypokalemia may predominate. Adrenocorticotropic hormone–dependent forms of Cushing syndrome result in bilateral adrenal enlargement.

Diagnosis

Exogenous GC intake by any route should be excluded (intra-articular injections and inhaled GC therapy need to be considered as sources of exogenous exposure). Indicators of GC excess, including weight gain, history of recurrent or chronic infections (especially candidal), worsening diabetic control, change in menses, or fractures should be assessed. Abnormal fat distribution (not just the presence of adipose tissue), particularly in the supraclavicular and temporal areas, proximal muscle weakness, or wide (>1 cm) purple striae should also be examined. In addition, physicians should check for physical features that support a specific cause of Cushing syndrome, such as feminization or virilization, an abdominal mass (adrenal tumor), or visual field losses (pituitary tumor). Examination of photographs over time can highlight otherwise subtle physical changes and provide an estimate of changes over time.

Figure 2 summarizes the evaluation of suspected Cushing syndrome. To diagnose hypercortisolism, a 24-hour urine free cortisol measurement, overnight 1-mg dexamethasone suppression test, or nighttime salivary cortisol level should be obtained. If a 24-hour urine free cortisol level is >3 times normal, the diagnosis of Cushing syndrome is confirmed. Inability to suppress serum cortisol following the overnight 1-mg dexamethasone suppression test also suggests the diagnosis. In healthy persons, cortisol secretion exhibits a diurnal rhythm whereby serum cortisol levels reach a nadir late at night and peak in the early morning. Because loss of this diurnal rhythm is a central feature of Cushing syndrome, and salivary levels correlate with free cortisol in serum, measurement of the nighttime salivary cortisol level can also be used as a diagnostic test.

Table 2. Characteristics of Adrenal Insufficiency

Deficiency	Type of Adrenal Insufficiency	Symptoms	Signs	Crucial Laboratory Findings	Additional Laboratory Findings
Cortisol	Primary and secondary (central)	Fatigue, nausea, anorexia, weight loss, abdominal pain, arthralgias, low-grade fever	Hyperpigmentation (in primary disease only),[a] slight decrease in blood pressure (unless cortisol deficiency is complete)	Low basal serum cortisol level (<5 μg/dL [138 nmol//L]) with suboptimal response (<18.0 μg/dL [497 nmol/L]) to cosyntropin; high plasma ACTH level (in primary disease only)	Hyponatremia; normal potassium level; azotemia; anemia; leukopenia, with high percentage of eosinophils and lymphocytes; hypoglycemia
Aldosterone	Primary	Salt craving, postural dizziness	Hypotension, dehydration	Low serum aldosterone level and high plasma renin activity	Hyponatremia; hyperkalemia
Adrenal androgen	Primary and secondary (central)	Decreased libido	Decreased pubic/axillary hair (only in women)	Low serum DHEA and DHEAS levels	—

ACTH = adrenocorticotropic hormone; DHEA = dehydroepiandrosterone; DHEAS = dehydroepiandrosterone sulfate.

[a] Results from increased secretion of ACTH and its precursor, proopiomelanocortin. An increase in the latter leads to increased secretion of one of its products, melanocortin-stimulating hormone, which causes hyperpigmentation.

Table 3. Glucocorticoid Replacement Therapy in Adrenal Insufficiency

Condition	Hydrocortisone	Prednisone	Dexamethasone
Physiologic daily dosing	15 mg/d orally in 2 divided doses at 8 AM (10 mg) and at 3 PM (5 mg)	3-5 mg/d orally in 1 dose	0.375 to 1 mg/d orally in 1 dose
Minor stress (such as cold symptoms)	30-50 mg/d orally in 2 to 3 doses for 2-3 days	8-15 mg/d orally in 1 dose or 2 divided doses for 2-3 days	1-2 mg/d orally in 2 divided doses for 2-3 days
Moderate stress (such as a minor/moderate surgical procedure)	45-75 mg/d orally or IV in 3 to 4 divided doses for 2-3 days	15-20 mg/d orally or IV (as prednisolone) in 2 or 3 divided doses for 2-3 days; hydrocortisone can be used instead	2-3 mg/d orally in 2 divided doses for 2-3 days; hydrocortisone can be used instead
Severe stress (such as a major surgical procedure, or sepsis)	100-150 mg/d IV in 3 to 4 divided doses for 1 day; taper to physiologic dose over 3-5 days once patient is stable and recovering	Follow hydrocortisone regimen; needs inpatient treatment	Follow hydrocortisone regimen; needs inpatient treatment
Septic shock, severe inflammatory process	150-200 mg/d IV in 3 to 4 divided doses; taper as clinically tolerated	Follow hydrocortisone regimen; needs inpatient treatment	Follow hydrocortisone regimen; needs inpatient treatment

IV = intravenously.

Table 4. Causes of Cushing Syndrome (Hypercortisolism)

Type of Cushing Syndrome[a]	Cause
Endogenous	
ACTH dependent (75%-80% of patients)	ACTH-secreting pituitary adenoma (60%-65% of patients)
	Ectopic ACTH secretion by tumors, such as small cell carcinoma of the lung, bronchial carcinoid tumor, pheochromocytoma, and medullary thyroid carcinoma tumors (10%-15% of patients)
	CRH-secreting tumors (rare)
ACTH independent (20%-25% of patients)	Adrenal adenoma (10%-15% of patients)
	Adrenal carcinoma (5%-10% of patients)
Exogenous	Prolonged administration of supraphysiologic doses of glucocorticoid therapy (such as prednisone, dexamethasone, or hydrocortisone)
	Administration of drugs with glucocorticoid activity (progestational agents, such as megestrol)

ACTH = adrenocorticotropic hormone; CRH = corticotropin-releasing hormone.

[a] Patients with ACTH-dependent Cushing syndrome have hypercortisolism associated with normal or elevated plasma ACTH levels; those with ACTH-independent Cushing syndrome have hypercortisolism associated with low or undetectable plasma ACTH levels. Patients with exogenous Cushing syndrome have low or undetectable plasma ACTH levels, and their serum cortisol levels are often low unless the glucocorticoid used crossreacts in the cortisol assay.

Obesity, alcohol abuse, kidney failure, and depression can cause false-positive results (pseudo–Cushing syndrome). An elevated 24-hour urine free cortisol measurement <3 times normal is likely due to pseudo–Cushing syndrome. If the test result is equivocal, confirmatory testing with another 24-hour urine free cortisol, dexamethasone suppression test, or nighttime salivary cortisol level should be performed. Typically, 2 to 3 of these tests are performed to confirm the diagnosis, and additional studies may be required in equivocal cases (see Figure 2).

Once unequivocal excess cortisol production is biochemically proven, plasma ACTH should be measured to differentiate between ACTH-dependent (pituitary or ectopic) and ACTH-independent (adrenal) causes of Cushing syndrome. Basal ACTH levels <6 pg/mL (1.3 pmol/L) are found in adrenal forms of Cushing syndrome, while levels >6 pg/mL (1.3 pmol/L) occur in ACTH-dependent disease.

Once the source of hypercortisolism (pituitary, adrenal, or ectopic) is biochemically determined, imaging studies are indicated. An adrenal computed tomography (CT) or MRI scan should be obtained to localize lesions in patients with suppressed ACTH values. In patients with nonsuppressed ACTH levels, a pituitary MRI scan should be obtained. The most common ectopic ACTH-secreting

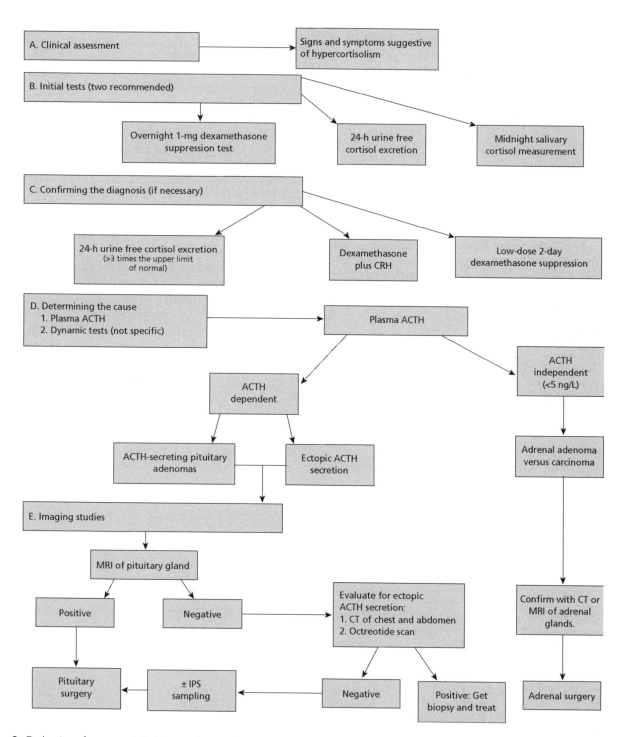

Figure 2. Evaluation of suspected Cushing syndrome. ACTH = adrenocorticotropic hormone; CRH = corticotropin-releasing hormone; CT = computed tomography; IPS = inferior petrosal sinus; MRI = magnetic resonance imaging.

tumors are small cell carcinoma of the lung, bronchial carcinoid tumor, pheochromocytoma, and medullary thyroid carcinoma. The evaluation should begin with a chest MRI or CT scan. If negative, an abdominal CT or MRI scan should be obtained to look for a pancreatic tumor or other mass.

Therapy

Surgical resection of an identified tumor (adrenal, pituitary, or ectopic) is the optimal therapy for Cushing syndrome. Pituitary radiation ("gamma knife") therapy can be used for patients with persistent or recurrent Cushing disease after transsphenoidal surgery or for those in whom pituitary surgery is contraindicated.

Drugs are used adjuvantly in patients undergoing surgery and as sole therapy for those with occult ectopic ACTH secretion or metastatic adrenal cancer to reduce cortisol production. Ketoconazole, mitotane, metyrapone, and aminoglutethimide reduce endogenous cortisol production and reverse most signs and symptoms of Cushing syndrome. Steroidogenesis inhibitors may be needed as adjuncts to pituitary radiation therapy in patients with Cushing disease, as radiation therapy can take 2 to 5 years to ablate the tumor.

Follow-Up

Following surgery, patients require daily GC replacement until the HPA axis has recovered, which can take up to 1 year. Recovery should be assessed with serial cosyntropin stimulation tests. Patients should be monitored for the development of pituitary deficiencies after pituitary irradiation or extensive pituitary resection. Patients with occult ectopic ACTH production should undergo imaging surveillance every 6 months the first year, then annually, to assess for recurrence. More than one-half of tumors are initially occult.

Hyperaldosteronism

Once thought to be a rare cause of hypertension, hyperaldosteronism (also called aldosteronism) has been recognized in up to 14% of unselected hypertensive patients. Depending on the cause, hyperaldosteronism is amenable to medical or surgical treatment.

Diagnosis

The diagnosis of hyperaldosteronism should be considered in patients with difficult-to-control or worsening hypertension despite multiple antihypertensive agents, spontaneous hypokalemia, severe hypokalemia after institution of low-dose diuretic therapy, or hypertension at a young age. Hypokalemia results when hyperaldosteronism causes excess distal renal tubule exchange of sodium for potassium. In the presence of an elevated aldosterone and suppressed renin level, a midmorning ambulatory plasma aldosterone concentration (PAC)/PRA ratio >20 to 30 suggests primary hyperaldosteronism. If 2 screening PAC/PRA ratios are positive, a confirmatory test should be performed, such as assessing for serum aldosterone suppression after dietary or intravenous sodium loading; if aldosterone secretion is not suppressed, hyperaldosteronism is confirmed.

Once unequivocal excess aldosterone production is proven, a dedicated adrenal CT scan should be obtained. Bilateral adrenal hyperplasia (also termed idiopathic primary hyperaldosteronism) is the most common cause of primary hyperaldosteronism, followed by unilateral aldosteronoma (Conn syndrome), and more rarely, unilateral hyperplasia or adrenal carcinoma.

Therapy

Adrenalectomy is the treatment of choice for aldosteronoma. Bilateral adrenal resection is not indicated for bilateral adrenal hyperplasia because of the risks associated with possible primary adrenal insufficiency. Hypokalemia usually resolves following surgery, but hypertension does not always resolve; long-standing hypertension results in permanent vascular changes, making normalization of BP difficult.

Spironolactone is the treatment of choice for idiopathic hyperaldosteronism, bilateral adrenal hyperplasia, and nonsurgical candidates with aldosteronoma. A more selective mineralocorticoid receptor antagonist, eplerenone, can be used in patients unable to tolerate side effects from spironolactone, such as decreased libido, impotence, or gynecomastia. Dietary sodium restriction will decrease urinary potassium wasting and help potentiate the effect of antihypertensive therapy.

Follow-Up

Postsurgical patients should be monitored for hypoaldosteronism (hypotension and hyperkalemia) due to long-term suppression of the contralateral zona glomerulosa. Patients taking spironolactone or eplerenone require titration of medication to maximal effect on potassium concentration and BP, as well as tapering of potassium supplementation with frequent BP checks and potassium measurement.

Table 5. Differential Diagnosis of Pheochromocytoma

Disease	Notes
Thyrotoxicosis (see Chapter 11)	Weight loss, tachycardia, tremor, and suppressed serum TSH concentration; evaluate T_4 and/or T_3 levels
Insulinoma	Whipple triad: neuroglycopenia (sympathetic symptoms alone are not enough), glucose <50 mg/dL (2.8 mmol/L) during the occurrence of symptoms, and prompt resolution of symptoms with administration of glucose
Essential hypertension (see Chapter 31)	Labile blood pressure is quite common and is associated with normal levels of catecholamines and metanephrine
Renovascular hypertension (see Chapter 31)	Paroxysmal hypertension can occur. Normal levels of metanephrines exclude pheochromocytoma
Anxiety, panic attacks, and hyperventilation	Panic disorder is frequently confused with pheochromocytoma. Normal levels of metanephrines exclude pheochromocytoma
Carcinoid syndrome	Typically presents with flushing, diarrhea, and cardiac-related symptoms. Symptoms are sometimes associated with eating. Elevated 24-h urinary excretion of 5-hydroxyindole acetic acid is diagnostic
Unexplained flushing spells	Diagnosis of exclusion. Signs and symptoms may be clinically indistinguishable from patients with pheochromocytoma, except that metanephrine levels are normal

T_3 = triiodothyronine; T_4 = thyroxine; TSH = thyroid-stimulating hormone.

Pheochromocytoma

Pheochromocytoma is a rare tumor of the adrenal gland that accounts for a small number of cases of secondary hypertension (0.1%-0.6%). Ten percent of pheochromocytomas are extra-adrenal, 10% are malignant, 10% recur, and 10% are asymptomatic. Up to 25% of pheochromocytomas are familial. These familial tumors are more likely to occur at a young age; to be bilateral, extra-adrenal, and malignant; and to recur. Genetic testing should be considered in suspected familial cases. Pheochromocytomas are paraganglioma tumors that arise in the chromaffin cells of the adrenal medulla. The tumors can produce, store, and secrete catecholamines (norepinephrine, epinephrine, and/or dopamine); most produce norepinephrine.

Diagnosis

Pheochromocytoma should be considered in patients with moderate-to-severe hypertension (sustained or paroxysmal) coupled with the classic triad of episodes of severe headache, diaphoresis, and palpitations. Table 5 describes some important disorders in the differential diagnosis of pheochromocytoma, and Table 6 describes particular history findings that may lead physicians to screen for pheochromocytoma.

Initial evaluation is by measurement of 24-hour urine catecholamine and metanephrine excretion or plasma free metanephrine level. Twenty-four-hour urine catecholamine and metanephrine collection is more specific and should be used to screen when pretest probability for pheochromocytoma is low. Plasma free metanephrines are more sensitive and best used when pretest probability is high. If positive, the diagnosis should be confirmed with 24-hour urine studies. Plasma catecholamine measurement (high false-positive rates) and urine vanillylmandelic acid (requires a special diet prior to collection) should be avoided. Testing should be avoided in the setting of acute illness, as catecholamine production is increased. Patients under marked psychological stress, or with anxiety or panic disorder, may have increased catecholamine production, but measured levels should be less than 2 to 4 times the upper limit of normal.

When the diagnosis of pheochromocytoma is biochemically proven, a dedicated adrenal CT or MRI scan should be obtained to localize the tumor. Intravenous contrast is contraindicated, as it can precipitate hypertensive crisis. If no adrenal abnormality is seen, CT scans of the chest, abdomen, and pelvis should be obtained to look for paragangliomas along the sympathetic chain.

Therapy

Surgical resection is the treatment of choice for pheochromocytoma. Patients must receive full α-adrenergic blockade prior to surgery to avoid a hypertensive emergency during the procedure. Phenoxybenzamine is a long-acting irreversible nonselective α-blocker that is classically used for preoperative management, but shorter-acting selective $α_1$-adrenergic antagonists (eg, terazosin, prazosin, or doxazosin) can also be used. If needed, β-blockade can follow α-blockade for additional control of BP (goal of ≤120/80 mm Hg) and heart rate (<100 beats per minute). β-Blockade prior to α-blockade is contraindicated because of the dangers of unopposed α-adrenergic activity.

Follow-Up

Patients should be screened for recurrence of preoperative symptoms and BP should be monitored. Plasma free metanephrine measurement should be performed after tumor resection to ensure normalization and if recurrence is suspected. Patients with a history of pheochromocytoma should be screened annually for recurrence. Blood pressure does not always normalize following resection because of the long-term vascular effects of hypertension.

Incidental Adrenal Nodules

Given the frequency of abdominal CT and MRI scanning, adrenal nodules are commonly incidentally noted on these images. When imaged for other conditions, 1% to 7% of patients are found to have adrenal "incidentalomas," and the incidence increases with age.

A careful history and physical examination should be performed on all patients with an incidentally discovered adrenal adenoma. Greater than 90% of incidentalomas are nonfunctional, but all patients should be screened for Cushing syndrome and pheochromocytoma. Patients with hypertension or spontaneous hypokalemia should be screened for hyperaldosteronism. If the patient is virilized (voice deepening or clitoral enlargement), DHEA, DHEAS, and testosterone levels should be checked.

If the nodule is >6 cm, the risk of malignancy is approximately 25%, and surgical resection is recommended. If the nodule is <4 cm, the risk of malignancy is approximately 2%, and surgery is not recommended. Certain imaging characteristics of an adrenal nodule can indicate a higher or lower risk of malignancy (metastatic disease or primary adrenal cancer). If the patient has a history of malignancy, an incidentally noted adrenal nodule is likely to represent metastatic disease, especially if bilateral nodules are present. Irregular borders or intranodular necrosis are especially worrisome for malignancy. To avoid hypertensive crisis, biopsy of an adrenal nodule should never be attempted until pheochromocytoma has been ruled out. Follow-up recommendations include repeat biochemical testing at 1 year, with additional testing if signs or symptoms of hormonal functionality develop, and repeat adrenal imaging (CT or MRI) at 6 to 12 months to assess for change in the size and imaging characteristics of the nodule, with additional imaging if a significant change is detected.

Table 6. Patient History Prompting Screening for Pheochromocytoma

Suggestive (hyperadrenergic) cyclic spells of hypertension, diaphoresis, palpitations, or headache

Familial predisposing syndrome (neurofibromatosis type 1, MEN2, succinate dehydrogenase subunit B mutation)

Previous vasopressor response to anesthesia or angiography

Incidentally discovered adrenal mass

Hypertension at a young age (<20 years)

Drug-resistant hypertension

Unexplained cardiomyopathy and atrial fibrillation

MEN2 = multiple endocrine neoplasia type 2.

Bibliography

Arnaldi G, Boscardo M. Adrenal incidentaloma. Best Pract Res Clin Endocrinol Metab. 2012;26(4):405-419. [PMID: 22863384]

Chakera AJ, Vaidya B. Addison disease in adults: diagnosis and management. Am J Med. 2010;123:409-413. [PMID: 20399314]

Prague JK, May S, Whitelaw BC. Cushing's syndrome. BMJ. 2013;346:f945. [PMID: 23535464]

Rossi GP. Diagnosis and treatment of primary aldosteronism. Rev Endocr Metab Disord. 2011;12(1):27-36. [PMID: 21369868]

Chapter 13

Diabetes Mellitus

Norra Kwong, MD
Erik K. Alexander, MD

Diabetes mellitus is a heterogeneous disorder with a common clinical phenotype of inappropriate glucose metabolism. Nearly 20 million people in the United States have been diagnosed with diabetes, and this number is rising in parallel with the obesity epidemic. Diabetes remains a major contributor to heart disease, blindness, kidney failure, and other complications, making it an important focus for public health initiatives.

Two processes are central to the development of all forms of diabetes: β-cell failure in producing sufficient insulin and/or insulin resistance of peripheral tissues (ie, muscle and liver). Type 1 diabetes mellitus (T1DM) is primarily a disease of β-cell failure resulting in lack of circulating insulin; insulin sensitivity usually remains normal, with insulin doses required to treat patients being similar to a healthy individual's daily endogenous insulin production (30-60 U/day). The pathophysiology of T1DM involves the production of autoantibodies against the pancreatic islet cells. These autoantibodies are often detectable, particularly during the early stages of the disease. Type 1 diabetes can occur at any time throughout life but most often presents in childhood or early adulthood. Because of the acute nature of the symptoms, most cases of T1DM are detected soon after disease onset.

Type 2 diabetes mellitus (T2DM) is often initially asymptomatic and therefore not typically diagnosed for several years after disease onset. It is almost always associated with significant insulin resistance. In insulin-treated patients, a total of 100 to 200 U/day of insulin is often required. Although initial resistance results in augmented insulin secretion from β-cells, this compensation is unsustainable over the long term. Over the course of 5 to 10 years, most patients with T2DM require increased medication (or insulin) to maintain glycemic control. The underlying etiology for T2DM likely involves a combination of genetic and environmental factors. The risk of developing T2DM increases with age, obesity, and sedentary lifestyle.

At times, it may be difficult to definitively classify a patient as having T1DM or T2DM. Rarely, patients who do not have T1DM and evidence of autoantibodies may present with ketoacidosis; such patients often develop insulin-independent diabetes. This illness is best classified as ketosis-prone diabetes. In contrast, patients with biochemical evidence of immune-mediated diabetes may present phenotypically with characteristics of T2DM during adulthood. Clinically, they demonstrate gradual β-cell failure though without insulin requirement for many years. Such patients are best classified as having latent autoimmune diabetes in adults, which is estimated to account for 10% of the current population of patients with T2DM. Diabetes can also be rarely attributable to other concurrent illness, other endocrine disorders, genetic syndromes, or medication use (Table 1).

Prevention/Delay of Diabetes

There are no data to suggest any known lifestyle or pharmacologic intervention can delay the onset of T1DM. However, lifestyle modifications and certain medications can reduce the incidence of T2DM. Dietary and exercise programs that lead to mild to moderate weight loss (5%-7% reduction) in overweight or obese patients are associated with the most impressive clinical outcomes. In addition, treatment of prediabetic patients using metformin results in mild reductions in the incidence of progression to diabetes, though pharmacologic intervention was significantly less effective than lifestyle changes.

Table 1. Classification of Diabetes Mellitus

Type 1 Diabetes — Autoimmune β-cell destruction, usually leading to absolute insulin deficiency
    Immune mediated
    Idiopathic (seronegative)

Type 2 Diabetes — Defect ranging from predominant insulin resistance with relative insulin deficiency to profound insulin deficiency and resistance

Gestational Diabetes Mellitus — Similar pathogenesis to that of type 2 diabetes

Latent Autoimmune Diabetes in Adults — Patient with type 2 diabetic phenotype combined with islet antibodies and slow progressive β-cell failure

Other Specific Types
    Genetic defects in β-cell function (includes the 6 types of maturity-onset diabetes of the young, characterized by impaired insulin secretion with minimal or no defect in insulin action)
    Genetic defects in insulin action
    Diseases of the exocrine pancreas (pancreatitis, pancreatic cancer, cystic fibrosis, hemochromatosis, pancreatectomy)
    Endocrinopathies (Cushing syndrome, acromegaly, glucagonoma, pheochromocytoma)
    Drug- or chemical-induced diabetes (glucocorticoids, niacin, diazoxide)
    Infections associated with β-cell destruction (cytomegalovirus infection, congenital rubella)
    Other genetic syndromes associated with diabetes (Down, Turner, Klinefelter, Prader-Willi, and Laurence-Moon-Biedl syndromes; myotonic dystrophy; Huntington chorea)

Data from American Diabetes Association. Diagnosis and classification of diabetes mellitus. Diabetes Care. 2010;33(suppl 1):S65. [PMID: 20042775]

Screening

Currently, there is no recommendation to screen individuals for T1DM. The US Preventive Services Task Force recommends screening for T2DM in asymptomatic adults with sustained blood pressure (BP; treated or untreated) >135/80 mm Hg. In contrast, the American Diabetes Association (ADA) recommends screening patients who are overweight or obese (body mass index >25 kg/m²) and who have risk factors (eg, BP >140/90 mm Hg, dyslipidemia [high-density lipoprotein levels <35 mg/dL (0.9 mmol/L) and/or triglyceride levels >250 mg/dL (2.8 mmol/L)], first degree relative with diabetes or member of a high-risk ethnic group, or polycystic ovary syndrome). Asymptomatic patients without risk factors should consider screening at age 45 years.

Diagnosis

Diagnostic evaluation is warranted in patients presenting with symptoms consistent with diabetes (eg, unexplained weight loss, frequent infections, polyuria, and/or erectile dysfunction) or relevant physical findings (eg, acanthosis nigricans, peripheral neuropathy, recurrent vaginal yeast infections, and proliferative retinopathy).

Fasting plasma glucose ≥126 mg/dL (7.0 mmol/L) and 2-hour plasma glucose ≥200 mg/dL (11.1 mmol/L) during the 75-g oral glucose tolerance test are highly specific for the diagnosis. However, a glycated hemoglobin (HbA_{1c}) value ≥6.5% is adequate to establish the diagnosis, as is a random plasma glucose level of ≥200 mg/dL (11.1 mmol/L) in a patient with classic symptoms of hyperglycemia or hyperglycemic crisis (Table 2). Once diabetes is diagnosed, HbA_{1c} measurement, fasting lipid profile, serum electrolyte panel, urinalysis (including testing for moderately increased albuminuria [microalbuminuria]), and electrocardiography are performed to screen for complications and establish baseline values.

Individuals whose glucose levels are higher than normal but do not meet the criteria for diabetes are considered prediabetic. An HbA_{1c} ranging from 5.7% to 6.4%, impaired fasting glucose (100 mg/dL [5.6 mmol/L] to 125 mg/dL [6.9 mmol/L]), or impaired glucose tolerance test (2-hour postprandial serum glucose level of 140 mg/dL [7.8 mmol/L] to 199 mg/dL [11.0 mmol/L]) can all be used to diagnose patients with prediabetes (see Table 2). Given their relatively high risk for developing diabetes, it is important to identify these patients to offer appropriate preventive measures. Patients with an HbA_{1c} between 5.5% and 6.0% have an incidence of diabetes ranging from 9% to 25% within a 5-year period, while those with an HbA_{1c} of 6.0% to 6.5% have an incidence of 25% to 50%.

Therapy

The ultimate goals of diabetes care are to control disease-related symptoms and prevent (or delay the progression of) diabetic complications. Improved control of blood glucose levels has been shown to reduce the incidence of microvascular complications (retinopathy, nephropathy, and neuropathy) in patients with T1DM and T2DM. However, there is conflicting evidence about whether improving glucose levels also benefits macrovascular complications (myocardial infarction, stroke, and peripheral arterial disease).

The most reliable assessment of overall glycemic status is a periodic measurement of the HbA_{1c} value. This test allows practitioners to determine the average degree of glycemia over the previous 2 to 3 months. Ideally, the HbA_{1c} value should be <7.0% (reference range, 4.0%-6.0%). Although more strict control (HbA_{1c} <6.0%-6.5%) may provide some benefit in patients in whom this level has been achieved shortly after diagnosis, in most patients it has been associated with increased hypoglycemia, no significant reduction in cardiovascular outcome or mortality, and possibly an increased overall mortality rate. However, glycemic goals need to be individualized for each patient. In patients with a shorter duration of diabetes and no significant cardiovascular disease or hypoglycemia, it may be reasonable to attempt an HbA_{1c} goal of 6.5%. **For patients with a history of hypoglycemia, a limited life expectancy, and advanced macrovascular complications, a target HbA_{1c} goal of 8.0% may be reasonable.**

Patient education and self-management are critical in the management of diabetes. Education should be individualized to a patient's specific needs and should include information about the disease process, its complications, its relationship to metabolic control, and the key role of diet and exercise in diabetes management. Glucose-monitoring techniques, proper administration of oral agents and/or insulin, treatment of hypoglycemia, and situations in which medical care should be sought must also be carefully reviewed. Home monitoring should be considered for all diabetic patients, particularly those receiving insulin therapy, as it allows patients and providers to assess glucose control in real time and longitudinally. Although fasting glucose concentrations are usually most helpful, postprandial measurements are also informative, especially in patients with an elevated HbA_{1c} despite normal fasting glucose levels. The desired fasting glucose and postprandial glucose levels

Table 2. Diagnostic Criteria for Diabetes Mellitus[a]

Criteria Number	Test	Normal Range	Increased Risk for Diabetes (Prediabetes[b])	Diabetes
1	–	–	–	Classic hyperglycemic symptoms plus a random plasma glucose ≥200 mg/dL (11.1 mmol/L)
2	Fasting plasma glucose	<100 mg/dL (5.6 mmol/L)	100-125 mg/dL (5.6-6.9 mmol/L)	≥126 mg/dL (7.0 mmol/L)
3	2-hour plasma glucose in 75-g OGTT	<140 mg/dL (7.8 mmol/L)	140-199 mg/dL (7.8-11.0 mmol/L)	≥200 mg/dL (11.1 mmol/L)
4	Glycated hemoglobin	<5.7%	5.7%-6.4%	≥6.5%

OGTT = oral glucose tolerance test.

[a]In the absence of hyperglycemic symptoms, criteria 2 through 4 should be confirmed by repeat testing for the diagnosis of diabetes. If 2 tests are performed and only 1 has abnormal results, the American Diabetes Association recommends repeating the test with abnormal results.

[b]Risk for prediabetes is continuous, extending below the lower limit of the range and becoming disproportionately greater at the higher ends of the range.

Data from American Diabetes Association. Standards of Medical Care in Diabetes–2013. Diabetes Care. 2013;36(suppl 1):S11-S16. [PMID: 23264422]

are 70 to 130 mg/dL (3.9-7.2 mmol/L) and <180 mg/dL (10.0 mmol/L), respectively.

Type 1 Diabetes

Insulin is the primary therapeutic intervention for patients with T1DM and is required to avoid ketoacidosis. Without insulin, patients will become hyperglycemic (and ultimately ketotic) within 24 to 48 hours. Insulin therapy most frequently consists of multiple daily subcutaneous injections of long- and short- or rapid-acting insulins (basal-bolus).

A further option for basal-bolus insulin delivery is the use of an insulin pump. With this therapy, a continuous infusion of short-acting insulin is delivered through a subcutaneous needle implanted under the skin. Patients are able to deliver standard basal rates of insulin throughout the day and bolus insulin at mealtimes. This strategy allows for greater flexibility and precision, but requires significant patient education, self-care, and follow-up.

Achieving the therapeutic goal of HbA_{1c} <7.0% commonly results in mild hypoglycemia. Patients need to be educated about how to avoid hypoglycemia and how to recognize and treat hypoglycemia if it occurs.

Type 2 Diabetes

Type 2 diabetes is conventionally treated first with diet, weight loss (for overweight or obese patients), and exercise. Such lifestyle modifications reduce insulin resistance and blood glucose levels and also improve cardiovascular risk factors. However, these steps are usually insufficient to attain glucose targets.

Noninsulin medications available to treat T2DM are summarized in Table 3, and available insulin preparations are described in Table 4.

Metformin is the preferred first-line monotherapeutic agent in patients with creatinine levels <1.6 mg/dL (141.4 µmol/L; men) and <1.5 mg/dL (132.6 µmol/L; women) and without known liver disease or alcohol abuse. Metformin must be discontinued before receipt of radiocontrast agents. Patients should be counseled about the risk of loose stools, bloating, gas, or other gastrointestinal side effects.

However, many patients fail to achieve optimal glucose control with monotherapy. Various pharmacotherapies are then available, which should be individualized based on a patient's known risk factors, comorbidities, medication side effects, and cost burden. Available therapeutic strategies include:

- Addition of sulfonylureas: Sulfonylureas can be given as first-line agents or in combination with metformin. Sulfonylureas are well tolerated and have few contraindications, although they

Table 3. Commonly Used Noninsulin Antihyperglycemic Agents for Type 2 Diabetes

Drug Class (Examples)	Mechanism of Action	Benefits	Risks/Concerns
Sulfonylureas (glyburide, glipizide, glimepiride)	Bind to sulfonylurea receptor on β-cells, stimulating insulin release; long duration of action	Long-term safety; can be once-daily oral pill; substantial HbA_{1c} reduction (1.0%-1.5%); low cost	Hypoglycemia; weight gain
Glinides (repaglinide, nateglinide)	Bind to sulfonylurea receptor on β-cells, stimulating insulin release; short duration of action	Target postprandial glucose	Only modest glycemic effect; potential hypoglycemia; weight gain; no long-term studies; expensive
Biguanides (metformin)	Decrease hepatic glucose production	Long-term safety; substantial HbA_{1c} reduction (1.0%-1.5%); no hypoglycemia; weight loss or weight neutral; possible macrovascular benefit; low cost	Loose stool, mild abdominal discomfort; lowers vitamin B_{12} levels; contraindicated when kidney disease is present (creatinine >1.5)
Thiazolidinediones (pioglitazone, rosiglitazone)	Activate the nuclear receptor PPARγ, increasing peripheral insulin sensitivity; may also reduce hepatic glucose production	No hypoglycemia; may improve lipid profile	Edema and heart failure risk; weight gain; possible increased myocardial infarction risk with rosiglitazone; expensive; increased risk for bladder cancer and fracture
Incretin modulators (exenatide, liraglutide)	Activate GLP-1 receptors, increasing glucose-dependent insulin secretion, decreasing glucagon secretion, delaying gastric emptying, and enhancing satiety	No hypoglycemia; weight loss; may prevent further β-cell decline (theoretical)	Injectable; nausea, vomiting; possible pancreatitis (rare); expensive
DPP-4 inhibitors (sitagliptin, saxagliptin, vildagliptin)	Inhibit degradation of endogenous GLP-1 and GIP, thereby enhancing the effect of these incretins on insulin and glucagon secretion	No hypoglycemia; weight neutral; once-daily oral dosing	Possible urticaria/angioedema (rare); no long-term studies; weight neutral; expensive
α-Glucosidase inhibitors (acarbose, miglitol, voglibose)	Inhibit polysaccharide absorption in the gut	No hypoglycemia; weight neutral	Minimal HbA_{1c} effect (~0.5%); flatulence, abdominal discomfort
SGLT2 inhibitor (dapagliflozin, canagliflozin)	Inhibit SGLT2 in proximal renal tubules to reduce renal reabsorption of filtered glucose resulting glucosuria	No hypoglycemia; weight neutral; possible lower blood pressure	Genital infection such as vulvovaginal candidiasis and possible urinary tract infection; long-term efficacy and safety data are pending

DPP-4 = dipeptidyl peptidase-4; GIP = gastric inhibitory peptide; GLP-1 = glucagon-like peptide-1; HbA_{1c} = hemoglobin A_{1c}; PPARγ = peroxisome proliferator-activated receptor-γ; SGLT2 = sodium glucose co-transporter 2.

Table 4. Pharmacokinetic Properties of Insulin Products

Human Insulins and Insulin Analogues	Onset	Peak	Duration
Rapid acting (lispro, aspart, glulisine)	10-15 min	1-2 h	3-5 h
Short acting (regular)	0.5-1 h	2-4 h	4-8 h
Intermediate acting (NPH)	1-3 h	6-10 h	10-16 h
Long acting			
Glargine	2-3 h	None	24+ h
Detemir	1 h	None	12-24 h

NPH = neutral protamine Hagedorn.

can cause hypoglycemia and should be used with caution in the elderly, especially in the presence of chronic kidney disease.

- Initiating an incretin-based therapy while continuing oral medications: Currently available incretin therapies include glucagon-like peptide-1 receptor agonists or dipeptidyl peptidase-4 inhibitors. This class of drug can reduce HbA_{1c} by approximately 0.5% to 1.5%. Glucagon-like peptide-1 agonists improve glycemic control without increasing the risk of hypoglycemia or weight gain and, in some patients, may promote modest weight loss. However, side effects include significant nausea, diarrhea, vomiting, and bloating. In addition, these agents require injections and are significantly more expensive than other medications. Dipeptidyl peptidase-4 inhibitors are oral agents that can similarly reduce HbA_{1c}, although without changes in body weight.

- Initiating a third oral medication: Thiazolidinediones (pioglitazone, rosiglitazone) can result in further reductions in HbA_{1c} of approximately 0.5% to 1.0%. However, current evidence suggests that rosiglitazone (and possibly pioglitazone) may not be optimal for treating T2DM. Rosiglitazone is associated with increased cardiovascular adverse events, and its use has been significantly restricted by the US Food and Drug Administration. These medications are contraindicated in patients with heart failure or liver dysfunction and have been associated with increased risk of bladder cancer and osteoporotic fracture. They may have a role in unique circumstances, although risks and benefits must be carefully weighed and discussed with the patients in advance.

- Most experts initiate insulin therapy if the desired level of glycemic control is not achieved with these other strategies. The most popular method is to begin with a single nighttime injection of basal (long-acting) insulin because this simple approach minimizes the risk of hypoglycemia. Basal insulin, although effective in many patients, does not address postprandial glucose excursions. To address this, a short- or rapid-acting insulin is added before each meal. Another method is twice-daily use of a premixed product that contains both intermediate- and short- or rapid-acting insulin in fixed ratios. Some oral agents can be continued with the initiation of basal insulin, although insulin secretagogues (sulfonylureas and glinides) are usually discontinued because of the additive risk for hypoglycemia. Regardless, patients should be counseled that consistency in their routine (both timing of insulin administration and eating patterns) is paramount to success in managing their diabetes. Insulin therapy is also considered the standard of care for treating diabetes during pregnancy, although some recent studies suggest certain oral agents may prove to be safe.

Chronic Complications and Their Prevention

Microvascular complications of diabetes involve the kidneys (diabetic nephropathy), the retina (diabetic retinopathy), and the peripheral nerves (diabetic neuropathy). To screen for nephropathy, it is recommended that all patients with T1DM and T2DM be tested for urine albumin excretion with a spot urine sample for albumin-creatinine ratio (see Chapter 66). The presence of moderately increased albuminuria (approximately 30-300 mg/g) should prompt initiation of an angiotensin-converting enzyme inhibitor or angiotensin-receptor blocker for its renoprotective effects. Optimizing glycemic control and BP control may reduce the risk and slow the progression of nephropathy.

The highly vascular retina is often affected in patients with long-standing diabetes mellitus, and diabetic retinopathy is responsible for most cases of legal blindness among adults in the United States. Hard exudates, microaneurysms, and minor hemorrhages (background diabetic retinopathy) are among the early changes. Although diabetic background retinopathy is not typically associated with any decline in visual acuity, it is associated with retinal infarcts and growth of abnormally fragile blood vessels (neovascularization) that predispose to retinal and vitreous hemorrhage resulting in visual loss. Macular edema may also occur. Laser photocoagulation can preserve sight in these individuals. In addition, BP reduction and glycemic control slow the progression of eye disease.

To prevent foot ulcers, foot-care strategies should be instituted for all patients with diabetes, particularly those with documented diabetic neuropathy. A foot ulcer, defined as any transdermal interruption of skin integrity, is predictive of amputation. Thus, patients must be educated about daily foot inspections, appropriate footwear and avoiding barefoot activities, and testing water temperature before bathing. Orthotic footwear should be prescribed for patients with foot deformities to cushion high-pressure areas. Testing sensation using a 5.07/10-g monofilament has been shown to predict ulcer and amputation risk (Plate 1) and have superior predictive value, compared with other sensory test modalities (tuning fork, pinprick, and cotton wisps), for the presence or absence of neuropathic symptoms.

Cardiovascular autonomic neuropathy is an often underdiagnosed autonomic neuropathy in diabetic patient that may present with nonspecific symptoms such as exercise intolerance, orthostatic hypotension, or cardiovascular lability. While often difficult to identify, cardiovascular autonomic neuropathy is associated with increased risk of silent myocardial ischemia and mortality. Gastrointestinal neuropathy, often manifesting as gastroparesis, is another cause of frequent hospitalization in patients with advanced diabetes. Gastroparesis should be suspected in a diabetic patient who has erratic glucose control with nonspecific gastrointestinal complaints and no other identifiable cause. Autonomic neuropathy can also involve the genitourinary tract, resulting in neurogenic bladder and, in men, erectile dysfunction and retrograde ejaculation. Erectile dysfunction has been reported to affect up to 35% to 75% of men with diabetes and is usually a marker for development of other microvascular complications. Like many other complications of diabetic patients, optimal glycemic control can prevent the development of neuropathies. However, once neuropathies are present, glycemic control can only slow progression but not reverse the disease process.

To reduce the risk of macrovascular complications, BP and cholesterol levels should be aggressively managed. Guidelines from the Eighth Report of the Joint National Committee on Prevention, Detection, Evaluation, and Treatment of High Blood Pressure recommend a target BP of <140/90 mm Hg, while the ADA recommends a target BP of <140/80 mm Hg. Lipid control is usually achieved with the assistance of statin therapy. The American Heart Association/ American College of Cardiology guidelines recommend moderate-intensity statin therapy (to lower the low-density lipoprotein cholesterol [LDL-C] concentration by 30% to <50%) in patients with diabetes, and high-intensity statin therapy (to lower the LDL-C concentration by ≥50%) if the 10-year cardiovascular risk is ≥7.5% in patients aged 40 to 75 years.

The ADA and American Heart Association recommend aspirin for secondary prevention in patients with a history of myocardial infarction, vascular bypass, stroke or transient ischemic attack, peripheral arterial disease, claudication, or angina. Aspirin is also recommended for primary prevention in patients with diabetes and a 10-year risk of cardiovascular disease >10% (based on the Framingham risk score), which would include most men aged >50 years and women aged >60 years who have at least 1 additional cardiovascular risk factor.

Hospital Management

Hyperglycemia in the hospitalized patient, with or without diabetes, is associated with poor outcome. However, the optimal level of blood glucose control in hospitalized patients remains unclear. Despite early evidence that intense glucose control (a target blood glucose of 80-110 mg/dL [4.4-6.1 mmol/L]) improved outcomes in surgical patients in the intensive care unit, subsequent studies showed significantly increased hypoglycemia and increased mortality in patients treated to this level. Therefore, current recommendations for critically ill, hospitalized patients are to initiate insulin therapy with persistent hyper-glycemia >200 mg/dL (11.1 mmol/L) and aim for a target goal of 140 to 200 mg/dL (7.8-11.1 mmol/L). There is no clear evidence for a glucose goal in non-critically ill patients, and the ADA recommends premeal blood glucose targets to be <140 mg/dL (7.8 mmol/L) and random blood glucose to be <180 mg/dL (10.0 mmol/L). The guidelines also emphasize the need to reconsider widespread use of sliding scale regular insulin as the sole antihyperglycemic therapy in hospitalized patients with diabetes. Instead, more proactive, physiologic insulin regimens, such as a basal-bolus approach, are advised. Currently, the data on the safety and efficacy of oral antihyperglycemic agents and other noninsulin, injectable agents are lacking. These agents are usually replaced by insulin while the patient is in the hospital to avoid the possibility of developing medication contraindications, especially given the unpredictable progression of acute illness and the necessity of tests or procedures while hospitalized. In selected situations, such as in anticipation of discharge of a clinically stable patient, medications without significant risk for hypoglycemia, such as metformin, may be appropriate. However, the patient's kidney and liver function and contrast use should be closely monitored.

Follow-Up

Glycemic control should be monitored with HbA_{1c} measurements every 3 to 6 months. Obtain an annual fasting lipid profile, including LDL-C, triglyceride, high-density lipoprotein cholesterol, and total cholesterol levels, and adjust treatment to meet goals. Screen annually for diabetic nephropathy with a spot urine test for moderately increased albuminuria (microalbuminuria). Perform a foot examination at each visit. Obtain an annual dilated funduscopic examination from a specialist, unless otherwise dictated by the specialist. Reinforce the key issues of diabetes self-management, hypoglycemia prevention and treatment, appropriate use of medications, blood glucose monitoring, and lifestyle measures.

Bibliography

American Diabetes Association. Standards of medical care in diabetes–2013. Diabetes Care. 2013;36(suppl 1):S11-S66. [PMID: 23264422]

Stenström G, Gottster A, Bakhtadze E, Berger B, Sundkvist G. Latent autoimmune diabetes in adults: definition, presentation, β-cell function, and treatment. Diabetes. 2005;54(suppl 2):S68-S72. [PMID: 16306343]

Vinik AI, Maser RE, Mitchell BD, Freeman R. Diabetic autonomic neuropathy. Diabetes Care. 2003;26(5):1553-1579. [PMID: 12716821]

Chapter 14

Diabetic Ketoacidosis and Hyperglycemic Hyperosmolar Syndrome

Norra Kwong, MD
Erik K. Alexander, MD

The most life-threatening acute complication of type 1 diabetes mellitus is diabetic ketoacidosis (DKA), occurring in 10% to 20% of patients at the initial presentation of their illness. Diabetic ketoacidosis develops when significant insulin deficiency is coupled with excess circulating levels of counter-regulatory hormones, including glucagon. Insufficient insulin prevents glucose uptake by muscle and liver cells, resulting in profound hyperglycemia and excessive hepatic glucose production. The hyperglycemia is responsible for osmotic diuresis and hypovolemia. The excess glucose is metabolized via the fatty acid degradation pathway to free fatty acids that are converted to β-hydroxybutyrate and acetoacetate by the liver, resulting in ketoacidosis, ketonuria, and electrolyte abnormalities.

Hyperglycemic hyperosmolar syndrome (HHS) is associated with type 2 diabetes. Although HHS shares similar pathophysiology to DKA, residual circulating insulin precludes the onset of ketosis; therefore, acidosis does not occur despite severe hyperglycemia (Table 1).

Prevention

Once type 1 diabetes has been diagnosed, patient education is paramount in preventing DKA. Patients should be instructed on how to manage their diabetes during illness. When ill, patients with type 1 diabetes must increase the frequency of home blood glucose monitoring, measure urinary or fingerstick ketones regularly, continue insulin (even if not eating), and maintain fluid and carbohydrate intake. Insulin deficiency of even 6 to 12 hours can lead to significant ketosis. Patients should be advised to seek emergent medical care if nausea or vomiting limits oral hydration or if ketone testing is positive.

Precipitating Factors

Once DKA or HHS is diagnosed, identification of the cause or precipitating factor(s) is an important next step as these conditions rarely occur de novo. Obtaining a thorough history and physical examination is essential to guide a diagnostic testing and treatment plan. DKA is most commonly caused by omission of insulin therapy, but both conditions may occur with concomitant infection or rarely with other clinical events such as silent myocardial infarction or cerebrovascular accident. Pancreatitis, trauma, alcohol abuse, and illicit drug (cocaine) use are other possible causes. Less often, drugs that affect carbohydrate metabolism may lead to DKA or HHS. These include the use of glucocorticoids, thiazide diuretics, sympathomimetic agents, or second-generation antipsychotics. In elderly patients, restricted access to water intake or altered thirst response increases risk of dehydration and, therefore, HHS.

Identification of the cause of DKA or HHS may be complicated by the manifestations of the disease process itself. For example, while infection is an important trigger to consider, typical signs and symptoms may be masked in the setting of DKA. Due to peripheral vasodilatation, patients can often be normothermic or mildly hypothermic despite having an ongoing infection. Conversely, leukocytosis is often seen in DKA in the absence of infection. Thus, when infection is suspected, additional diagnostic testing such as chest x-rays, urinalysis, blood cultures, or analysis of cerebrospinal fluid must be obtained accordingly. Another important consideration is neurologic pathology. While patients with HHS and a serum osmolality of >320 mOsm/kg (320 mmol/kg) are often obtunded or comatose, altered mental status is rarely seen in patients with a lower serum osmolality. In such cases, an alternative etiology such as cerebrovascular accident should be investigated. In addition, abdominal pain in DKA may correlate with the severity of acidosis. However, other causes of

Table 1. Comparison of Diabetic Ketoacidosis and Hyperglycemic Hyperosmolar Syndrome

	Diabetic Ketoacidosis	Hyperglycemic Hyperosmolar Syndrome
Diabetes mellitus association	Type 1	Type 2
Serum glucose	250-600 mg/dL (13.9-33.3 mmol/L); rarely >800 mg/dL (44.4 mmol/L)	>600 mg/dL (33.3 mmol/L); often >1000 mg/dL (55.5 mmol/L)
Serum and urine ketones	Positive	Negative
Anion gap	Elevated	Normal
Serum pH	<7.2	>7.3
Serum osmolality	Variable	>320 mOsm/kg (320 mmol/kg)
Serum bicarbonate	<18 mEq/L (18 mmol/L)	>18 meq/L (18 mmol/L)

abdominal pain should be explored when acidosis is minimal or absent, or when pain is disproportionate to the biochemical findings. Lastly, myocardial infarction may trigger HHS, particularly in older patients, and may be the only manifestation of cardiac ischemia in a diabetic patient.

Diagnosis

Diabetic Ketoacidosis

The development of DKA is usually a rapid process, culminating within a few hours after the inciting event. In contrast, the development of HHS is more insidious, evolving over days or weeks. Symptoms of DKA include polyuria, polydipsia, blurred vision, nausea, vomiting, and abdominal pain. If DKA is severe, patients may have altered mental status or be unresponsive. Physical examination will reveal signs of hypovolemia, including tachycardia, hypotension, dry mucous membranes, and poor skin turgor. Kussmaul respiration (deep and frequent breathing) is a sign of metabolic acidosis, and a fruity breath odor is often noted due to acetone elimination by the lungs.

The diagnosis of DKA is based on a triad of hyperglycemia (blood glucose level >250 mg/dL [13.9 mmol/L]), increased anion gap metabolic acidosis (arterial pH <7.30; serum bicarbonate <15 meq/L [15 mmol/L]), and positive serum or urine ketones. Blood urea nitrogen and serum creatinine levels are usually elevated secondary to hypovolemia.

The serum sodium level will often be low due to the hyperglycemia-induced osmotic shifts of fluid into the vascular system. Serum potassium may be elevated due to extracellular potassium shifts caused by acidosis, but total body potassium stores are often depleted because of urinary losses.

Hyperglycemic Hyperosmolar Syndrome

Hyperglycemic hyperosmolar syndrome is almost exclusively seen in patients with type 2 diabetes. Signs and symptoms often include altered mental status and evidence of hypovolemia. Common precipitating conditions include infection, trauma, and in some cases myocardial infarction.

Diagnostic criteria for HHS include plasma glucose >600 mg/dL (33.3 mmol/L); arterial pH >7.30; serum bicarbonate >15 meq/L (15 mmol/L); serum osmolality >320 mOsm/kg (320 mmol/kg); and absent urine or serum ketones. The anion gap is usually normal but can be increased in the setting of hypovolemia-induced prerenal azotemia.

Therapy

Diabetic Ketoacidosis

Diabetic ketoacidosis is a life-threatening condition. Patients require hospitalization, often in an intensive care unit. The goals of treatment are the resolution of ketosis (anion gap normalization), volume repletion, and restoration of electrolyte abnormalities. An intra-venous (IV) infusion of 0.9% saline is started immediately, along with IV regular insulin. From 2 to 6 L of IV fluid may be required to achieve euvolemic status. An initial IV bolus of regular insulin (0.15 U/kg) is administered, followed by a continuous IV infusion of approximately 0.1 U/kg/h. Blood glucose is monitored hourly, targeting a reduction in serum glucose of 50-100 mg/dL (2.8-5.6 mmol/L) per hour. When the serum glucose reaches 250 mg/dL (13.9 mmol/L), the IV solution is typically changed to 0.45% saline with 5% or 10% dextrose to avoid hypoglycemia. The insulin infusion is continued until the anion gap has normalized and ketones are no longer present. Premature discontinuation of insulin may lead to rebound acidosis. Once ketones are cleared and the anion gap is normalized, patients are started on subcutaneous insulin with a 2- to 6-hour period of overlapping subcutaneous and IV insulin before IV insulin is discontinued.

Insulin will cause substantial shifts of potassium and phosphorus from the extracellular to the intracellular space. Therefore, it is important to measure serum potassium every 1 to 2 hours and to replace potassium intravenously. Phosphate repletion is typically not required. Bicarbonate therapy is reserved for severe acidosis (pH <6.9).

The most dangerous complication of DKA treatment is the rare development of cerebral edema, signaled by symptoms of headache and altered mental status, which is most common during the treatment of children and can be fatal. The exact cause is unknown but may be due in part to aggressive hydration with hypotonic fluids.

Hyperglycemic Hyperosmolar Syndrome

Patients with HHS are often hemodynamically unstable and usually require care in an intensive unit care. The mainstay of treatment is correction of hypovolemia with 0.9% saline, infusing at least 1 L before the initiation of insulin. Half of the fluid deficit should be replaced during the first 24 hours, with the remainder replaced during the following 2 to 3 days (see Chapter 67). Intravenous insulin is initiated with a bolus of 0.1 U/kg and continued at a rate of 0.1 U/kg. The goal is to decrease serum glucose by 50-100 mg/dL (2.8-5.6 mmol/L) per hour until glucose is <200 mg/dL (11.1 mmol/L) and the patient is eating, at which point the patient is changed to subcutaneous insulin.

Potassium is monitored closely, as patients may become hypokalemic. Intravenous or oral potassium is provided to maintain serum potassium concentrations between 4.0 and 5.0 meq/L (4-5 mmol/L). Bicarbonate therapy is typically not required. Serum osmolality is monitored, with a goal of decreasing it by <3 mOsm/kg (3 mmol/kg) per hour.

Bibliography

Kitabchi AB. Hyperglycemic crisis in diabetes mellitus: diabetic ketoacidosis and hyperglycemic hyperosmolar state. Endocrinol Metab Clin North Am. 2006;35:725-751. [PMID: 17127143]

Kitabchi AE, Umpierrez GE, Murphy MB, et al; American Diabetes Association. Hyperglycemic crises in diabetes. Diabetes Care. 2004;27 (suppl 1):S94-S102. [PMID: 14693938]

Wilson JF. In the clinic. Diabetic ketoacidosis. Ann Intern Med. 2010;152: ITC1-ITC15. [PMID: 20048266]

Chapter 15

Osteoporosis

Mark D. Corriere, MD

Osteoporosis is a skeletal disorder characterized by compromised bone strength predisposing to an increased risk of fractures. Decreased bone strength occurs because peak bone mass is low, bone resorption is excessive, or bone formation is decreased during remodeling. All 3 mechanisms contribute to osteoporosis. The disease affects an estimated 57 million Americans. The prevalence of low bone mineral density (BMD) is particularly high in the elderly, approaching 80% in women aged >80 years. The disease can result in significant burden, with one-half of all postmenopausal women experiencing an osteoporosis-related fracture in their lifetime. Effective screening modalities and treatments are available.

Prevention

Measures to prevent bone loss are indicated whenever risk factors for bone loss are present or a dual-energy x-ray absorptiometry (DEXA) T-score is < –1 (see *Screening* below). Nonpharmacologic preventive measures include adequate daily calcium and vitamin D intake, regular exercise, and avoidance of tobacco products and excessive alcohol use. Exercise should focus on weight-bearing activities (eg, walking, jogging, or stair climbing) and muscle strengthening (eg, weight or resistance training). Excessive exercise may actually be counterproductive in the adolescent or young adult female patient, since this may lead to the "athlete's triad" of a restrictive eating disorder, amenorrhea, and osteoporosis. Reducing the risk of falls is particularly important for helping to prevent fracture in the frail elderly.

Screening

The goal of screening is to identify individuals at increased risk for osteoporosis who would benefit from lifestyle modifications or pharmacologic treatment to prevent fractures. Modifiable risk factors include low calcium or vitamin D intake, inadequate physical activity, low body mass index, tobacco use, and excessive alcohol use. Nonmodifiable risk factors include increasing age, female sex, race (white or Asian), impaired mobility, and a family history of fragility fracture in a first-degree relative. A fragility fracture is a spontaneous fracture or a fracture due to a fall from standing height or less.

All women aged ≥65 years should be screened regardless of risk factors. In addition, postmenopausal women aged <65 years with risk factors for low bone density should be screened. Several other specific populations also require screening (Table 1). Screening for osteoporosis should also be considered in patients with a known secondary cause of osteoporosis (Table 2).

The screening modality of choice is a DEXA scan. DEXA scans use x-rays at 2 different doses to create images used to estimate the mineral content of bone (also termed BMD). Measurements are usually made in the spine and hip. The reliability of these sites allows for repeat serial measurements to monitor disease progression over time. Results of DEXA scans are provided as T- and Z-scores.

- T-scores represent standard deviations from the mean BMD of young healthy adults. Measurements of BMD of 2.5 standard deviations or lower below the mean (T score ≤–2.5) are considered to be diagnostic of osteoporosis; scores between –1 and –2.5 define low bone mass.
- Z-scores represent the number of standard deviations from the reference mean value for age- and sex-matched controls. Z-scores are used in assessing osteoporosis risk in individuals aged <40 years, if indicated. In individuals aged >40 years, abnormally low Z-scores suggest the presence of a secondary cause of osteoporosis.

Diagnosis

Normal bone mass is defined as a BMD within 1 standard deviation of the reference mean. Low bone mass is diagnosed with a T-score between –1 and –2.5. The diagnosis of osteoporosis is made with a T-score of lower than –2.5 or the presence of a vertebral or hip fracture sustained with low trauma (fragility fracture) regardless of BMD.

In high-risk patients and in those with low bone mass or osteoporosis, the focused medical history in patients should include assessment of daily calcium and vitamin D intake, level of physical

Table 1. Indications for Measurement of Bone Mineral Density

Women aged ≥65 years (regardless of risk factors)
Postmenopausal women aged <65 years who have at least 1 risk factor for osteoporosis (other than menopause in women)
Women or men who have fractures on presentation
Radiographic findings suggestive of osteoporosis or vertebral deformity
Glucocorticoid therapy for more than 3 months
Primary hyperparathyroidism
Treatment for osteoporosis (to monitor therapeutic response and guide further therapy)

Table 2. Selected Causes of Secondary Osteoporosis

Endocrine disorders: hyperparathyroidism, Cushing syndrome, hypogonadism, hyperthyroidism, prolactinoma, acromegaly, osteomalacia

Hematopoietic disorders: multiple myeloma, sickle-cell disease, thalassemia minor, leukemia, lymphoma, polycythemia vera

Connective tissue disorders: osteogenesis imperfecta, homocystinuria

Renal disease: chronic kidney disease, renal tubular acidosis, hypercalciuria

Nutritional: malabsorption, total parenteral nutrition

Gastrointestinal disorders: gastrectomy, primary biliary cirrhosis, celiac disease

Medications: glucocorticoids, anticonvulsants, heparin

Genetic: Turner syndrome, Klinefelter syndrome

activity, tobacco or alcohol use, menstrual history, falls, and medication use. In patients without standard risk factors, the history should also review possible secondary causes (see Table 2).

Physical examination can provide critical information if osteoporosis is suspected. Height should be measured using a wall-mounted stadiometer, with serial measurements followed for possible height loss. A loss of ≥1.5 inches (3.81 cm) from peak adult height is suggestive of potential osteoporosis. The spine should be assessed for evidence of kyphosis or vertebral fractures. Physical findings predictive of osteoporosis include frail appearance and poor proximal muscle strength demonstrated by difficulty rising from a chair without pushing off with the arms.

Laboratory testing in patients with low bone mass or osteoporosis is focused on identifying potential underlying causes and may include a complete blood count, serum thyroid-stimulating hormone, calcium and phosphorus, creatinine, liver transaminases, alkaline phosphatase, erythrocyte sedimentation rate, serum 25-hydroxyvitamin D, serum testosterone (in men), and tissue transglutaminase antibodies (if celiac disease is suspected). Additional laboratory testing may be indicated based on assessment of the potential presence of a secondary cause of osteoporosis (see Table 2). Primary osteoporosis is associated with no abnormalities on laboratory testing.

Therapy

Nonpharmacologic treatment should be instituted in all patients with low bone mass and osteoporosis, while pharmacologic therapy is indicated in patients with osteoporosis. Use of medication in those with low bone mass is usually based on fracture risk. The World Health Organization has developed the Fracture Risk Assessment Tool (FRAX®; www.sheffield.ac.uk/FRAX), which estimates a patient's 10-year risk of hip and major osteoporotic fracture.

Ten-year risks >3% for hip fracture or >20% for major osteoporotic fracture are thresholds beyond which therapy in patients with low bone mass would likely benefit from pharmacologic therapy.

Nonpharmacologic Measures

Ensuring adequate oral calcium intake is an essential treatment for osteoporosis. The recommended daily calcium intake varies by age and sex (Table 3). It is most desirable to achieve oral calcium goals through regular dietary intake. Daily dietary calcium intake can be estimated by multiplying each serving of a dairy product (milk, yogurt, or cheese) by 300 mg and then adding 250 mg, representing the average calcium intake from other foods. Calcium supplements (calcium carbonate or calcium citrate) are recommended for patients who do not routinely consume adequate amounts of daily dietary calcium. Calcium carbonate requires stomach acid for absorption and should be taken with meals. Calcium citrate does not require an acidic environment to be absorbed and is more appropriate for elderly patients or those who are taking acid-suppression medications.

Vitamin D is required for small intestinal absorption of calcium. Vitamin D deficiency is common and has been linked to decreased bone density. However, the optimal serum concentration of 25-hydroxyvitamin D for optimal skeletal health is controversial, with the Institute of Medicine supporting concentrations above 20 ng/mL (50 nmol/L) but not chronically exceeding 50 ng/mL (125 nmol/L). Several trials support the use of calcium and vitamin D in prevention and reversal of postmenopausal bone loss. Dietary sources of vitamin D include fortified foods such as milk, juice, and cereals. Supplementation is accomplished with multivitamins (most contain 200-400 IU of vitamin D), combined calcium/vitamin D preparations, or oral vitamin D repletion. The recommended vitamin D intake is 600 to 800 IU/day for all adults aged >50 years (see Table 3). Vitamin D levels also rise with adequate sun exposure.

Table 3. US Institute of Medicine Daily Recommended Intake of Calcium and Vitamin D[a]

Group	Calcium Intake (mg)	Upper Limit of Calcium Intake (mg)	Vitamin D Intake (units)	Upper Limit of Vitamin D Intake (units)
Men and women (19-50 y, including women who are pregnant and lactating)	1000	2500	600	4000
Men (51-70 y)	1000	2000	600	4000
Women (51-70 y)	1200	2000	600	4000
Men and women (>70 y)	1200	2000	800	4000

[a]For adults aged 19 years and older.

Adapted with permission from The National Academies Press, Copyright 2011, National Academy of Sciences. Institute of Medicine of the National Academies. DRIs for Calcium and Vitamin D. 11/30/2011. www.iom.edu/Reports/2010/Dietary-Reference-Intakes-for-Calcium-and-Vitamin-D.aspx. Accessed June 13, 2012.

Table 4. Pharmacologic Therapy for Osteoporosis

Class/Agent	Notes
Oral bisphosphonates (alendronate, risedronate, and ibandronate)	Decrease bone resorption by attenuating osteoclast activity. First-line treatment of osteoporosis. Increase bone mass; decrease vertebral and nonvertebral fractures. May cause esophageal irritation. Must take in morning without food and with 8 oz of water and not recline for 30-60 min.
Intravenous bisphosphonates (zoledronate and ibandronate)	Decrease bone resorption by attenuating osteoclast activity. First-line treatment of osteoporosis. Increase bone mass; decrease vertebral fracture, hip fracture, and nonvertebral fractures. Flu-like symptoms after first dose. Zoledronate is given every 12 mo and ibandronate every 3 mo.
Raloxifene	Selective estrogen receptor modulator. Suppresses osteoclasts and decreases bone resorption; estrogen antagonist in uterus and breast. Increases bone mass; decreases vertebral fractures; decreases risk of breast cancer; increases thromboembolic risk and vasomotor symptoms; increases risk of fatal stroke. Not recommended for premenopausal women or women using estrogen replacement therapy.
Teriparatide	Recombinant parathyroid hormone. Stimulates bone formation. Increases bone mass; decreases vertebral and nonvertebral fracture rates. Treatment cannot exceed 24 mo. Contraindicated in patients with history of bone malignancy, Paget disease, hypercalcemia, or skeletal radiation.
Calcitonin	Decreases bone resorption by attenuating osteoclast activity. Increases bone mass slightly; decreases vertebral fracture rates. Decreases pain associated with vertebral fracture. Causes rhinitis. Not considered first-line treatment for osteoporosis.
Denosumab	Monoclonal antibody that inhibits the proliferation, differentiation, and maturation of preosteoclasts into active bone-resorbing cells. Decreases bone remodeling and increases bone mineral density. Can be used in patients with chronic kidney disease but may cause hypocalcemia.

Pharmacologic Therapy

Available pharmacologic therapies for low bone mass and osteoporosis are listed in Table 4.

Bisphosphonates are first-line agents. Bisphosphonate treatment results in a 30% to 60% decrease in fracture rates, with the greatest efficacy shown in the prevention of new vertebral fractures. Three oral bisphosphonates are currently available: alendronate, risedronate, and ibandronate. **There is no advantage of newer bisphosphonates compared to older forms available as generics (ie, oral alendronate).** These drugs reduce the risk of fracture by preventing bone resorption. Oral bisphosphonates are taken on an empty stomach with at least 8 oz (237 mL) of water, and patients must remain upright for at least 30 minutes (60 minutes for ibandronate) to prevent pill-induced esophageal ulceration. Bisphosphonates are contraindicated in patients with chronic kidney disease or esophageal disease. Intravenous ibandronate (administered once every 3 months) and intravenous zoledronate (administered once yearly) also have approval by the US Food and Drug Administration (FDA) for the treatment of osteoporosis in postmenopausal women. These may be particularly helpful with compliance or in patients where malabsorption is a concern. Bisphosphonate therapy (mainly intravenous) in patients with metastatic cancer has been associated with osteonecrosis of the jaw. There are reports of atypical subtrochanteric or diaphyseal femur fractures in patients taking long-term bisphosphonates. This rare side effect is thought to be due to long-term suppression of bone turnover. Alendronate, risedronate, and zoledronate all have FDA approval for treatment of osteoporosis in men.

Raloxifene is a selective estrogen receptor modulator. It has an estrogen agonist effect on bone and an antagonist effect in the breast and uterus and may be used in women who cannot tolerate bisphosphonate therapy. Side effects include increased risk of thromboembolism and increased vasomotor symptoms. The effect of raloxifene on bone mass is less than that of estrogen or alendronate, with efficacy in reducing the risk of vertebral but not hip fracture rates. Although estrogen is effective, it is no longer recommended for prevention or treatment of osteoporosis because of an overall unfavorable risk/benefit profile.

Teriparatide is a recombinant form of parathyroid hormone and is the first FDA-approved osteoporosis medication that stimulates bone formation rather than decreasing bone resorption. It is indicated for treatment of men and women with severe osteoporosis who have failed or cannot take other osteoporosis medications and is considered second-line therapy to bisphosphonates. Teriparatide reduces vertebral fractures by 65% and nonvertebral fractures by 53%, a reduction that continues even after therapy is discontinued. The drug is given as a subcutaneous injection once daily for 24 months. **Teriparatide is 10 times more expensive than other therapies for osteoporosis and cannot be continued beyond 24 months because of concern about a potential risk for osteosarcoma.**

Calcitonin is an antiresorptive agent administered as a nasal spray. It is indicated for patients with bone pain from osteoporotic fractures or patients with contraindications to other therapies. Calcitonin is not a first-line agent, as other therapies are typically more effective.

Denosumab is a monoclonal antibody that blocks osteoclast activation, leading to decreased bone resorption and increased bone density. It is given as a subcutaneous injection once every 6 months. Denosumab has been shown to reduce the risk of vertebral, nonvertebral, and hip fractures in women with osteoporosis. It is FDA approved for use in postmenopausal women with a history of osteoporotic fracture or multiple risk factors for fracture or who have failed or cannot take other osteoporosis medications, and may also be used in patients with chronic kidney disease who are unable to take bisphosphonates. Side effects may include an increased number of infections (ie, cellulitis, pneumonia, or viral infections) and hypocalcemia if used in patients with kidney failure. **Because of potential side effects and expense, denosumab is considered second-line therapy for patients unable to take or tolerate bisphosphonate therapy.**

Follow-Up

For patients with a normal or low normal BMD, repeat DEXA scans need not occur for 10 to 15 years. There is no consensus on follow-up BMD testing for patients with more significant bone loss or those started on pharmacologic therapy. For those with T scores of −2.0 to −2.5, repeat DEXA scanning in 2 years is reasonable. For those started on pharmacologic treatment, a repeat DEXA scan in 12 to 24 months to look for percent improvements in bone density to determine treatment efficacy and the T-score to assess current fracture risk is also reasonable. Possible secondary causes, poor adherence, and need for additional treatment should be considered in patients with continuing bone loss after 12 to 18 months of medical therapy. There is no consensus on the frequency of subsequent BMD testing after this time period.

Bibliography

Gourlay ML, Fine JP, Preisser JS, et al. Bone-density testing interval and transition to osteoporosis in older women. N Engl J Med. 2012;366: 225-233. [PMID: 22256806]

U.S. Preventive Services Task Force. Screening for osteoporosis: U.S. Preventive Services Task Force recommendation statement. Ann Intern Med. 2011;154:356-364. [PMID: 21242341]

Warriner AH, Saag KG. Osteoporosis diagnosis and medical treatment. Orthop Clin North Am. 2013;44:125-135. [PMID: 23544819]

Section 3
Gastroenterology and Hepatology

Associate Editor – Jonathan S. Appelbaum, MD, FACP

High Value Care Recommendations

- The diagnosis of gastroesophageal reflux disease is usually based on the clinical picture.

- Proton pump inhibitor (PPI) therapy is the treatment of choice for patients presenting with gastroesophageal reflux disease.

- Younger patients with mild to moderate epigastric pain consistent with peptic ulcer disease and no other associated symptoms can be treated empirically with a PPI and forgo endoscopy.

- Repeat liver chemistry studies are indicated in asymptomatic patients to confirm any abnormal test results.

- The duration of liver test abnormalities can often be determined through the history and laboratory records, and this is important information in interpreting abnormal liver studies.

- Asymptomatic patients with mild liver enzyme abnormalities require only follow-up with repeated laboratory studies.

- Liver biopsy is often not required to make the diagnosis of nonalcoholic fatty liver disease in a consistent clinical setting.

- Screening for gallstones in asymptomatic, average-risk individuals is not indicated.

- Measuring serum lipase alone is sufficient to confirm the diagnosis of acute pancreatitis in the appropriate clinical setting.

- Imaging of the pancreas in acute pancreatitis is not indicated in all patients but should be considered in those with moderate or severe pancreatitis or persistent fever and in those who do not improve clinically within 48 to 72 hours to confirm the diagnosis, exclude other intraabdominal processes, grade the severity of pancreatitis, and diagnose local complications (pancreatic necrosis, pseudocyst, abscess).

- Because most episodes of diarrhea are self-limited, diagnostic testing generally is reserved for patients with severe diarrheal illness characterized by fever, blood in the stool, or signs of dehydration (weakness, thirst, decreased urine output, orthostasis) or patients with diarrhea lasting >7 days.

Chapter 16

Approach to Abdominal Pain

Seth Politano, DO
Eric Hsieh, MD

Abdominal pain is a common symptom, accounting for 18% to 42% of hospital admissions. Although some patients have classic symptoms pointing to a particular diagnosis, in other patients the diagnosis is obscure. Pain in the abdomen is generally of visceral or peritoneal origin, originates from the abdominal wall, or is referred from other sites. Visceral pain is usually caused by stretching of the organ and is not associated with signs of peritoneal inflammation. In contrast, peritoneal pain is secondary to inflammation or irritation of the overlying peritoneum and is associated with tenderness, guarding, or rebound. Abdominal wall pain tends to be chronic and to be precisely located by the patient. Referred pain generally follows a dermatomal distribution and is not associated with underlying tenderness or signs of peritoneal inflammation.

Evaluation

The history and physical examination help develop a differential diagnosis (Table 1) and direct the relevant investigations. Important clues to the underlying diagnosis can be discovered through carefully characterizing the abdominal pain with respect to onset, duration, nature (intermittent or constant), relation to eating, association with bleeding, location, and radiation. Pain that is acute in onset generally points to acute inflammatory, infectious, or ischemic causes. Whereas upper abdominal pain is usually of gastric, hepatobiliary, or pancreatic origin, pain in the lower abdomen originates from the hindgut and genitourinary organs. The origin of periumbilical pain is the midgut and pancreas. Hematemesis definitely points to an upper gastrointestinal (GI) etiology, but melena, maroon stools, hematochezia, or occult blood can be from either upper or lower GI sources. General symptoms such as anorexia, nausea, or vomiting are insensitive in diagnosing abdominal pain. Associated medical problems can often suggest a diagnosis such as embolic or ischemic infarction due to cardiovascular disease, arrhythmia, or infective endocarditis. A history of multiple sexual partners, unprotected intercourse, or previous sexually transmitted disease highlights the possibility of pelvic inflammatory disease in women. The evaluation of abdominal pain is never complete until a physical examination, including pelvic and rectal examination, has been performed.

Acute Abdominal Pain

Acute abdominal pain is defined as pain lasting less than 1 week. The most common diagnoses are appendicitis, biliary disease, and nonspecific abdominal pain. Patients with acute abdominal pain, peritoneal signs, and hemodynamic instability require an urgent investigation and may need early surgical intervention. A chest radiograph and flat and upright abdominal radiographs should be obtained in every patient with significant acute abdominal pain to exclude bowel obstruction or perforation (free air under the diaphragm) and

intrathoracic processes that can present as abdominal pain (eg, pneumonia, pneumothorax, aortic dissection). In older patients and patients with diabetes, an electrocardiogram should be considered to exclude an atypical presentation of myocardial infarction.

Abdominal aortic aneurysms occur in 1% of all men older than age 65 years. The pain is often of acute onset, radiating to the back. A pulsatile mass may be palpated in the abdomen. Free rupture frequently presents with hemodynamic instability and cardiovascular collapse. Immediate treatment of these patients should include judicious fluid replacement because overaggressive fluid resuscitation can worsen hemorrhage.

Upper Abdominal Pain

Biliary pain is the most common cause of acute abdominal pain among patients older than age 50 years. Cholelithiasis should be suspected in patients with postprandial, right upper quadrant pain associated with ingesting fatty foods. Murphys sign (respiratory arrest on deep inspiration while palpating the right upper quadrant) suggests cholecystitis, and Charcots triad (pain, fever, jaundice) suggests cholecystitis or ascending cholangitis. Abdominal ultrasonography is the imaging modality of choice for cholelithiasis, with sensitivity and specificity both approaching 100%. Cholescintigraphy scans (e.g., hepatobiliary iminodiacetic acid [HIDA] scans) are an alternative to diagnose acute cholecystitis and can be used when ultrasonography is equivocal.

Peptic ulcer disease and gastritis commonly present as burning abdominal pain, but the pain may be vague or even cramping. In two thirds of cases, the pain is epigastric, with the remainder of cases involving pain in the upper right or upper left quadrant. Pain that radiates through to the back is unusual with peptic ulcer disease or gastritis and suggests pancreatitis or penetrating peptic ulcer disease; hematemesis or blood in the nasogastric aspirate excludes pancreatitis. In fewer than half of patients with confirmed peptic ulcer disease, digestion of food worsens gastric ulcer pain and improves duodenal ulcer pain.

Acute pancreatitis presents as acute epigastric pain, often radiating to the back. Vomiting occurs in more than 85% of cases; the absence of vomiting favors another diagnosis. Bending forward or lying curled up on one's side may relieve the pain, but many patients report no alleviating factors. The diagnosis of pancreatitis is confirmed by serum lipase (sensitivity, 90%–100%; specificity, 99%) concentrations that are at least three times the upper limits of normal. The degree of elevation does not correlate with the severity of disease. Serum amylase is less sensitive and specific and has a shorter half-life, so serum lipase is often favored. Jaundice frequently accompanies gallstone pancreatitis, and a history of alcohol abuse supports alcoholic pancreatitis. Occasionally, patients may have flank ecchymoses from retroperitoneal bleeding (Grey-Turner sign) or periumbilical ecchymosis (Cullen sign). Ultrasonography should be per-

Table 1. Differential Diagnosis of Acute Abdominal Pain

Disorder	Notes
Right Upper Quadrant (RUQ)	
Acute cholangitis (see Chapter 23)	RUQ pain, fever, jaundice; bilirubin generally >4 mg/dL (68.4 mmol/L), AST and ALT may be >1000 U/L; ALT usually > AST
Pneumonia (see Chapter 57)	Cough, shortness of breath, chest or upper abdominal pain, fever
Acute viral hepatitis (see Chapter 21)	Jaundice; AST and ALT generally >1000 U/L; ALT usually > AST
Acute alcoholic hepatitis	Recent alcohol intake, fever; leukocytosis, bilirubin generally >4 mg/dL (68.4 mmol/L); AST usually 2-3 times >ALT
Gonococcal perihepatitis (Fitz-Hugh-Curtis syndrome)	Pelvic adnexal tenderness, leukocytosis; cervical smear shows gonococci
Cholecystitis (see Chapter 23)	Epigastric and RUQ pain that radiates to right shoulder; mildly elevated bilirubin, AST, and ALT; ultrasonography shows thickened gallbladder and pericholecystic fluid
Midepigastric or Periumbilical	
Acute pancreatitis (see Chapter 24)	Midepigastric pain radiating to the back, nausea, vomiting; elevated amylase and lipase; usually secondary to gallstones or alcohol; pain from penetrating peptic ulcer may present similarly
Inferior myocardial infarction (see Chapter 3)	Chest or midepigastric pain, diaphoresis, shortness of breath; elevated cardiac enzymes; acutely abnormal electrocardiogram
Perforating peptic ulcer (see Chapter 19)	Postprandial abdominal pain, weight loss, abdominal bruit (chronic presentation); pain out of proportion to tenderness on palpation
Mesenteric ischemia	Possible anion gap metabolic acidosis; abdominal plain films may show classic thumbprinting sign (acute presentation)
Small bowel obstruction	Colicky pain; obstructive pattern seen on CT or abdominal series
Aortic dissection or rupture	Elderly patient with vascular disease and sudden-onset severe pain that radiates to the back and lower extremity
Diabetic ketoacidosis (see Chapter 14)	Blood glucose always elevated; anion gap always present
Celiac disease	Bloating, diarrhea, weight loss; may see osteopenia and anemia
Right Lower Quadrant (RLQ)	
Acute appendicitis	Midepigastric pain radiating to RLQ; ultrasonography and CT may confirm diagnosis; anorexia and nausea frequently present
Ectopic pregnancy, ovarian cyst or torsion	RLQ or LLQ abdominal pain, nausea, fever; leukocytosis; suspect in women with unilateral pain
Pelvic inflammatory disease	May be RLQ or LLQ; fever; abdominal tenderness, uterine or adnexal tenderness, cervical motion tenderness; cervical discharge
Nephrolithiasis	Right or left flank pain that may radiate to groin; hematuria
Pyelonephritis (see Chapter 60)	Fever, dysuria, and pain in right or left flank that may radiate to lower quadrant; urinalysis shows leukocytes and leukocyte casts
Left Lower Quadrant (LLQ)	
Acute diverticulitis	Pain usually in LLQ but can be RLQ if ascending colon is involved; CT can diagnose complicated diverticular disease with abscess formation
Toxic megacolon	Nonobstructive dilatation of transverse and descending colon; systemic toxicity; associated with inflammatory bowel disease and *Clostridium difficile* infection

ALT = alanine aminotransferase; AST = aspartate aminotransferase; CT = computed tomography.

formed to evaluate the biliary tract for stones. An abdominal computed tomography (CT) scan, ideally with oral and intravenous contrast, should be obtained when the diagnosis of acute pancreatitis is in question; to stage the severity; or to determine the presence of complications such as abscess, necrosis, or pseudocyst.

Central and Lower Abdominal Pain

Appendicitis is the most common cause of acute abdominal pain in patients younger than age 50 years. Despite sophisticated diagnostic techniques and algorithms, appendicitis is missed in at least 20% of cases. The pain classically begins in the periumbilical region and migrates to the right lower quadrant, is associated with anorexia, and may be followed by nausea and vomiting. The diagnosis of appendicitis is doubtful if nausea and vomiting are the first signs of illness. Physical examination will reveal tenderness over McBurney point (1/3 the distance from the anterior superior iliac spine to the umbilicus); abdominal rigidity and a positive psoas sign (pain elicited by extending the patient's right thigh while the patient is lying on his or her left side) increase the pretest probability of appendicitis. Leukocytosis and fever, although sensitive, are not specific for appendicitis. Abdominal CT with oral and intravenous contrast is the diagnostic test of choice in nonpregnant patients (sensitivity and specificity >92%; positive likelihood ratio, 18). Ultrasonography and plain abdominal radiography have poor sensitivity and specificity in the diagnosis of appendicitis.

Small bowel obstruction presents as central or generalized abdominal pain associated with vomiting or constipation. A history of prior abdominal surgery, hyperactive bowel sounds, and abdominal distension increase the probability of small bowel obstruction. Abdominal radiography shows multiple dilated bowel loops with air-fluid levels usually arranged in a stepladder pattern; this finding plus a lack of colonic gas is pathognomic. Strangulating small bowel obstructions are better visualized on CT. CT scans with contrast are also superior to plain radiographs in detecting complete small bowel obstruction, but early or partial obstruction may be missed by either modality. Other causes of small bowel obstruction include neoplasms, strictures, intussusception, and volvulus.

Acute colonic distension is most likely due to mechanical obstruction, toxic megacolon (a complication of inflammatory bowel disease or *Clostridium difficile* infection), and colonic pseudo-obstruction. Mechanical obstruction presents as crampy abdominal pain. On abdominal radiographs, dilated loops of small and large bowel, and lack of gas in the distal colon or rectum suggest mechanical obstruction but can also be seen in pseudo-obstruction. Mechanical obstruction is most commonly caused by tumors and sigmoid volvulus. Acute colonic pseudo-obstruction (Ogilvie syndrome) is characterized by dilatation of the cecum and right hemicolon in the absence of mechanical obstruction; the most common causes are trauma, infection, and cardiac disease (ie, myocardial infarction, heart failure). Toxic megacolon presents as fever, tachycardia, and abdominal tenderness, and there is usually a history of bloody diarrhea. Abdominal radiographs may show thumbprinting because of the presence of submucosal edema.

Acute diverticulitis presents as left lower quadrant abdominal pain and tenderness to palpation. Patients may have a history of chronic constipation and intermittent low-grade abdominal pain before an acute attack. Abscess formation should be suspected if guarding, rigidity, or a tender fluctuant mass is present. Abdominal and pelvic CT with contrast is the test of choice, and antibiotic therapy is the usual initial therapy.

Nonspecific abdominal pain is the third most common cause of acute abdominal pain presenting to the emergency department. It includes all causes of abdominal pain for which no specific surgical, medical, or gynecologic diagnosis can be made, including dyspepsia, constipation, irritable bowel syndrome (IBS), viral gastroenteritis, mesenteric adenitis, and dysmenorrhea.

Celiac disease presents as a constellation of bloating, diarrhea, and weight loss. It should be considered in any patient suspected of having IBS. Other manifestations include osteopenia, anemia (iron, folate, or vitamin B_{12}), peripheral neuropathy, and dermatitis herpetiformis. Complications include T-cell lymphoma. There is a higher prevalence of celiac disease in patients with diabetes and autoimmune thyroid disease. Workup begins with testing for tissue transglutaminase antibody. Confirmation can be made with small bowel biopsy

Kidney stones, acute urinary obstruction, and urinary tract infection (including pyelonephritis) are common causes of abdominal pain. Pain caused by a kidney stone is typically acute and colicky and may radiate from the flank to the groin, particularly as the stone travels down the ureter. Renal colic may be associated with hematuria and dysuria. Helical CT is the most sensitive and specific imaging study available for kidney stones and for investigating other causes of flank pain.

Acute urinary obstruction presents as suprapubic discomfort and oliguria or anuria. It is common in older men secondary to prostatic hypertrophy. A palpable bladder may be felt above the symphysis pubis. Insertion of a catheter relieves the obstruction and pain. Testicular torsion may cause referred pain to the lower abdomen. Physical examination classically reveals an asymmetrically high-riding testis. The cremasteric reflex (elevation of the ipsilateral testis after stroking the skin of the upper thigh) is usually absent. Color Doppler ultrasonography can help to confirm the diagnosis (absent blood flow).

Women of childbearing potential presenting with lower abdominal or pelvic pain *must* have a pelvic examination and a urine pregnancy test; pelvic inflammatory disease and ectopic pregnancy are often overlooked causes of lower abdominal pain. Ovarian cyst rupture, which is best diagnosed with ultrasonography, and endometriosis, which requires direct visualization of the implants for diagnosis, should also be considered in women with lower abdominal or pelvic pain.

Generalized Abdominal Pain

Diffuse abdominal pain is seen in acute peritonitis, ischemia of the mesentery and small bowel, and small bowel obstruction. The most common causes of ischemic small bowel is a mesenteric arterial embolism originating from the heart (50%) followed by mesenteric arterial thrombosis (25%) and mesenteric venous thrombosis (10%). Initially, abdominal pain is poorly localized and is more severe than the findings suggested by abdominal palpation. Peritoneal signs may signify bowel infarction. Selective mesenteric angiography is the diagnostic study of choice.

Colonic ischemia, also called ischemic colitis, is much more common than mesenteric ischemia. Although an underlying cause often is not identified, colonic ischemia can occur in association with colonic hypoperfusion in the setting of aortic or cardiac bypass surgery, prolonged physical exertion, and any cardiovascular event associated with hypotension. Medications such as oral contraceptives, illicit drugs such as cocaine, the vasculitides, and hypercoagulable states also are risk factors. Most patients with colonic ischemia are older than age 60 years. Colonoscopy is the primary diagnostic procedure.

Abdominal pain can be a presenting feature of metabolic disorders such as diabetic and alcoholic ketoacidosis, adrenal crises, sickle cell crisis, porphyria, and familial Mediterranean fever. Vasculitides (Henoch-Schönlein purpura, systemic lupus erythematosus, polyarteritis nodosa) also should be considered in the differential diagnosis, particularly if the abdominal pain is associated with extra-abdominal manifestations such as rash, arthralgias, pleuritic pain, hematuria, or kidney failure.

Chronic Abdominal Pain

Abdominal pain is chronic if it has persisted for more than 3 months. Chronic abdominal pain is a common cause of ambulatory care visits; within this category, IBS is one of the most common causes of chronic abdominal pain. Abdominal wall pain is an often overlooked cause of chronic pain and includes entities such as hernia and rectus sheath hematomas. The pain is precisely localized by the patient with one finger.

Irritable Bowel Syndrome

The pain of IBS is localized to the lower abdomen and may be associated with bloating, nausea, and diarrhea or constipation. Physical examination characteristically reveals only nonspecific tenderness over the sigmoid colon. IBS frequently coexists with other chronic conditions such as depression, fibromyalgia, and chronic pelvic pain syndrome. The pain of IBS often is exacerbated by psychological stress.

Irritable bowel syndrome is recognized to have three major subtypes: diarrhea predominant, constipation predominant, and mixed. Alternating between diarrhea and constipation or changing from constipation predominance to diarrhea predominance (or vice versa) over time is not uncommon.

Irritable bowel syndrome previously had been considered a diagnosis of exclusion, but this approach leads to unnecessary additional tests; the use of symptom-based diagnostic criteria can be used to discriminate the condition from other disorders and make diagnosis more effective with the use of appropriate testing. The Rome criteria (sensitivity, 48%; specificity, 100%) and the Manning criteria (sensitivity, 60%; specificity, 80%) are used to diagnose IBS (Table 2). The diagnostic accuracy of the Manning criteria is better in women, in younger patients, and when more criteria are present.

Patients can be diagnosed without additional testing and started on therapy as long as alarm symptoms are not present. Red flags, such as onset after 50 years of age, weight loss, anorexia, malnutrition, bleeding, or a family history of inflammatory bowel disease or cancer, should be investigated with well-thought-out tests. Because there is a higher prevalence of celiac disease in those with IBS, testing for celiac should be pursued in IBS patients with diarrhea.

The management of IBS focuses on managing symptoms rather than on cure. In the absence of alarm symptoms, those with constipation-predominant disease can be started on a trial of fiber. Those with diarrheal symptoms can be started on loperamide after celiac disease is excluded. A focus on a strong physician–patient relationship should be pursued. Because psychiatric disorders are common in those with IBS, patients should be screened for anxiety and depression and treated as indicated. Tricyclic antidepressants are helpful, especially with diarrhea-predominant disease, and selective serotonin reuptake inhibitors are helpful, especially with constipation-predominant disease. Benzodiazepines may be used in these patients with anxiety but offer minimal help for IBS symptoms and may lower the pain threshold. Studies support the short-term use of antispasmodics, such as hyoscyamine and dicyclomine. Lubiprostone (a chloride channel activator) and linaclotide (a guanylate cyclase-C agonist) can be used in select cases of constipation-predominant IBS. Alosetron, a 5-HT3 antagonist, can be used but is available only through a Food and Drug Administration–restricted program. Nonpharmacologic treatments for IBS include exercise, relaxation therapy, biofeedback, hypnotherapy, cognitive behavioral therapy, and psychotherapy. There currently are no data that dietary modification will improve IBS symptoms. However, if food triggers can be clearly identified, they should be eliminated or reduced from the patient's diet.

Pancreatic Disease

Pancreatic disease is an important cause of chronic abdominal pain. The four cardinal findings characterizing chronic pancreatitis are pain (90% to 95% of cases), diabetes mellitus, steatorrhea, and pancreatic calculi (best detected on CT scan). Periods of pain may be irregular, with weeks to months of remission. One third to half of patients with pancreatitis may become pain free, but this may take years. Pancreatic enzyme replacement is often ineffective for pain relief, and many patients require chronic opiates. Refractory pain in these patients sometimes necessitates sphincterotomy, stenting, or surgical resection, although evidence confirming the efficacy of these procedures is limited.

Age and tobacco smoking are the most important risk factors for pancreatic cancer. The most common symptom is constant epigastric pain that radiates to the back. Patients with tumors of the body and tail of the gland usually present with pain because these tumors tend to be large when detected. The most common location of pancreatic cancers is in the head of the gland; these tumors often are accompanied by painless jaundice caused by obstruction of the common bile duct. Physical examination often reveals weight loss, jaundice, and abdominal tenderness. Occasionally, there is a nontender palpable gallbladder (Courvoisier sign) in a jaundiced patient; rarely, migratory thrombophlebitis is noted. Pancreatic protocol contrast-enhanced spiral CT is the most effective diagnostic and staging tool for pancreatic cancer, with a sensitivity greater than 90%.

Table 2. Criteria for Diagnosis of Irritable Bowel Syndrome

Rome Criteria

≥3 months of continuous or recurrent symptoms of abdominal pain or discomfort that is:	Relieved with defecation and/or
	Associated with a change in frequency of stool and/or
	Associated with a change in consistency of stool
and ≥2 of these 5 symptoms on >25% of occasions or days:	Altered stool frequency (>3 bowel movements daily or <3 bowel movements weekly)
	Altered stool form (lumpy or hard, loose or watery)
	Altered stool passage (straining, urgency, feeling of incomplete evacuation)
	Passage of mucus
	Bloating or feeling of abdominal distention

Manning Criteria

The presence of abdominal pain and ≥2 of these 6 symptoms:	Pain relief with defecation
	Looser stools at pain onset
	More frequent stools at pain onset
	Abdominal distention
	Mucus per rectum
	Feeling of incomplete evacuation

Bibliography

American Gastroenterological Association medical position statement: irritable bowel syndrome. Gastroenterology. 2002;123:2105-2107. [PMID: 12454865]

Jacobs DO. Clinical practice. Diverticulitis. N Engl J Med. 2007;357:2057-2066. [PMID: 18003962]

Mayer EA. Clinical practice. Irritable bowel syndrome. N Engl J Med. 2008; 358:1692-1699. [PMID: 18420501]

Trowbridge RL, Rutkowski NK, Shojania KG. Does this patient have acute cholecystitis? JAMA. 2003;289:80-86 [published erratum appears in JAMA. 2009;302:739]. [PMID: 12503981]

Chapter 17

Dyspepsia

Chad S. Miller, MD

Dyspepsia is chronic or recurrent discomfort in the upper mid-abdomen (epigastrium) usually accompanied by fullness, early satiety, bloating, or nausea. The etiology and pathophysiology of dyspepsia are unclear; the disorder may be multifactorial. Potential causes or contributing factors include dysmotility, visceral hypersensitivity, *Helicobacter pylori* infection, acid peptic disease (damage from gastric acid and pepsin activity), food or drug intolerance, central nervous system dysfunction, and psychosocial factors. However, nearly 70% of patients with dyspepsia have no physiologic explanation for their symptoms and are designated as having *functional dyspepsia*. It is estimated that dyspepsia affects close to 25% of the general population and accounts for approximately 2% to 5% of all primary care visits.

Diagnosis

Table 1 summarizes the differential diagnosis of dyspepsia. The Rome III criteria are used to diagnose dyspepsia. The predominant symptom(s) must be one or more of the following: (1) bothersome postprandial fullness, (2) early satiety, (3) epigastric pain, or (4) epigastric burning. The patient should have symptoms for 3 months, with symptom onset at least 6 months before diagnosis. After the symptoms are confirmed by history and physical examination, the next step is to assess for alarm features. These include an onset of symptoms after the age of 50 years, unintentional weight loss, unexplained anemia, progressive dysphagia, odynophagia, persistent vomiting, a palpable abdominal mass, jaundice, a history of peptic ulcer disease, or a family history of proximal gastrointestinal (GI) cancer. If any alarm features are present, the patient should undergo upper endoscopy (Figure 1). Otherwise, the next step is distinguishing dyspepsia from gastroesophageal reflux disease (GERD). If

the predominant symptom is heartburn or acid regurgitation, the diagnosis of functional dyspepsia is excluded because the patient most likely has GERD and should be managed such (see Chapter 18). Next, medications should be thoroughly evaluated for potential dyspeptic side effects; nonsteroidal anti-inflammatory drugs (NSAIDs) are the most common offenders, but bisphosphonates, tetracyclines, and selective serotonin reuptake inhibitors are frequent causes. Finally, if the patient does not have alarm symptoms, does not have symptoms consistent with GERD, and is not taking medications associated with dyspepsia, the patient is diagnosed with dyspepsia and treated accordingly. However, if the patient has pain that improves with defecation, irritable bowel syndrome (IBS) should be considered because nearly a third of patients with dyspepsia have symptoms of IBS (see Chapter 16).

After a diagnosis of functional dyspepsia is established, the Rome criteria can be used to classify a patient by symptom category:

- Ulcer-like dyspepsia: predominant symptom is epigastric pain or burning
- Dysmotility-like dyspepsia: predominant symptom is epigastric discomfort associated with postprandial fullness, early satiety, bloating, or nausea
- Unspecified (nonspecific) dyspepsia: patients who do not fit into the previous two categories

Classifying patients into symptom subgroups can help guide therapy. For example, patients with ulcer-like functional dyspepsia have been shown to respond better to treatment with proton pump inhibitors (PPIs) compared with patients with dysmotility-like functional dyspepsia. A promotility agent such as metoclopramide may have efficacy in the dysmotility-like group.

Most patients presenting with dyspepsia do not need endoscopy. Many, especially those younger than 50 years, without alarm fea-

Table 1. Differential Diagnosis of Dyspepsia

Disorder	Notes
Functional dyspepsia	Up to 60% of epigastric pain; meet Rome III criteria
Gastroesophageal reflux disease (see Chapter 18)	Heartburn or acid regurgitation; 2%–29% of epigastric pain
Medication side effect	Examples: NSAIDs, aspirin, bisphosphonates, SSRIs, potassium supplements, tetracyclines, digoxin; 2%–8% of epigastric pain
Irritable bowel syndrome (see Chapter 16)	Symptoms of bowel dysfunction (diarrhea or constipation) associated with abdominal pain or discomfort in the absence of alarm features (Rome criteria)
Peptic ulcer disease (see Chapter 19)	Pain or distress centered in the upper abdomen; ulcerative lesions visualized with endoscopy; 7%–25% of epigastric pain
Pancreatitis (see Chapter 24)	Nausea or vomiting, pain radiating to the back, elevated amylase and lipase
Gastric or esophageal cancer	Alarm features present; 1%–3% of epigastric pain
Biliary disease (see Chapter 23)	Jaundice, dark urine, abnormal liver test results; <5% of epigastric pain

NSAID = nonsteroidal antiinflammatory drug; SSRI = selective serotonin reuptake inhibitor.

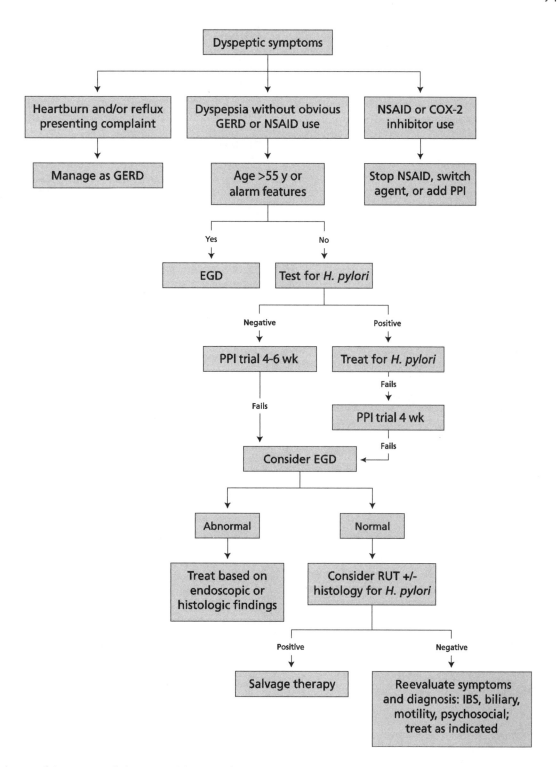

Figure 1. Evaluation of the patient with dyspepsia. COX-2 = cyclooxygenase-2; EGD = esophagogastric duodenoscopy; GERD = gastroesophageal reflux disease; *H. pylori* = *Helicobacter pylori*; IBS = irritable bowel syndrome; PPI = proton pump inhibitor; RUT = rapid urease test.

Adapted from Talley NJ; American Gastroenterological Association. American Gastroenterological Association medical position statement: evaluation of dyspepsia. Gastroenterology. 2005;129: 1754. [PMID: 16285970] Copyright 2005, Elsevier.

tures, should be treated empirically. Endoscopy is recommended only for patients with alarm features and patients 55 years or older who have new-onset symptoms because the incidence of GI malignancy is higher in this population. Finally, the diagnosis of *functional dyspepsia* is made only in patients with dyspepsia who have had endoscopy with no significant findings.

Therapy

For patients taking potentially offending medications (eg, NSAIDs, bisphosphonates), the medications should be stopped or changed to different agents. If medications cannot be changed, a PPI can be added. For patients younger than age 55 years without alarm features, a noninvasive "test and treat" approach for *H. pylori* is appropriate using serum antibody tests, the urea breath test, or stool antigen assay. If the patient tests positive, eradication of *H. pylori* may relieve symptoms. However, it is important to note that randomized controlled trials provide conflicting results as to the efficacy of *H. pylori* eradication in improving symptoms of dyspepsia. If the patient does not test positive for *H. pylori* or *H. pylori* treatment fails, a trial of a PPI is warranted. If symptoms persist after 4 to 6 weeks of PPI therapy, endoscopy is recommended for further evaluation.

For patients with dysmotility-like symptoms, consider a prokinetic agent such as metoclopramide. Note, however, that metoclopramide has significant side effects; the drug typically is reserved for patients with severe symptoms and is used only for short durations.

Patients older than 55 years old or patients with alarm features should always be evaluated with upper endoscopy. Treatment in these patients will ultimately depend on endoscopic or histologic findings.

Follow-Up

Patients who continue to have symptoms despite appropriate diagnostic investigations and therapy are difficult to manage. Reassessment of symptoms and potential offending agents is appropriate. Psychiatric illness, especially depression, may need to be considered.

Bibliography

Camilleri M. Functional dyspepsia: mechanisms of symptom generation and appropriate management of patients. Gastroenterol Clin North Am. 2007;36:649-664, xi-xx. [PMID: 17950442]

Chapter 18

Gastroesophageal Reflux Disease

Corina Ungureanu, MD

Gastroesophageal reflux disease (GERD) is a highly common disorder. Some degree of reflux is physiologic and typically occurs postprandially. Episodes are short-lived and asymptomatic. However, pathologic reflux, commonly referred to as GERD, is associated with symptoms of heartburn and regurgitation or mucosal injury.

GERD is multifactorial and results from increased esophageal exposure to gastric contents. The most common form is acid reflux, defined as the reflux of gastric contents with a pH <4.0. However, a small subset of patients has symptoms caused by reflux of non-acidic material. Non-acid reflux is reflux of gastric contents with a pH ≥4.0 (above the threshold used by conventional pH monitoring to identify acid reflux). This diagnosis is usually considered in patients who fail to respond to treatment for acid reflux.

Defects in the lower esophageal sphincter (LES) and the anti-reflux barrier located at the gastroesophageal junction contribute to prolonged exposure to gastric contents. Esophageal acid exposure is also increased when normal esophageal acid clearance is impaired. Normal acid clearance occurs through peristalsis and neutralization by saliva and alkaline esophageal secretions. Examples of extra-esophageal conditions that impair acid clearance include systemic disorders such as systemic sclerosis (scleroderma) and cigarette smoking. Although acid exposure is central to the pathogenesis of GERD, inappropriate, nonphysiologic relaxation of the LES is the most important etiologic factor in the development of reflux. Anatomic anomalies such as hiatal hernias are more commonly found in patients with GERD than in the unaffected population. Obesity, pregnancy, estrogen, and methylxanthine exposure are also associated with GERD because of LES tone.

The major complication of GERD is Barrett esophagus, which can progress to esophageal adenocarcinoma. Other potential complications include esophagitis and chronic bleeding, with resultant iron-deficiency anemia.

Diagnosis

The diagnosis of gastroesophageal reflux disease is usually based on the clinical picture. The typical patient presents with symptoms of heartburn and regurgitation that occur after meals; are aggravated by recumbency, bending, or physical exertion; and are relieved by antacids. Patients with classic symptoms rarely require confirmatory testing. Response to a 4-week trial of empiric proton pump inhibitor (PPI) therapy has a 78% sensitivity and 54% specificity when compared with pH probe testing. Up to 33% of patients have extraesophageal manifestations of GERD. Extraesophageal manifestations include wheezing, shortness of breath, chronic cough, hoarseness, chest pain, choking, halitosis, sore throat, hypersalivation, globus sensation, dental erosions, and chronic sinusitis. Physical examination findings are less prominent but may include wheezing, signs of pharyngeal irritation, and dental erosions.

Patients who require additional testing for gastroesophageal reflux disease include those who do not respond to a 4- to 8-week course of empiric PPI therapy or have alarm symptoms, including weight loss, dysphagia, odynophagia, recurrent vomiting, or evidence of gastrointestinal bleeding or anemia in association with reflux symptoms. All these symptoms raise concern of significant complications of GERD and are indications for upper endoscopy. Upper endoscopy should be used when visualization of the esophagus is desired (eg, when there is concern for esophagitis, stricture, ulceration, cancer, or Barrett esophagus).

Ambulatory esophageal reflux monitoring (24- or 48-hour pH or impedance-pH) is the only test that allows for determining the presence of abnormal esophageal exposure to gastric contents, reflux frequency, and association of symptoms with reflux episodes. Monitors that detect only pH are available, although some monitors combine pH and impedance testing. Monitoring of pH detects an acidic environment in the esophagus caused by reflux of gastric acid. The information provided by the pH electrode is used to classify reflux episodes into acid or non-acid with a cutoff pH of 4. The sensitivity for pH monitoring alone is 77% to 100% with a specificity of 85% to 100% in patients with erosive esophagitis. However, the sensitivity is lower in those with endoscopy-negative reflux symptoms (<71%). Impedance monitoring is based on detection of changes in resistance to electrical currents. Liquids refluxing from the stomach into the esophagus are detected by decreases in the electrical resistance to alternating current (impedance) progressing over time from distal to proximal (retrograde bolus movement). Impedance testing added to pH monitoring increases the sensitivity of reflux monitoring to close to 90%, and impedance testing is useful in the evaluation of non-acid reflux.

Barium studies, esophageal biopsy, and esophageal manometry are not indicated for diagnosing gastroesophageal reflux disease but can be used in specific clinical settings for testing for complications of reflux or alternative diagnoses. *Helicobacter pylori* testing is not indicated for diagnosing gastroesophageal reflux disease and does not need to be screened for in the setting of reflux disease.

GERD that presents atypically or is unresponsive to empiric therapy also warrants the consideration of alternative diagnoses, such as infectious esophagitis, medication-induced (pill) esophagitis (eg, alendronate, nonsteroidal anti-inflammatory drugs, iron, potassium supplements, doxycycline), esophageal motility disorders, esophageal cancer, nonulcer dyspepsia, peptic ulcer disease, cardiac disease, and biliary disease (Table 1).

Therapy

Treatment aims to eliminate symptoms, heal esophagitis, prevent complications, and maintain remission; an algorithm for managing GERD is presented in Figure 1.

PPI therapy is the treatment of choice for patients presenting with GERD. PPI therapy has been associated with superior healing

Table 1. Differential Diagnosis of Gastroesophageal Reflux Disease (GERD)

Condition or Disease	Notes
Achalasia	Dysphagia for liquids and solids; also may be associated with chest pain. Heartburn or chest pain in achalasia is not caused by reflux but by fermentation of retained esophageal contents or esophageal muscle spasm.
Coronary artery disease (CAD; see Chapter 3)	Chest pain in CAD may be clinically indistinguishable from chest pain associated with GERD. CAD should be ruled out in patients with CAD risk factors before evaluating GERD as a cause.
Diffuse esophageal spasm	Dysphagia for liquids and solids; also may be associated with chest pain; may be coincident with GERD
Esophageal cancer	Dysphagia for solids (initially) and liquids (later), weight loss; often in patients with long-standing GERD; usually incurable by the time it presents clinically
Infectious esophagitis	Dysphagia or odynophagia; often in immunocompromised patients with candidal, CMV, or HSV esophagitis
Medication-induced esophagitis	Dysphagia or odynophagia; history of offending pill ingestion
Peptic ulcer disease (see Chapter 19)	Pain or distress centered in the upper abdomen; relieved by food or antacids
Biliary disease (see Chapter 23)	Epigastric or right upper quadrant pain, jaundice, acholic stools, dark urine, abnormal liver test results

CMV = cytomegalovirus; HSV = herpes simplex virus.

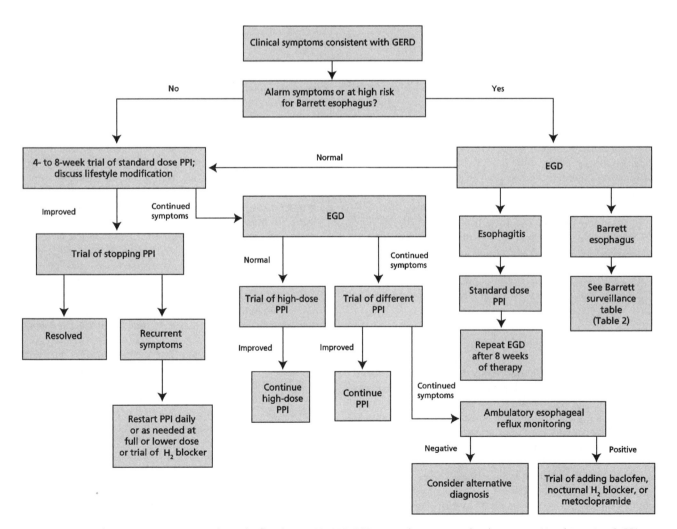

Figure 1. Algorithm for managing gastroesophageal reflux disease (GERD). EGD = esophagogastric duodenoscopy; H$_2$ = histamine-2; PPI = proton pump inhibitor.

rates and decreased relapse rates compared with histamine-2 (H_2)-receptor antagonists and placebo for patients with erosive esophagitis. For patients with nonerosive reflux disease, PPI therapy is superior to H_2-receptor antagonists and prokinetics for heartburn relief. Maintenance PPI therapy should be administered for patients with GERD who continue to have symptoms after PPI is discontinued and in patients with complications including erosive esophagitis and Barrett esophagus.

There are currently six available PPIs: omeprazole, lansoprazole, rabeprazole, pantoprazole, esomeprazole, and dexlansoprazole. There is also a combination capsule containing omeprazole and sodium bicarbonate; however, it has not been shown to be more effective than a single PPI. PPIs are administered once daily. For partial responders or nonresponders to this therapy, increasing the dose of PPI to twice daily or changing the PPI can offer additional improvement. There are no data to support switching PPIs more than once in partial responders or nonresponders. Baclofen, addition of night-time H_2-receptor antagonist, or prokinetic therapy with metoclopramide can also be used in refractory cases.

Recent studies showed that patients with known osteoporosis can remain on PPI therapy. Concern for hip fractures and osteoporosis should not affect the decision to use PPI for the long term except in patients with other risk factors for hip fracture. PPI therapy can be a risk factor for *Clostridium difficile* infection and should be used with care in patients at risk. Short-term PPI usage may increase the risk of community-acquired pneumonia. The risk does not appear elevated in long-term users. PPI therapy does not need to be altered in concomitant clopidogrel users.

H_2-receptor antagonist therapy can be used as a maintenance option in patients without erosive disease if patients experience heartburn relief.

There is no role for sucralfate in nonpregnant patients with GERD. Because antacids do not prevent GERD, their role is limited to intermittent use for relief of mild GERD symptoms.

Behavior modification is an adjunct to pharmacologic or surgical therapy. Improvement in GERD symptoms or reflux monitoring has been found with weight loss in obese patients or patients with recent weight gain. Elevation of the head of the bed and avoiding recumbency for 2 to 3 hours after eating should be recommended for patients with nocturnal GERD. Dietary modification should not be routinely recommended in all patients with GERD; rather, patients who note correlation between symptoms and certain dietary triggers (eg, alcohol, fatty or spicy foods, caffeine, chocolate, peppermint, carbonated drinks) should be advised to avoid them. Smoking cessation, sleeping in the left lateral decubitus position, and avoidance of tight fitting garments have not been shown to improve GERD.

Surgical intervention with a Nissen fundoplication is an option for patients who wish to avoid lifelong medication, but it is not likely to improve symptoms that were unresponsive to PPI therapy. Preoperative ambulatory pH monitoring is mandatory in patients without evidence of erosive esophagitis, and all patients should undergo preoperative manometry to rule out achalasia or scleroderma-like esophagus. Current endoscopic therapy or transoral incisionless fundoplication is not recommended as an alternative to medical or traditional surgical therapy. Obese patients contemplating surgical therapy for GERD should be considered for bariatric surgery.

Barrett Esophagus

Barrett esophagus is a premalignant change of the esophagus that has an increased risk of developing esophageal adenocarcinoma (approx-

Table 2. Practice Guidelines for Endoscopic Surveillance of Barrett Esophagus

Dysplasia Grade	Recommendation
None	Repeat endoscopy 3-5 years after diagnosis
Low grade	Confirmation by expert pathologist
	Repeat endoscopy 6-12 months after diagnosis
High grade	Confirmation by expert pathologist
	Endoscopic evaluation for any focal lesion (may indicate more advanced neoplasia): if present, focal lesion(s) should be removed by endoscopic mucosal resection for diagnosis and staging
	Options for further management: esophagectomy, endoscopic ablation, endoscopic mucosal resection
	In the absence of eradication therapy, repeat endoscopy at 3 months

imately 0.5% per year). The detection of intestinal metaplasia on esophageal biopsy indicates the presence of Barrett esophagus. Risk factors for developing Barrett esophagus are age older than 50 years, male gender, white race, presence of GERD, hiatal hernia, high body mass index, and an intra-abdominal distribution of body fat. Alcohol and smoking are not as strongly associated with Barrett esophagus. Moderate consumption of wine and a diet high in fruits and vegetables may protect against the disorder. Esophagitis can mask Barrett esophagus, and a repeat upper endoscopy after healing of esophagitis is indicated. The risk of adenocarcinoma in patients with Barrett esophagus is 30 to 40 times that of the general population. Table 2 indicates the recommended endoscopic follow-up for patients with Barrett esophagus.

PPI for treatment of GERD is recommended in these patients, but acid suppression with PPI in the absence of GERD will not reduce the risk of progression of Barrett esophagus to dysplasia. Aspirin is emerging as having a protective effect on progression of Barrett esophagus, but it is not recommended to use aspirin solely to prevent esophageal adenocarcinoma in the absence of other indications. Antireflux surgery has not been shown to be superior to medical treatment to prevent progression to Barrett esophagus.

Endoscopic eradication therapy with endoscopic ablation or endoscopic mucosal resection rather than surveillance is recommended for treatment of patients with confirmed Barrett esophagus with high-grade dysplasia. Esophagectomy should also be considered in this situation. However, it is not clear that the potential benefit of ablation in reducing the risk of cancer for patients who have Barrett esophagus without dysplasia or with low-grade dysplasia warrants the risks and substantial expense of the ablative procedures.

Bibliography

Katz PO. Guidelines for the diagnosis and management of gastroesophageal reflux disease. Am J Gastroenterol. 2013;108:1672. [PMID: 23419381]

Numans ME. Short-term treatment with proton-pump inhibitors as a test for gastroesophageal reflux disease: a meta-analysis of diagnostic test characteristics. Ann Intern Med. 2004;40:518-527. [PMID 15068979]

Spechler SJ. American Gastroenterological Association Technical Review on the Management of Barrett's Esophagus. Gastroenterology. 2011; 140:e18-e52. [PMID: 21376939]

Chapter 19

Peptic Ulcer Disease

Karen Szauter, MD

A peptic ulcer is an ulcer of the mucous membrane of the alimentary tract caused by gastric acid. Gastric acid is made by parietal cells in the stomach. Parietal cells have three stimulant receptors for gastric acid production: gastrin, acetylcholine, and histamine. Gastric acid production is inhibited by somatostatin and prostaglandins. Excessive gastric acid can cause peptic ulceration, esophagitis (in patients predisposed to reflux), and steatorrhea. Steatorrhea results from acid inactivation of pancreatic lipase, which aids in fat digestion. Gastric defenses include a mucous and bicarbonate layer, an epithelial barrier function, and adequate blood flow. Gastric acid aids in absorption of various nutrients (iron, vitamin B_{12}), defends against foodborne illnesses, and prevents small intestinal bacterial overgrowth.

The most common causes of peptic ulcer disease (PUD) are *Helicobacter pylori* infection and nonsteroidal anti-inflammatory drugs (NSAIDs), which together account for >90% of PUD. *H. pylori* expresses a host of factors that contribute to its ability to colonize the gastric mucosa and cause mucosal injury. NSAIDs likely cause ulcers by inhibiting the prostaglandin-mediated gastrointestinal (GI) release of the protective mucous and bicarbonate layer and through a direct toxic mucosal effect.

If neither *H. pylori* infection nor NSAID use is documented in a patient with PUD, consider other causes of PUD, including infectious agents, medications, gastric acid hypersecretory states, infiltrative diseases, and vascular compromise.

See Table 1 for additional entities in the differential diagnosis of PUD.

Prevention

Cigarette smoking, alcohol consumption, glucocorticoid administration, and psychological stress are not currently thought to be independent risk factors for the development of peptic ulcers in the absence of *H. pylori* infection or NSAID use. Although lifestyle modification for other health reasons may be advisable, there is no evidence that modification of diet or tobacco, alcohol, or caffeine use is helpful in PUD prevention. In patients who require NSAIDs for other health reasons, concomitant use of a proton pump inhibitor (PPI) (or, less commonly, misoprostol) can reduce the incidence of ulcer complications. Prophylactic treatment with a PPI is recommended for high-risk NSAID users, including patients with a history of ulcer disease or patients with multiple risk factors, including the use of high-dose NSAID therapy, concurrent use of anticoagulants or glucocorticoids, or age older than 65 years.

Diagnosis

Most patients with PUD do not have pain at diagnosis; ulcers usually are detected during an evaluation for potential ulcer-related complications, such as overt or obscure bleeding. When symptoms are present, they include dyspepsia or a nonspecific, gnawing epigastric

Table 1. Causes of Peptic Ulcer Disease

Common
Helicobacter pylori infection
Nonsteroidal anti-inflammatory drugs
Less Common
Malignancy
Stress ulcerations
Viral infections (herpes simplex virus type 1, cytomegalovirus)
Gastrinoma (Zollinger-Ellison syndrome)
Medication associated (bisphosphonates, glucocorticoids, sirolimus, selective serotonin reuptake inhibitors, chemotherapy)
Ischemia-related ulcers (cocaine or methamphetamine use)
Systemic mastocytosis
Myeloproliferative disorders with basophilia
Idiopathic (non-*H. pylori*) hypersecretory ulcers
Radiation therapy to the abdomen
Crohn disease
Sarcoidosis or amyloidosis

pain. Other presentations include bleeding, perforation (sometimes with penetration into adjacent organs), and gastric outlet obstruction. The most common complication of PUD is GI bleeding, which may manifest as hematemesis, melena, or hematochezia; occult bleeding presenting as iron-deficiency anemia is less common. Patients with perforation from PUD often present with sudden, severe abdominal pain and hemodynamic compromise. Affected patients may be febrile, hypotensive, and tachycardic; bowel sounds may be absent, and abdominal examination may show guarding and rebound tenderness. The ulcer may penetrate into the pancreas, resulting in a presentation similar to that of acute pancreatitis. Imaging often reveals free intraperitoneal air. Gastric outlet obstruction is a rare complication of PUD, typically from ulceration in the prepyloric region or pyloric channel. Patients with obstruction present with progressive nausea, vomiting, early satiety, and weight loss.

Upper endoscopy (esophagogastric duodenoscopy) is used to establish the diagnosis of PUD. Endoscopy is indicated for patients older than age 55 years with unexplained new-onset epigastric abdominal pain and for patients with abdominal pain and unexplained weight loss, GI bleeding, microcytic anemia, or recurrent vomiting. **Younger patients with mild to moderate epigastric pain consistent with peptic ulcer disease and no other associated symptoms can be treated empirically with a PPI and forgo endoscopy.** However, endoscopy is indicated in these patients if symptoms persist after an adequate PPI trial. Upper endoscopy is contraindicated in patients with perforation; these patients require emergent surgical consultation.

Endoscopy allows for both diagnostic and therapeutic interventions. Biopsies of the GI mucosa provide important information about underlying inflammatory changes as well as evidence for the presence of *H. pylori* infection, gastric cancer, or MALT (mucosa-associated lymphoid tissue) lymphoma. For ulcers with associated GI bleeding, endoscopy provides the option for direct visualization and management of the underlying cause.

Testing for *H. pylori* is indicated in patients with active PUD. The most commonly used endoscopic tests include histologic assessment and the rapid urease test. The sensitivity of the rapid urease test can be reduced up to 25% in patients who have taken a PPI within 2 weeks or bismuth or antibiotic therapy within 4 weeks of the endoscopy; histology is the endoscopic test of choice in such patients. Nonendoscopic studies include serum antibody tests, the urea breath test, and stool examination for *H. pylori* antigens. The sensitivity of the urea breath test and stool antigen test, similar to that of the rapid urease test, is reduced by medications that affect urease production; therefore, PPI therapy, bismuth, and antibiotic therapy should be held for the intervals previously noted. The urea breath test and stool antigen test can be used to confirm *H. pylori* eradication; confirmatory tests should be done at least 4 weeks after completion of therapy at a time that the patient is no longer taking a PPI.

Patients with refractory or recurrent ulcer disease, ulcers located in the distal duodenum, or ulcers and watery diarrhea should be evaluated for a gastrinoma. Gastrinomas are tumors that secrete an excess and unregulated amount of gastrin that in turn stimulates the parietal cells, leading to excess acid production. The acid leads to peptic ulcer formation and watery diarrhea, a clinical syndrome termed *Zollinger-Ellison syndrome*. The diagnosis is made by identification of a serum gastrin level >1000 pg/mL (1000 ng/L). Information about family history of PUD or evidence of other endocrine tumors should also be obtained because gastrinomas are associated with multiple endocrine neoplasia I syndrome (hyperparathyroidism, pancreatic islet cell tumor, pituitary adenoma).

Therapy

The mainstay of PUD treatment is to identify and manage the contributing factors and to reduce gastric acid to promote ulcer healing. Four to 6 weeks of treatment with a PPI is recommended. For patients on NSAID treatment, stopping the drug or decreasing the dose is essential. Continued use of PPI therapy is recommended if ongoing treatment with NSAIDs is needed. Alternatively, misoprostol can be used along with NSAIDs to prevent ulcer complications; however, side effects of misoprostol (diarrhea) may limit long-term adherence. For gastric or duodenal ulcers associated with *H. pylori*, treatment includes a PPI and antibiotics. A variety of drug combinations and dosing schedules have been tested, but current recommendations support the use of a PPI with amoxicillin and clarithromycin or a PPI with clarithromycin and metronidazole. Other regimens include bismuth, tetracycline, metronidazole, and a PPI. It is likely that recommendations will continue to evolve as resistant strains of *H. pylori* are recognized.

Surgery for PUD usually is reserved for patients whose disease fails to respond to medical therapy or for patients with life-threatening complications. The surgery typically involves a vagotomy with a drainage procedure but depends on the urgency, indication, and baseline anatomy.

Follow-Up

Follow-up for patients with PUD is determined by the location of the ulcer, the underlying cause, and associated symptoms. Ongoing treatment with a PPI is not recommended when an adequate treatment regimen has been completed and the patient is free of symptoms. All patients with *H. pylori*–associated ulcers should undergo follow-up testing to ensure that the organism is eradicated; persistence of *H. pylori* infection requires a second treatment course with an alternative antibiotic regimen.

Uncomplicated duodenal ulcers in asymptomatic patients do not require endoscopic follow-up. However, patients with complicated duodenal ulcers (bleeding, perforation, obstruction) should undergo follow-up endoscopy to ensure healing. Gastric ulcers associated with *H. pylori* infection or with worrisome features (eg, large ulcers, irregular borders) should be reassessed to verify healing and biopsied to confirm the absence of gastric cancer. Patients should be educated about symptoms of PUD, signs of GI bleeding, and medication-associated GI symptoms.

Bibliography

Lanza FL, Chan FKL, Quigley EMM, and the Practice Parameters Committee of the American College of Gastroenterology. Guidelines for prevention of NSAID-related ulcer complications. Am J Gastroenterol. 2009;104:728-738. [PMID: 19240698]

Malfertheiner P, Chan FK, McColl KE. Peptic ulcer disease. Lancet. 2009;374:1449-1461. [PMID: 19683340]

Scheiman JM. The use of proton pump inhibitors in treating and preventing NSAID-induced mucosal damage. Arthritis Res Ther. 2013;15(Suppl 3):S5. [PMID: 24267413]

Tytgat GN. Etiopathogenetic principles and peptic ulcer disease classification. Dig Dis. 2011;29:454-458. [PMID: 22095009]

Chapter 20

Approach to Liver Chemistry Tests

Jonathan S. Appelbaum, MD

Up to 4% of asymptomatic persons have abnormal results on liver chemistry tests. Standard tests that evaluate liver injury include serum alanine aminotransferase (ALT), aspartate aminotransferase (AST), alkaline phosphatase (ALP), and bilirubin. Two additional studies, γ-glutamyl transferase (GGT) and 5′-nucleotidase, are associated with bile duct injury and are useful in assessing conditions in which the ALP is elevated. Tests that reflect liver synthetic function include serum albumin and prothrombin time (PT)/international normalized ratio (INR). This chapter discusses the patterns of abnormal liver chemistry test results and addresses the approach to patients with hepatocellular and cholestatic liver injury tests, abnormal liver synthetic function test results, and drug-induced liver injury.

Liver Injury Test Patterns

Hepatocellular injury most often results in an elevation of serum ALT and AST. ALT and AST are released from injured hepatocytes. Whereas AST is also released from other tissues (heart, skeletal mus-

cle), ALT is minimally produced in nonhepatic tissues. Thus, ALT elevations are more specific for diagnosing liver disease. In alcoholic liver disease, 70% of patients have AST levels that are twice as elevated as ALT levels.

Cholestatic injury (cholestasis) is indicated by an elevation of serum ALP and, possibly, bilirubin. Cholestasis (impaired flow of bile from the liver) may occur without jaundice because the liver's capacity to continue to secrete bile sufficiently until injury to the bile ducts is significant. Profound disruption of the bile secretory mechanisms is likely to result in elevation of serum bilirubin and therefore jaundice. Bilirubin elevations may be due to increases in either conjugated (direct) or unconjugated (indirect) bilirubin. The predominance of unconjugated bilirubin may indicate overproduction (hemolysis) or impaired conjugation, which may be the result of a congenital defect such as Gilbert syndrome (Table 1). Hepatocyte dysfunction (hepatocellular injury) and impaired bile flow (cholestasis) are associated with conjugated hyperbilirubinemia (direct fraction >50%). ALP can be found in bone, intestine, placenta, and other organs. To confirm that an elevated ALP level is of liver origin, other bile duct enzymes (GGT, 5′-nucleotidase) will be elevated.

Table 1. Liver Chemistry Studies as Clues to the Diagnosis of Liver Inflammation

Disease	AST	ALT	Alkaline Phosphatase	Bilirubin	Other Features
Acute viral hepatitis	↑↑↑	↑↑↑	↑↑	Normal to ↑↑↑	Exposure history; constitutional symptoms
Chronic viral hepatitis	↑	↑↑	Normal to ↑	Normal	History of percutaneous, sexual, or perinatal exposure
Nonalcoholic steatohepatitis	↑	↑↑	Normal to ↑	Normal	Metabolic syndrome
Alcoholic hepatitis	↑↑	↑	Normal to ↑	Normal to ↑↑↑	History of alcohol abuse
Acute autoimmune hepatitis	↑↑↑	↑↑↑	Normal to ↑	Normal to ↑↑↑	Positive autoantibodies
Chronic autoimmune hepatitis	↑	↑↑	Normal to ↑	Normal	Positive autoantibodies
Wilson disease (acute or chronic)	↑↑	↑↑	↓	↑ (unconjugated)	Hemolysis, neuropsychiatric abnormalities, renal tubular acidosis
α_1-Antitrypsin deficiency (chronic)	↑	↑	Normal to ↑	Normal	Lung disease
Hemochromatosis (chronic)	↑	↑	Normal to ↑	Normal	Elevated ferritin
Primary biliary cirrhosis (chronic)	↑	↑	↑↑↑	Normal to ↑↑	Antimitochondrial antibodies
Primary sclerosing cholangitis (chronic)	↑	↑	↑↑↑	Normal to ↑↑	Presence of IBD
Large bile duct obstruction (acute)	↑↑	↑↑	↑↑	↑↑	Abdominal pain
Infiltrative liver disease (eg, lymphoma)	↑	↑	↑↑↑	Normal	Malaise, hepatomegaly
Ischemic hepatitis ("shock liver")	↑↑↑	↑↑↑	Normal to ↑	Normal	History of hypotension, rapid resolution of liver test results

ALT = alanine aminotransferase; AST = aspartate aminotransferase; IBD = inflammatory bowel disease.

Liver Synthetic Function Tests

Serum albumin and PT/INR reflect the liver's synthetic capacity. Serum albumin decreases only after significant liver damage; therefore, it is an insensitive test of early synthetic function. An elevated PT/INR may indicate impaired hepatic production of clotting factors; however, these parameters may also be elevated in the setting of vitamin K deficiency (malnutrition, malabsorption), so PT/INR is a nonspecific test of synthetic function.

Clinical Approach to Abnormal Liver Study Results

In a patient without known liver disease, abnormal liver test results must be interpreted in the context of the clinical presentation and the pattern, degree, and duration of the biochemical abnormalities. **Repeat liver chemistry studies are indicated in asymptomatic patients to confirm any abnormal test results.** Normal or minimally elevated liver chemistry test results do not exclude serious liver disease, such as hepatitis B or C. After confirming abnormal results, determine the pattern of liver study abnormality (hepatocellular,

cholestatic, or mixed) to narrow the differential diagnosis. Next, it is important to determine whether the patient has symptoms of liver disease, which may be constitutional (malaise, listlessness, weight loss, nausea) or more specific (jaundice, right upper quadrant pain). **The duration of liver test abnormalities can often be determined through the history and laboratory records, and this is important information in interpreting abnormal liver studies.** Whereas hepatocellular disorders present for less than 6 months are considered

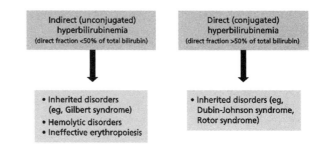

Figure 1. Evaluation of elevated bilirubin levels.

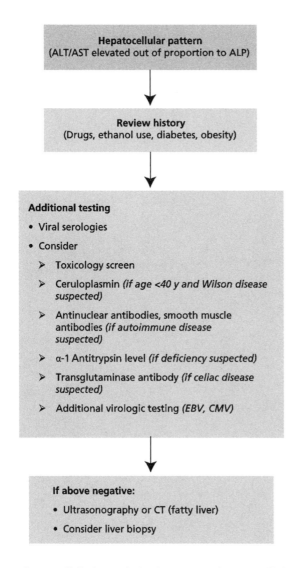

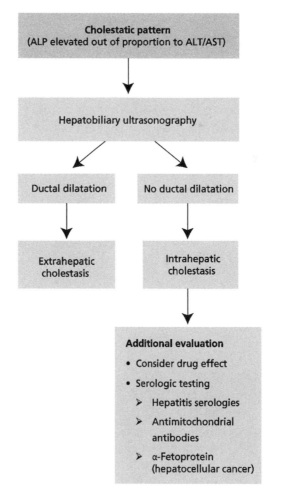

Figure 2. Evaluation of bilirubin and other liver test results. ALP = alkaline phosphatase; ALT = alanine aminotransferase; AST = aspartate aminotransferase; CMV = cytomegalovirus; CT = computed tomography; EBV = Epstein-Barr virus.

acute forms of hepatitis, hepatocellular abnormalities present longer than 6 months are considered chronic forms of hepatitis. A stepwise approach to evaluating abnormal liver studies based on the elevated liver test parameters is provided in Figure 1 and Figure 2.

Drug-Induced Liver Disease

Most drug-induced liver injury results in a hepatocellular pattern that may include jaundice. Cholestatic forms of liver injury are typical of hypersensitivity reactions and generally take longer to resolve than hepatitis syndromes. Patients who develop abnormal liver enzyme values while taking medications known to cause hepatotoxicity need to be evaluated carefully because the enzyme elevation may be due to a previously undiagnosed primary liver disease rather than to the medication. **Asymptomatic patients with mild liver enzyme abnormalities require only follow-up with repeated laboratory studies.** However, symptomatic patients require prompt evaluation and discontinuation of the possible hepatotoxic drug.

Bibliography

Krier M, Ahmed A. The asymptomatic outpatient with abnormal liver function tests. Clin Liver Dis. 2009;13:167-177. [PMID: 19442912]

Chapter 21

Hepatitis

Carlos Palacio, MD

Hepatitis can be acute or chronic. The laboratory hallmark of acute hepatitis is elevated serum aminotransferase levels; the clinical course ranges from asymptomatic disease to fulminant hepatic failure. Chronic hepatitis is an inflammatory process that persists >6 months and can progress to cirrhosis. Histologically, hepatitis is characterized by inflammatory cell infiltration involving the portal areas or the parenchyma, often with associated necrosis; significant fibrosis may be seen in chronic hepatitis.

Viral hepatitis is caused by infection with any of at least five distinct viruses, of which the most commonly identified in the United States are hepatitis A virus (HAV), hepatitis B virus (HBV), and hepatitis C virus (HCV). HAV is transmitted through the fecal–oral route, spreading primarily through close personal contact with an HAV-infected person. HBV is transmitted through exposure to the blood or body fluids of an infected person (eg, injection drug use, sexual contact, maternal–newborn transmission). HCV, also transmitted parenterally, is the most prevalent bloodborne infection in the United States. All three viruses can cause an acute illness characterized by nausea, malaise, abdominal pain, and jaundice. HBV and HCV also can produce a chronic infection that is associated with an increased risk for chronic liver disease and hepatocellular carcinoma. Hepatitis D virus (HDV; also called *delta hepatitis*) depends on the presence of hepatitis B surface antigen (HBsAg) for replication and therefore cannot survive on its own. In an HBV-infected patient, HDV infection may present as an acute hepatitis (in which case it is a coinfection) or an exacerbation of preexisting chronic hepatitis (in which case it is a superinfection). Patients with a history of injection drug use are at greatest risk for acquiring HDV infection. Hepatitis E virus (HEV) is most likely to occur in residents of or recent travelers to underdeveloped nations; it is transmitted via the fecal–oral route. Pregnant women with acute HEV infection are at greatest risk for developing severe hepatitis or liver failure.

Causes of nonviral hepatitis include alcoholic liver disease, drug- and toxin-induced liver injury, autoimmune hepatitis, genetic causes, and (occasionally) metabolic liver diseases.

Prevention

Administer hepatitis A vaccine to adults whose departure to endemic areas for HAV is >2 weeks away. These areas include Africa, Central and South America, the Middle East, and Asia (see www.cdc.gov/travel/default.aspx for relevant countries). If departure is <2 weeks away, immunoglobulin should be administered alone or in combination with the vaccine. Immunoglobulin ensures passive immunity for several months. Other risk groups that benefit from hepatitis A immunization include men who have sex with men (MSM), illicit drug users (oral and injection), persons with occupational risks (ie, sewage handlers, persons working with nonhuman primates), and persons who have chronic liver disease.

It is now universal practice to provide hepatitis B vaccine to all newborns. However, persons who were born before the onset of universal vaccination should be offered vaccination, especially if they are at risk of being exposed. Such persons include all children and adolescents who did not get the vaccine when they were younger. Others who should be vaccinated include MSM and others with high-risk sexual behavior, current or recent injection drug users, persons with chronic liver disease or with end-stage kidney disease on hemodialysis, health care workers and public safety workers exposed to blood or potentially infectious body fluids, household or sexual contacts of HBV carriers, clients and staff members of institutions for persons with developmental disabilities, travelers to countries endemic for HBV, and any adult seeking protection from HBV infection.

In nonimmunized patients who have been exposed to viral hepatitis, administer hepatitis A immunoglobulin as postexposure prophylaxis (within 2 weeks of exposure) to household, sexual, and day care contacts of persons with confirmed cases of hepatitis A and to individuals who have consumed HAV-contaminated products. Administer hepatitis B immunoglobulin, along with hepatitis B vaccine, for exposure to HBV-positive blood, sexual exposure to an HBV-positive person, or household exposure to a person with acute hepatitis B. There is no passive or active immunization for HCV.

Screening

Screen all pregnant women and persons at high risk for hepatitis B. The United States Preventive Services Task Force has recommended that all persons at high risk for infection be screened, as well as a one-time screening for all adults born between 1945 and 1965. Risk factors for hepatitis C include injection drug use, receipt of blood products before 1992, and needle-stick exposure to HCV-positive blood. Other potential exposures that may warrant screening for hepatitis C include high-risk sexual exposures, tattoos, body piercing, and non-injection illicit drug use. Screen patients with unexplained acute or chronic hepatitis for hepatitis B and C. Consider anti-HDV testing in patients with acute or chronic hepatitis B who are injection drug users or immigrants from HCV-endemic areas.

Diagnosis

Hepatitis A accounts for approximately half of all cases of acute hepatitis in the United States. Hepatitis A typically is associated with an abrupt onset of constitutional symptoms, such as fatigue, anorexia, malaise, nausea, and vomiting. Low-grade fever and right upper quadrant pain often are present as well. Skin, sclera, or urine color changes are particularly helpful findings. Approximately 50% of patients with hepatitis A have no identifiable source for their infection, so the absence of classic risk factors cannot exclude the diagnosis. Physical examination often reveals jaundice, hepatomegaly, and abdominal tenderness. Confirm the diagnosis with serologic testing, specifically IgM antibody to HAV. In most patients, IgM antibody is detectable by the time a person is symptomatic and becomes undetectable by 6 months. The IgG antibody indicates prior infection and immunity; there is no chronic state of hepatitis A. Hepatitis A is almost always self-limited but can rarely cause fulminant hepatic failure; therefore, test all patients with unexplained acute liver failure for hepatitis A.

Hepatitis B accounts for approximately one third of cases of acute viral hepatitis in the United States and approximately 15% of cases of chronic viral hepatitis. Symptoms of acute hepatitis B are similar to those of acute hepatitis A; however, approximately 70% of patients have anicteric or subclinical acute infection. Approximately 30% to 40% of patients with acute hepatitis B have no risk factors identified. A characteristic pattern of serologic tests usually is seen in acute hepatitis B (Table 1). During the course of acute infection, a "window period" exists when HBsAg levels have fallen but antibody to HBsAg (anti-HBs) has not yet become detectable; diagnosis is then based on the presence of antibody to hepatitis B core antigen (anti-HBc [IgM]). Test patients with evidence of chronic liver disease for chronic hepatitis B. Also test patients with glomerulonephritis, polyarteritis nodosa, or cryoglobulinemia because these are extrahepatic manifestations of chronic hepatitis B. Serologic assays can distinguish between chronic hepatitis B and the inactive carrier state (see Table 1). Obtain a liver biopsy to determine the grade and stage of liver injury in chronic hepatitis B, as well as to exclude additional causes of liver injury. Although rare, acute liver failure can occur in acute hepatitis B, and all patients with unexplained acute liver failure should have serologic testing.

Hepatitis C usually manifests as chronic liver disease because the acute infection is usually asymptomatic. Test patients with chronic liver disease for anti-HCV antibody. Consider testing patients with extrahepatic complications of hepatitis C, including cryoglobulinemia, glomerulonephritis, and porphyria cutanea tarda. A positive antibody test indicates only exposure, not immunity; therefore, HCV RNA must be measured to confirm ongoing infection. Up to 40% of patients with chronic hepatitis C have normal aminotransferase levels, and this finding cannot exclude the diagnosis. There is poor correlation between viral load and hepatic histology. For those with detectable viral loads, HCV genotype should be obtained in any patient being considered for therapy because genotype affects likelihood of treatment response and duration of therapy. Consider liver biopsy to evaluate the severity of disease, although this is not essential before initiating treatment.

Consider anti-HDV antibody testing in patients with acute or chronic hepatitis B who are injection drug users or immigrants from HDV-endemic areas. This test currently is available in reference laboratories. HEV infection can be confirmed by the presence of HEV antibodies.

Nonviral causes of hepatitis are discussed below.

Differential Diagnosis

Important conditions to consider in the differential diagnosis of hepatitis besides viral hepatitis include alcoholic liver disease; drug- and toxin-induced liver injury; autoimmune hepatitis; and, occasionally, metabolic liver diseases (Table 2). Acute alcoholic hepatitis is diagnosed by finding hepatic inflammation in a patient with recent heavy alcohol consumption. Inflammation is indicated by modest elevation of the serum aspartate aminotransferase (AST) concentration; the AST value usually is <400 U/L and approximately twice the serum alanine aminotransferase (ALT) value. Patients may present with leukocytosis, jaundice, hepatomegaly, and right upper quadrant pain suggesting acute viral infection.

Nonalcoholic fatty liver disease (NAFLD) consists of variable degrees of fat accumulation, inflammation, and fibrosis in the absence of significant alcohol intake. It is possibly the most common form of liver disease in the United States. The term steatohepatitis is used to describe patients with NAFLD in which there is prominent inflammation is present and is associated with increased risk for progression to advanced fibrosis. NAFLD is most commonly seen in patients with underlying consequences of obesity, including insulin resistance, hypertension, or hyperlipidemia. The diagnosis usually is made when patients with characteristic clinical risk factors are found to have mildly to moderately elevated serum aminotransferase concentrations. Imaging with ultrasonography, computed tomography, or magnetic resonance imaging can confirm the presence of steatosis. **Liver biopsy is often not required to make the diagnosis of nonalcoholic fatty liver disease in a consistent clinical setting.** Any drug can cause liver injury through such mechanisms as the formation of protein adducts that disrupt cell membranes, an immunologic response, or the generation of injurious free radicals. Drug-induced liver injury may be either dose dependent and predictable or idiosyncratic. Drug-induced liver injury can present with either a cholestatic or hepatocellular pattern of liver injury. There are many idiosyncratic hepatotoxins, but a few have become known for their "signature" patterns of hepatotoxicity (Table 3).

Autoimmune hepatitis is more common in women and usually presents in adulthood. Approximately 50% of patients are asymptomatic. The remainder of patients may have malaise, rash, and arthralgias. Findings on physical examination may include only hepatomegaly. Other findings include jaundice or signs of hepatic decompensation, such as ascites or encephalopathy. The presence of other autoimmune disorders may also be a clue to the diagnosis. In most cases, serum

Table 1. Serologic Diagnosis of Hepatitis B Infection

Test	Acute Hepatitis	Inactive Carriers	Chronic Hepatitis	Prior Exposure	Prior Vaccination
HBsAg	Positive	Positive	Positive	Negative	Negative
Anti-HBc	Positive (IgM)	Positive	Positive	Positive	Negative
Anti-HBs	Negative	Negative	Negative	Positive	Positive
HBV DNA	Positive	Negative	Positive	Negative	Negative
HBeAg	Positive	Negative	Positive or negative	Negative	Negative
Anti-HBe	Positive or negative	Positive	Positive or negative	Positive or negative	Negative

anti-HBc = antibody to hepatitis B core antigen; anti-HBe = antibody to hepatitis B e antigen; anti-HBs = antibody to hepatitis B surface antigen; HBeAg = hepatitis B e antigen; HBsAg = hepatitis B surface antigen; HBV = hepatitis B virus.

Table 2. Differential Diagnosis of Hepatitis

Disorder	Notes
Viral hepatitis	At least five distinct causes. Determined by serologic testing for hepatitis A, B, C, D, and E and confirmation of viral replication of hepatitis B and C. RIBA for HCV infection may also be used for confirmation.
Alcoholic liver disease	Common cause of chronic hepatitis and cirrhosis. History of excessive alcohol consumption. AST/ALT ratio >2. Improvement with alcohol cessation.
Autoimmune hepatitis	Typically women (90%); acute hepatitis in 25% of patients; other autoimmune disorders may be present. Test for ANA, ASMA, and elevated immunoglobulins; characteristic liver biopsy.
Drug-induced chronic hepatitis	Typically women and elderly adults but may affect men and women of all ages; history of drug consumption. Improvement with drug discontinuation.
Hemochromatosis	Most common genetic liver disease; iron overload usually not evident until midlife; cardiac dysfunction, diabetes, and arthritis. Elevated fasting serum iron, transferrin saturation, and ferritin. Quantitative hepatic iron index on liver biopsy and *HFE* genotyping assist with diagnosis.
Nonalcoholic fatty liver disease	Perhaps most common cause of chronic hepatitis in United States. Spectrum of liver disease ranges from steatosis to steatohepatitis to cirrhosis. Associated with diabetes mellitus, obesity, dyslipidemia, and insulin resistance.
Other metabolic liver disease	Wilson disease: rare; most cases diagnosed before age 40 y; may present as speech or gait difficulties; low serum ceruloplasmin, elevated urine copper, and Kayser-Fleischer rings on slit-lamp examination; quantitate hepatic copper for diagnosis. α_1-Antitrypsin deficiency: serum α_1-antitrypsin and phenotyping; PAS-positive inclusions in liver biopsy specimen.

ALT = alanine aminotransferase; ANA = antinuclear antibody; anti-HBc = antibody to hepatitis B core antigen; ASMA = anti–smooth muscle antibody; AST = aspartate aminotransferase; HCV = hepatitis C virus; PAS = periodic acid–Schiff stain; RIBA = recombinant immunoblot assay.

Table 3. Signature Pattern of Drug-Induced Hepatotoxicity

Signature Pattern	Specific Agents
Acute liver injury	Acetaminophen, isoniazid
Chronic liver injury	Nitrofurantoin, minocycline, methyldopa
Fibrosis and cirrhosis	Methotrexate, vitamin A
Jaundice	Erythromycin, amoxicillin–clavulanate, chlorpromazine, estrogens
Hypersensitivity (rash, fever, and multiorgan failure)	Phenytoin
Fatty liver	Amiodarone, tamoxifen, valproic acid, didanosine

aminotransferases are elevated, ranging from mild increases to values >1000 U/L. Hyperbilirubinemia may occur with a normal or near-normal serum alkaline phosphatase level. Certain autoantibodies may be elevated, including anti–smooth muscle antibody; antinuclear antibody; and, rarely, anti–liver-kidney microsomal antibody type 1 (anti-LKM1). In addition, serum IgG and IgM are elevated.

Hereditary hemochromatosis is a common genetic disorder in white persons characterized by excessive iron deposition in tissues, especially the liver, heart, pancreas, and pituitary gland. The iron overload can lead to cirrhosis, heart disease, and diabetes mellitus. The gene mutations leading to phenotypic hereditary hemochromatosis are the C282Y mutation and H63D mutation of the *HFE* gene. Initial evaluation involves fasting transferrin saturation and serum ferritin measurements. A fasting transferrin saturation >50% strongly suggests the diagnosis of hemochromatosis. Hepcidin, the iron regulatory hormone that is deficient in hemochromatosis, can now be measured in the urine and serum.

Wilson disease is a rare autosomal recessive disorder. It is characterized by the reduced excretion of copper into the bile secondary to a transport abnormality, leading to the pathologic accumulation of copper in the liver and other tissues, particularly the brain. Patients may present with fulminant disease characterized by elevated serum aminotransferase concentrations in the setting of hemolytic anemia.

α_1-Antitrypsin deficiency affects the liver, lungs, and skin. Disease in the liver is the result of abnormal accumulation of a vari-

ant protein in hepatocytes, which can be identified as inclusions with periodic acid–Schiff staining. The disease can manifest in early childhood or in adulthood and is associated with an increased risk of cirrhosis and hepatocellular carcinoma.

Therapy

In patients with acute hepatitis, be alert to the development of asterixis or any subtle changes in neurologic or mental status (eg, somnolence). Such clinical findings signal the onset of encephalopathy, which defines the patient as having fulminant hepatic failure (a rare complication of acute hepatitis A and B). A patient suspected of being at high risk for development of fulminant hepatic failure should be evaluated for potential liver transplantation.

All patients with acute or chronic viral hepatitis are counseled to avoid alcohol and acetaminophen and to eat a balanced, nutritionally adequate diet. Criteria for hospitalization in acute viral hepatitis include inability to maintain oral hydration and symptoms or signs of liver failure.

The treatment for hepatitis A is primarily supportive. No conclusive data show that bed rest or inactivity affects the course of hepatitis A.

Antiviral drug therapy is used in selected patients with chronic hepatitis B to reduce likelihood of progression to cirrhosis and hepatocellular carcinoma. The goals of therapy in chronic hepatitis B are suppression of viral replication, conversion from HBeAg-positive to HbBeAg-negative status, and mitigation of hepatic inflammation as evidenced by a reduction in serum liver enzyme concentrations. An additional goal is sustained suppression of viral replication, indicated by lack of recurrent HBV DNA after antiviral therapy is discontinued. The approved therapies for chronic, replicative hepatitis B are interferon (standard and pegylated), lamivudine, adefovir, tenofovir, entecavir, and telbivudine. The advantages of interferon are limited duration of therapy, lack of resistance, and high response rate. Interferon alfa is administered subcutaneously and is associated with frequent side effects, including flulike symptoms, myelotoxicity, depression, and exacerbation of autoimmune conditions. Pegylation of interferon, attaching it to polyethylene glycol to slow its metabolism, allows for less frequent administration than standard interferon and is more efficacious. Patients with advanced liver disease or decompensated cirrhosis should not be given interferon therapy because they may be at risk for decompensation of liver disease and infection. Other contraindications include severe preexisting bone marrow suppression and severe depression. In such patients, different available agents, sometimes in combination, are used; however, disadvantages of these agents are a limited ability to achieve sustained suppression of viral replication, cost, and propensity for drug resistance.

The goal of therapy for hepatitis C is achievement of sustained virologic response (SVR), defined as loss of HCV RNA 6 months after completion. SVR results in improved patient outcomes, including a decrease in all-cause mortality. The treatment of HCV is evolving rapidly. Patients with HCV had previously been treated primarily with pegylated interferon and ribavirin. However, the introduction of protease inhibitors effective against HCV (eg, boceprevir, simeprevir, telepravir) and direct-acting antiviral agents (eg, sofosbuvir) has markedly changed HCV therapy. Increasingly, interferon- and ribavirin-free regimens are being developed for both HCV genotype 1 (the most prominent genotype in the United States) and genotypes 2/3. Therefore, multiple treatment options are increasingly available for HCV based on genotype, the point in infection when therapy is started, and cost and side effect considerations.

Patients with alcoholic hepatitis should abstain from alcohol. The Maddrey discriminant function (DF) score, which helps to identify patients whose short-term survival is improved by glucocorticoid therapy, is calculated as follows:

DF = 4.6 (Prothrombin time [s] – Control prothrombin time [s]) + Serum bilirubin (mg/dL)

Patients with a DF score >32 have a >50% short-term (30-day) mortality risk. Such patients are candidates for therapy with prednisone. Pentoxifylline may be used as an alternative for patients with contraindications or early renal failure.

Treatment of drug-induced liver injury is primarily supportive and involves withdrawal of the suspected offending agent. However, there are a few specific antidotes, including *N*-acetylcysteine for acetaminophen intoxication and L-carnitine for valproic acid overdose. Treatment for autoimmune hepatitis consists of prednisone alone or, more commonly, in combination with azathioprine. Treatment can be discontinued when remission is achieved. There is no definitive treatment for NAFLD. Reduction of underlying risk factors is essential, including weight loss; exercise; and aggressive control of plasma glucose, lipids, and blood pressure. Treatment of Wilson disease is directed at reducing copper overload with the use of copper chelators (penicillamine, trientine) or agents that reduce copper absorption (zinc). Treatment of hereditary hemochromatosis involves therapeutic phlebotomy to extract excess iron or to prevent accumulation of iron before symptomatic overload occurs. Although there is no treatment for hepatic disease caused by α_1-antitrypsin deficiency, liver transplantation is an option for patients who develop hepatic decompensation.

Follow-Up

Patients on antiviral therapy must have regular laboratory and clinical monitoring to assess their response to treatment and development of side effects. Among patients with hepatitis C who develop cirrhosis, the risk for hepatocellular carcinoma is approximately 5% per year. Patients with established chronic hepatitis B must be monitored for the development of cirrhosis or hepatocellular carcinoma. Although cirrhosis seems to be the greatest risk factor for hepatocellular carcinoma in hepatitis B, 30% to 50% of cases occur without cirrhosis. Therefore, screening every 6 to 12 months with ultrasonography is generally recommended for patients with chronic hepatitis B or cirrhosis caused by hepatitis B or C. Patients with cirrhosis caused by hepatitis B or C should be screened for the presence of esophageal varices by upper endoscopy.

Bibliography

Brundage SC, Fitzpatrick AN. Hepatitis A. Am Fam Physician. 2006;73:2162-2168. [PMID: 16848078]

Ghany MG, Strader DB, Thomas DL, Seeff LB; American Association for the Study of Liver Diseases. Diagnosis, management, and treatment of hepatitis C: an update. Hepatology. 2009;49:1335-1374. [PMID: 19330875]

Lok AS, McMahon BJ. Chronic hepatitis B. Hepatology. 2007;45:507-539. [PMID: 17256718]

Navarro VJ, Senior JR. Drug-related hepatotoxicity. N Engl J Med. 2006;354:731-739. [PMID: 16481640]

Shiffman ML. Management of acute hepatitis B. Clin Liver Dis. 2010;14:75-91; viii-ix. [PMID: 20123442]

Chapter 22

Cirrhosis

Mark J. Fagan, MD

irrhosis (from the Greek *kirrhos*, referring to the yellow-brown appearance of the cirrhotic liver) is a pathologic state of the liver characterized histologically by extensive fibrosis and regenerative nodules. Liver fibrosis begins with the activation of hepatic stellate cells, which produce excess extracellular matrix proteins, including type I collagen. Failure to degrade the increased interstitial matrix leads to progressive fibrosis. In general, cirrhosis is irreversible. A variety of toxic, infectious, and inflammatory insults to the liver may result in cirrhosis (Table 1). Patients with cirrhosis may present with symptoms related to either hepatocyte dysfunction (jaundice, coagulopathy) or increased portal venous pressure (ascites, edema, spontaneous bacterial peritonitis, bleeding esophageal varices, hepatic encephalopathy, hypersplenism). Asymptomatic patients with cirrhosis may be initially identified through abnormal laboratory test results such as elevated aminotransferases or prolonged prothrombin time, thrombocytopenia, or the incidental finding of cirrhosis on abdominal imaging.

Prevention

Counsel patients who consume hazardous amounts of alcohol to stop or reduce their intake of alcohol. Alcohol cessation is effective in reducing the risk of cirrhosis. Also counsel patients with chronic hepatitis B or C to avoid alcohol because concomitant alcohol use increases the risk for cirrhosis. Antiviral treatment may reduce the risk of cirrhosis in some patients with hepatitis B or C. Administer hepatitis B vaccine to nonimmune patients with risk factors for hepatitis B (see Chapter 21).

Screening

Screen patients for hazardous drinking using validated questionnaires such as the Alcohol Use Disorders Identification (AUDIT) instrument (see Chapter 38). Screen patients born between 1945 and 1965 for hepatitis C; assess for other risk factors for hepatitis B or C and consider testing if present (see Chapter 21). Screen first-degree relatives of patients with hereditary hemochromatosis for evidence of iron overload.

Table 1. Differential Diagnosis of Cirrhosis

Disorder	Notes
Chronic exposure to drugs or toxins	Exposure history most commonly alcohol but may be medications (methotrexate, amiodarone, high-dose vitamin A) or chemicals (hydrocarbons). Long-term TPN can lead to cirrhosis.
Chronic viral hepatitis	Etiology most commonly hepatitis B or C. Diagnosis by typical viral hepatitis serology.
Autoimmune hepatitis	Typically young women with fatigue and jaundice and, later, aminotransferase elevations; hypergammaglobulinemia and other autoimmune diseases may be present. Look for specific autoantibodies (ANA, ASMA).
Primary biliary cirrhosis	Typically women in their 50s who are often asymptomatic at diagnosis (incidental finding of elevated alkaline phosphatase); otherwise, fatigue and pruritus. AMA typically positive (>90%).
Primary sclerosing cholangitis	Typically men in their late 30s who are asymptomatic (incidental finding of elevated alkaline phosphatase), particularly in patients with established ulcerative colitis. Diagnosis usually by endoscopic cholangiography.
Nonalcoholic fatty liver disease	Typically obese, women with diabetes and hyperlipidemia. Liver ultrasonography shows fatty infiltration. May require liver biopsy to identify steatohepatitis.
Hereditary hemochromatosis	Typically men; early findings include arthralgia and aminotransferase elevations; later findings may include diabetes, skin darkening, impotence, and heart failure. Diagnosis suggested by elevated transferrin saturation and ferritin and confirmed by hemochromatosis gene test.
Wilson disease	Variable presentation (fatigue, anorexia, abdominal pain, tremor, poor coordination, spastic dystonia, psychiatric conditions). Diagnosis suggested by low serum ceruloplasmin, elevated serum free copper levels, and Kayser-Fleischer rings on slit-lamp examination.
α_1-Antitrypsin deficiency	Typical presentation in first months of life, with jaundice and elevated aminotransferase levels. Some present in late childhood or early adolescence with hepatosplenomegaly and evidence of portal hypertension. Diagnosis by serum α_1-antitrypsin and phenotyping.
Cryptogenic cirrhosis	Typical clinical features of cirrhosis but no obvious cause after extensive evaluation.

AMA = antimitochondrial antibody; ANA = antinuclear antibody; ASMA = anti-smooth muscle antibody; TPN = total parenteral nutrition.

Diagnosis

Patients with cirrhosis may be asymptomatic for years before developing evidence of hepatocyte dysfunction or portal hypertension. Patients may report a change in skin, sclera, or urine color caused by jaundice, and they may develop pruritus related to cholestasis. The relative estrogen excess of the cirrhotic state may lead to symptoms of decreased libido, erectile dysfunction, or amenorrhea. Decreased hepatic production of clotting factors may lead to abnormal bleeding. Portal hypertension may cause esophageal varices, which may lead to hematemesis or melena. Patients may report weight gain, increased abdominal girth, or ankle swelling related to ascites and edema. Family members may report changes in the patient's behavior or mental status characteristic of hepatic encephalopathy.

Take a thorough history, including a detailed alcohol history. Question patients about risk factors for hepatitis C infection, such as date of birth between 1945 and 1965, intravenous (IV) drug use, blood transfusion before 1992, having a sexual partner who uses IV drugs, or incarceration. Similarly, ask patients about risk factors for hepatitis B infection, such as birth in an endemic country, having multiple sex partners, or IV drug use. Inquire about other diseases that may result in cirrhosis, such as right-sided heart failure, and about risk factors for nonalcoholic fatty liver disease (NAFLD) (obesity, diabetes, hyperlipidemia). Ask about the use of medications associated with increased risk for cirrhosis, such as methotrexate, amiodarone, and high-dose vitamin A. A family history of liver disease should prompt a consideration of genetic diseases that cause cirrhosis, such as hemochromatosis, α_1-antitrypsin deficiency, or Wilson disease.

Jaundice, which can be appreciated by most observers only when the bilirubin exceeds 2.5 to 3.0 mg/dL, usually is first noticed in the conjunctiva, with more severe degrees apparent in other mucous membranes or the skin. Spider angiomata, thought to be the result of an increased ratio of serum estradiol to testosterone, may be found over the face, neck, shoulders, and upper thorax. The lesions blanch with pressure and refill from the center outward. Palmar erythema, gynecomastia, and testicular atrophy are thought to be related to the same hormonal effects. The breath may have a characteristic odor (fetor hepaticus) caused by the presence of dimethyl sulfide due to portosystemic shunting. The liver may be palpable or reduced in size, and the spleen may be palpable because of engorgement from portal hypertension. Bulging flanks, flank dullness, shifting dullness, or a fluid wave suggests ascites. Of these findings, flank dullness has the highest sensitivity (84%), and fluid wave has the highest specificity (90%). Patients with ascites may have a palpable umbilical hernia. The presence of leg edema in patients with cirrhosis increases the likelihood that ascites is present. Rarely, portal hypertension causes markedly dilated abdominal wall veins (caput medusae). Impaired mental status, confusion, agitation, hyperreflexia, or asterixis (the inability to maintain a fixed posture) suggests hepatic encephalopathy. Other physical examination findings in cirrhosis include parotid enlargement, Dupuytren contracture, clubbing, axillary hair loss, and white nails.

Although liver biopsy is the definitive method of establishing a diagnosis of cirrhosis, laboratory tests and imaging studies, in combination with physical examination findings, can be used to estimate the likelihood of cirrhosis (Table 2). In clinical practice, liver biopsy is generally not performed if the history, physical examination, laboratory tests, and imaging studies strongly suggest cirrhosis. The serum albumin level, prothrombin time, total and direct bilirubin levels, and aminotransferase levels are useful in assessing hepatic function. Thrombocytopenia suggests hypersplenism caused by portal hypertension.

Use the history, along with laboratory tests, to establish the cause of cirrhosis. Alcoholic liver disease and chronic hepatitis C, the two most common causes of cirrhosis in the United States, are diagnosed from the history and the presence of antibody to hepatitis C virus, respectively. Chronic hepatitis B, a less common cause of cirrhosis in the United States, is indicated by the presence of hepatitis B surface antigen. In parts of the world with a high prevalence of chronic hepatitis B (sub-Saharan Africa, China, Southeast Asia), hepatitis B is an important and vaccine-preventable cause of cirrhosis.

Chronic cholestatic liver diseases such as primary biliary cirrhosis (PBC) and primary sclerosing cholangitis (PSC) can cause cirrhosis. PBC is a slowly progressive autoimmune liver disease that is five times more common in women than in men and usually affects those between 30 and 65 years of age. Fatigue and pruritus are the most common presenting symptoms, and other autoimmune disorders such as hypothyroidism, Sjögren syndrome, and systemic sclerosis (scleroderma) may coexist. In PBC, the alkaline phosphatase is usually markedly elevated, and more than 90% of patients have antimitochondrial antibodies. PSC is a chronic condition characterized by progressive bile duct inflammation and destruction and, ultimately, fibrosis of both the intrahepatic and extrahepatic bile ducts, leading to cirrhosis. PSC is strongly associated with ulcerative colitis and, similar to PBC, is associated with markedly elevated alkaline phosphatase. In contrast to PBC, PSC is not associated with antimitochondrial antibodies.

Autoimmune hepatitis can vary in severity from subclinical illness to fulminant hepatic failure and is associated with elevated γ-globulin levels as well as antinuclear antibodies, anti–smooth muscle antibodies, and anti–liver–kidney microsomal antibodies. The disease is more common in women. Approximately 50% of patients are asymptomatic and are diagnosed as a result of incidental findings on testing performed for other reasons.

NAFLD and nonalcoholic steatohepatitis (see Chapter 21) are also potential causes of cirrhosis.

Consider hereditary causes of cirrhosis in patients with a family history of liver disease. Hereditary hemochromatosis can be associated with diabetes, skin hyperpigmentation, pseudogout, and cardiomyopathy. A serum transferrin saturation ≥60% in men and ≥50% in women has 90% sensitivity for identifying patients homozygous for the hemochromatosis gene. Wilson disease, an autosomal recessive disorder affecting copper transport, is associated with neuropsychiatric symptoms and cirrhosis. A very low serum ceruloplasmin level strongly suggests the diagnosis. α_1-Antitrypsin deficiency affects the liver and lungs (emphysema). Liver disease is the result of abnormal accumulation of a variant protein in hepatocytes, which can be identified as inclusions with periodic acid–Schiff staining. The diagnosis is confirmed by a low serum α_1-antitrypsin level.

In patients with ascites, diagnostic paracentesis is an important tool for identifying the cause and determining if infection (spontaneous bacterial peritonitis [SBP]) is present. Thirty percent of patients with SBP do not have fever, and 40% do not have abdominal pain. Abdominal paracentesis is indicated in patients with newly identified ascites and in situations associated with an increased risk for SBP (hospital admission, signs of infection, clinical deterioration, gastrointestinal [GI] bleeding). Samples should be sent for albumin and protein concentrations, cell count, Gram stain, and culture. Bleeding complications from paracentesis are uncommon, even when the international normalized ratio (INR) is prolonged, so that pre-paracentesis plasma or platelet transfusions are not necessary. Calculate the serum-ascites albumin gradient to differentiate among causes of ascites (Table 3). A gradient ≥1.1 suggests that the ascites is due to portal hypertension; a gradient <1.1 indicates that another

Table 2. Laboratory and Other Studies for Cirrhosis

Test	Notes
Tests for Diagnosis	
AST/ALT ratio ≤1	Sensitivity, 44%; specificity, 94%
Platelets <100,000 μL (100 × 10⁹/L)	Sensitivity, 38%; specificity, 97%; suggests presence of splenomegaly
PT, bilirubin, albumin	Measures of liver function
Liver ultrasonography	Sensitivity, 71%–100%; specificity, 88% compared with liver histology
Abdominal CT	Sensitivity, 84%; specificity, 100%; based on caudate lobe-right lobe ratio >0.65
Abdominal MRI	Sensitivity, 93%; specificity, 92%; based on enlargement of hilar periportal space as sign of early cirrhosis
Serum-ascites albumin gradient	Sensitivity, 97%; specificity, 91%; gradient >1.1 compatible with cirrhosis
Tests to Determine Etiology	
Viral hepatitis studies	HBsAg, anti-HBs, anti-HBc, anti-HCV antibody
Alkaline phosphatase	Increased in PSC and PBC
Antimitochondrial antibody	Positive in PBC (>90% of cases)
Antinuclear antibody	Positive in autoimmune hepatitis and PBC
Anti-smooth muscle antibody	May be positive in autoimmune hepatitis
Anti-LKM antibody	May be positive in autoimmune hepatitis
Total protein, globulin	May be elevated in autoimmune hepatitis, viral hepatitis, and PBC
Iron studies	Transferrin saturation and ferritin increased in hemochromatosis
GGT	Elevated GGT may be only abnormality in NASH
Ceruloplasmin	Decreased in Wilson disease
α₁-Antitrypsin	Decreased in α₁-antitrypsin deficiency
Tests to Detect Complications	
α-Fetoprotein	Levels >500 ng/mL (500 μg/L) highly suggest HCC
Abdominal ultrasonography	Screening for HCC; gold standard for detection of ascites
Ascitic fluid granulocyte count	Count >250/μL (0.25 × 10⁹/L) suggests SBP
Serum electrolytes	Abnormal in cirrhosis caused by diuretic therapy for ascites or alcoholism
Serum BUN, creatinine	Elevated in hepatorenal syndrome
Upper endoscopy	Used to document (and treat) varices
Serum ammonia	Elevated serum ammonia may be helpful in unusual presentations of hepatic encephalopathy

ALT = alanine aminotransferase; anti-HBc = antibody to hepatitis B core antigen; anti-HBs = antibody to hepatitis B surface antigen; anti-LKM antibody = anti-liver-kidney microsomal antibody; AST = aspartate aminotransferase; BUN = blood urea nitrogen; CT = computed tomography; GGT = γ-glutamyl transpeptidase; HBsAg = hepatitis B surface antigen; HCC = hepatocellular carcinoma; HCV = hepatitis C virus; MRI = magnetic resonance imaging; NASH = nonalcoholic steatohepatitis; PBC = primary biliary cirrhosis; PSC = primary sclerosing cholangitis; PT = prothrombin time; SBP = spontaneous bacterial peritonitis.

process is present, such as nephrotic syndrome, tuberculosis, or cancer. An ascitic fluid neutrophil count >250/μL (250 × 10⁶/L) is compatible with infection. Patients with an ascitic fluid protein concentration <1 g/dL (10 g/L) are at increased risk for developing SBP.

About 30% to 50% of patients with portal hypertension will bleed from varices, and death from variceal bleeding is 30% to 50%. Patients with cirrhosis should undergo upper endoscopy to search for esophageal varices.

Therapy

The goals of therapy for cirrhosis are to slow the progression of the underlying liver disease, prevent further injury to the liver, prevent and treat complications (esophageal varices, ascites, hepatic encephalopathy, hepatocellular carcinoma), and evaluate the patient for liver transplantation. Protein-calorie malnutrition and hypermetabolism are common in patients with cirrhosis, and nutritional assessment is important. Patients with alcoholism should receive folate and thiamine supplementation, and patients with ascites should have dietary sodium restriction (<2 g/day). Abstinence from alcohol is critically important to reduce further liver injury. Vaccinate nonimmune patients against hepatitis A and B and administer pneumococcal and yearly influenza vaccines.

Nonselective β-blockers (propranolol, nadolol) are effective for primary prophylaxis of bleeding from high-risk varices and for secondary prophylaxis after an episode of variceal bleeding by lowering the portal pressure. The dose is titrated to produce a 25% reduction in resting heart rate. Endoscopic variceal band ligation or sclerotherapy is indicated for primary and secondary prophylaxis in patients with contraindications to or intolerance of β-blockers. Patients who

Table 3. Tests Performed on Ascitic Fluid

Test	Clinical Use
Cell count and differential	>250/μL neutrophils diagnostic for SBP
Albumin concentration	Used to calculate the SAAG, SAAG ≥ 1.1 g/dL 97% accurate for diagnosing ascites caused by portal hypertension
Total protein	Values <1 g/dL identify patients at high risk for SBP
Culture (in blood culture bottles)	Used to identify causative organisms of SBP
Glucose	Low glucose suggests peritonitis caused by infection, bowel perforation, or tumor
Lactate dehydrogenase (LDH)	An ascitic-serum LDH ratio >1 suggest peritonitis caused by infection, bowel perforation, or tumor
Acid-fast bacilli smear and culture	Smear has very low sensitivity for tuberculous peritonitis; culture sensitivity approximately 50%
Amylase	Elevated in ascites caused by pancreatitis
Cytology	Used when malignant ascites is suspected; sensitivity, 58%–75%

SAAG = serum ascites albumin gradient; SBP = spontaneous bacterial peritonitis.

rebleed despite variceal banding may be considered for alternative treatments such as a transjugular intrahepatic portosystemic shunt (TIPS) procedure or portosystemic shunt surgery. TIPS creates a low-resistance channel between the hepatic vein and the intrahepatic portion of the portal vein using angiographic techniques. The channel is kept open by an expandable metal stent. However, 30% of patients will develop hepatic encephalopathy after TIPS.

Diuretics and sodium restriction are the mainstays of treatment for ascites. Combination diuretic therapy with spironolactone plus furosemide is most effective; in one trial, this combination controlled ascites in 90% of patients. The drugs can be given together in once-daily dosing. Refractory ascites can be treated with repeat large-volume paracentesis. When >5 L of ascitic fluid is removed, intravenous (IV) albumin is administered to reduce the risk for hemodynamic instability, hyponatremia, and worsening kidney function. TIPS is an alternative when repeat large-volume paracentesis is impractical or ineffective.

SBP commonly develops in hospitalized patients with ascites and an ascitic fluid protein <1.0 g/dL (10 g/L), variceal bleeding, or prior SBP. Patients with an ascitic fluid neutrophil count >250/μL (250 × 10⁶/L) should be treated for SBP initially with antibiotics active against Enterobacteriaceae organisms, *Streptococcus pneumoniae*, and enterococcus. Patients with ascitic fluid neutrophil counts <250/μL (250 × 10⁶/L) but with risk factors for SBP (including GI bleeding or recurrent episodes of SBP and those with low ascites protein levels with kidney failure) benefit from short-term antibiotic prophylaxis (ie, trimethoprim–sulfamethoxazole, ciprofloxacin, norfloxacin) directed at the common organisms causing SBP. It is uncertain whether long-term antibiotic prophylaxis of SBP is superior to intermittent prophylaxis during hospitalizations.

Hepatorenal syndrome is the development of kidney failure in patients with portal hypertension, ascites, and normal renal tubular function. Vigorous diuretic therapy, large-volume paracentesis without volume expansion, and GI bleeding may precipitate hepatorenal syndrome. Other causes of kidney failure should be excluded, particularly SBP. Failure to improve after withdrawal of diuretics and volume expansion with IV albumin is indicative of hepatorenal syndrome. Dialysis is indicated for patients with significant volume overload or severe electrolyte abnormalities. Albumin and norepinephrine (or vasopressin) may improve renal arterial blood flow, but almost all patients will require liver transplantation.

The treatment of hepatic encephalopathy begins with a search for precipitating causes such as hypovolemia, electrolyte and acid–base disturbances, GI bleeding, infections (including SBP), and medica-

tion effects. Lactulose is the mainstay of drug treatment to lower serum ammonia levels and prevent or treat hepatic encephalopathy. The lactulose dose is titrated to produce two to three soft stools per day. For patients who do not respond to lactulose, a nonabsorbable antibiotics such as rifaximin can be added.

Patients with cirrhosis are at increased risk for hepatocellular carcinoma, although the magnitude of the risk varies with the cause of cirrhosis. With chronic hepatitis C, hepatocellular carcinoma generally occurs only in patients who have progressed to cirrhosis. In chronic hepatitis B, hepatocellular carcinoma can occur even without cirrhosis. Ultrasonography is the recommended screening test, performed every 6 to 12 months. The beneficial impact of screening on hepatocellular carcinoma–specific mortality has been best established for patients with chronic hepatitis B. Contrast-enhanced computed tomography is indicated for further evaluation of suspicious lesions identified on ultrasound screening.

Liver transplantation is the definitive treatment for patients with end-stage liver disease and complications such as variceal bleeding, ascites, or hepatic encephalopathy. Some patients with cirrhosis and hepatocellular carcinoma can also be treated with liver transplantation. The Model for End-Stage Liver Disease (MELD) scoring system uses the patient's bilirubin, creatinine, and INR to prioritize transplant candidates. Contraindications to liver transplantation include cardiopulmonary disease that constitutes prohibitive risk for surgery, non-skin malignancy outside of the liver within 5 years of evaluation or not meeting oncologic criteria for cure, and active substance abuse.

Follow-Up

Follow-up issues for patients with cirrhosis include counseling about substance abuse, monitoring for complications (bleeding, ascites, SBP, hepatic encephalopathy, hepatorenal syndrome), monitoring for medication side effects, screening for hepatocellular carcinoma, and assessing for liver transplantation. Cessation of substance abuse is critical for reducing further liver damage from toxins such as alcohol and to permit consideration for liver transplantation. Instruct patients to report any symptoms suggestive of cirrhotic complications, such as melena, weight gain, increased abdominal girth, edema, abdominal pain, change in mental status, or decreased urine output. For patients taking diuretics, careful monitoring of blood urea nitrogen, creatinine, and electrolytes is important to detect potential volume depletion, hyperkalemia, hypokalemia, or hyponatremia.

Bibliography

Garcia-Tsao G, Bosch J. Management of varices and variceal hemorrhage in cirrhosis. N Engl J Med. 2010;362:823-832. [PMID: 20200386]

Ginès P, Schrier RW. Renal failure in cirrhosis. N Engl J Med. 2009;361:1279-1290. [PMID: 19776409]

Runyon BA; AASLD. Introduction to the revised American Association for the Study of Liver Diseases Practice Guideline management of adult patients with ascites due to cirrhosis 2012. Hepatology. 2013;57:1651-1653. [PMID: 23463403]

Udell JA, Wang CS et al. Does this patient with liver disease have cirrhosis? JAMA 2012;307:832-842. [PMID: 22357834]

Chapter 23

Diseases of the Gallbladder and Bile Ducts

Nora L. Porter, MD

Gallstones are the most common cause of biliary disease in the United States. Ninety percent of gallstones in the United States are cholesterol or mixed cholesterol and bilirubin stones. Risk factors for the formation of cholesterol stones include estrogen (female gender, pregnancy, estrogen therapy), obesity, a diet high in simple carbohydrates, physical inactivity, impaired gallbladder emptying (total parenteral nutrition [TPN], biliary strictures), rapid weight loss (gastric bypass surgery), dyslipidemias, diabetes mellitus, cirrhosis, Crohn disease, resection of the terminal ileum, and medications (thiazide diuretics, ceftriaxone). Black pigment stones occur in hemolytic disease, including sickle cell disease. Brown pigment stones form in the setting of chronic biliary infection or cirrhosis.

Most patients with gallstones remain asymptomatic. When gallstones obstruct the cystic duct, symptoms of biliary colic develop. Prolonged obstruction can cause painful distension and inflammation of the gallbladder (cholecystitis). Gallstones may migrate into and obstruct the common bile duct (choledocholithiasis), potentially resulting in cholangitis (infection of the biliary tree) and pancreatitis. Untreated acute cholecystitis can progress to perforation, gangrenous cholecystitis (especially in patients with diabetes), and acute cholangitis. In cholangitis, bacterial infection proximal to a bile duct obstruction may result in bacteremia and septic shock.

Acalculous cholecystitis is inflammation and ultimately infection of the gallbladder in the absence of stones and without obstruction of the bile duct. Risk factors are critical illness (sepsis, mechanical ventilation, TPN), atherosclerotic vascular disease, HIV/AIDS, chronic salmonella infection, cytomegalovirus infection, polyarteritis nodosa, and systemic lupus erythematosus.

Biliary dyskinesia may cause symptoms similar to gallstones; causes include functional gallbladder dysmotility and biliary sphincter of Oddi dysfunction.

Primary biliary cirrhosis (PBC) and primary sclerosing cholangitis (PSC) are chronic diseases of the biliary system. The incidence of PBC is higher in first-degree relatives of patients with the disease. The major risk factor for PSC is ulcerative colitis.

Malignancies of the biliary tree include gallbladder cancer, cholangiocarcinoma, and ampullary adenocarcinoma. Risk factors for gallbladder cancer, the most common, include gallstones larger than 3 cm in size, gallbladder polyps larger than 1 cm in size, porcelain gallbladder, and women of Pima Indian ancestry. Risk factors for cholangiocarcinoma include PSC, ulcerative colitis, intrahepatic bile duct stones, biliary atresia, biliary cysts, and chronic liver flukes. Ampullary adenocarcinoma is a rare malignancy that occurs in patients with hereditary polyposis syndromes (familial adenomatous polyposis, Peutz-Jeghers syndrome).

Prevention

Primary prevention for gallstones includes a diet high in fiber and plant-based foods; increasing physical activity; maintaining normal body weight; and, if appropriate, lowering low-density lipoprotein cholesterol. Consider recommending small amounts of alcohol. In patients with asymptomatic gallstones, there are no prospective studies comparing cholecystectomy with observation; however, because most patients will remain asymptomatic, prophylactic cholecystectomy is not usually indicated.

Populations at increased risk for developing complicated gallbladder disease include those with sickle cell anemia, organ transplant candidates, and those undergoing rapid weight loss (eg, bariatric surgery patients). These at-risk individuals and those at increased risk of developing gallbladder cancer may be candidates for prophylactic cholecystectomy. Ursodeoxycholic acid may also be used to prevent gallstones in persons undergoing rapid weight loss.

Screening

Screening for gallstones in asymptomatic, average-risk individuals is not indicated. However, some patient groups (eg, Pima Indian women and those undergoing bariatric surgery) have a significantly increased risk of developing gallstones, so screening of selected patients should be considered.

Consider screening first-degree relatives of patients with PBC with serum alkaline phosphatase, aminotransferase, and antimitochondrial antibody measurement.

Diagnosis

No single symptom or sign is sensitive or specific enough to establish or rule out the diagnosis of biliary disease (Table 1). An appropriate history and physical examination, with selected laboratory and imaging studies, is required. Classic biliary colic is episodic, severe, constant epigastric or right upper quadrant abdominal pain that develops quickly, frequently after a meal or at night, radiates to the right scapula or shoulder, and subsides in several hours. The pain of acute cholecystitis is similar but lasts longer, usually more than 3 hours, and may be accompanied by fever. Nausea and vomiting are common in both. Cholecystitis may be asymptomatic in elderly patients, immunosuppressed patients, or patients with diabetes. A history of jaundice, pruritus, acholic stools, and dark urine indicates biliary obstruction caused by choledocholithiasis.

The physical examination in biliary colic may be benign, although the patient may have epigastric or right upper quadrant tenderness. A positive Murphy sign (inspiratory arrest when the gallbladder fossa is palpated during deep inspiration) has a 50% to 80% specificity for acute cholecystitis; infrequently, a tender right upper quadrant mass is palpable. Jaundice supports the diagnosis of choledocholithiasis and, in the presence of fever, cholangitis.

Suspect acute cholecystitis or cholangitis in patients with leukocytosis. Serum aminotransferase and bilirubin concentrations may be mildly elevated. A bilirubin concentration greater than 4 mg/dL

Table 1. Differential Diagnosis of Acute Cholecystitis

Disorder	Notes
Acute cholecystitis and acalculous cholecystitis	Epigastric and RUQ pain with Murphy sign. Bilirubin <4 mg/dL (68.4 mmol/L) unless complicated by choledocholithiasis; AST and ALT levels may be minimally elevated.
Biliary crystals (microlithiasis, sludge)	Typical biliary pain and no gallstones on imaging studies. If necessary, diagnosis made by aspiration of gallbladder bile from the duodenum or directly from the gallbladder during ERCP and microscopic examination. May cause pain, cholecystitis, or pancreatitis. Treated with cholecystectomy.
Biliary dyskinesia	Typical biliary pain, no gallstones on imaging studies, and a CCK-induced gallbladder ejection fraction <35%-40% on cholescintigraphy. Symptoms usually relieved with cholecystectomy.
Acute cholangitis	Charcot triad (RUQ pain, fever, jaundice) or Reynold pentad (Charcot triad plus shock and mental status changes). Bilirubin >4 mg/dL (68.4 mmol/L); AST and ALT levels may exceed 1000 U/L.
Acute pancreatitis	Midepigastric pain radiating to the back, nausea, and vomiting. Elevated serum amylase and lipase levels (amylase level more than two times normal). Vomiting and hyperamylasemia generally are more pronounced than in acute cholecystitis.
Pyelonephritis (right)	Costovertebral angle tenderness and evidence of UTI. Urinalysis helps to establish the diagnosis.
Peptic ulcer disease	RUQ or midepigastric pain. Free air on upright radiograph if perforated. Perforated ulcer can mimic acute cholecystitis.
Acute viral hepatitis	Prodromal syndrome and jaundice. AST and ALT levels generally >1000 U/L; bilirubin level generally >4 mg/dL (68.4 mmol/L) and often much higher.
Acute alcoholic hepatitis	Recent significant alcohol intake. RUQ pain, fever, and jaundice. Coagulopathy, leukocytosis; AST level usually two to three times greater than ALT level; bilirubin level generally >4 mg/dL (68.4 mmol/L).
Gonococcal perihepatitis (Fitz-Hugh–Curtis syndrome)	RUQ pain and pelvic adnexal tenderness; leukocytosis. Cervical smear shows gonococci.

ALT = alanine aminotransferase; AST = aspartate aminotransferase; CCK = cholecystokinin; ERCP = endoscopic retrograde cholangiopancreatography; RUQ = right upper quadrant; UTI = urinary tract infection.

(>68.4 mmol/L) is not a feature of cholecystitis and should prompt an evaluation for cholangitis. In cholangitis, serum alkaline phosphatase elevation is common, and aminotransferase levels may be significantly elevated.

Abdominal pain may be absent in critically ill or elderly patients with acalculous cholecystitis. Maintain a high index of suspicion in such patients who present with fever, leukocytosis, and abnormal aminotransferase levels. Ultrasonography is the most sensitive and specific test for detecting gallstones, has no risk or radiation exposure, is widely available, and is relatively inexpensive (Table 2). Ultrasonography shows dilatation of the cystic or biliary duct if there is an obstructing stone. In acute cholecystitis, ultrasonography shows pericholecystic fluid and a thickened gallbladder wall; a sonographic Murphy sign further supports the diagnosis. Findings in acalculous cholecystitis are the same as in acute cholecystitis but with no gallstones or obstruction. If ultrasonography is nondiagnostic, cholescintigraphy (eg, hepatobiliary iminodiacetic acid [HIDA] scans) should be obtained; nonvisualization of the gallbladder suggests cholecystitis. Abdominal computed tomography (CT) should be used when other studies are equivocal or when complications of cholecystitis (eg, perforation, cholangitis, gangrenous cholecystitis) are suspected. If bile duct stones are suspected, magnetic resonance cholangiography is preferred because it is more sensitive than ultrasonography and, unlike endoscopic retrograde cholangiopancreatography (ERCP), is noninvasive.

Symptoms of biliary dyskinesia are similar to those of biliary colic. Clinical diagnosis of biliary dyskinesia is suggested by characteristic abdominal pain with normal ultrasonographic imaging. Functional gallbladder dysmotility is diagnosed by finding a decreased cholecystokinin–induced gallbladder ejection fraction on cholescintigraphy. Sphincter of Oddi manometry may be required to diagnose sphincter of Oddi dysfunction.

Primary biliary cirrhosis is a slowly progressive autoimmune liver disease that is more common in women and typically affects persons age 30 to 65 years. It presents as chronic cholestasis with fatigue, pruritus without rash, hyperpigmentation, and sometimes xanthomas. Most patients have antimitochondrial antibodies and

Table 2. Imaging Studies for Acute Cholecystitis

Test	Notes
RUQ US	Sensitivity, 81%-98%; specificity, 70%-98%. Sonographic Murphy sign (maximal tenderness directly over the visualized gallbladder) is >90% predictive of acute cholecystitis.
HIDA scan	Sensitivity, 85%-97%; specificity, 90%; more sensitive and specific than US; higher cost and less availability limit its use.
CT	Most useful to diagnose complications (perforation, cholangitis, gangrenous cholecystitis); radiation exposure and expensive.
MRI or MRCP	95%-100% sensitive, 75%-95% specific for CBD stones. Less sensitive for stones in gallbladder, malignancy. Expensive.
Endoscopic US	Sensitivity and specificity for CBD stones similar to MRI; more sensitive for smaller stones and biliary sludge. Less invasive than ERCP.

CBD = common bile duct; CT = computed tomography; ERCP = endoscopic retrograde cholangiopancreatography; HIDA = hepatobiliary iminodiacetic acid; MRCP = magnetic resonance cholangiopancreatography; MRI = magnetic resonance imaging; RUQ = right upper quadrant; US = ultrasonography.

elevated serum IgM, γ-glutamyl transferase, and ALP levels; aminotransferase levels also may be elevated. Ultrasonography should be used to exclude extrahepatic bile duct obstruction. PBC frequently is associated with other autoimmune disorders, such as hypothyroidism, Sjögren syndrome, sicca syndrome, and systemic sclerosis.

Primary sclerosing cholangitis is characterized by progressive bile duct inflammation, destruction, and ultimately fibrosis of both the intrahepatic and extrahepatic bile ducts, which leads to cirrhosis. PSC is strongly associated with ulcerative colitis. The most common symptoms of PSC are pruritus and fatigue; as the disease progresses, most patients develop jaundice. PSC is associated with a markedly elevated ALP level and mildly elevated aminotransferase levels. The diagnosis of PSC depends on detecting multifocal strictures alternating with normal, dilated segment of the bile ducts leading to a "beaded" pattern on cholangiographic imaging. Cholangitis is a common complication of PSC. Cholangiocarcinoma occurs in approximately 10% of patients with PSC.

Gallbladder cancer usually is diagnosed at an advanced stage and therefore has a very poor prognosis. Presenting symptoms of nausea, abdominal discomfort, jaundice, weight loss, and anorexia usually occur when the cancer is advanced and unresectable. The diagnosis can be made with ultrasonography, CT, or magnetic resonance imaging (MRI).

Cholangiocarcinomas (sometimes referred to as Klatskin tumors) are rare tumors that arise from the biliary tract. Patients usually present with painless jaundice, pruritus, and weight loss. MRI with magnetic resonance cholangiopancreatography is the diagnostic imaging modality of choice because it can also assist in staging.

Ampullary adenocarcinoma typically presents with obstructive jaundice caused by blockage of the distal bile duct. The diagnosis is usually made by endoscopy and biopsy, with abdominal CT and sometimes endoscopic ultrasonography used for staging. The prognosis is good when diagnosed early.

Therapy

Surgery provides definitive management for most patients with symptomatic gallstone disease, which has a high rate of recurrence. In patients with uncomplicated cholecystitis, cholecystectomy within 24 to 48 hours is associated with fewer complications and earlier hospital discharge. Laparoscopic cholecystectomy results in shorter hospital stays, less pain, lower costs, and fewer complications than open cholecystectomy. ERCP is both diagnostic and therapeutic in choledocholithiasis. In patients with severe cholangitis, sepsis, or gallstone pancreatitis, urgent ERCP allows rapid removal of obstruction and biliary drainage.

In most patients with gallstone disease, drug therapy is supportive until definitive surgery can be performed. Diclofenac provides pain relief in biliary colic and decreases the risk of developing acute cholecystitis. Nonsteroidal antiinflammatory drugs also are helpful in patients with acute cholecystitis with mild to moderate pain; patients with more severe pain may require narcotic analgesia. Although cholecystitis is a primarily inflammatory disorder, secondary infection may occur because of cystic duct obstruction and bile stasis. Therefore, broad-spectrum antibiotics (ie, metronidazole plus ciprofloxacin or ampicillin–sulbactam) are appropriate for those who appear toxic or who have fever, leukocytosis, or possible cholangitis. Ursodeoxycholic acid may be used in selected symptomatic patients who are unable or unwilling to undergo surgery. Ursodeoxycholic acid should be used only in a patient with cholesterol stones smaller than 10 mm diameter, a patent biliary tract, and a functioning gallbladder.

Treatment of acalculous cholecystitis is similar to treatment of acute gallstone cholecystitis, including the use of supportive therapy and antibiotics. Because patients with acalculous cholecystitis often are too unstable for immediate surgical intervention, initial management usually is percutaneous cholecystostomy and drainage, with surgery deferred until the patient's other medical conditions have stabilized.

Treatment of functional gallbladder dysmotility is cholecystectomy. Treatment of sphincter of Oddi dysfunction is endoscopic sphincterotomy. This invasive procedure should be reserved for patients with severe symptoms who meet diagnostic criteria and in whom other diagnoses have been excluded.

PBC may be effectively treated with ursodeoxycholic acid if the medication is used early in the disease. Endoscopic dilatation of dominant strictures provides symptomatic relief in PSC, but definitive management is liver transplantation at the point when complications of end-stage liver disease become apparent. Pruritus in both PBC and PSC can be managed with bile acid resins.

Treatment for gallbladder cancer is surgical resection if localized; most studies report a 5-year survival rate of 0% to 10%. Palliative therapy is used for advance disease. Surgical resection may be an option with extrahepatic or hilar cholangiocarcinoma; however, even with successful resection, the 5-year survival rate is 20% to 35%. Ampullary adenocarcinoma is usually resectable by pancreaticoduodenectomy and has a good prognosis.

Follow-Up

Most patients with asymptomatic gallstone disease should be followed the development of symptoms. Patients who undergo cholecystectomy should have routine surgical follow-up. Use ultrasonography to follow patients being treated with ursodeoxycholic acid and those at high risk of malignancy who elect not to have cholecystectomy.

Monitor for disease progression in patients with PBC and PSC with periodic history, physical examination, and laboratory studies. Those who develop cirrhosis should have endoscopic evaluation for esophageal varices. Because of chronic biliary stasis, follow patients with PBC or PSC for deficiencies of vitamins A, D, E, and K. In addition, patients with PSC should have periodic tumor serology and abdominal imaging (ultrasonography, CT, or MRI) for early detection of malignancy.

Bibliography

Trowbridge RL, Rutkowski NK, Shojania KG. Does this patient have acute cholecystitis? JAMA. 2003;289:80-86. [PMID: 12503981]

Chapter 24

Acute Pancreatitis

Nora L. Porter, MD

Acute pancreatitis occurs when the pancreatic enzyme trypsinogen is prematurely activated to trypsin, which in turn activates pancreatic zymogens. The resulting pancreatic autodigestion leads to an inflammatory response that causes further pancreatic damage. Most cases of acute pancreatitis are mild (interstitial) and self-limited, but in severe cases, the inflammation may progress to a systemic inflammatory response that can lead to capillary leak syndrome, multiple organ failure, and death. Repeated episodes of acute pancreatitis may result in chronic pancreatitis and pancreatic endocrine and exocrine insufficiency.

The most common etiologies of acute pancreatitis in the United States are biliary obstruction caused by gallstones and alcohol abuse. Pancreatitis also may be caused by medications, very high serum triglyceride levels (>500 mg/dL [5.7 mmol/L]), hypercalcemia, sphincter of Oddi dysfunction, trauma, surgery, cystic fibrosis and other genetic disorders, or penetrating peptic ulcer or as a complication of endoscopic retrograde cholangiopancreatography (ERCP). Other causes of acute pancreatitis can be classified as obstructive, toxic or drug induced, infectious, or vascular. Approximately 10% of acute pancreatitis is idiopathic.

Prevention

The best preventive measures for pancreatitis involve avoidance of known etiologic agents (alcohol, smoking, medications) and medical or surgical management of other precipitating factors. Avoiding diagnostic ERCP and using noninvasive magnetic resonance cholangiopancreatography (MRCP) instead, when possible, decreases the risk of procedure-related pancreatitis. However, MRCP cannot replace ERCP for therapeutic drainage of the biliary system.

Diagnosis

The most common symptom of acute pancreatitis is the sudden onset of severe epigastric or diffuse abdominal pain radiating to the back. The pain usually may improve when the patient sits up or leans forward. Nausea, vomiting, and fever are common. Table 1 summarizes the differential diagnosis of pancreatitis. Diagnosis of acute pancreatitis requires at least two of the triad of clinical symptoms, elevated serum amylase or lipase, and typical findings on imaging.

Abdominal tenderness (diffuse or epigastric), guarding, and distension are common in acute uncomplicated pancreatitis. Diminished bowel sounds may point to an associated ileus. Several physical findings may suggest a specific etiology; for example, jaundice suggests biliary obstruction, and eruptive xanthomas suggest hypertriglyceridemia. Evaluate for hypovolemia (tachycardia, hypotension), infection, or gastrointestinal (GI) bleeding. Large pseudocysts may be palpable and painful. The Grey-Turner or Cullen sign (painless ecchymoses in the flank or periumbilical region, respectively) suggests retroperitoneal bleeding.

Serum amylase and lipase levels are elevated in approximately one third of patients with acute pancreatitis. The degree of elevation of pancreatic enzymes does not correlate with disease severity. Elevation to at least three times the upper limit of normal is consid-

Table 1. Differential Diagnosis of Acute Pancreatitis (AP)

Disorder	Notes
Perforated viscus (see Chapter 16)	Very sudden onset (in AP, pain gradually increases over 30 min to 1 h). Intraperitoneal air present on radiographs.
Acute cholecystitis and biliary colic (see Chapter 23)	Pain tends to be located in epigastrium and right upper quadrant and radiates to right shoulder or shoulder blade (in AP, pain tends to radiate to the back). Ultrasonography shows thickened gallbladder and pericholecystic fluid.
Intestinal obstruction (see Chapter 16)	Colicky pain (versus constant pain in AP). Obstructive pattern seen on CT or abdominal series.
Mesenteric vascular occlusion (see Chapter 16)	Classic triad for chronic mesenteric ischemia: postprandial abdominal pain, weight loss, and abdominal bruit. Acute mesenteric ischemia is characterized by pain out of proportion to examination findings and metabolic acidosis.
Dissecting aortic aneurysm (see Chapter 9)	Sudden-onset pain that may radiate to lower extremity (in AP, pain gradually increases over 30 min to 1 h and does not radiate to lower extremity).
Myocardial infarction (see Chapter 3)	Include in differential diagnosis in all patients with upper abdominal pain.
Appendicitis (see Chapter 16)	Pain may start in epigastrium but eventually migrates to right lower quadrant. CT very helpful for diagnosis.
Diabetic ketoacidosis (see Chapter 14)	Blood glucose always elevated; anion gap always present (blood glucose may be elevated in severe AP but usually develops later in the clinical course; acidosis may be present in severe AP).

CT = computed tomography.

Table 2. Nonpancreatic Causes of Elevated Serum Lipase Levels

Intestinal ischemia or obstruction

Duodenal ulcer

Ketoacidosis

Celiac disease

Macrolipasemia

Head trauma, intracranial mass

Kidney failure

Heparin

ered diagnostic but is not sensitive because many patients with acute pancreatitis do not have enzyme levels that reach this threshold. Serum lipase is more sensitive and specific than amylase and stays elevated up to 14 days after an episode of acute pancreatitis. **Measuring serum lipase alone is sufficient to confirm the diagnosis of acute pancreatitis in the appropriate clinical setting.** However, other conditions may also cause elevation of serum lipase (Table 2).

Pancreatitis may cause significant systemic complications, mediated primarily by the effect of tissue damage and the release of cytokines and inflammatory mediators. These include hypocalcemia, hyperglycemia, acute kidney injury, disseminated intravascular coagulation, and acute respiratory distress syndrome. In all patients with acute pancreatitis, obtain laboratory studies to evaluate for etiology and complications, including a complete blood count, electrolytes, calcium, blood glucose, blood urea nitrogen (BUN), creatinine, triglycerides, prothrombin time, and partial thromboplastin time, as well as pulse oximetry or, in more critically ill patients, arterial blood gases (Table 3).

Chest and abdominal (flat and upright) radiographs may be obtained to exclude bowel perforation or obstruction. Abdominal ultrasonography is performed if gallstones are suspected. Contrast-enhanced computed tomography (CT) of the abdomen is the preferred imaging study for defining the extent of disease. **Imaging of the pancreas in acute pancreatitis is not indicated in all patients but should be considered in those with moderate or severe pancreatitis or persistent fever and in those who do not improve clinically within 48 to 72 hours to confirm the diagnosis, exclude other intraabdominal processes, grade the severity of pancreatitis, and diagnose local complications (pancreatic necrosis, pseudocyst, abscess).** In acute interstitial pancreatitis, CT may show enlargement or irregular contour of the gland, peripancreatic inflammation, and fluid collections. Pancreatic necrosis is identified by areas of nonenhancement on a contrast CT. Magnetic resonance imaging is used if there is a contraindication to intravenous radiocontrast.

Age older than 70 years, the presence of multiple comorbidities, and a body mass index >30 are associated with more severe acute pancreatitis. The best predictors of outcome are clinical findings that are markers of severity of pancreatic inflammation and its effect on systemic function. Third spacing of fluid and hemoconcentration, identified by increased BUN, increased creatinine, and sometimes increased hematocrit, may predict morbidity and mortality because they reflect severity of capillary leak. Organ failure is defined by the presence of shock (systolic blood pressure <90 mm Hg), respiratory insufficiency (arterial Po_2 <55 mm Hg [7.3 kPa]), acute kidney injury (serum creatinine >2 mg/dL [176.8 mmol/L]), or GI bleeding (>500 mL/24 h). Most patients with multiple organ system involvement have pancreatic necrosis involving 30% to 50% of the pancreas, often with infection; these patients have a very high mortality rate.

Therapy

Therapy for acute pancreatitis depends on disease severity. Mild acute pancreatitis is usually self-limited and is treated with bowel rest,

Table 3. Laboratory and Other Studies for Acute Pancreatitis (AP)

Test	Notes
Amylase	Cutoff values just above normal: sensitivity, 90%; specificity, 70%. Cutoff values three times the upper limit of normal: sensitivity, 60%; specificity, 99%.
Lipase	Cutoff values three times the upper limit of normal: sensitivity, 90%–100%; specificity, 99%. More sensitive and specific than amylase; may be used alone to confirm diagnosis of AP.
AST/ALT	Elevated levels raise suspicion for biliary pancreatitis.
Triglycerides	Hypertriglyceridemia can cause AP.
Calcium	Hypercalcemia can cause AP. Hypocalcemia can be a complication of AP.
BUN and creatinine	Incidence of acute kidney injury: 4% in interstitial AP, 22% in noninfected necrotic AP, and 45% in infected necrotic AP. May be a marker for hemoconcentration.
Glucose	Hyperglycemia is a negative prognostic factor.
PT/PTT	May be elevated in AP complicated by DIC.
Abdominal and chest radiographs	Can exclude perforated viscous or obstructed bowel; obtain in patients with severe abdominal pain.
Abdominal ultrasonography	Evaluates for presence of gallstones; obtain if biliary pancreatitis is suspected or etiology of pancreatitis is unknown. Generally preferred study for uncomplicated acute pancreatitis.
CT	Test of choice to determine the presence of local complications; no indication for routine CT in all patients with AP; obtain if diagnosis is uncertain or complications are suspected.
Test for arterial hypoxemia	Pulse oximetry in mild cases of AP. Arterial blood gases in severe cases of AP.

ALT = alanine aminotransferase; AST = aspartate aminotransferase; BUN = blood urea nitrogen; CT = computed tomography; DIC = disseminated intravascular coagulation; PT = prothrombin time; PTT = partial thromboplastin time.

intravenous hydration, antiemetics, and opioid analgesics. Oral intake is withheld until there is clear clinical improvement. Initiate nasojejunal enteral feeding in patients who are not improving within 72 to 96 hours. Compared with parenteral nutrition, early jejunal enteral feeding may decrease the risk of complications, particularly infection. Use nasogastric suction only in patients with refractory vomiting caused by ileus.

Patients with interstitial (non-necrotizing) pancreatitis without evidence of infection do not require antibiotics. Use of prophylactic antibiotics in patients with significant pancreatic necrosis is controversial. Persistent fever, necrosis involving >30% of the pancreas by CT scan, and clinical instability are indications to consider antibiotics. If antibiotics are used, select agents for coverage of *Escherichia coli* and *Pseudomonas*, *Klebsiella*, and *Enterococcus* spp.

ERCP is indicated only if there is evidence of biliary obstruction (jaundice, common bile duct dilatation, or elevated liver enzymes) in a patient with cholangitis (right upper quadrant pain, fever, jaundice) or in a patient with biliary pancreatitis who is not improving clinically and whose liver enzymes are rising. Stone extraction with biliary sphincterotomy improves mortality, decreases the risk of cholangitis and biliary sepsis, and may prevent further attacks of acute biliary pancreatitis. Surgical debridement or percutaneous drainage is indicated for infected pancreatic necrosis. Cholecystectomy is indicated in patients with biliary pancreatitis to prevent recurrence.

Follow-Up

Acute pancreatitis typically is a self-limited condition that does not recur if the precipitating factor is removed. Because amylase and lipase typically remain elevated during the course of acute pancreatitis, do not correlate with disease severity, and may persist for several weeks after resolution of symptoms, there is no clinical utility in repeating them except in patients who fail to improve. Patients with alcohol abuse should be advised to abstain from alcohol or referred for counseling and appropriate treatment. Pancreatitis associated with other medical conditions such as hypertriglyceridemia or hypercalcemia should be treated to decrease the risk of recurrence. If a specific drug precipitated the pancreatitis, discontinue its use and substitute another as needed.

Patients with acute pancreatitis should be followed symptomatically for the development of complications. Pancreatic pseudocysts are the most common complication of acute pancreatitis and may present several weeks after an episode of acute pancreatitis. A pseudocyst is a collection of pancreatic fluid with a fibrous, non-epithelialized lining. Pseudocysts are usually asymptomatic and usually resolve spontaneously. Suspect a persistent pseudocyst if pain, anorexia, or weight loss persists for several weeks. Symptomatic pseudocysts require drainage (percutaneous, endoscopic, or surgical). Pancreatic abscess (infected pseudocyst) presents with worsening abdominal pain, fever, and leukocytosis. Treatment includes antibiotics and drainage.

Patients with recurrent episodes of acute pancreatitis may develop chronic pancreatitis. At least 80% of patients with chronic pancreatitis have chronic abdominal pain, characteristically constant midepigastric pain radiating to the back and exacerbated by food. Acute exacerbations of pain may occur. Destruction of exocrine pancreatic tissue may result in malabsorption, leading to steatorrhea and weight loss. Destruction of insulin-producing β-cells may lead to diabetes mellitus; concurrent destruction of glucagon-producing α-cells increases the risk of hypoglycemia in patients with diabetes. In chronic pancreatitis, pancreatic calcifications can be seen on abdominal radiographs and CT scans, which may also show parenchymal atrophy or ductal dilatation in the pancreas. Patients with chronic pancreatitis should be evaluated for diabetes and deficiencies of fat-soluble vitamins.

Bibliography

Gupta K, Wu B. In the clinic. Acute pancreatitis. Ann Intern Med. 2010;153: ITC51-5. [PMID: 21041574]

Chapter 25

Approach to Diarrhea

Lynda Misra, DO

Diarrhea is traditionally defined as more than 200 g of stool per day. In clinical practice, diarrhea is defined as more than three loose stools per day. Diarrhea may occur because of a variety of mechanisms, such as the presence of poorly absorbed solutes in the lumen of the gut (eg, lactose), disruption of intestinal mucosal ion transport and subsequent water secretion (eg, cholera), disruption in the mucosal barrier secondary to infection or inflammation (eg, ulcerative colitis, *Clostridium difficile* infection), malabsorption of fat from pancreatic or bile salt insufficiency (eg, chronic pancreatitis, obstructive jaundice), bowel resection, reduced mucosal surface area (eg, celiac disease), injury from radiation treatment, bacterial overgrowth (eg, surgical blind loop), intestinal ischemia (eg, chronic mesenteric artery insufficiency), and disorders of motility (eg, systemic sclerosis). Many patients confuse true diarrhea with three other conditions: pseudodiarrhea (the frequent passage of small volumes of stool), fecal incontinence, and overflow diarrhea caused by fecal impaction. A thorough history and physical examination can help distinguish true diarrhea from these alternative conditions. Evaluation usually begins by differentiating symptoms based on their time course; acute diarrhea is present for less than 14 days, persistent diarrhea has been present for at least 14 days but 4 weeks or less, and diarrhea is considered to be chronic if it has

been present for more than 4 weeks. Figure 1 presents an approach to diagnosis based on the type of diarrhea present.

Acute Diarrhea

The most common cause of acute diarrhea is an infectious agent (>90% of cases). Acute infectious diarrhea is transmitted predominantly through the fecal–oral route by ingestion of contaminated food or water. Diarrhea may result from ingestion of preformed bacterial toxins (food poisoning) or from ingestion of bacteria that subsequently produce exotoxins or invade the gastrointestinal (GI) mucosa (Table 1). Although the vast majority of episodes of acute diarrhea are caused by viruses and are self-limited, further clinical evaluation is indicated in those who have bloody stools, body temperature greater than 38.5°C (>101.3°F), significant abdominal pain, severe diarrhea causing symptomatic dehydration, recent antibiotic use, a history of inflammatory bowel disease, or immunocompromised states; food handlers; the elderly; or pregnant women.

Diagnosis

The first step in evaluation of patients with acute diarrhea is to obtain a detailed history and physical examination to assess the severity, qual-

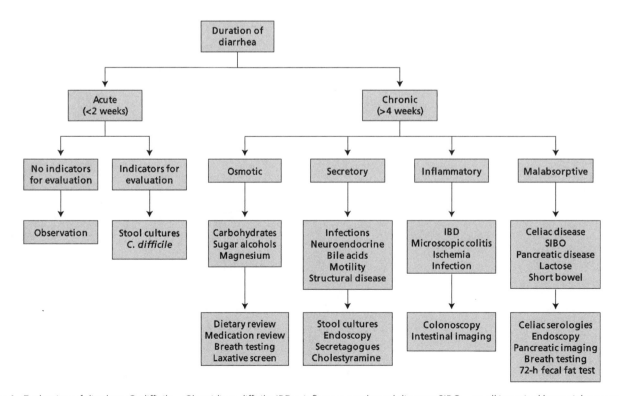

Figure 1. Evaluation of diarrhea. *C. difficile* = *Clostridium difficile*; IBD = inflammatory bowel disease; SIBO = small intestinal bacterial overgrowth.

Table 1. Causes of Noninfectious and Infectious Diarrhea

Pathologic Mechanism	Organism	Source or Diagnostic Clues	Incubation Period
Preformed toxin *(Toxins are ingested, and no intestinal microbial growth is required; symptoms occurs rapidly, within 2-12 hours)*			
	Staphylococcus aureus	Potato salad, mayonnaise, ham	1–8 h
	Bacillus cereus	Fried rice	1–8 h
	Clostridium perfringens	Beef, poultry	8–24 h
Enterotoxin *(Toxins produced by intestinal microbes that act directly on secretory mechanisms in the intestinal mucosa, causing watery diarrhea)*			
	Vibrio cholerae	Shellfish	8–72 h
	Enterotoxigenic *Escherichia coli*	Salads, cheese, meats	8–72 h
	Klebsiella pneumonia		8–72 h
	Aeromonas spp.		8–72 h
Enteroadherent *(Infecting organisms adhere to the gastrointestinal mucosa and compete with normal bowel flora)*			
	E. coli	Travel history	1–8 d
	Giardia lamblia		1–8 d
	Cryptosporidiosis	Acute or chronic watery diarrhea in an immunocompromised patient; outbreak in a nursing home or day care center or on a cruise ship	1–8 d
	Helminths		1–8 d
Enteroinvasive *(Infecting organisms invade and destroy intestinal mucosa, resulting in bloody diarrhea)*			
Minimal Inflammation	Norovirus	Outbreak in a nursing home, day care center, or on a cruise ship	1–3 d
	Rotavirus		
Moderate Inflammation	*Salmonella* spp.	Beef, poultry, eggs, dairy, travel history	12 h–11 d
	Campylobacter spp.	Poultry, raw milk, travel history	
	Aeromonas spp.	Travel history	
	V. parahaemolyticus		
	Yersinia spp.	Raw milk	
Severe inflammation	*Shigella* spp.	Travel history	12 h–8 d
	Enteroinvasive *E. coli*		
	Entamoeba histolytica		
Cytotoxin production *(Toxins produced by intestinal organisms cause destruction of mucosal cells and associated inflammation, resulting in dysentery: bloody stools containing inflammatory cells)*			
	Clostridium difficile	Health care facility or antibiotic exposure	1–3 d
	Enterohemorrhagic *E. coli*	Ground beef, raw vegetables	12–72 h

ity, and duration of diarrhea and to identify epidemiologic clues for potential diagnosis (see Table 1). Ask patients about recent food ingestion, antibiotic use, travel, and sick contacts. Ingestion of preformed bacterial toxins results in nausea and vomiting followed by diarrhea within 12 hours. Bacteria that require colonization to produce symptoms may not cause diarrhea until 2 to 3 days after ingestion of contaminated food. Outbreaks of diarrhea in families; on cruise ships and airplanes; and in day care centers, extended care facilities, or schools are commonly associated with norovirus. Traveler's diarrhea is most commonly caused by *Escherichia coli, Campylobacter, Shigella, Salmonella, Giardia,* and *Entamoeba* spp., although the exact causative agent varies depending on areas of travel and exposure risks. For hospitalized patients and those with recent antibiotic use, *C. difficile* infection should be considered because disruption of the intestinal flora by antibiotics and decreased gastric acidity caused by antacid therapy are recognized risk factors for *C. difficile* infection. *C. difficile*

infection is an inflammatory condition of the colon caused by the ingestion of the spore-forming, anaerobic, gram-positive bacillus. The inflammatory response is secondary to toxin-induced cytokines (toxins A and B) in the colon. Findings can range from watery diarrhea to ileus and life-threatening conditions (toxic megacolon, perforation, sepsis). Noninfectious causes of acute diarrhea include ischemic colitis, diverticulitis, and medications or ingestion of substances that can cause osmotic diarrhea (sorbitol, fructose, laxatives).

Because most episodes of diarrhea are self-limited, diagnostic testing generally is reserved for patients with severe diarrheal illness characterized by fever, blood in the stool, or signs of dehydration (weakness, thirst, decreased urine output, orthostasis) or patients with diarrhea lasting >7 days. For severe community-acquired or traveler's diarrhea, obtain stool cultures for *Salmonella, Shigella,* and *Campylobacter* spp. Routine stool culture cannot distinguish pathogenic *E. coli* from normal fecal flora. Therefore, in the setting of blood in the stool, test specifically for *E. coli* O157:H7 and Shiga toxin. If symptoms have persisted beyond 7 days, stool should be examined for ova and parasites. For health care–related diarrhea, test for *C. difficile* toxin. Fecal specimens collected after 3 days of hospitalization have a very low yield for standard bacterial pathogens, and routine stool culture is not indicated for inpatients with diarrhea unless there is evidence of a specific outbreak. In an immunocompromised patient, test for *Mycobacterium avium* complex (MAC) by sending stool for acid-fast bacillus stain and culture because disseminated MAC infections often involve the GI tract and cause diarrhea; also test for viruses (cytomegalovirus, adenovirus, herpes simplex virus) and protozoa (cryptosporidium, *Isospora* spp., microsporidia).

Therapy

Adequate hydration and avoidance of easily malabsorbed carbohydrates (lactose, sorbitol) often are sufficient treatments for otherwise healthy patients with acute noninflammatory diarrhea (ie, diarrhea without pain, fecal blood or pus, or fever) that is most likely secondary to a transient infection. Although prophylactic antibiotics are not recommended for traveler's diarrhea, empiric antibiotics (quinolones) may be appropriate for patients with symptoms. Untreated traveler's diarrhea usually resolves in 3 to 5 days, but treatment can improve symptoms and shorten the course. Antidiarrheal agents should be avoided in patients with suspected inflammatory diarrhea (eg, diarrhea due to ulcerative colitis, *C. difficile* infection, or Shiga toxin–producing *E. coli*) because of the association with toxic megacolon. New treatment guidelines for *C. difficile* infections have been published (Table 2). Relapse is common after initial treatment for *C. difficile* infection, occurring in up to 20% of patients.

Complications may occur after treatment of acute diarrhea. Chronic diarrhea may occur because of lactase deficiency after an acute diarrheal illness. Exacerbation of inflammatory bowel disease (IBD) or irritable bowel syndrome (IBS) may also occur after acute infectious diarrhea. Reactive arthritis can occur after *Shigella*, *Salmonella*, and *Campylobacter* infections. Guillain-Barré syndrome is associated with *Campylobacter* and *Yersinia* infections. Hemolytic uremic syndrome (hemolytic anemia, thrombocytopenia, acute kidney injury) can occur with Shiga toxin–producing *E. coli* or *Shigella* infection.

Chronic Diarrhea

A patient-centered approach to evaluation focuses on attributes that are most apparent to the patient, including duration of the diarrhea, severity of symptoms, and stool characteristics. Potential causes of chronic diarrhea are listed in Table 3.

Diagnosis

Ask the patient about stool frequency and characteristics, association of diarrhea with food, medications, previous surgery, and prior radiation treatment. Ask specifically about fecal incontinence because patients may not volunteer this symptom but instead report it as diarrhea; fecal incontinence is a common problem, especially in elderly patients. Diet history may reveal large quantities of indigestible carbohydrates (osmotic diarrhea) or intolerance to wheat products (celiac disease, Whipple disease). A patient's fixation on body image and weight loss may be a clue to laxative abuse. Frequent, high-volume, watery stools suggest a disease process affecting the small intestine. Whereas high-volume diarrhea that is exacerbated with eating and relieved with fasting or a clear liquid diet suggests carbohydrate malabsorption, persistent or nocturnal diarrhea suggests a secretory process. The presence of persistent, severe or aching abdominal pain suggests an invasive process associated with inflammation or destruction of the mucosa. Oral ulcers and arthritis could indicate IBD. Skin findings, when present, may provide significant diagnostic clues. For example, flushing may indicate carcinoid syndrome, dermatitis herpetiformis (grouped, pruritic, erythematous papulovesicles on the extensor surfaces of the arms, legs, central back, buttocks, and scalp) may occur in patients with celiac disease, and erythema nodosum (Plate 2) or pyoderma gangrenosum (Plate 3) may suggest underlying inflammatory bowel disease. Bloody diarrhea typically indicates an invasive process with loss of intestinal mucosal integrity. An oily residue or evidence of undigested food in the toilet bowl is more suggestive of malabsorption, which can be seen in pancreatic insufficiency or malignancy.

Consider IBS in patients with a long-standing history of abdominal pain, complaints of increased mucus in the stool, and abnormal bowel habits (constipation, diarrhea, or variable bowel movements) in the absence of other defined illnesses. The presence of weight loss, blood in the stool, or nocturnal diarrhea almost always indicates that the patient does not have IBS.

The number and variety of diagnostic tests available for patients with chronic diarrhea are extensive, and testing should be guided by information obtained from the history and physical examination. A complete blood count and chemistry panel can reveal anemia, leukocytosis, and electrolyte and nutritional status. Bacterial infections rarely cause chronic diarrhea in immunocompetent patients, but common infectious causes of acute diarrhea such as *Campylobacter* or *Salmonella* infection can cause persistent diarrhea in immunocompromised patients, as can *Cryptosporidium* infection. Infection should always be ruled out in patients with chronic diarrhea before proceeding with more extensive testing (Table 4).

A fecal fat study is usually indicated for evaluating a patient with noninvasive diarrhea. However, test results are valid only if the patient ingests an adequate amount of dietary fat (>100 g/d). Any cause of diarrhea may mildly elevate fecal fat values (6–10 g/24 h), but values in excess of 10 g/24 h almost always indicate primary fat malabsorption. False-positive test results can also occur in patients taking olestra, a weight loss drug that inhibits the absorption of fat; patients should be instructed to stop this medication if a fecal fat study is being performed.

The presence of fecal leukocytes or lactoferrin suggests an inflammatory process but rarely provides more specific clues about the cause of diarrhea. If infection is excluded in a patient with chronic inflammatory diarrhea, colonoscopy or flexible sigmoidoscopy with biopsies usually are required for diagnosis.

Measurement of stool electrolytes is valuable for only a subset of patients who remain a diagnostic challenge despite the exclusion of infectious, iatrogenic, and inflammatory causes of diarrhea. Stool electrolytes help differentiate osmotic from secretory diarrhea. If factitious diarrhea is suspected, a fresh liquid stool sample should be obtained for determination of total osmolarity and stool sodium and potassium concentrations, and the osmotic gap (290 mosm/kg – [2 × ([Na$^+$] + [K$^+$]) should be calculated. Whereas secretory diarrhea has an osmotic gap less than 50 mOsm/kg, the osmotic gap in osmotic diarrhea is often greater than 125 mOsm/kg.

Celiac disease (gluten-sensitive enteropathy) occurs in approximately one in 120 to one in 300 persons in the United States. Classic symptoms include steatorrhea and weight loss, but many patients have only mild or nonspecific symptoms that often result in an erroneous diagnosis of IBS. Serum anti–tissue transglutaminase antibodies are sensitive and specific for celiac disease; confirmation is by endoscopic small bowel biopsy showing intraepithelial lymphocytes, crypt hyperplasia, and partial to total villous atrophy. Celiac disease is associated with multiple extraintestinal manifestations as listed in Table 5.

Excessive bacterial colonization of the small bowel lumen may result in diarrhea and malabsorption. A clue to the presence of bacterial overgrowth is finding a low serum vitamin B_{12} level (bacteria

Table 2. Treatment Recommendations for *Clostridium difficile* Infection

Presentation	Severity	Antibiotic Regimen
Initial episode	Mild to moderate	Metronidazole, 500 mg PO every 8 hours for 10-14 days
Initial episode	Severe	Vancomycin, 125 mg PO every 6 hours for 10-14 days
Initial episode	Severe with multiorgan system failure or hypotension	Vancomycin, 500 mg PO or by nasogastric tube every 6 hours for 10-14 days plus metronidazole, 500 mg IV every 8 hours for 10-14 days
Initial episode	Severe with ileus or toxic megacolon	Same as for severe infection with multiorgan system failure with the addition of vancomycin by rectal tube
First recurrence		Treatment regimen based on severity, as in initial episode
Second recurrence		Vancomycin taper: vancomycin, 125 mg PO four times daily for 10-14 days, then 125 mg PO twice daily for 7 days, then 125 mg PO daily for 7 days, then 125 mg PO every 2-3 days for 2-8 weeks

IV = intravenous; PO = oral.

Data from http://www.idsociety.org/IDSA/Site_Map/Guidelines/Patient_Care/IDSA_Practice_Guidelines/Infections_by_Organ_System/Gastrointestinal_(GI)/Clostridium_difficile.aspx

Table 3. Causes of Noninfectious Diarrhea

Disorder	Clues or Risk Factors	Diagnosis
Medications	Acarbose, antibiotics, antineoplastic agents, magnesium-based antacids, metformin, misoprostol, NSAIDs, proton pump inhibitors, quinidine	Withhold suspected medications
Carbohydrate intolerance	Lactose or fructose intake, use of artificial sweeteners (sorbitol, mannitol), bloating, excess flatus	Dietary exclusion, hydrogen breath test, stool osmotic gap
Irritable bowel syndrome (diarrhea predominant)	No weight loss or alarm features	Chronic bloating, abdominal discomfort relieved by bowel movement
Inflammatory bowel disease (ulcerative colitis, Crohn disease)	Bloody diarrhea, tenesmus, weight loss, anemia, hypoalbuminemia	Colonoscopy with biopsy
Microscopic colitis	Chronic relapsing-remitting watery diarrhea	Normal colonoscopy, abnormal biopsy (includes collagenous colitis, lymphocytic colitis)
Celiac disease	Iron-deficiency anemia, dermatitis herpetiformis, family history	Antitissue transglutaminase antibodies, small bowel biopsy
Pancreatic insufficiency	Steatorrhea, chronic pancreatitis, pancreatic resection, weight loss	Tests for excess fecal fat, features of chronic pancreatitis on imaging (eg, pancreatic calcification on CT)
Enteral feedings	Osmotic diarrhea	Modify enteral feeding
Dumping syndrome	Postprandial flushing, tachycardia	History of gastrectomy or gastric bypass surgery
Small bowel bacterial overgrowth	Intestinal dysmotility (eg, systemic sclerosis), bloating, excess flatus, malabsorption	Duodenal aspirate for bacterial culture, response to empiric antibiotics, hydrogen breath testing
Bile acid malabsorption	Resection of <100 cm of terminal ileum	Empiric response to cholestyramine
Bile acid deficiency	Cholestasis, resection of >100 cm of terminal ileum	Tests for excess fecal fat, response to medium-chain triglyceride diet
Radiation exposure	History of radiation therapy (may begin years after exposure)	Bowel imaging, characteristic biopsy findings
Whipple disease	Arthralgia, neurologic or ophthalmologic symptoms, lymphadenopathy	Polymerase chain reaction for *Tropheryma whippelii*, small bowel biopsy
Common variable immune deficiency	Pulmonary disease, recurrent *Giardia* infection	Immunoglobulin assay
Factitious diarrhea	Psychiatric history, history of laxative abuse; diagnosis of exclusion	Low stool osmolality; stool magnesium >90 meq/L may be diagnostic

CT = computed tomography; NSAID = nonsteroidal antiinflammatory drug.

Table 4. Common Diagnostic Tests for Diarrhea

Test	Condition	Characteristics
Fecal leukocytes	Infectious or inflammatory diarrhea	Poor sensitivity and specificity (limited usefulness)
Stool culture	Infectious diarrhea	Used selectively because of low yield (<3%); detects *Salmonella*, *Shigella*, and *Campylobacter* spp.; specify if needed to test for *Escherichia coli* O157:H7 (if visible or occult blood)
Stool ova and parasites	Infectious diarrhea	Microscopic examination for *Giardia*, *Entamoeba*, *Cryptosporidium*, *Cyclospora*, and *Isospora* spp. and microsporidia if suspected
Stool enzyme immunoassays	Infectious diarrhea	Detect Shiga toxins 1 and 2 and antigens for *Giardia*, *Entamoeba*, *Campylobacter*, *Cryptosporidium* spp. if suspected
Qualitative fecal fat (Sudan stain)	Fat malabsorption	Sensitivity >90% for significant steatorrhea
Quantitative fecal fat (48- or 72-h collection)	Fat malabsorption	Values >10 g/24 h indicate fat malabsorption
Stool osmolarity	Factitious diarrhea	<250 mOsm/kg (250 mmol/kg) suggests factitious diarrhea
Stool electrolytes (sodium, potassium)	Differentiate osmotic from secretory diarrhea	Osmotic gap[a] >125 mOsm/kg (125 mmol/kg) suggests osmotic diarrhea; <50 mOsm/kg (50 mmol/kg) suggests secretory diarrhea
Stool magnesium	Magnesium-containing antacids, cathartics (factitious or iatrogenic diarrhea)	Spot magnesium sample >90 meq/L (37.1 mmol/L)
Stool pH	Carbohydrate malabsorption	pH <6.0 suggests carbohydrate malabsorption
Clostridium difficile toxin enzyme immunoassay	*C. difficile* infection	Should be performed if recent antibiotic use or hospitalization; sensitivity 70%–80% and specificity >97% for toxins A and B
Tissue transglutaminase antibody IgA	Celiac disease	Sensitivity (69%–93%), specificity (96%–100%); diagnosis confirmed by small bowel biopsy
Hydrogen breath test	Lactase deficiency	Lactose metabolized by bacterial flora in distal small intestine releases hydrogen, which is excreted by lungs
Duodenal aspirate	Small bowel bacterial overgrowth	Quantitative bacterial culture; responds to empiric antibiotic trial
Neuropeptide assays[b]	Neuroendocrine tumors	Useful if persistent diarrhea despite fasting

[a]Osmotic gap calculation (mOsm/kg (mmol/kg): 290 - [2 × (Na$^+$ + K$^+$)].

[b]Gastrin, vasoactive intestinal peptide, glucagon, somatostatin, pancreatic peptide, neurotensin, substance P, calcitonin, motilin, and urine 5-hydroxyindoleacetic acid.

bind vitamin B$_{12}$ and cleave it from intrinsic factor) and a high serum folate level (intestinal bacteria synthesize folate). Common conditions that predispose patients to bacterial overgrowth include diabetes, systemic sclerosis, and surgically created blind loops (ie, gastrojejunostomy). Although the gold standard is aspiration of duodenal luminal contents for quantitative culture at the time of upper endoscopy, many clinicians first attempt a trial of empiric antibiotics to assess if the patient's symptoms improve.

Therapy

Treatment of chronic diarrhea should be based on the underlying cause. Symptomatic therapy may be considered if a diagnosis is pending, if a diagnosis cannot be confirmed, or if the condition diagnosed does not have a specific treatment. Symptoms may be controlled with stool-modifying agents (eg, fiber, psyllium), opiate-based medications (loperamide), bile acid–binding agents (cholestyramine), and bismuth-containing medications.

Table 5. Extraintestinal Manifestations of Celiac Disease

Category	Examples
Hematologic	Anemia (low iron, vitamin B$_{12}$, folate), functional asplenia
Musculoskeletal	Osteopenia or osteoporosis, osteomalacia, arthropathy
Neurologic	Seizures, peripheral neuropathy, ataxia
Reproductive	Infertility, recurrent miscarriages
Skin	Dermatitis herpetiformis
Renal	Glomerular IgA deposition
Other	Enamel defects, abnormal liver chemistry tests, vitamin-deficient states

Bibliography

De Bruyn G. Diarrhea in adults (acute). Am Fam Physician. 2008;78:503-504. [PMID: 18756660]

Sandhu DK, Surawicz C. Update on chronic diarrhea: a run-through for the clinician. Curr Gastroenterol Rep. 2012;14:421-427. [PMID: 22903799]

Sellin JH. A practical approach to treating patients with chronic diarrhea. Rev Gastroenterol Disord. 2007;7 Suppl 3:S19-S26. [PMID: 18192962]

Chapter 26

Inflammatory Bowel Disease

Susan T. Hingle, MD

nflammatory bowel disease (IBD) is a group of inflammatory conditions of the colon and small intestine. Two distinct disorders account for the majority of IBD: ulcerative colitis and Crohn disease. Ulcerative colitis is characterized by diffuse mucosal inflammation that is limited to the colon and extends proximally and continuously from the anus. Crohn disease is characterized by focal, asymmetric, transmural lesions and by skip lesions rather than continuous disease. Rectal sparing is common in Crohn disease. As many as 10% of patients cannot be shown to have either Crohn disease or ulcerative colitis and are considered to have indeterminate colitis.

The pathophysiology of IBD appears to involve an imbalance between proinflammatory mediators (interleukin 1β, tumor necrosis factor, thromboxane A_2) and anti-inflammatory mediators (prostaglandin E_2, interleukin 10), resulting in an inflammatory response. Immunoregulatory cytokines also appear to be imbalanced in patients with IBD.

The cause and pathogenesis of IBD are unclear, although several epidemiologic associations and risk factors have been identified. There is no gender predilection for IBD; men and women are at similar risk. There is a bimodal age distribution for presentation, with the first and largest peak in the third decade of life and a second, smaller peak between age 50 and age 80 years. The incidence is highest in northern climates (Scandinavia, northern Europe, North America) and lowest in southern climates and underdeveloped regions (Asia, Africa, South America).

Both genetic and environmental factors appear to play a role in development of IBD. IBD is more common in those of Jewish descent. There also is a familial tendency for IBD. From 10% to 25% of patients with IBD have an affected first-degree relative, and twin studies show a higher concordance for identical twins than for fraternal twins. Numerous environmental factors also have been studied, including cigarette smoking, diet, oral contraceptives, nonsteroidal antiinflammatory drugs, and infections. It is likely that the interplay between genetics and environment is responsible for the development of IBD.

Diagnosis

Ulcerative colitis generally presents with bloody diarrhea associated with rectal urgency, discomfort, and cramping. Patients have profound tenesmus (feelings of urgency and incomplete evacuation), which is secondary to proctitis. Inflammation of the rectum can cause constipation to be a more prominent manifestation than diarrhea. Weight loss secondary to the inflammatory disease itself or to chronic diarrhea is common. Physical examination findings can range from mild lower abdominal tenderness to life-threatening nonobstructive colonic dilatation with systemic toxicity (toxic megacolon).

Crohn disease often presents with abdominal pain and large-volume diarrhea; whereas diarrhea is associated with both small and large bowel disease, hematochezia is almost always a sign of colonic disease. The transmural nature of Crohn disease results in three distinct types of lesions: inflammatory, fistulizing, and fibrostenotic. Inflamed tissue causes a secretory diarrhea and protein-losing enteropathy, as well as steatorrhea from fat malabsorption. Fistulae

Table 1. Extraintestinal Manifestations of Inflammatory Bowel Disease

Manifestation	Notes
Peripheral arthritis	Frequently classified as one of two types: type 1 affects large joints of arms and legs (elbows, wrists, knees, ankles); symptoms often acute and migratory; correlate with active bowel disease. Type 2 is symmetric, affects small joints, and is often chronic; unrelated to bowel disease activity.
Sacroiliitis	Pain and stiffness in lower spine and sacroiliac joints; may present before IBD symptoms.
Ankylosing spondylitis (see Chapter 104)	Rare complication; seen more in CD than UC.
Osteoporosis	More common in women with CD; related to IBD and therapy. Periodic screening important.
Erythema nodosum	Tender, red nodules over shins and ankles; more common in UC and women; related to IBD disease activity.
Pyoderma gangrenosum	Papules and pustules coalesce to form deep, chronic ulcers, often on shins and ankles; more common in UC; related to IBD disease activity.
Aphthous stomatitis	Small ulcers between gums and lower lip or along tongue; related to IBD disease activity.
Uveitis	Pain, blurry vision, photosensitivity, redness of eye. An ophthalmologic emergency.
Scleritis	Deep pain, redness of sclera. An ophthalmologic emergency.
Primary sclerosing cholangitis (see Chapter 21)	Severe inflammation and scarring of bile ducts; more common in UC and men, Jaundice, nausea, pruritus, weight loss. May be complicated by cholangiocarcinoma or colon cancer.

CD = Crohn disease; IBD = inflammatory bowel disease; UC = ulcerative colitis.

are abnormal connections between the bowel and adjacent organs. Fistulae around the anus (perianal fistulae) may drain fecal material, but those through the skin (enterocutaneous fistulae) may seep bowel contents. Feces may pass through fistulae to the vagina (rectovaginal fistulae), and fistulae to the bladder (enterovesical fistulae) may cause pneumaturia or recurrent urinary tract infections. Fistulae connecting to abscesses may drain pus. Patients with intestinal strictures present with signs of obstruction. Strictures may be secondary to severe inflammation or to fibrosis of the bowel and are relieved only by surgical resection.

Approximately 10% to 20% of patients with IBD have extraintestinal manifestations at some point in the course of disease. The musculoskeletal, dermatologic, ocular, and hepatobiliary systems may be involved (Table 1).

Approximately 75% of patients with ulcerative colitis but only 10% to 20% of patients with Crohn disease are positive for perinuclear antineutrophil cytoplasmic antibody (p-ANCA). Approximately 60% of patients with Crohn disease have anti–*Saccharomyces cerevisiae* antibody (ASCA) compared with 5% to 10% of patients with ulcerative colitis. Therefore, measuring serum p-ANCA and ASCA is reasonably reliable for the diagnosis of Crohn disease or ulcerative colitis. In patients with Crohn disease, an upper gastrointestinal barium study with small bowel follow-through is helpful in determining the extent of involvement and presence of strictures (demonstrating string signs) and fistulae. Colonic disease may be seen on barium enema. In patients with ulcerative colitis, abdominal radiography can be useful to diagnose toxic megacolon. Diagnosis of both ulcerative colitis and Crohn disease is made by colonoscopy and confirmed with biopsy. Table 2 lists essential differences between ulcerative colitis and Crohn disease. Table 3 summarizes the differential diagnosis of IBD.

Therapy

Medical therapy for IBD is based on the location and severity of disease. The goal of medical therapy is to achieve and maintain clinical remission. Induction therapy is a short course of therapy used to control active disease; induction usually requires higher or more frequent doses than are used after the disease is brought under control. Maintenance therapy is used long term to prevent relapse. Five classes of drugs are available to treat IBD: 5-aminosalicylates, antibiotics, glucocorticoids, immunomodulators, and biologic agents (Table 4).

Mild ulcerative colitis is treated with the 5-aminosalicylates. Moderate disease often requires steroids for induction therapy and immunomodulators (azathioprine, 5-mercaptopurine) for maintenance therapy. Severe ulcerative colitis requires intravenous (IV) glucocorticoids, immunomodulators, and biologic agents. Medically refractory ulcerative colitis can be treated surgically with colectomy, which is considered curative.

Patients with mild to moderate Crohn disease (no fever, weight loss, or abdominal pain) are treated with the 5-aminosalicyates, topical budesonide, or metronidazole. Patients with moderate to severe Crohn disease (fever, weight loss, dehydration, abdominal pain) receive oral glucocorticoids for induction therapy but require immunomodulators for maintenance therapy. Biologic agents also may be helpful. Patients with severe to fulminant (steroid-refractory) disease are treated with IV glucocorticoids and biologic agents. Cyclosporine also may be effective. Patients with fistulae respond well to infliximab and azathioprine.

There generally is no viable medical therapy for fibrostenotic stricturing disease that leads to bowel obstruction. Limited small bowel or ileocolic resection or bowel-sparing small bowel stricturoplasties are the only therapy. Recurrence of disease at the sites of previous surgery is common; therefore, surgery is not a preferred strategy for inflammatory Crohn disease. Metronidazole after surgery reduces the incidence of severe relapses, and 6-mercaptopurine is modestly effective for decreasing both endoscopic and clinical recurrences in patients with Crohn disease.

Follow-Up

Smoking should be avoided in all patients but particularly patients with Crohn disease. Patients with sclerosing cholangitis may benefit from therapy with ursodeoxycholic acid, which has been shown to reduce the risk of colon cancer in this setting. Colon cancer screening recommendations include colonoscopy every 1 to 2 years

Table 2. Differences Between Ulcerative Colitis and Crohn Disease

Characteristic	Ulcerative Colitis	Crohn Disease
Pathology		
Granulomas	No	Yes
Fissures or fistulae	No	Yes
Transmural inflammation	No	Yes
Continuous disease	Yes	No
Crypt abscesses	Yes	No
Clinical presentation	Diarrhea (prominent), hematochezia, weight loss, fever	Abdominal pain (prominent), diarrhea, inflammatory masses, fever, weight loss
Laboratory findings		
Anti-*Saccharomyces cerevisiae* antibody	10% of cases	60% of cases
Perinuclear antineutrophil cytoplasmic antibody	75% of cases	10% of cases
Smoking	Alleviates symptoms	Risk factor for disease
Colon cancer risk	High risk	High risk

beginning 8 years after diagnosis in patients with pancolitis and beginning 15 years after diagnosis in patients with left-sided disease only. Unlike sporadic colorectal cancer that develops primarily from colonic polyps, IBD-associated colon cancer can arise from flat dysplastic mucosa, which is not readily detectable from underlying inflammatory tissue; therefore, multiple random biopsies are per-

Table 3. Differential Diagnosis of Inflammatory Bowel Disease

Disease	Notes
Bacterial enteritis (see Chapter 25)	Acute-onset diarrhea with fever, chills, hematochezia, and/or pus in stool; positive stool culture (*Escherichia coli* or *Campylobacter*, *Shigella*, *Salmonella*, or *Yersinia* spp.)
Protozoan enteritis (see Chapter 25)	Acute diarrhea caused by *Entamoeba* or *Giardia* spp.; *Entamoeba* spp. may cause hepatic abscess and RUQ pain; history of travel or drinking untreated water; stool antigens detected by ELISA
Clostridium difficile infection (see Chapter 25)	Watery stool, lower abdominal cramping, fever, leukocytosis; recent antibiotic use, hospitalization, or stay in long term-care facility; *C. difficile* toxin in stool
Irritable bowel syndrome (see Chapter 16)	Altered bowel movements with pain; no nocturnal symptoms, fever, weight loss, or hematochezia; normal colonoscopy
Celiac disease	Abdominal pain, bloating, diarrhea; tissue transglutaminase antibody; avoidance of gluten-containing foods is curative
Microscopic colitis	Abdominal pain, bloating, chronic watery diarrhea; normal colonoscopy but abnormal biopsy with two subtypes (lymphocytic, collagenous); chronic NSAID use implicated in >50% of cases
Lactose intolerance (see Chapter 25)	Abdominal pain, bloating, diarrhea after lactose ingestion
Diverticulitis (see Chapter 16)	LLQ pain, fever, diarrhea; abdominal CT shows inflamed diverticula
Ischemic colitis (see Chapter 16)	Abdominal pain, diarrhea, hematochezia; elderly patients with vascular disease; imaging of mesenteric vessels confirms diagnosis
Infectious proctitis	Tenesmus, diarrhea, hematochezia; history of receptive anal intercourse; positive bacterial or viral cultures (*Neisseria*, *Chlamydia*, or *Treponema* spp.; HSV)

CT = computed tomography; ELISA = enzyme-linked immunosorbent assay; HSV = herpes simplex virus; LLQ = left lower quadrant; NSAID = nonsteroidal antiinflammatory drug; RUQ = right upper quadrant.

Table 4. Medical Therapy for Inflammatory Bowel Disease

Medication	Indication	Side Effects or Adverse Events
5-Aminosalicylates		
Sulfasalazine, olsalazine, balsalazide, mesalamine: oral, rectal	UC: induction or maintenance	Interstitial nephritis (rare)
	CD (mild) involving the colon: induction or maintenance	Diarrhea (olsalazine)
Antibiotics		
Metronidazole, ciprofloxacin	CD: perianal and colonic disease	Metronidazole: peripheral neuropathy, metallic taste, disulfiram (Antabuse) effect
		Ciprofloxacin: arthropathy, tendon injury, sun sensitivity
Glucocorticoids		
Oral, intravenous, rectal	UC or CD: induction; not maintenance	Acne, moon facies, truncal obesity, osteoporosis, osteonecrosis, diabetes mellitus, hypertension, cataracts, infection, adrenal insufficiency with rapid withdrawal
Budesonide	CD (ileal or right colon): induction	Minimal glucocorticoid effects
Immunomodulators		
Methotrexate	CD: induction or maintenance	Nausea, fatigue, hepatotoxicity, pneumonitis
Cyclosporine	UC: glucocorticoid refractory	Hypertension, nephro- and neurotoxicity
6-MP, azathioprine	UC or CD: glucocorticoid withdrawal, maintenance	Pancreatitis, fever, infection, leukopenia, hepatotoxicity, lymphoma
Biological Agents		
Anti-TNF-α (adalimumab, certolizumab pegol, infliximab)	UC or CD: induction or maintenance	Infusion or injection-site reaction, tuberculosis reactivation, demyelination, infection, heart failure, lymphoma
Natalizumab	CD: induction or maintenance for disease refractory to anti-TNF agents	Progressive multifocal leukoencephalopathy

ASA = aminosalicylate; CD = Crohn disease; MP = mercaptopurine; TNF = tumor necrosis factor; UC = ulcerative colitis.

formed. Patients with biopsies positive for dysplastic changes are encouraged to consider prophylactic colectomy.

Bibliography

Kornbluth A, Sachar DB; Practice Parameters Committee of the American College of Gastroenterology. Ulcerative colitis practice guidelines in adults: American College Of Gastroenterology, Practice Parameters Committee. Am J Gastroenterol. 2010;105:501-523; quiz 524 [published erratum appears in Am J Gastroenterol. 2010;105:500]. [PMID: 20068560]

Lichtenstein GR, Hanauer SB, Sandborn WJ; Practice Parameters Committee of American College of Gastroenterology. Management of Crohn's disease in adults. Am J Gastroenterol. 2009;104:465-483; quiz 464, 484. [PMID: 19174807]

Chapter 27

Approach to Gastrointestinal Bleeding

Gauri Agarwal, MD

Gastrointestinal (GI) bleeding refers to any bleeding in the lumen of the GI tract from the mouth to the anus and can range from microscopic levels to overt amounts of bleeding. Bleeding that originates proximal to the ligament of Treitz is referred to as upper gastrointestinal (UGI) bleeding. Lower gastrointestinal (LGI) bleeding refers to any bleeding distal to the ligament of Treitz, and there has been increasing use of the term "mid-GI bleeding" when a bleeding source is identified between the ligament of Treitz and the ileocecal valve.

Patients with acute GI bleeding typically present with melena (black, tarry, foul-smelling stools), hematochezia (bright red or maroon-colored stools), or hematemesis (vomiting blood or coffee ground–like material). Microscopic levels of bleeding (occult bleeding) may occur slowly over time and only be identified by fecal occult blood testing, the presence of iron-deficiency anemia, or symptoms caused by blood loss or anemia (fatigue, dyspnea, syncope, angina). Approximately 10% to 20% of patients with GI bleeding have "obscure" bleeding, defined as an unknown cause despite evaluation with esophagogastric duodenoscopy (EGD), colonoscopy, and radiographic small bowel imaging. Approximately half of these patients have recurrent or persistent bleeding and are further subclassified as obscure overt (passage of visible blood) or obscure occult (microscopic).

Common causes of UGI bleeding include peptic ulcer disease, esophageal varices, esophagitis, vascular abnormalities (eg, angiectasias, arteriovenous malformations, Dieulafoy lesions), Mallory-Weiss tears, and neoplasms. LGI bleeding can be caused by diverticuli, hemorrhoids, angiectasias, neoplasia, colitis, and other rarer causes. Management begins with assessment and stabilization of the patient's hemodynamic status, risk stratification, identifying and controlling the source of bleeding, and preventing a recurrence.

Differential Diagnosis

Upper Gastrointestinal Bleeding

UGI bleeding typically presents with melena or hematemesis. Peptic ulcer disease (secondary to *Helicobacter pylori* infection or nonsteroidal anti-inflammatory drugs [NSAIDs]) is the most common cause of acute UGI bleeding. *H. pylori* attaches to gastric epithelial cells and releases toxins that can cause mucosal injury and initiate an inflammatory response. NSAIDs block the enzyme cyclooxygenase and interfere with production of prostaglandins that play a central role in the defense and repair of gastric epithelium. The decreasing incidence of *H. pylori* infection, widespread use of proton pump inhibitors (PPIs), and increased awareness and implementation of ulcer prevention strategies in users of NSAIDs may have led to the overall decline in incidence of UGI bleeding in the Unites States. Esophageal or gastric varices are the second most common cause of acute UGI bleeding. Variceal bleeding often is brisk, can lead to hemodynamic instability, and carries a high mortality rate of 15% to

20%. Mucosal erosive disease (esophagitis and gastritis) is more likely to present as small-volume bleeding or occult blood loss. Erosive esophagitis usually is associated with symptoms of gastroesophageal reflux disease. Gastritis tends to develop in patients who use NSAIDs, have heavy alcohol intake, or are severely ill with other medical illnesses. Dieulafoy lesions are submucosal arteries that intermittently protrude through the mucosa and cause hemorrhage. Mallory-Weiss tears are mucosal lacerations near the gastroesophageal junction. A history of vomiting or retching followed by hematemesis suggests this diagnosis but is noted in only a minority of patients. Upper GI cancers (esophageal, gastric) may also result in UGI bleeding. Rarer causes include portal hypertensive gastropathy, gastric antral vascular ectasias (GAVE), Cameron lesions (see below), hemobilia, proximal Crohn disease, Zollinger-Ellison, Osler-Weber-Rendu disease, hemosuccus pancreaticus, and aortoenteric fistulas (seen in patients who have had recent aortic surgery).

Lower Gastrointestinal Bleeding

LGI bleeding typically presents with hematochezia or occult bleeding. The most common causes of acute, severe LGI bleeding are colonic diverticula, angiectasias (also known as angiodysplasia), colitis (eg, caused by inflammatory bowel disease, infection, ischemia, or radiation therapy), anorectal disease (hemorrhoids, anal fissures), and colonic neoplasia. Bleeding from a colonic diverticulum typically is acute and painless. Diverticulae are common with advancing age and tend to occur at the site of entry of the small arteries (vasa recta). These vessels may bleed at the base of the diverticular neck. Angiectasias are most common among elderly individuals and usually present as chronic or occult blood loss but can also cause acute painless, hemodynamically significant bleeding. Ischemic colitis is caused by a temporary interruption in mesenteric blood flow (more likely in the regions of the splenic flexure and rectosigmoid junction) and typically occurs in older individuals with significant cardiac and peripheral vascular disease. Patients present with abdominal pain followed by the passage of bloody stools. Acute small bowel (mesenteric) ischemia should be suspected in patients who have risk factors for embolism or thrombosis and who present with sudden-onset, severe abdominal pain that, in the early stage, is out of proportion to the physical examination findings. Although the stool is often positive for occult blood, brisk bleeding rarely is associated with early-stage acute small bowel ischemia. Infections, inflammatory bowel disease, and radiation colitis can also result in LGI bleeding. Hemorrhoids are the most common cause of minor LGI bleeding and are often associated with straining with bowel movements. Anal fissures typically present as intermittent, severe pain on defecation and, similar to hemorrhoids, may also cause a small amount of bright red blood on the toilet paper or in the toilet. Fissures and hemorrhoids can be diagnosed by direct rectal examination or by anoscopy. GI bleeding should not be attributed solely to hemorrhoids or fissures until other causes have been excluded. Colon cancer must always be considered in patients who are age >50 years or who have a recent change in bowel movements, constitutional symptoms, anemia, or a family or personal history of cancer or polyps. Bleeding from a colonic polyp or carcinoma usually is occult or small volume.

Immediate Assessment

The first step in the management of acute GI bleeding is hemodynamic stabilization. This begins with measuring routine vital signs. Resting tachycardia indicates a 15% to 30% blood loss, and hypotension indicates greater than 30% blood loss. Orthostatic changes in blood pressure and pulse indicate large-volume bleeding when routine vital signs are normal. Two large-caliber (18-gauge or larger) intravenous (IV) catheters should be inserted to allow volume replacement with normal saline and, if necessary, blood products. The goals of volume resuscitation are to restore normal intravascular volume and prevent complications from red blood cell loss, including myocardial infarction, heart failure, and stroke. There is no absolute hemoglobin value that determines when transfusions are appropriate. The decision to transfuse should incorporate an assessment of the patient's age and comorbidities, amount of ongoing blood loss, stability of vital signs, and adequacy of tissue perfusion. Endotracheal intubation may be necessary to prevent aspiration in patients who have ongoing UGI bleeding and altered level of consciousness.

While the hemodynamic status is being stabilized, a focused history and physical examination may suggest specific causes for the bleeding and can provide prognostic information (Table 1). Particular attention should be paid to:

- Nature, amount, and duration of the bleeding and whether it is ongoing and the character and frequency of stool output
- Presence or absence of abdominal pain and other symptoms, such as fever, diarrhea, retching before hematemesis, recent weight loss, constipation, or change in bowel habits
- Complications from bleeding, such as weakness, syncope, chest pain, dyspnea, or oliguria
- Medications and ingestions, such as the use of aspirin, NSAIDs, anticoagulants, and alcohol
- Conditions predisposing to bleeding, including known bleeding disorders, abdominal or pelvic radiation, and abdominal surgery
- Previous episodes of GI bleeding (eg, history of peptic ulcer disease or liver disease)
- Comorbid conditions that increase the risk of a poor outcome, such as diabetes and cardiopulmonary, kidney, or neurologic disease
- Stigmata of chronic liver disease, cardiopulmonary and abdominal examination, and digital rectal examination

Evaluation and Management

Initial studies include a complete blood count, blood type and crossmatch, partial thromboplastin time (PTT) and international normalized ratio (INR), serum electrolytes, blood urea nitrogen (BUN), creatinine, aminotransferase levels, and an electrocardiogram. Although

Table 1. Common Causes of Gastrointestinal Bleeding

Cause	Clues to Diagnosis
Upper Gastrointestinal Tract	
Gastric and duodenal ulcers	Dyspepsia, *Helicobacter pylori* infection, NSAID use, anticoagulation, severe medical illness
Variceal bleeding	Stigmata of chronic liver disease on examination and evidence of portal hypertension or risk factor for cirrhosis (heavy alcohol use, viral hepatitis)
Mallory-Weiss tear	Retching before hematemesis
Esophagitis	Heartburn, regurgitation, dysphagia; usually small-volume or occult bleeding
Gastritis or gastroduodenal erosions	NSAID use, heavy alcohol use, severe medical illness; usually small-volume or occult bleeding
Esophageal or gastric cancer	Progressive dysphagia, weight loss, early satiety, abdominal pain; usually small-volume or occult bleeding
Lower Gastrointestinal Tract	
Diverticula	Painless, self-limited hematochezia
Angiectasias or angiodysplasia	Chronic blood loss or acute painless hematochezia in elderly individual; frequently involves upper GI tract in addition to colon
Colonic polyp	Usually asymptomatic; stool may be positive for occult blood
Colon cancer	Age >50 y and usually asymptomatic; change in bowel pattern or microcytic anemia
Ischemic colitis	Risk factors for atherosclerosis and evidence of vascular disease in elderly individual; abdominal pain
Acute small bowel (mesenteric) ischemia	Severe abdominal pain out of proportion to physical findings; atherosclerotic or embolic risk factors; anion gap metabolic acidosis; bleeding a late finding
Hemorrhoids	Intermittent mild rectal bleeding associated with straining on bowel movement
Infectious colitis	Bloody diarrhea, fever, urgency, tenesmus; exposure history
Inflammatory bowel disease	History of condition and bloody diarrhea, tenesmus, abdominal pain, fever, extracolonic symptoms
Meckel diverticulum	Painless hematochezia in a young patient; normal EGD and colonoscopy

EGD = esophagogastric duodenoscopy; GI = gastrointestinal; NSAID = nonsteroidal antiinflammatory drug.

an isolated elevation of the BUN or elevated BUN-to-creatinine ratio suggests an UGI source of blood loss, neither finding reliably discriminates between UGI and LGI bleeding. In acute, severe bleeding, the initial hematocrit often is an unreliable indicator of the volume of blood loss; it may take 24 to 72 hours with adequate hydration before the hematocrit reveals the true reduction in oxygen-carrying capacity. Macrocytosis and an elevated INR may indicate underlying liver disease, and microcytosis may indicate chronic bleeding.

Clinical risk factors are used to assess the patient's risk for rebleeding and death. Risk assessment of patients is clinically useful to determine which patients are at higher risk of further bleeding or death and may inform management decisions such as the timing of endoscopy, time of discharge, and level of care (eg, general medical ward vs. intermediate care vs. intensive care). Presence of increased age, large-volume bleeding (as indicated by hemodynamic instability), significant comorbidities (diabetes, liver failure, heart failure, chronic kidney disease), and endoscopic characteristics determine risk of rebleeding. Several clinical scoring instruments are available to assess rebleeding risk. Early consultation with a gastroenterologist and a surgeon should be obtained for high-risk patients.

After hemodynamic stabilization, the next step is to distinguish UGI bleeding from LGI bleeding. Although melena and hematemesis generally are associated with UGI bleeding and hematochezia is more often a sign of LGI bleeding, these distinctions are not absolute. Melena indicates that blood has been present in the GI tract for at least 14 hours, but some patients with melena have bleeding distal to the ligament of Treitz, and 10% of patients with hematochezia may have UGI bleeding. Placement of a nasogastric (NG) tube had previously been standard protocol in such patients to rule out UGI bleeding. However, NG tubes are uncomfortable and can still miss up to 15% of actively bleeding lesions. If an upper GI source is considered in a patient with hematochezia, an EGD (upper endoscopy) would be the most appropriate procedure.

Most GI bleeding is self-limited. Emergent diagnostic studies usually are required only for patients with persistent, rapid bleeding or for those who are hemodynamically unstable. For most patients with UGI bleeding, EGD should be performed within the first 24 hours of admission. Prokinetic agents given before endoscopy have been proposed to improve visualization at endoscopy but have not been shown to improve clinical outcomes. In patients with peptic ulcer bleeding, PPI before endoscopy have been shown to decrease the likelihood of high-risk stigmata on subsequent endoscopy and to reduce the likelihood of requiring an intervention during endoscopy. Endoscopy identifies the bleeding source with considerable accuracy, provides important prognostic information, and allows for immediate treatment for many patients. Variceal or ulcer-related bleeding with specific features (ie, adherent clot, nonbleeding visible vessel, or active bleeding) has a higher risk for recurrent bleeding, need for surgery, and death. Endoscopic therapy reduces morbidity and mortality in these patients. Endoscopic therapy incorporates injection therapy (epinephrine, sclerosing agents), thermal techniques (probes, argon plasma coagulation), and mechanical modalities (clips). The type of lesion and the presence or absence of ongoing bleeding determine which technique is used.

In patients with a bleeding peptic ulcer, the use of IV PPI therapy has also been shown to reduce the risk of recurrent hemorrhage after endoscopic hemostasis. Histamine-2 blockers have not shown a similar effect. If bleeding persists despite endoscopic therapy, further options include endoscopic retreatment, angiographic embolization, and surgery. Surgery should be reserved for patients who have persistent bleeding that is unresponsive to medical and endoscopic therapy. In patients with variceal bleeding, prophylactic antibiotics are indicated to prevent spontaneous bacterial peritonitis. First-line therapies for varices are endoscopic band ligation or sclerotherapy and octreotide. When LGI bleeding is suspected, colonoscopy is recommended within the first 48 hours of admission. Colonoscopy may identify a bleeding diverticulum and permit endoscopic treatment with epinephrine, electrocautery, or both. It may also help identify other causes of bleeding, such as vascular angiectasis. Surgery is reserved for refractory bleeding. Ideally, when the site is known, a segmental resection can be done rather than a subtotal colectomy. In ischemic colitis, colonoscopy can reveal a well-defined segment of cyanotic or ulcerated mucosa. Computed tomography, which is increasingly used to make the diagnosis, may show segmental colitis. Most episodes of ischemic colitis resolve spontaneously with supportive care, such as IV fluids and pain control. In contrast, acute small bowel (mesenteric) ischemia is associated with a high mortality rate and requires an aggressive early approach to management, often involving angiography or laparotomy.

Ongoing rectal bleeding without an identifiable source despite upper endoscopy and colonoscopy can be evaluated with a technetium 99m pertechnetate-labeled red blood cell scan or angiography. Tagged red blood cell scanning is positive in 45% of patients with active bleeding and has an overall accuracy for localizing the bleeding of 78%. It can detect ongoing bleeding occurring at a rate of 0.1 to 0.5 mL/min. This is often the first radiologic test performed because it is much more sensitive than angiography in detecting bleeding, but it is not very specific with reference to localization. (For example, bleeding in a redundant sigmoid colon may appear as extravasated blood in the right lower quadrant, suggesting right colon bleeding.) Visualization of the bleeding site (usually a diverticulum or vascular angiectasis) by angiography necessitates a bleeding rate of at least 1 mL/min, but the advantage of angiography is the ability to provide selective embolization to control bleeding. Barium studies have low sensitivity, may interfere with subsequent testing, and should not be done in the setting of acute GI bleeding.

Patients age <40 years at low risk for colorectal cancer who present with small-volume, self-limited hematochezia may not require colonoscopy. If the bleeding consists of blood on toilet paper or a few drops of blood in the stool, a bleeding hemorrhoid is the most likely cause. Patients with pain on defecation may have an anal fissure. These patients often can forgo colonoscopy if a digital rectal examination and anoscopy confirm a benign anorectal process and there are no other concerning features, such as constitutional symptoms, anemia, change in bowel habits, or family history of colorectal polyps or cancer. Patients >50 years of age with small volume rectal bleeding should undergo colonoscopy even in the presence of identified anorectal disease.

Obscure Gastrointestinal Bleeding

Obscure gastrointestinal bleeding refers to recurrent or persistent bleeding from the GI tract without an obvious source on endoscopic studies. Many such patients have bleeding sources in the small intestine, now sometimes referred to as "mid-GI bleeding" (Table 2). Angiectasia is the most common cause of small bowel bleeding in the United States. Some causes, such as Dieulafoy lesions, produce brisk but intermittent bleeding, which makes it difficult to identify on EGD. Cameron lesions are erosions found in gastric folds within a large hiatal hernia and are thought to be caused by mechanical trauma as the hiatal hernia slides up and down. Cameron lesions are relatively common and often are incidental findings on upper endoscopy, but they may present as acute or chronic GI bleeding.

Table 2. Causes of Obscure Gastrointestinal Bleeding

Location	Differential Diagnosis	Age (y)	Clinical Clues
Proximal to the ligament of Treitz	Cameron erosion	20-60	Large hiatal hernia
	NSAID ulcerations	>20	Medication review
	Dieulafoy lesion	>40	Intermittent large-volume bleeding
	Crohn disease	20-60	Family history, extraintestinal manifestations; may also occur in small bowel and colon
	Gastric antral vascular ectasia	20-60	Female, autoimmune disease
Small bowel	Angiectasias	>60	Intermittent, usually occult bleeding; may also occur in colon
	Peutz-Jeghers syndrome	<20	Perioral pigmentation, obstructive symptoms
	Meckel diverticulum	20-60	Possible abdominal pain
	Hemangioma	<20	Possible cutaneous hemangiomas
	Malignancy	>50	Weight loss, abdominal pain
	Hereditary hemorrhagic telangiectasia	>50	Facial telangiectasias
Colon	Diverticulosis	>50	Intermittent, painless bleeding
	Malignancy	>50	Weight loss, family history of colorectal cancer

NSAID = nonsteroidal anti-inflammatory drug.

GAVE (commonly referred to as a "watermelon stomach" because of the characteristic striped appearance of the gastric vascular malformations on endoscopy) is an uncommon cause of UGI bleeding. Meckel diverticulum is a congenital anomaly that is located near the ileocecal valve. It often contains heterotopic gastric mucosa that can ulcerate and intermittently bleed. Technetium 99m pertechnetate has an affinity for gastric mucosa, and the Meckel scan identifies the heterotopic mucosa. Meckel diverticulum tends to cause bleeding in children and should be considered in younger patients presenting with GI bleeding of obscure origin. Small bowel tumors (eg, GI stromal cell tumor, lymphoma, carcinoid, adenocarcinoma, or polyp) should also be considered in the differential diagnosis.

The evaluation of GI bleeding of obscure origin usually begins with repeat endoscopy directed at the most likely site. If repeat endoscopy is unrevealing in a patient who is not actively bleeding, examination should focus on the small intestine using such tests as enteroscopy or capsule endoscopy.

Bibliography

Barkun AN, Bardou M, Kuipers EJ, et al; International Consensus Upper Gastrointestinal Bleeding Conference Group. International consensus recommendations on the management of patients with nonvariceal upper gastrointestinal bleeding. Ann Intern Med. 2010;152:101-113. [PMID: 20083829]

Kerlin MP, Tokar JL. Acute gastrointestinal bleeding. Ann Intern Med. 2013;159:793-794. [PMID: 24297203]

Section 4
General Internal Medicine

Associate Editors – Susan T. Hingle, MD, FACP and Robert Trowbridge, MD, FACP

High Value Care Recommendations

- An evidence-based estimate of the pretest probability of disease can guide clinicians on the utility of further testing because a very low or very high pretest probability may not change significantly regardless of a test's result.

- The goal of screening is to prevent or delay the development of disease by early detection; early detection may result in diagnosis at a more treatable stage or before the disease has caused complications.

- Screening electrocardiograms are not recommended because abnormalities of the resting electrocardiogram are rare, are not specific for coronary artery disease, and do not predict subsequent mortality from coronary disease.

- Although echocardiography is more sensitive in diagnosing ventricular hypertrophy, it is not routinely recommended in all patients with a new diagnosis of hypertension.

- Combined therapy with an angiotensin converting-enzyme inhibitor (ACEI) and angiotensin-receptor blocker (ARB) for treatment of hypertension is associated with increased adverse effects and no improvement in outcome and is not recommended.

- Evaluation for secondary hypertension is indicated only when the clinical situation is suggestive or a patient is adherent to a four-drug regimen without adequate control.

- Because statins can cause aminotransferase elevations, and fatal acute hepatic failure has occurred rarely in patients taking statins, aminotransferase levels should be obtained before starting statin therapy but do not need to be monitored during therapy.

- Imaging for acute nonspecific musculoskeletal pain is not recommended because there is poor correlation between a patient's symptoms and imaging findings.

- In patients with low back pain caused by suspected disc herniation or spinal stenosis, magnetic resonance imaging (MRI) is recommended only if the patient is a potential candidate for surgery and usually only after a trial of medication therapy.

- Electromyography and nerve conduction velocity tests and additional diagnostic studies are rarely indicated in the initial evaluation of low back pain.

- Most cases of acute low back pain (<4 weeks in duration) are self-limited; up to 90% of cases of acute low back pain should resolve with conservative treatment by 4 to 6 weeks.

- First-line medication therapy is analgesia with acetaminophen or nonsteroidal anti-inflammatory drugs (NSAIDs).

- Muscle relaxants and opioid analgesics have not been shown to be more effective than NSAIDs for treatment of low back pain, and both may have central nervous system side effects and addiction potential.

- Antiviral therapy for influenza is indicated only for hospitalized patients and those with severe, complicated, or progressive illness.

- There is little evidence to support the use of most over-the-counter and prescription antitussive medications for treatment of cough, with the effectiveness of most agents being similar to placebo.

- The history and physical examination identify a cause of syncope in 45% of cases.

- Patients with a history suggestive of neurocardiogenic syncope who are deemed at low risk may require no further evaluation.

- As many as two-thirds of patients with lymphadenopathy have an obvious self-limited cause, such as a recent upper respiratory tract infection, that does not require further evaluation.

- Because of the many potential causes of lymphadenopathy, the clinician must rely heavily on the patient's history and physical examination to focus the subsequent laboratory or imaging evaluation on the most likely diagnoses.

- Before pursuing additional testing in patients with unexplained weight loss, review prior medical studies such as age-appropriate cancer screening to help identify areas that may need further investigation.

- Cellulitis is a clinical diagnosis; cultures usually are not necessary, and results are seldom positive.

- Folliculitis often resolves spontaneously; therefore, systemic antibiotics should not be used routinely.

- Incision and drainage may be adequate therapy for skin abscesses, and systemic antibiotics are not routinely required.

- Attempted elimination of methicillin-resistant Staphylococcus aureus (MRSA) nasal carriage (decolonization) using intranasal mupirocin or from body surfaces using topical antiseptic cleansers is not recommended as a routine part of managing MRSA infections, although it may have a role in outbreaks, patients in intensive care units, and selected patients with recurrent S. aureus infections.

- Combination antifungal and glucocorticoid products should be avoided in treating fungal skin infections.

- Systemic glucocorticoids have not been shown to reduce the incidence of postherpetic neuralgia.

- In most cases, the history and physical examination are sufficient to diagnose acne.

Chapter 28

Diagnostic Decision Making

D. Michael Elnicki, MD

One of the most interesting and exciting aspects of medicine is the search for a diagnosis to explain a patient's symptoms. The clinician starts with a medical history and physical examination and uses the findings to order diagnostic tests to confirm clinical suspicions. The goal of diagnostic testing is to obtain additional information that helps refine the clinician's assessment that a specific condition is the cause of the patient's findings (the pretest probability of disease); each diagnostic intervention should help in either increasing or decreasing the likelihood that the disease is present until a threshold (a posttest probability of disease) is reached at which there is comfort in further evaluating or treating the patient for that condition or concluding that the disease is absent.

When considering using diagnostic tests in an evidence-based fashion, the clinician needs to ask a series of questions:

- Is there valid evidence that the test is accurate?
- Does the test accurately distinguish between patients with the disease in question and those without the disease?
- Does the test apply to this patient?

Table 1. Common Terms Used in the Interpretation of the Medical Literature for Diagnostic Tests

Term	Definition	Calculation	Notes
Prevalence (Prev)	Proportion of patients with disease in the population	$Prev = (TP + FN)/(TP + FP + FN + TN)$	
Sensitivity (Sn)	Proportion of patients with disease who have a positive test result	$Sn = TP/(TP + FN)$	
Specificity (Sp)	Proportion of patients without disease who have a negative test result	$Sp = TN/(FP + TN)$	
Positive predictive value (PPV)	Proportion of patients with a positive test result who have disease	$PPV = TP/(TP + FP)$	Increases with *increasing* prevalence
Negative predictive value (NPV)	Proportion of patients with a negative test result who do not have disease	$NPV = TN/(TN + FN)$	Increases with *decreasing* prevalence
Positive likelihood ratio (LR[+])	The likelihood that a positive test result would be expected in a patient with the disease compared with the likelihood that a positive test result would be expected in a patient without a disease	$LR(+) = Sn/(1 - Sp)$	LR(+) is used if result of test is positive
Negative likelihood ratio (LR[−])	The likelihood that a negative test result would be expected in a patient with the disease compared with the likelihood that a negative test result would be expected in a patient without a disease	$LR(−) = (1 - Sn)/Sp$	LR(−) is used if result of test is negative
Pretest odds	The odds that a patient has the disease before a test is performed	Pretest odds = Pretest probability/(1 − Pretest probability)	
Posttest odds	The odds that a patient has the disease after a test is performed	Posttest odds = Pretest odds × LR	
Pretest probability	Proportion of patients with the disease before a test is performed	Pretest probability can be estimated from population prevalence, clinical risk calculators, or clinical experience if no evidence-based tools exist	
Posttest probability	Proportion of patients with the disease after a test is performed	Posttest probability = Posttest odds/(1 + Posttest odds)	

FN = false negative; FP = false positive; TN = true negative; TP = true positive.

Evaluating Diagnostic Tests

For the evidence supporting the use of a new diagnostic test to be valid, the assessment of the test should follow certain steps. First, the study subjects should be recruited in a systematic fashion from a population that is appropriate for the disease being studied. All subjects should receive the reference ("gold standard") test. The gold standard test is not necessarily perfect but represents the current practice standard. The results of the new test are compared with the gold standard. Importantly, the results of the two tests (the gold standard and the new test) are assessed independently to avoid bias in their decisions about interpretations of the different studies. It is from this evaluation that the characteristics of diagnostic tests are derived.

Test Characteristics

Quantifiable terms are used to describe the accuracy of tests as shown in Table 1, with several of these measures based on a comparison of the test result with the gold standard study (Figure 1). *Sensitivity* and *specificity* describe the ability of a test, when compared with the gold standard, to detect or exclude a disease. Sensitivity is the proportion of patients with the disease who have a positive test result; specificity is the proportion of patients without the disease who have a negative test result. As illustrated in Figure 1, these proportions can be expressed as:

$$\text{Sensitivity} = a/(a + c)$$

$$\text{Specificity} = d/(b + d)$$

It is important to understand that sensitivity and specificity are characteristics of the test itself and do not change as the prevalence of the disease in the patient population being evaluated changes.

Because a highly sensitive test should detect most cases of a disease if it is truly present, it is very useful in excluding a disease when test results are negative. The mnemonic SNOUT is used to refer to this concept (ie, a SeNsitive test, when negative, rules OUT disease). Conversely, because a highly specific test is almost always positive if the disease is truly present, it is very useful in establishing the presence of a disease when test results are positive. The mnemonic SPIN refers to this concept (ie, a SPecific test, when positive, rules IN disease).

As with anything that is measured, sensitivity and specificity cannot be determined absolutely, so some uncertainty remains. For this reason, the precision of sensitivity and specificity often is expressed in terms of 95% confidence intervals (CIs). A way to conceptualize 95% CI is that if an experiment were performed 100 times, 95 times out of 100 the measured outcome value would fall within these parameters. For example, if a nuclear medicine scan has a sensitivity of 84% (95% CI, 76%–92%) for the diagnosis of a disease, a clinician can be 95% confident that the actual sensitivity of the scan is between 76% and 92%.

Compared with sensitivity and specificity, predictive values result from the application of a test of known sensitivity and specificity to a specific patient population. *Positive predictive value* refers to the proportion of patients who have a positive test result who actually have the disease. *Negative predictive value* refers to the proportion of patients with a negative test result who truly do not have the disease. As illustrated in Figure 1, these proportions can be expressed as:

$$\text{Positive predictive value} = a/(a + b)$$

$$\text{Negative predictive value} = d/(c + d)$$

Unlike sensitivity and specificity, predictive values are highly dependent on the prevalence of the disease in the population being tested; for a specific prevalence of disease, positive and negative predictive values are the same as posttest probability.

DISEASE

		Positive	Negative
TEST	Positive	a	b
	Negative	c	d

Sensitivity = a/(a + c)
Specificity = d/(b + d)
Positive predictive value = a/(a + b)
Negative predictive value = d/(c + d)

Figure 1. Test characteristics.

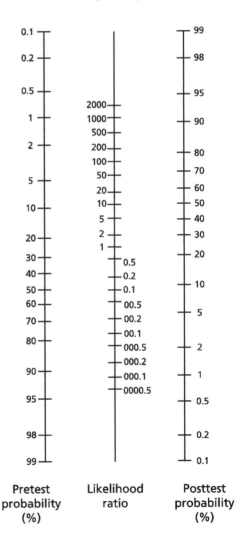

Pretest probability (%) — Likelihood ratio — Posttest probability (%)

Figure 2. Nomogram for using likelihood ratios.

Likelihood ratios are another useful tool in diagnostic testing. A likelihood ratio (LR) is a statistical indicator of how much the result of a diagnostic test will increase or decrease the pretest probability of a disease in a specific patient. LRs may be determined from the sensitivity and specificity of a diagnostic test. Separate LRs are calculated for use when a test result is positive (LR(+)) or when the test result is negative (LR(–)):

$$LR(+) = Sensitivity/(1 - Specificity)$$

$$LR(–) = (1- Sensitivity)/Specificity$$

The use of LRs may be seen graphically in Figure 2 and as an available online calculator (www.cebm.net/catmaker-ebm-calculators/). The pretest probability of disease is located on the left axis, the LR for the test is on the center axis, and the posttest probability of disease is on the right axis. To use a LR, the estimated pretest probability of a disease is anchored on the left column, with the positive or negative LR (depending on the test result) being indicated on the center axis; the posttest probability of disease is determined by connecting a line from the pretest probability of disease through the LR to the posttest probability of disease on the right axis.

As can be seen, LRs between 0.5 and 1 and between 1 and 2 do not change probability significantly. For ease of clinical use, several general LR rules apply. LR(+) values of 2, 5, and 10 correspond to an increase in disease probability by 15%, 30%, and 45%, respectively; LR(–) values of 0.5, 0.2, and 0.1 correspond to a decrease in disease probability by 15%, 30%, and 45%, respectively. Larger positive LRs and smaller negative LRs are more apt to affect clinical decisions.

Many test outcomes are continuous variables that clinicians arbitrarily divide into normal and abnormal values; the level at which abnormal is defined is termed the cutpoint. Some common examples of continuous variables are troponin and prostate-specific antigen (PSA) levels. It is important to realize that the process of deciding the cutpoint indicating the presence or absence of disease has significant implications. Decreasing the cutpoint to indicate an abnormal test result will help to detect more cases of the disease and decrease false-negative test results (by making the test more sensitive) but at the cost of increasing the number of false-positive test results (by decreasing the specificity). Conversely, increasing the cutpoint to indicate an abnormal result decreases the number of false-positive test results (by decreasing the sensitivity) but at the price of increasing false-negative results (by increasing the specificity). The relationship between sensitivity and specificity may be shown graphically by the receiver operator characteristic (ROC) curve as shown in Figure 3. It demonstrates how increasing sensitivity (moving up the

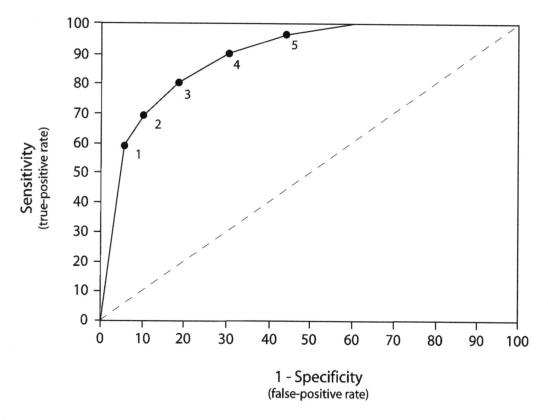

Cutpoint	Sensitivity	Specificity
1	60	95
2	70	90
3	80	80
4	90	70
5	95	60

Figure 3. Receiver operator characteristic curve.

y axis) can decrease specificity (moving across the x axis). In the example shown, changing the cutpoint for abnormal from 4 to 2 increases the specificity from 70% to 90% but decreases the sensitivity from 90% to 70%. The usual goal is to find a cutpoint that maximizes both sensitivity and specificity; in this case, a cutpoint of 3 is best with both a sensitivity and specificity of 80%.

This concept is particularly valuable when comparing two tests. The test with the greatest overall accuracy will have the largest area under the ROC curve. A perfect test (100% sensitive and 100% specific) would have an area of 1.0, so a good test might have an area of 0.9, and one that is less good would have an area of 0.8.

Applying Results to Patients

The first step in diagnosis is to estimate the pretest probability that a patient has a condition or disease. The pretest probability of disease is based on demographic variables and history and physical examination findings in addition to knowledge of the prevalence of disease in the population applicable to the patient. When screening large asymptomatic populations, the prevalence of disease often is used as the pretest probability. For many symptomatic conditions, pretest probabilities in varying populations have been calculated and published. For example, a 50-year-old man with atypical angina has a pretest probability of coronary artery disease (CAD) that is >60%, but a 30-year-old woman with the same chest pain has a <15% chance of having CAD.

The sensitivity and specificity of history and physical examination findings have been studied and published and can assist clinicians in estimating the likelihood of conditions. Constellations of findings can also be grouped to give an overall estimate of pretest probability that is more precise than any single element of the history or physical examination; these groups of findings are referred to as clinical prediction tools (see Chapter 56, Table 2 for an example of a clinical prediction tool used in the diagnosis of pharyngitis). **An evidence-based estimate of the pretest probability of disease can guide clinicians on the utility of further testing because a very low or very high pretest probability may not change significantly regardless of a test's result.**

Ultimately, a clinician needs to apply clinical judgment when applying test results to patient care decisions. The degree of certainty needed for deciding whether a condition is present or not will often vary based on consequences of the disease and the risks of treatment. A clinician may be comfortable with a degree of uncertainty when the risk of significant morbidity or mortality is low. For example, one might withhold antibiotics for pharyngitis with a 10% risk of streptococcal infection because the risk of serious complications is <1%. Conversely, a disease with significant risk of death, such as pulmonary embolism, might prompt further testing.

To illustrate the use of diagnostic testing data on clinical decision making, consider two 55-year-old men with chest pain. The first has typical angina, and the second has non-anginal chest pain. After considering their cardiac risk factors and normal electrocardiographic findings, you assess that the pretest probability of significant CAD to be 65% and 20% in these patients, respectively. The test characteristics for an exercise stress test include a sensitivity of 68% and specificity of 77%. These yield likelihood ratios of:

$$LR(+) = .68/(1 - (.77)) = 3.0$$

$$LR(-) = (1 - (.68))/.77 = 0.42$$

For the first patient, you recommend that he undergo cardiac catheterization to further investigate his chest pain. The reason you do not recommend a cardiac stress test is that his calculated posttest probability after a negative stress test result (using LR[−] data) would still be 43%. You would be uncomfortable with that level of uncertainty and would recommend a catheterization anyway. Because the patient would undergo catheterization for a positive test result as well, the stress test is not necessary for clinical decision making. However, for the second patient, you recommend having the stress test. This is because his estimated negative posttest probability (using LR[−] data) is 10%. At that level, you may be comfortable that the patient's pain is unlikely to be cardiac in origin and would recommend observation. If he had a positive stress test result (using LR[+] data), his posttest probability of ischemic heart disease as a cause of his chest pain would be 45%, and at that level you would likely proceed with additional testing for evaluation of possible CAD.

In many cases, sequential testing is used in the diagnostic process. If two tests are independent, the posttest probability after the first test can become the pretest probability for the second. This is the premise behind the Bayes theorem, which quantifies successive probabilities as testing unfolds and allows a precise estimate of certainty before treatment is started or a diagnosis is excluded. A strategy often used for sequential testing is the initial use of a noninvasive, sensitive test followed by a more specific (and often more invasive) confirmatory test if the first test result is positive (eg, PSA measurement followed by prostate biopsy).

As medical technology continues to advance at a rapid rate, clinicians will increasingly be confronted with new diagnostic tests. Various factors including cost, availability, and risks will compete in the clinical decision-making process. However, having a solid working knowledge of evidence-based clinical practices will enable clinicians to more easily assess new tests and appropriately apply them to patient care.

Bibliography

Akobeng AK. Understanding diagnostic tests 1: sensitivity, specificity and predictive values. Acta Paediatr. 2007;96:338-341. [PMID: 17407452]

Akobeng AK. Understanding diagnostic tests 2: likelihood ratios, pre- and post-test probabilities and their use in clinical practice. Acta Paediatr. 2007;96:487-491. [PMID: 17306009]

Akobeng AK. Understanding diagnostic tests 3: receiver operating characteristic curves. Acta Paediatr. 2007;96:644-647. [PMID: 17376185]

Gajulapalli RD, Aneja A, Rovner A. Cardiac stress testing for the diagnosis and management of coronary artery disease: a reference for the primary care physician. South Med J. 2012;105:93-99. [PMID: 22267098]

Chapter 29

Therapeutic Decision Making

Brian Heist, MD
D. Michael Elnicki, MD

After a diagnosis is made, the next step often includes determining appropriate treatment. Similar to the preceding chapter on diagnostic test interpretation (see Chapter 28), therapeutic decision making benefits from an evidence-based approach by systematically asking several questions:

- What is the evidence that a treatment is effective?
- Does the efficacy outweigh side effects?
- Is the research evaluating the treatment applicable to my patient?
- Am I practicing high value care?

Assessing Benefits and Risks

Study designs to evaluate therapies fall into two general categories, experimental and observational. Table 1 lists these designs, in decreasing order, in their ability to provide the strongest evidence of the effectiveness of a treatment. Recently developed therapies are commonly evaluated using the most rigorous method, a double-blinded randomized controlled trial (RCT). This method involves dividing the study patients randomly into groups and then administering a different treatment to each. One group serves as the control and generally receives a placebo or the current standard of care.

Table 1. Types of Study Designs

Study Design	Description	Strengths	Weaknesses	Key Threats to Validity
Experimental Studies				
Randomized controlled trial (RCT)	Patients receive one of two interventions, often one being a placebo	Strongest design for determining causation	Expensive, time consuming, not practical for many clinical situations Limited follow-up duration Limited number of outcomes that can be assessed Limited generalizability	If randomization is ineffective If data are not analyzed according to initially assigned group If key individuals are aware of group assignment (not blinded) If follow-up is incomplete
Cluster-randomized trial	Patients grouped by clusters (eg, nursing unit) rather than assigned randomly	Same as for RCTs Can be used if randomization of patients is not ethical or feasible	Same as for RCTs Challenging to analyze	Same as for RCTs If analysis does not account for clustering
Quasi-experimental design	Review of data collected before and after an intervention	Can be used if randomization of patients is not ethical or feasible	Patients not randomized	If no adjustment for possible confounding
Observational Studies				
Cohort study	Studies outcomes of groups using observed assignment	Able to detect associations, but these are not always cause-and-effect relationships Able to study multiple outcomes over a long period of time Large sample size	Requires complicated statistical techniques to minimize confounding Prospective designs can be expensive and take many years before results are available	Selection bias in cohort Bias in measurement of exposures and outcomes If important confounders not accounted for
Case-control study	Compares past exposures in patients with and without disease	Useful for rare diseases or exposuresInexpensive	High risk for bias High risk for confounding Cannot assess incidence or prevalence	Selection bias, especially in control participants Measurement bias, especially recall bias

Importantly, "double blinded" means that neither the patient nor the researcher knows who received which treatment. Adherence to these principles helps ensure a low risk of bias. Another way to express this would be to say the study has high *internal validity*, or high support for the study's conclusions.

Efficacy is the effect of the treatment within the trial and may differ from *effectiveness*, the effect of the treatment in clinical practice. Efficacy is determined by comparing the occurrence of important clinical outcomes in each study group. Common important differences between a clinical trial and clinical practice include the organization of clinical care; rigor of follow-up; and the application of *intention-to-treat* analysis, whereby trial dropouts are assumed to have failed therapy.

Consider the 55-year-old man with a high pretest probability of chest pain described in the preceding chapter (see Chapter 28). Cardiac catheterization reveals a significant stenosis in a single artery. This is consistent with his symptoms, and a drug-eluting stent is placed to open this artery. To help prevent stent occlusion, a common complication after stent placement, antiplatelet medication must be prescribed. Although clopidogrel has been historically used, a new, alternative antiplatelet medication is now available. A double-blinded RCT is available comparing this new medication with clopidogrel for preventing stent thrombosis in patients with acute coronary syndrome. This trial showed that 1 year from commencing treatment, 2.1% of patients receiving the new medication experienced stent thrombosis compared with 2.7% of patients prescribed clopidogrel. Additionally, 11.6% of the patients taking the new medication experienced significant bleeding during treatment compared with 11.2% of those taking clopidogrel. Specific statistical measures can help translate the results of this study into helpful form for clinical decision making.

Absolute and Relative Measures of Treatment Effect

Several measures of efficacy are commonly reported in experimental studies: *absolute risk*, *relative risk*, and *numbers needed*. Table 2 describes these measures and how they are calculated.

Measures of absolute risk refer to the simple difference in outcome rate of the intervention being studied (experimental event rate [EER]) in the treatment group compared with the group receiving either the control treatment or placebo (control event rate [CER]). Whether the absolute risk is reduced or increased depends on whether the EER is lower than or greater than the CER; if lower, it is termed absolute risk reduction (ARR), and if higher, absolute risk increase (ARI).

Measures of relative risk refer to the ratio of absolute risk to the rate of outcome occurrence in the control group; as with absolute measures, whether the relative risk is reduced or increased depends on whether the EER is lower than or greater than the CER; if lower, it is termed relative risk reduction (RRR), and if higher, relative risk increase (RRI).

Numbers needed are the number of patients who must receive the intervention being studied to cause one patient to experience the outcome being studied; if beneficial, it is termed the number needed to treat (NNT), and if detrimental, the number needed to harm (NNH).

Table 2. Common Terms Used in the Interpretation of the Medical Literature for Therapeutics

Term	Definition	Calculation	Notes
Absolute risk (AR)	The probability of an event occurring in a group during a specified time period	AR = Patients with event in group/Total patients in group	Also known as *event rate*; can be for benefits or harms. Often, an experimental event rate (EER) is compared with a control event rate (CER)
Relative risk (RR)	The ratio of the probability of developing a disease with a risk factor present (experimental event rate [EER]) to the probability of developing the disease without the risk factor present (control event rate [CER])	RR = EER/CER	Used in cohort studies and randomized controlled trials Any two ARs can be substituted for EER and CER
Absolute risk reduction (ARR) or absolute risk increase (ARI)	The difference in rates of events between the experimental group (EER) and control group (CER)	ARR or ARI = (EER − CER)	Any two ARs can be substituted for EER and CER
Relative risk reduction (RRR) or relative risk increase (RRI)	The ratio of ARR to the event rate among control participants	RRR or ARI = (EER − CER)/CER	Any two ARs can be substituted for EER and CER
Number needed to treat (NNT)	Number of patients needed to receive a treatment for one additional patient to benefit	NNT = 1/ARR	A good estimate of the effect size
Number needed to harm (NNH)	Number of patients needed to receive a treatment for one additional patient to be harmed	NNH = 1/ARI	ARI = absolute risk increase and equals (EER − CER) when the event is an unfavorable outcome (eg, drug side effect)
Odds ratio (OR)	Compares the odds (the ratio of the probability that the event will happen with the probability that the event will not happen) between study groups	OR = Odds of event in study group/Odds of event in control group	May be used with studies using nominal data; when the occurrence of the study condition is small, the OR will approximate RR Required for case-control and cross-sectional studies

In this study these measures can be used to compare the relative effectiveness of the new medication (EER = 2.1%) with clopidogrel (CER = 2.7%) in preventing stent thrombosis:

$$ARR = CER - EER$$

$$ARR = 2.7\% - 2.1\% = 0.6\%$$

$$RRR = (CER - EER)/CER$$

$$RRR = (2.7\% - 2.1\%)/2.7\% = 22.2\%$$

$$NNT = 1/ARR$$

$$NNT = 1/0.6\% = 167$$

It is important to note that whereas the ARR and NNT are absolute measures, the RRR is a relative measure of treatment effect. Because of this, the RRR will commonly be much greater than the ARR (particularly when the CER is low), seemingly indicating a more robust treatment effect than reflected in the absolute measures. For example, based on this trial's results, the new medication appears to reduce stent thrombosis by greater than 20%, although the absolute risk reduction is only 0.6%.

Using numbers needed is a convenient way of understanding the actual treatment effect that might be expected in practice. In this case, the NNT with the new medication compared with clopidogrel to prevent one additional stent thrombosis is 167, which means that 167 patients would need to be treated with the new medication to prevent an additional episode of stent thrombosis compared with those taking clopidogrel.

Numbers needed are also very helpful when balancing potential benefits and harms. For example, bleeding is a common side effect of antiplatelet therapy, and the risk of bleeding with the new medication compared with clopidogrel can also be assessed by calculating the NNH. In the study, major bleeding occurred in 11.6% of patients taking the new medication and 11.2% of those taking clopidogrel, representing an ARI of 0.4%. The NNH may be calculated based on this increased risk:

$$NNH = 1/ARI$$

$$NNH = 1/0.4\% = 250$$

This means that 250 people would need to be treated with the new medication to experience one additional episode of major bleeding compared with those taking clopidogrel, suggesting that the risk of bleeding with the new medication does not appear to be substantially higher compared with clopidogrel. Using the NNT and NNH together for a particular intervention is of great help in assessing the balance of potential benefits and risks when considering a particular therapy.

In addition to the measures described, some studies report their results as an *odds ratio* (OR). Conceptually, this is similar to relative risk, but rather than comparing the ratio of rates of occurrence of an event between study groups, the OR compares the odds (the ratio of the probability that the event will happen to the probability that the event will not happen) between study groups. To understand the difference between odds and risk, consider an event in which there are four outcomes of equal likelihood. The odds of any one of the events occurring would be one in three (0.33), but the risk of one of the events occurring would be one in four, or 0.25. The OR can be used in any with study that uses prospective data; when the occurrence of the study event is small, the OR will approximate the RR. However, use of the OR is required for studies using retrospective data, such as case-control studies in which the groups being compared may not have a similar risk for the condition; therefore, relative risk cannot be accurately calculated.

The *hazard ratio* (HR) measures the relative risk over time and is used primarily when we are interested not only in the total number of events but also in their timing, such as hospital readmission or death. It enhances understanding of the effect of a treatment in many trials because the relative risk at one point in time may not match the relative risk at another point in time, such when patients reach the outcome (eg, death) or otherwise drop out of the study.

Combining Results of Clinical Studies

In answering a clinical question, rather than performing a new study, investigators may collectively evaluate the research already performed. This involves a *systematic review* of the literature on a given topic, assessing each study's design strengths and limitations, and abstracting data. If the investigators determine the studies similar enough to quantitatively combine the respective data, they may perform a *meta-analysis*, with an understanding that the results depend on the quality of the data in the original studies. These analyses can be especially relevant when individual studies contain conflicting results, are not adequately powered to demonstrate statistically significant results, or are too small to draw conclusions. The highest quality evidence is generally considered to be a meta-analysis followed by a qualitative systematic review and then the individual clinical studies as listed in Table 1.

Applying Results to Patients

In clinical practice, selecting an appropriate treatment is a complex process. Not only does the physician need to clearly understand the potential benefits and risks of a therapeutic intervention, but the overall clinical status of the patient also needs to be considered in tailoring therapy to a specific individual. Additionally, patient preference and cost must be factored into clinical decision making. Shared decision making with the patient is usually recommended, and these measures of clinical effectiveness may be helpful in communicating the benefits and risks of treatment directly to patients.

High Value Care

Approximately 30% of healthcare costs in the United States are estimated to result from wasted care such as unnecessary hospitalizations, overuse of emergency department care, and the inappropriate use of diagnostic testing and treatments. In 2010, the American College of Physicians began a campaign to integrate physicians into cost reduction and quality enhancement through the practice of *high value care*. High value care is defined as care that balances the potential benefits of an intervention with its harms and costs.

The treatment for providing high value care consists of the following steps:

1. Understanding the benefits, harms, and relative costs of the interventions you are considering
2. Decreasing or eliminating the use of interventions that provide no benefits or may be harmful
3. Choosing interventions and care settings that maximize benefits, minimize harms, and reduce costs; using comparative effectiveness and cost effectiveness data when available
4. Customizing a care plan with each patient that incorporates the patient's values and addresses patient and family concerns
5. Identifying system-level opportunities to improve outcomes, minimize harms, and reduce healthcare waste

More information can be found at http://hvc.acponline.org/ and www.choosingwisely.org.

Bibliography

Qaseem A, Alguire P, Dallas P, et al. Appropriate use of screening and diagnostic tests to foster high-value, cost-conscious care. Ann Intern Med. 2012;156:147-149.[PMID: 22250146]

Smith CD; Alliance for Academic Internal Medicine–American College of Physicians High Value; Cost-Conscious Care Curriculum Development Committee. Teaching high-value, cost-conscious care to residents: the Alliance for Academic Internal Medicine–American College of Physicians Curriculum. Ann Intern Med. 2012;157:284-286. [PMID: 22777503]

Chapter 30

Health Promotion, Screening, and Prevention

L. James Nixon, MD
Briar Duffy, MD

The periodic health examination includes counseling to maintain health, screening for disease, and immunizing against future disease. All physicians should be familiar with the principles of preventive health care.

In general, interventions that address personal health practices have greater potential to improve health than does screening for disease. For example, a periodic health examination with a young woman is an opportunity to discuss healthy lifestyle choices, including dietary habits, exercise and activity levels, substance use (eg, tobacco, alcohol), psychosocial stresses, environmental risks (eg, seat belts, sun exposure), safe sexual practices, and contraception.

Although the value of the periodic health examination has been debated, it has been shown to improve delivery of preventive services and decreased patient worry. Additionally, brief, primary care–based interventions for changing identified risk behaviors, such as smoking and at-risk alcohol use, are effective in modifying long-term health habits.

Primary prevention is the deterrence of disease before its onset. Examples include immunizing patients against disease and reminding patients to wear seatbelts. Secondary prevention measures include most forms of screening, during which asymptomatic patients with risk factors for disease or preclinical disease are identified and managed. Examples include mammography for early detection of breast cancer and colonoscopy to screen for colon cancer. Tertiary prevention includes treating a disease with the goal of restoring the patient to his or her previous level of health, minimizing the negative effects of disease, and preventing complications. An example of tertiary prevention is treating a patient after a myocardial infarction with cholesterol-lowering drugs to prevent a second cardiovascular event.

Principles of Screening

The goal of screening is to prevent or delay the development of disease by early detection; early detection may result in diagnosis at a more treatable stage or before the disease has caused complications. The following principles of screening are essential in understanding the potential benefits and risks of screening:

- The disease should be clinically important (common and associated with substantial morbidity or mortality).
- The disease should have an asymptomatic period during which it can be detected.
- An effective screening method should be available that is accurate, readily available, affordable, and acceptable to both patient and provider.
- An acceptable and efficacious treatment should be available.
- Early treatment should be more beneficial than treatment once the patient is symptomatic.

Bias

Be aware of certain biases that have the potential to make a screening test appear to perform better than it actually does.

Lead-time bias is the artificial increase in survival time introduced with screening by simply diagnosing the disease earlier without necessarily increasing overall life expectancy. For example, the lead-time bias associated with prostate cancer screening is estimated at 5 to 10 years.

Length bias occurs with screening because testing is less likely to detect rapidly progressive diseases than slowly progressive, more indolent diseases. It will always appear that cancer detected by screening will have better outcomes than cancer detected by signs or symptoms. For example, lung cancer detected by computed tomography (CT) appears to have doubling times nearly twice as long as lung cancer detected by routine chest radiography.

An extreme form of length-biased sampling is *overdiagnosis*, in which the disease is so indolent that it probably would never have been detected during the screened person's lifetime had it not been for screening. For such a person, early detection and associated treatment can only do harm, yet the person seems to benefit because he or she is "cured."

Screening Guidelines

Screening guidelines change due to the availability of new evidence, and recommendations vary depending on the organization. The United States Preventive Services Task Force (USPSTF), a government agency, conducts scientific reviews of different screening interventions and publishes recommendation statements based on the strength of evidence for each (Table 1). In addition, many medical specialty organizations publish guidelines that may also include expert opinion, particularly in areas where there is not significant evidence to support clinical decision making. An excellent resource for guidelines is the National Guidelines Clearinghouse (www.guidelines.gov).

This section focuses on conditions for which screening is currently recommended. There are certain conditions for which the USPSTF recommends against screening, as the potential harm from follow-up testing or therapeutic interventions outweighs any potential benefit. These conditions include carotid artery stenosis, coronary artery disease in low-risk patients, prostate cancer, testicular cancer, and ovarian cancer. There are other conditions for which the USPSTF indicates there is insufficient evidence to recommend for or against screening. These conditions include hypothyroidism, glaucoma, and skin cancer.

Cancer

Cancers for which there is good evidence that screening is beneficial include breast, colorectal, and cervical. Mammograms are the test of

Table 1. Recommended Interventions for Preventive Care[a]

Screening

Height and weight (periodically)

Blood pressure

Alcohol and tobacco use

Depression (if appropriate follow-up is available)

Diabetes mellitus: type 2 diabetes in asymptomatic adults with sustained blood pressure (either treated or untreated) greater than 135/80 mm Hg

Dyslipidemia: Men ≥35 years and men and women aged ≥20 y who have cardiovascular risk factors

Colorectal cancer screening (men and women aged 50-75 y)

Mammogram every 2 y for all women aged 50-74 y; evaluation for *BRCA* testing in high-risk women only

Pap test (at least every 3 y in women aged 21-65 y) or Pap test with HPV testing (at least every 5 y in women aged 30-65 y)

Chlamydial and gonococcal infection (sexually active women aged ≤24 y and older at-risk women)

Routine voluntary HIV screening (patients aged 15-64 y)

Hepatitis C screening (once for adults born between 1945 and 1965)

Bone mineral density test (women aged ≥65 y and at-risk women aged <65 y)

AAA screening (one time in men aged 65-75 y who have ever smoked)

Lung cancer (only in patients ages 55 to 80 years who have a 30-pack-year smoking history and currently smoke or quit within the past 15 years with annual low-dose computed tomography)

Substance Abuse Counseling

Tobacco cessation counseling

Alcohol misuse: brief office-based behavioral counseling; alcohol abuse: referral for specialty treatment

Dietary and Exercise Counseling

Behavioral dietary counseling in patients with hyperlipidemia, risks for CHD, and other diet-related chronic disease

Regular physical activity (at least 30 min/d most days of the week)

Intensive counseling/behavioral interventions for obese patients

AAA = abdominal aortic aneurysm; *BRCA* = breast cancer susceptibility gene; CHD = coronary heart disease; HDL = high-density lipoprotein; HPV = human papilloma virus; Pap = Papanicolaou.

[a]Based on recommendations from the U.S. Preventive Services Task Force. A mobile application for applying recommended preventive services screening interventions in individual patients is available at: http://epss.ahrq.gov/PDA/index.jsp.

choice to screen for breast cancer; women ages 50 to 74 are recommended to have biennial mammograms routinely, but guidelines conflict about routine mammograms for women ages 40 to 50 or older than 74 (see Chapter 82). The average-risk person 50 years of age or older has several options for colorectal cancer screening: yearly fecal occult blood test or fecal immunochemical testing, sigmoidoscopy every 5 years with fecal occult blood tests every 3 years, or colonoscopy every 10 years. There is currently insufficient evidence regarding CT colonography as a screening test for the USPSTF to recommend it as an alternative screening option (see Chapter 83). Screening for human papillomavirus (HPV) infection in conjunction with routine Papanicolaou (Pap) anicolaou smear has been proposed as a method to improve detection of cervical cancer based on evidence that cervical cancer is linked to HPV infection. Although the typical Pap smear screening interval for women ages 21 to 65 years is every 3 years, the USPSTF now recommends that women 30 to 65 years old may have a Pap smear with HPV testing every 5 years if they wish to extend the time in between tests (see Chapter 84). Prostate cancer is common, but evidence regarding screening efficacy is still lacking, so the USPSTF now recommends against routine screening. The USPSTF also recommends against screening for testicular, ovarian, pancreatic, and bladder cancers due to lack of evidence showing benefit. The American Cancer Society, however, recommends examination of the thyroid, testicles, ovaries, lymph nodes, oral region, and skin during periodic health examinations.

Obesity

The periodic physical examination should include height and weight measurements. Patients with a body mass index >25 (overweight) or >30 (obese) should receive counseling regarding weight loss and lifestyle modification.

Depression

In general, screening for depression should be conducted in clinical practices where accurate diagnosis, effective treatment, and follow-up are available. A two-question screen for abnormal mood and anhedonia ("Over the past 2 weeks, have you felt down, depressed, or hopeless?" and "Over the past 2 weeks, have you felt little interest or pleasure in doing things?") is likely as effective as longer screening instruments.

Fall Prevention

Falls are a common cause of morbidity and mortality among persons aged >70 years. A minimum assessment includes inquiring about a history of falls and assessing risk for future falls. Although little direct evidence links fall screening with reduction of adverse outcomes in screened populations, screening in all at-risk populations is warranted given the combination of disease burden, available screening tools ("Get Up and Go" test), and available risk-intervention strategies.

Abdominal Aortic Aneurysm

One-time screening for abdominal aortic aneurysms (AAAs) with ultrasonography is recommended for all men aged 65 to 75 years who have ever smoked. Data from randomized clinical trials indicate that identification and repair of AAAs that are >5 cm reduces AAA-related mortality in older men.

Dyslipidemia

The USPSTF recommends that screening for dyslipidemia begin at age 35 in men at average risk for coronary artery disease; there are insufficient data to recommend screening in average-risk women at any age. In men and women who have risk factors for coronary vascular disease or who have a suspected heritable familial lipid disorder, screening should start at age 20 years. Repeat lipid screening every 5 years or when the patient's risk profile changes. Guidelines from the American Heart Association/American College of Cardiology recommend screening for dyslipidemia starting at age 20 years, with repeat reassessment of atherosclerotic cardiovascular disease risk every 4 to 6 years in average risk individuals. Usual screening consists of a fasting lipid profile.

Osteoporosis

The USPSTF recommends routine screening for osteoporosis in all women aged ≥65 years and in younger women who are at increased risk for osteoporotic fractures. This recommendation is based on evidence that bone density measurements accurately predict the risk for fractures in the short term, and that treating asymptomatic women with osteoporosis reduces their risk for fracture. Women at increased risk for low bone density include those with a smoking history, physical inactivity, secondary osteoporosis, prolonged glucocorticoid use, prolonged hyperthyroidism, celiac disease, a family history of osteoporosis, and inadequate calcium intake. The evidence is not as strong for men, but screening may be indicated in men with certain risk factors (eg, long-term glucocorticoid use, androgen deprivation). The preferred screening test for osteoporosis is dual-energy x-ray absorptiometry.

Type 2 Diabetes Mellitus

Although there is no direct evidence that screening for diabetes reduces adverse outcomes, screening for type 2 diabetes is recommended by the USPSTF in patients with sustained blood pressure (treated or untreated) of >135/80 mm Hg. The American Diabetes Association recommends screening all adults aged >45 years for diabetes every 3 years, citing the rationale that one-third of all people with diabetes may be undiagnosed and that early diagnosis may prevent complications. Also consider screening younger adults with risk factors for type 2 diabetes (eg, overweight or obese [BMI >25 kg m2], blood pressure >140/90 mm Hg, dyslipidemia, first degree relative with diabetes or member of a high-risk ethnic group, or polycystic ovary syndrome), with repeat screening every 3 years. Appropriate screening tests include fasting plasma glucose concentration, oral glucose tolerance test, and hemoglobin A_{1c} level. All patients who receive abnormal test results must repeat testing on a subsequent day.

Sexually Transmitted Infections

All sexually active women aged less than or equal to 24 years should undergo screening for chlamydial and gonorrhea infection; this recommendation is based on evidence that screening reduces the incidence of pelvic inflammatory disease by 50%. Additionally, any male or female deemed to have risk behaviors (eg, new or multiple sexual partners, history of a sexually transmitted infection, history of sex work, inconsistent condom use) should be screened for chlamydial infection, syphilis, and gonorrhea. Screening for herpes simplex virus infection is not recommended.

HIV Infection

The Centers for Disease Control and Prevention now recommends routine voluntary screening for HIV infection in all patients aged 15 to 64. Targeted screening should still continue in high-risk patients, including all patients initiating treatment for tuberculosis and patients seeking treatment for sexually transmitted diseases.

Hepatitis C Infection

Adults born between 1945 and 1965 are recommended to have one-time screening for hepatitis C because 75% of those with chronic hepatitis C infection are in this age group. Other patients who should be screened are individuals who are previous or current injection or intranasal drug users, have been incarcerated, had a blood transfusion prior to 1992, have been on long-term hemodialysis, received an unregulated tattoo, or were born to a mother with hepatitis C. Patients who are at continued risk of acquiring hepatitis C, such as those who continue to inject drugs, should be offered regular screening.

Coronary Artery Disease

Routine screening for coronary artery disease in asymptomatic persons without cardiovascular risk factors is not recommended. **Screening electrocardiograms are not recommended because abnormalities of the resting electrocardiogram are rare, are not specific for coronary artery disease, and do not predict subsequent mortality from coronary disease.** Exercise testing may identify individuals with coronary artery disease, but two factors limit routine testing in asymptomatic adults. First, the prevalence of significant coronary artery disease is low in this population, rendering the predictive value of a positive exercise test low (ie, false-positive results are common). Second, abnormalities of exercise testing do not accurately predict major coronary events in asymptomatic persons. There may still be a role for screening for coronary artery disease, however, in patients with diabetes before beginning an exercise program and in selected asymptomatic persons whose occupations may affect public safety or who engage in high-intensity physical activity. The role of coronary artery calcium scoring by CT is evolving. The American College of Cardiology believes it is reasonable to consider use of coronary artery calcium measurement in patients whose estimated 10-year risk of coronary events is 10% to 20% because these individuals might be reclassified to a higher risk status based on a high coronary artery calcium score, and subsequent patient management may be modified.

Hypertension

Early detection of hypertension is essential in reducing the likelihood of target organ damage. Cure of some secondary forms of hypertension (eg, primary aldosterone excess) is more likely if the duration of elevated blood pressure is short. Screen at every office visit, using the correctly sized blood pressure cuff. The average of two readings on two different occasions is used to classify the stage of hypertension.

Immunization

The Advisory Committee on Immunization Practices (ACIP) is a group of medical and public health experts that develops recommendations on how to use vaccines to control diseases in the U.S. Immunization recommendations change frequently; for up-to-date information regarding current recommendations, two excellent web sites are www.cdc.gov/vaccines and www.needletips.org; the ACP also makes available an Immunization Advisor application for mobile devices (http://immunization.acponline.org/). Most vaccines are safe and can be administered in the presence of a recent mild illness, including low-grade fever.

Influenza

The ACIP recommends yearly influenza vaccination for all persons aged ≥6 months. The trivalent or quadrivalent inactivated virus vaccine is given intramuscularly and is appropriate for all groups, including pregnant women. The intranasal live attenuated vaccine is approved for patients aged 2 to 49 years but should be avoided in pregnant women and in patients with diabetes, immunosuppression, and certain other long-term conditions. Persons with a history of Guillain-Barré syndrome should not receive either vaccine.

Pneumococcal Infection

Two versions of pneumococcal vaccine are available: a 23-valent pneumococcal polysaccharide vaccine (PPSV23) and a 13-valent conjugate vaccine (PCV13). PPSV23 is associated with substantial reductions in morbidity and mortality among the elderly and high-risk adults and, therefore, is recommended for all adults aged ≥65 years and for adults with other risk factors (eg, chronic heart disease, chronic lung disease, diabetes, cerebrospinal fluid leaks, cochlear implants, alcoholism, chronic liver disease, cigarette smoking smoking, asplenia, immunocompromising conditions). Patients who receive an initial PPSV23 vaccine at age <65 years should receive a second dose at age 65 years if at least 5 years have elapsed since the last PPSV13 immunization. One-time revaccination with PPSV23 is also recommended in 5 years for patients with asplenia or immunocompromising conditions. The PCV13 vaccine is also indicated as one-time therapy for all adults ≥65 years of age. The PCV vaccine is otherwise indicated primarily in patients <65 years of age with immunocompromising conditions, asplenia, cerebrospinal fluid leaks, or cochlear implants. To optimize immunogenicity in patients eligible for the PPSV23 and PCV13 vaccines, they are not administered together. For patients <65 years of age who have never received any pneumococcal vaccination, the PCV13 is usually given first, with the PPSV23 following at least 8 weeks later. Individuals age ≥65 years who have never received any pneumococcal vaccination should receive the PCV13 vaccine first followed by PPSV23 in 6 to 12 months, and those who have already received the PPSV23 before age 65 years should receive the PCV13 at age ≥65 years followed by the PPSV23 in 6 to 12 months.

Tetanus, Diphtheria, and Pertussis

Booster tetanus-diphtheria toxoid (Td) vaccinations are recommended every 10 years. Booster Td vaccination should also be given to any patient presenting with a wound who has received fewer than three doses of vaccine, whose vaccination status is unknown, or whose last vaccination was >10 years ago for a clean minor wound or >5 years ago for a more significant wound.

The ACIP recommends routine administration of a single dose of combined tetanus, diphtheria, and acellular pertussis (Tdap) vaccine for adults aged 19 to 64 years to replace one Td booster. This vaccine can be given regardless of the timing of the previous Td vaccine to provide the added pertussis protection. Subsequent vaccinations should be with the usual Td vaccine. As with other inactivated vaccines and toxoids, pregnancy is not considered a contraindication for Tdap vaccination and is in fact recommended for pregnant women during the third trimester to ensure antibodies are present in the newborn.

Measles, Mumps, and Rubella

Adults born before 1957 are generally considered immune to measles and mumps but not necessarily to rubella. Persons born after 1956 require measles, mumps, and rubella (MMR) vaccination unless there is documentation of prior administration, physician-confirmed disease, or laboratory evidence of immunity to all three diseases. It is important to ensure that women who are considering pregnancy have positive antibody titers for rubella. As with all live virus vaccines, women who are known to be pregnant should not receive the MMR vaccine, and pregnancy should be avoided for 4 weeks following vaccination. MMR vaccination should also be avoided in immunocompromised patients.

Human Papillomavirus

Bivalent and quadrivalent HPV vaccines are available. The ACIP recommends routine HPV vaccination of females ages 11 to 26 with either the bivalent or quadrivalent vaccines, and males ages 11 to 26 with the quadrivalent vaccine, regardless of sexual activity. HPV vaccination is also recommended for immunocompromised patients.

Hepatitis A

Hepatitis A vaccination is now routinely recommended in children. In addition, international travelers, persons relocating to areas of poor sanitation, day care staff, food handlers, military personnel, illicit drug users, men who have sex with men, persons with clotting factor disorders, and persons with hepatitis B and/or hepatitis C infection or other chronic liver disease should be vaccinated if not already immune. The safety of hepatitis A vaccine in pregnancy has not been established.

Hepatitis B

Children are routinely vaccinated against hepatitis B virus. All adolescents and young adults not immunized in childhood and those at increased risk for infection (eg, health care workers) should be immunized. Postvaccination testing is recommended only for those who are at occupational risk or are undergoing hemodialysis. To decrease the risk of perinatal hepatitis B virus transmission, all pregnant women are tested for hepatitis B surface antigen during an early prenatal visit. The hepatitis B vaccine is safe for pregnant women.

Varicella

Varicella vaccination (live attenuated virus) should be considered for any adult not previously immunized, particularly those working in high-risk environments (eg, schools), and for women who could become pregnant. Women who are known to be pregnant should not receive the varicella vaccine, and pregnancy should be avoided for 3 months following vaccination. Varicella vaccination should also be avoided in immunocompromised patients.

Zoster

Zoster vaccination is recommended by the ACIP for adults aged ≥60 years to prevent shingles and to reduce the incidence of postherpetic neuralgia. As patients can have a second herpes zoster outbreak, zoster vaccination is indicated regardless of a history of shingles. The vaccine is a live virus and is contraindicated in immunocompromised adults.

Meningococcal Infection

A single dose of meningococcal conjugate vaccine is recommended for young adults, particularly those living in dormitories. Others who should receive meningococcal immunization include patients with asplenia or terminal complement deficiency and persons traveling to areas of the world where meningococcal infection is endemic. The safety of meningococcal conjugate vaccine administration during pregnancy is unknown.

Bibliography

Boulware LE, Marinopoulos S, Phillips KA, et al. Systematic review: the value of the periodic health evaluation. Ann Intern Med. 2007;146: 289-300. [PMID: 17310053]

Chapter 31

Hypertension

Thomas M. DeFer, MD

Hypertension is extremely common, is often asymptomatic for many years, and may result in serious and sometimes mortal complications. Less than one-third of patients with hypertension in the U.S. have adequately controlled blood pressure (BP). In >90% of cases, hypertension has no specific underlying cause (referred to as *essential, primary,* or *idiopathic hypertension*) and arises from diverse factors, such as environmental influences, salt sensitivity, disorders of renin, cell membrane defects, insulin resistance, and genetic effects. *Secondary hypertension* refers to hypertension resulting from an identifiable structural, biochemical, or genetic defect (Table 1).

ommendations to lower BP consist of consuming a diet that emphasizes the intake of fruits, vegetables, and whole grains; includes poultry, fish, legumes, nuts, nontropical vegetable oils, and low-fat dairy products; and restricts the consumption of red meat, sweets, and sugar-sweetened beverages. The American Heart Association diet, the USDA food pattern, and the DASH (Dietary Approaches to Stop Hypertension) diet can help to achieve these goals. Dietary sodium should be restricted to <2400 mg/day (<1500 mg/day results in greater reductions) or by at least 1000 mg/day. Three to four sessions averaging 40 minutes in duration per week of moderate to vigorous aerobic physical activity may also lower BP.

Prevention

Lifestyle modifications should be instituted in all patients at risk for hypertension, including those with prehypertension. Dietary rec-

Screening

Early detection of hypertension is essential in reducing the risk of stroke, coronary artery disease, peripheral vascular disease, chron-

Table 1. Causes of Secondary Hypertension

Cause	Notes
Drug-induced hypertension	Possible causes include NSAIDs, amphetamines, cocaine, sympathomimetic agents (eg, decongestants, dietary supplements), oral contraceptives, antidepressants, bromocriptine, erythropoietin, and glucocorticoids.
Chronic kidney disease (see Chapter 71)	Late manifestations of kidney failure include elevated BUN, creatinine, potassium, and phosphate levels; low calcium level; and anemia. Most patients present at an earlier stage, with minimal signs and symptoms.
Renovascular disease (atherosclerotic and fibromuscular)	Characterized by onset of hypertension at a young age, especially in women (fibromuscular). Atherosclerotic disease is often associated with cigarette smoking, flash pulmonary edema, coronary artery disease, flank bruits, advanced retinopathy, elevated creatinine level (usually with bilateral renovascular disease), and an increase in creatinine level after treatment with an ACE inhibitor or ARB (ACE inhibitors or ARBs are preferred agents, if tolerated). Digital subtraction angiography is the diagnostic gold standard. Renal revascularization is indicated for most patients with fibromuscular dysplasia, but benefit is less clear with atherosclerotic stenosis.
Primary hyperaldosteronism (see Chapter 12)	Characterized by muscle cramping, nocturia, thirst, hypokalemia, and hypernatremia. Physical examination is normal.
Pheochromocytoma (see Chapter 12)	Characterized by sweating, heart racing, pounding headache, pallor, tachycardia, and elevated urine or plasma levels of catecholamines or metanephrine. Hypertension may be sustained or episodic, and orthostatic hypotension may also occur. Some patients with pheochromocytoma are normotensive.
Cushing syndrome (see Chapter 12)	Characterized by weight gain, menstrual irregularity, hirsutism, truncal obesity, abdominal striae, hypokalemia, metabolic alkalosis, and elevated urine or blood cortisol levels.
Thyroid disease (see Chapter 11)	Either hyper- or hypothyroidism may increase blood pressure. Hyperthyroidism is characterized by sweating, tachycardia, weight loss, tremor, and hyperreflexia. Hypothyroidism is characterized by cold intolerance, weight gain, goiter, and slowed reflexes.
Obstructive sleep apnea (see Chapter 94)	Characterized by daytime sleepiness, snoring, nonrestorative sleep, gasping or choking at night, witnessed apnea, morning headaches, obesity, large neck circumference, and crowded oropharyngeal airway. Diagnosis is established with polysomnography. Treatment with positive airway pressure may decrease blood pressure modestly in some patients.
Aortic coarctation	Fairly common cause in children. Characterized by headache, cold feet, leg pain, reduced or absent femoral pulse, delay in femoral compared with radial pulse, murmur (continuous systolic and diastolic) heard between the scapulae, and three sign on chest radiography.

ACE = angiotensin-converting enzyme; ARB = angiotensin receptor blocker; BUN = blood urea nitrogen; NSAIDs = nonsteroidal anti-inflammatory drugs.

ic kidney disease, and retinopathy. The United States Preventive Services Task Force recommends initiating blood pressure screening in all patients starting at 18 years of age. Screening should be done using sphygmomanometry using an appropriately sized cuff and proper technique. For patients who are normotensive and otherwise well, the optimal BP screening interval is unknown, although an interval of every 2 years is reasonable.

Diagnosis

Table 2 outlines the classification of blood pressures using the average of two or more readings obtained on each of two or more office visits. *Prehypertension* refers to patients with higher-than-normal blood pressures and indicates an increased risk for eventually developing hypertension. The diagnosis of hypertension is established by a systolic BP ≥140 mm Hg and/or diastolic BP ≥90 mm Hg, with the stage of hypertension determined by the degree of blood pressure elevation. Hypertension can also be diagnosed on the basis of an elevated systolic BP and a normal diastolic BP (referred to as *isolated systolic hypertension*).

Ambulatory BP monitoring should be performed if the diagnosis is uncertain, if white coat hypertension (elevated BP only in the office) is suspected, or if the clinical situation suggests an episodic cause of hypertension (eg, pheochromocytoma). Conversely, patients who are normotensive in the office may meet criteria for hypertension by ambulatory monitoring—a phenomenon referred to as *masked hypertension*. Masked hypertension is associated with increased cardiovascular risk; however, reasonable screening strategies for masked hypertension have not been defined. Self-performed and recorded BPs may be a reasonable alternative to ambulatory BP monitoring; patients should be instructed in technique and their device checked for accuracy if this is used.

Cardiovascular risk correlates directly with BP level and, beginning at 115/75 mm Hg, doubles with each increment of 20/10 mm Hg. In persons aged >50 years, systolic BP ≥140 mm Hg is a much more important cardiovascular risk factor than elevated diastolic BP. The risk from hypertension is compounded by each additional risk factor for cardiovascular disease. All patients should be assessed for cardiovascular risk factors, including smoking, obesity, physical inactivity, dyslipidemia, diabetes mellitus (DM), moderately increased albuminuria (microalbuminuria) or estimated glomerular filtration rate <60 mL/min/1.73 m², increased age, and family history of premature cardiovascular disease.

The history can help determine the likelihood of secondary hypertension (see Table 1) and to assess for evidence of end-organ damage, including angina, heart failure, stroke, transient ischemic attack, kidney disease, or claudication. Relevant physical examination findings include retinopathy, cardiac signs consistent with hypertensive changes such as a fourth heart sound or heart failure, bruits, neurologic signs consistent with stroke, and diminished or absent peripheral pulses.

Obtain the following studies in all patients: hematocrit, glucose, creatinine, electrolytes, urinalysis, fasting lipid profile, and electrocardiography. Blood or protein in the urine may indicate kidney damage or suggest secondary hypertension. An electrocardiogram showing left ventricular hypertrophy and/or signs of previous infarction is evidence of cardiovascular damage. **Although echocardiography is more sensitive in diagnosing ventricular hypertrophy, it is not routinely recommended in all patients with a new diagnosis of hypertension.** Specific laboratory tests are usually needed to confirm the presence of secondary hypertension suspected from the history or physical examination.

Some patients present with severely elevated BP. *Hypertensive emergency* is defined as markedly elevated BP (≥180/120 mm Hg) combined with symptoms or signs of end-organ damage, such as encephalopathy, papilledema, retinal hemorrhages or exudates, stroke, myocardial ischemia or infarction, aortic dissection, pulmonary edema, or acute kidney injury. *Hypertensive urgency* is a severe elevation in BP without acute end-organ damage.

Hypertension is relatively common in pregnancy. *Gestational hypertension* is defined as a blood pressure of ≥140/90 mm Hg on two occasions at least 6 hours apart in a previously normotensive woman presenting at >20 weeks' gestation. Hypertension arising at <20 weeks' gestation is considered evidence of previously undiagnosed chronic hypertension. The addition of proteinuria defines preeclampsia; therefore, the urine protein-creatinine ratio should be measured in all hypertensive pregnant women. Elevated BP that persists beyond 12 weeks postpartum should be considered chronic hypertension. Severe gestational hypertension (BP ≥160/110 mm Hg) and preeclampsia are associated with increased perinatal and maternal morbidity and mortality.

Therapy

The Eighth Joint National Committee (JNC-8) guidelines for the management of high blood pressure were published in 2014 and provide evidence-based recommendations for treating patients with hypertension.

Therapeutic lifestyle changes should be instituted in all patients with prehypertension and hypertension and should be continued even if drug therapy becomes necessary. Any modifiable risk factors, such as obesity or smoking, should be treated.

In the general adult population <60 years of age, pharmacologic treatment is recommended when the systolic BP is ≥140 mm Hg or the diastolic BP is ≥90 mm Hg. The goal of therapy should be <140/90 mm Hg. In patients ≥60 years of age, therapy is recommended if the systolic BP is ≥150 mm Hg or the diastolic BP is ≥90 mm Hg. The goal of treatment is <150/90 mm Hg, although patients with a BP of <140/90 mm Hg on well-tolerated therapy do not need to have their treatment changed.

The initiation threshold and goal for pharmacologic treatment in those ≥18 years with DM or chronic kidney disease is 140/90 mm Hg (which differs from the previously recommended level of 130/80 mm Hg). The American Diabetes Association, however, recommends a threshold and goal of 140/80 mm Hg in patients with DM.

In the general non-African American population, thiazide diuretics, angiotensin-converting enzyme inhibitors (ACEIs), angiotensin receptor blockers (ARBs), and calcium channel blockers (CCBs) may all be considered for initial treatment of hypertension, and all reduce the complications of hypertension. The Eighth Joint National Committee guidelines include patients with diabetes in this recommendation.

Table 2. Classification of Blood Pressure in Adults

Classification	Systolic Blood Pressure (mm Hg)		Diastolic Blood Pressure (mm Hg)
Normal	<120	*and*	<80
Prehypertension	120-139	*or*	80-89
Stage 1 hypertension	140-159	*or*	90-99
Stage 2 hypertension	≥160	*or*	≥100

For African Americans, initial therapy should be a thiazide diuretic or CCB, including those with diabetes. As a group, African Americans have less BP reduction with equivalent ACEI dosing compared with non-African Americans. Furthermore, African Americans initially treated with ACEIs rather than CCBs have about a 50% higher rate of stroke, and combined cardiovascular outcomes are better with a thiazide diuretic than with an ACEI.

For all patients (regardless of race or the presence or absence of diabetes) >18 years of age with chronic kidney disease (including those with and those without proteinuria), initial therapy should be an ACEI or ARB because these agents are renoprotective and improve renal outcomes. In blacks with chronic kidney disease but without proteinuria, the initial agent can be a CCB, thiazide diuretic, ACEI, or ARB. If the initial choice is not ACEI or ARB, then one of these should be the second drug added if necessary to lower the BP to target (<140/90 mm Hg).

Diuretics may equalize the response of black patients to ACEIs and ARBs. Loop diuretics are preferred for patients with chronic kidney disease and a serum creatinine level >1.5 mg/dL (132.6 µmol/L) or a glomerular filtration rate <30-50 mL/min/1.73 m^2. Thiazide diuretics are much more likely than loop diuretics to cause significant hyponatremia, particularly in elderly women. ACEIs and ARBs are similarly efficacious, but ARBs are less likely to cause cough.

Without compelling indications, β-blockers are not considered first-line therapy, particularly in older patients, due to the lack of data supporting an independent effect on morbidity and mortality. α-Blockers are not as effective as diuretics and should not be used as monotherapy for hypertension. Direct renin inhibitors (eg, aliskiren) are relatively new agents that effectively lower BP but lack outcome data; they should not be used as first-line therapy but may be useful in patients unsuccessfully managed with standard, evidence-based therapies. Other agents that effectively lower BP but lack data of improved cardiovascular outcomes include mineralocorticoid receptor antagonist diuretics (eg, spironolactone), loop diuretics (eg, furosemide), centrally acting α-$_2$ agonists (eg, clonidine), and direct vasodilators (eg, hydralazine).

Two or three antihypertensive agents are often needed to reach target BP levels. Typically, a single agent decreases systolic BP by 12 to 15 mm Hg and diastolic BP by 8 to 10 mm Hg. Therefore, in patients with untreated stage 2 hypertension (>160/100 mm Hg), drug therapy may be initiated with a combination of antihypertensive medications. **Combined therapy with an ACEI and ARB for treatment of hypertension is associated with increased adverse effects and no improvement in outcome and is not recommended.**

Compelling indications for certain antihypertensive agents include coronary artery disease, heart failure, stroke, diabetes, and chronic kidney disease, particularly with proteinuria (Table 3). In these instances, the preferred agents are used first and continued regardless of whether additional agents are needed to control BP. In patients with hypertension and coronary artery disease, β-blockers are the drugs of choice because they decrease cardiovascular mortality. The presence of asthma or chronic bronchitis may limit the use of β-blockers. ACEIs are preferred for use in patients with asymptomatic ventricular dysfunction and symptomatic heart failure because they decrease cardiovascular mortality. Compared with β-blockers, ARBs may be specifically beneficial in patients with left ventricular hypertrophy. Combination ACEIs and thiazide diuretic therapy reduces recurrent stroke rates. ACEIs and ARBs reduce albuminuria and the progression of chronic kidney disease, including diabetic nephropathy. ACEIs produce greater reductions in cardiac morbidity and mortality compared with calcium channel blockers. An increase of up to 33% in serum creatinine is acceptable and not a reason to discontinue ACEI therapy; however, hyperkalemia may limit the use of ACEIs.

Table 3. Antihypertensive Drugs: Compelling Indications, Contraindications, and Side Effects

Drug Class	Compelling Indications	Contraindications	Side Effects
Diuretics	Heart failure, systolic hypertension	Gout	Hypokalemia, hyponatremia, hyperuricemia, glucose intolerance, hypercalcemia, hyperlipidemia, orthostatic hypotension, sexual dysfunction, insomnia; metabolic effects less common with low-dose therapy
β-Blockers	Angina, heart failure, post-MI, tachyarrhythmia, migraine	Asthma, COPD, heart block	Bronchospasm, bradycardia, heart failure, impaired peripheral circulation, insomnia, fatigue, decreased exercise tolerance, hypertriglyceridemia, sexual dysfunction (uncommon), reduced awareness of hypoglycemia
ACE inhibitors	Heart failure, left ventricular dysfunction, post-MI, diabetic nephropathy, proteinuria	Pregnancy, bilateral renal artery stenosis, hyperkalemia	Azotemia, cough, angioedema, hyperkalemia, hypotension, rash, loss of taste, leukopenia
Angiotensin receptor blockers	ACE inhibitor cough, diabetic nephropathy, heart failure, post-MI but intolerant to ACE inhibitor	Pregnancy, bilateral renal artery stenosis, hyperkalemia	Azotemia, angioedema (rare), hyperkalemia, hypotension
Calcium channel blockers	Systolic hypertension, cyclosporine-induced hypertension, angina, coronary heart disease	Heart block and heart failure (verapamil, diltiazem, and short-acting dihydropyridines)	Edema, headache, dizziness, flushing, constipation
α-Blockers	Prostatic hypertrophy	Orthostatic hypotension	Headache, drowsiness, fatigue, weakness, postural hypotension

ACE = angiotensin-converting enzyme, COPD = chronic obstructive pulmonary disease, MI = myocardial infarction.

Patients with hypertensive emergencies are treated in the hospital setting with parenteral medications and intensive care unit monitoring. Nitroprusside is generally considered the most effective parenteral agent for most patients but can cause cyanide toxicity at high doses or with prolonged use (>24-48 hours). Other potentially useful intravenous drugs are nitroglycerine, labetalol, nicardipine, and fenoldopam. Overly aggressive BP lowering (ie, to a diastolic pressure <100-110 mm Hg within 2-6 hours) is undesirable and may result in ischemic injury due to autoregulatory changes. Caution in this regard is particularly advisable during the first 24 hours after a stroke, unless thrombolytic therapy is being considered. There are exceptions as well, including aortic dissection, for which aggressive BP lowering with a β-blocker (ie, to a systolic pressure <100-120 mm Hg) is indicated.

Parenteral drugs are usually not necessary in hypertensive urgency, unless symptoms or progressive end-organ damage is present. Initial treatment is with one or more rapid-onset oral antihypertensive drugs (such as clonidine or a short-acting ACEI such as captopril) followed by a longer-acting formulation once BP is <180/110 mm Hg. Clonidine may be given hourly until the desired BP is achieved, although care must be taken to not excessively lower the BP. BP should be rechecked within 48 hours. Avoid short-acting calcium channel blockers in patients with ischemic heart disease (such as nifedipine), because reflex adrenergic stimulation and tachycardia may lead to myocardial ischemia.

Mild gestational hypertension is often managed expectantly with frequent antepartum visits. Typical lifestyle modifications (eg, weight loss, sodium restriction) are inappropriate. The efficacy of bed rest is unclear. Severe gestational hypertension is typically treated with antihypertensive agents. Methyldopa, labetalol, and sustained-release nifedipine are generally recommended in pregnancy. The use of thiazide diuretics is controversial, because the resultant volume depletion is undesirable. ACEIs, ARBs, and direct renin inhibitors are contraindicated in pregnancy. Patients must be monitored frequently for progression to preeclampsia. Patients with preeclampsia, particularly if severe, are best referred to a high-risk obstetrician. When urgent BP lowering is required, intravenous labetalol, hydralazine, and nicardipine can be used. Nitroprusside is generally contraindicated in pregnancy. The cure for gestational hypertension is delivery.

Follow-Up

Follow-up should be individualized. Uncontrolled hypertension requires more vigilant follow-up, at least monthly, until control is achieved. Consider regular home BP monitoring in select patients. Patients should be questioned about medication side effects. At follow-up, if there has been a partial response to a submaximal dose of the initial agent, the dose should be increased. A second drug from a different class may be added if there is a partial response to an otherwise well-tolerated initial agent. Alternatively, some physicians may choose to start a second drug before maximizing the dosage of the initial agent. A thiazide diuretic may augment the effect of ACEIs and ARBs, particularly in African Americans, but as noted previously, in patients at high risk for cardiovascular events, the preferred combination may be ACEI plus a CCB. A third agent should be added if the target BP has not been reached. If not used first or second, a thiazide diuretic is the preferred third agent. β-Blockers are reasonable to add as a fourth agent when maximal doses of more preferred drugs are insufficient.

Resistant hypertension is BP that is not at target level despite maximal doses of three antihypertensive agents, one being a diuretic. Important causes include medication nonadherence, inadequate therapy, excessive alcohol consumption, and other drugs (eg, NSAIDs, sympathomimetic agents). White coat hypertension may also contribute to the apparent occurrence of refractory hypertension; ambulatory BP monitoring is useful if this is suspected. Treatment strategies include addressing potential reasons for resistance. If a typical β-blocker is being used, changing to a vasodilating or dual-acting β-blocker may be helpful. Aldosterone antagonists (eg, spironolactone, eplerenone) are potentially effective additions for resistant hypertension, even in the absence of hyperaldosteronism. The addition of hydralazine or clonidine may be necessary in a few patients. **Evaluation for secondary hypertension is indicated only when the clinical situation is suggestive or a patient is adherent to a four-drug regimen without adequate control (see Table 1).** Patients whose BP was previously well controlled and have an acute rise may also benefit from a secondary cause evaluation.

Only half of patients who start therapy remain on treatment after 1 year. Using once-daily therapy, maintaining close contact with patients, encouraging home BP monitoring, and using drugs with fewer adverse effects and lower cost may improve adherence.

Bibliography

American Diabetes Association. Standards of medical care in diabetes–2013. Diabetes Care. 2013;36:S11-S66. [PMID: 23264422]

Eckel RH, Jakicic JM, Ard JD, et al. 2013 AHA/ACC Guideline on Lifestyle Management to Reduce Cardiovascular Risk: A Report of the American College of Cardiology/American Heart Association Task Force on Practice Guidelines. Circulation 2013 Nov 12. [Epub ahead of print] [PMID: 24222015]

James PA, Oparil S, Carter BL, et al. 2014 Evidence-Based Guideline for the Management of High Blood Pressure in Adults: Report From the Panel Members Appointed to the Eighth Joint National Committee (JNC 8). JAMA. 2013 Dec 18. [Epub ahead of print] [PMID: 24352797]

Mancia G, Fagard R, Narkiewicz K, et al. 2013 ESH/ESC Guidelines for the management of arterial hypertension: the Task Force for the management of arterial hypertension of the European Society of Hypertension (ESH) and of the European Society of Cardiology (ESC). J Hypertens. 2013 Jul;31:1281-357. [PMID: 23817082]

Chapter 32

Dyslipidemia

Gary Tabas, MD
D. Michael Elnicki, MD

In 2013, the American College of Cardiology (ACC) and the American Heart Association (AHA) jointly released new cholesterol guidelines, supplanting the National Cholesterol Education Program Adult Treatment Panel III guidelines published in 2002. Compared to the Adult Treatment Panel III, these new recommendations base treatment of hyperlipidemia on an individual's risk for developing atherosclerotic cardiovascular disease (ASCVD) instead of the level of low-density lipoprotein cholesterol (LDL-C) or other lipid measurement.

This major change from previous cholesterol guidelines was prompted by the observation that the key studies showing the benefit of treating hyperlipidemia used fixed doses of statins and did not vary these doses to reach specific target LDL-C levels. These trials demonstrated that the beneficial effects of statin therapy were not related to pretreatment LDL-C levels, and those with the greatest benefit were those at high risk for ASCVD even if LDL-C was not high. For patients at low risk for ASCVD, benefit was limited even if the LDL-C was significantly elevated. Therefore, the new guidelines recommend that treatment decisions be based on the patient's likely benefit rather than on a pretreatment or target LDL-C level.

Statins lower the patient's risk of developing cardiovascular endpoints, including myocardial infarction and stroke, through multiple mechanisms in addition to lowering LDL-C cholesterol levels. These so-called pleiotropic effects include improved endothelial function, decreased oxidative stress, inflammation and thrombosis, and plaque stabilization.

Low-density lipoproteins are protein-bound lipids in the blood that comprise 60% to 70% of the total serum cholesterol and are considered the major atherogenic lipid particle. High-density lipoprotein (HDL) accounts for 20% to 30% of total serum cholesterol. The HDL level is inversely related to coronary heart disease (CHD) risk, but HDL is generally not a target of primary preventive therapy; there is no established goal for HDL. Very-low-density lipoproteins (VLDLs) are triglyceride-rich precursors of LDL that are produced by the liver and contain highly atherogenic remnant particles. Intermediate-density lipoproteins are also atherogenic and are also included in the LDL measurement. Chylomicrons are formed in the intestine, are rich in triglycerides, and when partially degraded are atherogenic.

Other lipoproteins are likely involved in the formation of an atheroma. Lp(a) lipoprotein is associated with increased risk for CHD, but treatment with statins does not lower Lp(a) lipoprotein levels or the associated risk. Small LDL particles and HDL subfractions are related to CHD, but measurement of these other lipoproteins is not routinely indicated.

Other nonlipid risk factors for atherosclerotic disease include age, gender, race, blood pressure, diabetes mellitus, and smoking.

Prevention

All patients should be advised about lifestyle measures to reduce risk for atherosclerotic disease. These actions include a healthy diet, regular exercise, weight control, avoiding tobacco, and moderating alcohol intake. A healthy diet is one that does not exceed caloric needs, contains less than 25% to 35% of calories from all fat sources (less than 7% from saturated fat), and includes less than 200 mg (5.2 mmol/L) of cholesterol per day. Increasing dietary intake of vegetables, fruits, and high-fiber foods will help lower lipid levels. Aerobic exercise has beneficial effects and should be performed most days for at least 30 minutes per session. Any amount of exercise is beneficial, however, and more is better. Body weight should be brought as close as possible to the ideal BMI. All forms of tobacco should be avoided, and alcohol intake should be moderated to ≤2 drinks per day for men and ≤1 drink per day for women.

Screening

The United States Preventive Services Task Force recommends that screening for dyslipidemia begin at age 35 in men at average risk for coronary artery disease; there are insufficient data to recommend screening in average-risk women at any age. In men and women who have risk factors for coronary vascular disease or who have a suspected heritable familial lipid disorder, screening should start at age 20. Repeat lipid screening every 5 years or when the patient's risk profile changes. Guidelines from the American Heart Association/American College of Cardiology recommend screening for dyslipidemia in all patients starting at age 21 years, with repeat reassessment of atherosclerotic cardiovascular disease risk every 4 to 6 years in average risk individuals.

Usual screening consists of a fasting lipid panel, although a non-fasting study may be used in patients who may not return for a fasting blood test. A fasting lipid profile consists of total and HDL cholesterol and triglyceride measurements and calculated LDL cholesterol. LDL cholesterol is calculated using the Friedewald formula:

$$LDL = [total\ cholesterol] - [HDL] - [triglycerides/5]$$
$$(all\ units\ are\ mg/dL)$$

An alternative way to calculate is:

$$LDL\text{-}C = total\ cholesterol\ minus\ HDL\text{-}C\ minus\ triglycerides/5$$
$$(all\ units\ are\ mg/dL)$$

Triglyceride levels >400 mg/dL (4.5 mmol/L) invalidate the Friedewald formula. In this case, LDL cholesterol should be directly measured.

Diagnosis

Perform a thorough history to identify other cardiovascular risk factors, such as cigarette smoking, hypertension, or a family history of premature heart disease. A variety of drugs can cause dyslipidemia, including estrogens, glucocorticoids, thiazide diuretics, β-blockers, and androgenic steroids. History can identify CHD risk equivalents such as diabetes mellitus, aortic aneurysm, peripheral vascular disease (claudication), stroke, or transient ischemic attack. Physical examination can also identify CHD risks or CHD equivalents. The examination should include measurement of blood pressure and BMI. Patients with existing cardiovascular disease may have abnormal cardiac examinations, diminished pulses, bruits, or other signs of peripheral vascular disease.

Patients with very high lipid levels often have cutaneous xanthomas. Eruptive xanthomas are small yellow papules on the trunk or extremities; they are seen when triglycerides are elevated, particularly in familial hypertriglyceridemia.

Tendinous xanthomas are nodules deposited within the extensor tendons; they are seen in patients with high LDL-C levels, particularly in those with familial hypercholesterolemia. Tuberous xanthomas are soft yellow papules or nodules that can form lobular masses on extensor surfaces; they are seen with elevations of LDL-C or triglycerides. Planar xanthomas are yellow plaques found in skin folds in the neck, face, upper trunk, and arms; they are seen with elevations of LDL or triglycerides. Xanthelasma are flat yellow papules or plaques around the eyelids seen in patients with familial hypercholesterolemia.

Secondary causes of dyslipidemia–important because they often are treatable (Table 1) include hypothyroidism, obstructive liver disease, nephrotic syndrome, alcoholism, uncontrolled diabetes, smoking, and kidney failure.

Before making the diagnosis of hyperlipidemia, obtain at least two measures of LDL-C at least 1 week apart. Triglycerides (triglycerides) are no longer considered as separate targets for therapy unless levels are very high. Triglyceride levels are classified as normal (<150 mg/dL [1.7 mmol/L]), borderline (150-199 mg/dL [1.7-2.2 mmol/L]), high (200-499 mg/dL [2.3-5.7 mmol/L]), and very high (>500 mg/ dL [5.7 mmol/L]). Very high triglyceride levels can cause pancreatitis and are treated regardless of cardiovascular risk. Low HDL cholesterol (<40 mg/dL [1.0 mmol/L] in men) is a CHD risk factor, but HDL is no longer considered a target for pharmacologic therapy.

Cardiovascular risk factors often occur in clusters. One example of particular importance is the metabolic syndrome, the diagnostic criteria for which are shown in Table 2. Adult Treatment Panel III recommendations state that the metabolic syndrome should be considered a secondary target for risk reduction therapy, but metabolic syndrome was not specifically addressed in the 2013 ACC/AHA Guidelines. Any person at high or moderately high risk who has lifestyle-related risk factors such as the metabolic syndrome is a candidate for therapeutic lifestyle changes to modify these risk factors. It is not clear, however, whether the metabolic syndrome in itself confers an independent risk beyond that associated with the specific individual risk factors that comprise this syndrome.

Therapy

In patients at low-to-moderate risk for CHD, dietary interventions to reduce LDL-C are appropriate. Switching to a diet low in saturated fat can result in a 5% to 15% reduction in LDL-C, and incorporating high-fiber foods can result in a 5% further reduction. Diets rich in fruits, vegetables, nuts, whole grains, and monounsaturated oils (eg, olive oil, canola oil) and low in animal fat reduce cardiovascular risk even without changing lipid levels. Diets rich in omega-3 fatty acids, from fish intake or supplements, improve lipid profiles and reduce risk of CHD by 20% to 30%.

Overweight patients should be encouraged to lose weight by reducing caloric intake, particularly calories from fats and simple carbohydrates. Regular physical activity is encouraged, and both weight loss and exercise are particularly encouraged for patients with a BMI >25. Regular aerobic exercise facilitates weight loss and improves lipid profiles. The beneficial effects are related to the amount of exercise, rather than exercise intensity or overall fitness. Patients should begin structured exercise programs lasting at least 30 minutes on most days. Smoking cessation reduces CHD risk and should be an integral part of lifestyle therapy.

The 2013 ACC/AHA guidelines identify four groups of patients for whom ASCVD risk reduction clearly outweighs the risk of adverse events. ASCVD is defined as acute coronary syndrome, myocardial infarction, angina, coronary or arterial revascularization, stroke, transient ischemic attack, or peripheral vascular disease.

Table 1. Laboratory Tests for Evaluating Dyslipidemia

Test	Notes
Fasting lipid profile with calculated LDL-C	Obtain two measurements at least 1 wk apart to confirm diagnosis. Results unreliable >24 h after myocardial infarction, major surgery, or trauma and for 6-8 wk after event onset.
Direct LDL-C measurement	Obtain if triglycerides >400 mg/dL (4.5 mmol/L), which makes Friedewald formula unreliable for calculating LDL-C.
Thyroid-stimulating hormone	Identify hypothyroidism as secondary cause.
FBG	Identify uncontrolled diabetes as secondary cause with FBG >126 mg/dL (7.0 mmol/L) on two fasting samples.
Direct bilirubin	Identify obstructive jaundice as a secondary cause if bilirubin >50% above normal.
Alkaline phosphatase, AST/ALT	Identify liver disease as contraindication to some lipid-lowering drugs.
Urine protein	Begin with urine dipstick for overt proteinuria to identify nephrotic syndrome as secondary cause.

ALT = alanine aminotransferase; AST = aspartate aminotransferase; FBG = fasting blood glucose; LDL-C = low-density lipoprotein cholesterol.

Table 2. Criteria for Diagnosis of Metabolic Syndrome

Any Three of the Following Risk Factors	Defining Level
Abdominal obesity (waist circumference)	Men, >40 in (102 cm) Women, >35 in (88 cm)
Triglycerides[a]	≥150 mg/dL (1.7 mmol/L)
High-density lipoprotein (HDL) cholesterol	Men, <40 mg/dL (1.0 mmol/L) Women, <50 mg/dL (1.3 mmol/L)
Blood pressure	≥130/85 mm Hg
Fasting glucose	≥110 mg/dL (6.1 mmol/L)

[a]Triglycerides ≥150 mg/dL (1.7 mmol/L) as a single factor correlates highly with presence of metabolic syndrome.

Data adapted from the National Heart Lung and Blood Institute. National Cholesterol Education Program. Third Report of the Expert Panel on Detection, Evaluation, and Treatment of High Blood Cholesterol in Adults (Adult Treatment Panel III): Executive Summary. www.nhlbi.nih.gov/guidelines/cholesterol/atp_iii.htm. Published May 2001.

Table 3. ACC/AHA Blood Cholesterol Guidelines Major Statin Benefit Groups

	ASCVD	Age (y)	LDL (mg/dL)	DM	Risk[b]	Statin Intensity
LDL≥190[a]		≥21	≥190			High
ASCVD	Yes	≥21				≤75 y = high
						>75 y = moderate
Risk		40 to 75	70 to 189		≥7.5%	Moderate to high
DM		40 to 75	70 to 189	Yes	<7.5%	Moderate
					≥7.5%	High

ACC/AHA = American College of Cardiology/American Heart Association; ASCVD = atherosclerotic cardiovascular disease; DM = diabetes mellitus; LDL = low-density lipoprotein.

[a]In mg/dL.

[b]Estimated using the Pooled Cohort Equations.

Source: Gary Tabas, MD

The four groups expected to benefit from statin therapy include patients who have any of the following:

1. Clinical atherosclerotic cardiovascular disease (ASCVD)
2. LDL-C ≥190 mg/dL
3. Diabetes and age 40 to 75 years with an LDL-C of 70 to 189 mg/dL and no ASCVD
4. No ASCVD or DM and estimated 10-year ASCVD risk ≥7.5%

The 10-year risk for ASCVD is estimated by using the Pooled Cohort Equations calculator, which was derived from data from multiple longitudinal study databases including the Framingham cohort. The calculator is available at www.cardiosource.org/en/Science-And-Quality/Practice-Guidelines-and-Quality-Standards/2013-Prevention-Guideline-Tools.aspx and is also available for mobile devices.

For patients in any one of the four statin benefit groups, therapy with a statin is indicated. The intensity of the recommended statin therapy is determined by specific group, age, whether the LDL-C is ≥190, and the 10-year risk for ASCVD (Table 3). High-intensity statin therapy is recommended for patients with LDL-C of ≥190 mg/dL if <75 years of age, ASCVD if <75 years of age, or diabetes if 40 to 75 years of age with an LDL-C level of 70 to 189 mg/dL and 10-year ASCVD risk ≥7.5%.

Moderate-intensity statin therapy is recommended for patients with ASCVD if >75 years of age or in patients with diabetes if 40 to 75 years of age with an LDL-C of 70 to 189 mg/dL and 10-year risk <7.5%. Patients without an LDL-C level of ≥ 190 mg/dL, ASCVD, or diabetes, but who have 10-year risk ≥7.5%, should be treated with moderate-to high-intensity statin therapy depending on comorbidities.

High-intensity statin therapy lowers LDL-C on average by approximately ≥50%. Moderate-intensity statin therapy lowers LDL-C on average by approximately 30 to ≤50%. Individual statins and the doses needed to provide moderate and intense therapy are listed in Table 4.

For patients with LDL-C levels <190 mg/dL who are not in one of the previously mentioned groups, additional risk factors as well as physician and patient preference may be considered to inform treatment decisions. For example, the physician and patient may decide together to initiate statin therapy if the patient has a strong family history of ASCVD, even if the patient was not in one of the four statin benefit groups.

Drug classes available for treating dyslipidemia include HMG-CoA reductase inhibitors (statins), fibrates, niacin, bile acid sequestrants, and intestinal cholesterol absorption blockers (Table 5). The guidelines emphasize that statins are preferred for therapy since they were used in the primary trials showing benefit from pharmacotherapy, and there is less evidence for using other lipid-lowering drugs including fibrates, niacin, bile acid sequestrants, and ezetimibe. Despite the limited evidence for the use of these nonstatin drugs, they are sometimes prescribed when patients cannot tolerate statins.

Fibrates are indicated to treat very high triglyceride levels (>500 mg/dL) to prevent pancreatitis. Nicotinic acid is no longer recommended for CHD patients taking statins who have low HDL-C and high TGs due to lack of effectiveness in reducing CHD endpoints.

Table 4. High-, Moderate-, and Low-Intensity Statin Therapy[a]

High-intensity Statin Therapy	Moderate-intensity Statin Therapy	Low-intensity Statin Therapy
Daily dose lowers LDL-C on average by approximately ≥50%	Daily dose lowers LDL-C on average by approximately 30% to <50%	Daily dose lowers LDL-C on average by <30%
Atorvastatin (40)–80 mg	**Atorvastatin 10** *(20)* **mg**	*Simvastatin 10 mg*
Rosuvastatin 20 *(40)* **mg**	**Rosuvastatin** *(5)* **10 mg**	**Pravastatin 10–20 mg**
	Simvastatin 20–40 mg	**Lovastatin 20 mg**
	Pravastatin 40 *(80)* **mg**	*Fluvastatin 20–40 mg*
	Lovastatin 40 mg	*Pitavastatin 1 mg*
	Fluvastatin XL 80 mg	
	Fluvastatin 40 mg twice daily	
	Pitavastatin 2–4 mg	

FDA = Food and Drug Administration; LDL–C = low-density lipoprotein cholesterol.

[a]Specific statins and doses that have been shown to be effective in randomized, controlled trials are indicated in bold; medications and doses in italics have been approved by the FDA for lipid treatment but have not been tested in randomized, controlled trials.

Adapted from: Goff DC Jr, Lloyd-Jones DM, Bennett G, et al. 2013 ACC/AHA Guideline on the Assessment of Cardiovascular Risk: A Report of the American College of Cardiology/American Heart Association Task Force on Practice Guidelines. J Am Coll Cardiol. 2013 Nov 12. [PMID: 24239921]

Statins can cause hepatotoxicity and myopathy, particularly when used in combination with other lipid-lowering drugs (Table 6). Patients should routinely be asked about symptoms such as nausea, abdominal pain, or myalgias. **Because statins can cause aminotransferase elevations, and fatal acute hepatic failure has occurred rarely in patients taking statins, aminotransferase levels should be**

Table 5. Medications for Treating Abnormal Lipid Levels

Agent	Changes in Lipid Values	Notes
Statins	LDL cholesterol ↓ 18%-55% HDL cholesterol ↑ 5%-15% TGs ↓ 7%-30%	Most effective agents for reducing LDL cholesterol. Higher doses increase risk for adverse events. Contraindicated in pregnancy.
Bile acid sequestrants[a]	LDL cholesterol ↓ 15%-30% HDL cholesterol ↑ 3%-5% No effect or possible ↑ in TGs	Avoid in patients with high TGs (>200 mg/dL [2.26 mmol/L]). Constipation, abdominal pain, and nausea are common side effects, but are seen less frequently with colesevelam.
Fibrates[a]	LDL cholesterol ↓ 5%-20% (↑ in patients with elevated TGs) HDL cholesterol ↑ 10%-35% TGs ↓ 20%-50%	Most effective agents for reducing TGs, but may raise LDL cholesterol. Combination therapy with statins reduces overall cholesterol profile but may increase risk for myopathy. Avoid in patients with gallstones or kidney disease.
Nicotinic acid[a]	LDL cholesterol ↓ 5%-25% HDL cholesterol ↑ 15%-35% TGs ↓ 20%-50%	Flushing is common, but may be less frequent with sustained-release formulations or with prior administration of aspirin. Other adverse events include hepatotoxicity, gout, and hyperglycemia.
Ezetimibe[a]	LDL cholesterol ↓ 18%	Can reduce LDL cholesterol by an additional 19% when added to statin therapy. May be associated with myopathy.
Omega-3 fatty acids[a]	TGs ↓ 30%-50%	Used as an alternative to fibrates for lowering TGs. Therapeutic doses range from 3-12 g/d.

CHD = coronary heart disease; HDL = high-density lipoprotein; LDL = low-density lipoprotein; TGs = triglycerides.

[a]Not recommended as first-line agents for patients in any of the four statin benefit groups according to the 2013 ACC/AHA cholesterol guidelines.

Table 6. Major Adverse Events Associated With Statin Use

Adverse Event	Definition	Incidence	Management Strategy
Myalgia	Muscle ache or weakness *without* an increase in CK	5%-10%	Investigate for other causes of muscle pain, including vitamin D deficiency, thyroid disease, fibromyalgia, medications, exercise, and strenuous work. Follow symptoms and CK levels weekly; discontinue statin or decrease dose if symptoms worsen or CK levels increase. Once symptoms resolve and CK levels return to baseline, consider use of a statin or alternative LDL cholesterol–lowering medications associated with less risk for myopathy: fluvastatin, rosuvastatin, pravastatin, ezetimibe, bile acid sequestrants. Consider supplementation with coenzyme Q10.
Myositis	Muscle ache or weakness *with* an increase in CK less than 10× ULN	NA	Same as for myalgia.
Rhabdomyolysis	Muscle ache or weakness *with* an increase in CK > 10× ULN and creatinine elevation, accompanied by myoglobinuria	0.09%	Discontinue statin therapy immediately. Monitor symptoms and CK levels. Statin may be restarted, preferably at a lower dose, once symptoms resolve completely and CK levels normalize.
Elevated aminotransferases	Incidental asymptomatic elevation of serum aminotransferase levels to less than 3× ULN with no associated histopathologic changes	3%	Continue statin therapy. Elevation is typically transient and occurs during the first 12 weeks of therapy. Recheck liver chemistry tests only if clinically indicated.
Hepatotoxicity	Alanine aminotransferase > 3× ULN with total bilirubin levels > 2× ULN	1%	Discontinue statin therapy and recheck liver chemistry test results. If liver chemistry test results normalize, consider rechallenge with the same statin at a lower dose or a different statin. If liver chemistry test results remain elevated, continue to withhold statin, screen for underlying liver disease, and consider drug interactions.

CK = creatine kinase; LDL = low-density lipoprotein; NA = not available; ULN = upper limit of normal.

obtained before starting statin therapy but do not need to be monitored during therapy. Patients who have aminotransferase levels greater than three times the upper limit of normal should not be started on a statin. Patients should be instructed to call their physician if there are signs of liver disease including jaundice, fatigue, or anorexia. If statin-induced myopathy is suspected, confirm the diagnosis by measuring serum creatine kinase. Consider substituting a different statin in patients who complain of myalgias but do not have creatine kinase elevation.

Follow-up

Repeat lipid testing every 4 to 12 months is indicated to ensure adherence to lipid-lowering medication. Lipid testing is no longer considered necessary to determine if a specific LDL target has been achieved.

Bibliography

AIM-HIGH Investigators, Boden WE, Probstfield JL, Anderson T, et al. Niacin in patients with low HDL cholesterol levels receiving intensive statin therapy. N Engl J Med. 2011 Dec 15;365:2255-2267. [Erratum in: N Engl J Med. 2012 Jul 12;367:189]. [PMID: 22085343]

Goff DC Jr, Lloyd-Jones DM, Bennett G, et al. 2013 ACC/AHA Guideline on the Assessment of Cardiovascular Risk: a Report of the American College of Cardiology/American Heart Association Task Force on Practice Guidelines. J Am Coll Cardiol. 2013 Nov 12. [PMID: 24239921]

Kopin L, Lowenstein C. In the clinic. Dyslipidemia. Ann Intern Med. 2010 Aug 3;153:ITC21. [PMID: 20679557]

Miller M, Stone NJ, Ballantyne C, et al.; American Heart Association Clinical Lipidology, Thrombosis, and Prevention Committee of the Council on Nutrition, Physical Activity, and Metabolism; Council on Arteriosclerosis, Thrombosis and Vascular Biology; Council on Cardiovascular Nursing; Council on the Kidney in Cardiovascular Disease. Triglycerides and cardiovascular disease: a scientific statement from the American Heart Association. Circulation. 2011 May 24;123:2292-2333. [PMID: 21502576]

Naci H, Brugts J, Ades T. Comparative tolerability and harms of individual statins: a study-level network meta-analysis of 246 955 participants from 135 randomized, controlled trials. Circ Cardiovasc Qual Outcomes. 2013 Jul;6:390-399.[PMID: 23838105]

Chapter 33

Obesity

L. James Nixon, MD
Briar Duffy, MD

Obesity results from an imbalance of energy intake versus energy expenditure and a disturbance in the factors that regulate the feedback process. The causes of obesity are multifactorial and can be considered in terms of the biopsychosocial model; biologic factors (eg, genetic, metabolic factors, comorbidities, medications), psychological factors (eg, eating behaviors, activity habits, health knowledge), and social factors (eg, socioeconomic status, food policy) all contribute to the current obesity epidemic. Obesity is linked with many illnesses, including structural (eg, obstructive sleep apnea, osteoarthritis), metabolic (eg, diabetes mellitus, nonalcoholic steatohepatitis, hypertension), and atherosclerotic (eg, coronary, cerebral, and peripheral vascular disease).

Obesity affects >30% of Americans and is currently the second leading cause of preventable deaths. Another 30% of Americans are overweight. Compared with persons with a normal body mass index (BMI), patients who are overweight have a 20% to 40% higher risk of death; the mortality risk is increased twofold to threefold in those who are obese. The best treatment for obesity is prevention. Obese patients require education about the health risks of obesity, treatment goals, and lifestyle interventions to achieve those goals. Some patients may require the addition of counseling about drug therapy or surgery to achieve weight goals.

Prevention

One goal for internists is to identify and counsel persons at risk for obesity. This approach, if successful, is ideal because it avoids the pitfalls associated with trying to treat obesity once it occurs. Inquire about a family history of obesity; obesity is influenced by both genetic and environmental factors. Also ask the patient about exercise and television viewing habits; persons with a more sedentary lifestyle are at greater risk for obesity. A medication history can provide important information, as many drugs are associated with weight gain (eg, glucocorticoids and some β-blockers; certain antipsychotic, antidepressant, anticonvulsant, and antidiabetic drugs). Also ask about any recent weight gain; a gain of >0.45 to 0.90 kg (1-2 lb) per year is a red flag for risk of future weight gain. Counsel patients who plan to stop smoking that they are at increased risk for weight gain. Other life events associated with increased risk for weight gain include pregnancy and short-term disability after surgery or injury. Additional risk factors for obesity include lower socioeconomic status and race/ethnicity (eg, Hispanic, black, Polynesian).

Counsel at-risk patients to exercise regularly; a minimum of 30 minutes of moderate physical activity 5 or more days per week is ideal, although there is benefit from any form of physical exercise (eg, taking stairs instead of an elevator). Beneficial dietary changes include controlling energy intake by using small portion sizes. Also counsel patients to reduce dietary fat intake, increase dietary fiber, drink fewer sugar-sweetened beverages, and eat breakfast to lower the risk of becoming overweight.

Educate patients about the adverse health effects of weight gain; this is particularly important for patients who have children. The rate of childhood obesity is increasing, and >50% of overweight children will become overweight adults. Internists have a role in preventing childhood obesity, because the children of overweight adults are more likely to become overweight themselves. Internists can also help by advising pregnant women about the risk that excessive weight gain poses to their health and the health of their unborn child, as intrauterine imprinting can affect long-term control of body weight. Higher maternal weight increases the risk for childhood weight above the 95th percentile and for the metabolic syndrome.

Screening

Measure height, weight, and waist circumference at each visit, and calculate BMI (ie, weight in kilograms divided by height in meters squared). *Overweight* is defined as someone who has a BMI of 25 to 29.9; *obesity* is a BMI ≥30. Obesity is further divided into class I (BMI = 30-34.9), class II (BMI = 35-39.9), and class III (BMI >40). BMI has good correlation with health risks associated with obesity and excess body fat, such as diabetes, heart disease, osteoarthritis, gallbladder disease, gastroesophageal reflux disease, and certain cancers (eg, breast, endometrium, prostate, colon, kidney, gallbladder).

Abnormal waist circumference (>102 cm [40 in] for males or >88 cm [35 in] for females) is a measure for central obesity, which is a surrogate estimate for visceral fat. Visceral fat is a more metabolically active fat that releases free fatty acids into the portal system, contributing to hyperlipidemia, hyperinsulinemia, and atherogenesis. In adults with a BMI of 25.0 to 34.9, an abnormal waist circumference is associated with a greater risk than that determined by BMI alone. For adults with a BMI >34.9, this measurement is less helpful. The coexistence of metabolic risk factors for both type 2 diabetes and coronary heart disease (ie, abdominal obesity, hyperglycemia, dyslipidemia, and hypertension) defines the metabolic syndrome (see Chapter 32).

Diagnosis

Assess all patients identified as overweight, obese, or having an abnormal waist circumference for obesity-associated conditions, including hypertension, metabolic syndrome, endocrine disorders (eg, hypothyroidism, diabetes, Cushing syndrome), and polycystic ovary disease. In all patients with a BMI >25.0, obtain a fasting blood glucose or hemoglobin A1$_c$ measurement, serum creatinine level, and fasting lipid profile (eg, high-density lipoprotein cholesterol, triglycerides, and low-density lipoprotein cholesterol levels) to assess for comorbidities. A sleep study may be indicated to confirm sleep apnea in patients with daytime somnolence, hypertension, plethora, or a history of snoring.

Therapy

Help patients with a high BMI and/or increased central obesity to develop a plan to prevent further weight gain and, ultimately, reduce body weight. Initial steps include addressing modifiable risk factors for obesity and setting goals for gradual, sustainable weight loss. A 10% reduction in body weight is associated with significant risk reduction. Although rates for weight loss vary, a reasonable goal is to lose 0.22 to 0.45 kg (0.5-1.0 lb) per week.

Weight loss can be achieved through alterations in both diet and physical activity level. Behavioral interventions generally involve self-monitoring of food intake, learning about and controlling stressors that trigger eating, slowing food intake during meals, learning about portion size and nutrient content of foods (meal planning), setting realistic goals, behavioral contracting, increasing physical activity, and establishing a supportive social network.

Reducing energy intake is essential for weight loss. At reduced energy intake under controlled conditions, diet composition is less important than calorie restriction. Calorie-restricted diets generally fall into three major categories: balanced low-calorie diets, low-fat diets, and low-carbohydrate diets. Low-carbohydrate diets produce slightly greater initial weight loss compared with other diets and may have a slightly more favorable effect on glucose control, blood lipids, and blood pressure; after 2 years, weight loss is independent of which diet patients follow. Increased intake of high-fiber foods may enhance satiety, as may diets higher in protein. Very-low-calorie diets (<800 kcal/d) are difficult to administer and can be associated with a higher incidence of adverse effects; they are not recommended for routine use.

Increasing energy expenditure through increased physical activity is also crucial for weight loss. Advise patients to engage in 30 to 60 minutes of moderate physical activity 5 or more days a week (eg, walking or other comparable activities). Once a lower weight is achieved, exercise is particularly helpful in maintaining weight loss. Sustained weight loss requires lifestyle changes, so consider referring obese patients to behavioral specialists, such as clinical psychologists or trained dietitians (Figure 1).

When lifestyle changes are ineffective in helping patients to lose excess weight, the addition of drug therapy may be helpful. Drug therapy is generally tried before surgical intervention and is usually considered for patients with a BMI ≥30.0 or for patients with a BMI ≥27.0 and comorbidities (eg, hypertension, diabetes, heart failure,

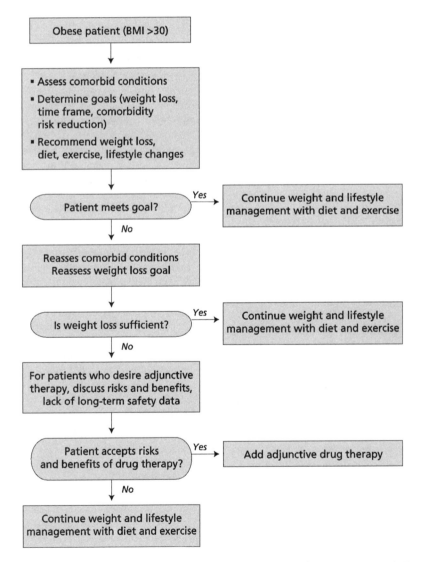

Figure 1. Medical management of obesity. BMI = body mass index. Adapted with permission from Snow V, Barry P, Fitterman N, Qaseem A, Weiss K; Clinical Efficacy Assessment Subcommittee of the American College of Physicians. Pharmacologic and surgical management of obesity in primary care: a clinical practice guideline from the American College of Physicians. Ann Intern Med. 2005;142:526-531. [PMID: 15809464]

coronary artery disease, obstructive sleep apnea, osteoarthritis). Criteria for success with drug therapy include weight loss >2 kg (4 lb) at 4 weeks, >5% weight loss at 6 months, and sustained weight loss (>5%) at 1 year. Orlistat (a drug that blocks lipase and, thus, fat absorption in the intestine) is available without a prescription; however, the FDA has recently added a warning about rare cases of liver toxicity. Orlistat use is often limited by abdominal discomfort and increased frequency of defecation. Diethylpropion, benzphetamine, phendimetrazine, and phentermine are noradrenergic sympathomimetic drugs that are available for short-term use as appetite suppressants; they may increase blood pressure, however. Topiramate, which causes appetite reduction and change in the taste of food, is approved in combination with phentermine, although it must be used with caution for women of child-bearing age due to teratogenic effects. Lorcaserin, a serotonergic agonist, is also approved for weight loss, as is the combination of buproprion (a novel antidepressant) and naltrexone (an opioid antagonist). The American College of Physicians clinical guidelines for obesity management include fluoxetine and bupropion as alternate drugs for the treatment of obesity. Exenatide, an injected drug that improves glycemic control by mimicking the action of the hormone incretin, is associated with weight loss among users. The weight loss may be related to delayed gastric emptying, causing patients to feel full faster and longer. Exenatide is approved by the FDA for use only in patients with diabetes. There is limited safety and efficacy information about the use of over-the-counter herbal preparations for weight loss. Ephedra-containing compounds have been removed from the market because of safety concerns.

Consider bariatric surgery for obese patients (BMI ≥35 plus serious obesity-related medical comorbidities, BMI ≥40 without comorbidities) who have not achieved weight loss despite lifestyle attempts and drug therapy. Surgery may also be recommended to patients with progressive obesity, such as individuals who have gained >5 kg (11 lb) per year before age 30. Bariatric surgery produces long-term weight loss that can be >25% of body weight at 1 year; after surgery, lost weight is regained slowly, if at all. The most common procedures target either early satiety (adjustable gastric banding) or a combination of early satiety and mild malabsorption (Roux-en-Y gastric bypass) (Figure 2). After surgery, patients are expected to follow a specific very-low-calorie program for 12 to 36 months and a low-calorie program thereafter. After bariatric surgery, many patients have significant improvement or resolution of obesity-related diseases, including diabetes, hypertension, sleep apnea, and hyperlipidemia, and recent studies suggest a decreased overall mortality up to 29%. Referral for bariatric surgery should not be done lightly, however. The operative mortality in most studies ranges from 0.1% to 1%. Complications after gastric banding include nausea and vomiting, band erosion, stomal obstruction, and severe gastroesophageal reflux disease. Gastric bypass complications include nutritional deficiencies (eg, vitamin B_{12}, folate, iron, micronutrients), marginal ulcers, stomal stenosis, gallstones, infections, vomiting, and dumping syndrome. Bariatric surgery is also associated with pulmonary embolism.

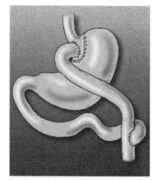
Roux-en-Y gastric bypass

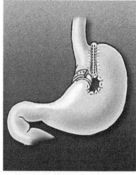
Vertical banded gastroplasty

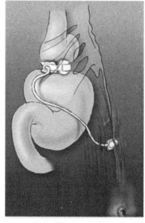
Adjustable gastric band

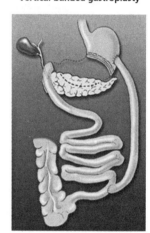
Biliopancreatic diversion with duodenal switch

Figure 2. Surgical procedures for obesity. Reprinted with permission from Maggard MA, Shugarman LR, Suttorp M, et al. Meta-analysis: surgical treatment of obesity. Ann Intern Med. 2005;142:547-559. PMID: 15809466 Copyright 2005, American College of Physicians.

Follow-Up

Schedule follow-up visits to monitor weight loss and comorbid conditions in all obese patients. Use ongoing office visits or ongoing behavioral therapy to reinforce or boost weight loss programs, as the recidivism rate is high for obesity. Generally, the more support the patient receives, the more successful the weight loss effort will be.

Bibliography

Eckel RH. Clinical practice. Nonsurgical management of obesity in adults. N Engl J Med. 2008;358:1941-1950. [PMID: 18450605]

Chapter 34

Approach to Low Back Pain

Sarita Warrier, MD

Low back pain is a common symptom in adults, with a lifetime prevalence approaching 80%. Most acute low back pain is of musculoskeletal origin and will resolve within a 2- to 6-week period. However, in some patients, back pain may be recurrent or chronic (defined as lasting >12 weeks), leading to significant disability. Rarely, low back pain may be related to a serious systemic illness. Evaluation is focused on looking for evidence of either neurologic involvement or systemic disease as the cause of the low back pain.

Prevention

Regular aerobic physical activity and maintenance of fitness and normal body weight may decrease the likelihood of low back pain, although there is no direct evidence to support this. Specific interventions to prevent low back pain in the workplace, such as educational interventions and the use of lumbar mechanical supports, have been studied in several randomized clinical trials but have not demonstrated significant benefit.

Diagnosis

In patients with low back pain, an appropriately directed history and physical examination is the first step in evaluation, with the goal of categorizing the pain as one of the following: nonspecific musculoskeletal low back pain, back pain associated with radiculopathy or spinal stenosis, back pain that may be caused by specific spinal pathology, or nonmusculoskeletal back pain (Table 1).

The most common cause of low back pain in adults is nonspecific musculoskeletal pain, although the precise biologic rationale for the symptoms is unknown. The history and physical examination should look for the precise mechanism of injury, although often there is not an identifiable precipitant. Musculoskeletal pain frequently is described as an ache or a cramp, with radiation across the back in a beltlike fashion. Musculoskeletal pain often radiates to the proximal thigh or hip but rarely further. Neurologic deficits are not observed in acute nonspecific musculoskeletal pain.

Low back pain caused by disc herniation results in radicular pain that follows a dermatomal distribution and extends below the knee. Pain exacerbation with Valsalva maneuver, defecation, or cough suggests disc herniation. Because 95% of all disc herniations occur at L4 to L5 or L5 to S1, careful attention should be paid to these nerve roots. Pain radiating to the anterolateral leg and great toe with weakness in the ankle and dorsiflexion of the great toe is consistent with L5 nerve impingement from the L4 to L5 disc. Pain radiating to the posterior leg with weakness in ankle plantar flexion and a decreased ankle jerk reflex suggests S1 nerve impingement from L5 to S1 disc herniation. The straight-leg raise test, in which the examiner passively raises the patient's leg off the table 30 to 70 degrees while the patient is in a supine position, will pull on the nerve, reproducing the pain on the affected side. This test has a high sensitivity (91%; LR[−] = 0.28) but a low specificity (26%; LR[+] = 1.3) for lumbar disc herniation. The

Table 1. Categories of Low Back Pain

Category	Notes
Nonspecific Musculoskeletal Back Pain	Degenerative joint disease, a common radiologic abnormality that may or may not be related to symptoms, may be seen on imaging.
Back Pain Associated with Radiculopathy or Spinal Stenosis	
Degenerative disc disease with herniation (radiculopathy)	Common cause of nerve root impingement and radicular symptoms. Disc bulging is also a common incidental finding on lumbar spine MRI in asymptomatic patients.
Spinal stenosis	Most common in elderly patients presenting with severe leg pain and pseudoclaudication aggravated by walking or standing.
Back Pain Caused by Specific Spinal Pathology	
Osteomyelitis (see Chapter 63), epidural abscess, or discitis	Associated with probable previous or ongoing source of infection and constitutional symptoms.
Cauda equina or cord compression	Most commonly from metastatic prostate, breast, or lung cancer; central disc herniation can also cause cord compression. Look for overflow incontinence, saddle anesthesia, and leg weakness.
Osteoporosis with compression fracture (see Chapter 15)	Osteoporotic compression fracture accounts for approximately 4% of back pain complaints.
Ankylosing spondylitis	Usual onset before age 40 y. Patients typically present with chronic low back pain that worsens with rest and improves with activity. Associated with decreased spinal range of motion.
Nonmusculoskeletal Back Pain	Gastrointestinal (peptic ulcer, pancreatitis), genitourinary (nephrolithiasis, pyelonephritis, prostatitis, pelvic infection, tumor), or vascular (abdominal aortic aneurysm, aortic dissection).

MRI = magnetic resonance imaging.

crossed straight-leg raise test, in which the examiner passively lifts the unaffected leg, reproducing pain in the affected leg, has a higher specificity (88%; LR[+] = 2.4) but is less sensitive (29%; LR[−] = 0.8).

Back pain caused by spinal stenosis is more common in elderly patients and typically presents as severe bilateral leg pain. The pain is described as *pseudoclaudication* because it is similar to the claudication of peripheral vascular disease. Unlike claudication, which occurs with exertion and is relieved with rest, pseudoclaudication may be worsened with prolonged standing or walking downhill (lumbar extension) and is alleviated by lying down or with hip and lumbar flexion when sitting. In patients with progressive neurologic deficits caused by spinal stenosis, physical examination findings may include numbness and decreased motor strength in the distal lower extremities bilaterally.

Back pain caused by specific spinal causes may present with certain "red flags" that suggest a systemic illness or more serious spinal pathology as the cause of back pain (Table 2) and may warrant early imaging and referral. Although these findings are very sensitive, they are not specific and do not automatically warrant a more exhaustive evaluation. The evaluation depends on the patient's description of the pain, associated symptoms, and elements in the patient's past medical history.

- Rapidly progressive neurologic deficits should alert the clinician to potential spinal cord compression, which is a surgical emergency. Bilateral lower extremity weakness with bowel or bladder dysfunction, decreased anal sphincter tone, and perineal sensory loss (saddle anesthesia) raise concern for cauda equina syndrome, which is compression of sacral nerves from a tumor or central herniated disc.
- A previous history of cancer, unexplained weight loss, age older than 50 years, pain that wakes the patient from sleep, or pain that is slowly progressive increases the likelihood of cancer.

- A history of injection drug use or chronic immunosuppression and the presence of fever, chills, night sweats, or weight loss suggest infection (osteomyelitis, septic discitis, epidural abscess).
- A history of trauma or risk factors for osteoporosis (prolonged glucocorticoid use, advanced age) raise suspicion for vertebral compression fracture.
- Morning stiffness, pain that is alleviated with exercise, onset of symptoms before age 40 years, slow onset of pain, and pain lasting longer than 3 months suggest ankylosing spondylitis.

Back pain may also be a reflection of nonmusculoskeletal processes. In a patient with atherosclerotic disease and hypotension, a leaking abdominal aortic aneurysm is a consideration, and ripping or tearing low back pain raises the rare possibility of aortic dissection with extension into a renal artery. Pancreatitis and peptic ulcer disease can cause pain that radiates to the back, and nephrolithiasis and pyelonephritis may cause flank pain that may be mistaken for musculoskeletal low back pain.

Most patients with low back pain do not require imaging at the time of presentation; however, patients with history or physical examination findings suggesting potentially serious underlying systemic illness require imaging for further evaluation. The American College of Physicians (ACP) Clinical Practice Guidelines on imaging for low back pain recommend a trial of therapy for patients with no neurological symptoms before obtaining plain radiographs of the lumbar and sacral spine, which are most useful to evaluate for vertebral fractures when such pathology is suspected. Anteroposterior pelvis plain radiography along with an elevated erythrocyte sedimentation rate (ESR) or C-reactive protein may be helpful in identifying ankylosing spondylitis in the appropriate clinical scenario. Otherwise, plain radiography adds little to a patient's evaluation. Magnetic resonance imaging (MRI) is most useful for the evaluation of systemic illness, infection, and cord compression or cauda equina

Table 2. "Red Flags" in the Evaluation of Low Back Pain

Key Features on History or Physical Examination	Possible Cause	Imaging
History of cancer with new onset of low back pain	Cancer	MRI
Unexplained weight loss, failure to improve after 1 mo; age >50 y	Cancer	Lumbosacral plain radiography after trial of therapy
Multiple risk factors present	Cancer	Plain radiography or MRI
Fever; injection drug use; recent infection	Vertebral infection	Emergent MRI
Urinary retention; motor deficits at multiple levels; fecal incontinence; saddle anesthesia	Cauda equina syndrome	Emergent MRI
History of osteoporosis; use of glucocorticoids; older age fracture	Vertebral compression fracture	Lumbosacral plain radiography
Morning stiffness; improvement with exercise; alternating buttock pain; awakening because of back pain during the second part of the night; younger age	Ankylosing spondylitis	Plain radiography of pelvis after trial of therapy
Back pain with leg pain in an L4, L5, or S1 nerve root distribution; positive straight-leg raise test or crossed straight-leg raise test	Herniated disc	None; MRI only if persistent progressive symptoms >1 mo and potential treatment with epidural steroid injection or surgery
Radiating leg pain; older age (pseudoclaudication a weak predictor)	Spinal stenosis	None; MRI only if persistent progressive symptoms >1 mo and potential treatment with surgery
Symptoms present >1 mo	Thorough reevaluation necessary to suggest cause before imaging	

AP = anteroposterior; CRP = C-reactive protein; ESR = erythrocyte sedimentation rate; MRI = magnetic resonance imaging.

Adapted with permission from Chou R, Qaseem A, Snow V, et al; Clinical Efficacy Assessment Subcommittee of the American College of Physicians; American College of Physicians; American Pain Society Low Back Pain Guidelines Panel. Diagnosis and treatment of low back pain: a joint clinical practice guideline from the American College of Physicians and the American Pain Society [erratum in Ann Intern Med. 2008;148:247-248]. Ann Intern Med. 2007;147:481. [PMID: 17909209] Copyright 2007, American College of Physicians.

syndrome and is required emergently when these conditions are suspected. **Imaging for acute nonspecific musculoskeletal pain is not recommended because there is poor correlation between a patient's symptoms and imaging findings.** In asymptomatic patients, a bulging disc can be seen in 60% of MRI studies, with true herniation present in 30%, so careful correlation between imaging studies and the patient's history and physical examination is necessary to prevent further unnecessary diagnostic and therapeutic maneuvers. **In patients with low back pain caused by suspected disc herniation or spinal stenosis, MRI is recommended only if the patient is a potential candidate for surgery and usually only after a trial of medication therapy.** Laboratory studies, including a complete blood count, urinalysis, and ESR, also are highly sensitive but not specific in systemic illness, especially infections. **Electromyography and nerve conduction velocity tests and additional diagnostic studies are rarely indicated in the initial evaluation of low back pain.**

The most important factor predicting the course of acute or chronic back pain is the presence of psychosocial distress. Psychosocial factors that predict a risk for chronic disability include depression, somatoform disorders, and job dissatisfaction. Low back pain associated with pain and weakness in a nondermatomal distribution raises concern for psychosocial issues exacerbating the patient's symptoms. Physical examination findings suggesting that psychosocial distress may be causing or exacerbating low back pain include nondermatomal distribution of pain, increase in pain with passive rotation of the spine, increase in pain on axial loading (ie, when the examiner applies a few pounds of pressure to the top of the patient's skull), and discrepancy in straight-leg test results between the supine and sitting positions or with distraction.

Therapy

Conditions that lead to rapid and potentially irreversible loss of neurologic function, such as spinal cord compression caused by a tumor or infection, are surgical emergencies that require immediate treatment. The greatest predictor of prognosis is pretreatment neurologic status. Treatment for spinal cord compression includes surgical decompression and, in cases of metastatic disease, radiation therapy. When cord compression is suspected, high-dose glucocorticoids are given immediately for pain relief and to prevent further loss of neurologic function. Surgical therapy also may be considered in patients with severe or progressive neurologic deficits secondary to disc herniation. Kyphoplasty and vertebroplasty, which involve the injection of bone cement into collapsed vertebrae under radiologic guidance, are sometimes used in cases of vertebral compression fractures caused by osteoporosis or other diseases affecting the spine. However, because the pain of acute osteoporotic compression fractures typically resolves with conservative therapy without intervention, these procedures are recommended only in patients with refractory pain.

Most cases of acute low back pain (<4 weeks in duration) are self-limited; up to 90% of cases of acute low back pain should resolve with conservative treatment by 4 to 6 weeks. Multiple systematic reviews have shown that bed rest is ineffective and can prolong low back pain. Early mobilization and continuation of normal activity is most beneficial, although back-specific exercise should not begin until there is resolution of acute pain. There is no evidence that any specific exercise program is more beneficial, but general exercise and weight control will help prevent future episodes of low back pain. Patients with subacute (4–12 weeks) or chronic (>12 weeks) low back pain may benefit from physical therapy, chiropractic manipulation, massage, yoga, or acupuncture, although there are conflicting data on the effectiveness of these modalities.

First-line medication therapy is analgesia with acetaminophen or nonsteroidal anti-inflammatory drugs (NSAIDs). Muscle relaxants and opioid analgesics have not been shown to be more effective than NSAIDs for treatment of low back pain, and both may have central nervous system side effects and addiction potential. Therefore, they are not recommended as first-line therapy. A short course of a muscle relaxant or opioid analgesic should be considered only in a patient with acute low back pain who has not responded to a first-line analgesic. Opioids should not be used long term to treat chronic back pain. Anticonvulsants, such as gabapentin, have demonstrated small short-term benefits in treating radiculopathy. Systemic glucocorticoid therapy has not been shown to improve acute or chronic low back pain. Glucocorticoid injection therapy has shown mixed results for the treatment of lumbar radiculopathy caused by disc herniation; studies show moderate short-term improvement (<3 months in duration) but no long-term benefits. Currently, there is insufficient evidence to support the use of glucocorticoid injections in the treatment of spinal stenosis and nonspecific low back pain.

Follow-Up

Patients with acute low back pain should have a scheduled follow-up office visit or telephone call at 2 to 4 weeks to determine whether recovery is consistent with the natural history of the condition. If recovery is delayed, reevaluation for more serious underlying causes of back pain should be considered. If no cause is found, the patient should be reexamined for possible psychosocial factors that may be exacerbating symptoms. It may be appropriate to consider consultation with a back specialist when patients with nonspecific low back pain do not respond to standard noninvasive therapy. In general, decisions about consultation should be individualized and based on assessment of the patient's symptoms and response to interventions and the availability of specialists with relevant expertise. For patients with back pain caused by radiculopathy or spinal stenosis, published guidelines suggest referral for surgery after 3 months to 2 years of failed nonsurgical interventions, although progressive neurologic deficits and severe pain that is not responsive to conservative treatment can lead to earlier consideration of surgery. Surgical treatment for radiculopathy caused by a herniated lumbar disc involves discectomy. Spinal stenosis may be surgically treated with decompressive laminectomy. Both surgical treatments have shown moderate short-term benefits (<3 months with discectomy, 1–2 years with laminectomy) compared with nonsurgical interventions. However, in both cases, there is no evidence of long-term benefits from surgical treatment. Current guidelines from the ACP and the American Pain Society recommend that decision making about surgical treatment for these conditions include a discussion between the physician and patient about the benefits and risks of surgical treatment.

Bibliography

Chou R, Loeser JD, Owens DK, et al; **American Pain Society Low Back Pain Guideline Panel.** Interventional Therapies, Surgery, and Interdisciplinary Rehabilitation for Low Back Pain: an evidence-based clinical practice guideline from the American Pain Society. Spine 2009;34:1066–1077. [PMID: 19363457]

Chou R, Qaseem A, Owens DK, et al; **Clinical Guidelines Committee of the American College of Physicians.** Diagnostic imaging for low back pain: advice for high-value health care from the American College of

Physicians.[published erratum appears in Ann Intern Med. 2012 Jan 3;156(1 Pt 1):71]. Ann Intern Med. 2011;154:181-189. [PMID: 21282698]

Chou R, Qaseem A, Snow V, et al; Clinical Efficacy Assessment Subcommittee of the American College of Physicians; American College of Physicians/American Pain Society Low Back Pain Guidelines Panel. Diagnosis and treatment of low back pain: a joint clinical practice guideline from the American College of Physicians and the American Pain Society [published erratum appears in Ann Intern Med. 2008;148:247-248]. Ann Intern Med. 2007;147:478-491. [PMID: 17909209]

Wilson JF. In the clinic. Low back pain. Ann Intern Med. 2008;148:ITC5-1-ITC5-16. [PMID: 18458275]

Chapter 35

Approach to Cough

Kendall Novoa-Takara, MD

Acute Cough

Acute cough is one of the most common presenting complaints in ambulatory practice. Acute cough lasts <3 weeks and usually is self-limited. The most common causes of acute cough are listed in Table 1. A cough lasting 3 to 8 weeks is termed a subacute cough and may represent a prolonged presentation of an acute cough or may be an early presentation of a chronic cough.

Viral upper respiratory tract infection is the most common cause of acute cough; however, acute viral airway infection can result in protracted bronchial hyperreactivity, with secondary cough lasting weeks to months. Airway cough receptors are located in the larynx, trachea, and bronchi, and cough in the setting of rhinitis, rhinosinusitis, and pharyngitis is attributed to reflex stimulation from postnasal drainage or throat clearing. Specific viruses most often associated with cough are those that produce primarily lower respiratory tract disease (ie, influenza A and B, parainfluenza virus, respiratory syncytial virus) as well as viruses that produce upper respiratory tract symptoms (ie, coronavirus, adenovirus, rhinovirus). Viral rhinitis or rhinosinusitis is characterized by rhinorrhea, sneezing, nasal congestion, and postnasal drainage with or without fever, headache, tearing, and throat discomfort. The chest examination findings in these patients are normal. Most viral causes of cough are treated symptomatically.

Influenza is characterized by the sudden onset of fever and malaise followed by cough, headache, myalgia, and nasal and pulmonary symptoms, particularly during the appropriate season. Clinical criteria suggesting the diagnosis of influenza include temperature ≥37.7°C (100.0°F) and at least one of the following symptoms: cough, pharyngitis, or rhinorrhea. A diagnosis of influenza can be established by viral cultures of secretions or by rapid diagnostic tests (immunofluorescence, polymerase chain reaction [PCR], enzyme immunoassays). These rapid tests are helpful in confirming disease if results are positive, although they have limited sensitivity, and negative results do not exclude the diagnosis; other studies are indicated if confirmation is necessary. **Antiviral therapy for influenza is indicated only for hospitalized patients and those with severe, complicated, or progressive illness.** The neuraminidase inhibitors oseltamivir and zanamivir are approved medications for treatment of influenza A and B. When indicated, treatment should be started within the first 2 days of symptom onset and may reduce the duration of illness and decrease the risk for serious complications. Because of increasing resistance, specific treatment guidelines are issued annually based on the sensitivities of the predominant circulating influenza strain. Although vaccination is the preferred preventive intervention, antiviral chemoprophylaxis provides immediate protection and may be useful in persons who have not been vaccinated or who are not expected to respond to a vaccine or until vaccine-induced immunity becomes effective (about 2 weeks after vaccination). Chemoprophylaxis should be restricted to residents in an assisted-living facility during an influenza outbreak, persons who are at higher risk for influenza-related complications and who have had recent household or other close contact with a person with laboratory-confirmed influenza, and unvaccinated health care workers who have had recent close contact with a person with laboratory-confirmed influenza. H1N1 virus ("swine flu") is an emerging influenza A virus. Symptoms (cough, fever, rhinorrhea) are similar to those occurring in seasonal influenza, as is the mode of spread, including person-to-person transmission. This virus is susceptible to neuraminidase inhibitors with oseltamivir and zanamivir, the drugs of choice for chemoprophylaxis of influenza- and H1N1-exposed high-risk adults.

Bordetella pertussis, Mycoplasma pneumoniae, and *Chlamydophila pneumoniae* are nonviral causes of uncomplicated acute bronchitis and cough in adults, accounting for 5% to 10% of total

Table 1. Differential Diagnosis of Acute and Chronic Cough

Acute Cough (<3 wk)	Chronic Cough (>8 wk)
Common cold or viral upper respiratory tract infection	Upper airway cough syndrome
Lower respiratory tract infections (bronchitis and pneumonia)	Asthma
Bacterial sinusitis	GERD
Rhinitis caused by allergens or environmental irritants	Nonasthmatic eosinophilic bronchitis
Asthma or COPD exacerbation	Bronchiectasis
Cardiogenic pulmonary edema	Medication reaction (eg, ACE inhibitor)
Aspiration or foreign body	Chronic bronchitis caused by smoking
Medication reaction (eg, ACE inhibitor)	
Pulmonary embolism	

ACE = angiotensin-converting enzyme; COPD = chronic obstructive pulmonary disease; GERD = gastroesophageal reflux disease.

cases. Because Gram stain and culture of sputum do not reliably detect *M. pneumoniae*, *C. pneumoniae*, or *B. pertussis*, these tests and other diagnostic tests are not recommended. Routine antibiotic treatment of acute bronchitis does not have a consistent effect on the duration or severity of illness or on potential complications and is not recommended. The one uncommon circumstance for which evidence supports antibiotic treatment is suspicion of pertussis. Unfortunately, no clinical features allow clinicians to distinguish adults with persistent cough caused by pertussis. Therefore, clinicians should limit treatment for suspected pertussis to adult patients

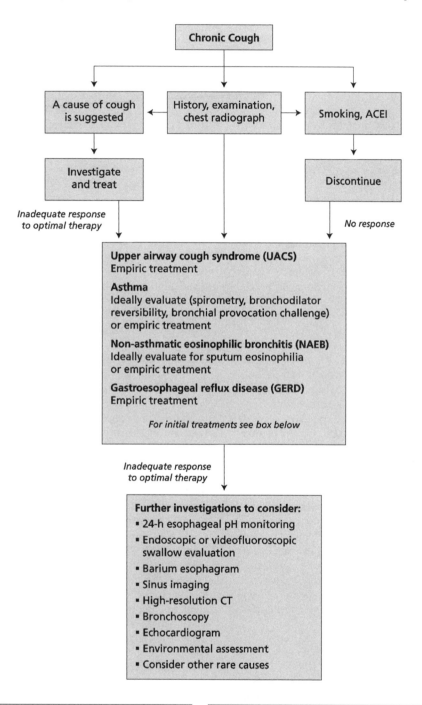

Figure 1. Evaluation of chronic cough. ACEI = angiotensin-converting enzyme inhibitor; CT = computed tomography; LTRA = leukotriene receptor antagonist.

with a high probability of pertussis (cough lasting ≥2 weeks without an apparent cause associated with one of the following symptoms: paroxysms of coughing, inspiratory whoop or posttussive emesis or cough ≥2 weeks during a documented outbreak of *B. pertussis,* known close contact to a confirmed case of pertussis). The diagnostic gold standard is recovery of bacteria in culture or by PCR. Antimicrobial therapy for suspected pertussis in adults is recommended primarily to decrease shedding of the pathogen and spread of disease because antibiotic treatment does not appear to improve resolution of symptoms if it is initiated beyond 7 to 10 days after the onset of illness.

Pneumonia is the third most common cause of acute cough illness and the most serious; therefore, the primary diagnostic objective when evaluating acute cough is to exclude the presence of pneumonia. The combined absence of abnormalities in vital signs (ie, heart rate ≥100/min (negative likelihood ratio [LR(–)] = 0.7), respiration rate ≥28/min [LR(–) = 0.8], oral temperature ≥37.8°C [100.0°F; LR(–) = 0.7]) or on chest examination (ie, crackles [LR(–) = 0.8], diminished breath sounds [LR(–) = 0.8]) sufficiently reduces the likelihood of pneumonia to the point where further diagnostic testing is unnecessary.

Asthma is a consideration in patients presenting with an acute cough illness. However, in the setting of acute cough, the diagnosis of asthma is difficult to establish unless there is a reliable previous history of asthma and episodes of wheezing and shortness of breath in addition to the cough. This is because transient bronchial hyperresponsiveness and associated abnormal results on spirometry are common to all causes of uncomplicated acute bronchitis. Postinfectious airflow obstruction on pulmonary function testing or bronchoprovocation testing (eg, methacholine challenge) may be present up to 8 weeks after an acute bronchitis episode, making the distinction from asthma difficult. Inhaled short-acting β-agonists should be used in patients with cough and wheezing but are of unclear benefit in those with acute cough without wheezing.

Acute exacerbation of chronic bronchitis and bronchiectasis presents as an abrupt increase from baseline in cough, sputum production, sputum purulence, and shortness of breath (discussed later).

Treatment of acute cough may include antitussive agents, expectorants, mucolytic agents, antihistamines, and nasal anticholinergic agents. The main indications for therapy are sleep disruption, painful cough, and debilitating cough. **There is little evidence to support the use of most over-the-counter and prescription antitussive medications for treatment of cough, with the effectiveness of most agents being similar to placebo.** Additionally, antitussive medications may cause significant adverse effects, including confusion, nausea, and constipation, particularly in elderly adults; among antitussive agents, codeine was no more effective than placebo; and evidence was mixed for dextromethorphan, with some evidence suggesting a benefit with guaifenesin.

Chronic Cough

Chronic cough lasts >8 weeks. The most common causes of chronic cough are listed in Table 1. Although the clinical evaluation of chronic cough includes a careful history and physical examination focusing on common causes, all patients should undergo chest radiography. Smoking cessation and discontinuation of angiotensin-converting enzyme (ACE) inhibitors should be recommended for 4 weeks before additional workup (Figure 1). The cause(s) of cough may be determined by observing which therapy eliminates the symptoms associated with cough. Because cough may be caused by more than one condition, a second or third intervention should be added in the event of partial initial response.

Upper airway cough syndrome (UACS), asthma, and gastroesophageal reflux disease (GERD) are responsible for approximately 90% of cases of chronic cough in patients who are nonsmokers, have a normal chest radiograph, and are not taking an ACE inhibitor. The patient's description of the cough, the timing of the cough (eg, when lying down), and the presence or absence of sputum production all have no predictive value in the evaluation of chronic cough. Chronic cough is caused by more than one condition in most patients.

UACS refers to a recurrent cough that occurs when mucus from the nose drains down the oropharynx and triggers cough receptors. The diagnosis is confirmed when drug therapy eliminates the discharge and cough. Most patients with UACS have symptoms or evidence of one or more of the following: postnasal drainage, frequent throat clearing, nasal discharge, cobblestone appearance of the oropharyngeal mucosa, or mucus dripping down the oropharynx. Nonsedating antihistamines, in combination with a decongestant, are the most consistently effective form of therapy for patients with UACS not caused by sinusitis. Additionally, the avoidance of allergens and the daily use of intranasal glucocorticoids or cromolyn sodium are recommended for patients with allergic rhinitis. When the cause of a chronic cough is unclear, the American College of Chest Physicians recommends initial treatment with a nonsedating antihistamine–decongestant combination to treat UACS. Patients who do not respond to empiric therapy should undergo sinus imaging to diagnose "silent" chronic sinusitis.

Cough-variant asthma is suggested by the presence of airway hyperresponsiveness and is confirmed when cough resolves with asthma medications. Cough-variant asthma (cough is the predominant symptom) occurs in up to 57% of patients with asthma. If the diagnosis is uncertain, bronchoprovocation testing should be considered. A negative test result is 100% sensitive in ruling out asthma, but a positive test result is less helpful because it is not specific for asthma; other conditions, such as chronic obstructive pulmonary disease, can be associated with a positive test result. The treatment of cough-variant asthma is the same as for asthma in general, but the maximum symptomatic benefit may not occur for 6 to 8 weeks in cough-variant asthma.

Although GERD can cause cough by aspiration, the most common mechanism is a vagally mediated distal esophageal-tracheobronchial reflex. There is nothing about the character or timing of chronic cough caused by GERD that distinguishes it from other causes of cough. Up to 75% of patients with GERD-induced cough may have no other GERD symptoms. The most sensitive (96%) and specific (98%) test for GERD is 24-hour esophageal pH monitoring; however, a therapeutic trial with a proton pump inhibitor is recommended before invasive testing. Symptom relief may not occur until 3 months after treatment is begun.

In patients with chronic cough who have normal findings on chest radiography, normal spirometry results, and a negative methacholine challenge test, the diagnosis of nonasthmatic eosinophilic bronchitis (NAEB) should be considered. NAEB is confirmed as a cause of chronic cough by the presence of airway eosinophilia (obtained by sputum induction or bronchial lavage during bronchoscopy) and improvement with treatment. Patients with NAEB should be evaluated for possible occupational exposure to a sensitizer. First-line treatment of NAEB is inhaled glucocorticoids and avoidance of responsible allergens.

Cough with sputum is the hallmark symptom of chronic bronchitis. Treatment is targeted at reducing sputum production and airway inflammation by removing environmental irritants, particularly cigarettes. An inhaled anticholinergic agent (ipratropium or tiotropium) can decrease sputum production, and systemic glucocorticoids and antibiotics may be helpful in decreasing cough during severe exacerbations. Bronchiectasis, a type of chronic bronchitis, causes a chronic or recurrent cough characterized by voluminous (>30 mL/day) sputum production with purulent exacerbations. Chest radiography and high-resolution computed tomography (CT) results may be diagnostic, showing thickened bronchial walls in a "tram line" pattern. Bronchiectasis should be treated with antibiotics selected on the basis of sputum culture and with chest physiotherapy.

Although most patients who smoke have a chronic cough, these are not the patients who commonly seek medical attention for cough. After smoking cessation, cough has been shown to resolve or markedly decrease in 94% to 100% of patients. In 54% of these patients, cough resolution occurred within 4 weeks of smoking cessation.

Cough caused by ACE inhibitors is a class effect, not dose related, and may occur a few hours to weeks or months after a patient takes the first dose of an ACE inhibitor. The diagnosis of ACE inhibitor–induced cough can be established only when cough disappears with elimination of the drug. The median time to resolution is 26 days. Substituting an angiotensin receptor blocker for the ACE inhibitor also can eliminate an ACE inhibitor–induced cough.

Hemoptysis

Hemoptysis is defined as coughing up blood, and it may be associated with either acute or chronic cough syndromes. The most commonly encountered causes of hemoptysis in ambulatory patients are infection (bronchitis or pneumonia) followed by malignancy. Elevated pulmonary pressures from left-sided heart failure or pulmonary embolism may cause hemoptysis, although hemoptysis alone is not sufficiently sensitive or specific to diagnose pulmonary embolism. In up to 30% of patients, the cause is not identified (cryptogenic hemoptysis). In addition to lower respiratory (tracheobronchial, pulmonary, and primary vascular) sources of hemoptysis, the differential diagnosis of hemoptysis must include upper airway (nasopharyngeal) sources of bleeding and gastrointestinal bleeding.

All patients with hemoptysis should undergo chest radiography. Factors that increase the risk of malignancy include male sex, age older than 40 years, a smoking history >40 pack-years, and symptoms lasting >1 week. These patients should be referred for chest CT and fiberoptic bronchoscopy if a clear cause of hemoptysis is not identified on the chest radiograph. Bronchoscopy is necessary in these patients because endobronchial lesions are not always visible on CT scans. Patients with history suggestive of a lower respiratory tract infection and a normal chest radiograph may be treated with an oral antibiotic and observed for recurrence; if hemoptysis recurs or persists, a referral for bronchoscopy should be made. A diagnosis of cryptogenic hemoptysis should not be made until the patient has undergone a thorough evaluation. Patients with mild hemoptysis (<30 mL/day) who are clinically stable may undergo outpatient evaluation and treatment.

Massive hemoptysis is blood loss greater than 200 mL/day. Massive hemoptysis requires urgent inpatient evaluation, early consultation with a pulmonologist, and intensive care. Airway management and ventilation is critical because death results from asphyxiation, not exsanguination. Urgent bronchoscopy should be considered in massive hemoptysis as well as bronchial artery embolization by interventional radiology. Surgical intervention is considered the last resort for the treatment of massive hemoptysis.

Bibliography

Braman SS. Postinfectious cough: ACCP Evidence-based clinical practice guidelines. Chest. 2006;129:138S-146S. [PMID: 16428699]

Dudha M, Lehrman SG, Aronow WS, Butt A. Evaluation and management of cough. Compr Ther. 2009;35:9-17. [PMID: 19351100]

Dudha M, Lehrman S, Aronow WS, Rosa J. Hemoptysis: diagnosis and treatment. Compr Ther. 2009;35:139-149. [PMID: 20043609]

Smith SM, Schroeder K, Fahey T. Over-the-counter (OTC) medications for acute cough in children and adults in ambulatory settings [review]. Cochrane Database Syst Rev. 2012(8):CD001831. [PMID: 22895922]

Chapter 36

Smoking Cessation

Nadia Ismail, MD

Smoking is the most common cause of avoidable disease, disability, and death in the United States. More than 400,000 people in the U.S. die from cigarette smoking each year, and an additional 8.6 million have a serious illness caused or exacerbated by smoking. Cigarettes are a known risk factor for coronary artery disease, chronic obstructive pulmonary disease (COPD), and other pulmonary diseases, aerodigestive cancers, genitourinary cancers, peptic ulcer disease, and complications of pregnancy.

The benefits of smoking cessation are well documented. People who quit smoking before age 50 years have half the risk of dying within the next 15 years compared with those who continue to smoke. The excess risk of death from coronary artery disease drops by 50% in the first year of abstinence and continues to decline thereafter. In patients with peripheral arterial disease, smoking cessation is associated with improved walking distance, decreased pain, and improved bypass graft patency. In people with sustained abstinence from smoking, forced expiratory volume in 1 second declines 72 mL over 5 years compared with 301 mL in people who continue to smoke. Within 5 to 15 years, stroke risk is reduced to that of a person who does not smoke. Smoking cessation also results in a 50% reduction in bladder cancer.

Despite strong evidence in favor of cessation, progress in reducing rates among young persons and adults has stalled. Adult smoking prevalence declined steadily from 1965 (42.2%) through the 1980s; however, the decline in smoking rates among adults began to slow in the 1990s, and the percentage of people smoking has remained relatively unchanged (around 20%) since the mid-2000s.

Up to 70% of people who smoke would like to quit, but only 5% to 8% can quit without therapy and usually only after several attempts. Every year, almost half of the 51 million smokers in the U.S. try to quit for at least 1 day, highlighting the need for all physicians to address smoking cessation with every patient during every visit.

Therapy

Nicotine is a naturally occurring alkaloid found primarily in tobacco and most commonly consumed via cigarette smoking. The half-life of nicotine is about 2 hours; the principal metabolite of nicotine, cotinine, has a half-life of up to 20 hours. Nicotine stimulates α- 4 β-

2 nicotinic acetylcholine receptors and, like other highly addicting drugs, increases dopamine release, producing a pleasurable effect. The central nervous system effects of nicotine are related to both blood level and rate of increase at nicotinic acetylcholine receptors. Cravings for nicotine are stimulated by low levels of central nervous system dopamine during periods of smoking abstinence, which leads to a loss of the euphoric effects and possibly withdrawal symptoms (insomnia, irritability, anxiety, shaking, hunger, and difficulty concentrating). These effects, coupled with the psychosocial factors associated with tobacco use make successful smoking cessation challenging for many patients.

Smoking status should be determined in all patients. The U.S. Public Health Service recommends asking all patients two questions: "Do you smoke?" and "Do you want to quit?" The U.S. Public Health Service clinical practice guideline on smoking cessation recommends brief interventions for tobacco use and dependence (Table 1). For patients who may be willing to quit, the "5 A's" provide a counseling strategy for clinicians to assist in the process. For patients who are unwilling to quit, the "5 R's" are recommended as a motivational technique to move patients from the precontemplation stage of behavior change (*I don't want to quit*) to contemplation (*I am concerned but not ready to quit now*) or preparation (*I am ready to quit*).

For those who wish to stop smoking, the success rate without assistance is low, estimated to be between 4% and 7% at 1 year. The advice of physicians alone can improve the smoking cessation rate by around 2.5% at 1 year. Although even brief interventions can be effective, high-intensity counseling (>10 min) is more likely to be successful. There is no apparent advantage of group therapy over individual therapy or gradual cessation over abrupt cessation. Some patients may benefit from self-help information (via printed material or electronic media), but the magnitude of benefit is small. The addition of self-help materials to personal counseling or drug treatment does not result in added benefit. Telephone counseling (ie, a system of individual help that includes consistent support and reminders provided over the telephone) can be particularly beneficial. Whether initiated by a physician or by the patient, telephone counseling is equally effective in helping patients who want to quit be successful. An example of a telephone counseling system is the

Table 1. Five-Step Brief Intervention for Smoking Cessation

The 5 A's: For Patients Willing to Quit	The 5 R's: To Motivate Patients Unwilling to Quit
Ask about tobacco use	Encourage patient to think of **R**elevance of quitting smoking to their lives
Advise to quit	Assist patient in identifying the **R**isks of smoking
Assess willingness to make a quit attempt	Assist the patient in identifying the **R**ewards of smoking cessation
Assist in quit attempt	Discuss with the patient **R**oadblocks or barriers to attempting cessation
Arrange follow-up	**R**epeat the motivational intervention at all visits

Table 2. Commonly Used Pharmacologic Therapies for Smoking Cessation

Agent	Mechanism	Effectiveness	Initial Prescription	Advantages	Disadvantages	Approximate Cost
Nicotine gum[a]	Prevents nicotine withdrawal[b]	Increases cessation rates about 1.5-2 times at 6 mo.	1 piece (2 mg) whenever urge to smoke, up to 30 pieces/d. Continuous use for >3 mo not recommended. Max dose: 24 pieces per day	Less expensive than other forms of nicotine replacement. Chewing replaces smoking habit. No prescription required. Associated with delay in weight gain.	Some patients find taste unpleasant.	$2.50-$6.00 per day for 10 pieces (depending on dose)
Nicotine patch (24 h)[a,c]	Prevents nicotine withdrawal[b]	Increases cessation rates about 1.5-2 times at 6 mo.	Most patients: 21-mg patch for 4-8 wk (remove and replace every 24 h), then 14-mg patch for 2-4 wk, followed by 7-mg patch for 2-4 wk. Max dose: 22 mg per day. Adults weighing <100 lb (45.5 kg), smoking fewer than 10 cigarettes/d, and/or with cardiovascular disease: 14-mg patch for 4-8 wk, then 7-mg patch for 2-4 wk.	Less expensive than other forms of nicotine replacement. No prescription required.	Can cause skin irritation.	$3-$5 per day per patch
Nicotine nasal spray[a]	Prevents nicotine withdrawal[b]	Increases cessation rates about 1.5-2 times at 6 mo.	1 spray (0.5 mg) in each nostril 1-2 times/h whenever urge to smoke, up to 10 sprays/h or 80 sprays/d. Initially, encourage use of at least 16 sprays/d, the minimum effective dose. Recommended duration of therapy is 3 mo. Max dose: 80 sprays per day; do not exceed 10 sprays per h.	Some patients prefer this delivery method.	More expensive than other forms of nicotine replacement. Requires a prescription. Safety not established for use >6 mo.	$5-$6 per day for 24 sprays
Nicotine inhaler[a]	Prevents nicotine withdrawal[b]	Increases cessation rates about 1.5-2 times at 6 mo.	6 to 16 cartridges (containing 4 mg)/d for up to 12 wk, followed by gradual reduction in dosage over a period up to 12 wk.	Some patients prefer this delivery method.	More expensive than other forms of nicotine replacement. Requires a prescription. Use >6 mo not recommended.	$9-$12 per day for 6 cartridges

(continued on next page)

Table 2. Commonly Used Pharmacologic Therapies for Smoking Cessation (cont.)

Agent	Mechanism	Effectiveness	Initial Prescription	Advantages	Disadvantages	Approximate Cost
Nicotine lozenge[a]	Prevents nicotine withdrawal[b]	Increases cessation rates about 1.5-2 times at 6 mo.	1 lozenge (2 mg or 4 mg) every 1-2 h during weeks 1-6, then lozenge every 2-4 h during weeks 7-9, then 1 lozenge every 4-8 h during weeks 10-12. Patients who smoke within 30 min of waking require 4-mg lozenge; those who have first cigarette later in the day require 2-mg lozenge. Recommended duration of therapy is 12 wk.	Some patients prefer this delivery method.	Some patients find the taste unpleasant. Side effects include nausea, dyspepsia, and mouth tingling. Avoid acidic beverages (juice, soda) 15 min before use.	$5 per day for 10 lozenges
Bupropion	Unclear	Increases cessation rates about 2 times at 1 y.	Begin 1-2 wk before quit date; start with 150 mg once daily for 3 days, then 150 mg twice daily through end of therapy (7-12 wk max). Max dose: 150 mg twice daily.	Some antidepressant activity; may be a good option for patients with a history of depression. Associated with a delay in weight gain.	Requires a prescription. Can interact with other drugs. Safety in pregnancy is unclear. Associated with hypertension. Avoid in patients with seizure disorder or at risk for seizure; also avoid in patients with eating disorders.	$3-$4 per day
Varenicline	Reduces cravings via nicotine receptor agonist.	Increases cessation rates >3.5 times and almost 2 times over bupropion at 12 wk.	Begin 0.5 mg once daily on days 1-3, then 0.5 mg twice daily on days 4-7, then 1 mg twice daily through end of therapy (12 wk). Consider additional 12 wk of therapy to prevent relapse. Max dose: 1mg twice daily.	No hepatic clearance. No clinically significant drug interactions reported.	Requires a prescription. Associated with hypertension. Side effects include drowsiness, fatigue, nausea, sleep disturbance, constipation, and flatulence. Safety in pregnancy is unclear. Avoid in patients with kidney disease.	$8 per day

[a]Avoid nicotine replacement in patients with recent myocardial infarction, arrhythmia, or unstable angina. Safety of nicotine replacement in pregnancy is unclear.

[b]A standard cigarette contains approximately 1 mg of nicotine.

[c]Several formulations of patches are available. Dosing guidelines are for patches designed to stay in place for 24 h and that come in doses of 21 mg, 14 mg, and 7 mg. Clinicians should check prescribing information on nicotine patches that come in other doses or that are designed for use <24 h/d.

Wilson JF. In the clinic. Smoking cessation. Ann Intern Med. 2007;146:ITC2-1-ITC2-16. [PMID: 17283345]

National Smoking Cessation hotline (1-800-QUITNOW), which is a free resource to patients.

Behavioral counseling is most efficacious when combined with pharmacotherapy (Table 2). Nicotine replacement therapy by any of the available delivery systems increases quit rates by alleviating symptoms of withdrawal. Nicotine replacement therapy is available over the counter (eg, gum, patch, lozenge) and by prescription (eg, inhaler, nasal spray, sublingual tablet). There is no evidence that one form of replacement is more effective or safer than another, and decisions should be based on patient preference, side effects, and cost. In severely nicotine-addicted patients, combining a nicotine patch with another form of replacement (eg, gum, inhaler, nasal spray, or lozenge) produced better results than the use of a single product. Nicotine replacement therapy is contraindicated in patients with a history of recent myocardial infarction, severe angina, or life-threatening arrhythmia and appears to be safe in patients with chronic stable angina. Nicotine replacement is likely safer than smoking for pregnant women but is recommended only after failure of behavioral programs. Unlike other nicotine replacement therapies, nicotine gum has been shown to delay the weight gain associated with smoking cessation.

When used as sole pharmacotherapy, bupropion doubled the odds of cessation compared with placebo, although its mechanism of enhancing smoking abstinence is unknown. Like nicotine gum, bupropion has been shown to delay the weight gain associated with smoking cessation. Bupropion provides a better 1-year quit rate (30%) than nicotine replacement therapy (16%); combination bupropion and nicotine replacement therapy may be superior to monotherapy. Bupropion may lower the seizure threshold and is contraindicated in patients with a history of seizure disorder or in other situations that increase the risk of seizures (eg, alcohol or benzodiazepine withdrawal) and recent monoamine oxidase inhibitor use. Bupropion is a category B drug for pregnancy (no evidence of risk in humans).

Varenicline has a higher affinity for the α-4 β-2 nicotinic receptor than nicotine, blocking nicotine binding and stimulating receptor-mediated activity. Varenicline therapy reduces the cravings felt by smokers. Varenicline given for 12 weeks increased the odds of long-term smoking cessation approximately threefold compared with placebo. When compared directly with bupropion or a nicotine patch, varenicline was more effective; the effectiveness and safety of using varenicline with nicotine replacement therapy has not been well studied. Varenicline has not been well studied in pregnancy (it is pregnancy category C); therefore, its use is considered only when the potential benefits outweigh the potential risks to the fetus.

Both bupropion and varenicline carry FDA "black box" warnings due to the risk for serious neuropsychiatric symptoms, including changes in behavior, hostility, agitation, depressed mood, suicidal thoughts and behaviors, and attempted suicide. Varenicline also carries a warning for a small increase in risk of cardiovascular events in patients with known disease; the significance of this potential adverse effect remains under investigation. Therefore, the balance of potential benefits versus possible risks of using varenicline in patients with cardiovascular disease needs to be carefully considered.

Other medications include nortriptyline, which remains second-line therapy, especially in smokers with depression in whom bupropion is contraindicated. Clonidine has been shown to increase the chance of quitting but is limited by a dose-dependent rise in adverse effects. Naltrexone has been studied for smoking cessation because of its blockade of opioid receptors that might decrease the rewarding effects of nicotine use; however, it has not been found effective and has no current role in smoking cessation.

Many smokers may use alternative therapies such as hypnotherapy and acupuncture for help in smoking cessation. Although there is insufficient evidence to support their use as effective smoking cessation therapies, up to 30% of smokers have considered acupuncture, and 40% of smokers have considered hypnotherapy.

Electronic cigarettes are aerosolizing delivery devices with a disposable cartridge that typically contains nicotine in solution in a solvent such as propylene glycol. Devices vary but are usually contained in a tubular structure made to resemble a cigarette. Despite being called a cigarette, these devices have more in common with nebulizers and metered-dose inhalers, which can be loaded with a drug. There is great variability in the amount of nicotine delivered depending on the device. These devices are currently not regulated by the FDA, and their role in smoking cessation remains to be defined.

Bibliography

Wilson JF. In the clinic. Smoking cessation. Ann Intern Med. 2007; 146:ITC2-1-ITC2-16. [PMID: 17283345]

Chapter 37

Depression

Karen E. Kirkham, MD

Depressive disorders are the most common psychiatric abnormality yet often go undiagnosed. In the United States, 15% of adults are affected by depression at some point during their lifetime. Depression is second only to hypertension as the most commonly encountered condition in primary care practices. Only about half of patients with depression receive treatment despite evidence that it improves quality of life. The spectrum of depressive disorders ranges from mild to severe and from brief to lifelong. Depression can occur alone or coexist with other mood or psychiatric disorders, impairing social and occupational functioning. The detrimental effects of depression on quality of life and daily function match those of heart disease and exceed those of diabetes mellitus and arthritis combined.

Demographic and socioeconomic risk factors for depression include older age (an independent risk factor, especially when associated with neurologic conditions), female sex, unemployment, lower socioeconomic status, lower level of education, alcohol dependence, nonmarried status, and stressful life events. Medical risk factors include a previous personal or family history of depression or other psychiatric disorder, the postpartum state, and chronic disease (eg, diabetes, dementia, coronary artery disease, cancer, stroke). Recent evidence has identified depression as an independent risk factor for increased mortality in patients with coronary artery disease, cancer, and stroke.

The biologic basis for depression involves imbalances in norepinephrine, serotonin, and/or dopamine in the prefrontal cortex, basal ganglia, hippocampus, and cerebellum. Serotonergic pathways are believed to function largely in mood, whereas norepinephrine is likely involved with drive and energy state. Both systems function in appetite, sleep regulation, and anxiety. Depression is strongly linked with stress, and stress systems in the brain are largely mediated by changes in norepinephrine transmission. There is also evidence of a genetic component with elevated rates of depression in those with first-degree relatives affected by depression and high rates of concordance among twins. However, no specific genes that provide increased susceptibility or resistance to depression have been identified.

Table 1. Differential Diagnosis of Major Depressive Disorder

Disorder	Notes
Major depressive disorder	Depressed mood or loss of interest or pleasure in almost all activities. In addition, symptoms must occur nearly every day for ≥2 wk, and at least five DSM-V depressive symptoms must be present.[a]
Grief reaction	Major depression may be transiently present in normal grief, although sadness without the complete syndrome is more common. Pervasive and generalized guilt and persistent vegetative signs and symptoms should raise concern for major depression.
Situational adjustment reaction with depressed mood	Subsyndromal depression (symptoms not severe enough to for a diagnosis of depression) with a clear precipitant. Usually resolves with resolution of the acute stressor and without medication.
Minor/subsyndromal depression	An acute depression that is less symptomatic than major depression and causing less impairment in social or occupational functioning.
Persistent depressive disorder (dysthymia)	Characterized by depressed mood or anhedonia at least half the time for ≥2 y, accompanied by two or more vegetative or psychological symptoms and functional impairment.
Seasonal affective disorder	A subtype of major depression occurring with seasonal change, typically fall or winter onset, and resolving with seasonal remission.
Premenstrual dysphoric disorder	Characterized by depressed mood, anxiety, and irritability during the week before menses, resolving with menses.
Bipolar disorder	Characterized by one or more manic or mixed episodes, usually accompanied by major depressive disorder.
Dementia	Characterized by impairment of memory, judgment, and other higher cortical functions; usually has an insidious onset. Assess mental status or perform neuropsychiatric testing if diagnosis is uncertain.
Hypothyroidism	Characterized by features that overlap with depression, including fatigue, decreased cognitive function, and depressive symptoms. Laboratory testing (elevated TSH level) confirms the diagnosis.
Medication effect	Symptoms may have a temporal relationship to medication initiation (eg, glucocorticoids, interferon, propranolol, levodopa, oral contraceptives).

DSM-V = *Diagnostic and Statistical Manual of Mental Disorders*, fifth edition; TSH = thyroid-stimulating hormone.

[a]DSM-V major depressive disorder symptoms include depressed mood, loss of interest or pleasure in most or all activities, insomnia or hypersomnia, change in appetite or weight, psychomotor retardation or agitation, low energy, poor concentration, thoughts of worthlessness or guilt, or recurrent thoughts about death or suicide.

Prevention

Identifying and counseling asymptomatic persons at higher risk for depression can prevent or mitigate the disorder's severity. Inquire about chronic disease, previous episodes of depression, recent stressful events, a family history of depression, and postpartum stress; offer counseling to asymptomatic adults with any of these risk factors. Antepartum counseling helps prevent postpartum depression in women with previous episodes of major depression, premenstrual dysphoric disorder, psychosocial stress, or inadequate social support during pregnancy.

Screening

Routine screening is currently recommended for all U.S. adults in settings where appropriate depression care supports are in place. The presence of risk factors or medical conditions associated with depression should heighten the clinician's application of screening for depressive disorders. A simple two-question screening tool has been shown to have a sensitivity of 96% and a specificity of 57%, similar to more comprehensive instruments studied. The questions are:

- "Over the past 2 weeks, have you felt down, depressed, or hopeless?"
- "Over the past 2 weeks, have you felt little interest or pleasure in doing things?"

An affirmative answer to one or both questions from a patient with depressed mood or anhedonia (the inability to experience pleasure in activities that are usually enjoyable) should precipitate additional diagnostic assessment for mood disorders using a more detailed depression screening tool. Validated instruments commonly ususing a more detailed depression screening tool. Validated instruments commonly used include the Patient Health Questionnaire-9 (PHQ-9), Beck Depression Inventory, Geriatric Depression Scale, and Edinburgh Postnatal Depression Scale, depending on the specific clinical situation.

Diagnosis

The diagnosis of clinical depression is based on patient history and exclusion of alternative diagnoses (Table 1); there are no additional tests that can confirm the diagnosis. The major symptoms of depression can be recalled by the mnemonic SIG-E-CAPS (Table 2). The interviewer must establish whether the patient meets established criteria for major depression, dysthymia, or a different psychiatric condition, as well as assess for the presence of coexisting substance abuse. Up to 72% of depressed patients also present with moderate to severe anxiety.

Table 2. SIG-E-CAPS Mnemonic for Major Symptoms of Depression

Sleep changes (increased or decreased)

Interest in previously pleasurable activities (decreased)

Guilt

Energy (decreased)

Cognition or concentration (decreased)

Appetite (increased or decreased)

Psychomotor agitation or retardation

Suicidal ideation or preoccupation with death

A diagnosis of depression requires differentiation from a grief reaction in which depressive symptoms may be seen. After a loved one dies, a person may experience symptoms of anger or bitterness over the death, a sense of disbelief in accepting the death, recurrent feelings of intense longing for and preoccupation with the deceased person, and a feeling that life is empty and the future has no meaning without the person who has died. Psychiatric referral for further evaluation and treatment should be considered if significant depressive symptoms persist for 10 weeks or longer following the loved one's death.

Once the diagnosis of major depression has been established, it is critical to assess symptom severity, functional impairment, and suicide risk. Although the PHQ-9 can be used as a screening tool, it has also been validated for initial severity assessment and for assessing response to treatment. It is readily available and takes from 1 to 5 minutes to administer. It uses self-reported responses to the presence and degree of nine diagnostic criteria for depression (Table 3) to generate a score that can be used to assess the severity of depression and can be followed with treatment.

Depressed patients must be asked about suicidal thoughts, intent, and plans. Such questioning does not increase the likelihood of committing suicide and is effective in detecting patients at risk for carrying out a planned suicide. Patients with suicidal ideation but without a plan or intent are begun on treatment, and suicidal ideation is closely monitored. Patients with a suicide plan are emergently referred to a psychiatrist or for hospitalization and psychiatric assessment, depending on the clinical situation.

There are other depressive disorders that can be revealed through screening but that fall short of meeting all the criteria for the diagnosis of major depression. These include minor depression, dysthymia, seasonal affective disorder, and premenstrual disorder.

It is important to screen the patient for a history of manic episodes (eg, unusually high energy, euphoria, hyperactivity, hypersexuality, intense drug use, spending sprees, or other manifestations of impaired judgment). The Mood Disorders Questionnaire is a formal tool used in defining a history of possible bipolar disorder. Should a patient with undiagnosed bipolar disorder be treated for depressive disorder alone, frank mania may be unmasked.

Table 3. Questions on the Patient Health Questionnaire 9 (PHQ-9)[a]

Little interest or pleasure in doing things

Feeling down, depressed, or hopeless

Trouble falling or staying asleep, or sleeping too much

Feeling tired or having little energy

Poor appetite or overeating

Feeling bad about self, or are a failure or have let self or family down

Trouble concentrating on things, such as reading the newspaper or watching television

Moving or speaking so slowly that other people have noticed. Or the opposite—being so fidgety or restless that the patient has been moving around a lot more than usual

Thoughts that would be better off dead or of hurting self in some way

[a]Patients are asked to indicate the presence of symptoms over the previous 2 weeks. Each variable is rated as "Not at all" (0 points), "Present on several days" (1 point), "Present on more than half the days" (2 points), or "Present nearly every day" (3 points). Responses for each variable are totaled. Scores 10 to 14 are consistent with minor depression or mild major depression; scores 15 to 19 indicate moderately severe major depression; scores ≥20 suggest severe major depression.

It is key that urgent consultation with a mental health professional be pursued in the case of suicidal or homicidal ideation, features suggesting bipolar disorder, psychotic symptoms, persistent symptoms despite therapy, or diagnostic uncertainty.

A physical examination at the time of a patient interview may be normal. Symptomatic patients may appear anxious or exhibit poor eye contact, depressed mood, decreased psychomotor activity, or tearfulness. In severe depression, affect is blunted or flat, and delusions may be present. In select cases, tests should be performed to exclude conditions associated with depression, such as hypothyroidism, anemia, and vitamin B_{12} deficiency.

Therapy

Mild to moderate depression can be effectively treated in a primary care setting while more severe forms are considered best managed by with psychiatric consultation. In patients with mild to moderate depression, psychotherapy and pharmacotherapy are equally effective treatment. In patients with severe depression, a combination of psychotherapy and antidepressant drug therapy is more effective than either treatment alone. Of the different psychotherapy modalities, cognitive behavioral therapy, interpersonal therapy, and problem-solving therapy have the greatest evidence of benefit. Cognitive behavioral therapy focuses on recognizing unhelpful patterns of thinking and reacting that lead to emotional distress, then modifying or replacing these patterns with more realistic or helpful ones. Multifaceted approaches that include readily accessible care, patient education, reminders, reinforcement, counseling, and additional supervision by a member of the care team are the most effective in improving adherence.

Initially, patients with major depression, dysthymic disorder, or both are started on single-agent antidepressant drug therapy. The choice of agent depends on tolerance, safety, cost, side effect profile, and evidence of previous effectiveness in the patient or a first-degree relative who has been treated for depression (Table 4). Rates of withdrawal from clinical trials suggest that second-generation antidepressants (eg, selective serotonin reuptake inhibitors, serotonin and norepinephrine reuptake inhibitors [SNRIs], selective serotonin and norepinephrine reuptake inhibitors) are better tolerated than tricyclic antidepressants and have less potential overdose lethality. Monoamine oxidase inhibitors have a longer list of restrictions and interactions, making them the least commonly prescribed category of antidepressants. Recent clinical practice guidelines from the American College of Physicians recommend second-generation antidepressants as first-line therapy in treating patients with acute major depression, noting that existing evidence does not support the choice of one agent over another on the basis of efficacy. In mild to moderate depression, St. John's wort is as effective as other antidepressant agents and rarely has side effects. Bupropion has been found to have less sexual side effects, but its use is contraindicated in patients with seizure risk due to its ability to lower the seizure threshold. There is some evidence that an SNRI may be more helpful in patients with concomitant pain syndromes. Breastfeeding is not a contraindication to the use of antidepressants, but they are a pregnancy category C in pregnancy and warrant the appropriate risk/benefit consideration.

Table 4. Frequently Prescribed First-Line Antidepressants

Agent	Advantages	Disadvantages
SSRIs		
Citalopram	Few drug interactions; safe in cardiovascular disease	
Escitalopram	Few drug interactions	
Fluoxetine	Effective for OCD, GAD, bulimia, PMDD. Long half-life (good for missed doses, poor adherence)	Long half-life (can lead to accumulation); affects cytochrome P-450 system, and drug interactions are common
Paroxetine	Effective for panic disorder, GAD, PTSD, OCD, social phobia	Highest risk (class D) in pregnancy; affects cytochrome P-450 system and drug interactions are common; weight gain
Sertraline	Few drug interactions; effective for panic disorder, PTSD, OCD, social phobia, PMDD; safe in cardiovascular disease	
SNRIs		
Venlafaxine	Effective for anxiety spectrum disorders; few drug interactions	Nausea; can exacerbate hypertension
Duloxetine	Effective in pain conditions and GAD	Nausea
Serotonin Antagonist (and Noradrenergic Enhancement)		
Mirtazapine (tetracyclic)	Facilitates improved sleep; few drug interactions	Weight gain; sedation
Tricyclic Antidepressant		
Nortriptyline	Drug levels can be monitored; analgesic effect	Anticholinergic side effects (eg, dry mouth, sedation, weight gain); cardiac toxicity with overdose
Norepinephrine and Dopamine Reuptake Inhibitor		
Bupropion	Effective in smoking cessation; less sexual side effects than SSRIs; less weight gain; lowest risk (class B) in pregnancy	Seizure risk

GAD = generalized anxiety disorder; OCD = obsessive compulsive disorder; PMDD = premenstrual dysphoric disorder; PTSD = posttraumatic stress disorder; SNRI = selective serotonin-norepinephrine reuptake inhibitor; SSRI = selective serotonin reuptake inhibitor.

The goal of treatment is to achieve complete remission within 6 to 12 weeks; once remission is achieved, treatment should continue for 4 to 9 months (maintenance drug therapy). The duration of treatment will be longer if the precipitating event or other stressors persist, if there is a history of previous depressive episodes, or if depression existed for a long time before starting therapy. Up to 50% of patients will experience recurrent symptoms and will require long-term maintenance pharmacotherapy.

Counsel patients about antidepressant drug therapy to improve adherence, and educate patients about the nature of their illness, the use of medications, strategies for coping, and the risks and benefits of treatment. Provide educational materials appropriate for the patient's health literacy skills, culture, and language. Specific points of emphasis should include the importance of taking the medication daily, the anticipated 2- to 4-week delay before noticing any improvement in symptoms, the need to continue the medication even if feeling better, and potential side effects. Of specific concern is the growing awareness that initiation of antidepressant therapy can transiently increase the risk of suicidal ideation in adolescents and young adults. This requires close monitoring, but the risk of suicide in untreated depression far outweighs this initial concern. Common side effects should be discussed, and patients should be encouraged to be in contact with their physician should side effects occur. Common adverse reactions to anticipate are sexual dysfunction (eg, decreased libido, anorgasmia, delayed ejaculation), weight gain, nausea/vomiting, sedation, or agitation, depending on the specific antidepressant used and the patient's individual response.

Referral to a psychiatrist is advisable for patients with severe depression, significant suicidal or homicidal ideation, psychotic symptoms (eg, delusions, disorganized speech, hallucinations, catatonia), substance abuse, suspected bipolar disorder, or inadequate response to standard treatments (two or more antidepressants). Some of these patients may require hospitalization, whereas others may need more complex management than is practical for the primary care physician to provide.

Follow-Up

Patients must be monitored at regular intervals during initiation of treatment, titration to remission, and maintenance. Therapy discontinuation as a result of drug side effects is common and occurs in up to 50% of patients; counseling helps prevent discontinuation. Patients should be seen 2 weeks and 4 weeks after initiating therapy (to assess for adherence, adverse drug reactions, and suicide risk) and again at 6 to 8 weeks (to assess for response to therapy). At this latter visit, patients should complete a formal questionnaire (eg, PHQ-9) to assess symptom severity; a ≥50% decrease in symptom score is considered evidence of a response to treatment. After severity assessment, patients can be classified as having a complete or partial response or no response. Patients with a complete response should continue on the same therapy for an additional 4 to 9 months.

Treatment options for patients with a partial response to medication include using a higher dose of the same agent, switching to an agent from a different class, or adding psychotherapy. Combining monoamine oxidase inhibitors with SNRIs or tricyclic antidepressants is contraindicated, because it may trigger the serotonin syndrome (ie, triad of mental status changes, autonomic hyperactivity, and neuromuscular abnormalities). For those on psychotherapy alone, a pharmacologic agent may be added. For some side effects (eg, insomnia, agitation), atypical antidepressants (eg, trazodone, mirtazapine) may be helpful alone or at low doses at bedtime, in combination with a second-generation antidepressant. Bupropion can be helpful in patients with particularly low energy levels related to the depression. Aripiprazole, a second-generation antipsychotic, is also available to add as adjunct therapy for severe depression. Patients with no response to medication are switched to a different category of drug or to psychotherapy. Any change in therapy requires periodic follow-up as previously outlined. Once patients achieve remission, they are monitored regularly and undergo continued counseling about medication adherence and risk of symptom recurrence.

Bibliography

Fancher TL, Kravitz RL. In the clinic. Depression. Ann Intern Med. 2010;152:ITC51-15; quiz ITC5-16. [PMID: 20439571]

US Preventive Services Task Force. Screening for depression in adults: U.S. preventive services task force recommendation statement. Ann Intern Med. 2009;151:784-92. [PMID: 19949144]

Chapter 38

Substance Abuse

Bipin Thapa, MD

Alcohol

Alcoholism is a broad, nonspecific term indicating problems with alcohol and in common usage is associated with a number of manifestations, including a craving or compulsion to drink, a loss of control, physical dependence, and alcohol tolerance. However, the misuse of alcohol typically represents a spectrum of specific conditions that can be defined by a patient's drinking pattern and its consequences (Table 1). These various gradations of alcohol use assist in defining the clinical significance of a patient's drinking and help determine appropriate interventions. For example, *at-risk* drinking involves a quantity of alcohol consumption that may lead to injuries from falls, depression, memory problems, liver and cardiovascular disease, cognitive changes, and sleep problems. *Hazardous drinking* is defined as a quantity or pattern of consumption that increases the risk for adverse consequences from alcohol use, and *harmful drinking* is defined as alcohol consumption that is actually causing physical, psychological, or social harm. *Alcohol abuse* is defined as a pattern of drinking that results in persistent, significant personal impairment or legal problems, and *alcohol dependence* indicates physiologic addiction to alcohol and maladaptive behavior and is best understood as a chronic disease with a peak onset by age 18 years.

Screening

Alcoholism may be difficult to diagnose. Patients often present with complaints that may be attributable to other medical conditions or associated only when actively consuming alcohol. These problems might include depression, insomnia, injuries, gastroesophageal reflux disease, uncontrolled hypertension, and important social problems. It is useful to inquire about recurrent legal or marital problems, absenteeism or loss of employment, and committing or being the victim of violence.

The U.S. Preventive Services Task Force (USPSTF) recommends screening all adults older than 18 years of age for alcohol use and abuse, identifying the quantity and frequency of drinking, adverse consequences, and patterns of use. The USPSTF considers any of three tools as the instrument of choice for screening: Alcohol Use Disorder Identification Test (AUDIT), the abbreviated AUDIT-Consumption (AUDIT-C), and single-question screening. AUDIT is

Table 1. Spectrum of Alcohol Abuse

Condition	Notes
Moderate drinking	Men, ≤2 drinks per day Women, ≤1 drink per day Patients age >65 y, ≤1 drink per day
At-risk drinking	Men, >14 drinks per week or >4 drinks on any day[a] Women, >7 drinks per week or >3 drinks on any day[a]
Hazardous drinking	At-risk for adverse consequences from alcohol
Harmful drinking	Alcohol is causing physical, psychological, and social harm
Alcohol abuse	One or more of the following events in a year: • Recurrent alcohol use resulting in failure to fulfill major role obligations • Recurrent alcohol use in hazardous situations • Recurrent alcohol-related legal problems • Continued use despite social or interpersonal problems caused or exacerbated by alcohol use
Alcohol dependence	Three or more of the following events in a year: • Alcohol tolerance • Increased amounts to achieve effect • Diminished effect from same amount • Withdrawal • Great deal of time spent obtaining alcohol, using it, or recovering from its effects • Important activities given up or reduced because of alcohol • Drinking more or longer than intended • Persistent desire or unsuccessful efforts to cut down or control alcohol use • Use continues despite knowledge of having a psychological problem caused or exacerbated by alcohol

[a]Both criteria represent alcohol consumption above the levels recommended by the National Institute on Alcohol Abuse and Alcoholism.

the most studied screening tool for detecting alcohol-related problems in primary care settings. It uses 10 questions and has a sensitivity of 84% to 85% and a specificity of 77% to 84% in detecting all forms of alcohol misuse. A modification of the AUDIT, AUDIT-C (Table 2), is reduced to three questions, is much easier to administer, and still performs relatively well in detecting alcohol misuse. Single-question screening ("How many times in the past year have you had 5 [for men] or 4 [for women and all adults older than 65 years] or more drinks in a day?") is the easiest screening tool to use and has a sensitivity of 82% to 87% and specificity of 61% to 79% for detecting alcohol misuse. The CAGE questionnaire, although easy to administer and has been used frequently, has comparatively poor sensitivity for identifying risky or hazardous drinking, particularly in young adults and pregnant women.

In the United States, one in 10 women has a drinking problem, which often is hidden. Women are more likely than men to develop long-term sequelae of alcohol abuse. With women, there is an increased risk of violence, sexual assault, and unplanned pregnancy. Persons older than 65 years represent the fastest growing segment of the United States population, and practitioners may miss alcoholism in this group by thinking of it as a young person's disease. Age-related complications and illnesses (falls, cognitive decline, depression) might present as similar symptoms. The average senior takes two to seven prescription medications, increasing the risk of a drug–alcohol interaction in those who drink. Fortunately, seniors are more likely to participate in and complete a treatment program when identified as having an alcohol problem.

There are no specific laboratory tests to screen for alcohol use. The main objective of the clinical evaluation is to look for physical and behavioral effects of alcohol, such as liver disease, pancreatitis, seizure disorder, and mood disorder. Abnormal laboratory study results, including elevated serum aminotransferases (sensitivity, 30%–50%; specificity, 80%) and macrocytic anemia (sensitivity, 30%–50%; specificity, 80%), although supportive of alcohol use, are not able to establish the diagnosis.

Therapy

Alcoholism can be treated but not cured. Nonpharmacologic intervention is rooted in behavioral treatment for the patient with at-risk alcohol use. Abstinence is essential to the maintenance of a successful treatment program. A patient is encouraged to set drinking goals (*I will start on* this *date*; *I will cut down by* this *many drinks*; *I will stop drinking by* this *date*), to use a diary to observe patterns of drinking, and to avoid situations that lead to alcohol use. Unfortunately, few patients are able to do this alone and therefore do best with the assistance of a counselor or support group.

The USPSTF recommends that clinicians provide brief behavioral counseling interventions to reduce alcohol misuse to persons engaged in at-risk or hazardous drinking. A brief intervention is a 10- to 15-minute session during which the patient receives feedback and advice, sets goals, and has follow-up assessments. The goal is to move the patient along the path of behavior change. Brief interventions need to be motivational, with the practitioner offering empathetic listening and autonomy for decisions. Unfortunately, because of the lack of longitudinal contact and the higher severity of disease in inpatients, brief intervention counseling has limited utility in the hospital setting.

Intoxicated patients should be observed until intoxication has resolved or admitted if a responsible adult is not available. In situations when there is physical dependence to alcohol, detoxification may be appropriate. Detoxification is defined as the forced abstinence with treatment of alcohol withdrawal, and it may be done in either ambulatory or inpatient settings. Patients who should not be considered for ambulatory detoxification include those with acute or chronic medical or psychiatric illness that would require hospitalization or that would be complicated by alcohol withdrawal; pregnant women; and individuals with a history of seizures or delirium tremens, the inability to follow up daily, or an inadequate social support system. These patients should be hospitalized for alcohol detoxification.

Withdrawal symptoms generally begin 6 to 24 hours after alcohol intake is substantially reduced or stopped. Symptoms include anxiety and tremulousness. Physical examination may show tachycardia, elevated blood pressure, and tremors. Other findings of chronic alcohol use such as spider angioma, hepatosplenomegaly, or peripheral neuropathy may be present. Delirium tremens, a severe complication of withdrawal characterized by fever, profound confusion, and hallucinations, and associated with a high level of morbidity and mortality, usually does not occur before the second to third day of abstinence. Clinicians should identify the severity of withdrawal and factors that may predict the onset of serious complications.

Benzodiazepines are first-line therapy for patients who require alcohol withdrawal treatment or prophylaxis. Patients with alcohol withdrawal who are treated with benzodiazepines have fewer complications, including a lower incidence of seizures and delirium tremens. Patients with a history of seizures should receive a prophylactic long-acting benzodiazepine on a fixed schedule even if they are asymptomatic during the acute alcohol withdrawal period. β-Blockers and clonidine can control tachycardia and hypertension, and haloperidol can treat agitation and hallucinosis. However, β-blockers have been associated with a greater incidence of delirium, and neuroleptic medications have been associated with a greater incidence of seizures during withdrawal.

For long-term management, a multidisciplinary approach may be necessary. Alcoholics Anonymous has been shown to be helpful in maintaining abstinence; the organization provides fellowship and a support group for patients. Cognitive behavioral therapy is conducted by a mental health practitioner. With this treatment

Table 2. Modified Alcohol Use Disorders Identification Test (AUDIT-C)[a]

	0 Points	1 Point	2 Points	3 Points	4 Points
How often did you have a drink containing alcohol in the past year?	Never	≤1 per month	2-4 per month	2-3 per week	≥4 per week
How many drinks did you have on a typical day when you were drinking in the past year?	0-2	3-4	5-6	7-9	≥10
How often did you have 6 or more drinks on one occasion in the past year?	Never	<1 per month	Monthly	Weekly	Daily or almost daily

[a]An optimal balance of sensitivity and specificity for detecting all forms of alcohol misuse occurs when a cutoff of 4 points in men or 3 points in women is used.

approach, patients learn skills to cope with situations that perpetuate drinking. Spousal involvement has been shown to improve the completion of the behavioral program.

Naltrexone, an opioid receptor antagonist, is effective for short-term treatment of alcohol dependence and may be coadministered with psychosocial support. Naltrexone can be used in patients who are still actively drinking and in cases when abstinence may be difficult. The drug reduces the frequency of relapse and the number of drinking days by attenuating craving and blocking the reinforcing effects of alcohol.

Disulfiram, an aldehyde dehydrogenase inhibitor, leads to the accumulation of acetaldehyde if alcohol is consumed, resulting in flushing, headache, and emesis. Administration of disulfiram under supervision of another person improves abstinence and adherence to therapy. Patients who use disulfiram must avoid all alcohol-containing products, including mouthwash and cold medications.

Acamprosate, a synthetic compound resembling homotaurine (a γ-aminobutyric acid analogue), has been successful in decreasing drinking days, enhancing abstinence, and helping to prevent withdrawal symptoms.

Drug Use

Although alcohol is the most commonly abused substance, illicit and legal drug use remains an important medical problem. Marijuana, cocaine, and opioid substances (including prescription drugs) are among the more frequently used drugs.

The USPSTF does not recommend for or against routine screening for drug abuse. Patients may be less likely to volunteer information on drug use (as opposed to alcohol use) given the potential legal ramifications. Although clinical screening tools for drug use are available, a careful history remains the primary method for assessing inappropriate drug use. When there is a heightened clinical suspicion, urine toxicology testing may play a confirmatory role. Certain medical problems may arise from the use of injected illicit drugs, including HIV infection, hepatitis C, and infective endocarditis. A history focused on the route of drug administration and coexisting medical problems is needed. High-risk patients should be screened with serologic testing for relevant diseases.

With cocaine use, the most serious health concerns associated with acute intoxication are myocardial infarction, unstable angina, uncontrolled hypertension, and seizures. β-Blockers should be avoided in patients using cocaine because the unopposed α-adrenergic stimulation may increase the vascular tone, thus worsening the cardiovascular effects. In the acute setting, benzodiazepines, vasodilators, and calcium channel blockers are the safest and most effective agents to treat hypertension or chest pain. Withdrawal from cocaine can produce dysphoria, sleep disturbance, anxiety, and depression. The symptoms of anxiety and depression suggest a role for antidepressants, but these agents have a delayed onset of action and may be useful only after the period of withdrawal is over. Benzodiazepines are used to terminate seizures related to acute drug toxicity; chronic antiseizure treatment is necessary only if seizures persist after detoxification.

All amphetamines, including the synthetic cathinones (commonly referred to as "bath salts"), cause an adrenergic syndrome from release of catecholamines, thus producing tachycardia, hyperthermia, agitation, hypertension, mydriasis, and acute psychosis. Myocardial ischemia, seizures, intracranial hemorrhage, stroke, and kidney failure can result. Overdose of the recreational drug "ecstasy" (3,4-methylenedioxymethamphetamine) is associated with bruxism, jaw clenching, and hyponatremia caused by an elevated antidiuretic hormone concentration, which may result in seizures, cerebral edema, and death in some users. Fulminant hepatic failure has also been reported. Treatment is supportive for all amphetamine ingestions, with a focus on correcting the hyponatremia and using benzodiazepines to manage extreme agitation.

Opioids can depress respiratory drive and cause sedation, requiring respiratory support with mechanical ventilation and naloxone to reverse the opioid effects. Opioid withdrawal syndrome is characterized by pupillary dilation, lacrimation, rhinorrhea, piloerection, anorexia, nausea, vomiting, and diarrhea. Opioid detoxification has three goals: initiating abstinence, reducing withdrawal, and retaining the patient in treatment. β-Blockers and clonidine may be used to reduce autonomic manifestations of opioid withdrawal. Longer term pharmacologic treatment involves substituting a long-acting oral agent (methadone, buprenorphine) for the abused drug and then gradually tapering its dosage. Methadone is used to treat acute withdrawal symptoms and may be used as maintenance therapy for weeks to years. Buprenorphine may be preferred over methadone because it is a partial opioid agonist that has superior ability in reducing withdrawal symptoms, and its combination with naloxone allows for less abuse potential and respiratory depression in overdose.

Patients may benefit from referral to a formal drug treatment center that addresses motivation, teaches coping skills, provides reinforcement, improves interpersonal functioning, and fosters compliance with pharmacotherapy. Patients with moderate to severe withdrawal symptoms, poor social support, or substantial medical or psychiatric conditions should be referred to specialized outpatient or inpatient programs. The U.S. Public Health Service has advocated use of the "five A's" construct in behavioral counseling interventions (Table 3).

Prescription drug abuse is use of prescription medication, usually self-administered, in a manner that deviates from the medical, legal, and social standard. Medications such as stimulants, anxiolytics, opioids, and dissociative anesthetics are the most frequently abused prescription medications. The incidence of prescription drug abuse in increasing rapidly in United States and has caused significant morbidity and mortality. Management for prescription drug abuse is agent specific.

Bibliography

Leikin JB. Substance-related disorders in adults. Dis Mon. 2007;53:313-335. [PMID: 17645897]

Moyer VA. Screening and behavioral counseling interventions in primary care to reduce alcohol misuse: U.S. preventive services task force recommendation statement. Ann Intern Med. 2013;159:210-218. [PMID: 23698791]

Saitz R. Clinical practice. Unhealthy alcohol use. N Engl J Med. 2005;352:596-607. [PMID: 15703424]

Table 3. The "Five A's" of Behavior Change Counseling

Assess	Ask about or assess health risks and factors affecting choice of behavior change.
Advise	Give clear, specific, and personalized behavior change advice.
Agree	Select appropriate treatment goals and methods based on patient interest and willingness to change.
Assist	Aid the patient in achieving agreed-upon goals with use of social or environmental support and adjunctive medical treatments when appropriate (including pharmacotherapy).
Arrange	Schedule follow-up contacts to provide ongoing support and referral as needed.

Chapter 39

Disorders of Menstruation and Menopause

Sara B. Fazio, MD

Disorders of menstruation are common and range from the complete absence of menstrual blood flow (amenorrhea) to irregular or heavy bleeding (abnormal uterine bleeding). The normal menstrual cycle depends on a tightly regulated system that includes the central nervous system, hypothalamus, pituitary gland, ovaries, uterus, and vaginal outflow tract. Disorders of menstruation can result from disruption at any level of the system (Table 1).

The menstrual cycle is regulated by the pituitary-hypothalamic axis. The hypothalamus secretes gonadotropin-releasing hormone in a pulsatile fashion, stimulating release of follicle-stimulating hormone (FSH) and leuteinizing hormone (LH) from the pituitary gland. FSH causes the development of multiple ovarian follicles, which in turn release estradiol. Estradiol inhibits FSH release, allowing only one or two dominant follicles to survive, and stimulates LH secre-

Table 1. Differential Diagnosis of Amenorrhea

Disorder	Present in Primary Amenorrhea?	Present in Secondary Amenorrhea?	LH	FSH	Estrogen	Notes
Hypothalamus						
Hypothalamic amenorrhea	Yes	Yes	↓ or normal	↓ or normal	↓	Exercise, weight loss, stress, and chronic illness
Hypogonadotropic hypogonadism	Yes	Yes	↓ or normal	↓ or normal	↓	Anosmia may be present
Hypothalamic tumor	Yes	Yes	↓ or normal	↓ or normal	↓	Brain imaging indicated
Pituitary						
Hypogonadotropic hypogonadism	Yes	Yes	↓ or normal	↓ or normal	↓	
Pituitary tumor (prolactinoma)	Yes	Yes	↓ or normal	↓ or normal	↓	Prolactin may be elevated; brain imaging
Pituitary infection or infiltration	Yes	Yes	↓ or normal	↓ or normal	↓	
Sheehan syndrome	No	Yes	↓ or normal	↓ or normal	↓	After delivery; can be acute or insidious
Ovary						
Gonadal dysgenesis	Yes	Yes	↑	↑	↓	45,XO karyotype
Pure gonadal dysgenesis	Yes	Yes	↑	↑	↓	46,XX or 46,XY karyotype
Premature ovarian failure	No	Yes	↑	↑	↓	Autoimmune syndromes
Polycystic ovary syndrome	Yes	Yes	↑ or normal	Normal	Normal	Hyperandrogenism, oligomenorrhea since menarche
Ovarian tumor	No	Yes	↓	↓	↑ or normal	Look for acute virilization
17α-hydroxylase deficiency	Yes	No	↑	↑	↓	Sexual infantilism
Uterus						
Müllerian agenesis	Yes	No	Normal	Normal	Normal	May have cyclical pelvic pain
Asherman syndrome	No	Yes	Normal	Normal	Normal	History of dilation and curettage (uterine synechiae)
Other						
Adrenal tumor	No	Yes	↓	↓	↑ or normal	Hyperandrogenism
Thyroid disease	Yes	Yes	Normal	Normal	Normal	
Testicular feminization	Yes	No	↑	↑ or normal	↑	XY karyotype

↑ = elevated; ↓ = decreased; DHEA = dehydroepiandrosterone sulfate; FSH = follicle-stimulating hormone; LH = luteinizing hormone.

tion. LH promotes progesterone production, which then causes a surge of LH secretion 34 to 36 hours before follicle rupture and ovulation. Once this occurs, progesterone is produced by ovarian granulose cells (the corpus luteum) for approximately 14 days, which then involutes unless pregnancy is established. Estrogen functions to increase the thickness and vascularity of the endometrial lining, whereas progesterone increases its glandular secretion and vessel tortuosity. The cyclical withdrawal of estrogen and progesterone results in endometrial sloughing and menstrual bleeding.

Amenorrhea

Primary amenorrhea is the absence of menarche in females aged ≥16 years. Secondary amenorrhea is the cessation of menstruation for three cycle intervals or 6 consecutive months in females who were previously menstruating regularly. Table 2 lists common tests used in the evaluation of primary and secondary amenorrhea.

Primary Amenorrhea

Approximately 50% of primary amenorrhea is caused by chromosomal disorders associated with gonadal dysgenesis and depletion of ovarian follicles. Turner syndrome is the most common disorder in this category and is classically associated with a 45,XO genotype. It is characterized by a lack of secondary sex characteristics, growth retardation, webbed neck, and frequent skeletal abnormalities. Hypothalamic hypogonadism accounts for approximately 20% of primary amenorrhea and includes both structural and functional hypothalamic disorders, such as developmental defects of cranial midline structures, tumors, and infiltrative disorders.

Less common causes of primary amenorrhea include developmental disorders (eg, Müllerian agenesis, imperforate hymen) and defects of the cervix or vagina. Such patients have normal secondary sex characteristics. Patients with androgen insensitivity syndrome (testicular feminization) have some female secondary sex characteristics but an absence of or minimal pubic and axillary hair, a shallow vagina, and often a labial mass (testes). Endocrine abnormalities such as prolactin excess, thyroid disease, and polycystic ovary syndrome, although more commonly associated with secondary amenorrhea, also cause primary amenorrhea.

Patients with primary amenorrhea should be examined for the presence of an intact uterus and vaginal outflow tract, secondary sex characteristics, and signs of hyperandrogenism. If evidence of characteristic developmental disorders is present, karyotyping should be considered. Primary ovarian failure of any cause can be diagnosed by an elevated serum FSH level. A low or normal FSH level warrants measurement of serum prolactin and thyroid-stimulating hormone (TSH) levels as well as brain imaging to exclude structural disease.

Secondary Amenorrhea

Secondary amenorrhea is much more common than primary amenorrhea. All previously menstruating women who present with amenorrhea should be tested for pregnancy, the most common cause. Premature ovarian failure may occur as a result of surgical oophorectomy, chemotherapy, radiation, or autoimmune destruction of ovarian tissue.

Diagnosis of secondary ovarian failure is made by an elevated FSH level. In such patients, vaginal bleeding will not occur with a progesterone challenge, because estrogen levels are low; however, bleeding will occur after estrogen priming followed by a progesterone challenge, demonstrating the integrity of the uterine lining and outflow tract. The presence of bleeding following a progesterone challenge suggests a serum estradiol level >40 pg/mL (146.8 pmol/L)

Table 2. Laboratory and Other Studies for Amenorrhea

Test	Notes
β-hCG	Use to confirm or exclude pregnancy.
FSH	Ovarian failure or menopause present when serum FSH levels are >20 mU/mL. Perform karyotyping in all patients aged <30 y with elevated FSH levels.
Prolactin	Serum prolactin levels can be elevated by stress, breast examination, and food intake; repeat analysis on a fasting morning sample before performing cranial imaging. Hypothyroidism, phenothiazines, tricyclic antidepressants, metoclopramide, and methyldopa can cause hyperprolactinemia. Values >200 ng/mL (200 µg/L) suggest pituitary tumor.
Thyroid-stimulating hormone	Hypothyroidism and, less commonly, hyperthyroidism are associated with menstrual cycle abnormalities and infertility.
Testosterone, DHEAS	May be helpful in a patient with hirsutism and acne. Total serum testosterone levels >200 ng/dL (6.9 nmol/L) and DHEAS levels more than three times the upper limit of normal suggest tumor (although no tumor is found in most cases).
17-hydroxyprogesterone	Beneficial in screening for congenital adrenal hyperplasia.
Estradiol	Decreased in hypothalamic and pituitary amenorrhea and in ovarian failure. Serum estradiol should always be assessed with serum FSH. Most useful in evaluating primary amenorrhea.
LH	Normal levels are 5-20 mU/mL (5-20 U/L), with midcycle peak three times the base level. The level is <5 mU/mL (5 U/L) in hypogonadotropic states (eg, hypothalamic or pituitary dysfunction) and >20-40 mU/mL (20-40 U/L) in hypergonadotropic states (eg, postmenopausal, ovarian failure). Serum LH measurement not needed to diagnose PCOS.
DEXA	May be required to evaluate amenorrhea in a patient who is estrogen deficient.
Brain MRI	Necessary to rule out hypothalamic or pituitary mass, infection, or infiltration; critical to consider in the setting of primary amenorrhea with hypogonadotropic hypogonadism.

DEXA = dual-energy x-ray absorptiometry; DHEAS = dehydroepiandrosterone sulfate; FSH = follicle-stimulating hormone; hCG = human chorionic gonadotropin; LH= luteinizing hormone; PCOS = polycystic ovary syndrome.

and obviates the need for estradiol measurement. Absence of bleeding following a progesterone challenge indicates either insufficient circulating estrogen or an anatomic abnormality that prohibits blood flow, such as Asherman syndrome (endometrial scar tissue development after dilation and curettage).

PCOS affects 6% of women of childbearing age and typically presents as oligomenorrhea and signs of androgen excess (eg, hirsutism, acne, alopecia [occasionally]). The cause is not fully understood but involves abnormal gonadotropin regulation, with subsequent overactivity of the ovarian androgen pathway. Insulin resistance is an important feature of the disorder, as is increased BMI, although only 50% of affected women are obese. PCOS is characterized by mildly elevated testosterone and dehydroepiandrosterone sulfate (DHEAS) levels and an LH/FSH ratio >2:1. Diagnosis requires two of the following: ovulatory dysfunction, laboratory or clinical evidence of hyperandrogenism, and ultrasonographic evidence of polycystic ovaries. If the evaluation does not support a diagnosis of PCOS and evidence of androgen excess is present, other causes must be excluded, including an ovarian or adrenal androgen-producing tumor (associated with serum testosterone levels >150-200 ng/dL [5.0-6.9 nmol/L]), congenital adrenal hyperplasia (elevated DHEAS and 17-hydroxyprogesterone levels), and Cushing syndrome (elevated serum cortisol level, abnormal dexamethasone suppression test). In the absence of findings suggesting Cushing syndrome (hypertension, large purple striae, dorsocervical fat pad, centripetal obesity, easy bruising), routine laboratory testing generally is not needed. Androgen-secreting tumors are most often associated with virilization, including hirsutism, acne, clitoromegaly, male-pattern balding, and deepening of the voice.

Hyperprolactinemia is a frequent cause of secondary amenorrhea and is commonly related to the use of certain medications. Drugs that reduce central catecholamine and dopamine production or release can cause hyperprolactinemia; tricyclic antidepressants, phenothiazines, and metoclopramide are among the most common causes. Primary hypothyroidism is associated with increased levels of hypothalamic thyrotropin-releasing hormone, which stimulates prolactin production. Tumors that secrete prolactin or that compress the pituitary stalk will lead to hyperprolactinemia (see Chapter 10). If the prolactin level is elevated and medication and hypothyroidism are excluded, brain imaging is warranted. Generally, a prolactin-producing adenoma is associated with serum prolactin levels >200 ng/mL (200 µg/L), whereas hyperprolactinemia caused by drugs and other nonpituitary tumor causes is usually associated with prolactin levels <150 ng/mL (150 µg/L). Hypothalamic amenorrhea involves disordered gonadotropin release, which may occur as a result of a tumor or an infiltrative lesion (eg, lymphoma, sarcoidosis) but more commonly is functional. The usual causative factors are stress, significant loss of body weight or fat, excessive exercise, or some combination thereof. Diagnosis is one of exclusion.

The initial evaluation of a patient with secondary amenorrhea should consist of serum FSH, TSH, and prolactin measurements; if signs of androgen excess are present, a serum testosterone and plasma DHEAS level should be obtained. When amenorrhea is associated with low or inappropriately normal FSH levels, secondary causes (eg, PCOS, androgen or prolactin excess, hypothyroidism) must be ruled out. If FSH, TSH, and prolactin levels are normal, the next step is to perform a progesterone challenge test to determine if there is an adequate circulating level of estrogen; absent withdrawal bleeding following progesterone challenge should prompt serum estradiol measurement and evaluation of the uterine outflow track with ultrasonography, MRI, or hysterosalpingography. If a functional cause is suspected, moderation of exercise, improvement in nutrition, and/or attention to stress factors may be helpful. Because lack of adequate estrogen predisposes to osteoporosis, it is important to initiate adequate estrogen and progesterone replacement until causative factors are resolved and menstruation can return to normal.

Abnormal Uterine Bleeding

Abnormal uterine bleeding is bleeding that is excessive or scanty or occurs outside the normal menstrual cycle. Similar to amenorrhea, the diagnosis is best approached in anatomic terms and can be further categorized by patient age (Table 3). Pregnancy always must be considered. Implantation, ectopic pregnancy, threatened or missed abortion, and gestational trophoblastic disease all can cause abnormal bleeding. In women of all ages, consider anatomic lesions of the uterus, including endometrial polyps, uterine leiomyomata (fibroids), and endometrial hyperplasia or carcinoma (particularly in peri- or postmenopausal women). Cervical polyps and cervical neoplasia commonly present as abnormal uterine bleeding, although typically with intermenstrual bleeding. All patients should have a speculum examination to assess for visible lesions, a Papanicolaou smear, and a bimanual examination to assess for structural abnormalities. Ultrasonography may be necessary to detect endometrial polyps or submucosal leiomyomata and can assess the endometrial thickness. The latter is particularly important in a peri- or postmenopausal woman with abnormal uterine bleeding, because an endometrial biopsy may be warranted if the endometrium is >4 to 5 mm in thickness or is heterogeneous. Risk factors for endometrial carcinoma include chronic unopposed estrogen (as seen in chronic anovulatory states), obesity, age >45 years, nulliparity, and tamoxifen use.

Anovulation is the most common cause of abnormal uterine bleeding. Estrogen is produced by FSH stimulation of the ovary, but because ovulation does not occur, progesterone is never produced, and the uterine lining builds up. This eventually leads to discoordinate menstrual bleeding, often presenting as bleeding at intervals shorter than the typical cycle length (metrorrhagia) or extended periods of heavy blood loss (menorrhagia). It is common for patients at extremes of the menstrual cycle (puberty and perimenopause) to be anovulatory. The most common cause of anovulatory bleeding in reproductive-aged women is PCOS. Anovulatory bleeding may precede amenorrhea in patients with functional hypothalamic disorders. Endocrine causes must also be considered in patients with abnormal uterine bleeding. Prolactin excess initially will cause anovulation. Menorrhagia may be reported in women with hypothyroidism. Cushing syndrome commonly causes menstrual irregularities, likely secondary to cortisol suppression of gonadotropin-releasing hormone.

Systemic illness, coagulopathy, and medication effect should also be considered as potential causes of abnormal uterine bleeding. Cirrhosis reduces the ability of the liver to metabolize estrogen and decreases clotting factor production. Kidney failure interferes with estrogen clearance and is associated with abnormalities in platelet function. In adolescents with menorrhagia, up to 20% have an inherited bleeding disorder, most commonly von Willebrand disease.

Hormone therapy can correct anovulatory bleeding. Options include combination oral contraceptives, cyclic progestins, or a progestin-containing intrauterine device. In most cases, regularity of menstrual flow can be reestablished, and control of heavy blood loss can be achieved. In patients who are at risk for endometrial hyperplasia or carcinoma, a biopsy should be obtained before initiating hormone therapy. Nonsteroidal anti-inflammatory drugs inhibit endometrial prostaglandins and decrease blood flow.

Table 3. Causes of Abnormal Uterine Bleeding by Age

Cause	Diagnostic Clues
Menarche to Teenage Years	
Pregnancy	Irregular or absent periods
Anovulation	Cycle length falls outside normal range or varies by ≥10 d
Stress	Physical or mental
Bleeding disorder	Other sources of abnormal bleeding (gums, nose)
Infection (cervical, vaginal)	Postcoital bleeding and/or vaginal discharge
Teens to 40s	
Pregnancy	Irregular or absent periods
Malignancy (uterine, cervical, vaginal, vulvar)	Postcoital bleeding and/or vaginal discharge
Infection (cervical, vaginal)	Postcoital bleeding and/or vaginal discharge
Polyps (cervical, endometrial)	Dysmenorrhea
Adenomyosis, leiomyomata	Dysmenorrhea
Anovulation	Irregular periods
Bleeding disorder	Other sources of abnormal bleeding (gums, nose)
Endocrine disorder	Signs of hypothyroidism, diabetes mellitus, hyperprolactinemia, or polycystic ovary syndrome
Ovarian or adrenal tumor	New-onset virilization or hirsutism
Perimenopausal	
Anovulation	Irregular periods
Endometrial hyperplasia and polyps, leiomyomata	Dysmenorrhea
Malignancy (uterine, cervical, vaginal, vulvar)	Postcoital bleeding and/or vaginal discharge
Postmenopausal	
Malignancy (uterine, cervical, vaginal, vulvar)	Postcoital bleeding and/or vaginal discharge
Atrophy of vaginal mucosa	Vaginal dryness, dyspareunia
Estrogen replacement therapy	Estrogen withdrawal bleeding

Menopause

Menopause refers to cessation of ovarian function. Because one-third of most women's lives encompasses the postmenopausal period, physicians who care for these patients must recognize the effects of estrogen deficiency. Elements that should be addressed in the patient's history include timing of change in menstrual cycle, hot flashes or night sweats, and mood fluctuations. Patients should be asked about symptoms of urinary incontinence, vaginal dryness, and changes in sexual function or desire. Examination should include evaluation for height loss and kyphosis (eg, signs of osteoporosis), breast examination (given increased incidence of breast cancer with advancing age), and evidence of vulvar or vaginal atrophy. Because the diagnosis of menopause can be made by history and physical examination without laboratory confirmation, serum FSH measurement is only indicated if the diagnosis is unclear or if the patient requires confirmation for reassurance.

Osteoporosis is a direct effect of estrogen loss at any age. Premenopausal women have less heart disease than men (in the absence of other risk factors), but this relative protection is lost at menopause. The role of hormone replacement therapy has become increasingly controversial. Although it clearly controls many of the symptoms of menopause (eg, vasomotor instability, vaginal dryness) and reduces the risk of osteoporotic fractures, research has demonstrated an increased the risk of coronary heart disease, venous thromboembolism, invasive breast cancer, and stroke. Thus, the approach to managing menopausal symptoms has become more individualized and involves an assessment of risks and benefits; if estrogen is prescribed, it should be used at the lowest dose and for the shortest duration possible to treat menopausal symptoms (treatment for longer than 5 years is not advised). Hormone therapy may be used to treat menopausal symptoms in women ages 50 to 59 or those within 10 years of menopause, as there is minimal coronary heart disease and minimal invasive breast cancer risk; hormone therapy should not be initiated in women older than 60 years of age. The increased incidence of breast cancer occurs with exposure in the early postmenopausal period, after 3 to 5 years of exposure. Estrogen still remains the most effective treatment for vasomotor instability (eg, hot flashes), reducing the severity and frequency of symptoms by 70%, usually within 1 month. Contraindications to hormone replacement therapy include unexplained vaginal bleeding or a history of venous thromboembolism, liver disease, coronary artery disease, stroke, breast cancer, or endometrial cancer.

Serotonin and norepinephrine reuptake inhibitors (most notably venlafaxine), serotonin reuptake inhibitors, clonidine, gabapentin, and black cohosh all may be helpful in controlling vasomotor symptoms in select patients. Soy preparations have minimal efficacy. Vaginal atrophy can be treated with lubricants or localized vaginal estrogen preparations, which have little systemic absorption and are the most effective. Patients should be educated about risk reduction for coronary artery disease. Bone density testing should be offered to all women aged ≥65 years as well as younger women who are at increased risk for osteoporosis based on risk factor assessment.

Perimenopausal patients frequently experience irregular bleeding secondary to anovulation. Shortened intermenstrual cycles (more frequent bleeding), longer duration of bleeding, episodes of heavy bleeding, or menstruation after ≥6 months of amenorrhea warrants further evaluation. For women with prolonged or excessively heavy perimenopausal bleeding, pelvic ultrasonography should be performed. If the endometrial lining is <4 mm in thickness, an endometrial biopsy may occasionally be deferred.

Postmenopausal bleeding almost always requires endometrial evaluation with both ultrasonography and biopsy. Although the most common cause is endometrial atrophy, the possibility of endometrial carcinoma must be excluded. Referral to a gynecologist is generally recommended in the context of abnormal peri- or postmenopausal bleeding and always in a patient who experiences bleeding while taking noncyclical estrogen replacement or tamoxifen.

Bibliography

Col NF, Fairfield KM, Ewan-Whyte C, Miller H. In the clinic. Menopause. Ann Intern Med. 2009;150:ITC4-1-15; quiz ITC4-16. [PMID: 19349628]

Chapter 40

Approach to Syncope

Gretchen Diemer, MD

Syncope is a common symptom in adults, with a lifetime prevalence of almost 40%. Syncope is defined as a sudden, transient loss of consciousness and postural tone caused by global cerebral hypoperfusion followed by spontaneous recovery. Presyncope is the sensation of impending syncope without loss of consciousness. Syncope accounts for up to 3% of emergency department visits and 6% of all hospital admissions. It is more common in women than in men. Syncope from cardiac causes has higher morbidity and mortality rates. A major purpose of the evaluation of a patient with syncope is to distinguish cardiac from noncardiac causes.

Diagnosis

In most cases, the cause of syncope is established by a combination of history and physical examination and simple diagnostic studies. The history and physical examination focus on a search for precipitating causes and associated symptoms. Causes of syncope can be divided into three main groups: cardiac causes (arrhythmias and obstructive causes), neurocardiogenic causes, and orthostatic hypotension. Table 1 delineates the potential causes within these groupings and other potential causes of syncope. Figure 1 is a diag-

Table 1. Differential Diagnosis of Syncope

Disorder	Notes
Cardiac	
Tachyarrhythmia (see Chapter 6)	May be associated with palpitations. Ventricular arrhythmias causing syncope typically occur in the setting of structural heart disease (myocardial infarction-associated ventricular tachycardia) or with a family history of sudden cardiac death (long QT syndrome, Brugada syndrome). Extended electrocardiographic recording, event monitoring, or electrophysiologic studies may be required to document arrhythmia.
Bradyarrhythmia (see Chapter 4)	May be associated with symptoms of near-syncope (transient) or signs of diminished cardiac output (persistent). Can be diagnosed by electrocardiography, extended electrocardiographic monitoring, or electrophysiologic studies. Includes both sinoatrial and atrioventricular node dysfunction, which may be drug-induced (β-blockers, calcium channel blockers, antiarrhythmic drugs).
Obstruction to outflow	May be related to exercise or associated with angina or heart failure. Can be diagnosed by physical examination, echocardiography, or specialized testing. Specific causes include aortic stenosis, hypertrophic cardiomyopathy, mitral stenosis, myxoma, pulmonic stenosis, massive pulmonary embolism, and pulmonary hypertension.
Neurocardiogenic	
Vasovagal syncope	Patients tend to be younger and have presyncopal symptoms, such as lightheadedness, nausea, warmth, diaphoresis, or blurred vision. Common triggers include micturition, defecation, cough, fear, pain, phlebotomy, and prolonged standing
Situational syncope	Syncope that occurs in association with specific activities (micturition, cough, swallowing, defecation). Generally can be diagnosed by history alone.
Carotid sinus hypersensitivity	Syncope precipitated by pressure on the carotid sinus (tight collar, sudden turning of head). Generally can be diagnosed by history. Carotid massage may be confirmatory.
Orthostatic Hypotension	
Orthostatic hypotension	Syncope occurs on assuming the upright position. May be caused by hypovolemia, drugs, or disorders of the autonomic nervous system (idiopathic hypotension, Shy-Drager syndrome).
Other Causes	
Seizure disorder	A history of a seizure disorder may be present. Additional findings include cyanosis or absence of pallor during the episode, frothing at the mouth, tongue biting, disorientation, postictal muscle aching and somnolence, age younger than 45 y, and duration of unconsciousness >5 min. Diaphoresis or nausea before the event and postsyncopal orientation argue against seizure.
Psychiatric disorder (eg, anxiety, depression, conversion disorder)	A high incidence (24%-35%) of psychiatric disorders has been reported in patients with syncope.
Cerebrovascular disease	Invariably associated with neurologic signs and symptoms. Carotid Doppler ultrasonography is not indicated because ischemia of the anterior cerebral circulation rarely causes syncope.

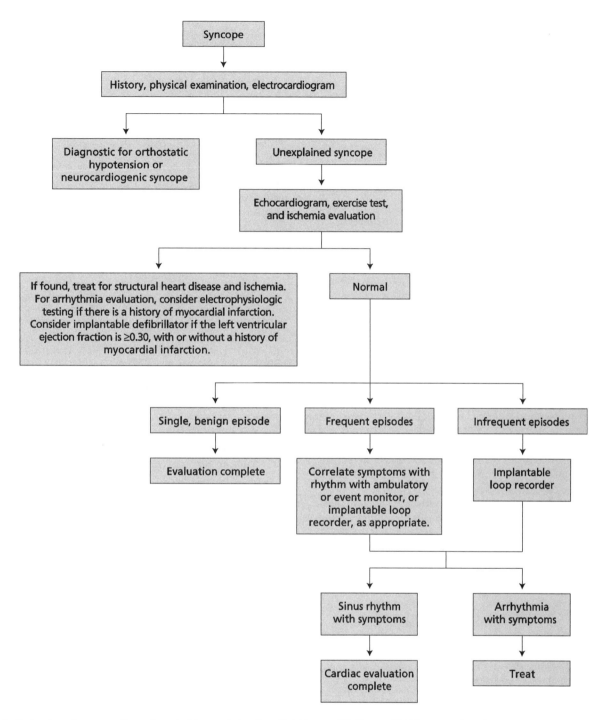

Figure 1. Evaluation of syncope. Reproduced with permission from Strickberger SA, Benson DW, Biaggioni I, et al; American Heart Association Councils on Clinical Cardiology, Cardiovascular Nursing, Cardiovascular Disease in the Young, and Stroke; Quality of Care and Outcomes Research Interdisciplinary Working Group; American College of Cardiology Foundation; Heart Rhythm Society; American Autonomic Society. AHA/ACCF Scientific Statement on the evaluation of syncope. Circulation. 2006;113:317. [PMID: 16418451]. Copyright 2006, American Heart Association, Inc.

nostic algorithm based on this classification. The history should distinguish true syncope from falls without loss of consciousness, stroke or transient ischemic attack (TIA), trauma-related loss of consciousness, intoxication, and hypoglycemia. Seizure is often mistaken for syncope, but generalized tonic-clonic movements, loss of continence, tongue biting, and postictal confusion are rare in syncope. Tonic posturing can be seen in both syncope and seizure.

The history and physical examination identify a cause of syncope in 45% of cases. In general, brain imaging, electroencephalography, and carotid Doppler ultrasonography play small roles in the workup of syncope. Hospital admission is appropriate when the cause of syncope is unknown or if the risk of illness or death from presumed cardiac disorders is high. Patients with underlying cardiac disease and syncope have a 5-year mortality rate of approximately 50%, so it is important to identify these individuals.

Cardiac Causes

Arrhythmias

Arrhythmias cause approximately 15% of cardiac syncope. Syncope with no warning or prodrome should raise the suspicion of an arrhythmia. Palpitations can occur in both tachycardia- and bradycardia-associated disorders, although syncope can also occur without presyncopal palpitations. Ventricular tachycardia, atrial arrhythmia, and bradyarrhythmia can cause syncope. Atrial tachyarrhythmia is more likely to cause palpitations and lightheadedness than syncope. Ischemic heart disease and systolic heart failure are risk factors for ventricular tachycardia. Syncope is unlikely to be caused by an acute coronary syndrome in the absence of an arrhythmia. Hospitalization and evaluation for acute coronary syndrome in patients with syncope is rarely indicated unless additional clues suggest active myocardial ischemia.

Syncope also may be associated with long (>3-second) sinus pauses and high-grade heart block. Regardless of heart rate, arrhythmias cause syncope by reducing cardiac output and reducing cerebral perfusion. Male sex, age older than 54 years, and syncope lasting only a few seconds are associated with an increased incidence of cardiac arrhythmia. Syncope without warning or in a supine position also should raise concern for arrhythmia. Patients who sustain facial or head injuries as a result of syncope also should be evaluated for potential arrhythmia. A family history of syncope or sudden death suggests long QT syndrome. Physical examination may reveal an abnormal heart rate or rhythm but typically is normal.

Obstructive Causes

Important structural cardiac causes include aortic stenosis; hypertrophic cardiomyopathy; and, less commonly, mitral stenosis. Syncope associated with these conditions usually is exertional and is caused by an inability to increase cardiac output in response to exercise and the associated decrease in systemic vascular resistance. More than 25% of patients with hypertrophic cardiomyopathy will have syncope from dynamic outflow obstruction during exertion; these patients also are predisposed to ventricular tachycardia. Physical examination should focus on listening for murmurs of aortic stenosis, mitral stenosis, or hypertrophic obstructive cardiomyopathy.

Pulmonary hypertension, particularly in the setting of an acute rise in pressure from a pulmonary embolism, can cause transiently decreased cardiac output and syncope. A careful examination revealing signs of right-sided heart failure (elevated central venous pressure, peripheral edema, and a normal pulmonary examination) suggests elevated pulmonary pressure.

Cardiac Evaluation

Diagnostic testing for a possible cardiac cause of syncope is based on the pretest probability for a particular cause of the syncope (Table 2). Unless a clear noncardiac cause can be established, a 12-lead resting electrocardiogram (ECG) should be obtained; however, a normal ECG does not rule out a cardiac cause unless it is obtained during an episode of presyncope or syncope. The ECG may reveal arrhythmias, a prolonged QT interval, a high-degree atrioventricular block, a delta wave (preexcitation syndrome), or evidence of structural heart disease (left ventricular hypertrophy, ST-segment elevation, Q waves suggesting current or previous ischemic heart disease).

If the cause of syncope is unexplained from the initial evaluation, continuous telemetry may be useful to screen for paroxysmal arrhythmias. If symptoms are frequent, 24-hour ECG monitoring may be useful to exclude an arrhythmia as a cause of symptoms. For situations in which arrhythmia is suspected but not frequent enough to be captured during the hospital stay, more prolonged ambulatory heart rhythm monitoring may be indicated. An external patient-triggered event monitor can capture the arrhythmia, provided the event lasts long enough for the patient to activate the recorder. A looping event monitor captures several seconds of the ECG signal before the device is triggered and is useful when episodes are accompanied by syncope or presyncope. For very infrequent events, a loop recorder implanted under the skin may be warranted.

If structural heart disease is suspected, an echocardiogram is indicated. If syncope occurs during exercise, a graded exercise test may reveal useful information. Specific testing for pulmonary embolism may be necessary in the appropriate clinical setting.

Neurocardiogenic Causes

Neurocardiogenic syncope is a broad term referring to a syndrome of either increased parasympathetic tone or decreased sympathetic tone resulting in transient loss of consciousness. Approximately one third of syncope will be "reflex mediated," or neurocardiogenic. Patients with neurocardiogenic syncope usually are younger and have presyncopal symptoms, such as lightheadedness, nausea, warmth, diaphoresis, or blurred vision. These presyncopal warning symptoms, if lasting >10 seconds, are highly sensitive for the diagnosis of neurocardiogenic syncope. Patients with neurocardiogenic causes of syncope do not have increased mortality rate compared with the general population. The physical examination typically is unrevealing.

Vasovagal syncope is the most common cause of neurocardiogenic syncope. Vasovagal syncope occurs because of sudden vasodilation and bradycardia, with resultant hypotension and cerebral hypoperfusion. In these patients, a sudden sympathetic surge may activate mechanoreceptors in the left ventricle and stretch receptors in the great vessels. Such stimulation may result in inappropriately increased vagal tone. Vasovagal syncope precipitated by a specific trigger is referred to as *situational syncope*. Common triggers include micturition, defecation, cough, fear, pain, phlebotomy, and prolonged standing. Eliciting the exact circumstances surrounding the event usually reveals the trigger. Patients with vasovagal syncope often give a history of previous episodes.

Carotid sinus hypersensitivity is a similar cardiac reflex provoked by carotid sinus massage or other factors that place direct pressure on the carotid sinus, such as a tight shirt collar. The association of presyncope or syncope with shaving or turning one's head to the side is consistent with carotid sinus hypersensitivity.

Patients with a history suggestive of neurocardiogenic syncope who are deemed at low risk may require no further evaluation. If the history suggests carotid sinus hypersensitivity, carotid sinus massage with monitoring can be attempted in patients without bruits or cerebrovascular disease and when other causes of syncope have been excluded. The massage attempts to reproduce index symptoms with a characteristic heart rate and blood pressure response. In patients with recurrent syncope and in those with a single episode who are at high risk based on their occupation (eg, pilots), a tilt table test can be useful; in this test, the patient is passively moved from the supine position to the head-up position (between 60 and 90 degrees). The tilt table test provides a diagnosis in up to 60% of cases when done with pharmacologic stimulation; however, the poor sensitivity, specificity, and reproducibility of the test must be considered when interpreting the results.

Table 2. Laboratory and Other Studies for Unexplained Syncope

Test	Notes
12-Lead ECG	Perform in all patients with unexplained syncope. Arrhythmias, conduction defects predisposing to complete heart block, and evidence of structural heart disease may be documented. Yields a diagnosis in approximately 5% of patients in whom the initial history and physical examination are nondiagnostic.
Routine blood tests	Not recommended because they rarely yield diagnostic information not suggested by the history and physical examination. Blood testing yields a diagnosis in approximately 0.5% of patients in whom the initial history and physical examination are nondiagnostic.
Echocardiography	Should be performed in patients with syncope and clinically suspected heart disease or with exertional syncope. Can diagnose and quantify obstructive lesions and can identify abnormalities that provide a substrate for malignant arrhythmias (ie, cardiomyopathy, valvular heart disease, and pulmonary hypertension).
Stress testing	Recommended in patients with exercise-associated syncope and patients whose clinical evaluation suggests the presence of ischemic heart disease.
Ambulatory electrocardiographic monitoring	Indicated in patients whose symptoms suggest arrhythmia, patients with known or suspected heart disease, and patients with abnormal ECG findings. Ambulatory (24-h) ECG monitoring correlates symptoms with an arrhythmia in only 4% of patients. Increasing the duration of monitoring (ie, to 48 or 72 h) increases the number of arrhythmias detected but not the diagnostic yield. Cardiac event monitors (patient triggered or looping) worn for longer periods of time (weeks to months) may be helpful in selected patients with infrequent episodes of suspected arrhythmogenic syncope.
Implantable loop recorders	Indicated in patients with recurrent, unexplained syncope. Long-term follow-up (median, 17 mo) led to diagnosis of the cause of syncope in 41% of patients compared with 7% of patients assigned to conventional evaluation.
Invasive electrophysiologic studies	Performed in patients with structural heart disease and syncope that remains unexplained after appropriate evaluation. The diagnostic yield in patients without organic heart disease is 10%.
Tilt table test	Poor sensitivity, specificity, and reproducibility; despite its limitations, the tilt table test is the only diagnostic tool available for determining susceptibility to neurocardiogenic syncope.

ECG = electrocardiogram.

Orthostatic Hypotension

Syncope with a change in posture or prolonged standing suggests orthostatic hypotension. Orthostatic hypotension is defined as a systolic blood pressure decrease of ≥20 mm Hg or diastolic pressure decrease of ≥10 mm Hg within 3 minutes of standing. Causes include hypovolemia, disorders of the autonomic nervous system, and drug effect (especially in elderly patients).

A careful history should be obtained, looking for reasons for volume loss, such as vomiting, diarrhea, bleeding, or limited oral intake. Adrenal insufficiency also can contribute to orthostasis. The physical examination is directed at identifying signs of hypovolemia (dry axilla and oral mucosa) and orthostatic blood pressure changes.

Drugs particularly prone to producing orthostatic syncope include vasodilatory antihypertensive medications and preload-reducing agents, such as diuretics, nitrates, and α-blockers. β-Blockers impair the compensatory increase in heart rate with positional changes and are common causes of orthostasis in elderly adults. Autonomic neuropathy can impair the blood pressure response to a change in position; diabetes is a common cause of autonomic neuropathy, but other conditions (alcoholic polyneuropathy, multiple system atrophy) can produce similar symptoms. Multiple system atrophy is a heterogeneous degenerative disorder that can be associated with parkinsonism, ataxia, and autonomic nervous system impairment.

Therapy

Treatment of syncope is directed at the underlying cause, with the goal of preventing recurrence and decreasing morbidity and mortality. Structural cardiac disease and arrhythmias are discussed in the Cardiovascular Medicine section. Pacemakers or implantable cardioverter-defibrillators can improve outcomes for some of these conditions.

If neurocardiogenic syncope is suspected, isometric muscle contraction to increase systemic vascular resistance and decrease venous pooling of blood at the onset of impending syncope may be useful. Prophylactic fluid loading before high-risk situations (eg, prolonged standing) also may be helpful. All patients should be educated regarding the pathophysiology of situational syncope and avoidance strategies. As a last resort, the placement of a pacemaker for neurocardiogenic syncope has been shown to reduce recurrence in up to 70% of cases.

If orthostatic hypotension is diagnosed as the cause of syncope, volume expansion is recommended to increase intravascular volume. For patients with chronic orthostatic hypotension unrelated to acute volume loss, liberal salt and fluid intake is appropriate. For syncope refractory to these measures, compression stockings or abdominal binders may decrease venous pooling. Additional treatment steps include elimination of drugs associated with orthostatic hypotension, including α- and β-blockers and anticholinergic agents, if possible. If orthostatic hypotension or neurocardiogenic syncope is insufficiently addressed by nondrug approaches, the addition of mineralocorticoids (to increase plasma volume by renal sodium retention) and α-adrenergic receptor agonists (to increase peripheral vascular tone) may be successful. Alternative agents may include nonsteroidal antiinflammatory drugs and caffeine. In elderly patients taking antihypertensive medications, dose modification can be useful in resolving symptoms of syncope or presyncope.

Bibliography

Parry SW, Tan MP. An approach to the evaluation and management of syncope in adults. BMJ. 2010;340:c880. [PMID: 20172928]

Chapter 41

Approach to Lymphadenopathy

Heather Harrell, MD

Lymphadenopathy, an enlargement of one or more lymph nodes, is a common condition that affects patients of all ages and backgrounds. Lymphadenopathy may be discovered incidentally as part of a physical examination or may be detected in an evaluation for a patient-reported mass or "swollen gland." The causes of lymphadenopathy are numerous, ranging from malignancy to a self-limited immunologic reaction, infection, or inflammation. This chapter reviews the evaluation of lymphadenopathy, with an emphasis on identifying findings that are more likely to be associated with underlying pathologic conditions requiring further evaluation.

Evaluation

The history and physical examination are critical in determining which patients need further evaluation for lymphadenopathy. The patient's age is one of the most helpful pieces of information; age >40 years is associated with a 20 times greater risk of malignancy or granulomatous disease compared with younger age. The setting in which the lymphadenopathy occurs is also important; acute onset following an infection suggests an infectious or reactive lymphadenopathy, whereas subacute onset in a person who smokes cigarettes suggests malignancy. Timing is another helpful clue, as most benign immunologic reactions resolve in 2 to 4 weeks, whereas more serious conditions are associated with persistent or progressive lymphadenopathy. Finally, the presence of systemic symptoms suggests a more serious underlying illness. For example, "B" symptoms (eg, fever, night sweats, weight loss) are sometimes present in patients with Hodgkin lymphoma, whereas rash is often associated with specific infectious or inflammatory diseases (eg, secondary syphilis, drug hypersensitivity reaction, systemic lupus erythematosus).

When evaluating a patient with lymphadenopathy, all lymph node regions should be carefully examined. Determine the location, size, consistency (eg, soft, rubbery, fluctuant, firm, hard), and mobility of any involved nodes; if multiple nodes are involved, also determine whether the nodes are discrete or matted. Features concerning for malignancy include size >2 cm, hard consistency, and fixed and/or matted nodes. The location and number of involved lymph nodes provide particularly helpful clues regarding cause. For example, supraclavicular lymphadenopathy is usually a sign of a serious underlying condition, whereas inguinal lymphadenopathy is very common and often benign. Characterizing whether the lymphadenopathy is localized (limited to one anatomic region) or generalized (involving more than two anatomic regions) may suggest which diagnoses are more likely; a single supraclavicular node suggests metastatic cancer, whereas generalized lymphadenopathy suggests a systemic inflammatory or infectious disease, such as syphilis or HIV infection. In the case of localized lymphadenopathy, the anatomic region that drains into the affected lymph node system should be examined for signs of infection or malignancy. For example, if an evaluation reveals axillary adenopathy suspicious for malignancy, a thorough breast examination and mammography should be performed. Signs of inflammation (eg, warmth, redness, tenderness, fluctuance) suggest an infectious cause. The presence of splenomegaly can be a helpful clue to the diagnosis of infectious mononucleosis, lymphoma, or leukemia. Table 1 highlights the signs and symptoms that help differentiate benign and pathologic causes of lymphadenopathy.

As many as two-thirds of patients with lymphadenopathy have an obvious self-limited cause, such as a recent upper respiratory tract infection, that does not require further evaluation. There are many other, more diagnostically challenging causes of lymphadenopathy, however. Table 2 presents a mnemonic, CHICAGO, useful in creating a differential diagnosis for lymphadenopathy. **Because of the many potential causes of lymphadenopathy, the**

Table 1. ALL STAGES Mnemonic for Lymphadenopathy Features Suggesting a Benign or Pathologic Cause

Feature	Greater Likelihood of Benign Cause	Greater Likelihood of Pathologic Cause
Age	<40 y	>40 y
Location	Cervical, axillary, inguinal	Supraclavicular, mediastinal, abdominal
Length of time present	<2 wk	>4 wk
Size	<2 cm	>2 cm
Texture	Soft, rubbery	Hard, matted
Associated signs	Tender, mobile	Nontender (unless massive), fixed
Generalized vs localized	Not helpful predictor but may be useful in identifying cause	Not helpful predictor but may be useful in identifying cause
Extranodal associations	Localized infection (eg, cellulitis, pharyngitis)	Splenomegaly, weight loss, arthritis, persistent fever
Setting	Recent illness or injury	Risk factors for malignancy

Table 2. Selected Differential Diagnosis of Lymphadenopathy: CHICAGO Mnemonic

Diagnostic Category	Example(s)
Cancer	Lymphoma, leukemia, metastatic cancer (numerous primary sites)
Hypersensitivity	Drug reaction, vaccine reaction, serum sickness
Infection	Viral (EBV, CMV, or HIV infection), bacterial (eg, cat scratch fever, staphylococcal or streptococcal infection, syphilis, chlamydia), mycobacterial (eg, tuberculosis, nontuberculous mycobacterial infection), parasitic (toxoplasmosis), fungal (histoplasmosis, coccidioidomycosis), rickettsial (typhus)
Connective tissue disease	Systemic lupus erythematosus, rheumatoid arthritis, Sjögren syndrome
Atypical lymphoproliferative disorder	Castleman disease (giant lymph node hyperplasia)
Granulomatous disease	Sarcoidosis, silicosis, berylliosis
Other unusual cause	Kikuchi disease (histiocytic necrotizing lymphadenitis)

CMV = cytomegalovirus; EBV = Epstein-Barr virus.

clinician must rely heavily on the patient's history and physical examination to focus the subsequent laboratory or imaging evaluation on the most likely diagnoses. A complete blood count with differential is a useful initial test, as it can provide clues regarding a possible infection (eg, atypical monocytosis in the case of Epstein-Barr virus infection), connective tissue disease (eg, anemia, thrombocytopenia, and leukopenia in the case of systemic lupus erythematosus), or malignancy (eg, blast cells in the case of leukemia). Blood cultures and serologic studies for the presence of specific antigens or antibodies are helpful when an infectious cause is suspected but should be done only when clinical factors make a specific infection likely. Chest radiographs are obtained when lymphoma, lung cancer, or granulomatous disease is in the differential diagnosis. Computed tomography and magnetic resonance imaging may be useful when assessing for the presence of intrathoracic or intra-abdominal lymphadenopathy. An empiric trial of antibiotics or glucocorticoids has no role in the evaluation of lymphadenopathy.

The evaluation of lymphadenopathy often centers on whether a lymph node biopsy is needed. Generally, the more high-risk criteria that are present (see Table 1), the more urgent the biopsy. Even in the absence of multiple risk factors, persistent (>4 weeks) unexplained lymphadenopathy usually requires biopsy. Biopsies can be excisional (entire node) or core (pieces of the node). Excisional biopsy is required to fully evaluate lymphoma (to demonstrate lymph node architecture and provide specimens for flow cytometry), whereas needle biopsy is sufficient for suspected squamous cell carcinoma secondary to head and neck cancers. Many such lymph node biopsies show only nonspecific reactive changes, however, and a directed biopsy of the suspected primary tumor may be required. Lymph node needle aspirates may also be cultured to diagnose an infection.

Bibliography

Bazemore AW, Smucker DR. Lymphadenopathy and malignancy. Am Fam Physician. 2002 Dec 1;66:2103-10. [PMID: 12484692]

Chapter 42

Approach to Involuntary Weight Loss

Danelle Cayea, MD

Involuntary weight loss is defined as the loss of >5% of total body weight over a 6-month period or >10% over a 1-year period. Involuntary weight loss is common and may be associated with significant illness, malnutrition, decline in physical function, reduced quality of life, and a twofold increase in mortality.

Terminology used to describe weight loss is confusing and betrays an incomplete understanding of the underlying pathophysiology of involuntary weight loss. Classic definitions of involuntary weight loss are derived from two syndromes first described in starving children (kwashiorkor and marasmus), both of which are reversible with feeding. Many adults with involuntary weight loss fail to respond to feeding, however. In adults, involuntary weight loss may result from several types of conditions that may overlap:

- Wasting, or starvation, is weight loss that occurs without an underlying inflammatory condition and may respond to increased calorie intake.
- Sarcopenia is age-related muscle loss that occurs without other precipitating causes.
- Cachexia is weight loss associated with an underlying inflammatory condition and characterized by increased cytokine production and possible muscle wasting; cachexia is associated with several chronic diseases (eg, cancer, AIDS, chronic obstructive pulmonary disease [COPD]).
- Protein-energy malnutrition is characterized by weight loss, reduced mid-upper arm circumference, and laboratory evidence of reduced dietary intake of protein and calories.
- Failure to thrive is weight loss and decline in physical and/or cognitive functioning associated with signs of hopelessness and helplessness.

Differential Diagnosis

Although few well-designed studies have been conducted on the causes of involuntary weight loss in adults, those studies have been relatively consistent in the proportion of patients reported with various causes. Approximately 50% to 70% of patients have a physical cause, 10% to 20% have a psychiatric cause, and 15% to 25% have no specific cause determined after a thorough evaluation and long-term follow-up (Table 1). Of note, the studies on which these proportions are based involved primarily referred inpatients, and some of the studies were performed at a time when body imaging techniques were less robust than today. Thus, it is reasonable to expect that among outpatient populations, the causes of involuntary weight loss may be different.

The most common physical cause of involuntary weight loss is cancer. Weight loss may be the presenting feature of cancer before other symptoms emerge. The second most common physical cause is nonmalignant gastrointestinal disease, including peptic ulcer disease, inflammatory bowel disease, malabsorption, oral disorders, dysphagia, and gallbladder disease. A broad spectrum of conditions accounts for the remainder of physical causes, including endocrine disorders (especially thyroid disorders and diabetes mellitus), infections (eg, tuberculosis, HIV infection), and chronic conditions that cause increased energy expenditure, such as late-stage heart failure, COPD, and movement disorders (eg, tardive dyskinesia, Parkinson disease). Kidney and liver disease may induce weight loss by causing nausea and decreased appetite.

Many medications can cause weight loss, especially among the elderly, by causing anorexia, dysgeusia (ie, distortion of the sense of taste), or nausea. Such drugs include angiotensin-converting enzyme inhibitors, nonsteroidal anti-inflammatory drugs, selective serotonin reuptake inhibitors, cholinesterase inhibitors, anticholinergic agents, and dopaminergic agents (eg, levodopa, metoclopramide). Additionally, polypharmacy can cause dysgeusia and anorexia.

Several psychiatric disorders are associated with weight loss, the most common being depression. Weight loss associated with dementia may precede the diagnosis of the underlying cognitive disorder. Eating disorders (anorexia) and substance abuse disorders (eg, alcoholism or drug use) also cause weight loss. Socioeconomic and functional factors may cause or exacerbate weight loss; examples include difficulty in obtaining food because of functional disabilities, lack of financial resources, or social isolation.

Evaluation

Involuntary weight loss may be identified by patient self-report. However, because a substantial proportion of patients who report weight loss may not have experienced it, use documented weight measurements or objective evidence of weight loss, such as a change

Table 1. Differential Diagnosis of Involuntary Weight Loss (IWL)

Cause	Percentage of Patients With IWL
Cancer	16%-38%
Gastrointestinal disorder	10%-18%
Endocrine disorder	~5%
Infection	~5%
Pulmonary disorder	6%
Medication effect	2%-9%
Cardiovascular disorder	~9%
Kidney disorder	4%
Neurologic disorder	2%-7%
Depression	9%-18%
Undetermined	5%-26%

in how clothes fit or corroboration by a trusted observer, before pursuing an evaluation. Then, confirm that changes in total body water are not the cause of weight loss. Dramatic weight changes can occur with gain or loss of total body water (such as with diuresis), which occur more quickly and erratically than changes in lean body mass.

Although the differential diagnosis of weight loss is wide ranging, it is clear from the literature that a carefully performed patient history and physical examination, followed by targeted use of diagnostic studies, is likely to reveal the cause. An often-overlooked clinical pearl is that the chief complaint frequently points to a specific cause. Look for information suggesting chronic disease (eg, cancer, gastrointestinal disease, endocrine disorder, infection, severe cardiopulmonary disorder). Patients with weight loss and an increased appetite may be more likely to have increased calorie loss (eg, type 2 diabetes, malabsorption) or energy expenditure (eg, hyperthyroidism). Take a careful medication history, with particular emphasis on medications known to affect appetite or to be temporally related to weight loss. Assess for affective and cognitive disorders; standard depression and cognitive function screening tools are helpful in this regard. Obtain a history of dietary practices, dietary intake, and use of nutritional supplements. Inquire about living environment, access to food, functional status, dependency, caregiver status, alcohol or substance abuse, social support, and resources. It is important to question relatives and caregivers.

Before pursuing additional testing in patients with unexplained weight loss, review prior medical studies such as age-appropriate cancer screening to help identify areas that may need further investigation. Initial diagnostic testing is limited to basic studies unless the patient's history and physical examination suggest a specific cause (Table 2). The following studies should be obtained in most patients: complete blood count; erythrocyte sedimentation rate or C-reactive protein; serum chemistry tests, includ-

Table 2. Laboratory and Other Studies for Involuntary Weight Loss (IWL)

Test	Notes
CBC	Anemia is present in 14% of patients with a physical cause of weight loss.
Electrolytes, blood urea nitrogen, creatinine, glucose, calcium level, liver tests	The combination of decreased albumin level and elevated alkaline phosphatase level has a sensitivity of 17% and specificity of 87% for cancer. Adrenal insufficiency is associated with electrolyte disturbances in 92% of patients.
ESR or CRP	Mean ESR is increased (49 mm/h) in patients with neoplasia compared with patients with a psychiatric or unknown cause of IWL (19 mm/h and 26 mm/h, respectively).
Thyroid-stimulating hormone	Look for "apathetic" hyperthyroidism.
Ferritin	Low ferritin may be an earlier sign of occult blood loss than other hematologic parameters. Among people with IWL, ferritin > 100 µg/L has a higher negative predictive value for colorectal cancer than other GI cancers.
Urinalysis	Asymptomatic microscopic hematuria may be the only abnormal test result in a patient with weight loss caused by renal or genitourinary malignancies.
Home fecal occult blood test	Six samples on three cards obtained by the patient at home may be helpful in detecting colonic malignancies.
Chest radiography	A useful test overall in patients with a physical cause of IWL.
HIV antibody	HIV antibody testing is indicated if the patient falls into a recommended screening group or if risk factors are present.
Upper GI radiography series, EGD, abdominal ultrasonography, or abdominal CT	Upper GI has the highest yield in disclosing a pertinent abnormality beyond basic screening tests among patients with a physical cause of weight loss if GI symptoms are present. Among patients diagnosed with cancer, the most useful follow-up tests include: • Patients with only an isolated abnormality on CBC: abdominal CT, abdominal ultrasonography, and endoscopy • Patients with only an isolated abnormality in liver tests: abdominal ultrasonography and abdominal CT • Patients with normal liver test results and CBC: upper endoscopy and abdominal CT

CBC = complete blood count; CRP = C-reactive protein; CT = computed tomography; EGD = esophagogastric duodenoscopy; ESR = erythrocyte sedimentation rate; GI = gastrointestinal.

Table 3. Clinical Prediction Rule for Malignancy as a Cause of Isolated Weight Loss

Test or Feature	Points[a]
Age >80 y	+1
Serum albumin >3.5 g/dL (35 g/L)	−2
Leukocyte count >12,000/µL (12 × 10⁹/L)	+1
Serum alkaline phosphatase >300 U/L	+2
Serum lactate dehydrogenase >500 U/L	+3

[a]A score of <0 indicates a low probability for malignancy (positive likelihood ratio = 0.07), a score of 0-1 indicates an intermediate probability (positive likelihood ratio = 1.2), and a score >1 indicates high probability (positive likelihood ratio = 28).

Adapted with permission from Hernández JL, Matorras P, Riancho JA, González-Macías J. Involuntary weight loss without specific symptoms: a clinical prediction score for malignant neoplasm. QJM. 2003;96:649-55. [PMID: 12925720]

ing calcium level, kidney and liver function tests, and thyroid-stimulating hormone level; urinalysis; chest radiography; and stool occult blood test. Among patients with a completely normal baseline evaluation, later diagnosis of a serious organic disorder is rare, and watchful waiting may be the preferred approach (Table 3). In patients with gastrointestinal symptoms or abnormalities on complete blood count or liver tests, obtain an upper gastrointestinal series or esophagogastric duodenoscopy, or abdominal ultrasonography or abdominal computed tomography (CT), as appropriate. High-risk smokers and ex-smokers (ages 55 to 74 with ≥30 pack-years of smoking and for ex-smokers who quit ≤15 years ago) may benefit from a low-dose chest CT instead of a plain chest radiography to evaluate for cancer. Indiscriminate imaging of the thorax and abdomen with CT or MRI in the absence of supporting findings on history, physical examination, or laboratory studies is not helpful or indicated. Truly occult malignancy is not common.

It may be difficult to establish a definitive diagnosis for weight loss, and perhaps a quarter of patients will not have a diagnosis after an appropriate initial evaluation. For such patients, careful reevaluation over time is appropriate; if serious disease is present, the cause is likely to become evident within 3 to 6 months. If a cause cannot be established over time, the prognosis is favorable.

Treatment

Once a specific diagnosis is made, directed treatment should alleviate weight loss in most cases. If weight loss continues, the putative diagnosis may not be correct or completely responsible. Consider medication and lifestyle changes for some patients. Change or eliminate medications that may be associated with anorexia and/or temporally related to weight loss. Address issues of social isolation and poor eating environment, if applicable. Ensure that oral health is adequate and that the patient has access to food and is able to eat it. Address personal and ethnic food preferences in the promotion of oral dietary intake. Assist those who need help with eating by seeking to improve functional status and making certain that patients obtain help to eat. Eliminate restrictive diets, where appropriate.

The proven benefit of oral nutritional supplementation for weight loss is limited. In fact, the amount of regular food intake is sometimes decreased by the use of oral nutritional supplements. Nutritional supplementation may be useful, however, when access to calories is an issue due to functional impairments. Appetite stimulants are often recommended but are of limited benefit in patients not responding to treatment of the primary cause of weight loss or if the cause is unknown. Appetite-stimulant therapy has been studied mainly in patients with cachexia related to cancer or AIDS. In these patients, certain agents (eg, megestrol acetate, human growth hormone) have been shown to promote weight gain. A survival benefit has never been demonstrated, however, quality- of-life benefits are modest, and in some trials, patients who received such agents have experienced an increase in mortality.

Bibliography

Vanderschueren S, Geens E, Knockaert D, Bobbaers H. The diagnostic spectrum of unintentional weight loss. Eur J Intern Med. 2005;16:160-164. [PMID: 15967329]

Chapter 43

Comprehensive Geriatric Assessment

Jenny Wright, MD
Anne Eacker, MD

The comprehensive geriatric assessment (CGA) expands upon the typical medical database collected in an adult patient to include an assessment of functional capacity and to evaluate for common conditions associated with aging, including hearing and vision loss, urinary incontinence, cognitive decline, and falls.

Benefits of the CGA and subsequent interventions include improved functional status and quality of life in frail elderly patients and, possibly, reduced mortality. In the inpatient setting, CGA and appropriate follow-up care have been found to increase a patient's likelihood of being alive and living in the community 1 year later. In the outpatient setting, CGA after an emergency department visit has been found to reduce subsequent hospital admission rates.

Potential barriers to completion and implementation of the CGA are significant and include the time required and lack of support from a multidisciplinary team. The CGA should be focused on high-risk patients, such as those with recent weight loss or multiple medication changes. In low-risk patients, the assessment can be done over several visits.

Medical Database

Geriatric patients often have multiple medical problems, take many prescription and nonprescription medications, and have several providers prescribing their medications. In addition, many medications are poorly tolerated in the geriatric population. Reducing the number of medications patients take significantly reduces the risk of drug interactions and falls; some studies show that mortality rates also are reduced. It is important to regularly review all prescription and nonprescription medications to check for possible drug interactions and to eliminate any unnecessary or unsafe medications. The Beers criteria are useful for identifying medications to avoid in elderly adults (www.americangeriatrics.org/health_care_professionals/clinical_practice/clinical_guidelines_recommendations/2012).

Important aspects of the social history include asking about family and community support and the frequency of social contact, obtaining the names and contact information for persons in the patient's support network, and screening for elder abuse by asking if the patient feels safe at home. If elder abuse is suspected, additional assessment should be done, and mandatory reporting is required in most states; the laws vary from state to state. If the cost of medical care is a burden to a patient, consult with a medical social worker about additional resources.

Undernutrition and dietary deficiencies, such as vitamin B_{12} deficiency, are more common in elderly adults. Several factors can contribute to undernutrition, including decreased enjoyment of eating because of an impaired sense of taste and smell, decreased access to food as a result of social isolation, and difficulty chewing because of poor dentition and age- or drug-related dry mouth.

Assessment of Functional Ability

A patient's ability to perform *basic* and *instrumental* activities of daily living (ADLs) offers insight into the patient's functional status. Basic ADLs include bathing, dressing, toileting, transferring, feeding, and maintaining continence; these are activities required for self-care. A patient who is unable to perform these functions is unlikely to be able to safely live independently. Instrumental ADLs include taking medications, using the phone, preparing food, housekeeping, managing household finances, and grocery shopping; these are activities that further enable a patient to function independently. A structured assessment is not required in all elderly patients or at each visit; however, it is useful if a change in function is noted, such as missing several appointments or appearing poorly groomed. If a patient does have declining ability to perform ADLs, it is important to establish the cause and to intervene before the patient develops significant disability.

End-of-Life Wishes

Discussions about end-of-life issues should take place when a patient is medically stable and cognitively intact to offer guidance for caregivers in the event of advanced or acute illness. Ask the patient who should make decisions if he or she is unable to do so, and ask about the patient's goals of care.

A living will or advanced directive outlines wishes regarding measures for prolonging life, such as artificial nutrition and prolonged ventilator support, if a patient becomes incapacitated and is unable to voice his or her wishes. A health care proxy, also referred to as a durable power of attorney for health care, makes decisions for the patient if the patient is incapacitated; this differs from full power of attorney in that it is limited to health care decisions and no longer applies when the patient's decision-making capacity is restored. If a health care proxy has not been appointed, the legal next of kin is empowered to make these decisions.

In many states, a POLST program exists; POLST stands for Physician Orders for Life-Sustaining Treatment (www.polst.org). In a patient who has a terminal illness or very advanced age, this form can be very helpful. It acts as a medical order that can guide emergency treatment if the patient is not able to voice his or her wishes because of an acute decompensation. The form outlines a patient's code status and other issues of immediate importance such as intubation, use of antibiotics, and admission to intensive care units. It is completed with the medical provider but remains with the patient.

A key issue in delivery of appropriate care in elderly patients is identifying those at a high risk of mortality in the next 6 months because of multiple or advanced medical conditions. In these patients, discussion regarding palliative care options, including hospice care, should be considered. Physicians often have difficulty predicting mortality; a question that has been found indicative of high mortality risk is to ask the physician, "Would you be 'surprised' if this patient died in the coming year?" If the answer to this question is "no," the provider should discuss end-of-life issues expeditiously with the patient and the family if available.

Cognitive Function

The most frequently used and extensively studied screening test for assessing mental status is the Mini–Mental State Examination (MMSE). Scores <24 correlate highly with cognitive dysfunction. Many other screening instruments can be used to identify cognitive dysfunction. The Mini-Cog is a quick test that has similar accuracy to the MMSE but takes less time. Patients are asked to recall three unrelated words after drawing a clock; if they are unable to recall any of the words or can recall one or two of the words but have an abnormal clock drawing, significant cognitive dysfunction is likely (see Chapter 76).

When cognitive dysfunction is identified, further evaluation should be performed to look for causes, particularly reversible conditions. Common reversible causes of cognitive dysfunction in eld-

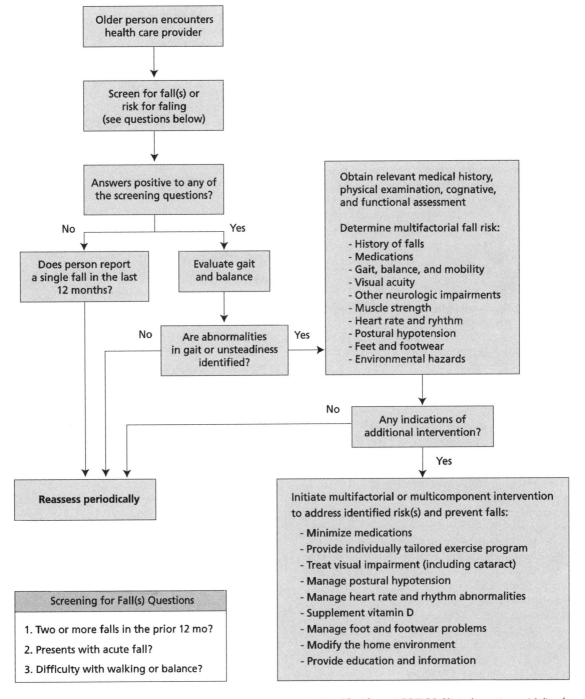

Figure 1. Algorithm for fall prevention in older persons living in the community. Modified from: AGS/BGS Clinical practice guideline for prevention of falls. J Am Geriatr Soc 2010, www.americangeriatrics.org/files/documents/health_care_pros/JAGS.Falls.Guidelines.pdf

erly adults include thyroid disorders, vitamin B_{12} deficiency, medication side effects, and hyponatremia. Early identification of patients with dementia, particularly Alzheimer disease, is important because some medications may have benefit and diagnosis may assist in long-term care planning (see Chapter 76).

Depression

Depression increases the risk of death in elderly patients with coronary artery disease and other chronic diseases. Elderly patients also are at higher risk for suicide than younger patients. Treatment of depression can have a positive impact on the quality of life of older patients as well as their caregivers. Diagnosis may be difficult because geriatric patients may present with somatic complaints rather than an alteration in mood. In addition, symptoms may be inappropriately attributed to comorbid conditions or medication side effects. A simple screening tool for depression consists of two questions: "Over the past 2 weeks, have you felt down, depressed, or hopeless?" and "Over the past 2 weeks, have you felt little interest or pleasure in doing things?" A positive response to both questions is highly sensitive for the diagnosis of depression.

Treatment options for depression include psychotherapy and pharmacotherapy; both are efficacious in elderly patients. Selective serotonin reuptake inhibitors are considered first-line pharmacotherapy. Tricyclic antidepressants (TCAs) usually are avoided because of side effects, including orthostatic hypotension, urinary retention, and cognitive impairment. Antidepressant medications are started at a lower dose in elderly patients, although the ultimate therapeutic dose is typically unchanged (see Chapter 37).

Sensory Impairment

Vision impairment is a common problem among elderly adults. As many as one third of geriatric patients have unrecognized severe vision loss, and up to 25% are wearing improper corrective lenses. The most common causes of vision impairment in older adults are presbyopia (diminished ability of the lens to accommodate), cataracts, primary open-angle glaucoma, age-related macular degeneration, and diabetic retinopathy, all of which are potentially treatable. There is consensus that accurate detection of the intraocular changes of age-related macular degeneration and glaucoma is difficult in a primary care setting; therefore, periodic examination by an eye care professional is prudent for patients older than age 65 years, especially patients with risk factors for these disorders.

Hearing loss affects one third of adults older than age 60 years and half of those older than age 85 years. Untreated hearing loss is associated with depression and decreased quality of life. The most common cause of hearing loss in elderly adults is presbycusis, a sensorineural hearing loss that initially affects high-frequency hearing. The best strategy for determining a need for formal audiometric testing is a combination of self-reported hearing loss (a positive answer to the question, "Do you have trouble hearing?") and the whispered voice test. The whispered voice test assesses the patient's ability to hear the whispered voice of the examiner as he or she stands behind the patient. Admission of hearing difficulties or the inability to repeat back numbers or letters accurately during the whispered voice test is an indication for referral for audiometry.

Falls

Falls are a major medical problem in elderly adults. Assessing fall risk is an essential component of the CGA (Figure 1). All geriatric patients should be screened for fall risk by asking about a history of falls in the past year or difficulty with gait or balance. The "get up and go" test is the recommended screening test for balance and gait difficulties. Patients are timed in their ability to rise from a chair without use of their arms, walk 10 feet, turn, and then return to the chair. Most adults can complete this task in 10 seconds; most frail elderly persons take 11 to 20 seconds to complete the test. Those requiring >20 seconds are at high risk for falls. A strong association exists between poor performance on this test and functional independence in ADLs.

Patients at high risk for falls should undergo a comprehensive fall evaluation, including assessment of visual acuity, medication use, basic and instrumental ADLs, and cognition; evaluation for orthostatic hypotension and gait abnormalities; and home safety assessment.

Interventions recommended by the U.S. Preventive Services Task Force for fall prevention include exercise or physical therapy and vitamin D supplementation. Vitamin D supplementation is associated with a lower risk of falls in elderly adults independent of bone health; this effect is strongest in those with low baseline vitamin D levels. Other interventions to consider include home safety modification directed by a trained professional, withdrawal of psychotropic medications, and tai chi group exercises.

Table 1. Types of Urinary Incontinence

Type	Characteristics	Pathophysiology	Therapy
Urge incontinence, overactive bladder	Daytime frequency, nocturia, bothersome urgency	Involuntary contraction of the bladder, decreased control of the detrusor muscle, decreased competence of the urethral sphincter (in men)	Biofeedback, bladder training, anticholinergic agents (oxybutynin, tolterodine)
Stress incontinence	Involuntary release of urine secondary to effort or exertion (sneezing, coughing, physical exertion)	Pelvic muscle laxity, nerve injury (eg, urologic surgery), poor intrinsic sphincter function	Pelvic floor muscle training (Kegel exercises), biofeedback, electrical stimulation, open retropubic colposuspension, suburethral sling procedure
Overflow incontinence	Associated with overdistention of the bladder	Underactive detrusor muscle or outlet obstruction	Pelvic floor muscle training with biofeedback in early postprostatectomy period, external penile clamp
Functional incontinence	Incontinence in patients with impaired mobility or cognition	Normal urge, bladder, and sphincter control but inability to get to the toilet in time	Regular voiding assistance, timed voiding, management of mobility impairment, bedside commode

In addition, if it is available, a multidisciplinary, multifactorial intervention program tailored to the patient's needs can be beneficial in preventing falls in elderly persons living in the community, reducing the relative risk of falls by as much as 20%. These programs have multiple interventions targeting identified risk factors, including exercise therapy, gait and balance training by physical therapists; prescription of and instruction using assistive devices by occupational therapists; review and modification of medications; modification of home hazards; and treatment of cardiac problems, including postural hypotension.

Urinary Incontinence

The incidence of urinary incontinence increases with age in both men and women. Urinary incontinence is a cause of caregiver burnout and can lead to social isolation for the patient. Patients often hesitate to report symptoms, making it important to periodically ask about them.

If incontinence is an issue, evaluation should begin by ruling out reversible causes. These are summarized by the mnemonic DIAPPERS (Delirium, Infection of the urinary tract, Atrophic urethritis/vaginitis, Pharmaceuticals, Psychological disorders [especially depression], Excessive urine output [associated with heart failure or hyperglycemia], Restricted mobility, and Stool impaction). Evaluation for reversible causes includes an cardiopulmonary examination for heart failure, pelvic examination in women and prostate examination in men, and urinalysis and blood chemistries.

Stress, urge, and mixed (stress plus urge) urinary incontinence are most common in women. In men, urge incontinence and incontinence as a result of prostate disease or surgery are common (Table 1). Of note, behavioral therapies, such as Kegel exercises and prompted (timed) voiding, are effective for treatment of incontinence and are good initial options in frail elderly patients. The medications used to treat urge incontinence (oxybutynin, tolterodine) have anticholinergic side effects (dry mouth, constipation, confusion), so they are best avoided in older patients.

Driving

Any reported incident involving an elderly driver should trigger an assessment of the person's driving capacity, and patients should be asked about their driving activities. Older patients with known cognitive or vision deficits, history of falls or ambulation difficulties, limited neck rotation, neurologic disease, history of motor vehicle accidents, or medication use known to impair cognition (eg, benzodiazepines, opi-oids, or TCAs) should be considered high risk and require careful evaluation. Patients with Alzheimer dementia who continue to drive, compared with similarly aged persons without Alzheimer dementia, have at least double the rate of collisions. The American Academy of Neurology advises that patients with even mild dementia should be advised to stop driving. States vary in their requirements to report patients with dementia to the Department of Motor Vehicles.

Pressure Ulcers

Risk factors for the development of pressure ulcers include increased age, limited mobility, sensory impairment, chronic illness, incontinence, vascular disease, and malnutrition. Older patients often have several of these risk factors. Prevention requires identification of risk factors and interventions to avoid continuous pressure, friction, and shear forces on the skin, all of which lead to ulcer formation. Pressure ulcers are described by stage (Table 2), which is useful for documenting the examination findings and for planning treatment. Treatment of pressure ulcers is best managed with an interdisciplinary team approach, with a care plan directed toward addressing the factors that predisposed to ulcer development. Dressings should be chosen to maintain a moist wound environment and manage exudates. When present, infection should be controlled with topical therapies and, when cellulitis is present, systemic antibiotics. The possibility of underlying osteomyelitis should be considered. Surgical or nonsurgical debridement of eschars and nonviable tissue may be needed. Protective creams or solid barrier dressings should be used to protect the skin surrounding the wound. Air-fluidized beds are likely to improve healing compared with other pressure-relief devices, although they make it harder for patients to get into and out of bed independently.

Bibliography

Carr DB, Ott BR. The older driver with cognitive impairment: "It's a very frustrating life". JAMA. 201028;303:1632-1641. [PMID: 20424254]

Ellis G, Whitehead MA, Robinson D, et al. Comprehensive geriatric assessment for older adults admitted to hospital: meta-analysis of randomized controlled trials. BMJ. 2011;343:d6553. [PMID: 22034146]

Michael YL, Whitlock EP, Lin JS, et al. Primary care-relevant interventions to prevent falling in older adults: a systemic evidence review for the U.S. Preventive Services Task Force. Ann Intern Med. 2010;153:815-825. [PMID: 21173416]

Rosen SJ, Reuben DB. Geriatric assessment tools. Mt Sinai J Med 2011;78:489-497. [PMID: 21748738]

Table 2. Classification of Pressure Ulcers

Pressure Ulcer Stage	Description
Suspected deep tissue injury	Purple or maroon localized area of discolored, intact skin or blood-filled blister caused by damage of underlying soft tissue from pressure or shear (or both). May be difficult to detect in persons with dark skin tones.
Stage I	Intact skin with nonblanchable redness of a localized area, usually over a bony prominence. Darkly pigmented skin may not have visible blanching; its color may differ from the surrounding area.
Stage II	Partial-thickness loss of dermis presenting as a shallow open ulcer with a red-pink wound bed, without slough. May also present as an intact or open or ruptured serum-filled blister.
Stage III	Full-thickness tissue loss. Subcutaneous fat may be visible, but bone, tendon, or muscle is not exposed. Slough may be present but does not obscure the depth of tissue loss. May include undermining and tunneling. Depth varies by anatomic location and may be extremely deep in areas of significant adiposity.
Stage IV	Full-thickness tissue loss with exposed bone, tendon, or muscle. Slough or eschar may be present on some parts of the wound bed. Often includes undermining and tunneling.
Unstageable	Full-thickness tissue loss in which the base of the ulcer is covered by slough (yellow, tan, gray, green, or brown) or eschar (tan, brown, or black) in the wound bed.

Adapted with permission from National Pressure Ulcer Advisory Panel. Pressure ulcer stages revised by NPUAP. www.npuap.org/resources/educational-and-clinical-resources/npuap-pressure-ulcer-stagescategories/. Published February 2007. Accessed May 9, 2014.

Chapter 44

Palliative Care

Susan Glod, MD

Palliative care is specialized medical care for patients with serious illnesses. It focuses on management of the symptoms and stress of serious illness, and interventions include comprehensive communication, appropriate goal setting, and pharmacologic and nonpharmacologic management of symptoms. The goal is to improve quality of life for both the patient and the family.

Palliative care is typically provided by an interdisciplinary team that works in conjunction with a patient's other providers. It is appropriate at any age and at any stage in a serious illness and can be provided along with treatment with curative intent.

Advance Care Planning

Discussions surrounding goals of care are best had longitudinally through periods of good health and early in the disease course. Unfortunately, in many cases, these discussions occur only in the setting of advanced disease, if at all.

Regardless of when these discussions occur, establishing goals of care should not be framed in terms of withholding or withdrawing treatments. Rather, discussions should begin by eliciting a patient's values and preferences in the event he or she becomes ill. For example, a patient may wish to maintain a certain level of functionality, experience good control over pain or other symptoms, or attend a specific family function. After a clear picture of the individual patient's values and goals emerges, a medical plan tailored toward meeting those goals can be developed.

Various documents have been developed to aid in advance care planning. A *living will* allows patients to indicate the extent to which they wish to receive life-sustaining treatment in the event they are terminally ill or in a persistent vegetative state and are unable to speak for themselves. A *durable healthcare power of attorney* is a legal document in which patients can designate another individual to make healthcare decisions for them through periods of time during which they are incapacitated. Although living wills focus mainly on the withholding or withdrawal of life-sustaining interventions, individuals who have been granted durable medical power of attorney have greater scope of decision making in both terminal and nonterminal situations. Physician Orders for Life-Sustaining Treatment (POLST) are sets of medical orders written by a physician after consultation with the patient, surrogate, or both that direct the type and extent of treatment that a patient will receive. Although living wills refer to hypothetical future situations in which patients develop terminal illness or permanent unconsciousness, POLST documents are applicable to the patient's current state of health. All advance care planning documents are applicable only when patients are unable to make their own decisions.

Symptom Management

Pain

Pain can be classified into two categories, nociceptive and neuropathic pain. Nociceptive pain is caused by activation of nociceptors, which are neurons that carry sensory information from the periphery to the brain. It may be further classified into somatic pain (on the body surface or musculoskeletal tissue) or visceral pain (caused by compression, obstruction, ischemia, or other damage to viscera). Neuropathic pain results from direct injury or disease on the somatosensory nervous system. It is less well understood than nociceptive pain and encompasses a broad range of categories, including focal neuropathies (eg, phantom limb pain), generalized neuropathies (eg, diabetic or alcoholic neuropathy), and central pain syndromes (eg, multiple sclerosis).

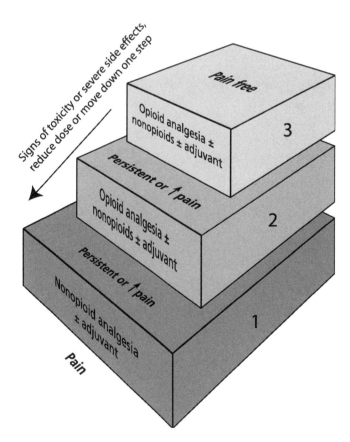

Figure 1. A three-step approach to pain control based on the World Health Organization's analgesic ladder. Adapted with permission from: Induru RR, Lagman RL. Managing cancer pain: frequently asked questions. Cleve Clin J Med. 2011;78:449-464.

Effective management of pain begins with a thorough assessment of pain characteristics, including the site, duration, type, and intensity. A variety of standardized scales, including visual analogue scales, verbal rating scales, and numerical rating scales, have been developed. The World Health Organization's three-step analgesic "ladder" represents a useful framework for pharmacologic treatment of pain (Figure 1). Mild pain (scores of 1–3 on the 0–10 pain intensity scale) is treated with nonopioid pain relievers (eg, aspirin, acetaminophen, nonsteroidal antiinflammatory drugs). Moderate pain (scores 4–6) is often treated with a conservatively dosed strong opioid. Severe pain (scores 7–10) is treated mainly with opioid analgesics. If an opioid is combined with acetaminophen in a single pill, care must be taken to avoid inadvertent overdosing of acetaminophen if the need for the opioid ingredient increases; the maximum daily dose of acetaminophen for adults is 4 g. Information on commonly used opioid medications, including starting doses, routes of administration, half-lives, and other considerations, is detailed in Table 1.

Effective pain management is often an ongoing process that requires repeated assessment of a patient's pain control; appropriate titration and choice of therapy based on available routes of delivery, side effects, and metabolic parameters; and attention to social, emotional, and spiritual components that may affect a patient's perception of pain.

Adjuvant analgesics are defined as drugs that have a primary indication other than pain but have been shown to have analgesic properties in specified conditions. They are appropriate for use at any step of the World Health Organization analgesic ladder. Bisphosphonates and calcitonin have been shown to improve pain related to metastatic disease and osteoporotic fractures. Tricyclic antidepressants, venlafaxine, and duloxetine may be especially useful in patients with both neuropathic pain and depression.

Gabapentin and pregabalin also are effective for neuropathic pain. Glucocorticoids can reduce edema and reduce the burden of certain tumors and are effective in the management of pain related to malignant infiltration of the brachial or lumbar plexus and spinal cord compression, as well as head pain related to intracranial peritumoral edema. Anticholinergic drugs such as glycopyrrolate may improve pain in patients with malignant bowel obstruction.

Dyspnea

Dyspnea, the subjective sensation of feeling short of breath, is a common symptom in patients with chronic or terminal illness. It is often related to direct cardiothoracic pathology, such as pleural effusion, heart failure, chronic obstructive pulmonary disease, pulmonary embolism, pneumonia, primary lung cancer, or metastatic disease, but can also be caused by systemic conditions such as anemia, muscle weakness, and conditions causing increased intraabdominal pressure. The patient's self-report of discomfort should be the driving factor for treatment and often has little correlation with respiratory rate, arterial blood gas levels, oxygen saturation, or use of accessory musculature.

The mainstay of dyspnea management in palliative care is the optimization of the underlying disease. Patients with chronic heart or lung disease may experience significant relief with continued maximal medical therapy. This may also include antibacterial treatment of pulmonary infections such as bronchitis or pneumonia. In patients for whom disease-modifying therapies are not available, temporizing measures such as airway stenting for obstructive bronchial lesions or pleural drainage via thoracentesis or catheter placement for malignant effusions are appropriate.

If the etiology of dyspnea cannot be modified, opioids are the mainstay of treatment. Opiates decrease oxygen consumption at rest

Table 1. Dosing and Conversion Chart for Opioid Analgesics

Medication	Usual Starting Dose[a,b]		Equianalgesic Dosing[c]	
	Oral	Parenteral	Oral	Parenteral
Hydrocodone	5.0 mg every 3-4 h	Not available	30.0 mg	Not available
Oxycodone	5.0-10.0 mg every 3-4 h (immediate release or oral solution)	Not available	20.0 mg	Not available
Morphine	5.0-15.0 mg every 3-4 h (immediate release or oral solution)	2.5-5.0 mg SC/IV every 3-4 h	30.0 mg	10.0 mg
Oxymorphone	10.0 mg every 4-6 h (immediate release)	1.0-1.5 mg SC/IM every 4-6 h	10.0 mg	1.0 mg
Hydromorphone	1.0-2.0 mg every 3-4 h	0.2-0.6 mg SC/IV every 2-3 h	7.5 mg	1.5 mg
Fentanyl	Sublingual tablets, lozenges, films, and buccal formulations available; appropriate consultation is advised for dosing of these agents	25.0-50.0 µg IM/IV every 1-3 h Transdermal patch 12 µg/hr every 72 h	Not available	100 µg (single dose) Initial patch dose based on 24-h oral morphine dose 30.0-59.0 mg — 12.0 µg/h 60.0-134.0 mg — 25.0 µg/h 135.0-224.0 mg — 50.0 µg/h 225.0-314.0 mg — 75.0 µg/h 315.0-404.0 mg — 100.0 µg/h

IM = intramuscularly; IV = intravenously; SC = subcutaneously.

[a]Adult, opioid-naïve patients >50 kg (110 lb).

[b]Dose should be reduced by half in older patients or those with liver or kidney disease.

[c]Estimated dose offering equivalent analgesia as other medications.

in healthy individuals, have a vasodilatory effect on pulmonary vasculature, and affect the ventilatory response to carbon dioxide and hypoxia, all of which likely contribute to their ability to decrease dyspnea. Relatively small doses of opioids (the equivalent of 10–20 mg of oral morphine daily in divided doses) have demonstrated efficacy in dyspnea reduction. Although morphine is commonly used for this purpose, there is little evidence to suggest that it is superior to other opiates. The data to support the use of oxygen therapy for palliation of dyspnea, particularly in the absence of hypoxemia, are mixed, and decisions to implement home oxygen therapy should only be made after careful weighing of the potential benefits of therapy with patient and caregiver burden. Nonpharmacologic interventions for the management of dyspnea may include invasive or noninvasive ventilation, facial cooling, external air movement with fans, body position change, and the implementation of strategies to conserve energy by spacing out daily activities. Anxiety reduction is often an important component of the management of dyspnea.

Nausea

Nausea is the sensation of abdominal discomfort often accompanied by the involuntary urge to vomit, and is thought to occur through stimulation of at least one of four stimulant pathways:

- Gastrointestinal (mechanical stretch, mucosal injury, toxins) – mediated by mechanoreceptors, chemoreceptors, and 5-hydroxytryptamine (5-HT3) receptors
- Cortical (increased intracranial pressure, meningeal irritation, anxiety)
- Vestibular (motion, labrynthine disorders) – mediated by muscarinic acetacholine receptors and histamine type 1 receptors
- Chemotactic trigger zone (drugs, toxins, metabolic products) – mediated by central dopamine type 2 (D2) receptors, 5-HT3 receptors, and neurokinin type 1 receptors

An initial evaluation of nausea should be directed at the prompt identification of any potentially life-threatening emergencies, such as cardiac ischemia or intracranial hemorrhage, followed by an assessment of any reversible etiologies, such as constipation, electrolyte abnormalities, or medications. Further therapy should be directed at identifying the most likely pathway involved and tailoring therapy appropriately. In general, patients who are actively vomiting will benefit from scheduled intravenous antiemetics.

Nausea originating in the gastrointestinal (GI) tract may improve with administration of a 5HT3 receptor antagonist such as ondansetron or palonosetron. These agents block both peripheral receptors found on the vagus nerve and enterochromaffin cells as well as central receptors in the chemoreceptor trigger zone. Metoclopramide is a prokinetic agent with central D2 antagonism at high doses that may improve nausea related to impaired proximal GI motility. If nausea is related to tumor obstruction or compression, glucocorticoids may decrease peritumoral edema and relieve the obstruction. Vestibular nausea may be treated with histamine antagonists such as promethazine or meclizine. If activation of the chemoreceptor trigger zone is implicated, a central dopamine antagonist such as haloperidol or prochlorperazine may be effective. Nonpharmacologic interventions will depend on the etiology of nausea and may include hydration; parenteral nutrition; small, frequent meals; or the elimination of strong or unpleasant odors.

Constipation

Constipation is described as a decrease in the usual frequency of bowel movements or stool that is hard or difficult to pass. Many factors contribute to constipation in patients with life-altering illnesses, including medications, immobility, metabolic abnormalities, and decreased oral intake. Because the frequency of defecation varies widely among normal individuals, it is helpful to ascertain an individual's baseline bowel function when assessing for constipation. The next step in management includes assessing for and possibly correcting reversible factors such as dehydration, fecal impaction, dietary issues, or mechanical obstruction. In patients at risk for developing constipation, particularly including those who are taking opioid medications, a preventive approach using a mild stimulant laxative such as senna is appropriate.

Additional oral agents for the management of constipation include bulking agents (psyllium, methylcellulose), which increase stool bulk by the addition of undigestible material. These agents are only efficacious in individuals taking adequate fluids and may worsen constipation in patients with poor oral intake. Polyethylene glycol is a nonabsorbable polymer that bulks stool and speeds transit time. Lactulose is a nondigestible sugar that exerts an osmotic effect on the small bowel and increases stool bulk by promoting microbial growth. Saline laxatives (magnesium hydroxide, magnesium citrate) stimulate peristalsis through irritation of the bowel wall. Rectal therapies are often used to soften or lubricate hard impacted stool within the rectal vault. Methylnaltrexone is a peripheral mu receptor antagonist that is used to treat refractory opiate-induced constipation.

Anorexia and Cachexia

The anorexia and cachexia syndrome is characterized by the progressive loss of skeletal muscle mass that is not fully reversible using nutritional support and that leads to progressive functional impairment. Cachexia is often associated with advanced cancer, although it has also been described in numerous chronic diseases. Decreased oral intake combined with altered energy metabolism related to a chronic release of proinflammatory cytokines lead to muscle wasting and fatigue.

If the prognosis is uncertain or death is clearly not imminent, appetite stimulants may be considered. In cancer-related anorexia, the most commonly studied medications are progestins, such as megestrol and medroxyprogesterone. These medications improve anorexia and promote weight gain but have an uncertain impact on quality of life. Glucocorticoids or dronabinol may also be used for appetite stimulation, but they have not been proven to increase lean body mass.

The use of enteral and parenteral feeding in terminally ill patients is controversial. The benefits of these modalities are most pronounced in patients with good functional status and with GI disease affecting nutritional intake. There is scant evidence for improved quality of life in patients with anorexia and weight loss caused by terminal disease. In addition, important risks are associated with enteral and parenteral feeding, such as line infection or dislodgement, hyperglycemia, electrolyte imbalances, and fluid overload. Discussing the expectation that anorexia and cachexia will occur, as well as patient nutrition preferences before the onset of weight loss and anorexia, is important to avoid emotional distress for the patient and family.

Hospice

Hospice is one way to provide comprehensive palliative care to patients who have a limited prognosis. In the United States, hospice services are usually covered by insurance when a patient is believed to have a prognosis of 6 months or less and has chosen a palliative route of care. Hospice care includes an interdisciplinary approach with mandatory contributions from physicians, registered nurses, chaplains, social workers, and volunteers. Most hospice care is provided in the patient's residence, whether it is their private home or a nursing facility. Patients are not required to have a Do Not Resuscitate order in place to enroll in hospice but are expected to forgo any treatment that does not primarily focus on symptom management.

Bibliography

Kamal AH, Maguire JM, Wheeler JL, et al. Dyspnea review for the palliative care professional: treatment goals and therapeutic options. J Palliat Med. 2012;15:106-114. [PMID: 22268406]

Ripamonti CI. Pain management. Ann Oncol. 2012;23(Suppl 10):x294-x301. [PMID: 22987980]

Strand JJ, Kamdar MM, Carey EC. Top 10 things palliative care clinicians wished everyone knew about palliative care. Mayo Clin Proc. 2013;88:859-865. [PMID: 23910412]

Chapter 45

Genetics and Genetic Testing

Robert Robinson, MD
Madhusree Singh, MD

The role of genetics in disease has long been recognized and is becoming increasingly important in medical practice. Clinical genetics has traditionally focused on identifying specific disease-causing mutations that typically follow a Mendelian pattern of inheritance. These diseases have historically been diagnosed and managed in the pediatric population. An increasing number of these genetic diseases are being diagnosed in adulthood (Table 1), however, and improved treatment and survival of many individuals with classic genetic disorders has extended the spectrum of clinicians who manage these disorders to include adult medicine physicians.

As opposed to single-gene abnormalities, identifiable genetic variants or groups of specific genetic polymorphisms that do not follow a Mendelian pattern of inheritance are increasingly associated with the development of complex diseases (eg, type 2 diabetes mellitus, neurologic, and psychiatric disorders). The understanding of the role of these genetic factors in predisposing an individual to certain diseases is rapidly evolving, although the predictive accuracy and appropriate use of this form of genetic testing remains to be established.

Additionally, genetic information is increasingly being used to individualize treatment for specific patients. For example, in hematology and oncology, genetic characteristics of certain blood disorders and tumors provide new strategies and targets for therapy. Pharmacogenetics is the use of genetic information to predict the likelihood of a patient's response or susceptibility to adverse events with specific drugs and is increasingly available for clinical use.

The growing availability and lowering cost of direct-to-consumer genetic testing has also added additional challenges to using genetic information in caring for patients, emphasizing the need for clinicians to understand the basics of detecting, diagnosing, and managing genetic diseases.

Assessing Risk for Genetically Associated Diseases

Assessing risk for genetically associated diseases starts with a comprehensive family history before formal genetic counseling or testing is considered. Obtaining a family history of two or more generations can provide information regarding potential risk for genetic disorders or predispositions. Family histories can be complicated, however, by incomplete information, uncertainty about the diagnosis in older family members, adoption, assisted reproductive technology, and misattributed maternity or paternity. Great care must be taken when exploring these issues because of the potential harm to the patient and his or her family if genetic testing reveals unexpected results that may be due to any of these factors. The family history shows the intersection of heredity, environment, and lifestyle with a person's health. Historical "red flags" are indications that there might be increased genetic risk in an individual or family (Table 2).

This information derived from the patient's family history may help determine whether further investigation, formal genetic counseling, and possible genetic testing may be indicated. Potentially modifiable risk factors may also be identified for diseases for which a patient may be at increased risk that may be used to develop a strategy to lower the risk.

Genetic Counseling and Testing

Genetic counseling is a detailed discussion with a patient (and often his or her family) about the risks, heritability, and management options for a genetic disorder. Genetic counseling can be a complex and lengthy process and includes both pretesting and posttesting discussions. Although some clinicians have the knowledge and experience to provide this service, most genetic counseling for high-risk

Table 1. Common Genetic Disorders That May Be Diagnosed in Adults

Disorder	Prevalence	Inheritance	Gene(s)	Consequences
Factor V Leiden	1/20	AD	Factor V	Increased risk of thrombosis
Breast/ovarian cancer	1/33	AD	*BRCA1, BRCA2*	Increased risk of breast and ovarian cancer
Hemochromatosis	1/200	AR	*HFE*	Increased risk of iron overload, diabetes, cirrhosis
Familial hypercholesterolemia	1/500	AD	*LDLR*	Early-onset atherosclerosis
α-1 antitrypsin deficiency	1/2,800	AR	*AAT*	Early-onset emphysema
Cystic fibrosis	1/3,000	AR	*CFTR*	Cystic fibrosis
Familial adenomatous polyposis	1/10,000	AD	*FAP*	Increased risk of colon cancer
Huntington disease	1/20,000	AD	*HTT*	Huntington disease

AD = autosomal dominant; AR = autosomal recessive.

Table 2. "Red Flags" Suggesting an Increased Genetic Risk in an Individual or Family

Family history of multiple affected family members with the same or related disorders
- Such a pattern indicates increased risk, whether through genetic or environmental risk factors, or a combination of genes and environment.
- Example: three family members in two generations with heart disease

Earlier age at onset of disease than expected
- Disorders that arise at a younger age than expected may occur because of a genetic predisposition that makes an individual more susceptible to environmental exposures.
- Example: heart disease occurring in the 4th decade of life

Condition in the less-often-affected sex
- A disorder that occurs in the less common sex may arise because of a genetic predisposition that overrides other hormonal, developmental and environmental factors that contribute to its occurrence.
- Example: breast cancer in a male

Disease in the absence of known risk factors
- Genetic predisposition may lead to the occurrence of a disorder in the absence of obvious environmental factors.
- Example: hyperlipidemia in an individual with an ideal diet and exercise regimen

Ethnic predisposition to certain genetic disorders
- Some genetic disorders are more common in certain ethnic groups. Awareness of a patient's ethnicity or ancestral background can aid in recommending genetic testing and evaluation of genetic conditions.
- Example: lactose intolerance in an individual of African ancestry

Close biological relationship between parents
- Consanguinity is a relationship by blood or a common ancestor. Because relatives are more likely to share the same genes, children from a consanguineous couple related as first cousins or closer have an increased risk of having an autosomal recessive condition.
- Example: cystic fibrosis

Adapted from: National Coalition for Health Professional Education in Genetics (www.nchpeg.org)

patients and their families is done by individuals with focused training in medical genetics and knowledge of the specific complex legal issues that may arise with genetic testing.

Genetic testing may be used for different purposes (Table 3). Before considering genetic testing, clinicians and patients should understand its limitations:

- Current testing methods may not detect all mutations that might occur in a particular gene.
- A mutation in one gene can cause different diseases.
- Genetic testing may not produce a clinically useful result if a variant of unknown clinical significance is identified.
- Genetic tests provide probabilistic, not deterministic, information and therefore are not able to necessarily determine clinical outcome.
- Genetic tests do not account for the interaction of hereditary and environmental factors.
- Multiple different genes may cause a particular disease, and not all involved genes may have been identified.

Table 3. Types of Genetic Testing and Indications

Diagnostic Testing	Used to confirm or support a diagnosis in a patient with clinical disease (eg, cystic fibrosis, sickle cell disease)
Predictive Testing	Used to identify individuals at risk for heritable disease: • Presymptomatic tests evaluate for conditions caused by single genes with a high degree of penetrance that will likely eventually cause disease (eg, Huntington disease). • Predisposition tests evaluate for genetic alterations known to significantly increase the risk of disease (eg, *BRCA* mutation). • Susceptibility tests evaluate for different genetic markers associated with complex diseases (eg, coronary artery disease)
Pharmacogenetic Testing	Tests for genetic factors influencing drug metabolism (eg, TPMT assay for azathioprine)
Tumor (somatic cell) testing	Involves testing tissue (usually cancer) for nonheritable mutations for diagnostic purposes or to assist in selecting a specific treatment (eg, *HER2*, *KRAS*)
Carrier Testing	Used to identify a specific genetic mutation in an asymptomatic family member, frequently for reproductive decision making; typically for the heterozygous state that presents with disease when homozygous (eg, cystic fibrosis, sickle cell disease)
Prenatal (Antenatal) Testing	Testing during pregnancy (by amniocentesis or chorionic villus sampling) to identify congenital conditions (eg, Down syndrome, Turner syndrome)
Newborn (Neonatal) Screening	Testing after birth for presence of disease for which preventive measures or treatment exist (eg, phenylketonuria); often legally mandated and varies by state

BRCA = breast cancer susceptibility genes 1 and 2; TPMT = thiopurine methyltransferase; HER2 = human epidermal growth factor receptor 2; KRAS = Kirsten rat sarcoma viral oncogene.

Common indications for which genetic testing may be appropriate include diagnosis of a condition in a person with signs and symptoms of a disease; to assess risk status for a family member who may be an asymptomatic carrier or at risk to develop a disease (eg, muscular dystrophy, familial cancer syndromes, cystic fibrosis, Huntington disease); concerns about cancer risk based on family history; an abnormal prenatal or newborn screening test that may indicate increased risk of a genetic disorder; concern regarding risk to a future pregnancy because of family history, maternal age, or a previous abnormal pregnancy outcome; maternal exposure to teratogens; or an ethnic background suggesting an increased risk for a genetic disease (eg, sickle cell disease, thalassemia, Tay-Sachs disease, or Fanconi anemia).

In recent years, tests have been developed that identify genetic polymorphisms that may be associated with specific diseases (eg, coronary heart disease, diabetes), and direct-to-consumer testing for these genetic variables has become available. It is also possible for patients to obtain a full sequencing of their personal genome. The concept behind this testing is to identify genetic risk factors for certain diseases and provide the opportunity for individuals to make lifestyle changes that may prevent or delay disease onset. This approach to testing is controversial, however, because many of the available tests are not FDA approved for diagnosis, the genetic associations with clinical disease and effectiveness of interventions to reduce risk based on identified factors have not been established, and there is no clear mechanism to help patients understand the results of testing. Physicians are increasingly likely to encounter patients who have had direct-to-consumer genetic testing who have questions about what to do with the results.

Many challenging ethical, legal, and social issues surround genetic diagnosis and testing, including fears about genetic discrimination, insurability, reproductive rights, and privacy. The rapid pace of the development and availability of genetic testing led to passage of the Genetic Information Nondiscrimination Act of 2008, a landmark federal law that bans the use of genetic information in health insurance coverage and employment decisions. This legislation does not prohibit the use of genetic information in life, disability, or long-term care insurance coverage decisions, however.

Genetic testing is also relatively expensive. Tests often cost hundreds or thousands of dollars, so shared decision making with patients and health care payers is essential before ordering testing. Although direct-to-consumer genetic testing may appear reasonable in cost, it does not factor in potential follow-up consultations, subsequent testing, and the harms of concern with being diagnosed with a genetic abnormality based on nonspecific test results.

Bibliography

Andermann A, Blancquaert I. Genetic screening: a primer for primary care. Can Fam Physician. 2010;56:333-339. [PMID: 20393090]

Berg AO, Baird MA, Botkin JR, et al. National Institutes of Health State-of-the-Science Conference Statement: Family History and Improving Health. Ann Intern Med. 2009;151:872-877. [PMID: 19884615]

National Human Genome Research Institute, National Institutes of Health. Genetic Information Nondiscrimination Act (GINA) of 2008. Available at www.genome.gov/24519851.

U.S. Preventive Services Task Force. Risk Assessment, Genetic Counseling, and Genetic Testing for BRCA-Related Cancer in Women: U.S. Preventive Services Task Force Recommendation Statement. AHRQ Publication No. 12-05164-EF-2. Available at www.uspreventiveservicestaskforce.org/uspstf12/brcatest/brcatestfinalrs.htm.

Chapter 46

Common Dermatologic Disorders

Matthew Burday, DO

Weighing in at about 8 lb and spanning 22 square feet, the skin is the largest organ in the body. A structured approach and the ability to recognize patterns are crucial to identify the many conditions that affect the skin.

Evaluation

A detailed and targeted history is obtained, including location of skin lesions, time of onset and evolution (acute or chronic), and any systemic symptoms (eg, fever). A rash accompanied by fever is common with disseminated infections (viral or bacterial, especially those caused by rickettsia), drug reactions, collagen vascular diseases, and vasculitis. External factors (new medications, foods, soaps, detergents) and occupational, environmental, and sun exposures should be investigated.

It is imperative to inspect the entire skin and mucosal surfaces. Patients should be undressed, wearing only a gown. Natural lighting is preferable. Skin palpation can help appreciate texture, depth, and tenderness of lesions. Learning how to describe skin lesions is critical to correctly communicate relevant findings. Several attributes of skin lesions are paramount, including location, color, border, type (Table 1), and arrangement.

Common Skin Infections and Nail Disorders

Bacterial Infections

Some of the most common skin infections seen in both inpatient and outpatient settings are cellulitis, erysipelas, and folliculitis. These infections are increasingly caused by community-acquired methicillin-resistant *Staphylococcus aureus* (MRSA).

Cellulitis is a rapidly spreading deep subcutaneous dermis-based infection. It is most often caused by *S. aureus* or group A streptococci and is characterized by a well-demarcated area of warmth, swelling, tenderness, and erythema (Plate 4), possibly accompanied by lymphatic streaking or fever and chills. Risk factors for lower extremity cellulitis include eczema, tinea pedis, onychomycosis, skin trauma (including insect bites, drug injection), chronic leg ulcers, long-standing diabetes mellitus, and edema. **Cellulitis is a clinical diagnosis; cultures usually are not necessary, and results are seldom positive.** Risk factors for MRSA infection include recent close contact with persons having a similar infection, recent antibiotic use, recent hospitalization, hemodialysis, injection drug use, diabetes, and previous MRSA colonization or infection. Treatment is based on the risk of MRSA infection and the severity of illness (Table 2).

Erysipelas is a superficial skin infection involving the upper dermis and superficial lymphatics. It is usually erythematous in appearance ("St. Anthony's fire") with well-demarcated borders and is almost always caused by group A streptococci. Treatment is usually a β-lactam antibiotic (eg, penicillin or amoxicillin).

Folliculitis is a pustular skin infection in the hair follicle and typically affects the beard, pubic area, axillae, and thighs (Plate 5). Causes include *S. aureus* and, less frequently, group A streptococci. **Folliculitis often resolves spontaneously; therefore, systemic antibiotics should not be used routinely.** Folliculitis often is effectively treated with local application of heat and a topical antibiotic (mupirocin, chlorhexidine cleanser).

Furuncles or "boils" (infection of the hair follicle that extends into the dermis and subcutaneous tissues) and skin abscesses (pus

Table 1. Dermatologic Lexicon[a]

Description	Definition	Example
Macule	Flat skin lesion <1 cm in diameter	Freckle
Patch	Flat skin lesion >1 cm in diameter	Tinea versicolor
Papule	Raised skin lesion <0.5 cm in diameter	Acne
Plaque	"Plateau-like" elevated lesion >0.5 cm in diameter	Psoriasis
Nodule	Raised sphere-like lesion >0.5 cm in diameter and depth; called a *cyst* when filled with liquid or keratin	Erythema nodosum
Vesicle	Blister filled with clear fluid <0.5 cm in diameter	Varicella
Bulla	Blister filled with clear fluid >0.5 cm in diameter	Poison ivy
Pustule	Vesicle filled with pus	Folliculitis
Crust (scab)	Dried pus, blood, and serum from breakage of vesicles, bullae, or pustules	Herpes zoster (shingles)
Scale	Dry, whitish, and flaky stratum corneum	Seborrheic dermatitis

[a]Other common terms include *induration* (dermal thickening), *lichenification* (epidermal thickening), *atrophy* (loss of epidermal or dermal tissue), *wheal* (dermal edema), *comedone* (acne lesion), *ulcer* (loss of epidermal tissue and some dermis), *erosion* (superficial loss of epidermis), and *fissure* (linear opening in epidermis).

Table 2. Empiric Treatment Options for Cellulitis

Cellulitis without Purulence[a]

Probable β-hemolytic streptococci or MSSA; MRSA unlikely	Oral
	Dicloxacillin
	Cephalexin
	Clindamycin
	Intravenous[b]
	Oxacillin
	Nafcillin
	Cefazolin
	Clindamycin

Cellulitis with Purulence[a]

Probable MRSA; risk factors for MRSA[c]; failure to respond to non-MRSA therapy	Oral
	Trimethoprim-sulfamethoxazole
	Clindamycin
	Doxycycline
	Minocycline
	Linezolid
	Intravenous[b]
	Vancomycin
	Linezolid
	Daptomycin

Relative Cost for Oral Medications

$ Cephalexin

$ Dicloxacillin

$ Doxycycline

$ Trimethoprim–sulfamethoxazole

$$ Clindamycin

$$ Minocycline

$$$ Linezolid

MRSA = methicillin-resistant *Staphylococcus aureus*; MSSA = methicillin-sensitive *Staphylococcus aureus*.

[a]Cellulitis with no purulent drainage or exudate and no associated abscess

[b]Consider intravenous therapy for complicated cellulitis (multiple infected sites, rapid progression, significant comorbid disease (eg, immunocompromise), difficult-to-drain areas (face, hand), or lack of response to incision and drainage).

[c]Risk factors for MRSA infection include recent close contact with persons having a similar infection, recent antibiotic use, recent hospitalization, hemodialysis, illicit injection drug use, diabetes, and previous MRSA colonization or infection.

collections in the dermis and deeper tissues) are acute, tender, pus-containing nodules that commonly appear on the neck or in the axillae or groin but may occur at any skin site; furuncles and abscess nearly always are caused by *S. aureus*. Warm compresses to facilitate drainage may be adequate therapy for small furuncles. Incision and drainage is required for larger furuncles and all abscesses. **Incision and drainage may be adequate therapy for skin abscesses, and systemic antibiotics are not routinely required.** However, they may be indicated if the patient is febrile or immunocompromised, has diabetes, or is at risk for MRSA or if there is a surrounding cellulitis. Cultures from purulent material can distinguish MRSA from methicillin-susceptible *S. aureus* (MSSA) and can guide treatment. **Attempted elimination of MRSA nasal carriage (decolonization) using intranasal mupirocin or from body surfaces using topical antiseptic cleansers is not recommended as a routine part of managing MRSA infections, although it may have a role in outbreaks, patients in intensive care units, and selected patients with recurrent *S. aureus* infections.**

Impetigo is a superficial infection of the skin (epidermis) characterized by a group of yellowish, crusted pustules (Plate 6). Impetigo is caused by staphylococci or streptococci. Predisposing factors include poor hygiene, neglected minor trauma, and eczema. Limited disease usually can be treated effectively with topical mupirocin or bacitracin; more extensive disease can be treated with a cephalosporin, penicillinase-resistant penicillin, or β-lactam–β-lactamase inhibitor.

Ecthyma is an ulcerative form of impetigo usually caused by streptococci or staphylococci. The classic findings are superficial, saucer-shaped ulcers with overlying crusts, typically on the legs or feet (Plate 7). Effective treatment consists of cleansing with an antibacterial wash followed by topical mupirocin plus oral cephalexin, dicloxacillin, or clindamycin. If MRSA is suspected or there is β-lactam allergy, one should consider other options (see Table 2).

Ecthyma gangrenosum is an ulcerative infection involving the dermis usually caused by *Pseudomonas aeruginosa*. It is usually seen in immunocompromised patients and may indicate pseudomonal sepsis. Classic findings are ulcers with a central gray-black eschar and erythematous halo, typically on the legs or feet (Plate 7). Initial therapy usually involves an antipseudomonal penicillin plus an aminoglycoside.

Fungal Infections

Dermatophytoses (tinea) are superficial infections caused by fungi that thrive only in nonliving components of the skin, hair, and nails and often cause pruritus but not invasive systemic infections. Predisposing factors include immunosuppression; hyperhidrosis; diabetes; glucocorticoids; direct contact (eg, towels); and hot, humid, occlusive environments. An expanding, ringlike (annular) lesion with a slightly scaly, erythematous, advancing edge and central clearing suggests a fungal infection; however, the presence of fungus should be confirmed by microscopic KOH examination before initiating treatment. *Tinea corporis* can occur on any part of the body, including the trunk and extremities. *Tinea pedis* is the most common dermatophyte infection, presenting as silvery scale and dull erythema on the soles and sides of the feet (moccasin type) (Plate 8) or may be characterized by interdigital scale and maceration. *Tinea cruris* typically presents as erythematous, arciform or polycyclic plaques with sharp margins and central clearing; the lesions may be located on the thighs, perineum, perianal region, buttocks, and intergluteal cleft (Plate 9). In contrast to candidiasis, tinea cruris typically spares the scrotum in males. Topical antifungal creams (clotrimazole, terbinafine) usually are effective in treating dermatophyte infections. **Combination antifungal and glucocorticoid products should be avoided in treating fungal skin infections.** Oral antifungal therapy (ketoconazole, terbinafine) is needed to treat widespread or severe tinea infection. It is essential to treat tinea pedis in patients with diabetes because tinea can create a portal of entry for bacteria and resultant cellulitis.

Tinea versicolor is caused by the yeast, *Malassezia*. Lesions typically are round or oval nonpruritic, macules, patches, or papules located on the trunk and proximal upper extremities (Plate 10). The diagnosis is confirmed by the classic microscopic appearance of both spores and hyphae in a "spaghetti and meatball" pattern. Treatment consists of topical selenium sulfide or ketoconazole (a single dose is effective). For those unresponsive to topical measures or with extensive disease, short-course therapy with ketoconazole, fluconazole, or itraconazole can be given.

Candida infections tend to occur in warm, moist skin folds and are often seen in obese patients and those with diabetes. The infection occurs frequently in the axillary, inframammary, and genital regions. *Candida* infections must be differentiated from *intertrigo*, an inflammatory condition of warm, moist skin folds related to rubbing or chafing; *Candida* infections are typically associated with satellite papules and pustules. Keeping the area as dry as possible is critical (zinc oxide cream is helpful) along with the use of a cream such as clotrimazole or a powder such as nystatin.

Erythrasma is a bacterial infection of the skin caused by *Corynebacterium minutissimum*. It is usually found between the toes as well as skin folds. It appears as a brownish plaque or patch that exhibits coral-red fluorescence with a Woods lamp. Treatment involves topical clindamycin or benzoyl peroxide for limited disease or oral clarithromycin.

Onychomycosis is an infection of the nail caused by dermatophytes, yeasts, or molds and characterized by a thickened yellow or white nail with scaling under the elevated distal free edge of the nail plate (Plate 11). Nail infections can be diagnosed by microscopic examination or culture. Most patients with toenail onychomycosis are asymptomatic and do not require treatment. However, treatment with oral terbinafine, itraconazole, or fluconazole is indicated in patients with symptomatic infection or peripheral arterial disease or diabetes who are at risk for complications from onychomycosis (cellulitis). Treatment efficacy is usually <75%, and recurrence rates can approach 40%. Topical antifungal lacquers generally are not effective.

Viral Infections

Herpes zoster (shingles) results from reactivation of latent varicella-zoster virus (VZV), which resides in the nerve ganglia after an initial varicella (chickenpox) infection; it typically affects persons older than age 60 years and patients who are immunosuppressed. Recurrent herpes zoster should trigger testing for possible associated HIV infection. Pain, tingling, or itching may precede the rash by 1 to 5 days. The classic morphology is grouped vesicles on an erythematous base; the vesicles occur in multiple plaques along one or several contiguous unilateral dermatomes. Although it typically stops at the midline (Plate 12), several vesicles may cross over. In immunosuppressed patients (HIV infection, chemotherapy), lesions may occur in multiple, widely separated dermatomes or may be disseminated. Vesicles become pustular and then crust with healing. Antiviral therapy with acyclovir, valacyclovir, or famciclovir, given within 48 to 72 hours of the onset of the rash, may speed healing, decrease acute pain, and possibly reduce the incidence and intensity of postherpetic neuralgia (PHN), a painful sequela of herpes zoster (see Chapter 77). **Systemic glucocorticoids have not been shown to reduce the incidence of postherpetic neuralgia.** Involvement of the eye, periorbital skin, or tip of the nose (trigeminal nerve) mandates urgent ophthalmologic consultation because of the risk of ocular complications. Vaccination (VZV vaccine) of immunocompetent adults older than age 60 years decreases the incidence and severity of herpes zoster and PHN (see Chapter 30).

Nail Disorders

Common nail disorders and their associated conditions are listed in Table 3.

Common Rashes

Atopic dermatitis is common in persons with a personal or family history of other atopic conditions, such as asthma or allergic rhinitis. The rash characteristically involves the antecubital and popliteal fossae and flexural wrists and, when acute, results in pruritic, erythematous, poorly demarcated, eczematous, crusted, papulovesicular plaques and excoriations. The skin becomes lichenified and

hyperpigmented in chronic atopic dermatitis (Plate 13). Atopic dermatitis is diagnosed clinically. Treatment consists of topical glucocorticoids, antihistamines, and emollients. A potential complication of atopic dermatitis is staphylococcal superinfection.

Contact dermatitis can be caused by an irritant or allergen. Irritant contact dermatitis is a nonimmunologic, toxic reaction that results from exposure to harsh conditions or chemicals. Allergic contact dermatitis (ACD) is a delayed hypersensitivity reaction that requires initial sensitization. Common allergens include plants (eg, poison ivy), neomycin, preservatives, and metals (eg, nickel). In ACD, the skin is itchy, red, edematous, weepy, and crusted, and there may be vesicles or bullae (Plate 14). The skin becomes lichenified (thickened epidermis with exaggeration of normal skin lines), scaly, and hyperpigmented as the dermatitis becomes chronic. Exposure history and the pattern of the rash may provide clues as to the causal allergen. Patch testing is the gold standard for diagnosis. Treatment of acute and chronic ACD usually consists of mid- to high-potency topical glucocorticoids; tapered systemic glucocorticoids are used for severe or extensive reactions. Avoidance of exposure to the offending allergen, if determined, is a key therapeutic principle.

Venous stasis dermatitis affects the skin on the lower legs, particularly around the medial malleolus, and results from venous hypertension, edema, chronic inflammation, and microangiopathy. Distinguishing stasis dermatitis from bacterial cellulitis can be difficult, but bilateral involvement, absence of fever or leukocytosis, and minimal pain suggest stasis dermatitis. The diagnosis of stasis dermatitis is clinical; edema, hyperpigmented skin caused by hemosiderin deposition (most prominent at the medial ankle), and varicose veins suggest the diagnosis (Plate 15). Ulceration is a potential complication. Stasis dermatitis is treated with topical glucocorticoids (if erythema and inflammation are present), leg elevation, and knee-level compression stockings; topical antibiotics are not recommended.

Seborrheic dermatitis affects areas of the body that are rich in sebaceous glands; the condition may be secondary to colonization with the yeast, *Malassezia furfur*. Lesions are erythematous, with a dry or greasy scale and crusts, and may be pruritic (Plate 16). Common areas of involvement include the scalp (dandruff), nasolabial folds, cheeks, eyebrows, eyelids, and external auditory canals. Frequent remissions and exacerbations are common. Severe seborrheic dermatitis is common in persons with HIV infection and Parkinson disease. Treatment consists of low-potency glucocorticoids (face), ketoconazole cream (face), or medicated shampoos that contain tar, ketoconazole, or selenium sulfide (scalp).

Psoriasis is a chronic, relapsing immune-mediated skin disorder and is one of the most common skin diseases. Exacerbating factors include stress, infection, injury to the skin, and certain medications (lithium, β-blockers). *Psoriasis vulgaris* can be limited or widespread. It is characterized by sharply marginated, erythematous, scaly papules and plaques covered by a silvery white scale on the extensor surfaces of the extremities, presacral skin, or scalp (Plate 17). *Guttate psoriasis* is characterized by small, droplike scaly plaques and is usually triggered by an upper respiratory infection with *Streptococcus pyogenes*. *Palmoplantar psoriasis*, although localized, may be difficult to manage and may interfere with activities of daily living. Generalized *pustular psoriasis* can be life threatening and frequently occurs after withdrawal of systemic glucocorticoids. Nail changes (pitting, onycholysis) often occur in patients with psoriasis and correlate with a greater risk of accompanying psoriatic arthritis (Plate 18).

The diagnosis of psoriasis is clinical and based on the appearance and distribution of the rash. Mild disease often responds to local therapy with topical agents (glucocorticoids, calcipotriene, taza-

Table 3. Common Nail Disorders

Nail Finding	Physical Exam Finding	Associated Conditions
Habit tic	Horizontal ridges extending the length of the nail resulting from picking at, playing with, or stroking the nails constantly; the thumbnails are usually damaged by another nail	Anxiety
Longitudinal lines or ridging	Discolored, often yellowish, longitudinal lines or ridges extending from the cuticle to the end of the nail; nails may be more fragile	May occur normally with aging
Terry nails	A white, "ground glass" appearance of >60% of the nail	Congestive heart failure, diabetes, liver disease, chronic kidney disease
Lindsay ("half-and-half") nails	The proximal portion of the nail is white and the distal half red, pink, or brown, with a sharp line of demarcation between the two halves	Chronic kidney disease (advanced)
Beau lines	Deep grooved lines that transverse the nail horizontally	Trauma, hypotension, chemotherapy, malnutrition causing altered nail production
Splinter hemorrhages	Tiny (1-2 mm) thin dark red or black lines	Trauma, systemic infection causing pinpoint bleeding beneath the nail
Melanonychia	Longitudinal black or brown pigment	May be normal but may be caused by melanoma (especially suggested if associated with proximal nail fold pigmentation [Hutchinson sign])
Koilonychia ("spoon nails")	Abnormally thin nails that have lost their convexity, becoming flat or even concave in shape	Iron deficiency
Muehrke nails	White, non-grooved lines that extend horizontally across the nail	Nephrotic syndrome, malnutrition, hypoalbuminemia
Nailfold telangiectasias	Variably shaped telangiectasias—often associated with a ragged cuticle; best seen via capillary microscopy	Connective tissue diseases such as systemic lupus erythematosus, dermatomyositis, rheumatoid arthritis, systemic sclerosis

rotene, anthralin), Moderate to severe or recalcitrant disease may also require phototherapy, systemic therapy (methotrexate, acitretin, cyclosporine, biologic agents), or both. Topical glucocorticoids should be discontinued slowly to avoid rebound of psoriasis. Systemic glucocorticoids have no role in the treatment of psoriasis.

Erythema multiforme (EM) is an acute, often recurrent mucocutaneous eruption characterized by circular erythematous plaques with a raised, darker central circle ("target lesions"). EM usually follows an acute infection, most often recurrent herpes simplex virus (HSV) infection. *Mycoplasma pneumoniae* is another frequently associated infection; it also may be drug related or idiopathic. Lesions generally are located on the extremities, palms, and soles (Plate 19). Painful oral mucosal erosions and bullae are common. The diagnosis is clinical. Treatment of EM is primarily symptomatic. Systemic glucocorticoids may provide symptomatic improvement. Antiviral therapy does not shorten the EM outbreak in HSV-associated cases.

Cutaneous drug reactions are common in both hospitalized patients and outpatients; most of these eruptions are self-limited and not severe. The most common causes are antibiotics (β-lactams, sulfonamides), anticonvulsants, nonsteroidal anti-inflammatory drugs (NSAIDs), thiazide diuretics, and allopurinol. Drug-induced cutaneous eruptions can mimic many different kinds of rashes and should be in the differential diagnosis in the sudden appearance of a symmetrical eruption. Pruritus may be mild, severe, or absent. The most common reaction patterns include morbilliform (Plate 20), urticaria, fixed drug eruption, photosensitivity, and EM-like reaction. Because drug reactions can occur within days or up to 2 months after exposure to the causative medication, a detailed history is essential to determine the cause. Treatment consists of stopping the offending drug, antihistamines, and systemic glucocorticoids if the reaction is severe or widespread.

Pityriasis rosea is a common papulosquamous eruption that has been linked to reactivation of human herpesvirus 6 or 7. The rash typically begins with a single thin, pink, oval, 2- to 4-cm plaque (herald patch) with a thin collarette of scale within the border of the plaque (Plate 21). This can help differentiate it from tinea, in which the scale is typically present at the periphery. A KOH analysis of the scale can also be helpful (results are negative in pityriasis rosea). Similar but smaller plaques subsequently erupt within days to weeks, usually on the torso along skin cleavage lines, in a Christmas tree–like distribution. The lesions can be asymptomatic or mildly pruritic. The eruption is self-limited and usually lasts 4 to 10 weeks. No treatment is needed, but topical glucocorticoids, oral antihistamines, or both may be used for pruritus.

Common Oral Lesions

Aphthous ulcers (aphthae, canker sores) are common, recurring, painful, round or oval oral ulcers; the causative factors are unknown. The diagnosis is clinical. Treatment typically consists of topical analgesics and topical glucocorticoids. Severe oral ulcers may be associated with inflammatory bowel disease, celiac disease, HIV infection, and Behçet syndrome (which is characterized by aphthous ulcers plus urogenital ulcerations and iridocyclitis).

HSV type 1 infection typically causes herpes labialis. The primary infection is asymptomatic in most patients but may present as acute, painful gingivostomatitis. Recurrent episodes result from reactivation of dormant virus in the neural ganglia. Recurrences often are characterized by a prodrome of burning, stinging, or pain approximately 24 hours before the onset of lesions, which typically occur on the lips ("cold sores"). The lesions consist of grouped vesicles on an erythematous, edematous base; the lesions rupture and leave behind clustered erosions that involute (Plate 22). The diagnosis usually is made clinically, but laboratory confirmation of infection with viral culture or by direct fluorescent antibody testing may be helpful. Treatment with an oral antiviral agent given at the onset of the prodromal symptoms and before the outbreak of vesicles decreases the duration of the rash by 1 to 2 days. Topical antiviral agents are not efficacious.

Leukoplakia is a common premalignant white patch or plaque adherent to the oral mucosa. Patients should be referred for biopsy and excision.

Acneiform Lesions

Acne vulgaris usually begins at puberty and involves several mechanisms, including hyperkeratinization of follicles, increased sebum production secondary to increased androgenic hormone levels, proliferation of *Propionibacterium acnes*, and resulting inflammation. Topical and systemic glucocorticoid therapy, hormone therapy, use of anabolic steroids, hyperandrogenism, and polycystic ovary syndrome may contribute to acneiform eruptions. Acne-prone sites include the face, neck, chest, upper back, and shoulders. **In most cases, the history and physical examination are sufficient to diagnose acne.** Acne is classified as either noninflammatory or inflammatory and by degree of severity. Noninflammatory acne involves open and closed comedones (occluded hair follicles); inflammatory acne consists of erythematous papules; pustules; and, occasionally, nodules. Topical retinoids and benzoyl peroxide are effective treatments for noninflammatory acne. Treatment of inflammatory acne requires an antibacterial agent (topical clindamycin or erythromycin) in addition to a comedolytic or keratolytic agent. Moderate to severe inflammatory acne often requires both topical treatment and an oral antibiotic (doxycycline, minocycline, erythromycin). Treatment with oral contraceptives and spironolactone, in addition to topical acne therapy, is effective for female patients with androgen excess. Isotretinoin (an oral retinoid) is used in patients with severe nodular acne that is unresponsive to oral antibiotic therapy and may result in prolonged remissions; however, because of teratogenicity, isotretinoin should be administered only by physicians who are trained in its use and registered with the Food and Drug Administration.

Acne rosacea (rosacea) is a chronic inflammatory skin disorder affecting the face, typically the cheeks and nose. The cause is unknown. Rosacea is characterized by erythema with telangiectasia, pustules, and papules; comedones are absent (Plate 23). In the early stages, rosacea can present as only facial erythema and resemble the butterfly rash of systemic lupus erythematosus (SLE); however, the rash of SLE typically spares the nasolabial folds and areas under the nose and lower lip. Rhinophyma (large, irregular hyperplastic nose) can develop in some patients with rosacea. Treatment may consist of topical agents (metronidazole gel, benzoyl peroxide, tretinoin) or oral antibiotics (tetracycline, erythromycin).

Perioral dermatitis is characterized by discrete papules and pustules on an erythematous base centered around the mouth (Plate 24). The eruption often follows the use of topical or inhaled glucocorticoids. Treatment consists of discontinuing the glucocorticoid or protecting the skin from the inhaled product. Initial treatment includes topical antibiotics and sulfur preparations.

Urticaria

Urticaria (hives) appears as raised, pruritic, erythematous wheals with sharp borders (Plate 25). The lesions can last from minutes to hours and usually involve the trunk and extremities, sparing the palms and soles. Lesions that persist >24 hours, burn, or resolve with purpura are suspicious for urticarial vasculitis and should be biopsied. Episodes of urticaria lasting <6 weeks are classified as acute and often are caused by acute infection, medication, food, or allergies. Episodes lasting >6 weeks are classified as chronic. Many patients with chronic urticaria have an IgG antibody to the IgE receptor; others are reacting to a chronic infection or ingestion. Approximately 50% of cases of chronic urticaria have no identifiable cause. Angioedema is localized swelling of the skin and mucosa caused by extravasation of fluid into the interstitium with propensity for mucosal surfaces and skin, including the lips, face, hands, feet, penis, or scrotum (Plate 26). Concurrent angioedema occurs in 40% of patients with urticaria and may be life threatening because of airway obstruction. Urticaria is a clinical diagnosis; a careful history and physical examination are essential to determine possible causes. First-line therapy is avoidance of triggers and administration of antihistamines (H_1-receptor blockers). Patients with severe acute urticaria that is unresponsive to antihistamines should be treated with a tapered dose of prednisone. Chronic urticaria may require the use of antiinflammatory or immunosuppressive agents.

Pruritus

Generalized pruritus without rash can be due to local or systemic causes. Dry skin (xerosis), exacerbated by poor hydration and dry winter weather, is the most common cause of pruritus in elderly patients. Treatment consists of the use of a humidifier, moisturizers, and occlusives. Persistent generalized pruritus in the absence of skin lesions suggests a possible systemic cause and should prompt evaluation for conditions such as cholestasis, chronic kidney disease, thyroid disease, infection (HIV), hematologic disease (polycythemia vera), and malignancy.

Infestations

Scabies is a skin infestation caused by the mite *Sarcoptes scabiei*, an obligate human parasite preferentially affecting impoverished, immobilized, and immunodeficient persons. Spread is through direct personal contact, especially sexual contact. Acquisition from bedding or clothes is rare. Scabies infestation causes intense pruritus, often worse at night, and a papular or vesicular rash; the papules often are tipped with blood crusts. Burrows are visible as short, wavy lines (Plate 27). The distribution of scabies often involves the interdigital webs, flexure surface of the wrists, penis, axillae, nipples, umbilicus, scrotum, and buttocks. Treatment is with permethrin or ivermectin.

Bed bugs are obligate parasites (of the Cimicidae family) and feed on the blood of humans and other animals. They are most active at night but may feed on a sedentary host during the day. Bed bug bites cause pruritic erythematous maculopapular lesions that are often grouped in a straight line. Infestations can be recognized by fecal spots on the bedding and exoskeletons. The smell of rotting raspberries can be distinctive but is usually seen with a chronic infection. Treatment involves supportive therapies such as antihistamines. Discarding infected items and heating the involved room to at least 113.0°F (45.0°C) for 90 minutes or more may be indicated. Insecticides are variably effective.

Pediculosis (lice infestation) typically presents as pruritus, possibly with excoriation. The identification of crawling lice in the scalp or hair establishes the diagnosis. Lice egg cases are called *nits* and are found sticking to the hair shaft in patients with lice. Treatment is with permethrin, although resistance to this agent may be increasing.

Benign Growths

Seborrheic keratoses are common benign, painless neoplasms that present as brown to black, well-demarcated papules with a waxy surface and a "stuck-on" appearance (Plate 28). Seborrheic keratoses are more common in older patients. Treatment is not indicated unless the growths are inflamed, irritated, or pruritic.

Verruca vulgaris (common wart) is caused by infection with a human papillomavirus. Common warts generally appear as 5- to 10-mm, rough-surfaced, skin-colored papules. The diagnosis is based on the typical verrucous appearance of a papule or plaque noted on the hands or feet. Spontaneous involution occurs in most patients within 3 years; thus, not treating cutaneous warts often is a reasonable option. Topical salicylic acid is the first-line therapy. Cryotherapy is used for warts that do not respond to initial topical management; cryotherapy should be avoided with subungual and periungual warts.

Dermatofibromas are firm, dermal nodules approximately 6 mm in diameter; the surface often is hyperpigmented (Plate 29). Dermatofibromas are most commonly seen on the legs of women but also occur on the trunk in both men and women. Excision is indicated only if the lesion is symptomatic, has changed, or bleeds.

The most common type of skin cyst is an epidermoid inclusion cyst. Usually present on the face, neck, or chest, this type of cyst is made up of epidermal cells that are present in the dermis. Patients usually note a nontender lump that may become painful if infected. In this case, treatment involves incision and drainage and removal of the cyst and cyst wall.

A lipoma is a group of fat cells encased in a thin fibrous capsule. These are typically softer and more pliable than cysts and can be single or multiple. Lipomas can be superficial or deep and usually do not need to be removed. However, if there is growth or pain, removal should be carried out.

Cutaneous Manifestations of Internal Disease

Up to 50% of patients infected with hepatitis C virus (HCV) develop mixed cryoglobulinemia. Mixed cryoglobulinemia consists of circulating immune complexes that deposit in postcapillary venules, causing inflammation and vessel damage, which present clinically as palpable purpura (Plate 30); the purpura may be accompanied by arthralgia, peripheral neuropathy, and glomerulonephritis. The diagnosis is confirmed by the presence of cryoglobulins (proteins that precipitate at <37.0°C [98.6°F]) and low complement levels; a skin biopsy will demonstrate leukocytoclastic vasculitis. Treatment is directed at the underlying HCV infection.

Porphyria cutanea tarda (PCT) is a hereditary or acquired blistering disease caused by excess circulating porphyrins resulting from deficiency or reduced activity of the enzyme, uroporphyrinogen decarboxylase. Iron overload, as seen with hemochromatosis, leads to decreased activity of this enzyme. Up to 50% of patients with sporadic PCT have HCV infection. Clinically, patients present with vesicles and bullae on sun-exposed skin surfaces, most commonly on the face, dorsal hands, and scalp (Plate 31). The diagnosis can be confirmed by elevated urine uroporphyrin levels. Treatment consists of phlebotomy, low-dose antimalarial agents, and erythropoietin for patients with chronic kidney disease. Treatment of underlying HCV infection is indicated.

Lichen planus is another skin finding associated with hepatitis C. However, it may be found in isolation or related to medication or autoimmune causes. It is found in many areas of the body. On the skin, it is often recognized by the "six Ps": polygonal, pruritic, papular, planar, purple, plaques. The treatment is usually topical or oral glucocorticoids.

Erythema nodosum is characterized by the sudden onset of deep, tender, palpable erythematous nodules, typically on the anterior lower legs (Plate 2); fever and joint pain also may be present. The condition usually is acute and self-limited. Erythema nodosum is the result of a hypersensitivity immune reaction to infection or systemic inflammation or may be secondary to drugs. Common causes include sarcoidosis, tuberculosis, inflammatory bowel disease, and streptococcal pharyngitis; at least 50% of cases are idiopathic. Management consists of treating the underlying disease. NSAIDs provide symptomatic relief; systemic glucocorticoids can be used if an infectious cause is ruled out.

Dermatomyositis is a condition with characteristic cutaneous manifestations combined with proximal inflammatory myopathy or muscle weakness; skin disease sometimes may be the only manifestation (see Chapter 105). The distinctive cutaneous features are heliotrope rash (a violaceous to dusky erythematous periorbital rash) and Gottron papules (slightly elevated, scaly, violaceous papules and plaques that arise over bony prominences, particularly the small joints of the hands). Poikiloderma (a combination of erythema, telangiectasias, hyperpigmentation and hypopigmentation) may occur on the V of the neck (V sign), hip (holster sign), and upper back (shawl sign). The cuticle may be ragged, and telangiectasias may be prominent. An increased risk of malignancy exists.

SLE is a multisystem disorder whose clinical spectrum ranges from a relatively benign cutaneous eruption to a severe, potentially fatal systemic multiorgan disease. Skin lesions are categorized as chronic (usually associated with scarring or atrophy), subacute, and acute; this classification helps predict systemic manifestations of the disease. Acute cutaneous lupus erythematosus is characterized by a confluent malar erythema or generalized red papular or urticarial lesions on sun-exposed skin surfaces and is usually is associated with systemic disease (Plate 32). Chronic cutaneous (discoid) lupus erythematosus consists of slowly progressive, scaly, infiltrative papules and atrophic red plaques on sun-exposed skin surfaces and is not associated with systemic disease (Plate 33). Patients with subacute cutaneous lupus erythematosus have bright red annular or papulosquamous (psoriasis-like) lesions that may be associated with the more benign manifestations of SLE, such as arthralgia, photosensitivity, and serositis (Plate 34). The diagnosis of cutaneous lupus erythematosus is based on the clinical lesions and findings on skin biopsy. Initial management includes sun protection, topical glucocorticoids, and antimalarial agents.

Pyoderma gangrenosum is a neutrophilic, ulcerative skin condition typically associated with an underlying systemic condition, such as inflammatory bowel disease, rheumatoid arthritis, spondyloarthitis, or a hematologic disease or malignancy (most commonly acute myelogenous leukemia). Lesions often are multiple and tend to appear on the lower extremities. They begin as tender papules, pustules, or vesicles that spontaneously ulcerate and progress to painful ulcers with a purulent base and undermined, ragged, violaceous borders (Plate 3). Treatment may include topical or systemic glucocorticoids, dapsone or cyclosporine.

Bibliography

Bershad SV. In the clinic. Acne. Ann Intern Med. 2008;149:ITC1-1–ITC1-16. [PMID: 18591631]

Stevens DL, Eron LL. Cellulitis and soft-tissue infections. Ann Intern Med. 2009;150:ITC11. [PMID: 19124814].

Tyring SK. Management of herpes zoster and postherpetic neuralgia. J Am Acad Dermatol. 2007;57(6 Suppl):S136–S142. [PMID: 18021865].

Williams HC. Clinical practice. Atopic dermatitis. N Engl J Med. 2005;352:2314-2324. [PMID: 15930422].

Section 5
Hematology

Associate Editor – Philip A. Masters, MD, FACP

High Value Care Recommendations

- Universal screening of unselected populations for inherited thrombophilias should be avoided.

- Routinely screening for inherited thrombophilias in patients undergoing high-risk surgical procedures (such as certain orthopedic surgeries) is not recommended.

- Testing for inherited causes of thrombophilia in the setting of an acute venous thromboembolism (VTE) may not be reliable since the acute phase reactants of the VTE may interfere with factor measurements.

- Most experts do not recommend testing for the congenital thrombophilias to determine the method, intensity or duration of treatment for patients presenting with their first venous thromboembolism unless there is a suggestive or known history of familial thrombophilia.

- Except to monitor the effectiveness of anticoagulant therapy, routinely checking laboratory studies once the diagnosis of thrombophilia has been established is not recommended.

- A more restrictive approach to transfusion in non-cardiac patients with a hemoglobin goal of 7 to 8 g/dL (70-80 g/L) is favored in most patients.

Chapter 47

Anemia

Reed E. Drews, MD

Anemia is a common condition encountered in clinical practice. Often identified incidentally in asymptomatic patients, anemia can be benign or related to serious underlying disease. The differential diagnosis is wide and includes congenital and acquired disorders. A structured approach is used to distinguish among the many causes of anemia and to determine management. This approach considers red cell morphology alongside other clinical and laboratory findings.

Because the life span of normal erythrocytes approaches 120 days, nearly 1% of circulating erythrocytes must be replenished daily to maintain a normal hematocrit level. Normal hematopoiesis, as well as heightened production during bleeding or hemolysis, requires a healthy bone marrow microenvironment, healthy hematopoietic stem cells, ample endogenous growth factors (eg, erythropoietin, thyroid hormone, and testosterone in the case of males), and ample and usable body stores of iron, folate, and cobalamin.

Defining Anemia

Anemia is defined as a reduction below normal in the number of erythrocytes in the circulation. The percentage of whole blood comprised of erythrocytes is the hematocrit level. Since erythrocytes contain hemoglobin (a complex of globin chains and heme that binds oxygen for delivery to tissues), anemia is also defined by the hemoglobin level, which is the concentration of hemoglobin in whole blood after lysing erythrocytes. Both hematocrit and hemoglobin levels are important parameters to be examined together, since certain conditions may yield low hemoglobin levels with normal hematocrits (eg, thalassemia; see below). Men have higher mean hematocrit and hemoglobin values than women, largely due to testosterone production in men and borderline iron stores in menstruating women. Hematocrit and hemoglobin levels have wide reference ranges, and changes in plasma volume can influence these measurements considerably, either by hemodilution or hemoconcentration. For example, in pregnant women, red blood cell mass rises; however, plasma volume increases to a greater extent. Therefore, pregnant women develop lower hematocrit and hemoglobin levels (physiologic anemia). The World Health Organization defines anemia as a hemoglobin level <13 g/dL (130 g/L) in men and <12 g/dL (120 g/L) in women.

Measuring Anemia

Automated multichannel analyzers directly assess the erythrocyte count, mean corpuscular volume (MCV), red cell distribution width (the degree of variation in erythrocyte size), and hemoglobin level while calculating the following parameters from these measurements: mean corpuscular hemoglobin (MCH; hemoglobin level divided by red blood cell count); and mean corpuscular hemoglobin concentration (MCHC; hemoglobin level divided by hematocrit). Examining all of these parameters together is important as they provide important clues to anemia etiology (Table 1). Automated analyzers may yield spurious findings in certain clinical circumstances (eg, high leukocyte counts, lipemia, precipitating monoclonal proteins, cold agglutinins, and hyperglycemia), and this should be suspected when measured hemoglobin levels do not approximate one-third of the calculated hematocrit value.

Clinicians should evaluate erythrocyte measurements alongside leukocyte counts, platelet counts, and leukocyte differential counts. Abnormalities in these other blood cell lines may suggest a disorder of trilineage hematopoiesis. Reticulocyte counts suggest whether or not the bone marrow responses to anemia are adequate. Appropriately increased reticulocyte counts (ie, >100,000/μL [100 × 10^9/L]) almost always reflect either erythrocyte loss (eg, bleeding,

Table 1. RBC Parameters Categorize Anemias and Suggest Anemia Etiologies

RBC Parameter	Category of Anemia	Subtypes of Anemia to Consider
Low MCV	Microcytic	Iron deficiency; inflammatory block to iron utilization; thalassemia; sideroblastic
Normal MCV	Normocytic	Aplasia; marrow infiltration; renal disease; inflammation; evolving microcytic or macrocytic anemia if MCV is declining or rising within normal range, respectively
High MCV	Macrocytic	Stress erythropoiesis with high reticulocyte count resulting in high MCV; nonmegaloblastic causes of increased MCVs resulting in increased RBC membrane in relation to RBC volume (eg, liver disease, asplenia, hyposplenia, hypothyroidism); megaloblastic causes of increased MCVs (eg, cobalamin deficiency, folate deficiency, certain drugs, alcohol, myelodysplasia)
Low MCH and/or low MCHC	Hypochromic	Disorders leading to decreased Hgb per RBC and/or HCT, including iron deficiency, inflammatory block to iron utilization, thalassemia, and sideroblastic causes
High MCH and/or high MCHC	Hyperchromic	Disorders leading to increased Hgb per RBC and/or HCT, implying loss of RBC membrane in relation to RBC volume (eg, hemolytic anemias, certain hemoglobinopathies)

HCT = hematocrit; Hgb = hemoglobin; MCH = mean cell hemoglobin; MCHC = mean cell hemoglobin concentration; MCV = mean cell volume; RBC = red blood cell.

Table 2. Peripheral Blood Smear Findings and Associated Conditions

Finding	Association
Acanthocytes (erythrocytes with a small number of spicules of variable size and distribution on the cell surface)	Liver disease
Bite cells (erythrocytes with a nonstaining, clear zone)	Oxidative hemolysis, which may be due to unstable hemoglobins or potent oxidants (with or without G6PD or pyruvate kinase deficiency)
Echinocytes (erythrocytes with a small number of spicules of uniform size and distribution on the cell surface)	End-stage kidney disease
Hypochromia (increase in central pallor of erythrocytes), anisocytosis, poikilocytosis	Iron deficiency anemia
Intraerythrocytic parasites (eg, *Plasmodium*, *Babesia*)	Hemolytic anemia
Rouleaux formation ("stacked-coins" appearance of erythrocytes)	Monoclonal protein, cold agglutinin, or increased fibrinogen (as in acute phase reaction)
Schistocytes (irregularly shaped, jagged fragments of erythrocytes)	Fragmentation hemolysis, as in micro- or macroangiopathic hemolytic anemia (eg, DIC, TTP, malfunctioning native or prosthetic heart valve)
Sickle cells (spindle- or crescent-shaped erythrocytes)	Sickle cell anemia
Small target cells (erythrocytes with area of central density surrounded by pallor and then a rim of density), teardrop cells (cells with round main body part and an elongated end), and basophilic stippling (cells with blue granules in the cytoplasm)	Thalassemia
Spherocytes (small, round erythrocytes that are uniformly dense)	Membrane loss (as in hereditary spherocytosis, immune hemolytic anemia) without central pallor
Teardrop cells, nucleated erythrocytes, and immature myeloid forms	Myelophthisic anemia (also known as leukoerythroblastosis)

DIC = disseminated intravascular coagulation; G6PD = glucose-6-phosphate dehydrogenase; TTP = thrombotic thrombocytopenic purpura.

Table 3. Laboratory Tests in Anemia Evaluation

Test(s)	Notes
Absolute reticulocyte count[a]	Values >100,000/μL (100 × 10⁹/L) signify increased erythropoiesis and a shift in reticulocyte pool from bone marrow to peripheral blood; compatible with bleeding, hemolysis, or response to treatment
Serum folate and vitamin B_{12} levels	Used to assess possible folate or vitamin B_{12} deficiency
Serum iron, TIBC, and ferritin	Low serum iron and high TIBC (iron/TIBC <10%-15%) characterize iron deficiency without inflammation (low ferritin). Low serum iron and low TIBC characterize anemia of inflammation (normal to high ferritin). Caveat: 20% of patients with "anemia of inflammation" have iron/TIBC <10%
Serum transferrin receptor concentration	Elevated in the setting of increased erythropoiesis or iron deficiency. If hemolysis or ineffective erythropoiesis is excluded, an elevated serum transferrin receptor concentration suggests iron deficiency
ESR, CRP fibrinogen and haptoglobin	Increased levels indicate acute phase reaction due to inflammatory cytokines, which decrease erythropoietin production, decrease responsiveness to erythropoietin, and block iron transport
Serum creatinine	High levels signify underproduction of erythropoietin, which is manufactured primarily by the kidneys
Erythropoietin	Should rise logarithmically above normal levels in relation to decreasing hematocrit. Levels >500 mU/mL (500 U/L) predict poor response to recombinant erythropoietin administration
Thyroid-stimulating hormone	Used to assess possible hypothyroidism, which may cause anemia
Serum testosterone	Used to assess possible hypotestosteronism in men, which may cause anemia
Serum LDH, bilirubin, and haptoglobin	Haptoglobin levels <20 mg/dL (200 mg/L) indicate hemolysis, supported by elevated LDH and total bilirubin levels
Urine hemosiderin and hemoglobin	Presence supports intravascular hemolysis
SPEP, UPEP, and quantitative immunoglobulins	Hypogammaglobulinemia, positive serum monoclonal proteins, and urine free kappa or lambda light chains suggest possible plasma cell myeloma or lymphoma

CRP = C-reactive protein; ESR = erythrocyte sedimentation rate; LDH = lactate dehydrogenase; SPEP = serum protein electrophoresis; TIBC = total iron-binding capacity; UPEP = urine protein electrophoresis.

[a] Absolute reticulocyte count = (erythrocyte count × reticulocyte count)/100, where erythrocyte count is expressed as n × 10⁶/μL.

hemolysis) or response to appropriate therapy (eg, iron, folate, and vitamin B_{12}). A lower-than-expected reticulocyte count indicates erythrocyte underproduction, including anemia due to deficient erythropoietin, nutritional deficiencies (eg, iron, folate, or vitamin B_{12}), inflammatory block, or a primary hematopoietic disorder (eg, red blood cell aplasia or myelodysplasia). Examination of the peripheral blood smear for morphologic features of erythrocytes, leukocytes, and platelets may provide important clues to the cause of anemia (Table 2). Results of various blood chemistry tests (Table 3) help to refine or confirm diagnostic considerations suggested by the complete blood count (CBC), reticulocyte count, and peripheral blood smear.

Reticulocyte counts are determined using the same automated multichannel technologies used to obtain CBCs. By microscopic examination of Wright-Giemsa–stained peripheral blood smears, reticulocytes appear larger than more senescent erythrocytes and somewhat purple (polychromatophilic) due to increased ribonucleoprotein and nucleic acid content from the extruded erythrocyte nucleus. Reticulocyte counts are expressed as percentages; methods for interpreting reticulocyte counts are summarized in Table 4. Absolute reticulocyte counts tend to be preferred because patients with anemia who have healthy bone marrow microenvironments, healthy hematopoietic stem cells, ample endogenous growth factors, and ample and usable body stores of iron and vitamins should have appropriately increased absolute reticulocyte counts (ie, >100,000/µL [100 × 10⁹/L]). An approach to using laboratory results for the evaluation of anemia is outlined in Figure 1.

Diagnosis

Anemia due to erythrocyte underproduction generally develops and progresses slowly over weeks to months. In contrast, anemia due to bleeding or hemolysis generally occurs rapidly over days to weeks. Because anemia may be hereditary rather than acquired, knowledge of a family history of anemia is useful when considering congenital and acquired causes of anemia as well as acquired contributors to worsened congenital anemia (eg, thalassemia).

Although symptoms and signs can offer important clues to the cause of anemia, physical examination is often normal or nonspecific. The history and physical examination are supplemented by a consideration of anemia categorized by erythrocyte size (ie, microcytic [MCV <80 fL], normocytic [MCV 80-100 fL], or macrocytic [MCV >100 fL]) and other morphologic abnormalities (see Table 2).

When routine laboratory test results, history, and physical examination fail to adequately explain the cause of anemia, bone marrow aspiration and biopsy help to evaluate disorders of marrow microenvironment (eg, infiltrative myelopathies from fibrosis, cancer metastasis, or infection), disorders of myeloid maturation (eg, leukemias or myelodysplastic syndromes), or aplasia.

Microcytic Anemia

Factors to consider in the differential diagnosis of microcytic anemia include a reduction in iron availability, globin chain production, and/or heme synthesis (Table 5); deficiency in one or more of these will result in hypochromic, often microcytic, anemia. Severe iron deficiency and inflammation reduce iron availability. Reduced globin production characterizes the thalassemias and other hemoglobinopathies. Certain toxins (eg, alcohol and lead) and drugs (eg, chloramphenicol and isoniazid) reduce heme synthesis. Decreased heme synthesis is also a characteristic of the congenital and acquired idiopathic sideroblastic anemias.

Iron Deficiency

The most common cause of microcytic anemia is iron deficiency, usually related to menstrual or gastrointestinal blood loss or malabsorption syndromes. Hypochromia (decreased MCH and/or MCHC) is the first morphologic sign of iron deficiency, followed by microcytosis (decreased MCV). As hemoglobin levels decline, erythrocytes become heterogeneous in size and shape (anisocytosis, poikilocytosis; Plate 35). Pica (a craving for ice or other unusual substances, such as clay or cornstarch) is a symptom of iron deficiency and quickly disappears with iron replacement. In men and postmenopausal women with iron deficiency, evaluation of the gastrointestinal tract for a source of blood loss is mandatory. In premenopausal women, evaluation also includes gynecologic examination. Chronic intravascular hemolysis with loss of iron in the urine is an uncommon cause of iron deficiency. Partial or total gastrectomy leads to decreased production of hydrochloric acid and diminished iron absorption. Celiac disease results in malabsorption of iron by the duodenum.

Serum ferritin levels are the most useful test in the diagnosis of iron deficiency. However, because ferritin is an acute phase reactant, it has less diagnostic value in patients with an infection or inflammatory disorder. Virtually all patients with serum ferritin levels <10 to 15 ng/mL (10-15 µg/L) are iron deficient. However, 25% of menstruating women with absent stainable bone marrow iron have fer-

Table 4. Interpreting the Reticulocyte Count

Method of Interpretation	Calculation	Notes
Corrected reticulocyte count	Reticulocyte percentage × (observed HCT/expected HCT)	Corrects for degree of anemia
Reticulocyte production index (RPI)	Reticulocyte percentage/ correction factor	Corrects for shortened reticulocyte maturation time as anemia worsens • HCT = 40 to 45; correction factor = 1.0 • HCT = 35 to 39; correction factor = 1.5 • HCT = 25 to 34; correction factor = 2.0 • HCT = 15 to 24; correction factor = 2.5 • HCT <15; correction factor = 3.0 • RPI value <2 implies inadequate bone marrow response
Absolute reticulocyte count	(Erythrocyte count × reticulocyte count)/100, where erythrocyte count is expressed as n × 10⁶/µL	In steady state conditions, absolute reticulocyte count is 25,000 to 75,000/µL (25-75 × 10⁹/L). Values >75,000 to 100,000/µL (75-100 × 10⁹/L) imply stress erythropoiesis

HCT = hematocrit.

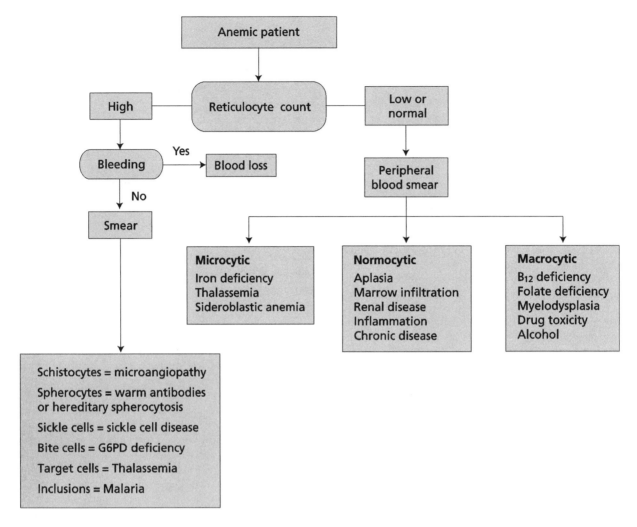

Figure 1. Laboratory diagnostic evaluation of the patient with anemia. G6PD = glucose-6-phosphate dehydrogenase.

ritin levels >15 ng/mL (15 µg/L). Assuming absence of inflammation, higher ferritin cutoff limits of 30 to 41 ng/mL (30-41 µg/L) improve diagnostic efficiency. **The treatment of choice for iron deficiency is almost always an oral iron preparation.** Iron salts (eg, ferrous sulfate) are preferred over iron polysaccharide complexes. Ascorbic acid enhances absorption of iron, whereas certain dietary substances, calcium, and inhibitors of gastric acid secretion decrease iron absorption. Treatment should be continued for 6 months to 1 year until hemoglobin levels and iron stores return to normal. Indications for parenteral iron therapy include (1) inability to tolerate oral iron compounds; (2) inability to absorb oral iron; (3) repeated failure to adhere to a regular schedule of oral iron administration; (4) circumstances when iron (blood) loss exceeds oral iron replacement and/or when oral iron exacerbates symptoms of the underlying disease (eg, inflammatory bowel disease); (5) autologous blood donation (in selected cases); and (6) hemodialysis.

Thalassemia

Thalassemias (Table 5) are congenital disorders involving imbalanced globin chain production or abnormal globin chain synthesis. Microcytic hypochromic erythrocytes in thalassemic states are accompanied by target cells (Plate 36), teardrop cells, and basophilic stippling. In contrast to patients with iron deficiency who have low

erythrocyte counts and mildly to moderately decreased MCV values, patients with thalassemia often have normal to high-normal erythrocyte counts with strikingly low MCV values. Although patients with thalassemia trait can develop iron deficiency, this is less likely among patients with severe thalassemia, where iron overload is a concern, particularly in patients who have had frequent blood transfusions.

Folic acid supplementation is a supportive therapy in all patients with thalassemia. However, other treatments vary according to the severity of the thalassemia. Patients with thalassemia trait do not require specific therapy. Patients with more severe thalassemia often require blood transfusions to maintain growth, manage symptomatic anemia, and prevent complications of extramedullary hematopoiesis. Iron chelation therapy prevents and manages iron overload. Hydroxyurea may benefit patients with β-thalassemia intermedia. Hematopoietic stem cell transplantation is an established treatment for severe β-thalassemia.

Macrocytic Anemia

Clinicians should first assess the reticulocyte count and rule out stress erythropoiesis (eg, from bleeding or hemolysis). Reticulocytes are larger than senescent erythrocytes; consequently, increased reticulocyte numbers elevate the MCV, but generally not to levels >110 to 115 fL. Macrocytic anemia may be megaloblastic or nonmegaloblastic (Table 6).

Hemolysis

When laboratory tests suggest hemolysis (see Table 3), the possible causes of anemia should be considered by type (spherocytic or nonspherocytic), site (intramedullary or extramedullary, intravascular or extravascular), and mechanism (immune-mediated or nonimmune-mediated, intrinsic vs extrinsic to the erythrocyte). For example, spherocytic hemolytic anemia implicates a membrane defect, either acquired (eg, warm autoimmune hemolytic anemia) or congenital (eg, hereditary spherocytosis). Nonspherocytic hemolytic anemias include "bite cell" hemolysis (eg, oxidant stress) and fragmentation hemolysis (eg, thrombotic microangiopathy). Intramedullary hemolysis is seen in various disorders associated with ineffective erythropoiesis, including thalassemia. Extramedullary hemolysis may be extravascular (eg, hemolysis mediated by the spleen) or intravascular (eg, hemolysis associated with cold agglutinin disease or thrombotic microangiopathy). Immune-mediated hemolysis is distinguished by the presence of antibodies (detected by the Coombs test) directed against erythrocytes; these antiglobulins, also referred to as "agglutinins," may be detected when bound to the surface of red blood cells (direct Coombs test) or circulating in serum (indirect Coombs test). They may also be further characterized by the body temperature at which they react, with "warm agglutinins" (usually IgG antibodies) reacting at body temperature, and "cold agglutinins" (usually IgM antibodies) reacting at temperatures below core body temperature. Hemolytic disorders "intrinsic" to the erythrocyte include membrane defects, enzymopathies, and hemoglobinopathies. Table 7 summarizes various causes of hemolytic anemia. In all cases, examining the peripheral blood smear is central to identifying erythrocyte morphologies that implicate certain mechanisms of hemolysis (see Table 2).

In oxidant hemolysis, a by-product is methemoglobin, which contains ferric ions. Methemoglobin has altered spectrophotometric properties from hemoglobin, which contains ferrous ions. As a consequence, patients with methemoglobinemia have arterial Po_2 values (reflecting the total concentration of oxygen in blood) that appear higher than expected in relation to the percent oxygen saturation (which specifically reflects the percent of oxygen bound to hemoglobin).

Megaloblastic Macrocytosis

Macro-ovalocytes suggest megaloblastic maturation of erythrocytes; hypersegmented neutrophils may also be present (Plate 37). Causes (see Table 6) include folate and/or vitamin B_{12} deficiency, drugs

Table 5. Differential Diagnosis of Microcytic Anemia

Disorder	Genotype	Notes
Iron deficiency anemia	N/A	Anemia with hypochromia, microcytosis, and increased RDW. Usually due to menstrual or GI blood loss; less commonly due to celiac disease or chronic intravascular hemolysis. Serum ferritin concentration and transferrin saturation are usuallye low. Search for a source of chronic blood loss
α-Thalassemia trait	-α/-α –/αα	Asymptomatic mild anemia with normal RDW due to homozygous single α-globin gene deletion or heterozygous double α-globin gene deletion. Seen in persons of African, Mediterranean, Middle Eastern, or Southeast Asian ancestry. Serum ferritin concentration and transferrin saturation are normal. Hgb electrophoresis shows a normal percentage of Hgb A_2 and Hgb F. Usually a diagnosis of exclusion. Treatment not needed
Hemoglobin H disease	–/-α	Moderate to severe anemia with splenomegaly. Intermittent transfusions may be needed with risk of iron overload. Hgb H = tetramers of β-globin chains.
Hemoglobin Barts	–/–	Usually lethal in utero, unless salvage is obtained with in utero transfusions. Hgb Barts = tetramers of γ-globin chains
β-Thalassemia minor	$β^{NL}/β^+$	Mild, asymptomatic anemia with normal RDW due to reduced expression of one β-globin gene. Seen in persons of African, Mediterranean, Middle Eastern, or Southeast Asian ancestry. Serum ferritin concentration and transferrin saturation are generally normal. Hgb electrophoresis shows an increased percentage of Hgb A_2 and a normal to slightly increased percentage of Hgb F. Treatment not needed
β-Thalassemia intermedia	$β^{NL}/β^0$ $β^+/β^+$	Moderate, asymptomatic to symptomatic anemia due to reduced but not absent expression of one or both β-globin genes. Typically, there is evidence of ineffective erythropoiesis, with a low serum haptoglobin and increased levels of indirect bilirubin and LDH in the setting of a normal reticulocyte count and increased iron stores. Serum ferritin concentration and transferrin saturation are increased. Hgb electrophoresis shows an increased percentage of Hgb A_2 and Hgb F. Intermittent transfusion and risk of iron overload requiring iron chelation therapy
β-Thalassemia major	$β^0/β^0$ $β^+/β^+$ $β^0/β^+$	Severe, symptomatic anemia due to reduced or absent expression of both β-globin genes. There is evidence of ineffective erythropoiesis, with a low serum haptoglobin and increased levels of indirect bilirubin and LDH in the setting of a normal reticulocyte count and increased iron stores. Serum ferritin concentration and transferrin saturation are increased. Hgb electrophoresis shows an increased percentage of Hgb A_2 Hgb F. Transfusions with iron overload requiring iron chelation therapy. Splenectomy may enhance RBC survival and reduce transfusion need. HSCT is an option to consider
Sickle cell-β-thalassemia	$β^S/β^+$	Seen in persons of African, Middle Eastern, Mediterranean, or Indian ancestry. Serum ferritin and transferrin saturation are usually normal. Hgb electrophoresis shows predominantly Hgb S but also variable amounts of Hgb A (5%-30%), an increased percentage of Hgb A_2 (>3.5%), and a normal to variably increased percentage of Hgb F (2%-10%)

$β^{NL}$ = Normal β-globin expression; $β^+$ = mutations causing decreased β-globin expression; $β^0$ = mutations causing ineffective β-globin expression; GI = gastrointestinal; Hgb = hemoglobin; HSCT = hematopoietic stem cell transplantation; LDH = lactate dehydrogenase; N/A = not applicable; RBC = red blood cell; RDW = red cell distribution width.

affecting folate metabolism and/or DNA synthesis, and acquired idiopathic causes of megaloblastic maturation (eg, myelodysplastic syndromes). An MCV >115 fL is almost always due to a megaloblastic cause. Because megaloblastic causes of anemia impact trilineage hematopoiesis, leukopenia and thrombocytopenia may accompany anemia. The myelodysplastic syndromes are stem cell clonal disorders characterized by ineffective hematopoiesis and various peripheral cytopenias (see chapter 50).

Patients with macrocytic anemia or specific neurologic symptoms should be screened for vitamin B_{12} deficiency. However, the MCV should not be used as the only indication to exclude vitamin B_{12} deficiency, which can be present despite a normal MCV or may be present in combination with microcytic causes of anemia (eg, iron deficiency or thalassemia), thereby yielding a normal MCV. Concomitant iron and vitamin B_{12} deficiencies can arise due to various causes, including celiac disease. Elevated serum levels of

Table 6. Differential Diagnosis of Megaloblastic Anemia

Disorder	Notes
Folate deficiency	Morphologically indistinguishable from vitamin B_{12} deficiency and drug-induced megaloblastosis. Inquire about excessive alcohol use, quality of diet, and history of small-bowel disease; consider evaluation for celiac disease
Vitamin B_{12} deficiency	Morphologically indistinguishable from folate deficiency. Loss of vibration or position sense favors vitamin B_{12} deficiency. However, neurologic disease due to vitamin B_{12} deficiency may occur without anemia or macrocytosis
Drug-induced changes in erythrocytes	Numerous drugs prescribed for cancer, HIV infection, psoriasis, SLE, rheumatoid arthritis, and post-transplantation immunosuppression cause macrocytic and sometimes megaloblastic changes in erythrocytes. History should be revealing
Myelodysplastic syndromes	Myelodysplastic syndromes (see chapter 50) are a spectrum of primary hematopoietic disorders characterized by hypercellular bone marrow and peripheral blood cytopenias due to ineffective myelopoiesis, abnormal maturation (including idiopathic acquired megaloblastic maturation of erythroid cells), and intramedullary apoptosis of myeloid cells

SLE = systemic lupus erythematosus.

Table 7. Differential Diagnosis of Hemolytic Anemia

Disorder	Notes
Membrane defect (hereditary spherocytosis, hereditary elliptocytosis)	Suspect in patients with a positive family history, splenomegaly, and spherocytes or elliptocytes on blood smear. Diagnosis is confirmed by osmotic fragility and negative direct antiglobulin (Coombs) test
Enzymopathy (G6PD deficiency, pyruvate kinase deficiency)	Common forms of G6PD deficiency usually cause only episodic moderate hemolysis, precipitated by oxidant drugs or infection. Variable blood smear findings include bite cells, spherocytes, fragments (rarely), and minimal abnormalities of erythrocytes other than polychromasia (from reticulocytosis). Common drugs and chemicals that are unsafe for use in patients with G6PD deficiency include dapsone, methylene blue, nitrofurantoin, phenazopyridine, phenylhydrazine, primaquine, sulfamethoxazole, and sulfapyridine. Pyruvate kinase deficiency is rare and causes moderately severe anemia; blood smear shows acanthocytes
Hemoglobinopathy (hemoglobin S, hemoglobin C, thalassemia, hereditary unstable)	Chronic or episodic hemolysis. Hgb A_2 level is increased with β-thalassemia; Hgb F also may be increased. No structural Hgb abnormality is detectable with α-thalassemia; diagnosis is based on hematocrit, MCV, blood smear, and family study. Abnormal Hgbs (eg, E and D) are uncommon in the United States. Blood smear changes suggest certain hemoglobinopathies; Hgb electrophoresis reveals the abnormal Hgb
Autoimmune hemolytic anemia	Spherocytes on blood smear; erythrocyte agglutination is seen with cold agglutinin disease. Diagnosis is confirmed by direct and indirect antiglobulin (Coombs) tests and cold agglutinin titer; direct antiglobulin (Coombs) test is positive for C3 in cold agglutinin disease. Most cases of warm antibody disease are drug induced or associated with an underlying disorder (eg, SLE, lymphoproliferative disorder). Cold agglutinin disease is also frequently associated with underlying disorders (eg, *Mycoplasma pneumoniae* infection, SLE)
Erythrocyte fragmentation (TTP, HUS, DIC; see Chapter 49)	TTP usually presents as neurologic symptoms and severe fragmentation anemia and thrombocytopenia. With HUS (children), kidney abnormalities predominate, and anemia and thrombocytopenia are milder. In other causes of microangiopathic anemia (DIC, malignant hypertension, scleroderma renal crisis), the anemia and thrombocytopenia are usually mild to moderate; these disorders are diagnosed by peripheral blood smear in the proper clinical context
Infection (malaria, babesiosis)	Symptoms of infection, particularly fever, usually dominate. Splenomegaly is the rule with malaria; babesiosis usually produces a milder malaria-like illness, unless patients are asplenic. Finding intraerythrocytic parasites on blood smear is diagnostic
Hypersplenism (see Chapter 22)	Splenomegaly (any cause) can cause hemolysis; hypersplenism may also decrease the number of leukocytes, platelets, or any combination of cell lines. Hypersplenism produces no erythrocyte morphologic changes in erythrocytes, but the blood smear may show changes related to the underlying cause (eg, target cells with liver disease)

DIC = disseminated intravascular coagulation; G6PD = glucose-6-phosphate dehydrogenase; Hgb = hemoglobin; HUS = hemolytic uremic syndrome; MCV = mean corpuscular volume; SLE = systemic lupus erythematosus; TTP = thrombotic thrombocytopenic purpura.

methylmalonic acid and homocysteine support vitamin B$_{12}$ deficiency in patients with slightly low or borderline serum vitamin B$_{12}$ levels (200-300 pg/mL [147.6-221.3 pmol/L]). Daily oral vitamin B$_{12}$ can be used to treat most vitamin B$_{12}$-deficient patients. Timed-release formulations may not reliably release their vitamin B$_{12}$ content and should be avoided.

Nonmegaloblastic Macrocytosis

Large target cells (MCV = 105-110 fL) and echinocytes (erythrocytes with a small number of spicules of uniform size and distribution on the cell surface) signify membrane changes associated with liver disease. Diminished spleen function (hyposplenism or asplenia) yields large target cells, acanthocytes (erythrocytes with a small number of spicules of variable size and distribution on the cell surface), Howell-Jolly bodies, and variable numbers of nucleated erythrocytes.

Normochromic Normocytic Anemia

When the MCV is normal (80-100 fL), assessing whether it is declining or rising over time may provide clues to an evolving microcytic or macrocytic pathology (see Table 1). Other causes of normocytic anemia (Table 8) include underproduction of erythropoietin (eg, kidney failure), deficiency of other growth factors (eg, thyroid hormone or testosterone), inflammation, and marrow infiltrative myelopathies, which yield teardrop cells, nucleated erythrocytes, and immature leukocytes. With the exception of acute blood loss, the most common cause is the anemia of inflammation. Aplastic anemia, a rare cause of normocytic normochromic anemia, is usually accompanied by severe granulocytopenia and thrombocytopenia due to deficient hematopoietic stem cells.

Anemia of Inflammation

Inflammatory cytokines impede erythropoiesis by decreasing erythropoietin production, decreasing responsiveness of maturing erythroid precursors to erythropoietin, and decreasing iron absorption by the gastrointestinal tract and iron release from storage pools (macrophages). Hepcidin, an acute phase protein that rises in response to certain inflammatory cytokines, is chiefly responsible for the effects on iron by causing internalization and degradation of the iron export protein ferroportin. Inflammatory cytokines also decrease transferrin production while increasing ferritin levels. Thus, the consequences of inflammation are lower serum iron and total iron-binding capacity levels (calculated from transferrin levels) and higher serum ferritin levels. With iron deficiency absent inflammation, transferrin and calculated total iron-binding capacity levels rise while ferritin levels decline (reflecting diminished storage pools of iron). Cytokines disrupt this physiologic response to iron deficiency, thereby confounding diagnosis of iron deficiency when inflammation is present. However, since cytokines increase serum ferritin levels by as much as 3 fold, serum ferritin levels <100 ng/mL (100 μg/L) may reflect iron deficiency in patients with inflammatory states. Reticulocyte counts are inappropriately low for the degree of anemia. Bone marrow biopsies are generally not indicated unless competing causes of anemia are suspected (eg, pure red cell aplasia, sideroblastic anemia, or other myelodysplastic syndromes).

The management of anemia of inflammation is treatment of the underlying inflammatory condition. When symptomatic anemia persists despite treatment of the chronic condition (eg, rheumatoid arthritis), administration of recombinant human erythropoietin can improve anemia and diminish the need for erythrocyte transfusion.

Table 8. Differential Diagnosis of Normocytic Anemia

Disorder	Notes
Acute blood loss	Anemia with variation in erythrocyte size (increased RDW) if iron deficiency is present. Reticulocyte count is usually increased; leukocyte count and platelet count may be slightly increased, depending on the rapidity of bleeding
Chronic kidney disease (see Chapter 71)	Anemia with a low reticulocyte count due to impaired erythropoietin production. Renal endocrine function does not correlate with renal exocrine function
Pure red cell aplasia	Anemia with severe reticulocytopenia. Diagnosis is made by examination of a bone marrow aspirate, in which erythroblasts will be absent or severely diminished. Red cell aplasia can be idiopathic or secondary to a thymoma, solid tumor, hematologic malignancy, collagen vascular disease, viral infection (particularly human parvovirus B19 infection, which is common in immunosuppressed patients), or drug (eg, phenytoin, azathioprine, isoniazid, chloramphenicol, mycophenolate mofetil). Red cell aplasia may also occur in patients with hemolytic anemia from any cause
Malignancy (solid tumor, lymphoma, myelofibrosis)	Anemia with a low reticulocyte count. With bone marrow involvement by tumor, leukoerythroblastosis and extramedullary hematopoiesis occur, and nucleated erythrocytes and myelocytes are seen in the peripheral blood. Peripheral blood smear may show rouleaux formation (if a plasma cell dyscrasia is present) or teardrop-shaped erythrocytes (if splenomegaly is present)
Alcoholic liver disease	Anemia with a low reticulocyte count. Target cells and acanthocytes may also be present. Leukocyte and platelet counts will be reduced if there is portal hypertension with splenomegaly, although thrombocytopenia in liver disease is chiefly due to underproduction of thrombopoietin by the liver
Anemia of inflammation (chronic disease)	A normocytic (but sometimes microcytic) anemia that occurs in association with another disease. The underlying disorder is usually infectious, inflammatory, or neoplastic and is characterized by distinct abnormalities of iron metabolism: low serum iron and transferrin with reduced transferrin saturation, normal or elevated serum ferritin, and normal or increased bone marrow iron stores
Hemolytic anemia	Anemia with an elevated reticulocyte count and spherocytes, sickle cells, bite cells, or fragmented erythrocytes. There may be hemoglobinuria. If the reticulocyte count is sufficiently elevated, the MCV may be high. The serum haptoglobin level will be low whether the hemolysis is intravascular or extravascular, and if the hemolysis is antibody-mediated, the direct antiglobulin (Coombs) test result will be positive. The essential laboratory test is the peripheral blood smear, which can distinguish between the different types of hemolysis: spherocytic hemolytic anemia, erythrocyte enzyme defect, erythrocyte fragmentation, cold agglutinin disease, hemoglobinopathy, heavy metal intoxication, and paroxysmal nocturnal hemoglobinuria. Urine hemoglobin and urine hemosiderin measurements are useful for detecting intravascular hemolysis

ESR = erythrocyte sedimentation rate; MCV = mean corpuscular volume; RDW = red cell distribution width.

Therapy of Anemia

Appropriate treatment is dictated by the underlying cause or causes of anemia. In view of the diverse causes of anemia, each dictating specific strategies for optimal management, an in-depth review of anemia treatments is not possible here. However, a few overarching principles apply.

Clinicians should always ensure intact nutritional, mineral, and vitamin stores. When anemia is due to bleeding, the source of bleeding should be eliminated as best as possible. When anemia relates to hemolysis, the cause should be identified. If hemolysis is due to a congenital hemoglobinopathy, it should be managed accordingly (eg, supplemental folic acid, hydroxyurea for sickle cell disease). If hemolysis is acquired, the cause should be identified and managed accordingly (eg, immunosuppression for autoimmune hemolytic anemia, plasmapheresis for thrombotic thrombocytopenic purpura, elimination of drugs causing oxidant stress, treatment of malaria or babesiosis, treatment of the underlying cause of disseminated intravascular coagulation, or replacement of a deteriorating native or mechanical heart valve).

When anemia relates to underproduction of erythropoietin (eg, in chronic or end-stage kidney disease), treatment with erythropoiesis-stimulating agents should be considered. In patients with primary hematopoietic disorders impacting normal bone marrow hematopoiesis (eg, aplastic anemia, myelodysplastic syndrome, leukemia, plasma cell myeloma, lymphoma, and myelofibrosis), clinicians should proceed with the most appropriate management of the underlying primary hematopoietic disorder. For management of anemia-associated symptoms (eg, fatigue, lethargy, and exertional dyspnea), supportive blood transfusions versus pharmacologic doses of erythropoiesis-stimulating agents should be considered. In some instances, allogeneic hematopoietic stem cell transplantation may be indicated.

Bibliography

Bain BJ. Diagnosis from the blood smear. N Engl J Med. 2005;353:498-507. [PMID: 16079373]

Chapter 48

Sickle Cell Disease

Reed E. Drews, MD

The sickle mutation is a single base change (GAT → GTT) in the sixth codon of exon 1 of the β-globin gene, resulting in replacement of the normal glutamic acid with valine at position 6 of the β-globin polypeptide. When both β-globin genes (homozygous) have this single amino acid substitution, deoxygenated hemoglobin S heterotetramers polymerize to form fibrils, causing erythrocytes to sickle and hemolyze (Plate 38). Sickle cells, forming in the relatively hypoxic regions of tissues, impede blood flow in the microvasculature and promote vaso-occlusion, resulting in profound, often disabling complications, including acute pain (crises), chronic pain, and organ dysfunction or failure (Table 1). When only one copy of the β-globin gene has this defect and is inherited along with a normal β-globin gene, patients have sickle cell trait and are asymptomatic. The prevalence of sickle cell trait varies widely worldwide and may be as high as 50% in certain regions, affecting individuals of African, Hispanic, Mediterranean, Asian, and Indian descent. Among persons of African ancestry, sickle cell disease is one of the most common genetic diseases; about 10% are carriers of the sickle gene, and 1 in 600 newborn infants have sickle cell disease.

Screening

The goal of newborn screening is to identify infants with sickle cell disease and to treat these patients for 5 years with prophylactic penicillin (or a macrolide, if there is an allergy to penicillin); antibiotic therapy has been shown to reduce both mortality and morbidity from pneumococcal infections in infants with sickle cell disease and sickle cell–β-thalassemia. Abnormal hemoglobin may be identified in white individuals; most reports indicate that universal screening is more cost effective than targeted screening. For possible future primary prevention, counseling the family of an affected infant should include screening of other family members, especially the parents.

Sickle trait is a benign carrier condition that can also be detected at birth. While individuals with sickle cell trait do not have an increased mortality rate compared with the general population, there are a number of complications associated with sickle trait that may arise, including increased risk of sudden death with intense physical activity and extreme exercise. Athletic and military groups may require mandatory testing for sickle trait with opt-out provisions. However, the American Society of Hematology opposes such mandatory screening, favoring universal interventions to reduce exertion-related injuries and deaths, since this approach can be effective for all athletes irrespective of sickle cell status.

Diagnosis

Sickle cell disease is inherited in an autosomal manner. If both parents carry sickle hemoglobin or another abnormal hemoglobin, there is a 25% risk that the fetus of each pregnancy will have sickle cell disease or another sickle cell syndrome. Prenatal diagnosis is possible, and genetic counseling is important for affected families to fully understand the diagnosis, its complications, and possible therapeutic interventions.

Most patients with sickle cell disease experience clinical manifestations in childhood, even as early as age 6 months. Aspects of the medical history that support the possibility of sickle cell disease or a related hemoglobinopathy include recurring episodes of acute pain, chronic pain, and symptoms and signs of anemia and its sequelae (see Table 1). The average hemoglobin level in patients with sickle cell disease is 7 to 8 g/dL (70-80 g/L); the anemia is normocytic normochromic, with high reticulocyte counts from stress erythropoiesis and chronic hemolysis. Microcytic hypochromic indices suggest sickle cell–β-thalassemia or coinherited α-thalassemia. High platelet and leukocyte counts relate to functional asplenia because of destruction of the spleen due to sickling (autoinfarction).

Hemoglobin electrophoresis distinguishes most structural variants of hemoglobin. High hemoglobin F levels are associated with less severe clinical disease. Elevated hemoglobin A_2 levels signify the presence of β-thalassemia. Knowledge of the molecular lesion in a patient with sickle cell disease may predict severity, assist with family counseling and planning, and guide use of aggressive therapeutic modalities (eg, allogeneic bone marrow transplantation).

Additional laboratory testing documents organ dysfunction caused by sickle cell disease. Urinalysis and serum creatinine level identify patients with proteinuria and kidney failure. In patients who have received multiple transfusions, indirect antibody testing detects alloantibodies relevant to future transfusions; liver enzymes, viral hepatitis serologies, and serum iron chemistries identify patients who have contracted viral hepatitis and/or developed iron overload. Pulmonary hypertension, correlating with older age and prior history of acute chest syndrome, is the most common abnormality on echocardiography, with electrocardiography demonstrating signs of right ventricular hypertrophy or strain. Physical examination findings associated with sickle cell disease are summarized in Table 2.

Therapy

Hydroxyurea augments levels of hemoglobin F, which inhibits intracellular polymerization of hemoglobin S. Hydroxyurea decreases the incidence of acute painful episodes by approximately 50% in responders; it also reduces the incidence of acute chest syndrome and the need for blood transfusion. Nine-year follow-up of adult patients taking hydroxyurea showed that hydroxyurea was associated with a 40% reduction in mortality. In addition to inducing fetal hemoglobin, other beneficial effects of hydroxyurea in sickle cell disease include improved erythrocyte hydration, macrocytosis, and lower neutrophil and reticulocyte counts with decreased adhesiveness and improved flow (rheology) of circulating neutrophils and reticulocytes. Together, these beneficial effects reduce intracellular sickling and result in reduced hemolysis and improved hemoglobin levels. There is growing evidence that hydroxyurea therapy also offers multiple benefits in children. Beginning hydroxyurea in childhood or adolescence may help to prevent chronic and long-term end-organ damage, thereby supplanting the need for chronic management strategies such as exchange transfusion and chelation therapy.

Exchange transfusions, a technique that removes the patient's blood while transfusing normal, crossmatched donor blood, should be considered to decrease hemoglobin S levels by <30% in managing specific acute complications, including cerebral infarction, fat embolism, acute chest syndrome, unresponsive acute priapism, and nonhealing leg ulcers. Incidence of iron overload requiring chelation therapy, which increases morbidity and mortality, is less in patients receiving exchange transfusions compared with those on simple blood transfusion.

Angiotensin-converting enzyme (ACE) inhibitors prevent progressive kidney disease by lowering intraglomerular pressures. In addition, ACE inhibitors can lower protein excretion and should be used in patients with sickle cell disease and albuminuria, even in the absence of hypertension. Recombinant erythropoietin stimulates

Table 1. Major Complications of Sickle Cell Disease

Complication	Notes
ACS vs pneumonia, fat embolism, VTE	ACS correlates with risk of pulmonary hypertension and is the most frequent cause of death. ACS is associated with chlamydia, mycoplasma, respiratory syncytial virus, coagulase-positive *Staphylococcus aureus*, *Streptococcus pneumoniae*, *Mycoplasma hominis*, parvovirus, and rhinovirus infections (in decreasing order of frequency)
	Pneumonia is usually a localized infiltration, whereas ACS is usually characterized by diffuse pulmonary infiltrates. Cultures of bronchial washings or deep sputum are usually positive in pneumonia
	Fat embolism presents as chest pain, fever, dyspnea, hypoxia, thrombocytopenia, and multiorgan failure. Fat embolism is a component of ACS and is usually associated with acute painful episodes. It is best differentiated by the presence of fat bodies in bronchial washings or in deep sputum and by multiorgan involvement (eg, stroke or kidney failure)
	The presence of lower-extremity thrombophlebitis may differentiate VTE from ACS, but pulmonary arteriography may be needed in some cases. Newer contrast agents may be safer than hypertonic contrast agents, which precipitate intravascular sickling
Avascular necrosis	Involves the hips and shoulders; may require surgery. More common in sickle cell–α-thalassemia than in other sickle cell syndromes
Stroke	Occurs in 8%-17% of patients. Infarction is most common in children; hemorrhage is most common in adults. Brain imaging and lumbar puncture establish the diagnosis
Cholecystitis vs hepatic crisis	Chronic hemolysis may result in gallstones and acute cholecystitis. Fever, right upper-quadrant pain, and elevated aminotransferase levels may also be due to sickle cell–related ischemic hepatic crisis. Abdominal ultrasonography can help differentiate the conditions
Dactylitis vs osteomyelitis	Dactylitis is associated with painful, usually symmetric swelling of the hands or feet, erythema, and low-grade fever; it is more common in children aged <5 y. Osteomyelitis usually involves one bone
Heart failure	Related to pulmonary and systemic hypertension and ischemia
Infection	Related to functional asplenia
Leg ulcers	Most common in hemoglobin S disease
Liver disease	Viral hepatitis and/or iron overload from transfusions and ischemia-induced hepatic crisis
Priapism	Prolonged or repeated episodes may cause permanent erectile dysfunction
Proteinuria and kidney failure	Prevalence of proteinuria and kidney failure is approximately 25% and 5%, respectively
Pulmonary hypertension	Risk of development correlates with increasing age and prior history of ACS. Electrocardiogram may show evidence of right ventricular hypertrophy or strain (marked right axis deviation, tall R waves in lead V_1, delayed precordial transition zone with prominent S waves in leads V_5 and V_6, inverted T waves and ST-segment depression in leads V_1 to V_3, and peaked P waves in lead II due to right-atrial enlargement)
Retinopathy	More common in patients with compound heterozygosity for hemoglobin SC
Sickle anemia vs aplastic crisis, hyperhemolysis	A hemoglobin level that decreases by ≥2 g/dL (20 g/L) during a painful crisis could be due to aplastic crisis or hyperhemolysis. Aplastic crisis could be idiopathic or due to coexistent infection (eg, parvovirus B19) or cytotoxic drugs. Hyperhemolysis could be due to infection (eg, mycoplasma), transfusion reaction, or coexistent G6PD deficiency. Reticulocyte count is decreased with aplastic crisis and increased with hyperhemolysis. Serum bilirubin, LDH, and aminotransferase levels are elevated in hyperhemolysis
Sickle cell pain syndrome vs MI, appendicitis	Sickle cell pain crisis involving the chest may suggest acute MI. The quality of pain of MI (central pressure) is different from that of sickle cell pain (sharp, pleuritic). Serial determination of cardiac enzymes will differentiate the conditions
	Abdominal pain, fever, and leukocytosis may suggest appendicitis. Elevated serum LDH level and normal bowel sounds support sickle cell pain syndrome
Splenomegaly and splenic sequestration	Common in children aged <5 y who afterward manifest asplenia from splenic infarction. Patients with hemoglobin SC often have splenomegaly persisting into adulthood

ACS = acute chest syndrome; G6PD = glucose-6-phosphate dehydrogenase; LDH = lactate dehydrogenase; MI = myocardial infarction; VTE = venous thromboembolism.

Table 2. Physical Examination Findings Associated With Sickle Cell Disease

Physical Examination Component	Notes
Temperature	Acute painful episodes are often associated with low-grade fever. If temperature is >38.3°C (101.0°F), rule out infection
Pulse	Anemia, infection, and pain are often associated with tachycardia
Respiration rate	Respiration rate is usually 16 to 20/min in the steady state. A rate <10/min suggests opioid overdose
Blood pressure	Blood pressure is usually low-normal. Hypertension increases morbidity and mortality risk
Cardiac examination	A systolic murmur due to anemia is common. The absence of a murmur is associated with mild anemia and no cardiomegaly. Findings associated with pulmonary hypertension and right ventricular hypertrophy or strain include increased intensity of the pulmonic component of S_2, right-sided murmurs and gallops (increased intensity with inspiration), and a prominent a wave in the jugular venous pulse
Pulmonary examination	The lungs are usually clear in the steady state. Rhonchi may be heard in patients with a history of recurrent ACS. Decreased breath sounds and/or pulmonary crackles in a febrile patient suggest pneumonia or ACS
Abdominal examination	With age and repeated episodes of sickling, the spleen becomes small, fibrosed, and devoid of any function (autosplenectomy). However, splenomegaly may persist into young adulthood, especially in patients with hemoglobin SC, sickle cell-β-thalassemia, or sickle cell-α-thalassemia. Hepatomegaly could be a sign of iron overload or heart failure. Tender hepatomegaly suggests hepatic crisis
Skin examination	Leg ulcers develop in 5% to 10% of patients; ulcers are most often located on the medial or lateral aspect of the ankle
Neurologic examination	Focal findings suggestive of stroke. Not all patients with a history of stroke have residual weakness

ACS = acute chest syndrome.

erythropoiesis to achieve hemoglobin levels similar to steady-state values (ie, 7-9 g/dL [70-90 g/L]) in patients who have kidney failure or to limit blood transfusions in patients who are alloimmunized and for whom crossmatch-compatible blood is difficult to find.

Supplemental folic acid prevents folate deficiency (arising from chronic hemolysis) and subsequent elevation of homocysteine levels, which may be a risk factor for stroke. Periodic retinal examinations are recommended for monitoring and managing (photocoagulation) progressive proliferative sickle retinopathy. Pneumococcal, *Haemophilus influenzae* type b, and influenza vaccines prevent infections. Relaxation and biofeedback methods, cognitive coping strategies, and self-hypnosis are techniques that reduce emergency department visits, hospital admissions, hospital days, and analgesic use. Goals of these interventions are to improve quality of life by increasing activity and enhancing normal function and to decrease dependence on opioid analgesics.

Patients are hospitalized when severe acute painful episodes (crises) do not resolve at home with oral analgesics after 1 to 2 days or do not resolve or improve significantly after a minimum of 4 to 6 hours of treatment with parenteral opioids. Effective pain relief is best achieved with combined use of acetaminophen, nonsteroidal anti-inflammatory drugs, opioid analgesics, and adjuvant therapies (antihistamines, antidepressants, and anticonvulsants). Meperidine is not recommended as opioid therapy, because it is less effective than morphine or hydromorphone and is associated with more side effects (eg, seizures). Nonsteroidal anti-inflammatory drugs should be avoided in patients with kidney failure.

In patients with sickle cell disease, supplemental oxygen should be used only in the presence of demonstrated hypoxia (oxygen saturation <92% or arterial P_{O_2} ≤70 mm Hg [9.3 kPa]). For severe symptomatic anemia or acute organ failure, blood/exchange transfusions improve blood oxygen-carrying capacity and microvascular perfusion by diluting circulating sickled erythrocytes. To avoid increased blood viscosity, transfusions should not yield hemoglobin levels >10 g/dL (100 g/L).

Allogeneic bone marrow transplantation (in patients aged <16 years with severe complications) may cure sickle cell disease, but its success depends on the availability of donors and the severity of the disease of the patient in question. Recipients of HLA-matched donor marrow have 75% to 85% event-free survival, 15% graft rejection, and 10% mortality.

Bibliography

Frenette PS, Atweh GF. Sickle cell disease: old discoveries, new concepts, and future promise. J Clin Invest. 2007;117:850-858. [PMID: 17404610]

Ware RE. How I use hydroxyurea to treat young patients with sickle cell anemia. Blood. 2010;115:5300-5311. [PMID: 20223921]

Chapter 49

Thrombocytopenia

Richard S. Eisenstaedt, MD

Thrombocytopenia occurs through 1 of 2 mechanisms: decreased platelet production or accelerated platelet destruction (Table 1). Most disorders that produce thrombocytopenia through inadequate bone marrow production also affect other marrow cell lines and cause additional cytopenias. Platelet production may be decreased due to bone marrow injury mediated by toxins (eg, alcohol) or idiosyncratic drug reaction, metastatic cancer, miliary tuberculosis or other infections, deficiency of vitamin B_{12} or folic acid, or bone marrow disease (eg, acute leukemia, myelodysplastic syndrome, or aplastic anemia). Accelerated peripheral platelet destruction occurs in patients with splenomegaly and hyper-splenism or disseminated intravascular coagulation. This chapter focuses on 3 other causes of accelerated platelet destruction: immune thrombocytopenic purpura (ITP), heparin-induced thrombocytopenia (HIT), and thrombotic thrombocytopenic purpura–hemolytic uremic syndrome (TTP-HUS).

Immune Thrombocytopenic Purpura

Although ITP was formerly known as *idiopathic* thrombocytopenic purpura, *immune* thrombocytopenic purpura is a more appropriate

Table 1. Differential Diagnosis of Thrombocytopenia

Disorder	Notes
Decreased Platelet Production	
Vitamin B_{12} or folate deficiency (see Chapter 47)	Associated with pancytopenia, macrocytosis, macro-ovalocytes, hypersegmented neutrophils, and possibly neurologic signs with B_{12} deficiency
Bone marrow disorder (eg, acute leukemia, aplastic anemia, myelodysplastic syndrome)	Associated with pancytopenia, abnormal blood smear (eg, nucleated erythrocytes, teardrop cells, immature leukocytes), and abnormal bone marrow examination
Toxin- or drug-related bone marrow injury	History of alcohol abuse, environmental or occupational exposures, or drug use. Mechanism may also include accelerated destruction. Often associated with anemia or pancytopenia
Infection	Thrombocytopenia is seen in HIV infection, hepatitis B and C, EBV infection, rubella, disseminated tuberculosis, and other infections. Mechanism may also include accelerated destruction
Accelerated Destruction	
Immune thrombocytopenic purpura (ITP)	Isolated thrombocytopenia in the absence of systemic disease, or a causative drug defines the idiopathic form of ITP. Associated with large platelets on peripheral smear and increased megakaryocytes on bone marrow evaluation (marrow evaluation is usually not required for diagnosis in the absence of other features listed for bone marrow disorders). ITP may also be drug induced or associated with underlying disease, such as HIV, SLE, or chronic lymphocytic leukemia
Heparin-induced thrombocytopenia	History of exposure to heparin. May be associated with modest thrombocytopenia and devastating arterial and venous thrombosis
Chronic liver disease (see Chapter 22)	Portal hypertension can lead to splenic sequestration of platelets and thrombocytopenia. Liver disease may be associated with target cells. Liver disease may be occult
Thrombotic thrombocytopenic purpura–hemolytic uremic syndrome (TTP-HUS)	Syndromes associated with hemolytic anemia and thrombocytopenia. HUS is characterized by more severe renal involvement, TTP by more frequent neurologic symptoms. Associated with elevated serum LDH level, decreased haptoglobin concentration, and schistocytes on peripheral blood smear
Disseminated intravascular coagulation (see Chapter 52)	Coagulopathy that typically occurs in the setting of sepsis, metastatic cancer, or obstetric catastrophe. Associated with prolonged prothrombin time and activated partial thromboplastin time, low fibrinogen level, and thrombocytopenia
HELLP syndrome (**H**emolysis, **E**levated **L**iver enzymes, **L**ow **P**latelets)	Late pregnancy complication of thrombocytopenia associated with microangiopathic hemolytic anemia, and elevated liver enzymes, and hypertension
Other	
Pseudothrombocytopenia	In vitro clumping of platelets caused by EDTA-dependent agglutinins leads to falsely decreased platelet counts. Excluded by examination of a peripheral blood smear; no therapy is needed
Gestational thrombocytopenia	Mild, asymptomatic thrombocytopenia first noted late in pregnancy; resolves following delivery without therapy

EBV = Epstein-Barr virus; EDTA = ethylenediaminetetraacetic acid; LDH = lactate dehydrogenase; SLE = systemic lupus erythematosus.

term. Thrombocytopenia in ITP occurs when antibodies targeting platelet antigens mediate accelerated destruction. Antibodies arise in 3 distinct clinical settings: in response to a drug, in association with a disease, and when neither an offending drug nor a related underlying disease process can be identified (idiopathic).

Almost any drug can trigger platelet-targeted antibody production, but the syndrome is most often linked to quinine or quinidine. Although these drugs are used infrequently, quinine-related compounds are found in diverse naturopathic or herbal products. Other drugs that are less often linked to ITP include ranitidine, trimethoprim-sulfamethoxazole, rifampin, phenytoin, and gold compounds. The glycoprotein IIb/IIIa platelet inhibitors, such as abciximab, have also been associated with an acute onset and severe thrombocytopenia. A careful drug history, including a review of all prescriptions, vaccines, over-the-counter drugs, herbal products, and supplements, is important to identify the offending agent. Stopping the drug hastens recovery from ITP.

Immune thrombocytopenic purpura may be part of a broader disease affecting immune regulation, such as HIV infection, systemic lupus erythematosus, and, especially in older patients, lymphoproliferative malignancy. Patients infected with HIV may develop ITP before the infection has been diagnosed and immunosuppression and opportunistic infections occur. Therefore, screening for HIV infection is warranted in all patients with ITP. Recent reports link ITP to *Helicobacter pylori* infection, although platelet count response to antibiotic therapy is unpredictable.

Patients with ITP commonly present with easy bruising or petechial rash. At times, asymptomatic thrombocytopenia is noted on routine blood tests. Immune thrombocytopenic purpura is a disease of exclusion; the diagnosis is most probable in patients with isolated thrombocytopenia. The leukocyte count should be normal, and the hemoglobin concentration is normal or reduced as a result of blood loss secondary to thrombocytopenia (Table 2). Measurement of platelet-associated antibody is not helpful because the test lacks both sensitivity and specificity. The physical examination is normal, with the exception of signs of bleeding, most often petechiae (punctuate red macular lesions that do not blanch with pressure) on the skin or mucous membranes. Patients may have ecchymoses on the skin or more overt bleeding, especially in the gastrointestinal tract. The presence of fever or hepatosplenomegaly suggests another diagnosis. The blood smear will show decreased platelets and occasional large platelets (megathrombocytes). Bone marrow aspirate, if necessary to exclude other diagnoses, will show increased numbers of megakaryocytes and normal erythroid and myeloid precursors. Hematology consultation is advised for patients with severe thrombocytopenia or an uncertain diagnosis.

Patients with ITP require emergent treatment when thrombocytopenia is severe (<10,000/µL [10×10^9/L]) or when active bleeding is present. Treatment is often recommended in newly diagnosed patients with more modest thrombocytopenia (<50,000/µL [50×10^9/L]), whether or not they are actively bleeding. Both glucocorticoids and intravenous immune globulin (IVIG) are effective therapies, but thrombocytopenia often relapses when treatment is discontinued. In patients with chronic ITP, the risks of prolonged therapy with glucocorticoids or IVIG must be balanced against the benefits. Some patients who remain asymptomatic or who have mild, easily controlled bleeding are best managed without immunosuppressive therapy. Alternative immunosuppressive agents may be used for patients who do not respond to or who have intolerable toxicity from glucocorticoids or IVIG. Rh_o(D)-positive patients with ITP may be treated with anti-Rh_o(D) immunoglobulin. Another second-line immunosuppressive agent, rituximab, a chimeric monoclonal

Table 2. Laboratory Tests to Support the Diagnosis of ITP

Test	Notes
CBC	Low platelet count with normal hemoglobin, hematocrit, and leukocyte count is evidence for the diagnosis of ITP
Peripheral blood smear	Exclude platelet clumping (pseudothrombocytopenia). Myeloid and erythroid morphology should be normal. Platelets should appear normal or large in size. Abnormal or immature leukocytes should be absent. The presence of schistocytes is associated with TTP, DIC, and HELLP syndrome and is evidence against ITP. The presence of polychromatophilia, poikilocytosis, and spherocytes suggests hemolytic anemia. Nucleated erythrocytes should be absent
Bone marrow	Consider bone marrow aspiration and biopsy to establish the diagnosis only in patients with atypical or nondiagnostic findings, especially with additional cytopenias or immature leukocytes or with additional abnormalities on peripheral blood smear. ITP will show normal or increased numbers of megakaryocytes, normal myeloid and erythroid morphology, and no malignant cells
HIV antibodies	Indicated in all patients
PT/aPTT	Coagulation studies should be normal; an abnormal PT or aPTT is evidence against ITP
ANA and other serologic tests	ANA is not recommended for routine diagnosis; however, consider ANA and other serologic tests (eg, rheumatoid factor, complement levels, anti-DNA) in patients with rash, synovitis, arthralgia, or other signs of rheumatologic disease

ANA = antinuclear antibody; aPTT = activated partial thromboplastin time; CBC = complete blood count; DIC = disseminated intravascular coagulation; HELLP = hemolytic anemia, elevated liver enzymes, low platelets; ITP = immune thrombocytopenic purpura; PT = prothrombin time; TTP = thrombotic thrombocytopenic purpura.

antibody directed against the CD20 surface marker on B lymphocytes, will lead to doubling of the platelet count in 40% of patients. Thrombopoiesis-stimulating agents, such as romiplostim or eltrombopag, are also effective in augmenting platelet counts in patients with ITP, but the expense of therapy and need for continued treatment to maintain response need to be considered.

Rarely, patients with significant bleeding unresponsive to immunosuppressive medication require splenectomy. Although platelet counts will improve, perioperative complications and long-term asplenia sequelae (ie, infection with encapsulated bacteria) must be anticipated. Pneumococcal, meningococcal, and *Haemophilus influenzae* vaccines are administered before splenectomy.

Heparin-Induced Thrombocytopenia

Heparin-induced thrombocytopenia is a unique, drug-triggered platelet disorder that develops in 1% to 2% of patients receiving unfractionated heparin. The incidence of HIT is 2 to 3 times lower in patients receiving low-molecular-weight heparin. Other patient-specific variables also influence the incidence of disease. For example, patients undergoing open-heart surgery have a higher incidence of HIT than do patients receiving heparin products for thromboembolism prophylaxis. Most patients develop clinical signs of HIT, including a decrease of approximately 50% in platelet count from baseline levels, 5 to 10 days after initiating heparin therapy. Perhaps 5% of patients will have delayed thrombocytopenia a mean of 14 days after heparin exposure, and those patients may have the first clinical signs of HIT noted after the heparin has been discontinued. Conversely, HIT may be detected as early as 10 hours after heparin administration in patients with prior heparin exposure in the last 1 to 3 months. Thrombocytopenia nadir in HIT is modest; mean platelet counts are approximately 60,000/µL (60 × 10^9/L), and patients typically do not bleed excessively. To the contrary, patients with HIT have a dramatic risk of thromboembolic complications, including deep venous thrombosis and pulmonary embolism, as well as unusual clotting problems such as portal vein thrombosis or acute arterial occlusion.

The early stages of HIT are asymptomatic; all patients receiving heparin should have periodic screening of platelet counts. In patients on heparin who develop thrombocytopenia, laboratory tests will reveal antibodies that cause heparin-induced serotonin release or platelet aggregation, although the clinical circumstances may suggest the diagnosis before confirmatory laboratory data are available.

Heparin must be discontinued and an alternative rapidly acting anticoagulant must be used instead. Warfarin is not a suitable alternative agent. Direct thrombin inhibitors (eg, lepirudin or argatroban) should be administered, often under a hematologist's guidance. Hospitalized patients may have a broad differential to explain thrombocytopenia. A clinical decision tool (4T scoring system) incorporates features of the magnitude of fall and timing of thrombocytopenia, along with the presence or absence of new thromboses or skin necrosis to prioritize the likelihood of HIT. This scoring system may be useful in considering whether heparin should be stopped and a costly and potentially risky anticoagulant alternative, such as argatroban, begun while awaiting more definitive laboratory assays for HIT (Table 3).

Thrombotic Thrombocytopenic Purpura–Hemolytic Uremic Syndrome

Patients with TTP-HUS develop consumptive thrombocytopenia and microangiopathic hemolysis from platelet thrombi that form throughout the microvasculature. The multisystem nature of this syndrome is unpredictable. Fever, acute kidney injury, and fluctuating neurologic abnormalities are components of the syndrome, but all are seldom present during earlier phases of the illness. Patients with little to no kidney involvement and prominent neurologic symptoms fall more into the TTP category, whereas those with acute kidney injury and fewer neurologic manifestations (often seen in children with significant diarrhea) fit better with HUS. Clinical features often overlap, and a precise distinction between TTP and HUS may be difficult to make. Thrombotic thrombocytopenic purpura–hemolytic uremic syndrome is a syndrome with diverse triggers and pathophysiology, including abnormal von Willebrand factor metabolism and very high-molecular-weight polymers that predispose to platelet microthrombi. Most patients with TTP have an autoantibody that inhibits a metalloproteinase (ADAMTS13) that normally cleaves unusually large von Willebrand factor multimers into smaller fragments. Pregnant women, HIV-infected patients, and patients receiving cancer chemotherapy or immunosuppressive agents following organ transplantation are at increased risk. Children develop HUS with prominent gastrointestinal symptoms from Shiga toxin-producing enteric bacteria (eg, *Escherichia coli* O157:H7).

Laboratory findings suggestive of TTP-HUS include microangiopathic hemolysis with prominent schistocytes on peripheral blood smear (Plate 39), decreased haptoglobin, elevated serum lactate dehydrogenase, and thrombocytopenia. Assays for ADAMTS13

Table 3. The "4T Score" for Diagnosis of HIT

Thrombocytopenia

1. Platelet count fall >50% and nadir >20,000/µL (20 × 10^9/L): 2 points
2. Platelet count fall 30% to 50% or nadir 10,000 to 19,000/µL (10-19 × 10^9/L): 1 point
3. Platelet count fall <30% or nadir <10,000/µL (10 × 10^9/L): 0 points

Timing of platelet count fall

Clear onset between days 5 and 10 or platelet count decrease at ≤1 day if prior heparin exposure within the last 30 days: 2 points

Consistent with platelet count decrease at 5 to 10 days but not documented (eg, missing platelet counts) or onset after day 10 or fall ≤ day with prior heparin exposure within the last 30 to 100 days: 1 point

Platelet count fall at <4 days without recent exposure: 0 points

Thrombosis or other sequelae

Confirmed new thrombosis, skin necrosis, or acute systemic reaction after intravenous unfractionated heparin bolus: 2 points

Progressive or recurrent thrombosis, nonnecrotizing (erythematous) skin lesions, or suspected thrombosis that has not been proven: 1 point

No thrombosis or sequelae: 0 points

Other causes for thrombocytopenia present

None apparent: 2 points

Possible: 1 point

Definite: 0 points

Test interpretation

A score is determined for each of the 4 categories, resulting in a total score from 0 to 8. Pretest probabilities for HIT are, as follows:

0 to 3: Low probability

4 to 5: Intermediate probability

6 to 8: High probability

HIT = heparin-induced thrombocytopenia.

activity may help to confirm the diagnosis, but the test is neither uniformly standardized nor easily available, and therapy should not be withheld while awaiting test results. Malignant hypertension, disseminated intravascular coagulation, and prosthetic heart valves can be associated with microangiopathic hemolysis, although the additional presence of thrombocytopenia and fever, kidney, and neurologic findings strongly supports the diagnosis of TTP-HUS.

Most patients with TTP-HUS should receive plasma exchange transfusion, although young patients with features suggesting enteric bacterial toxins as the etiology have a much better prognosis and may be managed supportively. Automated equipment and large-bore, secure intravenous access are needed for plasma exchange; plasma infusion therapy may be initiated in the interim. Glucocorticoids are also recommended. Patients with more severe disease, especially with prominent neurologic manifestations, or those with delayed response to plasma exchange and glucocorticoids, may be treated with alternative immunosuppressive agents (eg, rituximab). Platelet transfusions in patients with untreated TTP-HUS are associated with acute kidney injury, stroke, and sudden death.

Bibliography

George JN. Clinical practice. Thrombotic thrombocytopenic purpura. N Engl J Med. 2006;354:1927-1935. [PMID: 16672704]

Chapter 50

Hematopoietic Stem Cell Disorders

Richard S. Eisenstaedt, MD

Acquired injury to hematopoietic stem cells (HSCs) (Figure 1) may be clinically expressed as a range of disease from aplastic anemia, where the hematopoietic precursor cells fail to proliferate normally, leaving the bone marrow deficient in normal cells and replaced with fat, to acute leukemia, where leukocyte or lymphocyte precursor cells are arrested in the earliest stages of maturation and proliferate in an uncontrolled, neoplastic manner. Other manifestations of HSC injury include the myelodysplastic (or dysmyelopoietic) syndromes and the myeloproliferative neoplastic diseases. The HSC disorders may arise following exposure to ionizing radiation or drugs, such as alkylator agents used in chemotherapy, that cause genetic mutations or, in aplastic anemia, may be part of an autoimmune process. In most cases, a specific etiology cannot be identified.

Aplastic Anemia

Most patients with aplastic anemia have an autoimmune basis for their illness, although the trigger for immune dysregulation is usually inapparent and the precise pathophysiology is unknown. Symptoms usually result from underlying pancytopenia, including fatigue, dyspnea, bleeding, and infection. The peripheral blood will reveal anemia, thrombocytopenia, and leukopenia; blasts or other immature leukocytes, if present, will be small in number. Vitamin B_{12} and folate deficiency, which may lead to pancytopenia, must be excluded. Drug-induced marrow suppression should be considered; potential causative medications should be discontinued or switched to an alternative biochemical class. Bone marrow biopsy will reveal hypocellularity with increased fatty deposits and distinguish aplas-

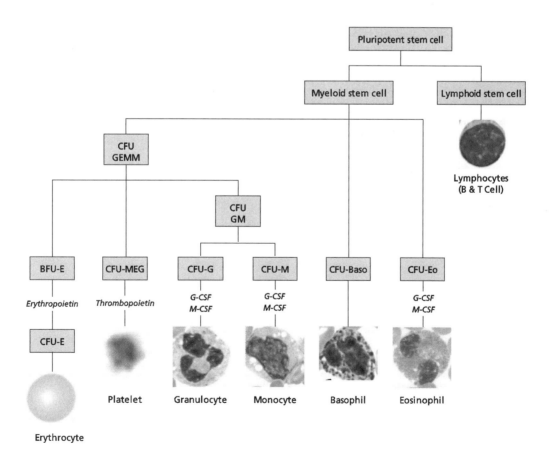

Figure 1. Regulation of hematopoiesis. The process of hematopoiesis is regulated by lineage-specific cytokines. These cytokines stimulate the proliferation and/or differentiation of pluripotent stem cells to committed mature peripheral blood cells. BFU-E = burst-forming unit–erythrocyte; CFU = colony-forming unit; CFU-Baso = CFU-basophil; CFU-E = CFU-erythrocyte; CFU-Eo = CFU-eosinophil; CFU-G = CFU-granulocyte; CFU GEMM = CFU-granulocyte, erythrocyte, megakaryocyte, monocyte; CFU GM = CFU-granulocyte, monocyte; CFU-M = CFU-monocyte; CFU MEG = CFU-megakaryocyte; G-CSF = granulocyte colony-stimulating factor; M-CSF = macrophage colony-stimulating factor.

tic anemia from myelodysplastic syndrome or acute leukemia that may present clinically in a similar fashion.

Allogeneic HSC transplantation (HSCT) is curative in >75% of patients and should be offered to individuals with aplastic anemia who are younger than 40 years, are otherwise healthy, and have an HLA-compatible sibling. Patients who are not eligible for allogeneic HSCT should receive immunosuppressive therapy with antithymocyte globulin and cyclosporine, with long-term survival expected in the majority of patients.

Acute Leukemia

Acute leukemias are clonal proliferations of myeloid or lymphoid cells that fail to differentiate beyond the blast or promyelocyte stage. These immature cells lack the functional capability of mature granulocytes or lymphocytes and replicate aggressively, displacing normal white cell, red cell, and platelet precursors, and cause bone marrow failure as well as infiltration of other organs. Although the clinical presentation of acute lymphoblastic leukemia (ALL) and acute myeloid leukemia (AML) may be similar, they are treated differently.

Acute Myeloid Leukemia

While AML most commonly occurs in patients with no antecedent risk factors, its incidence is increased in patients who are exposed to radiation or benzene or following therapy with chemotherapy, especially alkylating agents. AML also occurs as a result of transformation of a pre-existing myeloproliferative neoplasm (eg, CML, polycythemia vera) or in patients with a known myelodysplastic syndrome.

Patients with AML present with nonspecific symptoms of fatigue, pallor from anemia and bleeding manifestations, including bruising and petechiae, from underlying thrombocytopenia. Inadequate numbers of mature functioning leukocytes lead to infection. Patients have a variable degree of lymphadenopathy and hepatosplenomegaly. Leukemic cells may infiltrate extramedullary sites, such as the gingivae, skin, and meninges. When the leukocyte count is very high, patients may present with leukostasis syndrome, which is presumed to be secondary to leukemic blasts occluding the microcirculation and leading to respiratory failure and cerebral dysfunction.

Diagnosis

The diagnosis of AML is suggested by an elevated leukocyte count, anemia, thrombocytopenia, and blasts on the peripheral blood smear (Plate 40). At times, patients may have an "aleukemic" form of AML with severe leukopenia (often pancytopenia), and a scarcity of circulating immature blast forms. The diagnosis of AML is confirmed by bone marrow aspiration and biopsy showing >20% blasts. Typical myeloblasts demonstrate antigens found on immature cells, such as CD34 (a stem cell marker) and HLA-DR, as well as antigens more specific for granulocytic maturation, such as CD33 and CD13. Cytogenetic studies are crucial, because specific genetic abnormalities are associated with either a favorable or a poor prognosis. The morphology of the bone marrow cells combined with immunophenotype and results of cytogenetic studies are used to classify AML according to the World Health Organization and French-American-British (FAB) classification systems.

Acute promyelocytic leukemia is a special subset of AML characterized by a t(15;17) translocation (which disturbs a retinoic acid receptor) and by proliferation of promyelocytes, with their characteristic primary granules. Patients with acute promyelocytic leukemia have significant bleeding at the time of their presentation due to fibrinolysis and disseminated intravascular coagulation.

Therapy

Patients require immediate hospitalization for placement of durable venous access (Hickman catheter, subcutaneous port), initiation of chemotherapy, irradiated blood and platelet transfusion support, and, if febrile and leukopenic, antibiotics for presumed infection.

The standard chemotherapy induction regimen is 3 days of an anthracycline, such as idarubicin, and 7 days of a continuous infusion of cytarabine. With the initiation of chemotherapy, some patients are at risk for abrupt necrosis of a large mass of leukemia cells and release of their intracellular contents into the circulation causing the tumor lysis syndrome (see Chapter 88). After induction therapy, patients remain pancytopenic for many days, and infectious and bleeding complications are common. Patients with neutropenic fever should receive broad-spectrum antibiotics until the bone marrow recovers, regardless of whether cultures remain negative. Persistent neutropenic fever despite antibiotics warrants empiric antifungal therapy.

Younger patients and patients with favorable cytogenetic abnormalities achieve remission rates of 60% to 70%; remission is defined as normalization of the blood count, <5% bone marrow blasts, and normalization of the karyotype. Most of these patients will remain in remission and achieve 10-year disease-free survival. Older patients with significant comorbidities and high-risk cytogenetic abnormalities have much lower remission rates as well as a higher risk of treatment mortality; these patients may be better treated palliatively rather than with induction chemotherapy. In addition to advanced age, poor performance status, and certain cytogenetic abnormalities, AML that is related to prior cancer chemotherapy or a preexisting myeloproliferative neoplasm or dysmyelopoietic syndrome has a poor prognosis. Once remission is achieved, consolidation chemotherapy is given and patients with high-risk disease may be referred for allogeneic BMT.

Treatment for acute promyelocytic leukemia is initiated with all-trans-retinoic acid, which induces maturation of the promyelocyte and ameliorates disseminated intravascular coagulation.

Follow-Up

Patients with AML who relapse tend to do so within 18 to 24 months of achieving complete remission. Patients are seen monthly during the first 2 years after remission to perform an interim history, physical examination, and blood count; bone marrow aspiration is performed only if there are abnormalities in the CBC. Patients who have undergone allogeneic BMT should be monitored for posttransplantation complications, including opportunistic infections and graft-versus-host disease, usually at specialized treatment centers.

Acute Lymphoblastic Leukemia

ALL is a malignancy of B or T lymphoblasts and is more common in children although it may occur in adults, predominantly in the seventh decade of life. Patients frequently present with circulating lymphoblasts and progressive marrow failure with fatigue, dyspnea, bleeding, and infection-related fever. Lymphadenopathy and hepatosplenomegaly are common, and central nervous system involvement may occur. Severe cytopenias and metabolic derangements related to tumor lysis syndrome are common.

Diagnosis

Diagnosis requires the presence of 20% or more lymphoblasts on bone marrow examination. Cytochemical stains and flow cytometry can help distinguish ALL from AML and B-cell from T-cell ALL. Cerebrospinal fluid examination for evidence of central nervous system involvement is an essential part of the initial diagnostic evaluation.

Therapy

In adults, cure rates for ALL approach 30% to 40% with standard chemotherapy. Induction therapy commonly consists of an anthracycline, vincristine, L-asparaginase, and a glucocorticoid. Given the risk for central nervous system involvement in ALL, intrathecal chemoprophylaxis is routinely administered with or without cranial irradiation. Tumor lysis syndrome is common at diagnosis or shortly after institution of chemotherapy; consequently, all patients should receive intravenous fluid hydration and allopurinol.

Follow-Up

Patients who achieve complete remission receive further intensive chemotherapy with multiple chemotherapeutic agents for several months followed by 2 to 3 years of maintenance chemotherapy. Patients with high-risk disease who are otherwise healthy and have a suitable donor are considered for allogeneic hematopoietic stem cell transplantation in first remission.

Myeloproliferative Neoplasms

There are 4 myeloproliferative neoplasms (previously termed myeloproliferative disorders): polycythemia rubra vera (PRV) CML, essential thrombocythemia (ET), and myelofibrosis with myeloid metaplasia (MMM). While each has distinct clinical features, they have in common the excess production of one or more mature blood cell lines that occurs independent of any physiological stimulus. Each of these disorders has some likelihood of evolving into an acute leukemia, although that complication ranges from rare in young adults with ET to virtually all patients with CML.

Polycythemia Rubra Vera

Diagnosis

Patients with PRV often present with vague, nonspecific symptoms such as headache or malaise. Pruritus is a less common symptom that, unlike the pruritus associated with skin or liver disease, tends to worsen following a warm bath–a phenomenon attributed to release of histamine from an expanded pool of basophils. Patients may also note a burning pain in the hands or feet, termed erythromelalgia. Thromboembolic events or stroke are also known complications of the disease. Not uncommonly, asymptomatic patients are diagnosed from an abnormal CBC.

Physical examination may reveal plethora and hepatosplenomegaly. Erythrocytosis is the hallmark of PRV and is often accompanied by leukocytosis and thrombocytosis. The leukocyte differential includes increased numbers of bands and myelocytes, as well as increased eosinophils and basophils. These patients lack other conditions, such as severe hypoxic lung disease or cyanotic heart disease, that lead to a compensatory secondary erythrocytosis. The erythropoietin level will be low, although that test is not typically necessary to make the diagnosis. Measurement of the red blood cell mass was traditionally advised, but many laboratories no longer perform this test routinely and it is not necessary in patients with

erythrocytosis and a hemoglobin level of >16.5 g/dL (165 g/L). Virtually all patients with PRV have a mutation in the Janus kinase 2 (*JAK2*) gene, a tyrosine kinase involved in regulating proliferation. Examination of the bone marrow will reveal hypercellularity and a modest shift toward less mature blood cell precursors, but is rarely needed to establish the diagnosis.

Therapy

Patients with PRV are at significant risk for stroke, myocardial infarction, and other thromboembolic disease. Therapeutic phlebotomy is the mainstay of treatment, performed weekly when the diagnosis is first established, and less often, subsequently, to reduce the hemoglobin to <15 g/dL (150 g/L). Patients who are aged >60 years or who have had prior thromboembolic events remain at high risk for morbidity despite phlebotomy and should receive a myelosuppressive agent, such as hydroxyurea. Low-dose aspirin treatment has been controversial because these patients also have an increased risk of bleeding from qualitative platelet defects. Other interventions for stroke prevention independent of the polycythemia should be employed, such as blood pressure control, tobacco cessation, and management of hyperlipidemia.

Follow-Up

Patients with PRV receiving appropriate therapy have a median survival of >10 years. The frequency of follow-up visits is determined by how often they need phlebotomy to maintain a normal hemoglobin level and whether or not they require additional myelosuppressive drug therapy. While patients have a small risk of PRV evolving into an acute leukemia, there is no specific screening recommended.

Chronic Myeloid Leukemia

Diagnosis

Chronic myeloid leukemia is a clonal proliferation of mature granulocytes associated with a translocation between chromosomes 9 and 22, t(9;22)(q34;q11), which results in a truncated chromosome 22 (the Philadelphia chromosome). This reciprocal translocation results in the *BCR-ABL* fusion gene and the production of a unique tyrosine kinase protein. Although patients usually present in the chronic phase of disease and may do well for years, CML, if untreated, will invariably transform into acute leukemia (myeloid in two-thirds of patients, lymphoid in one-third). The transformation may be preceded by an "accelerated phase" of disease characterized by progressive leukocytosis and splenomegaly, extreme thrombocytosis or thrombocytopenia, and systemic symptoms, all of which are resistant to treatment. Patients with CML present with fatigue, lethargy, low-grade fever, and weight loss. Splenomegaly may be striking and may be associated with early satiety, abdominal distention, or left upper-quadrant pain. Physical examination may reveal pallor and splenomegaly, but lymphadenopathy is not common in the chronic phase.

Chronic myeloid leukemia is recognized by an elevated blood leukocyte count and increased number of granulocytic cells in all phases of development on the peripheral blood smear (Plate 41). The magnitude of the leukocytosis varies from 15,000/µL (15×10^9/L) to 50,000/µL (50×10^9/L), but is still within the range that could be triggered by an infectious process (termed a *leukemoid reaction*). In some patients, the leukocyte count will be >100,000/µL (100×10^9/L), which is more pathognomonic of a myeloproliferative neoplasm. Very immature cells, such as myeloblasts and promyelocytes, may be seen in small numbers in the peripheral blood smear, but myelocytes and metamyelocytes are more predictably found. Basophils and eosinophils are increased, as they are in other myeloproliferative neoplasms. The platelet count is often elevated, and striking thrombocytosis (>1,000,000/µL [1000×10^9/L]) may be seen. Patients often have anemia. The bone marrow aspirate tends to mirror findings in the peripheral blood, with marked expansion of myeloid cells and a shift toward less mature forms. When blasts represent >10% of leukocytes, the accelerated or blast phase should be considered. Increased megakaryocytes are seen, and increased collagen and reticulin fibrosis will be noted on bone marrow biopsy.

The diagnosis is confirmed by cytogenetic studies of the bone marrow aspirate showing a t(9:22) chromosomal abnormality or the presence of the novel *BCR-ABL* gene produced by the translocation. The *BCR-ABL* gene is detected and quantitated by polymerase chain reaction (PCR). Patients with abdominal pain or discomfort should undergo abdominal ultrasonography or computed tomography to identify splenomegaly or splenic infarction.

Therapy

The treatment of CML was revolutionized by the development of therapy targeting the novel tyrosine kinase produced by the *BCR-ABL* gene. Inhibition of this kinase by imatinib reduces the leukocyte count, shrinks the spleen, and clears the bone marrow of Philadelphia chromosome–positive cells. Imatinib treatment often achieves molecular remissions in which no *BCR-ABL* transcripts can be identified in the blood or bone marrow. Imatinib must be given indefinitely; BCR-ABL-positive cells will appear 3 to 4 months after discontinuation of therapy. Dasatinib and nilotinib are newer options that may work more rapidly and cause more noticeable inhibition of tyrosine kinase. These newer agents may be used to initiate therapy or to treat patients who become resistant to imatinib.

Allogeneic BMT was the preferred treatment option for patients with CML before the discovery of tyrosine kinase inhibitors. Allogeneic BMT remains the most definitive option to cure the disease, albeit at the cost of significantly greater treatment toxicity (including mortality) and subsequent complications from graft-versus-host disease. There are no randomized trials to compare BMT to tyrosine kinase inhibitors, and most experts recommend beginning therapy with a tyrosine kinase inhibitor. Allogeneic BMT might be used as initial therapy in very young patients with CML but is more typically used in patients showing signs of resistance to tyrosine kinase inhibitors. Once the disease has transformed into an accelerated phase or acute leukemia, the prognosis is poor, regardless of the treatment option.

Patients may require transfusion occasionally to treat anemia and rarely for thrombocytopenia. Massive splenomegaly with splenic infarction may require splenectomy for patient comfort.

Follow-Up

Patients are typically seen every 1 to 2 weeks during the initiation of treatment with imatinib. Once stable blood counts are achieved, patients are followed every month to monitor blood counts. Peripheral blood or bone marrow samples are obtained periodically to assess the efficacy of treatment; the best results are associated with a 4-fold reduction of *BCR-ABL* transcripts determined by quantitative PCR. Increasing leukocyte counts, basophilia, fever, and an enlarging spleen are signs of accelerated phase and blast crisis.

Essential Thrombocythemia

Diagnosis

Essential thrombocytopenia is another myeloproliferative neoplasm, the hallmark of which is thrombocytosis that cannot be explained by clinical conditions known to cause a reactive elevation in platelet count, such as iron deficiency, chronic bleeding, infection, cancer, or autoimmune inflammatory disease. Most patients are asymptomatic, with the diagnosis made by finding unexpected thrombocytosis on a blood count; however, some patients may present with headache and erythromelalgia, similarly to those with PRV. At times, the patient may present with a thromboembolic event or acute bleeding, which are known complications of the disease. The diagnosis is made by finding persistent platelet counts >600,000/µL (600 x 10^9/L), with no other condition present leading to reactive thrombocytosis. Occasionally, the platelet count is so high (>1,000,000/µL [1000 × 10^9/L]) as to exclude secondary thrombocytosis. Since thrombocytosis may also be seen in CML and PRV, and since approximately one-half of patients with ET have the *JAK2* mutation, the diagnosis further requires that the Philadelphia chromosome be negative and that the patient not have concomitant erythrocytosis.

Treatment

Patients with ET are at significant risk for both bleeding and thromboembolic complications. However, individuals who are aged <60 years, have no prior thromboembolic event, and whose platelet count is <1,000,000/µL (1000 × 10^9/L) have an excellent prognosis and should be followed without therapy. Those who are not in the low-risk category should be treated with the myelosuppressive agent hydroxyurea, as well as low-dose aspirin.

Myelofibrosis With Myeloid Metaplasia

Diagnosis

Myelofibrosis with myeloid metaplasia, the least common of the myeloproliferative neoplasms, results from excessive proliferation of dysplastic megakaryocytes that may or may not produce thrombocytosis but invariably secrete factors that stimulate collagen production that leads to bone marrow fibrosis. Consequently, extramedullary hematopoiesis occurs in the liver and spleen and, more rarely, in other unusual sites. Patients typically present with symptoms from anemia and may have prominent systemic features, such as fever, night sweats, anorexia, and weight loss. Splenomegaly may be massive and cause abdominal pain and compressive symptoms, such as early satiety. Physical examination reveals pallor, hepatomegaly, and dramatic splenomegaly that may extend to the pelvic brim. Patients are anemic, but while pancytopenia is not uncommon, the white blood cell and platelet counts may also be elevated. The peripheral smear reveals a typical, so-called myelophthisic or leukoerythroblastic picture with immature leukocytes, nucleated erythrocytes, and teardrop-shaped erythrocytes (Plate 42). The bone marrow is difficult to aspirate in these patients, leading to a "dry tap," but the diagnosis is established from bone marrow biopsy that shows increased collagen and reticulin fibrosis, increased numbers of dysplastic-appearing megakaryocytes, and osteosclerosis. Other conditions that cause secondary bone marrow fibrosis, such as metastatic cancer or miliary tuberculosis, need to be excluded. The *JAK2* mutation is found in 50% of patients.

Treatment

As there is no definitive therapy for MMM, symptom palliation is the goal of treatment. The attenuated anabolic steroid danazol has been used to treat anemia, although transfusions are often required. Myelosuppressive drugs, such as hydroxyurea, are used to control splenomegaly. Splenic radiation or splenectomy may be required to relieve symptoms arising from massive spleen enlargement. Complications usually arise from progressive pancytopenia.

Myelodysplastic Syndromes

Diagnosis

The myelodysplastic syndromes are invariably manifest by anemia (often macrocytic) that cannot be explained by vitamin B_{12} or folate deficiency, but instead arise from a stem cell defect that leads to ineffective erythropoiesis. The anemia may range from mild to severe and may be accompanied by leukopenia and thrombocytopenia. Patients are diagnosed while asymptomatic when otherwise unexplained macrocytic anemia is found on a routine CBC, or they may have symptoms of more severe anemia as well as bleeding and/or infection from pancytopenia. Examination of the bone marrow will establish the diagnosis and reveals dysplastic cell maturation, increased numbers of immature white blood cell precursors, and characteristic cytogenetic abnormalities. The myelodysplastic syndromes occur most often in the elderly, who may have other comorbidities that decrease their tolerance for pancytopenia. The myelodysplastic syndromes all have some propensity for evolving into an acute leukemia, although the likelihood and the rapidity of such transformation vary and can be predicted by whether the patient presents with anemia versus more severe pancytopenia, as well as the percentage of immature blasts in the bone marrow. The World Health Organization classification of the myelodysplastic syndromes reflects those prognostic features (Table 1).

Therapy

No treatment is needed for patients with mild and asymptomatic anemia. Patients with more severe anemia associated with fatigue and exercise intolerance may require chronic transfusion support, and a small percentage will respond to erythrocyte-stimulating agents. Similarly, symptomatic bleeding from thrombocytopenia requires platelet transfusion support, and patients who develop infections related to underlying granulocytopenia will need antibiotics. Chemotherapy with agents such as the pyrimidine nucleoside analogue azacitidine will prolong survival and delay the time of

Table 1. World Health Organization Classification of MDS

Category	Features	Median Overall Survival (Months)
Refractory cytopenias with unilineage dysplasia	Unilineage (ie, single cell line) dysplasia, <5% marrow blasts	69
Refractory anemia with ringed sideroblasts	Erythroid dysplasia, ≥ 15% ringed sideroblasts, <5% marrow blasts	69
MDS associated with isolated 5q deletion	<5% marrow blasts, increased megakaryocytes with hypolobated nuclei	116
Refractory cytopenia with multilineage dysplasia	<5% marrow blasts, dysplasia in ≥2 lineages, +/- ringed sideroblasts	33
Refractory anemia with excess blasts-1	5% to 9% marrow blasts, 5 unilineage or multilineage dysplasia, no Auer rods	18
Refractory anemia with excess blasts-2	10% to 19% blasts, unilineage or multilineage dysplasia	10
MDS, unclassified	<5% marrow blasts, does not fit other categories	Currently not known

MDS, myelodysplastic syndrome.

transformation to leukemia and should be used in patients with poor prognosis, symptomatic myelodysplastic syndrome. Allogeneic HSCT is potentially curative but is associated with considerable treatment toxicity and not often advised in elderly patients, who are the typical patient population with myelodysplastic syndromes.

Bibliography

Betz BL, Hess JL. Acute myeloid leukemia diagnosis in the 21st century. Arch Pathol Lab Med. 2010;134:1427-1433. [PMID: 20923295]

Goldman JM. Chronic myeloid leukemia: a historical perspective. Semin Hematol. 2010;47:302-311. [PMID: 20875546]

Gribben JG, O'Brien S. Update on therapy of chronic lymphocytic leukemia. J Clin Oncol. 2011;29:544-550. [PMID: 21220603]

Testa U. Leukemia stem cells. Ann Hematol. 2011;90:245-271. [PMID: 21107841]

Chapter 51

Multiple Myeloma

Richard S. Eisenstaedt, MD

Multiple myeloma (MM) is a malignant clonal proliferation of plasma cells. Most cases are believed to arise from an asymptomatic premalignant proliferation of monoclonal plasma cells in a condition referred to as *monoclonal gammopathy of unknown significance* (MGUS). Although most cases of MGUS remain stable for many years, approximately 1% to 2% per year transform into MM. Several chromosomal abnormalities have been implicated in the pathogenesis of MM, including translocation at a chromosome region involved in immunoglobulin synthesis, oncogene activation, and inactivation of kinase inhibitors. The net result of these abnormalities is a malignant expansion of a plasma cell clone that secretes a specific immunoglobulin (most often an intact IgG, less often IgA or IgM). In approximately 20% of cases, the malignant plasma cells secrete a monoclonal light chain (kappa or lambda). These monoclonal proteins, whether in the form of intact immunoglobulins or light chains, are termed *M proteins*. Multiple myeloma accounts for approximately 1% of cancer cases and typically occurs in the seventh decade of life. New chemotherapy options and the use of autologous stem cell transplantation have improved the outlook for what was a uniformly fatal disease. Today, approximately one-third of patients aged <60 years achieve a 10-year survival, although a lasting cure of the disease remains unusual.

In MM, the uncontrolled clonal proliferation of plasma cells leads to bone marrow failure, initially manifesting as a normocytic anemia and progressing to other cytopenias. The clonal expansion also results in inadequate numbers of normal plasma cells, with subsequent hypogammaglobulinemia predisposing to infection with encapsulated bacteria (eg, *Streptococcus pneumoniae*). Neoplastic proliferation within the marrow is also associated with osteoclast activation, resulting in hypercalcemia and bone damage that produces pain and increases the risk of compression fracture of the spine and pathologic fracture of weight-bearing bones. Some patients develop plasma cell tumors (plasmacytomas), which may arise adjacent to or directly from bony structures or in extramedullary sites. Clinical features vary with location, but plasmacytomas arising from the vertebrae increase the risk of spinal cord compression. The M protein, when filtered through the glomerulus, can cause renal tubular injury; large M proteins (eg, IgM or multimers of IgA) may also cause symptoms related to hyperviscosity. Symptoms of hyperviscosity include bleeding (hyperviscosity interferes with normal coagulation factor activation and platelet function), decreased vision and other neurologic symptoms, dyspnea, and heart failure.

The amyloidoses are a group of diseases that share a common feature of extracellular deposition of pathologic, insoluble fibrils in

Table 1. Differential Diagnosis of MM

Disorder	Notes
Monoclonal gammopathy of undetermined significance	M protein <30 g/dL; bone marrow plasma cells <10%; asymptomatic, normal hemoglobin, serum calcium, serum creatinine, and bone survey. May evolve to MM, but no therapy reduces the likelihood of malignant transformation
Polyclonal hypergammaglobulinemia	A nonclonal increase in serum immunoglobulins. No increased risk of evolving into MM. Associated with liver disease, connective tissue disease, chronic infections (eg, HIV), lymphoproliferative disorders, and nonhematologic malignancies
Plasma cell leukemia	Circulating plasma cells seen on peripheral blood smear. Worse prognosis than typical MM
POEMS syndrome	Rare variant of MM consisting of **P**eripheral neuropathy, **O**rganomegaly, **E**ndocrinopathy, **M**onoclonal plasma cell proliferative disorder, **S**kin changes, sclerotic bone lesions, papilledema, fingernail clubbing, edema, effusions, and, possibly, Castleman disease.[a] Not all features required for diagnosis; minimum of peripheral neuropathy, plasma cell dyscrasia, and either sclerotic bone lesion or Castleman disease. Better overall prognosis than MM
Primary systemic amyloidosis (AL amyloidosis)	A clonal plasma cell proliferative disorder in which fibrils of monoclonal light chains are deposited in the kidney and other tissues (liver, heart, peripheral nervous system), causing nephrotic syndrome, cardiomyopathy, orthostatic hypotension, cholestatic liver disease, peripheral neuropathy, macroglossia, and carpal tunnel syndrome. Most patients have small serum M proteins and approximately 5% bone marrow plasma cells; 6% to 15% of patients with AL amyloidosis have coexisting MM
Waldenström macroglobulinemia	An IgM monoclonal gammopathy characterized by anemia, hyperviscosity, lymphadenopathy, and bone marrow plasmacyte infiltration. More responsive to purine nucleoside analogues and anti-CD20 immunotherapy
Plasmacytoma	A localized collection of plasmacytes that may occur as a single lytic lesion in bone or extramedullary (upper respiratory tract, especially sinuses, nasopharynx, or larynx) sites. Patients may or may not have M protein in the serum or urine. No increase in bone marrow plasma cells, anemia, hypercalcemia, or renal insufficiency. Treated with local therapy (excision, radiation). Patients have increased risk for developing MM

MM = multiple myeloma.

[a] A lymphoproliferative disorder association with HIV and human herpesvirus 8.

various tissues and organs. Within this group of disorders, AL amyloidosis is the most common systemic amyloidosis associated with an underlying clonal plasma cell dyscrasia. The plasma cell burden in this disorder is usually low, at 5% to 10%, although AL amyloidosis is associated with overt MM in 10% to 15% of cases. Clinical manifestations are variable but most commonly include nephrotic syndrome, cardiomyopathy, hepatosplenomegaly, gastrointestinal dysmotility, orthostatic hypotension, and peripheral neuropathy. Table 1 summarizes the differential diagnosis of MM.

Diagnosis

Multiple myeloma should be suspected in patients with anemia, bone pain, osteopenia or osteoporosis, pathologic fracture, lytic bone lesions, hypercalcemia, recurrent infections (particularly pneumococcal infections), or kidney failure. Asymptomatic disease may be found in patients who have elevated total serum protein levels on routine laboratory screening, with subsequent electrophoresis revealing an M protein. Rarely, the uniform cationic electrical charge of M proteins may create a seemingly narrow anion gap on the basic metabolic panel. The large numbers of M proteins also alter blood rheology and lead to erythrocytes sticking to one another (rouleaux formation on peripheral blood smear).

Evaluation of MM (Table 2) begins with serum protein electrophoresis and urine protein electrophoresis on a 24-hour urine sample. Up to 20% of patients with MM secrete lambda or kappa light chains rather than an intact immunoglobulin. The smaller molecular weight of the light chains allows them to be filtered by the glomerulus and excreted in the urine. Thus, electrophoresis of the serum will not reveal an M protein, although it may reveal hypogammaglobulinemia. An M protein in either urine or serum would be further characterized by immunoelectrophoresis. Light chains in the urine (Bence-Jones proteins) are not detected in a routine urinalysis, emphasizing the need for urine protein electrophoresis and subsequent immunoelectrophoresis in patients in whom MM is suspected. Additional studies include a complete blood count (CBC), a radiographic bone survey (Figure 1), and serum creatinine, blood urea nitrogen, and serum calcium levels. Normochromic anemia is the most common CBC abnormality, whereas patients with more advanced disease may also have leukopenia and thrombocytopenia. Multiple myeloma may be associated with kidney disease ("myeloma kidney") caused by several mechanisms, most commonly the direct renal tubular toxicity of light chains. Associated hypercalcemia may cause acute kidney injury, and amyloidosis is often associated with nephrotic syndrome and azotemia. Although diffuse lytic bone lesions are more specific for MM, osteopenia is a more common finding. Bone scans are not obtained, because the myeloma lesions are usually lytic and lack the associated increase in osteoblast activity that leads to positive bone scans typical of other forms of metastatic cancer. A bone marrow aspirate and biopsy are performed to document the presence of increased plasma cells. Although excessive in number, plasma cells are normal in individual appearance in most patients; however, in some patients, binucleate or other frankly dysplastic plasma cell morphologies may assist in the diagnosis. Quantitative immunoglobulin measurement will show depressed amounts of nonmonoclonal immunoglobulins, aiding in the diagnosis and providing clinically relevant information (ie, depressed levels of normal immunoglobulins predisposes the patient to recurrent infection). Significant elevations in serum lactate dehydroge-

Table 2. Laboratory and Other Studies for Diagnosis of MM

Test	Notes
Complete blood count	Anemia is present in about 60% of patients at diagnosis and eventually develops in all patients. Thrombocytopenia and leukopenia are possible
Peripheral blood smear	Rouleaux formation, due to increased serum proteins
Serum calcium (see Chapter 68)	Hypercalcemia is initially seen in 15% to 20% of patients, due to cytokine-mediated destruction of bone
Serum creatinine	At diagnosis, 20% of patients have serum creatinine levels >2 mg/dL (176.8 μmol/L). Causes include hypercalcemia, "myeloma kidney," dehydration, and hyperuricemia
Serum protein electrophoresis	Characteristic M protein is seen in approximately 80% of patients; presence or absence does not guarantee or exclude the diagnosis. Note whether there is a spike or a diffuse increase in M protein levels. A spike in γ-globulin is more consistent with an M protein; a diffuse increase correlates with a polyclonal gammopathy. A polyclonal gammopathy almost never relates to MM
Immunofixation of serum	At diagnosis, 93% of patients have an M protein in the serum by immunofixation
Quantitative immunoglobulin measurement (IgA, IgG, IgM)	Confirms monoclonal gammopathy; >90% of patients also have suppression of at least one uninvolved immunoglobulin at diagnosis
β_2-Microglobulin	Important for prognosis; measures tumor burden
24-Hour urine protein electrophoresis with immunofixation	75% of patients have M protein in their urine by immunofixation. Because approximately 20% of patients have light chain only, the free monoclonal light chain may be missed in the serum in these patients; this test is essential, especially in this subgroup of patients
Radiographic bone survey	75% of patients have punched-out lytic lesions, osteoporosis, or fractures on conventional radiography. Because myelomatous bone lesions are lytic, conventional radiography is superior to technetium-99m bone scanning.
Bone marrow aspirate and biopsy	Essential but not sufficient for the diagnosis of MM. Plasma cells account for ≥10% of bone marrow cells
Bone marrow plasma cell labeling index	Specifically measures plasma cell proliferation. Prognostic for survival
Cytogenetic and FISH studies	Obtained at diagnosis. Certain chromosomal abnormalities (eg, deletion of the long arm of chromosome 13) are associated with shorter disease-free and overall survival

FISH = fluorescence in situ hybridization; MM = multiple myeloma.

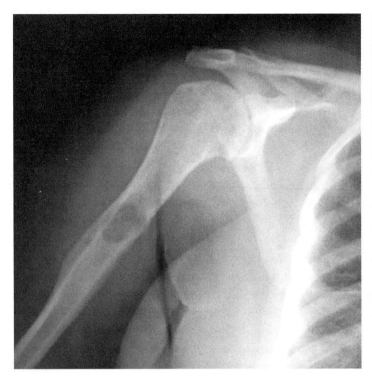 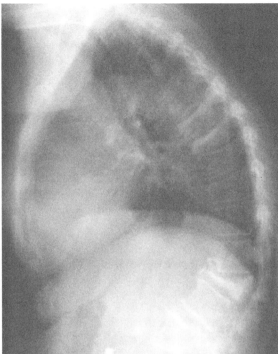

Figure 1. Lytic lesion of the right humerus (*left*) and osteoporosis and compression fracture of the thoracic spine (*right*) in a patient with multiple myeloma.

nase and β_2-microglobulin suggest a high myeloma tumor burden and are used to determine prognosis and guide therapy.

Patients found to have M proteins are stratified into 3 categories: MGUS (a premalignant condition that may remain stable for decades), MM, and an in-between condition termed *smoldering myeloma*. Patients with MGUS are asymptomatic. They have smaller amounts of M protein and normal amounts of the other immunoglobulins. Examination of the bone marrow reveals <10% plasma cells. These patients do not have signs of bone marrow failure, skeletal abnormalities, hypercalcemia, or kidney injury. Conversely, patients with MM have larger quantities of M protein associated with hypogammaglobulinemia. Most have anemia and/or bone pain or other radiographic signs of bone involvement. Hypercalcemia and kidney disease may be noted, and the bone marrow will show a higher percentage of plasma cells. Patients with smoldering myeloma have increased numbers of plasma cells in the bone marrow and a correspondingly larger amount of M protein, but they are otherwise asymptomatic. The differentiation of MM from MGUS is summarized in Table 3.

Therapy

Multiple myeloma is a heterogeneous illness, ranging from smoldering or asymptomatic myeloma, which requires no therapy, to rapidly progressive disease. The first goal is to determine whether therapy is needed. Patients with MGUS should not be treated, and patients with myeloma who lack any end-organ damage and who are asymptomatic should not be treated. The likelihood of MGUS or asymptomatic myeloma progressing to symptomatic disease can be predicted by the amount of monoclonal immunoglobulin and the percentage of plasma cells in the bone marrow (Table 4). Patients with myeloma that is causing symptoms and end-organ dysfunction require treatment, ideally involving autologous human stem cell transplantation.

Markers of poor prognosis include various cytogenetic abnormalities, such as deletion of chromosome 13 and certain chromosome translocations. Other high-risk markers include acute kidney injury, hypercalcemia, severe anemia, elevated β_2-microglobulin, hypoalbuminemia, and >50% plasma cells on bone marrow aspirate. A simple staging system considers patients with low serum β_2-microglobulin and normal serum albumin to be a good prognosis (Stage 1), those with β_2-microglobulin >5.5 mg/L poor prognosis (Stage III), and all others not Stage I or III to be intermediate in their prognosis.

Table 3. Diagnosis of MM[a] and MGUS

MM Major Criteria

1. Plasmacytoma on tissue biopsy
2. Bone marrow clonal plasma cells >30%
3. High M protein (IgG >3.5 g/dL [35 g/L], IgA >2.0 g/dL [20 g/L]) or Bence-Jones proteinuria >1.0 g/24 h

MM Minor Criteria

A. Bone marrow clonal plasma cells: 10%-30%
B. IgG <3.5 g/dL (35 g/L), IgA <2.0 g/dL (20 g/L)
C. Lytic bone lesions
D. Diminished levels of nonmonoclonal immunoglobulins (IgM <50 mg/dL [0.5 g/L], IgA <100 mg/dL [1 g/L], or IgG <600 mg/dL [6 g/L])

MGUS Criteria

• IgG <3.5 g/dL (35 g/L), IgA <2.0 g/dL (20 g/L)
• Bence-Jones proteinuria <1.0 g/24 h
• Bone marrow clonal plasma cells <10%
• No end-organ damage (no symptoms, bone lesions, or anemia; normal kidney function)

MGUS = monoclonal gammopathy of undetermined significance; MM = multiple myeloma.

[a]Diagnosis of MM is based on the presence of at least 1 major criterion + 1 minor criterion *or* the presence of at least 3 minor criteria that include A and B.

Table 4. Risk of Progression to Clinically Symptomatic Plasma Cell Dyscrasia

Diagnosis	Risk Factors	Progression[a]
MGUS	M protein ≥1.5 g/dL (15 g/L)	3 RFs: 58%
	Non-IgG M protein	2 RFs: 37%
	Abnormal serum FLC ratio[b]	1 RF: 21%
		0 RFs: 5%
Asymptomatic myeloma	M protein ≥3 g/dL (30 g/L)	M protein ≥3 g/dL (30 g/L) PCs ≥10%: 87%
	Bone marrow PCs ≥10%	M protein <3 g/dL, (30 g/L) PCs ≥10%: 70%
		M protein ≥3 g/dL, (30 g/L) PCs <10%: 39%

FLC = free light-chain ratio; MGUS = monoclonal gammopathy of undetermined significance; PCs = plasma cells; RFs = risk factors.

[a]Risk of progression at 20 years for MGUS, at 15 years for asymptomatic myeloma.

[b]The serum free light chain (FLC) test is an antibody-based assay that measures free kappa and lambda light chain antibodies not complexed to heavy chains; an increased about of kappa or lambda FLCs leads to an abnormal ratio of kappa to lambda FLCs, with an abnormal ratio associated with an increased risk of progression.

Patients aged <75 years with good performance status are candidates for autologous stem cell transplantation, which is now considered the best therapy for symptomatic MM. Contraindications to autologous stem cell transplantation beyond advanced age and poor performance status include unstable and progressive kidney disease, decompensated cirrhosis, and New York Heart Association class III or IV heart failure. Patients who are eligible for transplantation are treated with an induction chemotherapy regimen for 2 to 4 months to reduce the tumor burden and to demonstrate responsiveness to chemotherapy. In general, agents such as melphalan, which will be used during the transplantation, should be avoided during induction treatment. Initial treatment typically includes high-dose dexamethasone and thalidomide. Lenalidomide (which is related to thalidomide in its antineoplastic action) and bortezomib (a proteasome inhibitor) are newer agents used at some centers for induction therapy. Thalidomide and lenalidomide are potent teratogens and must be used cautiously in women of childbearing age, although most female patients are postmenopausal. Patients receiving either thalidomide or lenalidomide with dexamethasone as combination therapy have a very high risk for venous thromboembolism and require thromboprophylaxis with aspirin, low-molecular-weight heparin, or warfarin. The response to treatment is determined by monitoring serum protein electrophoresis and/or urine protein electrophoresis; the amount of immunoglobulin should decrease significantly after 3 to 4 months of treatment. If a response is achieved, the patient is referred for autologous stem cell transplantation. Patients who are not candidates for transplantation are treated with chemotherapy regimens similar to those used for induction therapy. Melphalan may also be used.

Beyond specific chemotherapy and stem cell transplantation, a number of interventions can prevent complications of MM. Although the immune response may be blunted, pneumococcal vaccine and annual influenza vaccine should be given to all patients. Trimethoprim-sulfamethoxazole should be administered to prevent *Pneumocystis* pneumonia in all patients receiving prolonged glucocorticoids, and acyclovir prophylaxis is recommended for patients receiving bortezomib to prevent varicella zoster virus reactivation. Bisphosphonates (pamidronate or zoledronate) should be given prophylactically to all patients, as such treatment has been proven to decrease subsequent bone fractures and bone pain. Bisphosphonates should also be used to treat hypercalcemia. Bisphosphonate therapy is limited to 2 years.

Radiation therapy can provide effective palliation of localized bone pain. Patients with MM and back pain need prompt radiographic evaluation, often with magnetic resonance imaging, to rule out spinal cord compression. The evaluation should be done even if there is no motor or sensory deficit or other neurologic manifestation of cord compression. Paralysis, sensory loss, or incontinence would be more worrisome, and once patients develop neurologic deficits, emergent management with glucocorticoids (typically dexamethasone), radiation therapy, or neurosurgery leads to neurologic recovery in only 50% of patients. Radiation therapy or surgery should be considered to treat impending long bone fracture unresponsive to chemotherapy.

Hydration should be maintained and nephrotoxic drugs and contrast dyes should be avoided in patients with MM to prevent acute kidney injury. Mild hypercalcemia may resolve with hydration alone, and early acute kidney injury may improve with hydration and treatment of hypercalcemia. Patients with severe kidney injury may require dialysis. Erythropoietic-stimulating agents will improve symptomatic anemia. Plasmapheresis should be initiated for symptomatic hyperviscosity.

Follow-Up

Patients with MGUS have a transformation rate to MM that is proportional to the size of the M protein peak in their serum or urine. For example, patients with IgG levels <1.5 g/dL (15 g/L) have a low risk of transformation than those with higher levels. Thus, patients with MGUS and low paraprotein concentrations are checked once a year, and those with larger concentrations are checked more often. Patients with MM are followed on a monthly basis to determine their response to therapy and to assess kidney function, blood cell counts, and calcium levels.

Bibliography

Palumbo A, Anderson K. Multiple myeloma. N Engl J Med. 2011;364:1046-1060. [PMID: 21410373]

Chapter 52

Bleeding Disorders

Joel Appel, DO

Bleeding disorders are characterized by defects in primary and secondary hemostasis. Primary hemostasis involves the formation of a platelet plug at the site of vascular disruption, a process that begins with adhesion of platelets to the exposed subendothelial matrix. Adhesion is mediated through interactions of specific platelet receptors, such as the collagen receptor and the glycoprotein Ib-IX-V complex, which binds von Willebrand factor (vWF) with the subepithelial matrix. Adhesion induces platelet activation, with attendant change in platelet shape, secretion of alpha granules and dense bodies, and exposure of fibrinogen receptors that mediate platelet aggregation through binding of the dimeric fib-

rinogen molecule to adjacent platelets. Platelet activation also leads to rearrangement of membrane phospholipid, with increased expression of anionic phospholipid on the platelet surface; anionic phospholipid provides a surface that supports secondary hemostasis. Secondary hemostasis is initiated by the exposure of tissue factor at the site of vascular damage; tissue factor binds activated factor VII and activates factor X and factor IX. Activated factor IX, in turn, activates additional factor X, leading to the generation of thrombin and cleavage of fibrinogen to form fibrin (Figure 1). It is important to note that some bleeding disorders feature pathophysiologic evidence of both processes.

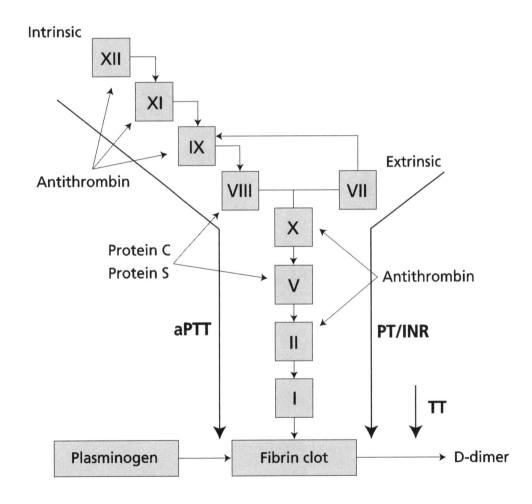

Figure 1. The coagulation cascade showing the pathways assessed by the prothrombin time/international normalized ratio (PT/INR), activated partial thromboplastin time (aPTT), and thrombin time (TT). The D-dimer results from the breakdown of fibrin by plasma.

Approach to the Patient

A detailed bleeding history should be obtained, including duration (> or <5 minutes), timing, (immediately after a procedure), and sites of bleeding (local or systemic); family history; medications (eg, aspirin, antiplatelet agents, nonsteroidal anti-inflammatory drugs [NSAIDs], or anticoagulants); and medical history (eg, liver disease, uremia, or poor nutrition). This information may provide clues to possible causes and help estimate bleeding risk.

A mucocutaneous bleeding pattern, often seen at multiple sites, is the hallmark of disorders of primary hemostasis. Petechiae, easy bruising, gingival bleeding, epistaxis, and menorrhagia are characteristic. Persistent oozing after an injury is common, because the initial platelet plug is not formed. Disorders of secondary hemostasis are characterized by more localized bleeding into the soft tissues (such as muscles) and joints (hemarthrosis). Delayed bleeding is common, because the platelet plug gradually succumbs to the pressures of blood flow without reinforcement from a strong fibrin mesh. Excessive bleeding after childbirth, surgery, or trauma can occur with disorders of primary or secondary hemostasis.

The laboratory analysis must begin with a complete blood count and a thorough review of the peripheral smear that might suggest other causes. Studies to assess for primary hemostasis disorders include a quantitative platelet count and platelet function analysis (PFA). Platelet function screening is most commonly performed with automated testing (ie, PFA-100), which measures the ability of activated platelets treated with collagen and epinephrine to occlude an aperture in vitro (the closure time) and is a sensitive method for assessing the effects of drugs or other disorders on platelet activity. This testing has replaced measurement of the in vivo bleeding time, which was difficult to interpret and is no longer used. Patients with evidence of abnormal platelet function may require additional testing for specific primary hemostatic disorders (such as von Willebrand disease [vWD]) and more detailed PFA. Screening for secondary hemostatic disorders is typically done with measurement of the prothrombin time (PT) and the activated partial thromboplastin time (aPTT), which detect clotting factor deficiencies as well as inhibitors that interfere with effective fibrin clot formation (Table 1). Clotting factor levels <30% of the reference range are needed to prolong the PT and aPTT, and reliance on these tests alone underestimates bleeding risk. A mixing study differentiates factor deficiency from presence of a factor inhibitor by mixing patient plasma with normal plasma; factor deficiencies correct with mixing. Thrombin time tests the rate of conversion of fibrinogen to fibrin. Levels of fibrinogen, fibrinogen degradation products, and D-dimer are used to identify excessive fibrinolysis. This is particularly useful as a measure of increased bleeding tendency in chronic liver disease, which is explained by decreased clearance of plasminogen activator.

Disorders of Primary Hemostasis

Disorders of primary hemostasis include abnormalities of platelets or the vascular endothelium. Quantitative platelet disorders may cause bleeding; spontaneous bleeding does not usually occur until the platelet count is <10,000 μL (10 × 10^9/L). Conditions causing abnormally low platelets are discussed in the Thrombocytopenia chapter (Chapter 49). Dysfunction of platelet adhesion occurs in vWD, Glanzmann thrombasthenia, Bernard-Soulier syndrome, and other hereditary disorders. Platelet activation can be limited due to drugs such as aspirin, antiplatelet agents, and NSAIDs, or in uremia.

Von Willebrand Disease

The most common inherited bleeding disorder is vWD, an autosomal dominant disorder that occurs in 1% of the population with random screening, but is not usually clinically evident. Patients have mild to moderate bleeding evidenced by nosebleeds, heavy menstrual flow, gingival bleeding, easy bruising, and bleeding associated with surgery or trauma.

Von Willebrand factor plays a critical role in platelet adhesion to injured vessels. It also functions as a carrier for factor VIII. Disorders of secondary hemostasis can occur due to low factor VIII levels in vWD; this distinction is important for treatment purposes. Diagnostic testing includes a PFA (although this may be normal in mild cases), vWF antigen level, vWF activity assay, factor VIII level (which may also be normal in mild cases), and a multimer study used to diagnose subtypes of vWD (Table 2). Desmopressin releases stored vWF and factor VIII from endothelial cells and is used as first-line therapy for most subtypes of vWD; in vitro documentation of a response to desmopressin with platelet function testing or vWF assay is performed prior to administration. It can readily be administered intravenously or intranasally. Intermediate-purity factor VIII concentrates, which contain vWF, can also be given. Cryoprecipitate is rich in vWF but carries the risk of transfusion-transmitted infection.

Disorders of Secondary Hemostasis

Disorders of secondary hemostasis are characterized by defects or deficiencies of coagulation factors and include inherited hemophilias, liver disease, vitamin K deficiency, acquired inhibitors of coagulation (antibodies), and consumptive processes (eg, disseminated intravascular coagulation) (Table 2). Medications such as warfarin,

Table 1. Causes of Prolonged PT, PTT, Thrombin Time, and PFA

Prolonged Laboratory Test	Causes
PT	Warfarin, factor VII deficiency or inhibitor, vitamin K deficiency (nutritional or antibiotic-related), liver disease
PTT	Heparin; lupus anticoagulant (predisposes to thrombosis); von Willebrand disease; factor VIII, IX, XI, or XII deficiency or inhibitor
Combined PT and PTT	Supratherapeutic dose of heparin or warfarin; DIC (PT prolonged first); liver disease; factor V or X, prothrombin, or fibrinogen deficiency; direct thrombin inhibitor
Thrombin time	Heparin, direct thrombin inhibitor, factor Xa inhibitor, fibrin degradation product, hypo- or dysfibrinogenemia
Platelet function analysis (PFA-100)	ASA, platelet dysfunction such as von Willebrand disease

ASA = acetylsalicylic acid; DIC = disseminated intravascular coagulation; PFA = platelet function analysis; PT = prothrombin time; PTT = partial thromboplastin time.

heparin, low-molecular-weight heparin, factor Xa inhibitors (eg, fondaparinux, rivaroxaban, and apixaban), and direct thrombin inhibitors (eg, argatroban, lepirudin, and dabigatran) also interfere with secondary hemostasis.

Hemophilia

Factor VIII deficiency (hemophilia A) and factor IX deficiency (hemophilia B) are X-linked disorders with clinical manifestations seen almost exclusively in males. Hemophilia A affects about 1 in 10,000 people, while hemophilia B occurs less frequently. All daughters of patients with hemophilia are obligate carriers, whereas all sons are normal. Sons of carrier mothers have a 50% chance of having hemophilia, and daughters have a 50% chance of being carriers. The spontaneous mutation rate is 3%. Fibrinogen deficiency and factor II, V, VII, X, and XI deficiencies are usually autosomal recessive disorders and are rare in comparison.

Both types of hemophilia are classified as mild, moderate, or severe according to baseline levels of clotting factors. Patients present in childhood with muscle hematomas, hemarthrosis, and persistent delayed bleeding after trauma or surgery. Mild hemophilia can be missed until adulthood. Assessing factor VIII and IX levels is indicated in any male who presents with a prolonged aPTT that corrects with a mixing study (see Table 1).

Factor VIII and IX deficiencies are treated with factor replacement (recombinant or purified). Fresh frozen plasma (FFP) is a diluted source of clotting factors with limited efficacy for high-level replacement.

Acquired Inhibitors

Although uncommon, acquired inhibitors are more likely to manifest as a life-threatening bleed than the deficiency of factor VIII. Patients may present with severe soft tissue bleeding, but not hemarthrosis. In addition, this disorder is seen in association with certain medications (phenytoin, sulfa drugs, and penicillin), malignancies, or autoimmune disorders (systemic lupus erythematosus and rheumatoid arthritis). The diagnosis is suggested in the proper clinical setting by the inability to correct the aPTT with the addition of normal plasma in a mixing study. Further testing can then quantify the inhibitor and guide therapy. Weak inhibitors may respond to factor VIII concentrates; stronger inhibitors may demand agents that bypass the inhibited factor, such as factor VIII inhibitor bypass activity or activated recombinant factor VII. Long-term management includes immunosuppressive therapy.

Liver Disease

The liver synthesizes almost all proteins involved in hemostasis, with exceptions being vWF and tissue plasminogen activator. The PT is a sensitive indicator of hepatic synthetic function due to the short half-life of factor VII (6 hours), which the failing liver cannot maintain. The PT and aPTT are both prolonged with more severe hepatic synthetic dysfunction. Fresh frozen plasma transiently replaces all coagulation factors but is short lived. Cryoprecipitate is useful if the fibrinogen level is <100 mg/dL (2.9 µmol/L).

Table 2. Coagulation and Platelet Function Test Results Found in Various Coagulation and Platelet Disorders

Coagulation or Platelet Disorder	PT/INR	aPTT	Mixing Study[a]	TT	Fibrinogen	D-dimer	Platelet Count	Platelet Function Analysis (PFA-100)	Platelet Aggregation	Blood Smear[b]	Notes
Liver disease	↑	↑	Corrects	↑	↓	↑	↓	↑ or →	Not indicated		Findings are often variable and most prominent in advanced liver disease with cirrhosis
Vitamin K deficiency	↑	↑	Corrects	→	→	→	→	→	Not indicated	Normal	The PT/INR rises before the aPTT because of the short half-life of factor VII
Disseminated intravascular coagulation	↑	↑	Corrects	↑	↓	↑	↓	↑	Not indicated	Schistocytes	Results vary depending on severity; some tests may be normal
Thrombocytopenia	→	→	Not indicated	→	→	→	↓	↑	Abnormal	Large platelets	Bleeding time and platelet size depend on the cause of thrombocytopenia
Qualitative platelet	→	→	Not indicated	→	→	→	→	↑	Abnormal	Normal	Platelet aggregation patterns vary depending on the defect
Von Willebrand disease	→	↑ or	Corrects	→	→	→	→	↑	Normal	Normal	The aPTT is dependent on factor VIII activity. Platelet aggregation does not detect abnormal adhesion; vWF level and ristocetin cofactor are abnormal. Ristocetin cofactor is a platelet aggregation study measuring the function of vWF. The structure of vWF can be determined by a vWF multimer assay

aPTT = activated partial thromboplastin time; INR = international normalized ratio; PFA = platelet function analysis; PT = prothrombin time; TT = thrombin time; vWF = von Willebrand factor; ↑ = increased; ↓ = decreased; → = normal.

[a]A mixing study is performed on the PT or aPTT, depending on which is prolonged.

[b]Findings on blood smear are variable, depending on the severity of the disorder, and may not be present.

Vitamin K Deficiency and Inhibition

Clotting factors II, VII, IX, and X, as well as protein C and protein S, require vitamin K-dependent gamma-carboxylation for full activity. Dietary vitamin K is obtained primarily from the intake of dark green vegetables and is modified by gut flora to the active form. Interruption of bile flow prevents absorption of vitamin K, and antibiotic-related elimination of enteric bacteria limits intestinal sources of vitamin K. Vitamin K antagonists (such as warfarin) used for therapeutic anticoagulation directly antagonize vitamin K activity.

The PT is first to prolong, but the aPTT will also lengthen with further factor deficiencies or inhibition. In adults with normal hepatic function, oral or subcutaneous vitamin K usually corrects the clotting times within 24 hours; however, the risk of anaphylaxis is increased with intravenous vitamin K. Fresh frozen plasma is used when urgent correction is required.

The management of a supratherapeutic international normalized ratio (INR) in patients taking vitamin K antagonists is challenging. Current guidelines suggest withholding the drug if the INR is <5, the addition of oral vitamin K in the presence of additional risk factors for bleeding with an INR ≥5 and <9, and the use of FFP or recombinant factor VII if the INR is ≥9 and there is a serious bleed or the patient is being prepared for surgery.

Other Anticoagulants

Newer-generation anticoagulants act at different points in the coagulation cascade (see Chapter 53). In cases of bleeding from direct thrombin inhibitors, it is important to recognize first that the aPTT or thrombin time are only reliable as an indicator that an effect of the anticoagulant is present, as they are not useful enough to guide therapy. Mild bleeding should warrant discontinuation of the drug, while moderate bleeding may require support with fluid and blood products. Hemodialysis may also be beneficial. Severe bleeding may respond to prothrombin complex concentrates (PCC) or activated recombinant factor VII. A similar approach holds for the new generation of factor Xa inhibitors. However, in this case, anti-Xa assays may be useful to detect the presence of the drug effect. A prolonged PT only indicates the drug was used in the last 7 hours. Minor bleeding demands discontinuation of the agent. Hemodialysis is not effec-tive with these agents. Moderate bleeding will require blood product support. As with the direct thrombin inhibitors, there is not a role for FFP; severe bleeding may be managed by PCC or recombinant factor VII.

Disseminated Intravascular Coagulation

Disseminated intravascular coagulation (DIC) is frequently considered to be both a disorder of primary and secondary hemostasis. It involves widespread activation of coagulation that leads to formation of fibrin clots. Some patients have a thrombotic disorder characterized by deep venous thrombosis or pulmonary embolism. Arterial thrombi and infarction may also occur rarely. In most patients, secondary fibrinolysis dissolves the fibrin clot, and consumption of platelets and coagulation factors causes thrombocytopenia, clotting factor deficiencies, bleeding, and vascular injuries. Disseminated intravascular coagulation most commonly occurs in patients with infection, cancer (typically mucin-producing adenocarcinoma), and obstetric complications. Gram-negative sepsis is the most common infection associated with DIC, although infection due to gram-positive organisms and viruses, including human immunodeficiency virus, may also be causative.

The diagnosis of DIC is based on the presence of a prolonged PT, aPTT, and thrombin time, a high D-dimer titer, and a reduced serum fibrinogen level and platelet count; in some cases, schistocytes may be seen on the peripheral smear. Serial fibrinogen levels are often helpful, but there remains no diagnostic test specific for DIC. The degree of these abnormalities depends on the extent of consumption of platelets and coagulation factors and the ability of the patient to compensate for these defects.

Treatment of DIC is focused on correcting the underlying cause. Patients may require FFP/cryoprecipitate to replace coagulation factors or transfusion of platelets or erythrocytes. Antithrombin III is occasionally useful. Unfractionated heparin and low-molecular-weight heparin are rarely used today because these formulations may increase the bleeding risk and do not improve outcomes.

Bibliography

Marks PW. Coagulation disorders in the ICU. Clin Chest Med. 2009;30:123-129, ix. [PMID: 19186284]

Chapter 53

Thrombophilia

Amy Hayton, MD
Lawrence Loo, MD

Thrombophilia refers to the increased likelihood to form clots (thrombosis). In 1856, Virchow hypothesized that thrombosis developed as a consequence of abnormalities in 3 distinct factors: blood flow, the blood vessel wall, or the blood itself. Today, we know these factors as stasis, injury to the endothelium, and a hypercoagulable state. A patient can be hypercoagulable from a genetically inherited condition or an acquired state that may be reversible (eg, immobilization) or persistent (eg, age) (Table 1). Patients often manifest their first clinical venous thromboembolic event (VTE) due to the interaction of multiple risk factors. For example, an older patient without a known inherited hypercoagulable condition might develop VTE if immobilized after surgery. Or, an asymptomatic woman heterozygous for factor V Leiden mutation may have a moderately increased risk for VTE compared with the general population, but her risk would increase substantially if she were to start an oral contraceptive (Table 2).

Clot formation is a homeostatic process that carefully balances procoagulation and anticoagulation pathways. In the normally functioning coagulation cascade, an initial disruption in the tissue activates platelets, which starts the process of clot formation. Clotting factors are activated, which results in fibrin being deposited along with the platelets. Protein C and S and antithrombin regulate clot formation by preventing excess thrombin production. If any of these naturally occurring anticoagulant pathways are disrupted, thrombin is increased, which leads to an abnormal state thrombophilia (Figure 1).

The process of finding the source of thrombophilia begins with a thorough evaluation of the patient's risk factors. A strong family history may point to an inherited condition. Many acquired thrombophilic states occur during hospitalization including surgery, immobilization, malignancy, and trauma. The pathogenesis of the acquired thrombophilic states varies depending on the condition. Surgery and immobilization activate the coagulation cascade by mechanisms that are not clearly understood beyond the associated increased stasis and possible vascular damage. Malignancy increases clot formation in multiple ways depending on the type of tumor. Multiple mechanisms have been studied involving tumor factors and production of substances with procoagulant activity by surrounding tissues. Comorbid factors such as prolonged bed rest, malnutrition, drugs, and infection also contribute.

The inherited thrombophilic disorders include deficiencies in coagulation factors and cofactors that allow thrombin to be produced in an unregulated manner. The most common of these disorders is factor V Leiden mutation, which causes activated protein C resistance. The mutation results in protein C being unable to inactivate factor V and VIII, which then leads to unregulated prothrombin activation. Heterozygosity of this gene increases the lifetime risk of thrombosis 7 fold, whereas homozygosity increases the risk 20 to 80 fold. This mutation is found in approximately 20% of individuals presenting with a VTE.

Protein C and protein S are vitamin K-dependent proteins. Protein C deficiency is inherited as an autosomal recessive trait, has a half-life of approximately 6 hours, and decreases to low levels soon after initiation of warfarin therapy; it is the cause of warfarin-induced skin necrosis in some patients. Protein S deficiency is inherited as an autosomal dominant trait; it is a cofactor of protein C, so decreased levels of this protein also lead to less protein C activity, resulting in increased fibrin formation. Protein S deficiency is very rare.

A mutation in the prothrombin gene at position G20210A causes increased levels of prothrombin that leads to excess thrombin for-

Table 1. Common Causes of Thrombophilia

Inherited

Resistance to activated protein C most commonly due to factor V Leiden

Prothrombin gene mutation 20210A

Antithrombin deficiency

Protein C deficiency

Protein S deficiency

Hyperhomocysteinemia

Elevated factor VIII

Acquired

Surgery - most commonly orthopedic (hip and knee replacement), cancer surgery

Malignancies - most commonly pancreas, GI, lung, ovaries, acute promyelocytic leukemia

Myeloproliferative disorders - most commonly polycythemia vera and essential thrombocythemia

Paroxysmal nocturnal hemoglobinuria

Trauma

Prolonged immobilization (eg, air travel >6 hours, bed rest for ≥3 days)

Pregnancy/postpartum

Nephrotic syndrome

Medication related - including oral contraceptives, hormone replacement therapy, tamoxifen/raloxifene, chemotherapy, thalidomide, heparin-induced thrombocytopenia, warfarin-induced necrosis

Presence of a central venous catheter or PICC line

Antiphospholipid syndrome

Acquired states of hyperhomocysteinemia, activated protein C resistance, and antithrombin deficiency

GI = gastrointestinal; PICC = peripherally inserted central catheter.

Table 2. Absolute Risk of VTE in Asymptomatic Carriers of Thrombophilia

Carrier Condition	Baseline Absolute Risk for VTE[a] (% per year)	Absolute Risk for VTE in the Presence of Specific Conditions		
		Surgery, Trauma, or Immobilization (% per episode)	Pregnancy (% per episode)	Oral Contraceptives (% per year used)
Factor V Leiden	0.5	2-3	2-3	1-3
Prothrombin G20210A	0.3	1-2	1-1.5	1-2
Protein C, protein S, antithrombin deficiency	1-3	6-8	4-5	4-5
Mild hyperhomocysteinemia	0.2	1	0.5	0.3

VTE = venous thromboembolic event.

[a]Reference ranges for VTE risk in the general population: adults <40 years = 0.01% per year; adults 40-70 years = 0.1% per year; adults >70 years = 1% per year.

mation. This condition occurs in approximately 3% of Caucasians in the United States and confers a 3- to 4-fold risk for VTE.

Antithrombin deficiency is an autosomal dominant genetic mutation associated with thrombophilia. It should be suspected in a patient whose clot does not respond to heparin therapy, since heparin requires the presence of antithrombin that is deficient in this condition.

Hyperhomocysteinemia can rarely be inherited through mutations of the *MTHFR* gene. Levels of homocysteine increase, leading to increased clot formation. Elevated plasma factor VIII coagulant activity (VIII:C) also increases thrombotic risk independently but not as strongly as the top 5 inherited thrombophilias (factor V Leiden, prothrombin gene mutation, and deficiencies of antithrombin, protein C, and protein S). The exact genetic mutation that causes this elevated factor is not yet known.

Antiphospholipid syndrome (APS) is the most common form of acquired thrombophilia resulting from the development of antibodies directed toward plasma proteins that are bound to phospholipids. Antiphospholipid antibodies may be detected in a number of different ways. Anticardiolipin antibodies are antiphospholipid antibodies that react with proteins associated with cardiolipin, and these antibodies are also responsible for false-positive tests for syphilis (such as the rapid plasma reagin test) that use cardiolipin in their assay. Lupus anticoagulants are antiphospholipid antibodies that, when bound to their target proteins, prolong clotting times (such as the prothrombin time and activated partial thromboplastin time); despite this clotting time prolongation, patients with lupus anticoagulants are actually thrombophilic. Because lupus anticoagulants act as inhibitors, these measures do not correct when a mixing study is performed in which the patient's plasma is combined with plasma that contains all of the normal clotting factors. Antiphospholipid autoantibodies may also be directed toward β_2-microglobulin, which is an inhibitor of coagulation and platelet aggregation. Some patients may have one or more of these antiphospholipid antibodies present. Although the mechanism is not completely understood, these antibodies may lead to disruption of normal coagulation and an increased risk of thrombosis. Antiphospholipid syndrome can present with one or more arterial or venous thrombosis in any tissue or organ, recurrent fetal loss, or premature births. The diagnosis of APS requires both clinical and laboratory criteria.

Acquired hyperhomocysteinemia has been associated with both arterial and venous thrombosis. The increased homocysteine can stem from vitamin B_6, vitamin B_{12}, and folate deficiencies. The thrombotic risk is most closely associated with the increased fasting plasma homocysteine level, regardless of etiology, and roughly doubles the risk of venous thrombosis.

Screening

Controversy exists as to whom and when to screen for inherited thrombophilias since the quality of evidence to support such recommendations is poor or conflicting. **Universal screening of unselected populations for inherited thrombophilias should be avoided.** However, a targeted selective screening strategy based on specific high-risk patient groups may be of some value. A careful discussion with a patient about the potential benefits and risks of screening may be necessary. For example, most experts do not recommend general screening for inherited thrombophilias in all women considering taking oral contraceptives. However, if a patient with a strong family history of thrombosis is considering the use of oral contraception or hormone replacement therapy, then screening may be helpful in this decision. Many consultants would advise against taking these hormones in patients who have factor V Leiden, prothrombin mutation, or protein C, protein S, or antithrombin deficiency because of a significant increased risk for thrombophilia (see Table 2). However, the avoidance of oral contraception may place the woman at increased risk of thrombophilia if she becomes pregnant. Most experts do not routinely recommend screening for inherited thrombophilias at the onset of pregnancy in all women without a history of VTE or recurrent pregnancy loss.

Routinely screening for inherited thrombophilias in patients undergoing high-risk surgical procedures (such as certain orthopedic surgeries) is not recommended. Instead, routine thrombo-

Table 3. Frequency of Inherited Thrombophilia Found in Patients With First VTE

Inherited Thrombophilia	Frequency, %
Heterozygous factor V Leiden[a]	12-20
Homozygous factor V Leiden	1-3
Prothrombin G20210A[b]	4-9
Protein C deficiency	2-6
Protein S deficiency	1-3
Antithrombin deficiency	1-3
Hyperhomocysteinemia[c]	10

VTE, venous thromboembolic event.

[a]Highest in Caucasians, lower in Hispanics (2%) and African Americans (1%), and lowest in Asians (0.5%).

[b]Highest in Caucasians and much lower in African Americans and Asians (0.3%).

[c]Hyperhomocysteinemia (>2.0 mg/L (15 umol/L)) is found in 5% of the general population without VTE.

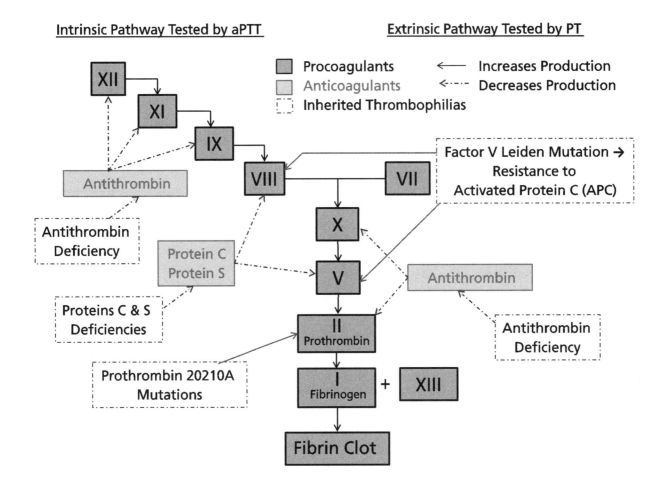

Figure 1. Mechanisms of thrombophilic conditions in the coagulation pathways. aPTT = activated partial thromboplastin time; PT = prothrombin time.

prophylaxis should be prescribed for all patients according to evidence-based guidelines without testing.

The cost of testing is a significant downside to undergoing universal population screening for inherited thrombophilias given the frequency found in the general population but the low absolute risk for VTE. For example, most experts recommend against testing for inherited thrombophilias in asymptomatic children younger than age 15, even if they have a parent with a known congenital thrombophilia, because of the low absolute risk (see Table 2). Other issues to consider when counseling about screening are the potential psychological impacts of being diagnosed an asymptomatic carrier.

Diagnosis

The decision to test for an inherited thrombophilia in all patients presenting with a VTE remains controversial. Epidemiologic studies have found an increased risk of inherited thrombophilia in patients presenting with a first-time VTE, although the percentage varies considerably on the selected population chose (Table 3). However, the evidence that identification of these disorders leads to improved clinical outcomes is limited or conflicting. Most experts do not recommend general screening to determine treatment duration of anticoagulant therapy, except perhaps for those with APS. Therefore, the decision should include a determination of the risk of recurrent thrombosis weighed against the benefit of long-term anticoagula-

tion. The factors that suggest an increased likelihood of a recurrent VTE are listed in Table 4.

Testing for inherited causes of thrombophilia in the setting of an acute VTE may not be reliable since the acute phase reactants of the VTE may interfere with factor measurements. When testing patients treated for a VTE while on heparin, antithrombin levels will be artificially decreased or look like a lupus anticoagulant. When testing patients on warfarin, levels of protein C and S may be artificially decreased. There is no ideal time to test for all of the inherited conditions, and the current recommendations suggest testing in multiple phases based on the risk factors present. Testing methods for the different inherited thrombophilias are outlined in Table 5. Finally, all test results should be confirmed before changing management decisions, as transient laboratory abnormalities are possible.

Therapy

Patients who have had a venous thromboembolism and are found to have a concomitant thrombophilia are at increased risk for recurrent VTE. **Most experts do not recommend testing for the congenital thrombophilias to determine the method, intensity or duration of treatment for patients presenting with their first venous thromboembolism unless there is a suggestive or known history of familial thrombophilia.** General guidelines are based on the estimate of VTE recurrence, the nature of the first VTE, and the

Table 4. Risk Factors for Inherited Thrombophilia

Thrombosis in ages <50 years, especially in the absence of acquired risk factors (idiopathic)

History of recurrent thrombosis, especially if idiopathic

First-degree relative(s) with thrombosis, especially if first VTE occurs at age <50 years

Unusual site of thrombosis (mesenteric, splenic, portal, hepatic, cerebral sinus, upper extremity in the absence of central lines)

Thrombotic event during pregnancy or postpartum

Thrombotic event while taking oral contraceptives

History of recurrent pregnancy loss

VTE = venous thromboembolism.

risk of bleeding with continued therapy. Some experts believe that lifelong anticoagulation is necessary for any patient who has had a VTE and has any of the following thrombophilias: lupus anticoagulant, anticardiolipin antibody, homozygosity for factor V Leiden mutation, homozygosity for prothrombin G20210A, combined heterozygosity for factor V Leiden mutation and prothrombin G20210A, and antithrombin deficiency. Others recommend a determination of the risk of recurrence and prescribe temporary anticoagulation when the patient is at higher risk, such as in surgery, immobilization, or pregnancy. Full-dose anticoagulation with warfarin must be weighed with the known risks including death from bleeding (0.1% per year) and major complications requiring hospitalization or blood transfusions (1%-3% per year).

The American College of Chest Physicians clinical practice guidelines recommend discontinuation of anticoagulation after 3 to 6 months in a patient with heterozygous factor V Leiden or prothrombin G20210A mutation. They advise extending therapy (1 year to lifetime) only in those with active cancer, persistently elevated anticardiolipin antibodies, or antithrombin deficiency. In patients with hyperhomocysteinemia, reducing levels with B vitamins or folic acid has not reduced the incidence of subsequent VTEs.

Follow-Up

Except to monitor the effectiveness of anticoagulant therapy, routinely checking laboratory studies once the diagnosis of thrombophilia has been established is not recommended. Platelet levels should be monitored in patients with anticardiolipin antibodies or lupus anticoagulant since these conditions may cause thrombocytopenia.

Bibliography

Bauer KA, Rosendaal FR, Heit JA. Hypercoagulability: too many tests, too much conflicting data. Hematology Am Soc Hematol Educ Program. 2002:353-368. [PMID: 12446432]

Kearon C, Akl EA, Comerota AJ, et al; American College of Chest Physicians. Antithrombotic therapy for VTE disease: Antithrombotic Therapy and Prevention of Thrombosis, 9th ed: American College of Chest Physicians

Evidence-Based Clinical Practice Guidelines. Chest. 2012;141(2 suppl): e419S-e494S. [PMID: 22315268]

Table 5. Laboratory Testing for Common Thrombophilic Conditions

Thrombophilia	Diagnostic Tests	Notes
APC resistance	APC resistance assay screen (sensitivity = 98%, specificity = 99%) All positive screening tests should be confirmed with direct genetic testing for factor V Leiden gene mutation	False-positive screening tests in pregnancy and oral contraceptive use
Prothrombin G20210A	Direct PCR gene test (sensitivity = 100%, specificity = 100%)	
Protein C deficiency	Consider both functional level and antigenic assays	Two abnormal results needed False-positive results seen with active thrombosis, warfarin use, and liver dysfunction
Protein S deficiency	Consider both functional level and antigenic assays	Two abnormal results needed False-positive results seen with active thrombosis, warfarin use, liver dysfunction, and pregnancy
Antithrombin deficiency	Consider both functional level and antigenic assays	Two abnormal results needed False-positive results seen with active thrombosis, heparin use, pregnancy, and nephrotic syndrome
Lupus anticoagulant	Requires a 3-step procedure including screening tests (eg, diluted Russell viper venom and sensitive aPTT); mixing studies; and confirmatory phospholipid tests	Avoid testing if the patient is on any anticoagulant therapy Positive tests must be repeated at least 12 weeks apart to confirm the diagnosis May be considerable variability among different laboratories
Anticardiolipin antibodies	ELISA testing for anticardiolipin and anti-β_2-glycoprotein-I (IgG and/or IgM) antibodies	Positive tests must be repeated at least 12 weeks apart to confirm the diagnosis May be considerable variability among different laboratories
Hyperhomocysteinemia	Fasting plasma homocysteine level (risk increases when levels >1.35 mg/L (10 μmol/L)	False-positive results with renal failure and vitamin deficiencies False-negative results sometimes seen in pregnancy

APC = activated protein C; aPTT = activated partial thromboplastin time; aPTT = activated partial thromboplastin time; ELISA = enzyme-linked immunosorbent assay; PCR = polymerase chain reaction.

Chapter 54

Transfusion Medicine

Dennis Chang, MD

More than 24 million blood components, including cellular products (erythrocytes and platelets) and plasma products (fresh frozen plasma [FFP], cryoprecipitate, intravenous immune globulin, and other plasma derivatives), are transfused each year. However, as with every treatment, transfusions have complications that range from mild to life threatening. Therefore, it is paramount that physicians fully understand the indications, benefits, and risks of each type of transfusion.

Cellular Products

Erythrocytes

The only true indication for erythrocyte transfusion is to improve tissue oxygen delivery. In the past, a more liberal approach to transfusion was common, with attempts to maintain hemoglobin concentration around 10 g/dL (100 g/L). **A more restrictive approach to transfusion in non-cardiac patients with a hemoglobin goal of 7 to 8 g/dL (70-80 g/L) is favored in most patients.** Randomized trials in both critically ill and surgical patients have shown similar outcomes when a hemoglobin transfusion threshold of 7 to 8 g/dL (70-80 g/L) is used as opposed to a threshold of 10 g/dL (100 g/L). Similarly, studies have also shown that, even in patients with coronary artery disease, there are not clear differences in outcomes when using 7 to 8 g/dL (70-80 g/L) as a hemoglobin transfusion threshold. However, if a patient has symptoms of poor oxygen delivery, active cardiac conditions, ongoing blood loss, and/or hemodynamic instability (Table 1), then transfusions should be given regardless of hemoglobin level.

The volume of one unit of packed red blood cells is about 250 to 300 mL and can be expected to increase the hemoglobin by 1 g/dL (10 g/L) in a nonbleeding adult. It should be transfused at about 60 to 120 mL/h, which should take about 3 to 4 hours, although faster transfusions are indicated in emergent situations.

Prior to erythrocyte transfusion, typing is performed to determine the patient's ABO and Rh phenotype, as well as for the presence of specific antibodies to other red cell surface antigens (termed alloantibodies). Crossmatching is also done by mixing a sample of the patient's blood with the donor blood to identify any additional compatibility issues not discovered with typing and screening.

The ABO and Rh erythrocyte membrane antigen groups are the most important because they are both highly immunogenic and their corresponding antibodies can cause severe and fatal transfusion reactions. Most deaths from erythrocyte transfusions are the result of transfusing ABO-incompatible blood.

The ABO system is a group of antigens on the surface of red cell membranes. If both AB antigens are present on a patient's erythrocytes, then that patient's blood group is AB; if neither is present on a patient's erythrocytes, then a patient's blood group is O (Table 2). An individual develops antibodies against the ABO antigens that are not present on their own erythrocytes.

The Rh system is another group of important erythrocyte membrane antigens, but the Rh(D) antigen is the most immunogenic; Rh positive and Rh negative refer to the D antigen only. Rh(D)-negative individuals should ideally only receive blood from Rh(D)-negative donors, whereas Rh(D)-positive individuals can receive erythrocytes from either Rh(D)-negative or -positive donors.

Therefore, blood group O-Rh(D)-negative (O-negative) patients are universal donors because they have no AB or Rh antigens on their

Table 1. Transfusion Indications[a]

Erythrocytes

- Acute blood loss, surgical or nonsurgical
- Anemia with hemodynamic compromise
- Patients with symptoms attributable to anemia[b]
- Critically ill patients with hemoglobin <7 g/dL (70 g/L)
- Critically ill patients with cardiopulmonary disease with hemoglobin <7 to 10 g/dL (70-100 g/L)[c]

Platelets (treatment)

- Active bleeding with platelet count <50,000 to 100,000/μL (50-100 × 10⁹/L)
- Active bleeding with dysfunctional platelets

Platelets (prophylaxis)

- Platelet count <10,000/μL (10 × 10⁹/L) in patients with leukemia with no other bleeding risk factors
- Platelet count <50,000/μL (50 × 10⁹/L) and planned surgery
- Platelet count <100,000/μL (100 × 10⁹/L) and planned intracranial surgery

Fresh frozen plasma

- Multiple clotting deficiencies with active bleeding (eg, DIC or liver disease)
- Thrombotic thrombocytopenic purpura
- Reversal of warfarin in patients with intracranial bleeding
- Factor replacement when specific factor concentrates not available
- Massive transfusion of packed red blood cells to avoid dilutional coagulopathy

Cryoprecipitate

- Hypofibrinogenemia or dysfibrinogenemia
- Factor XIII deficiency
- Hemophilia A or von Willebrand disease if factor concentrate not available

DIC = disseminated intravascular coagulation.

[a]This list is not all inclusive. Although this list should serve as a guideline, transfusion decisions need to be made on a case-by-case basis.

[b]When attributable to decreased tissue oxygenation, such as shortness of breath, exertional chest pain, worsened claudication, etc.

[c]The proper transfusion threshold remains controversial in patients with cardiopulmonary disease.

Table 2. ABO Compatibility Between Donor and Recipient Erythrocytes and FFP

| | Blood Type of Recipient | | | |
	A	B	AB	O
Erythrocyte antigen	A	B	A and B	None
Isohemagglutinins (ABO antibodies)	Anti-B	Anti-A	None	Anti-A, anti-B
Compatible donor erythrocytes	A, O	B, O	Any	O
Compatible donor FFP	A, AB	B, AB	AB	Any

FFP = fresh frozen plasma.

Note: Rh-negative patients should receive Rh-negative erythrocytes. Rh-positive patients can receive Rh-negative or Rh-positive erythrocytes.

erythrocytes to cause antibody reactions, and AB-Rh(D)-positive (AB-positive) patients are universal recipients because they do not possess any antibodies to the ABO or Rh antigens and are able to receive erythrocytes from any donor. Women of childbearing age who are Rh negative should not receive Rh-positive blood products to avoid the risk of anti-Rh(D) antibody production and neonatal hemolysis with subsequent pregnancy. Type O-negative blood should be given when emergent transfusion is indicated and the recipient's blood type is unknown or unavailable.

The last group of antibodies tested for are alloantibodies. They are typically directed against non-ABO blood group antigens and are formed after exposure to mismatched antigens during a previous blood transfusion or pregnancy. Screening for alloantibodies consists of mixing a patient's serum against panels of test erythrocytes for which the blood group antigens are known. The presence of alloantibodies may lead to difficulty in finding compatible blood for a patient.

Prior to erythrocyte transfusion, clinicians also have the option to treat red cells to minimize complications for certain patient populations (Table 3).

Platelets

In asymptomatic patients, platelets do not need to be transfused unless the count is <10,000/μL (10×10^9/L). However, in patients undergoing surgery or patients with active bleeding, the platelet target is >50,000/μL (50×10^9/L). For central nervous system bleeding or planned central nervous system surgery or ocular surgery, the platelet target is >100,000/μL (100×10^9/L). For minor procedures such as central line placement, lumbar puncture, and bone marrow aspiration, the platelet target is >20,000/μL (20×10^9/L).

Platelets may be provided as pooled random-donor units from several donors or from a single donor collected through apheresis. A single-donor unit is equal to approximately 6 random donor units and should raise the platelet count by at least 20,000 to 30,000/μL ($20-30 \times 10^9$/L). Whether transfusion of single-donor platelets leads to a decreased incidence of alloimmunization and transfusion reactions is uncertain.

ABO and Rh matching are generally not required for platelet transfusions because the number of erythrocytes in platelet transfusions is not significant. However, platelet transfusions do contain small numbers of leukocytes and a small amount of plasma. The leukocytes can lead to graft-versus-host disease (GVHD), febrile non-

hemolytic reactions, and alloantibodies, and the proteins in the plasma can lead to transfusion-related acute lung injury (TRALI) and anaphylactic reactions.

Platelets are stored at room temperature for a maximum of 5 days after collection as compared to erythrocytes, which are refrigerated for up to 42 days. The warmer storage conditions allow for proliferation of any contaminating bacteria that may occur during phlebotomy. Consequently, the risk for bacterial infection and sepsis is increased in patients receiving platelet transfusions compared with other blood products.

Transfused platelets typically survive 7 to 9 days, but this period may be much shorter in patients with acute illness or active bleeding. Checking the posttransfusion platelet count within 1 hour of transfusion is essential to properly evaluate for transfusion response and to evaluate for the presence of platelet refractoriness.

Platelet refractoriness is an inappropriately low increase in the platelet count following a transfusion, which occurs in 5% to 15% of chronic platelet recipients. A commonly used definition for platelet transfusion refractoriness is a post-transfusion platelet count increase of <10,000/μL (10×10^9/L). Nonimmune causes of platelet transfusion refractoriness are most common and should first be considered, including fever, disseminated intravascular coagulation (DIC), and drugs such as amphotericin B. Alloimmunization to HLA platelet antigens, specifically HLA class I antigens, accounts for about one-third of platelet refractoriness in multiply transfused patients and should be considered after other possible causes are excluded.

After platelet transfusion refractoriness has been identified, the freshest single-donor, ABO-matched platelets are transfused. If the transfusion is unsuccessful and HLA antibodies are identified, HLA-matched platelets or crossmatched compatible platelets should be administered.

Table 3. Pretransfusion Erythrocyte Treatments

Treatment	Notes
Leukoreduction	Reduces the number of leukocytes present in transfused erythrocytes. Reduces alloantibody production, FNHTR, and transmission of CMV, which resides in leukocytes. Performed on all erythrocyte transfusions in some institutions
Gamma irradiation	Radiation kills any living cells, particularly lymphocytes, in transfusion units. Used primarily used to prevent T-GVHD, which is mediated by donor lymphocytes. Indicated in patients with congenital immunodeficiencies, stem cell or organ transplantations, or hematologic (especially Hodgkin lymphoma) or solid organ cancers, in patients receiving chemotherapy, and in patients receiving transfusions from relatives. However, irradiation can weaken the red cell membrane, causing reduced cell viability and potassium leakage
Washed	Removes the proteins residing in the small amount of plasma of erythrocyte transfusions and is used in patients with a history of severe/recurrent allergic reactions, IgA deficiency, or complement-dependent autoimmune hemolytic anemia. Also reduces the amount of potassium transfused for use in patients who are at risk for hyperkalemia

CMV = cytomegalovirus; FNHTR = febrile nonhemolytic transfusion reaction; T-GVHD = transfusion-associated graft-versus-host disease.

Plasma Products

Fresh Frozen Plasma

Fresh frozen plasma contains all coagulation factors and proteins from circulating plasma. Indications are listed in Table 4. The prophylactic use of FFP in nonbleeding, nonsurgical patients remains unproven, and current evidence does not support the use of FFP to correct patient's international normalized ratio that is <1.6.

Fresh frozen plasma has a volume of 200 to 300 mL, and a typical effective dose of FFP is 10 to 15 mL/kg at a rate of approximately 1 to 1.5 hours per unit. The risk of transmitting intracellular viruses such as cytomegalovirus is somewhat lower than erythrocyte infusions, but the risk of most transfusion-transmitted infections from FFP is analogous to that associated with erythrocyte transfusion. Other risks include volume overload, TRALI, and febrile, allergic, and anaphylactic reactions.

Prior to receiving FFP, the recipient's ABO phenotype must be determined. Due to screening processes, the only red cell antibodies present in FFP are ABO antibodies. This is important to remember that, because FFP has no erythrocytes, transfusion reactions associated with FFP are caused by the donor FFP antibodies attacking the recipient erythrocyte ABO antigens, in contrast to erythrocyte transfusions where the recipient ABO antibodies attack the donor erythrocyte antigens. Recipients can receive either ABO-identical or ABO-compatible FFP (see Table 2).

Cryoprecipitate

Cryoprecipitate is the precipitated fraction of material remaining when FFP is thawed at 4.0°C (39.2°F). Cryoprecipitate contains a concentrated source of factor VIII, von Willebrand factor, factor XIII, fibronectin, and fibrinogen, and is the treatment of choice in bleeding patients with hypofibrinogenemia from liver disease, thrombolytic therapy, or DIC. (Other indications are listed in Table 1.) The recommended dose is typically 1 to 2 units per 10 kg. Although ABO compatibility is still performed with cryoprecipitate, transfusion reactions are extremely rare because of the small volume of plasma transfused. Cryoprecipitate has the same infectious risk as a unit of FFP.

Other Plasma-Derived Transfusion Products

Other plasma-derived transfusion products are manufactured from human plasma by plasma fractionation techniques. (The commonly used products are listed in Table 4.) Although specific isolation and viral inactivation techniques are used in the preparation of plasma-derived products, a small risk of infectious disease transmission remains.

Transfusion Complications

Hemolytic Reactions

Acute Hemolytic Transfusion Reaction

The acute hemolytic transfusion reaction (AHTR) is a rapid intravascular hemolysis that is the most feared complication of transfusion. It is almost always caused by ABO incompatibility between donor and recipient and, in most cases, results from a clerical or procedural error such as the mislabeling of a pretransfusion specimen. The classic presenting triad is fever, flank pain, and red or brown urine; however, often the only presenting features are fever and chills. The hemolysis may lead to DIC, shock, and acute renal failure due to acute tubular necrosis. When AHTR is suspected, the transfusion must be stopped immediately and a specimen sent to the blood bank to evaluate for incompatibility. Treatment is supportive.

Delayed Hemolytic Transfusion Reaction

A delayed hemolytic transfusion reaction (DHTR) occurs 3 to 10 days after erythrocyte transfusion. In contrast to AHTR, the DHTR is a gradual extravascular hemolysis caused by an amnestic minor, non-ABO erythrocyte antibody. Following a transfusion, there is a 1.0% to 1.6% chance of developing these minor non-ABO alloantibodies, and DHTR occurs when the patient is re-exposed to the same antigen with a subsequent transfusion. Clinical symptoms include an unexpected drop in hemoglobin, jaundice, and fever, although many patients will be asymptomatic. Life-threatening complications are rare, but patients with sickle cell disease may present with a worsening pain crisis. Treatment is supportive. A repeat type and screen

Table 4. Plasma Products and Indications

Plasma Derivative	Clinical Indication
Fresh frozen plasma	Warfarin reversal in actively bleeding patients (either alone or concomitantly with a 3-factor [II, IX, and X] prothrombin complex concentrate)
	Bleeding patients with deficiencies in several factors, such as in DIC or liver disease
	Dilutional coagulopathy during massive transfusion
	TTP either as infusion or plasma exchange
Intravenous immune globulin	Numerous indications including ITP, TTP, Kawasaki disease, specific autoimmune disorders, primary congenital hypogammaglobulinemia, Guillain-Barré syndrome
Prothrombin complex concentrates (contain factors II, VII, IX, X)	Warfarin reversal
Monoclonal factor VIII and IX	Hemophilia A and B, respectively
Protein C concentrate	Severe congenital protein C deficiency for prevention/treatment of venous thrombosis
Antithrombin III concentrates	Thromboembolism prophylaxis and treatment in hereditary antithrombin deficiency
α-1 antitrypsin	Congenital α-1-antitrypsin deficiency

DIC = disseminated intravascular coagulation; ITP = immune thrombocytopenic purpura; TTP = thrombotic thrombocytopenic purpura.

will identify the presence of a new alloantibody, and subsequent transfusions should be minimized, but not withheld, when indicated. All subsequent transfusions should be tested to ensure they do not have the identified antigen.

Nonhemolytic Reactions

Transfusion-Associated Circulatory Overload

Transfusion-associated circulatory overload (TACO) is a frequent and serious transfusion complication, which most commonly affects those with limited cardiopulmonary reserve, including the very young and the elderly. Presenting symptoms occur during or within 1 to 2 hours of a transfusion and include dyspnea, cough, tachycardia, cyanosis, edema, and chest tightness. Physical examination will typically reveal signs of fluid overload, and unlike TRALI, there will be an elevated N-terminal pro-B-type natriuretic peptide. Treatment consists of supplemental oxygenation and intravenous diuretics. The risk of TACO can be reduced by avoiding overly rapid transfusion rates.

Transfusion-Related Acute Lung Injury

Transfusion-related acute lung injury (TRALI) occurs in 1 of 5000 transfusions and is the most common cause of transfusion-related death, with a mortality rate of 5%. Transfusions containing higher concentrations of plasma, such as platelets and whole blood, pose the greatest risk. The pathogenesis of TRALI is not completely understood, but is thought to be due to the "priming" of neutrophils in the lung vasculature (by insults such as surgery, infection, or trauma) that make them vulnerable to activation, which occurs with exposure to an antineutrophil or HLA antibody contained in the transfusion. Upon activation, leukocyte sequestration occurs in the lung, and capillary leak ensues. The diagnostic criteria for TRALI includes the acute onset of dyspnea, hypoxia, and bilateral infiltrates on chest radiograph occurring within 6 hours of transfusion with no other cause for acute lung injury. The clinical and radiographic differential diagnosis includes TACO, acute respiratory distress syndrome, and heart failure. Unlike patients with acute respiratory distress syndrome, patients with TRALI typically improve within days. As such, treatment of TRALI is primarily supportive and prevention entails exclusion of the implicated donor from future transfusions.

Febrile Nonhemolytic Transfusion Reaction

The febrile nonhemolytic transfusion reaction (FNHTR) is the most common transfusion reaction and is benign. It presents with fever and chills 1 to 6 hours after erythrocyte or platelet transfusion. However, it cannot be clinically differentiated from the more severe and life-threatening AHTR. Recipient-derived leukoreactive antibodies and donor-derived cytokines are thought to represent the most common causes. When fever develops, the transfusion should be stopped immediately until AHTR can be excluded and causes of fever unrelated to the transfusion considered. After AHTR has been excluded, the transfusion can continue with close monitoring. Pretransfusion antipyretics such as acetaminophen, or leukoreduction of cellular blood products, may prevent recurrence.

Allergic Reactions and Anaphylaxis

Mild allergic reactions consisting of urticaria commonly occur, especially in multiply transfused patients. Most reactions are caused by donor plasma proteins reacting with preexisting IgE antibodies in the recipient and may not recur with subsequent transfusions. After stopping the transfusion, if the urticaria resolves without signs of anaphylaxis, the transfusion can resume. Rarely is urticaria the first sign of a more serious reaction. Pretreatment with antihistamines or washing of cellular blood products to remove plasma proteins is often effective in preventing recurrence.

Severe anaphylactic reactions are rare and typically occur in patients who are IgA deficient and have anti-IgA antibodies. These antibodies react to IgA contained in the transfused blood. When transfusing IgA-deficient patients, plasma products must be obtained from IgA-deficient donors and all subsequent cellular products should be washed thoroughly to remove plasma proteins. Clinically, patients present with rapid onset of hypotension, gastrointestinal symptoms, angioedema, stridor, and respiratory distress. Treatment requires prompt and rapid cessation of the transfusion, epinephrine, airway maintenance, and fluid resuscitation.

Transfusion Graft-Versus-Host Disease

Transfusion-associated GVHD (T-GVHD) is a rare, but often fatal, transfusion complication. It usually occurs in immunocompromised patients who receive a transfusion product that is contaminated with lymphocytes. Immunocompetent patients are not usually affected because their immune system destroys the lymphocytes in the donor transfusion. Patients at risk for T-GVHD include hematopoietic stem cell or solid organ transplant recipients, recipients of transfusions from first-degree relatives, and patients with immunosuppression associated with hematologic malignancies such as Hodgkin lymphoma. Affected patients experience severe pancytopenia, and, to a variable degree, diarrhea, skin rash, and liver chemistry test abnormalities. No treatment has proved effective; therefore, prevention is key. Gamma irradiation of cellular products virtually eliminates the risk for T-GVHD and should be performed before transfusion for all at-risk patients.

Infectious Complications

Given improved donor screening and pretransfusion testing, blood is currently safer than ever before. For example, the risk of HIV is less than 1 in 1,900,000 units; hepatitis C is less than 1 in 1,000,000 units; and hepatitis B is less than 1 in 205,000 units. However, infectious risk, including the transmission of West Nile virus, dengue virus, prions causing Creutzfeldt-Jakob disease, Chagas disease, and babesiosis, still remain, and new bloodborne pathogens will continue to emerge.

The risk for bacterial infection is higher than viral infection and can come from donor blood, donor skin, phlebotomists' skin, and environmental contamination. Because platelets are stored at room temperature, bacterial contamination occurs more commonly with platelet transfusions, with an estimated frequency of 1 in 3000 platelet units. There are other bacteria such as *Yersinia enterocolitica* that may survive refrigeration of erythrocyte units and can lead to fatal sepsis.

Bibliography

Boucher BA, Hannon TJ. Blood management: a primer for clinicians. Pharmacotherapy. 2007;27:1394-1411. [PMID: 17896895]

Goodnough LT, Levy JH, Murphy MF. Concepts of blood transfusion in adults. Lancet. 2013;381;1845-1854. [PMID: 23706801]

Sharma S, Sharma P, Tyler LN. Transfusion of blood and blood products: indications and complications. Am Fam Physician. 2011;83:719-724. [PMID: 21404983]

Section 6
Infectious Disease Medicine

Associate Editor – Susan T. Hingle, MD, FACP

High Value Care Recommendations

- Fever, as a symptom, does not always require treatment.

- Frequent hand washing has been proven to prevent transmission of common respiratory infections.

- Vaccination for influenza can reduce the risk of influenza-like illnesses by 36%.

- The use of vitamin C or echinacea to prevent common respiratory infections is not supported by strong evidence.

- Laboratory testing and imaging studies are unnecessary for diagnosis of common respiratory infections.

- Codeine and over-the-counter antitussive agents have not been proven to be effective for acute cough in patients with upper respiratory infections (URIs).

- Antibiotics are not indicated for uncomplicated URIs, even when purulent sputum or nasal discharge is present.

- Do not use prophylactic antibiotics in asymptomatic individuals with pharyngitis to prevent the spread of infection.

- Patients with 0 or 1 Centor criteria are at sufficiently low risk (<3%) that they should neither be tested for group A streptococcal pharyngitis nor treated with antibiotics.

- Avoid sinus imaging in uncomplicated acute sinusitis; patients with ophthalmic or neurologic symptoms or signs may need diagnostic imaging.

- Antibiotics have been found to have little if any role in the treatment of patients with acute sinusitis in the primary care setting, and in most cases, symptomatic treatment is first-line therapy.

- Sputum Gram stain and culture are not indicated in hospitalized patients with less severe pneumonia, but they should be obtained for any patient at risk for infection with drug-resistant or unusual pathogens or those with severe pneumonia.

- In hospitalized patients on intravenous antibiotics, switch to oral antibiotic therapy once symptoms improve and when patients have no fever on two occasions 8 hours apart and are able to take medications by mouth.

- Only obtain a chest radiograph after initial therapy for community-acquired pneumonia if the patient does not respond to treatment, or to document resolution of pneumonia with risk factors and suspicion of an underlying disease, such as malignancy.

- Screening is not needed for individuals at low risk of tuberculosis.

- Antibiotic prophylaxis for endocarditis is not indicated for patients with low- or moderate-risk cardiac conditions undergoing any type of procedure.

- Pathogen-directed therapy for endocarditis should be instituted once the microbiologic cause has been identified.

- Urinalysis should not be ordered as part of a routine well care examination in men and nonpregnant women.

- Urinalysis can be omitted for healthy women with acute cystitis if there are no complicating factors.

- A follow-up urinalysis or culture is not indicated after treatment for an uncomplicated upper respiratory tract infection (URI) with symptom resolution.

Chapter 55

Approach to Fever

Joseph T. Wayne, MD

Fever is a complex adaptive biologic response that alters the body's temperature set point. Fever results from the production of cytokines, including interleukins 1 and 6, tumor necrosis factor, interferons, and prostaglandin E_2. Normal body temperature ranges from 35.6°C (96.0°F) to 38.2°C (100.8°F), with a mean of 36.8°C (98.2°F). There is a diurnal variation, with a nadir near 6:00 AM and a peak near 4:00 PM. Fever is defined as a body temperature ≥37.2°C (99.0°F) in the morning or ≥37.7°C (100.0°F) in the afternoon. Hyperthermia occurs when thermoregulatory control is overwhelmed by the combination of exogenous heat exposure and excess heat production without a change in the hypothalamic set point or cytokine production.

Approach to the Patient

Fever can be a presenting sign or symptom in patients with infectious and noninfectious conditions. Subjective patient reports of fever are accurate only about 50% to 75% of the time. Body temperature can be measured with digital thermometers, infrared tympanic thermometers, and liquid crystal thermometers, which measure surface temperature of the skin. Digital thermometers are the most accurate, with rectal temperature the most reproducible. Infrared tympanic thermometers and liquid crystal thermometers can vary as much as 0.5°C to 1.5°C (0.9-2.7°F). Newer infrared thermometers measuring temporal artery temperatures are accurate and reliable. It is best to record body temperature from the same site every time (eg, all oral).

The approach to a febrile patient varies depending on clinical setting (outpatient or inpatient) and whether the patient is immunocompromised. For all patients, first determine the duration of the fever, rapidity of fever onset (abrupt or gradual), and the presence or absence of constitutional symptoms (eg, chills, rigor, sweating). Next, look for localizing clues (eg, cough, coryza, dyspnea, dysuria, diarrhea, localized pain, wounds, rash, unusual discharge, history of recent medical interventions or instrumentation), and focus the physical examination based on these findings. Medication history is always important. Drug reactions can cause confounding and recurrent fever, some with shaking chills. It is often possible to determine if a drug interaction is the cause of fever by eliminating the suspected drug and observing the patient for 48 to 72 hours.

Outpatient Fever

Most cases of fever seen in the outpatient setting are due to viral illness and will resolve in <2 weeks. If a patient is seriously ill (eg, pale, dyspneic, cool, clammy, hypotensive, tachycardic, cyanotic, confused or with an otherwise altered mental state), bacterial infection is more likely. If there are no localizing symptoms, a detailed history and thorough physical examination, including a pelvic examination in a female patient, are necessary. Address recent medication use or transfusions, implanted devices or prostheses, exposure to known illnesses, animal exposures, travel history, drug use, sexual habits, dietary habits (eg, consumption of raw seafood or undercooked meat), and family history of connective tissue disease. This process is repeated on subsequent visits if the fever persists to assess any new symptoms and to monitor for changes. If fever has been of short duration and no potential source for the fever is suggested at the first visit, testing should be directed at any potentially localizing symptoms or physical findings (eg, rapid antigen detection test for pharyngitis). A fever that persists for >3 weeks in an ambulatory patient despite three or more visits and appropriate investigation is designated a fever of unknown origin (FUO).

Inpatient Fever

Fever that occurs in the inpatient setting requires assessment for localizing signs and symptoms as well as potential sources of infection or fever, including intravascular catheters (bacteremia), urinary catheters (urinary tract infection), nasogastric tubes (sinusitis), foreign bodies (infected prosthetic joint, vascular graft, or pacemaker), and blood transfusions (febrile transfusion reaction). Problems due to prolonged immobility (deep venous thrombosis, decubitus ulcers, atelectasis) also should be considered.

Investigate any localized findings, check all invasive sites for signs of infection, inspect dependent parts of the body for skin breakdown (redness, warmth, tenderness, swelling, discharge), examine the legs for swelling, and look for medications associated with hyperthermia or fever. Examinations should be repeated daily until a source is found or the fever resolves. In addition, perform standard laboratory tests, chest radiography, and additional tests as directed by the physical findings. A fever that persists in a hospitalized patient without a diagnosis for >3 days in an immunocompromised inpatient or >1 week in an immunocompetent inpatient is designated FUO.

Fever of Unknown Origin

The most common categories of illness associated with FUO are infectious diseases, systemic inflammatory disorders, and malignancies. The most common infectious cause is tuberculosis; intraabdominal or pelvic abscess is another common cause. Vertebral osteomyelitis is occasionally characterized by FUO without localizing back pain or symptoms. When endocarditis causes FUO, it is usually associated with culture-negative organisms, such as *Coxiella burnetii*, *Bartonella quintana*, or the HACEK organisms (*Haemophilus* species, *Actinobacillus actinomycetemcomitans*, *Cardiobacterium hominis*, *Eikenella corrodens*, and *Kingella kingae*). Febrile illnesses are often associated with rash. The distribution of the rash (eg, extremities [Rocky Mountain spotted fever], trunk [eg, infectious mononucleosis, typhoid fever], or palms and soles [eg, syphilis]), the chronicity of the rash relative to fever, and the character of the rash (eg, vesicular [eg, smallpox, chickenpox] or petechial [eg, vasculitis]) are important in determining a potential cause. Some fever-associated skin lesions suggest serious underlying illnesses, such as Janeway lesions, Osler nodes, or subconjunctival petechiae, which occur in patients with infective endocarditis. In approximately 80% of patients with HIV infection, an additional infection is the cause of fever.

One of the more common vasculitides is temporal arteritis, which can present as FUO in adults aged >50 years, even in the absence of the classic symptoms of headache, jaw claudication, or polymyalgia rheumatica. Other vasculitides (eg, granulomatosis with polyangiitis [Wegener granulomatosis]) and systemic inflammatory disorders (eg, systemic lupus erythematosus, adult-onset Still disease) should also be considered.

The most common FUO-associated malignancy is non-Hodgkin lymphoma. Renal cell carcinoma, any malignancy that metastasizes to the liver, and leukemia are other common causes.

Patients with FUO require a thorough history, physical examination, and a thoughtful laboratory evaluation (Table 1). Imaging in patients with FUO usually begins with plain chest radiography. Subsequent imaging studies should be based on clinical suspicion and be part of a sequential diagnostic strategy. For example, echocardiography and computed tomography (CT) scans of the abdomen, chest, and pelvis may be appropriate depending on clinical considerations. Nuclear imaging studies may also be useful in identifying an inflammatory source of fever when the results of initial imaging studies are normal. Further evaluation, including biopsies, is dictated by abnormal test results. Bone marrow examination may be useful in patients with anemia and thrombocytopenia.

Immature neutrophils (band forms), toxic granulations, or Döhle bodies on a blood smear may indicate a bacterial cause of fever. Leukopenia is most often due to viral illness but may also be seen in patients with autoimmune or marrow infiltrative disorders. Lymphocytosis with atypical lymphocytes is associated with acute Epstein-Barr virus, cytomegalovirus, and HIV infections; monocytosis can be seen with typhoidal disease and tuberculosis. In stable patients with possible infection, there is no need to initiate antibiotic therapy until a diagnosis is established. If no infectious cause is identified, further evaluation is directed toward autoimmune diseases, connective tissue diseases, and granulomatous disorders (ie, sarcoidosis). In the miscellaneous category, thyroiditis, pulmonary embolism, drug fever, and factitious fever need to be considered. If inflammatory markers (eg, erythrocyte sedimentation rate or C-reactive protein) are normal at the time symptoms are present, factitious fever should be considered.

Despite an extensive workup, one-third to half of patients may not receive a specific diagnosis. These patients generally have a good prognosis, with resolution of fever in several months.

Management

Fever, as a symptom, does not always require treatment. When antipyretic agents are administered, studies have shown prolonged time to crusting in varicella and increased viral shedding and suppressed neutralizing antibody production in patients with herpes zoster and rhinovirus infections. Cooling blankets have been shown to increase oxygen consumption (by induced shivering) and to cause coronary artery vasospasm. Alternatively, animal studies suggest the febrile inflammatory response may be detrimental to survival depending on the organ system involved, with higher temperatures resulting in higher mortality in certain infections. This theory further supports the concept that fever treatment should be individualized depending on patient condition and perhaps the nature of the infections.

Also when deciding to treat fever, one must consider the potential adverse effects of antipyretic agents; aspirin is associated with gastrointestinal and renal adverse effects, and acetaminophen is associated with hepatic and renal adverse effects. Antipyretic therapy may be considered for patient comfort and is considered safe when appropriate dosing guidelines are followed. In stable patients without localizing signs, empiric antibiotic therapy is typically withheld. In unstable patients without localizing signs, empiric broad-spectrum antibiotics may be appropriate (see Chapter 64).

Hyperthermia

Hyperthermia is a noninfectious disorder of thermoregulation that results in elevation of body temperature above the normal range. Body temperatures >40.0°C (104.0°F) are life threatening, and brain death begins at 41.0°C (105.8°F). The most important causes of severe hyperthermia are heat stroke, malignant hyperthermia, neuroleptic malignant syndrome, and the serotonin syndrome.

Nonexertional heat stroke from impaired thermoregulation occurs in various cardiovascular, neurologic, and psychiatric disorders and in patients taking diuretics and anticholinergic agents, particularly with exposure to a hot environment. Exertional heat stroke results from strenuous exercise in very hot and humid weather. The first sign of serious heat stroke is the absence of sweating and warm, dry skin. Fans, cooling blankets, ice packs, cold intravenous fluids, and oxygen are used; for severe hyperthermia, cold gastric and peritoneal lavage is also used. Benzodiazepines decrease excessive shivering during treatment.

Malignant hyperthermia is an inherited skeletal muscle disorder characterized by a hypermetabolic state precipitated by exposure to volatile inhalation anesthetics (eg, halothane, isoflurane, enflurane, desflurane, sevoflurane) and depolarizing muscle relaxants (eg, succinylcholine, decamethonium). Malignant hyperthermia usually occurs on exposure to the drug. Increased intracellular calcium leads to sustained muscle contractions, with resultant skeletal muscle rigidity and masseter spasm, tachycardia, hypercarbia, hypertension,

Table 1. Typical Laboratory Evaluation for Persistent Fever
For all patients
Complete blood cell count with differential, peripheral blood smear
Comprehensive metabolic panel
Urinalysis and microscopy
Chest radiography
Blood and urine cultures
Antinuclear antibody and rheumatoid factor testing; ESR and total CRP
HIV antibody testing
For selected patients
Viral serology in patients with mononucleosis-like syndrome (cytomegalovirus, heterophil)
Q fever serology (if exposure to farm animals)
Hepatitis serology (if abnormal liver enzyme levels)

CRP = C-reactive protein; ESR = erythrocyte sedimentation rate.

hyperthermia, tachypnea, and cardiac arrhythmias. Rhabdomyolysis and acute kidney failure can develop. Malignant hyperthermia is life threatening if not treated immediately. Treatment includes discontinuing the offending drug and providing supportive care (eg, hydration, oxygen, cooling measures). Dantrolene sodium, a skeletal muscle relaxant, is the treatment of choice.

The neuroleptic malignant syndrome is a life-threatening disorder caused by an idiosyncratic reaction to neuroleptic tranquilizers and some antipsychotic agents. The most common offending neuroleptic agents are haloperidol and fluphenazine. The syndrome can occur with all drugs that cause central dopamine receptor blockade and usually occurs soon after starting a new drug or with dose escalation. Most patients with the syndrome develop muscle rigidity, hyperthermia, cognitive changes, autonomic instability, diaphoresis, sialorrhea, seizures, arrhythmias, and rhabdomyolysis within 2 weeks after initiating the drug. Death may occur from respiratory or cardiac failure, disseminated intravascular coagulation, or acute kidney failure. Drug therapy with dantrolene sodium and/or bromocriptine decreases mortality and symptom duration.

Patients with serotonin syndrome present with high fever, muscle rigidity, and cognitive changes. Unique findings include shivering, hyperreflexia, myoclonus, and ataxia. The serotonin syndrome is most often caused by the use of selective serotonin reuptake inhibitors. Stopping the offending medication(s) and supportive care are the mainstays of therapy.

Bibliography

Tolia J, Smith LG. Fever of unknown origin: historical and physical clues to making the diagnosis. Infect Dis Clin North Am. 2007;21:917-936, vii. [PMID: 18061082]

Hasday JD, et al. Fever, Hyperthermia, and the lung: It's all about context and timing. Trans Am Clin Climatol Assoc. 2011;122:34 -47. [PMID: 21686207]

Chapter 56

Common Upper Respiratory Infections

Jennifer Bierman, MD

This chapter addresses four common upper respiratory problems: upper respiratory infection (URI), pharyngitis, sinusitis, and otitis media (OM).

Upper Respiratory Infection

URI is an undifferentiated, usually viral syndrome that is benign and self-limited, lasting 3 to 10 days. Viruses (eg, rhinovirus, coronavirus, respiratory syncytial virus, metapneumovirus) cause infection by gaining entrance to epithelial cells of the upper respiratory tract, leading to host inflammatory responses, cholinergic stimulation, vasodilation, and increased vascular permeability.

Prevention

Contact with secretions is the most likely principal mode of transmission. **Frequent hand washing has been proven to prevent transmission of common respiratory infections. Vaccination for influenza can reduce the risk of influenza-like illnesses by 36%. The use of vitamin C or echinacea to prevent common respiratory infections is not supported by strong evidence.**

Diagnosis

Viral URIs have an incubation period of 24 to 72 hours and cause a combination of sore throat, cough, rhinorrhea, fever (body temperature ≤39°C [102°F]) lasting <72 hours, and/or laryngitis. Influenza is differentiated from a viral URI by a typically sudden onset of high fever (body temperature >39°C [102°F]), severe myalgia, and headache. Physical examination of the patient with a viral URI may reveal glassy-appearing nasal mucosa, nasal discharge, and mild oropharyngeal erythema. **Laboratory testing and imaging studies are unnecessary for diagnosis of common respiratory infections.** However, nasal swabs for influenza may be appropriate during flu season if the patient has a high fever. A small percentage of patients will develop secondary acute bacterial sinusitis. Upper respiratory viruses can cause lower respiratory tract infections in patients with underlying cardiopulmonary disease or immunosuppression. Viral URIs can also trigger exacerbation of symptoms in patients with asthma or chronic obstructive pulmonary disease. Pertussis should be considered in patients with a prolonged or harsh cough. Table 1 summarizes the differential diagnosis of URI.

Table 1. Differential Diagnosis of Upper Respiratory Infection

Disorder	Notes
Streptococcal pharyngitis	Fever, tonsillar exudates, and tender anterior cervical adenopathy; cough is absent. Trismus (reduced ability to open the jaw due to muscle spasm), unilateral tonsillar swelling, and deviation of the uvula suggest peritonsillar abscess.
Sinusitis	Purulent nasal discharge, unilateral sinus pain or tenderness, maxillary toothache, poor response to decongestants, and worsening illness after initial improvement.
Acute cough illness (bronchitis, pneumonia, pertussis)	Chest pain, wheezing, dyspnea, and fever. Consider evaluation for pneumonia if pulse is >100 bpm, respiration rate is >24 breaths/min, or temperature is >38.0°C (100.4°F). Consider pertussis with prolonged cough.
Epiglottitis	Severe sore throat with a benign-appearing oropharynx. Adults may have dyspnea, drooling, and stridor. Obtain urgent otolaryngology consultation, and do not attempt to examine the throat. A lateral neck film may show an enlarged epiglottis ("thumb sign").
Mononucleosis (EBV infection)	A 1- to 2-wk prodrome of fatigue, malaise, and myalgia followed by adenopathy (particularly of posterior cervical nodes), sore throat, fever, splenomegaly, hepatomegaly, and lymphocytosis (atypical lymphocytes).
Allergic rhinitis	Seasonal nasal symptoms, including clear rhinorrhea and watery, itchy eyes. Patients may have a history of asthma.
Asthma	Wheezing, dyspnea, and persistent dry cough. Symptoms may worsen at night and be triggered by cold air, exercise, or strong odors.
Influenza	Coryza, body temperature up to 41.0°C (105.8°F), myalgia, headache, and sore throat. Severity of symptoms associated with high fever and myalgia suggest influenza.
Otitis media	Ear pain, fever, decreased hearing acuity, and a tympanic membrane that is red, opaque, bulging, or retracted. Otitis media is more common in children than in adults.
Meningococcal disease	Patients with meningococcal disease may present with sore throat, rhinorrhea, cough, headache, and conjunctivitis before developing invasive disease.

EBV = Epstein-Barr virus.

Therapy

Inhaling heated vapor, such as steam from a hot shower, may decrease nasal symptoms. Other symptomatic measures include increasing fluid intake, gargling with salt water or using saline nasal spray, sucking on throat lozenges, and ensuring adequate rest. Although these measures lack good evidence of effectiveness, they are safe and inexpensive. For relief of nasal congestion, oral decongestants (eg, pseudoephedrine) or short-term (<3 days) use of topical nasal decongestants (eg, phenylephrine) is beneficial. In patients with rhinorrhea and sneezing, a short course of a first-generation antihistamine or intranasal ipratropium may be considered. In patients with a productive cough and wheezing, an inhaled β-agonist may reduce the duration of cough. Acetaminophen or an nonsteroidal anti-inflammatory drugs (eg, naproxen, ibuprofen) may be used for headache, myalgia, and malaise. **Codeine and over-the-counter antitussive agents have not been proven to be effective for acute cough in patients with URIs. Antibiotics are not indicated for uncomplicated URIs, even when purulent sputum or nasal discharge is present.** In the United States, antibiotics are overprescribed for URIs, leading to increased antibiotic resistance. Patients should be instructed to follow up if they develop persistent cough, shortness of breath, hemoptysis, chest pain, wheezing, dysphagia, trismus (inability to open the mouth), severe headache, persistent nasal discharge, or ear pain.

Pharyngitis

Pharyngitis is a common condition encountered in the ambulatory setting. Although viruses (eg, rhinovirus) are the most frequent cause of pharyngitis, infection caused by group A β-hemolytic streptococcus (GABHS) is a concern. GABHS is the major treatable pathogen of acute pharyngitis but causes only about 5% to 15% of cases in adults. Sequelae of GABHS pharyngitis include toxic shock syndrome, suppurative complications (eg, peritonsillar abscess, pneumonia, sepsis), and nonsuppurative postinfectious complications (eg, rheumatic fever, glomerulonephritis, reactive arthritis). Non-group A streptococcus (G and C), *Chlamydophila pneumoniae,* and *Mycoplasma pneumoniae* are other nonviral causes of pharyngitis, but treatment has not been proven to be beneficial. Much less common causes include Epstein-Barr virus infection and acute HIV infection. *Fusobacterium necrophorum* is an emerging cause of nonstreptococcal pharyngitis in adolescents and young adults, accounting for up to 10% of cases in some series. *F. necrophorum* is a gram-negative anaerobe that can cause suppurative complications; it is also the pathogenic agent of Lemierre syndrome (septic thrombophlebitis of the internal jugular vein). Lemierre syndrome has a mortality rate of approximately 4.4%.

Prevention

In the general population, proper diagnosis and treatment of patients who present with symptomatic group A streptococcal pharyngitis are usually sufficient to control the transmission and rapid spread of virulent GABHS strains. **Do not use prophylactic antibiotics in asymptomatic individuals with pharyngitis to prevent the spread of infection.**

Diagnosis

When diagnosing GABHS pharyngitis, it is important to consider the prevalence of GABHS in the community. GABHS is more common in the fall and winter and is associated with crowded living conditions and recent close contact with a person with a GABHS infection. Characteristic symptoms include sudden-onset sore throat, pain on swallowing, headache, fever, and malaise. Coryza (inflammation of the mucous membranes lining the nasal cavity), cough, and hoarseness are typically absent. Look for tonsillopharyngeal erythema with or without exudates, and examine for tender and enlarged anterior cervical lymph nodes. Non-GABHS pharyngitis is indistinguishable from GABHS pharyngitis, and the use of a clinical prediction tool such as the Centor score (Table 2) is recommended. In the diagnosis of GABHS pharyngitis, the rapid antigen detection test has comparable sensitivity (80%-90%) and specificity (95%) to throat culture and is supplanting culture in many settings. The throat swab for either culture or rapid antigen detection test should be obtained from both tonsils or tonsillar fossae and the posterior pharyngeal wall.

Therapy

Antimicrobial therapy should be used only when GABHS pharyngitis is highly likely. **Patients with 0 or 1 Centor criteria are at sufficiently low risk (<3%) that they should neither be tested for group A streptococcal pharyngitis nor treated with antibiotics.** Consider empirical antibiotic treatment for adults with four criteria, as they are at sufficiently high risk (>40%) of group A streptococcal pharyngitis. Evaluate adults with two, three, and perhaps four criteria with a rapid antigen detection test, prior to treatment with antibiotics. A 10-day course of oral penicillin is the treatment of choice; erythromycin is an alternative treatment for patients who are allergic to penicillin. Consider giving a single injection of intramuscular penicillin G benzathine to patients who are unlikely to complete a full 10-day course of oral therapy. Macrolides should be avoided in adolescents and young adults as they do not cover *F. necrophorum.* Advise patients to return if they do not respond to appropriate therapy within 12 to 24 hours or if they develop severe throat pain, dysphagia, drooling (epiglottitis), or unilateral neck swelling (Lemierre syndrome).

Sinusitis

Sinusitis, also referred to as *rhinosinusitis,* is inflammation of the paranasal sinuses and nasal mucosa. Rhinitis is a common symptom with a differential diagnosis that includes allergic, irritant, vasomotor, and infectious causes. Most sinus infections are viral in origin, with only 0.5% to 2% having a bacterial cause. If bacterial, typical

Table 2. Testing and Treatment Guidelines for Adult Pharyngitis

Centor Score[a]	Recommended Testing	Treatment
0-1	No test	No treatment
2-3	RADT	Penicillin V if test is positive
4	Consider RADT for confirmation	Empiric penicillin V

RADT = rapid antigen detection test.

[a]One point is given for each of fever (subjective or measured >100.5°F [38.1°C]), absence of cough, tender anterior cervical lymphadenopathy, and tonsillar exudates.

organisms include *Streptococcus pneumoniae*, *Haemophilus influenzae*, and occasionally *Moraxella catarrhalis*. Dental disease or instrumentation can cause anaerobic infections, whereas immunodeficiency may give rise to fungal infections. Symptoms may be classified as acute (<4 weeks), subacute (4-12 weeks), or chronic (>12 weeks). Complications are rare but include local spread (eg, osteitis of the sinus bones, orbital cellulitis) or metastasis to the central nervous system (eg, meningitis, brain abscess, infection of the intracranial venous sinuses).

Diagnosis

Ask the patient about allergies, systemic diseases, and exposure to irritants. The symptoms of acute sinusitis include nasal congestion, rhinorrhea, and facial pain; more severe infections may be associated with fever and malaise. Examine for rhinorrhea, purulent secretions in the nasal cavity, and local pain. Distinguishing viral rhinosinusitis from bacterial rhinosinusitis can be challenging. The probability of bacterial sinusitis is low (<25%) if only one of the following three diagnostic criteria is present: symptoms lasting >7 days, facial pain, and purulent nasal discharge. Diagnostic probability is higher (50%) when two or more criteria are present. **Avoid sinus imaging in uncomplicated acute sinusitis; patients with ophthalmic or neurologic symptoms or signs may need diagnostic imaging.**

Therapy

Antibiotics have been found to have little if any role in the treatment of patients with acute sinusitis in the primary care setting, and in most cases, symptomatic treatment is first-line therapy. Nonetheless, some guidelines conclude that antibiotics may be a reasonable option if the probability of bacterial rhinosinusitis is increased. This is suggested by rhinosinusitis symptoms lasting 7 or more days and any of the following: purulent nasal discharge, or maxillary tooth or facial pain, especially unilateral, or unilateral maxillary sinus tenderness, or worsening symptoms after initial improvement. If antibiotics are prescribed, amoxicillin-clavulanate is the first-line drug of choice, given increased resistance of *H. influenzae* and *S. pneumoniae*. Doxycycline or respiratory quinolones (eg, levofloxacin and moxifloxacin) are also reasonable treatment options. Macrolides and trimethoprim-sulfamethoxazole are no longer recommended given high rates of *S. pneumoniae* resistance to macrolides and *H. influenzae* resistance to trimethoprim-sulfamethoxazole. Nonmedical therapy includes saline nasal spray or sinus irrigation, which may help increase mucosal moisture and remove inflammatory debris and bacteria. Intranasal steroids may reduce inflammation, mucolytic agents (eg, guaifenesin) may reduce viscosity of nasal secretions, and topical decongestants (eg, xylometazoline) may reduce mucosal inflammation and improve ostial drainage. Although these therapies have not been proven to be efficacious in studies, they are often prescribed.

Otitis Media

Obstruction of the eustachian tube due to allergy or URI results in accumulation of secretions in the middle ear. Secondary bacterial or viral infection of the resulting effusion causes suppuration and the clinical features of OM. Risk factors for OM include age (eg, younger age for acute OM [AOM], older age for chronic OM), smoking, allergic rhinitis, and chronic eustachian tube dysfunction. Viruses responsible for OM include respiratory syncytial virus, influenza virus, rhinovirus, and adenovirus. The most common bacterial causes include *S. pneumoniae*, *H. influenzae*, and *M. catarrhalis*. Rare complications of OM include meningitis, epidural abscess, brain abscess, lateral sinus thrombosis, cavernous sinus thrombosis, and carotid artery thrombosis.

Diagnosis

OM must be differentiated from otitis externa, which is inflammation of the ear canal and is not associated with hearing changes or evidence of fluid in the middle ear. Symptoms of OM include ear pain and decreased conductive hearing. Typically allergy or URI symptoms precede signs of OM by several days. Examine for fluid in the middle ear and a retracted or bulging, erythematous tympanic membrane. The absence of tympanic membrane mobility on pneumatic otoscopy adds additional diagnostic information (sensitivity 89%, specificity 80%). Tenderness to palpation over the mastoid area may indicate extension of infection into the mastoid. Chronic OM may be suppurative or associated with formation of a cholesteatoma (a mass consisting of excess squamous epithelium), which can erode into surrounding structures and lead to otorrhea, pain, hearing loss, or neurologic symptoms.

Therapy

Managing AOM begins with decongestant therapy and pain control. Reserve antibiotic therapy for younger patients with evidence of purulent OM or for those whose symptoms (eg, congestion, eustachian tube dysfunction) do not respond to conservative treatment. Most adults with AOM should be managed with antibiotics. First-line therapy continues to include amoxicillin despite emerging resistance by *H. influenza* (or a macrolide for patients who are allergic to penicillin). Amoxicillin-clavulanate should be considered for patients with severe disease. Antibiotic treatment is usually for 7 to 10 days. Follow-up is not necessary unless symptoms persist or progress. Consider referral for ventilation tube insertion in patients with recurrent OM and/or associated hearing loss. There is no evidence to support the use of glucocorticoids for patients with AOM.

Bibliography

Centor RM. Expand the pharyngitis paradigm for adolescents and young adults. Ann Intern Med. 2009;151:812. [PMID: 19949147]

Chapter 57

Community-Acquired Pneumonia

Irene Alexandraki, MD

Community-acquired pneumonia (CAP) affects 4 million adults per year in the United States, 20% of whom will require hospitalization. CAP is the leading cause of death from infectious disease in the United States and the sixth-leading cause of death overall.

Host defense mechanisms keep the lower airways sterile. Pneumonia develops when there is a defect in host defenses, exposure to a particularly virulent organism, or an overwhelming inoculum. The pathogens descend from the oropharynx to the lower respiratory tract (90% of cases) or are acquired through inhalation (viruses), hematogenously (*Staphylococcus*), or directly from a contiguous infected site. Alterations in anatomic barriers and impairment of humoral or cell-mediated immunity or phagocytic function are risk factors for pneumonia.

Streptococcus pneumoniae is the most common pathogen isolated from patients with CAP; drug-resistant *S. pneumoniae* accounts for up to 40% of isolates. Other common bacterial pathogens include *Haemophilus influenzae* and atypical pathogens, such as *Mycoplasma pneumoniae*, *Chlamydophila pneumoniae*, and *Legionella*. Gram-negative bacteria may be a cause in patients with comorbidities (eg, chronic cardiopulmonary disease, chronic kidney or liver disease, diabetes mellitus, active malignancy, recent antibiotic therapy) and in extended care facility residents. *Klebsiella pneumoniae* causes severe pneumonia in patients with alcoholism. *Pseudomonas aeruginosa* is more common in patients with structural lung disease (eg, bronchiectasis) and after recent antibiotic therapy or hospitalization. When aspiration is a possibility, enteric gram-negative and anaerobic organisms should be considered. Viral pathogens (influenza virus, parainfluenza virus, adenovirus, respiratory syncytial virus) also cause CAP. Influenza increases the susceptibility of previously healthy persons to secondary invasive infections with pneumococcal or methicillin-resistant *Staphylococcus aureus* pneumonia, resulting in increased morbidity and mortality during influenza epidemics and pandemics.

Prevention

Influenza vaccine prevents or attenuates illness due to influenza and reduces pneumonia-related mortality during influenza season by 27% to 50%. The U.S. Advisory Committee on Immunization Practices recommends annual influenza vaccination with the 23-valent pneumococcal polysaccharide vaccine (PPSV23) for all persons aged ≥ 6 months. The vaccine should be administered as soon as it becomes available, usually in September. Consider empiric use of oseltamivir or zanamivir in unvaccinated high-risk persons during an influenza epidemic.

Two versions of pneumococcal vaccine are available: the PPSV23 and a 13-valent conjugate vaccine (PCV13). PPSV23 contains purified, capsular polysaccharide from 23 serotypes that cause 85% to 90% of invasive pneumonia in adults and children and is effective in preventing pneumococcal bacteremia and meningitis in healthy, immunocompetent adults. This vaccine should be administered to all adults aged ≥65 years and to all adults aged <65 years who live in long-term care facilities or who have coronary artery disease, heart failure, chronic obstructive pulmonary disease (COPD), diabetes, alcoholism, cirrhosis, cerebrospinal fluid leaks, or anatomic or functional asplenia, including sickle cell disease. Also immunize adults aged <65 years who are immunocompromised due to HIV infection, an immune disorder or malignancy, multiple myeloma, leukemia, lymphoma, Hodgkin disease, chronic kidney disease, nephrotic syndrome, or immunosuppressive therapy (including long-term glucocorticoids). Revaccinate immunocompromised patients once, 5 years after the initial vaccination, and revaccinate patients aged 65 years or greater if they received the PPSV23 vaccine at least 5 years earlier.

The PCV13 vaccine is also indicated as one-time therapy for all adults ≥65 years of age. The PCV vaccine is otherwise indicated only in patients with immunocompromising conditions, asplenia, cerebrospinal fluid leaks, or cochlear implants. To optimize immunogenicity in patients eligible for both vaccines, the PPSV23 and PCV13 vaccines are not administered together. For patients who have never received any pneumococcal vaccination, the PCV13 is usually given first, with the PPSV23 following at least 8 weeks later, and those who have already received the PPSV23, the PCV13 is usually given ≥1 year after that immunization.

Diagnosis

Consider pneumonia in a patient with cough, sputum, fever, chills, or dyspnea. Ask about the duration of symptoms and pleuritic chest pain, night sweats, and weight loss. Symptoms may develop abruptly or may gradually worsen over days. Patients with chronic illness may present with nonrespiratory symptoms or deterioration of their illness. Elderly patients may have confusion, weakness, lethargy, poor oral intake, or complaints of falling; older patients may be afebrile and remain undiagnosed until late in the course of illness.

Ask the patient about chronic heart and lung disease (eg, pneumococci, enteric gram-negative bacteria, *H. influenzae*); travel to the southwestern United States (eg, *Coccidioides*) or Southeast Asia (eg, *Mycobacterium tuberculosis*); alcohol abuse (eg, anaerobes, *K. pneumoniae*); injection drug use (eg, methicillin-resistant *S. aureus*, anaerobes, *M. tuberculosis*); and exposure to farm animals (eg, *Coxiella burnetii*), birds (*Chlamydophila psittaci*, *Cryptococcus*, *Histoplasma*), and bats (*Histoplasma*). Assess risk for aspiration, such as history of stroke, seizures, alcoholism, or poor dentition (eg, anaerobes). Information about residence and recent antibiotic therapy may also help predict likely pathogens.

Look for tachypnea, fever, crackles, bronchial breath sounds, and signs of pleural effusion, such as egophony and dullness to percussion with reduced breath sounds. Consider using the CURB-65 criteria (Confusion, blood Urea nitrogen >19.6 mg/dL [7.0 mmol/L],

Respiration rate ≥30 breaths/min, systolic Blood pressure <90 mm Hg or diastolic blood pressure <60 mm Hg, and age ≥65 years) to identify high-risk patients and to predict a complicated course. Patients who meet at least two criteria are usually admitted to the hospital, and those with at least three criteria are considered for intensive care unit (ICU) admission. Another prognostic model, the Pneumonia Severity Index, may be used to predict mortality risk based on patient age, comorbidities, physical examination findings, and laboratory data. Admit patients who have failed outpatient therapy, have decompensated comorbid illness, have complex social needs, cannot receive outpatient care or reliably take oral medications, or require intravenous antibiotics or oxygen. Although there is a need to reduce unnecessary hospitalizations for CAP, the decision for admission is complex, and no single rule can replace careful clinical assessment.

Obtain a chest radiograph in patients with clinical features suggesting CAP. Chest radiography documents the presence of pneumonia and complications, such as pleural effusion, lung abscess, cavitation, and multilobar illness. Limit directed laboratory testing in uncomplicated outpatient cases to chest radiography and pulse oximetry to assess oxygenation. The presence of cavities with air-fluid levels suggests abscess formation, whereas the presence of cavities without air-fluid levels suggests tuberculosis or fungal infection. If there is evidence of volume loss, bronchial obstruction must be excluded. Enlargement of mediastinal or hilar lymph nodes suggests fungal or mycobacterial infection. If a pleural effusion is present, obtain a decubitus film or chest CT scan. The presence of pleural fluid may indicate empyema possibly requiring thoracentesis.

For hospitalized patients, order chest radiography, two sets of blood cultures, a routine metabolic panel, pulse oximetry, and a complete blood count. Obtain arterial blood gases when carbon dioxide retention is suspected (eg, patients with COPD). **Sputum**

Gram stain and culture are not indicated in hospitalized patients with less severe pneumonia, but they should be obtained for any patient at risk for infection with drug-resistant or unusual pathogens or those with severe pneumonia. Use rapid antigen tests for influenza A and B during the appropriate season and during epidemics. Consider testing concentrated urine for pneumococcal and *Legionella* antigens in the appropriate clinical setting. Suspect *Legionella* in patients with risk factors (eg, age ≥50 years, smoking history, immunocompromising condition) who present with severe pneumonia and extrapulmonary symptoms (eg, headache, confusion, diarrhea, kidney failure). Hyponatremia occurs more often in individuals with Legionnaire disease than in other causes of pneumonia. The urine antigen test detects only *Legionella* serogroup 1.

Consider unusual pathogens (eg, *M. tuberculosis*, fungi, viruses, *Pneumocystis*) in patients who do not respond to empiric therapy within 48 to 72 hours. Also consider empyema, lung abscess, metastatic infectious complications (eg, endocarditis), and noninfectious processes (Table 1). In such circumstances, order additional diagnostic tests (eg, chest CT, pulmonary angiography, bronchoscopy) and consider obtaining infectious disease or pulmonary consultation.

Therapy

In the outpatient setting, treat patients without cardiopulmonary disease or other comorbidities with a macrolide or doxycycline. For patients with cardiopulmonary disease or modifying factors (Table 2), use a respiratory quinolone or a combination of a β-lactam and a macrolide or doxycycline. Macrolides, quinolones, and doxycycline will provide coverage of atypical organisms (Table 3).

For hospitalized patients, administer oxygen, titrating to an oxygen saturation level of ≥90%. Do not delay antibiotic therapy while awaiting sputum sampling for culture, if ordered. Give intravenous

Table 1. Differential Diagnosis of Community-Acquired Pneumonia

Disorder	Notes
Organizing pneumonia (see Chapter 95)	Subacute illness (4-6 wk) with fever and alveolar infiltrates (often peripheral). Diagnosis is based on biopsy (transbronchial or open lung) or characteristic clinical picture and response to glucocorticoids.
Lung cancer (see Chapter 81)	May cause postobstructive pneumonia. Suspect in patients who smoke, especially if there is hemoptysis and radiographic evidence of volume loss or a mass effect.
Eosinophilic pneumonia (see Chapter 95)	Presents as an acute illness with the radiographic "photo negative" of pulmonary edema, usually with peripheral eosinophilia. Biopsy may not be needed with a classic presentation.
Hypersensitivity pneumonitis (see Chapter 95)	Recurrent episodes of fever and dyspnea, with rapid resolution of infiltrates; chronic infiltrates after multiple episodes. Diagnose with precipitating antibodies to the antigen (molds etc.), characteristic history, or open lung biopsy.
Interstitial pneumonia (see Chapter 95)	A nonspecific radiographic pattern resulting from infection (viral, atypical pathogen), inflammation (usual interstitial pneumonia), or drug toxicity (amiodarone). A careful exposure history and duration of illness can help distinguish between several diagnostic possibilities, but open lung biopsy may be required.
Pulmonary embolism (see Chapter 96)	If infarction is present, there may be fever, lung infiltrate, dyspnea, and hemoptysis. Suspect in patients with appropriate risk factors (immobilization, heart failure, recent surgery). The infiltrate of infarction may "melt away" rapidly.
Sarcoidosis (see Chapter 95)	May present as lung infiltrate of any type, with or without mediastinal adenopathy. Suspect if the radiographic abnormalities in the lung parenchyma are extensive and the patient is not as ill as suggested by the radiographic pattern. Diagnosis can be made by transbronchial lung biopsy.
Granulomatosis with polyangiitis (Wegener) (see Chapter 106)	Associated with characteristic nodular and cavitary infiltrates, hemoptysis, and otitis media. May be limited to the lung or involve the kidneys (rapidly progressive glomerulonephritis). In general, diagnosis is based on the characteristic clinical picture, presence of c-ANCA, and absence of p-ANCA. If uncertain, perform open lung biopsy to document vasculitis.

c-ANCA = cytoplasmic antineutrophil cytoplasmic antibody; p-ANCA = perinuclear antineutrophil cytoplasmic antibody.

Table 2. Modifying Factors That Increase the Risk of Infection With Specific Pathogens

Modifying Factor	Pathogen
Age >65 y, β-lactam therapy (in previous 3 mo), alcoholism, immunosuppression (illness, glucocorticoids), multiple medical comorbidities, exposure to a child in a day care center	Penicillin-resistant and drug-resistant pneumococci
Residence in an extended care facility, underlying cardiopulmonary disease, multiple medical comorbidities, recent antibiotic therapy	Enteric gram-negative bacteria
Structural lung disease (bronchiectasis), glucocorticoid therapy, broad-spectrum antibiotic therapy for >7 d; malnutrition	*Pseudomonas aeruginosa*
Endobronchial obstruction (tumor)	Anaerobes, *Streptococcus pneumoniae, Haemophilus influenzae, Staphylococcus aureus*
Intravenous drug use	Anaerobes, *S. aureus, Mycobacterium tuberculosis, S. pneumoniae*
Influenza epidemic in the community	Influenza virus, *S. pneumoniae, S. aureus, H. influenzae*
COPD, smoking history	*S. pneumoniae, H. influenzae, Moraxella catarrhalis, P. aeruginosa, Legionella* species, *Chlamydophila pneumoniae*
Poor dental hygiene, aspiration, lung abscess	Oral anaerobes
Animal exposure	*Coxiella burnetii* (farm animals); *Chlamydophila psittaci, Cryptococcus* (birds); *Histoplasma* (birds, bats)

COPD = chronic obstructive pulmonary disease.

antibiotics within 6 hours of the patient's arrival to the hospital, after rapid assessment of oxygenation and blood work and cultures. Monitor oxygen therapy carefully in patients with COPD, who may further retain carbon dioxide. Provide intravenous hydration to patients with signs of dehydration and chest physiotherapy to patients with large volumes of respiratory secretions.

Give a respiratory quinolone or the combination of a β-lactam and a macrolide or doxycycline to hospitalized patients admitted to the medical ward (Table 4). Use clindamycin or a β-lactam/β-lactamase inhibitor (ampicillin-sulbactam, piperacillin-tazobactam) when aspiration is suspected. Treat a lung abscess secondary to aspiration with clindamycin, and consider surgery if there is inadequate response to medical therapy or concern for a noninfectious cause and a need for tissue diagnosis.

ICU admission is required for patients with severe pneumonia who are at increased risk for death (Table 5). Patients with respiratory failure requiring mechanical ventilation or with septic shock require ICU admission. Respiratory failure is defined as the inability to maintain an oxygen saturation level of >90% on maximal mask oxygen, or the presence of hypercarbia. Intubation may be required for patients with an inability to clear secretions or for airway protection. Alert and cooperative patients with isolated hypoxemia or hypercarbia might be candidates for noninvasive positive pressure ventilation. Treat patients in the ICU with a combination of antibiotics (see Table 4).

Treat patients with mild-to-moderate CAP for ≤7 days if there is a good clinical response, no fever for 48 to 72 hours, and no sign of extrapulmonary infection. Treat patients with *Legionella* infection for 5 to 10 days when a quinolone is used. Treat patients with severe illness, empyema, lung abscess, meningitis, or documented infection with pathogens such as *P. aeruginosa* or *S. aureus* for ≥10 days. Patients with bacteremic *S. aureus* pneumonia need 4 to 6 weeks of therapy and testing to rule out endocarditis, whereas patients with uncomplicated bacteremic pneumococcal pneumonia may need only a 7- to 10-day course of therapy if they have a good clinical response.

In hospitalized patients on intravenous antibiotics, switch to oral antibiotic therapy once symptoms improve and when patients have no fever on two occasions 8 hours apart and are able to take medications by mouth. Discharge patients once the switch to oral therapy is made.

Follow-Up

Follow-up is necessary to ensure that the pneumonia has resolved, to exclude other pulmonary disease, and to focus on prevention of future episodes. **Only obtain a chest radiograph after initial therapy for community-acquired pneumonia if the patient does not respond to treatment, or to document resolution of pneumonia with risk factors and suspicion of an underlying disease, such as malignancy.** Radiographic resolution lags behind clinical resolution, taking as long as 6 to 8 weeks; therefore, follow-up imaging should occur after 6 weeks if indicated. Lung cancer, inflammatory disease, or infection with unusual or resistant pathogens may be present if

Table 3. Antibiotic Therapy for Community-Acquired Pneumonia in Outpatients

Risk Factors	Treatment
Previously healthy and no risk factor(s) for drug-resistant *Streptococcus pneumoniae*	Macrolide (azithromycin, clarithromycin, or erythromycin) or doxycycline
Risk factor(s) for drug-resistant *S. pneumoniae* or underlying comorbidities	Respiratory fluoroquinolone (moxifloxacin, gemifloxacin, or levofloxacin) or β-lactam[a] plus a macrolide or doxycycline

[a]Amoxicillin, 1 g every 8 hours, or amoxicillin-clavulanate, 2 g every 12 hours (preferred), or cefpodoxime or cefuroxime, 500 mg twice daily (alternative).

Table 4. Empiric Antibiotic Therapy for Community-Acquired Pneumonia in Inpatients

Inpatient Setting	Treatment
Medical ward	β-lactam[a] plus a macrolide or doxycycline; or respiratory fluoroquinolone (eg, moxifloxacin, gemifloxacin or levofloxacin)
Intensive care unit	β-lactam[b] plus either azithromycin or a fluoroquinolone[c]; if penicillin allergic, a respiratory fluoroquinolone[d] plus aztreonam
If risk factor(s) for *Pseudomonas aeruginosa* or gram-negative rods on sputum Gram stain	Antipseudomonal β-lactam with pneumococcal coverage (eg, cefepime, imipenem, meropenem, or piperacillin-tazobactam) plus ciprofloxacin or levofloxacin (750 mg); or antipseudomonal β-lactam with pneumococcal coverage plus an aminoglycoside plus azithromycin; or antipseudomonal[e] β-lactam with pneumococcal coverage plus an aminoglycoside plus a respiratory fluoroquinolone
If risk factor(s) for CA-MRSA or compatible sputum Gram stain	Add vancomycin or linezolid to β-lactam[b] plus either azithromycin or a fluoroquinolone[c]

CA-MRSA = community-associated methicillin-resistant *Staphylococcus aureus*.

[a]Cefotaxime, ceftriaxone, or ampicillin; ertapenem is an alternative in patients with an increased risk of enteric gram-negative pathogens (not *P. aeruginosa*).

[b]Cefotaxime, ceftriaxone, or ampicillin/sulbactam.

[c]Moxifloxacin, gemifloxacin, ciprofloxacin, or levofloxacin.

[d]Moxifloxacin, gemifloxacin, or levofloxacin.

[e]Aztreonam can be used in a patient with a severe β-lactam allergy.

Table 5. IDSA/ATS Minor Criteria for Severe Community-Acquired Pneumonia

Clinical Criteria

Confusion (new-onset disorientation to person, place, or time)

Hypothermia (core temperature <36.0°C [96.8°F])

Respiration rate ≥30 breaths/min[a]

Hypotension necessitating aggressive fluid resuscitation

Multilobar pulmonary infiltrates

Laboratory Criteria

Arterial P_{O_2}/F_{IO_2} ratio ≤250[a]

Leukopenia (<4000 cells/μL [4.0×10^9/L])

Thrombocytopenia (<100,000 platelets /μL [10×10^9/L])

Blood urea nitrogen >20 mg/dL (7.1 mmol/L)

IDSA/ATS = Infectious Diseases Society of America/American Thoracic Society.

[a]A patient who requires noninvasive positive-pressure ventilation should be considered to meet this criterion.

Reprinted with permission from Mandell LA, Wunderink RG, Anzueto A, et al; Infectious Diseases Society of America; American Thoracic Society. Infectious Diseases Society of America/American Thoracic Society consensus guidelines on the management of community-acquired pneumonia in adults. Clin Infect Dis. 2007;44(suppl 2):S27-72. [PMID: 17278083] Copyright 2007, Oxford University Press.

the x-ray fails to resolve. Administer pneumococcal and influenza vaccines if they have not previously been given, and advise patients who smoke cigarettes to stop smoking.

Bibliography

Mandell LA, Wunderink RG, Anzueto A, et al. Infectious Diseases Society of America/American Thoracic Society Consensus Guidelines on the Management of Community-Acquired Pneumonia in Adults. Clin Infect Dis. 2007;44(suppl 2):S27-72. [PMID: 16983271]

Niederman M. In the clinic. Community-acquired pneumonia [published erratum appears in Ann Intern Med. 2009;151:827]. Ann Intern Med. 2009;151:ITC4-2-ITC4-14; quiz ITC4-16. [PMID: 19805767]

Tang KL, Eurich DT, Minhas-Sandhu JK, Marrie TJ, Majumdar SR.. Incidence, correlates, and chest radiographic yield of new lung cancer diagnosis in 3398 patients with pneumonia. Arch Intern Med. 2011;171:1193. [PMID: 21518934]

Chapter 58

Tuberculosis

Bipin Thapa, MD

Tuberculosis is a common infectious disease worldwide, with mortality rates up to 80% in untreated persons. Infection by *Mycobacterium tuberculosis* primarily involves the lungs but has the potential to affect nearly any organ. Inhalation of infected airborne droplets initiates a cell-mediated immunologic response. Macrophages initially engulf the inhaled bacilli but cannot arrest mycobacterial multiplication, and a granuloma forms. As immunity develops, the patient becomes reactive to the tuberculin skin test (TST) and positive to interferon-γ release assay (IGRA). If the infection is contained, a state of latent tuberculosis infection (LTBI) without systemic manifestations may ensue. Persons with LTBI are noninfectious. However, the risk for reactivation of dormant bacilli and resultant active infection remains for years. Treatment of LTBI, the most prevalent form of tuberculosis in the United States, decreases rates of reactivation tuberculosis by up to 90%. Reactivation tuberculosis is usually localized to the lungs.

In the case of an initial inadequate immune response, infection may spread to nearly every organ hematogenously or via lymphatics. HIV/AIDS is a major risk factor for both primary progression and reactivation of quiescent tuberculosis, but malnutrition and other immunosuppressed states also increase risk.

Recent challenges to tuberculosis control in the United States include the association with HIV infection, risks of reactivation (especially in settings of decreased cell-mediated immunity), spread of new disease (occasionally in epidemic form), and emergence of multidrug-resistant (MDR) strains. Multidrug resistance constitutes a major factor in mandating lengthy drug regimens monitored by a health care worker or public health program. Aggressive screening programs and a high index of suspicion form the cornerstone of control of active tuberculosis infection.

Prevention

Implement primary prevention of tuberculosis by isolating infected patients, and promote secondary prevention by treating patients with evidence of LTBI; the risk of reactivation tuberculosis is greatest in the first 1 to 2 years following initial infection. Hospitalized patients with suspected or confirmed active tuberculosis should be isolated in a private room with negative air pressure, the door should remain closed, all entering persons should wear masks with a filtering capacity of 95% (different from regular surgical masks), and the hospital infection control department should be notified. All cases of active tuberculosis must be reported to the public health department.

Offer LTBI treatment to all high-risk persons with a positive TST result or positive to IGRA regardless of age, unless prior treatment is documented or is medically contraindicated. Bacille Calmette-Guérin (BCG) vaccination has no role in tuberculosis prevention in the United States.

Screening

Screening is not needed for individuals at low risk of tuberculosis. Screen individuals at high risk for exposure to or contraction of tuberculosis using purified protein derivative with the Mantoux TST method or IGRA. Table 1 summarizes high-risk populations recommended for screening. A positive TST is defined by the diameter of the indurated area, not the size of the erythema; taking into account a person's risk profile increases the specificity of a TST test (Table 2). Educational outreach to health care workers improves the case detection rate of tuberculosis.

Skin tests do not always convert after BCG vaccination, and history of vaccination alters neither testing nor consideration of treatment in most adults. Because the skin test result may not become positive for up to 12 weeks after exposure to active tuberculosis, consider retesting or treating empirically, especially in high-risk persons (eg, those with HIV infection). Patients exposed to tuberculosis in the more distant past initially may have a negative skin test; a second skin test 7 to 21 days after the first may be helpful in reducing the false-negative response rate. Such two-step testing often "boosts" a negative test result to positive as the immune system recalls its previous exposure, thus uncovering a true-positive result. Two-step testing may be particularly helpful for regular testing programs (eg, nursing home resident/employee or hospital employee programs) to distinguish new from old exposure. An alternative screening option is the IGRA, which assesses the T-cell response to specific *M. tuberculosis* antigens. Although it is significantly more expensive than TST and may not be available in all areas, it is obtained with a single blood draw and does not require persons to return for the test to be inter-

Table 1. High-risk Populations Recommended for Tuberculosis Screening

Anyone who has close contact with a person with known or suspected active tuberculosis.

Persons who were born in areas with high rates of tuberculosis (Asia, Africa, Latin America, Eastern Europe, Russia).

Persons who reside or are employed in high-risk congregate settings.

Persons who provide health care to high-risk persons.

Medically underserved or low-income populations.

Populations with increased prevalence of tuberculosis (Asian and Pacific Islanders, Hispanics, blacks, American Indians, migrant farm workers, homeless persons).

Persons who use illicit injection drugs.

Persons with HIV infection or other immunocompromised state.

Patients who are on long-term immunosuppressive therapy (eg, glucocorticoids, TNF-α inhibitors, transplant recipients).

TNF-α = tumor necrosis factor-α.

Table 2. Criteria for Tuberculin Positivity by Risk Group

Induration ≥5 mm	Induration ≥10 mm	Induration ≥15 mm
Person with HIV infection	Person who recently (<5 y) arrived from a country with high TB prevalence	All others with no risk factors for TB
Person with recent contact with a case of active TB	Injection drug user	
Person with fibrotic changes on chest radiograph consistent with old TB	Resident or employee of a high-risk congregate setting (eg, prison, jail, nursing home or other long-term facility for the elderly, hospital or other health care facility, residential facility for patients with AIDS, homeless shelter)	
Person with an organ transplant or other immunosuppressive condition (eg, receiving equivalent of ≥15 mg/d of prednisone for >4 wk or those taking TNF-α antagonists)	Health care worker Employee of a mycobacteriology laboratory Person with a clinical condition associated with high risk for active TB Children age <4 y or exposed to adults in high-risk categories	

TB = tuberculosis; TNF-α = tumor necrosis factor-α.

preted, as does the TST. IGRA, unlike TST, does not give a false-positive result in BCG-vaccinated persons. Therefore, IGRA is the preferred screening method for those who are BCG vaccinated and those who are unlikely to return for TST interpretation. For children under 5 years of age, TST is preferred over IGRA. Generally, IGRA is used in place of and not in addition to TST in all situations where testing is recommended. Only in certain situations, such as when an initial test result is indeterminate or negative but the clinical suspicion is high, or when additional evidence of infection is required to improve compliance, both tests are considered. Choice of test depends on patient-specific factors, test availability, and cost. A positive skin test or positive IGRA test result suggest that the person has been infected with *M. tuberculosis*. Neither test, however, is able to differentiate between LTBI and active tuberculosis. Chest radiography, in addition to a history and physical examination, is mandatory to rule out active disease in all patients with a positive skin test or positive IGRA result being considered for LTBI treatment.

Diagnosis

Patients with pulmonary tuberculosis are often asymptomatic. Constitutional symptoms (eg, anorexia, fatigue, weight loss, chills, fever, night sweats), however, as well as local symptoms (eg, cough) may develop. Hemoptysis and chest pain from pleural involvement indicate advanced disease. The result of the pulmonary examination is often minimally abnormal. HIV-infected or otherwise immunocompromised patients have a greater likelihood of disseminated or extrapulmonary infection, but classic signs or symptoms of tuberculosis are often absent, and chest radiograph results may be normal. Maintain a high level of suspicion for active tuberculosis to enable rapid diagnosis. Gather information about active tuberculosis exposures, previous tuberculosis, and previous skin testing. Table 3 summarizes the differential diagnosis of tuberculosis.

Bacteriologic confirmation and susceptibility testing form the cornerstone of management. Obtain acid-fast bacilli smears and cul-

Table 3. Differential Diagnosis of Tuberculosis

Disorder	Notes
Nontuberculous mycobacterial infection	Signs and symptoms may be the same as for TB; patients usually have less fever and weight loss than patients with TB. Presence of multiple nodules with bronchiectasis on lung CT is highly specific for *Mycobacterium avium* complex.
Sarcoidosis (see Chapter 95)	Patients have dyspnea and cough. Chest radiography shows diffuse infiltrative lung disease with bilateral hilar adenopathy. Biopsy reveals noncaseating granulomas. Diagnosis is made after exclusion of other possibilities.
Aspiration pneumonia	May have an indolent course. Radiologic infiltrates are more common in dependent areas. Patients may have decreased mental status or evidence of reduced gag reflex.
Lung abscess	Frequently involves the posterior upper segments of the upper lobes; may be acute or indolent. Patients usually have foul-smelling sputum.
Histoplasmosis or coccidioidomycosis	Patients may have fever, cough, and night sweats. These diseases are usually geographically specific (eg, histoplasmosis, Midwest; coccidioidomycosis, Southwest). Chest radiography may show a miliary (eg, histoplasmosis) or cavitary lesion.
Granulomatosis with polyangiitis (Wegener granulomatosis)	Necrotizing granulomas in the lung and necrotizing glomerulonephritis. Patients have fever and cough. Chest radiography shows a cavitary lesion in up to 70% of cases. (see Chapter 106)
Actinomycosis	Characterized by cough, hemoptysis, and (eventually) draining sinuses. Has an indolent course; patients may have respiratory symptoms for up to 5 mo before diagnosis. Sulfur granules are seen in stained specimens from draining sinuses.
Lung cancer (see Chapter 81)	Symptoms may be the same as those in patients with TB (eg, weight loss, cough). Cytology or biopsy to rule out. Patients may have both lung cancer and TB.

CT = computed tomography; TB = tuberculosis.

tures (pulmonary and any suspected site of infection), chest radiographs, and skin tests or IGRA in patients suspected of having active tuberculosis (Table 4). In patients with infection, the TST result is usually positive within 48 to 72 hours. A false-negative skin test may occur in anergic patients and in up to 25% of those with active tuberculosis. On 3 separate days, send early-morning induced sputum (or early-morning gastric washings if voluntary sputum is unattainable) for rapid nucleic acid amplification testing, culture, and staining (Ziehl-Neelsen or Kinyoun). Nucleic acid amplification tests of sputum may be used to exclude tuberculosis in patients with false-positive sputum (nontuberculous mycobacteria) or to confirm the disease in some patients with false-negative smears. Patients with active disease may have only a single positive culture. For patients suspected of having pleural tuberculosis, consider thoracentesis to obtain fluid for testing (adenosine deaminase, microbiology, and cell count) or pleural biopsies. In persons with unknown human immunodeficiency virus (HIV) status, test for HIV infection.

Radiologic abnormalities of reactivation tuberculosis classically include lesions in the apical posterior segments of the upper lung and superior segments of the lower lobe. Primary progressive tuberculosis may manifest as hilar adenopathy or infiltrates in any part of the lung, similar to bacterial pneumonia. Atypical or absent radiologic findings are common in immunocompromised patients but may also be the case for immunocompetent patients. Bronchoscopy may aid in the diagnosis in certain circumstances.

Therapy

The standard treatment for suspected or confirmed active tuberculosis is at least 6 months of a four-drug regimen usually consisting of isoniazid, rifampin, pyrazinamide, and ethambutol. Base all treatment on resistance patterns in the area where the patient was likely exposed to tuberculosis. Directly observed therapy programs are ideal. A repeat sputum smear and culture after the initial 2-month phase of therapy may aid in determining whether the continuation phase of treatment requires 4 or 7 months of antibiotic therapy, especially in cavitary disease. These approaches decrease the incidence of acquired drug resistance, relapse, reactivation, and transmission. Consider the possibility of potential drug interactions (eg, with concurrent HIV drug therapy). MDR tuberculosis is resistant to at least isoniazid and rifampin. Extensively drug-resistant (XDR) tuberculosis is an MDR strain (therefore, resistant to isoniazid and rifampin) that is also resistant to fluoroquinolones and at least to kanamycin, amikacin, or capreomycin. Treatment of MDR or XDR tuberculosis requires an individualized regimen based on comprehensive drug susceptibility testing and consultation with an expert.

Patients with LTBI are treated with one of the following treatment regimens: isoniazid daily for 9 months or rifampin daily for 4 months, or the combination of rifapentine and isoniazid once weekly for 3 months via directly observed therapy. Therapy must be individualized. Before treatment is initiated, exclude active tuberculosis by history, physical examination, and chest radiography. Discuss with the patient the risks and benefits of drug therapy as well as the patient's perception of LTBI treatment to optimize adherence to treatment. Before starting therapy, obtain baseline blood tests specific to potential drug toxicities to detect abnormalities that might complicate treatment (eg, hepatic dysfunction complicated by isoniazid, pyrazinamide, or rifampin). Baseline or follow-up audiometry (eg, streptomycin toxicity) or visual acuity testing (eg, ethambutol toxicity) may also be required.

Table 4. Laboratory and Other Studies for Tuberculosis

Test	Notes
Complete blood count	Anemia is present in 10% of patients with TB, particularly if infection is disseminated. Leukocytosis is present in 10% of patients with TB.
Electrolytes	Hyponatremia is present in up to 11% of patients with TB.
Chest radiography	The classic appearance of reactivation TB is lesions in the apical posterior segments of the upper lung and superior segments of the lower lobe. Chest radiograph results may be normal in patients with endobronchial disease or in symptomatic HIV-infected patients with active TB. In disseminated disease, 50%-90% have a miliary pattern on chest x-ray.
TST	TST has a sensitivity of 59%-100% and a specificity of 44%-100%. Sensitivity and specificity change with specific patient risk factors and cutoff point (see Table 2). A positive test result may indicate latent TB. False-positive results can occur with exposure to nontuberculous mycobacteria and BCG vaccine. False-negative results occur in anergic patients and in up to 25% of patients with active TB.
IGRA	IGRA is more specific than and at least as sensitive as TST. It is preferred to TST in the setting of previous BCG vaccination and in individuals who are unlikely to return to have the test interpreted. Like TST, IGRA cannot distinguish between LTBI and active infection.
Sputum smear for acid-fast bacilli	Sputum smear has a sensitivity of 50%-80%; with multiple specimens, the sensitivity increases to up to 96%. At least 5000 to 10,000 organisms should be present for a smear to be positive. The more acid-fast bacilli seen, the more infectious is the patient. Induced sputum or gastric washings may be obtained if a patient does not have a productive cough. Nontuberculous mycobacteria may produce positive smears. *Nocardia* is acid fast on the modified acid-fast stain.
Sputum culture for acid-fast bacilli	Sputum culture has a sensitivity of 67%-82% and a specificity of 99%-100%. Solid media cultures in conjunction with liquid media are often the gold standard used for diagnosis. The only false-positive results that occur are as a result of laboratory error or contamination of the specimen. False-negative results do occur and are often due to nontuberculous mycobacterial overgrowth and antibiotic treatment.
Nucleic acid amplification of smear-positive sputum	Nucleic acid amplification has a sensitivity of 95% and a specificity of 98%. Results are available in a few hours. False-positive results occur only with laboratory contamination, although the test does not indicate if bacteria are alive or dead (ie, may remain positive for some time after treatment).

BCG = Bacille Calmette-Guérin; IGRA = interferon-γ release assay; LTBI = latent tuberculosis infection; TB = tuberculosis; TST = tuberculin skin test.

Isolation is paramount to limit the spread of disease. Hospitalization is especially appropriate in cases of respiratory distress, marked hemoptysis, or other indicators of systemic disease requiring hospital support or to remove the index case from an unstable housing situation or other high-risk setting (eg, extended care facility). Consider maintenance of isolation in patients with MDR tuberculosis until sputum cultures are negative. Surgical resection of diseased tissue is rarely required but may be considered in certain circumstances (eg, bronchopleural fistula, lack of response in MDR or XDR tuberculosis).

Follow-Up

Ensure careful monitoring for treatment adherence in patients with active tuberculosis or LTBI, and provide written information (including explanation of methods to limit spread of infection and factors that increase risk of liver damage) to improve adherence and avoid complications. Instruct patients to stop medications immediately in the event of adverse drug reactions and to report these events promptly. Consider monthly sputum cultures to monitor treatment response, and adjust the drug regimen based on susceptibilities and length of therapy. A tuberculosis expert should be consulted if the sputum culture remains positive or if the patient has not improved clinically after 3 months of therapy. Perform periodic (at least monthly) assessments for adverse reactions in patients on treatment, including evaluating for hepatitis, anemia, thrombocytopenia, visual changes, and gout. Assessment should focus on signs and symptoms surveillance rather than scheduled laboratory testing. Periodic laboratory monitoring is reasonable, however, in patients at higher risk for hepatitis (eg, elderly patients, patients with a history of alcohol abuse, patients with viral hepatitis, or HIV infection). Ensure that household members and other close contacts of patients with tuberculosis are tested for LTBI.

Bibliography

Escalante P. In the clinic. Tuberculosis [published erratum appears in Ann Intern Med. 2009;151:292]. Ann Intern Med. 2009;150:ITC61-614; quiz ITV616. [PMID: 19487708]

Chapter 59

Infective Endocarditis

Fred A. Lopez, MD

Most patients with infective endocarditis have an underlying cardiac lesion. Endothelial damage created by turbulent blood flow in this setting is the inciting event for formation of nonbacterial thrombotic endocarditis, which consists of fibrin, platelets, and other coagulation-associated proteins. Bacteria with adherence properties colonize nonbacterial thrombotic endocarditis lesions during episodes of transient bacteremia, forming infective vegetations. Bacteremia results from disruption of a mucosal surface during daily activities such as flossing and brushing the teeth and certain dental procedures. The ability of bacteria to avoid host-associated immune defenses by enveloping themselves within the vegetation contributes to the propagation and persistence of infection.

Staphylococci (eg, *Staphylococcus aureus,* coagulase-negative staphylococci), streptococci (particularly *Streptococcus viridans*), and enterococci are the most common organisms causing native valve infective endocarditis. Prosthetic valve infective endocarditis is categorized according to its temporal relationship to surgery. Infections within the first 2 months of valve implantation are most frequently due to coagulase-negative staphylococci; afterward, the microbiology is similar to native valve infective endocarditis. Due to virulence factors that facilitate adherence, colonization, persistence, tissue invasion, abscess formation, and dissemination, *S. aureus* can cause infective endocarditis in normal cardiac valves. *S. aureus* is also the most common cause of infective endocarditis in injection drug users (usually involving the tricuspid valve) and in patients on hemodialysis. Nosocomial infective endocarditis is usually caused by staphylococci or enterococci and is often associated with vascular catheters or invasive procedures. Increasingly recognized, recent health care-associated infective endocarditis represents about 25% of cases.

Suspect endocarditis when blood culture results are positive in a patient with valvular disease or in a patient with an unexplained febrile or chronic illness. The mortality rate is approximately 10% for patients with streptococcal endocarditis, 35% for staphylococcal endocarditis, and 25% to 50% for prosthetic valve endocarditis.

Prevention

Antibiotic prophylaxis for endocarditis is not indicated for patients with low- or moderate-risk cardiac conditions undergoing any type of procedure. Consider antibiotic prophylaxis only in patients with both an increased risk of infection and an increased risk of adverse outcomes, should infective endocarditis develop (Table 1) when undergoing high-risk procedures. High-risk procedures include dental procedures in which there is perforation of the oral mucosa or manipulation of the periapical region of the teeth or gingival tissue and respiratory tract procedures for which there is perforation of the respiratory mucosa (eg, tonsillectomy, adenoidectomy). Antibiotic prophylaxis is not necessary in patients undergoing low-risk procedures, regardless of his or her cardiac condition. Low-risk procedures include genitourinary and gastrointestinal procedures, cardiac catheterization, and incision of clean skin.

The goal of antibiotic prophylaxis is to achieve sufficiently high serum antibiotic concentrations to prevent attachment and growth of bacteria on predisposed cardiac structures. The choice of antibiotics is based on the predicted type of bacteremia. Because certain dental or respiratory tract procedures result in viridans group streptococcal bacteremia, a single dose of oral amoxicillin is given 30 to 60 minutes before the procedure. Clindamycin, azithromycin, and clarithromycin are options in patients with a history of anaphylaxis, angioedema, or urticaria with penicillins or ampicillin. Specific recommendations for preventing infective endocarditis are available in guidelines published by the American Heart Association.

Diagnosis

The diagnosis of infective endocarditis is established on the basis of specific clinical criteria or definitive histopathologic confirmation from involved valves. Risk factors for infective endocarditis include injection drug use, recent procedures associated with risk of transient bacteremia, presence of a prosthetic valve, and certain cardiac abnormalities (see Table 1).

Fever, malaise, and fatigue are sensitive but nonspecific symptoms associated with infective endocarditis. Symptoms suggesting septic emboli in patients with tricuspid valve endocarditis include shortness of breath, chest pain, and cough. Blindness, focal weakness, localized back or flank pain, hematuria, and gangrenous skin lesions may be embolic manifestations of left-sided infective endocarditis. Physical examination findings suggestive of infective endocarditis include a new cardiac murmur, new-onset heart failure, focal neurologic signs, splenomegaly, and cutaneous manifestations (eg, petechiae, splinter hemorrhages). The presence of Osler nodes (violaceous, circumscribed, painful nodules found in the pulp of the fingers and toes) or Janeway lesions (painless, erythematous, macular lesions found on the soles and palms) highly suggests infective endocarditis.

Nonspecific laboratory abnormalities associated with infective endocarditis include leukocytosis, normocytic normochromic ane-

Table 1. Cardiac Indications for Bacterial Endocarditis Antibiotic Prophylaxis

Prosthetic heart valve
Previous endocarditis
Heart transplant recipient with valvulopathy
Uncorrected complex cyanotic congenital heart disease
Corrected complex congenital heart disease (for 6 mo following correction)

Table 2. Modified Duke Criteria for the Diagnosis of Infective Endocarditis

Major Criteria

1. Microbiologic (any of the following):

    Typical microorganisms (including *Staphylococcus aureus*) grown from two blood cultures

    A microorganism grown from persistently positive blood cultures

    Positive serologic test or single positive blood culture for *Coxiella burnetii*

2. Evidence of endocardial involvement (either of the following):

    Echocardiogram: oscillating intracardiac mass, abscess, or new partial dehiscence of a prosthetic valve

    Physical examination: new valve regurgitation (change in pre-existing murmur is not sufficient)

Minor Criteria

1. Predisposing heart condition or injection drug use

2. Body temperature >38.0°C (100.4°F)

3. Vascular phenomena: major arterial emboli, septic pulmonary infarcts, mycotic aneurysm, intracranial hemorrhage, conjunctival hemorrhage, or Janeway lesions

4. Immunologic phenomena: glomerulonephritis, Osler nodes, Roth spots, positive rheumatoid factor

5. Microbiologic: serologic evidence of infection or positive blood cultures not meeting the major criteria (a single blood culture for coagulase-negative staphylococci is not sufficient)

Diagnosis

Definite endocarditis = 2 major criteria *or* 1 major + 3 minor criteria *or* 5 minor criteria

Possible endocarditis = 1 major + 1 minor criterion *or* 3 minor criteria

Adapted from Li JS, Sexton DJ, Mick N, et al. Proposed modifications to the Duke criteria for the diagnosis of infective endocarditis. Clin Infect Dis. 2000;30:633-8. [PMID: 10770721]

mia, electrocardiographic conduction defects (atrioventricular block from extension of infection into the conduction system), hematuria, and low serum complement levels (eg, glomerulonephritis). Radiologic findings suggesting heart failure or septic emboli from right-sided endocarditis (eg, multiple bilateral small nodules on chest radiograph) raise suspicion for infective endocarditis.

Obtain an echocardiogram to detect valvular abnormalities, particularly in bacteremic patients with underlying valvular disease, a history of infective endocarditis, injection drug use, or an unrecognized source of bacteremia. Transthoracic echocardiography is noninvasive and the usual initial diagnostic test of choice, but it has a sensitivity of only 50% to 80% for detection of valvular vegetations; use of transesophageal echocardiography increases both the sensitivity and specificity to approximately 95% and is often used in patients with moderate to high suspicion for infective endocarditis. Transesophageal echocardiography is particularly useful to better delineate the anatomy of a native valve and is essential to more accurately identify paravalvular abscesses and evaluate prosthetic valves.

Obtain blood cultures to identify the microbiologic cause of infective endocarditis. Additional serologic tests for *Coxiella burnetii* (Q fever) and for *Bartonella*, *Legionella*, *Brucella*, *Mycoplasma*, and *Chlamydophila* species can be obtained when there is a high clinical suspicion of infective endocarditis but blood cultures are negative in the absence of antibiotic therapy. Additional causes of culture-negative endocarditis include a group of gram-negative pathogens constituting the HACEK group (*Haemophilus*, *Actinobacillus*, *Cardiobacterium*, *Eikenella*, and *Kingella* species), nutritionally variant streptococci (eg, *Abiotrophia* species, *Trophermyma whippelii*), and fungi (eg, *Aspergillus* species, *Histoplasma capsulatum*).

Local extension of infection can result in paravalvular abscesses, heart failure due to valvular damage, pericarditis, and myocardial infarction from vegetation-associated emboli. Suspect a paravalvular abscess in patients with persistent fever despite appropriately targeted antibiotics and with electrocardiographic manifestations of

atrioventricular block. Neurologic complications include stroke (embolic or hemorrhagic), brain abscess, and meningitis. Emboli can result in renal and splenic infarction and abscesses and vertebral osteomyelitis. Mycotic aneurysm (ie, infection-induced dilatation of an artery) can occur anywhere in the vascular system. Right-sided infective endocarditis can result in pulmonary artery occlusion or multiple bilateral pulmonary abscesses. Immunologically mediated glomerulonephritis should be suspected in patients with low complement levels and hematuria, erythrocyte cell casts, or proteinuria.

The Duke criteria are validated clinical and laboratory criteria for the diagnosis of infective endocarditis, with a sensitivity >80% (Table 2). Consider other medical conditions that can mimic the syndrome of infective endocarditis, especially when patients with negative blood cultures do not respond to empiric antibiotic therapy or when transesophageal echocardiography is unrevealing (Table 3).

Therapy

Begin empiric antibiotic therapy in patients with proven or suspected infective endocarditis after at least three sets of blood cultures are obtained from separate sites. Empiric therapy for community-acquired native valve infective endocarditis includes vancomycin and gentamicin for streptococci (especially *S. viridans* and *Streptococcus bovis*), staphylococci (particularly in injection drug users and those with indwelling vascular catheters), and enterococci. Empiric therapy for early prosthetic valve infective endocarditis includes vancomycin, gentamicin, and rifampin for multidrug-resistant bacteria, particularly coagulase-negative staphylococci. **Pathogen-directed therapy for endocarditis should be instituted once the microbiologic cause has been identified**; recommended regimens are published in a scientific statement developed by the American Heart Association (http://circ.ahajournals.org/cgi/content/full/111/23/e394). Although vancomycin is used to treat methicillin-resistant *S. aureus*,

Table 3. Differential Diagnosis of Infective Endocarditis

Disorder	Notes
Pulmonary embolism (see Chapter 96)	Low-grade fever with pulmonary symptoms. Diagnosis is based on clinical algorithms using radiologic or nuclear medicine studies.
Bacteremic infections	Disseminated infection from a focal source. Transesophageal echocardiography result is negative.
Acute leukemia (see Chapter 50)	Fever, systemic symptoms, and splenomegaly. CBC and bone marrow examination are diagnostic.
Malignancy with metastases	Low-grade fever and systemic symptoms associated with known primary neoplasm. Imaging studies and biopsy are diagnostic.
Collagen vascular disease with angiitis (see Chapter 106)	Low-grade fever, systemic symptoms, and positive RF. Similar symptoms and a false-positive RF may be seen in patients with infective endocarditis. Specific immunologic tests help with the diagnosis.
Atrial myxoma	Low-grade fever, embolic phenomena, and specific imaging characteristics on echocardiogram. Blood cultures are negative.
Nonbacterial thrombotic endocarditis (see Chapter 103)	Fever and emboli. Blood cultures are negative.
Stroke (see Chapter 75)	Acute loss of motor function, speech or mental status changes. Patients are afebrile, echocardiogram result is normal; blood cultures are negative.

CBC = complete blood count; RF= rheumatoid factor.

it should not be used to treat methicillin-sensitive *S. aureus* (for which a β-lactam agent such as nafcillin or oxacillin is preferred) or penicillin-sensitive streptococci (for which penicillin or ceftriaxone is preferred), unless the patient is unable to tolerate a β-lactam antibiotic. Intravenous antibiotics are usually administered for at least 4 to 6 weeks. Oral antibiotics are not recommended due to unreliable absorption; oral agents are used only when patients refuse parenteral therapy or when parenteral therapy is not possible.

A distinct trend of improved outcomes has been documented with surgical resection of the infected valve in select patients with infective endocarditis. Absolute indications for surgical intervention of native valve infective endocarditis include valvular dysfunction with heart failure or infection refractory to antibiotic therapy. Relative indications include onset of atrioventricular block, extension of infection into perivalvular tissue, fungal endocarditis, relapse after prolonged antibiotic therapy, recurrent emboli despite antibiotic therapy, large vegetations (>1.0 cm), or persistent fever during empiric antibiotic therapy for culture-negative infective endocarditis. In patients with prosthetic valve endocarditis, relapse after prolonged therapy and the presence of *S. aureus* are indications for surgery.

Follow-Up

Most patients with infective endocarditis will be cured. With the exception of infection with *S. aureus*, fever resolves after 3 to 5 days of antimicrobial therapy. Outpatient treatment can be considered if vital signs are stable, symptoms are improving, and therapy is tolerated. Monitoring for refractory infection, development of heart failure, and antibiotic toxicity is important. An echocardiogram is obtained at the completion of therapy to establish a new baseline, because there is an increased risk for recurrent infective endocarditis. Valve replacement may be required months or years after successful medical therapy. All patients will require antibiotic prophylaxis for certain bacteremia-associated procedures.

Bibliography

Kang DH, Kim YJ, Kim SH, et al. Early surgery versus conventional treatment for infective endocarditis. N Engl J Med. 2012;366:2466-73. [PMID: 22738096]

Murdoch DR, Corey GR, Hoen B, et al. Clinical presentation, etiology, and outcome of infective endocarditis in the 21st century: the International Collaboration on Endocarditis-Prospective Cohort Study. Arch Intern Med. 2009;169:463-73. [PMID: 19273776]

Wilson W, Taubert KA, Gewitz M, et al. Prevention of infective endocarditis. Guidelines from the American Heart Association: a guideline from the American Heart Association Rheumatic Fever, Endocarditis, and Kawasaki Disease Committee, Council on Cardiovascular Disease in the Young, and the Council on Clinical Cardiology, Council on Cardiovascular Surgery and Anesthesia, and the Quality of Care and Outcomes Research Interdisciplinary Working Group [published erratum appears in Circulation. 2007;116:e376-e377]. Circulation. 2007; 116:1736-54. [PMID: 17446442]

Chapter 60

Urinary Tract Infection

Irene Alexandraki, MD

The majority of acute uncomplicated urinary tract infections (UTIs) occur in women 18 to 24 years of age. Urinary tract infections are unusual in men aged <50 years. Approximately 10% of adult women will have at least one UTI annually. UTIs may involve only the lower urinary tract or both the upper and lower urinary tracts. Infection limited to the bladder is termed *cystitis*, whereas infection involving the renal parenchyma is called *pyelonephritis*. Although most infections are uncomplicated and easily managed, a UTI in an individual with an indwelling urinary catheter, neurogenic bladder, kidney stones, obstruction, immunosuppression, pregnancy, renal disease, or diabetes is defined as complicated and may predispose to treatment failure or require modified approaches to management due to infection with antibiotic-resistant organisms. *Asymptomatic bacteriuria* is defined as ≥10^5 colony-forming units of bacteria per milliliter of urine in the absence of typical symptoms of UTI.

Bacteria typically gain access to the bladder via the urethra. In women, uropathogens from fecal flora can colonize the vagina and migrate to the bladder through the urethra. Pyelonephritis can develop if these organisms ascend to the kidneys via the ureters. Sexual intercourse and contraceptive use increase the risk for developing an uncomplicated UTI in women. In women with recurrent UTIs, genetic factors increase susceptibility to vaginal colonization with uropathogenic coliform bacteria that adhere to uroepithelial cells. In older men, bladder outlet obstruction due to benign prostatic hyperplasia may be associated with urinary stasis and an increased risk of UTI. Complications may range from acute prostatitis and cystitis to more complex infections, including pyelonephritis and urosepsis. Infection of the kidney, including abscess, can also occur hematogenously in patients with staphylococcal bacteremia or endocarditis.

Escherichia coli causes 80% of all UTIs. *Staphylococcus saprophyticus* accounts for 10% to 15% of acute symptomatic UTIs in young females. Typical causes of complicated UTIs include *S. aureus*, enterococci, and gram-negative bacilli, including *Proteus*, *Klebsiella*, *Serratia*, and *Pseudomonas* species. Isolation of *S. aureus* should raise suspicion of hematogenously acquired infection, which most often occurs in debilitated patients.

Prevention

Cranberry juice may decrease the incidence of acute cystitis in women, particularly those with recurrent UTIs. Postcoital antibiotic prophylaxis is considered in women with two or more episodes of postcoital UTIs per year. Intermittent patient-administered, symptom-directed antibiotics or chronic prophylactic antibiotic therapy may be indicated in selected patients with recurrent UTIs not responsive to other prophylactic measures. Long-term prophylactic antibiotic therapy is also beneficial in pregnant women with recurrent asymptomatic bacteriuria; if untreated, 20% to 40% of these cases will progress to symptomatic UTIs, including pyelonephritis, which is associated with low birth weight and prematurity.

Asymptomatic bacteriuria is treated only in the following circumstances: during pregnancy, in a patient with urinary tract obstruction or neutropenia, after removal of an indwelling urinary catheter, or before an invasive urologic procedure.

Screening

Urinalysis should not be ordered as part of a routine well care examination in men and nonpregnant women. Pregnant women should be screened for asymptomatic bacteriuria. Screening for asymptomatic bacteriuria is otherwise recommended only before transurethral resection of the prostate, urinary tract instrumentation involving biopsy, or other tissue trauma resulting in mucosal bleeding. Screening is not recommended for simple catheter placement or cystoscopy without biopsy.

Diagnosis

Table 1 summarizes the differential diagnosis of UTIs. Symptomatic cystitis is associated with dysuria, urinary frequency and urgency, and suprapubic pain. An abrupt onset of symptoms is more consistent with a UTI, whereas a gradual onset and vaginal symptoms suggest a sexually transmitted disease. The combination of dysuria and urinary frequency without vaginal discharge or irritation raises the probability of cystitis to >90%. A history of urologic abnormalities, underlying medical conditions (eg, diabetes), and modifying host factors (eg, advanced age) can predict infection with resistant organisms, delayed or incomplete response to therapy, relapse, and infectious complications (eg, kidney abscess, emphysematous pyelonephritis, perinephric abscess, sepsis).

Pyelonephritis is associated with an abrupt onset of fever, chills, sweats, nausea, vomiting, diarrhea, myalgia, and flank or abdominal pain; hypotension and septic shock may occur in severe cases. Urinary frequency and dysuria may precede pyelonephritis. Potential complicating conditions, such as recent instrumentation of the urethra and bladder, diabetes, pregnancy, or prior UTIs, should be assessed. Infection at distant sites suggests the possibility of hematogenous pyelonephritis.

Patients with acute prostatitis present with a rapid onset of fever, chills, low back and perineal pain, urinary frequency and urgency, nocturia, dysuria, and generalized malaise.

The physical examination in patients with cystitis generally reveals only tenderness of the urethra or suprapubic area. Pyelonephritis may be associated with fever, tachycardia, and marked costovertebral angle tenderness; unilateral abdominal tenderness may also be present. Pelvic examination may be indicated if the history suggests sexually transmitted disease. In men with suspected acute prostatitis, rectal examination may reveal a tender and

Table 1. Differential Diagnosis of Urinary Tract Infection

Disease	Notes
Cystitis	*History*: Dysuria, frequency, urgency, suprapubic pain, and sometimes without systemic symptoms (eg, fever, chills, nausea, vomiting). *Exam*: Suprapubic and/or lower abdominal discomfort. *Laboratory*: PMNs on urinalysis; urine culture with >10^4 CFU/mL of a typical uropathogen.
Pyelonephritis	*History*: Fever, malaise, sweats, headache; anorexia, nausea, vomiting, abdominal pain; back, flank or loin pain; ± voiding symptoms. *Exam*: Fever, tachycardia; costovertebral angle tenderness; possibly abdominal tenderness. *Laboratory*: Elevated leukocyte count, ESR, and/or C-reactive protein; urinalysis with PMNs and bacteria (as in cystitis), ± leukocyte casts; urine culture with >10^4 CFU/mL of a typical uropathogen. Imaging studies (not routinely indicated for uncomplicated pyelonephritis; may be indicated in specific circumstances (ultrasound, intravenous pyelogram, enhanced CT [looking for obstruction, stone]).
Vaginitis, cervicitis, or genital herpes (see Chapter 61)	*History*: Vaginal discharge, no urinary frequency or urgency, possibly new sexual partner or unprotected sexual activity; history of previous STDs, recurrent genital HSV, or vaginitis; gradual onset of symptoms (*Chlamydia*). Dysuria can result from urine coming into contact with inflamed and irritated vulvar epithelial surfaces in the absence of a bacterial UTI. Women may be able to differentiate between "internal" (UTI associated) and "external" (vulvovaginal) dysuria, which helps to guide evaluation. *Pelvic exam*: Vulvovaginal or cervical erythema, exudate, or ulcers; cervical discharge; adnexal tenderness or mass; cervical motion tenderness. *Laboratory*: Abnormal vaginal fluid findings; viral test from vulvovaginal ulcers positive for HSV; cervical swab with PMNs (± gram-negative diplococci) on Gram stain (if done), and positive by culture (or other test) for *Chlamydia* and/or *Neisseria gonorrhoeae* (if indicated); urinalysis with PMNs but no bacteria; urine culture negative or with low counts of nonpathogens.
Sexually transmitted urethritis (see Chapter 61)	*History*: New sexual partner, unprotected sexual activity, gradual symptom onset (*Chlamydia*); history of previous STDs or recurrent genital HSV, ± vaginal discharge; ± urinary frequency or urgency. Inflammation of urethra from sexually transmitted pathogens can mimic bacterial cystitis. Sexual history can suggest the diagnosis. Specific tests are needed for confirmation, in conjunction with the negative routine urine culture. *Pelvic exam*: Possibly normal, or evidence of coexistent vulvovaginitis or cervicitis/salpingitis. *Laboratory*: Urinalysis with PMNs but no bacteriuria; urine culture negative or low counts of nonpathogens; urine or urethral swab positive (by culture or other specific test) for *Chlamydia* or HSV (or *Mycoplasma genitalium* or *Ureaplasma urealyticum*).
Acute prostatitis	*History*: Spiking fever, chills, dysuria, pelvic or perineal pain, and cloudy urine; possible obstructive symptoms (dribbling, hesitancy, and anuria). *Exam*: Edematous (boggy) and tender prostate. *Laboratory*: Pyuria, positive urine culture.
Chronic prostatitis	*History*: Dysuria and frequency in the absence of the signs of acute prostatitis; recurrent urinary tract infections. *Exam*: Prostate tenderness and edema, but is frequently normal. *Laboratory*: Cultures of urine or expressed prostatic secretions are almost always positive.
Painful bladder syndrome/interstitial cystitis	*History*: Chronic bladder pain associated with bladder filling and/or emptying; urinary frequency, urgency, and nocturia. *Exam*: Diffuse tenderness in lower abdomen and pelvis. *Diagnosis*: Based on characteristic symptoms and exclusion of other conditions.

CFU = colony-forming units; CT = computed tomography; ESR = erythrocyte sedimentation rate; HSV = herpes simplex virus; PMNs = polymorphonuclear leukocytes; STDs = sexually transmitted diseases; UTI = urinary tract infection.

boggy prostate. Suspect UTI if there is evidence of bladder distention on physical examination, pericatheter leakage of urine (in catheterized patients), or decreased or absent urine output despite a sensation of bladder fullness.

Urinalysis can be omitted for healthy women with acute cystitis if there are no complicating factors. However, obtain a urine culture for women with suspected cystitis if (1) the patient is pregnant, (2) the diagnosis is not clear from the history and physical examination, (3) an unusual or antimicrobial-resistant organism is suspected, (4) therapeutic options are limited because of a history of medication intolerance, (5) the episode represents a suspected relapse or treatment failure after recent treatment for UTI, or (6) underlying complicating conditions are identified.

Proper urine specimen collection and handling is crucial to ensure that the microscopic examination and culture results are accurate. The presence of pyuria (defined as ≥4 leukocytes per high power field on microscopy) and ≥10^4 colony-forming units/mL of bacteria on quantitative urine culture confirm the diagnosis of UTI. If pyuria is absent, the diagnosis of UTI should be reconsidered.

When the diagnosis is not clear, a urine dipstick test for leukocyte esterase and/or nitrite is an acceptable screening tool but may be less sensitive than microscopic urinalysis with low-count bacteriuria. Gram stain of the urine sediment increases specificity, suggests the type of microorganism, and is particularly useful in patients with complicated UTIs.

Urinalysis in patients with chronic indwelling urinary catheters is difficult to interpret because collection systems concentrate normal urinary components and are frequently colonized with bacteria. Therefore, urinalysis in these patients should be limited to those with symptoms except in specific situations, such as pregnancy.

Obtain blood cultures in clinically ill patients; blood cultures are positive in 25% of patients with pyelonephritis. Obtain a complete blood count, urinalysis, and urine culture in patients with acute prostatitis; blood cultures are generally indicated only in immunosuppressed patients.

Use imaging studies only if an alternative diagnosis or a urologic complication is suspected. Kidney and bladder ultrasonography are usually the highest-yield initial imaging studies. Transrectal ultrasonography may be useful in the diagnosis of complicated prostatitis. Consider computed tomography (CT) and magnetic resonance imaging for patients with ultrasound findings suggesting an anatomic abnormality and for persistent or relapsing pyelonephritis despite normal findings on ultrasonography. CT may be useful in the diagnosis and drainage of a prostatic abscess and in ruling out other pelvic pathology mimicking prostatitis.

Therapy

Treat nonpregnant women who have uncomplicated cystitis empirically with trimethoprim-sulfamethoxazole (TMP-SMZ) for 3 days. Fluoroquinolones are also effective but are less preferred as initial therapy because of their additional cost and resistance concerns. If there is a high prevalence of resistance to TMP-SMZ or intolerance to the drug, substitute nitrofurantoin, a β-lactam, or a fluoroquinolone for 3 days. Fosfomycin as a single dose is another option, but it has lower efficacy compared with the other agents. Nitrofurantoin and fosfomycin should be avoided if pyelonephritis is suspected. See Table 2 for specific treatment recommendations.

Patients with underlying complicating conditions are more likely to have a drug-resistant infection, to exhibit a poor response to antimicrobial therapy even when the organism is susceptible, and to develop complications if initial therapy is suboptimal. For these patients, obtain a urine culture and treat empirically for 7 to 14 days with a fluoroquinolone or, if the organism is known to be susceptible, with TMP-SMZ. Acute cystitis in an elderly woman is not automatically considered complicated unless she has multiple comorbidities, was recently treated with antibiotics, or is a resident of an extended care facility. Obtain a urine culture and susceptibility testing for pregnant women with cystitis and treat for 3 to 7 days with an oral antimicrobial agent that is safe in pregnancy, such as amoxicillin or nitrofurantoin.

For women with recurrent uncomplicated UTIs, consider daily prophylaxis with nitrofurantoin or TMP-SMZ or self-treatment with 3 days of TMP-SMZ or a fluoroquinolone beginning at symptom onset. Recommend alternative contraception to women with recurrent UTIs who use spermicide-based contraception, as spermicides increase the risk of UTIs. Consider prophylaxis with single-dose TMP-SMX, nitrofurantoin, or ciprofloxacin after sexual intercourse for women with two or more episodes of postcoital UTIs per year. Daily topical application of intravaginal estrogen cream reduces the frequency of symptomatic UTIs in postmenopausal women. Young men with UTIs should be treated with short-course antibiotic regimens approved for women with cystitis. Consider evaluating these patients further to rule out urinary obstruction or other anatomic abnormalities.

Consider outpatient management for patients with pyelonephritis who are medically stable and able to take oral medication. Use fluoroquinolones as first-line empiric oral therapy (except in pregnancy) because of the higher urine drug concentrations achieved compared with TMP-SMX. Ampicillin, TMP-SMX, and first-generation cephalosporins are no longer used for empiric therapy because of unacceptably high resistance rates.

Patients with pyelonephritis who are acutely ill, hypotensive, nauseated, or vomiting are admitted to the hospital for intravenous fluids and parenteral antibiotics. If obstruction is present, catheter drainage of the bladder (or other drainage procedures) and replacement of an existing catheter are indicated in conjunction with antimicrobial therapy. Begin empiric therapy with a fluoroquinolone, an extended-spectrum cephalosporin or penicillin, or an

Table 2. Recommended Antimicrobial Agents for Urinary Tract Infections

Treatment of Acute Uncomplicated Cystitis in Women

Agent	Dose and Duration	Comments
Trimethoprim-sulfamethoxazole	160/800 mg (one double-strength tablet) orally twice daily for 3 d	Avoid if resistance rates to uropathogens are >20% or if used to treat a urinary tract infection in preceding 3 mo.
Nitrofurantoin monohydrate macrocrystals	100 mg orally twice daily for 5 d	Avoid if pyelonephritis is suspected.
Fosfomycin	3 g orally (single dose)	Has lower efficacy compared with some other agents; avoid if pyelonephritis is suspected.
Fluoroquinolones	Dose varies by agent; daily for 3 d	Reserved as an alternative when other agents cannot be used.
β-Lactams	Dose varies by agent; daily for 3-5 d	Avoid unless none of the above agents is appropriate.

Treatment of Acute Pyelonephritis

Outpatient treatment

Ciprofloxacin	500 mg twice daily for 7 d (± initial loading dose of ciprofloxacin, 400 mg IV, or a single dose of ceftriaxone 1 g IV, or a consolidated 24-h dose of an aminoglycoside)	Appropriate in geographic areas where fluoroquinolone resistance rates <10%.

Inpatient treatment

Intravenous fluoroquinolone; or an aminoglycoside ± ampicillin; or an extended-spectrum penicillin ± an aminoglycoside; or an extended-spectrum cephalosporin ± an aminoglycoside; or a carbapenem	Dose varies by agent; daily for 7 to 14 d	Choices should be based on local resistance data.

IV = intravenously.

aminoglycoside, and treat for 7 to 14 days; cephalosporins or aminoglycosides alone are insufficient for treating enterococci. Persistent fever and unilateral flank pain despite adequate treatment suggest perinephric or intrarenal abscess and the need for kidney CT.

Consider an intravenous fluoroquinolone or an extended-spectrum cephalosporin (with or without an aminoglycoside) for patients with acute prostatitis who are too ill for oral therapy. Patients who fail to respond within 72 hours should have a urologic evaluation and transrectal ultrasonography or CT to rule out a prostatic abscess. Treat patients with acute prostatitis for 4 to 6 weeks. In all cases of UTI, change from parenteral to oral therapy once the patient can tolerate oral intake.

Follow-Up

A follow-up urinalysis or culture is not indicated after treatment for an uncomplicated UTI with symptom resolution. In complicated cystitis in nonpregnant women, follow-up studies are indicated only with persistent symptoms within several weeks after completing an appropriate course of antibiotics. Following treatment of acute cystitis in pregnant women, obtain a urine culture to confirm eradication of bacteriuria, and repeat urinalyses or urine cultures at intervals through the time of delivery to confirm sterility of the urine. Treat recurrences with antimicrobial drugs based on susceptibility tests. Consider urologic evaluation for patients with complicated kidney infections, stones, prostatic abscess, or urinary tract obstruction.

Bibliography

Gupta K, Hooton TM, Naber KG, et al. International clinical practice guidelines for the treatment of acute uncomplicated cystitis and pyelonephritis in women: a 2010 update by the Infectious Diseases Society of America and the European Society for Microbiology and Infectious Diseases. Clin Infect Dis. 2011 Mar 1;52:e103-20. [PMID: 21292654]

Neal DE Jr. Complicated urinary tract infections. Urol Clin N Am. 2008;35:13-22. [PMID: 18061020]

Nicolle LE. Uncomplicated urinary tract infection in adults including uncomplicated pyelonephritis. Urol Clin N Am. 2008;35:1-12. [PMID: 18061019]

Ramakrishnan K, Salinas RC. Prostatitis: acute and chronic. Prim Care. 2010;37:547-63. [PMID: 20705198]

Chapter 61

Sexually Transmitted Diseases

Sara B. Fazio, MD

Sexually transmitted diseases (STDs) are common problems in both the inpatient and the outpatient setting. Diseases characterized by urethritis and cervicitis include gonorrhea and chlamydia, while herpes simplex, primary syphilis, and chancroid are the most common infectious diseases characterized by genital ulceration. Human papilloma virus (HPV) causes genital warts as well as cervical dysplasia. HIV infection is discussed in Chapter 62.

Prevention

Patient education regarding safe sexual practices is key to preventing STDs. All patients should be encouraged to use a latex condom for vaginal or anal intercourse and fellatio. Variables associated with STD acquisition include young age (<25 years), lower socioeconomic status, substance abuse, lack of or inconsistent use of a barrier method of protection, use of an intrauterine device, and douching. Additionally, new or multiple sexual partners and a history of an STD increases the risk of disease transmission. Consistent and correct use of condoms reduces transmission of all STDs as well as pelvic inflammatory disease (PID) and its sequelae (ie, chronic pelvic pain, infertility). Many STDs are spread asymptomatically. The presence of an ulcerative genital lesion greatly increases the risk of HIV transmission, making prevention much more critical. Partner treatment of patients diagnosed with an STD is an essential public health approach to prevention. HPV vaccination with either the 2- or 4-valent vaccine should be offered to all females between the ages of 11 and 26 years to prevent HPV infection and cervical dysplasia. Additionally, HPV vaccination with the 4-valent vaccine is recommended for males between ages of 11 and 21 years.

Screening

Any person who engages in high-risk sexual behavior should be screened for gonorrhea, chlamydia, syphilis, and HIV infection. All sexually active women aged <25 years should be routinely screened for chlamydia and gonorrhea, based on evidence that screening reduces the incidence of PID by >50%. Men who have sex with men should be screened for STDs on an annual basis or more frequently based on risk behavior. Pregnant women should be offered screening for HIV infection, syphilis, and chlamydia at the first prenatal visit, as well as screening for gonorrhea in areas of high prevalence. A repeat test for gonorrhea should be offered in the third trimester to women at continued risk to prevent neonatal conjunctivitis (eg, ophthalmia neonatorum). Prophylactic cesarean section is indicated in a woman with active herpes simplex virus (eg, HSV; human herpesvirus 3) lesions at the time of delivery to prevent infection in the newborn. The presence of one STD requires screening for other STDs. Papanicolaou (Pap) testing to screen for HPV infection and cervical dysplasia is discussed in Chapter 84. Although some experts recommend anal Pap smears for HIV-infected homosexual men, the current Centers for Disease Control and Prevention STD treatment guidelines do not recommend routine screening, given the limited data available on the natural history of anal squamous intraepithelial lesions and treatment efficacy.

Diagnosis

Genital herpes is suggested by the presence of multiple painful vesicular or ulcerative lesions (Plate 43) and is the most common cause of genital ulcers. The first episode of genital herpes is more severe than recurrent episodes and often involves systemic symptoms. Primary genital herpes outbreaks are characterized by fever, headache, and numerous painful, ulcerated, vesicular lesions. Grouped vesicles on an erythematous base are the classic clinical presentation. Recurrences often are unilateral and may be preceded by a neuropathic prodrome about 24 hours before lesions develop. Diagnosis is primarily with culture; direct fluorescent antibody testing and polymerase chain reaction (PCR) testing are useful when the diagnosis is unclear. A positive HSV type 2 antibody test indicates only previous infection and is not a clinically useful diagnostic test. Culture becomes less sensitive as genital lesions begin to heal. Use of the Tzanck test (showing multinucleated giant cells) is not recommended due to lack of sensitivity.

In primary syphilis, patients present with a painless ulcer (eg, chancre) with a clean base and raised indurated edges (Plate 44) as well as painless regional lymphadenopathy. Secondary syphilis typically occurs weeks to months after the onset of primary disease and is characterized by a generalized mucocutaneous rash that involves the palms and soles (Plate 45), generalized lymphadenopathy, and constitutional symptoms. Inflammation may develop in other organs, resulting in hepatitis, glomerulonephritis, aseptic meningitis, patchy alopecia, and mucous patches (Plate 46). Diagnosis of primary and secondary-stage mucocutaneous lesions can be established by darkfield microscopy visualization of motile *Treponema pallidum* in exudative fluid from the lesions. In a patient with suggestive clinical findings, a presumptive diagnosis can be based on reactive syphilis serology, which entails the use of a nontreponemal serologic test (eg, rapid plasma reagin [RPR] or VDRL test) followed by a more specific treponemal serologic test (eg, fluorescent treponemal antibody absorption test or *T. pallidum* particle agglutination assay). Tertiary syphilis, which occurs years to decades after the initial infection, is characterized by neurologic findings (eg, meningitis, tabes dorsalis, Argyll Robertson pupil, mental status changes), cardiac abnormalities (eg, thoracic aortic aneurysm), or gummatous disease. Latent syphilis is characterized by positive serology without symptoms. Patients with neurosyphilis require cerebrospinal fluid examination for diagnosis. Treponemal serologies typically remain positive for life, whereas nontreponemal serology titers regress after appropriate treatment and are used to assess disease activity.

Patients with chancroid (eg, *Haemophilus ducreyi* infection) present with one or more painful genital ulcers, often with unilateral suppurative inguinal lymphadenopathy. Diagnosis can be made by culture. Because chancroid is relatively rare in the United States, however, culture medium is often not readily available, and the diagnosis is often one of exclusion (Table 1).

Gonorrhea should be suspected in a man with purulent or mucopurulent urethral discharge or in a woman with mucopurulent cervicitis. *Neisseria gonorrhoeae* and *Chlamydia trachomatis* both cause cervicitis, urethritis, and proctitis (in persons who engage in anal receptive intercourse), but gonorrhea is characterized by a more exudative polymorphonuclear immune response and, consequently, a more visibly purulent discharge. However, diagnosis cannot reliably be based on clinical findings. *N. gonorrhoeae* and *C. trachomatis* are also common causes of epididymitis in sexually active men aged <35 years; patients with epididymitis typically present with testicular pain with or without dysuria. Infection at any site may be asymptomatic, most notably infection of the pharynx (causing pharyngitis) and rectum (causing proctitis), allowing for unrecognized sexual transmission. Most endocervical gonococcal or chlamydial infections are asymptomatic; thus, a high index of suspicion is necessary. Untreated gonococcal infection of mucosal sites can result in bacteremia and disseminated gonococcal infection, characterized by fever and the triad of dermatitis (eg, papular and pustular skin lesions that are typically few in number; Plate 47), tenosynovitis (eg, tendon sheath inflammation, usually involving the distal extremities), and mono- or oligoarthritis. Perihepatitis (eg, Fitz-Hugh–Curtis syndrome) and peritonitis may also occur with intraperitoneal extension of untreated pelvic infection in women. In the newborn, unrecognized perinatal acquisition of gonococcal infection may result in ophthalmia neonatorum. Chlamydial infection is the most commonly diagnosed sexually transmitted bacterial infection in the United States, with the highest prevalence among sexually active teenagers and adults aged <25 years. Women with chlamydia are frequently asymptomatic, and untreated infections can cause severe sequelae, including PID, infertility, ectopic pregnancy, and chronic pelvic pain. Men with chlamydia may have urethral discharge or may be asymptomatic. *C. trachomatis* can also cause conjunctivitis, which is most common in impoverished nations and is a leading cause of blindness worldwide.

Gonorrhea and chlamydia are best diagnosed by culture or PCR testing (eg, greater sensitivity). PCR testing using a sensitive and specific nucleic acid amplification test in both women and men may be performed with a urine specimen; alternatively, an endocervical specimen in women or urethral specimen in men may be obtained. In men with gonococcal urethritis, Gram stain reveals gram-negative intracellular diplococci in 95% of cases (Plate 48), allowing for a rapid, specific diagnosis. Gram stain of endocervical specimens is less sensitive, however, and thus should not be used to diagnose infection in women. Nongonococcal urethritis is defined by two criteria: the presence of urethritis (eg, dysuria or a thin mucoid discharge) and leukocytosis on Gram stain of the discharge. The failure of urethritis to respond to antibiotic treatment for gonorrhea and chlamydia suggests a less common cause, such as *Trichomonas vaginalis* or HSV. HSV also causes cervicitis and proctitis.

PID is a polymicrobial infection of the endometrium, fallopian tubes, and ovaries. The diagnosis is suggested by abdominal discomfort, uterine or adnexal tenderness, or cervical motion tender-

Table 1. Differential Diagnosis of Genital Ulcers

Disease	Characteristics
Syphilis (*Treponema pallidum*)	*Incubation*: 9-90 d. *Primary lesion*: papule. *Number of lesions*: usually one. *Pain*: none. *Size of lesion*: 5-15 mm. *Edges*: indurated. *Base*: clean. *Depth*: moderate. *Lymph nodes*: enlarged, nontender. *U.S. epidemiology*: Southeast, urban areas. The characteristics described are those seen in the classic presentation of infection. Atypical chancres may be small, nonindurated, or painful or have unusual shapes.
Herpes (herpes simplex virus types 1 and 2)	*Incubation*: days to years. *Primary lesion*: vesicle. *Number of lesions*: multiple. *Pain*: yes. *Size of lesion*: 1-2 mm. *Edges*: flat, red. *Base*: red, exudate. *Depth*: superficial. *Lymph nodes*: enlarged, tender. *U.S. epidemiology*: most common cause of genital ulcers. Herpes ulcers differ from primary syphilis in that they are much shallower, often appear in crops, begin as a vesicle, and are painful.
Chancroid (*Haemophilus ducreyi*)	*Incubation*: 1-14 d. *Primary lesion*: pustule. *Number of lesions*: one or many. *Pain*: exquisite. *Size of lesion*: 5-25 mm. *Edges*: ragged, undermined. *Base*: friable, purulent exudate. *Depth*: deep, excavated. *Lymph nodes*: tender, may suppurate/form buboes. *U.S. epidemiology*: rare, occasionally seen in warmer climates (many of these cases are imported from Mexico or the Caribbean). Chancroid differs from primary syphilis in that the ulceration is usually deeper and more destructive, the edges are ragged rather than punched out, and there is significant associated pain and tenderness as well as significant lymphadenopathy, which also is painful and tender.
Behçet disease	Behçet disease is an uncommon systemic disease with genital ulcers as one component; the ulcers are often painful. Other features include recurrent oral aphthous ulcers, uveitis, pathergy, arthritis, gastrointestinal manifestations, and central nervous system disease. In Behçet disease, serologic tests for syphilis will be negative.
LGV; *Chlamydia trachomatis* serovars L1, L2, and L3	LGV is extremely rare in the U.S. The infection can begin as a small papule, erosion, or ulcer in the genital or perineal region; the lesion usually is asymptomatic and heals quickly without scarring. Patients with LGV rarely, if ever, present in this early ulcerative stage. Subsequently, patients develop the painful lymphadenopathy and buboes. During this stage, patients may have fever and other constitutional symptoms and develop draining fistulae. The early ulcerative lesions of LGV differ from those of primary syphilis in that they are smaller and less destructive and heal promptly.
Granuloma inguinale (donovanosis; *Calymmatobacterium granulomatis*)	Granuloma inguinale (donovanosis) is extremely rare in the United States. Ulcers most commonly are large, nontender, and beefy red and bleed easily when touched. The lesions differ from the syphilitic chancre in that they are larger, may be multiple in number, and usually have a very beefy red base. The ulcers do not heal spontaneously and can be present chronically.

LVG= lymphogranuloma venereum.

ness. Other criteria include body temperature >38.3°C (101.0°F), cervical or vaginal mucopurulent discharge, leukocytes in vaginal secretions, and documentation of gonorrhea or chlamydia. PID is most likely to occur within 7 days of the onset of menses. Although *N. gonorrhoeae* and *C. trachomatis* are the primary causes of PID, more recent studies have implicated organisms associated with bacterial vaginosis. All women with suspected PID should be tested for gonorrhea and chlamydia and have a pregnancy test to rule out normal or ectopic implantation. In severe cases, imaging should be performed to rule out a tubo-ovarian abscess.

Most HPV infection is asymptomatic. Transmission of HPV can occur with skin-to-mucosa or skin-to-skin contact. HPV serotypes 6 and 11 are most often responsible for genital warts (eg, condylomata acuminata), whereas high-risk HPV serotypes (16, 18, 31, 33, and 35) are associated with cervical dysplasia and cervical cancer. Genital warts may be flat or pedunculated and are typically diagnosed by appearance alone, although biopsy can be used if necessary.

Therapy

Counsel all patients with active symptoms to abstain from sexual contact until at least 1 week of treatment has been completed. Because HSV persists in a dormant state, patients must be educated that treatment does not eradicate the virus and that asymptomatic shedding and transmission can occur, particularly during the first year of infection. Syphilis, gonorrhea, and chlamydia are reportable infectious diseases in every state. Table 2 summarizes the recommended treatments for common STDs.

Treat primary HSV infection for 7 to 10 days and recurrent disease for 3 to 5 days. Treatment decreases the duration of symptoms and reduces viral shedding. Suppressive therapy may be necessary to decrease the frequency of recurrences. Topical therapy is ineffective.

Chancroid is treated with a single dose of azithromycin or ceftriaxone, 3 days of ciprofloxacin, or 7 days of erythromycin base.

Primary or secondary syphilis is treated with one dose of intramuscular penicillin G benzathine. Late latent syphilis or tertiary nonneurosyphilis is treated with three weekly doses of intramuscular penicillin G benzathine. Doxycycline and tetracycline are alternative choices for penicillin-allergic nonpregnant patients. Failure of nontreponemal serologic titers to decline fourfold in the 6 to 12 months after treatment indicates treatment failure or reinfection. Neurosyphilis requires intravenous penicillin or ceftriaxone; in penicillin-allergic patients, desensitization is required. The Jarisch-Herxheimer reaction is an acute febrile illness occurring within 24 hours of treatment for any stage of syphilis and probably represents an immune response to cell wall proteins released by dying spirochetes.

Table 2. Recommended Treatment of Common Sexually Transmitted Infections

Clinical Situation	Recommended Regimen
Syphilis	
Primary, secondary, or early latent (<1 y) syphilis	Penicillin G benzathine 2.4 MU IM, given in a single dose
Late latent (>1 y) syphilis or latent syphilis of unknown duration	Penicillin G benzathine 7.2 MU total, given as three doses of 2.4 MU IM at 1-wk intervals
Neurosyphilis	Aqueous crystalline penicillin G 18-24 MU/d, given as 3-4 MU IV every 4 h or continuous infusion, for 10-14 d
HIV infection	For primary, secondary, and early latent syphilis, treat as previously described; some specialists recommend three doses. For late latent syphilis or latent syphilis of unknown duration, perform CSF examination before treatment.
Pregnancy	Penicillin is the only recommended treatment for syphilis during pregnancy. Women who report allergy should be desensitized and then treated with penicillin.
Gonococcal Infections[a]	
Infection of cervix, urethra, or rectum	Ceftriaxone 125 mg IM, given in a single dose, plus either azithromycin 1 g orally in a single dose *or* doxycycline 100 mg orally twice daily for 7 days
Chlamydial Infections	
Adults and adolescents	Azithromycin 1 g orally, given in a single dose *or* doxycycline 100 mg orally twice daily for 7 d
Pregnancy	Azithromycin 1 g orally, given in a single dose *or* amoxicillin 500 mg orally three times daily for 7 d
Nongonococcal urethritis	Azithromycin 1 g orally, given in a single dose *or* doxycycline 100 mg orally twice daily for 7 d
Pelvic inflammatory disease (outpatient management)	Ceftriaxone 250 mg IM, single dose, plus doxycycline 100 mg orally twice daily for 14 d
Pelvic inflammatory disease (inpatient management)	Cefoxitin 2 g IV, every 6 hours plus doxycycline 100 mg orally twice
Genital Herpes	
First clinical episode of genital herpes	Acyclovir 400 mg orally three times daily for 7-10 d *or* Acyclovir 200 mg orally 5 times daily for 7-10 d *or* famciclovir 250 mg orally three times daily for 7-10 d *or* valacyclovir 1 g orally twice daily for 7-10 d

CSF = cerebrospinal fluid; IM = intramuscularly; IV = intravenously; MU = million units.

[a]Treat also for chlamydial infection if not ruled out by a sensitive test (nucleic acid amplification test).

Table 3. Follow-Up for Patients With STD

Clinical Situation	Recommended Follow-Up
Primary HSV infection	Counsel patient regarding the natural history of herpes recurrence and use of barrier contraception.
Primary syphilis	Perform follow-up quantitative nontreponemal serologies at 6, 12, and 24 mo.
Tertiary syphilis, HIV-infected person with late latent syphilis, treatment failure	Perform lumbar puncture and cerebrospinal fluid analysis for neurosyphilis.
Sexual partner of patient with syphilis	Perform serologic testing if >90 d after sexual contact. Treat empirically if <90 d after sexual contact.
Gonorrhea or chlamydia	Repeat diagnostic testing if symptoms persist 3-4 d after treatment.
Sexual partner of patient with gonorrhea or chlamydia	Treat all sexual contacts of the last 60 d.
Pelvic inflammatory disease	Reevaluate within 48-72 h of initiating therapy and again at the end of antibiotic treatment. Patients not responding to therapy may require parenteral therapy or broader antibiotic coverage, additional diagnostic tests, drainage of an abscess or fluid collection, or surgical intervention.
Any patient with an STD diagnosis	Test for other STDs, including HIV and HBV infection.

HBV = hepatitis B virus; HSV = herpes simplex virus; STD = sexually transmitted disease.

Patients with documented or suspected gonorrhea, including men aged <35 years with presumed epididymitis, are treated for both gonorrhea and chlamydia, given the high frequency of coinfection. Fluoroquinolones and oral cephalosporins are no longer recommended in the treatment of gonorrhea due to the emergence of resistance. Men who have sex with men are increasingly vulnerable to antimicrobial-resistant gonorrhea; monitoring for treatment failure is important. Patients with chlamydia are effectively treated with a single dose of azithromycin, 7 days of doxycycline, or a fluoroquinolone.

In patients with suspected PID, the choice of antibiotic should cover gonorrhea, chlamydia, gram-negative rods, and anaerobic bacteria. The duration of treatment is 14 days. PID often can be treated on an outpatient basis. Hospitalization should be considered if there is no clinical improvement after 48 to 72 hours of antibiotic therapy, inability to tolerate oral antibiotics, severe illness (eg, nausea, vomiting, or high fever), suspected intra-abdominal abscess, pregnancy, or nonadherence with outpatient therapy.

Treatment of genital warts involves removal either by patient-applied regimens (eg, podofilox, imiquimod), provider-administered regimens (eg, cryotherapy, podophyllin resin, trichloracetic or bichloracetic acid), or surgery. Treatment may reduce, but does not eliminate, HPV.

Follow-up of patients with STDs is important to resolve infection and to ensure adequate partner management (Table 3).

Bibliography

Centers for Disease Control and Prevention. Sexually Transmitted Diseases Treatment Guidelines, 2010. www.cdc.gov/std/treatment/2010/pid.htm.

Wilson JF. In the clinic. Vaginitis and cervicitis. Ann Intern Med. 2009;151: ITC3-1-ITC3-15; Quiz ITC3-16. [PMID: 19721016]

Chapter 62

HIV Infection

Juan Reyes, MD

HIV, the cause of AIDS, slowly destroys the immune system and can lead to deadly opportunistic infections. Combination antiretroviral therapy (ART), however, offers many affected persons the chance to live for decades. Despite these advances, of the more than 1 million persons with HIV in the United States, one in five do not know they are infected. The greatest proportion of newly diagnosed cases of HIV/AIDS is made up of men who have sex with men, accounting for 63% of all new infections. Among adults infected through heterosexual contact, African Americans continue to bear the greatest burden. The effects of HIV/AIDS illness on the developing world remain devastating. In sub-Saharan Africa, the prevalence of HIV is 4.9% among adults, accounting for 69% of people living with HIV worldwide, which is currently estimated at 34 million individuals. All physicians must have a basic understanding of how HIV infection is acquired, diagnosed, and treated.

HIV is a retrovirus that enters the bloodstream via mucosal or blood contact. The virus enters cells through use of an external glycoprotein (gp120), which binds to the CD4 receptor on helper T cells. After fusion with the cell, facilitated by binding to a coreceptor (CCR5 or CXCR4), the virus inserts its core, and viral RNA is reverse-transcribed into DNA. It is then incorporated into the host cell DNA by its integrase enzyme. The reverse transcriptase has a high error rate, contributing to a large viral mutation rate, influencing the virulence of the virus and its response to host defenses and drug therapy. New virions leave the cell via exocytosis to infect other cells, and mature when protease cleaves its polypeptides into the functional core proteins. Infected T cells or virions enter the bloodstream and then multiply in gut-associated lymphoid tissue, the spleen, lymph nodes, and bone marrow. With this amplification, symptoms of acute HIV infection can result within days to weeks of infection. Initial host defenses to contain the spread of virus include CD8+ T-cell activation, which reduces viremia to a stable level. The virus causes destruction of CD4+ cells over a period of years. As the patient's CD4+ cell count declines, the risk for opportunistic infections increases. Knowledge of the replication cycle of HIV allows for understanding of the targets used for therapeutic intervention.

Prevention

Counsel all patients about the routes of HIV transmission and risk-reduction strategies. Teach patients that all forms of sexual contact involving mucosal exposure to genital secretions or blood, including oral sex, involve risk of HIV transmission. Condom use for men and women should always be recommended as a mode for prevention. Screening for other sexually transmitted infections, particularly genital ulcer diseases, is essential, because open lesions increase the likelihood of HIV transmission. Patients who use injection drugs should be counseled about risk-reduction behaviors (eg, not sharing needles and needle exchange programs). HIV transmission to health care workers can be prevented by educating those at risk for occupational exposures to HIV-infected blood or bodily fluids about safety precautions (eg, not capping used needles) and offering postexposure treatment in appropriate circumstances (eg, immediately after a high-risk needle-stick injury). Encourage compliance for patients already on ART, as this is associated with decreased transmission of HIV in discordant couples. Emerging evidence for male circumcision has arisen for the primary prevention of HIV as well as pre-exposure prophylaxis in high-risk individuals. The development of a safe and effective vaccine against HIV remains elusive and is a subject of ongoing research.

Screening

Early recognition of HIV infection facilitates effective counseling about ART, monitoring of disease progression, and prevention and treatment of opportunistic infections and other complications; it also reduces the risk of HIV transmission to others. The Centers for Disease Control and Prevention recommends screening all persons aged 15 to 64 years for HIV infection, with a similar recommendation endorsed by the U.S. Preventive Services Task Force. Screen all pregnant women; ART administered to an HIV-infected woman during pregnancy can significantly reduce maternal-fetal transmission. In an attempt to increase the number of persons tested, the Centers for Disease Control and Prevention does not recommend written consent for HIV screening.

Diagnosis

The presentation of HIV/AIDS can be protean and nonspecific. It is essential to maintain a high index of suspicion based on exposures, risk factors, symptoms, and findings on physical examination and diagnostic testing.

Certain diagnoses warrant HIV testing. These include severe or treatment-refractory herpes simplex virus infection, esophageal candidiasis, *Pneumocystis jirovecii* pneumonitis, cryptococcal meningitis, disseminated mycobacterial infection, cytomegalovirus retinitis or gastrointestinal disease, and toxoplasmosis.

HIV testing is indicated in any patient with signs or symptoms of immunologic dysfunction, weight loss, generalized lymphadenopathy, fever and night sweats of >2 weeks' duration, oral thrush, severe aphthous ulcers, severe seborrheic dermatitis, or oral hairy leukoplakia. Herpes zoster in a younger person, recurrent pneumonia, chronic diarrhea, or unexplained hematologic abnormalities (eg, anemia, leukopenia, thrombocytopenia, polyclonal gammopathy) should also prompt consideration of HIV infection.

The physician should suspect acute HIV infection as the cause of a febrile illness occurring within days to weeks of a potential exposure. Most persons with acute infection develop an acute symptomatic illness that may range from a simple febrile illness to a full-blown mononucleosis-like syndrome. Because patients lack an immune response during this period, virus levels tend to be very high, and a "window period" exists for 3 to 6 weeks, during which time seroconversion of the disease has not yet occurred, and results of HIV antibody testing are negative. Viral-specific tests, however, such as those for nucleic acid, are usually positive during this time frame and can be used to establish the diagnosis.

Obtain a detailed sexual history and ask about other risk factors, especially if fatigue, adenopathy, pharyngitis, mucocutaneous ulceration, rash, or headache is also present.

Traditional testing for HIV consisted of a highly sensitive enzyme-linked immunosorbent assay (ELISA) for antibodies directed toward HIV, or a rapid HIV antibody test (which may give results in less than 30 minutes); positive results on these tests required a more specific confirmatory test, such as the Western blot. However, current recommendations are for initial testing with a combination immunoassay that detects both HIV antibody and p24 antigen, a viral capsid protein that is elevated early in infection. This combination testing reduces the "window period" when false-negative results may occur and may diagnose HIV as early as 2 weeks after infection occurs. If negative, no further testing is indicated. If positive, supplemental testing is performed to determine virus type present (HIV-1 or HIV-2). If this follow-up testing is equivocal, HIV-1 nucleic acid testing is indicated. A positive rapid test should be followed by combination testing to confirm the result. In HIV-positive patients, assessing the viral load and CD4 cell count offers important prognostic information as well as being markers for monitoring response to therapy. The viral load is the most reliable marker for predicting clinical progression and treatment failure. The CD4 cell count is the most dependable marker for the current risk of opportunistic complications of HIV infection and ART initiation. Immunosuppression due to HIV infection can lead to several characteristic infectious and neoplastic conditions (Table 1).

The physician should suspect *P. jirovecii* pneumonia in patients with HIV/AIDS who have a CD4 cell count <200/μL (0.20×10^9/L) and who develop fever, dry cough, and dyspnea over days to weeks. Chest radiographs typically show diffuse interstitial infiltrates, but radiologic findings vary widely. Diagnosis is made by direct staining examination of sputum (eg, induced or obtained by bronchoscopy). Suspect toxoplasmic encephalitis in patients who have a CD4 cell count <100/μL (0.10 × 10^9/L), fever, and neurologic findings. Brain magnetic resonance imaging or head computed tomography will typically show multiple ring-enhancing lesions. Failure of the lesions to shrink after a trial of therapy for toxoplasmosis raises concern for primary central nervous system lymphoma. Primary central nervous system lymphoma tends to be periventricular in location and may also involve single or multiple ring-enhancing lesions.

Therapy

The primary goals for initiating ART are to reduce HIV-associated morbidity and mortality, restore/preserve immunologic function while reducing the viral load, and prevent HIV transmission. Suppressing the viral load slows disease progression, partially reconstitutes immune deficits, improves quality of life, and prolongs survival. Highly active antiretroviral therapy refers to a drug regimen of three or more active compounds that inhibit HIV and has become the standard of care for patients with HIV infection. Timing of the initiation of therapy has changed in recent years, as studies suggest a reduction in AIDS-related morbidity and possibly mortality when therapy is started at higher CD4 cell counts. Although ART had previously been initiated based on the specific level of CD4 cell count, the most recent U.S. Department of Health and Human Services Guidelines for the Use of Antiretroviral Agents in HIV-1-Infected Adults and Adolescents recommend starting ART in all HIV-infected individuals regardless of CD4 cell count to reduce the risk of dis-

Table 1. Complications of HIV Infection

Condition	Associated CD4 Count (cells/μL or cells × 10^9/L)	Key Characteristics
Mucocutaneous candidiasis	<200 (0.20)	Involves primarily the oropharynx and esophagus
Cryptococcosis	<100 (0.10)	Causes subacute meningitis; often associated with cryptococcemia
Cryptosporidiosis	Any, but <100 (0.10) with more severe disease	Persistent watery diarrhea
Cytomegalovirus	<50 (0.05)	Retinitis, esophagitis, colitis
Kaposi sarcoma	Any, but more often if <200 (0.20)	Nontender, raised discrete purplish lesions, often on the lower extremities or intraoral; primarily in homosexual men coinfected with human herpesvirus 8
Lymphoma	Any, but more often if <100 (0.10)	Burkitt, large B-cell NHL, or primary CNS lymphoma
Mycobacterium tuberculosis	Any	Pulmonary infection. Extrapulmonary manifestations more common if CD4 count <200 (0.20)
M. avium complex	<50 (0.05)	Disseminated infection, often with liver and bone marrow involvement and diffuse adenopathy
Pneumocystis pneumonia	<200 (0.20)	Subacute onset of dyspnea on exertion, hypoxia, nonproductive cough; diffuse interstitial infiltrates on chest radiograph
Progressive multifocal leukoencephalopathy	Any, but more often if <100 (0.10)	Caused by JC virus (a human polyomavirus); white matter lesions seen on imaging; patient presents with focal neurologic defects including altered mental status
Toxoplasmosis	<100 (0.10)	Fever, headache, focal neurologic deficits; multiple ring-enhancing lesions on CNS imaging; positive toxoplasma serology

CNS = central nervous system; JC = John Cunningham; NHL = non-Hodgkin lymphoma.

Table 2. Antiviral Agents and Common Side Effects

Drug Category and Examples	Notable Side Effects
Nucleoside/nucleotide reverse transcriptase inhibitors	Lactic acidosis, hepatic toxicity, lipoatrophy, pancreatitis, peripheral neuropathy
Abacavir *(preferred drug)*	Life-threatening hypersensitivity reaction, increased risk of myocardial infarction. Screen for HLA-B*5701 to reduce risk of hypersensitivity reaction.
Emtricitabine *(preferred drug)*	Lactic acidosis, severe hepatic steatosis
Tenofovir *(preferred drug)*	Nephrotoxicity: renal injury, Fanconi syndrome; osteopenia/osteoporosis
Nonnucleoside reverse transcriptase inhibitors	Hepatotoxicity, skin rash
Efavirenz *(preferred drug)*	Sleep disturbance, depression, vivid dreams or hallucinations, possible teratogenicity
Rilpivirine	Rare rash
Protease inhibitors	GI upset (diarrhea), lipodystrophy, hepatotoxicity, dyslipidemia
Atazanavir *(preferred drug)*	Jaundice (indirect hyperbilirubinemia), cholelithiasis, nephrolithiasis
Darunavir *(preferred drug)*	Hypersensitivity reaction (especially those with sulfa allergy)
Fusion inhibitors	
Enfuvirtide	Injection site reactions (itching/swelling/erythema), severe reactions (sometimes with eosinophilia and signs of allergy)
Coreceptor antagonists	
Maraviroc	Cough, fever, upper respiratory infections, rash, hepatotoxicity, musculoskeletal symptoms. Perform coreceptor tropism assay prior to use.
Integrase inhibitors	
Raltegravir *(preferred drug)*	Generally well tolerated. Commonly: headache, nausea, diarrhea. Rarely: rhabomyolysis, hypersensitivity reaction, depression
Dolutegravir	Headache, insomnia, hypersensitivity reaction

GI = gastrointestinal.

ease progression and transmission. This includes pregnant women, patients >50 years of age, and those coinfected with viral hepatitis, with the use of appropriate antiviral drugs in these specific situations. The strength of evidence on which this recommendation is based varies by the level of pretreatment CD4 T lymphocyte (CD4) cell count, with greater evidence of improved outcomes with lower CD4 cell counts.

Six classes of antiretroviral agents are currently available. Preferred initial combination therapy for treatment-naïve patients usually involves a "backbone" that consists of two nucleoside/nucleotide reverse transcriptase inhibitors. (The fixed combination of emtricitabine/tenofovir is often a first choice.) The backbone is combined with a "base" that consists of either a nonnucleoside reverse transcriptase inhibitor (typically efavirenz), an integrase strand transfer inhibitor (typically raltegravir), or one of two "boosted" protease inhibitors (typically atazanavir or darunavir combined with a second protease inhibitor ritonavir, which boosts the levels of the first by inhibiting the cytochrome P-450 system). Select a combination regimen based on drug characteristics (eg, interactions, pill burden), side effect profile, patient comorbidities, and viral resistance testing (eg, genotyping).

Drug selection for treatment-experienced patients who need to switch medications because of virologic failure or intolerable side effects should be based on ART history, concomitant use of medications to minimize interactions, and genotype testing for viral drug resistance. Combination therapy maximizes treatment efficacy by reducing the chance of resistance, but it increases the risk of drug interactions. Certain antiretroviral drugs are associated with rare but potentially fatal hepatotoxicity, hypersensitivity reactions, pancre-

atitis, and lactic acidosis (Table 2). In a small subset of patients, initiation of ART can lead to an inflammatory reaction as the immune system recovers and mounts a response to pathogens that may be present often subclinically. This is called the *immune reconstitution inflammatory syndrome*, and treatment is usually supportive.

Provide prophylaxis against certain opportunistic infections based on the level of immunosuppression and other clinical factors (Table 3). Treat patients with *P. jirovecii* pneumonia with trimethoprim-sulfamethoxazole, and add glucocorticoids for those with hypoxia (arterial P_{O_2}<70 mm Hg [9.3 kPa] or alveolar arterial gradient >35 mm Hg [4.7 kPa]). Vaccinate HIV-infected patients against influenza, pneumococcal pneumonia, and, if not already immune, hepatitis B. These should all be offered independent of CD4 count, although vaccination is likely more effective in patients with higher CD4 counts.

Follow-Up

The broad goal of ART is to achieve the lowest possible viral load while minimizing the adverse effects of treatment. Assess the viral load and CD4 count within 2 to 4 weeks after starting or modifying antiretroviral therapy and typically every 3 to 4 months thereafter. Generally, an effective antiretroviral regimen should achieve viral suppression within 3 to 6 months. Failure to do so suggests poor adherence, poor absorption, or viral resistance. Significant ongoing viral replication in the face of continuing therapy may contribute to the selection of multidrug resistance. Suspected viral resistance should prompt a change in the antiretroviral regimen, usually based on resistance testing and consultation with an infectious disease expert.

Table 3. Recommended Prophylaxis for Opportunistic Infections

Condition	Prophylaxis
Mycobacterium avium complex	*When*: CD4 count <50/μL (0.05 × 10^9/L) *What*: Weekly azithromycin *Discontinue*: CD4 count >100/μL (0.10 × 10^9/L) for >3 mo in response to ART
Toxoplasmosis	*When*: CD4 count <100/μL (0.10 × 10^9/L) and toxoplasma seropositive *What*: Daily trimethoprim-sulfamethoxazole DS *Discontinue*: CD4 count >200/μL (0.20 × 10^9/L) for >3 mo in response to ART
Pneumocystis pneumonia	*When*: CD4 count <200/μL (0.20 × 10^9/L) *What*: Daily trimethoprim-sulfamethoxazole DS *Discontinue*: CD4 count >200/μL (0.20 × 10^9/L) for >3 mo in response to ART
Mycobacterium tuberculosis	*When*: Induration of ≥5 mm on purified protein-derivative skin test or a positive interferon-γ release assay *What*: Isoniazid and pyridoxine. Alternative: Weekly isoniazid and rifapentine direct observed therapy if not on ART *Discontinue*: After 9 mo of therapy. Alternative regimen: 3 mo

ART = antiretroviral therapy; DS = double-strength.

Regular physical examinations and laboratory testing can help detect drug toxicities (eg, rash, fat redistribution, hepatic enlargement or tenderness, muscle tenderness, and/or peripheral neuropathy), opportunistic infections, and treatment failure due to resistance or nonadherence. Depending on the drug regimen, obtain a complete blood count, a chemistry profile, and liver-associated enzymes every 3 to 6 months to monitor for possible drug toxicities. Monitor a fasting lipid profile and glucose (or hemoglobin A1c) annually and more frequently if abnormal upon initiation of ART, especially if it is part of its side effect profile. Patients infected with HIV should be tested for hepatitis B and C viruses. Tuberculin skin testing using purified protein derivative (induration of ≥5 mm is considered positive) or an interferon–γ release assay should be performed in all patients with HIV at the time of diagnosis and annually for those at continued risk. A positive result of either test should prompt prophylactic therapy in the absence of active tuberculosis. It is critical for women to have regular gynecologic evaluations, including Papanicolaou testing; women with HIV infection have a much higher rate of cervical cancer than women who are not infected with HIV.

Bibliography

Panel on Antiretroviral Guidelines for Adults and Adolescents. Guidelines for the use of antiretroviral agents in HIV-1 infected adults and adolescents. Department of Health and Human Services. 2013. Available at http://aidsinfo.nih.gov/ContentFiles/AdultandAdolescentGL.pdf. Accessed May 10, 2014.

Thompson MA , Aberg JA, Hoy JF, et al; International Antiviral Society USA. Antiretroviral treatment of adult HIV infection: 2012 recommendations of the International Antiviral Society-USA panel. JAMA. 2012;308:387-402. [PMID: 22820792]

Chapter 63

Osteomyelitis

David C. Tompkins, MD

Osteomyelitis is an infection of bone caused by various bacteria and, less commonly, mycobacteria and fungi. Normal bone is highly resistant to infection, and the development of osteomyelitis often requires trauma, the presence of a foreign body, or inoculation with particular pathogens. *Staphylococcus aureus*, for example, expresses several receptors for bone components (eg, fibronectin, laminin, collagen) that allow adherence to bone and the establishment of infection.

Osteomyelitis can be characterized by the duration of illness (acute or chronic), mechanism of infection (eg, hematogenous spread, extension from a contiguous focus, direct contamination), affected bone, physiologic status of the host, and presence of orthopedic hardware. The clinical presentation and treatment vary depending on the type of osteomyelitis.

Hematogenous spread is responsible for <20% of cases of osteomyelitis in adults and occurs in patients at risk for bloodstream infections (including those on hemodialysis with long-term intravascular catheters) and in patients with high-grade bacteremia, endocarditis, or sickle cell disease. The intervertebral disc space and two adjacent vertebrae are the most common sites of hematogenous osteomyelitis in adults. Typically, only one microorganism is isolated in patients with hematogenous osteomyelitis; 40% to 60% of cases are caused by *S. aureus*.

Osteomyelitis from contiguous spread of infection is much more common in adults, particularly in persons aged >50 years who have diabetes mellitus or peripheral vascular disease. Patients with osteomyelitis from contiguous spread usually have a polymicrobial infection. Direct contamination of bone exposed by an open fracture or by surgery may lead to osteomyelitis, depending on the degree of contamination and associated soft tissue injury. Table 1 summarizes clinical risk factors and associated pathogens for osteomyelitis.

Prevention

Patients with diabetes or peripheral vascular disease are at increased risk for osteomyelitis, particularly involving the small bones of the feet. These patients should be educated about the importance of meticulous attention to foot care and proper management of minor foot injuries. In addition, patients with diabetes should have a yearly foot examination by a health care provider and custom-made footwear to accommodate foot deformities.

Hematogenous seeding of orthopedic implants following dental and other invasive procedures is very uncommon, except possibly within 2 years of prosthesis placement. Therefore, universal antimicrobial prophylaxis for immunocompetent patients undergoing dental, gastrointestinal, or urologic procedures is not recommended.

Diagnosis

Patients should be assessed for predisposing conditions (eg, diabetes, previous surgery, rheumatoid arthritis, peripheral vascular disease) and risk factors for bacteremia (eg, recent infections, illicit injection drug use, long-term intravenous catheters). The clinical hallmarks of osteomyelitis are local pain and fever, particularly in patients with acute hematogenous osteomyelitis; however, these findings may be absent in those with chronic or contiguous osteomyelitis. Patients with vertebral osteomyelitis often present with an insidious onset of progressively more severe, dull back pain. The infection can trigger paravertebral muscle spasm, with an associated decrease in mobility of the spine. On examination, there is often tenderness to percussion over the involved vertebral bodies. The presence of a sinus tract (fistula to the skin, draining pus from a deep tissue infection) overlying a bone and the palpation of bone when using a sterile, blunt,

Table 1. Clinical Risk Factors and Associated Bacterial Agents Causing Osteomyelitis

Risk Factor	Possible Organisms
Contiguous infection (eg, diabetic foot, wound)	Polymicrobial infection; most commonly *Staphylococcus aureus* and coagulase-negative staphylococci. May also include streptococci, enterococci, gram-negative bacilli (eg, *Pseudomonas* sp., *Enterobacter* sp., *Escherichia coli*, *Serratia* sp.) and anaerobes (eg, *Peptostreptococcus*, *Clostridium* sp., *Bacteroides fragilis*)
Contaminated open fracture	*Staphylococcus* sp., aerobic gram-negative bacilli (eg, *Pseudomonas* sp., *Enterobacter* sp., *E. coli*, *Serratia* sp.)
Dog bite, cat bite	*Pasteurella multocida*
Foot puncture wound (wearing sneakers)	*Pseudomonas aeruginosa*
Hematogenous (eg, bacteremia)	*S. aureus*
Illicit intravenous drug use	Varies in different communities but typically includes *S. aureus* and *Pseudomonas aeruginosa*.
Sickle cell disease	*Salmonella* sp.
Hemodialysis	*Staphylococcus* sp., *P. aeruginosa*

Table 2. Differential Diagnosis of Osteomyelitis

Disorder	Notes
Soft tissue infection	Imaging studies show sparing of the bone. Probe to bone test is negative.
Infectious arthritis (see Chapter 101)	Severe functional limitation and joint swelling are often present. Bone is not infected early in the disease course.
Metastatic malignancy to the bone	Usually associated with a primary lesion (eg, breast, prostate, lung). Metastasis is usually multifocal and tends to remain isolated to one vertebral body, whereas osteomyelitis often crosses the end plate.
Neuropathic arthropathy in diabetes	Radiologic features should be suggestive. Systemic signs and symptoms of infection are absent. May be difficult to distinguish from infection.
Osteoarthritis	Radiologic features should be suggestive. Systemic signs and symptoms of infection are absent. C-reactive protein level, erythrocyte sedimentation rate, and leukocyte count are normal.

stainless steel probe in the depth of a foot ulcer are almost always associated with osteomyelitis. In patients with diabetic foot infections, the presence of visible bone, an ulcer persisting for >2 weeks, and an ulcer >2 cm are correlated with the presence of osteomyelitis. Table 2 summarizes the differential diagnosis of osteomyelitis.

Prosthetic joint infection should be suspected in patients who have had joint pain since surgery. Prosthetic loosening in the first 2 years after arthroplasty should raise suspicion for a prosthetic joint infection.

Various bone imaging techniques can help to establish a diagnosis of osteomyelitis (Table 3). A plain radiograph has a low overall sensitivity but may reveal surrounding soft tissue swelling within the first days to first week of infection. Bone changes such as periosteal elevation, cortical erosion, and reactive sclerosis take several weeks to months to develop. Magnetic resonance imaging (MRI) has largely supplanted radionuclide bone scanning as an aid in the diagnosis of osteomyelitis. The inflammatory process associated with osteomyelitis results in bone marrow edema that can be shown on MRI, often within 1 week of the onset of infection. The absence of bone marrow edema in a patient with symptoms present for longer than 1 to 2 weeks has a high negative predictive value in ruling out osteomyelitis.

Laboratory values typically include a normal leukocyte count. Markers of inflammation, such as an elevated erythrocyte sedimentation rate and C-reactive protein level, can be helpful in supporting the diagnosis and monitoring the response to therapy. The erythrocyte sedimentation rate can be normal early in the disease process, becomes markedly elevated in established infections, and takes several months after therapy to normalize. The C-reactive protein level often rises and falls more quickly with the onset of infection and in response to effective therapy.

The choice of antimicrobial therapy is ideally based on identifying the infecting organism(s) and in vitro sensitivities. Blood cultures are obtained when signs and symptoms of infection are present. Superficial cultures obtained from drainage sites are often contaminated with skin flora and correlate poorly with deep cultures. If possible, obtain a bone biopsy (percutaneous or open) for cultures before initiating antibiotics. Open biopsy facilitates procurement of a larger piece of bone than that obtained through percutaneous biopsy, thereby increasing the diagnostic yield and facilitating debridement

Table 3. Laboratory and Other Studies for Osteomyelitis

Test	Notes
Leukocyte count	Absence of leukocytosis cannot be used as evidence against the diagnosis of infection (sensitivity 26%).
Erythrocyte sedimentation rate and C-reactive protein level	Most sensitive in patients with acute hematogenous osteomyelitis but often normal in early disease (sensitivity 50%-90%).
Sinus tract culture	Correlation is best for *Staphylococcus aureus* (sensitivity 80%). The association is poor for other microorganisms (sensitivity <40%).
Blood culture	Obtain in patients with fever or systemic signs of sepsis. Less sensitive in patients with chronic osteomyelitis and orthopedic implant–associated osteomyelitis (sensitivity <20%).
Plain bone radiography	Obtain in all patients. Soft tissue swelling earliest abnormality. Periosteal reaction and focal bony lysis may not be seen for 2 to 6 weeks (sensitivity 62%). Sclerotic changes with periosteal new bone formation suggest chronic infection. Plain radiographs also useful for identifying other causes of bone pain.
Radionuclide bone scan	High sensitivity (>90%). Specificity variable (38%-82%) because conditions with inflammation or increased bone turnover (eg, trauma, degenerative joint disease, surgery, malignancy) yield positive results. Specificity can be improved by pairing with a plain radiograph.
MRI	Excellent in distinguishing soft tissue infection from osteomyelitis. MRI is more sensitive than plain radiography and allows better identification of optimal areas for needle aspiration or biopsy (sensitivity 91%-95%).
Percutaneous bone biopsy	Not as invasive as an open biopsy. Mainly used in disc space infection or diabetic foot infection. Sensitivity 43%-87% varies and is lower with administrating antibiotics before biopsy.
Surgical bone biopsy	The gold standard for diagnosing osteomyelitis (sensitivity 100%, specificity 100%).

MRI = magnetic resonance imaging.

of the bone and surrounding tissues, if necessary. Biopsy material should be incubated in anaerobic and aerobic media. Bone biopsy may not be needed for patients with suspected osteomyelitis and a supportive imaging study in the setting of positive blood cultures. Table 3 also summarizes laboratory and other studies useful in the diagnosis of osteomyelitis.

Therapy

Surgical debridement is usually warranted in cases of chronic osteomyelitis, contiguous osteomyelitis, and orthopedic implant-associated osteomyelitis. Complete drainage and debridement of all necrotic soft tissue and resection of dead and infected bone is required. Failure to remove an infected orthopedic implant allows the offending microorganisms to form a biofilm and, therefore, escape the effect of antimicrobial agents. In patients with peripheral vascular disease, revascularization is extremely important to allow adequate oxygenation of soft tissues, promote bone healing, and increase access of antibiotics and the host humoral response to the infected area. The application of vacuum-assisted closure devices and use of hyperbaric oxygen exposure are adjunctive therapies, which may offer benefit for a selective group of patients.

Antibiotic treatment is typically begun immediately after appropriate cultures are obtained. Initial intravenous antimicrobial therapy is directed against the most common bacteria responsible for hematogenous osteomyelitis, including *S. aureus*. Nafcillin, cefazolin, or vancomycin is a reasonable empiric antibiotic choice for initial therapy. Patients with sickle cell disease have an increased risk for salmonella as well as streptococcal infection; illicit injection drug users are at increased risk for gram-negative infections. For both of these groups, levofloxacin plus nafcillin (or oxacillin) or vancomycin is a reasonable choice for empiric coverage. Surgical intervention should be considered in patients with acute hematogenous osteomyelitis and (1) femoral head involvement, (2) failure to make a specific microbiologic diagnosis with noninvasive techniques, (3) neurologic complications, (4) the presence of fragments of dead bone (sequestra), or (4) failure to improve while on appropriate antimicrobial therapy.

Osteomyelitis that complicates diabetic foot infections is usually polymicrobial in nature; initial antimicrobial therapy should target *S. aureus*, streptococci, enterococci, Enterobacteriaceae organisms, *Pseudomonas*, and anaerobes. Appropriate empiric antibiotic therapy includes a β-lactam/β-lactamase inhibitor (eg, piperacillin-tazobactam, ampicillin-sulbactam), a carbapenem (eg, imipenem, meropenem), or metronidazole with cefepime, ciprofloxacin, or aztreonam. In patients with diabetes, there is an increased risk of methicillin-resistant *S. aureus* infection because of recurrent infections and repeated use of antibiotics; therefore, vancomycin is often included in the initial antibiotic combination pending culture results.

The optimal duration of antibiotic therapy in patients with osteomyelitis is not clear; however, animal models and clinical experience have demonstrated a higher failure rate with a shorter duration of therapy (<4 weeks). Adult patients with uncomplicated acute hematogenous vertebral osteomyelitis are typically treated with 4 to 6 weeks of antimicrobial therapy.

In patients with chronic osteomyelitis without acute soft tissue infection or sepsis syndrome, withhold antimicrobial therapy until deep bone cultures have been obtained. Patients with chronic or contiguous osteomyelitis usually require a combination of surgical debridement and extended antimicrobial therapy based on culture results. Antimicrobial agents should be administered for 4 to 6 weeks to allow the debrided bone to be covered by vascularized soft tissue and to reduce the high relapse rate.

The duration of antimicrobial therapy in orthopedic implant-associated osteomyelitis is adjusted according to the surgical therapeutic modality. Following removal of all hardware and infected bone, administer 4 to 6 weeks of antimicrobial therapy. Antibiotic-impregnated polymethylmethacrylate can deliver high local levels of antimicrobial agents and sometimes is used at the time of surgical debridement. If removal of a foreign body is not possible (mechanical instability or contraindications to surgery), initial parenteral therapy is followed by prolonged suppression using an oral antimicrobial agent.

Follow-Up

Patients undergoing treatment for osteomyelitis require regular follow-up to monitor for drug-related toxicity, vascular access complications, and disease recurrence. A persistently elevated erythrocyte sedimentation rate or C-reactive protein level despite appropriate antibiotic therapy may reflect the presence of a persistent focus of infection. Interpretation of imaging studies is often difficult, particularly following surgical therapy for osteomyelitis; therefore, follow-up images are not routinely obtained.

Bibliography
Butalia S, Palda VA, Sargeant RJ, et al. Does this patient with diabetes have osteomyelitis of the lower extremity? JAMA. 2008;299:806-13. [PMID: 18285592]

Chapter 64

Sepsis Syndrome

Isaac O. Opole, MD

Sepsis syndrome is a continuum of four clinical entities of increasing severity that are associated with a stepwise increase in morbidity and mortality: systemic inflammatory response syndrome (SIRS), sepsis, severe sepsis, and septic shock. SIRS is defined by the presence of specific clinical findings (Table 1); sepsis is distinguished from other causes of SIRS by the presence of suspected or confirmed infection. Severe sepsis accounts for 20% of all admissions to intensive care units (ICUs) and is a leading cause of death. Approximately 750,000 cases of severe sepsis occur in the United States each year, with mortality rates of 20% to 50%. The incidence of sepsis rises exponentially after age 65 to 70 years, and age-specific mortality rates are much higher in patients with baseline comorbidities, such as diabetes mellitus or heart disease. Sepsis is most common in men, nonwhites, and the elderly, with gram-positive organisms accounting for >50% of all cases.

Mortality increases stepwise from SIRS through severe sepsis to septic shock. For patients with severe sepsis, the mortality rate increases by 15% to 20% for each sepsis-induced dysfunctional organ. Early diagnosis of sepsis syndrome and early goal-directed therapy significantly reduces mortality in severe sepsis, and routine screening in high-risk patients to enable early identification of the sepsis syndrome is recommended.

Sepsis represents a complex and variable host response to an infective trigger in which activation of both proinflammatory and anti-inflammatory mechanisms may lead to organ injury, further immunosuppression, and coagulation abnormalities. Primary cell injury may result directly from infection or occur when a toxic microbial stimulus initiates a host inflammatory response. A network of inflammatory mediators are generated, including tumor necrosis factor-α, interleukin-1 (IL-1), and other cytokines and chemokines that activate leukocytes and promote leukocyte vascular endothelial adhesion and damage. Endothelial damage leads to tissue factor expression and activation of the tissue factor–dependent clotting cascade and subsequent formation of thrombin. The result is the development of microaggregates of fibrin, platelets, neutrophils, and erythrocytes, which cause impaired capillary blood flow and decreased oxygen and nutrient delivery to tissues. The net result of the humoral, cellular, and microvascular changes results in hypotension and microvascular thrombosis, which mediate organ dysfunction through tissue hypoxemia and shock. Older patients may be particularly vulnerable to organ dysfunction in severe sepsis due to higher levels of inflammatory mediators such as tumor necrosis factor-α, IL-1, interleukin-6 (IL-6), and soluble adhesion molecules, which may explain in part the increased morbidity and mortality associated with sepsis in older patients.

Diagnosis

Diagnosis and timely intervention depend on early identification of the four clinical criteria for SIRS (see Table 1). Sepsis is defined as the presence of two or more SIRS criteria plus the presence of a suspected or known infection, whereas severe sepsis is defined as the presence of sepsis plus evidence of sepsis-induced dysfunction of at least one organ. Such evidence may include hypoxemia, shock, delirium, thrombocytopenia, acute kidney injury (rising serum creatinine level), or hepatic injury (rising bilirubin or aminotransferase level). Septic shock occurs when there is profound sepsis-induced hypotension and hypoperfusion despite adequate fluid resuscitation (Table 2). The differential diagnosis of septic shock should include other etiologies, such as cardiogenic shock, toxic shock syndrome, neurogenic shock, severe hypovolemia, adrenal insufficiency, and anaphylaxis (Table 3).

The initial evaluation of the patient with sepsis includes a rapid yet thorough history and physical examination, with an emphasis on identifying a possible source of infection. Screening of potential-

Table 1. Definition of Systemic Inflammatory Response Syndrome

Presence of two or more of the following in the absence of other known causes of these:

- Temperature >38.3°C (100.4°F) or <36.0°C (96.8°F)
- Heart rate >90/bpm
- Respiration rate >20 breaths/min or arterial P_{CO_2} <32 mm Hg (4.3 kPa)
- Leukocyte count >12,000/µL (12×10^9/L) or < 4000/µL (4×10^9/L) with 10% bands

Table 2. Spectrum of the Sepsis Syndrome

SIRS	Sepsis	Severe Sepsis	Septic Shock
Presence of two or more SIRS criteria	SIRS plus suspected or confirmed infection (positive cultures not required)	Sepsis with any evidence of organ dysfunction or tissue hypoperfusion	Sepsis-induced hypotension refractory to adequate fluid resuscitation

SIRS = systemic inflammatory response syndrome.

Table 3. Differential Diagnosis of Shock

Disorder	Notes
Septic shock	Persistent hypotension refractory to fluid resuscitation in the presence of severe sepsis. It is characterized by high cardiac output (early) that can become depressed (late), low systemic vascular resistance, and low filling pressures. Fever, leukocytosis, and source of infection are characteristically present.
Toxic shock syndrome	A form of septic shock caused by SA or GABHS. Diagnosis of staphylococcal TSS requires the presence of fever >38.9°C, systolic BP < 90 mm Hg, characteristic rash with desquamation, and involvement of any three organ systems (GI, muscular, mucous membranes, kidney, liver, blood, CNS) in the presence of positive SA cultures. Streptococcal TSS is diagnosed by the presence of GABHS from sterile sites (definite) or nonsterile site (probable), hypotension, and the presence of organ dysfunction in any two of the following systems: kidney, liver, skin, blood, and pulmonary.
Cardiogenic shock	Shock caused by inadequate cardiac output of any etiology (ischemia, infarction, cardiomyopathy, arrhythmia, etc.) to perfuse the tissues. Accompanied by a compensatory increase in SVR.
Hypovolemic shock	Characterized by decreased intravascular volume leading to low cardiac filling pressures, low cardiac output, and compensatory high systemic vascular resistance. Patients may have a history of hemorrhage or volume depletion from other causes (eg, severe diarrhea).
Anaphylactic shock	Results from release of inflammatory mediators (histamine, prostaglandins, cytokines, leukotrienes, etc.) resulting in systemic changes (eg, depressed myocardial contractility, vascular instability) and shock. Clinical presentation includes urticaria and/or angioedema, shortness of breath and wheezing, stridor due to laryngeal edema, pulmonary edema, and hypotension. Similar to severe sepsis, the systemic vascular resistance is typically low, and the cardiac output is elevated. Diagnosis is made when the typical signs and symptoms occur shortly after exposure to a suspected antigen and the absence of fever or infection. Treatment with epinephrine should be part of the initial management. Glucocorticoids and antihistamines are also indicated.
Neurogenic (spinal) shock	Occurs after injury to the spinal cord or other severe CNS injury; thought to be caused by autonomic nervous system dysfunction. It is associated with low systemic vascular resistance and, typically, bradycardia. Bradycardia and hypotension in a patient with spinal cord injury should raise suspicion for neurogenic shock.
Adrenal crisis	Caused by inadequate adrenal mineralocorticoid/glucocorticoid production that leads to vascular instability. Patients with adrenal crisis often have shock and abdominal symptoms (eg, tenderness, nausea, vomiting) and may have fever. In addition, weakness, fatigue, lethargy, and confusion are common. Patients may have hyponatremia and hyperkalemia. If adrenal insufficiency is suspected, glucocorticoid hormone with mineralocorticoid and glucocorticoid activity (eg, hydrocortisone) should be initiated without delay.
Obstructive shock	Causes of obstructive shock include cardiac tamponade, pulmonary embolism, tension pneumothorax and result in low cardiac output, hypotension, and tachycardia; may mimic septic shock. All of these diagnoses are rapidly life threatening.

ACS = acute coronary syndrome; CNS = central nervous system; ECG = electrocardiogram; GABHS = group A β-hemolytic streptococcus; GI = gastrointestinal; SA = *Staphylococcus aureus*; TSS = toxic shock syndrome; SVR = systemic vascular resistance.

ly infected seriously ill patients who are at high risk for sepsis is encouraged to enable early identification and intervention. Vital signs are crucial for screening and diagnosis as well as assessment of the patient's stability. Vital signs require continuous monitoring but are not always sensitive in older or immunosuppressed patients. For example, fever may be blunted or absent in approximately 15% of older patients with bacteremia. There must be a high index of suspicion (especially in older patients) when any of the following nonspecific clinical signs or symptoms of infection are present: delirium, weakness, anorexia, malaise, urinary incontinence, or falls.

Laboratory evaluation is focused on finding evidence of end-organ dysfunction related to sepsis, such as acute kidney injury, liver dysfunction, disseminated intravascular coagulation, or mental status changes, but should not delay initiation of therapy. Initial laboratory studies should include serum lactate levels and blood cultures, as well as a blood count with differential, serum electrolyte and creatinine levels, urinalysis, liver chemistry tests, and coagulation parameters. Serum lactate levels have been correlated with the degree of global tissue hypoxia, the severity of sepsis, and mortality risk, and goal-directed therapy should aim at normalization of serum lactate. Additional cultures from any sites of potential infection should be obtained as soon as the diagnosis of sepsis is suspected. If invasive *Candidia* or *Aspergillus* is suspected, 1, 3 beta-D-glucan, galactomannan, or anti-mannan assays may be helpful in identifying the presence of these infections. Various other biologic markers of sepsis have been studied (eg, procalcitonin, C-reactive protein, IL-

6), but have not been validated for routine clinical use. Radiography and other imaging studies should be obtained as directed by the patient's symptoms.

Therapy

Almost universally, patients are admitted to the hospital if they meet SIRS criteria. Patients with sepsis, severe sepsis, or septic shock are managed in the ICU. Most patients will require central venous access for fluid administration and invasive monitoring. Early goal-directed therapy aimed at restoration of hemodynamic stability should be instituted immediately on admission and continued until stabilization. The initial goal of therapy is to maintain tissue perfusion, balancing oxygen delivery with oxygen demand to prevent tissue hypoxia. The Surviving Sepsis Campaign and the Institute for Healthcare Improvement have advocated the use of management "bundles" (groups of interventions that result in better outcomes when they are implemented together) in patients suspected of having severe sepsis or shock. The standardized protocols in these "bundles" are central to improvement in patient outcomes. The "severe sepsis resuscitation bundle" includes early assessment of serum lactate, aggressive fluid resuscitation, blood culture before initiation of antibiotics, early broad-spectrum antibiotic administration, and vasopressor administration (Table 4). The resuscitation bundle should be initiated whenever indicated, and it should not be delayed by diagnostic procedures or pending ICU admission.

Table 4. Surviving Sepsis Campaign Care Bundles

To be completed within 3 hours

- Measure serum lactate level.
- Obtain blood cultures before administering antibiotics.
- Administer broad-spectrum antibiotics.
- Administer 30 mL/kg crystalloid for hypotension or lactate ≥4 mmol/L. (36 mg/dL)

To be completed within 6 hours

- Apply vasopressors (for hypotension not responding to initial fluid resuscitation) to maintain an MAP ≥65 mm Hg.
- In the event of persistent arterial hypotension despite volume resuscitation (septic shock) or initial lactate ≥4 mmol/L (36 mg/dL):
  - Measure CVP (target of 8-12 mm Hg).
  - Measure ScvO$_2$ (target ≥70%).
  - Remeasure lactate if original level was elevated.

CVP = central venous pressure; MAP = mean arterial pressure; ScvO$_2$ = central venous oxygen saturation.

Dellinger RP, Levy MM, Rhodes A, et al. Surviving sepsis campaign: international guidelines for management of severe sepsis and septic shock: 2012. Crit Care Med. 2013;41:580-637. [PMID: 23353941]

A serum lactate level >4 mmol/L (36 mg/dL) indicates inadequate tissue perfusion, and early therapeutic goals should aim to normalize the serum lactate. Aggressive fluid resuscitation with crystalloid should be initiated and continued until a central venous pressure of 8 to 12 mm Hg or a mean arterial pressure (MAP) ≥65 mm Hg is attained (Table 5). Adequate initial fluid resuscitation with resolution of lactic acidosis has been shown to be the most important factor in improving survival. An initial fluid challenge of 30 mL/kg crystalloid should be started and continued as long as there is hemodynamic improvement. Greater amounts of fluids may be needed in some patients, and albumin administration may be considered in selected cases. Routine use of colloids is discouraged, however, as there is no proven benefit over crystalloids despite the additional cost. The use of hydroxyethyl starches for fluid resuscitation is also discouraged, as they have been associated with adverse outcomes.

If a fluid challenge fails to achieve an MAP ≥65 mm Hg, vasopressors are added as part of early goal-directed therapy. Norepinephrine is recommended as the first-choice vasopressor. It is a potent peripheral vasoconstrictor effective in reversing the endotoxin-induced vasodilation that is the hallmark of septic shock. Epinephrine may be added to or substituted for norepinephrine, and vasopressin can also be added to raise MAP to target or reduce the amount of norepinephrine required. In patients with evidence of myocardial dysfunction or ongoing signs of hypoperfusion despite volume resuscitation and achievement of adequate MAP, an agent with cardiostimulatory properties may be added, such as dobutamine or high-dose dopamine (10-20 µg/kg/min), although both may be associated with significant tachycardia and arrhythmia (Table 6). All patients receiving vasopressors should be in the ICU with blood pressure monitoring through an arterial line and should be on a cardiac monitor.

Whenever possible and appropriate, source control, including removing sources of infection (eg, indwelling catheters), drainage of abscesses, and surgical debridement of wounds, should occur promptly upon diagnosis of sepsis. Empiric antibiotic therapy should be initiated within 1 hour of recognizing sepsis and after blood has been drawn and samples from other suspected sites of infection have been taken for culture. Inadequate initial antibiotic therapy is independently associated with poor outcomes, and initial empiric therapy should include agents with activity against all probable pathogens and with adequate tissue penetration into suspected infective sites. Because of increasing antibiotic resistance, broad and early antibiotic therapy must be balanced with de-escalation based on identified organisms and/or cessation of antibiotics once the infection has resolved. In selecting empiric antibiotics, recognize that gram-positive infections now cause most cases of sepsis; however, gram-negative infections are still prevalent, and fungal infections must be considered in high-risk patients (eg, neutropenic patients, those receiving immunosuppression therapy). In such patients and in individuals with severe infections associated with respiratory failure and septic shock, complex combination empiric therapy may be required.

Although patients with sepsis are believed to have some degree of relative adrenal insufficiency, glucocorticoid therapy is not currently indicated in sepsis or septic shock, except possibly for patients with adrenal insufficiency as defined by usual parameters (eg, a random cortisol level <18 µg/dL in a patient in shock) or in those with refractory hypotension despite all other therapeutic interventions. Serial

Table 5. Treatment of Sepsis

Agent(s)	Notes
Crystalloid	Restores intravascular volume, which is depleted in patients with severe sepsis. Improves cardiac output, organ perfusion, and mortality in patients with severe sepsis. Fluid challenge infusion of at least 30 mL/kg should be given and repeated until the patient shows a beneficial response without major adverse effects. Patients may require 4-6 L during initial stabilization.
Antibiotics (fourth-generation cephalosporin, extended-spectrum [antipseudomonal] penicillin, carbapenem)	Early appropriate antibiotic therapy is associated with improved outcomes. Appropriate empiric therapy should be initiated rapidly, even if the source of infection is unknown. A more appropriate, source-directed antibiotic selection should be initiated if the source is known or becomes known (eg, add vancomycin if MRSA is suspected, add double coverage with an intravenous fluoroquinolone or aminoglycoside if a highly resistant gram-negative pathogen is suspected, or add clindamycin if toxic shock syndrome is suspected); consider additional agents (eg, fluoroquinolones, macrolides, tetracyclines, antifungal agents, antiviral agents) depending on the clinical presentation.
Vasopressors: norepinephrine, epinephrine, dobutamine, dopamine, vasopressin phenylephrine	Improves blood pressure and cardiac output. Norepinephrine is associated with less tachycardia than other vasopressor agents with β-effects and is more effective than dopamine in refractory septic shock. Vasopressin works on receptors other than adrenergic receptors and may be useful in refractory septic shock treated with high-dose adrenergic vasopressors. Dobutamine may be used in combination with a vasopressor to increase cardiac output if it is inappropriately low.

MRSA = methicillin-resistant *Staphylococcus aureus*.

Table 6. Vasopressor Agents and Their Physiologic Effects

Agent (Dose)	Receptors	Clinical Use
Norepinephrine	$\alpha_1 > \beta_1$	First-line for septic shock, other refractory shock.
Epinephrine	$\alpha_1 = \beta_1$	Alternative/second-line for septic shock, other refractory shock.
Vasopressin	Vasopressin receptors	Second vasopressor for septic shock only, add to catecholamine vasopressor.
Dopamine (high dose: 10.0-20.0 µg/kg/min)	$\alpha_1 > \beta_1$	Used as second-line alternative for septic shock or other refractory shock in patients with low risk for arrhythmia.
Dopamine (medium dose: 2.0-10.0 µg/kg/min)	$\beta_1 > \beta_2$	Used as second-line alternative for septic shock or other refractory shock in patients with low risk for arrhythmia.
Dopamine (low dose: 0.5-2.0 µg/kg/min)	$DA > \beta_1$	Historically used for kidney failure, but no evidence of effectiveness for this indication.
Dobutamine	$\beta_1 > \beta_2$	Used primarily as an inotrope to increase cardiac output.
Phenylephrine	α_1	Used in patients in whom norepinephrine is contraindicated or not tolerated.

$\alpha_1 = \alpha_1$ adrenergic receptor; $\beta_1 = \beta_1$ adrenergic receptor; $\beta_2 = \beta_2$ adrenergic receptor; DA = dopaminergic receptor.

cortisol measurements or adrenocorticotropic hormone stimulation tests are not useful in stratifying or monitoring these patients and should not be performed.

Hyperglycemia and insulin resistance are common in patients who are critically ill. Blood glucose levels should be monitored through a protocolized approach, and insulin infusion dosing should be initiated following two consecutive blood glucose levels >180 mg/dL (9.99 mmol/L). Although blood glucose levels of 80-110 mg/dL (4.4-6.1 mmol/L) may be beneficial in patients with other forms of critical illness, tight glucose control does not have universal benefits and in some cases, may increase mortality. A glucose target of <200 mg/dL (1.0 mmol/L) results in lower mortality, and in septic patients, a modest goal of 140 to 200 mg/dL (7.8-8.3 mmol/L) is commonly recommended.

Low-dose unfractionated heparin or low-molecular-weight heparin is given for deep venous thrombosis prophylaxis. Mechanical compression devices should be used if anticoagulation is contraindicated. Proton pump inhibitors or H_2-receptor antagonists are given for stress ulcer prophylaxis. Erythrocyte transfusions should be considered conservatively. A target hemoglobin concentration of 7 to 9 g/dL (70-90 g/L) resulted in no additional mortality than the tradi-

tional target of 10 g/dL (100 g/L). Except in select cases, such as elderly patients with myocardial infarction, hemoglobin target concentrations of 7 g/dL (70 g/L) should be considered adequate. Erythropoietin, fresh frozen plasma, or antithrombin should not routinely be administered unless specifically indicated, for example, in bleeding patients or planned invasive procedures. Platelets may be administered prophylactically when counts are <10,000/µL (10×10^9/L), or when <20,000/µL (20×10^9/L) when there is active or significant risk of bleeding.

In patients requiring mechanical ventilation, such as sepsis-induced acute respiratory distress syndrome, a lung-protective strategy of ventilation is recommended (eg, tidal volume of 6 mL/kg predicted weight and an end-inspiratory passive recoil [plateau] pressure <30 cm H_2O). The head of the bed should be raised to 45° to reduce the risk of ventilator-associated pneumonia. Table 5 summarizes the various interventions used to treat sepsis.

Bibliography

Dellinger RP, Levy MM, Rhodes, A, et al. Surviving sepsis campaign: international guidelines for management of severe sepsis and septic shock. Intensive Care Med. 2013;39:2165-228. [PMID: 24067755]

Chapter 65

Health Care-Associated Infections

Gonzalo Bearman, MD

A health care–associated infection is a systemic or localized infection that was not present or incubating at the time of hospital admission, and it occurs 48 or more hours after admission to a hospital or within 48 to 72 hours of discharge. The most common health care–associated infections in medical patients are urinary tract infections, pneumonia (including ventilator-associated pneumonia), and bloodstream infections. *Clostridium difficile* antibiotic-associated diarrhea is on the rise in hospitals, long-term care facilities, and the community. More than 2.1 million health care–associated infections occur annually and cause significant increases in morbidity, mortality, and health care costs.

Many health care–associated infections can be prevented. Even with a growing body of literature on risk reduction practices, the single most important way to prevent health care–associated infections is by diligent hand hygiene with medicated soap and water or with an alcohol-based hand rub. The most important risk factor for a health care–associated infection is the presence of invasive devices such as urinary and vascular catheters and endotracheal tubes. Infection prevention programs perform surveillance of health care– and device-associated infections in high-risk patients and intensive care units to track their incidence and prevalence. Infection prevention programs also guide health care workers in the implementation of risk reduction practices across the health care setting. Patients with communicable diseases or drug-resistant pathogens should be appropriately and quickly isolated to minimize cross-transmission to patients, visitors, and health care workers (Table 1).

Catheter-Associated Urinary Tract Infections

Urinary tract infections (UTIs) are the most common health care–associated infection. Most are caused by indwelling urinary catheters. Bacteriuria occurs in 3% to 10% of catheterized patients daily, and incidence is directly related to the duration of catheterization. An estimated 5% of patients will become colonized for each day of catheterization beyond 2 days, and 10% to 25% of these will develop symptomatic UTIs. Urinary catheters pose the greatest risk for developing a catheter-associated urinary tract infection (CAUTI) because (1) bacteria can be inoculated directly into the bladder during insertion, (2) catheters are conduits to the bladder, (3) the glycocalyx that forms on the catheter surface protects bacteria from antibiotics and host defenses, and (4) residual urine serves as a reservoir for bacterial growth. Other risk factors for development of CAUTI include advanced age, female sex, diabetes, malnutrition, kidney dysfunction, and improper catheter care.

The most effective way to prevent CAUTIs is to decrease catheter use. Devices should be used for specific indications, not for convenience, and should be removed as soon as possible. Structured daily assessments of the ongoing need for patient urinary catheters and automatic catheter discontinuation orders are effective in limiting urinary catheter use. If a urinary catheter is needed, measures should be taken to decrease the risk of urinary colonization and infection. These actions include hand washing, aseptic catheter placement technique and sterile equipment for catheter insertion and care, securing the catheter properly, maintaining unobstructed urine flow with closed sterile drainage, and use of antibacterial-coated catheters. (Table 2). Manipulation and irrigation should be minimized, and urine specimens should be collected using the drainage bag valve. Prophylactic antibiotics should not be used to prevent CAUTIs.

Patients with CAUTIs often do not experience typical signs of urinary tract infection. If a patient develops fever or cloudy urine, or other systemic manifestations compatible with infection, blood and urine cultures should be obtained. If a CAUTI is suspected, manage-

Table 1. Infection Control Precautions for Health Care Institutions

Transmission Mode	Precautions	Indications
Airborne	Patient is isolated in a private room with negative air pressure, the door remains closed, and all entering persons wear masks with a filtering capacity of 95%. Transported patients must wear masks.	For patients with known or suspected illnesses transmitted by airborne droplet nuclei, such as tuberculosis, measles, varicella, or disseminated varicella-zoster virus infection.
Droplet	Patient is isolated in a private room, and hospital personnel wear masks when within 3 ft of the patient.	For patients with known or suspected illnesses transmitted by large-particle droplets, such as *Neisseria meningitidis* infections and influenza.
Contact	Patient is isolated in a private room or with patients who have the same active infection. Nonsterile gloves and gowns are required for direct contact with the patient or any infective material; gowns and/or gloves are removed before exiting isolation rooms.	For patients with known or suspected illnesses transmitted by direct contact, including infections due to vancomycin-resistant enterococci and methicillin-resistant *Staphylococcus aureus*.

Table 2. Best Practices to Prevent Health Care-Associated Infections

Practice	Notes
Hand hygiene	• Cleanse hands with soap and water or waterless alcohol product before and after contact with patients or contaminated surfaces. • Install alcohol-based waterless cleaning products inside and outside all patient rooms and in other locations where clinical care will be provided. • Do not allow clinical staff to wear artificial nails.
Prevention of catheter-related bloodstream infections	• Remove unnecessary vascular lines. • Use recommended hand hygiene before inserting or manipulating vascular lines. • Use maximal barrier precautions (eg, gowns, gloves, masks, head covers) for inserting vascular lines. • Apply appropriate skin antiseptics (chlorhexidine is the agent of choice) for inserting vascular lines, dressing changes, and reinsertion. • Use the subclavian site whenever possible, because this site is associated with the lowest risk for infection. • Maintain clean and dry dressings. • Do not use prophylactic antibiotics for insertion of vascular lines.
Prevention of urinary tract infections	• Remove all unnecessary catheters. • Use sterile technique for insertion of catheters. • Do not remove urine samples from lines or open systems. • Do not use antibiotics prophylactically.
Prevention of ventilator-associated pneumonia	• Sterilize and maintain respiratory equipment appropriately. • Raise the head of the bed to a 30° to 45° angle (use the semirecumbent position). • Use noninvasive ventilation techniques when possible. • Use oscillation or rotate the patient. • Use good oral care. • Use endotracheal tubes that allow for subglottic suctioning in high-risk patients.

ment includes removal of the catheter with catheter replacement only if necessary. A urine culture should be obtained before administering antibiotics. Common pathogens include *Escherichia coli*, *Klebsiella*, *Proteus*, *Enterococcus*, *Pseudomonas*, and *Staphylococcus*. Fungi (eg, *Candida*) are prevalent in patients with diabetes or chronic indwelling catheters. A third-generation cephalosporin (eg, cefotaxime, ceftriaxone), fluoroquinolone (eg, ciprofloxacin, levofloxacin) or carbapenem (eg, imipenem or meropenem) is used for suspected gram-negative infection and vancomycin for a suspected *Staphylococcus* or enterococcal infection. Antibiotics should be modified by pathogen susceptibility data obtained from the urine culture. Complications from CAUTIs include pyelonephritis and prostatitis. Secondary bacteremia occurs in about 3% of patients with CAUTIs.

Catheter-Related Intravascular Infections

Primary bloodstream infections (BSIs) occur without a recognizable focus of infection at another anatomic site. The increased use of intravascular catheters is believed to contribute to the large increase in BSIs in recent years. Approximately 50,000 catheter (or central) line–associated BSIs (CLABSIs) occur in the United States annually. Central venous catheters are percutaneously inserted into central veins (subclavian, internal jugular, or femoral) and account for the vast majority of primary bloodstream infections. Reported case fatality rates for primary bloodstream infections have ranged from 14% to 40%.

Use of central intravenous catheters should be reserved for patients with proven need, and the catheter should be removed as soon as clinically possible. Use of sterile technique and maximum sterile barriers (eg, full-body sterile drape, gown, mask, and gloves) during catheter insertion minimize risk. Chlorhexidine is the most effective agent for skin decontamination before catheter insertion and is the antiseptic of choice over povidone/iodine or alcohol alone (see Table 2). The highest risk for infection is associated with femoral placement, and the lowest risk is associated with subclavian placement.

The pathogenesis of CLABSI is contamination from skin flora, intraluminal or catheter hub contamination, and secondary seeding from other sources. Micro-organisms from the skin of the patient or health care workers migrate along the catheter and cause contamination. Thrombosis, contaminated intravenous products, and flushing of the line can cause contamination.

Antibiotic-coated catheters may decrease the risk of early central catheter-related infection and should be considered, and limiting the number of access events and using sterile technique when accessing the catheter help prevent hub contamination. Routine replacement of central venous catheters is not recommended. Central venous catheters should be dressed with chlorhexidine-gluconate impregnated sponges, as these dressings decrease the rate of CLABSI.

In any patient with fever and a central venous catheter, CLABSI is a diagnostic consideration. Purulence and cellulitis around the catheter site are frequently absent at the time of diagnosis. Clinical factors predicting CLABSI include placement duration >4 days, catheter thrombosis, prior positive blood cultures, respiratory infection, difficult or emergent insertion, a multiple lumen catheter, immunocompromised patients, and a high number of catheter manipulations per day.

Diagnosis typically relies on culture data, as clinical features are poor predictors. A CLABSI is defined as bacteremia or fungemia in a patient who has an intravascular device and at least one positive blood culture obtained from a peripheral vein, clinical manifestations of infection (eg, fever, chills, and/or hypotension), and no apparent source for bloodstream infection with the exception of the catheter. The organism isolated on the peripheral blood culture should be the same as the organism isolated either by blood culture drawn through a catheter or by culture of the catheter tip. In the absence of clinical features, positive catheter cultures often represent colonization or contamination. Persistent bacteremia strongly suggests endovascular infection. Endocarditis must be excluded in the setting of bloodstream infection and a heart murmur or previous valvular heart disease.

In nearly all cases, the central venous catheter must be removed as part of management. In cases of coagulase-negative staphylococcal catheter-related BSI, however, clearing the infection without removing the catheter may be attempted if the infection is uncomplicated, as defined by resolution of fever and clearance of blood cultures within 72 hours, the absence of endovascular hardware, such as prosthetic heart valves, and if there is no evidence of endocarditis. Begin empiric treatment with broad-spectrum antibiotics and then narrow the regimen once culture data are available. Coagulase-negative staphylococci, enterococci, *S. aureus*, and gram-negative rods (eg, *E. coli*, *Klebsiella*, and *Pseudomonas*) are common pathogens. Use vancomycin for empiric coverage given its activity against coagulase-negative staphylococci and *S. aureus*. Additional empirical coverage for enteric gram-negative bacilli and *Pseudomonas aeruginosa* with the use of a third (eg, ceftriaxone, ceftazidime) or fourth-generation cephalosporin (eg, cefepime) may be needed for severely ill or immunocompromised patients. Systemic antifungals should be prescribed when fungemia is suspected, as in patients with sepsis, on total parenteral nutrition or prolonged broad-spectrum antibiotic therapy, or those with a hematologic malignancy or transplant. Uncomplicated infections are treated for 10 to 14 days for most pathogens; coagulase-negative staphylococci may be treated for 5 to 7 days if the infected catheter is removed.

Complications of catheter-associated bloodstream infections include septic thrombosis, endocarditis, osteomyelitis, meningitis, and abscess. Patients with complicated infection require 6 weeks or more of antibiotic therapy.

Hospital-Acquired and Ventilator-Associated Pneumonia

Hospital-acquired pneumonia (HAP) is defined as pneumonia that develops at least 48 hours after hospitalization and includes ventilator-associated pneumonia, non–ventilator-associated pneumonia, and postoperative pneumonia. Pneumonia is the leading cause of death from hospital-acquired infection. Ventilator-associated pneumonia (VAP) is one of the most common types of HAP, affecting 9% to 27% of intubated patients, and is defined as occurring >48 hours after endotracheal intubation.

The most common cause of HAP is microaspiration of bacteria that colonize the oropharynx and upper airways in seriously ill patients. Gram-negative bacilli and *S. aureus* are common pathogens; however, the number of drug-resistant organisms continues to escalate. Endotracheal intubation with mechanical ventilation poses the greatest overall risk. Endotracheal intubation breaches airway defenses, impairs cough and mucociliary clearance, and facilitates microaspiration of bacteria-laden secretions that pool above the inflated endotracheal tube cuff. Consequently, 85% of all cases of HAP occur in ventilated patients. Major risk factors for postoperative pneumonia are age older than 70 years, abdominal or thoracic surgery, malnutrition, increased gastric pH, and reintubation.

Avoid intubation when possible; if required, prompt extubation (through frequent weaning trials) reduces the risk for infection. Minimizing manipulation of the endotracheal tube and ventilator tubing and performing meticulous hand hygiene before and after any contact with the system further prevents infections. While intubated, patients should be in a semi-upright or upright position, as this decreases aspiration of upper airway secretions. Mouth care may also reduce the risk of infection. Although ventilator circuits do not need to be changed regularly, any accumulating condensate should be drained carefully into patient-specific drainage containers (Table 2). Selective decontamination of the oropharynx or of the entire gastrointestinal tract is controversial and not uniformly recommended.

The diagnosis of VAP is based on clinical presentation, leukocytosis, and new or changing chest radiographic findings. A VAP is suspected if the patient has a radiographic infiltrate that is new or progressive, along with clinical findings suggesting infection (eg, fever, purulent sputum, leukocytosis) and decline in oxygenation. The presence of neutrophils or an organism on gram stain can refine the diagnostic accuracy for VAP.

If VAP is strongly suspected, empiric antibiotic therapy should not be delayed for the purpose of performing diagnostic studies. Antibiotic selection is based on the risk for multi-drug-resistant pathogens. These risk factors include prolonged duration of hospitalization (≥5 days), admission from a health care–related facility, and recent prolonged antibiotic therapy. Antibiotic selection is based on local antimicrobial susceptibility and anticipated side effects and takes into consideration which antibiotics were recently administered. Common pathogens include *Enterobacter*, *Pseudomonas*, *Klebsiella*, *E. coli*, *Streptococcus*, and *S. aureus* (including methicillin-resistant *S. aureus*). In patients with no risk factors, use ceftriaxone or levofloxacin. Patients with risk factors should be treated with an antipseudomonal agent and vancomycin.

C. difficile Antibiotic-Associated Diarrhea

C. difficile antibiotic-associated diarrhea occurs in about 20% of hospitalized patients taking antibiotics. The combination of health care associated exposure to *C. difficile* and loss of normal protective colonic bacteria leads to colonization. Colitis is produced by two toxins, A and B. These have different mechanisms of action, but both cause cytotoxicity at extremely low concentrations. Risk factors include use of antibiotics, enemas, intestinal stimulants, and chemotherapeutic agents that alter the colonic flora.

Limiting unnecessary antibiotic exposure is a key factor in preventing *C. difficile* infection. Routine infection control measures to prevent the spread of *C. difficile* include adherence to strict hand hygiene and use of universal precautions (see Table 2). Alcohol-based hand rubs are not sporicidal; therefore, hands should be washed with medicated soap and water after the care of a patient with presumed or confirmed *C. difficile* infection. Patients with known or suspected illness should be placed under contact isolation.

Consider *C. difficile* infection in patients with diarrhea who have received antibiotic therapy in the last 2 months or in those who have been recently hospitalized. Patients may complain of abdominal pain, fever, anorexia, malaise, or vomiting. Physical examination may demonstrate signs of volume depletion, abdominal tenderness, and, in severe cases, rigidity and rebound tenderness. Stool should be sent for nucleic acid amplification (polymerase chain reaction) testing of *C. difficile* toxin genes tcdA and tcdB. In select patients, colonoscopy may help establish diagnosis by demonstrating typical pseudomembranes. In severe cases, complications include toxic megacolon, colonic perforation, severe ileus, ascites, and death.

For an initial episode of *C. difficile* infection that is of mild to moderate severity, metronidazole is the first-line agent, administered orally or intravenously. For an initial episode that is severe, with a patient exhibiting a white blood cell count of 15,000/μL (15×10^9/L) or higher or a serum creatinine level 1.5 times greater than baseline, oral vancomycin is the drug of choice. Treat a first relapse with a second course of the initial antibiotic used for first-line therapy. For a second relapse, vancomycin in a tapered and/or pulsed regimen is preferred. Fidaxomicin, a new class of macrolide antibiotic, is efficacious for the treatment of severe *C.difficile* infection and may limit the frequency of recurrence.

Bibliography

Klompas M. Does this patient have ventilator-associated pneumonia? JAMA 2007;297:1583-93. [PMID: 17426278]

Mermel LA, Allon M, Bouza E, et al. Clinical practice guidelines for the diagnosis and management of intravascular catheter-related infection: 2009 Update by the Infectious Diseases Society of America. Clin Infect Dis. 2009;49:1-45. [PMID: 19489710]

Yokoe DS, Mermel LA, Anderson DJ, et al. A compendium of strategies to prevent healthcare-associated infections in acute care hospitals. Infect Control Hosp Epidemiol. 2008;29 Suppl 1:S12-21. [PMID: 18840084]

Section 7
Nephrology

Associate Editor – Thomas M. De Fer, MD, FACP

High Value Care Recommendations

- Because of its long half-life, measurement of serum $25(OH)D_2$ is the best indicator of total body vitamin D stores.

- Except for stone composition, additional studies for nephrolithiasis (such as 24-hour urine collections) are not done routinely and should be reserved for patients with recurrent stones in which they may be used to prescribe specific pharmacologic and dietary interventions.

Chapter 66

Approach to Kidney Disease

John A. Walker, MD

I n approaching a patient with kidney disease, two questions must be addressed: how long has the patient's kidney disease been present (ie, is it acute or chronic?), and what type of kidney disease does the patient have?

Acute kidney injury (AKI) is defined as an abrupt increase in the serum creatinine concentration or decrease in urine output over 48 hours (see Chapter 70), and chronic kidney disease (CKD) is defined as the presence of decreased kidney function or evidence of kidney damage that persists ≥3 months (see Chapter 71).

The two key components of the laboratory assessment used to characterize kidney disease are the glomerular filtration rate (GFR) and the quantitative and qualitative analysis of the urine.

Determination of Glomerular Filtration Rate

The GFR may be measured (mGFR) by the clearance of endogenous or exogenous filtration markers, although in clinical practice, it is usually estimated (eGFR) by the serum concentration of certain endogenous solutes.

Azotemia is defined as an increased concentration of blood urea nitrogen (BUN), which is an important indicator of a reduced GFR. BUN is a relatively poor indicator of eGFR because although urea is freely filtered at the glomerulus, it also undergoes tubular reabsorption. The BUN is also elevated by a high-protein diet, catabolic states, and gastrointestinal bleeding and reduced with liver failure and malnutrition. BUN often is measured simultaneously with serum creatinine. The normal BUN–creatinine ratio ranges from 10:1 to 15:1. Urea reabsorption is increased in states of decreased kidney perfusion. Therefore, prerenal conditions (eg, dehydration, heart failure) are associated with a disproportionate increase in the BUN–creatinine ratio, typically to 20:1 or higher.

Creatinine is generated by muscle at a relatively constant rate in proportion to muscle mass and is excreted by the kidneys. Because serum creatinine concentration increases as GFR falls, it is used to evaluate kidney function. However, serum creatinine concentration does not correlate linearly with GFR and thus is not an ideal marker for GFR for several reasons. A large change in GFR initially is required to raise the serum creatinine concentration significantly; in CKD, GFR may decrease as much as 50% before the serum creatinine concentration rises above the upper limit of normal (Figure 1). A reduction in muscle mass may cause a low serum creatinine concentration relative to the true GFR, which may result in an overestimation of GFR. Although freely filtered at the glomerulus, creatinine also is excreted via tubular secretion; in CKD, tubular secretion of creatinine may account for as much as a 50% of total creatinine excretion and thus lead to an overestimation of the true GFR.

Several estimating equations have been developed that use the serum creatinine in combination with other variables to provide more accurate quantitative information about the GFR.

The Cockcroft-Gault equation was developed to predict creatinine clearance (C_{Cr} [mL/min]) using the serum creatinine, age, and weight, adjusted for gender:

$$C_{Cr} = (140 - age\ [y]) \times weight\ [kg] / (S_{Cr} \times 72) \times 0.85\ [if\ female]$$

However, despite its long history and widespread use, it has been shown to be less accurate than newer estimation equations. Although it is not recommended for routine estimation of GFR in patients with CKD, it is still used for some drug-dosing calculations.

The Modification of Diet in Renal Disease (MDRD) equation was developed as part of a study of patients with CKD to estimate GFR (mL/min/1.73 m²). Consequently, it tends to be most accurate in this patient population and tends to underestimate GFR in patients with normal kidney function. Although it is used by some clinical laboratories, its limitations should be considered.

The Chronic Kidney Disease Epidemiology (CKD-EPI) equation provides the most reliable estimation of GFR (mL/min/1.73m²) in adult patients. In addition to the serum creatinine, it requires input of a patient's age, gender, and race (African American vs. all others). Although the equation is operationally complex, it is available for online calculation (www.kidney.org/professionals/kdoqi/gfr_calculator.cfm).

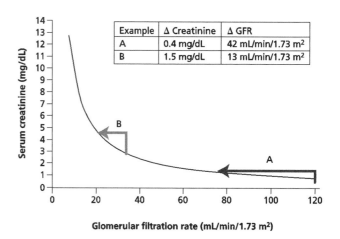

Figure 1. The relationship between serum creatinine and glomerular filtration rate. Example A illustrates that a small increase in the serum creatinine level in the reference range (in this case, 0.8 to 1.2 mg/dL [70.7-106 µmol/L]) reflects a relatively large change in GFR (120 to 78 mL/min/1.73 m²). Example B illustrates that a relatively greater increase in the serum creatinine level (in the high range of 3.0 to 4.5 mg/dL [265-398 µmol/L]) reflects a proportionately smaller change in GFR (35 to 22 mL/min/1.73 m²). GFR = glomerular filtration rate.

Many laboratories provide an eGFR when reporting serum creatinine concentration. However, eGFR equations are valid only when the serum creatinine concentration is at steady state; the equations should not be used in patients with AKI because the serum creatinine concentration changes rapidly in AKI.

A more accurate mGFR may be obtained by a urinary clearance study or by various radionuclide scanning techniques. Urinary clearance studies require an accurate, timed urine collection (usually over 24 hours), with creatinine being the most commonly measured endogenous solute. However, over- or undercollection of the urine sample will result in an inaccurate clearance calculation, and tubular secretion of creatinine may yield clearance values that exceed the true GFR. Radionuclide kidney clearance scanning is the gold standard for the measurement of GFR.

Urinalysis by Multireagent Dipstick

Urine pH may range between 4.5 and 8.0. Measurement of urine pH is useful when evaluating patients with suspected renal tubular disorders in whom kidney acid excretion may be impaired and the urine pH may be inappropriately high in the face of a systemic acidosis (eg, renal tubular acidosis).

Specific gravity quantifies the density of a solution. Urine specific gravity ranges between 1.003 and 1.035, with the specific gravity of normal serum being approximately 1.010; comparison of urine specific gravity to this value estimates the concentration or dilution of the urine. Excretion of urine with a persistently low specific gravity (<1.007) is called *hyposthenuria* and may indicate a loss of concentrating ability (eg, diabetes insipidus). High urine specific gravity may reflect an appropriate response to water loss or dehydration or may indicate a pathologic state of fluid retention (eg, heart failure). Excretion of urine with a specific gravity fixed at about 1.010 regardless of the state of hydration is known as *isosthenuria* and usually accompanies severe kidney damage involving disruption of both concentrating and diluting abilities.

Glycosuria occurs when the filtered load of glucose exceeds the reabsorptive capacity of sodium–glucose cotransporters in the proximal tubule. Glycosuria usually is detected by dipstick when blood glucose concentrations exceed approximately 200 mg/dL (11.1 mmol/L) and is seen most often in diabetes mellitus. Glycosuria without hyperglycemia usually is associated with proximal renal tubular dysfunction (eg, Fanconi syndrome, multiple myeloma).

Albumin is the only protein reliably detected by dipstick. The detection of proteinuria implies an albumin excretion rate (AER) of ≥300 mg/24 h. However, the detection of lesser but still abnormal degrees of albuminuria (albumin excretion rates of 30–300 mg/24 h) requires other quantitative methods. The dipstick protein indicator is insensitive to tubular proteins and immunoglobulins; identification of the latter (eg, Bence-Jones proteins secondary to multiple myeloma) is best accomplished by a 24-hour urine collection for total protein with protein electrophoresis and immunofixation.

The dipstick indicator is sensitive to intact erythrocytes but will also yield a positive reaction for blood in the setting of hemoglobinuria or myoglobinuria. If fewer than 3 erythrocytes per high-power field are reported for a urine sample that tests positive for blood, evidence for hemolysis or rhabdomyolysis should be sought.

Lysed neutrophils and macrophages release indoxyl esterase, which can be detected by multireagent dipstick technology (leukocyte esterase positive). A positive reaction for urine nitrite may indicate the presence of bacteria that reduce nitrate, most commonly gram-negative pathogens. Whereas a positive result for both urine leukocyte esterase and urine nitrites is 68% to 88% sensitive for urinary tract infection, a negative result for both assays has a high negative predictive value for urinary tract infection.

Microscopic Examination of the Urine Sediment

A freshly voided sample should be viewed because urine elements begin to lyse within 2 to 4 hours of urine collection. Among the most useful findings are casts; these cylindrical structures are composed of a Tamm-Horsfall glycoprotein matrix, which is secreted by the epithelial cells of the thick ascending limb of Henle, within which cells (erythrocytes, leukocytes, epithelial cells) may be trapped. Casts are formed only within the tubules. Thus, any cell contained within a cast is of renal parenchymal origin.

Microscopic hematuria is defined as the presence of ≥3 erythrocytes per high-power field. In patients with microscopic hematuria, the location of bleeding (glomerular or nonglomerular) should be identified to guide further diagnostic studies. Erythrocyte casts are specific for glomerular bleeding, but the sensitivity for glomerular pathology is poor (Plate 49). Glomerular hematuria also is characterized by the presence of dysmorphic erythrocytes (especially erythrocytes with blebs, termed *acanthocytes*). Transient glomerular bleeding has been noted in normal individuals after vigorous physical activity. However, the combination of microscopic hematuria and proteinuria usually signifies glomerular disease. Nonglomerular bleeding is suggested by the presence of isomorphic, normal-appearing erythrocytes and the absence of proteinuria. Figure 2 outlines a suggested evaluation of microscopic hematuria.

Up to 3 leukocytes per high-power field may be seen in normal urine. Greater numbers define pyuria, most often caused by a urinary tract infection. Pyuria in the face of a negative urine culture may reflect a viral or mycobacterial infection. However, sterile pyuria also may indicate noninfectious interstitial nephritis, in which the presence of leukocyte casts establishes the diagnosis of renal parenchymal disease and usually is associated with non-nephrotic proteinuria (Plate 50). Eosinophils may be seen in the urine of patients with AKI caused by drug-induced interstitial nephritis and in a variety of other conditions, including rapidly progressive glomerulonephritis, prostatitis, renal atheroemboli, and small-vessel vasculitis.

Renal tubular epithelial cell casts may be produced by desquamation of epithelial cells associated with acute tubular necrosis, proliferative glomerulonephritis, or interstitial nephritis. The broad, muddy brown casts associated with acute tubular necrosis are diagnostically helpful (Plate 51). Hyaline casts are composed of Tamm-Horsfall glycoprotein and normally may be seen in increased numbers in concentrated urine specimens. Granular casts are hyaline casts containing aggregated filtered proteins and may be seen in patients with albuminuria and proteinuria. Degenerated cellular casts may appear granular and upon further degeneration are described as *waxy casts*.

Lipiduria is associated with various glomerular diseases and usually is accompanied by heavy proteinuria. Lipids may be seen within tubular epithelial cells or macrophages. Lipids embedded within hyaline casts form fatty casts. When viewed under polarized light, lipid particles in the urine display a Maltese cross pattern (Plate 52).

Measurement of Total Protein Excretion and Urine Albumin

Normal daily urinary protein excretion, including all proteins (albumin and low-molecular-weight proteins, including immunoglobulin light chains), is <150 mg/24h, and the amount of albumin lost in the urine is normally <30 mg/24h. The gold standard for the quantitative measurement of protein in the urine is a 24-hour urine collection.

However, timed collections are inconvenient for patients and difficult to complete accurately. Therefore, two easier methods for quantifying proteinuria have been developed that correlate well with 24-hour

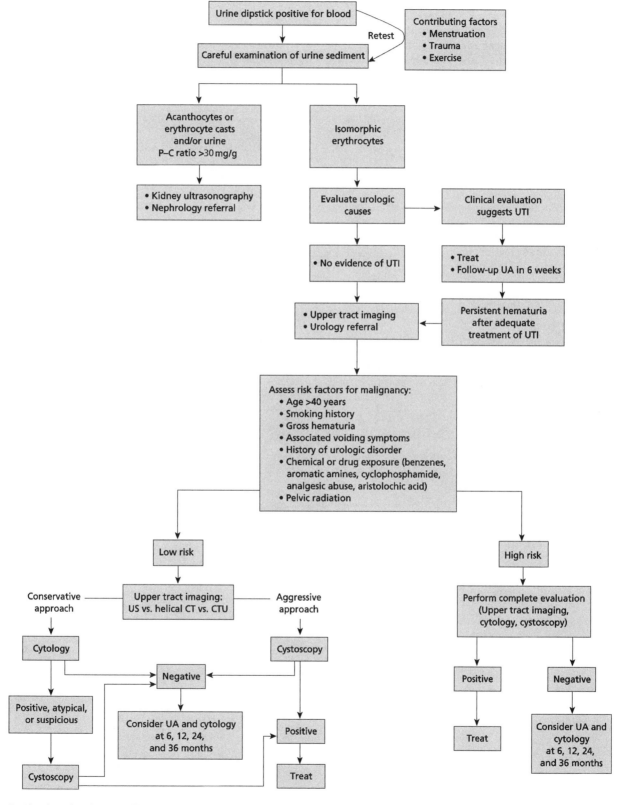

Figure 2. The clinical evaluation of hematuria. CT = computed tomography; CTU = computed tomography urography; eGFR = estimated glomerular filtration rate; P–C = protein to creatinine; UA = urinalysis; US = ultrasonography; UTI = urinary tract infection.

measurements. Both are performed on a single (spot) urine sample and use the ratio of the protein concentration to the creatinine concentration to estimate the amount of protein excreted or lost over 24 hours. A urine protein-creatinine ratio (PCR) is used to estimate total protein (albumin and non-albumin proteins) excretion, and a value of >150 mg/g is abnormal; a ratio >3.5 g/g is classified as nephrotic-range proteinuria. The albumin-creatinine ratio (ACR) is specific for albumin in the urine, and an ACR of >30 mg/g indicates albuminuria. The terminology for describing abnormal albumin excretion has changed. An albumin-creatinine ratio of 30 to 300 mg/g, previously termed microalbuminuria, is now referred to as *moderately increased albuminuria*, and levels above 300 mg/g, previously known as macroalbuminuria or overt proteinuria, are now termed *severely increased albuminuria*. Albuminuria is often the earliest sign of glomerular injury, and screening for albuminuria using the ACR is recommended in certain high-risk groups, such as patients with diabetes.

Electrophoresis can identify the types and relative quantities of urine proteins and may assist in distinguishing glomerular from tubulointerstitial disease. In proteinuria of glomerular origin, albumin constitutes 60% to 90% of the total urine protein. In tubular proteinuria, low-molecular-weight proteins typically predominate, and this may indicate either impaired tubular protein reabsorption or overproduction and filtration of low-molecular-weight proteins (eg, multiple myeloma).

Proteinuria does not always indicate significant kidney disease. Isolated or transient proteinuria (usually <1 g/24 h) may be associated with febrile illness or heavy exercise. This condition typically is benign and does not warrant further evaluation.

Orthostatic proteinuria refers to protein excretion that increases during the day but decreases to a normal value (<50 mg/8 h) during recumbency. The diagnosis is established by comparing the urine protein excretion rate during the day with that from a separate urine collection obtained during the night.

Nephrotic and Nephritic Syndromes

Glomerular disease can produce clinical patterns of kidney disease classified as either the nephrotic syndrome or the nephritic syndrome. Recognition of these syndromes can be helpful in the creation of a differential diagnosis for patients with kidney disease. Some patients have characteristics of both syndromes (Table 1).

The nephrotic syndrome is characterized by heavy proteinuria (>2+ protein by dipstick, urine PCR >3.5 g/g) and a relatively bland urine sediment, which may contain hyaline or hyaline-granular casts, lipids, and none to moderate numbers of erythrocytes. The nephrotic syndrome may be due to a primary glomerular disease or occur secondary to a systemic disease. Primary nephrotic syndrome usually is diagnosed when a secondary cause for the nephrotic syndrome has not been identified. Common causes of primary nephrotic syndrome include minimal change disease, membranous glomerulopathy, and focal segmental glomerulosclerosis. Diabetes is the most common cause of secondary nephrotic syndrome (diabetic nephropathy). Other causes include dysproteinemia (glomerulopathy caused by amyloidosis and multiple myeloma), HIV infection (focal segmental glomerulosclerosis), and hepatitis B (membranous glomerulopathy).

The nephritic syndrome is characterized by varying degrees of proteinuria and an active urine sediment, which may contain granular casts, moderate to large numbers of dysmorphic erythrocytes, and erythrocyte casts. Some patients with the nephritic syndrome have dermal inflammation that manifests as palpable purpura, necrosis, ulcers, or nodules. These patients may have renal–dermal syndromes, such as systemic lupus erythematosus, Henoch-Schönlein purpura, antineutrophil cytoplasmic antibody (ANCA)–associated vasculitis, and cryoglobulinemia. Pulmonary–renal syndrome also may develop in patients with the nephritic syndrome. Assays for anti–glomerular basement membrane antibody, ANCA, and markers for immune complex diseases (eg, antinuclear antibodies, anti–double-stranded DNA antibodies, cryoglobulins, antibodies to hepatitis B or C virus, complement concentrations) may further refine the diagnosis; low complement concentrations suggest lupus nephritis, postinfectious and membranoproliferative glomerulonephritis, and mixed cryoglobulinemia. Rapidly progressive glomerulonephritis is a clinical syndrome characterized by a swift loss of kidney function, hematuria, proteinuria, and glomerular crescent formation. The syndrome may be caused by many primary or secondary glomerular diseases, including those previously listed.

Table 1. Differentiating Features of Nephritic and Nephrotic Syndromes

	Nephritic	Nephrotic
Proteinuria (UPCR)	Variable; may be <3.5 g/g	Usually >3.5 g/g
Urine sediment	"Active" Dysmorphic RBCs RBC casts Granular casts	"Bland" Hyaline casts Lipiduria; oval fat bodies
Associated clinical features	Hypertension Oliguria Elevated serum creatinine	Hypoalbuminemia Hyperlipidemia Edema Hypercoagulability

Glomerular pathology	Inflammatory, eg,
	     Diffuse proliferative glomerulonephritis
	     Membranoproliferative glomerulonephritis
	     IgA nephropathy
	     Crescentic glomerulonephritis
		Noninflammatory, eg,
		     Minimal change disease
		     Focal segmental glomerulosclerosis
		     Membranous glomerulopathy
		     Amyloid

RBC = red blood cell; UPCR = urine protein–creatinine ratio.

Table 2. Use of Radiographic Imaging Studies in the Assessment of Kidney Function and Kidney Disease

Imaging Study	Indications
Kidney ultrasonography	Urinary tract obstruction, nephrolithiasis, cyst, mass lesion, location for kidney biopsy
Duplex ultrasonography, angiography	Renal artery stenosis
Abdominal CT	Urinary tract obstruction, nephrolithiasis, mass lesion
CT angiography	Renal artery stenosis, renal vascular lesion
MRI	Cyst, mass lesion, renal artery stenosis
Radionuclide kidney clearance scanning (GFR scanning)	GFR estimation, urinary tract obstruction, kidney infarction

CT = computed tomography; GFR = glomerular filtration rate; MRI = magnetic resonance imaging.

Imaging Studies

Assessment of kidney function often requires imaging of the urinary tract (Table 2). Because kidney ultrasonography is noninvasive and does not require the administration of contrast agents or radiation exposure, it is the imaging modality of choice in the initial diagnostic evaluation of most patients with kidney disease. Ultrasonography can identify simple and complex cysts, solid masses, and kidney stones; it also provides a reasonably reproducible estimate of kidney size and will reveal the uncommon patient with a solitary kidney. Ultrasonography detects hydronephrosis with a high sensitivity.

Kidney function should be evaluated before determining the most appropriate radiographic study. This evaluation is particularly important before performing studies that require use of radiocontrast agents to avoid contrast-induced nephropathy. Patients with AKI or with CKD (eGFR <60 mL/min/1.73 m^2) are at increased risk for contrast toxicity. Recently, nephrogenic systemic fibrosis, a systemic inflammatory process, has been identified in patients with reduced kidney function who are exposed to intravenous gadolinium contrast agents during magnetic resonance imaging; therefore, use of gadolinium contrast in these patients is contraindicated. Optimal selection of additional imaging modalities often is best informed by consultation with an experienced diagnostic or interventional radiologist.

Kidney Biopsy

Kidney biopsy is performed when histologic confirmation is needed to help diagnose kidney disease, implement medical therapy, or change medical treatment. Kidney biopsy is used predominantly to diagnose and categorize glomerular disease. The most common indications for kidney biopsy include the nephritic and nephrotic syndromes, AKI of uncertain etiology, and kidney transplant dysfunction.

Bibliography

Fogazzi GB, Verdesca S, Garigali G. Urinalysis: core curriculum 2008. Am J Kidney Dis. 2008;51:1052-1067. [PMID: 18501787]

Rosner MH, Bolton WK. Renal function testing. Am J Kidney Dis. 2006;47: 174-183. [PMID: 16377400]

Chapter 67

Fluid and Electrolyte Disorders

Mary Jane Barchman, MD

Total body water (TBW) constitutes approximately 60% of body weight in men and 50% in women. Two thirds of TBW is intracellular fluid (ICF); the remaining third is extracellular fluid (ECF), which is distributed 25% as intravascular volume and 75% as interstitial volume (Figure 1). The osmolality of the various fluid compartments is similar, but the solutes dictating the osmolality are not; the main extracellular osmole is sodium, and the primary intracellular osmoles are potassium and phosphates. Plasma osmolality is calculated as:

$$\text{Plasma osmolality} = (2 \times [\text{Sodium}]) + ([\text{Glucose}]/18) + ([\text{Blood urea nitrogen}]/2.8)$$

where blood urea nitrogen and glucose are in mg/dL.

Serum osmolality also can be measured indirectly by an osmometer, which determines the freezing point of the specimen; the lower the temperature needed to freeze the serum, the higher the osmolality. The difference between the measured and calculated values is the osmolal gap (normal osmolal gap = 10–15 mosm/kg [10-15 mmol/kg]). A large osmolal gap suggests the presence of added unmeasured osmotically active particles. Typically, this calculation

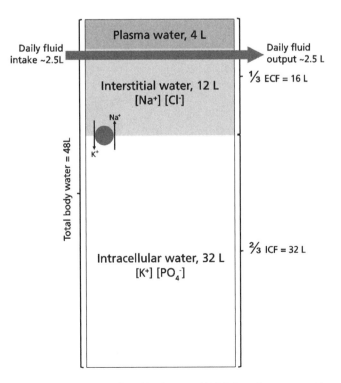

Figure 1. Partitioning of total body water (TBW). Based on a man with 80 kg of lean body mass. TBW constitutes approximately 60% of lean body mass. The osmolality of each compartment is similar. ECF = extracellular fluid; ICF = intracellular fluid.

is used to screen for ethylene glycol ingestion, but in practice, the most common cause of an osmolal gap is ethanol toxicity.

Water Metabolism

Normal plasma osmolality (285–295 mosm/kg [285–295 mmol/kg]) is maintained by thirst, renal handling of water, and antidiuretic hormone (ADH). The thirst center is located in the hypothalamus and is stimulated or suppressed by changes in plasma osmolality and effective intravascular volume. Water is filtered at the glomerulus, and 80% is absorbed isotonically in the proximal tubule. Water is then passively reabsorbed throughout the descending limb of the loop of Henle in response to the increasing osmolality in the medullary interstitium; this segment of the tubule is impermeable to sodium chloride. The ascending limb of the loop of Henle constitutes the diluting segment of the nephron; sodium chloride is reabsorbed to maintain the medullary gradient, but water is retained in the tubule, resulting in a minimum urine osmolality of 50 to 100 mosm/kg (50–100 mmol/kg). Water is reabsorbed in the distal tubule and cortical collecting duct under the influence of ADH. The hypothalamic osmostat has projections to the posterior pituitary gland, which stimulate or inhibit ADH release based on plasma osmolality and effective intravascular volume. Pain, nausea, emotional stress, psychosis, and several drugs also increase ADH levels. One of the most common drugs associated with hyponatremia is hydrochlorothiazide, which interferes with the function of the diluting segment of the nephron and causes mild intravascular volume depletion, leading to increased ADH release and thirst. The street drug "ecstasy" (3,4-methylenedioxymethamphetamine) stimulates ADH release and intense thirst and is increasingly being recognized as a cause of severe hyponatremia. When hypo-osmolality and hypovolemia occur together, low-volume stimulus overrides the inhibitory effect of the hypo-osmolality, and ADH secretion increases to protect volume preferentially.

Hyponatremia

Hyponatremia (serum sodium concentration <136 meq/L [136 mmol/L]) can be associated with high, normal, or low plasma osmolality. Hyponatremia with high plasma osmolality (hyperosmolal hypernatremia) occurs with accumulation of solutes in the ECF, which, in turn, causes movement of water from the intracellular space to the extracellular space. Hyperglycemia is the most common cause of a high solute load, and measured sodium concentration can be corrected by the following calculation:

$$\text{Corrected } [\text{Na}^+] = \text{Measured } [\text{Na}^+] + 0.016 \times ([\text{Glucose}] - 100)$$

where glucose is in mg/dL.

Other solutes capable of this effect include mannitol, radiographic contrast media, sorbitol, and glycine (sorbitol and glycine are used as irrigants during bladder or uterine surgical procedures).

Treatment is supportive until the solute is excreted; in extreme cases, dialysis may be required.

Hyponatremia with normal plasma osmolality (pseudohyponatremia) is characterized by a low serum sodium concentration caused by measurement in a falsely large volume (Figure 2); an interfering substance displaces water in the sample, similar to ice cubes in a pitcher. The most common space-occupying substances are lipids (eg, severe hyperlipidemia) and paraproteins (eg, multiple myeloma).

Hypo-osmolol hyponatremia is the most common form of severe hyponatremia. It may occur in patients with normal, increased, or decreased ECF volumes. The cause of hypotonic hyponatremia can be established by patient history, volume status, urine osmolality, and urine sodium level (Figure 3).

Evaluation of volume status is the first step in determining the cause of hyponatremia with hypo-osmolality. The most common cause is volume overload caused by heart failure, cirrhosis, or the nephrotic syndrome. In each of these edematous states, the kidney is conserving both sodium and water because renal perfusion is compromised (by poor cardiac output, arteriovenous shunting, or decreased intravascular oncotic pressure, respectively). Renal conservation of sodium and water is documented by a low urine sodium concentration (<10 meq/L [10 mmol/L]) and highly concentrated urine (frequently >450 mosm/kg [450 mmol/kg]). This results in water overload that is greater than sodium overload, but both are present. Symptomatic hyponatremia is uncommon, and aggressive treatment to raise the serum sodium level usually is unnecessary. The general approach to management is treatment of the underlying cause, dietary sodium restriction to 2 to 3 g/day, water restriction to 1 to 1.5 L/day, and adjunctive use of loop diuretics.

Hypo-osmolal hyponatremia associated with volume depletion manifests as dry mucous membranes, hypotension, and tachycardia. Volume loss can be gastrointestinal (GI) or renal or caused by third-space fluid shifts. The urine indices reflect renal sodium conservation (urine sodium concentration <10 meq/L [10 mmol/L]) and water conservation (urine osmolality greater than the serum osmolality and frequently >450 mosm/kg [450 mmol/kg]). If volume loss is due to vomiting, a low urine chloride concentration is corroborative. Treatment is intravenous (IV) normal saline as well as managing the condition that precipitated the volume loss. Hypertonic saline is reserved for symptomatic hyponatremia. As volume is restored, the stimulus for ADH release will decrease, potentially leading to correction of the serum sodium concentration too quickly; consequently, serum sodium levels must be monitored closely. Correcting hyponatremia too rapidly can lead to osmotic demyelination syndrome (previously known as central pontine myelinolysis), which is characterized by flaccid paralysis, dysarthria, and dysphagia. The rate of sodium correction must be 0.3 to 0.5 meq/L/h or less (0.3–0.5 mmol/L/h).

Hypo-osmolal hyponatremia with euvolemia is caused by either massive intake of water or an inability of the kidney to excrete a free water load. The normal renal capacity for water excretion is approximately 15 L/day. A massive increase in water intake occurs in psychogenic polydipsia or, rarely, in hypothalamic diseases. Urine indices are compatible with adequate intravascular volume (urine sodium concentration >20 meq/L [20 mmol/L]), and the urine is

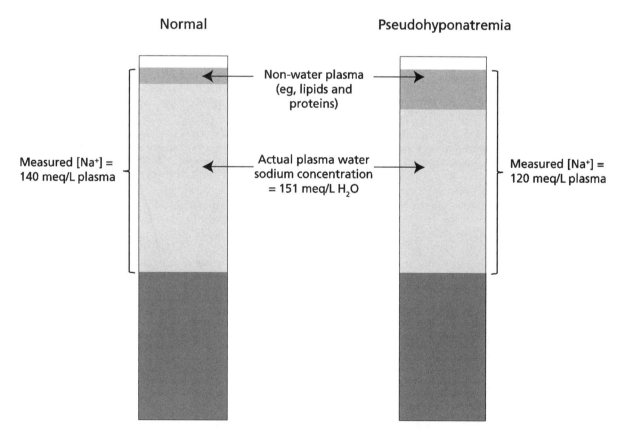

Figure 2. Mechanism of hyponatremia with normal plasma osmolality (pseudohyponatremia). Laboratory assessment of plasma sodium involves measurement of the sodium concentration in a specific volume, with expected displacement of a small amount of volume caused by normal levels of space-occupying substances in the blood (left). In pseudohyponatremia, an excessive amount of these substances displaces a significant volume of plasma, causing the reporting of an inaccurately low sodium concentration (right).

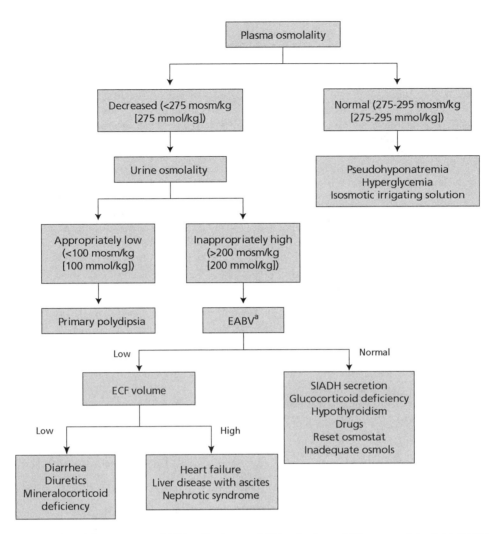

Figure 3. Approach to the patient with hyponatremia. EABV = effective arterial blood volume; ECF = extracellular fluid; SIADH = syndrome of inappropriate antidiuretic hormone secretion. [a]The clinical determination of EABV usually is straightforward. On physical examination, the best index of EABV is the pulse and blood pressure. Urine electrolyte levels also are extremely useful in assessing EABV. A low EABV is characterized by low urine sodium and chloride levels and low fractional excretion of sodium and chloride in the urine. In patients with normal serum creatinine levels, a high BUN (blood urea nitrogen) level suggests a low EABV, whereas a low BUN level suggests a high EABV.

maximally dilute (50–100 mosm/kg [mmol/kg]). Treatment is water restriction.

Hypothyroidism, adrenal insufficiency, reset osmostat, inadequate osmoles, and syndrome of inappropriate ADH secretion (SIADH) all are associated with hyponatremia caused by a renal defect in excreting free water. Thyroid and cortisol deficiencies lead to increased ADH release. The most common physiologic stimulus for reset osmostat is pregnancy, which contributes to the increase in plasma volume. At least 50 mosm (50 mmol) is needed to excrete 1 L of water via the urinary tract; malnourished patients may not have adequate osmoles to excrete excess free water. Treatment is water restriction until nutrition can be corrected. SIADH always is associated with hyponatremia but is a diagnosis of exclusion. Urine indices are compatible with euvolemia (urine sodium concentration >20 meq/L [20 mmol/L]), but the urine is inappropriately concentrated in the face of plasma hypo-osmolality. SIADH often is accompanied by very low serum uric acid and blood urea nitrogen levels, which help differentiate it from other causes of hyponatremia. Causes of SIADH include malignancy (eg, small cell carcinoma of the lung); medications; intracranial pathology; and pulmonary diseases, espe-

cially disorders that increase intrathoracic pressure and decrease venous return to the heart.

Symptoms occur at a serum sodium level of 110 meq/L (110 mmol/L) and include obtundation, coma, seizures, and death (if untreated). In general, symptoms tend to be worse when the hyponatremia develops quickly. Serum sodium level should be corrected to 120 meq/L (120 mmol/L) at a rate of 1 to 2 meq/L/h (1–2 mmol/L/h); when this level is achieved, the rate of correction is slowed to 0.3 to 0.5 meq/L/h (0.3–0.5 mmol/L). The quantity of sodium chloride required to increase the serum sodium concentration is calculated as:

$$TBW\ (L) \times (Desired\ serum\ [sodium] - Actual\ serum\ [sodium])$$

where the desired [sodium] is 120 meq/L (120 mmol/L).

Hypertonic saline should be used with caution and only for patients with symptomatic severe hyponatremia. The IV vasopressin receptor antagonist conivaptan and the oral vasopressin receptor antagonist tolvaptan are approved for the treatment of euvolemic and hypervolemic hyponatremia. These agents should not be used to treat hypovolemic hyponatremia. As with the administration of saline, care must be taken to prevent overly rapid correction of the serum sodium concentration. The efficacy of tolvaptan may be limited by stimulated thirst.

Hypernatremia

Hypernatremia is a serum sodium concentration >145 meq/L (145 mmol/L). All hypernatremia is associated with ICF contraction, and both thirst and ADH levels should be elevated. Therefore, severe hypernatremia indicates a defective thirst mechanism, inadequate access to water, or a renal concentrating defect. The brain generates idiogenic osmoles to protect the intracellular volume within 4 hours of development of hypernatremia, and the process stabilizes within 4 to 7 days. Symptoms of hypernatremia include weakness, lethargy, seizures, and coma. The approach to the patient with hypernatremia begins with assessment of volume status, as outlined in Figure 4. Hypernatremia associated with volume overload is unusual and often iatrogenic. Rarely, mild hypernatremia and volume overload occur with Cushing syndrome or primary hyperaldosteronism. Spontaneous diuresis often self-corrects volume overload hypernatremia, but on rare occasion, diuretic or dialysis therapy with simultaneous free water replacement is necessary.

Most commonly, hypernatremia is due to loss of hypotonic fluids with inadequate water replacement. Hypernatremia associated with volume depletion occurs with GI, renal, cutaneous, or pulmonary losses. Therapy includes sodium chloride replacement, free water replacement, and correction of the underlying problem leading to hypotonic fluid loss. The water deficit is estimated by the formula:

$$\text{Water deficit} = \text{TBW} - (\text{Desired [sodium]/Current [sodium]}) \times \text{TBW}$$

Because of the presence of idiogenic osmoles created by the brain to protect ICF volume, correcting hypernatremia too quickly can lead to cerebral edema. Extreme care must be taken to correct serum sodium concentration at a rate ≤1 meq/L/h (1 mmol/L/h), with a goal of 50% correction at 24 to 36 hours and complete correction in 3 to 7 days.

Central diabetes insipidus is a partial or complete deficiency of ADH production or release (or both), resulting in inadequate concentration of the urine. Provided the patient has access to water, the serum sodium concentration is normal. The presence of hypernatremia indicates loss of free water, and treatment is water replacement and administration of ADH (desmopressin, vasopressin) (see Chapter 10). Nephrogenic diabetes insipidus is an insensitivity of the cortical collecting duct to circulating ADH and can be caused by drugs (eg, lithium, foscarnet), hypokalemia, hypercalcemia, sickle cell disease and trait, and amyloidosis. Treatment requires adequate water intake; salt restriction; and, in some cases, a thiazide diuretic. Thiazide diuretics effectively block sodium reabsorption in the distal renal tubule, thereby causing natriuresis. Patients with an intact thirst mechanism do not develop significant hypernatremia unless their access to water is restricted by unconsciousness, immobility, or an altered mental status.

Potassium Metabolism

Serum potassium concentration is tightly regulated. Most of the body's potassium is intracellular and is maintained by the integrity of the cell membrane and sodium–potassium adenosine triphosphate (Na^+, K^+-ATPase). Because potassium is a steady-state ion, intake must equal output to maintain balance. Typical dietary intake of potassium is 50 to 100 meq/day (50–100 mmol/day), and renal excretion can be up to 1000 meq/day (1000 mmol/day). Potassium is excreted primarily (90%) by the kidneys. Normal renal handling of potassium depends on adequate glomerular filtration, aldosterone, intact distal tubular function, distal tubular flow, distal tubular sodium delivery, acid–base status, and intracellular potassium stores. Intracellular potassium balance is further affected by shifting of

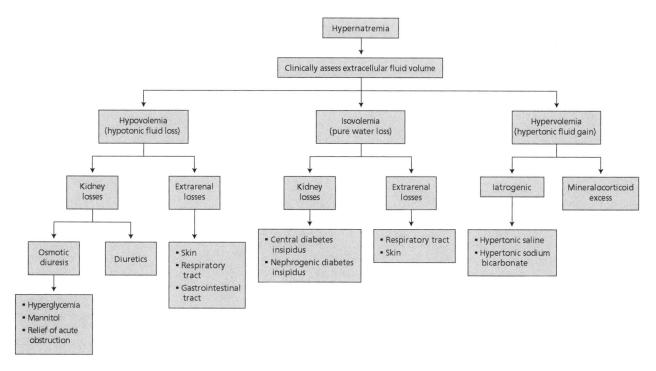

Figure 4. Approach to the patient with hypernatremia. All of these states are associated with impairment of thirst or access to water.

potassium between the ICF and ECF caused by circulating insulin, catecholamines, acid–base status, and plasma osmolality.

Hypokalemia

Hypokalemia (serum potassium concentration <3.5 meq/L [3.5 mmol/L]) can result from potassium loss or intracellular shift in potassium; it is rarely caused by inadequate potassium intake. The most common causes of potassium loss are GI and renal (diuretics). Rare causes include primary aldosteronism, Bartter syndrome, Gitelman syndrome, and periodic paralysis. Bartter syndrome is caused by various genetic mutations in the sodium–potassium–chloride (Na^+-K^+-$2Cl^-$) cotransporter in the thick ascending limb of the loop of Henle, which produce a clinical picture similar to that seen with chronic loop diuretic therapy (ie, hypokalemia, hypomagnesemia, and varying degrees of hypocalcemia). Gitelman syndrome is a milder disorder caused by mutations in the sodium–potassium (Na^+-Cl^-) cotransporter in the distal convoluted tubule, which lead to hypokalemia, hypomagnesemia, and metabolic alkalosis. Bartter and Gitelman syndromes differ from primary hyperaldosteronism (another cause of hypokalemia) in that patients are not hypertensive. Hypokalemic periodic paralysis is caused by a genetic defect leading to mutations in voltage-sensitive calcium or sodium channels. These patients have profound weakness, especially in proximal muscles, and are at risk for life-threatening cardiac arrhythmias due to hypokalemia caused by excessive intracellular shifting of potassium in response to a meal high in carbohydrates or sodium.

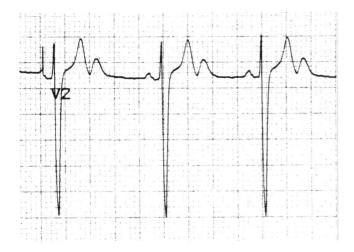

Figure 5. The characteristic electrocardiographic finding in hypokalemia is the appearance of a U wave after the T wave, eventually replacing the T wave.

Manifestations of hypokalemia are ileus, muscle cramps, paralysis, rhabdomyolysis, impaired insulin secretion, and cardiac arrhythmias. Electrocardiographic findings of hypokalemia include U waves and flat or inverted T waves (Figure 5). Hypomagnesemia should always be suspected in patients with hypokalemia because these ions often are lost together, and magnesium is necessary for renal conservation of potassium.

Hypokalemia is treated with oral or IV potassium salts. In severe cases, potassium is given intravenously at a rate of ≤20 to 40 meq/h (20–40 mmol/h) and at a concentration ≤40 meq/L (40 mmol/L). Although total potassium deficits are difficult to predict, a serum potassium level of 3 meq/L (3 mmol/L) is equivalent to a deficit of 200 to 400 meq (200–400 mmol), and a serum potassium level of 2 meq/L (2 mmol/L) is equivalent to a deficit of 400 to 800 meq (400–800 mmol).

Hyperkalemia

Excessive dietary intake of potassium rarely is a cause of hyperkalemia unless there is coexisting kidney disease. Potassium may shift out of cells secondary to tissue injury (eg, rhabdomyolysis, hemolysis), hyperosmolality, insulin deficiency, β-adrenergic blockade, metabolic acidosis, or inhibition of Na^+,K^+-ATPase activity (eg, by digoxin toxicity) and cause hyperkalemia. Decreased renal potassium excretion occurs if there is reduced glomerular filtration, poor distal tubular urine flow (eg, hypovolemia or reduced effective circulating volume), aldosterone deficiency, or tubulointerstitial disease leading to aldosterone unresponsiveness. Several medications (eg, angiotensin-converting enzyme inhibitors, angiotensin II receptor blockers, nonsteroidal anti-inflammatory drugs [NSAIDs], β-blockers) decrease aldosterone production by decreasing angiotensin II levels. Heparin and cyclosporine also decrease aldos-

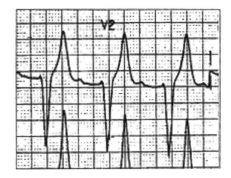

Figure 6. Electrocardiogram demonstrating tall, peaked T waves characteristic of hyperkalemia.

Table 1. Treatment of Acute Hyperkalemia

Treatment	Mechanism of Action
Calcium gluconate	Raises threshold for depolarization
Sodium bicarbonate	Shifts potassium intracellularly
Insulin/glucose	Shifts potassium intracellularly; monitor for hypoglycemia
β-Agonists (eg, inhaled albuterol)	Shifts potassium intracellularly
Loop diuretics	Increases renal excretion of potassium
Sodium polystyrene sulfonate	Ion exchange resin binding potassium in the gut; may be no more effective than laxatives and has been associated with intestinal necrosis
Dialysis	Extracorporeal removal of potassium

terone production. Potassium-sparing diuretics that inhibit aldosterone effect (eg, spironolactone) or block sodium channels in the collecting duct (eg, triamterene, amiloride) can lead to hyperkalemia. Trimethoprim and pentamidine similarly block sodium channels and can cause hyperkalemia.

Hyporeninemic hypoaldosteronism commonly causes mild hyperkalemia and is characterized by deficient angiotensin II production due to both decreased renin production and an intra-adrenal defect leading to aldosterone deficiency. This syndrome most commonly is associated with diabetic nephropathy but also may occur in patients with chronic interstitial nephritis, renal transplant recipients taking cyclosporine, patients with HIV infection, and patients using NSAIDs. Severe hyperkalemia is uncommon unless there is also renal insufficiency.

Acute hyperkalemia causes muscle weakness or flaccid paralysis. The cardiac toxicity is associated with peaked T waves, flattened P waves, and widened QRS complexes on electrocardiography (Figure 6). Ventricular arrhythmias result from an increased resting membrane potential that approaches the threshold for membrane depolarization. Emergent treatment is warranted in this setting, and options are discussed in Table 1 and are managed acutely with IV calcium gluconate, which raises the threshold for depolarization. Dialysis may be required in cases with severe cardiac changes caused by hyperkalemia to rapidly reduce the potassium level. Chronic hyperkalemia is managed with a low-potassium diet, loop diuretics, and avoidance of drugs known to increase serum potassium levels.

Bibliography

Ellison DH, Berl T. Clinical practice. The syndrome of inappropriate antidiuresis. N Engl J Med. 2007;356:2064-72. [PMID: 17507705]

Gennari FJ. Disorders of potassium homeostasis. Hypokalemia and hyperkalemia. Crit Care Clin. 2002;18:273-88, vi. [PMID: 12053834]

Lien YH, Shapiro JI. Hyponatremia: clinical diagnosis and management. Am J Med. 2007;120:653-58. [PMID: 17679119]

Chapter 68

Calcium and Phosphorus Metabolism

Mary Jane Barchman, MD

Calcium is a vital regulator of numerous cellular functions. An average daily diet contains 1000 mg of calcium, 200 to 400 mg of which is absorbed by the intestine when adequate vitamin D is present. The remainder is excreted in the urine and stool. Most of the total body calcium resides in bone. Calcium in the extracellular fluid (ECF) exists in three forms: ionized (the metabolically active fraction), bound to protein (primarily albumin), and complexed with organic ions. The protein-bound calcium fraction increases with alkalosis (ionized calcium decreases) and decreases with acidosis (ionized calcium increases).

Phosphorus is a critical component of cellular energy metabolism and bone formation. Bone mineral accounts for approximately 90% of total body phosphorus; 10% of phosphorus exists in the intracellular fluid, and <1% is present in the ECF. Approximately 70% of blood phosphorus is contained in phospholipids. The remaining inorganic phosphorus exists as either protein bound or free phosphorus or is complexed with circulating cations. Average daily dietary phosphorus intake varies between 800 and 1800 mg of phosphate, of which about half is absorbed in the small intestine.

Regulation of calcium and phosphorus metabolism are tightly linked through the action of parathyroid hormone (PTH); vitamin D; and, to a lesser extent, calcitonin (Figure 1). The primary role of PTH is to prevent hypocalcemia. The calcium-sensing receptor is located on cell membranes of the parathyroid gland and triggers release of preformed PTH into the circulation in response to low levels of ionized calcium. PTH returns ionized calcium levels to normal by rapidly mobilizing calcium and phosphate from bone stores and by increasing both gastrointestinal (GI) and renal absorption. PTH also upregulates 1α-hydroxylase expression in the kidney, resulting in increased production of 1,25-dihydroxyvitamin D_3 (1,25(OH)$_2D_3$; calcitriol), the most active form of vitamin D, further increasing GI absorption of calcium. Vitamin D_3 (cholecalciferol) is obtained from dietary sources but also is generated from cholesterol precursors by skin exposure to ultraviolet light, with ultimate conversion to 25-hydroxyvitamin D_3 (25(OH)D_3; calcidiol) by the liver. Vitamin D_2 (ergocalciferol) is obtained from dietary sources and undergoes hydroxylation similarly to vitamin D_3. **Because of its long half-life, measurement of serum 25(OH)D_2 is the best indicator of total body vitamin D stores.** Calcitonin is secreted by thyroid parafollicular C cells in response to hypercalcemia and inhibits osteoclast-mediated bone resorption. This effect is clinically insignificant in humans.

Hypocalcemia

Acute hypocalcemia leads to neuromuscular irritability (eg, cramping, paresthesia, tetany, seizure, laryngospasm, prolonged QT interval). Mild hypocalcemia is well tolerated, especially if the reduction in ionized calcium has been gradual. Precipitous development of

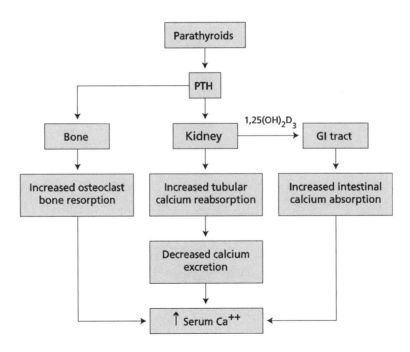

Figure 1. Overview of the metabolic systems that maintain calcium homeostasis. 1,25(OH)$_2D_3$ = 1,25-dihydroxyvitamin D_3; Ca^{++} = ionized calcium; GI = gastrointestinal; PTH = parathyroid hormone; ↑ = increased.

hypocalcemia is more likely to result in symptoms and may be detected by the presence of Chvostek sign (unilateral contraction of the facial muscles when the facial nerve is tapped just in front of the ear) and Trousseau sign (carpal spasm after occluding the brachial artery with an inflated blood pressure cuff).

In most cases, low total serum calcium levels are due to low albumin levels; the ionized calcium concentration is normal. In general, total calcium declines by 0.8 mg/dL (0.2 mmol/L) for each 1 g/dL (10 g/L) decrement in serum albumin concentration. The most common cause of acquired hypocalcemia is parathyroidectomy or vascular injury to the parathyroid glands. Other causes include autoimmune destruction and infiltrative diseases. Hypomagnesemia can cause hypocalcemia by impairing the release and activity of PTH. Patients who undergo subtotal parathyroidectomy may develop hungry bone syndrome postoperatively characterized by hypocalcemia and hypophosphatemia. Vitamin D deficiency or resistance can cause mild hypocalcemia. Hyperphosphatemia due to chronic kidney disease, rhabdomyolysis, or tumor lysis syndrome may result in hypocalcemia caused by formation and deposition of calcium–phosphate complexes. Hypocalcemia also may complicate pancreatitis when ionized calcium complexes with the free fatty acids are liberated by the action of pancreatic enzymes.

In patients with symptomatic hypocalcemia, treatment includes intravenous (IV) 10% calcium gluconate or calcium chloride. In less severe cases, calcium is replaced orally along with vitamin D; magnesium also must be replenished if serum values are low.

Hypercalcemia

Mild hypercalcemia (serum calcium level of 10.0–11.5 mg/dL [1.5–2.9 mmol/L]) usually is well tolerated and causes no symptoms. As serum calcium levels increase, more progressive symptoms occur, such as fatigue, weakness, polyuria, anorexia, nausea, vomiting, abdominal pain, pancreatitis, constipation, lethargy, and even coma. Serious cardiac dysrhythmias with a shortened QT interval may occur when serum calcium levels are >14 mg/dL (3.5 mmol/L). Chronic hypercalcemia caused by hyperparathyroidism can lead to osteopenia, osteoporosis, nephrolithiasis, nephrocalcinosis, hypertension, progressive renal failure, and soft tissue calcifications.

Causes for hypercalcemia are divided into PTH-mediated and non-PTH-mediated causes (Table 1). Non-PTH-mediated hypercalcemia is present when PTH is suppressed (<20 pg/mL [20 ng/L]). Malignancy is the most common cause and is responsible for most cases of hypercalcemia in hospitalized patients. The mechanism of hypercalcemia is related to humoral factors (PTH-related protein [PTH-rP]) or local osteolysis of bone. Granulomatous tissue (eg, sarcoidosis, tuberculosis, leprosy) may express 1α-hydroxylase activity, resulting in excess activated vitamin D production with subsequent development of significant hypercalcemia.

PTH-mediated hypercalcemia due to primary hyperparathyroidism is the most common cause of elevated calcium in outpatients. Effects of excess PTH include increased $1,25(OH)_2D_3$ levels; increased osteoclast-mediated bone resorption; enhanced distal tubular reabsorption of calcium; decreased proximal tubular reabsorption of phos-

Table 1. Differential Diagnosis of Hypercalcemia

Disorder	Notes
PTH Mediated	
Primary hyperparathyroidism	Often an incidental finding. Associated with elevated calcium, low phosphate, PTH in the normal range (20%) or elevated (80%), normal or elevated alkaline phosphatase, and normal or elevated urine calcium.
Non-PTH Mediated	
Suppressed PTH	
Humoral hypercalcemia of malignancy	Most common cause of hypercalcemia in patients with cancer even in those with skeletal metastases. Associated with elevated calcium, normal or low phosphate (elevated if GFR <35 mL/min/1.73 m²), normal or elevated PTHrP (not needed for diagnosis), normal or elevated alkaline phosphatase, and elevated urine calcium.
Metastatic bone disease	Hypercalciuria without hypercalcemia is most common. Associated with elevated calcium, normal or elevated phosphate, elevated alkaline phosphatase (most cases), and variable PTHrP.
Multiple myeloma	Common cause of hypercalcemia in patients with decreased GFR and anemia. Associated with elevated calcium, elevated phosphate, normal alkaline phosphatase, normal or low PTHrP, and abnormal serum protein immunoelectrophoresis.
Granulomatous disease (eg, sarcoidosis, tuberculosis)	Associated with elevated calcium, elevated phosphate, elevated alkaline phosphatase (but may not be of skeletal origin), elevated urine calcium, and elevated vitamin D.
Milk-alkali syndrome	Consider in healthy persons in whom primary hyperparathyroidism has been excluded. Excessive ingestion of calcium-containing antacids may be present. Associated with elevated calcium, elevated phosphate, elevated creatinine, normal alkaline phosphatase, elevated bicarbonate, and variable urine calcium.
Immobilization	Occurs in persons with high bone turnover before an immobilizing event (eg, untreated primary hyperparathyroidism, hyperthyroidism, Paget disease of bone). Associated with elevated calcium, elevated phosphate, elevated alkaline phosphatase, and elevated urine calcium.
Hyperthyroidism	Hypercalcemia is a frequent incidental finding in hyperthyroidism, which results from direct stimulation of osteoclasts by thyroxine or triiodothyronine.
Normal PTH	
Benign familial hypocalciuric hypercalcemia	Constitutive overexpression of the calcium-sensing receptor gene. Elevated calcium, low phosphate, and a calcium-creatinine clearance ratio <0.01 [calculated as (Urine calcium ÷ Serum calcium) × (Serum creatinine ÷ Urine creatinine)].

GFR = glomerular filtration rate; PTH = parathyroid hormone; PTHrP = parathyroid hormone–related protein.

phorus, hypercalcemia, hypophosphatemia; and increased urine phosphate and calcium levels. Primary hyperparathyroidism is caused by a solitary adenoma in about 85% of patients, with hyperplasia of all glands or multiple adenomas being less frequent. Multigland parathyroid hyperplasia should raise suspicion for multiple endocrine neoplasia (MEN) types 1 and 2a. Surgical resection of a hyperfunctioning adenoma may be curative in those patients with primary hyperparathyroidism and manifestations of chronic hypercalcemia. Parathyroidectomy generally is indicated in asymptomatic patients with any of the following criteria: serum calcium level >1 mg/dL (0.25 mmol/L) above the upper limit of normal; creatinine clearance (calculated) <60 mL/min; reduction in bone mineral density of the femoral neck, lumbar spine, or distal radius >2.5 standard deviations below peak bone mass (T-score <−2.5); or age younger than 50 years.

Secondary hyperparathyroidism is a normal physiologic response to chronically low calcium levels caused by chronic kidney disease, vitamin D deficiency, or GI malabsorption. In secondary hyperparathyroidism, PTH is elevated, but calcium levels are low to low-normal. Tertiary hyperparathyroidism occasionally develops in these patients, possibly because of parathyroid hyperplasia and loss of negative feedback; it is characterized by elevated serum PTH values despite elevated serum calcium levels.

Hypercalcemia requiring acute intervention is most common in the setting of malignancy. Because of the vasoconstrictive effects of calcium and a tendency toward nephrogenic diabetes insipidus with hypercalcemia, these patients usually are hypovolemic and require resuscitation with normal saline. Improved intravascular volume leads to improved glomerular filtration and increased sodium delivery to more distal nephron segments where calcium can be excreted. After generous volume resuscitation, calcium excretion can be further augmented by the addition of a loop diuretic; however, the variable utility and potential adverse effects of this measure (eg, hypokalemia, aggravation of hypovolemia) and the availability of bisphosphonate therapy have led to a recent reappraisal of this approach. Bisphosphonates, given intravenously, may be used to decrease bone resorption and may have a prolonged effect. Calcitonin may be used to inhibit osteoclast-mediated bone resorption in hypercalcemia of malignancy but is of only modest benefit, and tachyphylaxis occurs quickly. The treatment of hypercalcemia caused by granulomatous disease is directed at controlling the underlying process with glucocorticoids or antimicrobial therapy as appropriate.

If a neoplastic process results in increased active vitamin D levels, oral glucocorticoid therapy may be beneficial. In secondary hyperparathyroidism caused by chronic kidney disease, a combination of calcitriol and phosphate binders is used to suppress serum PTH values to no more than three to four times the normal level. Cinacalcet is another agent that may be used for treatment of secondary or tertiary hyperparathyroidism; the drug suppresses PTH secretion by acting primarily on the calcium-sensing receptor in the parathyroid glands. Cinacalcet may retard the development of renal bone disease while resulting in significantly less elevation in serum calcium and phosphorus levels. Its use is restricted to patients on hemodialysis.

Hyperphosphatemia

Hyperphosphatemia most often is due to phosphate retention caused by chronic kidney disease, but it also can occur with hypoparathyroidism, rhabdomyolysis, tumor lysis syndrome, acidosis, and overzealous phosphate administration. The symptoms of hyperphosphatemia are attributable to the attendant hypocalcemia. Most hyperphosphatemia is transient unless related to chronic kidney disease. Treatment of hyperphosphatemia associated with chronic kidney disease is a phosphorus-restricted diet, oral phosphate binders, saline diuresis, or dialysis (see Chapter 71).

Hypophosphatemia

Hypophosphatemia may result from impaired GI absorption, increased renal excretion, or intracellular shift of phosphorus (Table 2). Severe hypophosphatemia (serum phosphorus level <1 mg/dL [0.3 mmol/L]) usually indicates total body phosphate depletion and is characterized by muscle weakness, paresthesia, rhabdomyolysis, respiratory failure, heart failure, seizure, and coma; rarely, hemolysis, platelet dysfunction, and metabolic acidosis can occur. Moderate hypophosphatemia (serum phosphate level of 1.0–2.5 mg/dL [0.3–0.8 mmol/L]) is common in hospitalized patients but may not necessarily reflect total body phosphorus depletion. For example, insulin treatment of hyperglycemia will shift phosphate intracellularly. Refeeding syndrome is caused by a similar phenomenon; calories provided to a patient after a prolonged period of starvation serve as a stimulus for tissue growth, which consumes phosphorus in the form of phosphorylated intermediates such as adenosine triphosphate. Persons who chronically abuse alcohol frequently fall into this category, largely because of underlying poor nutrition. Acute respiratory alkalosis also can cause hypophosphatemia. Impaired absorption may be caused by excessive oral phosphate binders; chronic diarrhea or steatorrhea; and, rarely, inadequate intake. Persistent, moderate hypophosphatemia is treated with oral phosphorus replacement. Severe hypophosphatemia is treated with IV potassium phosphate or sodium phosphate. Patients who are hypophosphatemic often have associated hypokalemia and hypomagnesemia, which require correction.

Bibliography

Inzucchi SE. Management of hypercalcemia. Diagnostic workup, therapeutic options for hyperparathyroidism and other common causes. Postgrad Med. 2004;115:27-36. [PMID: 15171076]

Table 2. Causes of Hypophosphatemia

Kidney phosphate wasting
    Acetaminophen poisoning
    Vitamin D deficiency or resistance
    Hyperparathyroidism
    Osmotic diuresis
    Oncogenic osteomalacia
    Kidney transplantation
    Proximal (type 2) renal tubular acidosis (Fanconi syndrome)
        Tenofovir
        Ifosfamide
    Hypophosphatemic rickets

Chronic diarrhea

Decreased absorption
    Vitamin D deficiency or resistance
    Phosphate binders and antacids

Decreased intake

Intracellular uptake
    Refeeding syndrome
    Treatment of diabetic ketoacidosis with insulin
    Parathyroidectomy (hungry bone syndrome)
    Respiratory alkalosis

Chapter 69

Acid-Base Disorders

Joseph Charles, MD

A systematic approach to acid–base problem solving involves an analysis of arterial blood gases and electrolytes focused on answering five questions:

1. Is the patient acidemic or alkalemic?
2. Is the acid–base disorder primarily metabolic or respiratory?
3. Is there an anion gap?
4. If a metabolic acidosis exists, is there an appropriate respiratory compensation?
5. If an anion gap acidemia is present, is there an additional complicating metabolic disturbance?

Table 1 summarizes a differential diagnosis for the primary acid–base disorders.

Metabolic Acidosis

Metabolic acidosis is the most common acid–base disorder and can be life threatening. It results from excessive cellular acid production, reduced acid secretion, or loss of body alkali. The body has two buffering mechanisms to counteract an increase in acid. The initial response is to increase carbon dioxide excretion by increasing ventilation. The second response is increased renal excretion of acids and renal regeneration of bicarbonate. The adequacy of compensation can be assessed by the quick check method or the Winter formula (Table 2).

Metabolic acidosis can be classified into two categories using the anion gap. Each category has a distinct differential diagnosis.

Table 1. The Primary Acid-Base Disorders

Metabolic Acidosis ([serum bicarbonate] <22 meq/L [22 mmol/L]; pH <7.35)	Metabolic Alkalosis ([serum bicarbonate] >28 meq/L [28 mmol/L]; pH >7.45)
Increased serum anion gap (anion gap >12 meq/L [12 mmol/L])	Chloride responsive (urine [chloride] <10 meq/L [10 mmol/L])
• Ketoacidosis (diabetes, alcohol abuse, starvation)	• Vomiting
• Lactic acidosis (ischemia, sepsis, shock, drugs)	• Nasogastric suctioning
• Exogenous substances (methanol, ethylene glycol, salicylates, toluene)	• Thiazide and loop diuretic therapy
• Chronic kidney disease	• Contraction alkalosis
Normal serum anion gap (hyperchloremic)	• Exogenous bicarbonate in the setting of kidney dysfunction
• Positive urine anion gap	Chloride unresponsive (urine [chloride] >20 meq/L [20 mmol/L])
○ Type I RTA (normo- or hypokalemic)	• Elevated mineralocorticoid activity (primary hyperaldosteronism, Cushing syndrome)
○ Type II RTA (normo- or hypokalemic)	• Exogenous mineralocorticoid
○ Type IV RTA (hyperkalemic)	• Bartter, Gitelman, Liddle syndromes
• Negative urine anion gap	• Some forms of congenital adrenal hyperplasia
○ GI bicarbonate loss (severe diarrhea, ureterosigmoidostomy)	• Severe hypokalemia
○ Ingestion of acid	• Chronic licorice ingestion
Respiratory Acidosis (arterial P_{CO_2} >45 mm Hg [6 kPa]; pH <7.35)	**Respiratory Alkalosis (arterial P_{CO_2} <35 mm Hg [4.7 kPa]; pH >7.45)**
• Respiratory center depression (stroke, infection, tumor, drugs, COPD, OHS)	• CNS stimulation (stroke, infection, tumor, fever, pain)
• Neuromuscular failure (muscular dystrophy, ALS, Guillain-Barré syndrome, myasthenia gravis, COPD, OHS)	• Drugs (aspirin, progesterone, theophylline, caffeine)
• Decreased respiratory system compliance (kyphoscoliosis, interstitial lung disease)	• Anxiety, psychosis
• Increased airway resistance or obstruction (asthma, COPD, OHS)	• Hypoxemia (low atmospheric oxygen, severe anemia, lung disease, right-to-left shunt, heart failure)
• Increased dead space or ventilation-perfusion mismatch (pulmonary embolism, COPD, OHS)	• Pregnancy

ALS = amyotrophic lateral sclerosis; CNS = central nervous system; COPD = chronic obstructive pulmonary disease; GI = gastrointestinal; OHS = obesity hypoventilation syndrome; RTA = renal tubular acidosis.

Table 2. Compensation in Acid-Base Disorders

Condition	Expected Compensation
Metabolic acidosis	Acute (Winter formula): $P_{CO_2} = (1.5 \times [\text{Bicarbonate}]) + 8$
	Chronic: $P_{CO_2} = [\text{Bicarbonate}] + 15$
	Quick check: P_{CO_2} value should approximate last two digits of pH
	Failure of P_{CO_2} to decrease to the expected value indicates complicating respiratory acidosis; excessive decrease of P_{CO_2} indicates complicating respiratory alkalosis.
Metabolic alkalosis	For each 1 meq/L (1 mmol/L) increase in bicarbonate, P_{CO_2} should increase 0.7 mm Hg (0.09 kPa).
Respiratory acidosis	Acute: 1 meq/L (1 mmol/L) increase in bicarbonate for each 10 mm Hg (1.33 kPa) increase in P_{CO_2}
	Failure of the bicarbonate concentration to increase to the expected value indicates complicating metabolic acidosis; excessive increase in the bicarbonate concentration indicates complicating metabolic alkalosis.
	Chronic: 3.5 meq/L (3.5 mmol/L) increase in bicarbonate for each 10 mm Hg (1.33 kPa) increase in P_{CO_2}
Respiratory alkalosis	Acute: 2 meq/L (2 mmol/L) decrease in bicarbonate for each 10 mm Hg (1.33 kPa) decrease in P_{CO_2}
	Chronic: 4 to 5 meq/L (4 to 5 mmol/L) decrease in bicarbonate for each 10 mm Hg (1.33 kPa) decrease in P_{CO_2}
	Failure of the bicarbonate concentration to decrease to the expected value indicates complicating metabolic alkalosis; excessive decrease in the bicarbonate concentration indicates complicating metabolic acidosis.

Where P_{CO_2} is in mm Hg and bicarbonate in meq/L.

$$\text{Anion gap} = [\text{Sodium}] - ([\text{Chloride}] + [\text{Bicarbonate}])$$

Normally, the anion gap is approximately 12 ± 2 meq/L (12 ± 2 mmol/L). Most unmeasured anions consist of albumin. Therefore, the presence of either a low albumin level or an unmeasured cationic light chain, which occurs in multiple myeloma, results in a low anion gap. Increased hydrogen ion concentration or decreased bicarbonate concentration will increase the gap. When the primary disturbance is a metabolic acidosis, the anion gap helps to narrow the diagnostic possibilities to an increased anion gap acidosis or a normal anion gap acidosis.

Increased Anion Gap Metabolic Acidosis

Common causes include ketoacidosis (diabetes mellitus, alcohol abuse, starvation), lactic acidosis, chronic kidney disease, salicylate toxicity, and ethylene glycol and methanol poisoning. Diabetic ketoacidosis is the most common cause of an increased anion gap acidosis, but a normal anion gap acidosis may be present early in the disease course when the extracellular fluid (ECF) volume is nearly normal. Ketoacidosis also may develop in patients with a history of chronic alcohol abuse, decreased food intake, and (often) nausea and vomiting. The alcohol withdrawal, volume depletion, and starvation that occur in these patients significantly increase the levels of circulating catecholamines, which results in peripheral mobilization of fatty acids that is much greater than would be associated with starvation alone. Lactic acidosis develops when an imbalance occurs between the production and use of lactic acid and is most commonly associated with tissue ischemia. Lactic acidosis caused by increased production of lactic acid may occur in patients who engage in extreme exercise or who have tonic-clonic seizures and usually is of short duration. Aspirin poisoning leads to increased lactic acid production; the accumulation of lactic acid, salicylic acid, ketoacids, and other organic acids results in an increased anion gap metabolic acidosis. Salicylate poisoning manifests as either a respiratory alkalosis or an increased anion gap metabolic acidosis in adults, but affected children usually have only an increased anion gap metabolic acidosis.

Ethylene glycol and methanol poisoning are characterized by a severe increased anion gap metabolic acidosis accompanied by an osmolal gap. An osmolal gap is present when the measured plasma osmolality exceeds the calculated plasma osmolality by >10 mOsm/kg H$_2$O (10 mmol/kg H$_2$O). Plasma osmolality is calculated as:

$$\text{Plasma osmolality} = (2 \times [\text{Sodium}]) + ([\text{Glucose}]/18) + ([\text{BUN}]/2.8)$$

where glucose and blood urea nitrogen (BUN) are measured in mg/dL.

Ethylene glycol poisoning initially causes neurologic manifestations similar to those of alcohol intoxication, and seizures and coma can develop rapidly. Ethylene glycol poisoning also is associated with acute kidney injury and oxalate crystalluria. Clinical manifestations of methanol ingestion include acute inebriation followed by an asymptomatic period lasting 24 to 36 hours. Because formic acid, the metabolic end product of methanol, is toxic to the retina, blindness may result.

Normal Anion Gap Metabolic Acidosis

Normal anion gap metabolic acidosis is secondary to kidney or extrarenal disease. The clinical history usually helps to distinguish between kidney and extrarenal causes of metabolic acidosis, but the two categories can be reliably differentiated by measuring the urine anion gap:

$$\text{Urine anion gap} = (\text{Urine [Sodium]} + \text{Urine [Potassium]}) - [\text{Urine Chloride}]$$

The urine anion gap normally is 30 to 50 mEq/L (30–50 mmol/L). Metabolic acidosis of extrarenal origin (usually gastrointestinal) is suggested by a large, negative urine anion gap caused by significantly increased urine ammonium excretion, which is used as a measure of the kidney's ability to excrete acid. Metabolic acidosis of kidney origin is suggested by a positive urine anion gap related to the inability to excrete acid and the resulting minimal urine ammonium excretion. Severe diarrhea is the most common gastrointestinal cause. The most common kidney-related causes are renal tubular disorders causing renal tubular acidosis (RTA). Type 1 (distal) RTA, caused by impaired distal tubule acidification, should be considered in patients with a normal anion gap acidosis, hypokalemia, a positive urine anion gap, and a urine pH >5.5 in the setting of systemic acidosis; serum bicarbonate concentration may be as low as 10 mEq/L (10 mmol/L). Type 2 (proximal) RTA is caused by reduced proximal tubule bicarbonate reabsorption and should be suspected in patients with a nor-

Table 3. Renal Tubular Acidosis

Diagnosis	Metabolic Findings	Associated Findings
Type 1 (distal or classic)	Normal anion gap acidosis, hypokalemia, positive UAG, urine pH >5.5 (in the setting of systemic acidosis), serum [HCO_3] ≅ 10 mEq/L (10 mmol/L)	Nephrolithiasis and nephrocalcinosis, autoimmune disorders (SLE, Sjögren syndrome), amphotericin B use, urinary obstruction
Type 2 (proximal)	Normal anion gap metabolic acidosis, normal UAG, hypokalemia, urine pH <5.5, serum [HCO_3] ≅ 16–18 mEq/L (16–18 mmol/L)	Glycosuria, phosphaturia, uricosuria, aminoaciduria, and tubular proteinuria (Fanconi syndrome)
Type 4	Normal anion gap metabolic acidosis, hyperkalemia, positive UAG, urine pH <5.5	Diabetes mellitus, urinary tract obstruction

SLE = systemic lupus erythematosus; UAG = urine anion gap.

mal anion gap metabolic acidosis, a normal urine anion gap, hypokalemia, and an intact ability to acidify the urine to a pH of <5.5 while in a steady state. The serum bicarbonate concentration usually is 16 to 18 meq/L (16–18 mmol/L). Type 4 RTA should be suspected in patients with a normal anion gap metabolic acidosis associated with hyperkalemia and a slightly positive urine anion gap. Type 4 RTA occurs most often in patients with diabetes who have mild to moderate kidney insufficiency; the disorder is caused by hyporeninemic hypoaldosteronism, which is characterized by deficient angiotensin II production caused by both decreased renin production and an intraadrenal defect leading to aldosterone deficiency. Table 3 outlines the metabolic findings and associated clinical features. Figure 1 outlines an approach to patients with a low serum bicarbonate concentration.

Mixed Metabolic Disorders

To determine whether a complicating metabolic disturbance is present along with an anion gap metabolic acidosis, it is necessary to calculate the corrected bicarbonate level. The corrected bicarbonate level is obtained using the following formula:

$$\text{Corrected [Bicarbonate]} = \text{measured [Bicarbonate]} + [\text{Anion gap} - 12]$$

This formula is based on the assumption that the measured anion gap represents, in part, the bicarbonate that was consumed in attempting to compensate for the process producing the anion gap metabolic acidosis. If the measured anion gap is added to the measured bicarbonate concentration and the normal anion gap of 12 is subtracted, the result should represent the bicarbonate concentration if the anion gap acidosis were not present, hence the name "corrected bicarbonate."

If the corrected bicarbonate level is less than 24 ± 2 mEq/L (24 ± 2 mmol/L), a coexisting normal anion gap metabolic acidosis is present; conversely, if the corrected bicarbonate level is greater than 24 ± 2 meq/L (24 ± 2 mmol/L), a coexisting metabolic alkalosis is present.

Metabolic Alkalosis

A primary increase in bicarbonate concentration can result from loss of hydrogen chloride or, less commonly, addition of bicarbonate.

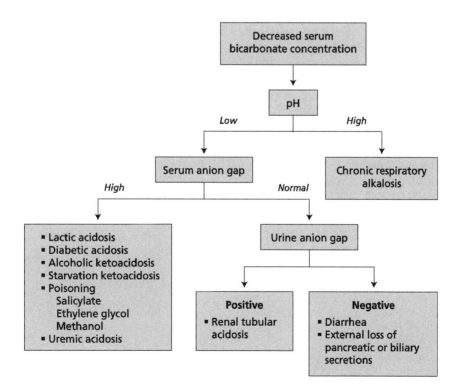

Figure 1. Approach to the patient with a decreased serum bicarbonate concentration.

Table 2 lists the expected respiratory compensation for metabolic alkalosis. After being generated, the metabolic alkalosis is corrected through urinary excretion of the excess bicarbonate. Alkalosis is maintained only when renal bicarbonate excretion is limited owing to a reduction in kidney function or stimulation of renal tubule bicarbonate reabsorption. Increased bicarbonate reabsorption is caused by ECF volume contraction, chloride depletion, hypokalemia, or elevated mineralocorticoid activity. Persistent delivery of sodium chloride to the distal tubule in the presence of high levels of aldosterone results in urinary loss of potassium and hydrogen, which maintains the metabolic alkalosis.

The most common causes of metabolic alkalosis are vomiting, nasogastric suction, and diuretic therapy. In these cases, which are classified as *chloride responsive*, administration of sodium chloride fluid reverses the alkalosis by expanding the intravascular volume and reducing the activity of the renin–angiotensin–aldosterone axis. Low urine chloride concentration suggests vomiting or remote diuretic ingestion; in either case, sodium chloride volume expansion will correct the alkalosis.

Less commonly, metabolic alkalosis is maintained in the absence of volume depletion. This condition is recognized by a high urine chloride level (>20 meq/L [20 mmol/L]) related to elevated mineralocorticoid activity and does not correct with sodium chloride volume replacement. Consequently, these disorders are classified as *chloride-unresponsive* or *chloride-resistant metabolic alkaloses*. Examples are primary hyperaldosteronism and Cushing syndrome.

Antacids (H_2-receptor blockers, proton pump inhibitors) may decrease hydrogen in patients with prolonged gastric aspiration or chronic vomiting. Potassium chloride almost always is indicated for hypokalemia, although potassium concentration may increase as the alkalosis is corrected.

Respiratory Acidosis

Primary respiratory acidosis develops as a result of ineffective alveolar ventilation and is suggested by an arterial P_{CO_2} >45 mm Hg (6.0 kPa). However, an arterial P_{CO_2} <45 mm Hg (6.0 kPa) may indicate respiratory acidosis in a patient with primary metabolic acidosis that is not adequately compensated by alveolar ventilation. This condition must be differentiated from primary respiratory acidosis (see Table 1). Respiratory acidosis is caused by a primary increase in arterial P_{CO_2}, which accumulates when ventilation is inadequate. Hypoventilation can result from neurologic disorders (eg, stroke) or medications (eg, opiates) that affect the central nervous system respiratory center, respiratory muscle weakness (eg, myasthenia gravis, Guillain-Barré syndrome) or chest wall deformity (eg, severe kyphoscoliosis), obstruction of airways (eg, COPD), or ventilation–perfusion mismatch (eg, pulmonary embolism). Respiratory acidosis may manifest as hypercapnic encephalopathy, a clinical syndrome that initially can present as irritability, headache, mental cloudiness, apathy, confusion, anxiety, and restlessness and can progress to asterixis, transient psychosis, delirium, somnolence, and coma. Severe hypercapnia may cause decreased myocardial contractility, arrhythmias, and peripheral vasodilatation, particularly when the serum pH decreases to <7.1. Patients with acute respiratory acidosis are primarily at risk for hypoxemia rather than hypercapnia or acidemia. Therefore, initial therapy should focus on establishing and maintaining a patent airway and improving ventilation to provide adequate oxygenation. Excessive oxygen may worsen hypoventilation in patients with chronic respiratory acidosis and should be used with caution in this population. The expected acute and chronic compensation for respiratory acidosis is indicated in Table 2.

Respiratory Alkalosis

Primary respiratory alkalosis is characterized by an arterial P_{CO_2} <35 mm Hg (4.7 kPa). Primary respiratory alkalosis must be differentiated from secondary respiratory alkalosis, which is a compensatory mechanism in the setting of primary metabolic acidosis (see Table 2). To maintain a normal ECF volume in the setting of increased urinary loss of sodium bicarbonate, the kidney retains sodium chloride. Therefore, patients with chronic respiratory alkalosis typically have hyperchloremia.

Common causes of respiratory alkalosis can be sorted by underlying pathology. Those involving the pulmonary vasculature include pulmonary hypertension and pulmonary embolism. Pulmonary parenchymal diseases are represented by pulmonary fibrosis, heart failure, and pneumonia. In patients with asthma, acute exacerbations of bronchospasm trigger an increased respiratory rate. Respiratory alkalosis also can result from conditions affecting ventilatory control (eg, anxiety, aspirin toxicity, sepsis, hypoxia, hepatic encephalopathy, pregnancy). Acute hypocapnia decreases cerebral blood flow and causes binding of free calcium to albumin in the blood. Mild respiratory alkalosis may cause lightheadedness and palpitations. More profound respiratory alkalosis may cause symptoms that resemble those of hypocalcemia, including paresthesias of the extremities and circumoral area and carpopedal spasm. Patients with ischemic heart disease may occasionally develop cardiac arrhythmias, ischemic electrocardiographic changes, and angina pectoris. In psychogenic hyperventilation, rebreathing air using a bag increases the systemic arterial P_{CO_2}. This method also may help to rapidly reduce the pH in patients with mixed, severe alkalosis.

Bibliography

Adrogué HJ, Madias NE. Secondary responses to altered acid-base status: the rules of engagement. J Am Soc Nephrol. 2010;21:920-3. [PMID: 20431042]

Chapter 70

Acute Kidney Injury

Harold M. Szerlip, MD

To better reflect the range of structural and functional changes that occur during acute injury to the kidney, the term *acute kidney injury* (AKI) is preferred over the older term *acute renal failure*. AKI is defined as an abrupt increase in the serum creatinine concentration or decrease in urine output, specifically as an absolute increase in the serum creatinine level of ≥0.3 mg/dL (26.5 µmol/L) over 48 hours, or an increase in the serum creatinine level of ≥50%, or urine output <0.5 mL/kg/h for >6 hours. AKI can be divided into three stages (Table 1). AKI may occur secondary to decreased perfusion from prerenal causes; intrarenal injury caused by ischemia, toxins, tubular obstruction, immunologic events, or allergic reactions; or postrenal obstruction of urine outflow (Figure 1). Because renal hypoperfusion and urinary outflow obstruction both can lead to renal parenchymal injury, it is paramount to

Table 1. Stages of Acute Kidney Injury

Stage	Serum Creatinine Criteria	Urine Output Criteria
1 (risk)	Increase of ≥150%-200%	<0.5 mL/kg/h for >6 h
2 (injury)	Increase of ≥200%-300%	<0.5 mL/kg/h for >12 h
3 (failure)	Increase of >300% or >4 mg/dL (353.6 µmol/L) with acute increase ≥0.5 mg/dL (44 µmol/L)	<0.3 mL/kg/h for >24 h or anuria for 12 h

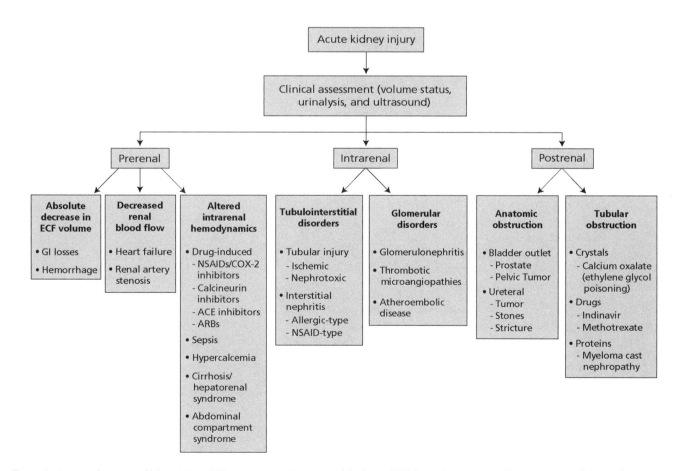

Figure 1. Approach to acute kidney injury. ARBs = angiotensin receptor blockers; COX-2 = cyclooxygenase-2; ECF = extracellular fluid; GI = gastrointestinal; NSAID = nonsteroidal anti-inflammatory drug.

295

promptly diagnose and correct these disorders.

Blood perfusing the corticomedullary portion of the kidney has a low oxygen content. As a result, the parts of the nephron that reside within this area (ie, the straight segment of the proximal tubule and the ascending loop of Henle) function under near-hypoxic conditions. In addition, these tubular segments use large amounts of energy-reabsorbing sodium. Insults that result in decreased renal perfusion or toxins that interfere with tubular cell energetics cause oxygen demand to exceed oxygen delivery. The resultant ischemia and subsequent reperfusion activate cellular processes that cause tubular cell apoptosis and necrosis. The loss of polarity of the tubular epithelial cells interferes with the transport of electrolytes out of the lumen back into the renal interstitium. The sloughing of these cells into the tubular lumen causes obstruction.

Prevention

An increase in serum creatinine concentration of as little as 0.3 mg/dL (26.5 μmol/L) is associated with an increase in morbidity and mortality; therefore, it is important to prevent AKI from developing. This is best accomplished by identifying patients who are at risk. AKI is most likely to occur in patients who already have decreased renal function or whose intravascular volume is depleted. Patients with hypertension or diabetes mellitus and elderly patients are especially at risk. The use of nonsteroidal anti-inflammatory drugs (NSAIDs), which can compromise renal hemodynamics, also places patients at risk. Routinely estimate glomerular filtration rate (GFR) in patients at risk for AKI. Serum creatinine concentration alone is a poor indicator of renal function. Validated equations for estimating GFR are available and are easy to use (see Chapter 66). A GFR <60 mL/min/1.73 m² represents significant renal dysfunction.

In at-risk individuals, if possible, avoid the use of nephrotoxins (eg, iodinated contrast, aminoglycoside antibiotics) and stop NSAIDs. In high-risk patients requiring imaging with contrast, use the smallest possible dose of a low-osmolality or iso-osmolality contrast agent and treat with isotonic saline or bicarbonate before and immediately after the procedure. The use of N-acetylcysteine also may be beneficial in some patients. All patients at high risk for AKI and any patient requiring a nephrotoxic drug should have an estimated GFR calculated. When prescribing aminoglycosides, consider once-daily dosing or follow peak and trough levels and discontinue the medications as early as possible. Avoid overdiuresis in patients with heart failure, the nephrotic syndrome, or cirrhosis. Patients who rely on an activated renin–angiotensin axis to maintain glomerular filtration are especially prone to develop AKI when angiotensin-converting enzyme (ACE) inhibitors or angiotensin II receptor blockers (ARBs) are added. This includes patients who are volume depleted from overdiuresis; patients with decompensated heart failure, hepatic dysfunction, chronic kidney disease (CKD), or renal artery stenosis; and patients who are using NSAIDs. In high-risk patients with poor oral intake or excessive fluid loss (eg, diarrhea, vomiting, burns), maintain intravascular volume using intravenous (IV) fluids.

Diagnosis

The diagnosis of AKI is made when there is an abrupt increase in serum creatinine concentration or decrease in urine volume (see Table 1). After establishing the presence of AKI, it is essential to determine the cause. Intrinsic AKI is divided into oliguric (≤400 mL/24 h) and nonoliguric (>400 mL/24 h) forms–the lower the urine output, the worse the prognosis. Prerenal and postrenal causes of AKI often are rapidly reversible and thus must be distinguished from intrinsic

Table 2. Differential Diagnosis of Acute Kidney Injury

Disorder	Notes
Prerenal	Characterized by BUN–creatinine ratio >20:1, urine sodium <10 meq/L (10 mmol/L) or FENa <1%, bland urine sediment, and urine specific gravity >1.018. Consider volume depletion, cirrhosis (including HRS), heart failure, sepsis, or impaired renal autoregulation.
Renal parenchymal	
Atheroembolic and thromboembolic disease	Atheroembolic disease characterized by urinary eosinophils; associated with recent manipulation of the aorta. May be associated with livedo reticularis or blue toe syndrome. Atrial fibrillation or recent myocardial infarction may be associated with thromboembolic disease.
Intrarenal vascular disease	Characterized by hematuria with erythrocyte or granular casts, mild proteinuria, and leukocytes. Consider vasculitis (ie, PAN), malignant hypertension, or TTP-HUS.
Acute glomerulonephritis	Characterized by hematuria with erythrocyte casts, mild or nephritic-range proteinuria, and FENa >1%. Consider SLE, IgA nephropathy, postinfectious glomerulonephritis, anti-GBM antibody disease, or Wegener granulomatosis.
Acute tubular necrosis	Characterized by muddy brown casts, tubular epithelial cell casts, and FENa >1%. Consider radiocontrast agents, drugs (aminoglycosides, amphotericin B), and episodes of hypotension. Aside from prerenal AKI, ATN is the most common cause of AKI in the hospital setting.
Acute interstitial nephritis	Characterized by pyuria, leukocyte casts, urine eosinophils, and nephritic-range proteinuria (in the case of drug- or NSAID-induced minimal change disease). Associated with medication use (methicillin or NSAIDs but can include nearly any drug) and rash. Discontinue any unnecessary or suspicious medications.
Intrarenal tubular obstruction	Characterized by coarse tubular casts (including muddy brown granular casts), crystalluria, and urinary light chains. Consider rhabdomyolysis, TLS, or multiple myeloma.
Renal vein obstruction	Characterized by hematuria and nephritic-range proteinuria. Consider nephrotic syndrome (membranous nephropathy), clotting disorder, malignancy, trauma, or compression.
Postrenal (Urinary tract obstruction)	Urinalysis usually is normal but depending on etiology may show microscopic or macroscopic hematuria, bacteriuria, pyuria, and crystals. Consider nephrolithiasis, malignancy, granuloma, pregnancy, hematoma, radiation, neurogenic bladder, benign prostatic hypertrophy, or retroperitoneal fibrosis.

AKI = acute kidney injury; ATN = acute tubular necrosis; BUN = blood urea nitrogen; FENa = fractional excretion of sodium; GBM = glomerular basement membrane; HRS = hepatorenal syndrome; NSAID = nonsteroidal anti-inflammatory drug; PAN = polyarteritis nodosa; SLE = systemic lupus erythematosus; TLS = tumor lysis syndrome; TTP-HUS = thrombotic thrombocytopenic purpura–hemolytic uremic syndrome.

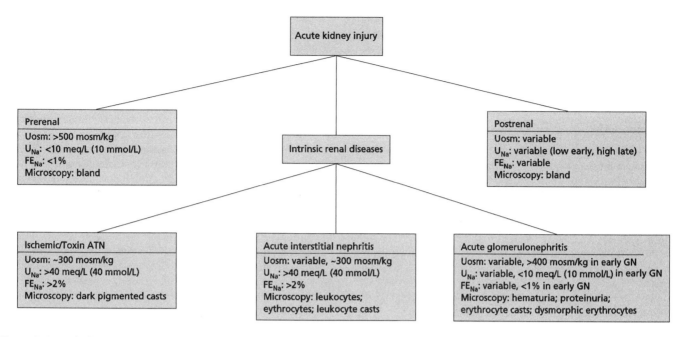

Figure 2. Urine findings associated with acute kidney injury. ATN = acute tubular necrosis; FE$_{Na}$ = fractional excretion of sodium; GN = glomeru-lonephritis; U$_{Na}$ = urine sodium; Uosm = urine osmolality.

renal parenchymal disease (Table 2). Selected urine characteristics of AKI are presented in Figure 2.

Prerenal

Important historical clues to prerenal causes of AKI include a history of volume loss (eg, vomiting, diarrhea), the presence of orthostatic symptoms, decreased urine volume, or urine that appears more concentrated. After abdominal surgery, patients may sequester large amounts of fluid within tissues and have reduced effective circulating volume. Look for a history of heart failure, liver disease, and the nephrotic syndrome, which are other conditions associated with decreased effective circulating volume. For hospitalized patients, review blood pressure records for evidence of prolonged hypotension, particularly in surgical patients. Obtain a complete list of all medications that can alter effective circulating volume, such as NSAIDs, ACE inhibitors, ARBs, diuretics, and vasodilators. An extreme form of prerenal failure is hepatorenal syndrome. This syndrome is seen in patients with acute liver failure or decompensated liver disease. Renal vasoconstriction is severe and cannot be reversed by intravascular volume repletion; the prognosis of this condition is quite poor.

On physical examination, look for signs of hypovolemia, such as tachycardia, a postural pulse rate increase of >30/min, dry axillae, flat neck veins, and dry oral mucosa. Decreased renal perfusion caused by decreased effective circulating volume is associated with heart failure; look for elevated jugular venous pressure, an S$_3$ gallop, and pulmonary crackles on lung examination. Spider telangiectasia, jaundice, and ascites support a diagnosis of liver disease. Increases in intraabdominal pressure from massive ascites or edematous bowel can lead to abdominal compartment syndrome, which limits both renal arterial perfusion and renal venous outflow. A distended, tense abdomen supports a diagnosis of abdominal compartment syndrome, which can be confirmed by placing a pressure transducer into the bladder.

Postrenal

Postrenal causes of AKI are most common in elderly men with prostatic hypertrophy, children with a history of congenital urinary tract abnormalities, and patients with a history of pelvic malignancy. Other causes include renal stone disease (particularly in patients with a solitary kidney), urinary tract malignancies, papillary necrosis or sloughing, retroperitoneal fibrosis, and neuropathic conditions affecting bladder emptying (eg, diabetic neuropathy). Medications with sympathomimetic and anticholinergic properties may contribute to urinary retention but are unlikely to be the sole cause of postrenal AKI. Historical clues may include difficulty passing urine, lower abdominal or flank pain, dysuria, or hematuria. Prostatic enlargement, suprapubic fullness, or an abdominal or pelvic mass suggests urinary obstruction. A so-called postobstructive diuresis may occur after relief of urinary tract obstruction, but this is more often a feature of chronic urinary retention.

Renal Parenchymal

Renal parenchymal disease is divided into processes that affect the tubules (acute tubular necrosis [ATN]), the interstitium (interstitial nephritis), the glomeruli (glomerulonephritis), or the vasculature (vasculitis, microangiopathic hemolytic anemia). The most common cause of ATN is sepsis. Also look for possible renal toxins (eg, aminoglycosides, amphotericin B, cisplatin, IV contrast), and review all medications, including over-the-counter preparations, herbal remedies, and illicit drugs, for potential renal toxicities. Patients who are using cocaine or who are found comatose from drug ingestion may develop rhabdomyolysis, which results in release of myoglobin, a renal tubular toxin.

Renal tubular obstruction and AKI can occur in patients with lymphoma or leukemia who develop tumor lysis after chemotherapy; these patients will have significantly elevated serum and urine uric acid concentrations. In patients with multiple myeloma, immunoglobulin light chains can precipitate within the renal tubules. The antiviral drugs acyclovir and indinavir and the sulfonamide antibiotics also can precipitate within the renal tubules and cause obstruction.

Inquire about recent invasive vascular procedures that may result in atheroembolic kidney disease (eg, angiography, aortic stenting, aneurysm repair). Clues to vasculitis include palpable purpura (Plate

30), petechiae, joint swelling, and skin rashes. The presence of a fine, reticular (netlike) red to purple rash (livedo reticularis) or blue toes ("blue toe syndrome") suggests atheroembolic disease (Plate 53). Underlying collagen vascular disease or chronic infection (eg, hepatitis B) may be associated with glomerular disease; ask about fever, joint pain, fatigue, rashes, and jaundice.

Diagnostic Studies

Examine the urine for casts, cells, and crystals (Table 3). Muddy brown granular casts (Plate 51) are consistent with renal injury secondary to tubular necrosis; erythrocyte casts (Plate 49) and proteinuria of >3 g/day are pathognomonic for glomerular disease; and leukocytes, leukocyte casts, and (rarely) eosinophils are associated with acute interstitial nephritis (Plate 50). Prerenal disease is associated with a normal urinalysis. Blood on urine dipstick analysis without erythrocytes detected on microscopic examination suggests the presence of myoglobin and supports a diagnosis of rhabdomyolysis; obtain a serum creatine phosphokinase concentration to confirm the diagnosis.

In all patients with AKI, routinely measure blood urea nitrogen (BUN) and serum electrolyte, creatinine, calcium, phosphorous, uric acid, glucose, and albumin concentrations and obtain a complete blood count with differential. Routinely measure urine sodium and creatinine concentrations and urine osmolality. The fractional excretion of sodium (FENa) indicates the percentage of filtered sodium that is excreted in the urine and is an indicator of sodium avidity of the kidney; it is useful in differentiating low perfusion states from other causes of AKI. It is most useful in patients who are oliguric. Recent use of diuretics will increase urinary sodium, in which case the fractional excretion of urea may be helpful (<35% suggestive of prerenal disease).

Low urine flow is associated with reabsorption of urea along the nephron, and patients with prerenal failure frequently have a BUN–creatinine ratio >20:1. Volume depletion leads to activation of hormonal systems aimed at conserving salt and water and is characterized by high urine osmolality and low urine sodium concentration (<10 meq/L [10 mmol/L]), with a fractional excretion of sodium of <1%. Acute glomerular disease can produce the same findings but is also associated with proteinuria, microscopic hematuria, and erythrocyte casts in the urine. If the history and physical examination suggest an underlying thrombotic or vasculitic process or the urinalysis shows erythrocytes, erythrocyte casts, or proteinuria suggesting glomerular disease, obtain assays for antinuclear antibodies, cytoplasmic and perinuclear antineutrophil cytoplasmic antibodies, anti–glomerular basement membrane antibody, hepatitis B surface antigen, hepatitis C antibodies, complement levels, and anti–double-stranded DNA antibodies. Look for schistocytes and decreased platelets on peripheral smear, which imply a thrombotic microangiopathy, such as hemolytic uremic syndrome or thrombotic throm-

Table 3. Laboratory and Other Studies for Acute Kidney Injury

Test	Notes
Urinalysis with microscopic examination	Significant proteinuria suggests glomerular disease. Dipstick hematuria without erythrocytes suggests rhabdomyolysis. Dysmorphic erythrocytes suggest acute glomerulonephritis.
BUN–creatinine ratio	BUN–creatinine ratio >20:1 suggests prerenal azotemia.
Fractional excretion of sodium (FENa)[a]	FENa >1 suggests ATN. FENa ≤1 suggests prerenal azotemia (when oliguria is present) and AGN.
Spot urine sodium	Urine sodium <10 meq/L (10 mmol/L) suggests prerenal azotemia and AGN
Serum phosphorus	Severe hyperphosphatemia suggests acute rhabdomyolysis or TLS.
Serum calcium	Hypercalcemia can cause AKI via several mechanisms.
Serum uric acid	Serum uric acid >15 mg/dL (0.9 mmol/L) suggests rhabdomyolysis or TLS.
Antinuclear antibody (ANA)	Indicated in acute nephritis or systemic disease (SLE).
Antineutrophil cytoplasmic antibody (ANCA)	c-ANCA (cytoplasmic ANCA) is more specific for Wegener granulomatosis. p-ANCA (perinuclear ANCA) is specific for microscopic polyangiitis or pauci-immune glomerulonephritis.
Anti-glomerular basement membrane antibody	Positive in 90% of patients with Goodpasture syndrome.
Complete blood count	Anemia can occur with severe AKI; decreased platelets suggest HUS-TTP.
Complement (C3) level	C3 level is decreased in 60%-70% of patients with type I or type II MPGN.
Cryoglobulins	Especially indicated for AKI in the setting of hepatitis C.
Anti-double-stranded DNA antibody	Sensitivity of 75% for SLE.
Hepatitis serology	AGN, hepatorenal syndrome.
Kidney biopsy	Biopsy is indicated when there is evidence of intrinsic renal disease; results will affect management or clarify diagnosis.
Serum and urine protein electrophoresis	Obtain in the setting of AKI, anemia, or hypercalcemia, especially in patients age >60 y or when serum anion gap is low to diagnose multiple myeloma.
Urine eosinophils	Suggest acute interstitial nephritis or atheroembolic disease.
Kidney ultrasonography	Sensitivity of 93%-98% for acute obstruction.

[a]Fractional excretion of sodium (FENa) = 100 x (Urine concentration of sodium/Plasma concentration of sodium) ÷ (Urine concentration of creatinine/Plasma concentration of creatinine).

AGN = acute glomerulonephritis; AKI = acute kidney injury; ATN = acute tubular necrosis; FENa = fractional excretion of sodium; MPGN = mesangioproliferative glomerulonephritis; SLE = systemic lupus erythematosus; TLS = tumor lysis syndrome; TTP-HUS = thrombotic thrombocytopenic purpura-hemolytic uremic syndrome.

bocytopenia purpura. If present, confirm hemolysis with serum lactate dehydrogenase and haptoglobin concentrations.

The first imaging test of choice is renal ultrasonography, which can show hydronephrosis from obstruction and demonstrate increased echogenicity or loss of size associated with CKD. A renal biopsy will diagnose acute glomerulonephritis and should be performed in patients with normal-appearing kidneys on renal imaging who do not improve with conservative therapy.

Therapy

In patients with prerenal and postrenal causes of AKI, therapy is aimed at increasing renal perfusion and relieving obstruction. Treat volume depletion with normal saline; if severe anemia is present, transfuse packed red blood cells. If the serum albumin level is extremely low or if a patient has portal hypertension and ascites, albumin may be beneficial as a volume expander in select patients. Discontinue all drugs that decrease renal perfusion (eg, NSAIDs) and stop all diuretics in volume-depleted patients. Reduce the dose of ACE inhibitors and ARBs or discontinue these mediations if the serum creatinine level increases >50%. If there is evidence of urinary obstruction, place a urinary catheter to relieve bladder outlet obstruction; if the obstruction is above the bladder, either retrograde or antegrade nephrostomy will be necessary.

For patients with suspected renal parenchymal disease, discontinue all nephrotoxins (eg, aminoglycosides, cisplatin, amphotericin B) unless absolutely necessary. In patients with rhabdomyolysis, IV normal saline may prevent renal toxicity from myoglobin. Whenever possible, identify and specifically treat the underlying cause of AKI. This may include treating collagen vascular diseases, vasculitides, or pulmonary–renal syndromes. Without significant volume overload, diuretics do not alter the outcome in ATN and are not recommended. Short of recovery of hepatic function, the treatment of the hepatorenal syndrome is challenging. In addition to albumin administration, measures to increase mean arterial pressure, including norepinephrine or midodrine plus octreotide, may improve renal function in these patients.

Most complications associated with AKI can be managed with dialysis; however, in patients who do not yet require dialysis or when dialysis is not promptly available, drug therapy is required. The treatment of metabolic acidosis is controversial, but many experts use sodium bicarbonate when the pH is <7.0. Immediately treat hyperkalemia with electrocardiographic changes (ie, peaking of T waves, lengthening of the PR and QRS intervals) with IV calcium gluconate to stabilize the myocardium. Shift potassium from the extracellular to the intracellular space with IV regular insulin and glucose (monitor for possible hypoglycemia); inhaled nebulized albuterol may be added if necessary. In patients with underlying metabolic acidosis, IV administration of sodium bicarbonate will also shift potassium into cells. These short-term measures must be followed by removal of potassium from the body. If the patient has normal intravascular volume and is making urine, administration of a loop diuretic will help with potassium excretion; otherwise, consider a cation-exchange resin (sodium polystyrene sulfonate in sorbitol) by mouth. Exchange resins are not immediately effective, may be no more effective than laxatives, and have been associated with intestinal necrosis (particularly in postoperative patients and those with ileus or obstruction). Initiate emergency hemodialysis if these measures are not successful in reducing the serum potassium level. In patients who develop hyperphosphatemia, begin phosphate binders, such as calcium carbonate, calcium acetate, aluminum hydroxide, lanthanum carbonate, or sevelamer hydrochloride.

Avoid overly aggressive treatment of hypertension. In patients with extremely elevated blood pressure, use IV nitroglycerin, labetalol, fenoldopam, nicardipine, or clevidipine to lower the mean arterial blood pressure by 10% to 15%. If there is evidence of volume overload, use loop diuretics. Avoid the use of ACE inhibitors or ARBs. When initiating or switching to oral medications for blood pressure control, use short-acting agents to avoid overtreatment and potential hypotension.

Adjust the dose of all medications that are excreted by the kidney. In patients with a rising serum creatinine level, assume a GFR <10 mL/min; GFR cannot be measured in non–steady-state conditions using any formulas. Confirm correct drug dosages by measuring drug levels if possible. Avoid drugs that have no proven benefit for the prevention or treatment of AKI, including loop diuretics (unless clinically volume overloaded), mannitol, and low-dose dopamine.

Begin renal replacement therapy (dialysis) in all patients with uremic signs or symptoms (nausea, vomiting, altered mental status, seizures, pericarditis) as well as patients who have hyperkalemia, metabolic acidosis, or volume overload that cannot be easily managed with medication. In patients who are critically ill and oliguric as well as nonoliguric patients whose serum creatinine level continues to rise without a readily reversible cause, begin renal replacement therapy before symptoms or laboratory findings make dialysis mandatory.

Bibliography

Abuelo JG. Normotensive ischemic acute renal failure. N Engl J Med. 2007;357:797-805. [PMID: 17715412]

Harel Z, Harel S, Shah PS, et al. Gastrointestinal adverse events with sodium polystyrene sulfonate (Kayexalate) use: a systematic review. Am J Med. 2013;126:e9-e24. [PMID 23321430]

McGee S, Abernethy WB 3rd, Simel DL. The rational clinical examination. Is this patient hypovolemic? JAMA. 1999;281:1022-9. [PMID 10086438]

Chapter 71

Chronic Kidney Disease

Matthew J Diamond, DO

Chronic kidney disease (CKD) is a worldwide epidemic and is associated with significant morbidity and increased utilization of health care resources. CKD is defined as the presence of decreased kidney function (glomerular filtration rate [GFR] <60 mL/min/1.73 m^2) or evidence of kidney damage that persists ≥3 months. Irrespective of the cause of CKD, several comorbidities may develop, including accelerated cardiovascular disease, anemia, disordered bone mineral metabolism, metabolic acidosis, malnutrition, and electrolyte disturbances. In the United States, the incident of CKD in the general population is estimated to be about 14%, and it affects an estimated 35% of people older than 60 years of age.

Diabetes mellitus, hypertension, and glomerular diseases account for most cases of CKD in the United States. In diabetes, hyperglycemia leads to pathologic changes in the kidney that usually follow a characteristic clinical course. Kidney disease manifests initially as moderately increased albuminuria (previously termed microalbuminuria), then as clinical proteinuria, and ultimately as loss of kidney function. Hypertensive nephropathy is characterized by long-standing hypertension, left ventricular hypertrophy, minimal proteinuria, and progressive kidney failure. Glomerular diseases are a heterogeneous group of disorders with a variable clinical course; the disorders are generically divided into the nephritic syndrome and the nephrotic syndrome (see Chapter 66). Recognition and early diagnosis of glomerular disease are vital because many forms progress to end-stage kidney failure. CKD occurring after kidney transplantation may be caused by chronic rejection, drug toxicity, or recurrence of the original kidney disease.

Prevention

Prevention of CKD focuses on aggressive management of the underlying cause. Guidelines from the Joint National Committee 8 (JNC-8) recommend reduction of blood pressure to <140/90 mmHg to prevent CKD, and patients with diabetes should target a hemoglobin A$_{1c}$ (HbA$_{1c}$) level <7% to prevent the development or progression of diabetic nephropathy.

Screening

Although the benefit of screening the general population for CKD is unclear, it is important to screen individuals at high risk. This includes elderly adults, patients with diseases that cause CKD (eg, hypertension, diabetes, systemic lupus erythematosus), and ethnic populations with increased risk (eg, blacks, American Indians, Hispanics, Asians, Pacific Islanders). All patients at risk for CKD should have their blood pressure measured and urine screened for proteinuria and cellular components (see Chapter 66).

Screen patients with diabetes for moderately increased albuminuria (microalbuminuria) with an albumin–creatinine ratio using a spot urine sample (normal albumin–creatinine ratio is <30 mg/g). Screen patients with type 1 diabetes beginning 5 years after diagnosis, at puberty, and yearly thereafter. Screen patients with type 2 diabetes at the time of diagnosis, and yearly thereafter.

If kidney disease is discovered, measure the serum creatinine concentration and calculate the estimated GFR (eGFR) (see Chapter 66). The stage of CKD based upon the estimated eGFR (Table 1 and Table 2).

Diagnosis

A thorough history and physical examination are paramount in the diagnosis of CKD (Table 3). Ask about diabetes, hypertension, and high-risk behaviors predisposing to infectious diseases associated with CKD and proteinuria (eg, HIV infection, hepatitis B and C, syphilis). Ask about a family history of kidney disease (eg, polycys-

Table 1. Stages of Chronic Kidney Disease

Stage	Description	GFR (mL/min/1.73 m^2)	Action
1	Kidney damage with normal GFR	≥90	Treatment of comorbid conditions, interventions to slow disease progression and reduce risk factors for cardiovascular disease
2	Kidney damage with mildly decreased GFR	60-89	Estimation of disease progression
3a	Moderately decreased GFR	45-59	Evaluation and treatment of disease complications (anemia, renal osteodystrophy)
3b	Moderately decreased GFR	30-44	Evaluation and treatment of disease complications (anemia, renal osteodystrophy)
4	Severely decreased GFR	15-29	Preparation for kidney replacement therapy (dialysis, transplantation)
5	Kidney failure	<15 (or dialysis)	Kidney replacement therapy if uremia is present

GFR = glomerular filtration rate.

Table 2. Proteinuria with Chronic Kidney Disease

Category	Albumin Excretion Rate (mg/24 h)	Albumin-to-Creatinine Ratio (mg/g)	Description	Likelihood of Early CKD Progression	Action
A1	<30	<30	Normal to mildly increased	Low with GFR >45; moderate with GFR <45	Control of proteinuria
A2	30–300	30–300	Moderately increased	Moderate with GFR >45; high with GFR <45	Optimization of RAAS blockade, HTN control, glycemic control
A3	>300	>300	Severely increased	High with GFR <45	Optimization of RAAS blockade, HTN control, glycemic control

GFR values expressed as mL/min/1.73 m². CKD = chronic kidney disease; HTN = hypertension; RAAS = renin-angiotensin-aldosterone axis

Table 3. Medical History and Historical Features Associated with Chronic Kidney Disease

Mechanism	Important Historical Features
Causing Direct Kidney Damage	
Diabetes mellitus	Duration
Hypertension	Duration
Glomerulonephritis	Autoimmune disease history
Multiple myeloma	History of treatment
AKI episodes	Episodes of kidney failure; dialysis
Chronic viral infections	History of hepatitis B, hepatitis C, or HIV infection
Kidney Damage from Treatment	
Cancer	History of chemotherapy use
Chronic pain	Pain medications and duration used
Infections	Antibiotics used
Genitourinary Abnormalities	
Kidney stones	Flank pain; hematuria
Kidney cancer	Kidney surgery or resection
Obstruction	Voiding issues; prostate issues; endometrial or pelvic cancers
Ureteral reflux	Urine infections; kidney infections
Exposures	
Contrast	Repeat imaging studies or angiography
Heavy metals	Exposure history
Herbal supplements	Nonprescription or OTC drug use
Increased Predisposition	
Patient demographics	Older age (>70 years); obesity (BMI >30)
Family history	Family history of dialysis, proteinuria, kidney failure, or genetic kidney diseases (eg, polycystic kidney disease)
Prior AKI even if baseline serum creatinine level is normal	Episodes of kidney failure; dialysis; prolonged hospitalizations; sepsis
Kidney transplant	Immunosuppressive drug use; episodes of rejection
Liver disease	Hepatitis; alcohol use

AKI = acute kidney injury; BMI = body mass index; CKD = chronic kidney disease; OTC = over the counter.

tic kidney disease, Alport syndrome). Inquire about symptoms of urinary obstruction and urinary tract infection. Obtain a detailed medication history because many medications may contribute to the development of CKD, and many require dose adjustment based on renal function. Specifically ask about nonsteroidal anti-inflammatory drugs (NSAIDs), acetaminophen, and herbal preparations. Ask about symptoms of fluid retention, such as leg swelling, orthopnea, or frequent nocturia. When eGFR declines to <20 mL/min/1.73 m², evaluate for symptoms of uremia, such as anorexia, nausea, vomiting, weight loss, dysgeusia, or itching.

A thorough physical examination may identify important clinical consequences and comorbidities. Look for signs of prolonged hypertension or volume overload, such as a cardiac gallop or lower extremity edema. The funduscopic examination is important for the detection of hypertensive or diabetic retinopathy. Check for signs of uremia, such as asterixis, or a pericardial friction rub.

A diagnostic algorithm for evaluation of CKD is shown in Figure 1. A kidney ultrasound is usually obtained to assess for any structural abnormalities. A urinalysis with microscopy (to evaluate for erythrocytes, leukocytes, and casts) and measurement of urine protein (protein–creatinine ratio) is critical in determining the cause and nature of the CKD. Other studies, including a complete blood count; serum electrolytes; a fasting lipid profile; and in patients with stage 3 or higher CKD, serum albumin and intact parathyroid hormone levels (Table 4), are indicated for CKD management. Use the eGFR to stage CKD and then classify CKD as diabetic, nondiabetic, or transplant-related kidney disease (Table 5). Patients in whom glomerular

disease is suspected or in whom the diagnosis is uncertain may require a renal biopsy.

Therapy

Patient lifestyle and dietary modification is an important step in the treatment of CKD (Table 6). Counsel patients about the importance of smoking cessation, regular exercise, and maintaining ideal body weight. Many patients with CKD have difficulty excreting sodium and potassium, and phosphorous balance can become compromised in later stages of their kidney disease. Many over-the-counter medicines and therapies are not medically appropriate for patients with CKD; instruct patients to avoid laxatives containing magnesium or phosphorus, NSAIDs, and cyclooxygenase-2 (COX-2) inhibitors.

Tight hypertension control is critical in preventing the early progression of CKD, and to decrease cardiovascular risk. The JNC-8 guidelines recommend a target blood pressure of <140/90 mmHg in

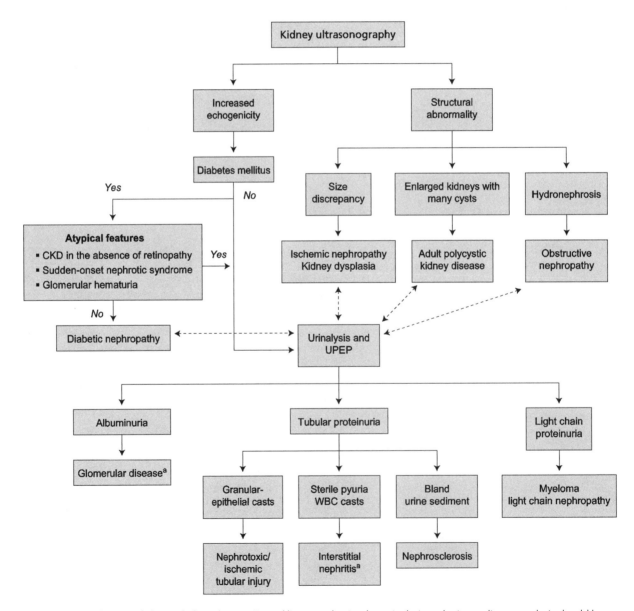

Figure 1. Diagnostic evaluation of chronic kidney disease. Dotted lines emphasize that urinalysis and urine sediment analysis should be performed in all patients. [a]Consider kidney biopsy. CKD = chronic kidney disease; UPEP = urine protein electrophoresis; WBC = white blood cell.

Table 4. Laboratory and Other Studies for Chronic Kidney Disease

Test	Notes
Spot urine protein-creatinine ratio	The preferred quantitative measure for diagnosing proteinuria; 24-h urine collections are inaccurate and not recommended. Urine dipsticks can be used to screen patients who do not have diabetes, but positive results should be followed with a quantitative measurement. Normal ratio is <150 mg/g. First morning urine specimens are preferred, but random specimens are acceptable. Patients with two or more positive quantitative test results 1–2 wk apart are diagnosed with persistent proteinuria and must undergo further evaluation and management.
Spot urine albumin-creatinine ratio	Normal ratio is <30 mg/g; 30–300 mg/g is defined as moderately increased albuminuria (microalbuminuria). In adults, albuminuria is a more sensitive marker than total protein for CKD caused by diabetes, hypertension, or glomerular disease.
Urinalysis	Hematuria, proteinuria, casts, and leukocytes are some of the abnormalities seen in CKD. The presence of dysmorphic erythrocytes suggests active glomerular disease.
Electrolytes	Hyperkalemia and metabolic acidosis often develop in CKD; hyponatremia may occur in edematous states associated with CKD.
Serum calcium	Hypocalcemia can be seen in patients with CKD. Corrected total calcium (mg/dL) = Total calcium (mg/dL) + 0.8 × (4 – Serum albumin [g/dL]).
Serum phosphorus	Phosphorus retention is common in CKD and leads to development of secondary hyperparathyroidism.
Serum intact PTH	PTH level is used to detect secondary hyperparathyroidism. Measure PTH in patients with stage 3 or higher CKD.
Albumin	Serum albumin level is a marker of nutritional status and an independent predictor of mortality in patients on dialysis.
Lipid profile	Patients with CKD are at high risk for cardiovascular disease.
Complete blood count	If the hemoglobin level is <11 g/dL (110 g/L), check erythrocyte indices, iron stores, reticulocyte count, and stool for occult blood to evaluate the need for iron replacement or an ESA.
Renal ultrasonography	Hydronephrosis may be found on ultrasonography in patients with urinary tract obstruction or vesicoureteral reflux. The presence of multiple discrete macroscopic cysts suggests autosomal dominant or recessive polycystic kidney disease. Increased cortical echogenicity and small kidney size are nonspecific indicators of CKD.
Other imaging studies	IVP, CT, MRI, or nuclear medicine scanning can be used for specific situations, such as stone disease, renal artery stenosis, or obstruction.

CKD = chronic kidney disease; CT = computed tomography; ESA = erythropoiesis-stimulating agent; IVP = intravenous pyelography; MRI = magnetic resonance imaging; PTH =parathyroid hormone.

Table 5. Classification of Chronic Kidney Disease

Disease	Notes
Diabetic kidney disease (see Chapter 13)	Diabetic kidney disease is the leading cause of CKD in the United States. Kidney disease in diabetes, particularly type 1 diabetes, usually follows a characteristic course, manifesting first as moderately increased albuminuria (microalbuminuria) followed by clinical proteinuria, hypertension, and declining GFR. Diabetic nephropathy often is accompanied by diabetic retinopathy, particularly in type 1 diabetes. In patients with type 2 diabetes, the presence of retinopathy strongly suggests coexisting diabetic nephropathy. Even in the absence of retinopathy, diabetic nephropathy is likely, but an evaluation for other causes of proteinuria is reasonable.
Glomerular disease	Patients may present with either nephritic or nephrotic syndrome. Nephritic syndrome is characterized by hematuria, variable proteinuria, and hypertension, often with other systemic manifestations. Common causes include postinfectious glomerulonephritis, IgA nephropathy, and membranoproliferative glomerulonephritis. Nephrotic syndrome is characterized by high-grade proteinuria (>3.5 g/24 h), hypoalbuminemia, and edema. Common causes include minimal change disease, focal glomerulosclerosis, membranous nephropathy, and amyloidosis. SLE commonly affects the kidneys and may cause nephritic or nephrotic syndrome. A kidney biopsy often is needed to make a specific diagnosis and to guide therapy.
Tubulointerstitial disease	Patients generally have a bland or relatively normal urinalysis but may have proteinuria, a concentrating defect, pyuria, casts, or radiologic abnormalities. Analgesic nephropathy, lead nephropathy, chronic obstruction, and reflux nephropathy are examples.
Vascular disease and vasculitis (see Chapter 106)	The clinical presentation depends on the type of blood vessels involved (small, medium, or large). Patients with small-vessel disease often have hematuria, proteinuria, and an associated systemic illness. Patients with vasculitis can present with rapidly progressive glomerulonephritis. Hypertension is an example of medium-vessel disease and is the second leading cause of CKD in the United States. Hypertensive disease generally is slowly progressive, leading to stage 5 CKD in a minority of patients. Blacks have more aggressive CKD caused by hypertension. Renal artery stenosis is an example of large-vessel disease.
Renal cystic disease	Patients can have normal findings on urinalysis. Diagnosis usually is made by imaging techniques and family history. Simple renal cysts are common, particularly in older persons. Autosomal dominant polycystic disease types I and II are the most common forms.
Transplant-related kidney disease	CKD in a renal transplant recipient may be due to chronic rejection, drug toxicity, or recurrence of native kidney disease. A careful history and serum drug levels and often a kidney biopsy are required for diagnosis.

CKD = chronic kidney disease; GFR = glomerular filtration rate; SLE = systemic lupus erythematosus.

Table 6. Lifestyle and Dietary Modifications in Chronic Kidney Disease

Lifestyle Modification	Smoking cessation
	Regular exercise: >30 minutes five times a week
	Limit alcohol consumption to <2 drinks/day for men and 1 drink for women
	Maintain a healthy body weight (BMI, 20-25)
Dietary Modification	Limit sodium intake to <2.4 g/day
	Limit potassium intake to <2 g/day in patients with hyperkalemia
	Limit phosphorous intake to <1 g/day when serum phosphorous is >4.6 mg/dL (1.49 mmo/L)
	Limit protein intake to <0.8 g/kg/day with stage 4 and 5 CKD

BMI = body mass index; CKD = chronic kidney disease.

all patients with CKD, irrespective of comorbidities. Other guidelines further delineate the blood pressure target by the presence of proteinuria or diabetes mellitus (<130/80 mmHg target).

Proteinuria is associated with a progressive decline in renal function and an increase in cardiovascular risk. Reduction in proteinuria is associated with slower progression of CKD. Agents that interfere with the renin–angiotensin–aldosterone axis (RAAS), specifically angiotensin-converting enzyme (ACE) inhibitors and angiotensin receptor blocking agents (ARBs), are of particular clinical benefit in patients with CKD because of their antihypertensive and antiproteinuric effects. They have been shown to slow the progression of CKD are considered to be renoprotective. Because of this, current guidelines recommend that ACE inhibitors or ARBs should be a part of regular hypertension control in patients with CKD, especially patients with diabetes and those with significant proteinuria. Additionally, CKD patients tend to have volume-sensitive hypertension; diuretic therapy, particularly loop diuretics, may be helpful in achieving appropriate hypertension targets.

Some guidelines also recommend that when used in patients with proteinuria that agents that interfere with the RAAS should be dosed to a goal of lowering the protein–creatinine ratio to <500 to 1000 mg/g. However, the use of dual blockade of the renin-angiotensin system (ie, ACE inhibitor plus ARB, ARB plus aliskiren, ACE inhibitor or ARB plus aldosterone antagonist) in patients with proteinuria is controversial and currently not recommended because of complications associated with this therapy. Nondihydropyridine calcium channel blockers can be used as second-line therapy to further lower blood pressure and reduce proteinuria.

In diabetic patients with CKD, hypertension control (<140/90 mmHg), preferably with an ACE inhibitor or ARB, and proteinuria control (<500-1000 mg/g) are the first goals of therapy. Afterwards, glycemic control becomes important with regard to CKD; maintain HbA_{1c} levels at <7% to slow progression of CKD.

Anemia is often present in patients with CKD and is multifactorial. As kidney disease progresses, erythropoietin production falls. Concomitant iron deficiency is common in patients with CKD and can be difficult to recognize because of the nature of the chronic inflammatory state of CKD. Serum ferritin is expected to be elevated in CKD patients and can give a false sense of adequate iron stores. A patient with CKD is considered to be iron deficient when the transferring saturation is <30% and serum ferritin <300 ng/mL (300 µg/L). Failure to meet one or both of these benchmarks should warrant evaluation to uncover potential sources of occult blood loss, namely via the alimentary tract. Because CKD-associated anemia of chronic disease is a diagnosis of exclusion, other forms of anemia should be ruled out (eg, hemolysis, vitamin deficiencies).

Treatment of anemia in patients with CKD involves correcting underlying causes (chronic infection, iron deficiency, vitamin deficiencies) and supplementation with erythropoiesis-stimulating agents (ESAs) (darbepoetin or recombinant erythropoietin) to maintain hemoglobin levels >10 g/dL (100 g/L). Iron deficiency is typically corrected with oral supplementation, but intravenous infusions may be necessary if the patient is refractory to oral therapy. Correction of hemoglobin to normal physiologic levels (>13 g/dL) is associated with an increased mortality rate and cardiovascular events and is not recommended. Furthermore, ESA supplementation is not without risk because it has been associated with an increased of stroke in patients with diabetes. ESAs may also allow progression of certain cancers in patients on therapy. Candidates for ESA therapy should be counseled about the specific indication for the therapy, goals of treatment, and potential adverse events.

Perturbation of bone mineral metabolism is a complex problem in CKD and leads to a myriad of bone and cardiovascular complications. Decreased kidney function leads to decreased phosphorous clearance and vitamin D activation. The latter results in secondary hyperparathyroidism caused by the resulting hypocalcemia. Secondary hyperparathyroidism may result in renal osteodystrophy, a mixture of multiple bone pathologies that includes osteitis fibrosa cystica, osteoporosis, osteomalacia, and adynamic bone disease. Secondary hyperparathyroidism also promotes vascular calcification, resulting in increased cardiovascular morbidity and mortality. The approach to treatment of mineral metabolism disease in CKD requires multiple medications aimed at lowering serum phosphorous, correcting vitamin D deficiency, and suppressing parathyroid hormone (Figure 2).

Other metabolic dysregulation occurs as kidney disease advances, namely non–anion gap metabolic acidosis or hyperkalemia. The kidneys handle the obligatory acid genesis that occurs as part of daily metabolism. Loss of functional nephrons results in the inability to properly buffer and excrete this acid load, resulting in non–anion gap metabolic acidosis. Metabolic acidosis commonly develops in advanced CKD (GFR <30 mL/min/1.73 m^2) and has become more important in the overall management of CKD over the past few years. Metabolic acidosis is linked to malnutrition, accelerates renal osteodystrophy, suppresses albumin synthesis, and causes a premature decline in overall renal function. Treating metabolic acidosis can slow the progression of CKD. Use oral sodium bicarbonate to maintain serum carbon dioxide levels within the range of 22 to 26 meq/L (22–26 mmol/L). Hyperkalemia may develop in advanced CKD and in certain forms of renal tubular acidosis. Restrict dietary potassium, ensure adequate hydration, and use loop diuretics as necessary. Severe hyperkalemia (>6.0 meq/L [6.0 mmol/L]) is associated with life-threatening cardiac dysrhythmias; patients with severe hyperkalemia require emergent hospitalization for medical management.

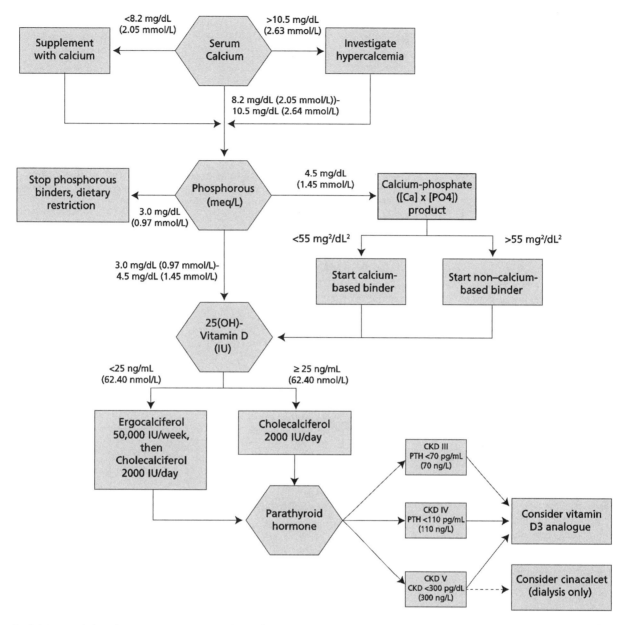

Figure 2. Calcium and phosphorous management in chronic kidney disease. CKD = chronic kidney disease; PTH = parathyroid hormone.

Follow-Up

Patients with CKD require close follow-up with laboratory measurements initially every 3 to 4 months and more frequently as CKD becomes more advanced. Consult a nephrologist for patients with CKD before eGFR decreases to <30 mL/min/1.73 m². Ensure medications are dosed appropriately for the eGFR. If administration of iodinated contrast is essential, give sodium bicarbonate or isotonic saline intravenously and consider using *N*-acetylcysteine before and after the procedure, closely monitoring fluid and electrolyte status to decrease the risk of contrast-induced nephropathy. Gadolinium, a contrast agent used with magnetic resonance imaging scanning, is contraindicated in patients when eGFR is <30 mL/min/1.73 m² because of an increased risk of nephrogenic systemic fibrosis (NSF). NSF causes thickening and hardening of the skin over the extremities and trunk but may also involve other organ systems and is associated with a high mortality rate. There is no treatment for NSF.

Patients with stage 5 CKD often become uremic and require renal replacement therapy (RRT). Options for RRT should be discussed when a patient reaches stage 4 CKD or 1 year before it is anticipated that the patient will reach stage 5 CKD. Options include outpatient hemodialysis, home hemodialysis, peritoneal dialysis, and renal transplantation. If hemodialysis is preferred, an arteriovenous fistula or graft should be placed well before initiation of RRT. RRT is indicated in patients with stage 5 CKD who have uremic signs or symptoms. For patients without uremic signs or symptoms, the optimal timing of RRT is unknown. Patients requiring RRT have high rates of cardiovascular events and are at increased risk for infectious complications. Discuss advanced directives and end-of-life issues. Evaluate for and treat depression when indicated.

Hemodialysis is performed at outpatient centers typically three sessions per week for approximately 4 hours per session. Hemodialysis is commonly associated with hypotension, nausea, vomiting, and chest pain; other symptoms during dialysis may include pruritus, muscle cramping, and restless legs. Providing hemodialysis in the home setting may be appropriate for selected patients. Peritoneal dialysis involves exchanging dialysis fluid within the abdominal cavity to remove toxins and reestablish fluid and electrolyte balance across the peritoneal membrane. Peritoneal dialysis is usually performed by patients at home, often nocturnally.

Transplantation is the treatment of choice for stage 5 CKD; however, donor organs are in short supply. Compared with hemodialysis, transplantation is associated with more favorable outcomes in all groups and allows for a more normal lifestyle. Refer patients early for transplantation evaluation to determine eligibility and to facilitate identification of potential living donors. Living donor kidneys afford better patient and graft survival. Furthermore, transplantation before or shortly after initiation of hemodialysis is associated with improved patient outcomes. Immunosuppression with both induction and maintenance therapy is needed to prevent rejection. Kidney transplant recipients are at increased risk for coronary vascular disease, infection, malignancy, recurrent kidney disease, graft loss, and bone disease associated with prolonged glucocorticoid use.

Bibliography

Abboud H, Henrich WL. Clinical practice. Stage IV chronic kidney disease. N Engl J Med. 2010;362:56-65. [PMID: 20054047]

Bhan I. Phosphate management in chronic kidney disease. Curr Opin Nephrol Hypertens. 2014;23:174-9. [PMID: 24445424]

James PA, Oparil S, Carter BL. 2014 evidence-based guideline for the management of high blood pressure in adults. Report from the Panel Members Appointed to the Eighth Joint National Committee (JNC8). JAMA. 2014;311:507-20. [PMID: 24352797]

Chapter 72

Nephrolithiasis

Scott Herrle, MD

Nephrolithiasis (kidney stones) is a common condition. It is estimated that up to 13% of men and 7% of women will have at least one symptomatic kidney stone during their lifetime. Furthermore, 50% of patients who experience a symptomatic calculus will have a second episode within 5 years, and 80% will do so within 20 years. Patients who have a family history of kidney stones have greater than a twofold higher risk of developing kidney stones compared with those lacking such a history.

Stone formation occurs when microscopic crystals aggregate together. Normally, proteins and other substances in urine inhibit this process; however, this balance can be easily disturbed. Low urine volume results in concentrated urine and favors stone formation. As such, individuals who spend time in hot climates are at an increased risk of developing kidney stones. Poor oral intake of fluids also increases the risk of kidney stone formation as do disorders associated with increased fluid losses (eg, ileostomy and short gut syndrome) leading to chronic volume contraction. Weight gain, obesity, diabetes mellitus, hypertension, and the metabolic syndrome are also risk factors for kidney stone formation. Additional risk factors for individual kidney stone types are discussed here.

Types of Kidney Stones

Approximately 80% of all kidney stones contain calcium, and of these calcium-containing kidney stones, 80% are composed mostly of calcium oxalate (Plate 54); the rest are composed of amorphous calcium phosphate. The most common metabolic abnormality seen in association with calcium oxalate stones is hypercalciuria. Hypercalciuria is most often idiopathic and frequently familial, although it can occur in the setting of hypercalcemia. Primary hyperparathyroidism and sarcoidosis both cause hypercalcemia. Whereas supplemental calcium and vitamin D also increase the risk of developing calcium oxalate stones, consumption of higher amounts of dietary calcium is associated with a lower risk. It is postulated that dietary calcium binds enteric oxalate, which prevents its absorption from the intestines and ultimately leads to less oxalate being excreted in the urine and a lower incidence of kidney stone formation.

Hyperoxaluria is associated with calcium oxalate stone formation and can be caused by intake of foods high in oxalate (eg, chocolate, tea, soy products, nuts, rhubarb, strawberries, dry beans, wheat bran, and spinach) and by consumption of excessive amounts of vitamin C. It can also be caused by gastrointestinal malabsorption, which occurs in inflammatory bowel disease and after bariatric surgery. In both of these conditions, an excess of enteric free fatty acids binds calcium, which allows oxalate to be absorbed and excreted into the urine. Primary hyperoxaluria, an autosomal recessive disorder, is an infrequent cause of hyperoxaluria.

Urine citrate reduces calcium stone formation by binding calcium, forming a water-soluble compound. Hypocitraturia due to increased citrate reabsorption in the proximal renal tubules can occur with the consumption of high protein diets and with type 1 (distal) renal tubular acidosis (RTA) (see Chapter 69).

Approximately 10% of kidney stones are composed of uric acid (Plate 55). The primary risk factor for developing uric acid stones is hyperuricosuria, which can occur with tumor lysis syndrome, gout, diabetes mellitus, the metabolic syndrome, and consumption of a high-protein diet.

Struvite stones account for fewer than 10% of all kidney stones and affect women more often than in men. They are composed of magnesium ammonium phosphate and calcium carbonate apatite (Plate 56). They form when a patient develops an upper urinary tract infection (UTI) with a urea-splitting organism such as *Klebsiella* or *Proteus* spp. These organisms produce ammonia, which raises urine pH and decreases the solubility of phosphorus, promoting aggregation of struvite crystals. Struvite stones usually do not cause any symptoms and are commonly discovered when the UTI that caused them becomes symptomatic. Struvite stones can grow rapidly over several weeks if not adequately treated and can eventually fill the entire renal pelvis, forming what is termed a staghorn calculus.

Cystine stones (Plate 57) account for 1% of all stones and are found in cystinuria, an autosomal recessive condition that occurs in one in 7,000 births.

Diagnosis

Clinical Presentation

Flank pain is the hallmark of nephrolithiasis and is caused by kidney stones that are lodged at the ureteropelvic junction. As the stone migrates down the ureter, the pain moves anteriorly into the abdomen and groin. When the stone is at the ureterovesical junction, the patient typically experiences urinary urgency and suprapubic discomfort. Infrequently, stones become lodged at the bladder neck and produce suprapubic discomfort and anuria. The pain associated with stones usually begins suddenly and is colicky (waxes and wanes). Passage of the stone is accompanied by sudden and dramatic pain relief. Nausea and vomiting are frequently present. The presence of fever should raise the suspicion for infection. Hematuria, either microscopic or gross, is usually, but not invariably, present. The physical examination is most useful for ruling out the possibility of other disorders. There are no specific physical examination findings seen with nephrolithiasis.

Imaging

Noncontrast computed tomography (CT) is the most frequently used method for diagnosing nephrolithiasis. It is both sensitive (95%-98%) and specific (95%) and can visualize all stone types. CT also allows for the diagnosis of other potential conditions or stone complications that could be causing the patient's symptoms, although it is associated with radiation exposure. Ultrasonography is also an option for diagnosis of nephrolithiasis. Although it may have somewhat lower sensitivity and specificity than CT, particularly for very small stones or those in the distal ureter, it does not involve radiation exposure. Ultrasonography is therefore the indicated diagnostic study for nephrolithiasis in pregnancy. However, it may be a reasonable initial study for other patients, with CT scanning reserved for those with a nondiagnostic or negative ultrasound study in the presence of a high clinical likelihood of kidney stones.

Other imaging modalities for diagnosing nephrolithiasis include plain radiography and intravenous pyelography (IVP). Plain radiography is limited to visualizing radiopaque stones and can miss stones that are <5 mm in size. Whereas calcium-containing stones are always radiopaque, cystine and struvite stones are only sometimes radiopaque. Pure uric acid stones are never radiopaque. IVP requires intravenous contrast, which, combined with its lower sensitivity and specificity, makes it less preferable than other forms of imaging. Magnetic resonance imaging is not a recommended modality for visualizing stones.

Biochemical Testing

In patients with suspected symptomatic nephrolithiasis, a urinalysis, complete blood count, and serum chemistries (electrolytes, blood urea nitrogen, creatinine, calcium, phosphorus and uric acid) should be obtained. The urinalysis evaluates for the presence of concomitant infection. Although usually present, the absence of hematuria does not preclude the diagnosis of nephrolithiasis. Serum chemistries can help detect the presence of renal dysfunction, which may indicate urinary tract obstruction in addition to alterations in intravascular volume. Whereas hypercalcemia suggests primary hyperparathyroidism or sarcoidosis, a low serum bicarbonate concentration with a urine pH >6.0 suggests RTA. A high urine pH in the setting of pyuria raises the possibility of struvite stones. Hypophosphatemia can be seen in patients with calcium stones who have a renal loss of phosphorus.

Determination of stone composition using either infrared spectroscopy or X-ray crystallography should be done in all patients at the time of initial diagnosis, if possible, as it is inexpensive and helps to guide future preventive therapy. **Except for stone composition, additional studies for nephrolithiasis (such as 24-hour urine collections) are not done routinely and should be reserved for patients with recurrent stones in which they may be used to prescribe specific pharmacologic and dietary interventions.**

Management

Acute Management

Most patients with symptomatic kidney stones can be managed in the outpatient setting. Table 1 lists indications for hospitalization.

All patients should be given a urine strainer to attempt to capture the stone or any fragments for analysis. Achieving adequate pain control is a key component to successfully managing nephrolithiasis. Both NSAIDs and opioids used either alone or in combination are effective for treating the pain associated with nephrolithiasis,

Table 1. Indications for Hospitalization in Patients with Nephrolithiasis
Kidney stone >5 mm in diameter if parenteral therapy is required to manage pain
Kidney stones of any size if pain or nausea and vomiting cannot be managed in the outpatient setting
Obstructed and infected urinary tract
Bilateral obstruction or obstruction in a solitary kidney if decreased renal function is present

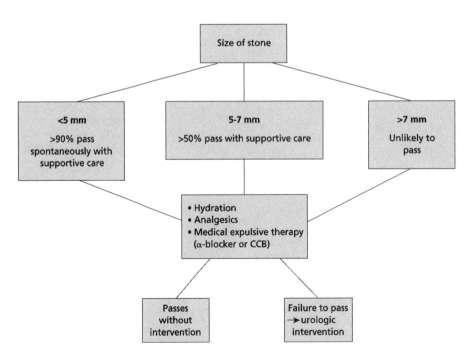

Figure 1. Acute management of uncomplicated symptomatic kidney stones. CCB = calcium channel blocker.

Table 2. Pharmacotherapy for Kidney Stone Prevention

Agent	Type of Stone Treated	Mechanism of Action	Comments
Hydrochlorothiazide	Calcium	Promotes proximal tubular calcium reabsorption. May inhibit bone resorption.	Use in patients with hypercalciuria. Sodium restriction maximizes effectiveness. Most patients require concomitant treatment with potassium citrate because of hypokalemia or decreased citrate excretion.
Potassium citrate	Calcium Uric acid Cystine	Citrate forms soluble complexes with calcium. Citrate increases urine pH after metabolism to bicarbonate by the liver, which dissolves uric acid crystals and makes cystine soluble.	May cause hyperkalemia, heartburn, and nausea.
Allopurinol	Uric acid	Xanthine oxidase inhibitor that reduces urinary uric acid excretion.	Adjunct to potassium citrate for treating uric acid stones because urinary alkalinization appears to be more important.

although nonsteroidal anti-inflammatory drugs (NSAIDs) are preferred because of their association with fewer side effects and for their purported role in helping stone passage by reducing ureteral tone and edema. NSAIDs should be avoided in patients with renal insufficiency and in cases of severe volume depletion.

The passage of distal ureteral stones <10 mm in diameter can be aided by using an α1-adrenergic antagonist (eg, tamsulosin) that functions as a spasmolytic to expulse ureteral stones. Alternatively, a calcium channel blocker (eg, nifedipine) that causes ureteral dilation can be used in combination with a glucocorticoid such as methylprednisolone. Glucocorticoids function by reducing ureteral edema. Intravenous fluids should be reserved for patients with evidence of intravascular volume depletion and should not be given routinely in an attempt to promote stone passage.

More than 90% of stones <5 mm in diameter will pass spontaneously, but only 50% of stones 5 to 7 mm in size will do so (Figure 1). A urologic consultation should be made when the likelihood of spontaneous stone passage is low (eg, with stones >7 mm in diameter), when medical management has failed to result in stone passage, or when nephrolithiasis is complicated by either infection or renal insufficiency. An obstructed and infected urinary tract is an absolute indication for emergent intervention as is the presence of renal insufficiency caused by obstruction. Struvite stones require both an appropriate antibiotic regimen and stone extraction.

Chronic Management

Patients with a history of nephrolithiasis should be encouraged to drink at least 2 to 2.5 L/day (64 to 72 oz) of fluids in an attempt to achieve a urine volume of approximately 2 L/day. Patients who are physically active or who work in hot environments, those who have conditions associated with stone formation, and those who have increased intestinal losses of fluid should consume even greater amounts.

All patients with calcium oxalate stones should be encouraged to consume 1200 mg/day of dietary calcium. Restriction of dietary sodium (<50 meq/L (50 mmol/L)/day) reduces urine calcium excretion, and restriction of dietary oxalate (<198 mg (2.2 mmol)/day) reduces urine oxalate excretion. Restriction of dietary protein (<93 g/day) helps to increase urine citrate concentration.

Although diet alone is unlikely to prevent uric acid stones, patients should be advised to limit their intake of animal protein. This leads to a reduction in intake of purines, a precursor of uric acid, and reduces uricosuria, which raises urine pH and reduces the amount of alkali needed to prevent stone formation. Weight is also inversely associated with urine pH and weight loss (other than by consumption of a high-protein diet) may decrease uric acid stone formation. Patients with cystine stones should limit their intake of both animal protein and sodium to increase urine pH and decrease urine cystine excretion.

Pharmacotherapy also plays an important role in stone prevention in patients with multiple episodes (Table 2).

Bibliography

Fink HA, Wilt TJ, Eidman KE, et al. Medical management to prevent recurrent nephrolithiasis in adults: A systematic review for an American College of Physicians Clinical Guideline. Ann Intern Med. 2013;158:535-43. [PMID: 23546565]

Hollingsworth JM, Rogers MA, Kaufman SR, et al. Medical therapy to facilitate urinary stone passage: a meta-analysis. Lancet. 2006;368:1171-79. [PMID: 17011944]

Worcester EM, Coe FL. Clinical practice. Calcium kidney stones. N Engl J Med. 2010;363:954-63. [PMID: 20818905]

Section 8
Neurology

Associate Editor – Jonathan S. Appelbaum, MD, FACP

High Value Care Recommendations

- Most primary headaches are benign and do not require routine laboratory evaluation or imaging studies.

- No one triptan for migraine headache has been shown to be superior to others, so treatment decisions should be made on prior experience and cost.

- Nonsteroidal anti-inflammatory drugs (NSAIDs), aspirin, and hormone replacement therapy have not been shown to prevent cognitive decline or dementia.

- Medications should be carefully reviewed at each visit to avoid unnecessary treatment that can cause delirium or exacerbate preexisting dementia.

- High-dose vitamin E, aspirin, and NSAIDs have not been found to slow the progression of symptoms in Alzheimer disease and should not be recommended.

- Brain imaging is usually unhelpful in the diagnosis of delirium unless there is a history of a fall or headache or evidence of focal neurologic impairment.

- Electromyography and nerve conduction studies may not be necessary when the history and examination point to a clear etiology of peripheral neuropathy (eg, classic carpal tunnel syndrome) or when an underlying condition exits that can explain the clinical presentation (eg, long-standing diabetes in a patient with a mild distal symmetric polyneuropathy).

- The benefit of antiviral therapy in treating Bell palsy has not been established.

- Opioids should generally be avoided in treating peripheral neuropathy but may be considered for acute, severe pain or when other treatments have been unsuccessful.

- The diagnosis of essential tremor is based on clinical features and the elimination of secondary causes.

- Patients who have had only a single seizure may not require treatment.

Chapter 73

Headache

Jonathan S. Appelbaum, MD

Effective diagnosis and management of headache depend on 1) recognizing the typical features, patterns, and prevalence of various headache syndromes; 2) attending to "red flags" in the history or physical examination; 3) using diagnostic studies wisely; and 4) developing an evidence-based strategy for treatment (Figure 1).

Primary headaches (eg, migraine, tension-type headache, and cluster headache) are headaches with no other known cause, whereas secondary headaches reflect an underlying structural, systemic, or infectious disorder (eg, meningitis or giant cell arteritis). Features that suggest a secondary cause include the development of progressively frequent and severe headaches within 3 months; the presence of neurologic symptoms, focal or lateralizing neurologic signs, papilledema, or systemic symptoms (eg, fever, night sweats, and weight loss); headaches aggravated or relieved by postural changes; headaches precipitated by a Valsalva maneuver (cough or sneeze); history of sudden-onset severe headache ("thunderclap"); and headache onset after age 50 years. Most patients who are evaluated for headache have a primary headache disorder, and more than 90% of these patients have a type of migraine (Table 1).

Evaluation

Most primary headaches are benign and do not require routine laboratory evaluation or imaging studies. However, it is important to identify the pattern of headache and seek any "red flags" suggesting a serious underlying condition (Table 2). Red flags on physical examination include focal or lateralizing neurologic findings, papilledema, fever, neck stiffness, meningeal signs, tenderness to palpation or diminished pulse over the temporal artery, diastolic blood pressure >120 mm Hg, and decreased visual acuity. Any red flag symptom or neurologic abnormality on physical examination is an indication for neuroimaging. Because it is effective in detecting intracranial bleeding, noncontrast computed tomography of the head is the procedure of choice when acute, sudden, severe headache suggests subarachnoid hemorrhage. A lumbar puncture is indicated if there is concern for meningitis (fever and neck stiffness) or encephalitis (focal neurologic signs, confusion, and altered mental status) or if subarachnoid hemorrhage is suspected but imaging studies are normal. Lumbar puncture with measurement of the cerebrospinal fluid opening pressure is used to diagnose benign intracranial hypertension.

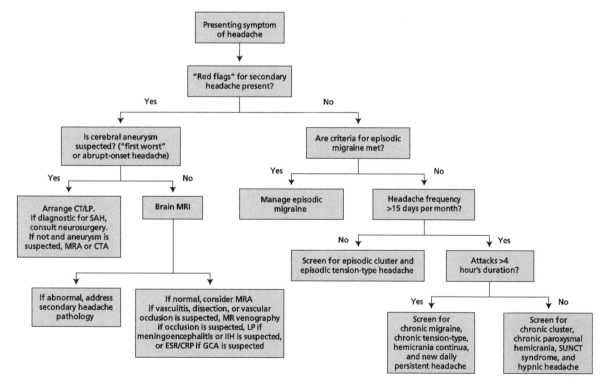

Figure 1. Algorithmic approach to a patient with headache. CRP = C-reactive protein level; CTA = CT angiography; ESR = erythrocyte sedimentation rate; GCA = temporal (giant cell) arteritis; IIH = idiopathic intracranial hypertension; LP = lumbar puncture; MRA = magnetic resonance angiography; MRI = magnetic resonance imaging; SAH = subarachnoid hemorrhage; SUNCT = short-lasting unilateral neuralgiform headache with conjunctival injection and tearing syndrome.

Table 1. Differential Diagnosis of Headache

Primary Headaches	Notes
Tension-type headache	One year prevalence of 40%. Lasts from 30 min to 7 d. Typically is bilateral, has a pressing or tightening quality, and is mild to moderate in intensity; not associated with nausea or vomiting. Headache is not aggravated by exertion and does not prohibit activity.
Migraine	One year prevalence of 13%. Lasts from 4 to 72 h. May be unilateral, pulsating in quality, and moderate to severe in intensity; associated with nausea or vomiting, photophobia, and phonophobia.
Trigeminal autonomic cephalalgias	Rare. Group of primary headache disorders characterized by excruciating unilateral headache that occurs in association with prominent cranial autonomic features (lacrimation, nasal congestion, rhinorrhea, and conjunctival injection). Disorders include cluster headache, paroxysmal hemicrania, and SUNCT syndrome.
Cluster headache	One form of trigeminal autonomic cephalalgia. One year prevalence of <1.0%. Sudden-onset headache lasting minutes to hours. Sometimes occurs several times per day (rare for migraine). Pattern repeats over a course of weeks, then disappears for months or years. Often associated with unilateral tearing and nasal congestion or rhinitis. Pain is severe, unilateral, and periorbital. More common in men but relatively uncommon overall.
Secondary Headaches	**Notes**
Frontal sinusitis	Usually worse when lying down. Associated with nasal congestion. Tenderness overlies affected sinus.
Medication-overuse headache	Chronic headache with few features of migraine. Tends to occur daily in patients who frequently use headache medications.
Subarachnoid hemorrhage (see Chapter 75)	Sudden, explosive onset of severe headache ("worst headache of my life"). Preceded by "sentinel" headache in 10%.
Meningitis or encephalitis (see Chapter 74)	Meningitis is associated with fever and meningeal signs. Encephalitis is associated with neurologic abnormalities, confusion, altered mental state, or change in level of consciousness.
Benign intracranial hypertension (pseudotumor cerebri)	Often abrupt onset. Associated with nausea, vomiting, dizziness, blurred vision, and papilledema. Neurologic examination is normal but may reveal sixth cranial nerve palsy. Headache aggravated by coughing, straining, or changing position. Cerebrospinal fluid pressure is elevated.
Intracranial neoplasm	Worse on awakening; generally progressive. Headache aggravated by coughing, straining, or changing position.
Temporal arteritis (see Chapter 106)	Occurs almost exclusively in patients aged >50 y. Associated with tenderness of the scalp and temporal artery, jaw claudication, and visual changes.

SUNCT = short-lasting unilateral neuralgiform headache attacks with conjunctival injection and tearing.

Table 2. Headache "Red Flag" Symptoms and Signs

First or worst headache

Abrupt onset or thunderclap

Progression or fundamental change in headache pattern

New abnormal findings on physical examination

Neurologic symptoms lasting more than 1 hour

New-onset headache in person aged >50 years

New-onset headache in patients with cancer, immunosuppression, or pregnancy

Headache associated with alteration in consciousness

Headache triggered by exertion, sexual activity, or Valsalva maneuver

Migraine

Although tension-type headache is the most common type of headache reported in community-based surveys, migraine is the most common primary headache disorder seen in clinical practice and is frequently missed or misdiagnosed as another type of headache (ie, tension-type or sinus headache). The criteria for diagnosis of migraine are well established and can be recalled with the mnemonic **POUND: P**ulsatile quality (headache described as pounding or throbbing), **O**ne-day duration (episode may last 4-72 hours if untreated), **U**nilateral in location, **N**ausea or vomiting, and **D**isabling intensity (altered usual daily activities during headache episode). The presence of ≥3 of these criteria is >90% predictive of migraine in patients consulting a physician for headache (Table 3). Fifteen percent to 20% of patients with migraine experience an aura. In >90% of these patients, the aura may consist of such visual symptoms as photopsia (sparks or flashes of light), fortification spectra (arcs of flashing light that often form a zigzag pattern), or a scotoma (an area of loss of vision surrounded by a normal field of vision). Paresthesia involving the hands, arms, and face or expressive or receptive language dysfunction can also occur.

Effective nonpharmacologic management includes trigger avoidance, biofeedback, cognitive behavioral therapy, stress management, and relaxation therapy. Many patients with migraine can identify specific dietary triggers; elimination diets may decrease migraine symptoms in some patients. Common dietary triggers include caffeine; nitrates or nitrite preservatives; phenylethylamine, tyramine, and xanthine in aged cheese, red wine, beer, champagne, and chocolate; monosodium glutamate (food additive); dairy products; and fatty foods. Relaxation training, thermal biofeedback with relaxation training, electromyographic biofeedback, and cognitive behavioral therapy reduce migraine frequency by 30% to 50%.

For acute attacks, treatment as soon as possible maximizes the likelihood of rapid and sustained relief and minimizes the need for backup and rescue medication. The treatment approach depends on several factors, including headache severity and frequency, associat-

Table 3. Estimating the Probability of Migraine Using the POUND Criteria

Number of Diagnostic Criteria[a]	Pretest Probability[b]		
	20%	50%	80%
0, 1, or 2	5	15	50
3	75	94	99
4 or 5	90	96	>99

[a]The 5 diagnostic criteria for migraine are: pulsatile quality, 1-day duration, unilateral location, nausea or vomiting, and disabling intensity.

[b]The pretest probability of migraine is 5% to 20% among the general population but at least 50% among persons consulting a physician for headache. Additional factors (eg, family history of headaches or migraine) can raise the pretest probability closer to 80%.

ed symptoms (eg, nausea or vomiting), and coexisting medical conditions. Intranasal, orally dissolving, and parenteral routes of drug administration should be used in patients with severe nausea or vomiting. Mild attacks are effectively treated with nonsteroidal anti-inflammatory drugs (NSAIDs) or acetaminophen; more severe attacks are treated with a triptan (selective serotonin receptor agonist) medication. Triptans have the highest overall efficacy rates for moderate to severe migraine, but they are contraindicated in the presence of ischemic vascular disease and uncontrolled hypertension. **No one triptan for migraine headache has been shown to be superior to others, so treatment decisions should be made on prior experience and cost.** Dihydroergotamine is an alternative to a triptan for acute migraine treatment but may not be as effective and is contraindicated in coronary artery disease and pregnancy; it should not be used concomitantly with a triptan. Acute therapies should not be taken more often than 2 to 3 days per week to avoid medication-overuse (rebound) headaches.

Taking a daily preventive medication typically reduces headache frequency by one-third to one-half. Preventive therapy may be indicated for patients with frequent disabling headaches (usually ≥2 headaches per week), poor relief from appropriately used acute therapies, or uncommon migraine, such as basilar or hemiplegic migraine. Other appropriate candidates are patients with a contraindication to acute therapy, failure or overuse of acute therapy, adverse effects from acute therapy, or a preference for preventive therapy. Avoiding migraine triggers, use of behavioral therapies, and cognitive behavioral therapy are nonpharmacologic methods to prevent migraines. The major medications shown to be effective for migraine prevention include β-blockers (such as propranolol, metoprolol, or timolol), tricyclic antidepressants (such as amitriptyline), and anticonvulsants (such as valproate, topiramate, or gabapentin). There is insufficient evidence to recommend acupuncture, chiropractic manipulation, oxygen therapy, occlusion adjustment, hypnosis, or nerve stimulation to prevent migraine. Some herbal products such as feverfew, butterbur root, the mineral magnesium, the vitamin riboflavin, and the antioxidant coenzyme Q_{10} may have some efficacy in migraine prevention.

Tension-Type Headache

Tension-type headaches may last minutes to days. Patients describe bilateral, pressing pain of mild to moderate intensity not aggravated by physical activities and without nausea. Stress and sleep deprivation are important triggers of tension-type headache. Chronic tension-type headache is present at least 50% of days and has a signifi-

cant impact on the patient's daily life. Nonpharmacologic treatments include biofeedback training and cognitive behavioral therapy. Drug treatment usually begins with NSAIDs. Prophylaxis, often with a tricyclic antidepressant, may be needed. The addition of caffeine to aspirin or NSAIDs increases treatment efficacy. There is no role for muscle relaxants or benzodiazepines.

Chronic Daily Headache

Chronic daily headache is a nonspecific term that refers to headache that is present >15 days per month for ≥3 months. The headache may be a primary or secondary headache. Risk factors for chronic daily headache include obesity, a history of >1 headache per week, caffeine consumption, and overuse of acute headache medications. Patients usually have significant disability secondary to pain, and many have depression, anxiety, panic disorder, or sleep disturbance requiring diagnosis and treatment.

Medication-Overuse Headache

Medication-overuse headache (previously referred to as analgesic rebound headache) is defined as daily or near-daily headache (≥15 days per month) in a patient with a primary headache disorder and medication overuse. Overuse is defined as the use of acute headache medications on a regular basis for more than 3 months. Examples of overuse include simple analgesics (eg, acetaminophen) or combination of drugs on ≥15 days a month. When the offending medication is withheld, "withdrawal" headaches ensue. There is agreement that opioids, butalbital combinations, isometheptene combinations, over-the-counter analgesic combinations, decongestants, ergotamine, and triptans can result in this pattern. Treatment is withdrawal of medication.

Cluster Headache

The trigeminal autonomic cephalalgias are a group of primary headache disorders characterized by excruciating unilateral headache that occurs in association with prominent cranial autonomic features, such as lacrimation, nasal congestion, rhinorrhea, and conjunctival injection. Cluster headache is the most common trigeminal cephalalgia, although it is much less common than migraine or tension-type headache. Prevalence is 3 times higher in men than in women. Smoking is a risk factor, and alcohol may trigger a cluster headache.

Cluster headaches are characterized by unilateral, severe, boring pain that is usually orbital, supraorbital, and/or temporal in location. The time from onset to peak intensity is usually minutes, with the pain lasting 15 minutes to 3 hours. Frequency ranges from 1 headache every other day to 8 per day. Accompanying autonomic symptoms include lacrimation, nasal congestion, rhinorrhea, miosis, ptosis, and conjunctival injection. The attacks occur in clusters that last weeks to months, with remissions lasting months to years. Oxygen inhalation delivered via a non-rebreather face mask at a flow rate of 6 to 12 L/min for 10 minutes is often effective in terminating the attack. Subcutaneous sumatriptan and nasal zolmitriptan are also effective in treating a cluster headache. Verapamil can be effective in preventing cluster headaches.

Bibliography

McGregor EA. In the clinic. Migraine. Ann Intern Med. 2013;159(9):ITC5-1-ITC5-16; quiz ITC5 16. [PMID: 24189604]

Chapter 74

Approach to Meningitis and Encephalitis

Fred A. Lopez, MD

Central nervous system (CNS) infections are medical emergencies classified by anatomic location and include the syndromes of meningitis (infection of tissues surrounding the cerebral cortex) and encephalitis (infection of the cerebral cortex). Bacterial meningitis requires early clinical recognition and differentiation from a viral etiology, an understanding of microbial causes, and an expedient diagnostic and therapeutic approach. Encephalitis is almost always caused by viral infection. Approximately 20,000 cases of encephalitis occur in the United States each year, with the predominant endemic cause being herpes simplex virus (HSV).

Bacterial Meningitis

More than 75% of cases of bacterial meningitis are due to either *Streptococcus pneumoniae* or *Neisseria meningitidis*. *S. pneumoniae* is the most common cause and may occur in patients with other foci of infection (eg, pneumonia, otitis media, mastoiditis, sinusitis, or endocarditis) or following head trauma with leakage of cerebrospinal fluid (CSF). The pneumococcal polyvalent polysaccharide and pneumococcal conjugate vaccines are both effective in prevention of invasive disease.

N. meningitidis is the second most common cause of bacterial meningitis in the United States, occurring primarily in children and young adults. An associated rash–often petechial, maculopapular, or purpuric in appearance and usually sparing the soles and palms–is characteristic. Patients with deficiencies in the terminal complement components (C5-C9) are at increased risk for recurrent infection by *N. meningitidis*. An unconjugated polysaccharide meningococcal vaccine against serogroups A, C, Y, and W-135 is available, as is a meningococcal polysaccharide diphtheria toxoid conjugate vaccine. However, neither vaccine affords protection against serogroup B, the causative agent in up to one-third of cases of bacterial meningitis in the United States.

Meningitis caused by *Listeria monocytogenes* is associated with extremes of age (neonates and adults aged >50 years), alcoholism,

Table 1. Differential Diagnosis of Meningitis

Disorder	Notes
Bacterial meningitis	Fever, severe headache, stiff neck, photophobia, drowsiness or confusion, nausea, vomiting. Neutrophil predominance on CSF evaluation.
Enteroviral infection	Fever, severe headache, stiff neck, photophobia, drowsiness or confusion, nausea, vomiting. Lymphocyte predominance on CSF evaluation. Most cases occur in the summer and early fall. Children are most often affected. Most frequently identified cause of aseptic meningitis. Primarily echovirus and coxsackievirus. PCR for enterovirus is available.
Arboviral infection	Most often presents as encephalitis but can present as meningitis or meningoencephalitis. Lymphocyte predominance on CSF evaluation. Seen in patients living in or traveling to areas of arboviral activity or epidemic. St. Louis encephalitis virus, California encephalitis virus, and West Nile virus are most common. Most cases occur in warmer months and when contact with mosquito vectors is most likely.
HSV infection	HSV-1 most often presents as temporal lobe encephalitis; HSV-2 causes aseptic meningitis. HSV meningitis is often associated with primary genital infection. Lymphocyte predominance on CSF evaluation. HSV accounts for approximately 0.5%-3.0% of all cases of aseptic meningitis. HSV meningitis is often self-limiting and does not require antiviral treatment. HSV encephalitis does require antiviral treatment.
HIV infection	HIV-associated aseptic meningitis generally follows a mononucleosis-like syndrome. Most commonly seen in acute HIV infection. Lymphocyte predominance on CSF evaluation. Viral load should be obtained to exclude acute HIV. Always a consideration in young adults and patients with high-risk behaviors.
Tubercular meningitis	Headache, nausea, vomiting, fever, mental status changes lasting more than 2 weeks. CSF abnormalities are nonspecific and generally show normal to slightly decreased glucose, elevated protein, and moderate pleocytosis with variable differential. CSF culture for *Mycobacterium tuberculosis* is low yield and may take several weeks to become positive. A negative TB PCR result on CSF evaluation does not exclude diagnosis of tubercular meningitis.
Lyme disease (*Borrelia burgdorferi*)	Associated with rash (erythema migrans) early, followed by aseptic meningitis approximately 4 wk after initial signs of disease. Lymphocyte predominance on CSF evaluation. Vector tick is endemic to northeastern United States and Great Lakes area, but cases seen in almost every state. Occurs most frequently in summer and autumn.
Cryptococcal meningitis	Subacute or chronic presentation. One-half of cases occur in HIV-negative patients. CSF pleocytosis of 40-400 cells/μL (0.04-0.4 x 10^9/L) with lymphocyte predominance and slightly low glucose is typical. India ink stain of CSF has limited sensitivity. CSF is positive for cryptococcal polysaccharide antigen in 90% of patients.

CSF = cerebrospinal fluid; HSV = herpes simplex virus; HSV-1 = HSV type 1; HSV-2 = HSV type 2; PCR = polymerase chain reaction; TB = tuberculosis.

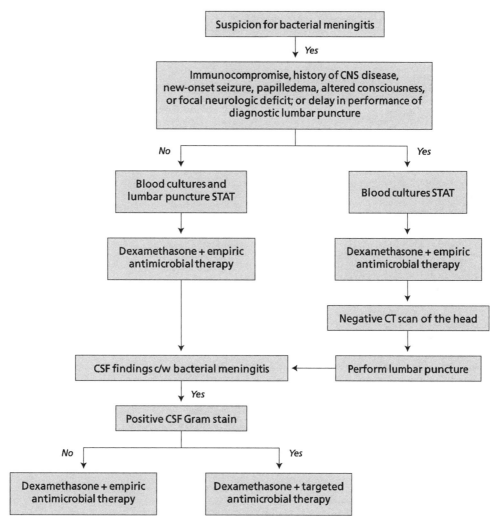

Figure 1. Management algorithm for adults with suspected bacterial meningitis. CNS = central nervous system; c/w = consistent with; CSF = cerebrospinal fluid; CT = computed tomography. Reprinted with permission from Tunkel AR, Hartman BJ, Kaplan SL, et al. Practice guidelines for the management of bacterial meningitis. Clin Inf Dis. 2004; 39:1267-84. Copyright 2004 Oxford University Press.

malignancy, immunosuppression, diabetes mellitus, hepatic failure, kidney failure, iron overload, collagen vascular disorders, and HIV infection. Group B streptococci, an important cause of meningitis in neonates, are seen in adults with underlying conditions such as diabetes, pregnancy, cardiac disease, malignancy, collagen vascular disorders, alcoholism, hepatic failure, kidney failure, glucocorticoid use, and HIV infection. Aerobic gram-negative bacilli (*Klebsiella* species, *Escherichia coli*, *Serratia marcescens*, and *Pseudomonas aeruginosa*), *Staphylococcus aureus*, and *Staphylococcus epidermidis* may cause meningitis in patients with head trauma or CSF shunts or following neurosurgical procedures. The differential diagnosis of bacterial meningitis is broad and includes other microbial agents (Table 1). An algorithm for the evaluation of suspected meningitis is included in Figure 1.

Viral Meningitis

Viruses are the major cause of the aseptic meningitis syndrome, defined as the presence of clinical and laboratory findings consistent with meningitis in a patient who has normal CSF stains and culture on initial evaluation. Enteroviruses are diagnosed in 85% to 95% of cases and are more common in the summer and fall months. Herpes simplex viruses account for 0.5% to 3.0% of cases of aseptic meningitis and are most often associated with primary genital infection due to HSV type 2 (HSV-2). In addition, HSV-2 is the most common cause of the syndrome of benign recurrent lymphocytic meningitis (previously termed Mollaret meningitis). Although encephalitis is the most common neurologic manifestation of West Nile virus infection (seen in fewer than 1% of patients), aseptic meningitis may also occur.

Diagnosis

Fever, headache, neck stiffness, and altered mental status are the cardinal symptoms of meningitis; the absence of these findings essentially rules out the diagnosis. Jolt accentuation of headache elicited with horizontal movement of the head is more sensitive for the diagnosis of meningitis than the Kernig or Brudzinski sign.

The clinical presentations of viral and bacterial meningitis are similar. The diagnosis is established by CSF analysis (Table 2). However, emergent lumbar puncture should not be performed in patients whose clinical presentation is consistent with a CNS mass lesion. A computed tomography (CT) scan of the head should be done before lumbar puncture in these patients, as well as patients who are immunocom-

Table 2. Typical CSF Findings in Patients With Acute Meningitis

CSF Parameter	Bacterial Meningitis	Viral Meningitis[a]
Opening pressure	200-500 mm H_2O[b]	≤250 mm H_2O
Leukocyte count	1000-5000/µL (1-5 × 10⁹/L)[c]	50-1000/µL (0.5-1 × 10⁹/L)
Leukocyte differential	Neutrophils[c]	Lymphocytes[d]
Glucose	<40 mg/dL (2.2 mmol/L)[e]	>45 mg/dL (2.5 mmol/L)
Protein	100-500 mg/dL (1000-5000 mg/L)	<200 mg/dL (2000 mg/L)
Gram stain	Positive in 60%-90%[f]	Negative
Culture	Positive in 70%-85%	Negative

CSF = cerebrospinal fluid.

[a]Primarily non-poliovirus enteroviruses (echoviruses or coxsackieviruses).

[b]Values >600 mm H_2O suggest cerebral edema, intracranial suppurative foci, or communicating hydrocephalus.

[c]Range may be <100 to >10,000 cells/µL (0.1-10 × 10⁹/L).

[d]Neutrophil predominance may occur early in infection but gives way to lymphocyte predominance over the first 6 to 48 h.

[e]The CSF/blood glucose ratio is ≤0.40 in most patients.

[f]Likelihood of a positive Gram stain correlates with number of bacteria in CSF.

promised, have a history of CNS disease, present with new-onset seizures, or have a decreased level of consciousness, focal neurologic deficits, or papilledema. Some experts also suggest delaying lumbar puncture in patients with clinical signs of impending brain herniation because of the risk of precipitating herniation even when CT findings are normal. Clinical signs of impending herniation include deteriorating level of consciousness, brainstem signs (including pupillary changes, posturing, or irregular respirations), and a seizure.

In the evaluation of patients with acute bacterial or viral meningitis, CSF findings that predict bacterial etiology with ≥99% certainty include:

- Protein concentration >220 mg/dL (2200 mg/L)
- Glucose concentration <34 mg/dL (1.9 mmol/L)
- CSF-blood glucose ratio <0.23
- Leukocyte count >2000/µL (2 × 10⁹/L)
- Neutrophil count >1180/µL (1.18 × 10⁹/L)

In patients with suspected viral meningitis, CSF polymerase chain reaction (PCR) testing should be considered for non-poliovirus enteroviruses (echoviruses and coxsackieviruses) and HSV, as well as enzyme-linked immunosorbent assay (ELISA) testing for arboviruses (West Nile virus, St. Louis encephalitis virus, California encephalitis virus, and eastern equine encephalitis virus).

Fungal, mycobacterial, HIV, mumps virus, tick-associated bacterial and spirochetal testing should be performed when clinically indicated (immunosuppression or exposure history).

Treatment

If CSF examination reveals purulent meningitis, and a positive Gram stain suggests a specific etiology, targeted antibacterial therapy is initiated. If the Gram stain is negative, empiric antibiotic therapy is initiated, based on the patient's age and underlying conditions (Table 3). Most adult patients with bacterial meningitis should be started on

Table 3. Empiric Antibiotic Therapy for Purulent Meningitis Based on Patient Age and Underlying Condition

Predisposing Factor	Common Pathogens	Antibiotic Therapy
Age 0-4 wk	Streptococcus agalactiae, Escherichia coli, Listeria monocytogenes, Klebsiella species	Ampicillin + cefotaxime **or** ampicillin + aminoglycoside
Age 1-23 mo	Streptococcus pneumoniae, Haemophilus influenzae, Streptococcus agalactiae, Neisseria meningitidis, Escherichia coli	Vancomycin + third-generation cephalosporin[a,b,c]
Age 2-50 y	Streptococcus pneumoniae, Neisseria meningitidis	Vancomycin + third-generation cephalosporin[a,b,c]
Age >50 y	Streptococcus pneumoniae, Neisseria meningitidis, Listeria monocytogenes, gram-negative bacilli	Vancomycin + ampicillin + third-generation cephalosporin[a,b]
Basilar skull fracture	Streptococcus pneumoniae, Haemophilus influenzae, group A beta-hemolytic streptococci	Vancomycin + third-generation cephalosporin[a]
Neurosurgery or head trauma	Staphylococcus aureus, coagulase-negative staphylococci (especially Staphylococcus epidermidis), gram-negative bacilli (including Pseudomonas aeruginosa)	Vancomycin + ceftazidime **or** cefepime **or** meropenem
Cerebrospinal fluid shunt	Staphylococcus aureus, coagulase-negative staphylococci (especially Staphylococcus epidermidis), gram-negative bacilli (including Pseudomonas aeruginosa), diphtheroids (including Propionibacterium acnes)	Vancomycin + ceftazidime **or** cefepime **or** meropenem

[a]Cefotaxime or ceftriaxone.

[b]Some experts would add rifampin if dexamethasone is given.

[c]Add ampicillin if the patient has risk factors for Listeria monocytogenes or infection with this organism is suspected.

adjunctive dexamethasone when empiric antimicrobial therapy is begun. Clinical trials have established the benefit of adjunctive dexamethasone on adverse outcomes and death in adults with suspected or proven pneumococcal meningitis. Dexamethasone administered with or just prior to the first dose of antimicrobial therapy attenuates the inflammatory response following antimicrobial-induced lysis of meningeal pathogens. There are insufficient data in adults with pneumococcal meningitis to know whether dexamethasone administration after antimicrobial therapy offers any outcome benefit. Once an etiologic agent is identified and antimicrobial susceptibility has been performed, specific antibacterial therapy should be started (Table 4).

Treatment of patients with viral meningitis is usually supportive. Whether antiviral therapy alters the course of mild HSV-2 meningitis is unclear.

Viral Encephalitis

Viral encephalitis presents as an acute-onset, febrile illness associated with headache, altered level of consciousness, seizures, and, occasionally, focal neurologic signs. Arboviral diseases such as eastern equine encephalitis, St. Louis encephalitis, and West Nile encephalitis have a low prevalence in humans but may be fatal or have significant morbidity; effective treatments and vaccines are not available. West Nile encephalitis is most severe in older patients, with the highest mortality and morbidity rates in those aged ≥65 years. The most common manifestations are encephalitis, meningitis, flaccid paralysis, and fever. Tremors and parkinsonism have also been reported.

Accounting for 5% to 10% of cases, HSV is one of the most common causes of identified sporadic encephalitis worldwide. While HSV type 1 occurs more commonly in adults, HSV-2 occurs more commonly in neonates. The encephalitis in adults results from reactivation of the latent virus in the trigeminal ganglion, which leads to inflammatory necrotic lesions in the temporal cortex and limbic system. Most cases occur in the absence of an antecedent illness.

Varicella zoster virus (VZV) should always be considered as a cause of encephalitis, particularly in the immunocompromised host. Though most often associated with aseptic meningitis, enteroviruses like coxsackieviruses and echoviruses can cause encephalitis.

Diagnosis

A CSF analysis (including PCR testing for HSV, enterovirus, and VZV, as well as arbovirus-associated IgM antibody capture ELISA), magnetic resonance imaging (MRI), and an electroencephalogram should

Table 4. Recommended Specific Antibiotic Therapy for Bacterial Meningitis Based on Pathogen and In Vitro Susceptibility Testing

Pathogen	Standard Therapy	Alternative Therapies
Streptococcus pneumoniae		
Penicillin MIC <0.1 µg/mL	Penicillin G or ampicillin	Third-generation cephalosporin,[a] chloramphenicol
Penicillin MIC 0.1-1.0 µg/mL	Third-generation cephalosporin[a]	Meropenem, cefepime
Penicillin MIC ≥2.0 µg/mL **or** cefotaxime or ceftriaxone MIC ≥1.0 µg/mL	Vancomycin + third-generation cephalosporin[a,b]	Fluoroquinolone[c]
Neisseria meningitidis		
Penicillin MIC <0.1 µg/mL	Penicillin G or ampicillin	Third-generation cephalosporin,[a] chloramphenicol
Penicillin MIC 0.1-1.0 µg/mL	Third-generation cephalosporin[a]	Chloramphenicol, fluoroquinolone, meropenem
Listeria monocytogenes	Ampicillin or penicillin G[d]	Trimethoprim-sulfamethoxazole
Streptococcus agalactiae	Ampicillin or penicillin G[d]	Third-generation cephalosporin,[a] vancomycin
Haemophilus influenzae		
β-Lactamase-negative	Ampicillin	Third-generation cephalosporin,[a] cefepime, chloramphenicol, fluoroquinolone, aztreonam
β-Lactamase-positive	Third-generation cephalosporin[a]	Chloramphenicol, cefepime, fluoroquinolone, aztreonam
Escherichia coli and other Enterobacteriaceae[e]	Third-generation cephalosporin[a]	Aztreonam, meropenem, fluoroquinolone, trimethoprim-sulfamethoxazole
Pseudomonas aeruginosa	Ceftazidime[d] or cefepime[d]	Aztreonam,[d] meropenem,[d] fluoroquinolone[d]
Staphylococcus aureus		
Methicillin-sensitive	Nafcillin or oxacillin	Vancomycin, meropenem
Methicillin-resistant	Vancomycin[f]	Trimethoprim-sulfamethoxazole, linezolid, daptomycin
Staphylococcus epidermidis	Vancomycin[f]	Linezolid

MIC = minimum inhibitory concentration.

[a]Cefotaxime or ceftriaxone.

[b]Addition of rifampin should be considered if the organism is sensitive and if the ceftriaxone MIC is >2 µg/mL.

[c]No clinical data available; would use newer fluoroquinolones with in vitro activity against *Streptococcus pneumoniae* (eg, moxifloxacin). Many experts would not use a fluoroquinolone as single-agent therapy but would combine with vancomycin or a third-generation cephalosporin such as cefotaxime or ceftriaxone.

[d]Addition of an aminoglycoside should be considered.

[e]Choice of specific antimicrobial therapy should be guided by in vitro susceptibility test results.

[f]Consider addition of rifampin.

be obtained. Analysis of CSF usually reveals an increased opening pressure, a lymphocytic pleocytosis, a modestly elevated protein level, and a normal or slightly low glucose level. The CSF may be completely normal in about 3% to 5% of patients with viral encephalitis. While CSF cultures for HSV and arboviruses are usually negative, PCR for HSV and IgM antibody capture ELISA for arboviruses both have a sensitivity exceeding 90%.

In HSV encephalitis, MRI demonstrates unilateral or bilateral abnormalities in the medial and inferior temporal lobes, which may extend into the frontal lobe. Electroencephalogram findings include focal delta activity over the temporal lobes, typically occurring between 2 and 14 days after symptom onset; periodic lateralizing epileptiform discharges may also be noted. Brain biopsy is reserved for patients who do not respond to acyclovir.

In patients with encephalitis caused by flaviviruses (Japanese encephalitis virus, St. Louis encephalitis virus, or West Nile virus) or eastern equine encephalitis virus, MRI may display a characteristic pattern of mixed-intensity or hypodense lesions on T1-weighted images in the thalamus, basal ganglia, and midbrain; the lesions are hyperintense on T2-weighted and fluid-attenuated inversion recovery imaging. These neuroimaging findings occur in about 30% of patients with West Nile encephalitis.

Therapy

Although various viruses may cause encephalitis, specific antiviral therapy is generally limited to disease caused by the herpes viruses, particularly HSV. In HSV encephalitis, prompt acyclovir reduces mortality to approximately 25% in adults and older children; however, >50% of patients who survive will have neurologic sequelae. Acyclovir is also recommended for treatment of VZV-associated encephalitis. There is no reliably effective therapy available for arbovirus-associated encephalitis.

Bibliography

Spanos A, Harrell FE Jr, Durack DT. Differential diagnosis of acute meningitis. An analysis of the predictive value of initial observations. JAMA. 1989;262(19):2700-07. [PMID: 2810603]

Tunkel AR, Glaser CA, Bloch KC, et al; Infectious Diseases Society of America. The management of encephalitis: clinical practice guidelines by the Infectious Diseases Society of America. Clin Infect Dis. 2008; 47:303-27. [PMID: 18582201]

van de Beek D, de Gans J, Tunkel AR, Wijdicks EF. Community-acquired bacterial meningitis in adults. N Engl J Med. 2006;354:44-53. [PMID: 16394301]

Chapter 75

Stroke and Transient Ischemic Attack

Jane P. Gagliardi, MD

Stroke, defined as irreversible neurologic symptoms caused by disrupted cerebral blood flow and cerebral ischemia, is the third leading cause of death in the United States and an important cause of disability. Most strokes are ischemic, resulting from thrombosis, embolism, or hypertensive vasospasm. Hemorrhagic stroke results from rupture of a blood vessel (in the case of subarachnoid hemorrhage) or from hypertensive or amyloid changes (in the case of intracranial hemorrhage). Transient ischemic attack (TIA), which results from temporary disruption of cerebral blood flow, mimics stroke but usually resolves within 30 minutes and is not associated with ischemic changes on brain imaging. Up to 40% of patients with TIA will eventually have a stroke, and up to 20% will have a stroke within 90 days. Within the first minutes to hours after the onset of cerebral ischemia, an irreversibly damaged area of brain develops (the "infarct core"). Potentially viable brain tissue (the "ischemic penumbra") surrounds this damaged area, and will eventually become part of the infarct core if blood flow is not restored quickly or even if blood pressure (BP) is lowered. The penumbra is the target of acute ischemic stroke therapy. Most damage occurs in the first 3 to 6 hours poststroke, so stroke is a time-critical medical emergency. The differential diagnosis of stroke includes seizure, hypoglycemia, metabolic abnormalities, complicated migraine, rapidly growing mass or brain tumor, and functional illness (Table 1).

Prevention

It is important to educate patients and families about symptoms of stroke and the critical need for immediate evaluation if these symptoms occur. Modifiable risk factors (eg, smoking, hypertension, and hyperlipidemia) should be addressed with appropriate management strategies, including treatment for hypertension and hyperlipidemia. For patients whose 10-year absolute risk of a first coronary artery event is ≥10% (see Chapter 2), it is reasonable to consider aspirin for primary prevention of stroke, provided there is no contraindication. Anticoagulation or antiplatelet therapy for atrial fibrillation should be initiated in patients for whom it is indicated (see Chapter 5). Asymptomatic carotid bruits are common, and their prevalence increases with age. Among selected patients aged <75 years with >70% carotid stenosis, carotid endarterectomy performed by a surgeon with low surgical morbidity (ie, <3% perioperative stroke or mortality rate) can reduce annual stroke risk by one-half (see Chapter 9).

Diagnosis

Successful stroke treatment requires rapid diagnosis, because the administration of thrombolytic therapy for ischemic stroke is beneficial only within a tight window of time (Figure 1). The abrupt or sudden onset of focal neurologic symptoms is a possible indicator of ischemic stroke or intracerebral hemorrhage. In the case of intracerebral hemorrhage, the sudden focal deficit will progress over minutes to hours and may evolve to include symptoms of increased intracranial pressure, such as headache, nausea, vomiting, and decreased level of consciousness. A sudden severe headache suggests subarachnoid hemorrhage; up to 40% of patients will have experienced a "thunderclap" or sentinel headache in the days to weeks leading up to the bleed. If the patient presents with a sudden severe

Table 1. Differential Diagnosis of Stroke and TIA

Disorder	Notes
Stroke	Abrupt onset. Fixed focal findings referable to arterial distribution (ie, hemiparesis of face, arm, or leg ± aphasia). Cannot distinguish stroke subtypes or infarct from hemorrhage without brain imaging
TIA	Same clinical features as for stroke, but lasting <30 min
Seizure	Abrupt onset and termination of ictus; usually decreased responsiveness during ictus; often involuntary movements during ictus; usually postictal lethargy or confusion; sometimes postictal focal findings that resolve over 24 h. May accompany stroke
Hypoglycemia	May look like stroke or TIA. Almost always a diabetic patient taking hypoglycemic medications. May or may not be accompanied by seizure
Complicated migraine (see Chapter 73)	Similar onset and focal findings as in stroke. Usually severe headache preceding or following attack. Sensory and visual disturbances often prominent; sensory symptoms often spread over affected area. Suspect in younger patients, more often women with history of severe headache. MRI usually normal. Stroke may accompany migraine
Mass lesion (tumor, abscess, subdural hematoma)	Focal symptoms occur over days, not minutes; may not be in one vascular territory. Primary cancer, fever, immunosuppression, and history of trauma often present. Can be distinguished from stroke by brain imaging
Encephalitis (see Chapter 74)	Onset over days, not minutes. Fever, followed by headache, possibly meningeal signs, and photophobia. Structural involvement suggested by mental status change
Functional	May look like stroke, but findings nonanatomic or inconsistent; normal MRI

MRI = magnetic resonance imaging; TIA, transient ischemic attack.

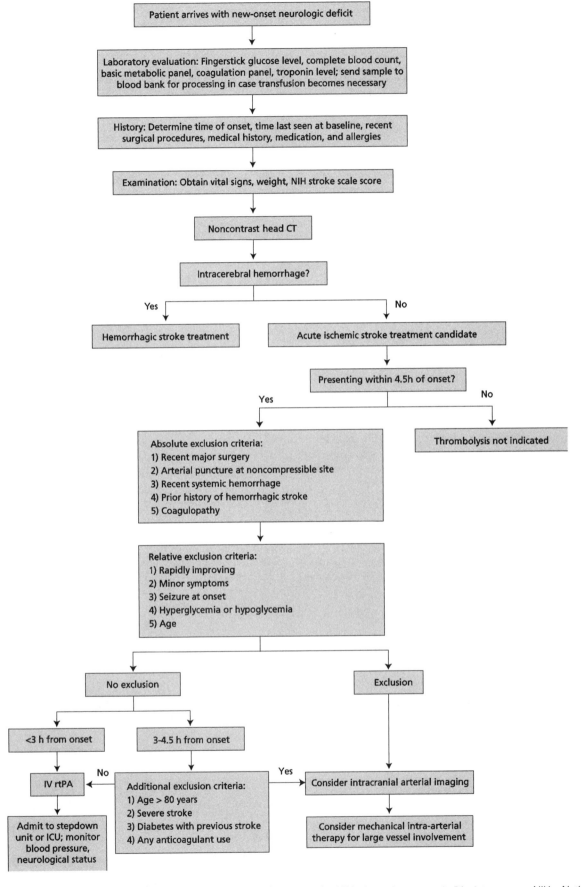

Figure 1. Algorithm for management of acute stroke. CT = computed tomography; ICU = intensive care unit; IV = intravenous; NIH = National Institutes of Health; rtPA = recombinant tissue plasminogen activator.

headache and computed tomography (CT) is negative for evidence of bleeding, it is necessary to perform lumbar puncture to assess the cerebrospinal fluid for evidence of erythrocytes or xanthochromia. Five percent of patients presenting with an acute subarachnoid hemorrhage may have a negative head CT scan, and management of subarachnoid hemorrhage is quite different from management of ischemic stroke.

A thorough neurologic examination is performed to localize the ischemic region (Table 2). The presence of facial paresis, arm drift, or abnormal speech is highly suggestive of stroke. Small, deep penetrating arteries that arise from the larger vessels may also be affected by stroke. Occlusion of these vessels may cause small infarctions with stereotypical "lacunar" syndromes, such as pure motor hemiparesis, pure sensory stroke, dysarthria-clumsy hand syndrome, and ataxic hemiparesis.

Urgent neuroimaging (within 30 minutes of the patient's arrival to the emergency department) is necessary to rule out intracerebral hemorrhage for patients presenting within the 3-hour timeframe during which thrombolysis may be considered. Noncontrast head CT is frequently employed for this purpose, although higher-resolution imaging with contrast CT or magnetic resonance imaging may be performed later to clearly define the area of ischemia or infarct. Duplex ultrasonography of the carotid arteries should be performed within the first 2 days to assess for stenosis warranting consideration of carotid endarterectomy; magnetic resonance and CT angiography may be used in the event of an equivocal carotid duplex result, although they should not be obtained routinely. Up to 40% of strokes may be idiopathic, and up to 50% of these may be caused by an atrial septal defect or patent foramen ovale. Echocardiography with testing for right-to-left shunting across the atrial septum is recommended in patients with stroke or in patients aged >45 years in whom an alternative explanation for TIA cannot be identified. Laboratory values should be obtained to define potential underlying conditions as dictated by the history and physical examination (Table 3).

Therapy

Patients with suspected stroke, high risk for stroke, or TIA lasting >10 minutes (which conveys a high risk for recurrent events, particularly if accompanied by limb weakness, speech disturbances, presence of diabetes mellitus, or age >60 years) should be hospitalized, preferably in a dedicated stroke unit with a multidisciplinary stroke team, unless monitoring in an intensive care unit is required. Specialized stroke units result in lower mortality and morbidity than conven-

Table 2. Cerebrovascular Territories and Syndromes

Artery	Major Clinical Features
Anterior cerebral artery	Contralateral leg weakness
Middle cerebral artery	Contralateral face and arm weakness greater than leg weakness; sensory loss, field cut, aphasia, or neglect (depending on side)
Posterior cerebral artery	Contralateral visual field cut
Deep penetrating arteries (lacunar strokes)	Contralateral motor or sensory deficit without cortical signs (eg, aphasia, apraxia, neglect, normal higher cognitive functions)
Basilar artery	Oculomotor deficits and/or ataxia with "crossed" sensory/motor deficits. Crossed signs include sensory or motor deficit on one side of the face and the opposite side of the body
Basilar artery (ventral pons)	Quadriplegia and speechlessness due to severe dysarthria with preserved consciousness; able to move eyes and wink
Vertebral artery	Lower cranial nerve deficits (eg, dysphagia, dysarthria, tongue or palate deviation) and/or ataxia with crossed sensory deficits

Table 3. Laboratory Studies for Transient Ischemic Attack and Stroke

Test	Rationale/Notes
In all patients	
Complete blood count	Ensure adequate oxygen-carrying capacity
PT/INR and aPTT	Baseline studies in anticipation of possible anticoagulation
Blood glucose, creatinine, and lipid profile	Define underlying risk factors
In selected patients	
Blood cultures	Obtain if patient is febrile, especially if endocarditis is suspected
Lupus anticoagulant, anticardiolipin antibody, factor V Leiden, protein C, protein S, antithrombin III	Screening for hypercoagulable states
Antinuclear antibody and related serologic studies, erythrocyte sedimentation rate	Obtain if vasculitis is suspected
Serologic test for syphilis	Neurosyphilis may present as acute stroke
Hemoglobin electrophoresis	Identify hemoglobinopathies causing stroke
Serum protein electrophoresis	Useful in defining lymphoproliferative diseases predisposing to brain hemorrhage

aPTT = activated partial thromboplastin time; INR = international normalized ratio; PT = prothrombin time.

tional ward settings. Cardiac, vital signs, blood glucose, and oxygen monitoring should be initiated. Given the risk of aspiration pneumonia and subsequent death, it is important to perform a bedside swallow evaluation to rule out evidence of dysphagia before permitting any oral intake.

The National Institutes of Health (NIH) Stroke Scale (Table 4) is a validated instrument that correlates with short- and long-term outcomes and may be helpful in stroke assessment. It consists of 11 items adding up to a possible total score of 42; a score ≥20 indicates a severe stroke.

For hemorrhagic stroke, management of BP and reversal of anticoagulants or coagulopathy is important. Early hemicraniectomy should be considered in patients aged <60 years with middle cerebral artery infarcts at risk for cerebral edema or herniation, as evidenced by a high initial NIH Stroke Scale value, early signs of swelling, or >50% middle cerebral artery hypodensity on imaging; early hemicraniectomy has been demonstrated to reduce fatality and improve functional outcomes at 1 and 3 years.

For ischemic stroke, the thrombolytic agent alteplase (recombinant tissue-type plasminogen activator) increases the chance of recovery from ischemic stroke when administered intravenously within 3 hours of symptom onset, or within 3 hours of when the patient was last seen awake and without symptoms. Brain imaging must be negative for hemorrhage. Thrombolysis is contraindicated in patients with intracerebral hemorrhage, a systolic BP >185 mm Hg or diastolic BP >110 mm Hg, or mean arterial pressure >130 mm Hg (the diastolic BP plus one-third of the pulse pressure–the difference between systolic and diastolic BPs). If thrombolytic therapy is administered after 3 hours, risk of hemorrhage and death increases. However, thrombolytic therapy may be appropriately used in selected patients (age <80 years and absence of severe stroke, diabetes mellitus, or anticoagulant use) between 3 and 4.5 hours after onset. It is important to hold aspirin and anticoagulants for 24 hours after thrombolytic therapy to prevent bleeding.

Because many patients may not qualify for thrombolytic therapy outside the 3-hour window, antiplatelet therapy may be the only therapy initiated; it should be started within 48 hours for stroke and TIA to reduce subsequent stroke risk. Aspirin has the greatest evidence of effectiveness, although clopridogrel is a reasonable alternative in patients who are intolerant of aspirin. The combination of aspirin and extended-release dipyridamole has also been shown to be effective. Dual antiplatelet therapy with aspirin and clopidogrel may also be of benefit in some patients, particularly in some patient populations. The optimal duration of dual platelet inhibition is not clear, although most experts recommend limiting dual antiplatelet therapy to 1 to 6 months.

As the small decrease in ischemia is completely offset by an increased risk of intracranial hemorrhage, even in instances of presumed cardioembolism (as with atrial fibrillation, intracardiac thrombus, or dilated cardiomyopathy), urgent anticoagulation with heparin is not recommended for patients with ischemic stroke unless cerebral venous thrombosis, basilar occlusion/stenosis, or extracranial arterial dissection is suspected.

Hypertension is a common finding in patients with acute stroke (whether hemorrhagic or ischemic), whether or not they have a preexisting history of hypertension. Any rapid decrease in BP can impair cerebral blood flow and lead to increased risk of cerebral ischemia. In the setting of acute stroke, hypertension should not be treated unless BP exceeds 220/120 mm Hg or there is another acute indication for lowering BP, such as acute coronary syndrome, heart failure, aortic dissection, hypertensive encephalopathy, or acute kidney injury. In these cases, BP should gradually be lowered by 15% over

the first 24 hours and cautiously thereafter with intravenous nicardipine or labetalol. If the patient is otherwise a candidate for thrombolytic therapy, BP must be stabilized and lowered to <185/110 mm Hg before initiation of thrombolysis and maintained at <180/105 mm Hg after initiation of therapy.

Antipyretics should be used to keep core body temperature <38.0°C (100.4°F). Supplemental oxygen should be used to maintain oxygen saturation at >95%. Persistent hyperglycemia during the first 24 hours after stroke is associated with poor outcomes; thus, patients with glucose levels >140 mg/dL (7.8 mmol/L) should be given insulin. To avoid exacerbation of hyperglycemia, normal saline (0.9%) should be used for intravenous fluid hydration rather than dextrose-containing fluids. Decubitus ulcers and deep venous thrombosis should be prevented through frequent repositioning and use of subcutaneous heparin or external compression devices. Oral nutrition should be held until swallowing is evaluated, and early nasogastric tube feeding should be considered if risk of aspiration is suspected or confirmed. In addition, physical, occupational, and speech therapists should be consulted.

Symptomatic patients with carotid stenosis may benefit from surgical treatment (see Chapter 9). Statin therapy may be of benefit early after TIA in patients with carotid stenosis to reduce subsequent stroke risk, and is indicated in all patients with atherosclerotic vascular disease to decrease disease progression.

Prognosis

Age, stroke type, stroke classification (based on symptoms and localization of lesion; lacunar, total anterior circulation, partial anterior circulation, or partial posterior circulation ischemia are possible classes of stroke), and premorbid disability are helpful in predicting inpatient and 7-day mortality from stroke. Prognosis after intracerebral hemorrhage is related to the volume of the hemorrhage and the patient's level of consciousness and may be improved with earlier hemicraniectomy to prevent edema and herniation. Prognosis after subarachnoid hemorrhage is related to severity of symptoms as well as localization and securing of the vascular anomaly (usually an aneurysm) within 72 hours.

Follow-Up

Patients hospitalized with acute stroke should be followed closely for the development of new neurological symptoms. Studies support early mobilization of patients with ischemic stroke to prevent complications. Patients should be referred for intensive rehabilitation (at home or in a facility) to improve function, with their progress monitored at least monthly after discharge. Clinicians should recognize and treat poststroke depression, which is common and can contribute to cognitive, functional, and social difficulties that impair rehabilitative efforts. Caregivers benefit from training in personal care and nursing techniques. Patients should be maintained on antiplatelet therapy indefinitely, although single-agent therapy after 1 to 6 months is most likely to confer the greatest benefit with less risk of significant bleeding than dual therapy. Patients with atrial fibrillation should receive appropriate anticoagulation or antiplatelet therapy (see Chapter 5). Antihypertensive treatment with diuretics and angiotensin-converting enzyme inhibitors is recommended for hypertensive patients beyond the hyperacute period to prevent recurrent stroke. Atherosclerotic cardiovascular disease as a cause of stroke is an indication for treatment with high-intensity statin therapy in patients ≤75 years of age, or moderate-intensity statin therapy if >75 years or not a candidate for high-intensity treatment. Patients with

Table 4. National Institutes of Health Stroke Scale[a]

Parameter (Testing Method)	Scores
1a. LOC	0 = normal 1 = not alert but arousable by minor stimulation 2 = not alert and requires constant verbal or painful stimuli to remain interactive 3 = unresponsive or responds with only reflexive movements
1b. LOC, questions (state month and age)	0 = answers both correctly 1 = answers one correctly 2 = answers neither correctly
1c. LOC, commands (close and open eyes; make fist or close one hand)	0 = performs both tasks correctly 1 = performs one task correctly 2 = performs neither task correctly
2. Gaze (track a finger in a horizontal plane)	0 = normal 1 = partial gaze palsy or isolated cranial nerve paresis 2 = forced gaze deviation or total gaze paresis
3. Visual fields (each eye tested individually)	0 = no visual loss 1 = partial hemianopia 2 = complete hemianopia 3 = bilateral hemianopia
4. Facial strength (show teeth, raise eyebrows, close eyes)	0 = normal 1 = minor paralysis (flattening of the nasolabial fold or asymmetry on smiling) 2 = partial paralysis (paralysis of the lower face only) 3 = complete paralysis (upper and lower face)
5. Arm strength (hold arm with palms down or lift arm for 10 s)	0 = no drift 1 = some drift but does not hit bed 2 = drifts down to bed 3 = no effort against gravity 4 = no movement
6. Leg strength (hold leg at 30 degrees for 5 s)	0 = no drift 1 = some drift but does not hit bed 2 = drifts down to bed 3 = no effort against gravity 4 = no movement
7. Limb ataxia (finger-nose-finger test, heel-knee-shin slide)	0 = absent 1 = present in 1 limb 2 = present in 2 limbs
8. Sensation (pinch/pinprick tested in face, arm, and leg)	0 = normal 1 = mild to moderate sensory loss or loss of sensation in only 1 limb 2 = complete sensory loss
9. Language (describe a picture, name 6 objects, and read 5 sentences)	0 = no aphasia 1 = mild to moderate aphasia (difficulty with fluency and comprehension; meaning can be identified) 2 = severe aphasia (fragmentary language, meaning cannot be clearly identified) 3 = global aphasia or mute
10. Dysarthria (repeat or read words)	0 = normal 1 = mild to moderate 2 = severe (speech not understandable)
11. Extinction/inattention (visual and tactile stimuli applied on right and left sides)	0 = normal 1 = visual or tactile extinction or mild hemispatial neglect 2 = profound hemi-inattention or extinction to more than one modality

LOC = level of consciousness.

[a]Maximum score = 42.

Data from www.ninds.nih.gov/doctors/NIH_Stroke_Scale.pdf.

diabetes mellitus require close monitoring and control of blood glucose and other cardiovascular risk factors. Modifiable risk factors that should also be addressed include cigarette smoking, excessive alcohol consumption, obesity, and lack of physical activity.

Bibliography

de Man-van Ginkel JM, Hafsteinsdóttir TB, Lindeman E, Ettema RG, Grobbee DE, Schuurmans MJ. In-hospital risk prediction for post-stroke depression: development and validation of the Post-stroke Depression Prediction Scale. Stroke. 2013;44:2441-5. [PMID: 23868275]

Goldstein LB, Simel DL. Is this patient having a stroke? JAMA. 2005; 293:2391-402. [PMID: 15900010]

van der Worp HB, van Gijn J. Acute ischemic stroke. N Engl J Med. 2007; 357:572-9. [PMID: 17687132]

Wang Y, Wang Y, Zhao X, et al; CHANCE Investigators. Clopidogrel with aspirin in acute minor stroke or transient ischemic attack. N Engl J Med. 2013;369:11-9. [PMID: 23803136]

Chapter 76

Altered Mental Status, Dementia, and Delirium

Jennifer S. Bequette, MD
Valerie J. Lang, MD

Altered mental status is a nonspecific term indicating an abnormality in intellect or behavior, which may be used to describe patients along the spectrum from mild cognitive impairment (MCI) to the persistent vegetative state (Table 1). Although dementia and delirium usually occur in similar patient populations and there may be overlap of some clinical features, they represent specific disorders with differing approaches to evaluation and management; therefore, distinguishing between them is critical. The evaluation of a patient with an alteration in mental status involves discriminating between dementia and delirium (Table 2) or other conditions, confirming the diagnosis, and searching for a potentially reversible cause.

Dementia

Dementia is defined as a progressive deterioration of cognitive function that leads to impairment in both social and occupational functioning. This acquired, persistent impairment of intellectual function results in compromise of at least 3 of the following spheres of mental activity: language, memory, visuospatial skills, emotion or personality, and cognition (abstraction, calculation, judgment, and executive function). It is important to recognize that the diagnosis of dementia is not based on memory loss alone. Alzheimer disease is the most common cause, accounting for up to 60% to 80% of cases (Table 3). Advancing age is the major risk factor for dementia. Because the population is living longer, dementia is increasingly a public health concern.

Dementia must be distinguished from MCI, which is defined as deficits in cognition that do not meet the criteria for dementia and do not interfere with the ability to carry out activities of daily living (ADLs). Almost all individuals older than 40 years of age report occasional forgetfulness, and there is a universal age-related decline in cognition that chiefly affects memory, learning, and problem solving. Mild cognitive impairment is considered an intermediate state between normal aging and dementia. Development of dementia in patients with MCI occurs at a rate of approximately 10% to 15% per year, with a positive family history for Alzheimer disease being a risk factor for progression. However, there is currently no clear benefit to

Table 1. Definitions of Impaired Attention and Cognition

Mild cognitive impairment	Deterioration in memory, learning, and problem solving that is greater than expected for age and educational level but does not interfere with occupational or social function
Dementia	Progressive deterioration of cognitive function measureable by standardized tests and sufficient to impair social or occupational function
Delirium	A state of fluctuating attention, impaired concentration, incoherence, disorientation (usually of acute onset), and hypoactive or agitated confusion in which excitement, hyperarousal, and disturbances of perception may be present
Persistent vegetative or minimally conscious state	A state of wakefulness lacking awareness of one's environment or purposeful activity, usually caused by severe injury to the cerebral hemispheres, with sufficient sparing of the diencephalon and brainstem to allow persistent autonomic and motor reflexes and sleep-wake cycles; complex reflexes are noted in some patients, including eye movements, yawning, and motor responses to noxious stimuli, but no awareness of self or environment

Table 2. Delirium and Dementia

Feature	Delirium	Dementia
Onset	Abrupt, with identifiable date	Gradual, cannot be dated
Duration	Acute, generally lasting days to weeks (rarely months)	Long duration, progresses over years
Clinical course	Usually reversible	Chronically progressive
Disorientation	Early finding	Late finding
Mental status	Variable moment to moment	Generally stable from day to day
Memory	Both short- and long-term loss	Short-term loss is greatest
Vital signs	Sometimes abnormal	Typically normal
Attention span	Strikingly short	Usually reduced
Sleep-wake cycle	Hour-to-hour variation	Day-night reversal
Psychomotor activity	Early psychomotor changes (hyper- or hypoactive)	Late psychomotor changes

Table 3. Causes of Dementia

Alzheimer Dementia

Alzheimer disease	Most common cause of dementia (60%-80% of cases). The result of structural neuronal changes with pathologic features including deposition of insoluble, neurotoxic β-amyloid protein in extracellular parenchymal plaques and intracellular accumulation of neurofibrillary tangles composed of abnormal tau protein

Non-Alzheimer Dementias

Frontotemporal dementia	Disproportionate atrophy of the frontal and anterior temporal brain regions. Characterized by language difficulties, personality changes, and behavioral disturbances
Dementia with Lewy bodies	Characterized by parkinsonism that is responsive to dopaminergic therapy, visual hallucinations, and/or fluctuating cognition. Intraneuronal Lewy body inclusions in the cerebral cortex
Vascular dementia	Consequence of progressive ischemic brain injury; stepwise deterioration
Normal pressure hydrocephalus	Triad of cognitive decline, gait impairment, and urinary incontinence in the setting of normal CSF pressure

Potentially Reversible Causes of Dementia

Nutritional	Vitamin B_{12} deficiency, thiamine deficiency
Inflammatory and autoimmune	SLE, CNS vasculitis, sarcoidosis, granulomatosis with polyangiitis, paraneoplastic disease
Infectious	Brain abscess, chronic meningitis, HIV, CNS Whipple disease, syphilis, viral encephalitis
Endocrine	Hypothyroidism, hyperthyroidism, hypoparathyroidism
Structural	Hydrocephalus, brain tumor, subdural hematoma, postconcussive syndrome
Toxic/metabolic	Drugs, heavy metal exposure
Psychiatric	Depression, catatonia, schizophrenia

CNS = central nervous system; CSF = cerebrospinal fluid; SLE = systemic lupus erythematosus.

early identification or treatment of MCI to decrease progression to dementia or improve clinical outcomes.

The clinical manifestations of dementia depend primarily on the location of pathologic changes. The clinical pattern of dementia can be divided into cortical and subcortical types. Alzheimer disease is a type of cortical dementia, with characteristic memory deficits and language impairment. Conversely, subcortical dementias include features of parkinsonism, apathy, bradyphrenia (slow response time), and depression.

Prevention

Treatment of hypertension, hyperlipidemia, and diabetes mellitus reduces the incidence of vascular dementia by decreasing risk factors for stroke. Specific lifestyle modifications, such as smoking cessation, engaging in regular physical exercise and mental activities (eg, solving puzzles), and avoiding head trauma, may also be beneficial. **Nonsteroidal anti-inflammatory drugs (NSAIDs), aspirin, and hormone replacement therapy have not been shown to prevent cognitive decline or dementia. Medications should be carefully reviewed at each visit to avoid unnecessary treatment that can cause delirium or exacerbate preexisting dementia.**

Screening

The U.S. Preventive Services Task Force has concluded that there is insufficient evidence of benefit for screening for dementia in the general population.

Because cognitive impairment may be difficult to detect clinically, multiple brief, standardized, office-based tests of cognitive function are available if screening is considered appropriate, such as in high-risk patients (eg, those with prior stroke or other neurologic conditions).

Two commonly used tests are the Folstein Mini–Mental State Examination (MMSE) and the Montreal Cognitive Assessment (MoCA). The MMSE contains items for testing memory, language, calculation, and executive function. Although the MMSE had been the most widely used, it is now proprietary and therefore less available. The MoCA (www.mocatest.org) is a more universally available assessment tool for testing the cognitive domains of executive function, visuospatial processing, and verbal fluency. Both tests may be administered in approximately 10 minutes and scores are reported on a 30-point scale.

When screening with any instrument, it is important to consider the level of education attained by the patient being tested. Low education levels might make successful completion of the screening tools difficult and can result in an unreliable score. In this situation, as with all patients being evaluated for dementia, it is important to gather accounts from the patient's family and/or friends to establish and confirm the time course and level of decline.

Diagnosis

The diagnosis of dementia is based primarily on the presence of cognitive deficits, the clinical pattern of the cognitive change, rate of progression, and the associated impairment in ADLs.

When taking a patient's history, clinicians should inquire about subjective memory loss and word-finding difficulties. In addition, they should ask about impaired instrumental ADLs, such as dressing, grooming, housework, laundry, using the telephone, food preparation, shopping, transportation, keeping appointments, finances, taking medications, and hobbies. Any potentially dangerous behaviors should also be assessed, such as failure to turn off the stove, wandering, or getting lost; having a caregiver or family member present for these questions is essential. Changes in personality, mood, decreased energy, decreased appetite, sleep disturbance, decreased enjoyment of activities, and agitation should be evaluated as well. Because many clinical features of depression mimic dementia, this should be ruled out.

The physical examination should focus on signs of acute or chronic illness that may be contributing to memory deficit. The neurologic examination should include assessment of the level of alertness, orientation, concentration, and mood, as well as evidence of gait abnormalities, clumsiness, sensory abnormalities, incontinence, and rigidity.

Office-based cognitive testing using a standardized instrument is used to more objectively evaluate cognitive deficits. For example, scores between 25 and 28 on the MMSE or MoCA (based on a 30-point scale) are associated with MCI, while scores <22 are supportive of a diagnosis of dementia. The clinical severity of dementia may also be estimated with these tools. For example, mild dementia implies that cognitive loss has progressed to the point of causing problems with normal ADLs, such as misplacing items, becoming lost in familiar places, and experiencing deterioration in personal care. Moderate dementia is characterized by impaired cognitive abilities (eg, language) and disability in performing basic ADLs such as running a household. Patients with severe dementia require assistance with all basic ADLs.

Neuropsychological testing is more extensive testing evaluating multiple cognitive domains, which is usually performed by clinicians with specific training in cognitive disorders. Although neuropsychological testing is not routinely performed on all patients, it may be helpful in patients with atypical findings or in those in whom the diagnosis of dementia is unclear based on office testing.

Diagnostic laboratory testing (Table 4) may disclose a reversible cause of the dementia. Neuroimaging with noncontrast computed tomography scans of the head should be considered and will help exclude a space-occupying neoplasia, intracerebral bleed, or hydrocephalus. If vascular dementia is considered, magnetic resonance imaging might be helpful. Cerebrospinal fluid examination is not indicated in the routine evaluation of dementia but is an important diagnostic test in special clinical circumstances: rapidly progressive dementia; age of onset less than 60 years; systemic cancer, infection, or inflammatory autoimmune disease; immunosuppressed or immunodeficiency state; and positive syphilis serology. Genetic testing is not part of the routine evaluation of dementia.

Patients with chronic dementia presenting with acute to subacute deterioration require further assessment for the cause of their decline. The differential diagnosis of this deterioration can include cerebral ischemia (stroke or vasculitis), infection (urinary tract infection, meningitis, or pneumonia), metabolic conditions (hyperglycemia, hepatic insufficiency, or kidney disease), intoxications (alcohol or medication side effect or overdose), trauma (concussion or subdural hematoma), and structural lesions (brain mass or obstructive hydrocephalus).

If a patient presents with rapidly progressive dementia, early age of onset, and prominent myoclonus, a diagnosis of Creutzfeldt-Jakob disease should be considered. In this case, electroencephalogram should be obtained and will show the characteristic pattern of triphasic sharp waves.

Therapy

The mainstay of therapy for dementia is proactive management to maximize functional status by assessing and treating psychiatric and behavioral symptoms with nonpharmacologic interventions (Table 5). Patients and caregivers should be educated about sleep hygiene, including sleep scheduling, nap restriction, daily physical activity, reduction of caffeine intake, and evaluation of nocturia. Cognitive stimulation through activities designed to stimulate thinking, cognition, and memory has been associated with an improved quality of life. Home-based education and exercise programs can help with

Table 4. Laboratory and Other Studies for Dementia

Test	Notes
Recommended Studies in All Patients	
Noncontrast head CT scan	Numerous expert consensus statements recommend neuroimaging to discover unsuspected structural lesions
Complete blood count	Leukocytosis, anemia, or thrombocytopenia may indicate a condition related to cognitive problems
Metabolic profile	Abnormal sodium, calcium, glucose, and liver or kidney function can be related to cognitive problems
Thyroid-stimulating hormone	Thyroid disease can cause cognitive problems
Vitamin B$_{12}$	If low-normal, measure methylmalonic acid and homocysteine
Folate	Consider particularly in the setting of very poor nutrition
Suggested Studies in Selected Patients	
HIV antibody	Advanced HIV disease can lead to dementia
Toxicology screen	Screen for benzodiazepines
Erythrocyte sedimentation rate	Consider vasculitis and systemic rheumatologic diseases, including systemic lupus erythematosus
Heavy metal screen	Useful when there is environmental exposure
Rapid plasma reagin (RPR)	Tertiary syphilis can cause dementia
Lyme serology	Consider in high-risk patients
Urinalysis	Look for infection, malignancy, or other systemic diseases
Lumbar puncture	Consider in the setting of a reactive RPR; patient aged <55 y; rapidly progressive dementia; immunosuppression; possible CNS metastatic cancer, infection, or vasculitis; possible hydrocephalus or Creutzfeldt-Jakob disease
Electroencephalogram	Obtain in the setting of delirium, seizures, encephalitis, or possible Creutzfeldt-Jakob disease
Neuropsychological testing	May be helpful in the differential diagnosis of Alzheimer disease, to distinguish from frontotemporal dementia, major depression, mild cognitive impairment, or normal aging

CNS = central nervous system; CT = computed tomography; RPR = rapid plasma reagin.

Table 5. Nonpharmacologic Treatment for Alzheimer Disease and Other Dementias

Ensure a safe, familiar, nonthreatening, well-lighted environment with simple routines, vigilance, and reassurance.

Address causes of frustration and irritability, such as pain, infection, and hunger.

Treat depression and anxiety.

Encourage frequent engagement and socialization.

Encourage exercise.

Encourage cognitive tasks.

Optimize hearing, vision, and orientation.

Avoid dehydration, falls, infections, and aspiration.

physical functioning of patients with dementia. Patients with vascular dementia should be counseled on the importance of smoking cessation, which may stabilize or improve cognition. Local and national organizations and support groups may be useful to clinicians and families.

The goal of pharmacotherapy is to delay cognitive and functional decline, although currently available medications are limited in effectiveness. Cholinesterase inhibitors (donepezil, rivastigmine, and galantamine) have been shown to improve the daily cognitive function of persons with all stages of dementia due to Alzheimer disease, dementia with Lewy bodies, Parkinson disease dementia, and mixed Alzheimer disease and vascular dementia. Treatment must be continuous and should be initiated once the diagnosis has been made. Memantine is a noncompetitive NMDA (N-methyl-D-aspartate) receptor antagonist that is indicated in moderate to advanced Alzheimer disease and vascular dementia, either in addition to or in place of a cholinesterase inhibitor.

Concomitant depression should be treated, but antidepressants with anticholinergic side effects, such as tricyclic antidepressants (amitriptyline and nortriptyline), should be avoided. Clinicians should consider using an antipsychotic medication in the treatment of hallucinations and delusions or behavioral disturbances (aggression, severe irritability, agitation, or explosiveness), if there is risk of harm to the patient or others or if patient distress is significant and nonpharmacologic treatments have been ineffective. These agents should be used cautiously because of the serious adverse effects including stroke and death. Likewise, the use of sedative-hypnotics, antihistamines, or benzodiazepines for sleep induction should be avoided in patients with dementia because of side effects and potential hazards, including exacerbation of delirium. **High-dose vitamin E, aspirin, and NSAIDs have not been found to slow the progression of symptoms in Alzheimer disease and should not be recommended.**

Follow-up

Patients who have been diagnosed with MCI should undergo reassessment of cognitive function at follow-up visits. In patients with dementia, each visit should include the evaluation of general health and hygiene and the level of functional abilities. In patients who still drive, clinicians should inquire about motor vehicle accidents or near accidents and changes in driving habits or patterns. Patients with potential driving impairment should undergo a driving evaluation or be advised to no longer drive. Caregivers should be educated about the natural history of the patient's dementia and referred to appropriate support programs. Assessment of the ability of the patient to be cared for independently should be ongoing.

Table 6. Precipitants of Delirium

Metabolic	Dehydration
	Alcohol withdrawal (delirium tremens)
	Hypothermia, hyperthermia
	Hyponatremia, hypernatremia
	Hypercalcemia
	Hypoglycemia, hyperglycemia (diabetic ketoacidosis or hyperosmolar syndrome)
	Hypothyroid, hyperthyroid
	Hypoxemia, hypercarbia
	Malnutrition, thiamine deficiency
Toxic	Medication side effect
	Other CNS toxins
Infection	CNS: meningitis, encephalitis, subdural empyema, brain abscess
	Outside CNS: urinary tract infection, pneumonia, and sepsis most common, although can occur with other infections
	Seizure (postictal state, status epilepticus)
Other	Altered environment (hospitalization, restraints, or invasive medical interventions)
	Pain
	Urinary retention, fecal impaction

CNS = central nervous system.

Delirium

Delirium is an acute state of confusion and may be either hypoactive, with a depressed level of consciousness, or hyperactive, with an increased level of alertness. Hypoactive delirium is more commonly overlooked, but both forms of delirium are associated with a higher risk of complications including prolonged hospitalization, impairment of physical function, increased rates of institutionalization, subsequent development of dementia, and death. Delirium often results from both underlying vulnerability and acute precipitating factors. Predisposing factors include advanced age, baseline cognitive impairment, multiple comorbidities, male sex, depression, alcohol abuse, and sensory impairment.

Prevention

Prevention of delirium includes interventions targeting specific risk factors, such as cognitive impairment, sleep deprivation, immobility, sensory impairment, and dehydration. Some measures that can help prevent delirium are providing access to glasses and hearing aids; frequent reorientation to place, time, and date; minimizing nocturnal disruptions and increasing daytime stimulation to facilitate a normal sleep-wake cycle; and minimizing medication use. These measures are also instituted for patients with delirium, in addition to addressing the specific precipitants (eg, hypoxemia, infection, or pain) and managing the symptoms of delirium.

Diagnosis

For patients with delirium, rapid detection, evaluation, and intervention are essential. The diagnosis of delirium is clinical. The Confusion Assessment Method tool is a 4-point bedside assessment instrument for delirium that has good sensitivity and specificity for detecting delirium. Although laboratory tests, imaging studies, or other studies may assist in determining an underlying cause, they are not helpful in making the diagnosis of delirium.

Identifying the precipitant is important for the management of delirium (Table 6). Clinicians should look for association of the onset of delirium with other events, such as medication changes or development of physical symptoms, as well as the presence of sensory deprivation (eg, absence of glasses or hearing aids) or uncontrolled pain. A medication history should be taken, with particular attention to sedative-hypnotic agents, barbiturates, alcohol, antidepressants, anticholinergic agents, opioid analgesics, antipsychotics, anticonvulsants, antihistamines, and antiparkinsonian agents, recognizing that drugs that are well tolerated in young patients can cause delirium in the elderly. The risk of delirium increases with the number of prescribed medications. Signs of infection, heart failure, myocardial ischemia, dehydration, malnutrition, urinary retention, and fecal impaction, or evidence of liver or kidney failure should be assessed.

The laboratory evaluation should be tailored to the specific clinical situation (Table 7). In most patients, a complete blood count, basic metabolic profile (including sodium, calcium, bicarbonate, glucose, blood urea nitrogen, creatinine, and glucose), and urinalysis should be obtained. The yield of additional tests and procedures is low unless a specific condition is suggested by the history or physical examination. **Brain imaging is usually unhelpful in the diagnosis of delirium unless there is a history of a fall or headache or evidence of focal neurologic impairment.**

Therapy

Treatment of delirium requires identifying and managing the underlying precipitant, decreasing sensory deprivation, frequent reorientation to place, time, and date, and facilitating a normal sleep-wake cycle.

Antipsychotic agents should be used only when behavioral measures have been ineffective for symptom control and are neces-

Table 7. Laboratory and Other Studies for the Evaluation of Delirium

Test	Notes
Recommended Studies in All Patients	
Complete blood count	Screen for infection and anemia
Serum electrolytes, calcium	Screen for hypernatremia, hyponatremia, hypercalcemia, and acid-base abnormality
BUN, creatinine	Screen for dehydration and kidney failure
Glucose	Screen for hypoglycemia, hyperglycemia, and hyperosmolar state
Urinalysis, culture	Screen for urinary tract infection
Pulse oximetry	Screen for hypoxemia
Suggested Studies in Selected Patients	
Aminotransferases, albumin, bilirubin, PT, ammonia	If liver failure and hepatic encephalopathy are suspected
Chest radiography	If pneumonia or heart failure is suspected or there is no obvious cause of delirium
Electrocardiography	If myocardial infarction or arrhythmia is suspected
Arterial blood gases	Helpful in patients with COPD, if hypercapnia or acid-base abnormality is suspected
Drug levels, toxin screen	If ingestion is suspected or patient is taking medication with narrow therapeutic window; keep in mind that delirium can occur with "normal" serum levels of a drug
Cerebral imaging	CT/MRI reserved for coma, patients with focal abnormalities on neurologic examination, head trauma, and other situations where suspicion is high or no cause is identified after initial evaluation
Lumbar puncture	Rarely helpful in the absence of high suspicion of meningitis, encephalitis, or subarachnoid hemorrhage
Electroencephalography	Rarely assists in the evaluation unless nonconvulsive status epilepticus is suspected

BUN = blood urea nitrogen; COPD = chronic obstructive pulmonary disease; CT = computed tomography; MRI = magnetic resonance imaging; PT = prothrombin time.

sary to prevent patient harm. Both conventional and atypical antipsychotic agents are equally effective in treating agitation associated with delirium. However, they are also associated with increased morbidity and mortality when used in the elderly to treat delirium, and these medications carry a "black box" warning for this indication. All antipsychotic agents may also pose a risk for ventricular arrhythmias and extrapyramidal side effects, as well as the neuroleptic malignant syndrome. The lowest dose of the least toxic agent that successfully controls the agitation should be used. Use of benzodiazepines may worsen or prolong delirium and should be reserved for patients with alcohol withdrawal, in which they are the treatment of choice.

Use of physical restraints is generally avoided, as they can increase patient agitation and risk of injury, but they may be used with caution if other measures to control a patient's behavior are ineffective or if an unrestrained patient may cause personal injury or injury to others.

Follow-Up

Delirium is distressing for significant others, and it is important to address their concerns and manage expectations. Delirium often resolves within days after the precipitating factor has been managed, but complete resolution may take weeks to months.

Bibliography

Blass DM, Rabins PV. In the clinic. Dementia. Ann Intern Med. 2008;148:ITC4-1-ITC4-16. [PMID: 18378944]

Han JH, Wilber ST. Altered mental status in older patients in the emergency department. Clin Geriatr Med. 2013;29:101-36. [PMID: 23177603]

Chapter 77

Peripheral Neuropathy

Christopher A. Klipstein, MD

Peripheral neuropathy is a general term for any disorder affecting the peripheral nerves. Peripheral neuropathies are common and may involve a single nerve (mononeuropathy), 2 or more nerves in different sites (mononeuropathy multiplex), or many nerves over a wide area, leading to a more generalized disorder (polyneuropathy). Clinical manifestations include various combinations of altered sensation, pain, weakness, and autonomic dysfunction. The history and examination, in combination with electrodiagnostic studies, are used to determine the type of neuropathy present, thereby narrowing the list of possible causes.

Differential Diagnosis

Peripheral neuropathies are classified as listed in Table 1. Mononeuropathies are most often caused by nerve entrapment or compression. Two common mononeuropathies include carpal tunnel syndrome and Bell palsy. Carpal tunnel syndrome involves median nerve compression at the wrist. Patients report paresthesias, pain, and, occasionally, weakness in the hand and wrist. Symptoms can radiate up the forearm at times. The paresthesias are often worse at night or when holding a book or steering a car. Pain and decreased grip strength can make it difficult to make a fist or grasp small objects. Examination may show sensory loss over the palmar surface of the first 3 digits (median nerve distribution), weakness of thumb abduction and opposition, and atrophy of the thenar eminence.

Bell palsy refers to unilateral facial muscle weakness due to acute dysfunction of the facial nerve. Growing evidence implicates facial nerve inflammation due to viral infection (especially herpes simplex virus type 1 infection) in the pathogenesis of Bell palsy. Other causes that should be considered are HIV and Lyme disease. Symptoms typically begin suddenly and peak over 1 to 2 days. Paralysis of the upper and lower face distinguishes Bell palsy from facial paralysis caused by stroke, which affects only the lower facial muscles (sparing the forehead and eye).

Mononeuropathy multiplex refers to simultaneous involvement of 2 or more separate, noncontiguous peripheral nerves. Mononeuropathy multiplex is often the result of a systemic disease (eg, diabetes mellitus, amyloidosis, vasculitis, or sarcoidosis); the mechanism of nerve injury may be a combination of compressive, ischemic, metabolic, and inflammatory factors. When successive acute involvement of individual nerves is accompanied by pain, a vasculitis should be suspected as the cause.

Polyneuropathy refers to diffuse, generalized, usually symmetric involvement of the peripheral nerves. Polyneuropathy is often a manifestation of systemic disease or exposure to a toxin or medication. Polyneuropathy presents in variable ways, depending on the pathophysiology of the underlying cause. Polyneuropathies can be characterized as axonal or demyelinating. Axonal polyneuropathies result from dysfunction of peripheral nerve cells and their axons, usually from metabolic or toxic causes (eg, diabetes or alcohol). Demyelinating polyneuropathies are due to dysfunction of the myelin sheath that encases many peripheral nerves.

Axonal polyneuropathies typically present as symmetric distal sensory loss, with or without burning, tingling, or muscle weakness. Because the longest nerves are affected earliest and most severely, initial symptoms are usually in the feet, beginning with numbness and paresthesias in the toes that gradually proceed up the limb, eventually resulting in depressed ankle reflexes and atrophy of the intrinsic foot muscles. As the sensory symptoms ascend, the fingers and hands become involved, resulting in the classic "stocking-glove" pattern of

Table 1. Classification of Peripheral Neuropathies

Category	Distribution/Pattern	Examples	Mechanism
Mononeuropathy	Focal (single nerve)	Carpal tunnel syndrome, Bell palsy	Entrapment, inflammation
Mononeuropathy multiplex	Asymmetric, multifocal (several noncontiguous nerves)	Vasculitis, diabetes mellitus, lymphoma, amyloidosis, sarcoidosis, Lyme disease, acute HIV infection, leprosy	Ischemia, infiltration, inflammation
Axonal polyneuropathy	Symmetric, distal, predominantly sensory symptoms, sometimes also motor symptoms	Alcohol, drugs, chronic arsenic exposure, diabetes mellitus, uremia, low vitamin B_{12} or folate, hypothyroidism, paraproteinemia, paraneoplastic syndrome, chronic HIV infection, Charcot-Marie-Tooth disease	Toxin, metabolic, neoplasm, hereditary defect, inflammation
Demyelinating polyneuropathy	Symmetric, often proximal, predominantly motor symptoms, spreading in ascending fashion	Acute arsenic toxicity, Guillain-Barré syndrome, chronic inflammatory demyelinating polyneuropathy, paraproteinemia	Toxin, immunologic dysfunction, neoplasm

Table 2. Peripheral Nerve Dysfunction in Diabetes Mellitus

Classification	Signs and Symptoms
Autonomic neuropathy	Constipation, early satiety, erectile dysfunction, hyperhidrosis or hypohidrosis, and orthostatic hypotension
Diabetic lumbosacral radiculoneuropathy (diabetic amyotrophy)	Pain in proximal leg (severe) followed by weakness, with or without sensory loss (proximal), and with or without weight loss
Mononeuropathy	Sensory loss with or without pain at onset, weakness in distribution of single nerve (such as the median or a cranial nerve)
Radiculopathy	Sensory loss or pain, thoracic levels often affected, weakness in distribution of nerve root(s)
Sensorimotor peripheral neuropathy	Asymptomatic (sometimes), distal sensory loss and weakness (length dependent), pain (often)
Small-fiber neuropathy	Burning extremity pain without weakness, usually distal or lower, may be non-length dependent

sensory loss, paresthesias, and sometimes burning pain. Long-standing diabetes (or impaired glucose tolerance) is the most common cause of axonal polyneuropathy, and the distribution of affected nerves may lead to a variety of symptoms and findings (Table 2). Other causes include alcoholism, vitamin B_{12} deficiency, and uremia.

In contrast, most patients with a demyelinating polyneuropathy initially present with motor symptoms. For example, hereditary motor sensory polyneuropathy (Charcot-Marie-Tooth) disease is a relatively common spectrum of hereditary demyelinating disorders caused by mutations in one of several genes associated with maintaining the structure and function of myelin. These disorders present with sensory deficits, distal leg weakness, and often foot deformities. Acquired demyelinating diseases, however, usually present with symmetric proximal weakness, with examples being Guillain-Barré syndrome (see Chapter 80) or chronic inflammatory demyelinating polyneuropathy.

A variety of other disorders may cause symptoms similar to those of a peripheral neuropathy. Myopathies (muscle disease) can cause muscle weakness, and diseases of the brain (eg, stroke, tumor, and multiple sclerosis) or spinal cord (eg, herniated disc and spinal stenosis) can cause sensory or motor symptoms or signs. Although the pattern of sensory and motor symptoms–along with the presence or absence of upper motor neuron signs (eg, hyperreflexia, Babinski sign, and clonus)–can often identify the location of the pathology, electrodiagnostic and neuroimaging studies may be needed to distinguish muscle and central nervous system disorders from peripheral neuropathies.

Evaluation

For patients with a peripheral neuropathy, the distribution of symptoms, combined with the characterization of the pathology (axonal or demyelinating), should be used to identify potential causes (see Table 1). Patients with severe or rapidly progressive symptoms or with no clear cause warrant prompt evaluation. Despite extensive diagnostic evaluation, no cause is found in approximately 20% of polyneuropathy cases.

Clinicians should focus the initial history on the distribution, time course, and nature of the deficit (sensory, motor, or both). In addition, they should ask about symptoms of systemic diseases that are associated with neuropathy (diabetes or uremia), exposure to medications (Table 3) or toxins that can cause a peripheral neuropathy (alcohol or heavy metals), and any family history of neuropathy. In the appropriate clinical context, they should also inquire about recent viral illnesses, HIV risk factors, foreign travel (leprosy), and the possibility of a tick bite (Lyme disease). The review of systems should be used to look for evidence of other organ involvement and symptoms of an underlying malignancy.

The physical examination should be used to confirm the distribution of nerve involvement and to determine the extent of motor and/or sensory involvement. Abnormalities detected in the distribution of a single nerve indicate a mononeuropathy. Strength in all major muscle groups should be measured, and all sensory modalities (ie, light touch, pinprick, temperature, vibration, and proprioception) should be tested. Deep tendon reflexes should be assessed, as hyporeflexia suggests peripheral pathology, whereas hyperactive reflexes imply a central cause. The patient's gait should be observed, and a Romberg test (afferent sensory pathways and posterior spinal column) should be performed. In addition, evidence of systemic disease (lymphadenopathy, organomegaly, rash, or arthritis) should be sought.

Electromyography and nerve conduction studies are often the most useful tests in the evaluation of peripheral neuropathies, especially when symptoms are severe or rapidly progressive. These tests augment the ability of the history and physical examination to distinguish neuropathies from myopathies and to differentiate mononeuropathies from polyneuropathies. For patients with polyneuropathies, electromyography and nerve conduction studies provide information as to the type of fibers involved (motor, sensory, or both) and characterize the pathologic process as primarily axonal or

Table 3. Drugs Associated with Peripheral Neuropathies

Amiodarone

Cisplatin

Colchicine

Dapsone

Hydralazine

Isoniazid

Leflunomide

Linezolid

Metronidazole

Nitrofurantoin

Nucleoside reverse transcriptase analogs

Oxaliplatin

Paclitaxel

Phenytoin

Vincristine

demyelinating. **Electromyography and nerve conduction studies may not be necessary when the history and examination point to a clear etiology of peripheral neuropathy (eg, classic carpal tunnel syndrome) or when an underlying condition exits that can explain the clinical presentation (eg, long-standing diabetes in a patient with a mild distal symmetric polyneuropathy).**

Laboratory tests for the most common causes of an axonal polyneuropathy often include measures of glucose metabolism (fasting blood glucose, hemoglobin A_{1c}, glucose tolerance testing), serum creatinine, thyroid-stimulating hormone, vitamin B_{12} level, complete blood count, erythrocyte sedimentation rate, serum protein electrophoresis, and urinalysis. In specific clinical contexts, other studies are potentially useful, including an antinuclear antibody test, HIV test, Lyme titer, and heavy metal screen.

When electromyography and nerve conduction findings suggest an acquired demyelinating neuropathy, the most common causes are Guillain-Barré syndrome and chronic inflammatory demyelinating polyneuropathy. Diagnosis is based on clinical recognition of progressive muscle weakness and reduced deep tendon reflexes, combined with abnormal electrodiagnostic studies. Cerebrospinal fluid evaluation in both conditions may show albuminocytologic dissociation, which is an elevation of the protein level with few or no leukocytes present.

Nerve biopsy (usually of the sural nerve) is indicated only for investigation of possible vasculitis, amyloidosis, sarcoidosis, leprosy, or tumor infiltration. Molecular genetic tests are commercially available for several hereditary neuropathies.

Therapy

Conservative treatment options for carpal tunnel syndrome include wrist splints and glucocorticoid injections. Steroid injections help symptoms acutely, but at 1 year there is no difference in symptoms compared to those who do not receive steroid injections, although the time to surgery is greater with steroid injections. Surgery should be considered for patients with severe sensory loss, hand weakness, moderate to severe electrodiagnostic findings, or failure to respond to conservative therapy.

Treatment of Bell palsy involves eye patching and lubrication to protect the cornea. Patients treated with glucocorticoids (such as prednisone) within 72 hours of symptom onset have improved outcomes. **The benefit of antiviral therapy in treating Bell palsy has not been established.** The prognosis is related to the severity of the initial symptoms; although most patients experience excellent recovery, those who present with complete unilateral facial paralysis may not recover full function of the facial nerve.

Treatment of axonal polyneuropathies is centered on removal of the toxic agent (eg, alcohol) or improvement of the underlying metabolic condition (eg, diabetes or vitamin B_{12} deficiency), which often halts the progression of symptoms. Pain and dysesthesias should be treated symptomatically using agents such as gabapentin, pregabalin, or duloxetine; venlafaxine and tricyclic medications are also effective. **Opioids should generally be avoided in treating peripheral neuropathy but may be considered for acute, severe pain or when other treatments have been unsuccessful.** Tramadol, a nonnarcotic centrally acting agent, can be used as an adjunct to control pain. Medications should be started at low dosages, slowly increased as tolerated, and continued for at least 4 weeks to determine effectiveness. Combined use of several medications with different mechanisms of action is often more successful than use of a single agent. Patients with diminished distal sensation should be educated about appropriate foot care to decrease the risk of foot ulcers and infections.

Vasculitic mononeuropathies and acute demyelinating polyneuropathies require prompt recognition and treatment with immunomodulating agents. Patients with Guillain-Barré syndrome should be treated with plasmapheresis or intravenous immune globulin; there is no evidence that glucocorticoids shorten the course or reduce residual deficits in Guillain-Barré syndrome. For chronic inflammatory demyelinating polyneuropathy, plasmapheresis, intravenous immune globulin, and glucocorticoids are effective. Most patients need long-term treatment with plasmapheresis or intravenous immune globulin every 4 to 6 weeks to prevent relapse.

Bibliography

Pascuzzi RM. Peripheral neuropathy. Med Clin North Am. 2009;93:317-42. [PMID: 19272511]

Chapter 78

Approach to Selected Movement Disorders

Bryan Ho, MD
Lianne Marks, MD, PhD

Movement disorders are a category of neurologic disease that leads to abnormalities in movement, specifically due to dysfunction in the extrapyramidal motor system. Depending on the type and degree of dysfunction, patients can present with a variety of clinical syndromes of too much movement (hyperkinesia) or too little movement (hypokinesia). Hyperkinetic disorders include tremor, tics, dystonia, chorea, myoclonus, and akathisia. Hypokinetic disorders are generally related to the basal ganglia (such as in Parkinson disease) or to mental disorders or debility. Distinctions between these different types of movement disorders are described in Table 1.

Tremor refers to involuntary oscillatory movements of a body part over a fixed axis, usually (but not always) a joint. Tremor is described in terms of its amplitude and frequency and the presence of resting, postural, or action components. Tremor is the most common type of movement disorder encountered in general clinical practice and can be a primary disorder or secondary to a variety of drugs and metabolic conditions.

Tics refer to movements that are stereotyped in nature but are temporarily suppressible. Generally, when suppressing these movements, patients describe a buildup of anxiety or internal discomfort that is released when the movements are allowed to occur. Tics are commonly associated with Tourette syndrome but can also be part of other hyperkinetic movement disorders.

Dystonia refers to involuntary, sustained contraction of agonist/antagonist muscles, which can often lead to uncomfortable or even painful twisting, bizarre-looking postures. Dystonia can be classified as focal (involving only one body part), segmental (2 or more contiguous body parts), multifocal (2 or more noncontiguous body parts), hemidystonic (one side of the body), or generalized. Primary dystonias are rare, while secondary dystonias are more common and can be due to drugs that block dopamine pathways.

Chorea refers to involuntary, random, purposeless movements that can involve the limbs, face, or trunk. Chorea is derived from the Greek word "to dance," and patients may have strikingly abnormal gaits due to random interruptions of voluntary movement as they walk. Patients

Table 1. General Classification of Abnormal Movements

Type of Movement	Clinical Features	Selected Causes
Hypokinetic		
Parkinsonism	Akinesia/bradykinesia, rigidity, tremor at rest, postural instability, gait freezing, and flexion posture	Parkinson disease, diffuse Lewy body disease, atypical neurodegenerative Parkinson-plus syndromes, hydrocephalus, vascular parkinsonism, neuroleptic-induced parkinsonism, Wilson disease, and toxic effect of drugs
Hyperkinetic		
Tremor	Repetitive oscillation of a body part that occurs at rest or with action or postural holding; intention tremor is an action tremor that increases toward the end of the action	Resting tremor: Parkinson disease Action or postural holding tremor: physiologic tremor, essential tremor, midbrain and cerebellar tremor, and dystonic tremor Intention tremor: cerebellar outflow tremor caused by disorders of the cerebellum (degenerative disorders, toxic disorders, or multiple sclerosis)
Tic	Stereotyped, automatic, purposeless movements and vocalizations	Tourette syndrome, cerebral palsy and other developmental delay syndromes, autism, and Huntington disease
Dystonia	Torsional movements that are partially sustained and produce twisting postures	Idiopathic or primary dystonia, dopa-responsive dystonia, anoxic/hypoxic injury, trauma, postencephalitic dystonia, and drug-induced acute or tardive dystonia
Chorea	Random, quick, unsustained, purposeless movements that have an unpredictable flowing pattern	Huntington disease, neuroacanthocytosis, postinfectious chorea, drug-induced chorea, vascular chorea, autoimmune chorea, and chorea gravidarum
Myoclonus	Sudden, shock-like movements of an isolated body part	Physiologic myoclonus, essential myoclonus, metabolic encephalopathy, postanoxic myoclonus, and progressive myoclonic epilepsy
Akathisia	Inner restlessness coupled with repetitive movements	Parkinsonism, drug-induced acute or tardive akathisia, and restless legs syndrome

with chorea have difficulty sustaining a fixed posture, such as tongue protrusion or persistent hand grip. Chorea can be due to neurodegenerative diseases (eg, Huntington disease), autoimmune diseases (eg, systemic lupus erythematosus), and medications, particularly drugs involved in dopamine pathways (eg, antipsychotic agents).

Myoclonus refers to rapid, jerk-like movements due to either sudden muscle contractions (positive myoclonus) or sudden interruption of sustained muscle contractions leading to loss of tone (negative myoclonus), as seen in asterixis. Similar to dystonia, myoclonus is classified by its distribution in the body (focal, segmental, multifocal, or generalized). Most people have some degree of physiologic myoclonus that can occur when falling asleep. Myoclonus may be a clinical component of epilepsy (ie, juvenile myoclonic epilepsy or myoclonic epileptic syndromes). Myoclonus can also be caused by toxic-metabolic derangements (eg, hepatic encephalopathy), severe anoxic brain injury, and certain medication exposures (eg, serotonin syndrome).

Akathisia refers to a sensation of restlessness that generally causes the individual to move the body. Dyskinesia is similar, with repetitive but involuntary movement of a specific area of the body; with akathisia the movement is thought to be at least initially voluntary, and individuals repeat motions to alleviate physical and mental discomfort. This symptom is most frequently associated with a drug, and is commonly related to antipsychotic medications.

Parkinson Disease

Parkinson disease, one of the more common neurodegenerative disorders, is associated with dopamine depletion from the basal ganglia. This loss of dopamine causes major disruptions in the connections to the thalamus and motor cortex, leading to the characteristic signs and symptoms of Parkinson disease. Most cases are idiopathic, although familial cases due to genetic mutations have been documented.

Parkinson disease is a clinical diagnosis based on 3 cardinal clinical features: bradykinesia, resting tremor, and postural instability. The diagnosis is established by the presence of bradykinesia and at least one other cardinal feature. The differential diagnosis of parkinsonism is summarized in Table 2. Parkinson disease presents asymmetrically, with clinical features more prominent on one side of the body. Findings that suggest an alternative diagnosis include symmetric symptoms or signs, early falling, rapid progression, poor response to levodopa, early dementia, early autonomic failure, and ataxia. There are many other nonmotor Parkinson symptoms, some of which can be quite disabling (Table 3).

The mainstay of drug therapy for Parkinson disease is dopamine replacement with levodopa or dopamine agonists. Levodopa is the most effective drug for symptom management. However, over time, patients on levodopa will inevitably develop motor fluctuations, including dyskinesia (excessive movements similar to chorea) and

Table 2. Differential Diagnosis of Parkinsonism

Disorder	Notes
Degenerative Parkinsonism	
Idiopathic Parkinson disease	Rest tremor, rigidity, bradykinesia, and gait disturbance
Multiple system atrophy	Ataxia, dysautonomia
Progressive supranuclear palsy	Early falls, impaired vertical eye movement
Corticobasal degeneration	Asymmetric spasticity and rigidity, alien limb movement, myoclonus
Dementia with Lewy bodies	Dementia, hallucinations
Secondary Parkinsonism	
Drug (antipsychotic agents, antiemetics, metoclopramide, reserpine, lithium, tetrabenazine, or flunarizine)	Exposure history
Toxin (manganese, MPTP, mercury, methanol, ethanol, or carbon monoxide)	Exposure history
Cerebrovascular disease	History; MRI showing stroke
Head trauma (including pugilistic encephalopathy)	History of head trauma
Hydrocephalus	Lower-body parkinsonism; MRI showing possible contusion
Creutzfeldt-Jakob disease	Rapidly progressive; signs/symptoms of ataxia, dementia, myoclonus, dystonia
Paraneoplastic syndrome	Rapidly progressive; signs/symptoms of ataxia, encephalopathy, myoclonus
Hepatocerebral degeneration	History of liver disease; MRI changes in basal ganglia
Hypothyroidism	Rare; resolves with treatment
Selected Hereditary Disorders Associated With Parkinsonism	
Wilson disease	Must be ruled out in patients aged <50 y; hepatic and psychiatric disease; tremor, dystonia, ataxia
Familial amyotrophy-dementia-parkinsonism	Cognitive/behavioral change; extremity weakness, atrophy; rigidity, bradykinesia
Spinocerebellar ataxia	Autosomal dominant; begins in early life; ataxia predominates
Huntington disease	Chorea, dystonia, psychiatric symptoms, dementia, ataxia
Fragile X-associated tremor/ataxia syndrome	Ataxia, tremor, dementia

MPTP = 1-methyl-4-phenyl-1,2,3,6-tetrahydropyridine; MRI = magnetic resonance imaging.

Table 3. Nonmotor Complications of Parkinson Disease

Type of Complication	Symptoms
Cognitive	Bradyphrenia, confusion, dementia
Behavioral	Depression, anxiety, hallucinations/delusions, psychosis, compulsive/addictive behaviors, hypersexuality, passivity, apathy
Sleep related	Sleep fragmentation, restless legs syndrome, rapid eye movement behavior disorder, excessive daytime sleepiness, sleep-wake reversal, drug-induced sleep attacks
Autonomic	Postural hypotension, bladder and sexual dysfunction, constipation, sialorrhea, seborrhea, excessive sweating
Musculoskeletal	Truncal and neck flexion, falls and fractures, arthritis and other mechanical complications of Parkinson disease
Pain related	Painful dystonia, pain due to mechanical factors, visceral ("off") painful sensations, primary central pain

"wearing-off" effect (sudden return of symptoms and gait freezing as a result of the levodopa losing effect before the next dose). Levodopa is always given in combination with carbidopa, which acts as a peripheral inhibitor of levodopa breakdown, allowing more of the drug to enter the central nervous system. Dopamine agonists (eg, ropinirole and pramipexole) are also effective for treating symptoms, although their effect is generally not as robust as that of levodopa. These agents are less likely to confer motor fluctuations, making them a good option for early disease. Side effects include somnolence, nausea, hallucinations, psychosis, and impulsive behavior.

Essential Tremor

Essential tremor is typically inherited in an autosomal dominant fashion and can involve the upper extremities and/or can cause head bobbing. This high-frequency tremor is present with both limb movement and sustained posture of the involved extremities (unlike the tremor associated with Parkinson disease, which typically occurs at rest). The tremor is characteristically bilateral, but there can be mild to moderate asymmetry. Tremor amplitude can worsen over time and become so severe that it interferes with writing, drinking, and other activities requiring smooth, coordinated upper-limb movements. Many patients report improvement in the tremor with ingestion of alcohol. **The diagnosis of essential tremor is based on clinical features and the elimination of secondary causes.** Patients with mild tremor may not require treatment. For more serious tremor, propranolol and primidone are first-line agents. Either drug may be initiated if the tremor interferes with activities of daily living or causes psychological distress.

Dystonia

All medications that block D_2 dopamine receptors can cause acute dystonic reactions. These movements most often affect the ocular muscles (oculogyric crisis) and the face, jaw, tongue, neck, and trunk. The limbs are rarely affected. Neuroleptic, antiemetic, and serotoninergic agents have been implicated. Treatment consists of parenteral diphenhydramine, benztropine mesylate, or biperiden.

Cervical dystonia, formerly known as torticollis, is the most commonly encountered primary dystonia. It is a focal dystonia that involves the cervical musculature and causes abnormal postures of the head, neck, and shoulders. Quick, nonrhythmic, repetitive movements, usually in a "no-no" pattern, can also occur and may be mistaken for tremor. The diagnosis is based on clinical features. Mild symptoms of cervical dystonia may not require therapy. However, dystonic movements that interfere with social or occupational functioning should be considered for pharmacotherapy or botulinum toxin injections. Botulinum toxin therapy is the treatment of choice. Anticholinergic medications result in improvement in up to 71% of patients with dystonia but can be limited by systemic side effects

Bibliography

Chou KL. In the clinic. Parkinson disease. Ann Intern Med. 2012;157: ITC5-1-ITC5-16. [PMID: 23128879]

Jankovic J. Medical treatment of dystonia. Mov Disord. 2013;28:1001– 12. [PMID: 23893456]

Zeuner KE, Deuschl G. An update on tremors. Curr Opin Neurol. 2012; 25:475-82. [PMID: 22772877]

Chapter 79

Seizures and Epilepsy

Martha Hlafka, MD

Seizures are one of the most common neurologic problems encountered in medicine. A seizure is defined as a sudden change in behavior as a consequence of an abnormally excessive or synchronous discharge of electrical activity in the brain. Most seizures are provoked by some inciting event. Approximately 5% to 10% of the population will have at least one seizure, with the highest incidence in childhood or late adulthood.

Epilepsy, defined as 2 or more seizures due to an underlying chronic process, is common. The prevalence of epilepsy in the United States is approximately 6 to 8 per 1000 persons. The annual incidence is approximately 26 to 40 per 100,000. About 70% of adults with new-onset epilepsy have focal seizures. In the majority of cases (62%), the cause is unknown.

A diagnosis of epilepsy can have a significant impact on a patient's quality of life. It can affect a patient's interpersonal relationships, ability to drive, employment, and mood. Patients must be discouraged from participating in activities that hold a high risk of injury or death in the case of seizure. This not only includes driving, but also the operation of high-risk power equipment, activities that include heights, swimming, or even bathing alone. Consequently, rates of depression among patients with epilepsy are high, with suicide rates tripled from the average population.

Clinical Presentation of Seizures

Whether a seizure is defined as focal or generalized usually depends on a description of behaviors that occurred before, during, and after the seizure. The International League against Epilepsy Commission on Classification and Terminology has developed a classification system for seizures based on these clinical features and associated electroencephalograph (EEG) findings.

Seizures are categorized as focal or generalized; seizures that were once described as "partial" are now described as "focal." The term "partial seizure" is no longer used. Focal seizures are categorized as aura, motor, autonomic; those involving changes in awareness or responsiveness; and those that evolve to a bilateral convulsive seizure. Generalized seizures are further classified as tonic, clonic, tonic-clonic, atonic, myoclonic, or absence (typical, atypical, or with special features, such as eyelid myoclonus). Some seizures may have elements of both focal and generalized seizures and may be difficult to categorize by using this system; these are considered unclassified seizures. Epilepsies are also usually further characterized by etiology: genetic, structural-metabolic, and unknown.

Focal Seizures

Focal seizures originate within a discrete neuronal network of the cortex (initiation phase), then spread to the neighboring regions (propagation phase), remaining localized to one cerebral hemisphere. The region of hyperexcitability may have developed secondary to injury, abnormalities in cortical development, or genetics. It is important to note that a seizure disorder secondary to central nervous system (CNS) injury such as trauma, stroke, or infection may not present for years after the initial insult. Structural remodeling over time eventually results in clinically apparent seizures.

Focal seizures may present with or without impairment of cognition (dyscognitive) features. They can evolve into generalized seizures, usually tonic-clonic in nature, which are often difficult to distinguish from primary generalized tonic-clonic seizures. Electroencephalography findings may be normal or show epileptiform spikes.

Focal Seizures Without Dyscognitive Features (Simple Partial Seizures)

In focal seizures without dyscognitive features, the individual remains aware of his or her surroundings and recollects the events of the seizure. The patient may experience localized motor, sensory, autonomic, or psychic symptoms.

Focal seizures with motor symptoms usually involve involuntary movements of the contralateral hand. The movements are typically clonic (repetitive flexion/ extension) and may include corresponding movements of the face. Patients who experience motor symptoms may also exhibit seizure progression ("Jacksonian march") in which the movements will start in a restricted region (such as the fingers) and progress to include a larger portion of the extremity, representing the spread of seizure activity over the motor cortex. Patients may also experience a temporary paresis following the seizure that can last for minutes to hours (Todd paralysis).

Sensory symptoms may result from disruption of somatic nerves (paresthesias), vision (flashing lights or hallucinations), equilibrium (vertigo or sense of falling), hearing, or olfactory sense. Seizures affecting the autonomic system can result in flushing, sweating, or piloerection. Higher cortical functioning could be affected resulting in psychic symptoms such as a sense of depersonalization or *deja-vu*.

Focal Seizures With Dyscognitive Features (Complex Partial Seizures)

Patients who experience focal seizures with dyscognitive features have transient inability to respond to external stimuli and have an impaired awareness of their seizure. The seizure often begins with a stereotypical aura that may be motor, sensory, autonomic, or psychic in quality. Impaired awareness often begins with an arrest of behavior with a motionless stare followed by involuntary automatisms. Automatisms are repetitive, nonpurposeful behaviors such as chewing, lip smacking, picking movements with the hands, repeating words or phrases, or more complex behaviors such as aimless walking or running, or undressing. The seizure duration is typically less than 3 minutes, after which patients may have a period of confusion or somnolence that may last up to an hour.

Generalized Seizures

Generalized seizures involve abnormal synchronous discharge of electrical activity in both cerebral hemispheres, generally with a loss of consciousness. Except for absence seizures, the mechanisms involved in seizure initiation and propagation are not well understood.

Absence Seizures

Typical absence seizures manifest as a sudden, brief lapse in consciousness without loss of postural control. Seizures typically last between 5 to 10 seconds, and consciousness immediately returns with no postictal confusion. Seizures can occur up to hundreds of times per day, mainly in association with boredom or hyperventilation. Motor signs may be subtle, with staring or blinking, small chewing movements, or small bilateral clonic movements of the hands. Onset is usually in childhood or adolescence, and 90% of patients have outgrown it by adulthood.

The hallmark finding on EEG for absence seizures is a generalized 3-Hz spike-and-wave discharge that begins and ends suddenly. These discharges appear to be related to normal rhythms generated during sleep by circuits connecting the thalamus and cortex, with evidence that mutations in this system contribute to familial forms of absence epilepsy.

Generalized Tonic-Clonic Seizures

Generalized tonic-clonic seizures are the most common type of seizure encountered in metabolic derangement, toxic ingestions, withdrawal, and infection. Approximately 10% of patients with epilepsy experience generalized tonic-clonic seizures as their primary seizure type.

Generalized tonic-clonic seizures usually begin without warning, sometimes with a shout ("ictal cry"). The initial seizure phase is usually tonic muscle contraction, including expiratory and laryngeal muscles. Respiration is impaired, resulting in cyanosis. The tonic phase will evolve into the clonic phase after about 10 to 20 seconds, in which there are periods of muscle relaxation between tonic contractions. The seizures typically last no more than 1 minute. During the postictal phase, the patient is generally unresponsive with flaccid musculature and excessive salivation that can compromise respiration. Bladder or bowel incontinence may also occur. The patient will gradually regain consciousness over minutes to hours, frequently with associated confusion.

Myoclonic Seizures

Myoclonus is a brief and sudden muscle contraction that can occur in one part or involve the entire body. Myoclonus is not always pathologic: normal myoclonus is the jerking movements that often occur when falling asleep. Pathologic myoclonus is seen most often in metabolic derangements, CNS disorders, and anoxic brain injury. Myoclonic seizures are the predominant feature in juvenile myoclonic epilepsy.

Approach to the Patient With a First Seizure

History and Physical Examination

A good history is the single most important factor in seizure diagnosis. Seizures most often occur outside of a clinical setting, so an in-depth history of symptoms before, during, and after the episode should be sought. If the patient experienced loss of consciousness, any witnesses to the event should be interviewed. The history should focus on excluding other potential diagnoses that may mimic seizures (Table 2). Any potential predisposing conditions such as a personal or family history of seizures, prior CNS trauma or infection, stroke, or tumor should be sought. Factors that may have precipitated a seizure should also be investigated: sleep deprivation, systemic diseases, potential metabolic derangement, medications that lower the seizure threshold, and alcohol or illicit drug use/withdrawal.

The physical examination should evaluate for signs of systemic illness or infection, chronic liver or kidney disease, cardiovascular disease, developmental disorders that may indicate underlying CNS disorders, or evidence of a neurocutaneous disorder such as tuberous sclerosis or neurofibromatosis. A thorough neurological examination is essential in order to help localize any focal areas of dysfunction.

In most cases of a new, unprovoked seizure, the physical examination and laboratory evaluation are normal.

Laboratory Evaluation

Laboratory studies (Table 3) are usually obtained to assess for the presence of any potential metabolic causes of seizures. These include evaluation for abnormalities in electrolytes, glucose, calcium, magnesium, kidney function, and evidence of liver failure. A toxicology screen may also be appropriate in patients with risk factors. A lumbar puncture is indicated if there is concern for CNS infection, and it is absolutely essential in any immunocompromised patient.

Imaging

All patients with new-onset seizures should have brain imaging (see Table 3) to determine if there is an underlying structural abnormality that may be a focus for developing seizures. In emergent situations where infection or tumor is suspected, computed tomography (CT) is an appropriate initial study. Otherwise, magnetic resonance imaging (MRI) is superior to CT in detection of lesions associated with epilepsy, including vascular malformations, tumors, and areas of sclerosis.

Electroencephalography

Patients with a first unprovoked seizure should undergo EEG to evaluate for evidence of epileptiform discharges (see Table 3). Electrographic seizure activity that is recorded at the time of an event establishes the diagnosis. However, as seizure onset is unpredictable and usually occurs outside of a clinical setting, most EEGs are not obtained at the time of the event. Consequently, EEGs are often normal, which does not rule out the possibility of a seizure disorder. Focal seizures may originate from an area of cortex that cannot be detected by scalp electrodes. In the case of generalized seizures, only about one-half of EEGs show any abnormalities, and only one-half of those are epileptiform in activity. For this reason, continuous, prolonged monitoring with video EEG for hospitalized patients or portable monitoring for 24 hours or more for ambulatory patients has become common. In situations in which the diagnosis of seizures is not clear, admission to an epilepsy monitoring unit with provocative studies may be diagnostically helpful.

Epilepsy Syndromes

An epilepsy syndrome is a constellation of seizure symptoms, EEG findings, and MRI findings in a given patient. There are more than 30 epilepsy syndromes, some of which present in adulthood or persist from childhood (Table 4). Many have been linked to gene mutations

Table 1. Differential Diagnosis of New-Onset Seizures in Adults

Disease	Characteristics
Syncope	Prodromal autonomic symptoms or palpitations followed by sudden loss of consciousness with rapid return to normal; clonic or tonic movements during syncope can be identical to generalized seizures
Migraine	Visual or sensory alterations associated with headache; can be problematic when not accompanied by headache
Pseudoseizure	Bizarre spells of altered or lost consciousness of prolonged duration (10-30 min); frequent pelvic thrusting; lack of response to antiepileptic drugs; only truly distinguishable from epileptic seizures by video-EEG monitoring
Movement disorders	Tics, nonepileptic myoclonus
Sleep disorders	Narcolepsy/cataplexy, sleep myoclonus
Seizures provoked by metabolic abnormalities and transient causes	Generalized tonic-clonic (not partial-onset) seizures associated with alcohol withdrawal, hypocalcemia, hyponatremia, hypoglycemia, drug overdose, recent head trauma; this diagnosis is dependent on identifying one of these conditions
Acute structural lesion-related seizures	Stroke: seizures are usually accompanied by neurologic deficits but seizure may be first manifestation Subarachnoid hemorrhage: usually associated with severe headache, nausea, and syncope Intracerebral hemorrhage: associated with headache, focal deficits A consideration only for new-onset seizures
CNS infection-related seizures	Meningitis is almost always associated with fever and meningeal signs. Encephalitis can have an insidious onset but is usually associated with altered mental status; a consideration only for new-onset seizures. CSF examination is always required if CNS infection is considered in the differential diagnosis
Chronic lesion-related seizures	Tumor: slowly growing masses may not cause neurologic deficits or the deficit may go unnoticed because of the gradual onset Developmental malformation: may not manifest with seizures until adulthood. Previous brain injury: history of any brain abnormality, especially stroke or head trauma, increases the risk of seizures A consideration in new-onset and chronic seizures. MRI is always necessary to exclude these diagnoses if partial-onset seizures are present

CNS = central nervous system; CSF = cerebrospinal fluid; EEG = electroencephalogram; MRI = magnetic resonance imaging.

Table 2. Evaluation of Seizures

Test	Notes
Laboratory studies (eg, complete blood count, comprehensive metabolic profile, glucose levels)	Indicated with a first seizure or if there is additional history to suggest infection or a metabolic abnormality
Brain MRI	Preferred study to evaluate for structural abnormalities associated with seizure activity, with a sensitivity of 95%
Head CT	Considered less sensitive than MRI for detecting potential structural causes of seizure activity
Routine (interictal) EEG	The first EEG is abnormal in only about one-half of patients with epilepsy and remains normal after multiple EEGs in about 40%; therefore, a normal EEG does not exclude epilepsy. Only 1%-2% of normal individuals have epileptiform discharges, so their presence strongly suggest epilepsy
Toxicology screen	Indicated in most patients with a first seizure and those with risk factors for possible substance ingestion
Lumbar puncture	Indicated when a CNS cause is suspected (infection or bleeding)

CNS = central nervous system; CT = computed tomography; EEG = electroencephalogram; MRI = magnetic resonance imaging.

or familial syndromes. Most new-onset seizure disorders that present in adulthood are focal seizures.

Treatment

The goal of treatment is to prevent recurrent seizures, and the use of antiepileptic drugs (AEDs) has been shown to reduce the rate of recurrence by 30% to 60%. However, the decision to initiate AEDs is a highly individualized one. Patients with a proven diagnosis of epilepsy almost always require treatment. **Patients who have had only a single seizure may not require treatment.** Of patients who do not have any risk factors associated with a high probability of recurrence (eg, abnormal EEG or known cause such as trauma or stroke), only about 25% will have another seizure within 2 years. In addition, AEDs have various side effects, drug interactions, and potential for adverse events such that a patient's sex, age, and comorbid conditions should be considered when choosing a treatment (Table 5).

Special consideration should be given to women of childbearing age, as well as patients with other comorbid conditions, prior to starting an AED. It is important to recognize that many AEDs can increase the clearance of oral contraceptives, rendering them less

Table 3. Common Epilepsy Syndromes Presenting or Persisting in Adulthood

Name	Age at Onset (y)	Seizure Types	Interictal EEG	Family History	Neuro-imaging	Natural History	Drugs of Choice
Temporal lobe epilepsy	10-30	FSD, 2° generalized	Temporal spikes	Negative	Mesial temporal sclerosis	Persists	Carbamazepine, oxcarbazepine, lamotrigine
Childhood absence epilepsy	4-10	ABS, GTC	3-Hz generalized spike and wave	Common	Normal	Resolves by age 14 in 70%	Ethosuximide, valproic acid, lamotrigine
Juvenile myoclonic epilepsy	12-18	MYO, GTC	Generalized 4.5-Hz multiple spike and wave	Common	Normal	Persists, but usually well controlled	Valproic acid, lamotrigine, topiramate, levetiracetam
GTC on awakening	10-20	GTC, ABS, MYO	Generalized epileptiform discharges	Variable	Normal	Variable	All except ethosuximide
Lennox-Gastaut	2-adult	Tonic, atonic, atypical ABS	Generalized slow spike and wave (<3 Hz)	Negative, depending on etiology	Variable depending on etiology	Persists, difficult to control	Valproic acid, lamotrigine, topiramate, felbamate

ABS = absence (seizure); EEG = electroencephalogram; FSD = focal seizure with dyscognitive features; GTC = generalized tonic-clonic (seizure); MYO = myoclonic.

effective. Many AEDs are potential teratogens, most notably valproate. Antiepileptic drugs can interact with a multitude of other medications that are metabolized in the liver, including cardiac, psychiatric, antineoplastic, immunosuppressive, and anti-infectious (most notably HIV) drugs.

The efficacy of AEDs against different seizure types and epilepsy syndromes has led to their classification as narrow spectrum or broad spectrum (see Table 5). Narrow-spectrum drugs should only be utilized in patients with focal seizures, as they are less effective and may sometimes exacerbate generalized seizure disorders. Broad-spectrum AEDs are effective in both generalized and focal epilepsy. About one-half of patients with newly diagnosed epilepsy become seizure-free with one AED. If the response to an AED is suboptimal, another AED may be substituted, or a second or third drug may be added as needed.

In cases in which seizures cannot be adequately controlled with AEDs alone, surgical options may be available. Implantation of a vagus nerve stimulator has been shown to be effective for patients with intractable focal epilepsy when used in conjunction with AEDs. Patients with uncontrolled mesial temporal lobe epilepsy are candidates for anterior temporal lobectomy, after which up to 70% to 80% of patients become seizure-free, although multiple potential neurologic deficits (eg, hemiparesis and memory problems) may result from this procedure.

Status Epilepticus

Status epilepticus (SE) is a condition in which a patient experiences a continuous generalized seizure or rapidly repeating seizures between which the patient does not regain consciousness lasting more than 30 minutes. Because generalized seizures rarely last more than a few minutes, any convulsive seizure lasting longer than 5 minutes should be treated as SE.

Status epilepticus is a medical emergency with an overall 30-day mortality rate of approximately 20%, with higher rates in those with hypoxia/anoxic brain injury and those with tumors, metabolic derangements, drug overdose, trauma, and stroke. Acute complications of SE include fever, lactic acidosis, cardiac arrhythmias, and

respiratory distress. Patients can also experience chronic, long-term effects including cognitive dysfunction and future seizures.

Although SE may be the presenting symptom with newly diagnosed epilepsy, the most common causes are subtherapeutic levels of AEDs, stroke, metabolic derangements, anoxic brain injury, or alcohol or drug intoxication or withdrawal. At onset, patients are unresponsive and usually have clinically obvious convulsions. Over time, however, the manifestations often become subtle, and some patients may have no observable motor activity; the detection of ongoing seizure activity may require EEG. First-line treatment of SE is intravenous lorazepam, followed by phenytoin or fosphenytoin. A third-line drug may also be necessary.

Bibliography

Schachter SC. Seizure disorders. Med Clin North Am. 2009;93:343-51. [PMID: 19272512]

Wilden JA, Cohen-Gadol AA. Evaluation of first nonfebrile seizures. Am Fam Physician. 2012 Aug 15;86:334-40. [PMID: 22963022]

Table 4. Commonly Used Antiepileptic Drugs (AEDs)

Drug	Common Side Effects	Serious Adverse Effects	Other Considerations
Narrow-Spectrum AEDs			
Carbamazepine	Dizziness, ataxia, diplopia, somnolence, nausea, weight gain, benign leukopenia	Agranulocytosis, aplastic anemia, hepatotoxicity, SJS, AV block, cardiac arrhythmias, hyponatremia	May decrease levels of other drugs through hepatic metabolism, including OCPs May aggravate generalized seizures
Ethosuximide[a]	Dizziness, ataxia, somnolence, nausea, vomiting	Agranulocytosis, aplastic anemia, SJS, drug-induced lupus	Potential teratogen Worsening of depression and suicidality in susceptible patients
Gabapentin	Somnolence, fatigue, dizziness, ataxia, mild weight gain	SJS, drug reaction with eosinophilia and systemic symptoms	Very few drug-drug interactions Well tolerated in older patients May aggravate generalized seizures or myoclonus
Lacosamide	Dizziness, nausea, diplopia	Cardiac arrhythmias, AV block, depression with suicidality	Increased risk of dizziness possible if used in conjunction with other sodium-channel blocking agents (phenytoin, carbamazepine, lamotrigine, and oxcarbazepine)
Oxcarbazepine	Dizziness, ataxia, diplopia, somnolence, headache, nausea, vomiting, abdominal pain	Agranulocytosis, SJS, suicidality, hyponatremia, anaphylaxis	May decrease levels of other drugs through hepatic metabolism, including OCPs Reduces T_4 and free T_4 levels May aggravate generalized seizures
Phenytoin[b]	Fatigue, dizziness, ataxia, diplopia, nausea, vomiting, confusion, gingival hyperplasia	Blood dyscrasias, SJS, hepatotoxicity, anaphylaxis, suicidality, drug-induced lupus	May decrease levels of other drugs through hepatic metabolism, including OCPs Reduces T_4 and free T_4 levels Potential teratogen
Pregabalin	Somnolence, fatigue, dizziness, ataxia, mild weight gain, edema	Jaundice, hypersensitivity reaction, increased creatinine kinase	Very few drug-drug interactions Well tolerated in older patients May aggravate myoclonus
Broad-Spectrum AEDs			
Lamotrigine	Dizziness, blurred vision, diplopia, ataxia, somnolence, headache, rash, diarrhea, nausea, tremor	SJS, hepatotoxicity, hypersensitivity	May help treat comorbid mood disorders Well tolerated in older patients Complex interactions with OCPs, potential teratogen Slow initiation of treatment required due to increased risk of SJS
Levetiracetam	Dizziness, headache, somnolence, depression, fatigue	SJS, pancytopenia, hepatotoxicity, suicidality, psychosis	Well tolerated in older patients Few drug-drug interactions Caution in patients with psychiatric disorders
Topiramate	Dizziness, confusion, somnolence, weight loss, metabolic acidosis	SJS, nephrolithiasis, glaucoma, hepatotoxicity, heatstroke	May decrease levels of OCPs May help treat comorbid migraine Increased risk of metabolic acidosis with metformin use
Valproic acid	Edema, alopecia, weight gain, diarrhea, nausea, dizziness, headache, somnolence, tremor	Thrombocytopenia, hyperammonemia, ototoxicity, pancreatitis	Significantly increased risk of teratogenicity Potential development of polycystic ovarian syndrome in women Multiple drug-drug interactions
Zonisamide	Ataxia, somnolence, weight loss, nausea, vomiting, headache, depression	Aplastic anemia, nephrolithiasis, SJS, heatstroke, psychosis	Caution in patients with psychiatric disorders

AV = atrioventricular; OCPs = oral contraceptive pills; SJS = Stevens-Johnson syndrome; T_4 = thyroxine.

aOnly effective for absence seizures.

bEffective for focal seizures and generalized tonic-clonic seizures. Not effective for generalized absence or generalized myoclonic seizures, and therefore classified as narrow spectrum.

Chapter 80

Other Neurologic Diseases

Amalia Landa-Galindez, MD

Multiple Sclerosis

Multiple sclerosis (MS) is the most common inflammatory demyelinating disease of the central nervous system (CNS), affecting approximately 400,000 people in the United States and more than 2.5 million individuals worldwide. Multiple sclerosis is twice as common in women and frequently presents between the ages of 20 and 50 years. The disease may vary from a mild illness to a more severe relapsing form with increasing disability between attacks or one with a progressive neurologic decline. The exact cause of MS is not known, but studies have suggested that environmental factors may trigger disease in genetically predisposed individuals.

Pathophysiology, Diagnosis, and Therapy

Multiple sclerosis is an autoimmune disorder where lymphocytes cross the blood-brain barrier and target myelin antigens in various parts of the nervous system causing inflammation, resulting in demyelination, neuroaxonal injury, and eventual neurodegeneration. Lesions primarily develop in the white matter where primary targets include the myelin sheaths, although gray matter lesions may also be seen. Pathologic changes in the axons include accumulation of amyloid precursor due to inflammation during the acute and progressive stages. The cumulative loss of axons directly correlates with progression to irreversible disability.

The hallmark of MS is that the symptoms vary in time and location and cannot be attributed to one CNS location. Symptoms may vary based on the locations of lesions within the brain. Lesions may develop within the optic nerve, brain stem, cerebellum, or spinal cord, leading to well-recognized syndromes that include optic neuritis, diplopia, changes in balance, and sensory and motor deficits. Symptoms may last for several weeks and subside. Several different patterns of the disease are commonly seen (Figure 1). Patients with the relapsing-remitting form of the disease will have recurrent episodes of variable frequency and severity, and may present with changes in sensation, muscle weakness, or visual problems. Over time, episodes may become more frequent and severe and encompass additional symptoms such as pain and bladder difficulties; while memory is often intact, lability in mood may be seen. Many patients with relapsing-remitting disease eventually develop a secondary progressive form of the disease in which there is steady accumulation of disability with minimal recovery. A small percentage of patients will have a progressive course from the time of onset of disease.

While there is no definitive diagnostic test for MS, diagnosis is made on the basis of clinical presentation combined with findings on magnetic resonance imaging (MRI), and if necessary, cerebrospinal fluid analysis and other supporting studies. The diagnosis is usually made after documentation of at least 2 distinct clinical episodes with supportive diagnostic findings. The McDonald criteria (lesions separated in time and location) provide objective clinical and MRI findings needed to establish the diagnosis.

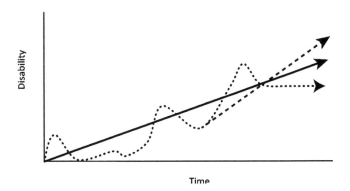

Figure 1. The 3 clinical phenotypes of MS. Most patients with MS follow a relapsing-remitting course (dotted line) at disease onset. Relapses do not initially result in significant permanent disability; with time, residual disability accrues. Some patients with relapsing-remitting disease eventually plateau at a consistent level of disability; some will transition to a secondary progressive course (dashed line), in which disability accrues over time without clear relapsing or remitting events. Primary progressive MS (solid line) demonstrates progressive disability from disease onset without relapsing-remitting events. MS = multiple sclerosis.

Early in its course, MS may remain subclinical, yet MRI will reveal active disease as evidenced by the development of lesions in various parts of the brain. Therefore, MRI is used both for initial diagnosis and to monitor progression of disease. In situations in which the diagnosis is inconclusive based on clinical presentation and neuroimaging studies, analysis of cerebrospinal fluid will reveal changes of chronic inflammation with a lymphocytic pleocytosis and frequently oligoclonal IgG bands on gel electrophoresis (Table 1). Other studies, such as electrophysiologic studies that measure the speed of neuronal conduction, such as visual evoked potentials, somatosensory evoked potentials, or brainstem auditory evoked responses, can provide indirect evidence of white matter lesions not evident on imaging.

High-dose glucocorticoids are typically used to treat severe acute exacerbations. While there is no definitive cure for the underlying disease, disease-modifying immunomodulatory agents reduce the relapse rate, slow disability progression, help lessen the severity of exacerbations, and improve quality of life. Disease-modifying agents include interferon, glatiramer acetate, dimethyl fumarate, teriflunomide, fingolimod, and natalizumab. Although there is no clear consensus on the use of these medications, the interferon-beta preparations (beta-1a and beta-1b) are usually considered first-line therapy for relapsing-remitting MS. Each of these medications has different side-effect profiles and may be helpful in specific cases. For refractory disease, the addition of other immunosuppressive agents such as glucocorticoids, cyclophosphamide, mitoxantrone, methotrexate, or azathioprine may be appropriate.

Table 1. Distinguishing Features of Selected Neurologic Disorders

Disease	Clinical Findings	Mechanism	Diagnostic Studies
Multiple sclerosis	Optic neuritis; diplopia; altered balance; ataxia; spastic weakness of the limbs; bladder and bowel dysfunction; depression or mood lability	Lymphocytes cross blood-brain barrier to target myelin antigens producing demyelination and axonal injury	MRI shows bright signal changes/plaques; elevated CSF protein with oligoclonal IgG bands
Myasthenia gravis	Diplopia, ptosis; slurred speech; difficulty swallowing	IgG antibodies against AChR block neuromuscular transmission; thymus may be site of abnormal antibody production	Repetitive nerve stimulation shows decremental responses; AChR antibodies and muscle-specific tyrosine kinase antibodies; edrophonium test shows transient improvement in deficits
Lambert-Eaton myasthenic syndrome	Proximal muscle weakness; decreased DTRs; autonomic dysfunction	Antibodies target voltage-gated calcium channels in neuromuscular junction	Repetitive nerve stimulation shows initial decrease followed by incremental response post exercise; evaluation to exclude small cell lung cancer
Guillain-Barré syndrome	Weakness and paresthesias; ascending pattern; respiratory muscle fatigue; autonomic dysfunction; decreased DTRs	Bacterial or viral infection induces autoantibodies to motor nerves with resulting demyelination and neuropathy	Nerve conduction studies show acute peripheral polyneuropathy; elevated CSF protein
Amyotrophic lateral sclerosis	Extremity weakness/atrophy; dysarthria and dysphagia; hyperreflexia; foot drop; muscle fasciculations; respiratory failure/aspiration	Toxic neuromodulators lead to degeneration of neurons at all levels of motor system	EMG reveals acute denervation in 2 or more extremities

AChR = acetylcholine receptor; CSF = cerebrospinal fluid; DTRs = deep tendon reflexes; EMG = electromyography; MRI = magnetic resonance imaging.

Myasthenia Gravis

Myasthenia gravis (MG) is an autoimmune disease of the neuromuscular junction that leads to muscle weakness and fatigability. The fluctuating muscle weakness usually worsens with use and improves with periods of rest. Affected muscles include the eye, facial, oropharyngeal, axial, and limb muscles. Although the incidence has been increasing, MG is a relatively rare disease, with a prevalence of 100 to 200 per million. Females with MG most often present in their 20s to 30s, whereas males present between 50 to 70 years of age. There are differences in presentation between ethnic groups, as Asian individuals often present with MG confined to the extraocular muscles at a younger age.

Pathophysiology, Diagnosis, and Therapy

Over 80% of patients have IgG type antibodies against the acetylcholine receptors (AChR). Patients who do not have AChR antibodies often have other antibodies such as muscle-specific tyrosine kinase, which can correlate with more severe symptoms. Numerous studies have revealed involvement of the thymus gland in the pathogenesis of MG with AChR antibodies. Patients who present with thymoma have more severe disease compared to patients without thymoma. Thymectomy often results in complete remission in a large number of cases. Several viruses have been implicated in the development of MG, including measles, Epstein Barr, and herpes viruses.

The fluctuating skeletal muscle weakness of MG varies from day to day and usually worsens as the day progresses. Muscle bulk is usually normal, and involuntary smooth muscles are not involved. Deep tendon reflexes are usually normal, and sensation remains intact. Abnormalities of the eye muscles are common but may not be noticeable upon first awakening. Patients will often complain of photophobia, stating that bright light makes their eye muscles weak. Ptosis is usually asymmetric in MG and may alternate between eyes. On physical examination the patient is often unable to keep the upper eyelid closed against the examiner's efforts to open it. However, pupillary responses remain normal. Patients may be unable to whistle, sip through a straw, or blow up balloons. If the tongue is involved, slurred speech and trouble swallowing may be seen. Vocal cord muscle weakness heralded by stridor can signal a rapidly developing medical emergency leading to intubation. Involvement of the intercostal muscles and diaphragm will lead to the need for mechanically assisted ventilation.

Diagnosis is made by electrophysiologic studies that show decremental responses in myasthenic muscles with repetitive nerve stimulation. Immunologic testing for AChR antibodies confirms the diagnosis of MG; if negative, the presence of muscle-specific tyrosine kinase antibodies should be assessed. Although not commonly used at present, administration of edrophonium chloride (Tensilon), a short-acting anticholinesterase, will produce a measurable change in signs such as ptosis and grip strength (see Table 1).

Treatment usually begins with recommendations for adequate rest and avoidance of exertion. Drugs that block acetylcholinesterase at the neuromuscular junction leading to increased levels of acetylcholine will help improve function. Pyridostigmine bromide (Mestinon) is given orally, usually 3 times a day. Use of these medications should be kept as low as possible to avoid cholinergic toxicity such as excess perspiration, salivation, or muscle cramps. More aggressive treatments include plasmapheresis with removal of the offending antibodies (useful in a severe crisis such as respiratory failure) and intravenous immunoglobulin therapy, which has a suppressive effect on the immune system.

Lambert-Eaton Myasthenic Syndrome

The Lambert-Eaton myasthenic syndrome (LEMS; previously referred to as the Eaton-Lambert syndrome) is a neuromuscular autoimmune disease that is classically associated with tumors, especially small cell lung carcinoma. LEMS is a rare disorder, with an incidence of less than 50 per million. The median age at presentation is usually 60 years, with the majority of patients being men, although one-half of patients with nontumor-associated LEMS are women. In patients with non-tumor-associated LEMS, small cell lung cancer with neuroendocrine characteristics is the predominant tumor type.

Pathophysiology, Diagnosis, and Therapy

Pathogenic autoantibodies directed toward the voltage-gated calcium channels on presynaptic nerve terminals produce the clinical symptoms of LEMS. These antibodies are found in up to 90% of patients and in almost 100% of patients with associated small cell lung cancer. It is postulated that an immune reaction on the tumor's surface triggers the autoantibody production.

The clinical presentation of LEMS usually includes proximal muscle weakness, autonomic symptoms, and loss of reflexes. The first symptom noted by patients is usually proximal leg muscle weakness (80%), followed by weakness of the arms. The weakness normally spreads distally and upwardly, eventually involving the oculobulbar region. In contrast to MG, isolated involvement of the eye muscles is rare. Autonomic dysfunction includes dry mouth, constipation, and erectile dysfunction. Deep tendon reflexes are usually decreased or absent. A unique phenomenon is postexercise facilitation, where there is short-term return of normal tendon reflexes and muscle strength after periods of exercise.

Patients with small cell lung cancer who present with LEMS are more likely to have limited disease and may present with neuromuscular symptoms before the lung cancer is detected. In any patient who presents with LEMS, particularly men with a smoking history, a thorough investigation to exclude underlying cancer is recommended. Although the diagnosis of LEMS is often clinical, radioimmunoassay for voltage-gated calcium channels has an excellent sensitivity of about 90% with a specificity of 99% to 100%. Electrophysiologic study with repetitive nerve stimulation is useful in diagnosing LEMS. There is usually an initial decrease in compound muscle action potential followed by an incremental response postexercise (see Table 1).

The most commonly used treatment for LEMS is 3,4-diaminopyridine, which potentiates neuromuscular transmission. If symptoms do not improve, glucocorticoids and azathioprine may be used. Treatment of the underlying cancer will alleviate the symptoms.

Guillain-Barré Syndrome

Guillain-Barré syndrome is an autoimmune neuropathic syndrome that usually has a dramatic presentation with an areflexic paralysis. It is the most frequent cause of acute flaccid paralysis in the world and is a neurologic emergency. Twenty percent of affected patients may be afflicted with severe disability, and mortality rates of 5% may be seen. The disorder is more prevalent in men. History is important in diagnosing Guillain-Barré syndrome, as two-thirds of cases are preceded by either upper respiratory infections or diarrhea. The most frequently associated pathogen is *Campylobacter jejuni*, although cytomegalovirus, Epstein-Barr virus, varicella zoster virus, and mycoplasma pneumonia have also been implicated.

Pathophysiology, Diagnosis, and Therapy

A proposed mechanism for Guillain-Barré syndrome involves the triggering of an immune response by an antecedent infection that cross-reacts with peripheral nerve components that leads to nerve damage and an acute polyneuropathy.

The first symptoms may include paresthesias in the legs followed by progressive bilateral and symmetric weakness of the limbs, which progresses in an ascending pattern. Patients classically have loss of reflexes followed by paralysis. The most serious complications include paralysis of the respiratory muscles requiring mechanical ventilation, autonomic dysfunction with arrhythmias, and hypotension. Hallucinations and psychosis may occur. The syndrome usually progresses for several weeks before a remission ensues. Two-thirds of patients will be unable to ambulate, and 25% will develop respiratory insufficiency. Nerve conduction studies confirm the acute peripheral neuropathy. A lumbar puncture is usually performed to exclude Lyme disease or malignancy, such as lymphoma. Cerebrospinal fluid will contain normal cell counts and elevated protein levels (see Table 1).

Nonambulatory patients with Guillain-Barré syndrome should be treated with plasmapheresis or intravenous immune globulin. There is no evidence that glucocorticoids shorten the course or reduce residual deficits in Guillain-Barré syndrome. Ventilatory support (needed in up to 30% of cases), infection surveillance, prophylaxis of venous thrombosis, pain management, and nutritional and psychological support contribute to reduced morbidity and mortality. The overall prognosis in patients with Guillain-Barré syndrome is good, with 80% of patients achieving recovery with little or no disability. Poor prognostic features include rapidly progressive weakness and the need for mechanical ventilation.

Amyotrophic Lateral Sclerosis

Amyotrophic lateral sclerosis (ALS) is a devastating neurodegenerative disorder that involves progressive degeneration of the motor system at all levels. The incidence is approximately 2 cases per 100,000 people per year. An autosomal dominant pattern of inheritance has been identified in 5% to 10% of cases. The disorder is progressive, and disease management strategies focus on counseling on end-of-life issues and palliative care.

Pathophysiology, Diagnosis, and Therapy

The pathophysiology of ALS is not well understood, but current studies suggest that toxicity from neuromodulators such as glutamate precipitate neuronal death by triggering excessive calcium influx in motor neurons. Since ALS involves loss of neurons at all levels of the motor system, physical signs of the disorder include both upper and lower motor neuron findings. Electromyography often reveals acute denervation in 2 or more extremities (see Table 1). The disorder is rapidly progressive, and 50% of patients die within 3 years of onset. Symptoms may include dysarthria, dysphagia, and facial weakness along with proximal and distal limb weakness. Upper and lower extremities may have profound wasting with hyperreflexia, foot drop, and prominent fasciculations. Dysphagia and dysarthria rapidly progress and lead to loss of normal alimentation and communication. The terminal phase of the disease is heralded by respiratory failure and aspiration of thick mucus secretions.

Because of the poor prognosis associated with ALS and the limited therapeutic interventions available, current treatment focuses on relief of symptoms and palliative care. The only available pharmacologic treatment for ALS is riluzole, a glutamate-release inhibitor that has been shown to prolong survival by 3 months. Current investigations include delivery of disease-modifying agents such as insulin-like growth factor and vascular endothelial growth factor using viral vectors or intrathecal administration.

Bibliography

Mitchell JD, Borasio GD. Amyotrophic lateral sclerosis. Lancet. 2007; 16;369:2031-41. [PMID: 17574095]

Querol L, Illa I. Myasthenia gravis and the neuromuscular junction. Curr Opin Neurol. 2013;26:459-65. [PMID: 23945282]

Titulaer MJ, Lang B, Verschuuren JJ. Lambert-Eaton myasthenic syndrome: from clinical characteristics to therapeutic strategies. Lancet Neurol. 2011;10:1098-107. [PMID: 22094130]

Wingerchuk DM, Carter JL. Multiple sclerosis: current and emerging disease-modifying therapies and treatment strategies. Mayo Clin Proc. 2014;89:225-40. [PMID: 24485135]

Yuki N, Hartung HP. Guillain-Barré syndrome. N Engl J Med. 2012; 14;366:2294-304. [PMID: 22694000]

Section 9
Oncology

Associate Editor – Philip A. Masters, MD, FACP

High Value Care Recommendations

- In patients with incidentally discovered pulmonary nodules, obtain prior chest radiographs or imaging scans if possible to determine stability over time. No follow-up is recommended for nodules that are ≤4 mm in patients who have never smoked and who have no other known risk factors for malignancy (history of a first-degree relative with lung cancer or significant radon or asbestos exposure).

- Routine screening for *BRCA1* and *BRCA2* mutations is not recommended in women who are at low risk for developing breast cancer.

- Screening for cervical cancer may be discontinued at age 65 years if the patient has been adequately screened, has had normal Pap smears, and has no other risk factors.

- Screening for cervical cancer is not indicated or necessary in patients who have had a total hysterectomy (with removal of the cervix) for benign disease.

- Serum carcinoembryonic antigen (CEA) should not be used as a screening test for colorectal cancer due to its poor sensitivity and specificity

Chapter 81

Lung Cancer

Alyssa C. McManamon, MD

Lung cancer is the leading cause of cancer-related death in both men and women in the United States at about 160,000 deaths per year. Despite being less common, lung cancer accounts for more cancer deaths than the three most common cancers (breast, prostate, and colon) combined. Lung cancer mortality correlates with the prevalence of cigarette smoking. Lung cancer will occur in 15% of lifetime smokers; the majority will die of the disease. Approximately 85% of lung cancer cases in the United States are attributable to smoking, and former smokers remain at risk. The World Health Organization (WHO) divides lung cancer into two major classes based on histology and biology. The majority (85%) are non-small cell lung cancer and the remainder are small cell lung cancer. Although many subtypes are known to be strongly linked to smoking, small cell lung cancer is diagnosed almost exclusively in smokers and behaves most aggressively as evidenced by a more rapid doubling time and metastases common at initial presentation.

Prevention

Abstinence from smoking remains the best method of preventing lung cancer. All patients should be screened for current or prior tobacco use; current smokers should be encouraged to stop smoking; and all patients should be advised to avoid second-hand smoke exposure. Smoking cessation could prevent up to 90% of all lung cancers. Retinol (vitamin A), β-carotene, *N*-acetylcysteine, and selenium supplementation do not prevent lung cancer.

Screening

There is no proven role for routine screening for lung cancer in the general population. However, the U.S. Preventive Services Task Force (USPSTF) recommends low-dose computed tomography (LDCT) scans to screen for early-stage lung cancer in a specific group of current or former smokers. Patients to be considered for screening LDCT are those 55 to 80 years of age who have a ≥30 pack-year smoking history either as current smokers or as former smokers who have quit within the past 15 years. The USPSTF estimates this screening strategy will lead to a 14% to 16% reduction in overall lung cancer mortality. As with any screening modality, patients must be counseled appropriately regarding related risks and benefits. In this case, there is risk of false positive LDCT results, associated radiation exposure from repeat screenings, and risks commonly associated with biopsy or surgery, if indicated based on screening.

Diagnosis

Carefully evaluate new pulmonary or chest complaints, particularly in smokers or former smokers. Be alert for symptoms such as hemoptysis, pulmonary infections, dyspnea, cough, or chest pain. Patients with small cell lung cancer often present with metastatic disease and paraneoplastic syndromes (Table 1).

In patients with new or persistent pulmonary symptoms, look for findings suggestive of a primary tumor (abnormal lung findings),

Table 1. Paraneoplastic and Other Syndromes Associated with Lung Cancer

Syndrome	Notes
Acromegaly	Growth hormone-releasing hormone (small cell carcinoma)
Cushing syndrome	Adrenocorticotropic hormone (small cell carcinoma)
Lambert-Eaton myasthenic syndrome	Proximal limb weakness and fatigue due to antibodies to voltage-gated calcium channels (small cell carcinoma)
Hypercalcemia	Parathyroid hormone-related peptide [more common with non-small cell carcinoma (squamous or adeno)]
Hypertrophic pulmonary osteoarthropathy	Painful, new periosteal bone growth and clubbing (most common with adenocarcinoma)
Hyponatremia	Syndrome of inappropriate antidiuretic hormone (small cell carcinoma)
Pancoast syndrome (superior sulcus tumor)	Shoulder pain, lower brachial plexopathy, and Horner syndrome from apical lung tumor (typically non-small cell/squamous)
Superior vena cava syndrome	External compression of superior vena cava causing face and arm swelling (more common with small cell)
Trousseau syndrome (migratory superficial thrombophlebitis)	Hypercoagulable state (most common with adenocarcinoma)
Vocal cord paralysis	Entrapment of recurrent laryngeal nerve

intrathoracic spread (hoarse voice, Horner syndrome, brachial plexopathy, chest wall tenderness), extrathoracic spread (wasting, lymphadenopathy, focal neurologic findings, bone tenderness, skin nodules, hepatomegaly), and paraneoplastic syndromes. Obtain a chest radiograph to look for masses, lymphadenopathy, and pleural effusions. Smaller lung cancers may require CT for detection.

Histologic confirmation is necessary for diagnosis. To guide patient management, tissue should be obtained by an approach that furthers disease staging. For example, the best approach to a patient with a lung mass in the setting of weight loss and unilateral supraclavicular lymph node enlargement is to obtain a peripheral node biopsy, which will simultaneously diagnose and stage the lung cancer. Alternatively, tissue can be obtained by percutaneous lung biopsy, pleural cytology, or transbronchial biopsy. Sputum cytology is reserved for patients with poor pulmonary function who cannot tolerate invasive procedures. Treatment and prognosis vary based on whether the patient has non–small cell lung cancer (adenocarcinoma, large cell carcinoma, or squamous cell carcinoma) or, less commonly, small cell lung cancer. In select non–small cell lung cancer cases (eg, adenocarcinoma), the molecular characterization of tumors may identify subsets of patients with different prognoses and treatment options. For example, the presence of a mutation or gene rearrangement (such as the oncogenes EGFR, KRAS and ALK) suggest the level of susceptibility to directed therapies such as tyrosine kinase inhibitors (eg, erlotinib and crizotinib).

In staging non–small cell lung cancer, the task is to find evidence of metastatic disease, which eliminates surgery as a therapeutic option. The staging evaluation should include CT of the chest and abdomen and a combined positron emission tomography and CT (PET-CT) scan to assess for malignant mediastinal lymphadenopathy. PET-CT may identify advanced disease and can preclude unnecessary thoracotomy. Brain imaging is generally indicated only to evaluate neurologic signs or symptoms, although it may be considered in patients with clinical disease stage II or higher (Table 2) in whom aggressive therapy is being contemplated to rule out occult intracranial involvement. If the patient is not otherwise a candidate for aggressive therapy, a bone scan is indicated if there is bone pain or an elevated serum calcium or alkaline phosphatase level. Other laboratory studies, such as a complete blood count, serum calcium, alkaline phosphatase, and aminotransferase levels, are obtained to detect evidence of advanced disease.

Small cell lung cancer generally is viewed as a systemic disease at diagnosis, as most patients have widespread organ involvement. Small cell tumors are exquisitely sensitive to radiation and chemotherapy. A simplified and accepted method of staging is described in terms of whether a tumor is limited to inclusion within a tolerable radiation therapy field. For example, a small cell tumor localized to one hemithorax, which could safely be radiated in one "port site," is termed limited-stage disease in contrast to the usual presentation of extensive-stage disease (more than one "port site"). Extensive-stage disease typically is associated with metastases involving the liver, bone, bone marrow, brain, adrenal glands, retroperitoneal lymph nodes, pancreas, and subcutaneous soft tissues. In patients who are considered eligible for treatment, extensive imaging and laboratory testing is performed to evaluate for the presence of metastatic disease. These studies usually include CT imaging of the chest and abdomen, PET-CT scanning, MRI of the brain, bone scanning (optional if PET-CT scan is obtained), and serum electrolytes, aminotransferase, and lactate dehydrogenase levels.

Incidentally discovered pulmonary nodules are common. Incidental pulmonary nodules are defined as an asymptomatic, discrete radiographic density ≤3 cm that is completely surrounded by aerated lung. Two features characterize benign pulmonary nodules: (1) no growth in 2 years and (2) calcification in a diffuse, central, or laminar pattern. Malignant nodules typically are >2 cm, have spiculated edges, and are located in the upper lobes. The probability of malignancy increases with age >40 years, past or current smoking status, asbestos or radon exposure, and previous diagnosis of cancer. The general approach to management of pulmonary nodules is to determine behavior over time and stratify risk. **In patients with incidentally discovered pulmonary nodules, obtain prior chest radiographs or imaging scans if possible to determine stability over time. No follow-up is recommended for nodules that are ≤4 mm in patients who have never smoked and who have no other known risk factors for malignancy (history of a first-degree relative with lung cancer or significant radon or asbestos exposure).** Nodules >4 mm in any patient require follow-up at an interval determined by whether the patient is considered to be at high or low risk for malignancy. Solid nodules ≥1.5 to 2.0 cm in high-risk patients require consideration for immediate biopsy; close interval CT scanning is another option in low-risk patients.

Therapy

Tumor staging dictates prognosis and management of any lung cancer. For non–small cell lung cancer, tumor size (T), regional node status (N), and presence or absence of metastatic disease (M) are used to assign patients to a stage of I to IV (see Table 2). Surgery is the mainstay of treatment for patients with stage I or II disease and select patients with stage III disease; the use of adjuvant chemotherapy has improved survival for patients with stage IB (tumors >3 cm) and higher disease. The use of adjuvant radiation therapy in patients with

Table 2. Staging, Treatment, and Prognosis for Patients with Non–Small Cell Lung Cancer

Stage	Definition	Treatment	Prognosis
I	Tumor surrounded by lung or pleura, more than 2 cm from carina	Surgery and, in selected cases, adjuvant chemotherapy; radiotherapy if not a surgical candidate; intent is cure	60% to 70% long-term disease-free survival
II	Locally advanced disease (ie, ipsilateral peribronchial, hilar, or intrapulmonary lymph nodes) without mediastinal involvement	Surgery and adjuvant chemotherapy; radiotherapy if not a surgical candidate; intent is cure	40% to 50% long-term disease-free survival
III	Mediastinal involvement, or two separate tumor nodules in same lobe without mediastinal involvement	Combined modalities of chemotherapy, radiotherapy, and/or surgery	5% to 20% long-term disease-free survival
IV	Metastatic (including malignant pleural nodules and pleural/pericardial effusions)	Chemotherapy	Median survival 7 months

early-stage non–small cell lung cancer has not been associated with a survival benefit, but radiation therapy can be considered as primary local treatment for patients with early-stage but inoperable disease. Patients with stage III disease represent a heterogeneous group. Most have mediastinal lymphadenopathy, and survival rates depend on extent of mediastinal disease. For patients with potentially resectable cancer with minimal mediastinal lymphadenopathy, neoadjuvant chemotherapy (with or without radiation) is often administered to shrink the tumor prior to surgery. For patients with unresectable disease, chemoradiation is superior to radiation alone. Encourage all patients who smoke to quit smoking before surgery or radiation to improve lung function and reduce iatrogenic morbidity.

Metastatic, inoperable (stage IV) non–small cell lung cancer necessitates consideration of a combined treatment approach including local radiation for a symptomatic mass or metastatic sites and/or palliative chemotherapy. Patients with good performance status but disease progression after one chemotherapy regimen may benefit from treatment with alternate single-agent regimens. Treatment has not been shown to be beneficial in patients with poor performance status (eg, patients who are bed bound, have weight loss >10%, or have severe symptoms). Monthly intravenous bisphosphonate therapy (eg, pamidronate, zolendronate) or monthly subcutaneous dosing of the RANK ligand inhibitor denosumab decreases skeletal complications in patients with bony metastases.

For small cell lung cancer, combination chemotherapy with a platinum-based agent (eg, cisplatin) and etoposide is the mainstay of treatment; tumor radiation is given concurrently or sequentially. Treatment markedly improves survival; even elderly patients with poor initial performance status may tolerate standard regimens. If small cell tumors respond to initial therapy, subsequent prophylactic cranial irradiation increases survival and decreases symptomatic brain involvement. Unfortunately, despite initial response to chemotherapy and radiotherapy, most patients relapse and die of their disease. In patients with good performance status despite documented relapse, consider second-line chemotherapy while educating the patient and family that tumor response is often short-lived.

Palliative treatment is important in cases of advanced disease (see Chapter 44). Severe pain typically requires scheduled administration of opioid analgesics. Use glucocorticoids for patients with brain metastases to decrease intracranial edema. Use thoracic radiation for airway obstruction or superior vena cava syndrome. Use targeted radiation to relieve bone pain, visceral pain secondary to capsular distention, or pain due to nerve compression or spinal cord metastases. Early referral to comprehensive palliative care services along with standard oncologic care has been shown to lengthen overall survival in patients with metastatic non–small cell lung cancer, improve quality of life, and lower rates of depression.

Follow-Up

Continue comprehensive, ongoing follow-up of patients for detection of recurrence, management of disease and treatment complications, and symptom palliation. Most patients with lung cancer will develop recurrent disease. In long-term survivors, surveillance may lead to the detection of a second primary tumor, most commonly of the lung. Schedule follow-up at frequent intervals, and evaluate for recurrent disease using clinical examination and appropriate laboratory testing. Patients with advanced, metastatic disease should be seen monthly to assess for and address new symptoms.

Bibliography

Sculier JP, Berghmans T, Meert AP. Update in lung cancer and mesothelioma 2009. Am J Respir Crit Care Med. 2010;181:773-81. [PMID: 20382800]

Chapter 82

Breast Cancer

Kathleen F. Ryan, MD

Breast cancer is the most frequently diagnosed cancer and the second most common cause of cancer death in women. Each year, >200,000 people are diagnosed with invasive breast cancer; >39,000 of these people will die from their disease. Most cases involve women, but nearly 2000 cases each year involve men. In women, the main risk factor for breast cancer is age. Other risk factors are a personal history of breast cancer, a family history of breast cancer (particularly in first-degree relatives), prior biopsy showing atypical ductal or lobular hyperplasia, prolonged estrogen exposure (ie, early menarche, late menopause, nulliparity, pregnancy after age 30, postmenopausal obesity), and inherited mutations of the *BRCA1* or *BRCA2* gene. Only age shows a strong enough correlation to target women for screening.

Prevention

Routine screening for *BRCA1* and *BRCA2* mutations is not recommended in women who are at low risk for developing breast cancer. Although *BRCA1* and *BRCA2* mutations are highly associated with cancer risk (>60% by age 50 years), they account for only a small percentage of all breast cancers (<5%). The U.S. Preventive Services Task Force (USPSTF) has identified several family history risk factors associated with increased likelihood of having a BRCA1/2 mutation:

- Breast cancer diagnosis before age 50 years
- Bilateral breast cancer
- Family history of breast and ovarian cancer
- Presence of breast cancer in ≥1 male family member
- Multiple cases of breast cancer in the family
- One or more family members with 2 primary types of *BRCA*-related cancer
- Ashkenazi Jewish ethnicity

To simplify screening, the USPSTF recommends that for women who have at least 1 family member with breast, ovarian, or other types of *BRCA*-related cancer, primary care providers use 1 of several brief familial risk stratification tools to determine the need for in-depth genetic counseling. These include the Ontario Family History Assessment Tool, Manchester Scoring System, Referral Screening Tool, Pedigree Assessment Tool, and the FHS-7 instrument. These tools are easy to administer in clinical settings and are equally effective in eliciting information about factors that are associated with increased likelihood of *BRCA* mutations. If identified as being at increased risk, referral for formal genetic counseling and testing is indicated.

Prevention strategies are available for women at high risk for breast cancer. Breast cancer risk may be calculated by using the Breast Cancer Risk Assessment Tool (Gail model) available at the National Cancer Institute Web site (www.cancer.gov/bcrisktool). It estimates a woman's risk of developing invasive breast cancer within the next 5 years and incorporates factors such as current age, age at menarche, age at first live birth, breast cancer in first-degree relatives, previous breast biopsy, and ethnicity. Women with a calculated 5-year risk ≥1.7% (risk of an average 60-year-old woman) are classified as being at high risk. In women aged 35 to 60 years at high risk for breast cancer in the next 5 years based on the Gail model, antiestrogen therapy with a 5-year course of a selective estrogen receptor modulator (SERM) (eg, tamoxifen, raloxifene) has been shown to reduce the risk of developing estrogen receptor (ER)-positive cancer. The risks of these medications are not insignificant and include thrombosis, endometrial cancer, and hot flashes, and the benefits of therapy therefore need to be weighed against the risks of treatment.

In women carrying the *BRCA1/2* genes the benefits of SERMs have not yet been defined. Screening this high-risk group should include both annual mammograms and breast MRI. Prophylactic mastectomy is another option for women at increased risk for breast cancer, especially women found to have a genetic predisposition. Women with a known *BRCA1* or *BRCA2* mutation should be referred to a genetic counselor for discussion of the risks and benefits of prophylactic mastectomy and oophorectomy.

Screening

There are differing screening recommendations for breast cancer. The American Cancer Society (ACS) recommends that all women aged ≥20 years should be taught and encouraged to perform breast self-examination (BSE) and to report any breast changes to their health care provider. The ACS also recommends that women should have a clinical breast examination (CBE) performed by a health professional every 3 years between age 20 and age 39 years and annually after age 40. Per ACS, mammograms should start at age 40 years and continue as long as the woman is in good health. However, it is important to note that BSE has not been shown to improve cancer-specific or all-cause mortality, and CBE may only modestly improve the detection of breast cancer and may increase the risk of false positive findings that may require further evaluation. The USPSTF recommends against teaching BSE and notes insufficient evidence for the benefit of CBE. The USPSTF recommends screening all women aged 50 to 74 years every other year using mammography, with the decision to start regular, biennial screening mammography before the age of 50 years being individualized and taking into account the clinical context and the patient's values regarding specific benefits and harms of screening. The American College of Physicians also recommends that physicians should perform an individualized assessment of risk in women 40 to 49 years of age to help guide the decision on initiating mammography.

There is no consensus on what age to stop screening because shortened life expectancy results in less benefit from breast cancer screening. The USPSTF concludes that the current evidence is insufficient to assess the additional benefits and harms of screening mammography in women 75 years or older. It is reasonable to continue screening for breast cancer as long as life expectancy is ≥10 years.

Specialized breast imaging techniques (eg, ultrasonography, scintigraphy with technetium 99m sestamibi) should be reserved for women with abnormal or inconclusive mammograms or clinical examinations. MRI should be used as an adjunct and not a replacement for mammography. It is best used when there is a high suspicion for breast cancer and other modalities are inconclusive.

Diagnosis

Women reporting new breast symptoms or new abnormalities on BSE should be carefully evaluated. The history should include an assessment of risk factors (age, family history of breast or ovarian cancer, use of hormone replacement therapy or oral contraceptives, age at menarche, number of pregnancies, menopausal status) and a detailed account of the patient's symptoms and concerns. Inquire about breast pain, nipple discharge, abdominal discomfort, bone pain, and respiratory or neurologic symptoms. Knowing the results of prior imaging studies or biopsies also is important.

The physical examination should include a detailed examination of both breasts and complete lymph node evaluation. Most often, breast cancer presents as a new lump, nipple discharge, or skin changes (retraction, dimpling). Erythema, scaliness, and edema with enlargement of pores and change in skin color (peau d'orange) are signs of inflammatory breast cancer, which often is misdiagnosed as eczema or mastitis. Younger women may have denser breasts, making detection of a mass more challenging than in older women, who tend to have more fat content in their breasts. Standardization of the CBE improves examiner accuracy. Four variables important for proper examination of the breast are:

- proper positioning of the patient (to flatten the breast against the chest)
- accurate identification of breast boundaries
- finger position (palpating along vertical strips) and palpation pressure
- duration of the examination (3 minutes per breast)

Axillary adenopathy may indicate more advanced disease, whereas supraclavicular or cervical adenopathy usually means metastatic disease.

For nipple discharge, cytology is an excellent diagnostic tool. All patients with new breast symptoms or abnormal CBE findings should undergo mammography or ultrasonography. Women aged <40 years are likely to have benign findings; following the abnormality through one menstrual cycle rather than imaging immediately is a reasonable option. Obtain a tissue diagnosis in women with a suspicious abnormality on mammography and in all women with a suspicious palpable mass, even if an imaging study is not abnormal (Table 1). The differential diagnosis of a breast mass is summarized in Table 2.

If surgery is planned to treat confirmed breast cancer, a preoperative evaluation consisting of bilateral mammography, chest radiography, and laboratory studies based on age and comorbidities is performed. Evaluation of ER and progesterone receptor (PR) status is important, as it predicts benefit from endocrine therapy. HER1-4 (human epidermal growth factor receptors 1-4) is a family of membrane-bound proteins with tyrosine kinase activity, which act as epidermal growth factors. Overexpression of HER2 occurs in up to 40% of breast cancers and is associated with a poorer prognosis. However, it allows for targeted adjuvant therapy to be used.

CT scan and bone scan will need to be done if the tumor is large or there are palpable lymph nodes. Staging of breast cancer is based on the TNM staging system, which is based on tumor size (T), axillary node status (N), and presence or absence of metastatic disease (M). Staging determines prognosis and therapeutic options (Table 3). The two most important prognostic factors are tumor size and axillary node status. In the future, genomic testing may replace staging systems.

Breast cancer usually metastasizes locally to axillary lymph nodes. Breast cancer also commonly spreads to the bones, lungs, liver, or brain. Some women have been found to have cancer of unknown primary origin and have adenocarcinoma or poorly differentiated carcinoma in the axillary lymph nodes and no evident primary breast lesions or distant disease spread after completion of the routine staging evaluation. These patients have been found to be potentially curable when managed according to standard guidelines for stage II breast cancer.

Table 1. Evaluation of Clinical Breast Abnormalities

Breast Abnormality	Diagnostic Approach
Palpable lump or mass (patient aged <30 y)	Consider observation to assess for resolution within 1 or 2 menstrual cycles. If persistent, perform ultrasonography. If asymptomatic and cystic on ultrasonography, observe. If symptomatic or not clearly cystic on ultrasonography, aspirate. If aspirate fluid is bloody or a mass persists following aspiration, biopsy or excise for diagnosis. If solid on ultrasonography, obtain mammogram and tissue diagnosis (fine-needle aspiration, core biopsy, or surgical excision). If not visualized on ultrasonography, obtain mammogram and tissue diagnosis.
Palpable lump or mass (patient aged ≥30 y)	Obtain mammogram. If BI-RADS category 1-3,[a] perform ultrasonography and follow protocol described for patient aged <30 y. If BI-RADS category 4-5, obtain tissue diagnosis.
Nipple discharge, no mass (any age)	If discharge is bilateral and milky, perform pregnancy test. If test is negative, conduct endocrine evaluation. If discharge is persistent, spontaneous, unilateral, serous/bloody, or involves one duct, obtain mammogram and surgical referral for duct exploration; cytology is optional.
Thickening or asymmetry (patient aged <30 y)	Consider unilateral mammogram. If normal, reassess in 3-6 mo. If abnormal, obtain tissue diagnosis.
Thickening or asymmetry (patient aged ≥30 y)	Obtain bilateral mammogram. If normal, reassess in 3-6 mo. If abnormal, obtain tissue diagnosis.
Skin changes[b] (patient aged <30 y)	Consider mastitis and treat with antibiotics (if appropriate) and reevaluate in 2 wk. Otherwise, evaluate as described for patient aged ≥30 y.
Skin changes[b] (patient aged ≥30 y)	Obtain bilateral mammogram. If normal, obtain skin biopsy. If abnormal or indeterminate, obtain needle biopsy or excision (also consider skin punch biopsy).

BI-RADS = Breast Imaging Reporting and Data System.

[a]BI-RADS 1 = negative. BI-RADS 2 = benign finding. BI-RADS 3 = probably benign finding; short-interval follow-up suggested. BI-RADS 4 = suspicious abnormality; consider biopsy. BI-RADS 5 = highly suggests malignancy; take appropriate action.

[b]Erythema, peau d'orange, scaling, nipple excoriation, eczema.

Table 2. Differential Diagnosis of a Breast Mass

Disorder	Notes
Fibrocystic changes of the breast	Excessive nodularity and general lumpiness. Pain may be exacerbated premenstrually.
Fibroadenoma	Tender, discrete, mobile, well-circumscribed mass. Confirmed by examination, ultrasonography, and fine-needle aspiration biopsy.
Breast cyst	Severe localized pain associated with rapid expansion of a cyst. Ultrasonography usually is diagnostic and is the test of choice in women aged <40 y.
Breast hematoma	Tender mass, usually in association with breast trauma or after biopsy.
Breast cancer	Pain in 5%-20% of patients. Firm, irregular mass and axillary nodes may be present. Skin thickening and erythema suggest an underlying neoplasm or inflammation. Examination, mammography, ultrasonography, and fine-needle aspiration are indicated. Associated bloody discharge is more suggestive of cancer.
Breast abscess	Erythema, pain, and fever. More common in lactating breast.
Ductal papilloma	Unilateral bloody discharge. Mass may not be detectable. Refer for duct exploration.
Ductal carcinoma in situ	Noninvasive lesions usually identified by mammogram. They can, however, present as a palpable breast mass.

Table 3. Staging, Treatment, and Survival for Patients with Breast Cancer

AJCC Stage	Definition	Treatment	5-Year Survival (%)
Carcinoma in situ (DCIS)	Noninvasive also called Stage 0. A malignant population of ductal or lobular cells that have not broken through the basement membrane.	Breast-conserving treatment (lumpectomy plus radiation therapy) or mastectomy. Lymph node evaluation is not typically recommended. For hormone receptor-positive DCIS, the standard of care is to discuss the use of tamoxifen for 5 years to reduce both the risk of recurrence and the development of a new primary tumor in the ipsilateral or contralateral breast. No data exist on the use of aromatase inhibitors in patients with DCIS. There is also currently no role for adjuvant chemotherapy, trastuzumab, or raloxifene.	100
I	Invasive carcinoma < 2 cm with negative lymph nodes	Lumpectomy and sentinel lymph node evaluation followed by whole-breast radiation therapy[a] Chemo if reoccurrence risk high Endocrine therapy if receptor positive	100
II	Invasive carcinoma < 2 cm with 1-3 positive lymph nodes Invasive carcinoma 2-5 cm with 0-3 positive lymph nodes Invasive carcinoma > 5 cm with no positive lymph nodes	Lumpectomy/mastectomy and sentinel lymph node evaluation followed by possible chemo if reoccurrence rate is high and possible radiation* Endocrine therapy if receptor positive	86
III	Invasive carcinoma > 5 cm with 1-3 lymph nodes positive 4 or more positive lymph nodes Tumor extending to chest wall or skin	Lumpectomy/mastectomy and sentinel lymph node evaluation followed by adjuvant chemo and possible radiation* Endocrine therapy if receptor positive	57
IV	Distant metastases	Palliative resection, multiagent chemotherapy	13

AJCC = American Joint Committee on Cancer; DCIS = ductal carcinoma in situ.

[a]Breast-conserving therapy is less suitable for most women with tumors greater than 5 cm (or for smaller tumors if the breast is small), tumors involving the nipple and areola complex, and multicentric tumors.

Therapy

Surgery is a mainstay of treatment for breast cancer. Lumpectomy (breast-conserving surgery) followed by radiation is an option for patients with focal disease (tumor <5 cm) or ductal carcinoma in situ; survival rates are similar to mastectomy. For more extensive ductal carcinoma, modified radical mastectomy with radiation is the best option to lower recurrence rates. Mastectomy is indicated for patients with very large tumors or with contraindications to radiation (eg, prior radiation). Radiation carries the risk of future cardiovascular damage and lymphoma. Surgery may be used as palliative therapy for metastatic disease (eg, to prevent complications such as infection).

Lymph node sampling is done as part of staging. Because aggressive removal of all axillary nodes does not improve survival and leads to limb lymphedema, sentinel node dissection often is used instead. Dye or tracer is injected into the tumor, and the first draining lymph node is biopsied and examined for tumor presence. If tumor is absent, no further dissection is needed; if tumor is noted, further lymph node dissection is performed.

Adjuvant systemic therapy with hormonal therapy, chemotherapy, or biologic agents is indicated for patients with early-stage breast cancer at significant risk for recurrence in a distant metastatic site. The purpose of adjuvant systemic therapy is to reduce the burden of clinically undetectable, distant micrometastatic disease. The most important prognostic factors used to determine the need for adjuvant therapy in patients with breast cancer are lymph node involvement and tumor size.

Endocrine therapy is beneficial only in patients with ER- or PR-positive tumors. In premenopausal women with ER- or PR-positive tumors, 5 years of tamoxifen is the standard adjuvant endocrine therapeutic regimen; treatment longer than 5 years is not recommended. Aromatase inhibitors (eg, anastrozole, letrozole, exemestane) appear to be more effective than tamoxifen in reducing risk for breast cancer recurrence in postmenopausal women with ER-positive breast cancer. Although aromatase inhibitors do not increase the risk for thromboembolic disease or endometrial cancer, they are associated with postmenopausal symptoms (hot flashes), musculoskeletal symptoms (arthralgia), and an increased risk for osteoporosis. The American Society of Clinical Oncology has suggested including an aromatase inhibitor as adjuvant therapy for postmenopausal women with hormone receptor–positive breast cancer to lower the risk of tumor recurrence. Postmenopausal women with hormone receptor–positive breast cancer should take a 5-year course of an aromatase inhibitor as primary treatment or for an additional 5 years after completing a 5-year course of tamoxifen therapy. In women who are initially treated with tamoxifen, an aromatase inhibitor may be started following 2 to 3 years of tamoxifen therapy to complete a total of 5 years of hormonal therapy. Aromatase inhibitors are contraindicated in premenopausal women, because reduced feedback of estrogen to the hypothalamus and pituitary gland leads to an increase in gonadotropin secretion, with potential adverse effects.

The decision to use systemic chemotherapy is based on the risk for recurrent disease. The presence of invasive disease within the biopsy is the most powerful prognostic factor for recurrence. Typical chemotherapy regimens include methotrexate, cyclophosphamide, doxorubicin or epirubicin, and 5-fluorouracil and the taxanes. Chemotherapy may cause short- and long-term side effects. Short-term effects include hair loss, mouth sores, vomiting, diarrhea, anorexia, fatigue, increased risk of infection, and easy bruising and bleeding. Long-term side effects include infertility, peripheral neuropathy, osteoporosis, myocardial damage (with doxorubicin or trastuzumab), decreased cognitive function, and leukemia.

Trastuzumab is a humanized monoclonal antibody to the HER2 receptor. In patients with HER2-positive tumors, adjuvant trastuzumab therapy reduces the risk for breast cancer recurrence by approximately 50% and improves overall survival.

For patients with metastatic disease, therapy is palliative. Patients with ER/PR-positive tumors and bone or visceral disease are initially treated with tamoxifen. Aromatase inhibitors are used in postmenopausal women with tamoxifen-resistant disease. For patients with lytic bone disease, radiation therapy is used to reduce pain or prevent pathologic fractures. Bisphosphonates, such as pamidronate, clodronate, risedronate (given orally) and zoledronate (given intravenously), are used to treat hypercalcemia from bone involvement in breast cancer. Bisphosphonate-related osteonecrosis of the jaw has been associated with high-dose bisphosphonate use in cancer patients.

Follow-Up

For at least 5 years after treatment, breast cancer survivors should undergo detailed histories and physicals every 6 months. After 5 years this can be done annually. They should undergo annual mammography of the preserved and contralateral breast. Breast MRI is currently not recommended. In the absence of specific symptoms, routine blood tests or imaging procedures looking for metastatic disease should not be performed.

Bibliography

Maughan KL, Lutterbie MA, Ham PS. Treatment of breast cancer. Am Fam Physician. 2010;81:1339-46. [PMID: 20521754]

Warner E. Breast-cancer screening. N Engl J Med. 2011;365:1025-32. [PMID: 22236238]

Chapter 83

Colorectal Cancer

Kathleen F. Ryan, MD

Colorectal cancer is the second leading cause of cancer death affecting both men and women in the United States. Each year >130,000 new cases of colorectal cancer are diagnosed and more than 51,000 people die from the disease. Death is preventable by using effective, safe, and relatively inexpensive screening methods.

Colorectal cancer arises from adenomatous polyps, and polyp removal reduces the risk of colorectal cancer. The main risk factors for malignant transformation are polyp size (>1.0 cm), number, and histologic type.

It is important to note that approximately 75% of colorectal cancers arise in individuals who have no obvious cancer risk. In these patients, a stepwise accumulation of epithelial genetic abnormalities results in polyp and colorectal cancer development. In some cases, however, colorectal cancers are related to inherited genetic abnormalities.

At least three molecular patterns that lead to colorectal tumorigenesis have been delineated: chromosomal instability (CIN), microsatellite instability (MSI), and island methylator phenotype (CIMP). In most sporadic cancers and some familial syndromes, CIN causing mutations in the *APC* gene–an important tumor suppression gene–occur. When both copies (alleles) of *APC* within a cell are mutated, cell growth becomes dysregulated. *APC* mutations, which tend to occur early in the process of colon carcinogenesis, are the cause of most cases of familial adenomatous polyposis (FAP). Mismatch repair genes assist in the repair of errors in DNA that occur during replication. When these genes are defective, small abnormal sequences of DNA called *microsatellites* are inserted into the genetic code, resulting in MSI, which predisposes the cell to malignant transformation. The extent of promoter hypermethylation in select growth-regulating genes defines CIMP. Newer data suggests that CIMP-positive tumors may come from serrated polyps involving inactivation of the *BRAF* gene, which differs from the classic adenoma-to-carcinoma pathway.

Inherited colon cancer syndromes include autosomal dominant FAP and its variants, autosomal dominant hereditary nonpolyposis colorectal cancer (HNPCC [also called Lynch syndrome]), and the autosomal dominant hamartomatous polyposis syndromes (eg, Peutz-Jegher syndrome, juvenile polyposis). FAP accounts for 1% of all colorectal cancers; in FAP, the mucosa of the colon is covered with polyps. HNPCC accounts for 5% to 10% of colorectal cancers, is seen in younger patients, and usually involves the right colon. Patients with HNPCC also have an increased risk of other cancers (endometrial, ovarian, urologic, gastric, small bowel, pancreatic, biliary, skin, brain). Lastly, the very rare hamartomatous polyposis syndromes present in children and are associated with pigmentation of the lips.

Prevention

Although the precise pathologic mechanisms of colorectal cancer have not been identified, patients should be counseled to stop smoking, avoid excess alcohol intake, maintain a normal body weight, keep physically active, and eat red meat in moderation. A diet rich in fresh fruits and vegetables can be recommended for general health purposes, but definitive evidence linking such a diet with colorectal cancer prevention is lacking. Aspirin has been shown to be effective

Table 1. Screening Recommendations for Average-Risk Persons

	ACP 2012	USPSTF 2008	ACG 2008	ACS 2013
Screening guidelines	Adults 50-75 y; do not screen >75 y	Adults 50-75 y; individualized decision for ages 76-85 y	Adults ≥50 y; start at age 45 y in African Americans	Adults ≥50 y
FOBT (two samples each from 3 spontaneously passed stools) or FIT[a]	FOBT annually	FOBT annually	FOBT and FIT annually	FOBT or FIT annually
Sigmoidoscopy	Every 5 y	Every 5 y with FOBT	Every 5-10 y	Every 5 y
FOBT combined with sigmoidoscopy	No recommendation	FOBT every 3 y plus sigmoidoscopy every 5 y	No recommendation	No recommendation
Double-contrast barium enema	No recommendation	No recommendation	No recommendation	Every 5 y
Colonoscopy	Every 10 y	Every 10 y	Every 10 y	Every 10 y
CT colonography (virtual colonoscopy)	No recommendation	No recommendation	Every 5 y in patients declining colonoscopy	Every 5 y

ACG = American College of Gastroenterology; ACP = American College of Physicians; ACS = American Cancer Society; CT = computed tomography; FIT = fecal immunochemical test; FOBT = fecal occult blood test; USPSTF = U.S. Preventive Services Task Force.

[a]If positive proceed to colonoscopy.

for primary prevention of colorectal cancer in women aged >45 in low doses, and in higher doses for secondary prevention in patients with a history of adenomas or colorectal cancer. Bleeding risk must be taken into account before aspirin is initiated.

Screening

Screening recommendations are based on risk. All adults aged 50 to 75 at average risk for colorectal cancer can be screened by one of several acceptable methods (Table 1). Persons at high risk are screened more intensely with colonoscopy, usually beginning at age 40 years and every 5 years thereafter (Table 2). High risk is defined as having multiple first-degree relatives with colorectal cancer or a first-degree relative diagnosed with colonic adenomatous polyps or colorectal cancer at age <60 years. Persons with a personal history of an ade-

nomatous polyp larger than 1.0 cm require a repeat colonoscopy within 3 years. **Serum carcinoembryonic antigen (CEA) should not be used as a screening test for colorectal cancer due to its poor sensitivity and specificity.** Computed tomographic (CT) colonography ("virtual colonoscopy") is a new screening modality that uses helical CT to capture two-dimensional axial images that can be converted into a three-dimensional view. The current guidelines suggest using CT colonography as a second line to traditional colonoscopy. Some reasons are that a full bowel preparation is required, only polyps greater than 1 cm can be visualized, and if identified these polyps cannot be removed during the procedure. Also there is a radiation exposure associated with this testing modality. When fecal occult blood testing is used, a positive reading in even one slide window should be evaluated with colonoscopy.

Table 2. Screening Recommendations For High-Risk Persons

Risk	Recommendation
Inflammatory bowel disease	Begin surveillance:
UC-pancolitis, distal colitis	Every 1-2 y starting 8 y after disease onset
UC-proctitis	Every 10 y starting 8 y after disease onset
Crohn's disease > 1/3 colon involved	Every 1-2 y starting 8 y after disease onset
with PSC	At PSC diagnosis and every y after
One first-degree relative with colorectal cancer or adenomatous polyps diagnosed at age <60 y or ≥2 second-degree relatives with colorectal cancer diagnosed at any age	Any modality screening beginning at age 40 y or 10 y younger than the earliest diagnosis in the family, whichever comes first
Two or more first-degree relatives with colorectal cancer at any age or one first-degree relative with colorectal cancer or adenomatous polyps at age <60 y	Colonoscopy every 5 y, beginning at age 40 y or 10 y younger than the earliest diagnosis in the family, whichever comes first. Double-contrast barium enema may be substituted, but colonoscopy is preferred.
Second- or third-degree relatives with colorectal cancer	Screen as described for average-risk person (see Table 1)

PSC = primary sclerosing cholangitis; UC = ulcerative colitis.

Table 3. Differential Diagnosis of Colorectal Cancer

Clinical Finding	Notes
Hematochezia (see Chapter 27)	Blood on toilet tissue and bright red or maroon stool characterizes hemorrhoids; diverticulosis and arteriovenous malformations usually exhibit massive bleeding. These nonmalignant conditions account for more than 95% of visible rectal bleeding, although evaluation to rule out cancer is always necessary.
Positive FOBT	Approximately 3%-5% of persons with a positive FOBT will have colorectal cancer; up to 50% will have polyps. Other causes of positive FOBT include NSAIDs, upper GI lesions, and false-positive results.
Iron deficiency anemia (see Chapter 47)	Menstrual blood loss is a frequent cause of iron loss in women of childbearing age but should not be presumed to be the diagnosis. Other causes include IBD, GERD, and causes listed for positive FOBT. Sprue causes iron malabsorption and is characterized by diarrhea and fat malabsorption. A substantial fraction of persons aged >50 y with iron deficiency anemia will be found to have colorectal cancer.
Change in bowel habits	IBS is characterized by abdominal pain plus diarrhea, constipation, or both. Changes in diet and bed rest may decrease bowel frequency. Many medications affect bowel frequency. Colorectal cancer accounts for <5% of cases of change in bowel habits but nonetheless must be considered.
Abdominal mass or hepatomegaly	Abdominal masses found on physical examination may have many causes. Abdominal and bowel imaging are the next steps. These findings are extremely rare presentations of colon cancer, although a rectal mass on rectal examination is quite specific for colon cancer or polyp.
Hypogastric abdominal pain (see Chapter 16)	Consider IBS, diverticulitis, IBD, ischemic colitis, colonic volvulus, and uterine or ovarian disease. Bowel, abdominal, and genitourinary imaging should follow physical examination for evaluating these possible conditions and for ruling out colon cancer. Colon cancer accounts for abdominal pain in <5% of patients.

FOBT = fecal occult blood test; GERD = gastroesophageal reflux disease; GI = gastrointestinal; IBD = inflammatory bowel disease; IBS = irritable bowel syndrome; NSAID = nonsteroidal anti-inflammatory drug" after "syndrome.

Diagnosis

Common signs and symptoms of colorectal cancer are influenced by the site of the primary tumor and may include a change in bowel habits, diarrhea, constipation, a feeling that the bowel does not empty completely, bright red blood in the stool, melanotic stools, and stools that are narrower in caliber than usual. Other signs include general abdominal discomfort (frequent gas pains, bloating, fullness, cramping), unintentional weight loss, fatigue, and vomiting. Findings of iron deficiency anemia in persons aged >40 years require careful evaluation for colorectal cancer (Table 3). Colonoscopy is performed when colorectal cancer is suspected. The sensitivity and specificity of colonoscopy are each >95%, and colonoscopy is the reference standard for detecting cancer or polyps. If colonoscopy is unavailable, a double-contrast barium enema can be used; sensitivity and specificity are 85% and 80%, respectively, for detecting cancer, but the test is much less sensitive in detecting polyps. If an inherited colorectal cancer syndrome is suspected when there is a dominant pattern of cancer occurrence in family members, both the patient and family members should be referred for genetic testing. Also suspect an inherited syndrome if hamartomatous polyps or >10 adenomatous polyps are found on colonoscopy. If undetected, colorectal cancer tends to spread to the liver, lungs, pleural space, bone, or brain.

Therapy

Surgery is an integral component of colorectal cancer treatment. Surgery usually is followed by chemotherapy in cases of advanced-stage colon cancer and in most cases of rectal cancer. There is debate over the usefulness of preoperative staging, but many experts agree that the initial evaluation should include a complete blood count, serum CEA and aminotransaminase measurements, chest radiography, and abdominal and pelvic CT. In rectal cancer, endoscopic ultrasonography is done to determine depth of tumor invasion.

For stage I or stage II colon cancer, tumor resection is performed for cure (Table 4). For stage III disease, the cancer is resected, and adjuvant chemotherapy is initiated. For advanced metastatic disease (stage IV), removal of the primary tumor is indicated for palliative relief of obstruction or to stop bleeding. Isolated hepatic metastases can be resected, depending on the patient's overall functional status.

For rectal cancers beyond stage I, radiation therapy in addition to surgery (with or without chemotherapy) is first-line treatment. The addition of radiation therapy to surgery and chemotherapy has been shown to decrease the risk of recurrence and death.

Chemotherapy is used as both adjuvant and palliative therapy in colon and rectal cancer after surgery to decrease relapses and increase survival. First-line agents for stage III colorectal cancer include 5-fluorouracil and leucovorin for 6 months, oral capecitabine for 24 weeks, or 5-fluorouracil, leucovorin and oxaliplatin for 24 weeks. In metastatic colorectal cancer, multiagent chemotherapy increases median survival compared with standard chemotherapy. In selected cases of advanced disease, other treatments such as the antiangiogenesis monoclonal antibody bevacizumab or monoclonal antibodies directed at specific molecular targets, such as cetuximab, may have a role.

In advanced disease, palliative surgical resection is sometimes needed to prevent obstruction. In addition, a palliative care consult can be helpful in assisting with pain management, navigation of the complex health care system, and psychosocial support for the patient and family.

Follow-Up

Colorectal cancer survivors are at increased risk for future adenomatous polyps and new colorectal cancers. The most common sites of recurrence of colorectal cancer are the site of initial removal as well as the liver, bone, and brain. Follow-up surveillance is based on tumor stage. For stage I, colonoscopy should be repeated within a year and then at 3 years. If results are normal the patient can be placed on a 5-year cycle. For stage II and III the recommendation for colonoscopy is the same as for stage I; however, CT scans of the abdomen and pelvis should be done annually for the first 3 years. For stage IV, CT scans of the chest, abdomen, and pelvis should be done as directed by the patient's symptoms. The percentage of patients with stage I or II colorectal cancer who will develop metastases ranges from 5% to 20%. Some metastatic disease can be surgically resected (salvage surgery), resulting in a substantial cure rate. When a curative approach is not appropriate, palliative care is instituted. Patients with stage III disease are followed for both recurrence of the tumor and adverse effects of chemotherapy. Periodic serum aminotransaminase and CEA measurements and chest radiography are often done but have not been shown to improve survival.

Bibliography

Markowitz SD, Bertagnolli MM. Molecular origins of cancer: Molecular basis of colorectal cancer. N Engl J Med. 2009;361:2449-60. [PMID: 20018966]

Rex DK, Johnson DA, Anderson JC, et al. American College of Gastroenterology guidelines for colorectal cancer screening 2009 [corrected]. Am J Gastroenterol. 2009;104:739-50 [published erratum appears in Am J Gastroenterol. 2009;104:1613]. [PMID: 19240699]

Table 4. Staging, Treatment, and Survival for Patients with Colon Cancer

AJCC Stage	Definition	Treatment	5-Year Survival (%)
I	Confined to muscularis propria	Resection for cure	>90
II	Extends into subserosa or directly invades other structures	Resection for cure	>70
III	Metastatic to regional lymph nodes	Resection and adjuvant chemotherapy	>35
IV	Distant metastases	Palliative resection, multiagent chemotherapy	3

AJCC = American Joint Committee on Cancer.

Chapter 84

Cervical Cancer

Asra R. Khan, MD

Cervical cancer is the second most common cancer in women worldwide and in the United States; its incidence has decreased dramatically with screening and management of premalignant conditions. Women in their teens to age 30 years typically present with dysplasia, whereas invasive cancer is more commonly seen after age 45 years. Persistent infection with high-risk human papillomavirus (HPV) subtypes (HPV-16 and HPV-18) can cause cervical dysplasia, and subsequently, cancer. Dysplastic lesions can progress to cellular intraepithelial neoplasia, which in turn can evolve into well-differentiated low-grade lesions and then undifferentiated high-grade lesions. These precancerous lesions may regress spontaneously at any point or may progress to invasive cancer.

Prevention

HPV infection is sexually transmitted and can cause cervical dysplasia and cervical cancer. Having multiple sexual partners increases exposure to HPV, and intercourse at an early age exposes the cervix to HPV when it is most vulnerable to infection. Using condoms helps decrease exposure to HPV. Therefore, patients should be advised to limit their number of sexual partners, avoid intercourse at an early age (age <13-15 years), and use condoms to decrease the risk of acquiring HPV infection. Patients who smoke should also be advised about smoking cessation; women who smoke have an increased risk of developing cervical dysplasia and cancer because of the carcinogenic and immunosuppressive effects of smoking.

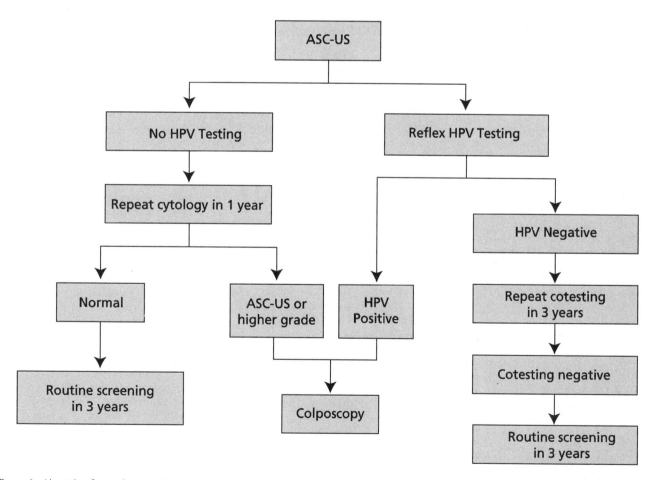

Figure 1. Algorithm for evaluating ASC-US in women aged >24 years. ASC-US = atypical squamous cells of undetermined significance; HPV = human papillomavirus.

Both bivalent and quadrivalent HPV vaccines are available. Both vaccines protect against high-risk HPV subtypes (HPV-16 and HPV-18) and the quadrivalent additionally protects against subtypes that cause genital warts (HPV-6 and HPV-11). Routine vaccination with either vaccine is recommended for girls aged 11 to 12 years but can be given as early as 9 years of age. Vaccination should be offered to females aged 13 to 26 years who have not previously received or completed the vaccine series. Both vaccines are administered in three doses: time zero, 1-2 months later, and 6 months after the initial dose. Ideally, the vaccine should be administered prior to the onset of sexual activity. Pregnant women should not receive the vaccine because there is a lack of safety data in this population. In 2011, the Advisory Committee on Immunization Practices recommended that males aged 11 to 12 years receive the quadrivalent vaccine, although the vaccine may be given to boys as young as 9 years of age. Males may be vaccinated up to age 26.

Both vaccines are very effective against HPV-16 and HPV-18; however, they do not protect against all types of HPV. They also do not treat existing HPV-related infections, warts, or precancerous lesions. Roughly 30% of cervical cancers will not be prevented by the vaccines, so women should continue to receive recommended cervical cancer screening. Moreover, the length of immunity from vaccination is not yet known, so a booster may be needed.

Screening

Pap anicolaou (PAP) smear screening has significantly decreased the risk of death from cervical cancer. Screening is initiated at age 21 years and is not recommended in younger females regardless of age at onset of vaginal intercourse. The screening interval is every 3 years starting at age 21 unless there is a history of diethylstilbestrol exposure or the patient is HIV-positive or immunocompromised. These

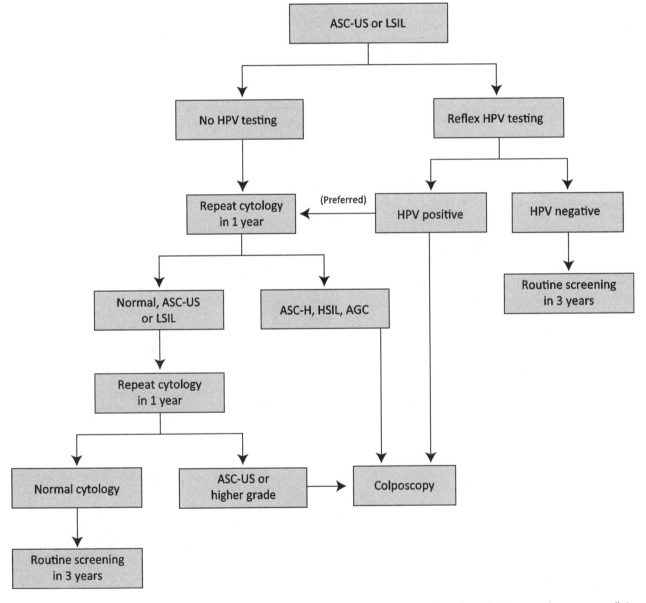

Figure 2. Algorithm for evaluating ASC-US in women aged 21 to 24 years. AGC = atypical glandular cells; ASC-H = atypical squamous cells/cannot exclude HSIL; ASC-US = atypical squamous cells of undetermined significance; HPV = human papillomavirus; HSIL = high-grade squamous intraepithelial lesion; LSIL = low-grade squamous intraepithelial lesion

high-risk women should undergo screening every 6 to 12 months. Women at average risk aged >30 years can be screened with a combined Pap smear and HPV DNA testing (also referred to as cotesting). If both tests are negative, the screening interval can be increased to every 5 years. If the cytology is negative, but high-risk HPV DNA testing is positive, both tests should be repeated at 12 months. **Screening for cervical cancer may be discontinued at age 65 years if the patient has been adequately screened, has had normal Pap smears, and has no other risk factors. Screening for cervical cancer is not indicated or necessary in patients who have had a total hysterectomy (with removal of the cervix) for benign disease.**

Results of cervical cytology are reported using the standard 2001 Bethesda System. Pap smears are reported as satisfactory if they contain an adequate sample, including an endocervical component. If the cytology result is unsatisfactory, usually due to scant cellularity, a Pap test should be repeated after 2 to 4 months. If the cytology result is atypical squamous cells of undetermined significance (ASC-US), the preferred management strategy is to order an HPV test when obtaining a Pap smear (Figure 1). Termed "reflex HPV testing," an HPV test will be performed on any Pap smear that is reported as ASC-US. If results are positive for high-risk HPV, the patient should be referred for colposcopy. The colposcope is a low-powered magnification device that permits the identification of mucosal abnormalities characteristic of dysplasia or invasive cancer and guides selection of tissue for biopsy. If results are negative for high-risk subtypes, the Pap smear and HPV test are repeated in 3 years. Alternatively, if the HPV test was not performed, the cytology can be repeated in 1 year. If the repeat cytology is negative, the patient resumes routine screening in 3 years. If the repeat cytology is ASC-US or worse, the patient should be referred for colposcopy. The preceding recommendations apply to both pre- and postmenopausal women older than 24 years with ASC-US. Women aged 21 to 24 years with ASC-US or low-grade squamous intraepithelial lesion (LSIL) are managed differently (Figure 2). The Pap test should be repeated in 12 months; if the result is negative, ASC-US, or LSIL, cytology is repeated again 12 months later. If a repeat test at 12 months is ASC-H (high-grade ASC-US) or worse, the patient should also be referred for colposcopy. If the cytology is negative × 2 or the initial reflex HPV test was negative, the patient can resume routine screening. If the cytology is ASC-US or greater at 24 months, the patient should be referred for colposcopy. The following cytology findings in pre- or postmenopausal women should be referred for colposcopy or further evaluation, even if HPV testing is negative: LSIL (unless aged 21 to 24), high-grade squamous intraepithelial lesion (HSIL), atypical squamous cells/cannot exclude HSIL (ASC-H), squamous cell cancer, adenocarcinoma, atypical glandular cells, or endometrial cells in women aged >40 years (Table 1).

Diagnosis

Table 2 summarizes the differential diagnosis of cervical cancer. Symptoms of cervical cancer may include postcoital bleeding, foul-smelling vaginal discharge, change in urinary or bowel habits, right upper quadrant abdominal pain, back pain, or leg swelling. The first symptom often is bleeding after intercourse. Large exophytic tumors and large ulcerative lesions can become necrotic and produce a foul-smelling vaginal discharge. Advanced cervical cancer may impinge on the urinary bladder, ureters, or rectosigmoid colon, causing change in urinary or bowel habits. Cancer can invade through the parametrium to the pelvic sidewall and obstruct the ureter, infiltrate nerves along the uterosacral ligament and sacrum, and compress the iliac vessels. The "terrible triad" of advanced cervical cancer is sciatic back pain, hydroureter, and leg swelling.

On physical examination, look for an exophytic or ulcerative lesion on the cervix, foul-smelling vaginal discharge, firmness in the

Table 1. The 2001 Bethesda System for Reporting Results of Cervical Cytology

Specimen adequacy
Satisfactory
Unsatisfactory
Interpretation/result
Negative for intraepithelial lesion or malignancy
Epithelial cell abnormalities
Squamous cell
ASC-US
ASC-H
LSIL
HSIL
Squamous cell carcinoma
Glandular cell
Atypical glandular cells
Atypical glandular cells, favor neoplastic
Endocervical adenocarcinoma in situ
Adenocarcinoma
Other malignant neoplasms

ASC-H = atypical squamous cells/cannot exclude a high-grade squamous intraepithelial lesion; ASC-US = atypical squamous cells of undetermined significance; HSIL = high-grade squamous intraepithelial lesion; LSIL = low-grade squamous intraepithelial lesion.

Table 2. Differential Diagnosis of Cervical Cancer

Disorder	Notes
Dysplasia	Abnormal Pap test result. Needs colposcopy and biopsy.
Nabothian cysts	Nabothian cysts are formed when glandular tissue is covered by squamous epithelium. Nabothian cysts are common and can become quite large. If diagnosis is questionable, needs biopsy.
Cervicitis (see Chapter 61)	May cause postcoital bleeding. There are no discrete lesions on the cervix, but the cervix is red and inflamed. Needs biopsy if Pap smear result is abnormal.
Cervical ectopy	Presence of columnar epithelium on the ectocervix is a normal variant appearing as a red, beefy area; occasionally mistaken for cervicitis. Close inspection reveals the demarcation where the squamous epithelium begins.
Cervical atrophy	May cause postcoital bleeding. Vagina and cervix tend to be pale and atrophic. Obtain Pap smear.
Cervical polyp	Finger-like mass protruding from os. Needs biopsy or excision.
Cervical cysts	Tend to be well-circumscribed bubble-like lesions on the cervix. If diagnosis is questionable, needs biopsy.

parametrium, leg swelling, and supraclavicular lymphadenopathy (Virchow node). Metastatic disease to the liver may present as tenderness or a mass in the right upper quadrant.

A Pap smear can detect cervical dysplasia and microinvasive and small invasive cancers of the cervix; a Pap test is indicated for any patient with postcoital bleeding. Cervical dysplasia and some early cancers are not visible to the naked eye and require colposcopic examination of the cervix for detection. Biopsies are taken of any grossly visible abnormality of the cervix to determine the histologic diagnosis and to exclude invasive cancer.

Table 3. Laboratory and Other Studies for Cervical Cancer

Test	Notes
Pap smear	Pap smears reduce the risk of death from cervical cancer by 95% when used appropriately.
HPV DNA	Testing for high-risk HPV DNA identifies more women with high-grade dysplasia than does Pap smear.
Colposcopy	Used to direct cervical biopsies after Pap smear that shows high-grade squamous intraepithelial lesion or cancer.
Cervical biopsy	Helps differentiate cervical dysplasia from microinvasive and invasive cancer.
Chest radiography	Used in staging to detect asymptomatic lung metastasis (1%).
Kidney ultrasonography	Used to detect hydroureter in patients with pelvic spread of cancer.
Abdominal and pelvic CT	May be used to help direct therapy but is not used as a part of staging.
Examination under anesthesia, with cystoscopy and proctoscopy	Used to detect regional spread to help determine stage.

CT = computed tomography; HPV = human papillomavirus.

Table 4. Staging, Treatment, and Prognosis for Patients with Cervical Cancer

Stage	Definition	Treatment	Prognosis (5-Year Survival Rate)
Stage 1A			93%
Stage IA1	Microscopic cervical cancer measuring <3 mm depth of invasion and <7 mm horizontal spread	LEEP or cervical conization, or abdominal or vaginal hysterectomy, or modified radical hysterectomy If not a surgical candidate: consider primary radiation therapy with radiation-sensitizing chemotherapy	
Stage IA2	Microscopic cervical cancer with a depth of 3 to 5 mm and <7 mm horizontal spread	Modified radical hysterectomy If not a surgical candidate: consider primary radiation therapy with radiation-sensitizing chemotherapy	
Stage IB			80%
Stage IB1	Microscopic cervical cancer with dimensions >stage 1A2 or any gross lesion <4 cm in width	Radical hysterectomy If not a surgical candidate: consider primary radiation therapy with radiation-sensitizing chemotherapy	
Stage IB2	Gross lesion >4 cm in width	Radical hysterectomy If not a surgical candidate: consider primary radiation therapy with radiation-sensitizing chemotherapy	
Stage IIA	Cervical cancer extending to the upper two-thirds of the vagina	Radical hysterectomy If not a surgical candidate: consider primary radiation therapy with radiation-sensitizing chemotherapy	63%
Stage IIB	Cervical cancer extending into the parametrium but not to the pelvic sidewall	Primary radiation therapy with radiation-sensitizing chemotherapy	58%
Stage IIIA	Cervical cancer extending to the lower one-third of the vagina	Primary radiation therapy with radiation-sensitizing chemotherapy	35%
Stage IIIB	Cervical cancer extending to the pelvic sidewall and/or causing hydronephrosis	Primary radiation therapy with radiation-sensitizing chemotherapy	32%
Stage IVA	Cervical cancer extending into the mucosa of the bladder or the rectum	Primary radiation therapy with radiation-sensitizing chemotherapy	16%
Stage IVB	Cervical cancer with metastatic spread to distant organs	Chemotherapy	15%

LEEP = loop electrosurgical excision procedure.

Used with the permission of the American Joint Committee on Cancer (AJCC), Chicago, Illinois. The original source for this material is the AJCC Cancer Staging Manual, Seventh Edition (2010) published by Springer New York, Inc.

The following tests should be obtained in all patients with cervical cancer: chest radiography, abdominal and pelvic CT, and pelvic examination under anesthesia with cystoscopy and proctoscopy (Table 3). Proper staging of cervical cancer (FIGO [International Federation of Gynecology and Obstetrics] system) helps with prognosis and tailoring of treatment and provides a small survival advantage (Table 4).

Therapy

Stage 1A1 cancers (microscopic, confined to cervix, depth of invasion <3 mm, horizontal spread <7 mm) have a small chance of recurrence and lymph node metastasis. Women with this diagnosis who wish to retain fertility may be treated with a loop electrosurgical excision procedure (LEEP) or cervical conization instead of hysterectomy. Women who do not wish to retain fertility may undergo vaginal, abdominal, or modified radical hysterectomy to decrease the chance of recurrence. Once cervical cancer has extended to stage 1A2 (microscopic, confined to cervix, depth of invasion 3 to 5 mm, horizontal spread <7 mm) or beyond, LEEP, cervical conization, or abdominal or vaginal hysterectomy alone cannot cure the patient; these patients require modified radical hysterectomy. If a tumor is stage 1B or 2A (microscopic cancer with dimensions >stage 1A2, any gross cervical lesion, or cancer extending to the upper two-thirds of the vagina), a radical hysterectomy is required to ensure that the tumor is removed en bloc with an adequate margin including regional lymph nodes.

Patients with early cervical cancer who are not surgical candidates or who do not wish to have surgery may undergo chemoradiation therapy. Once a tumor has grown into the parametrium or lower vagina (stages 2B to 4A), adequate margins cannot be obtained by surgery, and chemoradiation therapy is the treatment of choice.

Radiation-sensitizing chemotherapy increases the response to radiation by facilitating additional tumor cell death. However, systemic chemotherapy after chemoradiation treatment is usually not effective because radiation fibrosis prevents adequate drug delivery.

Total pelvic exenteration consists of resection of the uterus, vagina, bladder, and rectosigmoid colon and is reserved for patients with recurrent or persistent cancer after radiation therapy, provided the patients are good surgical candidates with no evidence of metastatic disease.

Once cervical cancer has spread from the pelvis, pelvic surgery and radiation therapy are no longer options, and chemotherapy is needed to treat distant disease. Cisplatin is the most active chemotherapeutic agent with which to treat cervical cancer.

Of cancers occurring during pregnancy, cervical cancer is one of the most common. Treatment is based on stage, but the timing of treatment is influenced by the duration of the pregnancy.

Follow-Up

Routine examination may allow for early detection of cancer recurrence. Schedule regular follow-up visits every 3 months for the first year, every 4 months for the second year, and every 6 months until 5 years. At follow-up visits, include history, physical examination, and Pap smear of the vaginal cuff. Patients with advanced disease may require additional imaging studies.

Bibliography

Massad LS, Einstein MH, Huh WK, et al. 2012 ASCCP Consensus Guidelines Conference. 2012 updated consensus guidelines for the management of abnormal cervical cancer screening tests and cancer precursors. Obstet Gynecol. 2013;121:829-46. [PMID: 23635684]

Chapter 85

Prostate Cancer

Eric H. Green, MD

Prostate cancer is the most common cancer in men and is second only to lung cancer as a cause of cancer-related deaths. Tumor growth can be slow or moderate in pace but occasionally is quite rapid. Prostate cancer is strongly associated with age, its incidence rising from near zero in patients younger than 40 years to 1 in 8 men in their 70s. Prostate cancer also is more common in black men and in men with a family history of the disease. Although the lifetime risk of developing prostate cancer is 1 in 6, the risk of death from prostate cancer is 1 in 30. Given the older age at which many patients are diagnosed and the slowly progressive nature of low-grade tumors, many patients with prostate cancer die of other illnesses.

Prevention

Because prostate cancer is common, slow-growing, and usually dependent on testosterone for growth, it is a potentially good target for chemoprophylaxis. Prophylactic use of 5α-reductase inhibitors (finasteride, dutasteride), agents that inhibit conversion of testosterone to the more active dihydrotestosterone, reduce the incidence of prostate cancer. However, these agents do not change 10-year survival, in part because the cancers that do develop are higher grade. Furthermore, these agents have significant side effects, including decreased libido, erectile dysfunction, and gynecomastia. The use of the drugs for chemoprophylaxis is controversial, and these drugs have not been approved by the FDA for this indication.

Screening

Although prostate cancer would seem to be an ideal disease for screening given a presumed prolonged treatable preclinical disease state, screening is controversial because of the imperfect sensitivity and specificity of the screening test (serum prostate-specific antigen [PSA] measurement), morbidity of treatment, and the unclear natural history of untreated disease. There is conflicting evidence from both large randomized controlled trials and epidemiologic studies regarding the efficacy of prostate cancer screening. This data suggest that screening may take more than 10 years to show a difference in mortality, if at all.

There are conflicting recommendations regarding screening. The U.S. Preventive Services Task Force recommends against screening. The American College of Physicians also recommends against screening individuals at average risk unless a patient expresses a desire to pursue testing following a discussion of the potential risks and benefits of screening. If pursued, screening should not be performed before age 50 years, after age 69 years, or if the life expectancy is <10 to 15 years.

Diagnosis

Most prostate cancer is discovered after screening. Early prostate cancer usually is asymptomatic, although some patients may present with hematospermia, painful ejaculation, or symptoms of bladder outlet obstruction, such as urinary hesitancy and frequency. Patients with metastatic disease may present with bone pain, back pain, weight loss, or fatigue. Although it has low sensitivity, digital rectal examination is without risk and is inexpensive, and should be performed in patients with clinical suspicion for prostate cancer. Any abnormality on digital rectal examination requires biopsy, regardless of serum PSA level. More advanced disease may present as signs of metastatic spread, including pelvic lymphadenopathy, or signs of spinal cord compression. In addition, men with metastatic disease from an unknown primary source should be evaluated for the possibility of prostate cancer. Table 1 describes important conditions in the differential diagnosis of prostate cancer.

Serum PSA measurement is the best available noninvasive test to diagnose prostate cancer. The normal range of PSA values varies with age and race, with older men and white men having higher PSA values. PSA testing is avoided immediately after prostatitis, which can raise PSA levels for up to 8 weeks. Although digital rectal examination also can elevate PSA values, this change rarely is clinically significant. Serum PSA values >4.0 ng/mL (4 μg/L) generally are considered abnormal. Serum PSA measurement has imperfect sensitivity: Only 25% of men with PSA values between 4.0 ng/mL (4 μg/L) and 10.0 ng/mL (10 μg/L) have prostate cancer, although most of these cancers are early stage and, therefore, potentially curable. Because the PSA value rises very slowly over time, an increase of >0.75 ng/mL (0.75 μg/L) in 1 year, regardless of the initial value, is considered abnormal.

Refer any patient with an abnormal PSA value for transrectal ultrasound-guided prostate biopsy. This outpatient procedure usually consists of six to twelve random needle biopsies. Random biopsies have a high false-negative rate and often need to be repeated if negative. Tumors detected on these biopsies are further classified according to their histology, using the Gleason score. In the Gleason histologic scoring system, tumors are graded from 1 to 5 based on the degree of glandular differentiation and structural architecture, with 1 being the most and 5 being the least differentiated. The composite Gleason score is derived by adding together the grades of the two most prevalent differentiation patterns on the biopsy (termed the primary and secondary grade). The resulting Gleason score (up to 10) reflects the biological characteristics of the tumor and correlates well with tumor behavior, with lower scores (2, 3, or 4) being considered well-differentiated or low-grade cancers, and higher scores (8.9. or 20) representing poorly differentiated or high-grade cancers.

This score, along with initial PSA level, tumor size, and the presence of nodal or distal metastases (TNM), is used to assign a clinical stage to the cancer. In general, patients with stage I cancer have low-risk disease limited to the prostate. Stage II disease is also limited to the prostate but has features that increase the risk for spread. Stage III disease is locally advanced outside of the prostatic capsule, and stage IV disease has positive regional lymph node involvement or distant metastases. Patients with Gleason score >7, serum PSA level >10

Table 1. Differential Diagnosis of Prostate Cancer

Disorder	Notes
Abnormal Findings on Prostate Examination	
Benign prostatic hyperplasia (BPH)	BPH is characterized by symptoms of urinary outflow obstruction (nocturia, urinary urgency and hesitancy) and may result in elevated serum PSA levels. Prostate cancer and BPH can coexist, but there is no causal association between the diseases. BPH results in a generalized and symmetric enlargement of the prostate, whereas prostate cancer may manifest as a palpable lump, induration, or asymmetric enlargement. Biopsy distinguishes between the two entities.
Acute prostatitis	Acute prostatitis can result in elevated serum PSA levels but also fever, chills, dysuria, pelvic or perineal pain, and possible obstructive symptoms (dribbling, hesitancy, anuria). DRE reveals edematous and tender prostate. Urine shows pyuria and positive urine culture.
Metastatic Skeletal Disease	
Osteomyelitis	Osteomyelitis results in increased uptake on bone scans and can be confused with metastatic disease. Osteomyelitis is not associated with an elevated serum PSA level, and metastatic prostate cancer in the context of a normal PSA level is very unusual. Metastatic prostate cancer tends to be multifocal, whereas osteomyelitis tends to be unifocal. Prostate cancer and osteomyelitis have very different appearances on CT and MRI scans.
Paget disease	Paget disease of the bone can look like sclerotic bone metastases. Paget disease is not associated with an elevated serum PSA level.
Other cancers	Many other cancers spread to the pelvic and retroperitoneal lymph nodes and the bones, including bladder cancer, colorectal cancer, testicular cancer, renal cell carcinoma, carcinoma of the ureter and renal pelvis, and penile cancer. Prostate cancer can generally be distinguished from other malignancies on the basis of histopathologic examination of biopsy specimens and presence of elevated serum PSA level.

CT = computed tomography; DRE = digital rectal examination; MRI = magnetic resonance imaging; PSA = prostate-specific antigen.

Table 2. Laboratory and Other Studies for Prostate Cancer

Test	Notes
Prostate-specific antigen (PSA)	A serum PSA level >4.0 ng/mL (4 µg/L) has a PPV for prostate cancer of 30%-37%; most men with PSA level of 4-10 ng/mL (4-10 µg/L) do not have prostate cancer. BPH, prostatitis, urinary tract infection, prostatic stones, manipulation of the prostate or lower urinary tract, and ejaculation can result in elevated serum PSA level. A serum PSA level >50 ng/mL (50 µg/L) has a PPV for prostate cancer of 98%-99%. In men with prostate cancer, the initial PSA level carries important prognostic information, with lower levels predicting localized and less aggressive tumors.
Bone alkaline phosphatase	Not used in diagnosing prostate cancer. Elevated levels in patients with prostate cancer suggest bone metastases.
Transrectal ultrasonography	Transrectal ultrasonography has a PPV of 7%-34% and an NPV of 85%. The test is used to guide prostate biopsies; it is not used to screen for or stage prostate cancer.
Prostate biopsy	Biopsy is the only way to definitively diagnose prostate cancer.
CBC	Metastatic cancer to the bone marrow is common and can result in anemia.
Abdominal and pelvic CT	CT is helpful in evaluating for pelvic or retroperitoneal lymph node metastases or bone metastases. Bone or lymph node metastases are rare in men with serum PSA levels <20 ng/mL (20 µg/L), especially if the Gleason score is <8.
Bone scan	Bone is the most common site of metastatic prostate cancer, and bone scans are useful for detection. Osteoarthritis, other degenerative changes, trauma or fracture, osteomyelitis, and Paget disease also can result in increased uptake on bone scans. Ambiguous bone scan results often lead to additional bone imaging studies (radiography, CT, MRI). A biopsy is performed for ambiguous radiologic imaging results.

BPH = benign prostatic hyperplasia; CBC = complete blood count; CT = computed tomography; MRI = magnetic resonance imaging; NPV = negative predictive value; PPV = positive predictive value.

ng/mL (10 µg/L), large tumors, or the presence of bone pain may require a bone scan and/or abdominal and pelvic computed tomography (CT) to evaluate for metastatic disease. Table 2 reviews laboratory and other studies for prostate cancer.

Therapy

Three major treatment strategies exist for localized prostate cancer: surgery, radiation therapy, and active surveillance. To date, the optimal treatment is not defined, and the choice should be governed by clinical stage and anticipated life expectancy, with more aggressive therapy offered to patients with either long life expectancy or high-risk tumors (Table 3).

Radical prostatectomy usually is reserved for patients with at least a 10-year life expectancy. Radical prostatectomy usually is curative in patients whose disease is confined to the prostate (stages T1 and T2) and who lack high-risk features, such as a high serum PSA level or Gleason score. Historically, radical prostatectomy was associated with a high rate of erectile dysfunction, but surgical advances, including robotic assistance, have reduced this risk.

Table 3. Initial Treatment of Prostate Cancer

Risk	Life Expectancy	Treatment Options
Low	<10 years	Observation
	>10 but <20 years	Observation or Radiation therapy or Radical prostatectomy
	≥20 years	Radiation therapy or Radical prostatectomy
Intermediate	<10 years	Observation or Radiation therapy or Radical prostatectomy
	≥10 years	Radiation therapy or Radical prostatectomy
High	<5 years	Observation with hormonal therapy
	≥5 years	Radiation therapy with hormonal therapy or Radiation therapy alone or Radical prostatectomy

Data from NCCN Clinical Practice Guidelines in Oncology: Prostate Cancer. National Comprehensive Cancer Network.

Radiation therapy can be delivered using external beam radiation or by implanting radioactive "seeds" around the prostate (brachytherapy). Radiation therapy has a similar cure rate as surgery for localized disease. In comparison to surgery, radiation carries lower risks of urinary incontinence and erectile dysfunction at the expense of risks for radiation proctititis and cystitis. Radiation therapy also does not confer the added risks of general anesthesia and surgery, although therapy may take months to complete. Palliative external beam radiation is effective for painful bone metastases.

Given that the natural history of most prostate cancer is characterized by slow growth and a long lag between detection and metastatic spread, watchful waiting or active surveillance is often used for patients with low-risk local disease and some patients with higher-risk disease but a low life expectancy. Active surveillance is distinguished from watchful waiting in that the former requires intermittent measurement of PSA, prostate imaging, and rectal biopsy while the latter relies on patient-reported symptoms of metastatic disease. Active surveillance maintains a focus on curative intent, with options for surgery or radiation therapy if there is cancer progression, albeit with risk and expense of frequent testing. Watchful waiting institutes palliative therapy if/when metastatic disease is present. Both approaches recognize that many patients with prostate cancer die from other diseases, and thus reduce the impact of side effects of prostate cancer therapy.

Prostate cancers are dependent on testosterone for growth; thus, androgen deprivation therapy (ADT) often is used with other therapies to treat higher-risk localized cancers and is the primary therapy in patients with local treatment failures (defined by a rise in serum PSA level after surgery or radiation therapy). Although some patients undergo surgical orchiectomy, most rely on a luteinizing hormone-releasing hormone analog (eg, leuprolide, goserelin) for "chemical castration." When these agents are initiated, there often is a transient testosterone surge, and patients with painful bone metastases or epidural metastases need additional short-term androgen blockade (usually using bicalutamide or flutamide). ADT has significant side effects, including hot flashes, loss of libido, gynecomastia, impotence, and osteoporosis. Patients with progressive disease despite ADT often are treated with added androgen blockade, diethylstilbestrol, or ketoconazole. Patients whose disease continues to progress may require chemotherapy. In patients with prostate cancer metastatic to bone, annual infusions of the bisphosphonate zoledronate can decrease the risk for skeletal complications.

Follow-Up

Patients are monitored at least annually for recurrent disease after definitive local therapy. Evaluation includes serum PSA levels and an interval history and examination to evaluate for signs or symptoms of relapse. Patients undergoing active surveillance are reevaluated more frequently, with PSA measurements sometimes done at 3-month intervals. Digital rectal examinations or imaging studies (eg, bone scan, CT) are not routinely performed unless specifically indicated by signs or symptoms of recurrence. Patients undergoing ADT should receive supplemental calcium and vitamin D and undergo surveillance for osteoporosis with bone density scans. Bisphosphonates can be used in patients who develop osteoporosis. The primary complication of prostate cancer is metastatic spread, most commonly to regional lymph nodes and bone. Bone metastases can cause severe pain as well as spinal cord compression. Back pain in a patient with prostate cancer may represent the first sign of spinal cord compression from epidural metastases and requires urgent evaluation with a spine magnetic resonance imaging.

Bibliography

Hoffman RM. Clinical practice. Screening for prostate cancer. N Engl J Med. 2011;365:2013-9. [PMID: 22029754]

Mohan R, Schellhammer PF. Treatment options for localized prostate cancer. Am Fam Physician. 2011;84:413-20. [PMID: 21842788]

Qaseem A, Barry MJ, Denberg TD, Owens DK, Shekelle P. Screening for prostate cancer: a guidance statement from the Clinical Guidelines Committee of the American College of Physicians. Ann Intern Med. 2013;158:761-9. [PMID: 23567643]

Chapter 86

Skin Cancer

Monica Ann Shaw, MD

More than 2 million cases of skin cancer are diagnosed annually in the United States. Basal cell carcinoma and squamous cell carcinoma make up the majority of these cases. Melanoma, the most serious form of skin cancer, is increasing at a rate of 3% to 6% annually. The lifetime risk of melanoma in the United States for persons with light skin is estimated to be 1 in 50. Melanoma is the most common cancer among people aged 25 to 29 years.

Prevention

Ultraviolet (UV) radiation from sunlight and man-made sources (tanning beds) is the most important environmental factor predisposing to skin cancer. Children and adults should limit sun exposure and prevent sunburn by wearing protective clothing, avoiding exposure during peak hours, wearing sunscreen with SPF 15 or higher, and avoiding sunburning. Nonmelanoma skin cancers, particularly squamous cell carcinoma, are associated with cumulative sun exposure and occur more frequently in areas maximally exposed to the sun, such as the face, forearms, and back of the hands. Melanomas are associated with intense intermittent sun exposure and tend to occur in areas exposed to the sun sporadically, such as the lower legs in women and the back in men. Studies suggest that sunscreen has a direct protective effect against acute UV-related skin damage and nonmelanoma skin cancer, but studies have failed to find a clear association between the use of sunscreen and the incidence of melanoma. Studies have shown that exposure to UV radiation from indoor tanning devices is associated with a significant increase in risk of melanoma. Risk increases with number of sunbed sessions and exposure before age 35 years. The increased risk is reported to be as high as 75%. Studies also demonstrate an increased risk of squamous cell and basal cell carcinomas with tanning bed use.

Screening

The U.S. Preventive Services Task Force (USPSTF) recommends counseling children, adolescents, and young adults aged 10 to 24 years who have fair skin about minimizing their exposure to ultraviolet radiation to reduce risk for skin cancer. The USPSTF concludes that the current evidence is insufficient to assess the balance of benefits and harms of counseling adults older than 24 years about minimizing risks to prevent skin cancer.

Risk factors for melanoma include UV radiation exposure, large number (≥50) of nevi, dysplastic nevi, history of blistering sunburns, poor tanning ability (fair skin, freckles, blonde or red hair, blue eyes), and personal or family history of melanoma. Approximately 10% of melanomas are familial. Patients should be encouraged to examine their own skin for changes in moles (nevi) and have regular clinical examinations. Individuals at high risk for melanoma benefit most from clinical examinations and should have a skin exam every 6 to 12 months by an experienced clinician. In the United States, the incidence of melanoma is at least 10 to 20 times greater in white populations than in black populations. Among white individuals, rates are >50% higher in men than in women. The trunk is the most common primary tumor site for persons who are white or American Indian, whereas the lower extremity is the most common primary site for persons who are Hispanic, black, Asian, or Pacific Islander.

Risk factors for basal cell carcinoma include chronic exposure to UV radiation, fair skin, immunosuppression, exposure to ionizing radiation, chronic arsenic exposure, previous basal cell carcinoma, and basal cell nevus syndrome. For white individuals in the United States, the lifetime risk of developing basal cell carcinoma is 30%.

The most important risk factors for squamous cell carcinoma include cumulative UV radiation exposure and increasing age. Other risk factors include skin that does not tan, exposure to ionizing radiation, immunosuppression, chronic inflamed skin resulting from scars or burns, arsenic exposure, family history, smoking, and inherited skin disorders (eg, xeroderma pigmentosum, epidermolysis bullosa, albinism). Actinic keratoses are precursors of squamous cell carcinoma; the lesions present as 1- to 3-mm, tan to red, raised, scaling "rough spots" on sun-exposed areas (eg, head, neck, dorsum of forearms and hands, legs). Patients with risk factors, sun-damaged skin, and actinic keratoses should be screened for basal cell and squamous cell cancers at least once yearly.

Diagnosis

Diagnose melanoma by carefully evaluating any skin lesion that is new, suspicious, or changing in size, shape, or color (Table 1, Plate 58). Review the history of the lesion and the patient's risk factors and perform a complete skin examination including scalp and soles. An increase in lesion size and a change in lesion color are the most common signs of melanoma.

There are four major subtypes of melanoma (Table 2, Plate 59, Plate 60, Plate 61, Plate 62). Melanoma can also be nonspecific in appearance or present as an amelanotic lesion that mimics basal cell

Table 1. ABCDE of Melanoma

Asymmetry: a lesion that is not regularly round or oval.

Border irregularity: a lesion with notching, scalloping, or poorly defined margins.

Color variegation: a lesion with shades of brown, tan, red, white, or blue-black, or combinations thereof.

Diameter: a lesion >6 mm in diameter; although a high level of suspicion exists for a lesion >6 mm in diameter, early melanomas may be diagnosed at a smaller size.

Evolution: a lesion that changes in size, shape, symptoms (itching, tenderness), surface (bleeding), or shade of color.

Table 2. Major Subtypes of Melanoma

Subtype	Notes
Superficial spreading melanoma (Plate 59); ~70% of cases	Presents as a variably pigmented plaque with an irregular border and expanding diameter ranging from a few millimeters to several centimeters. Can occur at any age and anywhere on the body, although most commonly seen on the back in men and on the legs in women. Most superficial spreading melanomas appear to arise de novo.
Nodular melanoma (Plate 60); ~15% of cases	Presents as a dark blue or black "berry-like" lesion that expands vertically (penetrating skin). Most commonly arises from normal skin. Most often found in people aged ≥60 y. Often fails to fulfill the ABCDE criteria (Table 1).
Lentigo maligna melanoma (Plate 61); ~10% of cases	Presents initially as a freckle-like, tan-brown patch. When confined to the epidermis, the lesion is called "lentigo maligna type." May be present for many years before it expands and becomes more variegated in color. Once it invades the dermis, it becomes melanoma. Most often arises in sun-damaged areas (face, upper trunk) in older people.
Acral lentiginous melanoma (Plate 62); ~5% of cases	Presents as an unevenly darkly pigmented patch. Can appear as a bruise or nail streak. Most often arises on the palmar, plantar, or subungual surfaces. Most common type among Asian and dark-skinned people, with a predilection for the soles of the feet.

cancer clinically. Biopsy is the gold standard to diagnose melanoma and to distinguish it from other pigmented lesions (Table 3). The biopsy must include sufficient tissue to establish the diagnosis and to allow accurate assessment of tumor thickness/extension, tumor ulceration, mitotic rate, and adequacy of surgical margins. An excisional biopsy is preferred for all subtypes of melanoma with the exception of lentigo maligna, for which a paper-thin shave biopsy offers the highest yield. For undiagnosed pigmented lesions, removal/destruction by laser, cryosurgery, or electrodessication is inappropriate, because the ability to diagnose and stage a potentially lethal skin cancer is lost. After diagnosis of melanoma, staging involves a complete history and physical examination, emphasizing complete skin and regional lymph node examination to determine the extent of disease and presence or absence of metastases.

Staging is based on tumor thickness (T), regional lymph node involvement (N), and presence or absence of metastatic disease (M) for the basis of the TNM staging system. Other features, mitotic rate and presence or absence of ulceration, also influence prognosis and staging. Proper staging is important for guiding further management.

Biopsy of the sentinel lymph node (the primary lymph node draining the site of the melanoma) should be considered in patients with primary melanomas >1 mm thick. Although currently there is no evidence of a survivor benefit from sentinel lymph node mapping, sentinel node involvement is a powerful prognostic indicator and stratifies patients for trials of adjuvant therapy.

To assess for potential basal cell or squamous cell carcinomas, ask about skin lesions that fail to heal or that bleed, itch, are painful, or are slowly enlarging. A basal cell cancer classically presents as a pink, pearly or translucent, dome-shaped papule with telangiectasias, but it can also appear as a flat or scar-like lesion (Plate 63).

The most readily recognized clue to the diagnosis of basal cell carcinoma is a changing skin lesion, including ulceration or erosion, that spontaneously bleeds (Table 4).

Cutaneous squamous cell carcinoma presents as a firm, isolated, keratotic macule or patch, commonly on the scalp, neck, pinna, or lip (Plate 64). Keratoacanthoma is a rapidly growing skin cancer thought to be a form of squamous cell cancer. These early lesions present as solitary round nodules that grow rapidly. As the lesions mature, a central keratotic plug becomes visible, and the lesion becomes crater-like. Keratoacanthoma rarely progresses to invasive or metastatic cancer and often involutes within months (Plate 65).

Therapy

Surgery is the mainstay of therapy for patients with melanoma. Because melanoma cells extend beyond the visible borders of the tumor, removal of tumor plus wide excision of surrounding skin including underlying subcutaneous tissue down to the fascia is necessary to ensure that all melanoma is removed. The extent of surgery depends on the thickness of the primary melanoma. For melanoma in situ, excision with a 0.5-cm margin is recommended; for melanomas <1 mm thick, 1-cm margin; for melanomas 1 to 4 mm thick, 2-cm margin; and for melanomas thicker than 4 cm, at least a 2-cm margin. It is important to confirm that surgical margins have negative histologic results after the wide-excision procedure. Several studies show that 80% of patients with melanoma are cured with wide-margin surgical resection. Melanomas that are <1 mm thick are associated with a 90% long-term overall survival. Patients with melanomas between 1 and 4 mm thick have a long-term survival that

Table 3. Differential Diagnosis of Melanoma

Lesion	Notes
Common nevi (moles)	Tend to be small macules or papules; most are <5 mm. Border is regular, smooth, and well defined. Coloration is homogeneous; usually no more than 2 shades of brown. Can be found at any site.
Dysplastic nevi	Occur predominantly on the trunk. Usually >5 mm, with a flat component. Border is characteristically fuzzy and ill-defined. Shape can be round, oval, or asymmetric. Color usually is brown but can be mottled with dark brown, pink, and tan. Some individuals have only 1-5 lesions, whereas others have >100 lesions. Some clinical features of dysplastic nevi are similar to those of melanoma. Significant asymmetry and heterogeneity of color should prompt a biopsy to rule out melanoma. Recognized as a precursor to melanoma.
Melanoma	Often >10 mm. Border is more irregular. Significant heterogeneity of color ranging from tan-brown, dark brown, or black to pink, red, gray, blue, or white. Can be found at any site.

Table 4. Differential Diagnosis of Basal Cell Carcinoma

Lesion	Notes
Nodular BCC (~60% of BCC)	A skin-toned to pink, pearly translucent, firm papule with telangiectasias. May have rolled borders and a central depression with ulceration. Often found on the head or neck.
Superficial BCC (~30% of BCC)	A well-defined, erythematous, scaling plaque or occasional papules with a thin pearly border. Larger lesions often have hemorrhagic crusts and occur predominately on the trunk. A complete skin examination to find other similar plaques may help distinguish the solitary lesion of superficial BCC from psoriasis.
Morpheaform BCC (~5-10% of BCC)	A skin-colored, waxy, scar-like area that slowly enlarges. Usually develops on the head or neck of an older person. The name is based on its resemblance to morphea (scleroderma).
Common nevi (moles)	Nevi can become elevated and may be irritated by clothing, causing inflammation and bleeding. Nevi can undergo progressive loss of color over time. By age 60 y, nevi may be flesh-colored, dome-shaped, soft papules. Even inflamed nevi do not have overlying telangiectasias.
Sebaceous hyperplasia	Benign, 2- to 4-mm papules with a characteristic yellow color and central umbilication. Occur in clusters on the face without telangiectasia or bleeding.
Actinic keratosis	Early lesions (1-3 mm) often are felt, not seen, and have a rough sandpaper texture. Color ranges from skin-colored to pink to red to brown. Occur on sun-damaged skin. Early superficial BCC may look like early actinic keratosis. With time, superficial BCC develops a rolled border and actinic keratoses get a thicker keratotic scale.
Bowen disease (SCC in situ)	A solitary, sharply demarcated, pink to fiery red scaly plaque that resembles superficial BCC, psoriasis, or eczema. May have a keratotic surface. Most commonly occurs on sun-exposed areas.
Psoriasis	A chronic skin condition in young adults. In the early phase, the sharply demarcated erythematous plaques with slight scale may resemble superficial BCC. As the psoriatic area matures, a silvery-white scale develops that has characteristic pinpoint bleeding when removed. Plaques are symmetrically distributed and usually occur on scalp, extensor elbows, knees and back.
Nummular eczema	Round, well-demarcated, eczematous patches (1-10 cm) found on the extremities and trunk. Pruritus may be intense, which results in scratching. The scratch marks may be the best way to discriminate nummular eczema from superficial BCC. Onset is usually spontaneous with no inciting event.
Tinea	Scaly patch with central clearing and an active border of erythema, papules, and vesicles. Tinea is more erythematous than BCC and usually has a larger area of central clearing.

BCC = basal cell carcinoma.

ranges from 50% to 85%. Patients with metastatic melanoma have an estimated 5-year overall survival of 6% to 10%.

Node dissection is performed in patients with clinically palpable regional lymph nodes. Patients with node-positive disease have potentially curable melanoma and should be treated aggressively with surgery. Tumor thickness and number of positive nodes are the most important prognostic factors in patients with melanoma. Many patients with melanoma are at low risk for recurrence (primary tumor <4 mm thick or negative nodes) and do not require postsurgical treatment. For patients with primary melanomas >4 mm thick or positive nodes, adjuvant treatment with high-dose interferon therapy is beneficial, but toxicity is considerable. Interferon is the only adjuvant therapy approved by the FDA for the treatment of high-risk patients to prevent disease recurrence and possibly improve overall survival rates. Experimental clinical trials with vaccines may be available for patients with melanomas thicker than 1.5 mm. Consider surgical resection in patients with metastatic melanoma (ie, melanoma that has spread beyond regional lymph nodes) with solitary metastases in skin, lung, gastrointestinal tract, and brain after a careful diagnostic work-up for metastases at other sites. Melanoma can metastasize to virtually any organ of the body.

Chemotherapy, immunotherapy, and clinical trials of new drugs may also be considered for patients with metastatic disease.

Nonmelanoma skin cancers can be categorized as low-risk or high-risk based on lesion and host characteristics. Lesion characteristics include anatomic location, size, cell type, border (well- or ill-defined), and whether the tumor is primary or recurrent; host characteristics include history of previous radiation therapy to the tumor site and immunosuppression. Basal cell carcinoma rarely metasta-

sizes, but its growth and treatment can be a source of morbidity. With squamous cell cancer, the thickness of the lesion is an important prognostic indicator. Squamous cell cancer metastases are seen in 1% to 5% of cases and are associated with a poor prognosis.

Surgery is the mainstay of therapy for nonmelanoma skin cancers. The goal is complete excision with cosmetic preservation. For actinic keratoses and low-risk basal cell or squamous cell skin cancers, treatment options include cryosurgery, electrodessication and curettage, topical therapy with fluorouracil or imiquimod, and surgical excision. For high-risk skin cancers, traditional surgical excision or Mohs surgery is preferred. Mohs micrographic surgery is the treatment of choice for many high-risk situations (eg, cancers with risk factors for recurrence, tumors located in the central face or periorificial area, tumor recurrence following previous treatment, incompletely excised tumor, high-risk pathology, large tumor, tumor with poorly defined borders). Mohs surgery involves excision of the tumor and immediate preparation of tissue to allow histologic examination at the time of the procedure to ensure that all margins are clear of tumor, thus reducing the chance of recurrence. Radiation therapy can be an option in older patients who cannot tolerate surgery or with large tumors.

Follow-Up

Patients with a history of melanoma have a 4% to 6% increased risk of developing a second primary melanoma as well as an increased risk of developing a basal cell or squamous cell cancer. Patient education regarding monthly skin self-examination, clinical characteristics of melanoma, safe-sun strategies, and careful lifelong surveillance by a dermatologist is an integral part of the management of patients with melanoma. Most recurrences of melanoma occur within 10 years.

Patients with squamous cell or basal cell carcinoma are at an increased lifelong risk of developing another skin cancer. Approximately 50% of patients with one nonmelanoma skin cancer develop another in the next 5 years. Patients need to do skin self-examination, reduce sun exposure, and have follow-up annual clinical examinations.

Bibliography

Boniol M, Autier P, Boyle P, Gandini S. Cutaneous melanoma attributable to sunbed use: systematic review and meta-analysis. BMJ. 2012;345: e4757. [PMID: 22833605]

Madan V, Lear JT, Szeimies RM. Non-melanoma skin cancer. Lancet. 2010;375:673-85. [PMID: 20171403]

Moyer VA. Behavioral counseling to prevent skin cancer: U. S. Preventive Services Task Force recommendation statement. Ann Intern Med. 2012;157:59-65.

Thompson JF, Scolyer RA, Kefford RF. Cutaneous melanoma. Lancet. 2005;365:687-701. [PMID: 15721476]

Chapter 87

Lymphoid Malignancies

Merry Jennifer Markham, MD

Lymphoid malignancies account for about 5% of all cancer cases in the United States, and they account for approximately 3% of cancer deaths. Lymphoid malignancies, also known as lymphomas, are broadly classified as either Hodgkin lymphoma (HL) or non-Hodgkin lymphoma (NHL). Lymphomas represent a diverse group of cancers that are derived from cells that would, under normal conditions, develop into mature T-lymphocytes or B-lymphocytes. While Hodgkin lymphomas are B-cell derived, the non-Hodgkin lymphomas may arise from any stage of the B-cell, T-cell, or NK-cell lineage (Table 1). The clinical behavior of the lymphomas varies by subtype of lymphoma, by histologic grade, and from patient to patient. General characteristics of HL, NHL, and chronic lymphocytic leukemia are reviewed below.

Hodgkin Lymphoma

Hodgkin lymphoma has a bimodal age distribution with the initial peak at age 15 to 34 years and a second peak at age 55 to 70 years. Although the etiology is unclear, there is a suggested association between HL and the Epstein-Barr virus (EBV). People with a history of infectious mononucleosis are more likely to develop HL, and EBV genomic material is often found within HL nodes. Later onset of HL may be a consequence of latent virus reactivation with age-related decline in immunity. Hodgkin lymphoma is also seen with increased frequency in patients with HIV or AIDS; however, HL is not an AIDS-defining illness.

Hodgkin lymphoma is divided by the World Health Organization (WHO) into two major categories: classical HL and nodular lymphocyte predominant HL (NLPHL) (Table 2). Classical HL is the most common form of HL and is characterized by the Reed-Sternberg cell, the malignant cell of origin. There are four histologic subtypes of classical HL, each named for the appearance of the background infiltrate of inflammatory cells: nodular sclerosis (the most common), mixed cellularity, lymphocyte rich, and lymphocyte depleted. The prognosis of classical HL varies by stage of disease and individual patient risk factors. However, cure rates for early-stage disease are in excess of 90%. For patients with advanced-stage HL, the cure rates are between 60% to 70%. NLPHL typically affects men between ages 30 and 50, behaves in an indolent fashion, and is distinguished from classical HL by distinct immunohistochemical markers.

Diagnosis and Staging

Painless peripheral lymphadenopathy is the primary clinical presentation in patients with HL. The most common site of enlarged nodes is in the cervical and/or supraclavicular region. Axillary lymphadenopathy is found in 10% to 20% of patients, and inguinal lymphadenopathy is rare. The second most common presentation is a mediastinal mass identified on chest x-ray. Up to half of patients, especially those with advanced-stage disease, may experience "B symptoms": body temperatures >100.4°F (38.0°C), weight loss of >10% of body weight, or drenching night sweats. An unusual but relatively common symptom is generalized pruritus.

The diagnosis of HL can only be made with a tissue biopsy. Within an HL tumor mass or involved lymph node, the characteristic malignant Reed-Sternberg cells (Plate 66) comprise only a small minority of the cellular makeup. The majority of the tumor mass is composed of a background of inflammatory cells and/or fibrosis of the nodal tissue; therefore, a fine needle aspirate (FNA) is inadequate for diagnosis due to potential sampling error. The preferred method of biopsy is an excisional biopsy. The biopsy material should be examined for histologic morphology and with immunohistochemical staining for the characteristic immunophenotype of HL.

HL is staged using the Ann Arbor staging system (Table 3). Staging for HL is clinical rather than pathologic. Computed tomography (CT) and positron emission tomography (PET) imaging are important in the initial staging of HL. Bone marrow biopsy and aspirate for the evaluation of bone marrow involvement is also commonly used.

Because the treatment of HL involves the use of chemotherapy with an anthracycline and bleomycin, a baseline cardiac function study (such as echocardiography) and pulmonary function testing are recommended. Patients of childbearing potential should receive fertility preservation counseling.

Treatment

The goal in the treatment of HL is to choose a treatment that is aggressive enough to achieve a cure while minimizing unnecessary toxicity from treatment, including both immediate toxicity and late treatment effects (such as secondary cancers and cardiac toxicity). The treatment of HL has evolved to include a decrease in radiation fields and total dose, the use of combination chemotherapy administered in conjunction with radiation (to allow for less total chemotherapy), and the use of multiagent chemotherapy alone (to avoid radiation exposure in patients with a high risk of late effects due to radiation). Prognostic risk factors are used to guide treatment choice and length of therapy. Adverse risk factors vary for disease stage; however, some common risk factors include elevated erythrocyte sedimentation rate (ESR), male gender, age 40 years or greater, stage IV disease, and bulky mediastinal lymphadenopathy.

The most commonly used chemotherapy regimen is the four-drug ABVD regimen, which contains doxorubicin, bleomycin, vinblastine, and dacarbazine. Patients with early-stage disease usually receive an abbreviated course (2 to 3 months) of chemotherapy followed by a course of radiation therapy to the involved region, especially if bulky mediastinal disease is present. Those with advanced-stage disease or with additional risk factors often receive a longer course (6 months) of chemotherapy alone. Radiation may be offered to select patients with advanced-stage disease as consolidation.

Table 1. World Health Organization 2008 Classification of Hodgkin and Non-Hodgkin Lymphomas

Mature B Cell	Mature T cell and NK Cell
Chronic lymphocytic leukemia	T-cell prolymphocytic leukemia
B-cell prolymphocytic leukemia	T-cell large granular lymphocytic leukemia
Splenic marginal zone lymphoma	Chronic lymphoproliferative disorder of NK cells[a]
Hairy cell leukemia	Aggressive NK-cell leukemia
Splenic lymphoma/leukemia, unclassifiable	Systemic EBV+ T-cell lymphoproliferative disease of childhood
Lymphoplasmacytic lymphoma (Waldenström)	Hydroa vacciniforme-like lymphoma
Heavy chain diseases (α, γ, μ)	Adult T-cell leukemia/lymphoma
Plasma cell myeloma	Extranodal NK/T-cell lymphoma, nasal type
Solitary plasmacytoma of bone	Enteropathy-associated T-cell lymphoma
Extraosseous plasmacytoma	Hepatosplenic T-cell lymphoma
Extranodal marginal zone B-cell lymphoma of mucosa-associated lymphoid tissue (MALT lymphoma)	Subcutaneous panniculitis-like T-cell lymphoma
Nodal marginal zone B-cell lymphoma	Mycosis fungoides
Follicular lymphoma	Sézary syndrome
Primary cutaneous follicle center lymphoma	Primary cutaneous CD30+ T-cell lymphoproliferative disorder
Mantle cell lymphoma	Primary cutaneous aggressive epidermotropic CD8+ cytotoxic T-cell lymphoma[a]
DLBCL, not otherwise specified	Primary cutaneous $\gamma\delta$ T-cell lymphoma
DLBCL (EBV+) of the elderly	Primary cutaneous small/medium CD4+ T-cell lymphoma
Lymphomatoid granulomatosis	Peripheral T-cell lymphoma, not otherwise specified
Primary mediastinal (thymic) large B-cell lymphoma	Angioimmunoblastic T-cell lymphoma
Intravascular large B-cell lymphoma	Anaplastic large cell lymphoma (ALK+)
Primary cutaneous DLBCL, leg type	Anaplastic large cell lymphoma (ALK−)[a]
ALK+ large B-cell lymphoma	
Plasmablastic lymphoma	
Primary effusion lymphoma	
Large B-cell lymphoma arising in HHV-8-associated multicentric Castleman disease	
Burkitt lymphoma	
B-cell lymphoma, unclassifiable with features intermediate between DLBCL and Burkitt lymphoma	
B-cell lymphoma, unclassifiable, with features intermediate between large B-cell lymphoma and classic Hodgkin lymphoma	
Hodgkin lymphoma	
Nodular lymphocyte-predominant Hodgkin lymphoma	
Classic Hodgkin lymphoma	
Nodular sclerosis	
Lymphocyte rich	
Mixed cellularity	
Lymphocyte depleted	

[a]Provisional subtypes and entities.

DLBCL = diffuse large B-cell lymphoma; EBV = Epstein-Barr virus; HHV-8 = human herpesvirus 8.

Reprinted with permission from Swerdlow SH, Campo E, Harris NL, et al. (Eds). World Health Organization Classification of Tumours of Haematopoietic and Lymphoid Tissues, IARC Press, Lyon 2008.

Follow-Up

During treatment, patients are monitored for side effects and toxicity of the treatment regimen. After completion of treatment, follow-up is performed regularly to assess for relapse. For the first 3 years, patients are seen every 3 to 6 months for clinical evaluation, every 6 months in the fourth and fifth year, and annually thereafter. Imaging studies (chest x-ray, CT scans) are often performed regularly during the first 2 to 3 years, although the optimum use and frequency of CT imaging is unclear.

Because HL survivors are at risk for developing secondary complications (late effects) from treatment, long-term follow-up is important. Examples of late effects include secondary cancers (acute leukemia, non-Hodgkin lymphoma, lung cancer, breast cancer) and organ dysfunction (cardiac disease, radiation-induced thyroid dysfunction). Women who received mediastinal radiation for HL between the ages of 10 and 35 are at the greatest risk for breast cancer.

Long-term follow-up for HL survivors should include annual visits with a complete blood count (CBC) to screen for bone marrow dysfunction, thyroid function testing in patients who received radiation to the neck, and annual influenza vaccination in patients who received bleomycin or chest irradiation. Women who received mediastinal radiation prior to age 35 should undergo breast cancer screening with annual mammography and breast magnetic resonance imaging beginning 8 to 10 years post-treatment or at age 40, whichever comes first.

Table 2. Features of Classical Hodgkin Lymphoma (HL) and Nodular Lymphocyte Predominant Hodgkin Lymphoma (NLPHL)

Characteristic	HL	NLPHL
Average age at diagnosis	First peak: 15-34 y Second peak: 55-70 y	30- 40 y
Tumor cell	Reed-Sternberg cell	Lymphocytic and histiocytic ("L & H") or "popcorn" cell
Background surrounding the tumor cells	Lymphocytes, histiocytes, eosinophils, plasma cells	Lymphocytes, histiocytes
Fibrosis	Common	Rare
Epstein-Barr virus in tumor cells	Positive in 40% to 100% of cases	Negative
Immunohistochemical (IHC) staining		
CD 15	Positive	Negative
CD 30	Positive	Negative
CD 20	Positive or negative	Positive
CD 45	Negative	Positive

Non-Hodgkin Lymphomas

Non-Hodgkin lymphoma represents a diverse set of malignancies. The various lymphomas that comprise NHL are classified by ontogeny (B cell, T cell, NK cell) and stage of differentiation. Approximately 80% to 85% of NHLs in adults are of B-cell origin, with the remainder derived from T cells or, more rarely, natural killer (NK) cells.

Generally, the incidence of NHL increases with age. Autoimmune disease and immunodeficiency states (patients with HIV/AIDS or chronic immune suppression after organ transplantation) have a known association with NHL. Infectious agents (EBV, *Helicobacter pylori*, *Chlamydia psitacci*, hepatitis C) have also been associated with some types of NHL. However, in most patients the etiology is not known.

Diagnosis and Staging

The patient presentation in NHL varies depending on the aggressiveness of the lymphoma type. The various histologic subtypes of NHL are classified by their level of aggressiveness into three categories: indolent (low-grade), aggressive (intermediate-grade), or highly aggressive (high-grade). Indolent lymphomas often present with slowly growing lymphadenopathy, enlarged spleen or liver, or with abnormalities in the CBC such as anemia, thrombocytopenia, or leukopenia. Aggressive lymphomas present more acutely, with rapidly enlarging lymph nodes or a rapidly growing mass. Patients with aggressive lymphomas are more likely to have B symptoms (fevers, weight loss, and night sweats), elevated lactate dehydrogenase (LDH), and elevated uric acid.

A tissue biopsy is crucial in the diagnosis of NHL and should be performed urgently if an aggressive lymphoma is suspected. Enlarged peripheral lymph nodes are preferred for biopsy due to the ease of obtaining a specimen; however, enlarged intrathoracic, intraabdominal, or retroperitoneal lymph nodes or masses may be biopsied through image-guided techniques or laparoscopy. Bone marrow biopsy and aspirate may also be helpful in diagnosis, especially in patients with advanced disease or cytopenias. While FNA may yield a diagnosis of NHL, it is usually inadequate to determine the type of lymphoma. As with HL, the lymph node architecture and morphology are important in subclassifying NHL; thus, an excisional biopsy is preferred.

The diagnosis of NHL is based on evaluation of morphology, immunophenotype, and genetic studies. Histologic examination may reveal a nodular or follicular pattern (as seen in follicular NHL), a diffuse pattern (as seen in diffuse large B-cell lymphoma), and the grade of the lymphoma (higher grade correlates to more aggressiveness). Immunophenotype is determined by flow cytometry on a fresh (not fixed) lymph node sample or through immunohistochemical staining. For example, all B-cell–derived NHLs are CD19 and CD20 positive, and T-cell lymphomas express CD3. Characteristic cytogenetic markers may be found in patients with some forms of NHL, such as a translocation in the c-MYC oncogene (most commonly the t(8;14) translocation) in highly aggressive Burkitt lymphoma.

Table 3. Ann Arbor Staging System for Lymphomas

Stage I	Involvement of a single lymph node region (I) or single extranodal organ or site (IE).
Stage II	Involvement of two or more lymph node regions or lymphatic structures on the same side of the diaphragm (II) or with involvement of limited, contiguous extranodal tissue (IIE).
Stage III	Involvement of lymph node regions or lymphoid structures on both sides of the diaphragm (III). May involve the spleen (IIIS) or limited, contiguous extranodal tissue (IIIE).
Stage IV	Diffuse or disseminated involvement of one or more extranodal organs or tissues, with or without lymphatic involvement.
Stage Modifiers	A = Absence of B symptoms[a] B = Presence of B symptoms[a] E = Extranodal site or organ X = Bulky disease (more than 10 cm)

[a]B symptoms include associated constitutional symptoms including body temperatures >100.4°F (38.0°C), weight loss of >10% of body weight, or drenching night sweats.

Once the diagnosis of a specific type of NHL has been made, staging is performed using the Ann Arbor staging system (Table 3). All patients should have laboratory studies performed to include a CBC, comprehensive metabolic panel (including blood urea nitrogen, creatinine, albumin, electrolytes, and liver function tests), serum calcium, serum uric acid, and LDH. Because of the association of NHL with HIV and with viral hepatitis, patients with NHL should be tested for HIV and hepatitis B and C. Imaging studies with CT scans of the chest, abdomen, and pelvis should be performed, and in some cases, integrated PET/CT scans are useful. Bone marrow biopsy and aspirate is used to identify NHL within the bone marrow, and lumbar puncture with cytologic evaluation of the cerebrospinal fluid is important in highly aggressive NHL (eg, Burkitt lymphoma) and in some types of aggressive NHL (eg, testicular diffuse large B-cell lymphoma).

Prior to receiving treatment that may affect the cardiovascular or pulmonary systems, patients should undergo baseline functional testing such as with echocardiography or pulmonary function studies. All patients of childbearing potential should receive fertility preservation counseling prior to the initiation of chemotherapy or radiation therapy.

Treatment

Treatment and prognosis generally depend on whether a patient has indolent, aggressive, or highly aggressive NHL. Indolent subtypes of NHL may often be observed without treatment, and they nearly always respond to chemoimmunotherapy when treatment is indicated. For B-cell lymphoid malignancies, chemoimmunotherapy most often consists of cytotoxic chemotherapy used concurrently with the anti-CD20 monoclonal antibody, rituximab. Despite their responsiveness to treatment, indolent lymphomas are generally considered incurable, but patient survival may be long. Aggressive and highly aggressive NHLs are curable with chemoimmunotherapy, with cure rates varying depending on the underlying biology of the disease as well as prognostic factors, such as the patient's age and overall health status, tumor stage, and serum LDH level. T-cell lymphomas typically have a worse prognosis than B-cell-derived lymphomas, and T-cell lymphomas are more likely to relapse. In addition, because only B-cell lymphomas express CD20, rituximab is not used in the treatment of T-cell lymphomas. Table 4 reviews clinical characteristics, general treatment overview, and prognosis for some of the more common B-cell NHL subtypes.

Follow-Up

Patients should be seen frequently during initial therapy to assess for side effects. After treatment, the frequency of follow-up often depends on the indolence or aggressiveness of the lymphoma. Patients are usually seen every 3 to 6 months for clinical evaluation for the first 3 to 5 years after treatment and annually thereafter. Imaging of the chest, abdomen, and pelvis with CT scans is often performed regularly during the first 2 years; however, the optimum use and frequency of CT imaging is unclear.

Table 4. Characteristics of the Most Common Subtypes of B-Cell Non-Hodgkin Lymphoma

Type of NHL	Clinical Characteristics	Treatment	Prognosis
Follicular lymphoma	Indolent. Second most common type of NHL. Average age at diagnosis is 60, and 80% have advanced disease at presentation.	Observation in asymptomatic patients. When symptoms occur, options include chemotherapy, immunotherapy, or chemoimmunotherapy. Some patients may receive radiation therapy.	Incurable. Average survival may exceed 8 to 10 years.
Marginal zone lymphoma	Indolent. Derives from the marginal zone of lymph nodes or spleen. Average age is 60. Includes splenic marginal zone lymphoma, mucosa-associated lymphoid tissue (MALT) lymphoma, and nodal marginal zone lymphoma.	Same as for follicular lymphoma.	Same as for follicular lymphoma.
Small lymphocytic lymphoma	Indolent. Characterized by an excess of small, mature-appearing lymphocytes in the blood, bone marrow, or lymph nodes. When a peripheral blood lymphocytosis is seen, it is also called chronic lymphocytic leukemia (CLL).	Same as for follicular lymphoma.	Same as for follicular lymphoma.
Mantle cell lymphoma	May be indolent or aggressive. Associated with the cyclin D1 protein overexpression. Most patients have widely advanced disease at presentation.	Chemoimmunotherapy.	Incurable. Average survival is 3 to 5 years.
Diffuse large B-cell lymphoma	Aggressive. Most common type of NHL. May occur outside the lymph nodes in up to 40% of patients, including within the CNS, the gastrointestinal tract, genitourinary tract, or bones.	Chemoimmunotherapy for all patients. The R-CHOP regimen is the primary treatment used. Radiation therapy is used after chemoimmunotherapy for patients with localized or bulky disease.	Curable. 5-year overall survival rate ranges from 30% to 50% for all stages. Early-stage, low-risk patients may have overall survival rates up to 90%.
Burkitt lymphoma	On histology, the "starry sky" pattern is classic and all cases have a translocation of the c-myc oncogene. Often associated with tumor lysis at the time of, or even before, treatment.	Chemoimmunotherapy. Prophylactic intrathecal chemotherapy is given to reduce the likelihood of relapse within the CNS.	Curable. 5-year overall survival rate in adults is 50% to 70%.

CNS = central nervous system; R-CHOP = rituximab, cyclophosphamide, doxorubicin, vincristine, and prednisone.

Similar to patients with HL, survivors of NHL are at risk for late treatment effects. Second malignancies occur with higher frequency in NHL survivors than the average population, including acute leukemia, various solid tumors, and second lymphoid malignancies. Survivors who received anthracycline-based chemotherapy and/or radiation are at higher risk for late cardiovascular complications. The risk for infertility and gonadal dysfunction depends on both the type and amount of chemotherapy received and whether radiation therapy to the pelvis was received. Patients who received radiation therapy to the neck often develop hypothyroidism.

Chronic Lymphocytic Leukemia

Chronic lymphocytic leukemia (CLL) is the most common leukemia encountered in adults. CLL is classified as a chronic lymphoproliferative disorder (a lymphoid malignancy). It is considered to be the same disease process as small lymphocytic lymphoma (SLL), one of the indolent B-cell NHL subtypes; the two lymphoid malignancies are often referred to singularly as CLL/SLL.

The median age of diagnosis is approximately 70 years, and the disease affects males more than females. CLL is characterized by clonal proliferation of mature B-lymphocytes within the blood, bone marrow, lymph nodes, and spleen. Though the disease is incurable, survival may be long.

Diagnosis and Staging

Patients may be asymptomatic in 25% of cases, usually diagnosed after the incidental finding of lymphocytosis on a CBC, with or without lymphadenopathy. Some patients have symptoms related to bulky lymph node enlargement or may have symptoms related to splenomegaly (early satiety, abdominal fullness). Patients also may have systemic symptoms, including fever, malaise, night sweats, and weight loss.

Patients with CLL may develop various immune defects that predispose to infectious complications, the most common being infection with encapsulated organisms (eg, *Streptococcus pneumoniae*), due to inadequate B-cell function or hypogammaglobulinemia. Patients may also have cell-mediated immune defects that predispose to recurrent herpes simplex virus infections. Patients with CLL also are at increased risk for autoimmune disease, most commonly autoimmune thrombocytopenia; autoimmune hemolytic anemia is less common. Management of the underlying autoimmune disorder often requires concomitant treatment of CLL.

Physical exam may reveal signs of anemia (pallor, tachycardia), lymphadenopathy, and hepatomegaly or splenomegaly. Key laboratory findings include a peripheral leukocytosis due to increased numbers of mature lymphocytes and "smudge" cells (lymphocytes that appear flattened or distorted) during the process of preparing the peripheral smear (Plate 67).

The diagnosis of CLL is made when there is (1) an absolute increase in mature lymphocytes (>5000/μL [5×10^9/L]) in the absence of an acute viral illness or other trigger of reactive lymphocytosis, and (2) the demonstration on flow cytometry of clonality of the circulating B-lymphocytes. Immunophenotyping by flow cytometry will show a monoclonal proliferation of mature B-lymphocyte phenotype with expression of CD19 and CD20, along with expression of a T-lymphocyte antigen (CD5). Immunophenotyping distinguishes CLL from reactive lymphocytosis and identifies less common variants of CLL, including those arising from clonal T-lymphocytes. Bone marrow biopsy is not required for the diagnosis of CLL; flow cytometry on a peripheral blood sample is adequate.

Staging of CLL is based on the physical examination and CT imaging to assess lymphadenopathy and hepatosplenomegaly. Two staging schemes are used:

- The Rai staging system ranges from asymptomatic patients with lymphocytosis (stage 0); these patients account for about 25% of the population and have a mean survival of >10 years. Patients with stage I CLL (lymphocytosis plus lymphadenopathy) or stage II CLL (lymphocytosis, lymphadenopathy, and hepatosplenomegaly) account for 50% of the population and survive 6 to 9 years. Patients with stage III (anemia) or stage IV (thrombocytopenia) CLL account for the remaining 25% and have a more lethal course, with a mean survival of <2 years.
- The Binet system is based on the number of lymph node sites involved. For example, bilateral cervical lymph node enlargement is counted as one site, bilateral cervical and axillary lymphadenopathy is counted as two sites, and an enlarged liver and enlarged spleen each count as one lymph node site. Stage A has fewer than three sites involved, and survival is comparable to that in age-matched controls without CLL. Stage B has three or more sites involved, with survival of 7 years. Stage C, defined as the additional presence of either anemia or thrombocytopenia, is associated with survival of approximately 2 years.

Treatment

Patients with asymptomatic, early-stage disease require only observation. Later-stage disease, often associated with symptoms, requires active treatment. Specialized testing, such as cytogenetic studies to assess for genetic mutations and determination of the mutational status of the immunoglobulin variable (V) gene, is becoming increasingly important in establishing risk for disease progression.

Complications associated with CLL may require treatment. About 10% of patients will develop autoimmune thrombocytopenia or hemolytic anemia, and they may respond to chemotherapy for CLL, prednisone, or anti-CD20 treatment. Recurrent bacterial infections and hypogammaglobulinemia are frequently treated with intravenous immunoglobulin (IVIG) infusion therapy; however, the use of IVIG to restore immune globulin levels to normal remains controversial. Pneumococcal and yearly influenza vaccinations are recommended for all those with CLL due to the risk for infectious complications. About 10% of patients experience a transformation of their chronic leukemia to a very aggressive and difficult-to-treat diffuse large B-cell lymphoma; this is known as *Richter transformation*.

The goal of therapy for CLL is not cure, but rather to slow the rate of progression, induce a period of remission, and control symptoms or complications. There is no consensus on initial therapy for CLL. Choices include the purine analogs (eg, fludarabine and pentostatin), alkylating agents (such as chlorambucil, bendamustine, and cyclophosphamide), and monoclonal antibodies against CD20 (including rituximab and ofatumumab). Treatment choice is made only after carefully considering patient factors such as functional status, comorbid conditions, age, and patient preferences. Young patients with high-risk genetic features (eg, 17p deletion or 11q deletion) may be considered for hematopoietic stem cell transplantation.

Follow-Up

For those patients who have not yet required treatment for their CLL or those achieving remission through chemoimmunotherapy, routine monitoring of the CBC every 3 to 6 months is recommended to assess the lymphocyte count or the development of anemia or thrombocytopenia. Physical examination should include a full lymph node examination and careful assessment of liver and spleen size. History should focus on new disease-related symptoms, such as fatigue, fevers, night sweats, or weight loss. Routine imaging is generally not recommended but is instead symptom-directed or used to evaluate response to treatment.

Bibliography

Ansell SM. Hodgkin lymphoma: 2012 update on diagnosis, risk stratification, and management. Am J Hematol. 2012;87:1096-103. [PMID: 23151980]

Gribben JG, O'Brien S. Update on therapy of chronic lymphocytic leukemia. J Clin Oncol. 2011;29:544-50. [PMID: 21220603]

Hallek M. Chronic lymphocytic leukemia: 2013 update on diagnosis, risk stratification, and treatment. Am J Hematol. 2013;88:803-16. [PMID: 23720127]

Chapter 88

Oncologic Urgencies and Emergencies

Maria Dungo, MD
Liana Nikolaenko, MD

Patients with cancer are at risk for certain conditions that require timely recognition to reduce morbidity and mortality. These oncologic urgencies and emergencies may be either structural or metabolic in nature.

Structural Urgencies and Emergencies

Structural abnormalities are caused by primary or metastatic tumor growth leading to significant impairment of normal function of vital organs due to obstruction or compression.

Superior Vena Cava Syndrome

Superior vena cava (SVC) syndrome is caused by obstruction of venous blood return from the head, neck, upper torso, or extremities. Lung cancer accounts for up to 72% of all cases, with lymphoma and germ cell tumors being less frequent causes.

SVC syndrome onset is typically insidious. Most patients develop progressive dyspnea, facial swelling, and cough. Swelling of the upper extremities, chest pain, and dysphagia occur less often. Physical examination findings include distention of the neck and chest veins, facial edema, cyanosis, facial plethora, and upper extremity edema. Pemberton sign (Plate 68) may be present, which is the onset of symptoms (facial flushing, distended neck and head superficial veins, inspiratory stridor, and elevation of the jugular venous pressure) upon raising both arms, which exacerbates the obstruction. Approximately 60% of patients present with SVC syndrome as the initial manifestation of a previously undiagnosed malignancy.

Diagnostic techniques include plain chest radiography and contrast chest CT scan. Findings on a chest radiography may include mediastinal widening but may be normal in as many as 16% of patients. Mediastinoscopy is generally used to obtain tissue biopsy samples for histologic diagnosis, although percutaneous computed tomography (CT)-guided needle biopsy appears to be a safer alternative to mediastinoscopy with reasonable diagnostic sensitivity.

Specific therapy is based on treatment of the causative tumor and can usually be delayed in stable patients while a tissue diagnosis is obtained to guide therapy. Primary therapy using chemotherapy, radiation therapy, or combined chemotherapy and radiation therapy is usually associated with rapid and complete resolution of symptoms and physical findings of SVC syndrome. Glucocorticoids are helpful in decreasing the inflammation if the tumor is steroid sensitive, such as in hematologic malignancies. When only partial patency is reestablished, anticoagulation may be appropriate in some patients. Endovascular stenting, angioplasty, surgery, and thrombolytic therapy are generally limited to use if emergent treatment is indicated or primary therapy is ineffective.

Central Nervous System Metastases

Central nervous system (CNS) metastases occur in 10% to 30% of solid tumors and may cause neurologic deficits or increased intracranial pressure. The most commonly involved cancers are lung, breast, kidney, colon, and melanoma. Patients may present with an acute change in mental status, headaches, nausea and vomiting, focal neurologic deficits, ataxia, seizures, or symptoms associated with increased intracranial pressure (ICP). Increased ICP results from a mass effect by the occupying lesion. Primary brain tumors and central nervous system lymphomas are also frequently associated with increased ICP. Immediate CT or magnetic resonance imaging (MRI) of the head is required to confirm the diagnosis and prevent potential complications, including brain stem herniation and permanent neurologic dysfunction. Lumbar puncture is contraindicated in patients with an increased ICP as the procedure may precipitate catastrophic brain stem herniation.

Glucocorticoids, such as dexamethasone, are the initial treatment of choice and can be administered orally or intravenously. When primary CNS lymphoma is suspected, a tissue biopsy should be performed to establish the diagnosis before initiation of glucocorticoid therapy in a stable patient as treatment may lead to a nondiagnostic biopsy because of the high susceptibility of most lymphomas to glucocorticoid treatment. When the effects of increased ICP are more severe, osmotic diuresis with mannitol may be used in addition to glucocorticoids. Anticonvulsants are indicated to treat seizures, which are a presenting symptom in 10% to 20% of patients with brain metastases. Obstructing hydrocephalus usually requires surgical drainage. In patients with an isolated brain metastasis, surgical resection followed by stereotactic or whole-brain radiation therapy may be appropriate. Patients with multiple brain metastases usually require whole-brain radiation therapy with or without chemotherapy.

Spinal Cord Compression

Spinal cord compression develops in 5% to 10% of patients with cancer and is one of the most debilitating complications of this disease. Patients with breast, lung, and prostate cancer are most likely to be affected. Rapid diagnosis before development of motor deficits allows treatment that can prevent most, if not all, of the potential adverse consequences. Growing metastatic lesions lead to vertebral collapse or venous congestion and edema of the spinal cord. Neurologic structures can be compressed by tumor growth within the vertebral body posteriorly, by anterior growth from the dorsal elements, or by invasion of the vertebral foramen, leading to neuronal cell damage, demyelination, and cord infarction. Multiple metastatic deposits may also occur along the spinal cord.

Pain is the most frequent initial symptom. A feeling of "heaviness" in the legs and difficulty climbing stairs or rising from a sitting position are also common. Leg weakness and bowel or bladder dysfunction usually develop later in the disease course. Physical examination findings are sometimes nonspecific but may include pain on palpation of the involved vertebral body, hyperreflexia, and decreased muscle strength.

MRI is used most often for rapid diagnosis. The entire spine should be imaged to avoid overlooking asymptomatic lesions. Immediate administration of high-dose glucocorticoids is indicated

Table 1. Paraneoplastic Syndromes

System Involved	Syndrome	Associated Malignancy	Mechanism	Clinical Manifestations
Endocrine	Cushing syndrome	SCLC	Ectopic secretions of ACTH	Hypertension, weakness, purple striae, moon facies, central obesity, hypokalemia, metabolic alkalosis
	SIADH	SCLC	Ectopic secretions of vasopressin	Hyponatremia, altered mental status, seizures
	Carcinoid syndrome	Carcinoid tumor	Large amount of serotonin release by the tumor	Flashing, diarrhea, wheezing, pellagra
	Hypercalcemia	Multiple myeloma, squamous cell carcinoma (lung), breast and kidney cancers	PTHrP production, bone turnover	Altered mental status (confusion, stupor, coma), nausea and vomiting, muscle weakness, cardiac arrhythmias
	Hypoglycemia	Insulinoma	Increased production of insulin	Palpitations, sweating, headache, confusion and seizures if severe
Neurologic	Lambert-Eaton myasthenic syndrome	SCLC	Autoantibodies against presynaptic voltage-gated calcium channels at the neuromuscular junction	Proximal muscle weakness improves with repetitive stimulation, transient cranial nerve palsies, upright presyncopal symptoms
	Myasthenia gravis	Thymoma	Autoantibodies against nicotinic acetylcholine receptor in the motor end plate for the neurotransmitter acetylcholine	Progressive muscle weakness
	Paraneoplastic cerebellar degeneration	Lung, ovarian, and breast cancers, Hodgkin lymphoma	Anti-Purkinje cell antibodies	Rapidly progressive disease, dysarthria, truncal, limb and gait ataxia, vertigo, nausea, vomiting, nystagmus and diplopia
	Paraneoplastic opsoclonus-myoclonus syndrome	Neuroblastoma, breast carcinoma or SCLC	Unknown	Irritability and malaise precede lethargy, nausea, vomiting, opsoclonus, myoclonus, cerebellar ataxia
Hematologic	Polycythemia	Renal cell carcinoma, brains tumors, hepatoma, pheochromocytoma	Erythropoietin overproduction	Hypertension, pruritis, joint pain, headaches, weakness
	Disseminated intravascular coagulation	APML	Cytokine release	Thrombosis in the setting of widespread bleeding
	Venous thromboembolism	Any malignancy	Hypercoaguable state	Pain and swelling of the involved extremity, signs and symptoms of PE
Mucocutaneous	Acanthosis nigricans	Gastrointestinal and genitourinary malignancies	Unknown, possibly immunologic	Thickened, hyperpigmented skin, velvety texture usually over neck and axilla
	Dermatomyositis	Chronic myelogenous leukemia or essential thrombocytosis, ovarian, lung, and pancreatic cancer	Anti-Jo1 antibody	Gottron nodules over knuckles, heliotrope eye rash, proximal muscle weakness, muscle pain
	Polymyositis	Non-Hodgkin lymphoma, lung and bladder cancers	Unknown, possibly immunologic, anti-signal recognition particle antibodies (anti-SRP antibodies), may have positive anti-Jo1 antibody	Proximal muscle weakness and muscle pain
	Hypertrophic pulmonary osteoarthropathy	Lung cancer	Unknown	Clubbing of the fingers, arthritis

ACTH = adrenocorticotropic hormone; APML = acute promyelocytic leukemia; PE = pulmonary embolism; PTHrP = parathyroid hormone-related protein; SCLC = small-cell lung cancer; SIADH = syndrome of inappropriate antidiuretic hormone secretion.

to minimize or prevent ongoing spinal cord injury and is continued at lower maintenance doses until definitive therapy is completed. Neurosurgical intervention is appropriate when rapid decompression is required. Radiation therapy is appropriate for most patients, and concurrent chemotherapy is often used for patients with chemosensitive malignancies such as lymphoma.

Malignant Pleural and Pericardial Effusions

A malignant pleural effusion may be the initial presentation in patients with previously undiagnosed cancer, although more commonly, as with malignant pericardial effusions, it reflects advanced malignancy that is incurable. Malignant pleural and pericardial effusions are most often caused by lung and breast cancer, lymphoma, and less frequently by cancer of unknown primary site.

Patients with a malignant pleural effusion usually have a history of increasing dyspnea on exertion. Some patients report cough and dull aching or stabbing chest pain. Diagnosis is confirmed by chest radiography or CT scan of the chest. After radiologic confirmation, a pleural fluid sample is obtained to confirm a malignant effusion, exclude an infectious cause, and assess for the presence of malignant cells through cytologic studies.

Thoracentesis is required for immediate palliation. Malignant pleural effusions recur in 70% of patients without additional treatment. Chest tube drainage and pleurodesis (obliteration of the pleural space) with antibiotics (tetracycline), cytotoxic agents (bleomycin), or talc are all effective in reducing recurrences. Indwelling pleural catheters provide additional control; pleurectomy or insertion of a pleuroperitoneal shunt is rarely required.

Patients with pericardial effusion are initially asymptomatic and have an enlarged cardiac silhouette on chest radiographs and low voltage on electrocardiography. Progression of the effusion causes early symptoms and signs of cardiac tamponade, including dyspnea, orthopnea, chest pain, and hypotension. Echocardiography is essential to establish the diagnosis before development of hemodynamic instability.

Urgent subxiphoid cardiocentesis with drainage alleviates cardiac chamber compression. Partial pericardiectomy or pericardial window placement may provide long-term relief. Radiation therapy or chemotherapy is appropriate for patients with radiosensitive or chemosensitive malignancies.

Metabolic Urgencies and Emergencies

Certain cancers may cause potentially life-threatening metabolic abnormalities, including tumor lysis syndrome and hypercalcemia, that require prompt recognition and treatment.

Tumor Lysis Syndrome

Tumor lysis syndrome occurs most often in patients with malignancies associated with rapid cell turnover, those associated with a high leukocyte count, high tumor burden, and cancers that are highly sensitive to chemotherapy. Specific cancers associated with tumor lysis include leukemia, lymphoma, and testicular tumors. Tumor lysis syndrome may be spontaneous or treatment induced. When lysis of tumor cells occurs, there is rapid cell breakdown; the consequent electrolyte abnormalities that may result include hyperkalemia, hyperphosphatemia, hyperuricemia, and hypocalcemia. Concomitant disseminated intravascular coagulation and acute kidney failure may also occur as part of the syndrome.

Prevention and treatment require aggressive hydration with normal saline to maintain a high level of urine output to avoid adverse effects of hyperuricemia and hypercalcemia. Monitoring for volume overload and replacement of electrolytes lost due to hydration are important parts of management. Treatment with allopurinol to decrease the formation of uric acid is given to prevent hyperuricemia. However, in patients with significantly elevated uric acid levels, a recombinant urate oxidase (rasburicase) can be given as it is able to actively break down existing uric acid. Additional treatment, including hemodialysis, may be indicated in patients with hyperphosphatemia, hyperkalemia, fluid overload, and uremia.

Hypercalcemia of Malignancy

Hypercalcemia occurs in 10% to 20% of patients with cancer and is associated with a poor prognosis. Increased serum calcium levels are due to direct bone destruction in 20% of patients and humoral effects caused by parathyroid hormone–related protein (PTHrP) released by tumor in 80% of patients. Patients with multiple myeloma, breast, kidney, and lung cancer are at greatest risk. The classical presentation includes kidney stones, bony pain (due to osteolytic or osteoblastic lesions), gastrointestinal complaints (nausea, vomiting, constipation), and mental status changes such as confusion ("Stones, bones, moans, and groans"). Weakness is a common symptom, and untreated, hypercalcemia may ultimately lead to cardiac arrhythmias.

Treatment requires immediate rehydration with normal saline followed by forced diuresis with a loop diuretic. Bisphosphonates, including zoledronic acid and pamidronate, may be administered parenterally. Glucocorticoids may also be used in patients with steroid-responsive tumors, such as multiple myeloma. Treatment of the underlying malignancy, if possible, is a more definitive therapy.

Paraneoplastic Complications

Various oncologic and hematologic malignancies are known to be associated with the development of rare but peculiar syndromes as a result of overstimulation of hormonal system or autoimmune activity by cancer cells. Paraneoplastic syndromes are estimated to affect 8% of patients with cancer. These cancer-specific syndromes are termed paraneoplastic syndromes, and their associated complications, mechanisms and tumor sites are outlined in Table 1.

Bibliography

Cairo MS, Coiffier B, Reiter A, et al. TLS Expert Panel. Recommendations for the evaluation of risk and prophylaxis of tumour lysis syndrome (TLS) in adults and children with malignant diseases: an expert TLS panel consensus. Br J Haematol. 2010 May;149:578-86. [PMID: 20331465]

Clines GA. Mechanisms and treatment of hypercalcemia of malignancy. Curr Opin Endocrinol Diabetes Obes. 2011;18:339-46. [PMID: 21897221]

Graus F, Dalmau J. Paraneoplastic neurological syndromes. Curr Opin Neurol. 2012;25:795-801. [PMID: 23041955]

Lewis MA, Hendrickson AW, Moynihan TJ. Oncologic emergencies: pathophysiology, presentation, diagnosis, and treatment. CA Cancer J Clin. 2011;61:287-314. [PMID: 21858793]

Section 10
Pulmonary Medicine

Associate Editor – T. Robert Vu, MD, FACP

High Value Care Recommendations

- A serum B-type natriuretic peptide (BNP) level <100 pg/mL helps exclude heart failure in the setting of acute dyspnea.

- The key to the workup of chronic dyspnea is a detailed history, approached in a systematic way to guide the search for the underlying cause in an efficient manner.

- Thoracentesis can be deferred in those patients with a small amount of pleural fluid and associated heart failure, pneumonia, or heart surgery (<1 cm thick on decubitus radiography or ultrasonography).

- Pleural fluid amylase should be measured only when pancreatic disease, esophageal rupture, or malignancy is considered.

- Omalizumab is a monoclonal antibody that binds to IgE and is useful for reducing exacerbations in patients with severe persistent asthma who have evidence of allergies. Because severe anaphylaxis has been reported with the drug use and it is extremely expensive, it is used only in selected patients who remain symptomatic despite other therapies.

- Smoking cessation is the most clinically effective and cost-effective way to prevent and slow the progression of chronic obstructive pulmonary disease (COPD) as well as improve disease-related survival.

- Screening for airway obstruction in asymptomatic patients is not recommended as there is little evidence that making the diagnosis in this setting is beneficial.

- A metered-dose inhaler (MDI), with proper instruction and good technique, is as effective as a nebulizer.

- The use of alternative home respiratory tests for the diagnosis of sleep apnea, even when interpreted by a certified sleep specialist, may provide inaccurate results.

- Inferior vena cava filters should not be used routinely for perioperative prophylaxis for pulmonary embolism.

- Screening for either deep vein thrombosis (DVT) or pulmonary embolism (PE) in asymptomatic patients at risk for venous thromboembolism (VTE) is not indicated as noninvasive diagnostic tests are insensitive and not associated with improved clinical outcomes.

- In clinically stable patients (eg, outpatients without hemodynamic compromise) with a low probability of PE, a normal D-dimer value effectively rules out PE and is correlated with an excellent outcome without further workup or treatment.

Chapter 89

Interpretation of Pulmonary Function Tests

Mysti D.W. Schott, MD

Pulmonary function tests are measurements of lung function used for diagnosing lung disease and managing patients with known pulmonary disorders. Although pulmonary function tests are effort-dependent, they are more precise than using symptoms or physical examination findings to gauge the severity of underlying lung disease. Specific indications for pulmonary function tests include (1) assessment of patients at risk for lung disease; (2) evaluation of respiratory symptoms, such as cough, wheezing, or dyspnea; (3) monitoring the benefits and risks of therapeutic interventions; and (4) assessment of pulmonary risk before surgery.

The four pulmonary function tests commonly used to measure lung function are spirometry, lung volumes, flow-volume loops, and diffusing capacity for carbon monoxide (D_{LCO}). Spirometry can be performed in the office, but measurement of lung volumes, flow-volume loops, and D_{LCO} requires a pulmonary function laboratory (Table 1).

Spirometry

Spirometry measures airflow rate and expired volume over time during forced breathing. Spirometry is useful in differentiating obstructive from restrictive lung disease (Table 2). Spirometry results are compared with reference values that are stratified by height, weight, sex, and ethnicity, with the measured value expressed as a "percent of predicted" (ie, percent of the predicted value for persons with similar characteristics). The most useful measures of expired volume over time are the forced vital capacity (FVC) and the forced expiratory volume in 1 second (FEV_1). FVC is the volume of air held by the lungs, measured from peak inspiration to maximum expiration. The FEV_1 is the volume of air exhaled in the first second of the FVC maneuver. FEV_1 and FVC values ≥80% of predicted are considered normal. The ratio of the absolute (not percent of predicted) values for FEV_1 and FVC is calculated. Patients with normal airflow will have an FEV_1/FVC ratio of approximately 75%. Spirometry also directly measures airflow as a function of time, with the most useful measure being the peak expiratory flow rate (PEFR), which is the maximum flow rate generated by the patient during the FVC maneuver.

If initial spirometry results are abnormal and suggest obstructive disease, the test is repeated following administration of an inhaled bronchodilator. An increase in FEV_1 of >12% and a minimum of 200 mL increase in FEV_1 after bronchodilator use establishes the presence of airflow reversibility and the diagnosis of asthma. A lack of response to bronchodilators is compatible with COPD but does not preclude a therapeutic trial of bronchodilator therapy.

Patients with a history suggestive of asthma (eg, dyspnea, cough) but with normal spirometry findings can be evaluated for reactive airway disease by bronchial challenge testing. Spirometry is repeated following inhalation of a medication that provokes bronchocon-

Table 2. Common Causes of Obstructive and Restrictive Lung Disease

Obstructive Lung Disease	Restrictive Lung Disease
Asthma	Chest wall deformities
Bronchiectasis	Interstitial lung disease
Chronic bronchitis	Neuromuscular disease
Emphysema	Obesity, pregnancy, ascites
Upper airway obstruction	Pain
	Pleural effusion

Table 1. Pulmonary Function Tests

Test	Notes
Spirometry	FEV_1 and FVC are the main measures. FEV_1/FVC ratio distinguishes obstructive from restrictive airway disease. A reduced ratio suggests obstructive disease (eg, asthma, COPD); a normal ratio suggests restrictive disease (eg, IPF) if lung volumes are reduced.
Lung volumes	Reduced lung volumes suggest restrictive airway disease if FEV_1/FVC ratio is normal. Increased lung volumes suggest obstructive airway disease if FEV_1/FVC ratio is decreased. Mixed restrictive and obstructive disease can occur and is diagnosed with spirometry and lung volumes.
Diffusing capacity for carbon monoxide (D_{LCO})	Decreased D_{LCO} and restrictive pattern on spirometry suggests intrinsic lung disease (eg, IPF), whereas normal D_{LCO} accompanied by restrictive pattern on spirometry suggests a nonpulmonary cause of restriction (eg, severe kyphoscoliosis, morbid obesity). Markedly decreased D_{LCO} and obstructive spirometry pattern suggests emphysema, whereas normal or mildly decreased D_{LCO} suggests other obstructive airway disease (eg, asthma).
Flow-volume loops	Flow-volume loops can identify upper airway obstruction. A characteristic limitation of flow (ie, a flattening of the loop) during inhalation suggests variable extrathoracic obstruction (eg, vocal cord dysfunction); limitation of flow during forced exhalation suggests variable intrathoracic obstruction (eg, asthma, COPD). Fixed upper airway obstruction (eg, tracheal tumor) causes flow limitation during both forced inhalation and forced exhalation.

COPD = chronic obstructive pulmonary disease; FEV_1 = forced expiratory volume in 1 second; FVC = forced vital capacity; IPF = idiopathic pulmonary fibrosis.

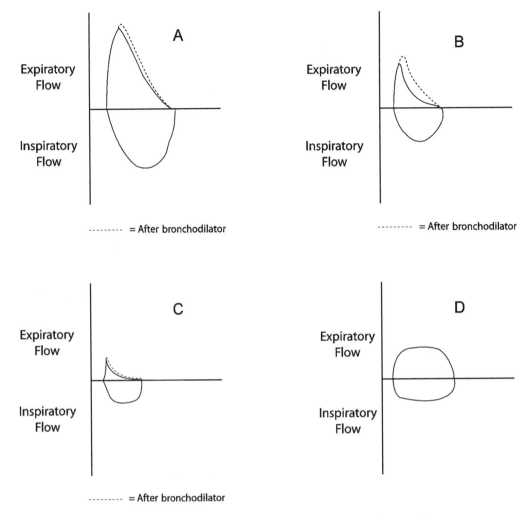

Figure 1. Flow-volume loop. Loop A: normal. Loop B: asthma. Loop C: COPD. Loop D: fixed extrathoracic obstruction.

striction, such as the cholinergic agent methacholine, histamine, or mannitol. A ≥20% decrease in at least two flow parameters establishes the diagnosis of asthma. Methacholine challenge is not performed in patients with known obstructive lung disease. Other contraindications include recent myocardial infarction or stroke, aortic or cerebral aneurysm, and uncontrolled hypertension.

Lung Volumes

Lung volumes are static measurements obtained through a dilution technique involving breathing either helium or nitrogen in a closed system or through body plethysmography with the patient in a sealed box. The most useful lung volume measurements are total lung capacity (TLC) and residual volume (RV). The TLC is the total amount of air in the lungs. It is equal to the vital capacity (VC) plus RV. The RV is the air remaining in the lungs after a full exhalation. Like spirometry measurements, lung volume measurements are compared with reference values and reported as percent of predicted values. TLC and RV values between 80% and 120% of predicted are considered normal. Lung volumes may also be useful in differentiating obstructive from restrictive lung disease and, thus, lend additional support to spirometry findings.

Flow-Volume Loops

Flow-volume loops plot forced inspiratory and expiratory flow in liters per second (y-axis) as a function of volume (x-axis). The normal expiratory portion of the flow-volume loop (above the x-axis) is characterized by a rapid rise to the peak flow rate, followed by a nearly linear fall in flow as the patient exhales. The inspiratory curve (below the x-axis) appears as a semicircle. If the flow-volume loop appears normal and FVC is normal, pulmonary function almost always is normal. Patients with obstructive disease have a "scooped out" expiratory curve (nonlinear) with a reduced slope. If the slope of the expiratory flow-volume loop appears normal or increased but FVC is reduced, restriction may be present. Flow-volume loops also are useful in assessing dynamic upper airway obstruction, which causes a plateau (flattening) in the inspiratory curve. Flow-volume loops demonstrating a decrease in both inspiratory and expiratory flow (flattened curves above and below the x-axis) are compatible with fixed obstruction outside the chest (eg, tracheal stenosis). An isolated decreased peak expiratory flow (decreased slope of the curve above the x-axis) is compatible with an obstruction within the chest (eg, COPD). Figure 1 shows examples of normal and abnormal flow-volume loops.

Table 3. Interpreting Pulmonary Function Tests

Measurement	Normal Range	Obstructive/ Parenchymal (eg, COPD)	Obstructive/ Nonparenchymal (eg, Asthma)	Restrictive/ Parenchymal (eg, Pulmonary Fibrosis)	Restrictive/ Nonparenchymal (eg, Obesity)
FEV$_1$	≥80% of predicted	Decreased	Decreased	Decreased	Decreased
FVC	≥80% of predicted	Normal or decreased	Normal or decreased	Decreased	Decreased
FEV$_1$/FVC ratio	75%	≤70%	≤70%	>75%	>75%
TLC	80%-120% of predicted	Normal or increased	Normal or increased	Decreased	Decreased
RV	80%-120% of predicted	Normal or increased	Normal or increased	Decreased	Decreased
D$_{LCO}$	≥80% of predicted	Decreased	Normal	Decreased	Normal

COPD = chronic obstructive pulmonary disease; D$_{LCO}$ = diffusing capacity for carbon monoxide; FEV$_1$ = forced expiratory volume in 1 second; FVC = forced vital capacity; RV = residual volume; TLC = total lung capacity.

Diffusing Capacity for Carbon Monoxide

The D$_{LCO}$ is a measurement of the rate of diffusion of carbon monoxide across the alveolar-capillary membrane. The patient inhales a minute amount of carbon monoxide, some of which diffuses across the membrane while the patient holds his or her breath for a specified amount of time, typically 10 seconds. The remaining carbon monoxide is exhaled and measured to determine the diffusing capacity (difference between inhaled and exhaled carbon monoxide). This value is compared with a standard and reported as a percent of predicted value. A D$_{LCO}$ value ≥80% of predicted is considered normal.

D$_{LCO}$ is used to determine the possible presence of parenchymal lung disease. D$_{LCO}$ is normal in conditions associated with abnormal spirometry measurements and lung volumes but normal lung parenchyma (eg, asthma, neuromuscular disease). D$_{LCO}$ is reduced in diseases associated with decreased alveolar-capillary membrane surface area (eg, emphysema) and thickened alveolar-capillary membranes (eg, interstitial lung disease, pulmonary fibrosis). Extrapulmonary conditions such as anemia (fewer red blood cells to transport carbon monoxide), pulmonary embolism (ventilation-perfusion mismatch), and pulmonary edema (interstitial edema is a barrier to gas flow) are associated with a decreased D$_{LCO}$.

Diagnostic Use of Pulmonary Function Tests

Obstructive lung disease results in a reduced ability to move air out of the lungs. This can be due to actual airway resistance or loss of elastic recoil. Obstructive lung disease causes a marked reduction in FEV$_1$ and a lesser reduction in FVC, resulting in a reduced FEV$_1$/FVC ratio. The inability to move air out of the lungs results in hyperinflation, causing an increase in TLC and RV.

Restrictive lung disease results in a reduced ability to maintain normal lung volumes due to reduced movement of air into the lungs. This can be due to parenchymal lung disease (infiltrative disease, fibrosis), abnormalities of the chest wall (scoliosis, extreme obesity), or muscle weakness (neuromuscular disease). Restrictive lung disease causes a proportional reduction in FEV$_1$ and FVC, a normal or elevated FEV$_1$/FVC ratio, and a reduction in TLC and RV.

D$_{LCO}$ is decreased in parenchymal lung disease; D$_{LCO}$ is normal in conditions affecting the chest wall and in neuromuscular disorders.

Patients with mixed obstructive and restrictive disease will have a decreased FEV$_1$/FVC ratio and reduced lung volumes. Table 3 summarizes the diagnostic use of pulmonary function tests.

Bibliography

Anderson SD. Indirect challenge tests: airway hyperresponsiveness in asthma: its measurement and clinical significance. Chest. 2010;138(2 Suppl):25S-30S. [PMID: 20668015]

Cockcroft DW. Direct challenge tests: airway hyperresponsiveness in asthma: its measurement and clinical significance. Chest. 2010;138(2 Suppl):18S-24S. [PMID: 20668014]

Pellegrino R, Viegi G, Brusasco V, et al. Interpretative strategies for lung function tests. Eur Respir J. 2005;26:948-68. [PMID: 16264058]

Chapter 90

Approach to Dyspnea

Nina Mingioni, MD

Dyspnea is the term used to describe a subjective experience of breathing discomfort. Because dyspnea is a symptom, clinicians have to rely on patients' self-description to assess for its presence and distinguish it from the physical exam signs of respiratory distress. Dyspnea usually is a combination of symptoms of awareness of work and effort of breathing, tightness, and unsatisfactory inspirations ("air hunger"). Patients frequently use phrases such as "my breath is short," "can't get enough air," and "trouble breathing" to describe their discomfort.

While the mechanisms of dyspnea are complex and its causes vast, it is clear that the sensation of dyspnea originates from the cere-bral cortex as it receives sensory input from the afferents of the respiratory muscles and lungs. Two main mechanisms leading to the sensation of dyspnea are impaired ventilatory mechanics and an increase in respiratory drive. However, in most cardiopulmonary conditions these mechanisms coexist.

Impaired ventilatory mechanics may be due to airflow obstruction (such as asthma and chronic obstructive pulmonary disease [COPD]), muscle weakness (myasthenia gravis, Guillain-Barré syndrome, myopathies), or decreased chest wall compliance (kyphoscoliosis, obesity). Impaired respiratory drive may be due to parenchymal or pulmonary vascular lung disease, congestive heart failure,

Table 1. Selected Differential Diagnosis of Acute Dyspnea

Disorder	History Clues	Physical Examination Clues
Pulmonary Causes		
Anaphylaxis	Allergen exposure	Urticaria, facial edema, wheezing
Asthma (may also present as chronic dyspnea)	Episodic cough, chest tightness, related to exercise, nocturnal symptoms	Wheezing
Pneumonia	Fever, cough, sputum	Fever, crackles, dullness to percussion
Pneumothorax	History of trauma, pleuritic chest pain	Absent breath sounds, deviated trachea (tension pneumothorax)
Pleural effusion/hemothorax	History of trauma or pneumonia	Dullness to percussion, absent breath sounds
Pulmonary embolism	Risk factors for thromboembolism, pleuritic chest pain, hemoptysis	Normal examination, possible unilateral leg swelling
Aspiration	Observed aspiration, symptoms start during or shortly after eating or vomiting. Patient with altered mental status or abnormal gag reflex at baseline	Unilateral, and sometimes bilateral, crackles, more commonly on the right, fever
Cardiovascular Causes		
Heart failure (acute)	Cardiovascular risk factors, paroxysmal nocturnal dyspnea	Jugular venous distention, S_3, pulmonary crackles, possible murmur, edema
Myocardial infarction	Cardiovascular risk factors, chest pain, nausea, diaphoresis	S_3 and/or S_4, jugular venous distention, possible mitral regurgitant murmur, pulmonary crackles
Pericardial tamponade	History of trauma, preceding "flu" symptoms, collagen vascular disease	Jugular venous distention, clear lungs, pulsus paradoxus, hypotension
Upper Airway Causes		
Tracheal stenosis, tracheomalacia	Prolonged mechanical ventilation and intubation	Stridor, clear lungs, normal cardiac examination
Vocal cord dysfunction	Previous normal spirometry results, history of immediate improvement following intubation	Stridor, clear lungs, normal cardiac examination
Vocal cord paralysis	History of thyroid or neck surgery	Single frequency wheezing localized to throat, dysphonia
Psychiatric Causes		
Panic attack	Rapid onset of chest pain, dyspnea that resolve without specific treatment	Normal cardiac and pulmonary examinations

chemoreceptor stimulation (hypoxemia, hypercapnia, acidemia), impaired gas exchange, pregnancy, and behavioral factors (hyperventilation, anxiety, panic attacks).

Dyspnea may be acute or chronic. Diagnosis of either is heavily reliant on history and physical exam to guide evaluation. Vital signs should be reviewed to ensure clinical stability. Patients with significant tachypnea, accessory muscle use, or conversational dyspnea should be transferred to an acute care setting for evaluation.

Acute Dyspnea

Acute dyspnea develops relatively rapidly over minutes to a day and has a limited differential diagnosis. Cardiovascular causes are related to acute decreases in left ventricular function, or any event that increases pulmonary capillary pressure (acute coronary syndrome, tachycardia, cardiac tamponade). Respiratory causes are related to airway dysfunction (bronchospasm, aspiration, obstruction), disruption of gas exchange by parenchymal disease (pneumonia, acute respiratory distress syndrome), vascular disease (pulmonary embolism), or disturbance of the ventilatory pump (pleural effusion, pneumothorax, respiratory muscle weakness). Panic disorder and hyperventilation syndrome should be considered diagnoses of exclusion.

In a patient who presents with acute dyspnea, vital sign assessment and stabilization of patient should be performed. Heart rate, blood pressure, respiratory rate, and pulse oximetry should be measured. Adequate respiratory support, in the form of either supplemental oxygen or, if needed, invasive or noninvasive ventilation should be provided before further evaluation.

Once a patient is stabilized, history and physical examination will provide important clues to the differential diagnosis of acute dyspnea. Some conditions are associated with well-defined, predictive findings that should be specifically sought (Table 1). Low oxygen saturation suggests abnormalities of respiratory gas exchange and points to processes such as asthma, acute exacerbation of COPD, acute respiratory distress syndrome, heart failure, pulmonary fibrosis, or pulmonary vascular disease.

Chest radiography is the primary initial diagnostic tool; results frequently indicate the cause, or assist in guiding further evaluation. For example, focal infiltrates suggest pneumonia, air in the pleural space indicates a pneumothorax, or the presence of a basal opacity with a meniscus represents a pleural effusion. Cardiomegaly and vascular congestion support a diagnosis of heart failure.

Depending on the clinical situation, other helpful diagnostic tests may include chest computed tomography (CT) angiography or ventilation-perfusion lung scanning to evaluate for pulmonary embolism.

High-resolution chest CT may be useful when chest radiography is nondiagnostic and suspicion for parenchymal lung disease is high. **A serum B-type natriuretic peptide (BNP) level <100 pg/mL helps exclude heart failure in the setting of acute dyspnea.** Laryngoscopy and bronchoscopy are useful in the diagnosis of suspected foreign body aspiration, airway obstruction, and vocal cord dysfunction. Bronchoscopy with bronchoalveolar lavage can be helpful in the diagnosis of certain cases of pneumonia (eg, pneumocystis).

Chronic Dyspnea

Dyspnea becomes chronic when symptoms persist longer than 1 month. In two-thirds of patients, chronic dyspnea results from COPD, asthma, interstitial lung disease, or heart failure. Less common causes include pulmonary vascular disorders, valvular and pericardial heart disease, anemia, and thyroid disease.

The key to the workup of chronic dyspnea is a detailed history, approached in a systematic way to guide the search for the underlying cause in an efficient manner. The history should assess the quality of dyspnea, precipitating events (including the degree of exertion and positional changes), associated features, and risk factors for cardiac and pulmonary disease (Table 2). Asking open-ended questions to help patients describe the quality of their dyspnea will also provide diagnostic clues to the etiology. Patients with dyspnea due to chronic heart failure tend to characterize their dyspnea as air hunger or suffocating, whereas those with asthma often describe chest tightness.

In patients who have a chronic condition that could cause dyspnea, the possibility of an exacerbation of that illness as a cause of symptoms should be explored, while the potential of a new condition responsible for the symptoms should be considered.

The common causes for worsening symptoms of chronic conditions that were previously stable are natural disease progression, medication noncompliance, and exposure to environmental or dietary factors (ie, continued smoking in a patient with COPD or high salt intake leading to fluid overload in a patient with congestive heart failure).

In individuals with no known chronic conditions that could cause dyspnea, potential cardiac-related symptoms should be sought, including the presence of orthopnea, edema, or exertional symptoms (including chest pain). Positive answers should prompt an evaluation for presence of volume overload on physical examination (jugular venous distension, hepatojugular reflux, murmurs, S_3 or S_4 gallop, and pulmonary and peripheral edema). Echocardiography should be performed to evaluate systolic and diastolic function, as well as valvular competency.

Table 2. Dyspnea Evaluation Based on Clinical Presentation

History	Review of Systems	Physical Examination Findings	Diagnostic Studies to Evaluate
History of prior cardiac disease (congestive heart failure, ischemic cardiomyopathy, valvulopathy) No known heart disease history but risk factors for cardiovascular disease	Exertional symptoms, chest pain, paroxysmal nocturnal dyspnea, orthopnea Assess dietary and medication compliance	Jugular venous distention, hepatojugular reflux, lung crackles, cardiac S_3, peripheral edema	Echocardiography Consider cardiac stress testing if ischemic disease suspected
History of asthma, COPD, smoking (current or past) No known lung disease but risk factors for pulmonary disease	Wheezing, cough, current or past smoking history, environmental exposures Assess medication compliance, new exposures, timing of medications	Wheezing, increased anterior-posterior chest diameter, distant heart sounds, decreased breath sounds, prolonged expiratory phase Dry lung crackles	Chest radiography Pulmonary function testing High-resolution CT
History of thyroid disease	Weight loss, palpitations, diarrhea	Goiter, thyroid bruit	Thyroid function testing

COPD = chronic obstructive pulmonary disease; CT = computed tomography.

In the absence of a likely cardiac cause, potential pulmonary symptoms should be assessed, including wheezing, cough, smoking history, and environmental exposures to pulmonary toxins. The lung examination should focus on the presence or absence of wheezing, distant breath sounds, a prolonged expiratory phase, and increased anterior-posterior chest diameter suggestive of hyperinflation. Dry crackles on lung examination can signify the presence of pulmonary parenchymal disease. To further assess suspected pulmonary causes of chronic dyspnea in patients with a suggestive history or examination, chest imaging (plain chest radiography or CT) and pulmonary function testing may be appropriate.

For patients in whom the review of systems is not suggestive of either cardiac or pulmonary etiology, further clinical information should be obtained and appropriately directed testing should be pursued (Table 3). For example, the presence of conjunctival pallor, tachycardia, and a flow murmur is suggestive of anemia, and a goiter and tachycardia may lead to consideration of hyperthyroidism and high output heart failure. Skeletal abnormalities, such as kyphoscoliosis, may indicate pulmonary restriction as a cause of dyspnea. Global weakness can suggest a muscular disorder. The presence of significant ascites or other cause of increased intra-abdominal pressure may be contributing to the sensation of dyspnea. Further diagnostic testing should be tailored to evaluate these specific diagnostic possibilities.

In patients whose history, exam, and initial workup are unrevealing, cardiopulmonary exercise testing should be considered to provide further diagnostic information. Cardiopulmonary exercise testing is performed with the patient exercising on a treadmill or stationary bicycle with continuous oximetry and electrocardiography and measurement of exhaled gases. This test quantifies the patient's exercise tolerance and provides evidence of abnormal cardiac or pulmonary responses to exercise that may suggest a diagnosis. Arterial blood gas measurements can be useful in further evaluating these patients. Low maximum oxygen uptake in the absence of an identifiable abnormality often indicates deconditioning as a cause of dyspnea.

Bibliography

Parshall MB, Schwartzstein RM, Adams L, et al. American Thoracic Society Committee on Dyspnea. An official American Thoracic Society statement: update on the mechanisms, assessment, and management of dyspnea. Am J Respir Crit Care Med. 2012;185:435-52. [PMID: 22336677]

Table 3. Selected Differential Diagnosis of Chronic Dyspnea

Disorder	History Clues	Physical Examination Clues
Pulmonary Causes		
COPD	Smoking history, cough, sputum	Diminished breath sounds, wheezing, prolonged expiration, large chest
Interstitial lung disease	Possible exposure history (silica, asbestos, smoking); collagen vascular disease (scleroderma)	Possible clubbing (pulmonary fibrosis), dry crackles (pulmonary fibrosis)
Pulmonary hypertension	May be idiopathic or related to other disease, such as interstitial lung disease (scleroderma) or cardiac shunts (atrial septal defect)	Jugular venous distention, increased P_2, fixed split S_2, tricuspid regurgitant murmur, clear lungs or crackles depending on cause
Pleural effusion/hemothorax	History of cancer, possible chest pain	Dullness to percussion, absent breath sounds
Hepatopulmonary syndrome	Cirrhosis, platypnea (dyspnea sitting up, relieved lying down)	Findings of chronic liver disease, normal pulmonary examination
Cardiovascular Causes		
Aortic stenosis	History of heart murmur, chest pain, syncope, dyspnea; history of rheumatic fever; history of aortic coarctation	Crescendo-decrescendo systolic murmur at right upper sternal border cardiac base with radiation to carotid arteries
Mitral stenosis	History of rheumatic fever, heart murmur	Opening snap followed by diastolic murmur with presystolic accentuation
Mitral regurgitation	History of heart murmur, mitral valve prolapse, or myocardial infarction	Holosystolic murmur at cardiac base
Chronic constrictive pericarditis	History of pericarditis, possible chest pain	Elevated jugular venous pressure, clear lungs, edema, tricuspid regurgitation, pulsatile liver
Other Causes		
Anemia	History of blood loss or hemolytic disease	Conjunctival pallor
Thyrotoxicosis	Heat intolerance, weight loss, nervousness	Possible goiter
Neuromuscular disease	Known neuromuscular disease	Normal cardiac and pulmonary examinations, neuromuscular findings
Deconditioning	Situations leading to decreased exercise tolerance	Normal cardiac and pulmonary examinations

COPD = chronic obstructive pulmonary disease; P_2 = pulmonic component of S_2.

Chapter 91

Pleural Effusion

Roderick Go, DO

A pleural effusion is created by an imbalance between the production and removal of fluid from the pleural space. Two major mechanisms lead to the accumulation of excessive fluid in the pleural space: increased capillary hydrostatic pressure (eg, heart failure, superior vena cava syndrome, constrictive pericarditis) and/or decreased plasma oncotic pressure (eg, cirrhosis, nephrotic syndrome, hypoalbuminemia). Pleural effusions may be caused by various disease processes, including heart failure, cirrhosis, nephrosis, infection, cancer, trauma, collagen vascular disease, venous thromboembolism, or aortic rupture.

The evaluation of pleural effusion requires a systematic history and physical examination and pertinent laboratory and imaging tests. The leading causes of pleural effusion in the United States are heart failure, pneumonia, and cancer.

Diagnosis

Symptoms of pleural effusion may include fever, dyspnea, and chest pain. Fever suggests an underlying infection, malignancy, or associated collagen vascular disease. Chest pain and dyspnea may be caused by the space-occupying effect of a large effusion or associated parenchymal lung disease. Small pleural effusions, such as those caused by nephrotic syndrome or rheumatoid arthritis, often are asymptomatic. On physical examination, large accumulations of fluid in the pleural space block transmission of sound between the lung and the chest wall; therefore, percussion over an effusion is dull, and tactile (vocal) fremitus is diminished or absent. On auscultation, the most common findings are decreased to absent breath sounds over the effusion and bronchial breath sounds toward the top of the

Table 1. Pleural Fluid Laboratory Studies

Test	Notes
Erythrocyte count	>100,000/μL (100 x 10⁹/L): malignancy, trauma, parapneumonic effusion, pulmonary embolism
Leukocyte count	>10,000/μL (10 x 10⁹/L): parapneumonic effusion >50,000/μL (50 x 10⁹/L): complicated parapneumonic effusion or empyema
Neutrophils	>50%: parapneumonic effusion, pulmonary embolism, abdominal disease
Lymphocytes	>80%: tuberculosis (most common), lymphoma, coronary artery bypass surgery, rheumatoid pleuritis, sarcoidosis
pH	<7.20: complicated parapneumonic effusion or empyema, malignancy (<10%), tuberculosis (<10%), esophageal rupture
Glucose	<60 mg/dL (3.3 mmol/L): complicated parapneumonic effusion or empyema, tuberculosis (20%), malignancy (<10%), rheumatoid arthritis
Adenosine deaminase	>40 U/L: tuberculosis (>90%), complicated parapneumonic effusion (30%) or empyema (60%), malignancy (5%)
Cytology	Positive: malignancy
Culture	Positive: infection
Useful in certain circumstances:	
Hematocrit fluid to blood ratio	≥0.5: hemothorax
Amylase	>Upper limit of normal for serum: malignancy, pancreatic disease, esophageal rupture
Triglycerides	>110 mg/dL (1.2 mmol/L): chylothorax

Table 2. Pleural Fluid Characteristics of Transudative and Exudative Pleural Effusions

Criteria for Differentiation	Transudate	Exudate
Ratio of pleural fluid protein to serum protein	≤0.5	>0.5
Ratio of pleural fluid lactate dehydrogenase (LDH) to serum LDH	≤0.6	>0.6
Pleural fluid LDH	≤2/3 upper limit of normal for serum	>2/3 upper limit of normal for serum

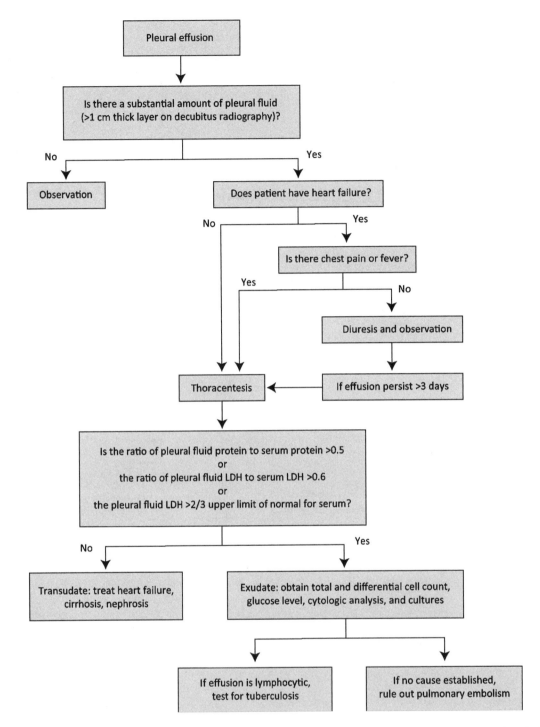

Figure 1. Evaluation of a patient with pleural effusion. LDH = lactate dehyrogenase. Data from Light RW. Clinical practice. Pleural effusion. N Engl J Med. 2002;346:1971-77; with permission. Copyright © 2002 Massachusetts Medical Society.

effusion. A pleural friction rub (harsh, rubbing, scratchy sound heard predominantly during expiration) may be auscultated.

Figure 1 is a diagnostic algorithm for pleural effusion. Chest radiography is usually the first study and can identify and quantify the amount of fluid and may demonstrate underlying diseases responsible for the effusion (eg, pneumonia, cancer) or suggest aortic dissection (widened mediastinum). Approximately 250 mL of pleural fluid is needed to blunt the costophrenic angle on a plain chest radiograph; greater amounts of fluid opacify the lower thorax and create a "meniscus sign."

After the presence of an effusion is documented, decubitus films (radiographs taken while the patient lies on the affected side) are usually obtained to evaluate whether the effusion is free-flowing or loculated (non-free flowing) and whether a sufficient quantity of fluid is present to perform thoracentesis. A 1-cm distance measured from the pleural fluid line to the chest wall on a decubitus radiograph is indicative of adequate pleural fluid to perform thoracentesis (Figure 2). Chest computed tomography (CT) is a valuable adjunct to chest radiography because it can more effectively define the size and

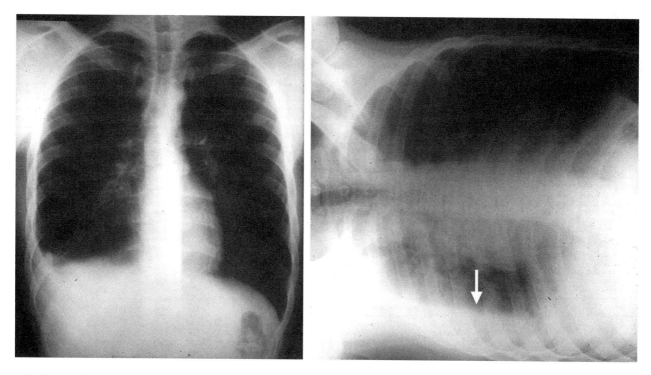

Figure 2. Chest radiograph showing a right-sided pleural effusion (left panel) that layers out along the right thorax when the radiograph is repeated with the patient in the right lateral decubitus position (right panel).

location of the pleural effusion and distinguish parenchymal from pleural disease. A spiral chest CT with contrast is highly sensitive for pulmonary embolism and may be indicated if the pretest probability of pulmonary embolism is moderate to high. Ultrasonography can be used to detect loculations, guide thoracentesis, and detect pleural abnormalities that are not apparent on chest radiographs.

A massive effusion, occupying the entire hemithorax, increases the likelihood of an underlying lung cancer or cancer involving the pleura (metastatic, mesothelioma). Bilateral transudative effusions are commonly associated with heart or liver failure. Bilateral exudative effusions suggest malignancy but also occur in patients with pleuritis due to systemic lupus erythematosus and other collagen vascular diseases. An empyema, or infection in the pleural space, is suggested by the presence of a loculated effusion on upright and decubitus chest radiography or by obvious loculation on chest CT.

Thoracentesis should be considered in all patients with a newly discovered, unexplained pleural effusion to assist in diagnosis and management. **Thoracentesis can be deferred in those patients with a small amount of pleural fluid and associated heart failure, pneumonia, or heart surgery (<1 cm thick on decubitus radiography or ultrasonography).** In those with congestive heart failure, thoracentesis should be performed in the setting of asymmetrical pleural effusions, chest pain, fever, or persistence despite diuresis. Caution is advised when considering performing a thoracentesis in patients with severe coagulopathy, thrombocytopenia, hemodynamic compromise, or on mechanical ventilation. Pneumothorax is the major complication of thoracentesis.

Pleural fluid analysis typically narrows the diagnostic possibilities but may not be definitive. Laboratory studies useful in pleural fluid analysis are listed in Table 1. Pleural fluid evaluation should include measures of pH, glucose, lactate dehydrogenase (LDH), protein, bacterial and acid-fast bacilli stains and culture, and leukocyte count with differential. If tuberculosis is suspected based on clinical

presentation and lymphocytic predominance on leukocyte count, adenosine deaminase activity and polymerase chain reaction assays can be useful adjuncts to diagnosis. Gross pus in the pleural space is diagnostic of empyema.

Comparing pleural fluid and serum levels of LDH and protein is used to distinguish transudative and exudative pleural effusions (Table 2). Exudative pleural effusions are predominantly caused by inflammatory, infectious, and malignant conditions and less commonly by collagen vascular disease, intra-abdominal processes, and hypothyroidism. Venous thromboembolic disease may cause either an exudative (particularly in the case of pulmonary infarction) or, less commonly, a transudative effusion. Transudative pleural effusions are caused by unbalanced hydrostatic forces and are associated more commonly with heart failure and cirrhosis and less commonly with nephrotic syndrome and constrictive pericarditis. Table 3 summarizes the causes of transudative effusions.

Cell counts may also be helpful in pleural fluid analysis. Transudative effusions typically have a low leukocyte count (<1000/μL). The most likely diagnoses associated with a pleural fluid leukocyte count >10,000/μL (10 × 10⁹/L) include parapneumonic effusion (a noninfected effusion occurring in the pleural space adjacent to a bacterial pneumonia); acute pancreatitis; splenic infarction; and subphrenic, hepatic, and splenic abscesses. A pleural fluid leukocyte count >50,000/μL (50 × 10⁹/L) is always associated with complicated parapneumonic effusions (a parapneumonic effusion with persistent bacterial invasion) and empyema (established infection with pus in the pleural space) but occasionally occurs with acute pancreatitis and pulmonary infarction. Malignant disease and tuberculosis typically present as a lymphocyte-predominant exudate. Additionally, although transudates may be blood-tinged, a grossly bloody effusion may be associated with cancer, tuberculosis, or trauma.

Normal pleural fluid pH is 7.60 to 7.66. Transudates are associated with a pleural fluid pH of 7.45 to 7.55. A limited number of diag-

Table 3. Causes of Transudative Effusions

Cause	Notes
Atelectasis	Small effusion caused by increased negative intrapleural pressure; common in patients in the intensive care unit
Constrictive pericarditis	Bilateral effusions with normal heart size; jugular venous distention present in 95% of cases
Duropleural fistula	Cerebrospinal fluid in the pleural space; caused by trauma and surgery
Extravascular migration of central venous catheter	With saline or dextrose infusion
Heart failure	Most common cause of transudates; diuresis can increase pleural fluid protein and lactate dehydrogenase, resulting in discordant exudate
Hepatic hydrothorax	Occurs in 6% of patients with cirrhosis and clinical ascites; up to 20% do not have clinical ascites
Hypoalbuminemia	Small bilateral effusions; edema fluid rarely isolated to pleural space
Nephrotic syndrome	Typically small and bilateral effusions; unilateral effusion with chest pain suggests pulmonary embolism
Peritoneal dialysis	Small bilateral effusions common; rarely, large right effusion develops within 72 h of initiating dialysis
Superior vena cava obstruction	Acute systemic venous hypertension
Trapped lung	Unexpandable lung; unilateral effusion as a result of imbalance in hydrostatic pressures from remote inflammation
Urinothorax	Unilateral effusion caused by ipsilateral obstructive uropathy

noses are associated with a pleural fluid pH <7.20; the most common causes are complicated parapneumonic effusion or empyema, tuberculous pleurisy, esophageal rupture, rheumatoid pleuritis, and malignancy.

Pleural fluid amylase should be measured only when pancreatic disease, esophageal rupture, or malignancy is considered. A chylous effusion (milky white fluid) is highly likely if the serum triglyceride level is >110 mg/dL (1.2 mmol/L). A chylous effusion (chylothorax) is commonly caused by leakage of lymph, rich in triglycerides, from the thoracic duct due to trauma or obstruction (eg, lymphoma).

When malignancy is suspected but initial thoracentesis is nondiagnostic, cytologic evaluation of a second, large-volume pleural fluid sample may be helpful. The sensitivity of cytologic analysis of pleural fluid ranges from 40% to 90% in patients with known malignancy. One reason for the variation is that the effusion may be associated with the malignancy, but malignant cells are not detected in the pleural fluid; these are termed paramalignant effusions, the causes of which include impaired lymphatic drainage, postobstructive pneumonia, and pulmonary embolism. Other factors affecting the sensitivity of pleural fluid cytology include the type of tumor (high positivity with adenocarcinoma and low positivity with Hodgkin lymphoma), the number of specimens submitted, the stage of pleural involvement (the more advanced the stage, the higher the sensitivity), and the expertise of the cytopathologist.

Approximately 25% of pleural effusions remain undiagnosed after analysis of one or more pleural fluid samples. Additional diagnostic evaluations are undertaken if the effusion is persistently symptomatic or if a progressive disease is suspected, such as malignancy, tuberculosis, or pulmonary embolism.

Therapy

Treatment of pleural effusions is dictated by the underlying cause. However, large effusions should be evacuated. For massive effusions associated with mediastinal shift, 2.0 L or more can be removed safely during a single procedure. Otherwise, therapeutic thoracentesis should be limited to removal of no more than 1.5 L at a time to minimize the likelihood of reexpansion pulmonary edema.

In pleural effusions associated with pneumonia, the presence of loculated pleural fluid, pleural fluid pH <7.20, pleural fluid glucose level <60 mg/dL (3.3 mmol/L), positive pleural fluid Gram stain or culture, or the presence of gross pus in the pleural space predicts a poor response to antibiotics alone; such pleural effusions are treated with drainage of the fluid through a catheter or chest tube. Thoracic empyema develops when antibiotics are not given and the pleural space is not drained in a timely manner. With multiloculated empyemas or uniloculated empyemas that fail to resolve with antibiotics and chest tube drainage, video-assisted thoracoscopic surgery is indicated for debridement. The use of intrapleural therapy with a combination of tissue plasminogen activator and DNase has been shown to improve fluid drainage, decrease the frequency of surgical referral, and decrease the duration of hospital stay.

Patients with recurrent, symptomatic malignant pleural effusions not responsive to chemotherapy require drainage for relief of dyspnea. Drainage can be accomplished either by placing a chronic indwelling pleural catheter or by performing chemical pleurodesis (obliteration of the pleural space) using a chemical agent (eg, large-particle talc) as a slurry through a chest tube.

Bibliography

Hooper C, Lee YC, Maskell N; BTS Pleural Guideline Group. Investigation of a unilateral pleural effusion in adults: British Thoracic Society Pleural Disease Guideline 2010. Thorax. 2010;65 Suppl 2:ii4-ii17. [PMID: 20696692]

Rahman NM, Maskell NA, West A, et al. Intrapleural use of tissue plasminogen activator and DNase in pleural infection. N Engl J Med. 2011;365:518-26. [PMID: 21830966]

Thomsen TW, DeLaPena J, Setnik GS. Videos in clinical medicine. Thoracentesis. N Engl J Med. 2006;355:e16. [PMID: 17035643]

Chapter 92

Asthma

Patricia Short, MD

Asthma is a disease of intermittent and reversible airway obstruction associated with chronic inflammation and a disordered immune response. Asthma affects 5% to 10% of the U.S. population and is steadily increasing in prevalence. The underlying cause of asthma remains unknown. Eosinophils are increased in the airway of patients with asthma, especially those with active disease, and neutrophils are increased during exacerbations and in severe disease; the role of neutrophils in the pathogenesis remains unclear. Th2 cells, a subtype of CD4 T cell, appear to play a central role in activation of the inflammatory response in asthma. Airway inflammation contributes to airway hyperresponsiveness and narrowing. Structural alterations occur in the lungs of some patients (a process known as airway remodeling) and consist of subepithelial fibrosis, increased smooth muscle mass, angiogenesis, and hyperplasia of mucous gland and goblet cells. Effective management of asthma involves use of objective measures of lung function to assess disease severity and to monitor therapeutic efficacy, identification and avoidance of environmental triggers that exacerbate symptoms, long-term use of medications that decrease airway inflammation, and use of medications to treat acute exacerbations.

Diagnosis

The diagnosis of asthma is based on episodic symptoms of airflow limitation and/or airway inflammation, evidence of reversible airflow obstruction, and exclusion of alternative diagnoses. Symptoms of airflow obstruction include wheezing, dyspnea, cough, and chest tightness. Symptoms that are intermittent and worsen in the presence of aeroallergens, irritants, cold air, or exercise are typical, as are nighttime symptoms that awaken the patient from sleep. The diagnosis of asthma should be considered in all patients with a chronic cough, especially if the cough is nocturnal, seasonal, or related to a workplace or an activity; coughing may be the only manifestation of asthma. A history of atopic dermatitis or eczema and a family history of asthma are additional risk factors for development of the disease.

Physical examination may be normal in the absence of an acute exacerbation. Findings of asthma may include wheezing during normal breathing or with forced expiration, chest hyperexpansion, and a prolonged expiratory phase. Accessory muscle use may be seen during an acute exacerbation. Additional findings may include nasal mucosal thickening, nasal polyps, or rhinitis manifested by cobblestoning of the oropharynx. Patients also may have evidence of atopic dermatitis or eczema on skin examination.

Spirometry should be performed in all patients suspected of having asthma (Table 1). Spirometry measurements, including forced expiratory volume in 1 second (FEV_1) and forced vital capacity (FVC), are taken before and after bronchodilator use. A reduced FEV_1 or a reduced FEV_1/FVC ratio documents airflow obstruction. An increase in FEV_1 of >12% with a minimum increase of 200 mL in FEV_1 after bronchodilator use establishes the presence of airflow reversibility and the diagnosis of asthma. However, normal measurements do not exclude the diagnosis. Patients suspected of having asthma who have normal spirometry results should proceed with a bronchoprovoca-

Table 1. Laboratory and Other Studies for Asthma

Test	Notes
Spirometry	Abnormal spirometry results (reversible obstruction) can help to confirm an asthma diagnosis, but normal results do not exclude asthma.
Peak flow variability	A patient with normal spirometry results but marked diurnal variability (based on a peak-flow diary kept for >2 wk) may have asthma, which may warrant an empiric trial of asthma medications or bronchoprovocation testing.
Bronchoprovocation testing	In a patient with a history highly suggestive of asthma and normal baseline spirometry results, a low PC_{20} (concentration of inhaled methacholine needed to cause a 20% drop in FEV_1) on methacholine challenge testing supports a diagnosis of asthma. A normal bronchoprovocation test essentially excludes asthma.
Chest radiography	Chest radiography may be needed to exclude other diagnoses but is not recommended as a routine test in the initial evaluation of asthma.
Allergy skin testing	There is a strong association between allergen sensitization, exposure, and asthma. Allergy testing is the only reliable way to detect the presence of specific IgE to allergens. Skin testing (or in vitro testing) may be indicated to guide the management of asthma in selected patients, but results are not useful in establishing the diagnosis of asthma.

Studies not helpful in the diagnosis of asthma:
- CBC with differential
- Sputum evaluation
- Serum IgE level
- Quantitative IgE antibody assays or specific IgE immunoassays (RAST)

CBC = complete blood count; FEV_1 = forced expiratory volume in 1 second; RAST = radioallergosorbent test.

tion test, such as a methacholine challenge. The lower the concentration of inhaled methacholine needed to cause a 20% drop in FEV_1, the more likely the patient has asthma. Methacholine challenge has a high sensitivity and a high negative predictive value for the diagnosis of asthma. Other bronchoprovocation tests include histamine and exercise; however, methacholine challenge remains the test of choice in patients for whom there is clinical suspicion for asthma despite normal spirometry results.

For patients with a smoking history who present with respiratory complaints consistent with asthma, consider obtaining a diffusing capacity for carbon monoxide (D_{LCO}) to differentiate between asthma and chronic obstructive pulmonary disease (COPD) (ie, chronic bronchitis, emphysema). D_{LCO} is normal or increased in asthma and decreased in COPD. Patients with COPD also do not demonstrate reversibility with bronchodilators on spirometry.

Exposure to high-level irritants (eg, chlorine gas, bleach, ammonia) can result in significant airway injury, which can lead to persistent airway inflammation and dysfunction with airway hyperresponsiveness and obstruction. A chronic cough, shortness of breath, and chest tightness may develop a condition known as reactive airways dysfunction syndrome (RADS). The symptoms of RADS may resolve with time but can persist for years in some patients.

Occupational asthma is an important consideration in patients with asthma symptoms. Patients should be asked about exposure to irritants, sensitizing chemicals, and allergens. Improvement of symptoms during weekends or vacations is an important historical clue in making this diagnosis.

Cough variant asthma presents with cough as the only symptom. This should be distinguished from other common causes of chronic cough such as allergic rhinitis, sinusitis, or gastroesophageal reflux disease. Alternative diagnoses should be considered when symptoms are difficult to control or if signs and symptoms are atypical. Vocal cord dysfunction, COPD, heart failure, interstitial lung disease, pulmonary hypertension, cystic fibrosis, Churg-Strauss syndrome, allergic bronchopulmonary aspergillosis, mechanical obstruction of the airway (endobronchial tumor or foreign body), obstructive sleep apnea, and medication-induced symptoms (particularly angiotensin-converting enzyme inhibitor use) are in the differential diagnosis of asthma (Table 2).

Acute Management

Short-acting β-agonists and consideration of a short course of systemic glucocorticoids are the drugs of choice for management of acute moderate to severe asthma exacerbations. Spirometry and/or peak expiratory flow rate (PEFR) are very useful objective measures to assess severity. PEFR 40% to 69% of predicted is considered moderate and PEFR <40% is considered severe. Patients with severe exacerbations should be treated with short-acting β-agonists and systemic glucocorticoids. Although anticholinergic agents are generally used primarily in COPD, short-acting anticholinergics (such as ipratropium) have been used to enhance the bronchodilator effect of short-acting β2-agonists in acute asthma exacerbations. Bronchodilators (β-agonists and ipratropium) should be given via nebulizer.

When evaluating a patient for an acute asthma exacerbation, look for historical features that identify high risk for a difficult course or complications, including (1) a history of intubation, intensive care unit admission, or unscheduled hospital admission for asthma; (2) β-agonist dispensing frequency exceeding one canister per month; (3) poor adherence to inhaled glucocorticoids; or (4) a history of depression, substance abuse, personality disorder, unemployment, or recent bereavement. Objective features that raise a red

Table 2. Differential Diagnosis of Asthma

Disorder	Notes
COPD (see Chapter 93)	Less reversibility of airflow obstruction; associated with a history of tobacco use. COPD may coexist with asthma in adults.
Vocal cord dysfunction	Abrupt onset of severe symptoms, often with rapid improvement. Monophonic wheeze heard loudest during either inspiration or expiration. The preferred diagnostic test is direct visualization of the vocal cords during symptoms. May closely mimic asthma, particularly in young adults.
Heart failure (see Chapter 7)	Spirometry results may or may not be normal; wheezing may be a sentinel manifestation. Consider when there is not prompt improvement with asthma therapy. Heart failure always is a consideration for persons with underlying cardiac disease.
Medication side effect	Chronic cough may occur with certain medications (eg, ACE inhibitors).
Bronchiectasis	Bronchiectasis is the permanent and abnormal dilatation and destruction of bronchi and bronchiolar walls associated with impaired drainage and recurrent infection that leads to chronic inflammation. Voluminous sputum production, often purulent and sometimes blood tinged. Suspect if physical examination reveals crackles with wheezing or clubbing or if chest radiograph shows peribronchial thickening.
Pulmonary infiltrates with eosinophilia (ABPA, eosinophilic granulomatosis with angiitis (Churg-Strauss), Loeffler syndrome, chronic eosinophilic pneumonia)	Wheezing may be seen in ABPA, chronic eosinophilic pneumonia, and eosinophilic granulomatosis with angiitis (Churg-Strauss). Note that in uncomplicated asthma, chest radiographs are normal. Findings of infiltrates, striking peripheral blood eosinophilia, and constitutional symptoms (eg, fever, weight loss) suggest chronic eosinophilic pneumonia. Asthma with eosinophilia, markedly high serum IgE levels, and intermittent pulmonary infiltrates is characteristic of ABPA. Difficult-to-treat asthma, upper airway and sinus disease, and multisystem organ dysfunction suggest eosinophilic granulomatosis with angiitis (Churg-Strauss).
Obstructive sleep apnea (see Chapter 94)	Excessive snoring and daytime fatigue; the patient's sleep partner may offer a history of noisy, labored, or erratic breathing. Obstructive sleep apnea is more common in obese patients.
Mechanical airway obstruction	Respiratory noises may be more pronounced in the inspiratory or expiratory phase of respiration, depending on location of obstruction. Diagnosed via flow-volume loop.
Cystic fibrosis	Associated with thick, purulent sputum containing bacteria and with GI symptoms due to pancreatic insufficiency. Recurrent respiratory infections may be present without GI or other system involvement.

ACE = angiotensin converting enzyme; ABPA = allergic bronchopulmonary aspergillosis; COPD = chronic obstructive pulmonary disease; GI = gastrointestinal.

flag include FEV_1 <50% of predicted, PEFR <50% of predicted, pulse oximetry <95%, arterial P_{CO_2} >40 mm Hg (5.3 kPa), arterial P_{O_2} <75 mm Hg (10 kPa), leukocyte count with >5% eosinophils or a total eosinophil count >1000 to 1500/μL (1000 to 1500 × 10⁶/L), respiration rate >30/min, and pulse rate >120/min. These patients are more prone to respiratory compromise and may require more intensive monitoring.

Chronic Management

The goal of asthma therapy is to achieve good long-term control, which is defined as infrequent asthma symptoms, unrestricted level of activity, normal or near-normal lung function, and rare asthma attacks requiring emergency care.

Encourage patients with asthma to reduce exposure to factors that worsen their asthma. Advise those who are allergic to dust mites to use measures to reduce mite allergen exposure at home, including (1) covering mattresses and pillows in allergen-proof fabric and laundering all bedding materials weekly in hot water (≥54.4°C [130°F]); (2) using air conditioning to maintain humidity at <50%;

(3) removing carpets; and (4) limiting fabric-covered items (eg, upholstered furniture, drapes, soft toys). Sensitive individuals may also benefit from other environmental control measures aimed at reducing potential reservoirs of common allergens in the home, such as exterminating cockroaches, removing cats, and reducing dampness. Advise patients to minimize exposure to tobacco smoke, wood-burning stoves, fireplaces, and unvented gas stoves. Other irritants to avoid include perfume, cleaning agents, sprays, dust, and vapors. There is no clear evidence regarding the value of high-efficiency particulate air filters (HEPA filters), air duct cleaning, or dehumidifiers in the control of asthma. Dehumidifiers may actually increase allergen levels if they are not properly cleaned and maintained.

Up to 20% of people may experience bronchoconstriction after taking aspirin or nonsteroidal anti-inflammatory drugs (NSAIDs). Patients with a history of nasal polyps are at increased risk, and aspirin and NSAIDs must be avoided if sensitivity to these medications exists. β-Blockers, even topical β-blockers, may exacerbate symptoms in susceptible individuals. Sulfite-containing foods (eg, processed potatoes, shrimp, dried fruit, beer, wine) should be avoided in patients with a history of sulfite sensitivity.

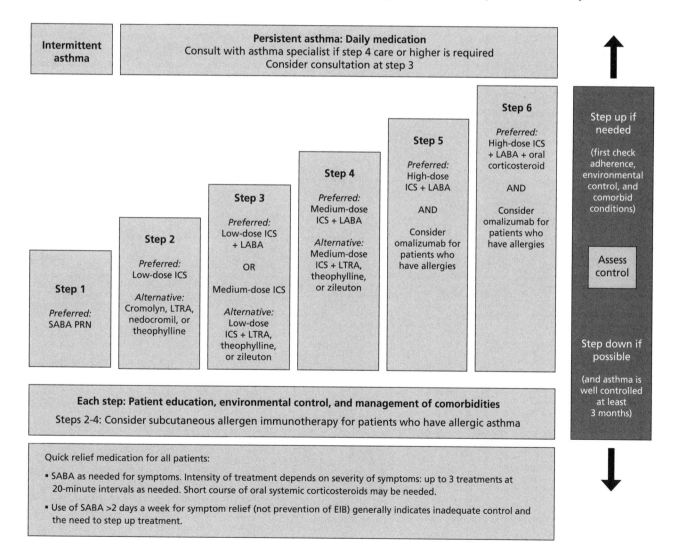

Figure 1. Stepwise approach to asthma therapy. EIB = exercise-induced bronchospasm; ICS = inhaled corticosteroids; LABA = long-acting β₂-agonist; LTRA = leukotriene receptor antagonist; PRN = as needed; SABA = short-acting β₂-agonist. Source: National Heart, Lung, and Blood Institute; National Institutes of Health; U.S. Department of Health and Human Services. National Asthma Education and Prevention Program. Expert Panel Report 3 (EPR-3): Guidelines for the Diagnosis and Management of Asthma-Summary Report 2007. J Allergy Clin Immunol. 2007;120(5 suppl): S94-138. [PMID: 17983880]

Medical management of asthma uses a step-wise approach based on asthma severity (Figure 1). Asthma severity is classified, based on spirometry measurements and frequency of symptoms, into one of four categories: intermittent, mild persistent, moderate persistent, or severe persistent (Table 3). Each category is defined by frequency of rescue inhaler use and nighttime symptoms as well as FEV_1 or PEFR measurement.

Regardless of disease severity, all patients are prescribed a short-acting, inhaled β-agonist medication. Short-acting β-agonists are the drugs of choice for reversal of acute symptoms of bronchoconstriction and are safe, well tolerated, and easy to use. All patients should be instructed on proper use of meter-dosed inhalers and be advised to have the medication available at all times in case symptoms arise. Patients with intermittent asthma do not need daily controller medication and are treated as needed with a short-acting β-agonist. If short-acting bronchodilators are needed for symptom relief more than twice a week for daytime symptoms or twice a month for nighttime awakenings, a long-acting controller medication is indicated. Use of more than one canister of short-acting β-agonist per month may be a clue to poor control of asthma and warrants further investigation.

Mild persistent asthma is treated with a single long-term controller medication. Patients with this level of disease activity are more prone to disease exacerbations and have underlying inflammation. A low-dose inhaled glucocorticoid is the preferred long-term controller medication; alternatives include a mast cell stabilizer, leukotriene modifier, or sustained-release methylxanthine. Inhaled glucocorticoids reduce bronchial hyperresponsiveness, decrease use of short-acting β-agonists, and control symptoms. Patients should be advised to rinse their mouth carefully after using inhaled glucocorticoids to reduce the risk of complications (thrush, dysphonia, cough, sore throat). Patients with moderate to severe disease should be taught how to use a peak-flow meter to self-monitor disease severity.

Moderate persistent asthma is treated with one or two long-term controller medications. Use either low doses of inhaled glucocorticoid and a long-acting β-agonist (preferred) or medium doses of a single inhaled glucocorticoid. In patients who remain symptomatic while taking medium doses of inhaled glucocorticoids, the addition of a long-acting bronchodilator (eg, salmeterol) results in improved lung physiology, decreased use of short-acting β-agonists, and reduced symptoms when compared with doubling the dose of inhaled glucocorticoid. Patients on long-acting β-agonists seem to obtain the same quick relief from a short-acting β-agonist when needed, although some mild tachyphylaxis does occur. However, a long-acting β-agonist should not be used alone; it should be used in conjunction with an inhaled glucocorticoid based on studies suggesting increased mortality associated with long-acting β-agonist monotherapy for asthma, including exercise-induced asthma.

Patients with severe persistent asthma may require at least three daily medications to manage their disease (ie, high doses of an inhaled glucocorticoid plus a long-acting bronchodilator and possibly oral glucocorticoids). These patients are highly prone to disease exacerbations and have underlying inflammation. The addition of a leukotriene modifier can improve FEV_1, decrease daytime symptom scores, and reduce nighttime awakenings. Patients with asthma who are obese, smoke cigarettes, or have aspirin sensitivity also may benefit from the use of a leukotriene modifier.

Omalizumab is a monoclonal antibody that binds to IgE and is useful for reducing exacerbations in patients with severe persistent asthma who have evidence of allergies. Because severe

Table 3. Classification of Asthma Severity

Components of Severity	Intermittent		Persistent	
		Mild	Moderate	Severe
Impairment				
Symptoms	≤2 days/week	>2 days/week but not daily	Daily	Throughout the day
Nighttime awakenings	≤2 ×/month	3-4 ×/month	>1 ×/week but not nightly	Often 7 ×/week
SABA use for symptom control (not prevention of EIB)	≤2 days/week	>2 days/week but not more than 1 ×/d	Daily	Several times a day
Interference with normal activity	None	Minor limitation	Some limitation	Extremely limited
Lung function[a]	Normal FEV_1 between exacerbations; FEV_1 >80% of predicted; FEV_1/FVC normal	FEV_1 >80% of predicted; FEV_1/FVC normal	FEV_1 >60% but <80% of predicted; FEV_1/FVC reduced 5%	FEV_1 <60% of predicted; FEV_1/FVC reduced >5%
Risk				
Exacerbations (consider frequency and severity)[b,c]	0-2/year		>2/year	
Recommended step for initiating treatment [d]	Step 1	Step 2	Step 3; consider short courses of systemic corticosteroids	Step 4 or 5; consider short courses of systemic corticosteroids

EIB = exercise-induced bronchospasm; FVC = forced vital capacity; FEV_1 = forced expiratory volume in 1 second; SABA = short-acting β-agonist.

[a]Normal FEV_1/FVC: 8-19 years old, 85%; 20-39 years old, 80%; 40-59 years old, 75%; 60-80 years old, 70%.

[b]Frequency and severity may fluctuate over time for patients in any severity category.

[c]Relative annual risk for exacerbations may be related to FEV_1.

[d]In 2 to 6 weeks, evaluate the level of asthma control that is achieved and adjust therapy accordingly.

National Asthma Education and Prevention Program, Third Expert Panel on the Diagnosis and Management of Asthma. Expert Panel Report 3: Guidelines for the Diagnosis and Management of Asthma. Bethesda (MD): National Heart, Lung, and Blood Institute (US); 2007 Aug. Available from: www.ncbi.nlm.nih.gov/books/NBK7232/.

anaphylaxis has been reported with its use and the drug is extremely expensive, it is used only in selected patients who remain symptomatic despite other therapies.

Poorly controlled asthma during pregnancy can lead to low birth weight, preeclampsia, premature labor, and increased infant mortality. Asthma treatment should continue during pregnancy. Short-acting β-agonists are safe during pregnancy. Inhaled glucocorticoids also are considered safe and should be used for long-term control of asthma during pregnancy; cromolyn sodium, montelukast, zafirlukast, and theophylline can be used if necessary but are considered less-preferred alternatives to inhaled glucocorticoids for daily control. For acute severe asthma exacerbations during pregnancy, oral glucocorticoids are recommended, even though a small risk of congenital malformations has been reported.

Exercise-induced bronchospasm typically begins at the start of exercise and peaks 5 to 10 minutes after exercise. Several therapeutic options are available for patients with asthma symptoms during exercise, particularly vigorous exercise in cold, dry air. Patients should be advised to use a short-acting β-agonist such as albuterol 15 to 30 minutes before the start of exercise. Cromolyn sodium or nedocromil 15 to 30 minutes before exertion also can be used. Leukotriene modifiers are useful for patients with chronic asthma and exercise-induced asthma. Patients with chronic asthma and poorly controlled exercise-induced asthma are candidates for a long-acting β-agonist added to an inhaled beta glucocorticoid or leukotriene modifier.

Management of comorbid conditions such as gastroesophageal reflux disease (GERD), allergic rhinitis, and chronic sinusitis may result in improved asthma control. Allergy tests, nasal examination, and assessment for GERD should be considered in all patients with asthma, particularly those who remain poorly controlled on long-term medications. Immunotherapy can be useful in patients with allergic rhinitis or insect hypersensitivity. Patients may need a "step up" in controller therapy during an acute upper respiratory infection. Obese or overweight patients should be advised that weight loss might improve asthma control. Obstructive sleep apnea (OSA) should also be considered as a possible comorbid condition in patients who are not well controlled.

Follow-Up

Patients should be reassessed regularly (experts suggest every 3 to 6 months) to determine whether their asthma classification has changed and whether therapy with controller medications should be increased ("stepped up") or decreased ("stepped down"). Monitor pregnant patients with asthma more frequently, as asthma symptoms can improve, worsen, or stay the same during pregnancy. Ensuring good asthma control during pregnancy is important as pregnancy-related complications (preeclampsia, low birth weight or intrauterine growth restriction, premature labor, infant mortality) are more common in patients with severe, poorly controlled disease.

For all patients, develop an individual self-management plan, taking into consideration the patient's underlying disease severity and ability to adapt to self-management. Have all patients demonstrate proper use of prescribed inhaler devices; improper use can be a cause of difficult-to-control asthma. For patients with intermittent or mild persistent asthma, provide a simple plan outlining how to handle exacerbations, including health care contacts in cases of emergency. Patients with moderate to severe persistent asthma should keep a daily diary and have a detailed written action plan with specific objective or subjective markers for self-directed changes in therapy. Ensure that all patients with moderate to severe persistent asthma have a peak-flow meter at home and know how to use it. Provide instruction in symptom-based monitoring to patients who are not using a peak-flow meter.

Bibliography

Panettieri RA Jr. In the clinic. Asthma. Ann Intern Med. 2007;146:ITC6-1-ITC6-16. [PMID: 17548407]

Chapter 93

Chronic Obstructive Pulmonary Disease

Carlos Palacio, MD

Chronic obstructive pulmonary disease (COPD) is characterized by airflow limitation that is not fully reversible. Chronic bronchitis and emphysema are the predominant conditions included in COPD; either or both may be present in a given patient. Chronic bronchitis is defined as a productive cough for 3 months in each of 2 successive years in a patient in whom other causes of chronic sputum production have been excluded. Chronic bronchitis is associated with an increase in the volume of tissue in the bronchiolar wall and an accumulation of inflammatory exudate in the airway lumen. Emphysema is defined as permanent enlargement of airspaces distal to the terminal bronchioles, with destruction of the bronchiolar walls without obvious fibrosis. Loss of alveolar attachments and elasticity contributes to small airway collapse during expiration. Chronic bronchitis and emphysema both result in peripheral airway obstruction, parenchymal destruction, and pulmonary vascular abnormalities that reduce the capacity for gas exchange, producing arterial hypoxemia, hypercapnia, and cor pulmonale. Hyperinflation causes respiratory muscle inefficiency and increased work of breathing.

Other conditions characterized by airflow limitation that is not fully reversible (eg, bronchiectasis, cystic fibrosis, bronchiolitis) should be differentiated from COPD (Table 1). The distinction between COPD and asthma can be challenging, as some overlap may be seen.

Risk factors for COPD include host factors and environmental exposures. Hereditary deficiency of α_1-antitrypsin (AAT) is the best-documented genetic risk factor. AAT is an antiproteolytic enzyme that neutralizes neutrophil elastase. AAT deficiency results in excessive amounts of neutrophil elastase in the lung, which destroys elastin, causing early-onset obstructive pulmonary disease, typically panacinar emphysema. Some individuals with AAT deficiency may develop liver and skin disorders. Also implicated in COPD are genes responsible for the production of enzymes involved in detoxification of cigarette smoke (eg, microsomal epoxide hydrolase, glutathione S-transferase). Developmental risk factors (eg, low birth weight) and childhood illness have a profound effect on lung growth. Important environmental exposures include tobacco smoke, occupational dust, chemical agents, and air pollution (including smoke from indoor burning of biomass fuels – often seen in developing countries).

Prevention

Eighty percent to 90% of the risk of developing COPD is attributable to cigarette smoking. Cigarette smoke is responsible for the development of bronchial mucous gland hypertrophy and goblet cell metaplasia with inflammatory cell infiltrates. Airway changes include squamous epithelial metaplasia, ciliary loss and dysfunction, and increased proliferation of smooth muscle and connective tissue. These smoking-related changes result in an accelerated decline in lung function. Smoking cessation slows the accelerated decline in forced expiratory volume in 1 second (FEV_1) and reduces all-cause mortality. Advise patients not to start smoking and to stop if they have started. **Smoking cessation is the most clinically effective and cost-effective way to prevent and slow the progression of COPD as well as improve disease-related survival.**

Screening

Screening for airway obstruction in asymptomatic patients is not recommended as there is little evidence that making the diagnosis in this setting is beneficial. Patients with early-onset COPD (age ≤45 years) and patients with a strong family history of lung or liver disease should be screened for AAT deficiency.

Table 1. Differential Diagnosis of COPD

Disorder	Notes
Asthma	Onset typically in childhood, although may occur at any age; history of allergy often is present. Lability of symptoms, with overt wheezing and rapid response to β-agonist bronchodilators, is typical. Asthma may be present in ~10% of cases of COPD.
Bronchiectasis	Bronchiectasis is the permanent and abnormal dilatation and destruction of bronchi and bronchiolar walls associated with impaired drainage and recurrent infection that leads to chronic inflammation. Often associated with excessive sputum production with purulent exacerbations. Chest radiograph and CT scan may be diagnostic, showing thickened and cystic airways. Often a specific inciting event may be recognized, such as pneumonia in childhood.
Cystic fibrosis	Onset usually at birth but in rare cases may be in adulthood. Positive sweat chloride test; cystic fibrosis transmembrane conductance regulator test is abnormal in many cases.
Bronchiolitis	Onset often follows respiratory infection; may be idiopathic or associated with other diseases (eg, rheumatoid arthritis). Postviral bronchiolitis usually is self-limited over a period of up to 3 mo. Bronchiolitis is poorly responsive to bronchodilators; oral glucocorticoids may be helpful in some cases.
α_1-Antitrypsin deficiency	Early-onset COPD, usually age <45 y. Family history of COPD; COPD and liver disease; emphysema affecting the lower lobes. Measure α_1-antitrypsin levels.

COPD = chronic obstructive pulmonary disease; CT = computed tomography

Diagnosis

Assess for the presence of cough, sputum production, and dyspnea. Inquire about exercise tolerance, energy level, and frequency and severity of exacerbations. A detailed smoking history is essential, and a history of exposure to other inhalation exposures should be noted. Self-reported history of COPD, >40 pack-year smoking history, age ≥45 years, and maximum laryngeal height ≤4 cm are most predictive of COPD (positive likelihood ratio >200). Laryngeal height is the distance between the top of the thyroid cartilage and the suprasternal notch.

Look for signs of hyperinflation, including barrel chest, a hyper-resonant percussion note, distant breath sounds, and prolonged expiratory time. Pursed-lip breathing, paradoxical chest or abdominal wall movements, and use of accessory muscles are all signs of severe airflow limitation. Cardiac examination may show cor pulmonale (increased intensity of the pulmonic sound, persistently split S_2, and a parasternal lift due to right ventricular hypertrophy). Extracardiac signs of cor pulmonale include neck vein distention, liver enlargement, and peripheral edema. Nonspecific radiographic signs of emphysema are flattening of the diaphragms, irregular lung lucency, and reduction or absence of pulmonary vascular markings.

COPD is confirmed and staged with spirometry (Table 2). The presence of a postbronchodilator FEV_1 <80% of predicted and an FEV_1 to forced vital capacity (FEV_1/FVC) ratio <70% confirms the presence of nonreversible airflow obstruction. Severity of COPD also can be graded using the BODE index, which consists of Body mass index, airflow Obstruction, Dyspnea, and Exercise capacity (the 6-minute walk distance). This index is useful in evaluating the risk for hospitalization and estimating long-term prognosis in COPD patients; higher BODE scores are associated with a greater risk of death.

Static lung volumes, including total lung capacity, residual volume, and functional residual capacity, are increased in advanced COPD. Diffusing capacity for carbon dioxide is reduced, particularly in emphysema. Obtain an oxygen saturation measurement and arterial blood gas measurement if oximetry testing suggests hypoxemia (<94% on ambient air) or if there is suspicion of hypercapnia.

AAT deficiency should be suspected with early-onset COPD, especially panacinar emphysema. When suspected, measure the serum AAT level; severe deficiency of AAT is associated with serum AAT levels <50 to 80 mg/dL (0.5 to 0.8 g/L).

Therapy

Stable COPD

Smoking cessation slows the decline in pulmonary function and should be reinforced at each visit. Administer annual influenza vaccine to all patients unless contraindicated because of hypersensitivity to egg protein. Administer pneumococcal vaccine to all patients and revaccinate those aged ≥65 years who were immunized more than 5 years ago and were younger than 65 years at the time of vaccination.

Management of stable COPD is characterized by a stepwise increase in treatment based on spirometry results (see Table 2). Medications are used to alleviate symptoms, improve pulmonary function, and prevent complications (Table 3). Inhaled therapy is preferred over systemic agents. **A metered-dose inhaler (MDI), with proper instruction and good technique, is as effective as a nebulizer.** A spacer device, which holds the medicine in a chamber and allows the patient to inhale the drug fully, reduces oropharyngeal deposition of the drug and decreases subsequent local side effects. Nebulizers may be helpful for patients who cannot use MDIs because of severe dyspnea, difficulties with coordination, or physical problems such as arthritis.

Three types of bronchodilators are used to treat patients with stable COPD: β-agonists, anticholinergic agents, and methylxanthines (eg, theophylline). These medications all work by relaxing airway smooth muscle, thereby improving lung ventilation.

Short-acting β-agonists (eg, albuterol, levalbuterol)–also known as "rescue" medications–act within a few minutes of administration, and their effect lasts approximately 4 to 6 hours. Give these medications as needed for relief of persistent or worsening symptoms and to improve exercise tolerance. Long-acting β-agonists (eg, salmeterol, formoterol, arformoterol) achieve sustained and more predictable improvement in lung function than the short-acting agents. They improve health status, reduce symptoms, decrease the need for rescue medication, and increase the time interval between exacerbations. Long-acting β-agonists, which typically are given every 12 hours, can be used as monotherapy or combined with other bronchodilators and/or inhaled glucocorticoids for better control of chronic symptoms. The most common side effects of β-agonist therapy are increased heart rate and tremor.

Table 2. Classification and Management of COPD[a]

Stage	Characteristics
I: Mild	FEV_1/FVC <70%; FEV_1 ≥80% of predicted
	With or without chronic symptoms (cough, sputum production)
	Add short-acting bronchodilator when needed
II: Moderate	FEV_1/FVC <70%; 50% ≤FEV_1 <80% of predicted
	With or without chronic symptoms (cough, sputum production)
	Add regular treatment with one or more long-acting bronchodilators; add pulmonary rehabilitation
III: Severe	FEV_1/FVC <70%; 30% ≤FEV_1 <50% of predicted
	With or without chronic symptoms (cough, sputum production)
	Add inhaled corticosteroids if repeated exacerbations
IV: Very severe	FEV_1/FVC <70%; FEV_1 <30% of predicted **or** FEV_1 <50% of predicted plus chronic respiratory failure
	Add long-term oxygen therapy if chronic respiratory failure; consider surgical treatments

COPD = chronic obstructive pulmonary disease; FEV_1 = forced expiratory volume in 1 second; FVC = forced vital capacity.

[a]Classification based on postbronchodilator FEV_1.

Data from the Global Initiative for Chronic Obstructive Pulmonary Disease, Executive Summary: Global Strategy for the Diagnosis, Management, and Prevention of COPD, 2014, www.goldcopd.com

Table 3. Criteria and Classification of Acute COPD Exacerbation

Major Criteria

Increase in sputum volume

Increase in sputum purulence (generally yellow or green)

Worsening of baseline dyspnea

Additional Criteria

Upper respiratory infection in the past 5 days

Fever of no apparent cause

Increase in wheezing and cough

Increase in respiration rate or heart rate 20% above baseline

Various nonspecific signs and symptoms may accompany these findings, such as fatigue, insomnia, depression, and confusion

Degree of Exacerbation

Mild exacerbation = 1 major criterion + 1 or more additional criteria

Moderate exacerbation = 2 major criteria

Severe exacerbation = all 3 major criteria

COPD = chronic obstructive pulmonary disease.

Vagal stimulation in the lung is mediated via muscarinic receptors. Anticholinergic drugs used to treat COPD include short-acting inhaled agents (eg, ipratropium) and tiotropium, a long-acting inhaled bronchodilator used in stable outpatients. Tiotropium selectively blocks the M3 muscarinic receptor. Short-acting anticholinergic agents are less potent than long-acting β-agonist or long-acting anticholinergic agents. Anticholinergic agents are especially useful in COPD when combined with short- or long-acting β-agonists and/or theophylline. Tiotropium should not be combined with short-acting anticholinergic drugs. The primary side effect of the inhaled anticholinergic agents used for COPD is dry mouth. Anticholinergic agents should be used with caution in patients with urinary obstruction and narrow-angle glaucoma.

Theophylline is a nonspecific phosphodiesterase inhibitor that increases intracellular cyclic adenosine monophosphate within airway smooth muscle and inhibits intracellular calcium release. The role of theophylline in treatment of COPD exacerbations is controversial; it may be used as an adjunct to inhaled bronchodilators and inhaled glucocorticoids. Some patients with COPD may benefit from a trial of theophylline for 1 to 2 months. Theophylline has a narrow therapeutic index, and toxicity therefore is a risk; maintain serum theophylline levels at 5 to 12 µg/mL (27.8 to 66.6 µmol/L). Side effects include nausea, vomiting, and cardiac arrhythmias. Discontinue theophylline if side effects develop or objective benefit is not evident within several weeks. Roflumilast is an oral phosphodiesterase-4 inhibitor that may be used in select patients with severe COPD to reduce risk for exacerbations.

The role of glucocorticoids in the management of stable COPD is limited. However, regular use of inhaled glucocorticoids in patients with recurrent exacerbations reduces the frequency of further exacerbations. Inhaled glucocorticoids should not be used alone. Combinations of inhaled glucocorticoids and long-acting bronchodilators are more effective than either therapy alone in reducing exacerbations and improving health status. The long-term safety of inhaled glucocorticoids in COPD is unknown. The use of inhaled glucocorticoids in elderly patients must be carefully monitored

because of the risk of adverse effects such as osteopenia, cataracts, hyperglycemia, and pneumonia.

Oxygen therapy is a major component of therapy for very severe (stage IV) COPD and usually is prescribed for patients with arterial Po_2 ≤55 mm Hg (7.3 kPa) or oxygen saturation ≤88% with or without hypercapnia. Patients with arterial Po_2 of ≤59 mm Hg (7.8 kPa) or oxygen saturation ≤89% also qualify for oxygen therapy if they have pulmonary hypertension, evidence of cor pulmonale or edema as a result of right-sided heart failure, or a hematocrit <55%. Oxygen treatment should be administered ≥15 hours per day. Long-term oxygen therapy improves survival in patients with chronic respiratory failure and has a beneficial effect on hemodynamics, exercise capacity, and mental status.

Pulmonary rehabilitation improves quality of life in patients with moderate to severe symptoms that persist despite optimal medical management. Exercise improves cardiovascular conditioning and increases ability to perform daily activities. Intensive counseling improves patient adherence and reinforces the proper use of pulmonary medications. Early pulmonary rehabilitation after hospitalization for an exacerbation leads to improved exercise capacity and health status.

Surgical interventions, including bullectomy, lung volume reduction surgery, and lung transplantation, may improve symptoms in highly selected patients. Lung volume reduction surgery improves exercise capacity, lung function, dyspnea, and quality of life; patients with predominantly upper lobe emphysema and low baseline exercise capacity may have improved survival.

COPD Exacerbation

COPD exacerbation is characterized by a sudden change in the patient's baseline dyspnea, cough, and/or sputum production that is beyond the typical day-to-day variation in symptoms. Various nonspecific signs and symptoms also may be present, such as fatigue, insomnia, depression, and confusion. Exacerbations commonly are caused by infection and air pollution. Exacerbations may be classified as mild, moderate, and severe (see Table 3). Mild to moderate exacerbations can be managed at home. Mild exacerbations require treatment with short-acting bronchodilators; moderate exacerbations require short-acting bronchodilators and systemic glucocorticoids and/or antibiotics. Severe exacerbations are treated in the hospital; severe exacerbations are characterized by loss of alertness or a combination of two or more of the following parameters: dyspnea at rest, respiration rate ≥25/min, pulse rate ≥110/min, or use of accessory respiratory muscles.

Oxygen therapy is the cornerstone of hospital management of COPD exacerbations, with a goal of adequate levels of oxygenation (arterial Po_2 >60 mm Hg [8.0 pKa] or oxygen saturation >90%). Arterial blood gas levels should be measured 30 to 60 minutes after oxygen therapy is started to ensure that oxygenation is adequate without carbon dioxide retention or acidosis.

Bronchodilator therapy with short-acting β-agonists is preferred for treating exacerbations. An anticholinergic agent should be added if the patient does not respond promptly to the β-agonist. In addition, systemic (oral or intravenous) glucocorticoids are used for hospital management of acute exacerbations of COPD to improve symptoms and lung function and to reduce the length of hospitalization. The effective dose is unknown, but high doses are associated with a significant risk of side effects. Prolonged treatment does not result in greater efficacy and increases the risk of side effects.

There is a significant benefit to using antibiotics in patients who have moderate or severe COPD exacerbations. The predominant bacteria recovered are *Haemophilus influenzae*, *Streptococcus pneu-*

moniae, and *Moraxella catarrhalis*. Generally, antibiotic regimens for community-acquired infection include coverage with a third-generation cephalosporin in combination with a macrolide or monotherapy with a fluoroquinolone. Sputum Gram stain and culture usually is unnecessary.

In patients with COPD exacerbations, adjunctive nonpharmacologic therapies help alleviate dyspnea and decrease sputum production. The following interventions may be considered:

- Percussion, vibration, and postural drainage to enhance clearance of sputum
- Relaxation techniques to reduce anxiety from dyspnea
- Control of breathing, pursed-lip breathing, and diaphragmatic breathing to alleviate dyspnea

Noninvasive intermittent ventilation alleviates respiratory acidosis and decreases respiration rate, severity of dyspnea, and length of hospital stay; importantly, mortality also is reduced. Indications for noninvasive ventilation include moderate to severe dyspnea with the use of accessory muscles of breathing and paradoxical abdominal motion, moderate to severe acidosis (pH <7.35) and/or hypercapnia (arterial P_{CO_2} >45 mm Hg [6.0 kPa]), and respiration rate >25/min. Exclusion criteria include respiratory arrest, cardiovascular instability (hypotension, arrhythmias, myocardial infarction), change in mental status (lack of cooperation), high aspiration risk, viscous or copious secretions, recent facial or gastroesophageal surgery, craniofacial trauma, fixed nasopharyngeal abnormalities, burns, and extreme obesity.

Invasive mechanical ventilation is indicated for patients who cannot tolerate noninvasive ventilation and patients with severe dyspnea with a respiration rate >35/min, life-threatening hypoxia, severe acidosis (pH <7.25) and/or hypercapnia (arterial P_{CO_2} >60 mm Hg [8.0 kPa]), respiratory arrest, somnolence or impaired mental status, cardiovascular complications (hypotension, shock), or other complications (eg, metabolic abnormalities, sepsis, pneumonia, pulmonary embolism, barotrauma, massive pleural effusion).

Follow-Up

After severe acute exacerbation, most patients experience reduced quality of life, and nearly 50% are readmitted more than once in the ensuing 6 months. Therefore, the goal is to reduce the number and severity of exacerbations through smoking cessation, preventive vaccination, adherence with maintenance medications, and early attention to mild exacerbations and side effects of treatment. Weight loss, muscle wasting, and weakness are common in severe COPD as a result of deconditioning and malnutrition. As patients age, the comorbid conditions associated with COPD increase and require concurrent management along with COPD in internal medicine settings.

Ensure that patients participate in disease self-management by understanding the causes, management, course, and prognosis of COPD. At follow-up visits, observe patients' use of inhalers and reinforce proper inhaler technique. Monitor pulmonary function periodically to determine the need for a change in or addition to treatment, including possible oxygen therapy. After hospitalization for a COPD exacerbation, early follow-up is important to reduce hospital readmission rates.

Bibliography

American College of Physicians; American College of Chest Physicians; American Thoracic Society; European Respiratory Society. Diagnosis and management of stable chronic obstructive pulmonary disease: a clinical practice guideline update from the American College of Physicians, American College of Chest Physicians, American Thoracic Society, and European Respiratory Society. Ann Intern Med. 2011;155:179-91. [PMID: 21810710]

Fromer L, Goodwin E, Walsh J. Customizing inhaled therapy to meet the needs of COPD patients. Postgrad Med. 2010;122:83-93. [PMID: 20203459]

Global Strategy for the Diagnosis, Management and Prevention of COPD, Global Initiative for Chronic Obstructive Lung Disease (GOLD) 2014. Available from: www.goldcopd.org/.

Littner MR. In the clinic. Chronic obstructive pulmonary disease. Ann Intern Med. 2011;154:ITC4-1-ITC4-15; quiz ITC4-16. [PMID: 21464346]

Chapter 94

Obstructive Sleep Apnea

David V. Gugliotti, MD

Obstructive sleep apnea (OSA) is the most common chronic respiratory sleep disorder. It is estimated that as many as 26% of the American population is at risk for sleep apnea; OSA affects 24% of adult men and 9% of adult women. However, OSA remains undiagnosed in a large proportion of patients. Therefore it is imperative to recognize patients at risk for the disorder.

OSA is characterized by recurrent episodes of partial (hypopnea) or complete (apnea) upper airway obstruction during sleep. Manifestations include impaired daytime attention and memory and significantly increased risk for motor vehicle accidents. The pathophysiology is not clearly understood; however, patients with OSA have more narrowed airways, which are vulnerable to collapse during sleep. Recurrent arousals from sleep, in addition to hypoxemia and hypercapnia, constitute the likely physiologic mechanism for the characteristic daytime somnolence and other sequelae of the disorder. Symptomatic OSA contributes to secondary hypertension, likely related to peripheral vasoconstriction from arousal-prompted sympathetic discharge. In addition, patients with severe OSA accompanied by marked hypoxemia may develop secondary polycythemia and related complications. Hemodynamic consequences include increased left and right ventricular afterload, decreased left ventricular compliance, and increased myocardial oxygen demand; heart failure and stroke are important sequelae of untreated OSA.

Diagnosis

Excessive daytime sleepiness is the most common manifestation of OSA, but patients may have a variety of symptoms (Table 1). It is important to obtain a sleep history from the patient and bed partner. Specifically address disruptive snoring, witnessed apnea, excessive daytime sleepiness (including while driving), fatigue, nasal congestion, weight gain, morning headaches, and number of hours slept per night (to rule out a contribution from sleep deprivation). Patients often do not report excessive daytime sleepiness because they accommodate to these symptoms. Consider using a validated questionnaire such as the Epworth Sleepiness Scale, which assesses the level of somnolence during daytime activity to help determine the need for diagnostic testing for sleep disorders. In addition, a sleep apnea screening tool can be used to assess a patient's likelihood of having significant OSA. The STOP-BANG questionnaire has been shown to have a high sensitivity and negative predictive value, particularly for moderate or severe sleep apnea.

Excess body weight is the most important risk factor for OSA, and the prevalence of OSA increases with greater weight and obesity. The majority of patients with OSA are obese, and obesity is associated with an 8- to 12-fold increased risk of OSA in middle-aged adults. However, thinner patients also may be affected. Postmenopausal women are at risk for OSA, and other risk factors include family history, male sex, aging, and race (African-Americans, Mexican Americans, Asians, and Pacific Islanders are at increased risk). Although prevalence is higher in men, OSA is likely underdiagnosed and undertreated in women. Other anatomic features associated with OSA include increased waist-hip ratio, self-reported large neck circumference (eg, >17 inches (43.2 cm) in men, >16 inches (40.6 cm) in women), crowded pharynx (due to long, low-lying uvula/soft palate, macroglossia, or enlarged tonsils/adenoids), nasal obstruction, retrognathia, or overbite. Further physical examination findings may include systemic hypertension, decreased oxygen saturation, nasal congestion, wheezing, an accentuated pulmonic component of S_2 (suggesting pulmonary hypertension), or S_3 gallop (suggesting heart failure).

Polysomnography (PSG) is needed for the diagnosis of OSA as clinical features are neither sufficiently sensitive nor specific enough for diagnosis. Electroencephalogram is often performed with the PSG for sleep staging and assessment for other causes of apnea and to most accurately confirm the diagnosis. The PSG measures respiratory events and hours of sleep to derive the apnea-hypopnea index (AHI), which is the average number of apnea and hypopnea events per hour. An AHI of >5 per hour confirms OSA, and a combination of AHI, degree of sleepiness, and presence or absence of cardiovascular problems (eg, hypertension, stroke, heart failure) determines the severity of disease. **The use of alternative home respiratory tests for the diagnosis of sleep apnea, even when interpreted by a certified sleep specialist, may provide inaccurate results.** Continuous positive airway pressure (CPAP) titration, if indicated, may be conducted in the same session as the diagnostic polysomnography or in a separate study (termed a "split-night study").

Consider additional testing to assess for possible contributing factors or complications based on the history and clinical suspicion (Table 2). Perform daytime awake pulse oximetry; if a patient with suspected OSA demonstrates hypoxemia in this setting, measure

Table 1. Clinical Features of Obstructive Sleep Apnea

Symptoms	Physical Findings
Habitual snoring	Obesity
Reports of witnessed apnea	Large neck circumference
Nighttime awakening with gasping or choking	Nasal obstruction
Insomnia	Enlarged tonsils
Nighttime diaphoresis	Low-lying soft palate
Morning headaches	Narrow oropharynx
Erectile dysfunction	Macroglossia
Daytime fatigue or sleepiness	Retro- or micrognathia
Alterations in mood	
Neurocognitive decline	

Table 2. Laboratory and Other Studies for Obstructive Sleep Apnea

Test	Notes
Polysomnography	Considered the gold standard test for OSA.
Reduced channel polysomnography (usually includes respiratory monitoring and oximetry)	Sensitivity 82%-94%, specificity 82%-100%. Less expensive and less accurate than polysomnography but may offer increased access to diagnosis.
Overnight oximetry	Sensitivity 87%, specificity 65%. Overnight oximetry is not an accurate test for OSA.
Serum TSH level	Obtain in patients with recent weight gain and fatigue. TSH level is elevated in 2%-3% of patients with OSA.
Complete blood count	Polycythemia can be a complication of severe OSA with accompanying severe hypoxemia.
Chest radiography	Obtain if coexisting heart failure is suspected based on physical examination. Heart failure can be a complication of OSA.
Electrocardiography	Obtain if coexisting heart failure is suspected based on physical examination.
Arterial blood gas analysis	Obtain if obesity hypoventilation syndrome is suspected, to look for hypercapnia and hypoxemia.

OSA = obstructive sleep apnea; TSH = thyroid-stimulating hormone.

arterial blood gases to assess for obesity hypoventilation syndrome (awake P_{CO_2} >45 mm Hg). Consider chest radiography or electrocardiography if cardiopulmonary disease is suspected.

The broad differential diagnosis of OSA includes other primary sleep disorders (eg, central sleep apnea, periodic limb movements of sleep, narcolepsy), and medical conditions or other factors that can disturb sleep (Table 3).

Therapy

Treatment of OSA aims to improve daytime sleepiness and cognitive performance and to prevent long-term sequelae. Lifestyle changes and CPAP form the cornerstones of therapy. Oral devices or upper airway surgical procedures may play a role in selected cases. Advise patients to defer driving or other potentially dangerous activities until OSA and alertness improve.

Table 3. Differential Diagnosis of Obstructive Sleep Apnea

Disorder	Notes
Central sleep apnea	Most commonly seen in patients with heart failure and stroke. Polysomnography shows an absence of respiratory effort during apnea, distinguishing central from obstructive apnea. Central sleep apnea sometimes is induced by opioid medications.
Upper airway resistance syndrome	Most commonly seen in loud snorers who complain of excessive sleepiness. Polysomnogram with EEG shows a normal AHI (<5/hr) and reveals that increased respiratory effort is causing frequent EEG interruptions during sleep. Symptoms and treatment are the same as for OSA.
Periodic limb movements of sleep	A neurologic disorder of unknown cause, characterized by frequent episodes of leg kicking during sleep. Most common in patients on dialysis. Limb movements are not associated with respiratory events on polysomnogram.
Narcolepsy	Severe excessive sleepiness and cataplexy (episodes of muscle weakness in response to emotion); onset peaks at age 15-25 y. Polysomnogram does not show OSA or periodic limb movements, but multiple sleep latency (the time required to fall asleep) tests are abnormal (patient falls asleep quickly and has REM sleep during short naps).
Obstructive or restrictive lung disease (see Chapter 94 and Chapter 95)	Shortness of breath or cough may disturb sleep. Pulmonary function tests establish the diagnosis and can guide specific therapy.
GERD (see Chapter 18)	Cough or choking may disturb sleep. Acid or burning taste in the throat is helpful for diagnosis but may be absent. A successful trial of empiric GERD therapy may confirm the diagnosis.
Sinusitis	Cough and drainage may disturb sleep. Clinical symptoms (nasal congestion, postnasal drip) suggest the diagnosis.
Heart failure (see Chapter 7)	Dyspnea and cough may disturb sleep. Symptoms and examination usually suggest heart disease. Central sleep apnea may be seen in patients with severe heart failure and indicates a worse prognosis.
Epilepsy (see Chapter 79)	Seizures may occur only at night, with or without motor activity. Obtain neurology consultation and EEG.
Sleep deprivation or short sleep schedule	Inadequate hours of sleep can cause daytime sleepiness; naps usually are refreshing, which is not typical for OSA. Review of sleep schedule is essential, and a trial of longer sleep hours may be helpful.
Hypothyroidism (see Chapter 11)	Only 2%-3% of patients with OSA have hypothyroidism. Suspect in patients with weight gain and fatigue, and screen with a serum TSH level.
Acromegaly (see Chapter 10)	Screen patients with compatible signs and symptoms. Treatment of acromegaly may significantly reduce OSA severity.

AHI = apnea-hypopnea index; EEG = electroencephalogram; GERD = gastroesophageal reflux disease; OSA = obstructive sleep apnea; REM = rapid eye movement; TSH = thyroid-stimulating hormone.

Crucial lifestyle changes include weight loss of at least 10% in obese patients (this may increase airway size), avoidance of alcohol and sedatives 3 to 4 hours before bedtime (to maintain muscle tone of airway dilators), and lateral sleeping position (to render airways less collapsible). Nasal obstruction or congestion may be improved with nasal glucocorticoids and decongestants.

If moderate to severe OSA persists despite these interventions, or if the changes cannot be instituted, nocturnal CPAP should be started. CPAP is effective in pneumatically splinting the entire airway, preventing collapse during sleep. CPAP raises intraluminal airway pressure and increases functional residual capacity. Regular use of CPAP may dramatically improve quality of life by increasing daytime alertness, decreasing hypertension, and eliminating apneic episodes. However, adherence to CPAP can be challenging due to discomfort from the device or due to air pressure and flow. Measures shown to improve adherence include early patient education, follow-up, heated humidification, and establishing a comfortable interface for the CPAP device. Patients still uncomfortable with CPAP (or with hypoventilation) may benefit from a trial of bi-level positive airway pressure nasal ventilation or auto-titrating positive pressure devices that modify airflow pressure to a more comfortable level. The role of supplemental oxygen is not yet determined in patients without a clear indication for oxygen therapy.

Consider the use of mandibular advancement devices (oral appliances that open the posterior airway space, usually by protruding the lower jaw or holding the tongue forward) as an alternative therapy; however, these devices eliminate the need for CPAP in only mild to moderate disease. Surgical intervention is another option for patients unable or unwilling to use CPAP. Resection of enlarged, obstructing tonsils may be beneficial in some patients. Other surgical procedures for OSA, most commonly uvulopalatopharyngoplasty, alleviate obstruction of the hypoglossal space. Surgical procedures have variable success rates depending on complex factors, including BMI, severity of OSA, and individual anatomy. A follow-up polysomnogram is recommended to document the effect of a mandibular advancement device or surgical procedure.

Follow-Up

Arrange follow-up at 1-month and then 6-month intervals to assess adherence to treatment and change in symptoms, particularly daytime sleepiness, and continue to emphasize weight loss in obese patients. Nonadherence, erroneously titrated CPAP, failure to wear CPAP every night, or coexisting periodic limb movements in sleep may contribute to persistent sleepiness. Perform a repeat sleep study if significant lifestyle goals have been attained to assess whether OSA is resolved or if CPAP should be adjusted. Monitor patients with moderate to severe OSA for potentially related cognitive, cardiovascular, metabolic, or obesity-related metabolic conditions.

Bibliography

Basner RC. Continuous positive airway pressure for obstructive sleep apnea. N Engl J Med. 2007;356:1751-8. [PMID: 17460229]

Guilleminault C, Abad VC. Obstructive sleep apnea syndromes. Med Clin North Am. 2004;88:611-30, viii. [PMID: 15087207]

Olsen EJ, Park JG, Morgenthaler TI. Obstructive sleep apnea-hypopnea syndrome. Prim Care. 2005;32:329-59. [PMID: 15935189]

Chapter 95

Diffuse Parenchymal Lung Diseases

Feroza Daroowalla, MD

The term *diffuse parenchymal lung disease* (DPLD), sometimes referred to as interstitial lung disease, is a convenient way to group a diverse set of conditions that have several basic features in common: the involvement of the distal lung parenchyma on histopathology, and some shared clinical, radiographic, and physiological characteristics. It is a term that does not include chronic obstructive pulmonary disease (COPD), lung malignancy, lung infections or pulmonary hypertension.

While the distal lung parenchyma is always involved, other parts of the lungs such as the small airways, vasculature, and/or pleura may also be involved in these conditions. Many of the conditions affect large areas of the lung (hence the designation "diffuse"), but this is not always the case. Additionally, not all lung areas may be affected uniformly.

Table 1 provides one useful way of classifying the diffuse parenchymal lung diseases, by one of two histopathologic (ie, lung response) categories: those that demonstrate primarily inflammation and fibrosis, and those that show granulomatous changes. Within each category, the diseases are further defined as those with a known cause or a disease known to cause DPLD, and those that are of unknown etiology. However, this is a simplified classification scheme, and there is considerable overlap of histopathology in many conditions.

With an inflammation and fibrosis pattern, it is believed that epithelial surface injury in the alveoli leads to spreading fibrotic change into the interstitium and vasculature, which can ultimately progress to interstitial fibrosis. There are several specific histopathologic patterns of interstitial involvement, some of which are detailed below: usual interstitial pneumonitis nonspecific interstitial pneumonitis, bronchiolitis obliterans organizing pneumonia, respiratory bronchiolitis-interstitial lung disease, desquamative interstitial pneumonia, and diffuse alveolar damage.

- Usual interstitial pneumonitis (UIP): The hallmark of this histologic pattern is a heterogeneous involvement of the lung with different stages of progression of fibrosis in adjacent areas of the lung. The disease starts in the subpleural regions and honeycombing is seen. This pattern is associated with several diseases or exposures, including pneumoconioses, radiation injury, end-stage hypersensitivity pneumonitis, and advanced sarcoid. If no underlying process is identified, a diagnosis of idiopathic pulmonary fibrosis (IPF) is made. In most cases of UIP, progression is likely and the likelihood for reversing disease is very poor.
- Nonspecific interstitial pneumonitis (NSIP): In this pattern, there is uniform involvement of lung parenchyma with cellular infiltration or fibrosis. The process is often bilateral, subpleural, with correlating ground-glass infiltrates on CT imaging and little honeycombing. This pattern is typically seen in association with an underlying disease process such as an autoimmune connective tissue disorder. Cases of NSIP may have remissions.

- Bronchiolitis obliterans organizing pneumonia (BOOP)/cryptogenic organizing pneumonia (COP): This pattern shows small-airway bronchiolitis with granulation tissue and organizing pneumonia.

With a granulomatous pattern, T cells, macrophages and epithelioid cells accumulate to form granulomas in the lung parenchyma. Granulomas are a hallmark of these diseases but are not the sole finding, and fibrotic change may be seen in the same patient. Granulomas can take several forms, and the histologic characteristics can help with diagnosis. For instance, well-formed noncaseating granulomas are typical for sarcoidosis; loosely formed granulomas are more commonly seen in hypersensitivity pneumonitis.

Diagnosis

Because DPLD is a very heterogeneous group of disorders, the clinical diagnosis of DPLD should be based on a thorough investigation that includes the history, physical examination, laboratory and imaging studies, and sometimes open lung biopsy. Table 2 provides some clinical clues to the diagnosis of DPLD.

A patient presenting with progressive dyspnea (over months), reduced exercise tolerance, and a persistent dry cough should raise the possibility of DPLD. Although most have a gradual onset, this is not universally true.

The history should focus on looking for potential underlying causes for possible DPLD. For instance, important elements of the history include medication use in the past or present, workplace or environmental exposures (eg, dusts, fibers, mold, or birds), symptoms of relevant systemic disease (connective tissue disease), exposure to radiation (timing, site on body), and family history of fibrosis or autoimmune disease.

The physical examination should include evaluation of oxygenation status, particularly desaturation with exertion, which is frequently an early sign, basilar inspiratory crackles on lung examination, digital clubbing, signs of autoimmune disease such as systemic sclerosis or rheumatoid arthritis, and evidence of right-sided heart failure (due to pulmonary hypertension), which can be a consequence of DPLD.

Plain chest radiography usually shows increased interstitial reticular or nodular infiltrates, often in the bases but the distribution can vary. Upper lung zone disease is characteristic of certain diseases.

High-resolution computed tomography (HRCT) is a crucial tool in the diagnostic evaluation of DPLD by providing detail about the distribution and extent of disease. In many cases the history, physical exam, serologies, and certain characteristic HRCT patterns can lead to a diagnosis without the need for a biopsy. Table 3 lists some of the expected CT findings (pattern of findings, distribution of the involved parenchyma of disease) and associated findings that give clues to underlying conditions.

Laboratory evaluation might include evaluation for underlying connective tissue disorders or serologic evidence of an immune reaction to exposure to inhaled antigens if indicated by the clinical history.

Pulmonary function testing (PFT) in DPLD is characterized by decreased lung volumes (total lung capacity, residual volume, and functional residual capacity) and decreased diffusing capacity. Many patients have a mixed picture of airflow obstruction and restriction due to airway involvement (such as with sarcoidosis) or coexisting COPD. Oxygenation is reduced, especially with exercise, and this frequently occurs before resting hypoxemia.

A lung biopsy is sometimes required to confirm a diagnosis. This is best performed via an open procedure using a thoracoscopic approach (video-assisted thoracoscopic biopsy), with sampling of multiple areas of the lung to improve diagnostic yield.

Table 1. Classification and Distinguishing Features of Select Forms of Diffuse Parenchymal Lung Disease (DPLD)

DPLD Causing Inflammation and Fibrosis

Known Causes

Drug-induced	Examples: amiodarone, methotrexate, nitrofurantoin, chemotherapeutic agents (see www.pneumotox.com for a complete listing)
Smoking-related	"Smoker's" respiratory bronchiolitis characterized by gradual onset of persistent cough and dyspnea. Radiograph shows ground-glass opacities and thickened interstitium. Smoking cessation improves prognosis. Desquamative interstitial pneumonitis and Langerhan cell histiocytosis are other histopathological patterns associated with smoking and DPLD.
Radiation	May occur 6 weeks to months following radiation therapy
Chronic aspiration	Aspiration is often subclinical
Pneumoconioses	Asbestosis, silicosis, berylliosis
Connective tissue diseases	
Rheumatoid arthritis	10%-20% of patients with rheumatoid arthritis (mostly men) are affected. May affect the pleura (pleuritis and pleural effusion), parenchyma, airways (bronchitis, bronchiectasis), and vasculature. The parenchymal disease can range from BOOP-type pattern to usual interstitial pneumonitis.
Progressive systemic sclerosis	Nonspecific interstitial pneumonia pathology; may be progressive in 50% of patients. May be exacerbated by aspiration due to esophageal involvement; antibody to Scl-70 or pulmonary hypertension portends a poor prognosis. Monitoring of diffusing capacity for early involvement is warranted.
Polymyositis/dermatomyositis	Many different types of histology; poor prognosis
Other connective tissue diseases	Sjögren syndrome, Behçet disease

Unknown Causes

Idiopathic interstitial pneumonias	
Idiopathic pulmonary fibrosis (IPF)	Chronic, insidious onset of cough and dyspnea, usually in a patient aged >50 y. Usual interstitial pneumonia pathology (honeycombing, bibasilar infiltrates with fibrosis). Diagnosis of exclusion.
Acute interstitial pneumonia	Dense bilateral acute lung injury similar to acute respiratory distress syndrome; 50% mortality rate.
Cryptogenic organizing pneumonia (COP)	May be preceded by flu-like illness. Radiography shows focal areas of consolidation that may migrate from one location to another.

DPLD Causing Granulomatous Changes

Known Causes

Hypersensitivity pneumonitis	Immune reaction to an inhaled low-molecular-weight antigen; may be acute, subacute, or chronic. Noncaseating granulomas are seen. Chronic hypersensitivity pneumonitis has a poor prognosis.

Unknown Causes

Sarcoidosis	Variable clinical presentation, ranging from asymptomatic to multiorgan involvement. Stage 1: hilar adenopathy. Stage 2: hilar adenopathy plus interstitial lung disease. Stage 3: interstitial lung disease. Stage 4: fibrosis. Noncaseating granulomas are hallmarks.
Granulomatosis with polyangiitis (Wegener)	May be associated with upper airway involvement and other systemic findings.

Rare DPLD with Well-Defined Features

Lymphangioleiomyomatosis	Affects women in their 30s and 40s. Associated with spontaneous pneumothorax. Chest CT shows cystic disease.
Langerhans cell histiocytosis	Affects younger men who smoke. Improves with smoking cessation.
Anti-GBM disease (Goodpasture syndrome)	Associated with anti-glomerular basement membrane antibody. Hemoptysis and glomerular disease are hallmarks.
Chronic eosinophilic pneumonia	Chest radiograph shows "radiographic negative" of heart failure, with peripheral alveolar infiltrates predominating. Other findings may include peripheral blood eosinophilia and eosinophilia on bronchoalveolar lavage.
Pulmonary alveolar proteinosis	Slowly progressive disorder affecting patients in their 20s to 50s (predominantly men). Diagnosed via bronchoalveolar lavage, which shows abundant protein in the airspaces. Chest CT shows "crazy paving" pattern.

BOOP = bronchiolitis obliterans organizing pneumonia; CT = computed tomography; GBM = glomerular basement membrane.

Table 2. Clinical Clues to Causes of Diffuse Parenchymal Lung Disease

Finding or Factor	Notes
Patient age	Idiopathic pulmonary fibrosis often occurs in patients aged >50 y, but interstitial lung disease associated with connective tissue disease, sarcoidosis, lymphangioleiomyomatosis, and Langerhan cell histiocytosis usually occurs in patients aged 20-40 y.
Female sex	Lymphangioleiomyomatosis.
Smoking history	Respiratory bronchiolitis–associated interstitial lung disease, desquamative interstitial pneumonia, and Langerhan cell histiocytosis.
Exposure history	Consider asbestosis and silicosis if occupational exposure. Consider hypersensitivity pneumonitis if exposure to birds, hay, or mold (and other organic material).
Acute onset (days to weeks)	Consider acute interstitial pneumonia, acute eosinophilic pneumonia, cryptogenic organizing pneumonia, hypersensitivity pneumonitis, drug-induced interstitial lung disease, and diffuse alveolar hemorrhage syndrome.
Clubbing	Common in idiopathic pulmonary fibrosis (30%). Rare in respiratory bronchiolitis–associated interstitial lung disease, cryptogenic organizing pneumonia, and connective tissue disease.
Erythema nodosum	Associated with sarcoidosis, connective tissue diseases.
Uveitis/conjunctivitis	Associated with sarcoidosis, connective tissue diseases.
Lacrimal/salivary gland enlargement	Associated with sarcoidosis and Sjögren syndrome.
Lymphadenopathy, hepatosplenomegaly	Associated with sarcoidosis.
Arthritis	Associated with connective tissue disease, sarcoidosis.
Muscle weakness	Associated with polymyositis and dermatomyositis.

Table 3. Distribution of High-Resolution CT Findings in Diffuse Parenchymal Lung Disease

Distribution	Lung Disease
Basal predominant	IPF, asbestosis, NSIP
Upper-lobe predominant	Hypersensitivity pneumonitis, sarcoidosis, silicosis
Peripheral	IPF, chronic eosinophilic pneumonia, cryptogenic organizing pneumonia
Central	Sarcoidosis, pulmonary alveolar proteinosis
Mosaic attenuation	Small-airways disease (hypersensitivity pneumonitis, respiratory bronchiolitis-associated interstitial lung disease)

CT = computed tomography; IPF = idiopathic pulmonary fibrosis; NSIP = nonspecific interstitial pneumonia.

Selected DPLD Conditions

Inflammation and Fibrosis Lung Response

Drug-Induced Parenchymal Lung Disease

Multiple drugs result in lung disease, and the time course to disease after initiating the medication can vary. The pattern of involvement can vary from a bronchiolitis with an organizing pneumonia, to a hypersensitivity reaction, to fibrotic changes.

Amiodarone is a common cause of lung disease. It is widely used in older patients who may be more susceptible to lung effects. The effects are dose dependent but can occur anytime between initiation to several years after starting the drug. Discontinuation is the primary therapeutic intervention, although the drug remains in the lung parenchyma even after it has been stopped. Glucocorticoids may also be of benefit.

Other common drugs associated with DPLD include methotrexate and nitrofurantoin. Methotrexate is used as treatment for connective tissue disease and as an immune system modulator in other conditions. Nitrofurantoin is as an antimicrobial often used over long courses.

Smoking-Related DPLD

Interstitial disease in smokers can take several forms. These range from asymptomatic to more extensive disease. These include respiratory bronchiolitis-interstitial lung disease, desquamative interstitial pneumonitis, and Langerhans cell histiocytosis. Smoking cessation alone may result in stabilization or remission of each of these diseases.

Connective Tissue-Associated DPLD

Diffuse parenchymal lung disease is associated with rheumatoid arthritis, progressive systemic sclerosis, polymyositis/dermatomyositis, Sjögren syndrome, and Behçet disease. The lung involvement is primarily due to the underlying autoimmune disease, or complications of the underlying disease such as aspiration in progressive sclerosis, or due to the medications used to modify the disease. The histopathology is usually NSIP (see beginning of chapter). Sometimes the lung manifestations precede any other manifestations of the connective tissue disease. Management is focused on the underlying connective tissue disease and supportive care for the lung manifestations (such as prevention of reflux in systemic sclerosis and supplemental oxygen in those who need it).

Pneumoconiosis

DPLD may be seen with exposure to asbestos, silicon, and beryllium. Interstitial pulmonary fibrosis associated with asbestos exposure is termed asbestosis. It typically presents decades after significant exposure and may be progressive. The clinical presentation includes dyspnea on exertion, dry cough, and exercise intolerance. Imaging shows an increase in basilar and subpleural bilateral, linear interstitial markings. Pleural plaques, which are often calcified and have a characteristic appearance, suggest previous exposure to asbestos; if present in a patient with DPLD, asbestos should be considered a potential cause. PFT findings show restriction and low diffusing capacity. The clinical course is progressive and there are no effective treatments.

Idiopathic Pulmonary Fibrosis

IPF is a common form of idiopathic DPLD. A diagnosis is important because of its poor prognosis. Clinical presentation is characterized by dyspnea on exertion, exercise intolerance, dry cough, and crackles on inspiration. In typical cases, imaging shows lower lung zone and subpleural linear reticular markings, volume loss, honeycombing and traction bronchiectasis. Histopathology of open lung biopsy shows UIP. The clinical course may be punctuated by acute declines due to exacerbations of underlying disease or overlay of infection, heart failure or other comorbidity. No medical treatment has shown consistent improved mortality for IPF, and overall prognosis is poor. Patients with acute exacerbations should be evaluated for underlying and treatable infection or volume overload. Many immunosuppressive treatments have been investigated and not found to provide a mortality benefit. Many patients require supplemental oxygen and may even benefit from treatment of pulmonary hypertension.

Acute Interstitial Pneumonia

Also called the Hamman-Rich syndrome, this is a rare illness of acute and abrupt onset, which can lead to fulminant respiratory failure after a prodrome of fever, cough, and shortness of breath. Imaging shows bilateral alveolar disease with ground-glass changes. Diagnosis is accomplished with an open lung biopsy. Histopathology shows a pattern of diffuse alveolar damage. The outcomes for these patients are poor.

Organizing Pneumonia

Organizing pneumonia is a histopathologic description of findings seen on tissue biopsy that includes small-airway bronchiolitis with granulation tissue. Clinically it can present with a flu-like illness and has a radiographic appearance characterized by peripheral opacities that change over time, among other findings. When a proximate cause is identified, this syndrome is called BOOP; when an inciting cause cannot be found, it is called COP. The majority of patients show a good response to systemic glucocorticoids.

Granulomatous Lung Response

Hypersensitivity Pneumonitis

Hypersensitivity pneumonitis (HP) occurs in people with repeated episodes of inhalation of antigens (organic or chemical) with an immunologic reaction to these antigens. Examples are exposure to fungal elements and bird droppings. History of exposure preceding symptoms can sometimes be difficult to elicit but should be sought by thorough questioning. HP can present as an acute flu-like syndrome after exposure but most often occurs over time with the patient presenting for medical care after a subacute course. Patients can present with crackles on physical exam, and labs may show a leukocytosis. HRCT imaging usually shows ground-glass opacities with centrilobular nodules and can include fibrotic changes, depending on how far the disease has progressed. Histopathology shows noncaseating granulomas. Treatment is primarily based on avoidance of the causative antigen, which requires that the antigen be identified. Avoidance can be challenging when the etiologic agent is part of the patient's home or work environment. Systemic steroids may be needed in patients with chronic symptoms.

Sarcoidosis

Sarcoidosis is a granulomatous disease of unclear cause that affects multiple organs, including the lung. The incidence of sarcoidosis is bimodal with peaks among young people aged > 18 years and among people aged 50 to 60 years. In the United States, blacks are overrepresented among patients. Although the disease can be asymptomatic, those with lung involvement commonly present with cough, dyspnea, and chest heaviness. PFT can show restriction, reduced diffusing capacity, and obstruction because airway involvement as well as interstitial abnormalities may be present. Imaging may show bilateral hilar adenopathy and/or interstitial infiltrates (nodular, peribronchial), or patchy alveolar infiltrates. Histopathology shows bronchocentric noncaseating granulomas involving the lung and other organs such as the liver, skin, eye, and, more rarely, the heart and nerves. The course of the disease can be one of remission and exacerbation or ongoing progression. Treatment is guided by symptoms and ranges from observation to systemic glucocorticoids.

Therapy

In addition to specific treatments focused on the diagnosed DPLD in an individual patient, all patients who smoke should be encouraged to stop. Many patients may require supplemental oxygen, usually initially only with exercise and sleep but eventually continuously. An evaluation should be done for all patients to determine this need with follow-up assessment in those with progressive disease. Symptomatic treatment for reactive airways or cough, maintenance of nutrition and fitness, and treatment of infections are also part of standard management. Whenever possible, environmental exposures that are either suspected to be causative or exacerbating of DPLD should be eliminated, including in the workplace.

Many patients with severe or chronic DPLD develop pulmonary hypertension. In addition to oxygen therapy, specific treatments (such as vasodilating agents) can be given to reduce right-sided vascular resistance and pressures.

Bibliography

Meyer KC, Raghu G, Baughman RP, et al. American Thoracic Society Committee on BAL in Interstitial Lung Disease. An official American Thoracic Society clinical practice guideline: the clinical utility of bronchoalveolar lavage cellular analysis in interstitial lung disease. Am J Respir Crit Care Med. 2012;185:1004-14. [PMID: 22550210]

Raghu G, Collard HR, Egan JJ, et al. ATS/ERS/JRS/ALAT Committee on Idiopathic Pulmonary Fibrosis. An official ATS/ERS/JRS/ALAT statement: idiopathic pulmonary fibrosis: evidence-based guidelines for diagnosis and management. Am J Respir Crit Care Med. 2011;183:788-824. [PMID: 21471066]

Vij R, Strek ME. Diagnosis and treatment of connective tissue disease-associated interstitial lung disease. Chest. 2013;143:814-24. [PMID: 23460159]

Chapter 96

Pulmonary Vascular Disease

Alpesh N. Amin, MD

The lungs have dual circulation, receiving blood flow from both the pulmonary and systemic circulations. The pulmonary arteries deliver mixed-venous blood from the right ventricle to the pulmonary capillary-alveolar membrane where gas exchange occurs, while the bronchial arteries deliver oxygenated blood directly from the aorta. Both of these circulation systems can be affected by a wide variety of conditions. This chapter will focus on pulmonary embolism and pulmonary (precapillary) hypertension. Other conditions affecting the pulmonary vasculature, such as pulmonary vasculitis and postcapillary pulmonary hypertension (causing pulmonary edema), are addressed elsewhere.

Pulmonary Embolism

Pulmonary embolism (PE) and deep venous thrombosis (DVT) are different manifestations of the same disease, often collectively referred to as venous thromboembolism (VTE). An estimated 2 million cases of DVT, 600,000 cases of symptomatic PE, and 300,000 VTE-related deaths occur annually in the United States. DVT is discussed in the Vascular Diseases chapter (see Chapter 9). PE is the result of DVT formation and subsequent embolization into the pulmonary arteries. The thrombotic material obstructing blood flow through the pulmonary arteries has several physiologic consequences, including ventilation-perfusion aberrations and relative ischemia of the peripheral lung tissues. Pulmonary infarction is relatively uncommon due to the lungs' dual circulation. In some cases, the amount of thrombotic material may be large enough to cause an acute increase in pulmonary vascular resistance, increasing demand on the right ventricle and possibly lowering cardiac output. In its extreme form, this combination of effects can cause right ventricular dysfunction, infarction, and even cardiac arrest. The differential diagnosis of PE is reviewed in Table 1.

Prevention

Patients with known thrombophilic conditions but without contraindications should receive prophylaxis for VTE (see Chapter 53), and all hospitalized patients with VTE risk factors and no significant contraindications should receive risk-appropriate prophylaxis to decrease their risk of venous thromboembolism (see Chapter 9). **Inferior vena cava filters should not be used routinely for perioperative prophylaxis for pulmonary embolism.**

Screening

Screening for either DVT or PE in asymptomatic patients at risk for VTE is not indicated as noninvasive diagnostic tests are insensitive and not associated with improved clinical outcomes.

Diagnosis

The diagnosis of lower extremity DVT is discussed in the Vascular Diseases chapter (see Chapter 9). The most common symptoms of PE are dyspnea, pleuritic chest pain, cough, and hemoptysis; tachypnea, crackles, tachycardia, and accentuated pulmonic component of S_2 are the most common findings. Although these symptoms and signs are sensitive, they lack specificity. Laboratory studies may be suggestive but lack adequate sensitivity and specificity to confirm a diagnosis of PE. Chest radiography may show atelectasis, a small pleural effusion, focal oligemia (lack of vascularity distal to the pulmonary embolus, termed Westermark sign), a peripheral wedge-shaped density above the diaphragm (Hampton hump), or an enlarged right descending pulmonary artery. An electrocardiogram

Table 1. Differential Diagnosis of Pulmonary Embolism

Disorder	Notes
Acute coronary syndrome (see Chapter 3)	Chest pain associated with specific dynamic ECG and echocardiographic changes. Elevated cardiac enzymes can be seen in both acute coronary syndrome and large pulmonary emboli.
Pericarditis (see Chapter 1)	Substernal pain that is sharp, dull, or pressure-like, often relieved with sitting forward; usually pleuritic. ECG usually shows ST-segment elevation (usually diffuse), PR-segment depression, and sinus tachycardia.
Aortic dissection (see Chapter 9)	Substernal chest pain with radiation to the back or mid-scapular region. Chest radiograph may show a widened mediastinal silhouette, a pleural effusion, or both.
Acute pulmonary edema (see Chapter 7)	Elevated venous pressure, S_3, bilateral crackles, and characteristic chest radiograph.
Pleurisy	Sharp, localized chest pain and fever. Pleural effusion may be present. Diagnosis of exclusion.
Pneumothorax	Sudden onset of chest pain and dyspnea. Chest radiograph establishes the diagnosis.
Asthma or chronic obstructive pulmonary disease exacerbation	Dyspnea and wheezing; positive response to bronchodilator (asthma). History of these disorders with a compatible course of illness is helpful.
Panic attack	Diagnosis of exclusion. Patient may have a history of somatization.

ECG = electrocardiogram.

often shows sinus tachycardia but this is a nonspecific finding. Electrocardiographic signs of right-sided heart strain (P-pulmonale, right axis deviation, right bundle branch block, and the combined presence of an S wave in lead I, Q wave in lead III, and T wave inversion in lead III [the S1Q3T3 pattern]) are uncommon but can suggest the presence of a hemodynamically significant embolus. Arterial blood gases are frequently abnormal, but the distributions of arterial PO_2 and the alveolar-arterial oxygen gradient are similar in patients with and without PE; approximately one of every four patients with PE has an arterial PO_2 ≥80 mm Hg.

Because of this, clinical prediction rules have been developed to estimate the pretest probability of PE. Similar to a prediction rule for DVT, there is also a set of Wells criteria specifically for PE (Table 2). **In clinically stable patients (eg, outpatients without hemodynamic compromise) with a low probability of PE, a normal D-dimer value effectively rules out PE and is correlated with an excellent outcome without further workup or treatment.** However, in patients with a higher probability of PE or clinical instability, D-dimer testing should not be used to confirm or exclude the diagnosis, and further testing is indicated (Table 3).

As an initial imaging test for PE, contrast-enhanced CT (also called CT angiography) or ventilation-perfusion (V/Q) scanning is appropriate. Either test can reliably diagnose a large PE; however, only a totally normal V/Q scan excludes PE. CT scans that do not disclose intraluminal filling defects or V/Q scans with matched or small defects are nondiagnostic, and the decision about whether to pursue further workup should be based on a consideration of the pretest probability. If the patient's pretest probability is moderate or high, additional diagnostic tests are required, such as lower extremity ultrasonography or pulmonary angiography.

Because a V/Q scan detects alterations in pulmonary blood flow rather than providing a direct image of a clot (as does contrast-enhanced CT), there are many more indeterminate studies because many cardiopulmonary diseases affect pulmonary blood flow. However, V/Q scans have several favorable characteristics. There is no radiocontrast agent load; therefore, renal failure and low perfusion states are not a contraindication. V/Q scans are also less affected by obesity than contrast-enhanced CT. Contrast-enhanced CT has excellent specificity and ability to provide alternative diagnoses but may not visualize small subsegmental pulmonary emboli.

Table 2. Wells Criteria for Pulmonary Embolism

Clinical Characteristic	Score
Clinical signs/symptoms of DVT	3
No alternative diagnosis more likely than PE	3
Pulse rate >100/min	1.5
Immobilization or surgery in the prior 4 weeks	1.5
Previous history of DVT or PE	1.5
Hemoptysis	1
Cancer actively treated in the prior 6 months	1

A score of <2 points indicates low probability of PE; 2 to 6 points indicates moderate probability of PE; >6 points indicates a high probability of PE.

DVT = deep vein thrombosis; PE = pulmonary embolism.

Table 3. Laboratory and Other Studies for Pulmonary Embolism (PE)

Test	Notes
Plain chest radiography	Sensitivity 84%, specificity 44%. Atelectasis and parenchymal abnormalities are most common (68%), followed by pleural effusion (48%), pleural-based opacity (35%), elevated diaphragm (24%), decreased pulmonary vascularity (21%), prominent central pulmonary artery (15%), cardiomegaly (12%), and pulmonary edema (4%).
Electrocardiography (12-lead)	Sensitivity 50%, specificity 88%. Most common abnormalities are ST-segment and T-wave changes (49%). P pulmonale, right axis deviation, right bundle branch block, and right ventricular hypertrophy occur less frequently. T-wave inversions in precordial leads may indicate more severe right ventricular dysfunction.
Arterial PO_2 and alveolar-arterial oxygen gradient	Sensitivity 81%, specificity 24%. Distributions of arterial PO_2 and alveolar-arterial oxygen gradient are similar in patients with and without PE.
D-dimer assay (ELISA)	Sensitivity 80%-100%, specificity 10%-64%. D-dimer levels <500 ng/mL (500 µL/L) have a high negative predictive value and are useful to exclude PE in patients with low pretest probability or a nondiagnostic lung scan. D-dimer measurement is less useful in patients with malignancy, recent surgery or trauma, and liver disease, because only a few have D-dimer levels <500 ng/mL (500 µL/L).
Ventilation-perfusion lung scan	Normal scan excludes PE. High-probability scan with high pretest clinical probability almost certainly confirms PE. Other scan results should be considered nondiagnostic and indicate need for further testing. PE is present in 87% of patients with a high-probability scan, 30% of patients with an intermediate-probability scan, and 14% of patients with a low-probability scan. Independent assessment of pretest probability is combined with lung scan results to improve diagnostic accuracy.
Pulmonary angiography	Indicated when noninvasive evaluation is nondiagnostic and clinical suspicion is high. Considered the gold standard.
Contrast-enhanced spiral CT of the chest (CT angiography)	Sensitivity (53%-100%) and specificity (81%-100%) of CT are higher for main, lobar, and segmental vessel emboli. An advantage of CT is the diagnosis of other pulmonary parenchymal, pleural, or cardiovascular processes causing or contributing to symptoms.
Echocardiography	Echocardiography is most useful in the evaluation of acute cardiopulmonary syndromes to help diagnose or exclude pericardial tamponade, aortic dissection, myocardial ischemia or infarction, valvular dysfunction, intracardiac shunts, and myocardial rupture.

CT = computed tomography; ELISA = enzyme-linked immunosorbent assay.

Therapy

The pharmacologic treatment options for DVT and PE are similar (see Chapter 9). Some carefully selected patients with PE but without hemodynamic and gas exchange compromise may be candidates for outpatient therapy. Otherwise, most patients with PE are managed in the hospital until stable with supportive care, including treatment of hypoxia and management of hemodynamic instability, if present. Hemodynamic changes resulting from acutely elevated pulmonary arterial resistance suggest a large clot burden and are associated with a high mortality rate. Therefore, a more intensive approach may be justified. Thrombolytic therapy may be effective in patients with circulatory shock due to PE and in patients with acute embolism and pulmonary hypertension or right ventricular dysfunction but without arterial hypotension or shock. Rapid clot lysis may lead to hemodynamic improvement and resolution of right ventricular dysfunction.

Surgical embolectomy for massive PE is indicated if the patient is unstable and thrombolytic therapy is contraindicated or if drug therapy has been unsuccessful. Surgical embolectomy requires the immediate availability of cardiopulmonary bypass; the operative mortality ranges from 10% to 75%.

Inferior vena cava filters prevent PE in patients with DVT within the first 2 weeks of filter placement. Indications include failure of medical therapy (evidence of PE despite adequate anticoagulation) and contraindications to anticoagulant therapy due to unacceptably high bleeding risk. After 1 year, patients may have a higher incidence of postphlebitic syndrome and increased risk of recurrent lower extremity thromboses.

Follow-Up

Once a patient is on stable anticoagulation, therapy should be continued for a duration based on the individual risk factor profile (see Chapter 9, Table 5).

Pulmonary Hypertension

Pulmonary hypertension (PH) is defined by an elevation of mean pulmonary artery pressure of 25 mm Hg (3.3 kPa) or greater during rest. The pulmonary vascular tree is normally a low-pressure, low-resistance system, and when PH develops it may lead to secondary effects on right-sided heart function and patient symptoms.

PH encompasses five distinct disease groups that differ in pathology, cause, and treatment (Table 4). In group 1 (pulmonary arterial hypertension [PAH]), the underlying pathophysiology relates to restricted flow through the pulmonary vasculature with elevation in vascular resistance. An uncommon but important subgroup is idiopathic PAH, which has an approximately 2-to-1 female-to-male predominance and an estimated prevalence of only about 6 cases per million adults. Management of PAH differs from most other causes of PH because treatment is focused on vasodilator therapy.

Over 80% of cases of PH are due to conditions causing elevation of left-sided heart filling pressures or pulmonary disease (groups 2 and 3, respectively). Treatment in these cases typically consists of addressing the underlying cause.

PH is associated with substantial morbidity and mortality. PH usually portends a worse prognosis when it complicates the diseases

Table 4. Classification of Pulmonary Hypertension

1. PAH (resting mPAP ≥25 mm Hg [3.33 kPa] and PCWP ≤15 mm Hg [2.0 kPa])

Idiopathic PAH

Heritable (including *BMPR2*, *ALK1*, endoglin with or without hereditary hemorrhagic telangiectasia)

Drug- and toxin-induced (eg, anorexigens, methamphetamine, rapeseed oil)

Associated with connective tissue diseases (eg, scleroderma), HIV infection, portal hypertension, congenital heart diseases, schistosomiasis, chronic hemolytic anemia

1'. Pulmonary veno-occlusive disease and/or pulmonary capillary hemangiomatosis

2. Pulmonary hypertension owing to left-sided heart disease (mPAP >25 mm Hg [3.33 kPa] with elevated PCWP and left-sided heart dysfunction)

Systolic dysfunction

Diastolic dysfunction

Valvular disease

3. Pulmonary hypertension owing to lung diseases and/or hypoxia (mPAP >25 mm Hg [3.33 kPa] with underlying lung disease)

COPD

Interstitial lung disease

Other pulmonary diseases with mixed restrictive and obstructive pattern

Sleep-disordered breathing

Alveolar hypoventilation disorders

Chronic exposure to high altitude

4. Chronic thromboembolic pulmonary hypertension

5. Pulmonary hypertension with unclear or multifactorial causes

Hematologic disorders: myeloproliferative disorders, sickle cell disease

Systemic disorders: sarcoidosis, pulmonary Langerhans cell histiocytosis, vasculitis

Metabolic disorders: glycogen storage disease, Gaucher disease, thyroid disorders

Others: tumoral obstruction, fibrosing mediastinitis, chronic kidney failure on dialysis

ALK1 = activin receptor-like kinase type 1; *BMPR2* = bone morphogenic protein receptor type 2; COPD = chronic obstructive pulmonary disease; mPAP = mean pulmonary artery pressure; PAH = pulmonary arterial hypertension; PCWP = pulmonary capillary wedge pressure.

Modified from Simonneau G, Robbins IM, Beghetti M, et al. Updated clinical classification of pulmonary hypertension. J Am Coll Cardiol. 2009;54(1 Suppl):S43-54. [PMID: 19555858] With permission from Elsevier. Copyright 2009, Elsevier.

in each of groups 2 through 5. The prognosis among the types of PAH (group 1) varies. Right-sided heart function and functional status (as determined by tests such as the 6-minute walk test) are better predictors of prognosis than the actual value of pulmonary artery pressure. With mild PH, right ventricular function may be preserved and patients may be asymptomatic. As disease worsens, however, right-sided heart function deteriorates and symptoms progress.

Diagnosis

Fatigue and dyspnea with exertion are the most common symptoms. Patients may have palpitations or chest pain that may be ill-defined or angina-like. With advanced PH, symptoms and signs of right ventricular decompensation, including syncope, edema, ascites, and hepatomegaly, may be noted. Depending on the severity of the PH, the cardiac examination may show a left parasternal lift; augmented jugular *a* wave and pulmonic component of S_2 or a single S_2; murmurs of tricuspid regurgitation or pulmonic insufficiency; and right ventricular S_3 or S_4 gallops.

The evaluation is similar for most patients with PH, but certain considerations may require special studies. Chest imaging studies suggest the diagnosis when pulmonary artery enlargement is noted. A diagnosis of PH can be confirmed only by right heart catheterization and direct measurement of mean pulmonary artery pressure. Echocardiography, with an estimated mean systolic pulmonary artery pressure of 40 mm Hg or greater, is highly suggestive. However, echocardiography may underestimate pulmonary artery pressures, particularly in the setting of advanced diffuse parenchymal lung disease. Right heart catheterization is required to confirm the diagnosis and to assess its cause if therapy for PH is to be considered.

Once PH is confirmed, evaluation is generally directed at determining the specific cause and the anatomic location and extent of vascular involvement. An array of studies (such as imaging of the chest to assess parenchymal lung disease; V/Q scanning to assess potential chronic thromboembolic disease; pulmonary function testing with DLCO; serologic studies for connective tissue disease, liver disease, and HIV; and sleep studies) may be helpful in selected patients. Biomarkers such as B-type natriuretic peptide or troponins may also provide prognostic information. Some patients with PH and all patients suspected of having PAH should be considered for right heart/pulmonary artery catheterization to confirm the diagnosis and guide therapy.

Six-minute walk studies provide a simple and important functional assessment. Repeat 6-minute walk, echocardiography, and/or catheterization studies are useful in assessing progression of disease and response to therapy.

Therapy

Treatment of most forms of PH without isolated PAH (see groups 2, 3, 4, and 5 in Table 4) is directed at the underlying condition. This may include optimal treatment of systolic and diastolic heart failure; oxygen therapy for patients with resting, exercise, or sleep-related desaturation; appropriate treatment of chronic obstructive pulmonary disease; and evaluation and management of obstructive sleep apnea.

In rare instances, despite aggressive treatment of underlying heart and lung disease, PH may persist and cause significant patient morbidity. The benefits of vasodilator therapy in this population remain unproved, and potential adverse effects of vasodilator therapy (including fluid retention, hypotension, and worsening hypoxemia from V/Q mismatch) underscore the need for careful patient selection and referral to a specialist with expertise in this area.

Bibliography

Agnelli G, Becattini C. Acute pulmonary embolism. N Engl J Med. 2010; 363:266-74. [PMID: 20592294]

Forfia PR, Trow TK. Diagnosis of pulmonary arterial hypertension. Clin Chest Med. 2013;34:665-81. [PMID: 24267297]

Section 11
Rheumatology

Associate Editor – Thomas M. De Fer, MD, FACP

High Value Care Recommendations

- Nonspecific rheumatologic tests (eg, rheumatoid factor, antinuclear antibodies, erythrocyte sedimentation rate) should be ordered only to confirm a diagnosis suggested by the history and physical examination and not for general evaluation of nonspecific joint pain.

- Obtain radiographs in patients with acute knee pain only in those who fulfill ≥1 of the Ottawa knee rules.

- In chronic knee pain syndromes, radiographs are often unlikely to alter management. Advanced imaging (such as magnetic resonance imaging [MRI]) should be used only in selected patients with knee pain, often in consultation with a specialist.

- Arthroscopic surgery has not been shown to improve outcomes as compared with pharmacologic and physical therapy for non-osteoarthritis-related knee pain.

- Imaging of the shoulder for acute pain should be based on the clinical presentation; except for specific indications (such as a rotator cuff tear), radiography has a limited role in the diagnosis and management of chronic shoulder pain.

- In clinical practice, the diagnosis of osteoarthritis should be based primarily on history and physical examination findings. Laboratory tests are not helpful for diagnosis.

- Due to low sensitivity, the absence of findings on plain radiography does not rule out symptomatic disease in any joint.

- Therapy for osteoarthritis should begin with and always include nonpharmacologic measures.

- Acetaminophen is first-line pharmacologic therapy for osteoarthritis because it is safe, effective, and inexpensive.

- Although cylcooxygenase-2-selective nonsteroidal anti-inflammatory drugs (NSAIDs) are somewhat less likely to cause gastrointestinal ulcers, they are not more effective than nonselective NSAIDs, are significantly more expensive, and are associated with an increased risk for adverse cardiovascular events.

- Opiate analgesics may play an additional role in the treatment of patients whose pain is refractory to other treatments but should not be used routinely due to potential side effects and dependency.

- Asymptomatic hyperuricemia itself is not an indication for uric acid-lowering therapy.

- Uric acid levels alone are inadequate to confirm or exclude a diagnosis of gout.

- Allopurinol is typically safe and effective and is considered first-line therapy for most patients with an indication for uric acid lowering treatment.

- There is no evidence to support the use of antibiotic prophylaxis to prevent infectious arthritis in patients with prosthetic joints undergoing procedures.

- No adequate screening test for rheumatoid arthritis (RA) currently exists and there are no screening recommendations, including testing for rheumatoid factor (RF), for otherwise healthy individuals.

- Antinuclear antibodies (ANA) may be positive in 40% of patients with RA and is a nonspecific finding.

- Magnetic resonance imaging and ultrasonography are more sensitive imaging modalities for early erosive disease compared with radiography. However, their roles in diagnosis have not been established and they are not obtained routinely.

- Testing for HLA-B27 positivity generally is not helpful diagnostically in patients suspected of having spondyloarthritis because most HLA-B27–positive persons do not develop disease.

- Routine testing for ANA or rheumatoid factor in patients with suspected fibromyalgia is not indicated and may be confusing as these tests often are abnormal in normal individuals.

- Opioid analgesics and glucocorticoids have no demonstrated efficacy in fibromyalgia and should be avoided.

Chapter 97

Approach to Joint Pain

Thomas M. DeFer, MD

Joint pain can be characterized in several overlapping ways that are helpful in formulating a differential diagnosis, including whether the source of pain is articular or periarticular, the specific joints involved, the number and symmetry of involved joints, the time course and pattern of joint involvement, and whether the process is inflammatory or noninflammatory. The presence or absence of extra-articular manifestations also can provide important diagnostic clues to joint pain.

In some clinical situations, the cause of joint pain can be determined quickly, but in other cases the patient will need to be seen multiple times before the diagnosis becomes apparent. This is particularly true in the early stages of systemic conditions that may initially present solely as joint pain. A flow diagram for the evaluation of joint pain is presented in Figure 1. **Nonspecific rheumatologic tests (eg, rheumatoid factor, antinuclear antibodies, erythrocyte sedimentation rate) should be ordered only to confirm a diagnosis suggested by the history and physical examination and not for general evaluation of nonspecific joint pain.** Specific serologic studies associated with particular rheumatologic conditions in which joint pain may be a major manifestation are presented in Table 1. These tests also have limited diagnostic utility in the setting of low pretest probability. Likewise, plain radiographs are indicated only when there is a likelihood that the results will change management (see Table 2). In patients with joint effusion, joint fluid analysis can establish the diagnosis of infection or narrow the differential diagnosis. Table 3 categorizes joint fluid findings.

Location and Pattern

The particular joint or joints involved may suggest certain diagnoses, such as the first metatarsophalangeal joint, gout; the knee, osteoarthritis; and the metacarpophalangeal joints, rheumatoid arthritis. The spondyloarthritides are overlapping conditions that characteristically involve the axial skeleton (ie, spine and sacroiliac, sternoclavicular, and manubriosternal joints) and large appendicular joints (see Chapter 104). Ankylosing spondylitis is the most common example of a spondyloarthritis; others include reactive arthritis, psoriatic arthritis, and enteropathic arthritis (associated with inflammatory bowel disease). Joint pain can affect a single joint (monoarticular), two to four joints (oligoarticular), or multiple joints (polyarticular). Common monoarthropathies include gout, calcium pyrophosphate dihydrate crystal deposition disease (pseudogout), septic arthritis, and avascular necrosis. The spondyloarthritidies are characteristically oligoarticular. Rheumatoid arthritis, systemic lupus erythematosus (SLE), and osteoarthritis usually are polyarticular. Acute gout occasionally can present in a polyarticular manner, which may cause diagnostic confusion. Determine symmetry if more than one joint is involved; joint involvement in rheumatoid arthritis, SLE, and osteoarthritis typically is symmetric. Table 4 presents a differential diagnosis of inflammatory arthritides based on the pattern and location of joint involvement.

Table 1. Disease Associations of Certain Serologic Studies in Patients with Joint Pain

Test	Association	Sensitivity/Specificity
ANA, centromere pattern	Limited PSS (CREST syndrome)	10%-30% sensitivity
ANA, nucleolar pattern	Systemic sclerosis (scleroderma)	20% sensitivity
ANA, peripheral pattern	Systemic lupus erythematosus	95% sensitivity, nonspecific
ANA, speckled and diffuse patterns	Nonspecific	
Anti-CCP antibody	Rheumatoid arthritis	70% sensitivity, more specific than rheumatoid factor
Anti-dsDNA antibody	Systemic lupus erythematosus	60% sensitivity
Antihistone antibody	Drug-induced lupus erythematosus	95% sensitivity
Anti-Jo-1 antibody	Polymyositis/dermatomyositis	20%-30% sensitivity
Anti-Ro (SSA)/Anti-La (SSB) antibodies	Sjögren syndrome; systemic lupus erythematosus	Sjögren syndrome: 70% sensitivity; lupus: 30% sensitivity
Anti-U1-RNP antibody	Mixed connective tissue disease	100% sensitivity
Anti-Scl-70 (anti-topoisomerase I) antibody	Systemic sclerosis (scleroderma)	10%-30% sensitivity
Anti-Smith antibody	Systemic lupus erythematosus	30% sensitivity, 99% specificity
Rheumatoid factor	Rheumatoid arthritis	70% sensitivity, nonspecific

ANA = antinuclear antibody; CCP = cyclic citrullinated peptide; CREST = calcinosis, Raynaud phenomenon, esophageal dysmotility, sclerodactyly, telangiectasia; dsDNA = double-stranded DNA; RNP = ribonucleoprotein; PSS = progressive systemic sclerosis.

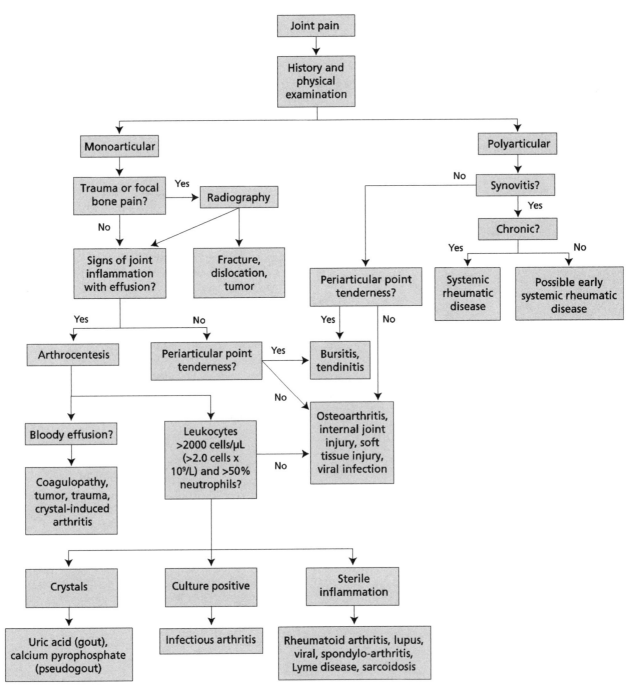

Figure 1. Algorithm for evaluation of joint pain.

Articular and Nonarticular Disorders

Differentiate articular from nonarticular sources of joint pain. Articular disorders are characterized by internal/deep joint pain that is exacerbated by active and passive motion and by reduced range of motion; joint pain may be accompanied by joint effusion, synovial thickening, joint deformity or instability, crepitations, clicking, popping, or locking. Periarticular disorders are associated with greater joint pain with active rather than passive motion; in addition, range of motion often is preserved, and tenderness and signs of inflammation are removed from the actual joint. Common periarticular disorders include bursitis, tendinitis, polymyalgia rheumatica, fibromyalgia, and enthesopathies (inflammation of tendinous or lig-

amentous attachments to bone). Enthesopathies are characteristic of spondyloarthritis; the most common are Achilles tendonitis and plantar fasciitis. Dactylitis ("sausage digits") is another classic feature of spondyloarthritis, particularly psoriatic arthritis and reactive arthritis; dactylitis is caused by synovitis and enthesitis of the fingers and toes (Plate 69). Pain also may be referred or radiate to the joints from nonarticular sources (eg, shoulder pain associated with cervical radiculopathy) or other local pathology.

Time Course and Development

Determine the time course and pattern of development of the joint pain. Some arthropathies present in an acute manner (eg, infection,

Table 2. Radiographic Findings of Common Rheumatic Conditions

Rheumatic Condition	Radiographic Findings
Rheumatoid arthritis	Bony erosions; periarticular osteopenia; subluxations; soft-tissue swelling; MCP and PIP involvement on hand radiograph
Psoriatic arthritis	Destructive arthritis with erosions and osteophytes; DIP involvement; "pencil-in-cup" deformity on hand radiograph; arthritis mutilans
Osteoarthritis	Asymmetric joint-space narrowing; osteophytes; subchondral sclerosis and cystic changes; degenerative disk disease with collapse of disks; degenerative joint disease with facet joint osteophytes; these findings lead to spondylolisthesis (anterior/posterior misalignment of the spine) and kyphosis
Ankylosing spondylitis	Sacroiliitis; squaring of the vertebral bodies; bridging vertical enthesophytes
Diffuse idiopathic skeletal hyperostosis	Calcification of the anterior longitudinal ligament; bridging horizontal syndesmophytes
Calcium pyrophosphate deposition disease	Chondrocalcinosis, most commonly of the knees, shoulders, wrists, pubic symphysis

DIP = distal interphalangeal; MCP = metacarpophalangeal; PIP = proximal interphalangeal.

gout, pseudogout); all patients with acute monoarticular arthritis require arthrocentesis and joint fluid analysis to establish the diagnosis. Other arthropathies have subacute or chronic presentations, such as osteoarthritis. Occasionally, some chronic arthropathies, such rheumatoid arthritis, may have an abrupt onset.

Ongoing development of joint pain follows one of three major patterns: additive, migratory, or intermittent. With an additive pattern, new joints become involved while the previous sites remain affected (eg, osteoarthritis, rheumatoid arthritis). A migratory pattern describes a sequential arthritis, in which a newly inflamed joint appears simultaneously with or immediately after a prior joint's improvement (eg, gonococcal arthritis, rheumatic fever). With an intermittent pattern, affected joints improve completely, and then at a later time the same or different joints become affected in a similar manner (eg, gout, pseudogout, SLE).

Inflammatory and Noninflammatory Pain

Joint pain is divided into inflammatory and noninflammatory categories (Table 5). Inflammatory joint pain is characterized by the presence of synovitis (soft-tissue swelling, tenderness, warmth, and effusion) and defines true arthritis. Inflammatory arthritides include septic arthritis, gout, pseudogout, rheumatoid arthritis, SLE, and the spondyloarthropathies. Inflammatory conditions are notable for more severe and prolonged (often ≥1 hour) morning stiffness and gelling (stiffness after a period of inactivity) that improve with activity. Inflammatory signs also are present in some periarticular conditions (eg, bursitis, tenosynovitis, enthesopathies) but are less pronounced. Noninflammatory conditions are associated with less morning stiffness, typically <30 to 60 minutes. Osteoarthritis is by far the most common noninflammatory joint disorder.

Inflammatory arthropathies can be accompanied by systemic symptoms, including malaise, fatigue, weight loss, and fever. Laboratory manifestations indicative of inflammation also are seen (eg, elevated erythrocyte sedimentation rate and/or C-reactive protein, anemia).

Extra-articular Manifestations

Focal signs of inflammation or organ dysfunction beyond the joints have important diagnostic value (see Table 4). Concomitant findings involving the skin, eyes, mucous membranes, nervous system (central or peripheral), kidneys, gastrointestinal system, or heart all are suggestive of systemic inflammatory disease. For example, in addition to rheumatoid nodules, the major extra-articular manifestations of rheumatoid arthritis are pulmonary (pleuritis, interstitial lung disease, pulmonary nodules), cardiac (pericarditis, carditis), and ocular (scleritis, episcleritis). SLE can have renal, hematologic, neurologic, and serosal manifestations. Psoriatic arthritis occurs in 5% to 8% of patients with psoriasis. Reactive arthritis appears 1 to 4 weeks

Table 3. Joint Fluid Categories

Characteristic	Normal	Group I[a] (Noninflammatory)	Group II[b] (Inflammatory)	Group III[c] (Infectious)
Volume (knee)	<3.5 mL	>3.5 mL	>3.5 mL	>3.5 mL
Viscosity	Very high	High	Low	Variable
Color	Clear	Straw	Straw to opalescent	Variable with organism
Clarity	Transparent	Transparent	Translucent, opaque at times	Opaque
Leukocyte count (cells/µL and cells × 10⁹/L)	200 (0.2)	200-2000 (0.2-20)	2000-100,000 (20-100)	>50,000 (50.0) (usually >100,000 [100])
Neutrophils (%)	<25	<25	>50	>75
Culture	Negative	Negative	Negative	Usually positive

[a]Examples include osteoarthritis, avascular necrosis, hemochromatosis, and sickle cell disease.

[b]Examples include crystal-induced arthritis, rheumatoid arthritis, spondyloarthritis, and systemic lupus erythematosus.

[c]Infectious arthritis (eg, staphylococcal infection, gonococcal infection, tuberculosis).

Table 4. Patterns of Joint Involvement in the Differential Diagnosis of Inflammatory Arthritis

Differential Diagnosis	Pattern of Joint Involvement							Common Locations and Presentations	Extra-articular Manifestations
	Symmetric	Asymmetric	Spinal	Monoarticular	Oligoarticular	Polyarticular	Migratory		
Bacterial (non-GC) infection	–	++++	++	++++	+++	+	–	Knee, hip, shoulder, wrist	Infective endocarditis
Disseminated gonococcal infection		++++			++++		++++	Knee, wrist, ankle, tenosynovitis	Painless pustular skin lesions
Crystal-induced arthritis									
Gout		++++	+	+++	+++	+	+	First MTP joint, top of foot, heel, ankle, knee	Tophi, nephrolithiasis, nephropathy
CPPD (pseudogout)	++	+++	–	+++	++	++		Knee, wrist, shoulder, ankle, elbow	
Rheumatoid arthritis	++++	–	+++	–	+	++++		Wrist, MCP joints, PIP joints, MTP joints, ankle, knee, elbow, shoulder, cervical spine	Nodules, sicca syndrome, interstitial lung disease, Felty syndrome (splenomegaly and leukopenia)
Spondyloarthritis									
Psoriatic arthritis	++	+++	+	++	+++	++		Knee, DIP joints, spondylitis, sacroiliitis, dactylitis, enthesitis	Psoriasis
Enteropathic arthritis	++	+++	+	++	+++	++		Spondylitis, sacroiliitis, knee, MCP joints	Crohn disease, ulcerative colitis
Reactive arthritis	–	++++	+	++	+++	+	–	Knee, ankle, enthesitis, dactylitis, Achilles tendinitis, plantar fasciitis, sacroiliitis	Urethritis, gastroenteritis, circinate balanitis, keratoderma blenorrhagicum, conjunctivitis, uveitis, oral ulcers
Lyme disease		++++			++++		++++	Knee, shoulder, ankle, elbow, wrist, temporomandibular joint	Erythema migrans, carditis, meningitis, neuropathy, conjunctivitis
Acute rheumatic fever		++++			++	+++	++++	Knee, ankle, elbow, wrist	Pharyngitis, carditis, nodules, erythema marginatum, chorea

CPPD = calcium pyrophosphate deposition disease; DIP = distal interphalangeal; GC = gonococcal; MCP = metacarpophalangeal; MTP = metatarsophalangeal; PIP = proximal interphalangeal.

after a genitourinary or gastrointestinal infection (ie, urethritis, cervicitis, or diarrhea). Sponndyloarthritis can be associated with ulcerative colitis and Crohn disease. Adult-onset Still disease is an uncommon systemic inflammatory disorder characterized by quotidian fever, evanescent rash, and multisystem involvement in which arthritis is a prominent feature.

Bibliography

Mies Richie A, Francis ML. Diagnostic approach to polyarticular joint pain. Am Fam Physician 2003;68:1151-60. [PMID: 14524403]

Table 5. Features of Inflammatory Versus Noninflammatory Arthritis

Feature	Type of Arthritis	
	Inflammatory	Noninflammatory
Physical examination findings	Joint inflammation (warmth, erythema, soft-tissue swelling, effusion)	No signs of inflammation; bony proliferation in osteoarthritis
Morning stiffness	>1 h (generally)	<1 h
Systemic symptoms	Low-grade fever, fatigue, rash	None
Synovial fluid findings	Leukocyte count >2000/µL [2.0 × 10^9/L], predominantly neutrophils	Leukocyte count <2000/µL [2.0 × 10^9/L], <50% neutrophils
Other laboratory studies	ESR and/or CRP often (but not always) elevated, anemia of inflammation, positive rheumatoid factor or anti-CCP antibody	Normal findings
Plain radiographs	Erosions, periostitis, joint-space narrowing	Joint-space narrowing, osteophytes, subchondral sclerosis

CCP = cyclic citrullinated peptide; CRP = C-reactive protein; ESR = erythrocyte sedimentation rate.

Chapter 98

Approach to Knee and Shoulder Pain

Joseph Rencic, MD

Knee Pain

Osteoarthritis is by far the most common cause of chronic knee pain in older persons. Acute knee pain may be due to inflammation (eg, crystal-induced arthritis, rheumatoid arthritis), trauma, overuse syndromes, or infection. The knee is the most commonly infected joint, and septic arthritis must be considered in all patients with unilateral knee pain.

Evaluation

Determine location, duration, and precipitating and relieving factors. Ask about a locking (meniscus tear) or "popping" sensation (ligament rupture). Consider the direction of force on the knee in traumatic knee pain to predict the most likely structural injury. Joint effusion occurring <2 hours after trauma suggests anterior cruciate ligament rupture or tibial fracture.

Inspect the knee for structural changes or swelling both in the standing and supine positions, then palpate for warmth, tenderness, and effusion. Palpate the medial and lateral joint line for collateral ligament injury. Also palpate the anserine bursa and popliteal fossa if symptoms are present in these areas. Small effusions may be noted by "milking" joint fluid into the suprapatellar pouch and then pushing medially on the lateral knee just inferior to the patella with the knee extended. A fluid wave or bulge will be apparent in the medial compartment. Observe gait and assess range of motion, which is normally 160 degrees of flexion to full extension. Check for stability of major ligaments by performing stress maneuvers. Ask the patient to squat and walk in the squatting position; if this can be performed, even if painful, the integrity and stability of the joint are intact. Arthrocentesis should be performed when diagnostic uncertainty exists or when symptomatic relief will result (Table 1).

Knee Pain Syndromes

The most common cause of knee pain in patients aged <45 years, especially in women, is patellofemoral syndrome. The pain is peripatellar and exacerbated by overuse (eg, running), descending stairs, or prolonged sitting. Diagnosis is confirmed by firmly compressing the patella against the femur and moving it up and down along the groove of the femur, reproducing pain or crepitation. The condition is self-limited; minimizing high-impact activity and use of nonsteroidal anti-inflammatory drugs (NSAIDs) improve symptoms.

Prepatellar bursitis is associated with anterior knee pain and swelling anterior to the patella; it often is caused by trauma or repetitive kneeling. Range of motion is not limited. Infectious prepatellar bursitis can be subtle; if warmth and erythema are present, aspirate to rule out infection. Located medially, about 6 cm below the joint line, the anserine bursa also can cause pain, which is worse with activity and at night. In general, treatment of bursitis includes avoidance of the inciting activity, ice, NSAIDs, and local glucocorticoid injection for persistent symptoms.

Iliotibial band syndrome is a common cause of knife-like lateral knee pain that occurs with vigorous flexion-extension activities of the knee (eg, running). Treat with rest and stretching exercises.

Trauma may result in fractures or ligament tears, which produce a noticeable "popping" sensation in 50% of patients. Typically, a large effusion collects rapidly after trauma. **Obtain radiographs in patients with acute knee pain only in those who fulfill ≥1 of the Ottawa knee rules** (Table 2).

Anterior cruciate ligament tears occur with sudden twisting (cutting or pivoting) resulting in valgus stress and hyperextension injuries. Collateral ligament tears occur with medial or lateral force without twisting. Posterior cruciate ligament tears occur with trauma to a flexed knee (eg, dashboard injury). Check for stability of major ligaments by placing the knee in 160 degrees of extension and performing medial and lateral stress maneuvers; normal knees will have minimal give. Flex the knee 20 degrees. Grasp the patient's thigh above the patella with one hand, and with the opposite hand placed behind the patient's knee exert forward pressure to the back of the knee in an attempt to move the tibia forward (Lachman test). A full tear of the anterior cruciate ligament is associated with joint laxity (compared with the other knee) without a firm end point (positive likelihood ratio [LR(+)] = 25; negative likelihood ratio [LR(-)] = 0.1). With the knee in 90 degrees of flexion with the patient's foot resting on the examination table, check for posterior cruciate rupture by applying posterior force to the leg. Posterior movement of the leg with respect to the thigh, joint laxity, and lack of a firm end point support a diagnosis of posterior cruciate ligament rupture.

Table 1. Indications for Arthrocentesis

Unexplained monoarthritis
Suspected joint infection
Unexplained joint effusion
Suspected crystal-induced arthritis
Suspected hemarthrosis
Symptomatic relief from large painful effusion

Table 2. Ottawa Knee Rules

Obtain a knee radiograph following trauma for:

1. Patient aged >55 y
2. Isolated tenderness of the patella
3. Tenderness at the head of the fibula
4. Inability to flex knee to 90 degrees
5. Inability to bear weight immediately after injury or in the emergency department

Table 3. Common Causes of Shoulder Pain

Disorder	Notes
Rotator cuff tendonitis	Lateral shoulder pain aggravated by reaching, raising the arm overhead, or lying on the side. Subacromial pain to palpation and with passive/resisted abduction.
Rotator cuff tear	Shoulder weakness, loss of function, tendonitis symptoms, and nocturnal pain. Similar to tendonitis examination, plus weakness with abduction and external rotation. Positive drop arm test; in this test, the patient lowers the arms from a fully abducted position; inability to lower the affected arm smoothly is highly specific (but not sensitive) for rotator cuff tear.
Bicipital tendonitis/rupture	Anterior shoulder pain with lifting, overhead reaching, and flexion; reduced pain after rupture. Bicipital groove tenderness and pain with resisted elbow flexion. "Popeye" lump in antecubital fossa following rupture.
Adhesive capsulitis	Progressive decrease in range of motion, more from stiffness than from pain. Loss of external rotation and abduction (unable to scratch lower back or fully lift arm straight overhead).
Acromioclavicular syndromes	Anterior shoulder pain and deformity, usually from trauma or overuse. Localized joint tenderness and deformity (osteophytes, separation); pain with adduction.
Glenohumeral arthritis	Gradual onset of anterior pain and stiffness. Anterior joint-line tenderness, decreased range of motion, and crepitation.

Meniscus tears present as pain, locking, and clicking. The most common traumatic cause involves twisting with the foot planted. Tenderness usually localizes to the joint line on the affected side, with pain elicited with tibial rotation as the leg is extended. No physical examination maneuver reliably rules in or rules out the diagnosis.

Referred hip pain due to L_5-S_1 radiculopathy can cause knee pain. In this case, the knee examination will be normal, but findings consistent with radiculopathy (eg weakness, sensory abnormalities, and/or diminished deep tendon reflexes) may be present.

Whether knee imaging should be obtained is based primarily on the clinical presentation. **In chronic knee pain syndromes, radiographs are often unlikely to alter management. Advanced imaging (such as magnetic resonance imaging [MRI]) should be used only in selected patients with knee pain, often in consultation with a specialist.**

Treatment

Treatment of knee pain depends on the severity and extent of injury. For most tendinous, bursal, or acute arthritic pain syndromes, standard therapy consists of Rest, Ice, Compression, and Elevation (RICE) for the first 24 to 48 hours. For more severe or chronic pain, pharmacologic options range from acetaminophen and NSAIDs to local glucocorticoid injections; tramadol and opioids may be appropriate in select patients. Although acetaminophen's efficacy is limited in moderate to severe pain, its low risk profile in appropriate doses, especially in the elderly, make an initial trial appropriate. Physical therapy is an important adjunct to any pharmacologic approach. Weight loss, quadriceps strengthening, and aerobic exercise are recommended for chronic knee osteoarthritis. **Arthroscopic surgery has not been shown to improve outcomes as compared with pharmacologic and physical therapy for non-osteoarthritis-related knee pain.** For severe osteoarthritis, total knee replacement improves both quality of life and functional ability.

Shoulder Pain

Shoulder pain occurs in up to 35% of the general population. It often evolves into a chronic, disabling problem (Table 3). The most common cause is irritation of the subacromial bursa or rotator cuff tendons from mechanical impingement between the humeral head and the coracoacromial arch, which includes the acromion, coracoacro-mial ligament, and the coracoid process (Figure 1). Chronic overhead activity may contribute to narrowing of this space, which can lead to recurrent microtrauma and chronic local inflammation of rotator cuff tendons.

Evaluation

Determine whether the pain is acute or chronic, and investigate possible mechanisms of injury (eg, trauma, occupational, or recreational activities). Ask for precipitating and relieving factors. Stiffness or loss of motion suggests glenohumeral arthritis or adhesive capsulitis, whereas referred pain is not exacerbated by shoulder movement.

Inspect the shoulder; asymmetry indicates a possible dislocation. Palpate the major anatomic landmarks, including the subacromial space below the tip of the acromion process, the acromioclavicular joint, the biceps tendon groove, the cervical spine, and the scapula. Ask the patient to raise both arms straight above the head (testing flexion and abduction), put both hands on the back of the

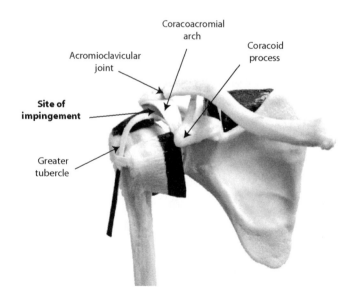

Figure 1. Shoulder anatomy as it relates to impingement syndrome.

head (testing external rotation), and put both hands behind the back (testing extension and internal rotation). The ability to perform all these maneuvers, even if painful, indicates normal joint anatomy and muscle strength. If the patient cannot perform these maneuvers actively, check passive range of motion; inability to perform passive maneuvers suggests an articular (glenohumeral or capsular) rather than a periarticular cause. Perform a neurologic examination to rule out radiculopathy as a cause of referred pain.

Imaging of the shoulder for acute pain should be based on the clinical presentation; except for specific indications (such as a rotator cuff tear), radiography has a limited role in the diagnosis and management of chronic shoulder pain.

Shoulder Pain Syndromes

Patients with rotator cuff tendonitis and subacromial bursitis typically have gradually worsening pain that limits motion, is worse at night, and may extend down the arm but rarely extends below the elbow.

On examination, use one hand to passively raise the arm in forward flexion while depressing the scapula with the other hand. This action pushes the greater tuberosity into the anterior acromion process and will elicit pain when impingement is present (impingement sign). The circumduction-adduction shoulder maneuver (Clancy test) is helpful for diagnosing acromioclavicular disease and rotator cuff pathology (LR(+) = 19, LR(-) = 0.05). The patient stands with the head turned to the contralateral (uninvolved) shoulder. The affected shoulder is circumducted and adducted across the body to shoulder level, with the elbow extended and the thumb pointing toward the floor. Exert a uniform downward force on the patient's distal forearm/wrist while the patient resists the movement. Anterolateral shoulder pain and/or weakness constitutes a positive test. Pain without weakness is consistent with tendonitis; pain with weakness is consistent with tendon tear. Check internal rotation by having the patient move the thumb up the spine as far as possible, looking for pain or restricted movement.

Severe pain and frank weakness (inability to maintain the arm at 90 degrees of abduction, drop arm sign) suggest complete rupture of the rotator cuff tendons. MRI is the most sensitive and specific imaging modality for complete or partial rotator cuff tears, although ultrasonography is quite good and more cost effective.

Other causes of shoulder pain include glenohumeral instability, inflammatory arthropathies (eg, rheumatoid arthritis), septic arthritis, acromioclavicular degeneration, and myofascial pain (eg, trapezius strain). Shoulder pain in the setting of a normal shoulder examination suggests referred pain from a nerve injury, such as a spinal nerve root compression syndrome (eg, cervical spondylosis, herniated disc) or brachial plexus pathology (eg, viral infection, superior sulcus tumor). A careful neurologic examination may demonstrate weakness, decreased sensation, or altered deep tendon reflexes, which support the diagnosis of cervical radiculopathy. Osteoarthritis of the glenohumeral joint is relatively uncommon. These other causes of shoulder pain may require input from a rheumatologist or orthopedist; therapy is based on the specific pathology.

Treatment

Treatment of shoulder pain depends on the severity and extent of injury. A 2-week trial of an NSAID and rest is reasonable initial therapy for tendinitis or bursitis. If no improvement occurs within 4 to 6 weeks, physical therapy, subacromial glucocorticoid injection, or (rarely) surgery may be helpful. Several small studies suggest that glucocorticoid injections as compared with a placebo may improve pain in the short to medium term. If there is no response to conservative therapy in 6 to 12 weeks, consultation with a rheumatologist or an orthopedist is the appropriate next step.

Bibliography

Matsen FA 3rd. Clinical practice. Rotator-cuff failure. N Engl J Med. 2008; 358:2138-47. [PMID: 18480206]

Schraeder TL, Terek RM, Smith CC. Clinical evaluation of the knee. N Engl J Med. 2010;363:e5. [PMID: 20660399]

Chapter 99

Osteoarthritis

Robert Pargament, MD

Osteoarthritis, the most common form of arthritis, is characterized by breakdown of articular cartilage, subchondral bone alterations, meniscus degeneration, and bone repair (osteophytes) with minimal synovial inflammatory response. Loss of articular cartilage causes pain and loss of joint mobility. Osteoarthritis can involve any joint but most often affects the weight-bearing joints (knee, hip, spine) as well as the distal and proximal interphalangeal and first carpometacarpal joints of the hand. The prevalence of osteoarthritis is increasing; the lifetime risk of development of osteoarthritis of the knee, for example, is somewhere between 40% and 50%. Risk factors for development of osteoarthritis include advanced age, female gender, obesity, prior joint injury and genetic factors.

Prevention

Obesity and repetitive joint strain may be modified to decrease the risk of developing osteoarthritis. Counsel patients with a body mass index >25 to lose weight. For each additional pound of body weight, the force across the knee increases by 0.9 to 1.4 kg (2 to 3 lb), thus increasing the risk of cartilage damage. Avoiding repetitive knee bending and heavy lifting helps reduce excessive loading of the knee and may reduce osteoarthritis. Advise athletes to follow graduated training schedules to build muscle strength, which helps improve joint stability and avoid intrinsic damage.

Diagnosis

In clinical practice, the diagnosis of osteoarthritis should be based primarily on history and physical examination findings. Laboratory tests are not helpful for diagnosis.

Osteoarthritis pain is a poorly localized, deep, aching sensation. Pain initially occurs with joint use; as the disease progresses, pain occurs at rest. Morning stiffness typically lasts <30 minutes. Joint examination findings may include tenderness, swelling, crepitation, bony enlargement or deformity, restricted motion, pain with passive movement, and instability.

In the hands, bony enlargement of the distal interphalangeal joints (Heberden nodes) and proximal interphalangeal joints (Bouchard nodes) is particularly characteristic of osteoarthritis (Plate 70). Osteoarthritis of the first carpometacarpal joint is very common. It causes pain at the base of the thumb and bony enlargement, producing a squared appearance to the base of the hand. Crepitation and pain may be elicited with passive circular motion of the carpometacarpal joint ("grind test").

For the knee, diagnostic criteria developed by the American College of Rheumatology include age >50 years, morning stiffness <30 minutes, crepitation, bony tenderness, bony enlargement, and no palpable warmth. The combination of knee pain plus at least 3 of these criteria is associated with a sensitivity of 95% and specificity of 69% for diagnosis of knee osteoarthritis. Some patients with knee osteoarthritis may have intermittent acute exacerbations with evidence of inflammation (ie, effusion and minor warmth), which can initially be challenging to differentiate from another inflammatory process (eg, pseudogout, infection).

Due to low sensitivity, the absence of findings on plain radiography does not rule out symptomatic disease in any joint. Osteophytes, subchondral sclerosis, and joint-space narrowing seen on radiographs are indicative of osteoarthritis (Figure 1, Figure 2, and Figure 3). Radiographs are most helpful in diagnosing osteoarthritis in the hip but only help to confirm osteoarthritis in the knee; they have lower sensitivity and specificity than physical examination for osteoarthritis of the hand. If these findings are seen in the knee, specificity for diagnosis increases from 69% to 86%.

Joint aspiration should be considered if an effusion is present and the diagnosis is in question or a concomitant infection is suspected. Synovial fluid typically is clear, with a leukocyte count <2000/µL (2.0 ×10^9/L).

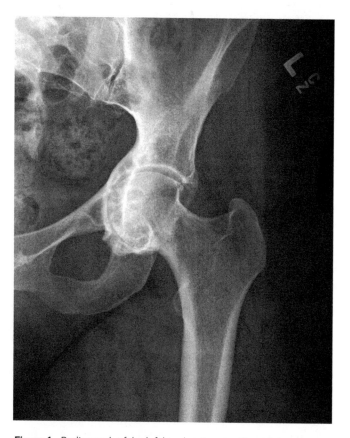

Figure 1. Radiograph of the left hip showing significant joint-space narrowing and subchondral sclerosis.

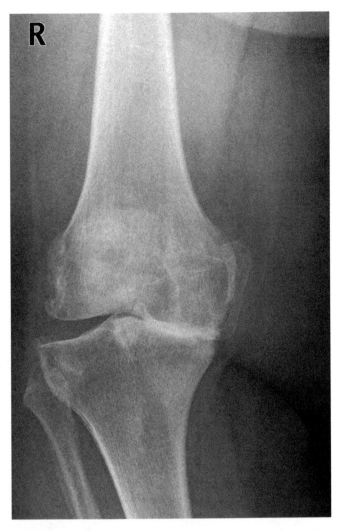

Figure 2. Radiograph of the right knee showing significant medial compartment joint-space narrowing and both medial and lateral osteophyte formation, consistent with osteoarthritis.

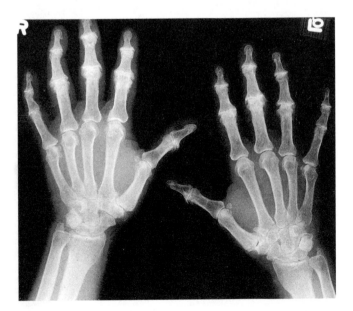

Figure 3. Radiograph of the hands showing joint space narrowing, subchondral sclerosis and osteophyte formation, indicating osteoarthritis.

Symptoms or symptoms consistent with inflammatory arthritis, such as symmetric peripheral polyarthropathy, soft-tissue swelling, morning stiffness >1 hour, or significant spine and sacroiliac joint involvement, should be evaluated for other causes of arthritis (Table 1). Secondary causes of osteoarthritis must be considered in patients who present with osteoarthritis in an unusual joint, at a young age, or with other symptoms (Table 2).

Therapy

Therapy for osteoarthritis should begin with and always include nonpharmacologic measures. In patients with inadequate response to these lifestyle measures, pharmacologic therapy can be added, progressing from lower-risk medications (ie, acetaminophen) to those with more side effects and higher risks (ie, nonsteroidal anti-inflammatory drugs [NSAIDs]). Ultimately, surgical intervention can be considered in those who have not responded to other measures.

Nonpharmacologic Therapies

Clinical guidelines from the American College of Rheumatology strongly recommend weight loss for overweight or obese patients with lower extremity osteoarthritis coupled with both aerobic exercise as well as exercise to strengthen muscles proximate to the involved joint (ie, quadriceps muscle strengthening for knee osteoarthritis). More specifically, medial knee compartment osteoarthritis may benefit from heel inserts (5-10 degrees of lift), which help relieve the pressure on the medial compartment. Adaptive devices such as a cane in the hand contralateral to the painful joint may help by unloading forces on the knee or hip. Knee taping or bracing improves knee alignment, thus improving pain. Referral to physical or occupational therapy for active and passive range of motion exercise instruction or joint protection education may be helpful.

Pharmacologic Therapies

Consider pharmacologic agents when conservative measures fail to relieve pain and improve function. **Acetaminophen is first-line pharmacologic therapy for osteoarthritis because it is safe, effective, and inexpensive.** Patients with an inadequate response can be started on NSAIDs, preferably at the lowest effective dose to limit side effects (eg, gastrointestinal and renal toxicity, exacerbation of congestive heart failure and hypertension). **Although cylcooxygenase-2-selective NSAIDs are somewhat less likely to cause gastrointestinal ulcers, they are not more effective than nonselective NSAIDs, are significantly more expensive, and are associated with an increased risk for adverse cardiovascular events.** Concomitant use of a proton pump inhibitor with an NSAID should be considered in patients with risk factors for gastrointestinal bleeding (eg, age >65 years, history of peptic ulcer disease or gastrointestinal bleeding, anticoagulant use).

Substance P has been implicated in the pathogenesis of osteoarthritis pain. Topical capsaicin depletes substance P and may be used in addition to or as an alternative to oral medications. For full efficacy, capsaicin should be applied 3 times daily for 3 weeks. Topical NSAIDs are an option for patients who should not take or cannot tolerate oral NSAIDs. Tramadol is a centrally acting synthetic opioid agonist that has comparable efficacy to NSAIDS in treating hip and knee pain due to osteoarthritis. Significant abuse has not been identified with tramadol, although nausea, constipation, and drowsiness may limit its use. **Opiate analgesics may play an additional role in the treatment of patients whose pain is refractory to other treatments**

but should not be used routinely due to potential side effects and dependency. Glucosamine and chondroitin do not appear to have clinically meaningful effects on knee or hip osteoarthritis.

Pain unresponsive to systemic medications may respond to local therapy. Intra-articular glucocorticoids injections are particularly effective in relieving pain from an acute exacerbation of osteoarthritis

in a specific joint. The benefit from intra-articular glucocorticoids for knee osteoarthritis varies, but statistically significant pain relief has been documented only up to 1 week after injection. In patients with osteoarthritis of the hip, intra-articular glucocorticoids therapy has been shown to effectively relieve pain for up to 3 months. The efficacy of this therapy in treating osteoarthritis of joints other than the knee

Table 1. Differential Diagnosis of Osteoarthritis

Disorder	Notes
CPPD deposition disease (see Chapter 100)	Chondrocalcinosis of the knee, triangular fibrocartilage of the wrist, and symphysis pubis; attacks of pseudogout; and osteoarthritis in the second and third MCP joints. CPPD crystals may be identified in synovial fluid.
Rheumatoid arthritis (see Chapter 102)	Soft tissue (synovial) swelling rather than bony enlargement of the PIP and MCP joints (rarely involves the DIP joints); inflammatory signs (fatigue, prolonged morning stiffness), rheumatoid nodules, and inflammatory synovial fluid. Marginal erosions and juxta-articular osteopenia seen on radiographs.
Psoriatic arthritis	Synovial and entheseal swelling; may involve the DIP joints; dactylitis (sausage digits) present. Erosions and periostitis seen on radiographs.
Trochanteric bursitis	Pain and tenderness over the greater trochanter; pain may radiate down the lateral aspect of the thigh. Hip range of motion is normal.
Anserine bursitis (see Chapter 98)	Pain and tenderness over the anteromedial aspect of the lower leg below the joint line of the knee. May be a confounding cause of knee pain in patients with knee osteoarthritis.
Osteonecrosis	Joint pain out of proportion to radiographic changes. Risk factors include glucocorticoids, alcohol abuse, systemic lupus erythematosus, and hemoglobinopathies. Usually involves the hip or knee. Diagnosis confirmed by MRI.
Gout (see Chapter 100)	History of acute attacks of monoarthritis with joint erythema. Bony enlargement of joints and tophi may be present on examination. Radiographs show large erosions with overhanging edges. Uric acid crystals may be identified in synovial fluid. Chronic tophaceous gout may involve the DIP and PIP joints and first MTP joint, causing deformities and bony enlargement akin to osteoarthritis.

CPPD = calcium pyrophosphate dihydrate; DIP = distal interphalangeal; MCP = metacarpophalangeal; MTP = metatarsophalangeal; PIP = proximal interphalangeal.

Table 2. Secondary Causes of Osteoarthritis

Cause	Notes
Trauma	Injury may predispose a joint to development of osteoarthritis. This is especially true for intra-articular fractures but also is true for fractures at distant sites that result in altered joint loading, such as fracture of the femoral shaft (hip), scaphoid (wrist), tibia (ankle), or humerus (shoulder).
Hemochromatosis	Hemochromatosis occurs due to iron overload and predominantly affects men aged 40-60 y. Osteoarthritis in the second and third MCP joints and radiographs showing hook-like osteophytes are characteristic. Early findings include arthralgia and elevated aminotransferase levels. Late findings may include hepatomegaly, bronze skin coloration, pituitary insufficiency, and diabetes. Serum transferrin saturation >60% in men or >50% in women suggests the diagnosis.
Wilson disease	Some patients with Wilson disease develop an arthropathy and, occasionally, chondrocalcinosis, most commonly in the knee. Laboratory findings include elevated aminotransferase levels. Diagnosis is suggested by a low serum ceruloplasmin level, high serum copper level, and Kayser-Fleischer rings on slit-lamp examination.
Ochronosis	In ochronosis, deficiency of homogentisic acid oxidase causes excretion of excess homogentisic acid in the urine and deposition of dark pigment in connective tissues. When the urine stands or is alkalinized, it turns dark (alkaptonuria). Associated arthropathy involves large joints and spares hands and feet; patients may present with early-onset lumbar spondylosis and calcification and ossification of the lumbar disks.
Acromegaly	In addition to increased size of the hands, feet, nose, and jaw, disease of the knee, hip, shoulder, and elbow joints occurs in 60% of patients with acromegaly; spine disease also is common. Radiographs may show widened joint space followed later by typical features of osteoarthritis.
Hyperparathyroidism	Most patients are asymptomatic but musculoskeletal symptoms may include proximal weakness, bone pain, nontraumatic fractures.
Neuropathic joints	Most commonly associated conditions are syringomyelia, diabetes, and neurosyphilis. Patients may present with massive joint swelling. Pain is less severe than would be expected from the appearance of the joint. Radiographs show large unusually shaped osteophytes, transverse fractures, osteolysis, and large loose bodies. Synovial fluid is noninflammatory or bloody.
Ehlers-Danlos syndrome	Several subtypes exist but all have in common hyperelastic skin and joint hypermobility. Other features (depending on the subtype) include keratoconus, scoliosis, and sudden death secondary to rupture of large blood vessels.

MCP = metacarpophalangeal.

and hip remains uncertain. Infection should be excluded before administering intra-articular glucocorticoids. Glucocorticoid injections should not be given more frequently than every 4 months due to the risk of tendon rupture. Viscosupplementation with intra-articular hyaluronic acid injection for knee osteoarthritis has not been shown to provide clinically meaningful benefit and is not recommended.

Total joint arthroplasty should be considered for patients who do not adequately respond to nonsurgical methods. Replacement of the damaged joint restores normal biomechanics and often results in dramatic improvements in quality of life. Arthroscopic lavage with or without debridement is not beneficial. Joint fusion is an option that may successfully alleviate osteoarthritis pain; it is typically reserved for joints not critical for mobility (eg, spine, small joints of the hand and foot). Although meniscus tears are almost universally present in knee osteoarthritis, they are not necessarily a cause of increased symptoms, and surgery is not recommended unless a patient experiences significant knee locking or loss of knee extension.

Bibliography

Abhishek A, Doherty M. Diagnosis and presentation of osteoarthritis. Rheum Dis Clin N Am. 2013;39:45–66. [PMID: 23312410]

Brand CA. Chronic disease management: a review of current performance across quality of care domains and opportunities for improving osteoarthritis care. Rheum Dis Clin North Am. 2013;39:123-43. [PMID: 23312413]

Hochberg MC, Altman RD, April KT, et al. American College of Rheumatology 2012 recommendations for the use of nonpharmacologic and pharmacologic therapies in osteoarthritis of the hand, hip, and knee. Arthritis Care Res.2012;64:465–74. [PMID: 22563589]

Hunter DJ. In the clinic. Osteoarthritis. Ann Intern Med. 2007;147:ITC8-1-ITC8-16. [PMID: 17679702]

Chapter 100

Crystal-Induced Arthritis

Sean Whelton, MD

The two most common forms of crystal-induced arthritis are gout and calcium pyrophosphate dihydrate (CPPD) deposition disease. These disorders present typically with episodic severe joint pains.

Gout (monosodium urate deposition disease) refers to the group of clinical disorders associated with hyperuricemia, which is variably defined as a serum urate level greater than 6.8 (0.405 mmol/L) or 7.0 (0.416 mmol/L) mg/dL (Table 1). If the serum uric acid concentration increases above this level, urate deposits may develop in synovial tissue, bursae, tendon sheaths, kidney interstitium, and the urinary collection system. It is important to note that many more people have asymptomatic hyperuricemia than have gout.

Gout attacks occur when urate crystals are released from preexisting tissue deposits. Typically a patient has had years of elevated uric acid prior to the first gout attack. Gout includes a group of clinical disorders ranging from acute, exquisitely painful, monoarticular arthritis to chronic, crippling, destructive polyarthritis. The risk of developing gout is directly related to the level and duration of elevated serum uric acid. Uric acid levels increase with increasing age, weight, and serum creatinine concentration. These increases may be accelerated by secondary factors including chronic kidney disease, alcohol consumption, dietary choices, diuretics, and low doses of aspirin. Hyperuricemia more often is related to underexcretion (90%) than to overproduction (10%) of uric acid. Polymorphisms of several different genes related to renal handling of uric acid play an important role in underexcretion. Acute attacks often are triggered by events that precipitously raise or lower serum uric acid level, such as dehydration, postoperative fluid shifts, or initiation of uric acid–lowering agents.

Gouty arthritis progresses through three distinct stages: asymptomatic hyperuricemia, which may last several decades; acute intermittent gout; and chronic tophaceous gout (Plate 71), which usually develops only after years of acute intermittent gout. Estrogen promotes uric acid excretion, so women typically do not develop gout until the postmenopausal period. Men typically develop gout in the fourth or fifth decade. During intercritical periods (asymptomatic periods between gout attacks), crystals may still be detected in the synovial fluid. Therefore, the presence of crystals in synovial fluid is not always sufficient to provoke an attack.

CPPD deposition disease, termed pseudogout, is caused by crystallization of calcium pyrophosphate dihydrate in articular tissues. The cause of this crystallization is unknown but is related to aging, and some cases are associated with specific metabolic abnormalities. Many patients with CPPD deposition disease are asymptomatic. Symptom presentation varies and may include pseudogout, pseudo-osteoarthritis, and pseudo-rheumatoid arthritis. Pseudogout causes acute mono- or pauciarticular inflammatory joint attacks that mimic acute attacks of gout. Pseudogout attacks may be precipitated by surgery or illness. Pseudo-osteoarthritis, which is a more common presentation than pseudogout, mimics osteoarthritis but involves the wrist, metacarpophalangeal, shoulder, ankle, hip, and knee joints. Pseudo-rheumatoid arthritis is a rare presentation of CPPD deposition disease that manifests as a symmetric polyarticular disease accompanied by morning stiffness, fatigue, and joint swelling.

Prevention

There are no primary prevention measures for gout or CPPD deposition disease. Administration of uric acid–lowering drugs to patients receiving chemotherapy for hematologic malignancies is recommended to prevent tumor lysis syndrome (see Chapter 88), which may cause acute hyperuricemia, hyperphosphatemia, hypocalcemia, hyperkalemia, and acute kidney injury. Effective secondary prevention of gout involves the use of drugs to lower uric acid. Indications for uric acid-lowering therapy include repeated attacks (≥2 attacks

Table 1. Disorders Associated with Hyperuricemia

Disorder	Clinical Presentation	Cause
Gouty arthritis	Inflammatory erosive arthritis	Inflammatory response to monosodium urate crystals deposited into synovial tissue, bursae, and tendon sheaths due to chronic uric acid supersaturation of serum; urate deposits cause joint and tissue destruction over time.
Tophi	Painless, persistent, generally noninflammatory nodules, which develop in tissues and tendons and are palpable on physical examination but also may occur as nodular lesions within joints or tissues	Tophi develop concomitantly with progressive gouty arthritis; although typically noninflammatory, an acute inflammatory response and local damage can occur at these sites
Nephrolithiasis	Formation of uric acid and calcium oxalate kidney stones	Increased uric acid levels in the urinary collecting system can serve as a nidus for both uric acid and calcium oxalate stone formation
Nephropathy	Loss of kidney function secondary to severe, typically acute increases in serum uric acid levels, such as occur in patients with tumor lysis syndrome	Deposition of monosodium urate crystals in the kidney interstitium

per year), the presence of tophi, or the presence of uric acid kidney stones. **Asymptomatic hyperuricemia itself is not an indication for uric acid-lowering therapy.**

Diagnosis

Gout is diagnosed by obtaining a history of intermittent severe episodes of arthritis and assessing for other potential causes on the differential diagnosis (Table 2). In the case of gout, frequently (75%) the first episode occurs in the great toe metatarsophalangeal joint (commonly referred to as *podagra*). It is important to note that the most common form of arthritis at this site is osteoarthritis. An active gouty joint is notable for warmth, swelling, and significant pain. At times there may be mild desquamation of the overlying skin. Pseudogout attacks may be as severe but typically are milder in presentation.

A definitive diagnosis may be made by performing arthrocentesis. Arthrocentesis is performed in patients presenting with acute monoarticular arthritis to diagnose infection or crystal-induced arthritis. It is possible for both infection and crystalline arthritis to coexist; thus, the finding of intracellular crystals does not eliminate the possibility of joint infection. A definitive diagnosis of gout is made by demonstrating negatively birefringent monosodium urate crystals within synovial fluid leukocytes. Arthrocentesis of a joint during the intercritical period also may establish the diagnosis of gout. If joint fluid cannot be obtained, clinical criteria can be used. Rapid symptom onset, intense joint inflammation, complete resolution between attacks, involvement of the first metatarsophalangeal joint, and radiographs demonstrating subcortical erosions are distinguishing features of gout.

Uric acid levels alone are inadequate to confirm or exclude a diagnosis of gout. Serum uric acid is typically elevated in patients with gout. During an acute attack the serum uric acid may be "falsely" low and can complicate the diagnosis. Furthermore, it is common to have asymptomatic elevations of uric acid.

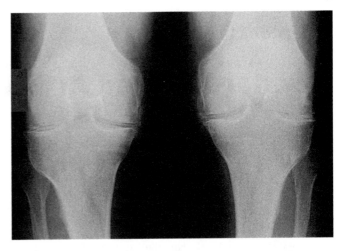

Figure 1. Linear calcification of the menisci and articular cartilage characteristic of calcium pyrophosphate dihydrate deposition disease.

The diagnosis of CPPD deposition disease is made by finding positively birefringent rhomboid intracellular crystals in the synovial fluid. Radiographs can reveal chondrocalcinosis (linear calcifications along the articular cartilage and fibrocartilage, Figure 1), degenerative changes, and osteophytes. Screen patients aged <50 years with CPPD deposition disease for associated metabolic conditions (eg, hemochromatosis, hyperparathyroidism, hypothyroidism, gout, hypomagnesemia, hypophosphatasia, familial hypocalciuric hypercalcemia, acromegaly).

Therapy

Advise patients with gout to avoid alcohol, because alcohol increases uric acid production and may impair uric acid excretion. Foods high in purines (eg, organ meats, red meat, seafood) also should be

Table 2. Differential Diagnosis of Gout

Disorder	Notes
Calcium pyrophosphate dihydrate (CPPD) deposition disease	May be asymptomatic or have a varied presentation resembling rheumatoid arthritis, osteoarthritis, or gout-like inflammation. Cartilage calcification termed chondrocalcinosis, especially in the knee, symphysis pubis, shoulder, hip, and triangular cartilage of wrist, are pathognomonic. Osteoarthritis in unusual places (wrist, elbow, metacarpophalangeal joints, shoulder) without a history of trauma suggests CPPD deposition. Defined by finding CPPD crystals in synovial fluid and by chondrocalcinosis on radiographs.
Osteoarthritis (see Chapter 99)	Characterized by joint-space narrowing with associated bony enlargement (osteophytes) with no acute signs of inflammation. Patients may have acute exacerbation of joint symptoms, especially after use. Radiographs may show focal joint-space narrowing, bony repair with osteophytes, and subchondral sclerosis.
Psoriatic arthritis (see Chapter 104)	Characterized by joint distribution and appearance similar to that of reactive arthritis. Predilection for distal interphalangeal joints, often with concomitant nail changes.
Reactive arthritis (see Chapter 105)	Presents as inflammatory oligoarthritis, most often involving weight-bearing joints; may include tendon insertion inflammation (enthesitis). Extra-articular manifestations include conjunctivitis, urethritis, stomatitis, and psoriaform skin changes. Infection with *Salmonella, Shigella, Yersinia, Campylobacter,* or *Chlamydia* species within 3 wk prior to onset of initial attack.
Rheumatoid arthritis (see Chapter 102)	Symmetric polyarthritis most often involving small joints of the hands and feet. About 30% of patients have subcutaneous rheumatoid nodules. Radiographic changes include soft-tissue swelling, diffuse joint-space narrowing, marginal erosions of small joints, and absence of osteophytes. Acute rheumatoid arthritis sometimes mimics gout. The greater the number of joints involved, the more likely that rheumatoid arthritis is the diagnosis.
Infectious arthritis (see Chapter 101)	Characterized by fever, arthritis, and exquisite joint tenderness. May occur as a complication of other arthritis syndromes. The source of infection (skin, lungs) often is evident. Usually occurs in previously abnormal joints.

Table 3. Drug Treatment of Gout

Agent	Notes
Acute Gout	
NSAIDs	Block formation of inflammatory prostaglandins and have analgesic effects. Effective within 12-24 h of onset. The NSAID used is less important than the rapidity with which the NSAID is started. Any NSAID *except* aspirin is appropriate. Start at high dose and taper rapidly over several days.
Colchicine (oral)	Colchicine decreases L-selectin expression by neutrophils, making them less able to adhere to vascular endothelium and egress into tissues. Nausea, vomiting, and diarrhea are dose related. Bone marrow suppression can be life-threatening if maximum doses are exceeded. Myopathy and neuropathy can occur at any dose. Modify dose according to kidney function. Colchicine is not removed by dialysis; therefore, it should be avoided in patients on dialysis. For acute gout, oral colchicine is given at a dose of 1.2 mg followed by 0.6 mg in one hour. Thereafter it is given twice daily or daily as appropriate, with dose adjustments downward for patients with kidney disease.
Glucocorticoids (oral)	Suppress inflammation by several mechanisms. Useful when NSAIDs are contraindicated (chronic kidney disease). Relative contraindication in active peptic ulcer disease. May interfere with control of diabetes.
Glucocorticoids (intra-articular)	Especially useful if only one joint is inflamed and patient has contraindications to other agents. Rule out infectious cause before administering injection.
Chronic Gout	
Allopurinol	Xanthine oxidase inhibitor; inhibits uric acid synthesis. Dose is increased over several weeks to minimize acute gout attacks that may occur with abrupt fluctuations in serum uric acid levels. Initial dose is modified according to creatinine clearance. Target serum uric acid levels ≤6.0 mg/dL (0.35 mmol/L). May cause a hypersensitivity reaction in 1 in 1000 patients treated.
Febuxostat	Xanthine oxidase inhibitor useful in patients allergic to allopurinol. Does not appear to cause hypersensitivity reactions. Concern exists for possible cardiovascular risk from the drug. Currently more expensive than allopurinol.
Probenecid, sulfinpyrazone	Uricosuric agents effective in long-term treatment of chronic gout if sodium urate levels are maintained at ≤6.0 mg/dL (0.35 mmol/L). Require adequate renal function so less effective or ineffective in chronic kidney disease.

NSAID = nonsteroidal anti-inflammatory drug.

avoided. Dietary interventions rarely are adequate to reverse hyperuricemia and prevent attacks of gout.

Gout treatment is focused on either dealing with an acute attack or preventing disease in the future. Effective treatment of acute attacks of gout involves therapy with nonsteroidal anti-inflammatory drugs (NSAIDs), glucocorticoids, or colchicine. The choice of agent for acute gout depends on patient characteristics and on the presence or absence of concomitant disease (Table 3). NSAIDs are effective but should be avoided in patients who are older, who have chronic kidney disease, heart failure, peptic ulcer disease, or are on anticoagulation therapy. In these situations, intra-articular or systemic glucocorticoids are preferred. Oral colchicine is also an effective treatment for acute gout if initiated within 36 hours of an attack.

Patients with recurrent episodes of gout who are at risk for joint damage are candidates for uric acid-lowering therapy. Management or prevention of recurrent gout and chronic tophaceous gout requires drug therapy to achieve and maintain serum uric acid levels below 6 mg/dL (0.35 mmol/L). First-line therapy is with xanthine oxidase inhibitors (allopurinol or febuxostat). **Allopurinol is typically safe and effective and is considered first-line therapy for most patients with an indication for uric acid lowering treatment.** It is rarely associated with a potentially severe hypersensitivity syndrome. Febuxostat can be used in patients with allopurinol allergy. Initiate uric acid-lowering therapy agent after resolution of an acute attack. As uric acid-lowering therapy can precipitate an attack, it is recommended that prophylactic therapy with colchicine or low-dose NSAIDs be used in the first 3 to 6 months of uric acid-lowering therapy. Uricosuric agents (eg, probenecid, sulfinpyrazone) are occasionally effective in patients with low uric acid excretion (<600 mg [35.4 mmol] daily) but are not effective in patients with a glomerular filtration rate <40 mL/min/1.73 m². In rare situations when there is very refractory tophaceous gout, IV pegylated uricase can be used to deplete uric acid stores.

Treatment of CPPD deposition disease is symptomatic. There is no agent that successfully reverses formation or deposition of CPPD crystals. NSAIDs, colchicine, glucocorticoids, and intra-articular glucocorticoids are useful in managing an acute attack. NSAIDs or colchicine may be used, as in gout, as prophylaxis following an acute attack.

Bibliography

Khanna D, Fitzgerald JD, Khanna PP, et al. 2012 American College of Rheumatology guidelines for management of gout. Arthritis Care Res (Hoboken). 2012;64:1447-61. [PMID: 23024029]

Neogi T. Gout. N Engl J Med. 2011;364:443-52. [PMID: 21288096]

Wilson JF. In the clinic. Gout. Ann Intern Med. 2010;152:ITC2-1-ITC2-16. [PMID: 20124228]

Zhang W, Doherty M, Pascual E, et al. EULAR recommendations for calcium pyrophosphate deposition. Part II: management. Ann Rheum Dis. 2011;70:571-5. [PMID: 21257614]

Chapter 101

Infectious Arthritis

Thomas M. De Fer, MD

nfectious (septic) arthritis is a medical emergency. Failure to promptly diagnose a joint infection can rapidly lead to joint destruction, chronic disability, or death.

Approximately 80% of joint infections are monoarticular; any joint can be affected. Acute monoarthritis, particularly of a large joint such as the hip, knee, ankle, or wrist, should prompt consideration of infectious arthritis. Infectious arthritis is more likely to have a polyarticular presentation in patients with preexisting rheumatoid arthritis than in other patients.

Many pathogens can cause infectious arthritis, including fungi and mycobacteria, but bacterial infections are the most significant, and nongonococcal infections are the most serious. Infectious arthritis is typically a result of hematogenous spread. The synovium lacks a basement membrane, and bloodborne bacteria can easily access the joint space, where they deposit in the synovial membrane and incite a vigorous inflammatory response. Infectious arthritis may be a presenting feature of bacterial endocarditis. Joint infection may also result from direct inoculation of bacteria into the joint space follow-

ing surgery, trauma, or arthrocentesis or from contiguous infection from soft tissue or bone. Within days, cytokines and proteases can cause cartilage degradation and bone erosion. Delay in diagnosis or misdiagnosis of infectious arthritis as rheumatoid arthritis or an acute gout flare not only postpones appropriate treatment but also may result in poor functional outcomes and even death.

Prevention

Preexisting arthritis, particularly rheumatoid arthritis, and prosthetic joint replacement predispose to infectious arthritis. Treatment of rheumatoid arthritis with glucocorticoid also increases a patient's vulnerability to infection. Other risk factors include age >80 years, injection drug use, indwelling catheters, alcoholism, diabetes mellitus, and an immunocompromised state (eg, HIV infection). Skin and wound infections are frequent sources of bacteria that seed diseased or prosthetic joints, resulting in infectious arthritis. Treat all skin and wound infections promptly and vigorously in patients pre-

Table 1. Differential Diagnosis of Infectious Arthritis

Disorder	Notes
Crystal-induced synovitis (see Chapter 100)	In gout, the first metatarsophalangeal joint most often is affected, and monosodium urate crystals are present in the synovial fluid. In CPPD deposition disease (pseudogout), the knee or wrist is the most common site of acute synovitis, and CPPD crystals are present in the synovial fluid. Consider the possibility that crystal-induced arthritis and infectious arthritis may coexist.
Rheumatoid arthritis (see Chapter 102)	Rheumatoid arthritis usually is a symmetric polyarthritis affecting large and small joints; it rarely presents as monoarthritis. Rheumatoid factor is positive in 80% of cases. Flares may be monoarticular and present as pseudoinfectious arthritis. Synovial fluid analysis including Gram stain and culture usually will distinguish a flare from infectious arthritis.
Systemic lupus erythematosus (see Chapter 103)	Acute arthritis, especially monoarthritis, in an immunosuppressed patient with systemic lupus erythematosus requires a diligent workup to rule out infectious arthritis. Search for opportunistic infections in addition to the common pathogens.
Reactive arthritis (see Chapter 104)	Reactive arthritis can be precipitated by gastroenteritis or a genitourinary infection. Patients may present with urethritis, conjunctivitis, and arthritis; heel pain with enthesitis; keratoderma blennorrhagicum on the palms or soles; or circinate balanitis on the penis. Upon initial presentation, initiating antibiotic therapy is reasonable until culture results are known and the diagnosis of reactive arthritis can be substantiated. Can easily be confused with disseminated gonococcal infection.
Sickle cell disease (see Chapter 48)	Acute joint pain is seen with a painful crisis. Arthralgia is common, but frank arthritis can be encountered. In the event of an acute inflammatory arthritis, infectious arthritis, bone infarction, and osteomyelitis must be considered. In addition to arthrocentesis, joint and bone imaging may be helpful in establishing a diagnosis.
Hemarthrosis	Blood in a joint may lead to an intense inflammatory reaction that mimics infectious arthritis. The source of the blood may be from trauma, over-anticoagulation, hemophilia, or another bleeding disorder (eg, thrombocytopenia, severe liver disease, acquired clotting factor deficiency).
Other causes of infectious arthritis	Although subacute or chronic in many cases, infectious arthritis can be caused by fungi, viruses, parasites, tuberculosis, and Lyme disease.
Overlying cellulitis	Tender and erythematous skin possibly with skin edema and/or induration and peau d'orange changes, not associated with joint effusion, less pain with range of motion; cellulitis and infectious arthritis may coexist.

CPPD = calcium pyrophosphate dihydrate.

disposed to infectious arthritis, particularly patients with inflammatory arthropathies and on treatment with immunotherapy or biologic agents. **There is no evidence to support the use of antibiotic prophylaxis to prevent infectious arthritis in patients with prosthetic joints undergoing procedures.**

Diagnosis

Acute monoarthritis should prompt a thorough history and physical examination and arthrocentesis for synovial fluid analysis. Consider infectious arthritis when a patient with rheumatoid arthritis has a monoarticular flare and in patients with acute gouty arthritis; crystal-induced arthritis and infectious arthritis may coexist. Large joints most often are affected, with the knee involved in about 50% of cases; however, any joint can be involved. Infectious arthritis may affect the axial skeleton, including the sternoclavicular and sacroiliac joints and symphysis pubis. Clues such as fever, joint pain, joint swelling, and recent trauma can be helpful but may be absent, particularly in elderly patients with multiple comorbidities and in immunosuppressed patients. Examine all joints for redness, warmth, swelling, and limitation of movement. Distinguish joint involvement from other causes of pain around a joint (eg, bursitis, tendonitis) and from referred pain. Infectious arthritis usually results from bacteremia; look carefully for potential sources, such as wound, skin, urinary tract, and intra-abdominal infections and pneumonia. Table 1 summarizes the differential diagnosis of infectious arthritis.

The definitive diagnostic test in all cases of suspected infectious arthritis is identification of bacteria in the synovial fluid. Therefore, it is necessary to obtain a joint fluid specimen for culture, Gram stain, polarized microscopy for crystals, and leukocyte count and differential (Table 2). In most patients, the synovial fluid leukocyte count is approximately ≥50,000/μL (50×10^9/L) with 90% neutrophils. A synovial fluid leukocyte count near 100,000/μL (100×10^9/L) with 90% neutrophils is specific for acute bacterial infection. However, patients who are immunosuppressed, have infection caused by *Mycobacterium* or *Neisseria* species, or have a prosthetic joint infection may have a lower synovial fluid leukocyte count. A count between 10,000/μL and 30,000/μL (10 and 30×10^9/L) with 50% neutrophils suggests mycobacterial or fungal arthritis. Confirm the diagnosis of nongonococcal infectious arthritis by isolation of microor-

ganisms from the synovial fluid; *Staphylococcus aureus* and *Streptococcus pneumoniae* are the most common causative organisms. Culture the blood and any extra-articular sites of possible infection to establish a microbiologic diagnosis. Synovial biopsy occasionally is indicated for patients with an indolent infection who have persistently negative cultures and a poor response to empiric therapy. Overlying cellulitis is a relative contraindication to arthrocentesis.

Plain radiographs of the infected joint are indicated to identify joint damage and possible concomitant osteomyelitis. Computed tomography (CT) or magnetic resonance imaging (MRI) may be more sensitive than radiography for diagnosing early osteomyelitis and are particularly useful in the evaluation of the hip, sternoclavicular, and sacroiliac joints. CT helps to guide aspiration of the hip; MRI helps to reveal adjacent soft-tissue edema and periarticular abscesses and to facilitate adequate debridement and drainage.

Acute arthritis in a sexually active young adult raises the suspicion of disseminated gonococcal infection. There are two common presentations of disseminated gonococcal infection: purulent arthritis without dermatitis, and a syndrome of polyarthralgias (without purulent arthritis), tenosynovitis, and dermatitis. The infectious arthritis form generally is monoarticular (occasionally involves two joints), most often in the knee, wrist, ankle, or elbow. In the syndromic form, arthralgias often involve the knees and elbows, and tenosynovitis typically affects multiple locations including the wrists, ankles, fingers, and toes. Skin lesions, which number about 5 to 40, can have a variety of appearances but are usually pustular and painless (Plate 47). Fever is much more common in the polyarthralgias form. Confirm the diagnosis by detection of the microorganism in synovial fluid, blood, urethra, cervix, rectum, or throat or from a skin pustule. Patients with the polyarthralgias form most often have negative synovial fluid cultures but are more likely to have positive blood cultures. Most patients will deny local symptoms of gonorrhea but gonococcal infection can often be detected (genitourinary, anorectal, pharyngeal cultures). Patients suspected of having disseminated gonococcal infection should also be tested for other sexually transmitted diseases including HIV.

Maintain a high index of suspicion for joint infection in patients with prosthetic joints. Although infections are uncommon (1% to 3%), they can be difficult to manage because bacterial organisms propagate as biofilms on the inorganic surfaces of prostheses and can

Table 2. Laboratory and Other Studies for Infectious Arthritis

Test	Notes
Complete blood count	The lack of leukocytosis does not rule out infectious arthritis.
Synovial fluid leukocyte count	Synovial fluid leukocyte counts vary in infectious arthritis. Most fall into the moderately (10,000-50,000/μL [10-50 × 10⁹/L]) to highly (50,000 to >100,000/μL [50 to >100 × 10⁹/L]) inflammatory range.
Synovial fluid Gram stain	The rate of finding gram-positive cocci varies from 50%-75%; these organisms are more easily seen than gram-negative organisms. The rate of finding gram-negative bacilli is only 50%. From 70% to 90% of synovial fluid specimens show positive culture results in cases of infectious arthritis not due to *Neisseria gonorrhoeae*; <50% of synovial fluid specimens are positive for *N. gonorrhoeae* arthritis. In the remaining cases, the diagnosis is established by culturing *N. gonorrhoeae* at an extra-articular site (eg, blood, skin pustule, urethra, cervix, rectum, throat).
Synovial fluid culture	Gram-positive organisms cause 75%-80% of cases of infectious arthritis. *Staphylococcus aureus* accounts for 50% of all cases; streptococci, 25%; gram-negative organisms, 20%; and other organisms (eg, *Staphylococcus epidermidis*, *Haemophilus influenzae*), 5%.
Blood culture	Culture blood and extra-articular sites of possible infection to establish a microbiologic diagnosis.
Radiography and MRI	Changes seen on joint radiographs and bone damage due to infection are relatively late findings. In acute infectious arthritis, soft-tissue fullness and joint effusions often are the only initial findings on radiographs. MRI of the affected joint is especially useful in detecting avascular necrosis, soft-tissue masses, and collections of fluid not appreciated by other imaging modalities.

MRI = magnetic resonance imaging

Table 3. Empiric Antibiotic Therapy for Septic Arthritis in a Native Joint

Gram Stain Results	Likely Pathogens	First-Line Therapy
Gram-positive cocci	*Staphylococcus aureus*; other staphylococcal species (eg, *Streptococcus pneumoniae*)	Vancomycin (if MRSA suspected) Nafcillin, oxacillin, cefazolin (if MRSA less likely)
Gram-negative cocci	*Neisseria gonorrhoeae*	Ceftriaxone (add azithromycin for possible concurrent *Chlamydia* infection)
Gram-negative bacilli	Enteric gram-negative bacilli	Ceftriaxone, ceftazidime, or cefotaxime Ceftazidime plus an aminoglycoside if *Pseudomonas aeruginosa* suspected
Gram stain negative	At risk for *N. gonorrheae* infection	Ceftriaxone, ceftazidime, or cefotaxime
	No risk for *N. gonorrheae* infection; *S. aureas* or gram-negative bacilli likely	Vancomycin plus ceftriaxone, ceftazidime, or cefotaxime

MRSA = methicillin-resistant *Staphylococcus aureus*.

be practically impossible to eradicate while the artificial joint is in place. Prosthetic joints may become infected during implantation; such infections are initially asymptomatic but become apparent ≤3 months after surgery. Alternatively, prosthetic joints may become infected after implantation (>3 months to years) via hematogenous spread. In either case, the joint may be swollen and inflamed or only painful. Most patients with infectious arthritis will be febrile; however, chills and spiking fevers are uncommon. Elderly patients frequently do not develop a fever. Failure to diagnose infection may lead to excess morbidity, prosthesis removal, and death. *Staphylococcus epidermidis* is much more common in prosthetic joint infections than in native joint infections. Leukocyte counts, erythrocyte sedimentation rate, and C-reactive protein levels are usually elevated. Radiographs may reveal erosion or loosening around the implantation site. Diagnosis requires synovial fluid aspiration or open debridement, along with Gram stain and culture.

Therapy

Hospitalize patients with suspected infectious arthritis to confirm the diagnosis, initiate prompt intravenous antibiotic therapy, and closely monitor response to treatment. Management is directed toward drainage of the purulent joint fluid, preservation of joint integrity and function, and initiation of antibiotic therapy.

Use repeated needle aspiration to drain purulent joint fluid as completely as possible; arthroscopic drainage may be necessary when needle aspirates fail. Prosthetic joint infections almost always require removal of the infected hardware. An antibiotic spacer is usually inserted, and long-term antibiotic therapy is initiated. Only after complete resolution of the infection can reimplantation be considered. If the patient is not a candidate for this process, surgical debridement and chronic antibiotic suppression may minimize morbidity and mortality.

Empiric antibiotic therapy of infectious arthritis is usually guided by Gram stain results, although there is little data regarding the optimal treatment regimens. Because of increasing prevalence of community-associated methicillin-resistant *S. aureus*, many experts recommend initiating vancomycin if the synovial fluid studies show gram-positive cocci, unless the local prevalence is low, where other β-lactam antibiotics may be appropriate. If synovial fluid studies reveal gram-negative cocci, ceftriaxone is an appropriate first choice to treat *N. gonorrhoeae*; also treat empirically with azithromycin for concurrent *Chlamydia* infection. If the initial Gram stain shows gram-negative bacilli, a third-generation cephalosporin (ceftriaxone, ceftazidime, or cefotaxime) are reasonable empiric choices to cover enteric organisms. If *Pseudomonas* infection is possible (eg, injection drug use), a third-generation cephalosporin with activity against *Pseudomonas* (such as cefotaxime) with an aminoglycoside (such as gentamicin) is indicated. If the initial Gram stain is negative, appropriate empiric therapy in patients at low risk for *N. gonorrhoeae* may include vancomycin and a third-generation cephalosporin; in those at high risk for *Neisseria* infection, coverage for *Neisseria* should be primary therapy with possible treatment for gram-positive bacteria. Table 3 summarizes an empiric treatment approach for infectious arthritis. As culture results become available, the antibiotic choice can be narrowed.

Duration of treatment is based on the initial response to antibiotic treatment, the specific microorganism, and patient characteristics. Shorten the duration of antibiotic administration to 2 weeks or less when the microorganism is exquisitely sensitive to the drug used (eg, *N. gonorrhoeae*) and the patient responds promptly. Administer antibiotics for 4 weeks or longer for virulent microorganisms (eg, *S. aureus*) or difficult-to-treat pathogens (eg, *P. aeruginosa*). Consider chronic suppressive antibiotic treatment of an infected prosthesis without removal only under certain circumstances, such as if the prosthesis is not loose or the patient is a poor surgical candidate.

Follow-Up

Perform serial synovial fluid examinations to help monitor the response to therapy. Serial synovial fluid specimens usually show a decrease in total leukocyte count, conversion to a negative culture result, and a decrease in the amount of fluid reaccumulation, findings that parallel other clinical signs of response. Pain with range of motion should decrease, and function of the joint should improve or be regained.

Bibliography

Carpenter CR, Schuur JD, Everett WW, Pines JM. Evidence-based diagnostics: adult septic arthritis. Acad Emerg Med. 2011;18:781-96. [PMID: 21843213]

Margaretten ME, Kohlwes J, Moore D, Bent S. Does this adult patient have septic arthritis? JAMA. 2007;297:1478-88. [PMID: 17405973]

Mathews CJ, Weston VC, Jones A, Field M, Coakley G. Bacterial septic arthritis in adults. Lancet. 2010;375:846-55. [PMID: 20206778]

Chapter 102

Rheumatoid Arthritis

Alda Maria Gonzaga, MD

Rheumatoid arthritis (RA) is a chronic, systemic inflammatory disease. Without treatment it leads to joint damage, disability, and premature death. RA affects 1% to 1.5% of the worldwide population. The incidence increases during adulthood and peaks between the fifth and seventh decades. Women are affected 2 to 4 times more frequently than men. The hallmark features of RA are symmetric polyarthritis affecting the hands and feet, although any joint can be affected, and the formation of autoantibodies. Patients may experience constitutional symptoms (weight loss, low-grade fever, malaise, fatigue) and develop rheumatoid nodules and other extra-articular manifestations.

The cause of RA is unknown, although several factors have been associated with development of the disease, including genetic susceptibility, cigarette smoking, hormones, and autoantibodies. Infections have long been suspected as triggers for RA, but no studies have confirmed this association. Once RA is established, proinflammatory cytokines (eg, tumor necrosis factor alpha [TNF-α] trigger the production of degradative enzymes and osteoclast activation leading to joint damage and bone erosion.

Early recognition and aggressive, proactive treatment to control inflammation have improved the prognosis of RA over the past two decades. Patients with longstanding disease who did not receive aggressive treatment often have the classic findings associated with altered joint alignment and joint deformity (eg, ulnar deviation, swan neck deformity, boutonniere deformity, and flexion contractures of knees and elbows).

Screening

No adequate screening test for RA currently exists and there are no screening recommendations, including testing for rheumatoid factor (RF), for otherwise healthy individuals. However, as symptoms in early RA are difficult to distinguish from other forms of arthritis or inflammatory disease, a reasonable index of suspicion for

---

Table 1. The 2010 ACR/EULAR Classification Criteria for Rheumatoid Arthritis

Target population consists of patients who:

1. Have at least 1 joint with definite clinical synovitis (swelling) *and*
2. The synovitis is not better explained by another disease

Classification Criteria	Score
Add score of categories A-D; a score of ≥ 6/10 is needed for classification of a patient as having definite rheumatoid arthritis	
A. Joint involvement (swollen or tender)	
1 large joint[a]	0
2-10 small joints[b]	1
1-3 small joints (with or without involvement of large joints)	2
4-10 small joints (with or without involvement of large joints)	3
>10 joints (at least 1 small joint)	5
B. Serology (at least 1 test result needed for classification)	
Negative RF and anti-CCP antibody	0
Low-positive RF or low-positive anti-CCP antibody	2
High-positive RF or high positive anti-CCP antibody	3
C. Acute-phase reactants (at least 1 test result needed for classification)	
Normal CRP and normal ESR	0
Abnormal CRP or abnormal ESR	1
D. Duration of symptoms[c]	
<6 wk	0
≥6 wk	1

ACR/EULAR = American College of Rheumatology/European League Against Rheumatism; CCP = cyclic citrullinated peptide; CRP = C-reactive protein; ESR = erythrocyte sedimentation rate; RF = rheumatoid factor.

[a]Large joints refers to shoulders, elbows, hips, knees, and ankles.

[b]Small joints refers to metacarpophalangeal joints, proximal interphalangeal joints, second through fifth metatarsophalangeal joints, thumb interphalangeal joints, and wrists.

[c]Duration of symptoms refers to patient self-report of the duration of signs and symptoms of synovitis of joints that are clinically involved at time of assessment.

Data from Aletaha D, Neogi T, Silman AJ, et al. 2010 Rheumatoid arthritis classification criteria: an American College of Rheumatology/European League Against Rheumatism collaborative initiative. Arthritis Rheum. 2010;62:2569-81. [PMID: 20872595]

RA should exist for those with risk factors (eg, typical age of onset, positive family history, female gender, and cigarette smoking) who have suggestive symptoms.

Diagnosis

Classically, RA is associated with the following findings: symmetric arthritis involving seven characteristic sites (proximal interphalangeal [PIP], metacarpophalangeal [MCP], wrist, elbow, knee, ankle, and metatarsophalangeal [MTP] joints) (Plate 72), associated synovitis, morning stiffness for longer than 60 minutes, and subcutaneous rheumatoid nodules over bony prominences or extensor surfaces. In 2010, the American College of Rheumatology in collaboration with the European League Against Rheumatism developed a score-based classification scheme for RA (Table 1) in an effort to detect early disease and initiate early therapy. The classification scheme takes into consideration the number and size of joints involved, presence of anti-cyclic citrullinated peptide (anti-CCP) antibody, and erythrocyte sedimentation rate (ESR) and C-reactive protein (CRP) measurements.

The initial presentation of RA may be insidious or acute; symptoms lasting more than 6 weeks make RA more likely. Patients usually present with joint pain and swelling, prolonged morning stiffness, and difficulty performing activities of daily living. While RA typically presents with symmetric arthritis, it may be asymmetric in distribution early in the disease course. Small joints are classically

involved, although any size joint can be affected. PIP, MCP, and MTP joints are almost always involved; the distal interphalangeal (DIP) joints and the lumbar spine are spared. The presence of C1-C2 subluxation in advanced disease can cause spinal instability and cord impingement, and is a risk factor for general anesthesia due to the need for neck hyperextension associated with intubation. Over time, patients are at increased risk of osteoporosis, both from their disease as well as its treatment.

On examination of the affected joints, synovitis (soft or "boggy" joint swelling and tenderness) is often found. There is often pain on range of motion. Acute inflammation, or joint deformity in chronic disease, can cause entrapment neuropathies, most commonly carpal tunnel syndrome.

Diagnostic testing for RA includes obtaining RF and anti-CCP antibody titers. RF is present in more than 70% of patients with RA. However, RF also is found in patients with other conditions (eg, infections, malignancies, other autoimmune diseases) as well as 10% of the normal population. Anti-CCP antibody is positive in 60% of patients with RA and is highly specific (95%) for RA, which is far greater than that of RF (approximately 80%). The presence of both RF and anti-CCP antibody greatly increases the likelihood a patient has RA. While their presence strongly supports the diagnosis, normal values of RF and anti-CCP do not rule out disease. **Antinuclear antibodies (ANA) may be positive in 40% of patients with RA and is a nonspecific finding.**

Other laboratory studies may show evidence of systemic inflammation, including elevated ESR and CRP, normocytic anemia, and thrombocytosis. These markers typically parallel the degree of joint inflammation. Plain radiographs may not reveal articular erosions early in the disease. The earliest radiographic abnormalities include soft-tissue swelling, uniform joint-space narrowing, and periarticular osteopenia in the wrists or feet. **Magnetic resonance imaging and ultrasonography are more sensitive imaging modalities for early erosive disease compared with radiography. However, their roles in diagnosis have not been established and they are not obtained routinely.**

Extra-articular features of RA include rheumatoid nodules and pulmonary, cardiovascular, ocular, hematologic, and neurologic manifestations (Table 2). Rheumatoid nodules, associated with more severe disease, occur in 30% of patients. These may be clinically indistinguishable from gouty tophi and are best identified by aspiration and analysis of the aspirate with a polarizing microscope; monosodium urate crystals indicate tophi, whereas cholesterol crystals indicate rheumatoid nodules. Accelerated coronary artery disease is a common cardiac manifestation. Extra-articular manifestations of RA are associated with increased mortality.

The differential diagnosis of RA includes the spondyloarthropathies (eg, ankylosing spondylitis, reactive arthritis, psoriatic arthritis), virally mediated arthritis (eg, Epstein-Barr virus, parvovirus B19, HIV, hepatitis C), bacterial infections (eg, endocarditis, gonococcal infection, Lyme disease), metabolic disorders (e.g., gout, calcium pyrophosphate dihydrate deposition disease, hemochromatosis), connective tissue diseases (eg, systemic lupus erythematosus, systemic sclerosis, dermatomyositis/polymyositis), sarcoidosis, amyloidosis, and malignancy. Osteoarthritis may present as joint swelling but generally is characterized by bony joint enlargement and morning stiffness lasting less than 30 minutes (Table 3).

Table 2. Extra-Articular Manifestations of Rheumatoid Arthritis

System	Findings
Constitutional	Fatigue
	Weight loss
Dermatologic	Rheumatoid nodules
	Leg ulcers
	Rheumatoid vasculitis
Ophthalmologic	Episcleritis
	Scleritis
	Keratoconjunctivitis sicca
Hematologic	Anemia of chronic disease
	Thrombocytosis
	Pancytopenia and splenomegaly (Felty syndrome)
	Large granular lymphocyte syndrome
Cardiovascular	Premature coronary artery disease
	Chronic heart failure
	Pericarditis
	Secondary amyloidosis
Pulmonary	Exudative pleural effusionsInterstitial fibrosis
	Pulmonary nodules
	Bronchiolitis obliterans organizing pneumonia
	Bronchiectasis, bronchiolectasis
	Cricoarytenoid disease producing stridor
Gastrointestinal	Dry mouth
Renal	Secondary amyloidosis
Neurologic	C1-C2 subluxation
	Peripheral neuropathy
	Mononeuritis multiplex (vasculitis)

Therapy

The goal of treatment is to proactively and aggressively suppress inflammation and preserve joint structure and function. It is the

Table 3. Differential Diagnosis of Rheumatoid Arthritis

Disease	Notes
Ankylosing spondylitis (see Chapter 104)	Inflammatory disorder of the axial skeleton; may have peripheral involvement; apical pulmonary fibrosis; back pain. Differs from rheumatoid arthritis because ankylosing spondylitis uncommonly has peripheral involvement and usually involves the lumbar spine.
CPPD deposition disease (see Chapter 100)	Deposition of CPPD crystals in and around joints, most commonly the wrist, MCP joints, shoulder, and knee. May be monoarticular or acute oligoarticular, with hot and red joints; may be chronic polyarticular in 5% of cases. CPPD deposition disease can have a pseudo–rheumatoid arthritis pattern. Polarized microscopy reveals weakly positive birefringent crystals in synovial fluid. Radiographs show chondrocalcinosis.
Gout (see Chapter 100)	Deposition of monosodium urate crystals in and around joints. Initial attack is monoarticular, most commonly in the first MTP joint. Chronic form may have symmetric involvement of small joints of the hands and feet, with tophi. Gout can have a pseudo–rheumatoid arthritis pattern. Polarized microscopy reveals strongly negative birefringent crystals in synovial fluid or tophi. Gout is highly uncommon in premenopausal women with normal kidney function.
Infective endocarditis (see Chapter 59)	Characterized by involvement of large proximal joints, fever with leukocytosis, and heart murmur. Obtain blood cultures in all patients with fever and polyarthritis. RF is a common finding in patients with endocarditis.
Lyme disease	Multisystem inflammatory disease caused by *Borrelia burgdorferi*. Early disease: erythema migrans rash and cardiac abnormalities. Late disease: intermittent monoarthritis or oligoarthritis that may become chronic. Rash and tick exposure or travel to an endemic area are important for the diagnosis. Obtain ELISA test; confirm a positive result with Western blot.
Osteoarthritis (see Chapter 99)	Degeneration of articular cartilage, most often affecting the DIP, PIP, first CMC, first MTP, hip, and knee joints and the cervical and lumbar spine. Pain occurs with use; minimal soft-tissue swelling and morning stiffness. Radiographs show osteophytes with joint-space narrowing. Laboratory studies are normal.
Psoriatic arthritis	Multiple presentations: monoarthritis, oligoarthritis (asymmetric), polyarthritis (symmetric), arthritis mutilans, and axial disease. Common involvement of DIP joints, with fusiform swelling of digits and skin and nail changes consistent with psoriasis. Psoriatic arthritis can have a pseudo–rheumatoid arthritis pattern but tends to be RF-negative.
Peripheral arthritis associated with IBD	Up to 20% of cases of IBD involve arthritis. The arthritis usually is nondestructive, involves the lower extremities, and reflects active bowel disease. May be indistinguishable from ankylosing spondylitis.
Reactive arthritis (Reiter syndrome)	Can be precipitated by infection (usually gastroenteritis or genitourinary infection) with one of several bacterial organisms. Patients may present with urethritis, conjunctivitis, and arthritis; heel pain with enthesitis; keratoderma blennorrhagicum on the palms or soles; or circinate balanitis on the penis. Differs from rheumatoid arthritis in that it is oligoarticular and asymmetric.
Infectious arthritis (see Chapter 101)	Usually monoarticular but may be oligoarticular; may be migratory; more often affects large joints. Patients present with hot, red, and swollen joints with limited range of motion. Joint fluid analysis is essential. Septic arthritis may develop in joints affected by rheumatoid arthritis.
Systemic lupus erythematosus (see Chapter 103)	Clinically indistinguishable from the arthritis of rheumatoid arthritis; however, the arthritis in systemic lupus erythematosus is non-nodular and nonerosive.
Viral arthritis	Possible causes include Epstein-Barr virus, adenovirus, human parvovirus B19, rubella, HIV, HBV, and HBC. Patients may have morning stiffness, with symmetric involvement of the hands and wrists; they also may be RF-positive (a pseudo–rheumatoid arthritis pattern). Most cases (except those caused by human parvovirus B19) resolve in 4-6 wk.

CMC = carpometacarpal; CPPD = calcium pyrophosphate dihydrate; DIP = distal interphalangeal; ELISA = enzyme-linked immunosorbent assay; HBV = hepatitis B virus; HCV = hepatitis C virus; IBD = inflammatory bowel disease; MCP = metacarpophalangeal; MTP = metatarsophalangeal; PIP = proximal interphalangeal; RF = rheumatoid factor.

standard of care to start disease-modifying anti-rheumatic drugs (DMARDs) at time of diagnosis and as early in disease course as possible. DMARDs are immunosuppressive agents that slow or block autoimmune damage to joints and organs. DMARDs are divided into two categories: nonbiologic and biologic (Table 4).

Nonbiologic DMARDs include methotrexate (MTX), leflunomide, hydroxychloroquine, sulfasalazine, and minocycline. MTX is the preferred initial therapy as it is highly effective, well tolerated, associated with high rates of adherence, and has a relatively low cost compared with other DMARDs. Low-dose MTX has anti-inflammatory effects while higher doses induce the antimetabolic effects used in treating cancer. In women of childbearing age, MTX must be stopped at least 3 months prior to conception. Leflunomide has similar efficacy and is frequently used if MTX is not tolerated. Either can be used effectively as initial monotherapy in patients with RA of any degree or duration. Regular use of alcohol and presence of hepatitis B or C are contraindications to the use of MTX or leflunomide.

Monotherapy with hydroxychloroquine, sulfasalazine, or minocycline can be considered as initial therapy to treat early, mild, and nonerosive disease; however, these agents are usually used as add-on therapy to MTX. Combination therapy tends to be more effective than monotherapy, especially for patients with high disease activity, and may include the use of 2 or 3 nonbiologic DMARDs. Hydroxychloroquine is an antimalarial agent effective in patients with symptoms that overlap with lupus. Sulfasalazine is an aspirin-like agent that is considered in patients who have had an inadequate response to initial treatment.

Table 4. Drug Treatment of Rheumatoid Arthritis

Drug	Mechanism	Indication	Notes
DMARDs			
Methotrexate	Folic acid antimetabolite	DMARD that is most likely to provide durable long-term response; often the initial choice	Takes 1-2 mo for full effect; frequently used in combination with other medications. Contraindicated in pregnancy and use with caution in patients who may become pregnant, have underlying liver or lung disease, immunosuppression, or infection. Folic acid supplementation prevents toxicity without interfering with efficacy.
Hydroxychloroquine	Antimalarial agent with lysosomotropic action that affects immune regulation and inflammation	Early, mild, and nonerosive disease; in combination with methotrexate or when methotrexate is contraindicated	Takes 2-6 mo for full effect; frequently used in combination regimens. Use with caution in patients who are pregnant or who have antimalarial allergy, G6PD deficiency, or retinal disease. Perform annual ophthalmologic examination.
Sulfasalazine	Unknown	Early, mild, and nonerosive disease; in combination with methotrexate or when methotrexate is contraindicated	Takes 1-2 mo for full benefit. Use with caution in patients with sulfonamide or aspirin allergy, G6PD deficiency, kidney or liver disease, blood disease, or asthma.
Leflunomide	Pyrimidine synthesis inhibitor	In combination with methotrexate or when methotrexate is contraindicated for progressive disease	Contraindicated in pregnancy; use with caution in patients who may become pregnant (known teratogen) or have liver disease.
Biologic Agents			
TNF inhibitors (adalimumab, etanercept, certolizumab pegol, golimumab, infliximab)	Immunomodulation	Uncontrolled disease despite use of DMARDs	Testing for latent tuberculosis required before starting therapy.
Interleukin-1 receptor antagonist (anakinra)	Immunomodulation	Uncontrolled disease despite use of DMARDs	Testing for latent tuberculosis required before starting therapy.
T-cell costimulatory blocker (abatacept)	Immunomodulation (down-regulation of T cells)	Uncontrolled disease despite use of DMARDs	Testing for latent tuberculosis required before starting therapy.
B-cell depleting agent (rituximab)	Monoclonal antibody against CD20	Uncontrolled disease despite use of DMARDs	Testing for latent tuberculosis required before starting therapy.
Anti-inflammatory Agents			
NSAIDs	Inhibit cyclooxygenase	Mild disease without erosions; as an adjunctive analgesic in more serious disease	NSAIDs do not prevent disease progression. Use with caution in patients with chronic kidney disease or ulcer disease.
Glucocorticoids	Suppress inflammation at multiple points along the inflammatory cascade	Low-dose or intra-articular injections when NSAIDs do not control symptoms and when DMARDs have not yet produced an effect	High-dose glucocorticoids are useful in treating serious extra-articular manifestations (eg, vasculitis).

DMARD = disease-modifying anti-rheumatic drug; G6PD = glucose-6-phosphate dehydrogenase; NSAIDs = nonsteroidal anti-inflammatory drugs; TNF = tumor necrosis factor.

Biologic DMARDs are considered when the response to MTX (alone or in combination with other nonbiologic DMARDs) has not resulted in tight control of inflammation or remission. They are powerful immunosuppressants that significantly increase the risk of infection. Screening for tuberculosis is mandatory prior to initiating treatment with a biologic DMARD, and they should be withheld in patients with active infections. All biologics have better efficacy when used in combination with MTX rather than as monotherapy.

Biologic therapy usually begins with a TNF-α inhibitor (adalimumab, etanercept, certolizumab pegol, golimumab, infliximab) generally added to MTX therapy, as combination therapy has been shown to decrease radiographic progression. There are no proven differences in efficacy between the different TNF-α inhibitors. Patients may respond to a different biologic DMARD if a trial of one agent is unsuccessful. Other available biologic DMARDs include a B-cell depleting agent (rituximab), the T-cell costimulatory blocker (abatacept), the interleukin-1 receptor antagonist (anakinra), and the interleukin-6 receptor antagonist (tocilizumab).

Nonpharmacologic modalities such as heat and joint range-of-motion exercises can help to alleviate joint symptoms but do not alter the disease course. Physical and occupational therapy and psychological support may be helpful to patients with RA. Counseling regarding joint protection techniques, use of assistive devices, and therapeutic exercises are essential. Surgical therapy may be indicated for patients with destructive RA that cannot be managed pharmacologically. End-stage disease of the hip or knee often is treated with total joint arthroplasty.

Follow-up

Patients on MTX or leflunomide therapy should have liver aminotransferase, albumin, creatinine levels, and a complete blood count checked every 4 to 8 weeks. Aggressive treatment of the underlying inflammatory process in RA has been shown to decrease the development of atherosclerotic disease. Because coronary artery disease is the leading cause of death in patients with RA, management of traditional cardiovascular risk factors (smoking, hyperlipidemia, diabetes, hypertension, obesity) is also recommended.

Bibliography

Aletaha D, Neogi T, Silman AJ, et al. 2010 Rheumatoid arthritis classification criteria: an American College of Rheumatology/European League Against Rheumatism collaborative initiative. Arthritis Rheum. 2010;62:2569-81. [PMID: 20872595]

Huizinga TW, Pincus T. In the clinic. Rheumatoid arthritis. Ann Intern Med. 2010;153:ITC1-1-ITC1-15; quiz ITC1-16. [PMID: 20621898]

Chapter 103

Systemic Lupus Erythematosus

Kimberly Tartaglia, MD

Systemic lupus erythematosus (SLE) is an autoimmune disease characterized by immune complex deposition, autoantibody formation, and organ inflammation. In patients with SLE, autoantibodies can take the form of immune complexes that deposit in tissues or bond to target cells. Autoantibodies can cause damage by fixing complement on the surface of a cell (causing cell lysis), by binding to Fc receptors on circulating cells (leading to cell clearance in the liver or spleen), or by binding to Fc receptors on macrophages (initiating cell-mediated inflammation). SLE is most common in women of childbearing age; women are 9 times more likely than men to be affected by SLE. People of certain races (eg, African, Asian, Hispanic) also are more commonly affected by SLE. The clinical course of SLE is variable and may be characterized by alternating periods of remission and relapse (with either acute or chronic onset).

Although the cause of SLE is unknown, the disease appears to be multifactorial. A genetic association exists, with more than 40 susceptibility genes identified. Environmental influences (eg, ultraviolet [UV] light), infection by the Epstein-Barr virus, smoking, stress, and hormonal factors likely contribute to SLE development or disease flares. Additionally, many drugs can trigger an SLE-like illness or autoantibody formation. However, drug-induced lupus erythematosus tends to be milder than SLE and is temporally related to the causative drug. The most common agents associated with drug-induced lupus are procainamide, hydralazine, isoniazid, and quinidine.

SLE commonly involves the blood components, skin, kidneys, lungs, joints, serosal tissues, and central and peripheral nervous systems. The most characteristic laboratory abnormality is the presence of antinuclear antibody (ANA) in serum.

Screening

Screening for SLE in asymptomatic patients with a family history of SLE or in patients with atypical symptoms is not indicated. ANA is found in 95% to 99% of patients with SLE but lacks specificity. ANA also is found in patients with viral and bacterial infections, other autoimmune diseases, malignancies, and cirrhosis and in up to 10% of the normal population.

Clinical Manifestations

Nonspecific constitutional symptoms are common in SLE and include fatigue, fever, and weight loss. Mucocutaneous findings, such as nasal and oral ulcers, alopecia, or rash (malar or discoid) are found in up to 90% of patients with lupus. Additionally, greater than 90% of patients with SLE have polyarthralgias or polyarthritis. Symmetric wrist or hand (metacarpophalangeal [MCP], proximal interphalangeal [PIP] joints) involvement is most common.

SLE is associated with Raynaud phenomenon, which is characterized by the fingers or toes becoming white or blue when cold and

Table 1. American College of Rheumatology Criteria for the Diagnosis of Systemic Lupus Erythematosus

Criteria[a]	Definition
Malar rash	Fixed erythema, flat or raised, over the malar eminences
Discoid rash	Erythematous, circular, raised patches with keratotic scaling and follicular plugging; atrophic scarring may occur
Photosensitivity	Rash after exposure to ultraviolet light
Oral ulcers	Oral and nasopharyngeal ulcers (observed by physician)
Arthritis	Nonerosive arthritis of ≥2 peripheral joints, with tenderness, swelling, or effusion
Serositis	Pleuritis or pericarditis (documented by electrocardiogram, rub, or evidence of effusion)
Kidney disorder	Urinalysis: 3+ protein or >0.5 g/d; cellular casts
Neurologic	Seizures or psychosis (without other cause)
Hematologic	Hemolytic anemia or leukopenia (<4000/μL [4.0 × 10⁹/L]) or lymphopenia (<1500/μL [1.5 × 10⁹/L]) or thrombocytopenia (<100,000/μL [100 × 10⁹/L]) in the absence of offending drugs
Immunologic	Anti–double-stranded DNA, anti-Smith, and/or antiphospholipid antibodies
Antinuclear antibodies (ANA)	An abnormal titer of ANA by immunofluorescence or an equivalent assay at any point in the absence of drugs known to induce ANA

[a]Any combination of 4 or more of the 11 criteria, well documented at any time during a patient's history, makes it likely that the patient has systemic lupus erythematosus (specificity and sensitivity are 95% and 75%, respectively).

Data from Hochberg MC. Updating the American College of Rheumatology revised criteria for the classification of systemic lupus erythematosus. Arthritis Rheum. 1997;40:1725. [PMID: 9324032]

then red when warmed (Plate 73). SLE is also associated with Sjögren syndrome, as evidenced by dry eyes and dry mouth.

Diagnosis

The diagnosis of SLE depends on obtaining an appropriate history and physical examination and supportive laboratory data. A patient is classified as having SLE if 4 of the 11 American College of Rheumatology criteria for SLE diagnosis are confirmed by a physician (Table 1). Patients may present with an explosive onset of multiple findings or have a more subtle presentation over a long period of time. To establish the diagnosis of SLE, patients need not manifest all the diagnostic criteria simultaneously; the criteria can be fulfilled over time. The differential diagnosis of SLE is broad and is summarized in Table 2.

Physical Examination and Laboratory Studies

A patient suspected of having SLE requires a thorough physical examination to identify specific organ involvement, with emphasis on the diagnostic criteria. Nonspecific findings (eg, fever, tachycardia, lymphadenopathy) are common but must not automatically be attributed to SLE. The most common cause of fever in SLE is infection, which may result from chronic immunosuppression caused by the disease or medications used to treat the disease. Closely inspect nasal and oral mucous membranes for painless ulcers. Photosensitive rashes spare the nasolabial folds and under the lower lip (Plate 32). Discoid rashes (Plate 33) commonly occur on the external ear, forearm, and scalp; scalp lesions may cause alopecia. Pleuritis or pericarditis may be detected by auscultating a friction rub or by identifying signs of a pleural effusion. Hepatosplenomegaly may be seen in SLE. On musculoskeletal examination, patients may have joint tenderness or synovitis. Tendon inflammation may lead to joint rupture or Jaccoud arthropathy (Plate 74). Neurologic deficits, seizures, or confusion may indicate central nervous system infection, ischemia, brain or spinal cord inflammation (cerebritis or transverse myelitis), or the more subtle neuropsychiatric manifestations of SLE. Sensory or motor symptoms may be due to peripheral neuropathy, muscle inflammation, or ischemia caused by vasculitis.

Renal disease is common in SLE, and the incidence of kidney involvement is higher in Asian, Hispanic, and African-American patients. A patient satisfies this criterion by having a 24-hour urine protein excretion >500 mg/d, by urinalysis showing >10 erythrocytes per high-power field or erythrocyte or leukocyte casts in a sterile urine sample (proven by culture), or by kidney biopsy. Lupus nephritis results from immune-complex deposition in glomeruli. There are 6 subtypes of lupus nephritis (Table 3), each with a different prognosis; treatment varies with the subtype.

Autoantibodies are a hallmark of SLE. A positive ANA is sensitive but not specific. A persistent ANA titer >1:640 is more likely to be suggestive of SLE. Anti-double stranded DNA (dsDNA) and anti-Smith antibodies are specific for SLE. Other antibodies, such as anti-Ro/SSA, anti-La/SSB, and anti-RNP, can be seen in SLE but may also be associated with Sjögren syndrome, rheumatoid arthritis, or overlap syndromes. In active SLE, the circulating immune complexes activate complement, causing their consumption and resulting in a decrease of C3, C4, and total hemolytic complement (CH50). Serial C3 and C4 or CH50 measurements may help determine whether SLE is becoming more active or is responding to therapy. In addition, the level of anti-dsDNA antibody may reflect disease activity, with higher levels corresponding to more active disease.

Hematologic disorders in lupus commonly include cytopenias and, less commonly, thrombophilia or antiphospholipid syndrome. In patients with SLE, anemia is most often due to chronic disease, but can also occur as a result of autoimmune hemolytic anemia

Table 2. Differential Diagnosis of Systemic Lupus Erythematosus (SLE)

Disorder	Notes
Fibromyalgia, chronic fatigue syndrome	About 30% of patients with SLE may have fibromyalgia; most patients with SLE have chronic fatigue syndrome. Fibromyalgia diagnosis requires characteristic tender points, with chronic pain above and below the waist.
Rheumatoid arthritis (see Chapter 102)	Rheumatoid arthritis causes symmetric polyarthritis, similar to SLE, but deforming arthritis and erosions are more common. Patients with SLE may be seropositive for rheumatoid factor.
Drug-induced lupus	Certain drugs (hydralazine, procainamide, isoniazid, quinidine) may cause a syndrome of fever, serositis, and arthritis.
Essential mixed cryoglobulinemia (see Chapter 106)	Essential mixed cryoglobulinemia can cause palpable purpura, nephritis, and neuropathy. Although 30% of patients with SLE have mildly elevated aminotransferase levels, these findings should lead to a search for hepatitis B or C in which this disorder frequently occurs.
Granulomatosis with polyangiitis (Wegener) (see Chapter 106)	Sinus disease, lung nodules, and kidney disease. Patients usually are seropositive for ANCA.
Polyarteritis nodosa (see Chapter 106)	Vasculitis, kidney disease, and mononeuritis multiplex. Biopsy shows medium-vessel vasculitis.
Erythema infectiosum (fifth disease)	Can cause a symmetric polyarthritis, usually self-limited. May be associated with fifth disease outbreak in the local school system.
Serum sickness	May mimic SLE, with fever, joint pain, rash, and complement consumption.
Thrombotic thrombocytopenic purpura (see Chapter 49)	May mimic SLE, with fever, CNS changes, thrombocytopenia, and kidney failure. Finding schistocytes on peripheral smear is a major clue.
Malignancy	May be associated with positive ANA, anemia, high ESR, polyarthritis, pleural effusions, fever, and other symptoms.
HIV/AIDS (see Chapter 62)	Can lead to production of antiphospholipid antibodies, a positive Coombs test, and thrombocytopenia. Some patients with SLE will have false-positive results for HIV infection on ELISA; confirmation on Western blot is essential.

ANA = antinuclear antibody; ANCA = antinuclear cytoplasmic antibody; CNS = central nervous system; ELISA = enzyme-linked immunosorbent assay; ESR = erythrocyte sedimentation rate.

Table 3. Classification of Glomerulonephritis in Systemic Lupus Erythematosus

Class	Histopathology	Comments
I	Minimal mesangial glomerulonephritis	Normal in light microscopy, but immune-complex deposits with immunofluorescence microscopy and/or electro-dense deposits by electron microscopy; good prognosis
II	Mesangial proliferative glomerulonephritis	Mesangial hypercellularity on light microscopy; mesangial immune-complex deposits; good prognosis
III	Focal proliferative glomerulonephritis	Involves <50% of all glomeruli with intracapillary proliferation, segmental or global active lesions; subendothelial immune-complex deposits; bad prognosis without adequate management
IV	Diffuse proliferative glomerulonephritis	Involves ≥50% of all glomeruli with intracapillary proliferation, segmental or global active lesions; subendothelial immune-complex deposits; bad prognosis without adequate management
V	Membranous glomerulonephritis	Characterized by thickening of the basement membrane, subepithelial immune-complex deposits. It can occur in combination with class III or IV; bad prognosis without adequate management
VI	Advanced sclerosing glomerulonephritis	≥90% of glomeruli globally sclerosed without residual activity; the results of progressive unresponsive severe glomerulonephritis

Data from Weening JJ, D'Agati VD, Schwartz MM, et al. The classification of glomerulonephritis in systemic lupus erythematosus revisited. J Am Soc Nephrol. 2004;15:241-50. [PMID: 14747370]

(AIHA) or anemia of kidney disease. Lymphopenia in SLE may be caused by anti-lymphocyte antibodies, and mild thrombocytopenia occurs in up to 50% of patients with lupus. Idiopathic thrombocytopenic purpura (ITP) may be the first presenting symptom of SLE. Evans syndrome, which is the occurrence of two or more immune-mediated cytopenias (usually AIHA and ITP), may also be a manifestation of SLE.

Antiphospholipid syndrome (see Chapter 53) can be associated with SLE or can occur in isolation. Diagnosis includes both clinical and laboratory criteria (Table 4). Antiphospholipid syndrome is associated with venous thromboembolism (59%), arterial thromboembolism (28%), pregnancy loss, vasculitis, and cardiac valvular abnor-malities. Diagnosis of antiphospholipid syndrome may be initially considered when a patient has unexplained thrombocytopenia or the activated partial thromboplastin time (aPTT) is prolonged and does not improve with a mixing study. Positive anticardiolipin antibodies (IgG or IgM) or lupus anticoagulant in the setting of previous arterial or venous thromboembolism or pregnancy morbidity make the diagnosis of antiphospholipid syndrome.

Therapy

Pharmacologic therapy for SLE depends on the manifestations in a particular patient. Musculoskeletal complaints should be treated

Table 4. Diagnostic Criteria for Antiphospholipid Syndrome (APS)[a]

Clinical Criteria	Definitions
Vascular events	One or more objectively confirmed symptomatic episodes of arterial, venous, or microvascular thrombosis. Histopathologic specimens must demonstrate thrombosis in the absence of vessel wall inflammation.
Pregnancy morbidity	One or more unexplained fetal deaths at or beyond the 10th week of gestation, with normal fetal morphology; or One or more premature births of a morphologically normal neonate before the 34th week of gestation because of eclampsia, severe preeclampsia, or placental insufficiency; or Three or more unexplained, consecutive, spontaneous abortions before the 10th week of gestation in the absence of maternal anatomic, chromosomal, or hormonal abnormalities or paternal chromosomal abnormalities

Laboratory Criteria	Definitions
Lupus anticoagulant	Positive result for a lupus anticoagulant using a phospholipid-dependent clotting assay (aPTT, dilute Russell viper venom assay, kaolin clotting time, dilute PT) with evidence of phospholipid dependence present on two or more occasions at least 12 weeks apart; or
Anticardiolipin antibody	Medium- or high-titer IgG or IgM anticardiolipin antibody measured using a standardized ELISA on two or more occasions at least 12 weeks apart; or
β_2 glycoprotein I antibody	High-titer anti-β_2 glycoprotein I IgG or IgM antibody measured using a standardized ELISA on two or more occasions at least 12 weeks apart

aPTT = activated partial thromboplastin time; ELISA = enzyme-linked immunosorbent assay; PT = prothrombin time.

[a]Definite APS requires one clinical criteria and one laboratory criteria.

Data from Miyakis S, Lockshin MD, Atsumi T, et al. International consensus statement on an update of the classification criteria for definite antiphospholipid syndrome (APS). J Thromb Haemost. 2006;4:295-306. [PMID: 16420554]; and Devreese K, Hoylaerts MF. Laboratory diagnosis of the antiphospholipid syndrome: a plethora of obstacles to overcome. Eur J Haematol. 2009;83:1-16. [PMID: 19226362]

with NSAIDs or hydroxychloroquine. Hydroxychloroquine may be continued indefinitely to prevent disease reactivation, even if the disease has been quiescent for many years, and is associated with decreased mortality. Methotrexate or, occasionally, low-dose glucocorticoids may be necessary if a patient fails to respond to initial therapies or the initial manifestations are more severe.

Photosensitive rashes can be treated conservatively with a sunscreen that blocks UVA and UVB radiation, hydroxychloroquine, and topical glucocorticoids. Intralesional glucocorticoids may be helpful to treat discoid lupus erythematosus until hydroxychloroquine therapy becomes effective.

High-dose or pulse-dose (high doses over a short period of time) glucocorticoids (such as methylprednisolone) and other immunosuppressive agents (eg, cyclophosphamide, mycophenolate mofetil, azathioprine) are used for the more severe manifestations of SLE, including nephritis, cerebritis, vasculitis, and life-threatening hematologic abnormalities.

Cyclophosphamide is generally reserved for lupus nephritis, given its serious side effect profile. Recent studies suggest that mycophenolate mofetil is effective for lupus nephritis with a more favorable side effect profile.

Prior to or at the time of initiation of systemic glucocorticoids or immunosuppressants, a tuberculin skin test or a *Mycobacterium tuberculosis* interferon-γ release assay must be performed to establish whether the patient is at risk for reactivation of latent tuberculosis. Because patients with SLE may have functional asplenia, vaccination against pneumococcal illness, *Haemophilus influenzae* infection, influenza, and, possibly, meningococcal infection is indicated.

Patients with antiphospholipid syndrome are at high risk for venous or arterial thromboembolism. Patients with SLE and positive antiphospholipid antibodies should be treated with low-dose aspirin (81 mg daily). Patients who have an episode of venous thromboembolism should be anticoagulated indefinitely.

Patient education is fundamental to the management of SLE and is directed toward understanding the disease and its treatment. Patients should try to avoid stress and UV radiation (ie, sun exposure) and strive to maintain good nutrition. Patients with SLE are at increased risk for premature atherosclerosis and glucocorticoid-induced osteoporosis. To help reduce these risks, patients should eat a balanced diet low in saturated fats, exercise regularly, take calcium and vitamin D supplements, and avoid cigarettes.

Follow-Up

Recent data indicate 80% to 90% survival rates for patients with SLE 10 years after diagnosis. Early deaths are seen in patients with active disease and in patients who require high doses of glucocorticoids and intense immunosuppression, whereas later deaths often are due to cardiovascular disease. Although SLE is not curable, extended periods of remission with no clinical activity frequently occur.

Patients need regular follow-up to detect disease flares. A complete blood count, serum creatinine level, C3 and C4 measurement, and urinalysis with culture and sensitivity should be performed at routine follow-up visits to screen for anemia, leukopenia, thrombocytopenia, and evidence of nephritis. Lifestyle modifications and pharmacologic therapies to reduce cardiovascular risk factors must be instituted, because cardiovascular disease is a major cause of death in patients with SLE.

Bibliography

Crow MK. Developments in the clinical understanding of lupus. Arthritis Res Ther. 2009;11:245. [PMID: 19849817]

Ruiz-Irastorza G, Crowther M, Branch W, Khamashta MA. Antiphospholipid syndrome. Lancet. 2010;376:1498. [PMID: 20822807]

Chapter 104

Spondyloarthritis

Thomas M. De Fer, MD

Spondyloarthritis (SpA) refers to a heterogeneous group of related disorders that include ankylosing spondylitis (AS), reactive arthritis (ReA) (formerly known as Reiter syndrome), psoriatic arthritis (PsA), and enteropathic arthritis (EA). Manifestations vary widely among these conditions and there may be overlap between different conditions (Figure 1), but common features include a genetic predisposition, the potential for an infectious trigger, the presence of enthesitis (inflammation at the attachment site of tendon to bone), and extra-articular involvement. Undifferentiated spondyloarthritis (USpA) refers to the clinical features of SpA in patients who do not meet the criteria for an individual disease process and applies to a significant minority of patients. The results of serologic studies, including rheumatoid factor (RF) assays, are characteristically negative in affected patients.

Various cytokines mediate the local inflammatory and destructive processes affecting the synovium, entheses, and bone. The significant efficacy of tumor necrosis factor α (TNF-α) inhibitors in the treatment of the SpAs suggests that TNF-α is a key mediator in this inflammatory process. T-cell activation is characteristic of the pathogenesis of the SpAs, particularly PsA.

The class I histocompatibility antigen HLA-B27 is a significant risk factor for AS and ReA, but is not as strongly associated with EA and PsA. Less than 5% of HLA-B27–positive persons actually develop AS. **Testing for HLA-B27 positivity generally is not helpful diagnostically in patients suspected of having spondyloarthritis because most HLA-B27–positive persons do not develop disease.** In addition, not all patients with AS have this allele.

Infectious triggers have been suspected in all of the SpAs. These triggers include the potential immunostimulatory properties of gastrointestinal flora in EA and the bacteria harbored in psoriatic skin plaques. Nongonococcal genitourinary tract infections (primarily caused by *Chlamydia*) and infectious diarrhea (caused by *Shigella*, *Salmonella*, *Yersinia*, and *Campylobacter*) can be associated with ReA. However, antibiotic treatment does not alter the course of arthritis in patients with nongonococcal disease. Patients with HIV infection have an increased incidence of ReA, psoriasis, and PsA. Testing for HIV infection is indicated for patients newly diagnosed with severe psoriatic or reactive arthritis.

Diagnosis

The clinical features of the different forms of spondyloarthritis are listed in Table 1. The most characteristic feature of SpA is enthesitis, with subsequent reactive new bone and spur (osteophyte) formation. Spinal manifestations include sacroiliitis and spondylitis, which typically cause insidious-onset pain in the gluteal region. In affected patients, pain often persists for >3 months and may progress over time to involve the rest of the spine. Unlike mechanical back pain, pain and stiffness associated with the SpAs are characteristically worse in the morning or after sedentary periods and are alleviated with exercise.

In patients with SpA, progressive limitation in spinal mobility may occur over years and ultimately result in spinal fusion (ankylosis), often in a forward-flexed position, with decreased chest expansion. Prior to fusion, sacroiliac joints may be tender to palpation. Patients also may have a loss of cervical spinal mobility. Inflammation of the ligamentous attachments erodes the corners of the vertebral bodies, which produces a squared-off appearance. Ossification of spinal ligaments leads to the development of a rigid "bamboo spine," named because the vertebrae resemble bamboo on radiography (Figure 2). Magnetic resonance imaging (MRI) is the most sensitive method for detecting early inflammatory changes in the sacroiliac joints and spine.

Enthesitis and bone spurs can occur at any site of tendon attachment. Commonly seen in the plantar fascia and Achilles tendon, involvement at these sites often causes episodes of inflammation and heel pain. However, most cases of isolated plantar fasciitis are not related to SpA. Enthesitis contributes to dactylitis, which can cause the characteristic sausage-shaped digits associated with psoriatic and reactive arthritis (Plate 75).

The pattern and degree of peripheral joint involvement among the SpAs vary widely, with the most common pattern being an asym-

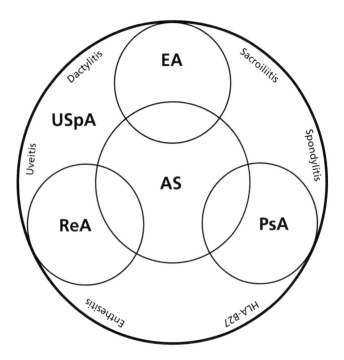

Figure 1. The spondyloarthitidies. The size and degree of overlap of the circles are not intended to be proportional to incidence or prevalence. Rather, they indicate the shared clinical features and potential challenges differentiating these diseases.

Table 1. Clinical Features of Spondyloarthritis

	Ankylosing Spondylitis	Psoriatic Arthritis	IBD-Associated Arthritis	Reactive Arthritis
Musculoskeletal				
Axial involvement	Axial involvement predominates; initially symmetrically involves the SI joints and lower spine, progressing cranially; does not skip regions		May be asymptomatic but can follow a course similar to ankylosing spondylitis; SI involvement often asymmetric; arthritis does not parallel IBD activity	Less common than in other forms of spondyloarthritis
Peripheral involvement	Enthesitis (eg, Achilles tendinitis) with or without asymmetric large-joint oligoarthritis; hip involvement can cause significant functional limitation; shoulders can be involved	Various patterns, most commonly polyarticular; DIP involvement is associated with nail involvement; dactylitis, enthesitis and tenosynovitis; arthritis mutilans	Two patterns: mono/oligoarticular large joint lower extremity (parallels IBD activity), and polyarticular small joint upper extremity (does not parallel IBD activity); dactylitis and enthesitis may occur	Enthesitis and asymmetric large-joint oligoarthritis; usually self-limited; non-erosive; some patients experience recurrent or persistent arthritis; may develop features of other forms of spondyloarthritis
Dermatologic	Psoriasis may coexist	Psoriasis typically precedes joint involvement; nail pitting; onycholysis	Pyoderma gangrenosum; erythema nodosum	Keratoderma blenorrhagicum; circinate balanitis
Ophthalmologic	Uveitis (typically anterior, unilateral, recurrent)	Conjunctivitis more common than uveitis (anterior, can be bilateral, insidious, or chronic)	Uveitis (anterior, can be bilateral, insidious, or chronic); conjunctivitis, keratitis, and episcleritis are rare	Conjunctivitis is more common than uveitis
Gastrointestinal	Asymptomatic intestinal ulcerations	–	Crohn disease; ulcerative colitis	Prior GI infection in some patients
Genitourinary	Urethritis (rare)	–	Nephrolithiasis	Prior GU infection in some patients; sterile urethritis, prostatitis, cervicitis, and salpingitis
Cardiovascular	Aortic valve disease; aortitis; conduction abnormalities; CAD	Association with traditional CAD risk factors	Thromboembolism	–
Pulmonary	Restrictive lung disease from costovertebral rigidity; apical fibrosis (rare)	–	–	–
Bone quality	Falsely elevated bone mineral density from syndesmophytes; increased risk of spine fracture	Increased risk of fracture; multifactorial	High risk for vitamin D deficiency, low bone density, and fracture	Localized osteopenia

CAD = coronary artery disease; DIP = distal interphalangeal; GI = gastrointestinal; GU = genitourinary; IBD = inflammatory bowel disease; SI = sacroiliac.

metric oligoarthritis that predominantly involves the large joints of the lower extremities. However, PsA may potentially manifest as a predominantly peripheral arthritis that involves the small joints.

Extra-articular manifestations of the SpAs include inflammatory disease involving the skin, eyes, lungs, gastrointestinal and genitourinary tracts, and vascular system. The most noticeable skin manifestation is psoriasis, but other mucocutaneous manifestations can include oral ulcers, keratoderma blennorrhagicum (pustular psoriasis on the soles and palms), and circinate balanitis (plaques or ulcers involving the glans and shaft of the penis), all of which are most typical in ReA. Erythema nodosum (Plate 2) and pyoderma gangrenosum (Plate 3) are typical in enteropathic arthritis. Inflammatory eye disease (conjunctivitis, uveitis, keratitis) can be recurrent and is the most common extra-articular manifestation of the SpAs.

Genitourinary manifestations of the SpAs include noninfectious urethritis, prostatitis, cervicitis, and salpingitis. Inflammatory bowel

disease (IBD) is a form of gastrointestinal involvement. Pulmonary fibrosis, when present, characteristically involves the lung apices. Aortitis with aortic root dilatation, conduction abnormalities, and myocardial dysfunction may occur. Both pulmonary and cardiac complications are rare and more characteristic of AS than of other types of SpA.

Ankylosing Spondylitis

AS is the prototypical SpA. The prevalence of this condition in the United States is less than 1%. Males are affected 2 to 3 times more often than females; however, the disease tends to be milder in females and may go undiagnosed.

The onset of AS is marked by persistent low back pain and occurs in the teenage years or twenties. Although inflammatory spinal disease in AS may be limited to the pelvis and sacroiliac joints, it typi-

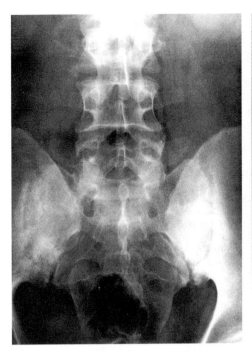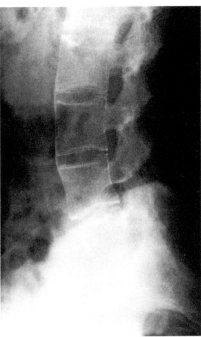

Figure 2. Radiographic findings in ankylosing spondylitis. The initial radiographic findings of ankylosing spondylitis include irregularities along the margins of the sacroiliac joints leading to eventual ankylosis and fusion. Inflammation of the ligamentous attachments erodes the corners of the vertebral bodies, which produces a squared-off appearance. Over time, ossification of these ligaments leads to the development of a rigid "bamboo spine," named because the shape of the vertebrae resemble bamboo on radiography.

cally progresses cephalad resulting in a characteristic stooped posture and loss of spinal mobility seen in late disease. Fractures, including those caused by minor trauma to the rigid spine, and spinal cord and nerve root impingement (eg, cauda equina syndrome), may complicate spinal involvement. Arthritis of the hips is common in this disease and further worsens function. Relatively common extra-articular manifestations of AS include uveitis, aortic regurgitation, chest wall restriction, and apical pulmonary fibrosis.

Early diagnosis has become particularly important with the availability of newer therapeutic agents that can alter the debilitating course of this disease. Early in the disease course, plain radiographs of the pelvis and spine often are normal. Symptomatic patients with suspected AS should undergo MRI of the sacroiliac joints to detect early inflammatory and erosive changes.

Reactive Arthritis

ReA is an uncommon inflammatory arthritis occurring within 2 months of an episode of bacterial gastroenteritis or nongonococcal urethritis or cervicitis. Precise estimates of incidence and prevalence are not known, and diagnosis is more difficult when there is no history of a preceding infection, as occurs in asymptomatic sexually transmitted diseases. It is generally accepted that ReA following a genitourinary infection is much more common in men but that men and women are affected equally after gastroenteritis. ReA is less strongly associated with HLA-B27 than AS. The arthritis in these patients is sterile but bacterial DNA has been isolated in some cases. Clustering of cases of ReA have been documented following single source infections.

ReA typically has an acute onset and presents as an asymmetric oligoarthritis predominantly of the lower extremities (knees, ankles), inflammatory back pain, or a combination of these symp-

toms. Symptoms of enthesitis (heel pain, dactylitis) may be present. Extra-articular manifestations, particularly ocular (conjunctivitis, anterior uveitis), genitourinary (urethritis, cervicitis), and mucocutaneous (oral ulcers, keratoderma blennorrhagicum, circinate balanitis), are common and may precede the development of the arthritis. Only a minority of affected patients have the classic triad of arthritis, urethritis/cervicitis, and conjunctivitis, previously referred to as Reiter syndrome.

Acute episodes of reactive arthritis typically resolve within 4 to 6 months. In some patients, these episodes recur or evolve into a chronic destructive arthritis or progressive spinal disease. As many as 50% of affected patients have recurrent or progressive disease.

Enteropathic Arthritis

About 20% of patients with IBD (Crohn disease, ulcerative colitis) develop inflammatory arthritis. IBD-associated peripheral arthritis may manifest as either a polyarticular arthritis resembling rheumatoid arthritis (RA) or an asymmetric oligoarthritis predominantly of the lower extremities, resembling ReA. The peripheral arthritis may precede the development of gastrointestinal symptoms. The course of arthritis often fluctuates with the activity of the underlying bowel inflammation.

Approximately 10% to 20% of patients with IBD have spinal involvement ranging from asymptomatic sacroiliac disease seen on radiographs to a clinical presentation identical to that of AS, with progressive spinal fusion. Unlike the peripheral arthritis, the progression of spinal involvement in EA is independent of the course of the bowel disease. The association of HLA-B27 with EA appears to be much less significant than it is with AS.

Additional extra-articular manifestations of EA include inflammatory eye disease and erythema nodosum, which occur in up to

20% of patients with this condition. The course of the extra-articular manifestations typically parallels peripheral joint and bowel inflammation.

Psoriatic Arthritis

Psoriasis affects approximately 1% to 2% of the general population, and about 15% to 30% of affected patients develop arthritis (though estimates range broadly). The highest incidence of arthritis occurs in patients with extensive skin involvement. However, arthritis can develop even in patients with minimal skin disease, such as psoriasis that is limited to the nails. In PsA, psoriasis typically predates arthritis, whereas arthritis develops before skin disease in 15% of patients.

PsA should be considered in patients with dactylitis, marked distal interphalangeal (DIP) joint involvement, asymmetric joint involvement, symptoms of enthesitis, or joint ankylosis. In these patients, a thorough skin examination should be performed to verify the diagnosis, looking for nail changes or undetected small patches of psoriasis in areas such as the scalp, periumbilical region, and intertriginous skin folds.

PsA often presents as a symmetric polyarticular arthritis resembling RA in distribution, with the exception that PsA also is associated with involvement of the DIP joints. In some patients, the arthritis is limited almost exclusively to the DIP joints, often with associated psoriatic nail changes, such as pitting and onycholysis (Plate 69). Other patterns of arthritis also occur, including the destructive arthritis mutilans (see Table 1). The so-called "pencil in cup" deformity may be seen on radiographs of the hand (Figure 3). Typical nonarthritic manifestations are enthesitis, dactylitis, and tenosynovitis. Uveitis occurs in a small percentage of patients.

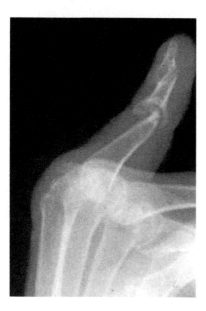

Figure 3. Psoriatric arthritis and "pencil in cup" finding.

Therapy

Many of the treatments used in RA also suppress inflammation in the joints and extra-articular structures and provide long-term prevention of joint damage and functional loss in spondyloarthritis. Current treatment emphasizes aggressive use of immunosuppressive, disease-modifying agents such as methotrexate or sulfasalazine and, more recently, use of TNF-α inhibitors. NSAIDs are used as adjunctive therapy for joint inflammation and pain; they do not alter the disease course or prevent progression. NSAIDs also may exacerbate IBD and should be used with caution in patients with enteropathic arthritis.

Ankylosing Spondylitis

TNF-α inhibitors are first-line therapy for ankylosing spondylitis. TNF-α inhibitors (eg, etanercept, infliximab, adalimumab) significantly suppress inflammation in the axial skeleton, improve back pain, and potentially halt progressive ankylosis and subsequent loss of mobility and function. TNF-α inhibitors also are effective for peripheral arthritis and extra-articular disease. Traditional immunosuppressants (eg, methotrexate, sulfasalazine) benefit patients with peripheral joint and extra-articular disease but are not effective for spinal involvement.

Reactive Arthritis

Antibiotics are indicated for treatment of the acute infection only and generally are of little benefit for treating reactive joint disease. NSAIDs are first-line therapy for symptom management in reactive arthritis. Disease-modifying agents such as sulfasalazine or methotrexate may be beneficial in recurrent or chronic inflammatory disease. TNF-α inhibitors should be considered if other interventions are ineffective or if patients have significant axial skeletal involvement or severe disease.

Enteropathic Arthritis

The immunosuppressive therapies that benefit IBD also have efficacy in the treatment of the associated peripheral joint and extra-articular manifestations of EA. These therapies include glucocorticoids, sulfasalazine, azathioprine, methotrexate, and TNF-α inhibitors. In patients with axial skeletal disease, TNF-α inhibitors should be considered as first-line therapy.

Psoriatic Arthritis

The therapeutic options in PsA are similar to those in RA. Generally, immunosuppressive agents that have efficacy in psoriatic skin disease also benefit patients with joint disease. Methotrexate is beneficial for both skin and joint disease and has dominated therapy for many years. TNF-α inhibitors increasingly have been shown to be effective in psoriatic arthritis and are the preferred intervention for patients with predominant axial skeletal disease.

Bibliography

Poddubnyy D, Rudwaleit M. Early spondyloarthritis. Rheum Dis Clin North Am. 2012;38:387-403. [PMID: 22819091]

Chapter 105

Other Rheumatologic Conditions

Kevin M. McKown, MD

Polymyositis and Dermatomyositis

Polymyositis and dermatomyositis are autoimmune inflammatory disorders that affect muscle and other tissues and typically present as subacute-onset, symmetric proximal weakness. Polymyositis and dermatomyositis are associated with significant morbidity and mortality and always need to be considered in a patient with proximal weakness. Other causes of proximal weakness also must be considered, especially medications (Table 1).

The causes of polymyositis and dermatomyositis are unknown, but the disorders are thought to be triggered by environmental factors (eg, viral infection) in genetically susceptible individuals. Dermatomyositis (less frequently polymyositis) also may occur as a paraneoplastic phenomenon. Myositis-specific autoantibodies may also play a role in disease pathogenesis. Involved muscles demonstrate muscle fiber necrosis, regeneration, and inflammatory infiltrates; histopathologic differences between polymyositis and dermatomyositis are thought to reflect differences in the pathophysiology of these disorders. In polymyositis the lymphocytic infiltration occurs within muscle fascicles, whereas in dermatomyositis, inflammation occurs predominantly around the muscle fascicles and in the interfascicular and perivascular areas. Because of vascular involvement in dermatomyositis, muscle damage may be due to infarction of small blood vessels supplying the muscle.

Diagnosis

Proximal weakness is suggested by difficulty rising from a chair, walking, and raising the arms or head. Pharyngeal and respiratory involvement is associated with higher mortality and is suggested by difficulty swallowing, nasal regurgitation, and dyspnea. Evidence of a neuropathic cause of weakness, such as dysesthesia, numbness, tremor, stiffness, focal or asymmetric neurologic findings, or distal weakness is absent.

Look for weakness raising the arms against resistance or rising from a chair, along with relative sparing of distal strength (eg, grip strength). Oculomotor muscles are spared, sensation and reflexes are normal, and significant muscle tenderness is unusual, as is muscle atrophy. Look for scaly, purplish papules and plaques located on the extensor surfaces of the metacarpophalangeal and interphalangeal joints (Gottron papules) (Plate 76) and an edematous, heliotrope (dusky purple) discoloration of the upper eyelids and periorbital tissues; both of these rashes are diagnostic for dermatomyositis (Plate 77). Patients also may have an erythematous rash in a V-shaped area over the lower neck and upper chest (V-sign) (Plate 78) or over the upper back, back of the neck, and shoulders (shawl sign). A pertinent hand finding is rough, cracked, dirty-appearing skin on the lateral surfaces and tips of the fingers (mechanic's hands).

Serum creatine kinase (CK), aldolase, and aspartate aminotransferase (AST) usually are elevated to at least twice the normal levels (Table 2). Electromyographic and nerve conduction velocity studies can suggest a myopathic process and can help exclude neuropathic conditions, although they are not adequate for definitive diagnosis. Muscle imaging with MRI is not routine and is nonspecific, although it will show evidence of a myopathy and may be helpful if a biopsy cannot be obtained, a specific biopsy site in need-

Table 1. Differential Diagnosis of Polymyositis and Dermatomyositis

Disorder	Notes
Hypothyroidism (see Chapter 11)	Can cause weakness, stiffness, and elevated CK level. Screen with serum TSH measurement.
Diabetes mellitus (see Chapter 13)	Can cause fatigue and generalized muscle weakness. Diabetes may also cause neuropathies and plexopathies.
Drug- and alcohol-induced muscle disease	Can cause weakness and possibly pain and elevated CK levels. Consider glucocorticoids, statins, fibric acid derivatives, and organophosphate poisoning.
Inclusion body myositis	Also an inflammatory muscle disease that causes asymmetric proximal and distal weakness; more common than polymyositis in older people; does not respond well to glucocorticoids and immunosuppressants. Biopsy showing evidence of filamentous inclusions is diagnostic.
Infections	Viruses often cause pain and may cause frank myositis. Consider bacterial infection, trichinosis, and other parasitic infections.
SLE, systemic sclerosis, Sjögren syndrome, amyloidosis, vasculitis, rheumatoid arthritis	May mimic myositis, have an element of myositis, or coexist independently of polymyositis.
Critical illness neuromyopathy	Profound generalized weakness following prolonged therapeutic paralysis in an intensive care unit; caused by a combination of muscle and nerve dysfunction.
Rhabdomyolysis	Acute muscle necrosis with myoglobinuria leading to acute kidney injury; caused by drugs, alcohol, trauma, seizures, and muscle disease. CK level usually is >10,000 U/L.

CK = creatine kinase; SLE = systemic lupus erythematosus; TSH = thyroid-stimulating hormone.

Table 2. Laboratory and Other Studies for Polymyositis and Dermatomyositis

Test	Notes
Creatine kinase (CK)	Elevated CK level is one of the diagnostic criteria; levels are 10 to 50 times normal. Myocardial muscle isoforms may be elevated. Exclude hypothyroidism, alcohol, medications, exercise, cardiac disorders, and muscular dystrophy as alternative causes for an elevated CK level.
Aldolase, aspartate aminotransferase (AST), alanine aminotransferase (ALT), lactate dehydrogenase (LDH)	AST, ALT, and LDH may be elevated in muscle disease but proportionately less than CK. Elevated AST, ALT, and LDH levels may mistakenly suggest liver dysfunction.
Electromyography	It may support the diagnosis of a muscle disorder or, alternatively, a neuropathic or spinal cord disorder.
Anti-Jo-1 antibody	Anti-Jo-1 antibody is the most commonly seen of several antisynthetase antibodies that may be detected. It is present in 20%-25% of adult patients, and is associated with higher likelihood of interstitial lung disease and higher mortality rates. The "antisynthetase syndrome" consists of acute onset of dermatomyositis or polymyositis with fever, rash, Raynaud phenomenon, arthritis, and interstitial lung disease.
Anti-Mi-2 antibody	Anti-Mi-2 antibody is present in 5%-10% of patients and is associated with good response to therapy. Seen in dermatomyositis in association with V-sign and shawl sign.
Anti-SRP antibody	Anti-SRP antibody are seen in approximately 5% of patients with inflammatory myopathy, mostly polymyositis. Associated with severe disease that is difficult to treat.
Antinuclear antibody (ANA) and rheumatoid factor (RF)	ANA and RF are positive in a fraction of patients with polymyositis but have no predictive value.
Muscle MRI	MRI helps to localize inflammation and to indicate a biopsy site and may be corroborative when the diagnosis cannot be confirmed by other criteria. Conversely, a negative MRI of a weak muscle makes polymyositis unlikely.
Muscle biopsy	A positive muscle biopsy is the definitive criterion for inflammation.
Chest imaging	Interstitial lung disease may be present before, at, or long after the onset of muscle disease and can follow a variable course.
Pulmonary function studies	In polymyositis and dermatomyositis, respiratory dysfunction can be caused by respiratory muscle weakness or, more often, by interstitial lung disease.

MRI = magnetic resonance imaging.

ed, or the results of a biopsy are nondiagnostic due to the patchy nature of muscle involvement.

Biopsy is the most definitive test to classify a myopathy as polymyositis, inclusion body myositis, or another less common disease. Inflammatory infiltrates of lymphocytes invading non-necrotic muscle cells (or interstitial and perivascular areas) will be seen in about 80% of cases of polymyositis or dermatomyositis. A clinically weak muscle that has not been damaged by electromyography should be chosen for biopsy. Myositis-specific autoantibodies may help predict manifestations (eg, interstitial lung disease) as well as responsiveness to therapy and mortality (see Table 2).

Interstitial lung disease, cardiomyopathy, arthritis, and photosensitive rashes are associated with polymyositis and dermatomyositis. Malignancies are increased in adults with dermatomyositis and in adults aged >45 years with polymyositis. The most commonly associated malignancies are adenocarcinomas of the cervix, lung, ovary, pancreas, bladder, and stomach. For most patients, age- and gender-appropriate cancer screening tests are performed initially to evaluate for possible malignancy, with additional evaluation based on additional individual risk factors.

Therapy

Therapy consists of a glucocorticoid prednisone and immunosuppressive agents. Prednisone typically is started at doses of 1 mg/kg/day and is tapered as the patient responds. Methotrexate or azathioprine is used with prednisone to improve the response rate and to act as a glucocorticosteroid-sparing agent.

Follow-Up

Monitor serum CK level and muscle strength to assess response to treatment and follow for treatment-induced toxicities. Glucoglucocorticoid-induced myopathy can occur during treatment and should be suspected when a patient on a moderate to high dose develops worsening proximal muscle weakness in the presence of a normal or minimally elevated CK level. Patients on high-dose or long-term glucocorticoids need to be observed for infection and treated appropriately to prevent accelerated bone loss. Patients also need to be monitored for the development of cardiac or pulmonary manifestations, malignancy, and other autoimmune disease.

Systemic Sclerosis

Systemic sclerosis is a disease of unknown cause. The hallmarks of this condition are microangiopathy and fibrosis of the skin and visceral organs. Common pathophysiologic findings include endothelial cell dysfunction, abnormal fibroblast function, and autoantibody production. Systemic sclerosis most commonly affects women and has a peak initial presentation in the third to fourth decade of life.

Classification

Systemic sclerosis is classified according to the extent and pattern of skin involvement. Limited cutaneous systemic sclerosis (lcSSc) is characterized by skin thickening distal to the elbows or knees but can also involve the face and neck. A subset of this condition is the CREST syndrome (calcinosis, Raynaud phenomenon, esophageal dysmotility, sclerodactyly [Plate 79], and telangiectasia). A major cause of disease-related mortality associated with lcSSc is pulmonary arterial hypertension. Diffuse cutaneous systemic sclerosis (dcSSc) is characterized by skin thickening proximal to the elbows and/or knees. The major causes of disease-related mortality associated with dcSSc are interstitial lung disease and kidney disease.

Diagnosis

The diagnosis of systemic sclerosis is established in patients with sclerodermatous skin changes (tightness, thickening, and nonpitting induration) and sclerodactyly (sclerodermatous skin changes limited to the fingers and toes). In the absence of these findings, the diagnosis of systemic sclerosis may be established in patients with 2 of the following features: sclerodactyly, digital pitting (soft-tissue defects and scarring in the pulp space of the distal phalanges), or basilar fibrosis visible on chest radiography (Table 3).

Antinuclear antibody (ANA) is present in >95% of patients with systemic sclerosis; a centromere pattern is associated with lcSSc and with a lower incidence of interstitial lung disease. The presence of anti-topoisomerase I (anti-Scl-70) antibody is associated with dcSSc and with an increased risk for interstitial lung disease (Table 4).

Early physical findings include puffiness or swelling in the hands and fingers. Later findings include hypo- or hyperpigmentation, telangiectases, and subcutaneous calcinosis. Raynaud phenomenon due to arterial vasospasm is the initial clinical manifestation in 70% of patients and eventually occurs in >95%. Episodes of Raynaud phenomenon usually are triggered by cold exposure. Look for sequelae of Raynaud phenomenon, such as digital pitting, ulceration, and gangrene (Plate 80). Inflammatory arthritis and inflammatory myositis are uncommon.

At least 80% of patients have esophageal dysfunction due to smooth muscle dysfunction resulting in dysphagia and gastroesophageal reflux disease (GERD). Mucosal telangiectases in the stomach may cause significant blood loss. Small- and large-bowel involvement may cause a functional ileus that manifests as symptoms of bowel obstruction. Bacterial overgrowth due to dysmotility may cause chronic diarrhea, alternating diarrhea and constipation, and/or malabsorption. Patients with lcSSc also may develop biliary cirrhosis.

Scleroderma renal crisis is a life-threatening condition characterized by the acute onset of hypertension, kidney failure, and microangiopathic hemolytic anemia. Scleroderma renal crisis usually is seen with dcSSC and may be precipitated by glucocorticoids therapy. Cardiac disease in patients with systemic sclerosis may be clinically silent or manifest as cardiomyopathy, pericarditis, or arrhythmias.

Therapy

No therapy has been shown to modify the underlying disease process involved in systemic sclerosis; therefore, treatment is directed at the clinical manifestations of the disease. There is no clearly effective treatment for skin thickening. Raynaud phenomenon is treated by avoiding cold exposure and with the use of vasodilators, such as dihydropyridine calcium channel blockers. Antiplatelet agents, such as aspirin and dipyridamole, also are used. The phosphodiesterase type 5 inhibitor sildenafil reduces the development of digital ulcers. Surgical revascularization, sympathetic nerve blockade or sympathectomy, prostacyclin analogues, or endothelin antagonists may be indicated in severe, refractory cases.

Gastric acid suppression with proton pump inhibitors is indicated for nearly all patients, as most will have symptomatic GERD. Extended courses of antibiotics may be useful in patients with small-bowel bacterial overgrowth. Scleroderma renal crisis is a medical emergency, and patients should be hospitalized for aggressive blood pressure control with angiotensin-converting enzyme inhibitors, which should be continued even in patients with significant renal insufficiency, as kidney function may improve even after months of dialysis.

Cyclophosphamide may improve pulmonary symptoms in patients with interstitial lung disease and has been shown to modestly improve lung function in this setting. Treatment for isolated pulmonary arterial hypertension is vasodilation (eg, sildenafil, bosentan, epoprostenol) and, if needed, oxygen.

Follow-Up

Screen patients for end-organ involvement, including interstitial lung disease, pulmonary arterial hypertension, and chronic kidney

---

Table 3. Differential Diagnosis of Systemic Sclerosis

Disorder	Notes
Primary Raynaud disease	Patients have cold-induced vasospasm without an associated underlying disease. ANA test is negative.
Systemic lupus erythematosus (see Chapter 103)	Among other disease characteristics, patients have fatigue, arthralgia, and a positive ANA test.
Inflammatory myopathy	Patients have proximal muscle weakness caused by muscle inflammation, elevated muscle enzymes (creatine kinase, aldolase), abnormal electromyography results, and a positive ANA test.
Eosinophilic fasciitis	Eosinophilic fasciitis causes woody induration of the skin with thickening of the fascia, often with associated peripheral eosinophilia; the hands and feet typically are spared. Internal organs are not affected, Raynaud phenomenon is absent, and ANA test is negative. Full-thickness skin-to-muscle biopsy is helpful in making the diagnosis.
Generalized morphea	Confluence of plaques of morphea (localized scleroderma), with sparing of the hands and feet. Internal organs are not affected, and Raynaud phenomenon is absent. ANA test may be positive.
Idiopathic pulmonary fibrosis (see Chapter 95)	Patients have restrictive lung disease with pathologic changes identical to those seen in systemic sclerosis. However, Raynaud phenomenon, gastrointestinal and musculoskeletal symptoms, and systemic sclerosis-specific autoantibodies are absent.
Nephrogenic systemic fibrosis	Brawny hyperpigmentation, papular lesions; occurs in patients with chronic kidney disease exposed to gadolinium-containing contrast agents used for MRI procedures.

ANA = antinuclear antibodies; MRI = magnetic resonance imaging.

Table 4. Laboratory and Other Studies for Systemic Sclerosis

Test	Notes
Antinuclear antibody (ANA)	ANA is present in >95% of patients with systemic sclerosis.
ANA, centromere pattern	Typically associated with lcSSc. Patients tend to have a reduced frequency of pulmonary, renal, and cardiac involvement.
Anti-Scl-70 (anti-topoisomerase I) antibody	Most commonly seen in patients with dcSSc. Associated with interstitial lung disease.
Blood urea nitrogen, serum creatinine	Used to monitor kidney function, particularly in patients with dcSSc. Patients with dcSSc are at risk for scleroderma renal crisis.
Complete blood count with peripheral smear	Scleroderma renal crisis (a microangiopathic process) is associated with anemia, schistocytes on peripheral blood smear, and thrombocytopenia.
Chest imaging	Chest imaging may reveal basilar pulmonary fibrosis.
Pulmonary function tests	Reduced forced vital capacity occurs in interstitial lung disease. Reduced diffusion capacity occurs in both interstitial lung disease and pulmonary hypertension. An isolated reduction of diffusion capacity may be indicative of pulmonary hypertension.
Doppler echocardiography	May reveal evidence of pulmonary hypertension.
Nailfold capillaroscopy	Wide-field magnification of the nailfold capillaries shows characteristic changes in patients with systemic sclerosis.

dcSSc = diffuse cutaneous systemic sclerosis; lcSSc = limited cutaneous systemic sclerosis.

failure. Judicious follow-up can aid in detecting internal organ involvement at an early stage.

Sjögren Syndrome

Sjögren syndrome is a chronic autoimmune inflammatory disorder associated with mononuclear cell infiltration of the exocrine glands, with resultant decreased lacrimal and salivary gland function. There is a 9:1 female predominance, and onset typically is in midlife. Although Sjögren syndrome may be a primary disorder, it commonly occurs secondary to another autoimmune disease. Secondary Sjögren syndrome can be seen in association with rheumatoid arthritis, systemic lupus erythematosus, systemic sclerosis, inflammatory myopathy, autoimmune liver disease, and autoimmune thyroid disease.

Diagnosis

The combination of the sicca complex (ie, dry eyes [xerophthalmia] and dry mouth [xerostomia]), an abnormal Schirmer test (confirming dry eyes), and positive anti-Ro/SSA and anti-La/SSB antibodies has both a sensitivity and a specificity of 94% for the diagnosis of primary Sjögren syndrome. Clues to this condition include a patient report of a dry, gritty feeling in the eyes or use of hydrating eye drops multiple times daily. Patients with dry mouth typically awaken at night to drink water and often keep water at their bedside.

Look for red sclerae, a decreased salivary pool, periodontal disease, dental caries, and parotid gland enlargement. Other possible features include an inflammatory polyarthritis, cutaneous vasculitis, interstitial lung disease, interstitial nephritis with associated distal renal tubular acidosis, vasculitis associated with mononeuritis multiplex, and peripheral neuropathy. Pathologic diagnosis of Sjögren syndrome can be confirmed if biopsy specimens of a labial salivary gland reveal focal lymphocytic infiltration. Because Sjögren syndrome is associated with B-cell clonal expansion, affected patients have an increased risk for developing lymphoma (5% lifetime risk), which typically involves the salivary glands.

Therapy

Frequent use of lubricant eye drops (artificial tears) is the primary treatment for symptomatic dry eyes. Saliva substitutes and parasym-

pathomimetic agents (pilocarpine or cevimeline) can be helpful for dry mouth symptoms. Aggressive dental prophylaxis can reduce the incidence of periodontal disease and dental caries. NSAIDs or hydroxychloroquine may be helpful for arthralgias. Systemic glucocorticoids therapy or other immunosuppressants may be warranted in patients with severe extraglandular manifestations.

Follow-Up

Regularly scheduled follow-up visits are needed to monitor the lymphatic system and to consider biopsy of persistently enlarged parotid or submandibular glands, to look for malignant lymphoproliferation.

Fibromyalgia

Fibromyalgia is a noninflammatory condition characterized by chronic, widespread musculoskeletal pain. Affected patients almost always have fatigue and nonrestorative sleep; they also have an increased prevalence of anxiety and major depression. Fibromyalgia affects women more frequently than men and typically has an onset between the ages of 20 and 50 years. The cause of fibromyalgia is unknown but may be related to central nervous system (CNS) mechanisms, such as dysregulation of neurotransmitter function and central pain sensitization.

Diagnosis

Patients with fibromyalgia demonstrate widespread tenderness, but the number of tender points may vary from day to day. The location of tender points is arbitrary and expert opinion holds that the presence of specific tender points is not essential in the diagnosis of fibromyalgia. Table 5 summarizes a differential diagnosis of fibromyalgia. Fibromyalgia can occur in association with autoimmune disorders, such as rheumatoid arthritis, systemic lupus erythematosus, and Sjögren syndrome. Laboratory studies are useful only in excluding conditions that may mimic fibromyalgia and generally should include a complete blood count and measurement of serum thyroid-stimulating hormone level, erythrocyte sedimentation rate or c-reactive protein level, and alanine and aspartate aminotransferase levels (chronic hepatitis). **Routine testing for ANA or rheumatoid factor in**

Table 5. Differential Diagnosis of Fibromyalgia

Disorder	Notes
Rheumatoid arthritis, osteoarthritis	Patients with arthritis have objective joint swelling. Look for findings related to the specific type of arthritis (eg, positive rheumatoid factor and bony erosions in rheumatoid arthritis; characteristic crepitation and radiographic findings in osteoarthritis).
Polymyalgia rheumatica (see Chapter 106)	Patients generally are older (>60 y) and have diffuse pain (mostly in hip and shoulder girdles), prominent stiffness, constitutional symptoms (fever, malaise, loss of appetite and weight), and elevated ESR (usually >50 mm/h).
Hypothyroidism (see Chapter 11)	Patients have fatigue, lethargy, muscle stiffness or cramping, constipation, dry skin, delayed relaxation phase of deep tendon reflexes, low T_4, and elevated TSH. Tender points are uncommon in hypothyroidism.
Myopathy	Patients have muscle weakness and fatigue, objective muscle weakness on examination, increased muscle enzymes, and typical electromyographic and muscle biopsy findings.
Ankylosing spondylitis (see Chapter 104)	Patients (most often males) have back pain, decreased mobility of the lumbar spine, characteristic radiographic findings of sacroiliitis, and elevated ESR.
Chronic fatigue syndrome	Patients have severe fatigue, postexertional malaise, musculoskeletal pain, impaired memory or concentration, sore throat, and tender cervical or axillary lymph nodes.

ESR = erythrocyte sedimentation rate; T_4 = thyroxine; TSH = thyroid-stimulating hormone.

patients with suspected fibromyalgia is not indicated and may be confusing as these tests often are abnormal in normal individuals.

Therapy

Patient education and nonpharmacologic interventions form the cornerstone of therapy. Educating patients with fibromyalgia about the nature and course of the disease is imperative. Regular low-impact aerobic exercise, such as walking and water aerobics, has demonstrated effectiveness. Cognitive behavioral therapy has been shown to be beneficial. Tricyclic antidepressants are the most-studied pharmacologic agents in the treatment of fibromyalgia and may be beneficial. Pregabalin, which disrupts neuronal signaling in the CNS, and the serotonin-norepinephrine reuptake inhibitors duloxetine and milnacipran are approved by the U.S. Food and Drug Administration for the treatment of fibromyalgia. All of these agents have been shown to decrease pain and, to various degrees, improve fatigue, sleep, depression, and quality of life compared with placebo. NSAIDs may provide some patients additional pain relief when used in combination with these agents. Opioid analgesics and glucocorticoids have no demonstrated efficacy in fibromyalgia and should be avoided.

Follow-Up

A therapeutic physician-patient relationship is an important component of treatment for fibromyalgia to determine progress, reinforce positive health behavior, and appropriately diagnose any new disease or condition that might have developed since the last visit.

Other Conditions

Mixed Connective Tissue Disease

This is a disorder with characteristics associated with elements of other specific rheumatologic diseases (such as systemic sclerosis, systemic lupus erythematosus and polymyositis) but does not meet the clinical or diagnostic criteria for a particular condition. Raynaud phenomenon, arthralgias, puffy hands, and fatigue are typical findings. All patients have high titers of anti-U1-ribonucleoprotein (RNP) antibodies. Treatment is based on active disease manifestations.

Undifferentiated Connective Tissue Disease

These patients have strong clinical and immunologic evidence of a systemic autoimmune disorder, but their clinical manifestations are very nonspecific for any particular rheumatologic condition. Patients may go on to develop a more well-defined rheumatic disorder, or may remain unchanged for years, or may go into remission.

Adult-Onset Still Disease

This is an uncommon inflammatory condition seen primarily in young adults and is characterized by daily spiking fevers, arthralgia or arthritis, and an evanescent salmon-colored rash. Laboratory abnormalities include leukocytosis, anemia, thrombocytosis, elevated liver chemistry tests, and elevated ESR. Ferritin levels are often markedly elevated (>1000 ng/mL). Initial treatment is with glucocorticoids. Methotrexate and inhibitors of interleukin (IL)-1, IL-6 and tumor necrosis factor-α are used in refractory or chronic disease.

Relapsing Polychondritis

Relapsing polychondritis is a very uncommon inflammatory disorder that manifests as inflammation of cartilaginous structures (eg, ears, nose, eyes, airways, joints) and less commonly other tissues (eg, heart, kidneys, skin, gastrointestinal tract, and nervous system). A significant minority of cases are associated with other rheumatologic conditions and malignancy. Treatment is mostly empiric and related to the degree of organ involvement. Chondritis may be treated with NSAIDs, prednisone, and dapsone. Additional therapy such as cyclophosphamide may be necessary in patients with more vasculitis and organ involvement.

Bibliography

Arnold LM, Clauw DJ. Fibromyalgia syndrome: practical strategies for improving diagnosis and patient outcomes. Am J Med. 2010;123:S2. [PMID: 20569735]

Gabrielli A, Avvedimento EV, Krieg T. Scleroderma. N Engl J Med. 2009;360:1989-2003. [PMID: 19420368]

Mammen AL. Dermatomyositis and polymyositis: Clinical presentation, autoantibodies, and pathogenesis. Ann N Y Acad Sci. 2010;1184:134-53. [PMID: 20146695]

Chapter 106

Systemic Vasculitis

Ernie L. Esquivel, MD

The systemic vasculitides are a heterogeneous group of disorders characterized by destructive inflammation within blood vessel walls. The clinical manifestations of vessel wall inflammation result from tissue ischemia or hemorrhage due to vessel occlusion, narrowing, or aneurysm formation. The vasculitides are classified according to the size of the predominant blood vessels involved. Large vessel (aorta and major branches) vasculitis can manifest with limb claudication, asymmetric blood pressures, renovascular hypertension, bruits or aortic dilation. Patients with medium vessel (smaller than aortic branches, but large enough to be visible by angiography) vasculitis may develop ulcers, cutaneous nodules, digital gangrene, mononeuritis multiplex, livedo reticularis or renovascular hypertension. Vasculitis involving small vessels (arterioles, capillaries and postcapillary venules) present with purpura, splinter hemorrhages, urticarial or vesiculobullous lesions, glomerulonephritis, alveolar hemorrhage, uveitis, or scleritis. Fever, weight loss, malaise and arthralgia/arthritis are common presentations of all the vasculitides.

A careful, stepwise diagnostic approach is indicated to establish the diagnosis of vasculitis. Risk factors for vasculitis, including age, gender and ethnic origin, need to be assessed. Environmental and occupational exposures have been linked to vasculitis, in particular, cigarette smoking and silica dust exposure. A thorough history of medication use and use of illicit drug, including cocaine, amphetamines, and ephedra alkaloids, should be obtained. As other systemic diseases (such as systemic lupus erythematosus, rheumatoid arthritis, sarcoidosis, chronic viral hepatitis) may manifest with vasculitis, these diseases must be considered.

Because the manifestations of vasculitis are highly variable, other processes that can mimic vasculitis should be ruled out. These include infectious endocarditis, atrial myxomas and arteriovenous occlusive diseases, such as disseminated intravascular coagulation, antiphospholipid antibody syndrome, or thrombotic thrombocytopenic purpura. Atheroembolic phenomena occur after angiography, aortic surgery, or thrombolytic therapy and can present with livedo reticularis, petechiae and purpuric lesions. Although a variety of studies may be useful in the diagnostic process (Table 1), a tissue biopsy is often required to make a definitive diagnosis. Classification of vasculitis depends upon the pattern of organ involvement, the presence of granulomatous inflammation, evidence of immune complex deposition and detection of antineutrophil cytoplasmic antibodies (ANCA). The most recent classification of vasculitis is shown in Table 2.

Large Vessel Vasculitis

Giant Cell Arteritis/Polymyalgia Rheumatica

Giant cell arteritis (GCA) is the most common systemic vasculitis in adults, frequently affecting adults aged >50 years. Inflammation with lymphocytic infiltration affects extracranial branches of the aorta in a segmental fashion, with the presence of multinucleated giant cells seen in half of biopsy specimens. The most common manifestations of GCA are new-onset headache, with temporal artery tenderness or enlargement. Visual symptoms, including diplopia and loss of vision, may be irreversible and reflect occlusive arteritis of the posterior ciliary artery. Other common symptoms include jaw claudication, transient ischemic attacks or stroke and fever and malaise. Although not classified as a vasculitis, there is abundant evidence that polymyalgia rheumatica (PMR) is related to GCA because they share the same inflammatory cytokines and associations with age, ethnicity, and HLA class II alleles. However, fever is uncommon and malaise and weight loss are frequent in patients with PMR. Patients complain of arthralgias and myalgias involving the proximal limbs, axial musculature, and tendinous attachments. Pain is worse with

Table 1. Diagnostic Studies for Suspected Vasculitis

To exclude mimics or secondary causes of vasculitis

Blood cultures

Echocardiography

HIV serology

Hepatitis B and C serologies

Antinuclear antibody

Rheumatoid factor

Antiphospholipid antibodies

Coagulation studies

Urine toxicology screen

To assess extent of organ involvement

Metabolic panel and complete blood count with differential

Urinalysis and microscopy

Chest X-ray and/or chest computed tomography scan

Nerve conduction studies/electromyography

To establish diagnosis of vasculitis

Erythrocyte sedimentation rate, C-reactive protein

Anti-neutrophil cytoplasmic antibodies

Cryoglobulins

Complement levels (C3, C4, C1q)

Anti-glomerular basement membrane antibody

Tissue biopsy with immunofluorescence staining

Angiography

Table 2. Classification Scheme and Characteristics of Systemic Vasculitides

Condition	Key Features
Large vessel vasculitis	
Giant cell arteritis (GCA)/polymyalgia rheumatica (PMR)	Headache, jaw claudication, vision loss, diplopia, scalp tenderness (GCA); diffuse proximal limb and axial muscle (PMR), elevated ESR, positive temporal artery biopsy
Takayasu arteritis	Limb claudication, vascular bruits, aortic regurgitation, young Asian women, vascular stenosis/occlusion/aneurysm on CT angiography
Variable vessel vasculitis	
Behçet disease	Oral and genital ulcers, uveitis, pathergy, cutaneous lesions
Cogan syndrome	Aortic aneurysm or regurgitation, interstitial keratitis, sensorineural hearing loss
Medium vessel vasculitis	
Polyarteritis nodosa	Abdominal pain, new onset hypertension, renal insufficiency, mononeuritis multiplex, cutaneous lesions, aneurysms on angiography
Kawasaki disease	Mostly in children, but also in HIV-infected adults, conjunctivitis, strawberry tongue, erythematous rash, cervical lymphadenopathy, arthritis, acute coronary syndrome, aneurysms
Small vessel vasculitis	
ANCA-associated vasculitis	
Granulomatosis with polyangiitis (Wegener)	Upper respiratory (otitis media, nasal ulcers, saddle-nose deformity, sinusitis), lower respiratory tract (pulmonary infiltrates, cavitary lesions and nodules, hemoptysis), renal insufficiency with crescentic glomerulonephritis, positive c-ANCA (95% specific)
Eosinophilic granulomatosis with polyangiitis (Churg-Strauss)	Asthma, allergic rhinitis and sinusitis, peripheral eosinophilia, crescentic glomerulonephritis, pulmonary infiltrates, mononeuritis multiplex, positive p-ANCA
Microscopic polyangiitis	Rapidly progressive glomerulonephritis, pulmonary hemorrhage, positive p-ANCA
Immune-complex mediated vasculitis	
Anti-glomerular basement membrane (Goodpasture) disease	Necrotizing glomerulonephritis, pulmonary hemorrhage, anemia, rash, circulating anti-GBM antibodies
IgA vasculitis (Henoch-Schönlein purpura)	Antecedent upper respiratory infection, abdominal pain, palpable purpura, arthralgias, glomerulonephritis
Cryoglobulinemic vasculitis	Arthralgias, myalgias, palpable purpura, common in hepatitis C infection, membranoproliferative glomerulonephritis, mononeuritis multiplex, low C3 and C4 levels, presence of serum cryoglobulins, positive rheumatoid factor
Cutaneous leukocytoclastic angiitis (hypersensitivity vasculitis)	Palpable purpura, maculopapular rash, offending drug or infectious agent, no systemic involvement
Hypocomplementemic urticarial vasculitis (anti-C1q vasculitis)	Painful urticarial lesions, glomerulonephritis, arthritis, COPD, uveitis, positive ANA, positive C1q precipitin, low C3 and C4 levels

ANA = antinuclear antibody; ANCA = anti-neutrophil cytoplasmic antibody; C-ANCA = cytoplasmic ANCA; COPD = chronic obstructive pulmonary disease; CT = computed tomography; ESR = erythrocyte sedimentation rate; P-ANCA = perinuclear ANCA.

Data from: Jennette JC, Falk RJ, Bacon PA, et al. 2012 revised International Chapel Hill Consensus Conference Nomenclature of Vasculitides. Arthritis Rheum. 2013;65:1-11. [PMID: 23045170]

movement, but muscle strength is preserved. Laboratory abnormalities in GCA and PMR include an elevated erythrocyte sedimentation rate, seen in 96% of patients. A mild normocytic anemia may be seen. The diagnosis of GCA requires a temporal artery biopsy, which has a sensitivity of 90% to 95%. In some patients a contralateral second biopsy is necessary. Given the risk of irreversible vision loss in patients with GCA, prompt initiation of glucocorticoid therapy (1 mg/kg/day of prednisone) is warranted. Biopsy results should not be influenced by steroids within the first 4 weeks of therapy. Up to 4 weeks of steroid therapy is needed until symptoms and laboratory abnormalities resolve, followed by a slow taper. Patients with PMR tend to respond to 10 to 20 mg/day of prednisone, with rapid improvement in musculoskeletal pain and stiffness.

Variable Vessel Vasculitis

Behçet Disease

Behçet disease is a chronic multisystem disease characterized by painful oral and genital ulcerations (Plate 81), uveitis, skin lesions, gastrointestinal or CNS involvement, and oligoarthritis, commonly found in Asians and people of Mediterranean origin. Cutaneous manifestations include erythema nodosum, pyoderma gangrenosum, Sweet syndrome-like lesions or pustules. Pathergy, the appearance of a pustule or papule 48 hours after the skin is pricked with a 20- to 21-gauge needle, is present in some patients. Ocular involvement, including uveitis and hypopyon (purulent exudate in the anterior chamber), is common. Treatment includes topical, intraocular or systemic glucocorticoid, and addition of immunosuppressive agents when severe.

Medium Vessel Vasculitis

Polyarteritis Nodosa

Polyarteritis nodosa (PAN) is a necrotizing vasculitis involving medium-sized arteries of the mesenteric circulation, kidney, heart, and peripheral nerves. Necrosis leads to widespread aneurysm formation, detectable by angiography. Patients present commonly with muscle pain or weakness, abdominal pain due to mesenteric ischemia, new onset hypertension, renal insufficiency, or testicular pain. Mononeuritis multiplex is seen in nearly half of patients and involves large, mixed-motor and sensory nerves. In 80% of patients, a sural nerve biopsy is diagnostic. Cutaneous manifestations include palpable purpura, skin ulceration, livedo reticularis, and splinter hemorrhages. Diagnosis is reached by biopsy or radiographic evidence of aneurysm formation. PAN is universally fatal if left untreated. Treatment consists of prednisone initially, with cyclophosphamide or alkylating agents added in patients with severe or life-threatening organ involvement. With this approach, 80% of PAN patients survive, with most entering long-term remission.

Small Vessel Vasculitis

ANCA-Associated Vasculitis

Antineutrophil cytoplasmic antibodies (ANCA) are defined by indirect immunofluorescence performed on neutrophils with 2 patterns of staining observed: cytoplasmic (c-ANCA) or perinuclear (p-ANCA). c-ANCA are targeted to serine proteinase-3 (PR3); whereas, p-ANCA positivity indicates antibodies mostly against myeloperoxidase (MPO). The ANCA-associated vasculitides affect small- to medium-sized vessels and do not involve immune complex deposition ("pauci-immune"). The diagnostic value of ANCA testing is well established, but antibody titers do not correlate with disease activity.

Granulomatosis with Polyangiitis (Wegener Granulomatosis)

Granulomatosis with polyangiitis (GPA) predominantly affects the upper and lower respiratory tracts and, in most cases, the kidneys. GPA may present in an indolent manner or be rapidly progressive. Constitutional symptoms include fever and weight loss. Upper airway involvement includes otitis media, nasal ulcers, saddle-nose deformity, sinusitis and subglottic stenosis. Pulmonary manifestations include hemoptysis, cough, fleeting pulmonary infiltrates and bilateral, occasionally cavitary, pulmonary nodules. Limited GPA refers to the absence of renal involvement. Glomerulonephritis occurs in up to 80% of patients and is suggested by the findings of urine red blood cell casts, hematuria, and proteinuria. Up to 40% of patients ultimately develop chronic renal insufficiency. The detection of a positive c-ANCA is 95% specific and has a sensitivity of 90% in patients with active GPA. Diagnosis is best established by lung or kidney biopsy. Treatment of GPA requires a combination of glucocorticoids and daily oral cyclophosphamide. Newer studies have shown efficacy of rituximab as an alternative to cyclophosphamide. Plasma exchange is used as adjunctive therapy with life-threatening disease. Although about 90% of patients achieve remission, up to 30% will relapse, requiring maintenance therapy with an immunosuppressant.

Eosinophilic Granulomatosis with Polyangiitis (Churg-Strauss syndrome)

Eosinophilic granulomatosis with polyangiitis (EGPA) is a necrotizing small vessel vasculitis with eosinophilic infiltration that occurs in the setting of antecedent asthma, allergic rhinitis and sinusitis. Patients present with migratory pulmonary infiltrates, mononeuritis multiplex, necrotizing crescentic glomerulonephritis, palpable purpura, cardiomyopathy and gastrointestinal disease. Peripheral eosinophilia occurs in the prodromal stages. Only 40% of patients will be p-ANCA-positive; therefore, biopsy is frequently necessary. Limited cases respond well to glucocorticoid therapy alone, but addition of cyclophosphamide is needed with kidney involvement (azotemia, proteinuria >1 g/day), cardiomyopathy, gastrointestinal disease, or neurologic manifestations. Full remission is achieved in 80% to 90% of patients.

Microscopic Polyangiitis

Microscopic polyangiitis (MPA) is a necrotizing vasculitis, which frequently presents with rapidly progressive glomerulonephritis and pulmonary capillaritis. Pulmonary manifestations range from mild dyspnea and anemia to massive alveolar hemorrhage, with patchy to diffuse infiltrates noted on chest radiography. Similar to other ANCA-associated vasculitides, arthralgias, myalgias, and fever are common, along with palpable purpuric skin lesions. p-ANCA is present in 60% to 85% of patient. The diagnosis is best made by biopsy of skin, kidney, or lung lesions. Combined therapy with glucocorticoids and cyclophosphamide (or rituximab) is used to induce remission, but risk of relapse is high.

Immune Complex-Mediated Vasculitis

Development of antibody-antigen (immune) complexes (IC) is called the Arthus reaction; deposition of these complexes in blood vessel walls initiates complement activation, an influx of inflammatory cells, thrombus formation, and hemorrhagic infarction. In the skin, palpable purpura, the most common cutaneous finding in IC-mediated vasculitis, results from extravasation of erythrocytes through damaged vessel walls (Plate 82). These nonblanching lesions are distributed symmetrically in dependent areas of the body, where tissue hydrostatic pressure is increased (eg, lower extremities, buttocks). On light microscopy, cellular infiltrates consisting predominantly of neutrophils within and around vessel walls are seen, along with endothelial swelling and proliferation and neutrophil degranulation; hence, the term leukocytoclastic vasculitis.

Cutaneous Leukocytoclastic Angiitis (Hypersensitivity Vasculitis)

This disease is defined by exposure to an offending agent, usually a medication or infectious agent, and is characterized by palpable purpura and/or maculopapular rash. No systemic involvement is noted. Biopsy shows neutrophilic infiltration around a blood vessel. Therapy involves discontinuation of the medication, with systemic glucocorticoids used only when disease is extensive.

IgA Vasculitis (Henoch-Schönlein Purpura)

Henoch-Schönlein (HSP) usually presents in children younger than 5 years. It presents less frequently in adults. It is usually associated with an upper respiratory tract infection followed by rash, abdominal pain, arthralgias and glomerulonephritis. Biopsy shows a predominance of IgA deposition on immunofluorescence. The disease can be self-limited when mild. In adults, a more prolonged disease course is likely. When kidney involvement is present, aggressive immunosuppressive therapy including systemic glucocorticoids and cyclophosphamide is prescribed.

Cryoglobulinemic Vasculitis

Cryoglobulins are immunoglobulins (IgG or IgM), so called because of their tendency to precipitate from serum below body temperature conditions. Type I cryoglobulinemia is associated with an isolated monoclonal immunoglobulin, typically Waldenström macroglobulinemia (IgM) or multiple myeloma (usually IgG). Such patients most commonly present with hyperviscosity and thrombosis, but vasculitic symptoms can occur. In type II cryoglobulinemia, monoclonal IgM and polyclonal IgG (mixed cryoglobulinemia) are present, and about 90% are associated with hepatitis C infection. When type II cryoglobulinemia is not associated with hepatitis C, the disease is called essential mixed cryoglobulinemia. Type III cryoglobulinemia is characterized by the presence of polyclonal IgG and polyclonal IgM and is frequently seen in patients with chronic infections, Sjögren syndrome, and systemic lupus erythematosus. Vasculitis manifests in types II and III cryoglobulinemic patients with a triad of arthralgias, myalgias, and palpable purpura. Involvement of medium-sized vessels results in cutaneous ulcers, digital ischemia, and fixed livedo reticularis. Severe involvement leads to membranoproliferative glomerulonephritis and mononeuritis multiplex. Laboratory abnormalities include high titers of rheumatoid factor, a low serum complement C4 level (out of proportion to the decreased C3 level), and the detection of serum cryoglobulins.

In patients with hepatitis C-associated cryoglobulinemic vasculitis, treatment is based on suppression of viral replication (see Chapter 21). Patients with severe involvement, such as mononeuritis and glomerulonephritis, require immunosuppressive therapy (glucocorticoids and rituximab) and plasma exchange to reduce circulating cryoglobulins.

Anti-Glomerular Basement Membrane (Goodpasture) Disease

Anti-glomerular basement membrane (GBM) disease is a vasculitis caused by the deposition of autoantibodies reactive against type IV collagen found in basement membranes of the glomerular and pulmonary capillaries. Necrotizing glomerulonephritis or pulmonary hemorrhage are devastating manifestations. The diagnosis is established by the detection of circulating anti-GBM antibodies in serum or detection of linear IgG deposits to GBM on kidney biopsy. Treatment involves plasma exchange and use of immunosuppressants.

Bibliography

Jennette JC, Falk RJ, Bacon PA, et al. 2012 revised International Chapel Hill Consensus Conference nomenclature of vasculitides. Arthritis Rheum. 2013;65:1-11. [PMID: 23045170]

Morris A, Grudberg S, Levy BD, Loscalzo J. Clinical problem-solving. A sleeping giant. N Engl J Med 2011;365:72-7. [PMID: 21732839]

Seo P, Stone JH. The antineutrophil cytoplasmic antibody-associated vasculitides. Am J Med. 2004;117:39-50. [PMID: 15210387]

Suresh E. Diagnostic approach to patients with suspected vasculitis. Postgrad Med J. 2006;82:483-88. [PMID: 16891436]

Index

Color Plates

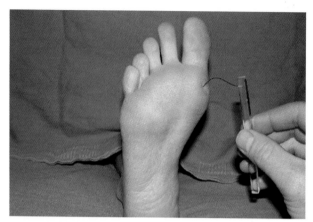

Plate 1. Testing for sensory neuropathy with a 5.07/10g monofilament.

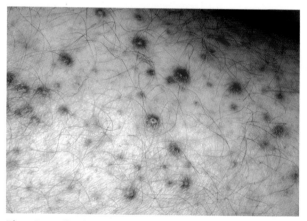

Plate 4. Cellulitis is a rapidly spreading subcutaneous-based infection characterized by a well-demarcated area of warmth, swelling, tenderness, and erythema.

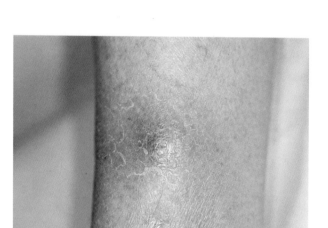

Plate 2. The typical clinical presentation of erythema nodosum is the sudden onset of one or more tender, erythematous nodules on the anterior legs.

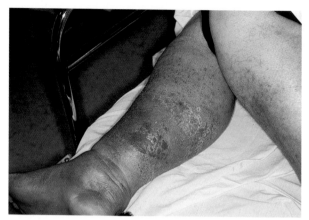

Plate 5. Folliculitis is characterized by pink papules and pustules centered on hair follicles.

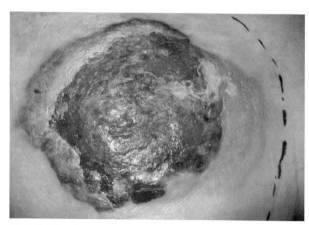

Plate 3. Pyoderma gangrenosum presents as a painful ulcer with a purulent base and undermined, ragged, violaceous borders.

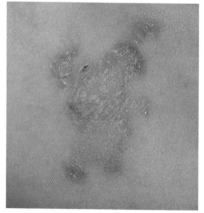

Plate 6. Impetigo is a superficial skin infection characterized by a yellowish, crusted surface. The infection may be caused by staphylococci or streptococci.

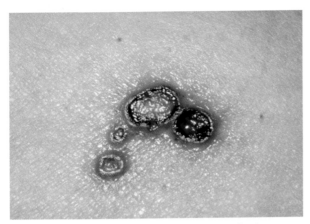

Plate 7. The classic lesions of ecthyma are superficial, saucer-shaped ulcers with overlying crusts.

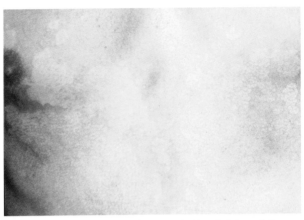

Plate 10. Tinea versicolor is characterized by slightly scaly hyper- or hypopigmented macules on the trunk and upper extremities.

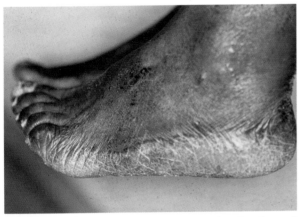

Plate 8. Tinea pedis is characterized by interdigital scaling and maceration or by blisters of the plantar arch, sides of the feet, and/or heel.

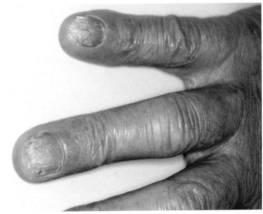

Plate 11. Onychomycosis usually is characterized by a thickened, yellow or white nail with scaling under the elevated distal free edge of the nail plate.

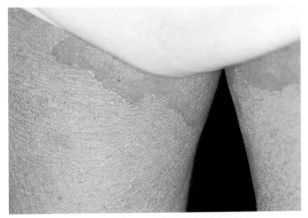

Plate 9. Tinea cruris characteristically presents as an annular lesion with a slight scale, an erythematous advancing edge, and central clearing.

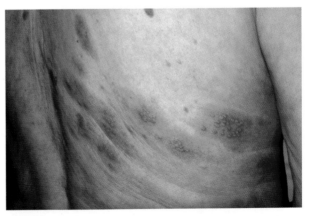

Plate 12. The classic herpes zoster morphology is grouped vesicles on an erythematous base.

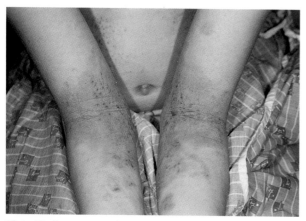

Plate 13. Acute atopic dermatitis is pruritic and red with poorly demarcated, eczematous, crusted, papulovesicular plaques and excoriations.

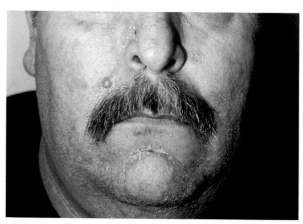

Plate 16. Seborrheic dermatitis is characterized by pink to red skin lesions with greasy scale, crusts, and, occasionally, small pustules.

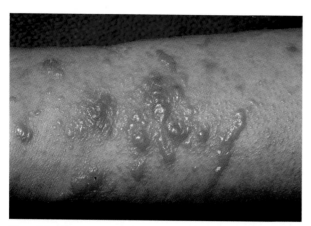

Plate 14. Allergic contact dermatitis usually is intensely pruritic. In acute reactions, the skin is red, edematous, weepy, and crusted, and there may be vesicles or bullae.

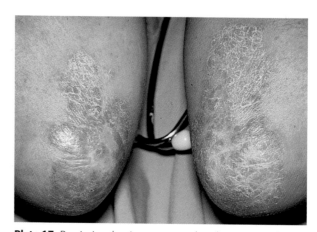

Plate 17. Psoriasis vulgaris appears as sharply marginated plaques with a thick, adherent, silvery scale.

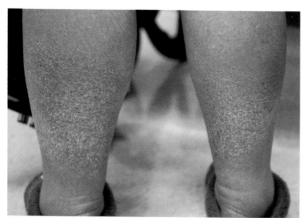

Plate 15. In acute venous stasis dermatitis, the skin is red, warm, and scaly.

Plate 18. Nail pitting is a classic diagnostic finding associated with psoriasis.

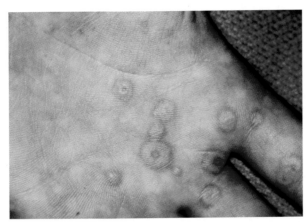

Plate 19. Erythema multiforme lesions range in size from several millimeters to several centimeters and consist of erythematous plaques with concentric rings.

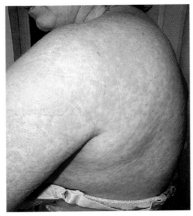

Plate 20. A morbilliform (measles-like) drug eruption consists of symmetrically arranged erythematous macules and papules, some discrete and others confluent.

Plate 21. Pityriasis rosea begins as a single thin, pink, oval, 2- to 4-cm plaque with a thin collarette of scale at the periphery; similar lesions subsequently develop.

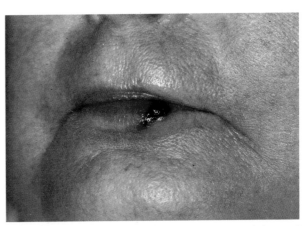

Plate 22. Orofacial herpes simplex lesions appear as a cluster of grouped, painful, pink papules that rapidly become vesicular and typically heal with crusting.

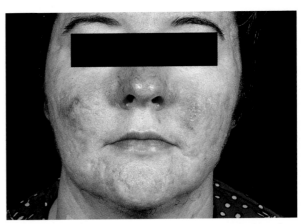

Plate 23. Rosacea is characterized by persistent central facial redness with telangiectasia, pink papules, pustules, and nodules.

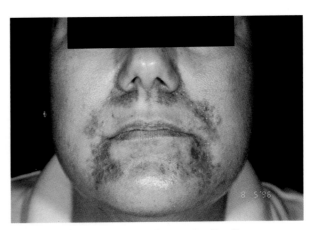

Plate 24. Perioral dermatitis is characterized by discrete papules and pustules on an erythematous base, centered around the mouth.

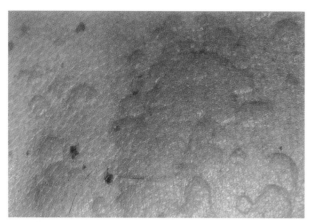

Plate 25. Urticaria presents as episodes of pruritic, red wheals with sharp borders; lesions can last from minutes to hours.

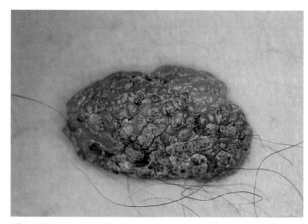

Plate 28. Seborrheic keratoses appear as yellow, tan, or brown to black, well-demarcated papules with a "stuck on" appearance.

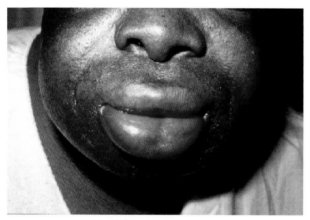

Plate 26. Angioedema, a severe, life-threatening form of urticaria, is characterized by localized edema of the skin or mucosa, usually involving the lips, face, hands, feet, penis, or scrotum.

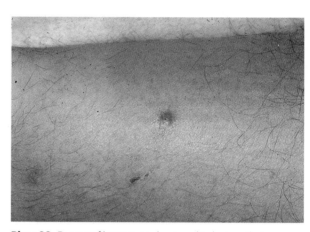

Plate 29. Dermatofibromas are benign skin lesions that appear as firm dermal nodules about the size of a pencil eraser.

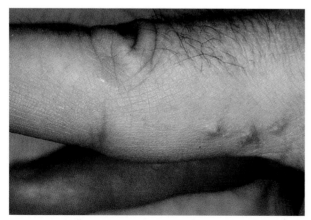

Plate 27. Scabies infestation causes intense pruritus and a papular or vesicular rash.

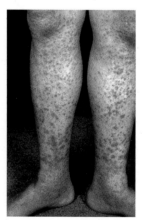

Plate 30. Leukocytoclastic vasculitis is characterized by palpable purpura.

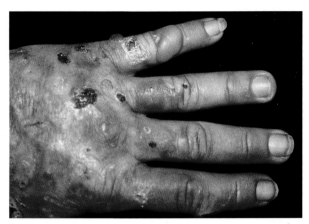

Plate 31. Porphyria cutanea tarda presents as vesicles and bullae on sun-exposed skin surfaces.

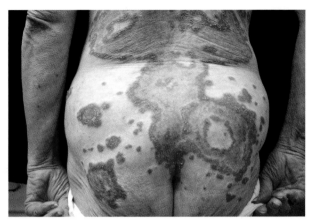

Plate 34. Subacute cutaneous lupus erythematosus is characterized by annular or papulosquamous (psoriasis-like) lesions on sun-exposed skin surfaces.

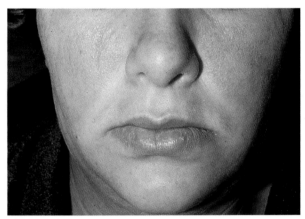

Plate 32. Acute cutaneous lupus erythematosus can present as the classic "butterfly rash," which is characterized by confluent malar erythema.

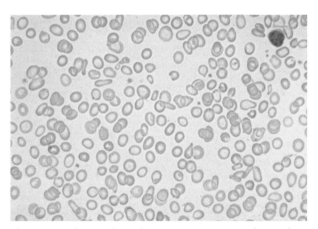

Plate 35. Erythrocyte hypochromia, anisocytosis, and "pencil cells" characteristic of iron deficiency anemia.

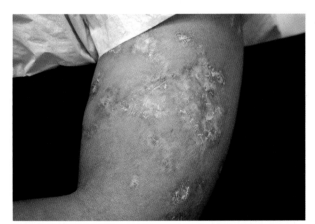

Plate 33. Chronic cutaneous (discoid) lupus erythematosus consists of slowly progressive, scaly infiltrative papules and plaques or atrophic red plaques on sun-exposed skin surfaces.

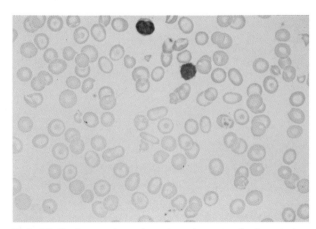

Plate 36. Erythrocyte hypochromia and target cells characteristic of thalassemia trait.

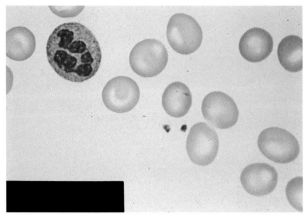

Plate 37. Macro-ovalocytes and a hypersegmented neutrophil characteristic of megaloblastic anemia.

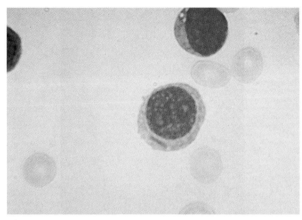

Plate 40. Peripheral blood smear showing an immature granulocyte with a rod-shaped inclusion body (Auer rod) characteristic of acute myeloid leukemia.

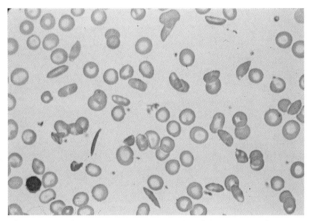

Plate 38. Erythrocyte anisocytosis and poikilocytosis with several sickle cells.

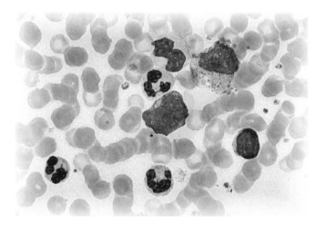

Plate 41. Increased number of granulocytic cells in all phases of development on the peripheral blood smear characteristic of chronic myeloid leukemia.

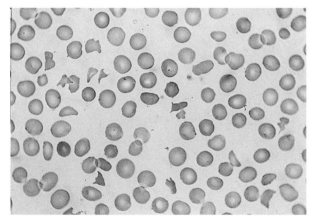

Plate 39. Marked anisocytosis and poikilocytosis with prominent schistocytes.

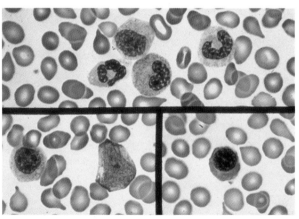

Plate 42. Left-shifted granulopoiesis and nucleated and teardrop-shaped erythrocytes in a patient with primary myelofibrosis.

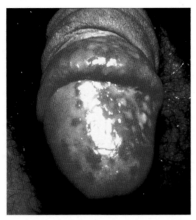

Plate 43. Genital herpes (herpes simplex virus infection) usually presents as a cluster of painful, pink papules that rapidly become vesicular.

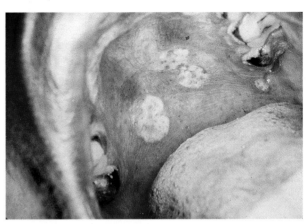

Plate 46. The mucous patches of secondary syphilis appear on mucous membranes and are highly infectious.

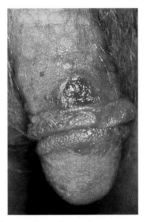

Plate 44. The primary ulcerative lesion (chancre) in syphilis has a clean appearance with heaped-up borders. The lesion usually is painless.

Plate 47. Disseminated gonococcal infection is associated with painless pustular or vesiculopustular skin lesions.

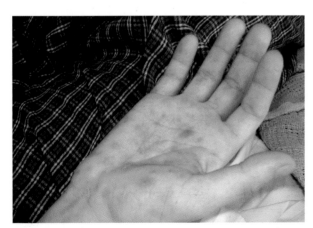

Plate 45. The skin findings of secondary syphilis consist of a generalized mucocutaneous rash (including palms and soles), generalized lymphadenopathy, and constitutional symptoms.

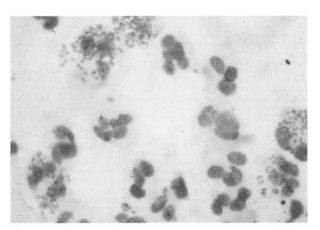

Plate 48. This image demonstrates gram-negative intracellular tubular necrosis.

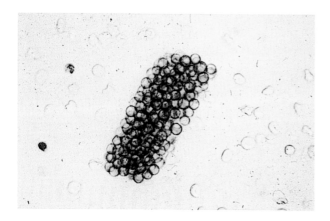

Plate 49. An erythrocyte cast indicative of glomerular disease.

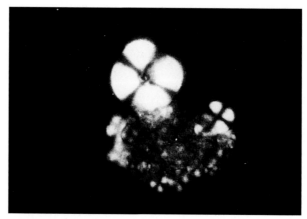

Plate 52. A fat droplet (oval fat body) seen with polarized microscopy indicative of lipiduria and giving a Maltese cross appearance.

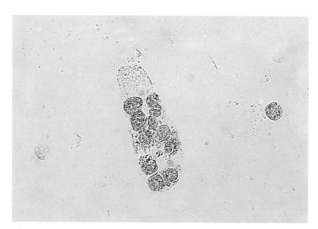

Plate 50. A leukocyte cast indicative of kidney interstitial disease.

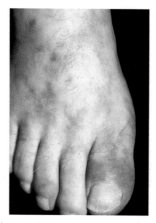

Plate 53. Livedo reticularis is a mottled discoloration of the skin that occurs in a netlike pattern and can be a manifestation of atheroemboli.

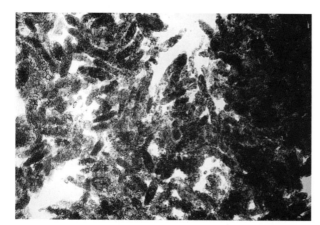

Plate 51. Muddy brown casts indicative of acute diplococci, an appearance characteristic of Neisseria gonorrhoeae.

Plate 54. Envelope-shaped calcium oxalate crystals.

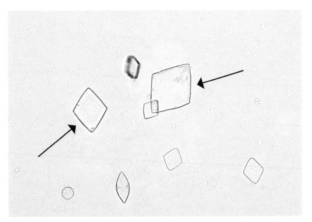

Plate 55. Diamond- and rhomboid-shaped uric acid crystals.

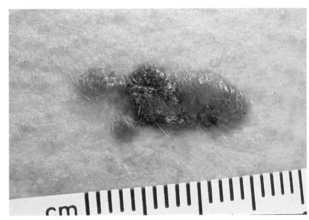

Plate 58. Malignant melanoma with characteristic asymmetric shape, irregular borders, and variegated coloration.

Plate 56. Coffin-shaped struvite (triple phosphate) crystals.

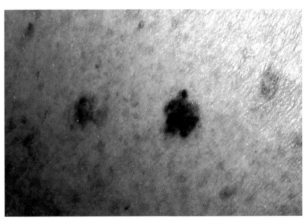

Plate 59. Superficial spreading melanomas typically are >6 mm, with irregular borders and pigmentation.

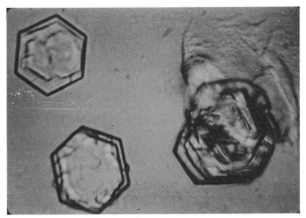

Plate 57. Hexagonal-shaped cystine crystals.

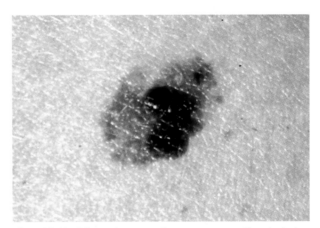

Plate 60. Nodular melanomas often present as uniformly dark blue or black "berry-like" lesions that most commonly originate from normal skin. Nodular melanomas, which expand vertically rather than horizontally, can also arise from a preexisting nevus, as did this melanoma.

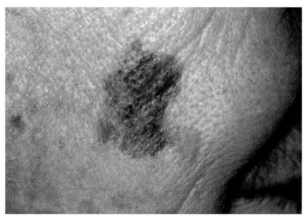

Plate 61. Lentigo maligna melanoma presents as a slowly enlarging, variegated, pigmented patch on sun-damaged skin.

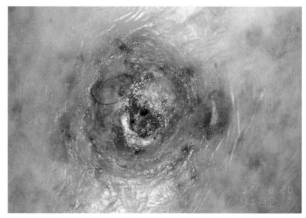

Plate 64. Squamous cell carcinomas present as hyperkeratotic scaly or crater-like lesions.

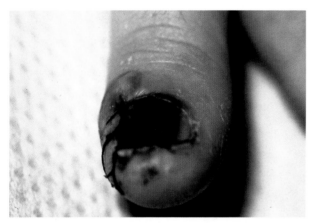

Plate 62. Acral lentiginous melanoma, with pigmentation involving the proximal nail fold and cuticle.

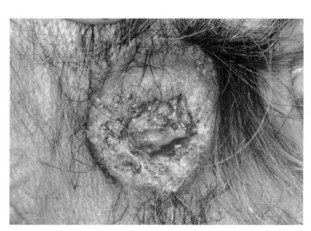

Plate 65. Fully developed keratoacanthoma, with a visible central keratotic plug.

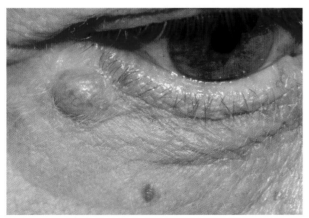

Plate 63. Basal cell carcinomas typically present as pearly papules with telangiectasias.

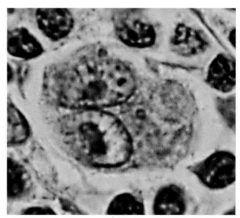

Plate 66. Reed-Sternberg Cell Characteristic of Hodgkin Lymphoma

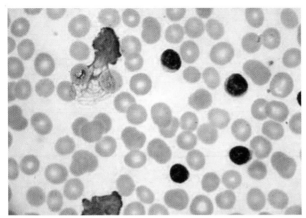

Plate 67. Increased number of mature lymphocytes and two "smudge" cells on peripheral smear (center and bottom) characteristic of chronic lymphocytic leukemia.

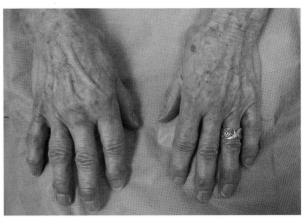

Plate 70. Heberden nodes in osteoarthritis are bony spurs at the dorsolateral and medial aspects of the distal interphalangeal joints.

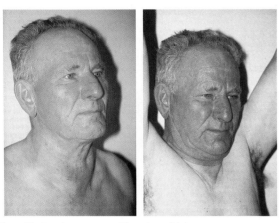

Plate 68. Pemberton sign. Elevation of the arms causes impaired venous return to the thoracic cavity due to a space occupying lesion, resulting in elevated jugular venous pressure, distended neck and head superficial veins, and facial flushing.

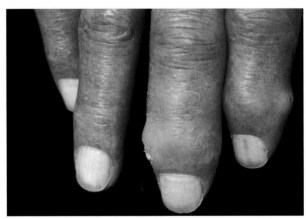

Plate 71. Milky white nodules characteristic of chronic tophaceous gout.Aspiration of the nodules will show sheets of monosodium urate crystals that are negatively birefringent and needle-shaped.

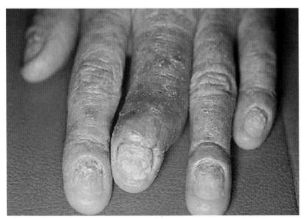

Plate 69. Small-joint polyarthritis with typical psoriatic skin lesions and nail pitting characteristic of psoriatic arthritis.

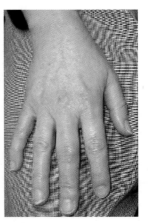

Plate 72. Typical fusiform swelling of the proximal interphalangeal joints with sparing of the distal interphalangeal joints characteristic of rheumatoid arthritis.

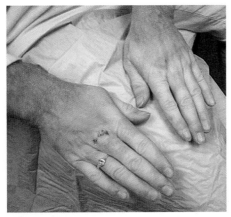

Plate 73. A typical episode of Raynaud phenomenon is precipitated by cold exposure, which is soon followed by distinctive color changes: white (ischemic phase), blue (cyanotic phase), and then red (with rewarming).

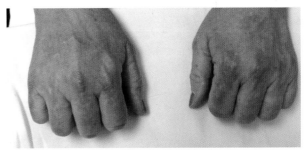

Plate 76. Scaly, purplish papules and plaques on the extensor surfaces of the metacarpophalangeal and interphalangeal joints are diagnostic for dermatomyositis.

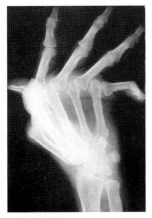

Plate 74. Subluxation of joints in Jaccoud arthritis associated with systemic lupus erythematosus.

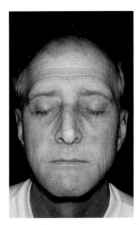

Plate 77. A dusky purple (heliotrope) rash on the eyelids characteristic of dermatomyositis.

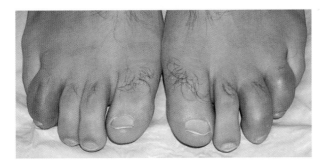

Plate 75. "Sausage digits" (dactylitis) in a patient with reactive arthritis.

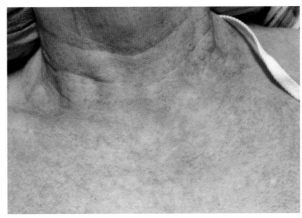

Plate 78. Erythematous rash (V-sign) associated with dermatomyositis.

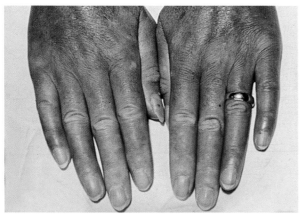

Plate 79. Sclerodactyly (skin thickening over the fingers) extending proximal to the metacarpophalangeal joints in a patient with systemic sclerosis.

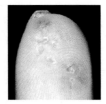

Plate 80. Digital pitting (soft-tissue defects and scarring in the pulp space of the distal phalanges) in a patient with systemic sclerosis.

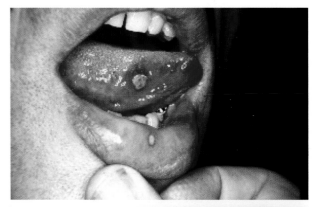

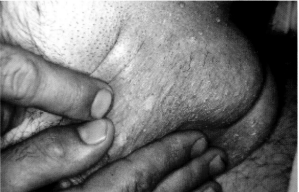

Plate 81. Oral aphthous and genital ulcerations in a patient with Behçet disease.

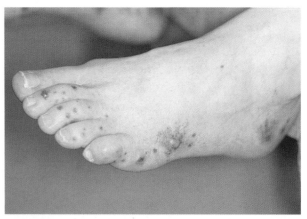

Plate 82. A typical rash of leukocytoclastic vasculitis due to immune complex deposition in small vessels.